Sex & Gender

An Introduction

SIXTH EDITION

Hilary M. Lips

Radford University

McGraw-Hill
Higher Education

Boston   Burr Ridge, IL   Dubuque, IA   New York   San Francisco   St. Louis
Bangkok   Bogotá   Caracas   Kuala Lumpur   Lisbon   London   Madrid   Mexico City
Milan   Montreal   New Delhi   Santiago   Seoul   Singapore   Sydney   Taipei   Toronto

McGraw-Hill
Higher Education

SEX & GENDER: AN INTRODUCTION
Published by McGraw-Hill, an imprint of The McGraw-Hill Companies, Inc., 1221 Avenue of the
Americas, New York, NY 10020. Copyright © 2008. All rights reserved. No part of this publication may
be reproduced or distributed in any form or by any means, or stored in a database or retrieval system,
without the prior written consent of The McGraw-Hill Companies, Inc., including, but not limited to,
in any network or other electronic storage or transmission, or broadcast for distance learning.

This book is printed on acid-free paper.

2 3 4 5 6 7 8 9 0 DOC/DOC 0 9 8 7

ISBN: 978-0-07-340553-7
MHID: 0-07-340553-1

Editor in Chief: *Emily Barrosse*
Publisher: *Beth Mijia*
Sponsoring Editor: *Michael J. Sugarman*
Marketing Manager: *Sarah Martin*
Director of Development: *Dawn Groundwater*
Developmental Editor: *Katherine Russillo*
Project Manager: *Amanda Peabody*
Manuscript Editor: *Kay Mikel*
Design Manager: *Cassandra Chu*
Cover Designer: *Ayelet Arbel*
Art Editor: *Emma Ghiselli*
Photo Research: *Brian Pecko*
Supplements Producer: *Meghan Campbell*
Production Supervisor: *Randy Hurst*
Composition: *10.5/12 Palatino by Laserwords Private Limited*
Printing: *45# New Era Matte, R. R. Donnelley & Sons/Crawfordsville, IN*

Library of Congress Cataloging-in-Publication Data

Lips, Hilary M.
    Sex & gender : an introduction / Hilary Lips. — 6th ed.
      p. cm.
    Includes bibliographical references and indexes.
    ISBN-13: 978-0-07-340553-7
    ISBN-10: 0-07-340553-1
    1. Sex role.   2. Sex differences (Psychology)   I. Title.   II. Title: Sex and gender.
HQ1075.L58 2008
305.3—dc22

2007011115

The Internet addresses listed in the text were accurate at the time of publication. The inclusion of a
Web site does not indicate an endorsement by the authors or McGraw-Hill, and McGraw-Hill does
not guarantee the accuracy of the information presented at these sites.

www.mhhe.com

In memory of Justine Mary Lips,
Hilaire John Lips,
Delores Janet Nielsen,
and Bill Nielsen
with love and gratitude

Contents

Chapter *3*
Researching Sex and Gender:
Exploring the Whys and Hows   *105*

PART II: *Behavior & Experience:*
Female–Male Similiarities and Differences

Chapter *4*
Worlds Apart?
Gender Differences in Social Behavior and Experience   *148*

Chapter 5
Biology and Environment:
The Process of Becoming Female or Male   *177*

Chapter 6
Perceptual and Cognitive Abilities:
Gender Similarities and Differences   *219*

Chapter 7
Sexual Lives and Orientations   256

Chapter *11*
Family and Friends: Attachment, Intimacy, and Power *438*

Chapter *12*
Economic and Political Life:
Power, Status, and Achievement *477*

Chapter *13*
Issues in the Workplace *510*

Chapter *14*
Justice, Equity, and Social Change   551

Epilogue
The Ties That Bind:
The Future of Sex and Gender   585

Preface

Dramatic changes have been wrought over the past century in female–male relationships, in the ways women and men think of themselves and each other, and in the societal norms for feminine and masculine behavior. For example, at the beginning of the 1900s, women did not have the right to vote in any country except New Zealand. With the exception of a few strong monarchs, such as Queen Victoria, women had been largely absent from high-profile political leadership positions. They had, until the last few years of the 19th century, been barred from institutions of higher education and were believed to be unsuited for great intellectual efforts. Women regularly died in childbirth, often as a result of a pregnancy they did not choose but were powerless to prevent.

Today women hold voting rights in most nations of the world and have held the roles of president or prime minister in more than 30 countries. Women have gained access to higher education in large numbers, currently making up the majority of university students in the United States. Advances in medical technology and changes in the laws surrounding contraception and abortion have made unwanted pregnancies less inevitable and far less dangerous, allowing choices for women that were unthinkable 100 years ago.

Yet, in the face of so many transitions, one thing has changed little: the notion that gender is an important dimension in human life, that it is a category to be reckoned with. The division of the human race into females and males has, in many ways, assumed an importance that overshadows other divisions. From culture to culture, the male–female distinction has been assigned meanings and significance that have implications for work, family, leisure, and ritual—virtually all aspects of social life. Yet it is only within fairly recent history that we have begun to stand back from and question the meaning that cultures have placed on femaleness and maleness, femininity and masculinity. It is this process of questioning that both leads to and is nourished by the study of sex and gender.

The study of the differences and similarities between women and men is compelling for both its personal and its political implications. Issues of femininity and masculinity are emphasized strongly in our culture and can be important aspects of individual identity and self-concept. But such issues go far beyond questions of personal self-awareness. Feminist scholarship over the last three decades has made it increasingly apparent that beliefs about the differences and similarities between women and men are both rooted in and help to perpetuate particular social and political arrangements. To appreciate both the personal and political dimensions of gender, it is useful to examine what we know and do not know about the similarities and differences between women and men, where that knowledge comes from, and how that knowledge may itself be shaped and limited by cultural perceptions of femininity and masculinity. It is precisely to this type of examination that this book is dedicated.

Any one person's attempt to summarize a body of knowledge must necessarily reflect her own values and biases; this book is no exception to that rule. As a feminist social psychologist, I have a conviction that many of the differences in the ways female and male human beings behave can be traced to social factors such as stereotyping, self-fulfilling prophecy, conformity to social pressure, expectancy effects, and different socialization practices for the two genders. Furthermore, although I believe empirical research—research that tests theories against observable facts—is one of the best tools for unmasking and discrediting false assumptions and inaccurate stereotypes about sex and gender, I am also well aware that researchers shape their own truths to some extent and that the biases built into the research process itself affect investigators' findings and can perpetuate faulty theories and sexist interpretations of data. Thus this book emphasizes empirical research but takes a critical approach to that research.

Knowledge is gathered and opinions formed in a social context. Early research on male–female differences took place in a context in which, for instance, it was often taken for granted that women's chief purpose in life was to bear children and that men were naturally better suited than women to take on public roles outside the family. Had I written this book 30 years ago, it would have been difficult to find and include a substantial amount of research that examined the social underpinnings of gender roles or challenged the assumption that sex differences in temperament were the inevitable outcome of the anatomical and physiological differences between females and males. It is largely under the impetus provided by the feminist movement that social scientists have begun to consider gender as something that is socially constructed rather than biologically inevitable. Yet our present social context continues to limit the study and understanding of sex and gender, and important gaps remain in the information that is available. Two of these gaps have been particularly noticeable to me as I compiled information for successive editions of this book. The first is the small proportion of research on sex and gender that focuses on or even includes perspectives other than those of Western, White, middle-class females and males. Most of the research is based at universities, and universities have been much more accessible to this group than to any other. This gap is hardly cause for surprise, but it is cause for concern. If we shape our "feminine" or "masculine" behavior largely in response to social cues and social pressure, it stands to reason that, to the extent that different groups emphasize or are subjected to different patterns of social cues and social pressure, femininity or masculinity in those groups will be associated with different experiences and behavior. For example, although some commonalties certainly exist, the female experience may differ in important ways for African American women, Asian American women, and European American women in the United States; the male experience may differ in important ways for Native American men or for men of

Indo-Pakistani or European descent in Canada. Where possible in this book I have tried to include information that broadens the perspective on gender beyond that of White middle-class culture. Such inclusiveness has been easier in this sixth edition because of a burgeoning emphasis on diversity in feminist scholarship. However, information on every group for every topic is not readily available.

A second gap in the knowledge base about sex and gender stems from a tendency on the part of social scientists to ignore the experience of anyone whose sexual orientation is not heterosexual. Thus research on the development of sexual feelings and relationships and research on couples and families have until recently all but ignored the experiences of lesbians and gay men and bisexual and transgendered individuals. Although many gaps still remain in this area, some excellent studies now exist. I have tried to include this perspective wherever information is available.

The book is divided into three parts. Part I, *Myths, Theories, and Research,* focuses on the stereotypes of femininity and masculinity and on the ways theory and research in psychology and the other social sciences have been influenced by and have affected these stereotypes. Part II, *Behavior and Experience: Female–Male Similarities and Differences,* pits the gender stereotypes against the research evidence. It examines the evidence for male–female similarities and differences in a wide range of domains, from aggression to altruism, from mathematical performance to sexuality, from the experience of reproduction to mental and physical health. Throughout this section, the emphasis is on evaluating the evidence for gender differences and, when differences appear, on trying to understand the reasons for them. Part III, *Sex and Gender in Social Relationships,* examines the reciprocal links between gender roles and the structure of relationships, in the social world, and in areas ranging from friendships to families and from work relationships to politics and law. This section stresses the position of individuals in their social context. Feminine and masculine gender roles are not simply sets of qualities developed by individuals; they are part of the rules of a social system in which these individuals live. Built into that system is a hierarchy in which males, in general, hold more power than females. The power difference cannot be ignored, and it is not easy for an individual to break away from it or to change it. Its consequences can be very negative for women, and there are negative side effects for men as well. An understanding of how gender, as an aspect of social relationships, is a reflection of a status hierarchy in which males outrank females leads back to an understanding of why gender stereotypes are the way they are, thus completing the circle that was begun in the first chapter of the book.

A primary emphasis of this sixth edition is to evaluate and resituate the major issues of every chapter in the context of the most current research literature. Strangely, one of the most important reasons for doing this is not due to advances in gender equity or understanding in the early 2000s but rather to the necessity to document via the most recent sources the lack of such advances. In business, in education, in politics, and in media stereotyping of females and males, women and men still receive different messages and are encouraged in different directions. Men are disproportionately represented in political leadership positions, in corporate boardrooms, and at the top levels of academic institutions. Little girls still encounter more barriers than do little boys when they explore mathematics, science, or computing. Rape and sexual harassment continue to be major issues confronting women in their daily environments—including on college campuses. The research I reviewed for this edition makes it abundantly clear that we must continue to pay attention to gender-related issues.

On a more positive note, frequent revisions of this book are necessary because of the explosion in scholarship on gender in recent years. Many issues have been rethought and reanalyzed: Are sex and gender really two different things? How malleable is gender identity? Should we emphasize gender differences, or is that the wrong question? When should we call a gender difference "small"? Are women really "nonaggressive," or does that label stem from stereotyping? How does subtle or "modern" sexism work on its targets? It is heartening to see the attention researchers are paying to these questions; it is difficult for an author to keep up with and include all the important scholarship being generated. Of course, not everything has been included. This edition does, however, convey some of the flavor of the interesting data gathering and debate that have focused on gender in the last 3 years.

Many people have provided me with help and encouragement. I thank the following people for insightful comments and suggestions on all or part of the manuscript or proposal for the first edition: Katherine Schultz, Dena Davidson, Nina Colwill, Jane Prather, Rhona Steinberg, Jeanne Kohl, Jeanne Maracek, Anne Peplau, and Ann Costain. Nina Colwill, my coauthor for Chapter 13 (*Issues in the Workplace*), provided welcome expertise and inspiration on many occasions. A book that she and I coauthored more than two decades ago, *The Psychology of Sex Differences*, provided some of the groundwork for this one, and I am indebted to her for the ideas that have been carried over from that earlier work to this.

For the second edition, I extend my circle of thanks to include the following reviewers: Judy Rollins Bohannon, East Carolina University; Claire Etaugh, Bradley University; Lisa Judd, Winona State University; Faye D. Pascak-Craig, Marian College; Gwendolyn T. Sorrell, Texas Tech University; Michael R. Stevenson, Ball State University; Gail A. Thoen, University of Minnesota; and Mary Roth Walsh, Harvard University.

For the third edition, I thank the following reviewers: Cathleen Callahan, John Carroll University; Claire Etaugh, Bradley University; and John R. McCarthy, University of Albany, State University of New York.

For the fourth edition, I thank reviewers Kristine Anthis, University of Nebraska, Omaha; Mary M. Brazier, Loyola University New Orleans; Barbara Peters, Southampton College; Gwendolyn T. Sorell, Texas Tech University; Gail A. Thoen, University of Minnesota.

For the fifth edition, Betty Dorr, Fort Lewis University; Tara Cornelius, Western Michigan University; Alice Eagly, Northwestern University; Marion Mason, Bloomsburg University; and Janet Melnick, Penn State University.

For this edition, I thank Isabelle Cherney, Creighton University; Genevieve D. Stevens, Houston Community College; Kimberly D. Brown, Ball State University; Gabbie Smith, Elon University; and Judith A. McLaughlin, Montana State University-Billings.

I am grateful to Frank Graham, my sponsoring editor at Mayfield Publishing Company, for his support, suggestions, and encouragement through the first four editions. In the editing and production of the sixth edition, I much appreciated the careful help of Katherine Rusillo, Mike Sugarman, Amanda Peabody, Kay Mikel, and Meghan Campbell. The students who have worked with me at Radford University's Center for Gender Studies have been an important source of inspiration and support as I worked through this edition. My students and colleagues in the Psychology Department and the Women's Studies Program also deserve thanks for sharing their ideas with me and keeping me on my toes. Finally, I am deeply indebted to Wayne Andrew for his patience and care, his ideas and encouragement, the many late nights, and for help in a multitude of ways large and small.

Hilary Lips

Masculinity and Femininity
Myths and Stereotypes

Jazz musician Billy Tipton lived life as a man, developed a thriving public career, married, adopted three sons, and spent a lifetime playing piano and saxophone in nightclubs. In death, at age 74, Billy Tipton was revealed to be a woman. In life, Tipton's secret was kept from everyone but his spouse, who said that Tipton had taken on a male identity to remove barriers to a musical career. Tipton's sons, as well as his former musician colleagues, were surprised and shocked to learn that he was female. "I'm just lost," said one son. "He'll always be Dad, but I think that he should have left something behind for us, something that would have explained the truth" ("Jazzman," 1989, p. 3A).

Ms. magazine carried a story about an "electronic imposter" (Van Gelder, 1985). This individual, a man, had presented himself as a woman on one of the large computer communication networks and had interacted for months with other users of the network under this assumed identity. When his deception was unmasked, the man's electronic "pen pals" were furious and hurt, not only because he had lied to them but also because they felt they had been tricked into relating to him in ways that they would not have done had they known he was male.

The labels *female* and *male* carry powerful associations. We use the information the labels provide to guide our behavior toward other people and to interpret their behavior toward us. We also use the label applied to ourselves to create guidelines for our own activities. Not sure whether you believe this? Ask yourself these questions: If I heard footsteps behind me in a lonely, dark alley, would I care whether they were those of a man or a woman? If I were boarding a transatlantic flight and found that the pilot was a woman, would I feel a touch of extra anxiety? If a bright, articulate male friend decided to postpone finishing college in order to get married and raise children, would I be more surprised than if a bright, articulate female friend made the same decision? More disapproving? If you can give an unhesitating "no" to all of these questions, it is just possible that you have evaded the effects of the stereotyping on the basis of sex that is prevalent in North American society. Most of us, however, have not.

In this chapter, we examine the ideas about femaleness, maleness, femininity, and masculinity that affect our judgments about and interactions with others. In particular, we tackle these questions:

- What are sex stereotypes and how are they shaped and maintained by society?
- Is there a difference between *sex* and *gender?*
- What exactly do stereotypes say about what women and men are like?
- Do gender stereotypes encompass issues beyond personality traits?
- To what extent do gender stereotypes imply that women and men are valued differently—that one group is "better" than the other?
- How do gender stereotypes interact with stereotypes about race, class, age, appearance, sexual orientation, and disability?
- How does the process of stereotyping work?
- How does it feel to be the target of gender stereotypes and prejudice?
- Do gender stereotypes affect research on sex and gender?

SEX STEREOTYPES

Sex stereotypes are socially shared beliefs about what qualities can be assigned to individuals based on their membership in the female or male half of the human race. Stereotyping individuals can proceed on the basis of race, age, religion, height, social class, or any other distinction that can be used to divide people into groups. Sex stereotyping, though, has the relatively unique aspect of being based on a distinction that divides human beings into two groups: male and female. As a result, many of our sex stereotypes are based on the notion of opposites. Indeed, our custom of referring to "the opposite sex" in discussions of female–male relationships springs from this tradition. In various cultures, the nature of the opposites has been specified. In some, the male principle has been represented by the sun, the female by the moon; the male by rationality and logic, the female by emotion and intuition; the male by light and clarity, the female by darkness, mystery, and magic. Some researchers suggest that the notion of the two sexes as opposites and of femininity and masculinity as two opposing poles on a continuum may be one of the basic organizing principles human beings have learned to use when thinking about gender (Deaux & Lewis, 1984; Foushee, Helmreich, & Spence, 1979). It is not necessarily natural to think of women and men as opposites, however. Historians have noted that in Western culture the "opposites" tradition succeeded an equally strong "hierarchical" one in which women and men were considered to be similar, with women less advanced than men along the same continuum of perfection (Laqueur, 1990).

An implication of stereotyping two groups as polar opposites is that any movement away from the stereotype of one group is, by definition, a movement toward that of the other group. For instance, a man who acts less rational than the male stereotype is seen not only as less masculine but as more feminine; a woman who acts less emotional than the female stereotype is viewed not only as less feminine but as more masculine. Thus it is that, for example, women doing competent intellectual work have been told, "You think like a man," and men showing reluctance to enter dangerous situations have been taunted with the epithet "old woman."

Another implication of the opposing stereotypes of masculinity and femininity is the notion that women and men should be separate from each other in a variety of contexts. A lone male or female in the midst of a group of the other sex is often made to feel like an invader or is obviously excluded, and individuals may scrupulously avoid situations they feel are geared for the other sex.

The ludicrous lengths to which such avoidance may be carried were demonstrated in an old episode of the television show *Candid Camera*. The crew labeled two adjacent telephone booths with the signs *Men* and *Women*, placed a man in the "men's" booth, and waited to see what would happen as male passersby came along wanting to make a phone call. Remarkably, men ignored the empty "women's" phone booth and paced around impatiently waiting for their turn to use the one labeled *Men*.

Another example that reflects both the arbitrariness of gender stereotypes and the phobia about violating them is provided by Tonkinson (1974), writing about the Aboriginal people of Australia. He tells of encountering a group of rural Aboriginal men who had been given some used clothing by a White station owner traveling through the area: "When our patrol arrived at the spot, the men in the group were wearing not only the trousers they had been given, but also the dresses. Our Aboriginal guide was quite embarrassed and quickly informed the men of their mistake; within seconds they discarded the female attire" (p. 104). To these men, who had not grown up with Western European customs, wearing dresses seemed just as appropriate as wearing pants—*until* the dresses were labeled as "for women."

Sex stereotypes, then, are culturally shaped beliefs about what men and women are like and how they do and should behave—and we often try to conform to these stereotypes to fit in with our social surroundings.

The Social Context of Stereotypes

Stereotypes about women and men, like stereotypes about ethnic, racial, religious, or other groups, do not exist in a social vacuum. To understand why stereotypes persist in a particular form, we must know something about the social relations between the groups in question. Many cultures, including our own, have a long history of a hierarchical relationship between men and women: Men have held more social power than women; men have been dominant and women subordinate (for comprehensive overviews of power and gender, see Lipman-Blumen, 1984; and Lips, 1991).

One function of stereotypes is to bolster the status quo, so it is not surprising that dominant groups are stereotypically credited with more competence and intelligence than subordinate groups are, and that groups with low social power are more likely to be stereotyped as emotional and incompetent than their higher power counterparts are. This pattern, which can be seen in the stereotypes for Blacks and Whites in the United States and for francophone and anglophone Canadians, is also evident in stereotypic beliefs about women and men. Indeed, stereotypes are often perpetuated simply because they justify prejudice against a subordinate group. In the discussion of stereotyping that follows, and indeed for the remainder of this book, it is important to remember that the behaviors and traits attributed to women and men have been observed in particular social contexts—contexts in which men have, in many ways, held greater social power than women have.

Because stereotypes are linked to social context and to individuals' observations of what is going on around them, they are dynamic. Amanda Diekman and Alice Eagly (2000) suggested that people adjust their stereotypes of women and men by taking into consideration the roles they occupy: If women tend to be in roles that demand nurturing behavior and men tend to be in roles that demand decision making and taking charge, observers will assume that women and men have the qualities required for such roles. But what if roles for women and men change? Diekman and Eagly predicted that stereotypes would change along with them. In fact, they argued that stereotypes have a dynamic component: that one aspect of a stereotype is the perception of whether and how characteristics are changing.

They tested their prediction by asking respondents to rate the likelihood that the average man and woman in 1950, 2000, and 2050 would possess each of a list of stereotypical characteristics. They also asked them to estimate the percentage of women and men in these 3 years who would be in occupations (e.g., lawyer, physician, flight attendant, automobile mechanic) and who would perform household tasks (e.g., taking care of the car, mowing the lawn, laundry, cooking). Respondents perceived women and men as becoming more and more similar in their characteristics over the years—this perception of increasing similarity went hand in hand with the perception that women's and men's roles, in terms of occupations and household tasks, were converging. Interestingly, respondents perceived most of the changes as occurring in women's characteristics: women were seen as progressively taking on more stereotypically masculine qualities and giving up some stereotypically feminine ones. Changes in men's characteristics were seen as much less dramatic. The researchers argued that this was because women's roles are changing more quickly than men's; for instance, women have moved into the paid labor force in large numbers since 1950, but relatively fewer men have chosen to become homemakers.

Because stereotypic views of females and males are dynamic and depend on social context, sex stereotypes and ideals of femininity and masculinity vary somewhat across social/cultural groups and historical periods. For a White woman in the American South of the 1950s, femininity might have meant emphasizing one's frailty and forswearing smoking on the street. For an African American urban woman in the United States in the 21st century, the notions of acceptably "feminine" behavior might be quite different. For a contemporary middle-class Japanese man in Tokyo, masculinity might involve working an intense 80-hour week without complaint, rarely taking vacations, and squeezing in time with his family when he can. For his North American counterpart, however, masculinity might imply having the leisure and means to do things with his family. Thus there is no *single* stereotype of masculinity or of femininity. Rather, these constructs are specific to time and place and are continually being reworked and their boundaries renegotiated. Movable though the boundaries are in theory, however, we often experience them as daunting in our own culture, time, and place. We sense that transgressing them may involve negative reactions from others.

SEX OR GENDER: MORE THAN A QUESTION OF TERMINOLOGY?

In the past, the words *sex* and *gender* were often used interchangeably. However, many psychologists, stimulated by an appeal from Rhoda Unger (1979), adopted more precise definitions of the two terms. **Sex** was used to refer to a person's biological maleness or femaleness and **gender** to the nonphysiological aspects of being female or male—the cultural expectations for femininity and masculinity. The distinction seemed a useful one because it kept us focused on the fact that many female–male differences in behavior or experience do not spring naturally or automatically from biological differences between the sexes.

We cannot cleanly and clearly separate "sex" and "gender," however. Cultural expectations for women and men (gender) are not separable from observations about women's and men's physical bodies (sex). Thus cultural constructions of gender include sex, in some sense. Conversely, history illustrates that even the most obvious biological "facts" about sex are susceptible to misperception and misinterpretation when they violate investigators' assumptions about gender. For example, the distinguished anatomist Herophilus of Alexandria, working under the assumption that women were essentially unperfected men, "saw" in his dissections of human bodies that women had testes with seminal ducts that connected to the neck of the bladder, just as men did (Laqueur, 1990). What he saw were ovaries and fallopian tubes—which clearly do *not* connect to the bladder. However, his expectation that women and men should be anatomically similar guided his perceptions, encouraging him to see similarities even where the evidence favored differences. Thus our understanding of biological sex differences is likely to be shaped by our culture's notions of gender.

We cannot, then, use the terms *sex* and *gender* to represent separate, nonoverlapping concepts. Often we do not know whether a particular difference between females and males arises from biology or culture. In fact, what we do know is that many differences are the result of biology–environment interactions (Hyde, 1994; Unger & Crawford, 1993). In this book, *gender* is used as the more inclusive term when discussing female–male differences that may be caused by any combination of environment and biology. *Sex* is reserved for discussions of anatomy and the classification of individuals based on their anatomical category. *Gender* is also used as a label for the system of expectations held by societies with respect to feminine and masculine roles.

"SUGAR AND SPICE" OR "SNIPS AND SNAILS": THE CONTENT OF GENDER STEREOTYPES

Personality Traits

Aggressive. Sensitive. Ambitious. Emotional. Which of these adjectives would you say are typically associated with men? With women? It is on questions such as these that much of our knowledge of the content of gender stereotypes is based.

Almost three decades ago, two researchers asked students at an American university to categorize 300 adjectives as being typically associated with women or men (J. E. Williams & Bennett, 1975). Seventy-five percent of the students agreed on 30 adjectives describing women and 33 describing men. These adjectives are shown in Table 1.1. They are not atypical of the findings of current research on gender stereotypes (B. P. Allen, 1995; Chen, 2005). Researchers in Canada (Edwards & Williams, 1980), Britain (Burns, 1977), and India (Gupta, 1991) have found similar if not identical patterns, and a study of gender stereotyping in 30 countries has shown considerable cross-cultural uniformity in

Table 1.1 Adjectives stereotypically associated with women and men.

Women

Affected	Emotional	High-strung	Sentimental
Affectionate	Excitable	Meek	Softhearted
Appreciative	Feminine	Mild	Sophisticated
Attractive	Fickle	Nagging	Submissive
Charming	Flirtatious	Prudish	Talkative
Complaining	Frivolous	Rattlebrained	Weak
Dependent	Fussy	Sensitive	Whiny
Dreamy	Gentle		

Men

Adventurous	Cruel	Jolly	Severe
Aggressive	Daring	Logical	Stable
Ambitious	Disorderly	Loud	Steady
Assertive	Dominant	Masculine	Stern
Autocratic	Enterprising	Rational	Strong
Boastful	Forceful	Realistic	Tough
Coarse	Handsome	Robust	Unemotional
Confident	Independent	Self-confident	Unexcitable
Courageous			

Source: Based on Williams & Bennett, 1975.

these descriptions (J. E. Williams & Best, 1982, 1990). Studies of adults in 25 countries showed agreement on a core of adjectives typical of women and men by 75% of the countries studied and that 6 (of a possible 300) items were associated with men in every country: *adventurous, dominant, forceful, independent, masculine,* and *strong* (J. E. Williams & Best, 1990). Only 3 items were associated with women in every country: *sentimental, submissive,* and *superstitious.* When Williams and Best scaled the items for affective meaning along the dimensions of favorability, strength, and activity, they found that in all countries the male stereotype items were more active and stronger, and the female stereotype items were more passive and weaker.

Depending on how they ask the question, researchers have found both stability and change in the content of gender stereotypes. One meta-analysis of seven surveys between 1974 and 1997 showed that stereotypes were stable over this time period, except for an increase in the perceived femininity of females (Lueptow, Garovich-Szabo, & Lueptow, 2001). However, another study of the self-descriptive responses of same-age college students at different points in time between 1973 and 1993 indicated that women's endorsement of masculine-stereotyped items increased over the 20-year period, while men's

Are gender stereotypes changing? It depends on how you ask the question

Type of Study	Changes Found
Self-description (Twenge, 1997)	Women's attribution of "masculine" qualities to themselves increased over time.
Seven surveys involving description of "typical" woman/man (Lueptow, Garovich-Szabo, & Lueptow, 2001)	The perception of women as having "feminine" qualities increased over time.
Description of "typical" woman/man in the past, present, and future (Diekman & Eagly, 2000)	Women's and men's roles were seen as converging, mainly because women were perceived as taking on more "masculine" qualities over time.

endorsement of feminine-stereotyped items remained stable (Twenge, 1997). The latter study is consistent with the findings of Diekman and Eagly (2000) that women were perceived as changing more than men over time.

Although the existence of both female and male stereotypes can be demonstrated, the male stereotype seems to be the more rigidly defined of the two. When 400 undergraduates were asked to use lists of trait and appearance adjectives to describe personal (How do you personally see males?), social (How does society view males?), and ideal (How do you see the ideal male?) views of males and females, all three perspectives on males were more stereotypic than the comparable perspectives on females (Hort, Fagot, & Leinbach, 1990). An important component of the masculine stereotype seems to be a belief that males do not express the emotions they feel (Fabes & Martin, 1991; Hayes & Mahalik, 2000).

Gender stereotypes are not only **descriptive** (describing what the typical woman and man *are* like) but also **prescriptive** (saying what women and men *should be* like). Deborah Prentice and Erica Carranza (2002) have shown that the prescriptive aspect of gender stereotypes can be broken down into four categories of traits that differ in how desirable they are deemed for women and men. In the first category are *gender-intensified prescriptions:* traits that are seen as desirable for everyone but especially desirable for people of a certain gender. In the second category are *gender-relaxed prescriptions:* traits that are considered desirable, but in which persons of one gender are allowed more leeway and forgiven more easily for falling short than are persons of the other gender. The third category, *gender-relaxed proscriptions,* contains traits that are not considered socially desirable but that are accorded more desirability for one gender than the other. The fourth category, *gender-intensified proscriptions,* is made

Table 1.2   Examples of intensified and relaxed prescriptions and proscriptions for women and men in American society.

Intensified Prescriptions		**Relaxed Prescriptions**	
For Women	*For Men*	*For Women*	*For Men*
Warm and kind	Having a business sense	Intelligent	Happy
Interested in children	Athletic	Mature	Friendly
Loyal	Having leadership ability	Having high self-esteem	Helpful
Sensitive	Self-reliant	Having common sense	Clean
Friendly	Dependable	Having a sense of humor	Warm and kind
Clean	Ambitious	Concerned for the future	Enthusiastic
Attentive to appearance	Having high self-esteem	Principled	Optimistic

Relaxed Proscriptions		**Intensified Proscriptions**	
For Women	*For Men*	*For Women*	*For Men*
Yielding	Rebellious	Rebellious	Emotional
Emotional	Solemn	Stubborn	Approval seeking
Impressionable	Controlling	Controlling	Impressionable
Childlike	Stubborn	Cynical	Yielding
Shy	Promiscuous	Promiscuous	Superstitious
Naive	Self-righteous	Arrogant	Childlike
Superstitious	Jealous		Shy

Source: Adapted from Tables 2 and 3 in Prentice & Carranza (2002).

up of traits that are considered undesirable in general and especially undesirable for one gender or the other. Table 1.2 provides some examples of traits that fell into the four categories in this research.

Both women and men can sometimes get trapped between the descriptive and prescriptive aspects of gender stereotypes. For example, if a woman has performed successfully in a stereotypically masculine occupation, she is seen as having the necessary qualities to succeed in a man's job. Thus people judging her will not assume she fits the descriptive stereotype of femininity and will conclude that, even though she is a woman, she is a good "fit" to the job. However, even though she may be viewed positively as fitting the job and performing it well, she may still be viewed negatively as violating prescriptive stereotypes of what a women "should" be like (Heilman, 2001). Similarly, a man who performs well in a feminine-stereotyped job may be viewed positively in terms of being a good fit to the job, but negatively in terms of prescriptive stereotypes of masculinity.

In trying to describe the themes inherent in gender stereotypes, psychologists have relied on a dichotomy—instrumentality versus expressiveness—first proposed by two family sociologists (T. Parsons & Bales, 1955). The masculine stereotype is said to be characterized by expectations of **instrumentality:** an orientation toward action, accomplishment, and leadership. The feminine stereotype combines attributes that add up to **expressiveness:** an orientation toward emotion and relationships. Although this dichotomy focuses only on positive qualities and fails to capture completely the stereotypic beliefs about female–male differences (for example, the masculine traits "loud" and "disorderly" do not really seem to depict instrumentality, whereas the feminine traits "weak" and "whiny" bear no obvious relation to expressiveness), it does help to provide a framework for studying these stereotypes. Researchers continue to find that women and men are rated differently on traits classified as *instrumental* and *expressive,* although women's and men's *self-ratings* on instrumental traits are more similar now than they used to be (Spence & Buckner, 2000). But how is such study carried out? What do researchers really mean when they claim to have delineated the existence of a certain stereotype about a particular group among members of a particular population?

Measuring Stereotypes

Researchers using key attributes to define *masculinity* and *femininity* may end up with findings that overestimate the strength of stereotypes and underestimate the overlap in the popular perceptions of females and males. The

Overview   The content of gender stereotypes

Gender	Traditional Theme	Most Agreed-Upon Traits Across Cultures	Affective Meanings
Female	Expressiveness	Sentimental, submissive, superstitious	Weaker, more passive
Male	Instrumentality	Adventurous, dominant, forceful, independent, masculine, strong	Stronger, more active

question comes with a built-in assumption that each adjective may be classified as more typical of either women or men. People answering such a question are thus subtly encouraged to provide stereotypic answers, and the results may yield an exaggerated view of the stereotypes. Moreover, respondents in these studies have usually been asked to indicate whether certain traits are "typically associated" with women or men, not whether they personally believe a particular set of adjectives actually reflects what women and men are like. Finally, a fact often overlooked in discussions of stereotypes is that the average ratings obtained for males and females in these studies, although significantly different from each other, do not usually represent opposite extremes. For instance, on a 10-point scale ranging from passive (1) to active (10), males might be rated at 7.2 and females at 6.1. Indeed, the mean ratings of males and females on such scales rarely fall on opposite sides of the midpoint (Spence, Helmreich, & Stapp, 1974).

Researchers using different methods to assess stereotypes have found less evidence for their pervasiveness and for their bipolarity. When measures are used that allow respondents to describe males and females on the basis of overlapping as well as differentiating characteristics, respondents indicate that the "most feminine" and "most masculine" persons they can imagine possess many of the same desirable traits (Jenkin & Vroegh, 1969).

Stereotypes are more than catalogs of adjectives, and researchers now recognize that, for example, some "masculine" adjectives are considered more representative of the category *Men* than are others. Studies using a method that allows participants to rate the degree to which traits characterize both the typical woman and the typical man suggest a tendency for the clusters of traits seen to characterize each to overlap (De Lisi & Soundranayagam, 1990). Gender stereotypes represent categories composed of "core" or **prototypical traits** (those most strongly linked with each category) surrounded by peripheral traits (those less strongly associated with each category). The core traits for women generally belong to a niceness/nurturance dimension, whereas those for men belong to a potency/power dimension. Overlap between the two categories is seen in that core adjectives for one gender tend to fall in the periphery for the other gender. One intriguing finding is that female respondents add to the niceness/nurturance qualities that constitute the female core a second group of adjectives: *capable, competent, dependable, intelligent,* and *responsible.* Male respondents do not include these adjectives in the female core; rather, they tend to add *attractive, good-looking, sexy,* and *soft* (De Lisi & Soundranayagam, 1990).

Accuracy of Stereotypes

When people describe women and men according to gender stereotypes, are they overestimating the differences, seeing differences that do not exist, or giving an accurate report of real gender differences? To find out, some researchers have examined gender stereotypes using a ratio method (B. P. Allen, 1995; C. L. Martin, 1987). For each trait on a list, respondents estimate the proportion of men and women who have the trait and also report on whether they themselves possess the trait. Using this method, both C. L. Martin (1987) and B. P. Allen (1995) found that people tend to overestimate the differences between women and men in comparison to the differences between women and men in their self-reports. Similarly, Beyer (1999) found that college students believed more strongly in academic gender stereotypes than they should have, overestimating the GPAs of male students and underestimating those of females students, particularly for masculine-stereotyped majors. In contrast, Janet Swim (1994) compared respondents' estimates of gender differences to research findings of behavioral gender differences on the same traits. She found that, compared with past research results rather than self-reports, her respondents tended to be accurate or to underestimate gender differences rather than to overestimate them.

There is considerable controversy in the field of psychology about the appropriate criteria to use when measuring the accuracy of stereotypes. Researchers will no doubt continue to produce conflicting findings about the extent to which people's perceptions of group differences between women and men parallel or exaggerate "real" differences, especially since the "real" differences can change across time and place. As Swim (1994) noted, it is important to remember that, even if people have a roughly accurate idea of the direction and size of gender differences on particular traits, it does not mean they understand the reasons for the differences or that they will apply the knowledge accurately to individual women and men. In Swim's research, her respondents underestimated the power of particular situations to produce gender differences. Yet research shows that the appearance of gender differences in behavior often seems to depend heavily on the social context (e.g., Maccoby, 1990).

BEYOND PERSONALITY TRAITS: THE MANY FACES OF GENDER STEREOTYPES

If you had to choose the qualities that most clearly make people seem "feminine" or "masculine" to you, would you focus on personality traits? Or might you concentrate instead on other things about the person: physical appearance, perhaps, or certain behaviors, occupation, or sexual preference? Researchers have come to realize that gender stereotypes are multifaceted, encompassing a variety of expectations about how people will look, act, think, and feel. Moreover, it is becoming apparent that there is more than a single "typical" male and female; rather, many people hold sets of stereotypes about different "types" of males and females.

Kay Deaux and Laurie Lewis (1984) showed that a number of separate **components of gender stereotypes** can be identified—traits, role behaviors, occupations, and physical appearance—each of which has a masculine and a feminine version. People see these components as independent to some extent. For example, a person could have a very masculine appearance but not necessarily be in a masculine occupation or show many masculine personality traits. However, information about one component influences people's assumptions about the others, in the absence of conflicting information. For a hypothetical person, these researchers gave participants a sex label (*male* or *female*) and information about specific role behaviors (masculine, feminine, or mixed) and asked the participants to estimate the likelihood that the person possessed particular masculine and feminine traits, pursued particular male- or female-associated occupations, and was heterosexual or homosexual. For example, participants were given the following description: "A woman has been described in terms of the following characteristics and behaviors: source of emotional support, manages the house, takes care of children, responsible for decorating the house. Consider these characteristics carefully and think about what type of woman this would be." The participants concluded that this woman was more likely to show feminine traits such as emotionality, gentleness, and understanding of others and to be in a feminine occupation such as occupational therapist or elementary school teacher than to show masculine traits or be in a masculine occupation. They also indicated a high probability that the woman was heterosexual.

In general, the participants apparently relied more heavily on the information they were given about role behaviors than on the male–female labels to estimate the probability of masculine or feminine traits or occupations. A person described in terms of the masculine role behaviors—head of household, financial provider, a leader, and responsible for household repairs—was judged much more likely to possess masculine traits such as independence, activity, and competitiveness and to be in male-associated occupations such as truck driving, insurance, or urban planning than was a person described in terms of female role behaviors, regardless of whether the person was labeled *female* or *male*. Also noteworthy is the finding that role behavior that is counterstereotypic for an individual's biological sex is linked to speculation that the person is homosexual. When feminine role behaviors were described for a hypothetical man, the estimated probability of homosexuality reached 40%. It is clear that gender stereotypes and stereotypes about homosexuality are linked, despite the lack of evidence that a person's sexual preference is related to gender-role behavior.

In a follow-up experiment, these researchers found that physical appearance cues (masculine: tall, strong, sturdy, broad-shouldered; feminine: quiet voice, dainty, graceful, soft) always outweighed sex labels when participants were making inferences about a hypothetical person's traits, occupation, or role behaviors. Other researchers have subsequently found that the masculinity or femininity of facial appearance can have an impact on judgments about a person's sexual orientation: Individuals with feminine male faces and masculine female faces were more likely than others to be judged as gay or lesbian (Dunkle & Francis, 1990). Furthermore, raters presented with a photograph or a verbal description of an individual whose physical appearance was not clearly masculine *or* clearly feminine rated the person as less likely to be gender-typed in behaviors or personality traits and more likely to be homosexual than individuals whose physical appearance was obviously either masculine or feminine (Madson, 2000). It is quite likely that appearance is a core aspect of gender stereotyping, judging by the level of dismay that greets deviations from "appropriate" feminine and masculine physiques. It is instructive to note that a common reaction to female bodybuilders, for example, is not to marvel at their achievement of a muscular body but to bemoan their lack of feminine appearance. In the women's bodybuilding championship depicted in the documentary film *Pumping Iron II*, the woman with the biggest, most well-defined muscles was given low scores because she "didn't look like a woman," despite one judge's argument that penalizing a contestant for having muscles that were too big was akin to telling a female skier that she would be disqualified if she went too fast!

The notion that people's ideas about gender are composed of several dimensions is underscored by Mary Ann Cejka and Alice Eagly (1999), who factor-analyzed a list of trait adjectives used in earlier gender stereotype research. Their analysis yielded three dimensions of gender stereotypes: personality, cognitive, and physical characteristics. Table 1.3 shows the adjectives that fell into these dimensions for women and men.

The research just described underscores another important point: Despite our tendency to think of females and males as opposites, stereotyping by sex is not an all-or-nothing affair. Clearly, respondents do not believe that *only*

Table 1.3   Dimensions of gender stereotypes (with examples of traits) for women and men in American society.

Dimensions	Physical	Personality	Cognitive
Feminine	Pretty	Affectionate	Imaginative
	Sexy	Sympathetic	Intuitive
	Gorgeous	Gentle	Artistic
	Dainty	Sensitive	Expressive
	Soft voiced	Nurturing	Perceptive
	Cute	Sentimental	Verbally skilled
	Petite	Sociable	Creative
	Beautiful	Cooperative	Tasteful
Masculine	Athletic	Competitive	Analytical
	Burly	Daring	Mathematical
	Rugged	Unexcitable	Good with numbers
	Muscular	Dominant	Exact
	Tall	Adventurous	Good at reasoning
	Physically vigorous	Aggressive	Good at abstractions
	Brawny	Courageous	Good at problem solving
	Physically strong	Resistant to pressure	Quantitatively skilled

Source: Adapted from Table 1 in Cjeka & Eagly (1999).

Table 1.4   Probability judgments of male and female stereotypic characteristics.

Characteristic	Judgment[a]	
	Men	Women
Trait		
Independent	.78	.58
Competitive	.82	.64
Warm	.76	.77
Emotional	.56	.84
Role behavior		
Financial provider	.83	.47
Takes initiative with opposite sex	.82	.54
Takes care of children	.50	.85
Cooks meals	.42	.83
Physical characteristic		
Muscular	.64	.36
Deep voiced	.73	.30
Graceful	.45	.68
Small boned	.39	.62

[a]Subjects' estimate of the probability that the average person of either sex would possess a characteristic.

Source: Adapted from Deaux (1984).

males can be aggressive, drive trucks, or act as leaders or that *only* females can be nurturant, have soft voices, and be elementary school teachers. Rather, the stereotypes are an expression of the perceived *probability* that a person will have certain qualities, given that she or he is female or male. Table 1.4 shows the probability judgments that respondents made about whether men and women would have particular characteristics. Although they assigned a higher probability to the possession of stereotypic characteristics by men and women, the table shows that they always acknowledged some probability that each characteristic could be displayed by an individual of either sex.

One final note on the complexity of gender stereotypes: Not only do they seem to be made up of different components, but they also seem to be organized in terms of specific *types* of men and women (Coats & Smith, 1999; Six & Eckes, 1991). People can quite easily list several types of women and men, along with descriptions that differentiate among the types. Sample types of males obtained from respondents in one study included the career man (well-dressed, self-confident, calculating, materialistic, eloquent) and the softy (sympathetic, able to show weakness, sensitive, unconventional, frank), along with such others as the egoist, the intellectual, the macho type, the cool type, and the playboy. Female types included the feminist (self-confident, cunning, intolerant, unlikely to show feelings) and the housewife (unattractive, "good girl," obsequious, selfless, having no interests of her own), along with such others as the society lady, the maternal type, the vamp, and the secretary (Six & Eckes, 1991).

Even when gender stereotypes have been narrowed down to such subtypes of women and men, they are still likely to vary in response to the examples of such subtypes that an individual has recently observed. Coates and Smith (1999) found that, depending on which of two examples of gender subtypes they showed to their research participants, participants listed different characteristics as descriptive of those subtypes. For example, participants who had, earlier in the study, been asked to fill out questionnaires about either television character Murphy Brown or news anchor Connie Chung (both examples of the female subtype "professional woman") later provided different descriptions of the professional woman subtype. People who had been asked to think about Murphy Brown later described the subtype "professional woman" as higher on an index of characteristics that included independent, dedicated, unfriendly, opinionated, impolite, and insensitive than did participants who had earlier been asked to think about Connie Chung. Similarly, participants who earlier had been asked to think about either tennis star Andre Aggasi or boxing great Muhammad Ali gave different ratings on a list of characteristics for the subtype

Overview   The many faces of gender stereotypes

Gender stereotypes are complex. Researchers have analyzed them in terms of the following categories.

Components	Different aspects of the individual, such as appearance, personality traits, occupation, and sexual orientation
Dimensions	Themes that emerge from lists of qualities stereotypically attributed to women and men, such as personality and cognitive and physical qualities
Types of Women/Men	Categories of "typical" women (e.g., housewife, feminist) and men (e.g., career man, playboy) considered to have different qualities
Examples Within Types	Specific examples of "types" of women and men, which elicit different descriptions of such types from respondents

"athletic man." Those who had answered questions about Andre Aggasi later described the athletic man subtype as more outgoing, attractive, feminine, sexual, confident, and conceited and less aggressive than did those who had answered questions about Muhammad Ali. It appears that the exemplars of a particular subtype a person has seen lately affect the way that person thinks about that category of individuals.

Why do gender stereotypes matter? Gender stereotypes affect the judgments people make about others—and those judgments can have consequences for how people are treated. For example, researchers interviewed staff members of one nursing home to find out their explanations for the aggressive, challenging behavior sometimes exhibited by their clients. The staff members believed their reactions to such behavior were not affected by the clients' gender. However, the way they spoke about their clients suggested otherwise. Perhaps because aggression falls outside the stereotype of femininity, staff tended to explain women's aggressive behavior as resulting from their menstrual cycle or from character flaws. On the other hand, they were more likely to explain men's aggressive behavior as due to circumstances, perhaps because such behavior fits more neatly with masculinity stereotypes (Wilcox, Finlay, & Edmonds, 2006).

Another example of how gender stereotypes have a real-world impact comes from a study of referees' decisions about soccer players' aggressive actions. Researchers examined French soccer referees' decisions in 26 games (13 women's and 13 men's). Although male players displayed more aggression than female players, researchers found that the referees penalized women more than men for such behavior (Coulomb-Cabagno, Rascle, & Souchon, 2005). Apparently, in light of gender stereotypes, women's aggression was less expected and thus appeared more serious to these referees.

Gender stereotypes, then, can have practical implications for the way we are judged and the way we judge others. As we will see in the following sections, these stereotypes can also be linked to prejudice and discrimination.

DIFFERENT AND UNEQUAL? THE EVALUATIVE ASPECTS OF GENDER STEREOTYPES

Stereotypes imply only beliefs about group differences and are not necessarily accompanied by positive or negative judgments about the groups in question, but there is some evidence that such evaluative judgments *do* accompany gender stereotypes. The negative evaluation of persons or their activities because of their membership in a particular group is known as **prejudice,** and the brand of prejudice that is based on a person's sexual category is called **sexism.** By definition, sexism can be used against either females or males; both women and men can be judged harshly, not be taken seriously, or be deprived of opportunities *because* they are women or *because* they are men.

The evidence that sexism plays a role in reactions to and treatment of women is long-standing and comprehensive. One need not be familiar with the psychological research literature to detect evidence of sexism either in our history or in our everyday lives. For years, women in the United States and Canada (among other countries) were denied the vote, denied equal access to higher education, and routinely and openly discriminated against in hiring and salary. Women who fought their way into institutions of higher education found that, when they had completed the requirements for advanced degrees, those degrees were withheld (Furomoto & Scarborough, 1986). Women who marched in public protest over their lack of voting rights were beaten by police and imprisoned in the United States and in Britain. Popular stereotypes of women emphasized their helplessness and compared them to children, and such views were enshrined in a multitude of laws and legal practices that restricted women's access to jobs and required a woman to have the permission of her husband or father to apply for a loan, own property, or change her name. The length and bitterness of the struggle for women's suffrage in so many countries, the necessity for Canadian women in the 1920s to go to court to have women declared "persons" under the law,* and the continuing controversy over issues such as gender pay equity bear strong testimony to the pervasiveness of sexism in the treatment of women.

Does all this mean that people do not like women as much as men? Not necessarily. In fact, researchers have found that women are evaluated more favorably than men—perhaps because women are stereotyped as more likely to be helpful, gentle, and understanding (Eagly, Mladinic, & Otto, 1991). In fact, some research tends to show a "women are wonderful" effect. Both women and men evaluate women more favorably than men (Eagly & Mladinic, 1989, 1994), but there are two important qualifications to this finding. First, favorability ratings can vary dramatically, depending on what *kind* of woman is on the mind of the evaluator. One study showed, for example, that among right-wing authoritarian respondents women were evaluated most negatively when they were viewed as "feminists" but most positively when they were viewed as housewives (Haddock & Zanna, 1994). Second, being liked apparently does not necessarily translate into being respected or being treated fairly.

Researchers have found that discrimination against women can be based on ambivalence, not just hostility toward women (Glick & Fiske, 1997). Men who

*In 1927 a group of prominent Canadian feminists known as the Famous Five (Henrietta Muir Edwards, Emily Murphy, Louise McKinney, Irene Parlby, and Nellie McClung) petitioned Parliament for an interpretation of a clause in the Constitution that referred to the eligibility of "persons" for appointments to the Senate. The Supreme Court of Canada ruled that women were not to be considered as persons under this clause and so did not qualify for Senate appointments. This decision was reversed by Britain's Privy Council in 1929—an event that is still celebrated by Canadian feminists on "Persons Day" in October. The "Women Are Persons" monument, comprising bronze statues of the five women celebrating their victory, was placed on Parliament Hill on October 18, 2000. It is the first statue in that location that does not commemorate either royalty or a prime minister of Canada.

have ambivalent, or mixed, feelings about women may display two different kinds of sexism: **hostile sexism** (dominance-oriented paternalism, derogatory beliefs about women, and heterosexual hostility) and **benevolent sexism** (protective paternalism, idealization of women, and desire for intimate relations). Even though the latter type of sexism sounds more positive, it still acts as a justification for keeping women in subordinate positions and traditional roles. Men who score high on the Ambivalent Sexism Inventory, which measures the hostile and benevolent components of sexism, are more likely than nonsexist men to classify women into polarized subgroups: those who belong on a "pedestal" and those who belong in the "gutter" (Glick, Diebold, Bailey-Werner, & Zhu, 1997). Yet women tend to underestimate the likelihood that benevolent and hostile sexism can exist in the same person, and many women fall into the trap of "wanting it both ways": approving of benevolent sexism while condemning hostile sexism (Kiliansky & Rudman, 1998).

Men, too, can be the targets of both hostile and benevolent sexism. Peter Glick and Susan Fiske (1999) developed the Ambivalence Toward Men Inventory, which measures both hostility and benevolence toward men. Using this scale, hostility toward men reflects resentment of paternalistic control by men, the belief that men have some qualities that are inferior to women's (e.g., that men are incompetent in certain areas), and the belief that male–female relationships tend to be adversarial. Benevolent sexism directed toward men includes maternalism (the idea that men need to be taken care of), the belief that men are naturally better at some things (e.g., more willing to take risks), and beliefs regarding heterosexual attraction (e.g., that women need romantic partnerships with men to be fulfilled). Women respondents tend to indicate more hostility and less benevolence toward men than men do (Glick & Fiske, 1999; Yakushko, 2005). As with sexism directed at women, benevolent sexism directed at men may not, at first glance, appear harmful. However, men who do not live up to the expectations of traditional masculinity enshrined in benevolent sexism (e.g., men who do not like to take risks or take charge in an emergency) may find themselves the target of disapproval. Indeed, scores on both benevolence toward men and benevolence toward women have been found to be positively related to respondents' espousal of traditional values (Feather, 2004).

Not all sexism is obvious. In fact, since so many people are aware of the disapproval that may greet the expression of gender stereotypes, they often express such stereotypes in subtle ways. Researchers in the United States and Canada have identified a constellation of attitudes they label **modern sexism** (Swim, Aikin, Hall, & Hunter, 1995) or **neosexism** (Tougas, Brown, Beaton, & Joly, 1995). Old-fashioned sexism openly endorses stereotypic judgments about and differential treatment of women and men. Modern sexism is more subtle and is characterized by a denial that women are still targets of discrimination, by antagonism toward women's demands, and by a lack of support for policies designed to improve women's status. Men who hold neosexist attitudes are more likely to show a pro-male bias in the evaluation of competence and are less likely to support women (Beaton, Tougas, & Joly, 1996).

What of sexism in the treatment of men? Although men are privileged over women in many respects, they also can be victims of sexist assumptions (New, 2001). Sexism cuts both ways; for example, the other side of the prejudiced attitude that bars women from combat positions in the military is the attitude that it is somehow less upsetting to have male soldiers killed than to have female soldiers killed. Small but active organizations of men have identified ways in which stereotypic expectations of men can result in negative consequences for them. Men's organizations—both liberal, feminist (e.g., National Organization for Changing Men) and conservative, masculinist (e.g., National Congress for Men)—note that the stereotype of men as tough, unemotional, and aggressive can result in harsh treatment of men and in male alienation. They cite society's lack of support for fathering, the expectation that men will do the fighting and dying in wartime, and ways in which the protector and provider roles have damaged and dehumanized men (C. W. Franklin, 1988).

With respect to the evaluation of men, some research shows that men may be more rigid than women in their insistence on stereotypical masculinity. Male college students describe the "ideal" man in more stereotypic terms than female students do (Hort, Fagot, & Leinbach, 1990). When female college students were given the opportunity to "listen in" on scripted interviews in which the male interviewees portrayed either traditional masculine or nontraditional

Overview   Sexism: prejudice based on an individual's sex

Old-fashioned sexism	Openly endorses stereotypic judgments about and differential treatment of women and men
Modern sexism	Is subtle and characterized by a denial that women are still targets of discrimination
Hostile sexism	When directed against women, includes dominance-oriented paternalism, derogatory beliefs about women, and heterosexual hostility; when directed against men, includes resentment of paternalism, derogatory beliefs about men, and heterosexual hostility
Benevolent sexism	When directed against women, includes protective paternalism, idealization of women, and desire for intimate relations; when directed against men, includes maternalism, idealization of men, and desire for intimate relations

Reflections : The Impact of Gender Bias

How much impact does gender bias have on human social life? Perhaps more than we think. Researchers Shelly Lundberg and Elaina Rose (2003) recently reported a surprising finding: An unmarried mother is 42% more likely to marry the father of her child if that child is a boy than if the child is a girl.

Is that because fathers place more importance on sons than daughters and so are more likely to commit to a family that includes a son? Or do mothers place more pressure on men to marry because they think a son needs a father? Researchers are not sure, but the intriguing finding fits with several others.

Earlier work by Lundberg and Rose (2002) showed that fathers seem to be more concerned with providing for sons than daughters. They work longer hours and come up with ways to earn more money per hour after the birth of a boy than after the birth of a girl. Sociologist Philip Morgan and his colleagues (Morgan, Lye, & Condran, 1988) even demonstrated that parents of girls were more likely than parents of boys to divorce. Does this all add up to a strong, lingering preference for sons over daughters?

Maybe, but Morgan argued that fathers' preference for boys has been eroding over the past several decades as the experience of parenting a girl has become more similar to that of parenting a boy. Decades ago, it was mainly boys who were groomed for careers, who played sports, and who engaged in a variety of active and intellectual pursuits. Girls were taught to be ladies and prepared to be homemakers and mothers, so some fathers may have felt they had little potential for common ground with daughters. All that has changed, Morgan said: "Fathers are just as excited about their daughters playing soccer as they are about their sons playing football" (*Seattle Post-Intelligencer,* 2003). In support of his argument, he noted that the "divorce gap" between parents of girls and boys now seems to have disappeared (Morgan & Pollard, 2002).

The "marriage gap," however, may still be in place. If so, girls are more likely than boys to grow up in single-parent families. Lundberg and Rose's data end with children born in 1993, and it remains to be seen whether the difference between marriage rates for single mothers of girls and single mothers of boys persisted over the next decade. Could changes in gender roles change gender bias by subverting the long-standing preference for sons over daughters?

androgynous roles, they consistently rated the nontraditional male more favorably (more appropriate, likable, moral, adaptive, conscientious, tactful, and reliable and less conventional, conceited, and jealous) than his traditional counterpart (Cramer, Dragna, Cupp, & Stewart, 1991).

There is apparently a silver lining for men in their experience of sexism. As Peter Glick and his colleagues (2004) noted, "negative stereotypes of men may reinforce the idea that men are designed for dominance (even as they reduce overall evaluations of men as a group" (p. 714). Remember the notion that "women are wonderful"? These researchers argue that, to capture the breadth and ambivalence of gender stereotypes, that phrase should be expanded to

"Men are bad but bold, and women are wonderful but weaker." According to this analysis, people may assign unfavorable traits (such as aggressiveness, rudeness, harshness) to men, but they still respect and admire the men who have these traits. Why? Although such traits do not render a person likeable, they *are* associated with power and respect. The saying "boys will be boys," these researchers argued, reveals that many people view men's stereotypically bad behavior as natural and inevitable correlates of dominance—and male dominance is expected and accepted.

Sexism in the Evaluation of Work

One of the most obvious manifestations of sexism directed against women is undervaluing their work. In a now classic study, P. H. Goldberg (1968) gave college women articles to evaluate. The same article was rated more favorably when attributed to a man than to a woman, leading Goldberg to suggest that women were prejudiced against other women.

Similar research carried out years later by Paludi and Strayer (1985) indicated that a pro-male bias could still be found, in both men and women, in reactions to written work. They asked 300 women and men to evaluate an article that was supposedly written by a man, a woman, an author with a sexually ambiguous name, or an anonymous author. The articles used were chosen to represent areas of stereotypically masculine expertise (politics), stereotypically feminine expertise (the psychology of women), or a neutral field (education). Raters judged the articles, even in the feminine and neutral fields, to be better written, more insightful, more persuasive, and higher in overall quality when they were told they were written by a man. Moreover, when presented with the "neutral" article attributed to either an anonymous author or to one whose name was sexually ambiguous, most respondents thought that the author was a man and rated the article more favorably than did those few who assumed the author was a woman. Such a tendency to evaluate men's work more favorably than women's is not always found; however, when differences in evaluation are found, they tend to favor men (Top, 1991). An antifemale bias is most likely to occur in domains that are stereotypically masculine when gender-neutral (rather than feminine or masculine) material is being rated, when participants have less information about the people being rated, and when participants are rating a job application or résumé rather than material such as written work or a biography (Swim, Borgida, Maruyama, & Myers, 1989). Research based in real-world settings rather than in the lab shows that discrimination against women in performance ratings is more likely when raters are male and when the measures used to obtain ratings contain gender-stereotypic items (Bowen, Swim, & Jacobs, 2000).

Prejudice against women is more likely to be found in studies outside the lab, in which respondents believe their ratings have real consequences (Top, 1991). Job applications seem particularly likely to trigger prejudiced evaluations. Although this effect is not always found, experimental studies of the impact of gender and qualifications on hiring recommendations show that males tend to be preferred over females (Davison & Burke, 2000; Harvie, Marshal-McCaskey, & Johnston,

1998; Olian, Schwab, & Haberfeld, 1988). For example, when confronted with male and female applicants with equivalent qualifications, studies have demonstrated that respondents favor the male over the female applicants for positions in university-level psychology teaching (Bronstein, Black, Pfenning, & White, 1986), newswriting (Etaugh & Kasley, 1981), sports photography (Heilman, Martell, & Simon, 1988), accounting (Zickmund, Hitt, & Pickens, 1978), and Congress (E. J. Katz & Madden, 1984). In addition to receiving unfavorable judgments of performance, women receive negative evaluations with respect to their competence: Their success is often devalued by being explained as "luck," and competent women are sometimes described as "unfeminine" and as less likable than competent men (Lott, 1985).

Clearly, the stereotypes about women as a group pave the way for the inference that women will not perform as well as men in a variety of arenas. Such an inference can be countered, however, by specific information about a job applicant—information that preempts stereotypic characterization. When specific, unambiguous information of direct relevance to job performance is presented about applicants, it tends to undermine discrimination against women (Davison & Burke, 2000).

We have seen that women's workplace performance is sometimes undervalued because of gender stereotypes, but what happens when the work being evaluated is related to home and family? Is men's work in the home undervalued in a similar way? There is little research addressing this question, but one recent study suggests that mothers and fathers are sometimes rated differently for the same parenting behaviors—and the lower ratings go to fathers. Krislea Wegner (2005) exposed groups of judges, psychologists, and college students to vignettes in which mothers and fathers interacted with their children in the same way. All three groups gave higher ratings to mothers than fathers on overall parenting skills and empathic parenting behaviors. Could it be, then, that sexism in the evaluation of work is not simply directed against women but against anyone working in an arena where his or her gender is deemed less likely to be competent?

DISCRIMINATION BASED ON PERCEIVED SUITABILITY?   Perhaps the reason for discrimination against women is not simply bias against women but bias against people behaving or trying to behave in ways incongruent with gender stereotypes. After all, many of the activities just mentioned, from writing articles to accounting, demand professional, competent, instrumental behavior—a type of behavior that forms part of the masculine stereotype. If the job or task in question requires more expressive than instrumental qualities or is classified as more suitable for a woman than a man, would men be the victims of discrimination? The parenting research cited here suggests that they would. Professional personnel consultants judging the suitability of applicants for two male sex-typed jobs (automobile salesperson and hardware shipping and receiving clerk), two female sex-typed jobs (telephone operator and receptionist), and two neutral jobs (motel desk clerk and darkroom assistant) judged male and female applicants as more suitable for their respective sex-typed occupations and showed no significant preference for male or female applicants on the neutral jobs (Cash, Gillen, & Burns, 1977). Since that early study, many others have substantiated that both women and men are discriminated against when they apply for or are being evaluated in jobs that are counterstereotypic for their sex. Women are discriminated against for masculine-stereotyped jobs, and men are discriminated against for feminine-stereotyped jobs (Davison & Burke, 2000).

A more elaborate theory of how gender stereotypes influence perceived suitability for particular jobs was proposed by Felicia Pratto and her colleagues (Pratto, Sidanius, & Siers, 1997). They argued that women are stereotyped as holding values that are hierarchy attenuating (challenging to the often male-dominated organizational power structure), whereas men are assumed to hold values that are hierarchy enhancing (supportive of the power structure). Thus managers are likely to hire women and men for jobs that seem to fit these value systems: women for jobs that require trying to change the system or help people who have been marginalized in the system and men for jobs that require supporting and strengthening the status quo. Indeed, when given the task of placing applicants in positions with different levels of hierarchy-attenuating or -enhancing features, participants favored women for the hierarchy-attenuating jobs and men for the hierarchy-enhancing jobs. This pattern held, even when the applicants' résumés showed a consistent violation of the stereotypes.

Can competence in a "gender-inappropriate" endeavor ever work to one's advantage? Perhaps. In 2005 Danica Patrick was the first female driver to lead the Indianapolis 500 for many laps. She came fourth in the race, but it was her picture—not that of the male winner of the race—that graced the cover of *Sports Illustrated* after the event. Some researchers argue that persons presented as very competent in a field that is extremely unusual for their gender can be *over-evaluated.* In one study, females identified as finalists in a football photography contest (a strongly male sex-typed field) were judged as more competent than male finalists in the same contest, but a similar overevaluation of females did not occur in the more moderately male sex-typed field of tennis photography (Heilman et al., 1988). In a similar vein, raters awarded the highest presentation marks, among two female and two male speakers, to a man who spoke on a strongly female sex-typed topic: "sex bias in the counseling of women" (Gilbert, Lee, & Chiddix, 1981). At least under some conditions, women who are good at "men's" work and men who are good at "women's" work are the beneficiaries of more positive evaluations than are their more traditional counterparts. What is going on here? Researchers speculate that, when behavior contrasts so sharply with stereotypical expectations that it exceeds a critical threshold, it creates a boomerang effect (Weber & Crocker, 1983). The individual is characterized as an exception who does not fit the stereotype or as a member of a "subtype" of the larger group ("career woman," "sensitive man") whose qualities are different from those of the larger group. These individuals may be given positive evaluations simply because their good performance is so surprising for their gender— gender bias works *for* them instead of against them.

Unfortunately for people entering nontraditional jobs, they cannot usually count on this positive effect of gender bias. Such an effect occurs, at least with respect to women, under very specific conditions: Information about high performance ability must be present, and the job in question must be very atypical for a woman to pursue (Heilman et al., 1988). When these conditions are not met, gender bias works *against* women (and perhaps against men) pursuing nontraditional occupations. Even when these conditions *are* met, it may be dangerous to succeed in a gender-atypical occupation. Women who are acknowledged to have been personally successful in a masculine gender-typed job run a real risk of being disliked—and being disliked can have a negative effect on one's career (Heilman, Wallen, Fuchs, & Tamkins, 2004).

One of the clearest illustrations that the prejudice against women involves something more than their perceived suitability to do particular work is that occupations undergoing a transition from being dominated by men to being dominated by women lose status, sometimes drastically. When secretarial positions were held mainly by men, they were reasonably high-status positions whose occupants had reasonable chances for advancement (Davies, 1975). Now that virtually all secretaries are women, the job is low status and often a dead end. A similar pattern has been noted for bank tellers (Prather, 1971) and teachers (Oppenheimer, 1970). In a laboratory demonstration of this phenomenon, Touhey (1974a) gave participants descriptions of five high-status professions: architect, college professor, lawyer, physician, and scientist. On the information sheet describing each profession, half the participants were told that the percentage of women in the profession was expected to remain stable and low for the next 25 to 30 years. The other half were told that the percentage of women would increase dramatically over the same time period. When told to expect an increasing proportion of women in these professions, participants consistently rated them lower in prestige. In a second study, Touhey (1974b) showed that the reverse was also true: raters who were told to expect an increasing number of men in feminine-stereotyped occupations (home economist, kindergarten teacher, librarian, nurse, social worker) assigned higher prestige and desirability ratings to these occupations than did raters not told to expect more men.

Do these 30-year-old studies still have relevance today? The answer seems to be yes. In 1991 Peter Glick found that, when raters believed masculine traits were required for a job, they assigned higher prestige and salary to that job. He also found that the greater the percentage of women raters perceived to be in an occupational category, the lower the salary they assigned to that occupation. A more recent study showed that not only are masculine personality traits linked to occupational prestige but virtually *all* highly prestigious jobs are male dominated (Glick, Wilk, & Perreault, 1995).

Although both women and men are subject to the restrictions of gender stereotypes, it is safe to conclude that the masculine stereotype is associated with higher status. Moreover, although members of either sex may suffer discrimination based on views that their gender renders them unsuitable for a task or position, women are the targets of more discrimination in this respect than men. Not only are almost all the high-status jobs defined as more suitable for men, but high-status jobs that become female dominated quickly lose their prestige.

GENDER AND OTHER STEREOTYPES:
RACE/ETHNICITY, CLASS, AGE, APPEARANCE,
SEXUAL ORIENTATION, DISABILITY

When someone completing a questionnaire to measure male–female stereotyping is asked about the "typical" woman or man, what kind of person do you suppose comes to that individual's mind? An elderly Black woman? A middle-aged Native American man confined to a wheelchair? A young woman who has trouble finding stylish clothing because she weighs 200 pounds? Most likely, the image is influenced by the person's tendency to define "typical" with reference to him- or herself and to the people most visible in the environment. Probably, as Hope Landrine (1985) suggested, research participants cannot imagine a woman (or man) "without attributing a race, a social class, an age, and even a degree of physical attractiveness to the stimulus" (p. 66). The image among North American college students, whose responses have formed much of the basis for research on gender stereotypes, is likely to be of someone who is relatively young, White, able-bodied, neither too fat nor too thin, neither too short nor too tall, and of average physical attractiveness. Thus our studies of the stereotypes that accompany gender are most likely limited by their reliance on generalizations that systematically exclude groups such as old people, Blacks, Latinos, native peoples, Asians, disabled people, fat people, lesbians and gay men, and people whose appearance diverges markedly from the norm.

These study limitations remind us of the necessity to think of gender as a category that interacts with other categories. To keep such interactions in view, psychologists Nancy Russo and Kim Vaz (2001) argued that, in thinking about or researching the psychology of gender, we should cultivate **diversity-mindfulness,** a mindset that includes openness to differences among people, the appreciation of and receptiveness to varied perspectives, and respect for others. Diversity-mindfulness does not mean considering every dimension of diversity all the time and in every research study. However, Russo and Vaz argued that it does mean "the consistent recognition of the potential limitations of one's approach and humility about generalizations drawn from one's own work" (p. 281). To start developing diversity-mindfulness, we will examine the interaction of gender stereotypes and race/ethnicity.

Gender Stereotypes and Race/Ethnicity

Researchers have tried to understand the interactive workings of racism and sexism by comparing the experiences of different gender–race groups. For example, the forms of racism directed at African American women or Latinas and African American men or Latinos may differ, and sexism may be expressed toward and experienced by a woman differently as a function of her ethnicity or race. An examination of gender stereotypes cannot ignore the way race and gender stereotypes interact or the ways in which racial ethnic groups may differ in the images and ideals they hold for femininity and masculinity.

FEMININITY   In an attempt to determine whether the often-reported stereotype of women is actually just a stereotype of middle-class White women, Landrine (1985) asked undergraduates to describe the stereotype of each of four groups of women—Black and White middle-class women and Black and White lower-class women—based on a list of 23 adjectives. She found that, although the stereotypes differed significantly by both race and social class, with White women and middle-class women being described in ways most similar to the dominant culture's traditional stereotypes of women, all four groups were rated in ways consistent with this feminine stereotype. White women were described more often than Black women by the most stereotypical terms: *dependent, emotional,* and *passive.* However, both groups were rated similarly on many other adjectives: *ambitious, competent, intelligent, self-confident,* and *hostile,* for example. The findings suggest that race and social class are implicit in what have been described as gender stereotypes but that a set of expectations for women transcends these variables to some extent.

According to the stereotypes held by the dominant White society, Black women may be judged as less "feminine" than White women. The history of Black women in the United States makes it clear that they have not, as a group, been conditioned toward the helpless, delicate, and even frail image of femininity historically cultivated in their White counterparts. As slaves, women were expected to endure backbreaking physical labor and hardships and were denied the security in their marital lives that White women took for granted. Angela Davis (1981) noted that, under slavery, Black women constructed a definition of *womanhood* that included "hard work, perseverance and self-reliance, a legacy of tenacity, resistance, and an insistence on sexual equality" (p. 29). Long after slavery ended, Black women continued a tradition of hard work that is at odds with any stereotypically feminine notions of helplessness or dependence. Of all American married women, African American women have consistently been the most likely to be in the paid labor force, as illustrated in Figure 1.1.

According to some African American women theorists, another legacy among American Black women that sets them apart from White models of femininity is their strong tradition of speech rather than silence, of oratory, preaching, and storytelling rather than subservient listening (P. H. Collins, 1991). One view within the African American community is that "blacks have withstood the long line of abuses perpetrated against them ever since their arrival in this country mainly because of the black woman's fortitude, inner wisdom, and sheer ability to survive" (Terrelonge, 1989, p. 556). Indeed, a persistent stereotype of Black women in the social science literature encompasses strength, self-reliance, and a strong achievement orientation (Fleming, 1983a; Greene, 1994a). However, Black women have also been stereotyped as sexually promiscuous, sexually aggressive, and morally loose (Greene, 1994a).

In contrast to Black women, Latinas (a group that includes Mexican Americans, Puerto Ricans, Cubans, and women from Central and South America and the Caribbean) have traditionally faced cultural ideals of femininity that glorified motherhood, subservience to men, and long-suffering endurance (Ginorio,

Figure 1.1   Labor force participation rates of married (spouse present) women and men by race or ethnicity, annual averages, 1989–2005.

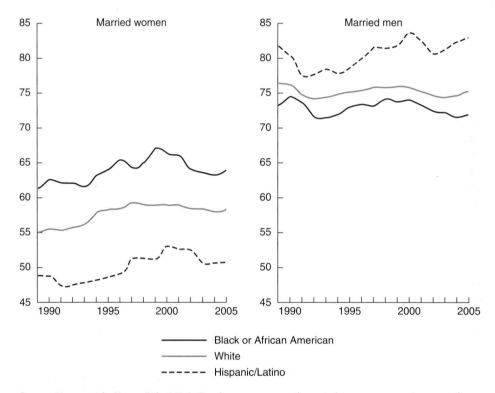

Source: Kosanovich, Karen (July, 2006). Employment status of married (spouse present) men and married women by race and Hispanic or Latino ethnicity, annual averages 1989–2005. Current Population Survey, Bureau of Labor Statistics.

Gutiérrez, Cauce, & Acosta, 1995). A woman was supposed to gain fulfillment by loving and supporting her husband and nurturing her children, and her place was unquestionably in the home (Astrachan, 1989). Latinas, socialized to place highest importance on family ties and obligations and to be nurturing to others, may feel intense conflict between these values and the demands of school or work (Vasquez, 2002). One result can be the decision to stay close to home during college or to take care of their families or communities rather than pursue such things as higher education goals for themselves (Ginorio & Huston, 2001). Such behavior may form the basis for the (untrue) stereotype that Latinas do not value education (Ginorio & Huston, 2001).

And what about European American women? Although much of the research on gender stereotyping was, until the past decade, done specifically on White women, relatively few White women think of race/ethnicity as an important aspect of their identity. Whereas women of color often think of race/ethnicity as intersecting with gender (and other categories) in complex and multilayered ways, White women often focus on gender as an identity that is more central than such other identities as race/ethnicity and class (Russo & Vaz, 2001). For example, in one study of African American and European American women firefighters, most of the European American women did not list their race as part of their self-description and said that race did not affect the way they were treated. Only a few recognized that being White conferred subtle privileges and made it more likely that they would be accepted by the (mostly White) male firefighters (Yoder & Berendsen, 2001).

One of the reasons for race-related differences in gender-role attitudes is that members of different racial groups frequently live in different social conditions. For example, in the United States, Black women have been more likely than White women to have to work for economic reasons; thus working for wages has been a normative aspect of their womanhood, and they see it as compatible with traditional family roles (Blee & Tickamyer, 1995). For White women, however (and perhaps even more for Latina women, who have only recently joined the labor force in such large numbers), the movement into paid work is more likely to provoke a questioning of traditional views of gender because it represents a break with past traditions (Dugger, 1991).

MASCULINITY   The interaction of masculinity stereotypes with race is similarly complex. Black, White, and Latino males in the United States, for example, hold and face differing, though overlapping, images of what it means to be masculine. The differences probably stem from variations in the social structural conditions currently facing the three groups and from their differing cultural heritage (Baca Zinn, 1989; Levant, 1996).

The status of Black males in American society has been in flux for the last several decades. Long after legal racial segregation ended, the effects of racism are still obvious in the White society's treatment of Black men. For example, Black men were often referred to not as *men* but as *boys*. Some writers have argued that it was not until the advent of the Black Power movement in the late 1960s that adult Black males were recognized as *men* by most of American society (C. W. Franklin, 1984). As a group, Black males live a hazardous existence as they try to maintain the competitive, success-oriented, aggressive aspects of masculinity in the face of discrimination and a lack of economic opportunities to pursue the "protector/provider" role. The result, according to some authors, is channeling attempts to be masculine into a cluster of behaviors that emphasize physical toughness, violence, and risk taking, especially among *young* Black men (C. W. Franklin, 1984). A tragic result is that the death rate from violence is frighteningly high in this group. Homicide is the leading cause of death among young American Black men; they are far more likely than any other age/gender/race group to be victims and perpetrators of homicide (Fox & Zawitz, 2001).

Latino men have also developed a tradition that places strong importance on masculinity—sometimes expressed in an ideology of male dominance labeled *machismo*. Machismo, Oliva Espín (1997) noted, "is nothing but the Hispanic version of the myth of male superiority supported by most cultures"

(p. 89). Although some have argued that machismo is a myth used to stereotype Latinos negatively and rationalize their lack of success in the dominant society, there seems little doubt that a male-dominant ideology of masculinity has played an important role in relations between Latinos and Latinas (Espín, 1997; Mirandé, 1997). The core aspect of machismo is men's dominance over women. The stereotypical macho male expects to be considered the head of his household and demands deference and respect from his wife and children. He may feel strongly that his wife's place is in the home and that his manhood is demonstrated by the number of children he has (Astrachan, 1989). A Chicano man may behave in an aggressive, macho way partly as "a conscious rejection of the dominant society's definition of Mexicans as passive, lazy, and indifferent" (Baca Zinn, 1989, p. 95). Yet machismo appears to be, in its own way, a public pose. Researchers find that actual decision making in Chicano families is as likely to be egalitarian as male dominant and that Chicano fathers are nurturant and expressive rather than distant and authoritarian with their young children. Even in egalitarian families, however, patriarchal ideology is strong, as expressed in statements that the father is the head of the house, the boss, the one in charge (Baca Zinn, 1989).

It is possible that in a society that values masculinity over femininity, gender may take on a special significance for men of color and other men who have little access to socially valued roles. They may emphasize and act out the toughness and dominance aspects of masculinity, both as a defense against put-downs from the larger society and because "being male is one sure way to acquire status when other roles are systematically denied" (Baca Zinn, 1989, p. 94).

GROUP DIFFERENCES IN STEREOTYPING   Studies of gender stereotyping and gender-role attitudes within racial/ethnic groups show mixed results. When a sample of Black and White male and female university students was asked to rate various qualities as characteristic of the "ideal man," the Black males placed significantly higher emphasis on aggressiveness than did the other groups (Cazenave & Leon, 1987). Black males also ranked highest among the groups in their rating of being comfortable with children as an ideal male quality. White females ranked highest among the groups in their rating of warmth and gentleness as essential characteristics of an ideal man. In a comparison of the gender-role attitudes of American Black and White women, Dugger (1991) found that Black women more often rejected culturally dominant views of the female role. For example, they were more likely than their White counterparts to indicate that they noticed sex discrimination; supported the women's movement; admired intelligent, outspoken women; and accepted nontraditional family structures. But these same Black women were *more* likely than White women to accept that girls and boys should be brought up to be feminine and masculine, respectively.

A few studies that compared the masculinity ideology of Black and White men have found that African American men endorse more traditional perspectives (e.g., Levant & Majors, 1997; Levant, Majors, & Kelley, 1998). In a similar vein, a study of machismo among different groups of men found higher levels of machismo among African American and Mexican American men than among European American men (Neff, Prihoda, & Hoppe, 1991). One study suggested that, in young African American, Latino, and European American men, the feeling of ethnic belonging (the sense of pride in and identification with one's ethnic group) is a strong predictor of traditional masculinity ideology (Abreu, Goodyear, Campos, & Newcomb, 2000).

Alison Konrad and Claudia Harris (2002) examined women's and men's reactions to adjectives categorized as *feminine* or *masculine* on the Bem Sex Role Inventory (a self-report questionnaire that aims to measure how closely respondents fit the social expectations that certain traits are associated with gender roles). These researchers found that European American women from the northeastern United States were the least traditional; they rated only 4 of the 40 items as differentially desirable for women and men. European American men from the same area were more traditional, rating 13 of 20 masculine adjectives as more desirable for men than women. The traditionality of African American men varied with geographical location: those in the Northeast rated only 4 of the 20 masculinity items (aggressive, dominant, individualistic, masculine) as more desirable for men than women, while those in the rural South rated 11 masculinity items as more desirable for men than women. Southern African American women rated "forceful" more desirable for women than men, while rating five other traits (ambitious, assertive, athletic, competitive, and masculine) more desirable for men than women.

Interpreting group comparisons that are based on the endorsement of particular items, such as *feminine, independent,* or *passive,* must be done with caution. Hope Landrine and her colleagues (Landrine, Klonoff, & Brown-Collins, 1995) showed that, even when diverse groups of women rate themselves identically on such terms, what they actually mean by the terms may be quite different. Their samples of European American women and women of color did not differ in how strongly they agreed that the terms *passive, assertive,* and *feminine* described themselves. However, the groups did differ significantly in the definitions they chose for these three terms. For example, the largest percentage of women of color, when asked to choose a definition for the term *passive,* selected "am laid back/easy-going," whereas the largest percentage of European American women chose "don't say what I really think." Thus it may be quite difficult to interpret data comparing the gender stereotypes of different groups.

Gender Stereotypes and Social Class

In a television advertisement for plastic wrap, a male chef—obviously very refined, very "cultured"—is shown debating what brand of wrap to use for his creation. In the background, a pudgy man in coveralls and a dirty face waits to take the package. The chef asks, appalled, "Is he going to *touch* it?" then hurriedly decides, presumably to avoid contamination of his food, to use the advertised brand of wrap. In this example, the two men are stereotyped according to social class: The chef (clearly portrayed as middle class) is apparently educated, intelligent, and sensitive and has an appreciation of the finer things in life; the man in coveralls (presumably a working-class man) is portrayed as dumb and dirty. The pro-middle-class bias is obvious, as is the difference between the notions of masculinity embodied in the two portrayals.

Social class is measured through socioeconomic indicators such as education, income, and occupation. The stereotypes applied to women and men differ somewhat according to their perceived social class. For example, one study among middle-class college students found that the stereotype of lower-class women was significantly higher than that of middle-class women for the traits *confused, dirty, hostile, illogical, impulsive, incoherent, inconsiderate, irresponsible,* and *superstitious* (Landrine, 1985). Working-class males, in the view of many middle-class social scientists, have been stereotyped as exemplars of old-fashioned, defiant, aggressive masculinity (Ehrenreich, 1983).

When gender stereotypes interact with social class, the result can be different levels of favorability for women and men. For example, Catherine Cozzarelli, Michael Tagler, and Anna Wilkinson (2002) found that college students held more positive stereotypes of poor women than of poor men. Poor women were viewed as more hardworking, proud, family oriented, friendly, responsible, loving, nice, and healthy than poor men. Poor men, on the other hand, were rated as more dirty, criminal, and alcoholic than poor women. In addition, respondents attributed men's poverty mainly to a lack of initiative and motivation and an inability to manage money. They attributed women's poverty to a lack of effort too, but they also listed having too many children as a cause. Perhaps, according to the researchers, these respondents did not view poor women as violating gender stereotypes; but they did view poor men as failing to live up to standards of masculinity.

Members of different social classes may differ in their notions of masculinity and femininity. Lillian Rubin (1976) argued that professional men, with more access to status and prestige outside the home, are more able than working-class men to assume a less authoritarian role within the family. Anthony Astrachan (1989) suggested, however, that the apparent differences between middle-class and working-class men may be partly just a matter of honesty:

> Blue-collar men feel the contradiction between their physical power and their place at the bottom of the male hierarchy, and they are more obvious than men in other classes about their need to treat women as underlings to compensate. They are more honest, or quicker to voice their anger and their fear, about changes in the balance of power and in sex roles, at work and at home. (p. 63)

Finally, Barbara Ehrenreich (1983) warned that

> patterns of working-class behavior may be formed, in part, in response to middle-class behavior and observation. . . . The middle-class "gaze" . . . can be an uncomfortable one—associated, in lower classes, with workplace supervision and negative judgments by teachers and other authorities. What appears to be a lack of "interpersonal skills" can be a withdrawal from middle-class discourse; what looks like residual "physical aggression" can be actual and ongoing hostility; and . . . "working-class male chauvinism" might be an expression of class, rather than gender, antagonism. (p. 135)

Gender Stereotypes and Age

The stereotypes of femininity and masculinity seem to apply most strongly to the young. There is scattered evidence that both women and men describe themselves in less stereotypic terms as they age (Cooper & Guttmann, 1987). There are some indications that women become more powerful as they move into older adulthood (Helson & Mitchell, 1990). There is, however, little evidence that self-reported investment in male or female role behavior changes between young adulthood and midlife (B. E. Carlson & Videka-Sherman, 1990).

Perhaps gender stereotypes become less pronounced for older people because age stereotypes replace them. For example, elderly women are often assumed to be disabled in some way (Healey, 1993). In one study in which respondents were asked to list the traits of 35-year-old and 65-year-old women and men, age stereotypes were more evident than gender stereotypes. Respondents described 65-year-old women and men similarly as *lonely, hard of hearing, rigid, experienced,* and *interesting* (Kite, Deaux, & Miele, 1991). Older people are expected to be more conservative than younger people on most issues, and women, in particular, are thought to decline steeply in their support for feminist issues as they age (Grant, Button, Hannah, & Ross, 2002).

Many writers have noted a "double standard" of aging, however, that places older women at a disadvantage with respect to older men (I. P. Bell, 1989). In contemporary North American society, much of a woman's worth is defined in terms of her physical attractiveness to men, whereas a man's worth is tied to success and wealth. The aging woman may find that, along with her "femininity," she is losing her value as a person. The changes in physical appearance that accompany aging, which are often considered acceptable or even "distinguished" in men, move women further and further from current definitions of female beauty. One study found that ratings of an individual's attractiveness decreased with age when the individual was a woman but not when the individual was a man (Mathes, Brennan, Haugen, & Rice, 1985). An examination of 100 top-grossing popular films from the 1940s to 1980s found that in these movies older female characters were underrepresented and more negatively portrayed than older males (Bazzini, McIntosh, Smith, Cook, et al., 1997). On the whole, these aging women were portrayed as unattractive, unfriendly, and unintelligent—hardly positive images! Perhaps it is not surprising, then, that women are more anxious than men about their aging process (Cummings, Kropf, & De Weaver, 2001).

Yet older women sometimes resist and challenge ideals of feminine attractiveness that emphasize youth and slimness. The elderly women interviewed in one study said they preferred female bodies to be more rounded than thin and that thin older women looked "scrawny." They emphasized inner beauty, and some said they viewed their facial wrinkles as badges of honor (Clarke, 2002).

For North American women, who often have few other sources of power and prestige than their attractiveness, acceptance of the idea that beauty requires youth can signify a slide into decreasing social worth. Older men, who are less likely to have to rely on their appearance for power and prestige, may have wider access to sources of social worth—through occupational achievement, money, and even relationships with younger women. However, the link between masculinity and success means that men who retire from or lose their jobs may also face diminished status with age. Indeed, recent research suggests that raters may see larger differences in competence between older and younger men than between older and younger women, showing that a double standard of aging cuts both ways (Kite, Stockdale, Whitley, & Johnson, 2005).

Gender Stereotypes and Appearance

Psychologists have become increasingly aware that physical appearance is a critical aspect of stereotyping. In terms of gender stereotypes, physical appearance may have strong implications for how masculine or feminine a person is thought to be. Many a tall, broad-shouldered woman has slouched and crouched through life in a futile effort to appear petite and "feminine," and many a short man has quietly cursed his diminutive stature because it seemed to detract from his ability to project a "masculine" image. Women who describe themselves as having "feminine" personality traits and men who describe themselves as having "masculine" personality traits are especially likely to feel dissatisfied with their bodies (Forbes, Adams-Curtis, Rade, & Jaber, 2001).

Although physical appearance is important to both males and females, beauty is generally defined as a peculiarly feminine attribute, and preoccupation with one's appearance is seen as part of the feminine stereotype (Rodin, Silberstein, & Striegel-Moore, 1985). In an exploration of the concept of femininity, Susan Brownmiller (1984) illustrated the powerful role played by physical appearance in cultural definitions of femininity. In various times and places, aspects of the female anatomy have become supposed signals of how feminine and how sexual a woman is. For example, Brownmiller notes the way that others react to a young woman's breast development: "Parents and relatives mark their appearance as a landmark event, schoolmates take notice, girlfriends compare, boys zero in; later a husband, a lover, a baby expect a proprietary share. No other part of the human anatomy has such semipublic, intensely private status" (pp. 40–41). Why all the fuss? Brownmiller argued that breasts are used as a prime cue to a woman's sexuality. She noted the myth that a flat-chested woman is nonsexual and that a woman with large breasts is flaunting her sexuality and seeking attention. Small wonder that women sometimes become intensely self-conscious about this part of their anatomy.

Stereotypical masculinity, too, is reflected in physical appearance, particularly in strength and muscularity. Muscles are equated with masculinity, and entrepreneurs have made fortunes playing on men's insecurity about their bodies. Bernarr MacFadden, originator of the physical culture movement of the 1900s, warned men that they must choose "whether you shall be a strong virile animal . . . or a miserable little crawling worm" (quoted in Glassner, 1989), and Charles Atlas enticed thousands of men into his exercise program in the 1950s with the promise, "I manufacture weaklings into MEN."

Studies show that many men express dissatisfaction with some aspect of their body shape (Prybock, 2000) and that gay men are significantly less satisfied with their bodies than are heterosexual men (McFadden, 2000). College men say that they want to be muscular, lean, and tall, and their specific concerns about muscularity include the desire for their muscles to be well-defined, large (but not too large), and contribute to an overall bodily appearance that is strong and athletic. They do not want to be short, fat or flabby, too skinny or weak (Ridgeway & Tylka, 2005). Men also do not want to be bald (Franzoi, Anderson, & Frommelt, 1990). This image of ideal physical masculinity is reinforced in popular media, especially in fitness magazines (Morry & Staska, 2001; Vartanian, Giant, & Passino, 2001), and researchers have found that young men who are exposed to such idealized media images of men show increased dissatisfaction with their bodies (Baird & Grieve, 2006). Furthermore, evidence from the study of male action figures suggests that the ideal male body has become progressively larger and more muscular over the past 25 years—making the ideal even more difficult to achieve (Baghurst, Hollander, Nardella, & Haff, 2006).

Perhaps no aspect of appearance is the cause of more grief in our own society right now than weight. When female Canadian university students were asked what kinds of activities or situations would make them feel less feminine, by far the most frequently checked item was "being overweight," which was endorsed by more than 50% of the sample (Lips, 1986). So highly charged is the issue of weight for women that, according to Hatfield and Sprecher (cited in Rodin et al., 1985), women respondents in the early Kinsey surveys of sexual practices were more embarrassed when asked their weight than when asked "How often do you masturbate?" or "Have you ever had a homosexual affair?"

In the context of the current concern with the "obesity epidemic," dieting—long a North American obsession—has become even more visible in popular culture. Television's *The Biggest Loser* drew high audience ratings, physicians warn of an upsurge in diabetes to accompany the rise in obesity, and diet gurus clash over what approaches (if any) would work for people who want to lose weight. Dieting is much more common among women than men: twice as many women as men are regularly or almost always on a diet (Kiefer, Rathmanner, & Kunze, 2005).

Tests on college undergraduates have indicated that weight and body shape, although important to men, were the *central* determinants of women's perception of their physical attractiveness (Rodin & Striegel-Moore, 1984; Stake & Lauer, 1987). Self-perceived heavy weight is linked to feelings of low self-esteem—and the link is stronger among women than among men (C. T. Miller & Downey, 1999).

Dissatisfaction with body shape and weight seem to be at epidemic proportions and rising for women—perhaps because the average North American woman's body size is increasing while the idealized female images presented in fashion magazines, *Playboy* centerfolds, Miss America pageants, and other media models are becoming smaller (Forbes et al., 2005). About 60% of adolescent women are dissatisfied with their weight and shape, and this body dissatisfaction does not seem to disappear as they mature (Smolak, 2006). A survey of a representative sample of 803 adult women in the United States revealed that almost half evaluated their appearance negatively, and there was a great preoccupation with being or becoming overweight (Cash & Henry, 1995). A more recent survey of women and men aged 35 to 75 found that women were significantly less satisfied with both their body appearance and their body function than were men (Reboussin et al., 2000).

An interesting finding that emerged in Cash and Henry's (1995) survey was a difference in body satisfaction between African American women and their White Anglo and Hispanic counterparts. African American women held more positive body images and were less concerned with being or becoming overweight. African American women, like other women of color in North America, live in a culture in which the predominant images of feminine beauty presented in the media are White (K. Russell, Wilson, & Hall, 1992). Do these findings of less body dissatisfaction among African American women mean they are successfully resisting the notion that they should match these images? The answer may be complicated. Some research showed that African American women with a strong positive racial identity report less dissatisfaction with their bodies (S. M. Harris, 1995). Another study provided a new clue to the difference between African American and European American women in their concern about weight: the women's perceptions of what men want. Beth Molloy and Sharon Herzberger (2002) found that, compared to their European American counterparts, African American women believed that men preferred heavier women. Since women's preferred weight correlated with their perception of men's preferences for female body size, the African American women were less concerned about heavy weight. African American women's resistance to body size dissatisfaction may be changing, however. One recent study illustrated that younger African American women reported thinner body ideal size goals than older women—suggesting that the thin ideal is gradually being accepted in this population (Williamson, White, Newton, Alfonso, & Stewart, 2005).

Women's concern about their body shape and size can be so profound that it preoccupies them and interferes with their performance at school or elsewhere. Barbara Fredrickson and her colleagues (Fredrickson, Roberts, Noll, Quinn, & Twenge, 1998) asked female and male undergraduate students in their lab to put on either a sweater or a swimsuit and then complete a questionnaire that measured body shame and take a math test. Women wearing swimsuits often reported feeling shame and disgust with their bodies, whereas men reported simply that they found the situation "silly." More disturbing, however, was that women wearing bathing suits tended to score much lower than men on the math test—a difference that was considerably narrower when participants were attired in sweaters. It appears that when wearing swimsuits the women were so distracted by disturbing thoughts about their bodies that they could not concentrate on the math problems. Men, by contrast, found the situation funny rather than disturbing and were easily able to turn their attention to math.

Women have good reason to be concerned about their weight and shape as obesity seems to trigger more negative evaluations for women than for men. Women who are "marketing themselves" for a male partner receive a consistent message that appearance, especially thinness, is a crucial selling point. Males placing personal ads for dating relationships in singles magazines and newspapers are more likely than women to emphasize the desired partner's physical appearance (S. Davis, 1990; J. E. Smith, Waldorf, & Trembath, 1990) and are far more likely than females (33.6% versus 2.2%) to specify that they are looking for someone who is thin (J. E. Smith et al., 1990). The stigma associated with obesity in women can be so strong that a male job applicant receives lower favorability ratings when he is pictured sitting next to a heavy woman (rather than an average-weight woman)—even if the woman is described as a stranger to him (Hebl & Mannix, 2003).

Gender Stereotypes and Sexual Orientation

As just noted, gender stereotypes are linked with social notions of sexuality: A "feminine" woman is supposed to be attractive to men; a "masculine" man is thought to be desirable to women. A major aspect of the stereotypes surrounding gay and lesbian individuals is that they do not fit the accepted stereotypes for their own gender. According to the dubious logic of stereotypes, a really feminine woman would not be sexually attracted to other women; a "real" man would not be sexually attracted to other men. Thus, in a reversal of gender stereotypes, lesbians are often characterized as masculine, and gay men are described as feminine. We have already seen that facial and other physical features that are stereotyped as feminine are linked, when found in males, with attributions of homosexuality, as are masculine features when found in females.

Since same-sex attraction is seen as a violation of gender roles, it is not too surprising that the people most likely to hold negative attitudes toward homosexuality are men who are hypermasculine and women who are hyperfeminine (Whiteley, 2002). A concern with "policing" gender roles is apparent, especially among heterosexual males, who often learn from their peers in childhood that any label associated with homosexuality implies a lack of masculinity and can be used as a term of derision and contempt (Plummer, 2001). Even among gay men, there is a strain of attitudes that can be labeled "anti-effeminate"; in other words, some gay men feel contempt and hostility toward their peers who behave in ways that are seen as too feminine (Taywaditep, 2001).

Stereotyped views of lesbian women often center on the notion that lesbians are not feminine. In one study, the predominant stereotypes of lesbian women included an aura of masculinity and the idea that lesbians would try to seduce heterosexual women (Eliason, Donelan, & Randall, 1992). In another, heterosexual college students rated lesbians as significantly less attractive, more insecure, more masculine, less loving, less emotional, less stable, and less mentally healthy than a sample of lesbians rated themselves (Viss & Burn, 1992). The stereotype of gay men incorporates the notion of femininity (Deaux

& Lewis, 1984) and also shares with the lesbian stereotype the notion of insta-bility (Simon, Glässner-Bayerl, & Stratenwerth, 1991).

Lesbian and gay male relationships are also stereotyped, often as mimick-ing heterosexual relationships. For instance, one widely held (and inaccurate) view of lesbian couples is that one member of the couple must be a "butch" and the other a "femme," imitating male-female relationships (Weitz, 1989).

Stereotyping lesbians and gay men is linked with antihomosexual preju-dice. For example, Janet Swim and her colleagues showed that heterosexual women were less willing to self-identify as feminists when doing so would ally them with a lesbian in front of others. The heterosexual women were appar-ently trying to avoid "stigma by association" (Swim, Ferguson, & Hyers, 1999). Research on university campuses in the United States shows that at least two-thirds of lesbian and gay students report that they have been verbally insulted, almost all have overheard derogatory antilesbian/antigay comments on cam-pus, and many report that they have been threatened with physical violence (Herek, 1993). Perhaps because the masculine role is more highly valued by so-ciety and gay males are seen to be deviating from that role, such prejudice is often more obvious in relation to gay men than to lesbians (Herek, 1988; Morin & Garfinkle, 1978).

Gender and Disability

Although the general stereotype of persons with disabilities involves victimiza-tion, helplessness, dependence, social isolation, and suffering, this stereotype seems to be moderated by the gender of the person with the disability (Fairchild, 2002). For women, already stereotyped as more passive and dependent than men, the disability stereotype can reinforce the image of dependence (Fine, 1991). In-deed, newly disabled women are far more likely than their male counterparts to be advised by their physicians to retire from paid employment (S. Russell, 1985) and less likely than their male counterparts to find a job postdisability (Fine, 1991; S. A. Fulton & Sabornie, 1994). For men, the dependence on others that many dis-abilities enforce is perceived as a threat to their masculine image. Indeed, one analysis suggested that people may view men with disabilities less positively than women with disabilities because disabilities imply weakness and a necessity to rely on others—and men are supposed to be strong, powerful, and indepen-dent (Stone & Colella, 1996). Even health professionals have different expectations for women and men who become disabled. They expect women to "express grief, feel shame, be cheerful and optimistic, talk about their feelings, request help, ac-cept curiosity, and be compliant and proactive during rehabilitation" and men to "express anger, be pessimistic, be upset by their dependency, conceal their feel-ings, reject sympathy and help, and avoid others" (Westbrook, 1997, p. 27).

Physical attractiveness is another area in which gender and disability stereotypes interact. We have already noted that physical attractiveness is more central to femininity than to masculinity; it is also apparent that a woman who is visibly disabled, even if not disfigured in any way, falls short of the cultural ideal of beauty. Here, for example, is the reaction of a former executive of the

Miss Universe contest to the notion of a paraplegic woman as a contestant: "Her participation in a beauty contest would be like having a blind man compete in a shooting match" (Matthews, 1985, p. 49). However, 1987 saw the first entry of a wheelchair-using woman, Maria Serrao, in a major American beauty contest (*Winnipeg Free Press*, 1987). In 1994 a deaf woman, Heather Whitestone, won the Miss America pageant, and actress Marlee Matlin, who appeared regularly on *The West Wing*, demonstrated that a deaf woman can become a media star.

The stereotypic expectations about femininity that many women find oppressive may be experienced as more complex by disabled women. For example, the automatic expectation that a woman will have children may be greeted with resentment by a woman who has no physical barriers to such a choice, but a woman with a disability that interferes with this choice may resent the automatic expectation that she will *not* have children (Waxman, 1994). Similarly, although many women object strongly to the casual sexual harassment they encounter on the street, some disabled women may object just as strongly to the assumption that they are not "harassable" (Fine, 1991).

Like the elderly, persons with disabilities are often stereotyped as asexual (Rousso, 1986). However, even the slowly growing public awareness that disability does not imply a lack of sexual needs or interest has been channeled by gender stereotypes that say sex is more important to men than to women. Much more has been studied and written on the subject of sexuality among disabled men than among disabled women. When the stereotypes about women's "weaker" sexual needs are combined with stereotypes about disability, the results can be ludicrous. Michelle Fine (1991) tells the story of a newly disabled woman who, when she asked her physician whether her disability would preclude a satisfying sex life, was "reassured" that her vagina would be tight enough to satisfy any man!

Statistics indicate that the popular presumption that disabled women are asexual does not protect them from sexual assault. In fact, disabled women may be more likely than other women to be assaulted sexually (Furey, 1994). Children of both sexes are at high risk for sexual abuse if they are disabled because it is often harder for them to get away from an abuser or to communicate to others about what is happening (Randall, Parilla, & Sobsey, 2000).

Gender stereotypes are pervasive, interacting with other stereotypes to shape social perceptions of persons of various races, ages, abilities, and appearances. Gender stereotyping both grows out of and reinforces the social relations between women and men and, as seen in the following section, does so in ways that are both complex and subtle.

THE PROCESS OF STEREOTYPING

Despite the pervasiveness of gender stereotyping, almost everyone can, if given a good reason to do so, summon up example after example of people, personalities, and actions that do not fit the stereotypes. Yet even in the face of counterexamples, the stereotypes persist.

Why do stereotypes persist to such an extent despite lack of support and even countervailing evidence? To answer this question, it is necessary to look beyond the content of specific stereotypes to the process of stereotyping itself. In recent years, psychologists have focused on two approaches in attempts to understand and describe how stereotyping works: information processing and self-fulfilling prophecy.

Stereotypes and Information Processing

Psychologists think of stereotypes not simply as sets of beliefs about specific groups of people but as knowledge structures that guide the way individuals process information: what they notice, what they remember, what kinds of information they seek out, and how they explain and make sense of what they see (D. L. Hamilton, 1979). These knowledge structures, often called *schemas,* act as self-perpetuating channels or filters of information, guiding the individual to pay attention to information that fits the schema or stereotype and to ignore or explain away things that do not fit. Such schemas are useful in that they allow for more efficient handling of the vast amount of information to which most of us are exposed, but inevitably they produce and perpetuate blind spots. Thus, for example, research participants' searching for information to explain an automobile accident of which they are given a vague description can apparently be guided by their schemas for young and elderly men, respectively. Participants told that the driver of the car was an elderly man tended to ask for information about the man's health and eyesight, whereas those told the driver was a young man requested information about whether he was speeding or drinking (Carver & de la Garza, 1984). This example illustrates how stereotypes can perpetuate themselves by orienting the individual toward information that confirms the stereotype and away from information that is irrelevant or disconfirming.

All this processing of information does not necessarily take place at a conscious level. In fact, much stereotyping takes place without either intention or awareness. Stereotyping on the basis of sex (as well as other categories such as age and race) can be activated automatically when an individual is merely exposed to a person, picture of a person, label, or verbal description of a person in a particular gender category. For example, researchers asked college students to decide whether certain occupations (e.g., engineer, secretary) and certain roles (father, sister) could describe the same person (Oakhill, Garnham, & Reynolds, 2005). Respondents more often rejected pairs of terms that went against gender stereotypes (such as electrician-sister or housekeeper-uncle), and even when they accepted such they took longer to do so than for pairs that fit neatly with gender stereotypes (such as receptionist-mother or butcher-aunt). These results persisted even when the researchers warned participants ahead of time that gender stereotypes might influence their responses. The researchers concluded that gender stereotypes about occupations are activated immediately when people are trying to form mental images of the people in those occupations—and that this stereotype-driven information is very difficult to suppress.

Through activation of a stereotype, the information a person has stored about a particular category of person (e.g., African American women) becomes accessible. However, just because a stereotype is *activated* does not mean it will be *applied* (used to perceive or evaluate the person). Indeed, some research shows that, if motivated to do so, people can learn to avoid applying stereotypes, even if the stereotypes are activated (e.g., Macrae, Bodenhausen, & Milne, 1995). It may even be possible, through persistent practice, to inhibit the automatic activation of stereotypes in response to particular categories (Kawakami, Dovidio, Moll, Hermsen, & Russin, 2000). However, in the absence of such practice and of conscious effort, the stereotypes we have learned tend automatically to shape our judgments of others and the way we make sense of information about them.

Women and men whose behavior is at odds with prevailing gender stereotypes are often startled by the apparent inventiveness observers use in linking this behavior to "normal" roles for their sex. For instance, one woman was puzzled to discover that the men at the gym where she was working out with weights in an effort to develop her strength and fitness were convinced that what she was really trying to develop was her bust. And a man who had chosen to stay home with his young daughter while his wife worked outside the home was dismayed one day at the playground to overhear two mothers of other children speculating that the reason he was caring for his daughter was that his wife was dead. Such apparently creative explanations are probably the result of stereotype-guided information processing that makes it difficult or impossible for the observer, without a conscious effort, to use incoming information in ways that are not in accord with preexisting gender stereotypes. Behavior that appears to disconfirm the stereotype, if it is noticed at all, is attributed to external forces (as in the assumption that the man would not be caring for his daughter if his wife were alive) or to internal motives that can be subsumed under the stereotype (as in the assumption that the woman in the gym was striving for sexiness rather than strength). Thus stereotypes guide the individual to interpret information in ways that keep stereotypes intact—even in the face of contradictory evidence.

But not all the evidence *is* contradictory. In fact, social psychologists have begun to show that the cognitive aspects of stereotyping are helped along considerably by a social-behavioral phenomenon known as the *self-fulfilling prophecy.* In many cases, people sense others' expectations of them and, in the interest of smooth interactions, act in such a way as to fulfill those expectations.

Self-Presentation and Self-Fulfilling Prophecy

Male–female differences are more likely to be observed in interactive situations than in less social, individualistic ones (Deaux, 1977; Maccoby, 1990). The explanation for this finding may reside partly in people's sensitivity to the expectations of others. For example, Darley and Fazio (1980) described the way social interaction might result in behavior that confirms the expectations of the participants: The perceiver holds a particular expectation for the target person's behavior and acts in accordance with that expectation, the target person interprets the perceiver's actions and responds accordingly, and the perceiver uses the target's response to confirm or reevaluate the original expectation. If the target's action is very discrepant from the original perception, the perceiver may attribute it to situational constraints or may even end the interaction to avoid taking in information that is counter to expectations.

Thus the implicit pressure on the target to play out the expected role is very strong; failure to do so may result in "bungled" or strained interaction. Moreover, if there is a motivation to be liked or approved of by the other participant, there are even stronger reasons to conform to that person's expectations. Women present themselves in a more or less stereotypically feminine manner depending on how they think a male job interviewer or potential date with whom they are interacting views women (von Baeyer, Sherk, & Zanna, 1981; Zanna & Pack, 1975). Similarly, Fried and Major (1980) found that males adjusted the way they presented themselves according to what they believed an attractive female partner would prefer.

Other aspects of the situation may also affect the likelihood of a self-fulfilling prophecy: the strength of the social desirability cues provided by the situation in which the interaction takes place, whether the situation is public or private, the target person's concern with looking good or with being true to her- or himself, the strength and certainty of the perceiver's expectation, and the power of the perceiver over the target (Deaux & Major, 1987).

A good demonstration of the way people adopt gender-role behaviors in response to the implied expectations of others was provided in laboratory research by Berna Skrypnek and Mark Snyder (1982). They asked individual male research participants to divide a series of tasks between themselves and a partner. The partners were located in separate rooms and communicated only by means of a signal system. In each case, the hidden partner was a woman, but some of the men were led to believe that their partner was male. The men who thought that their partner was female divided the tasks in a more gender-stereotyped way than those who thought the partner was male. Moreover, when the female partners, unaware of what the men had been told about them, were subsequently given the opportunity to choose tasks, they themselves chose more feminine-stereotyped tasks when paired with a man who had been expecting a female partner. All of this happened without the participants ever seeing or talking to each other.

A factor that may play a large part in the expectation-confirmation sequences for gender roles is physical appearance (Deaux, 1984). A person's appearance is a powerful influence on the initial impressions and expectations that others form of her or him. Thus a person who looks the part of the masculine stereotype—tall, strong, sturdy, broad shouldered—may, before having done or said anything, be the object of a set of perceiver expectations for masculine role behavior and may find himself falling into step with them. Indeed, big, strong-looking men and petite, fragile-looking women may have more trouble than anyone else in trying to break out of the confines of gender-role expectations.

Overview　　The process of stereotyping

Information Processing

Incoming information about a particular category of person (e.g., Latina women) is organized into a schema. When the person encounters someone in this category, this schema is activated automatically, shaping the way information about this new person is processed (e.g., if "family oriented" is part of the schema, the person will tend to notice and remember the family-oriented qualities of this woman). If the person does not want to make stereotyped judgments, she or he must make a conscious effort not to apply the stereotype.

Self-Fulfilling Prophecy

A person has a set of beliefs about a certain category of individuals (e.g., Asian American men). When this person meets a new person in this category, she or he behaves in a way that elicits the expected behavior from that person. For example, if the person expects Asian American men to be quiet and shy, he or she may not try very hard to converse with him, thus sending him signals that he is expected to be quiet. Because the person presents the Asian American man with few opportunities to talk, he will probably behave as expected, thus fulfilling expectations and confirming the stereotype.

HOW GENDER STEREOTYPES AND PREJUDICE AFFECT US

Women university students report experiencing nearly twice as many sexist events (directed against themselves or against women in general) as do their male counterparts (Swim, Cohen, & Hyers, 1998; Swim, Hyers, Cohen, & Ferguson, 2001). For both women and men, sexist events are most likely to involve sexist comments about gender roles and stereotypes, such as remarks about women's or men's lack of ability in particular areas, remarks about supposedly characteristic traits (such as weakness or passivity for women, insensitivity or aggressiveness for men), or assertions that women or men should restrict themselves to certain arenas (e.g., that women should stay at home or should not go into politics or that men should not interfere in women's affairs). The second most likely category of sexist event involved derogatory comments or behavior (e.g., sexist name-calling or insults, sexist jokes, and exclusion from conversation or activities based on gender). Least frequent, but still experienced almost twice a week on average by women (and far less frequently by men), were experiences of sexual objectification: offensive comments about one's body parts or clothes, street harassment, references to or threats of sexual acts, unwanted flirting, staring, or touching. For both women and men the experience of sexist incidents was related to feeling angry, anxious, and depressed and to reporting lower social self-esteem.

In general, do people notice and react to these sexist events? Do they feel angry and make judgments about the perpetrators, or do they simply shrug off the experience? There is no research on men's reactions, but it appears that women are not complacent about such events, even if they do not respond publicly to them. Janet Swim and Lauri Hyers (1999) brought participants to their lab to work with others on a task that required group discussion and decision making. During the discussion, male confederates of the researchers made several scripted comments that were sexist. The researchers monitored the female participants' public responses to these comments, administered a measure of self-esteem, and also asked the women to review a tape of the session later and record their feelings. Whether or not the women made a public response to the remarks, most women found the sexist remarks objectionable, viewed the person making the remark as prejudiced, and felt anger toward him. In addition, women who held traditional gender-role attitudes showed lower self-esteem after hearing sexist remarks than after hearing similar remarks that were not sexist.

As for responding publicly, women were cautious. Although most women (81%) in a simulated version of the study (in which they imagined themselves in the situation rather than actually being exposed to the situation) said that they would confront the person making sexist remarks, in the actual study only 45% did so, as seen in Table 1.5. Women who were the only members of their gender in the group and who held a committed, activist stance toward resisting sexism were most likely to confront the speaker. When confronting the speaker, women were most likely to use less risky, more polite strategies such as questioning the response (e.g., "What did you just say?!") than direct comments (e.g., "You can't pick someone for that reason") or exclamations (e.g., "I can't believe you said that!").

The results of this research suggest that women's caution about responding publicly to sexist events may not be justified. Most of the women found the comments objectionable, and it is likely that anyone who spoke up to object would not be viewed as impolite and would be supported by other women in the group. Confrontation serves the potentially valuable purpose of raising awareness that certain kinds of behavior are not acceptable. As the researchers point out, a person who sees that others do not tolerate sexist behavior may well become less tolerant of that behavior too and perhaps more likely to confront it.

Confrontation takes a lot of energy, however, and research shows that members of groups who are targets of stereotypes and prejudice often prefer simply to avoid situations in which they think they will be exposed to such attitudes. Thus women may choose to avoid taking classes from a professor who holds the reputation of being sexist or may steer away from career or academic paths, such as engineering, in which women form a small minority. Women who are "solos" (the only women in the group) are more likely than nonsolos to want to change groups or to change the gender composition of the group unless they

Table 1.5   The difference between what women actually do and what they think they would do in response to a sexist remark by a male group member: Comparison between actual and anticipated public responses.

Response	Percentage Who Actually Gave the Response (Study 1) (N = 44)	Percentage Who Anticipated Definitely Giving a Response (Study 2) (N = 109)
No response		
1. Ignore the comment[a]	55	1
2. Wait to see what others do	55	4
Confrontational responses		
3. Question the response	25	47
4. Task-related response	20	22
5. Comment on inappropriateness	16	48
6. Sarcasm or humor	16	37
7. Surprise exclamation	16	40
8. Grumbling	2	10
9. Hit or punch	0	8
Gave at least one confrontational response	45	81

[a]Whether the lack of responses was a result of ignoring the comment and waiting to see what others would do was not differentiated in Study 1.

Source: From Swim & Hyers (1999, p. 82).

have high confidence in their performance ability. If they do have high confidence, it seems to help them deal with the expectation of being stereotyped—perhaps by anticipating that they will perform well enough to disconfirm the stereotype (L. L. Cohen & Swim, 1995).

What effect does it have on a person to be in a situation in which he or she has to perform well but stereotypes about the group suggest that the person will perform poorly? Chances are that the person's performance will suffer. In a series of studies researchers have shown that **stereotype threat,** an individual's awareness that he or she may be judged by or may fulfill negative stereotypes about her or his gender or ethnic group, can have a dramatic negative effect on performance. In one study, women and men who had demonstrated high math ability were brought to the lab to complete a difficult math test. In one condition, participants were told that the test was one on which gender differences in performance usually appeared. In a second condition, the test was described as not producing gender differences. When the test was described as likely to produce gender differences—that is, when stereotype threat was high—the women performed substantially worse than the men did. However, when participants were led to expect *no* gender differences, women performed at the same level as men. This occurred even though both conditions used the same math test (Spencer, Steele, & Quinn, 1999). Even White men, who generally do not contend with a stereotype that they cannot do math, can be made vulnerable to stereotype threat by putting them in a situation in which they are made aware of the stereotype that Asian students are better at math than White students are. A group of White college men were brought to the lab and randomly assigned to conditions in which they either were or were not exposed to a packet of materials about the high math performance of Asian students and told that the study was an effort to understand why Asians tend to outperform other students on tests of math ability. When later given a math test, men who had been exposed to the stereotype (stereotype-threatened men) performed significantly worse than men who had not been exposed to the stereotype threat (Aronson et al., 1999). Men can also experience stereotype threat when performing feminine-stereotyped tasks. In one study, men performed worse on a test when they believed it measured the "feminine" quality of social sensitivity than when they believed it measured information processing (Keonig & Eagly, 2005).

The various stereotypes about femininity tend to clump together to form a coherent picture. Thus, mere exposure to *some aspect* of the feminine stereotype rather than a direct reminder of the specific notion that women are not competent in math will produce the impact of stereotype threat on math performance. One group of researchers (Davies, Spencer, Quinn, & Gerhardstein, 2002) showed students one of two 3-minute sets of actual television commercials. Both sets included four neutral commercials that did not depict any people or advertise any gender-stereotypic products. However, one set (the stereotypic set) also contained two commercials that displayed women in stereotypic ways: One showed a woman overjoyed about a new acne medication, and the other portrayed a woman wild with anticipation at the prospect of trying a new brownie mix. The other set (the counterstereotypic set) instead included one commercial in which an attractive woman demonstrated her knowledge of automotive engineering to an admiring man, and the other showed a woman discussing health care issues in an intelligent manner. Women exposed to the stereotypic commercials later performed more poorly on math problems than did men in either condition or women exposed to the counterstereotypic ads—even though neither set of commercials made any mention of women's competence in math. It appears that media reminders of the feminine stereotype can undermine women's performance even in areas not directly addressed by such media portrayals. The same researchers also demonstrated that women exposed to the stereotypic commercials were more likely than other women or than men to avoid math problems in favor of less-threatening verbal problems and to indicate lower preference for pursuing educational or vocational interests related to quantitative skills.

Clearly, stereotypes have real consequences with respect to performance. Researchers have argued that they also have consequences for life choices. It is painful to be in a perpetual battle with negative stereotypes, to be faced continuously with evaluative threat as one attempts to perform well. Under such conditions, as just illustrated, people show a tendency to disengage or "disidentify" with the domain in which the stereotype occurs—to move away from that domain as a basis for identity or self-esteem (Major, Spencer, Schmader, Wolfe, & Crocker, 1998; Steele, 1997). For example, women may stop taking math classes and decide that math is unimportant or boring, thus removing themselves from arenas in which they can be judged on their math performance. In doing so, they may inadvertently reinforce the stereotype. Similarly, men may shy away from situations that they perceive require interpersonal sensitivity—thus inadvertently reinforcing the stereotype of male incompetence in this arena.

GENDER STEREOTYPES
AND THE RESEARCH PROCESS

Researchers who study gender have not been immune to the effects of stereotypes. In an early article on "the fantasy life of the male psychologist," Naomi Weisstein (1971) sounded a stinging challenge for scholars interested in discovering the truth about human behavior to examine their own discipline for sexism. In a few pungent pages, she produced example after glaring example of cases in which researchers had accepted without question the notion that observed male–female differences in behavior were the inevitable result of natural, inborn differences in inclination or temperament. She railed against what she saw as the general failure of psychologists to consider the social context as an important contributor to gender differences and against the tendency to consider "natural" or "normal" any behavior that fit easily into gender stereotypes. Her analysis pointed to a conclusion with which all students of behavior should still be concerned: It is all too easy to be uncritical of research questions, findings, and interpretations that fit one's own preconceptions.

The history of psychology shows that it has indeed been far too easy to frame research questions and to interpret findings in ways that are consistent with gender stereotypes. For instance, at one period a vast amount of research energy was expended to study the possible existence of a "maternal instinct" in women, whereas the possibility of a "paternal instinct" in men was ignored. Countless studies of achievement motivation were carried out on boys and men before anyone thought of seriously studying it in women. Perhaps the most clear-cut example of the biasing effects of gender stereotypes on the research process can be found in the history of psychology's attempts to measure femininity and masculinity.

Psychology and the Measurement of Masculinity
and Femininity: A Comedy of Errors

The field of psychology, along with the larger culture, has held historically to the implicit assumption that adherence to gender stereotypes is normal and desirable: that women should be feminine and men masculine. This assumption has shaped psychological conceptions of masculinity-femininity (M-F) and attempts to measure it. In particular, it has until recently trapped psychologists in the idea that masculinity and femininity must be thought of as opposing poles of a single dimension.

The notion that such apparently intangible concepts as masculinity and femininity could be measured first became prominent through the work of Lewis Terman and his one-time student and colleague, Catherine Cox Miles. Convinced that the "real" mental differences between the sexes were in nonintellectual mental traits, they created the 456-item Attitude Interest Analysis Survey (AIAS; Terman & Miles, 1936) to measure the differences. This test and its authors' attempts to validate it are described at length by Miriam Lewin (1984), and the following discussion owes much to her account.

The AIAS, like most of the tests that followed it, was based not on coherent theories about the "essence" of masculinity or femininity but on statistically typical gender differences in the way respondents answered particular questions. Large numbers of items were given to a sample of junior high and high school students. Items on which girls and boys tended, on average, to answer differently were included in the test; those that showed no gender differences were dropped. In its final form, the test consisted of items for which the typical male and female were expected to choose different response alternatives. People taking the test received Femininity (F) points for all answers corresponding to the typical female choice and Masculinity (M) points for all answers corresponding to the typical male choice. To obtain the total M-F score, the F score was subtracted from the M score.

It is interesting to note the kinds of answers that produced high femininity and masculinity scores, respectively, using this method. On the information subtest, Femininity points were achieved through ignorance, such as indicating that Goliath was killed by Cain or that the earth turns once on its axis every 12 hours. Masculinity points were gained by giving the correct answers. On the emotional and ethical attitudes subtest, femininity was associated with greater anger at seeing others treated unfairly; masculinity was connected with anger at "being disturbed when you want to work." On forced-choice items, boys indicated they preferred to "command others" and to do "uninteresting work with a large income," whereas girls preferred to "persuade others" and do "interesting work with a small income"—so Masculinity points were assigned to the former and Femininity points to the latter. Femininity points were also achieved by indicating a dislike for "people with loud voices," "argumentative people," and "bald-headed men" or a liking for "very forgiving people," "washing dishes," and "being alone." Masculinity points were given for reporting a dislike of "tall women," "mannish women," "thin women," or "women cleverer than you." In retrospect, it is quite clear that the items included in the test, based as they were on gender differences in the self-reports of American junior high and high school students, simply reflected the gender stereotypes of a particular group in a particular time and place. What self-respecting junior high school girl of that era, knowing full well how ladies were supposed to behave, would admit, for example, that she liked to "command others"? What young boy could face his peers after an admission that he liked women cleverer than himself? The meanings assigned to femininity and masculinity using this test, then, are not at all universal but reflect a particularly American (White? Judeo-Christian? middle-class? urban?) pre–World War II set of biases. Had a similar test been developed using a sample of rural Mexican adolescents or of elderly Chinese office workers, the items associated with masculinity and femininity might have been quite different.

Terman and Miles found masculinity-femininity ratings to be less reliable (that is, less stable from one administration of the test to another) than those of almost any other personality trait. Moreover, they were unable to show that their test scores correlated with any other criteria of masculinity and femininity. For example, in keeping with the then prevalent assumption that feminine women were weak and masculine men were strong, the researchers correlated masculinity-femininity scores on the AIAS with the self-rated health ("robust" to "frail") of 533 adults. The robust men scored as slightly less masculine than the others, and the frail women were not conclusively more feminine. Other research was equally discouraging. The idea that a highly masculine husband and a highly feminine wife should make the happiest couple was tested and found wanting. Ratings of a person's attractiveness to or interest in the other sex showed no relationship with M-F scores. The researchers were undaunted, however, because they believed basing the test on observed gender differences in their original sample had ensured it was a valid test of masculinity and femininity. Their confidence in the test was not shaken even by the discovery that both women and men were very good at faking their scores to make themselves look masculine or feminine when instructed to do so.

Terman and Miles were not the only psychologists to become mired in imprecision while trying to define and measure M-F. Constantinople (1973), reviewing the literature on M-F measurement, searched in vain for a definition of the two terms that went beyond the idea of "whatever distinguishes males from females." Lewin (1984) described the series of erroneous assumptions of the AIAS and most subsequent M-F tests up to the 1970s. Among these are the notion that M-F is a static trait that does not change from an early age (hence the use of schoolchildren as a criterion group for developing the test), the idea that homosexual men and feminine women will give equivalent responses (the femininity dimension of the M-F scale of the well-known MMPI personality test was "validated" on 13 gay men!), and the belief that the gender norms of mid–20th-century America were universal and fixed rather than linked to changing social, economic, and political conditions.

Researchers currently developing or working with measures of femininity and masculinity are less likely to make these assumptions. In fact, they tend to view such tests not so much as measures of fixed personality traits but as indicators of gender-relevant aspects of a person's self-concept or of the degree to which a person's self-image conforms to gender-role stereotypes (Lewin, 1984). Their approach has changed in another way: They have abandoned the assumption that femininity and masculinity are at opposing ends of the same continuum and have accepted androgyny as a healthy option.

Androgyny

Earlier, we noted the tradition of considering the sexes as opposites—of conceptualizing masculinity and femininity as extreme poles of the same dimension. Researchers developing measures of femininity and masculinity adopted this assumption without questioning it and designed tests to accommodate it. By definition, then, a low masculinity score automatically meant high femininity and vice versa. But there is another tradition in human thinking about sex and gender: the idea that femininity and masculinity are two complementary halves of a single whole, each one needed to complete the other. According to this tradition, not only do women and men need each other but each individual can achieve wholeness only by developing both the feminine and the masculine aspects of her- or himself. This notion is a basic aspect of the ancient Chinese philosophy of Taoism, in which the male and female principles, yin and yang, are thought to be the archetypal poles of nature.

Many myths of the origin of the sexes contain elements of this tradition: the biblical account of the creation of Eve from Adam's rib, the Hindu myth of the separation of the Supreme Self into male and female, and Plato's story of Zeus's decision to cut all beings in two. Much mythology and literature contains themes of striving to reunite the two halves—male and female—into a being or state of androgyny (see C. Heilbrun, 1973, for an overview of this literature). **Androgyny** (deriving from the union of the Greek terms *andro* for "man" and *gyne* for "woman") refers to the psychological merging of the masculine and feminine principles. An androgynous person, by this definition, is one who has reconciled femininity and masculinity within her- or himself, one who has both feminine and masculine qualities.

An examination of the procedures used to score traditional M-F tests is sufficient to show that if there is such a thing as an androgynous person these tests could not identify that person. An androgynous individual would have substantial feminine *and* masculine qualities and so should score high on both masculinity and femininity on an M-F test. But the design of these tests makes such a score impossible: One cannot score high on femininity without scoring low on masculinity, and vice versa. An androgynous person would end up looking like a zero on an M-F test—as someone who was neither like men nor like women—instead of looking like someone who is like *both* men and women.

Psychologist Sandra Bem was the first to design a test that would allow an individual to score as androgynous. The Bem Sex Role Inventory (BSRI; Bem, 1974) treats femininity and masculinity as two separate, independent dimensions. A respondent can score high on both, low on both, or high on one and low on the other. This change was significant, not just for conceptual reasons but because masculinity and femininity are such highly charged concepts. On the BSRI, a male who admits to some feminine qualities need not fear for his masculinity score, for instance, and people of both sexes who show a mixture of "feminine" and "masculine" traits are classified as androgynous, not maladjusted or deviant.

Besides its treatment of femininity and masculinity as two separate dimensions, the BSRI also differs from traditional M-F tests in another way. Items for the masculinity and femininity scales were developed not by using the old approach of picking the items on which males and females answered differently but by picking the items that a pool of male and female respondents rated as most desirable "for an American man or woman." Twenty items rated as highly desirable for men were selected for the masculinity scale, and 20 items rated highly desirable for women formed the femininity scale. Another 20 neutral items were chosen for the social desirability scale. People taking the test are asked to indicate on a 7-point scale how well each of the adjectives describes them. Based on their responses, they can be classified in one of four ways: Masculine (high on masculinity, low on femininity), Feminine (high on femininity, low on masculinity), Androgynous (high on both femininity and masculinity), or Undifferentiated (low on both femininity and masculinity). Using the test with samples of California college students, Bem found that about one-third of the subjects scored as "sex-typed" (Feminine females and Masculine males), one-third scored as Androgynous, and fewer than 10% scored as "cross–sex-typed" (Masculine females and Feminine males). Other researchers have also developed scales that allow for the measurement of psychological androgyny, such as the Personal Attributes Questionnaire (Spence et al., 1974) and the PRF Andro scale (Berzins, Welling, & Wetter, 1975). Like the original Terman and Miles (1936) scale, all of these scales reflect the particular biases of the samples (usually middle-class American college students) on which they were developed.

Abandoning the notion that femininity and masculinity were two ends of a bipolar continuum and incorporating the idea of androgyny into psychological tests of gender have been important steps, but they have not solved the problems inherent in trying to measure masculinity and femininity. Several issues in designing the tests remain unresolved: the assumption that femininity and masculinity are unidimensional constructs rather than constellations of several dimensions, the difficulty of scaling the test items so that each one is "worth" the same amount of masculinity or femininity, and the problem of sex specificity— the possibility that a given item may count more heavily toward self-perceived femininity or masculinity for one sex than for the other (Colwill & Lips, 1978).

Underlying all these problems is one major theme: Psychologists are still not sure what they are trying to measure. A major limitation of the notion of androgyny is that it is based on the combination of masculinity and femininity, and it forces attention to these concepts and to the stereotypes on which they are based. In a way, then, it tends to "reproduce precisely the gender polarization that it seeks to undercut" (Bem, 1993, p. 125). Masculinity and femininity are still defined only as the two sets of qualities that distinguish males from females, and since these distinctions vary a great deal across time and place, trying to devise standard criteria with which to assess them appears to be a hopeless task. People's perceptions of masculinity and femininity appear to be far more complex than implied by the collection of items on these scales. When ordinary people are asked to describe what femininity or masculinity

Traditional Tests	*Modern Tests*
Femininity and masculinity were conceptualized as opposite ends of a single continuum. A high femininity score implied a low masculinity score.	Femininity and masculinity are conceptualized as separate, independent dimensions. Thus an individual can obtain a score that is both highly feminine and highly masculine. This allows for an individual to be categorized as androgynous.
Femininity and masculinity were defined according to the differences in the responses typically given by females and males.	Femininity and masculinity are defined as the degree to which an individual's self-description matches a set of traits categorized as typical or desirable for women or men.

means to them, their answers bear little resemblance to the items on the most widely used psychological tests (Lippa, 2005; Lips, 1986; Myers & Gonda, 1982). Psychologists are left with a dilemma: On one hand, masculinity and femininity are such slippery concepts that it seems fruitless to waste any more time trying to measure them; on the other hand, it is clear that they are experienced by people as important concepts against which to measure themselves and others. Popular conceptions of femininity and masculinity are complex and multidimensional and probably cannot be represented adequately by single scores on a personality test.

Disarming the Stereotypes: Approaches to Empowerment

Approaches to gender in psychology over the last 25 years have often rested on the desire to free people from the constraints of stereotypes based on biological sex. The freedom to be or behave in a particular way without worrying about whether one is being "appropriately masculine" or "feminine enough" allows individuals to seek out their own strengths, to use their energy where it will do the most good. Making gender stereotypes less rigid and inclusive of fewer aspects of behavior should be empowering for both women and men—increasing their sense of effectiveness and self-actualization and reducing the number of situations in which individuals experience stereotype threat. The process should also unleash new sources of human energy for societies, adding to a collective sense of power and accomplishment. Finally, by removing the justification for segregation of society's institutions and occupations by sex, dismantling gender stereotypes may ultimately help to reduce the power imbalance between women and men and foster an era of greater equality.

Are the approaches to gender in psychology really having this empowering effect? The answer is controversial, and you must judge this for yourself at the end of this book. Many people have argued that the concept of psychological androgyny, although initially liberating, became simply another prescription against which people must measure themselves. Now people can feel inadequate not only because they are not masculine enough or feminine enough but also because they are not androgynous enough. Even more serious, because androgyny is built on the concepts of femininity and masculinity, it continues to impart a sense that these are real entities rather than cultural constructions, and it can never transcend them. Androgyny pushed back the limitations imposed by a bipolar conception of masculinity-femininity, but it contains its own built-in limitations.

Sandra Bem (1993) has more recently argued that, as children are enculturated with the notion of a gender-polarized world, they are absorbing cultural messages not only about difference but about power. It is no simple matter to dismantle gender stereotypes when those stereotypes help to define the way power and status are arranged in a society. Her analysis suggests, however, that the connection between gender stereotypes and power is exactly the reason that disarming those stereotypes is empowering—especially for women.

SUMMARY

Labeling an individual as female or male has a powerful impact on others' perceptions of and reactions to that individual. Stereotypically, we expect different behaviors, personal qualities, and physical appearance from women and men. When we categorize people by sex (their biological femaleness or maleness), we tend to assume that we have also categorized them according to the set of cultural expectations for femininity and masculinity, although on many dimensions there is no necessary relationship between biological sex and cultural expectations for women and men.

Our conceptions of femininity and masculinity are framed in the language of opposites. Men are thought to be task oriented and independent; women to be relationship oriented and affiliative. Such gender stereotypes are more than just a random collection of groundless beliefs about women and men. Rather, they represent cultural constructions of femininity and masculinity, sometimes based tenuously on physical differences, that serve as underpinnings for the social relations between women and men as groups and as individuals. However, human beings have often failed, and still do, to recognize the extent to which gender stereotypes are products of the social context in which they exist, how resistant they are to disconfirmation, and how easily they can act as self-fulfilling prophecies. We react negatively to individuals who violate the stereotypes, as if they were acting in an "unnatural" way when, in fact, they are simply violating *cultural norms*. Individuals who, in defiance of cultural expectations, move into domains that are thought to be the province of the other gender can find themselves suffering from the performance decrements and disengagement that accompany stereotype threat.

The history of attempts by psychologists to measure femininity and masculinity reveals all too clearly that psychology as a discipline has not been exempt from gender stereotyping or from the mistaken belief that observed differences between the sexes automatically represent the natural state of affairs.

Psychologists used the concept of androgyny in an effort to deal with issues of masculinity and femininity without invoking the stereotypic notion of "opposite sexes." These attempts were only partially successful, but they provided a framework for new thinking about sex and gender.

This book revolves around three central questions: What do we know and not know about gender similarities and differences? Where does that knowledge come from? How is that knowledge itself shaped and limited by cultural perceptions of femininity and masculinity? Cultural perceptions of femininity and masculinity have been the main focus of this chapter. What should be clear at this point is just how strongly our expectations about women and men are shaped by our culture—and how significantly those expectations affect what we *observe* about gender similarities and differences. We will explore this theme further in the next chapter as we examine the ways scientific theories about sex and gender have gained and lost favor in conjunction with popular attitudes about women and men.

KEY TERMS

sex stereotypes
sex
gender
descriptive stereotypes
prescriptive stereotypes
instrumentality
expressiveness

prototypical traits
components of gender
  stereotypes
prejudice
sexism
hostile sexism
benevolent sexism

modern sexism
neosexism
diversity-mindfulness
stereotype threat
androgyny

Theoretical Perspectives on Sex and Gender

*D*uring the latter part of the 19th century, the idea flourished that educating women in the same way as men was dangerous and damaging. The danger supposedly arose from the energy needs of women's reproductive processes: menstruation and preparation for child-bearing. Physicians theorized that the womb exercised a dominating influence over a woman's personality and ability, almost as if the "Almighty, in creating the female sex, had taken the uterus and built a woman around it" (physician quoted in Smith-Rosenberg & Rosenberg, 1976, p. 56). Women who, during puberty, used up too much precious energy on the brain function required for advanced education would enfeeble their bodies, ruining their health and crippling their capacity to bear children. These dire warnings, sounded most prominently by Dr. Edward Clarke (1873), were based on a theory of thermo-dynamics: All physical systems, including the human body, followed the principle of conservation of energy, so that force expended in one function would be unavailable to any other. Men, whose passage into puberty supposedly did not place such a heavy strain on their bodies, could safely turn their energies to demanding intellectual tasks without endangering their physical well-being.

It is clear that ideas about sex and gender have had an impact on popular and scientific views of women and men. How have such ideas shaped what people have noticed and ignored about female and male behavior? In this chapter, we examine the theories that have influenced both research and popular thought about what women and men are—and are supposed to be—like. In particular, we ask these questions:

- What were the earliest theories about sex and gender?
- How have psychoanalytic/identification theories shaped our thinking about how and why girls and boys grow up the way they do?
- How have gender theorists worked notions about social structure and culture into their ideas about women and men?
- What about evolution? Are women and men biologically programmed to behave differently? How might culture and biology interact to produce female–male differences in behavior?
- What role does learning play in the development of gender roles?
- How does a child's cognitive development and maturity affect her or his ideas and behavior with respect to gender?
- When theorists put ideas about learning and cognitive development together, what theories about gender emerge?
- What social interaction processes seem to maintain continuity in gender-related behavior?
- Should theories about gender be focusing on female–male differences or similarities?

EARLY THEORIES ABOUT SEX AND GENDER

In the history of the study of sex and gender, the role played by theory has been substantial. But what exactly is a theory? Basically, a **theory** is a set of ideas about how and why things happen. In the realm of science, the role of a theory is to guide research: to generate hypotheses (propositions) that can be tested against observed reality. For example, if one subscribed to the theory already mentioned that women's personality is dominated by the uterus, one should be able to think of some testable hypotheses—things that should occur if the theory were true and should not occur if it were false—and then test them. Such testing might involve comparing women who had borne children with those who had not or comparing groups of same-age women who had or had not undergone hysterectomies.

It is easy to see how the acceptance of a particular theory can have a major impact on the kind of research that gets done: what questions are asked, what issues are investigated or ignored, what findings are considered important or trivial. It is also easy to see that a theory that did not lend itself to being checked against reality in some way might linger in people's imagination for a long time without being either proven or disproved and laid to rest, particularly if it had some popular appeal. A requirement for a good and useful theory, then, is that it can be tested.

The history of the study of sex and gender provides many examples of a problem that always besets the scientific process: Theories that fit well with the accepted assumptions at a particular time and place tend to receive a lot of attention and generate research, whereas those that seem to be at odds with accepted notions are frequently ignored. Indeed, we scientists are such creatures of our culture that our theories often incorporate as presuppositions untested aspects of the "conventional wisdom" of our time and place. For example, the basic cultural notion that men are intellectually superior to women was frequently accepted as a given by psychologists, who then set out to construct theories to explain *why* this was so. In the words of the eminent psychologist William James (1890), "It is astonishing what havoc is wrought in psychology by admitting at the outset apparently innocent suppositions that nevertheless contain a flaw" (p. 224).

Before anyone had ever heard of psychology, theories about gender were being offered by the early philosophers. Within these early theories lies an idea that influenced psychologists for years afterward—woman as incomplete man.

The idea of equality between the sexes can be found in the early writings of the Greek philosopher Plato, who described women and men as having the same nature and worth and deserving the same education and legal treatment. This idea fades out in his later writings, however, in which female weakness and inferiority are used as justification for assigning different social roles to men and women (Dickason, 1976). Later, in the writings of Aristotle, the idea of feminine inferiority and "incompleteness" was developed in detail. Aristotle claimed that the female state was an "ordinary" deformity and that a woman was, in some respects, a defective man (Whitbeck, 1976). Female inferiority lay in the fact that women supposedly had less "soul heat" than men and so could not process their menstrual blood to what he deemed the "final stage," semen. Women's inability to produce semen meant that they could contribute nothing but formative material to the embryo in the process of conception and that they made no genetic contribution to its distinctive character.

The Aristotelian notion that women were inferior because of a shortage of intrinsic heat received a later expression in the work of Juan Huarte, a 16th-century Spanish writer expounding on individual intellectual differences. He argued that the testicles were responsible for maintaining the "heat and dryness" characteristic of the male principle. Since "dryness of spirit" was necessary for intelligence and since the testicles maintained this quality, obviously men, who had testicles, were more intelligent than women, who did not (S. A. Shields, 1975).

Theories that viewed women as lesser beings than men—because of their inability to produce enough heat to process body fluids into semen—did not view women as *opposites* to men. Women and men were thought to be similar but differently developed. In fact, proponents of these theories often argued that women and men had similar bodies: There were many early medical references, for instance, to the male uterus, to female testicles, and to the "fact" that the female reproductive organs were the same as the male's—only "inside out," with the scrotum equivalent to the uterus, the penis to the cervix and vagina (Laqueur, 1990). Thomas Laqueur quotes a bit of popular verse from the early 19th century:

> . . . though they of different sexes be,
> Yet on the whole they are the same as we,
> For those that have the strictest searchers been,
> Find women are but men turned outside in. (p. 4)

The second-century anatomist Galen used the simile of the eyes of a mole to describe female genitalia. As he explained it, the eyes of the mole appear the same as those of other animals, except that they do not open and thus do not allow the animal to see. The mole's eyes remain closed, as if the animal were still in the uterus. Similarly, the female's genitalia remain unopened and undeveloped after birth, as if still in the womb, whereas the male's project outward and develop fully (Laqueur, 1990).

The "woman as defective man" motif affected theories of gender inside and outside the field of psychology for centuries, appearing in the writings of men from Thomas Aquinas to Sigmund Freud. The strength of the idea is not surprising, given that these theorists, encountering women mainly in subordinate positions, developed their theories to explain and justify what seemed to them a natural and inevitable situation. However, by the 19th century, the hierarchical approach to male–female differences had been supplanted to some extent by the "opposites" approach, an approach that treated the two sexes as irreconcilably different. Echoes of both approaches can be found in psychological theories of gender.

Seven general types of theories have emerged in the field of psychology to explain the differences and similarities between human males and females. Psychoanalytic/identification theories focus on personality development. Social structural theories concern social structures and culture, concentrating on how intergroup relations between women and men are linked to gender roles and stereotypes. Evolutionary theories attempt to explain gender issues with reference to the evolution of the human species. Biosocial theory focuses on how the physical attributes of women and men interact with the social contexts in which they live. All of these theoretical approaches put a heavy emphasis on the origins of gender, focusing on *why* the sexes may differ. The next three approaches—social learning, cognitive development, and social interaction process theories—focus more heavily on *how* gender differences occur, stressing the processes through which males and females may be led to adopt different or similar ways of behaving.

PSYCHOANALYTIC/IDENTIFICATION THEORIES

Sigmund Freud

Sigmund Freud, an Austrian physician whose work spanned the late 19th and early 20th centuries, was the father of **psychoanalytic theory,** perhaps the first theory of human personality to assign a central role to sexuality. His writings and the controversies they have generated fill volumes and have had a profound impact on ideas about male–female differences. Reaction to his work on gender has ranged from assertions that he has done more than anyone else to set back the cause of women to praise for his brilliant analysis of a patriarchal society.

Freud's theory was predicated on the idea that the human mind, like an iceberg that floats with only a small tip showing above the surface of the water, is only partially available to our awareness. The part of the mind available to awareness, referred to as the region of **consciousness,** contains the thoughts and feelings people know they have. The much larger part, the **unconscious,** contains the unacceptable urges, passions, ideas, and feelings that people cannot acknowledge. This notion of the unconscious arose from Freud's experience in trying to explain and treat symptoms for which there was no discernible physical cause. Many of his patients were women who, although there was nothing physically wrong with them, exhibited symptoms such as paralysis and shortness of breath—symptoms that usually led to a diagnosis of hysteria. Freud came to believe that the symptoms were not meaningless; rather, they were expressions of feelings that the women could not acknowledge any other way. Thus a woman might develop these symptoms instead of becoming aware of the unacceptable deep anger and resentment she felt over having to care for her dying father (L. C. Bell, 2004).

The contents of the unconscious can be explored only indirectly through dreams, free association, symptoms, mistakes (now sometimes called "Freudian slips"), or other "leaks" of the unconscious into conscious awareness. The unconscious was the cornerstone of Freudian theory, for he felt that the motives hidden in the unconscious are often the driving force behind conscious thoughts and deeds. The notion of the unconscious is also what makes this theory difficult to verify or disprove, however, because, by definition, the contents of the unconscious cannot be investigated with traditional objective methods for assessing people's thoughts and feelings.

Freud proposed that the personality is composed of three structures—id, ego, and superego—and that a person's behavior is produced by the interaction among these systems (Freud, 1924/1960). In his theory, the **id,** consisting of the individual's biological heritage, including sexual and aggressive instincts, provides a reservoir of psychic energy that powers the other two systems. A nonrational system, it operates strictly on the pleasure principle: Uncomfortable tension must be discharged and needs must be satisfied. The **ego** is a rational system that works on the reality principle: Discharge of tension or satisfaction of needs should be prevented until an appropriate situation is found. This second system handles transactions between an individual's subjective needs and the objective world of reality, helping to keep the individual out of trouble and ensure survival. Finally, the **superego** acts as the moral aspect of the personality, striving for perfection rather than pleasure and persuading the ego to substitute moralistic goals for realistic ones. The superego, also nonrational, was described by Freud as the internal representative of society's values and ideals as taught to the child by parents and enforced by rewards and punishments. The three systems should be balanced in an individual's personality, and domination of the personality by one of them can cause problems. A very strong id, combined with a weak ego and superego, creates a person who is impulsive, hedonistic, and unfettered by the demands of conscience; an overdeveloped superego produces one who is inhibited from most forms of self-expression by the crippling fear of imperfection.

Freud did not view gender as developing automatically but rather as a response to early interactions with caretakers. He argued that personality development, and especially gender development, were importantly influenced by the body and by sexuality. As Leslie Bell (2004) explains it, "The earliest physical and sensual handling and tending of the infant are the first ways the baby comes to know him- or herself in relation to an other. This has implications for gender in that experiencing one's body in relation to an other contributes to one's sense of self and gender. So in very basic and fundamental ways, one's experience of gender, the body, and sexuality are linked" (p. 149).

According to Freud's theory, personality development occurs in a series of five psychosexual stages. In each stage, strong pleasurable feelings, attributed by Freud to the satisfaction of sexual instincts, are associated with particular body zones. In the **oral stage,** during the first year of life, pleasure is centered in the mouth and sucking. During the second year, the child passes through the **anal stage,** in which pleasure is linked to defecation. Next comes the **phallic stage,** in which erotic pleasure is obtained from the penis for boys and the clitoris for girls. This is followed by the **latency phase,** in which erotic impulses are repressed until just before puberty. Puberty ushers in the **genital stage,** that of mature sexuality.

It is during the phallic stage, which lasts from about age 3 to age 6, that the development of boys and girls is theorized to diverge. This divergence, and consequent formation of appropriate masculine or feminine identification, is precipitated by the development and resolution of the **Oedipus complex,** a system of feelings named by Freud for the mythical Greek character who unwittingly killed his own father and married his own mother.

Boys at this stage develop an intense attachment to the mother and a desire to possess her sexually. The boy begins to see his father as a rival—a competitor for the mother's affections—and he wishes to replace him. Unable to acknowledge his strong negative feelings toward his father, the boy unconsciously projects the feelings onto the father, thus coming to believe that his father sees *him* as a rival. He then worries about what his father may do to him, and the fear that begins to haunt him is the fear of castration. Why castration? This is the phallic stage, the stage at which the penis is the source of a great deal of pleasure and pride for the little boy. It is a time when he has discovered masturbation and perhaps has been threatened by his parents that if he does not stop, they will "cut it off." Most important, according to Freud, it is a time when the boy discovers with chagrin that not everybody has a penis. His first glimpse of a naked girl or woman leaves him shocked and perturbed because it gives reality to his parents' threats and his own fears: Some people have apparently already been castrated! So intense does his fear become that he is literally forced to resolve the Oedipus complex to allay his fear. He achieves this end by identifying with his father (accepting his father as a model and incorporating many features of his father's personality into his own) and crushing his desire for his mother. Freud believed boys emerged from the Oedipus complex with either a contempt for or fear of women, based on the danger associated with attraction to the mother.

For a girl, the road to feminine identification begins, according to Freud, when she first notices that boys have something she does not: a penis. The realization produces what Freud labeled **penis envy:**

> She has seen it and knows she is without it and wants to have it. . . . The hope of someday obtaining a penis in spite of everything and so of becoming like a man may persist to an incredibly late age and may become a motive for the strangest and otherwise unaccountable actions. Or again, a process may set in which might be described as a "denial" . . . a girl may refuse to accept the fact of being castrated, may harden herself in the conviction that she *does* possess a penis and may subsequently be compelled to behave as though she were a man. (Freud, 1925/1974, pp. 31–32)

Seeing herself to be lacking such an important organ, the girl develops a sense of inferiority and contempt for her own sex. Gradually, her penis envy becomes a more general attitude of jealousy. She blames her mother, her original love object, for her lack of a penis and starts to withdraw her affection from her. She tries to suppress the tendency to masturbate because her clitoris is so inferior to the boy's penis. Her penis envy eventually leads her to enter the female version of the Oedipus complex, called the **Electra complex,** after the mythical Greek personage who urged her brother to slay their mother, who had murdered their father. "She gives up her wish for a penis and puts in place of it a wish for a child: and *with this purpose in view* she takes her father as a love object. Her mother becomes the object of her jealousy" (Freud, 1925/1974, p. 34). Gradually, she realizes that she can never possess her father. By facing this frustration, she accepts the link between pain and pleasure that is inherent in the female role and becomes masochistic. She replaces "active" clitoral sexuality with "passive" vaginal sexuality. Grudgingly, although still harboring some contempt and anger toward her mother (and the belief that she is inferior to her father), she reestablishes her feminine identification with her mother and concentrates on becoming an attractive love object so that she will be adored by some other man. Sexual attractiveness becomes her primary source of self-esteem and identity.

Females, unlike males, do not have a powerful fear motivation to resolve the Electra complex. For them, after all, the worst has already happened: They have been castrated. Freud felt that, in their case, the complex was slowly abandoned or repressed, rather than smashed, as it was for boys. For boys, the necessity to destroy the Oedipus complex results in the formation of a strong superego. For girls, the more gradual abandonment of the Electra complex makes strong superego development less necessary.

Thus the different courses followed by boys and girls in forming and resolving the Oedipus/Electra complex have far-reaching consequences in Freudian theory for the development of psychological gender differences. Among males, the result of resolution is masculine identification, contempt for or fear of women, and a strong superego. Among females, the upshot of the complex is feminine identification, a sense of inferiority, contempt for other women, a tendency toward jealousy, a rejection of clitoral sexuality, masochism, a wish for a child, an obsession with sexual attractiveness, and a weaker superego. See Figure 2.1.

Figure 2.1 Development of gender identification in boys and girls, according to Sigmund Freud's psychoanalytic theory.

Boy: Oedipus Complex

Has intense attraction to mother

Sees father as his rival and feels hostile toward him

Projects these hostile feelings onto the father, thus believing that his father sees *him* as a rival

Fears his father will castrate him (castration anxiety)

To resolve this overwhelming fear, identifies with his father and stamps out his own desire for his mother

Results:
- Masculine identification
- Contempt or fear toward women
- Strong superego

Girl: Electra Complex

Is originally bonded emotionally with mother

Notices her own lack of a penis

Has penis envy, sense of inferiority

Blames her mother for the lack of a penis and so withdraws affection from her

Eventually replaces her wish for a penis with a wish for a child

To obtain a child, takes her father as a love object and so becomes jealous of her mother

Gradually realizes she cannot possess her father

Reestablishes feminine identification with her mother and tries to become an attractive love object for another man

Results:
- Feminine identification
- Sexual attractiveness as main source of self-esteem
- Rejection of clitoral sexuality
- Feelings of inferiority
- Contempt for other women
- Wish for a child
- Weak superego

Two of Freud's conclusions in particular have had negative consequences for women. The first is his idea that the rejection of clitoral sexuality is a normal part of female development. Freud believed the suppression of sexual activity focused on the clitoris is necessary for the emergence of true feminine (vaginal) sexuality. In psychoanalytic theory, the clitoral orgasm is considered immature and not truly satisfying; a "real woman" finds satisfaction only in vaginal orgasms achieved during intercourse. This element of Freudian doctrine is puzzling in light of the complete lack of evidence that erotic sensitivity is transferred from the clitoris to the vagina during women's maturation. Nineteenth-century medical books made it abundantly clear that the clitoris has far more nerve endings than the vagina does, and Freud, as a doctor, could hardly have been unaware of this. So powerful was his theory's hold on the popular imagination, however, that scientists "forgot" what had been well known to doctors and to ordinary women and men for centuries—that the female orgasm is almost entirely clitoral (Laqueur, 1990). When researchers in the second half of the 20th century "discovered" what 17th-century women would have thought to be common knowledge—that the clitoris has as many nerve endings as the penis and that all female orgasms originate there (see Chapter 7)—many women who had been suffering guilt and inadequacy over their inability to have "proper" vaginal orgasms suddenly realized they had been duped. Resentment still simmers against Freudian-based psychiatry for its complicity in orienting women toward denial rather than trust of their own experience of sexuality.

The second Freudian concept that has been used against women is penis envy. Because the pressure to resolve the Oedipus complex is weak in women, Freud suggested that no resolution may be achieved. In this event, the adult woman is a neurotic victim of penis envy. She may try to be masculine, become resentful and jealous of men, and reject the feminine fulfillment of pregnancy—all the while completely unaware that it is her unconscious wish for a penis that is making her so cranky. If women take offense at this aspect of the theory, it is little wonder, for it implies that any woman who is not satisfied with her socially defined feminine role is neurotic and psychosexually immature. Freud himself was not above using the penis envy concept as a weapon against female psychoanalysts who broke ranks and criticized his theory: "We shall not be very surprised if a woman analyst who has not been sufficiently convinced of her own desire for a penis also fails to assign an adequate importance to that factor in her patients" (quoted in Garrison, 1981).

Because Freudian theory acknowledged the importance and pervasiveness of sexual feelings and desires—experiences that were largely denied or minimized in the Victorian era in which he worked—it opened the door for consideration of some hitherto undiscussed sexual behaviors. In one such case, incest, the door was opened slightly, then hastily closed. In another, homosexuality, some light was allowed to shine on a subject that had been shrouded in disapproval.

Many of Freud's women patients told him that they had been seduced by their fathers. At first Freud believed these accounts and attributed the women's neurotic symptoms to repressed horror over the incest. Later, however, he began to feel uneasy about the large number of his female patients who claimed to have been sexually molested by their fathers and male relatives. Refusing to accept the possibility that daughters were sexually victimized with such high frequency, he asserted in his public writings that the women's accounts (and their symptoms) were based on fantasies rather than real occurrences. In fact, he came to describe the fantasy of being seduced by the father as the expression of the Oedipus complex in women.

Unbelievable though it may have seemed to Freud, evidence suggests that most of his women patients were telling the truth. The occurrences of sexual abuse were, in many cases, confirmed by the abuser or other reliable witnesses (Sulloway, 1979). Surveys have now placed the occurrence of father-daughter incest at 1.3% to 4.5% and the occurrence of sexual abuse of girls in general at 6% to 62% (Finkelhor, 1986; D. E. H. Russell, 1983). Moreover, documentation of the widespread character of sexual abuse of girls is not new and was apparently available to Freud and known to him through medical colleagues in Paris. Some of his unpublished letters seem to suggest that, long after he had publicly discounted his patients' seduction stories, he continued to believe that at least some of the stories were true (Masson, 1984). The damage done by Freud's public refusal to believe his female patients lingers. Victims of sexual abuse who seek help still encounter disbelief or the charge that their accusations are an outcome of their own unconscious incestuous wishes (Sheffield, 1995).

Freud's legacy with respect to homosexuality was more positive. He argued that neither masculinity and femininity nor heterosexuality and homosexuality are polar opposites; rather, every individual displays a mixture of these qualities. He wrote the following to a woman concerned about her son's homosexuality:

> Homosexuality is assuredly no advantage, but it is nothing to be ashamed of, no vice, no degradation; it cannot be classified as an illness; we consider it to be a variation of the sexual function. . . . Many highly respectable individuals of ancient and modern times have been homosexuals, several of the greatest men among them. . . . It is a great injustice to persecute homosexuality as a crime—and a cruelty too. . . .
>
> What analysis can do for your son runs in a different line. If he is unhappy, neurotic, torn by conflicts, inhibited in his social life, analysis may bring him harmony, peace of mind, full efficiency, whether he remains homosexual or gets changed. (Freud, 1961, pp. 419–420)

Freud's theory opened new possibilities for debate in the whole area of sexuality and gender—and a debate is exactly what happened.

Challenging Freud's Phallocentrism: Horney's Gynocentric View

Almost from the first, some critics felt that in looking at psychosexual development from the male point of view Freud had created a theory that overemphasized the role played by the penis in the development of both sexes. An early proponent of this viewpoint was Karen Horney, a member of Freud's circle who had a reputation as one of the foremost training analysts in Europe. She questioned the idea that women see their bodies as inferior, and she argued that masculine narcissism is the only basis for the assumption that half the human race is automatically discontented with the sex assigned to it. Although accepting the possibility of penis envy in girls and castration anxiety in boys, she noted that males are also envious of females:

> From the biological point of view, woman has in motherhood, or in the capacity for motherhood, a quite indisputable and by no means negligible superiority. This is most clearly reflected in the unconscious of the male psyche in the boy's intense envy of motherhood. We are familiar with this envy as such, but it has hardly received due consideration as a dynamic factor. When one begins, as I did, to analyze men only after fairly long experience of analyzing women, one receives a most surprising impression of the intensity of this envy of pregnancy, childbirth, and motherhood, as well as of the breasts and the act of suckling. (Horney, 1926/1973, p. 10)

Horney also believed rejection of the female role in girls is mainly caused not by envy of the penis but by an unconscious fear of vaginal injury through penetration, aroused by guilt over masturbation. Thus she proposed that a girl's psychosexual development centers on her own anatomy rather than that of the male. Furthermore, she argued, rejection of the feminine role is partially a response to a society that views women as inadequate and inferior and gives them few opportunities outside the home. She was one of the first psychoanalysts to draw attention to the possibilities for interaction between cultural and inner dynamic forces in shaping the personality. Although both she and her views were rejected in orthodox Freudian circles, her work had considerable impact, and she herself became respected and renowned despite the controversy she created (Garrison, 1981).

Freudian theory can be labeled **phallocentric**—centered on the male penis. The perspective taken by Horney and a group of other psychoanalysts has been labeled **gynocentric**—centered on the female womb (Stockard & Johnson, 1979). This latter approach emphasizes the importance of both boys' and girls' pre-Oedipal relationship with the mother and links male dominance of women to that early mother-child tie. The bases proposed for the link are unconscious fear and envy of the mother and the necessity for boys but not girls to switch their identification from the mother to the father.

Horney suggested that men's desire to achieve and create is an overcompensation for their unconscious sense of inferiority in the creative process of reproduction. Furthermore, she proposed, men depreciate women because of this unconscious envy, rather than the recognition that the female lacks a penis. On this point she was echoed by Melanie Klein (1932/1960), who asserted that boys' pride in and emphasis on the penis compensate for feelings of anxiety, envy, and inferiority regarding the mother.

Horney's critique of Freud reclaimed the primacy of women's own body, rather than envy of the male body, in women's psychological development. Rather than challenge the Freudian notions of instinctual sexual drives or of female–male differences based on anatomy, she simply exposed the masculine bias in the way Freud had used these notions to describe female psychology (Kimball, 1995). In Horney's early writing on female development, she worked within the psychoanalytic framework to undermine its male-centered bias, using anatomical differences and sexual drives as her conceptual tools. In her later work, Horney rejected the notion that human behavior springs from instinctual drives (sex, aggression) and developed instead the notion that behavior is a product of experience in its cultural context (Westkott, 1986). She postulated that human beings are guided by needs for safety (inner security) and satisfaction and that a child's social environment determines whether these needs can be met easily or whether the child must develop a neurotic "solution" (such as dependency) to the anxiety and hostility that arise from an insecure environment.

According to Horney's (1939) theory, the environment presents two potential dangers to the young child: **devaluation** (parents' lack of respect for the child as unique, worthwhile) and **sexualization** (a sexual approach to the child, an emotional "hothouse" atmosphere). She argued that the clinging to one parent and jealousy toward the other that characterized what Freud had called the Oedipus complex is a child's anxious response to the abuse of parental power: devaluing or sexualizing treatment of the child (Westkott, 1986).

It is clear from Horney's writings that she felt the cultural pattern of preference for sons over daughters made girls more vulnerable than boys to devaluation and the development of a sense of inferiority. She also noted the pervasive cultural tendency for families to treat girls as if their sexuality were the most important aspect of their identity. Thus, although theoretically applicable to both boys and girls, in a society that values males over females the experiences of devaluation and sexualization are more likely to characterize the childhood of girls than of boys. Girls might, then, be more likely than boys to develop neurotic personalities characterized by the submissiveness and self-directed hostility that arise in response to parental devaluation. However, this gender difference is based not in anything biological but in a culture that values one sex more than the other.

Feminism and Psychoanalytic Theory

During the last three decades, much theorizing has been done about the aspect of development virtually ignored by Freud and highlighted in Horney's early writings—the early bond between mother and child. Writing in the gynocentric tradition of Karen Horney, Melanie Klein, and other pioneering analysts, Dorothy Dinnerstein (1976) argued that society allows men to hold the power outside the mother-child relationship precisely because the power held by the mother over the infant is so awesome. The relationship produces a fear of female power and authority in both men and women, Dinnerstein says. In the process of growing up, the individual flees from the power of the mother and finds it easier to accept male than female authority. Men end up with a particular fear of becoming overly dependent on women, whereas women carry a sense of inadequacy throughout their lives because they can never live up to the magically powerful mother image they experienced as infants. The result is a society that accepts and encourages male dominance.

Sociologist Nancy Chodorow (1978), taking a similar perspective about the overwhelming effect of the mother-child relationship, has argued that exclusively female parenting produces men and women with very different emotional needs. Women, having been parented by an adult with whom they could identify, try unsuccessfully to reexperience this sense of unity in their sexual relationships with men.

> But families organized around women's mothering and male dominance create incompatibilities in women's and men's relational needs. In particular, relationships to men are unlikely to provide for women satisfaction of the relational needs that their mothering by women and the social organization of gender have produced. The less men participate in the domestic sphere, and especially in parenting, the more this will be the case. (p. 199)

Furthermore, Chodorow (1989) noted, families in which women do the primary caregiving produce different problems for males and females. Contrary to Freud, whose analysis of the Oedipal trauma emphasized the difficulties faced by girls in forming a positive gender identity, Chodorow argues that boys face the most problems in initially forming their identity as males. Because of the early, close attachment between mother and child,

> [u]nderlying, or built into, core male gender identity is an early, nonverbal, unconscious, almost somatic sense of primary oneness with the mother, an underlying sense of femaleness that continually, usually unnoticeably, but sometimes insistently, challenges and undermines the sense of maleness. (p. 109)

Because boys initially identify with the mother, forming a masculine identity is a negative process that involves separation and denial. Males must form their gender identity by defining themselves as "*not* women." For girls, such drastic separation is not necessary. However, girls develop difficulties with identity later; these center on the problems of identifying with "a negatively valued gender category, and an ambivalently experienced maternal figure, whose mothering and femininity, often conflictual for the mother herself, are accessible, but devalued" (pp. 110–111).

Why is feminine identity negatively valued? Chodorow (1989) explained that men devalue it in their flight from it. Moreover, because men have more power than women, they have been able to "define maleness as that which is basically human, and to define women as not-men" (p. 111).

The attention paid to the mother-child relationship in the gynocentric branch of psychoanalytic theory makes it quite different from orthodox Freudian theory, in which the father-child relationship is the crucial one. An interesting implication that both Dinnerstein and Chodorow have drawn from their theoretical work is that society would be better off with a family system in which parenting was more equally shared between women and men. Such sharing of roles would presumably reduce the internalization of a perception of mothers as "all-powerful," paving the way for more egalitarian and intimate relationships between adult women and men. However, this implication may be too simplistic. As Ellyn Kaschak (1992) noted, only a small minority of families in North America now fit the model of a dual-parent family in which the mother is the main caregiver and the father is absent for most of the day. Most mothers work outside the home and are away from their children for a good part of the time. Many children are being raised by single parents or by slightly older siblings. Yet there is no convincing evidence that children not raised in the kind of nuclear family described by Chodorow and Dinnerstein differ from other children in terms of gender roles, relational orientation, or resentment of female power. Kaschak argued that the general social context—the collection of messages about gender that surround the child in the culture—weighs more heavily than particular family arrangements in the meanings children learn to associate with gender.

Contemporary theorists continue to debate and refine psychoanalytic theories, often moving beyond the notion that gender is "set" by childhood Oedipal experiences in particular kinds of family structures. For example, Chodorow (1995) explored the idea that outwardly similar mother-daughter relationships may be experienced quite differently by the persons involved—and argued that unconscious feelings push people to make sense of their cultural experiences in different ways. And Benjamin (1995) posited that holding fast to the well-defined either-or gender identity achieved through resolution of the Oedipal complex requires people to be "stuck" in a rigid, immature position. Adults, she said, must continue to develop, moving toward a more fluid understanding of gender as they mature, or risk splitting off an important part of themselves. These and other theorists have as Bell (2004) noted, "returned to Freud's most compelling early observations of gender—that it is related to but not determinate of sexuality, that it is influenced by but not determined by sex, that it is informed by but not caused solely by the body, and that it is always mediated by the personal unconscious" (p. 165).

Masculine Gender Role and Identity

Chodorow's description of the difficulties associated with masculine identity echoed the ideas of other theorists who have been concerned with the male role. The idea that gender-role acquisition was based on early identification with the appropriate parent led some theorists on a quest for the explanation of "masculinity problems." Freud felt that girls encountered the most difficulties on the road to proper gender identification, but these later theorists argued that boys faced greater obstacles. Joseph Pleck (1981) described the historical context that led to special concern with masculinity: the disqualification of large numbers of American males as mentally or physically unfit for the draft in World Wars I and II, the incidence of emotional breakdowns among men in battle, the erosion of the male breadwinner role through the Great Depression and women's wartime entry into the labor force, and such examples of "hypermasculinity" as wartime aggression and the rise of juvenile delinquency.

In trying to explain such "failures" of masculinity, theorists looked again to notions of identification and focused on the same critical issue identified by Chodorow: Boys, like girls, initially identify with the mother. Thus, these theorists reasoned, males have more difficulty than females in forming the appropriate gender-role identity, and overcoming their initial feminine identification is a central problem in males' psychological development.

Why should identification with the appropriate gender role be especially difficult for boys? First, the boy must *switch* identifications from his mother to his father, something the girl does not have to do. Second, the father is usually so much less available than the mother or other female caregiver as a model that the boy may have trouble knowing precisely what being masculine entails.

The general concern that boys need a male, heterosexual parent in the home to form a proper masculine gender-role identity now appears to have been misguided. Evidence does not support the idea that boys need a heterosexual male parent to establish a masculine identity (Pleck, 1995). Researchers now believe a wide variety of family structures can support good child development, as long as those structures include at least one responsible caretaking adult (of any sex) who has a consistent, positive emotional connection to the child (Silverstein & Auerbach, 1999). In fact, these researchers argued that the problems sometimes experienced by boys in single-mother households have little to do with father absence and everything to do with the way societies treat women and men:

> We speculate that the larger cultural context of male dominance and negative attitudes toward women may interfere with the ability of many single mothers to establish an authoritative parenting style with male children. Within patriarchal culture, boys know that when they become adult men, they will be dominant to every woman, including their mother. This cultural context, unmediated by a male presence, may undermine a single mother's authority with her sons. (p. 403)

Developments in research and changes in public attitudes have created some new perspectives on male gender-role identity. Some theorists now argue that the difficulties males face with respect to masculinity have more to do with role expectations than with identity conflicts. Pleck (1981, 1995), in his **gender-role strain** paradigm for understanding the social construction of masculinity, argued that the very behavior *expected* of males (for example, aggression, emotional constriction) can be dysfunctional, causing problems for males even when they conform to their masculine role. Furthermore, he noted, gender roles are contradictory and inconsistent, so it is difficult not to violate them (witness the simultaneous demands on modern men to be both sensitive and tough). Gender-role strain may be especially important for men because violating gender roles often has more severe consequences for males than for females. In North America, men are under increasing pressure to participate in child care and domestic work, yet men who do so are sometimes judged to be unmasculine. Men are encouraged to overcome their reluctance to take on "feminine" jobs, yet men who are nurses and secretaries may be the brunt of jokes. Some men may feel caught in a societal double bind in which they are being urged to abandon the old masculine roles yet punished when they try to do so.

Pleck's analysis alerts us to the difference between masculine identity and masculine role. One of the most important outcomes of the debates over the difficulties associated with masculinity has been just that: an increased awareness of the distinctions among gender identity, gender role, and sexual orientation.

Gender Identity, Gender Role, and Sexual Orientation: Distinct Issues

The "identification" theories just described make few explicit distinctions among *gender identity, gender role,* and *sexual orientation.* All three are considered aspects of identification with the same-sex parent. Researchers now acknowledge, however, that the three issues are conceptually separate and, in fact, not necessarily correlated. **Gender identity** is defined as the individual's private experience of the self as female or male—a powerful aspect of the self-concept that is formed early in childhood and, in most adults, is extremely resistant to change. Only a tiny percentage of people form a gender identity that is incongruent with their biological sex when no physiological abnormalities are present. **Gender role** refers to the set of behaviors socially defined as appropriate for one's sex. It is now quite clear that an individual can refuse to conform to society's gender-role prescriptions without experiencing any conflict about underlying gender identity. For example, a man can reject the masculine stereotype of aggressiveness and toughness without experiencing any serious doubts about whether he is actually male. **Sexual orientation** refers to an individual's preference for sexual partners of the same or other sex. A person with a heterosexual orientation is attracted to partners of the other sex; one with a homosexual orientation is attracted to partners of the same sex. Despite the early theorists' equation of male homosexuality with femininity, sexual orientation does not necessarily correlate with either gender identity or gender role. For example, a woman who is sexually attracted to other women usually has no conflict or uncertainty about whether she is indeed female, and she may or may not adhere to aspects of the traditional feminine gender role (see Chapter 7 for an extended discussion of sexual orientation). Theories of gender developed subsequent to the psychoanalytic/identification theories tend to draw clearer lines between gender identity and gender roles than the psychoanalytic approach does, and sexual orientation is often treated as a separate issue.

The debate over the merits of the psychoanalytic/identification approach to gender contains the seeds of another, quite different type of viewpoint, one that emphasizes social structure and culture as important determinants of the way females and males develop. As some of Freud's critics noted, the observations he made about parent-child relationships and sexuality were embedded in a particular culture that emphasized male dominance and had a particular, rigid set of ideas about male and female sexuality. Horney's ideas, too, were developed in the context of a society that had strong norms about female–male relationships, a society in which a cult of domesticity for women flourished and men and women were expected to occupy different, complementary spheres. Likewise, the more recent theories of Chodorow and Dinnerstein have not escaped the influence of their cultural context. As Nancy Chodorow (1989) commented after interviewing a number of the women who were pioneers in the psychoanalytic movement in the 1930s,

> I began to realize how much my perceptual and analytic categories had been shaped by my coming of age in the women's movement and my immersion in the recent literature of gender theory. Only with this recognition, that the salience

and meaning of gender were products of one's time and place, could I come to understand gender within the fabric of my interviewees' lives. (p. 217)

What if the cultural context that is treated as background in psychoanalytic theory were moved to the foreground? The next theoretical approach,

---

Overview — Psychoanalytic/identification theorists on gender

Theorist	Perspective on Gender Identification	Important Concepts
Sigmund Freud	In the resolution of the Oedipus/Electra complex, child identifies with same-sex parent. Is more difficult for girls because they must identify with the sex they perceive as inferior (lacking a penis).	Penis envy, castration anxiety, Oedipus complex, Electra complex
Karen Horney	Child identifies with same-sex parent. May be difficult for girls because females are often valued less in society. May be difficult for boys because they envy the mother and because they must switch identification from the mother to the father.	Womb envy, devaluation, sexualization
Nancy Chodorow	Child identifies with the mother because she is the primary caretaker. Boys must later switch their identification to the father, and they devalue femininity in their flight from it. Because of the power wielded by the mother in the early mother-child relationship, both males and females grow up to feel uneasy about female power.	Necessity for male to switch identification from mother to father; power of the mother
Joseph Pleck	Male difficulties are caused not so much by problems with gender identity as problems with gender roles. Masculine gender roles are contradictory and inconsistent, making it difficult for boys to settle into a comfortable gender role.	Gender-role strain

instead of focusing on anatomy and early parent-child relationships, concentrates the search for an understanding of gender on the culture in which these things exist.

SOCIAL STRUCTURE/CULTURAL THEORIES OF GENDER

Psychologists have often focused on identification theories as explanations for the origins and maintenance of gender roles, but the **social structure theories** have long been popular among sociologists and anthropologists. Such an approach stresses not the mechanisms through which children develop gender identity or acquire gender roles but the overarching social arrangements that define and support gender. In other words, instead of focusing on how boys acquire the notion that it is especially important for them to be tough and competent and how girls learn that it is especially important for them to be pretty and nice, it focuses on *why* society supports their learning of this message and, in its search for answers, emphasizes the different social positions of women and men. Two themes have been the focus for much of this discussion: power and status and the division of labor.

Power and Status

Many theorists now argue that most of the differences between feminine and masculine gender roles come about because of the greater power and status accorded to males than to females in most societies. In most societies, a gender hierarchy exists such that men hold most of the more powerful, high-status positions. For instance, in the United States, Canada, and around the world, women are drastically underrepresented at the top levels of business and politics and in highly paid, high-status positions generally, whereas they are overrepresented in the lower paid, lower-status service occupations (Lopez-Claros & Zahidi, 2005; Wirth, 2001). According to social structure theory, men develop more dominant (i.e., controlling, assertive, directive) behaviors as an accommodation to more powerful roles, and women develop more subordinate (i.e., compliant, less aggressive, more cooperative and conciliatory) behaviors as a way of accommodating to available roles with less power and status (Eagly & Wood, 1999). Researchers in a number of areas have demonstrated that "typical" gender differences hold only or most strongly when the sexes are in the common male dominant–female subordinate relationship and that much so-called feminine behavior is actually powerless behavior (Lips, 1991). These findings lead to the hypothesis that if women and men were accorded equal status in society many of the differences in behavior we attribute to gender would disappear. Although this idea will come up at many points in later chapters, let us look briefly now at some examples of how power and status differences can be confused with or can affect gender differences.

WOMEN IN ORGANIZATIONS   Rosabeth Moss Kanter's (1975, 1976) pioneering research on women in the workplace began as an attempt to discover the gender differences that would explain the stereotype that women make poorer leaders than men. Her conclusion was that people in token or dead-end positions, whether women or men, show poor leadership and success skills. They are rigid and hostile toward outsiders and powerful superiors, and they have more concern with socializing than with career advancement. It is the nature of the position rather than the gender of the person occupying it that is linked to these behaviors. The problem is that many more women than men are stuck in such positions.

> I could find nothing about women in my own research, and that of others, that was not equally true of men in some situations. For example, some women do have low job aspirations, but so do men who are in positions of blocked opportunity. Some women managers are too interfering and coercive, but so are men who have limited power and responsibility in their organizations. Some women in professional careers behave in stereotyped ways and tend to regard others of their sex with disdain, but so do men who are tokens—the only member of their group at work. (1976, p. 56)

Thus, Kanter concluded, many of the apparent gender differences in leadership and organizational behavior have no necessary relationship with gender. Instead, they can be traced to the social structure: women's more precarious positions in organizations and their lack of power relative to men.

Researchers who have followed up on Kanter's work have discovered that the perceptions by others of token female leaders—high visibility, contrast with other workers, and the rigid limiting of roles—do not happen to just anyone who holds a token position. Rather, these effects are more likely to happen to women who hold token positions in occupations deemed gender inappropriate for them (Yoder, 1991, 1994). Apparently, the organizational environment cannot be isolated from the more general social context of discrimination against women. Yoder (1991) also argued that merely increasing the number of women (so that women are no longer token representatives of their sex) will not remove gender discrimination in the workplace. As women increase in numbers, they are more likely to be perceived as a threat and treated in ways designed to hold them back: sexual harassment, salary inequities, and limited opportunities for advancement. Such a reaction would be a direct response to the possibility of a change in women's power relative to men.

"RAPE-PRONE" VERSUS "RAPE-FREE" SOCIETIES   Gender differences in rape and sexual assault are also linked to power differences. One gender difference to which people often point as an example of the inevitability of a "war" between the sexes is sexual aggressiveness. In its ultimate form, rape, sexual aggressiveness does differentiate the sexes: Men rape; women, by and large, do not. Yet even this difference is attenuated or magnified by the power relations between women and men in a given society. After studying 186 societies, Sanday (1981b) concluded that those in which rape was prevalent were characterized by interpersonal violence, male dominance, and separation of the sexes, whereas those in which rape was a relatively rare occurrence were societies in which male and female qualities were equally valued.

SOCIAL DOMINANCE THEORY   A recent, sophisticated approach to analyzing male–female behavioral differences in terms of power and status, **social dominance theory** (Pratto, 1996; Pratto & Walker, 2004) aims to explain the observation that men often seem to be more social-dominance-oriented than women (that is, more interested than women in having their group dominate others). Like the examples discussed previously, this theory suggests that male–female differences develop from contextual social differences: gender differences in social dominance orientation are most likely to be found in societies that emphasize group dominance and that are organized hierarchically. The theory posits that societies in which group dominance is important develop methods to maintain their dominance structures. In such societies the two sexes tend to be socialized toward and adopt different kinds of values. Women tend to adopt hierarchy-attenuating values— values emphasizing equality and reducing the power and status difference between groups. Men, on the other hand, tend to adopt hierarchy-enhancing values—values that emphasize protecting and promoting the interests of elite, powerful groups. These differences parallel those between other dominant and subordinate groups in such societies: for example, U.S. Blacks and Hispanics are lower in social dominance orientation than Whites, and gays, lesbians, and bisexuals are lower in social dominance orientation than straights (Pratto, 1996).

A gender difference in dominance orientation might emerge in dominance-oriented societies for several reasons. Because women have been targets of such beliefs, they (and other subordinate groups) may become suspicious of cultural beliefs that appear to legitimize the subordination of particular groups. This suspicion may lead them to question the hierarchies that support social dominance. On the other hand, because certain classes of men have benefited from cultural beliefs that support their dominant position, they may feel better about such beliefs and be willing to support them. Finally, these men's knowledge that they are able, ambitious, and hard-working (and their lack of knowledge about the abilities and efforts of other groups) may lead them to accept that their high status is normal and deserved (Pratto, 1996).

How are these gender differences in dominance orientation expressed? In part, expression is through the roles men and women adopt. Felicia Pratto (Pratto & Walker, 2004) argued that in dominance-oriented societies the roles associated with each of four forms of power are gendered—tilted toward men or women—and that this gendering of power-related roles helps to maintain social inequalities between the sexes and between racial, ethnic, class, sexual orientation, or other groups. Men in dominant groups use their greater access to powerful roles based on force, resource control, and ability to influence cultural ideologies to take a disproportionate share of societal resources. They also establish relationships with women in which women have the primary social obligation to provide care for them and for their children—and women depend on men for access to many resources. Such arrangements maintain societal organization, and they also mean that men (at least men in dominant groups) will have some vested interest in protecting social hierarchies and women will have some vested interest in undermining them. Table 2.1 shows some of the ways in which powerful and caretaking roles are gendered in the United States. According to social dominance theory, the preponderance of men in powerful, hierarchy-enhancing roles and women in caretaking, hierarchy-attenuating roles reflects not simply gender differences in preferences for such roles but a social structure that makes them differentially available to men and women.

Table 2.1   Percentage of women and mean annual wages associated with various hierarchy-enhancing and hierarchy-attenuation occupations, United States.

Relation to Power	*Occupation*	*Percent Women*	*Median Weekly Earnings*
Hierarchy-Enhancing Occupations			
Wields forceful power	Lawyers	30%	$ 1,354
	Police	14	738
Wields economic power	Securities sales	29	733
	Chief executives	24	1,413
Wields ideological power	Marketing managers	41	990
	Editors	58	794
Hierarchy-Attenuating Occupations			
Undoing harm	Social workers	80%	$ 982
	Counselors	70	728
	Volunteers	46	na
Empowering with information	Teachers	72	768
	Librarians	85	826
Cares for others	Child-care providers	95	330
	Registered nurses	92	930
Provides personal services	Secretaries	97	559
	Wait staff	78	332
	Cleaners, servants	90	328

Note: Percentage for volunteers is from the Independent Sector (2001). All other percentages and wages are from U.S. Bureau of Labor Statistics (2005a).

Source: Adapted and updated from Pratto & Walker (2004).

The Division of Labor

The approaches just discussed suggest that one important aspect of the status differences between the sexes is that they do different kinds of work: Women are the secretaries, men are the executives; women are the lab technicians, men are the scientists; men are the hunters and warriors, women stay home with the children. Anthropologists have been embroiled for years in controversies over whether the sexual division of labor is a cause or a consequence of the status differences between women and men; most likely, the process is a kind of vicious circle. However, the way work is divided between women and men in our own society practically guarantees that women will have less control over economic resources than men do. Men's greater control over economic resources, achieved through better jobs with higher salaries and through more continuous participation in the paid labor force, creates the expectation that women (and children) will depend on men for support. Under this set of expectations, which is communicated to children long before they understand the economic realities on which it is based, it is little wonder that girls and boys and women and men tend to make choices that emphasize different aspects of their skills, aspirations, and preferences. These choices lead males and females into different types of work, and the cycle repeats itself. This is one way in which the division of labor by sex and the parallel male–female difference in control over resources contribute to gender differences in behavior.

SOCIAL ROLE THEORY   There is another way in which the division of labor may contribute to gender differences in behavior: "Women and men seek to accommodate sex-typical roles by acquiring the specific skills and resources linked to successful role performance and by adapting their social behavior to role requirements" (Eagly & Wood, 1999, pp. 412–413). Women and men know what they are expected to do, so they try to learn the skills they need to do it properly, to fit in with social expectations.

According to **social role theory** (Eagly, 1987), women and men are expected to have the qualities that fit them for the tasks they normally carry out. For example, in North America women normally do much of the child care, nursing, and social work and are expected to be nurturing and compassionate. Men normally fill most of the roles involving military service, political office, and executive positions and are expected to be tough and decisive. Thus the qualities that are required to perform tasks typically assigned to women or men become stereotypic of women and men. In a circular fashion, the gender stereotypes make it easier for women and men to prepare for, be selected for, and perform roles that are gender stereotypic.

We seem to be caught in a vicious circle: We expect women and men to be different because we observe that they tend to do different things, and this very expectation then leads us to react negatively to those whose behavior does not match our original observations. Moreover, our expectations encompass not only stereotypical differences between women and men but also a hierarchy of occupational roles. Mary Ann Cejka and Alice Eagly (1999) examined the relationship between the distribution of women and men in 80 occupations and research participants' beliefs that six dimensions of gender-stereotypic qualities contribute to success in these occupations. They found that participants' beliefs that an occupation demanded feminine or masculine physical or personality traits predicted the extent to which that occupation was female or male dominated. Participants' beliefs that occupations required masculine personality or cognitive characteristics for success also predicted the prestige of occupations.

Social structure theories do not assume that gender roles are completely arbitrary, depending only on the whims of particular societies. Rather, they assume that societies shape gender roles in response to factors such as men's greater size and strength, women's reproductive activities, and the activities necessary for social and economic stability in a particular culture (Eagly & Wood, 1999; Wood & Eagly, 2002). Some of these factors (e.g., the fact that women are the ones who bear and breast-feed children) are common across societies and so should help to shape gender roles in similar ways in different cultures. This, according to social structural theorists, is why certain kinds of female–male differences in behavior are more common than others. For example, it is more common to find societies in which women do more of the work of child care than men do than the reverse.

Not all social scientists emphasize culture as the driving force behind the construction of gender, however. Some theorists argue that the why of female–male differences can be found in biology.

EVOLUTIONARY THEORIES OF GENDER

One set of theories about differences between women and men has stressed the possible genetic bases for behavioral differences between the sexes. According to this approach, the power differences between the sexes are not the result of learning and culture but the natural and inevitable outcome of our genetic heritage. **Evolutionary theories** were popular in North America at the beginning the 20th century, and they have gained visibility again.

Functionalism

The functionalist school of psychology was concerned with how an organism's behavior and consciousness are functional for its survival (Shields, 1975). Men and women, it was thought, have different and complementary functions for the survival of the human race and probably evolved somewhat differently to fulfill these functions. Psychologists using this theoretical approach came up with generalizations about sex differences in temperament that have implications for a wide range of behaviors. Perhaps the best known of these generalizations is the notion of a "maternal instinct" in women.

Many functionalists held that women evolved with an inborn emotional tendency toward nurturance—a tendency that could be triggered by contact with a helpless infant. Because the biological tasks of pregnancy, childbirth, and lactation are fulfilled by women, these theorists reasoned that the presence of a maternal instinct in women but not in men makes evolutionary sense. The behavioral differences thought to result from the differential presence of such an instinct, however, go far beyond those directed specifically toward infants. Herbert Spencer (1891, cited in Shields, 1975), for example, felt that women devote most of their energy to preparation for pregnancy and lactation, with the result that they have little energy left over to develop other qualities. His ideas, along with those of Clarke (1873), were used to justify excluding women from higher education, as discussed at the beginning of this chapter.

Edward L. Thorndike (1914, cited in Shields, 1975), an eminent American psychologist, contended that a number of instincts are relevant to the female reproductive role. He described, for example, a nursing instinct manifested in a strong tendency to nurture others. This instinct, he suggested, is the source of women's general moral superiority to men. He also felt that women have an instinctive tendency to submit to mastery by men. Thus Thorndike conceived of women as naturally both more nurturant and more submissive than men— a viewpoint that has gathered little empirical support but that lingers on in many people's assumptions about male–female differences.

Sociobiology and Evolutionary Psychology

The 1970s and '80s saw the emergence of sweeping claims about male–female differences by proponents of human sociobiology. **Sociobiology** emphasizes the comparison of animal and human behaviors and seeks evidence about how animals and humans have developed similar social behaviors in response to similar selection pressures. **Evolutionary psychology,** a more recent approach, adds to this an emphasis on the evolution of the mind and mental abilities, a focus on species-typical adaptations, and the explicit acknowledgment that selection pressures produce *tendencies*—not the necessity—to respond in particular ways (A. Campbell, 2002; Tooby & Cosmides, 2005). The differences between these two approaches are too complex to go into here, but both share the assumption that, in the interests of the survival of their own particular genes, women and men have evolved different strategies of sexual selection and reproduction. Men, who can produce millions of sperm with relatively little investment of energy, have evolved with an innate tendency to devote energy to short-term mating, fertilizing as many women as possible and maximizing the chances that their own genes will survive. Women, for whom reproduction (both the production of eggs and the gestation of embryos) involves a greater and more time-consuming commitment, have evolved with a tendency to be sexually selective, choosing only the best mates and trying to trick them into monogamy. Proponents of evolutionary approaches have argued that a variety of sex differences in behavioral dispositions have evolved because of these differing sexual strategies of women and men (Buss, 1995). For instance, because men have competed with men for sexual access to women, men have evolved to favor violence and competition. Because women have had to emphasize long-term mating, they have evolved to seek out men who are particularly successful and able to provide resources for their children.

The claims of sociobiology and evolutionary psychology are couched in the language of Darwin's (1871/1967) theory of evolution—a theory developed to explain the way the physical characteristics of animals changed over successive generations to favor those that were most conducive to species survival. This theory postulates that a physical characteristic is adaptive if it contributes to the *maximum fitness* of the species, where "maximum fitness" means being able to reach sexual maturity and leave healthy descendants. Thus, for example, if a certain skin or fur coloration enables a particular type of animal to avoid being eaten by predators and thus to reach sexual maturity and to reproduce, the genes for that particular coloration are more likely to be passed on to the next generation than are the genes for alternative colorations. Over successive generations, then, the protective color will become increasingly common in that species, a process known as *adaptation through natural selection.* By similar logic, if a male animal of a certain species is more likely to have surviving offspring by mating with as many females as possible and if a female animal is more likely to have surviving offspring by being *sexually selective* and mating with only the best available male, then those propensities toward male promiscuity and female selectivity will be passed on at higher rates than male selectivity and female promiscuity, and they will become increasingly common in that species.

This account of the development of sex differences seems plausible in certain respects. However, evidence in support of certain aspects of the approach is not uniformly convincing. For example, evolutionary theories predict that stronger, more competitively successful men would have more children than other men. Indeed, there are a number of reported cases in which highly powerful men in polygynous societies (societies in which one man may have several wives) produced huge numbers of offspring. For example, the *Guinness Book of World Records* asserts that a 17th-century tyrant, Ismail the Bloodthirsty of Morocco, maintained 500 concubines at a time and produced 888 children (McWhirter & McWhirter, 1975). However, there is no clear evidence that across all types of human societies, or in societies that emphasize monogamy, the physically stronger, more aggressive, smarter, or more economically successful men have fathered more children.

Evolutionary theories also predict that men should be more interested than women in casual sex, and researchers do indeed find differences between human females and males in their sexual behavior: Males hold more permissive attitudes toward casual sex than females do, and males tend to have more partners than females do (Oliver & Hyde, 1993). These findings are consistent with evolutionary theories, but they are also consistent with the predictions of other theories (such as social learning theory, to be discussed next) that emphasize learning attitudes and roles from cultural models and the media. Yet evolutionary approaches to social behavior claim that underneath our cultural trappings lie genetically based human universals: sexual aggressivity among men, a sexual division of labor that assigns child care to women, and an innate desire for sexual variety among men but not women. Moreover, the proponents of this approach argue that the genetic basis of these social patterns makes them more or less inescapable, not for individuals but for humans as a species.

Although behavior always reflects some inherent limits in physical capacity imposed by the genes (e.g., humans cannot fly), the idea that such complex human behaviors as competitiveness, the selection of sexual partners, and altruism are genetically encoded aspects of human nature that have evolved through Darwinian natural selection is a still dubious extrapolation of the theory. In fact, Darwin himself was skeptical about the usefulness of sexual selection processes for explaining behavior in modern human societies, arguing that modern humans were more guided by foresight and reason than by an instinctive pull toward genetic fitness in mate selection. He noted that, under conditions of civilization, men are attracted to women by their mental charms, wealth, and social position (Eagly & Wood, 1999). However, Darwin's successors have swept aside such doubts and argued strongly for the applicability of evolutionary theory to human social behavior and, in particular, to human sex differences.

In an attempt to demonstrate that human mating preferences are consistent with the predictions of evolutionary theory, Donald Buss and his colleagues (Buss, 1989; Buss et al., 1990) conducted a large-scale study across 37 cultures in which respondents were asked to specify the characteristics they desired in a mate. Evolutionary theory predicts that men would be more likely than women to specify youth and attractiveness in a mate and women would be more likely to specify that their mate be older and have significant resources. These predictions were upheld across cultures, leading evolutionary psychologists to point to such universality as evidence for powerful "built-in" sex differences that have evolved over time and become an innate part of human nature. This interpretation has been challenged, however. Alice Eagly and Wendy Wood (1999) argued that male–female differences in mate selection criteria stem from the division of labor by sex. In their view, a social structural approach predicts that in societies in which the roles and status of women and men are relatively equal there would be fewer differences between the sexes in the criteria for selecting a mate than in societies in which the roles and status of women and men are very different. In more egalitarian societies, both women and men would place less emphasis on selecting mates whose qualities matched a sexual division of labor because there would be less expectation of such a rigid division. A man does not select a woman only on the basis of her reproductive capacity if he expects her to have two children and then return to the workforce. A woman does not select a man only on the basis of his ability to be a good provider if she expects to have her own career.

Eagly and Wood were able to test their prediction by reanalyzing the data from Buss's 37-culture study. When all the cultures were considered as a group, they found that men showed a reliable tendency to value *physical attractiveness* and *good cooking and housekeeping skills* in a potential mate more than women did. They also found that women placed more importance than men did on *good earning capacity* in a mate. As well, women showed a preference for older men, and men showed a preference for younger women across all 37 cultures. However, the most interesting findings with respect to their predictions occurred when they rated the sample of 37 cultures according to the level of gender equality, using indices of Gender Empowerment and Gender-Related Development available from the United Nations: As the gender equality in societies increased, the tendency to pick mates on the basis of a gendered division of labor decreased. Thus, in more egalitarian cultures, the tendency for women to select men on the basis of their earning capacity and for men to select women on the basis of their domestic skills was weaker than in cultures in which there were large power and status differences between women and men. These findings are compatible with a social structural explanation of female–male differences and suggest that the apparent universality of certain mate selection preferences (and with it, the notion that such preferences are biologically built in to our species through evolution) can be challenged. Eagly and Wood (1999) called for future research that is "systematically designed to represent cultures with differing forms of social organization and levels of gender equality" (p. 420).

Biologist Anne Fausto-Sterling (1992) suggested that the apparent universality of a behavior is, in fact, no guarantee that it is genetic rather than learned. Her counterexamples include the story of a troop of Japanese macaques who came to feast on grain that had been spread on a sandy beach. Researchers observing the monkeys noted that at first they slowly picked out the food from the sand, grain by grain. Eventually, however, one young female monkey picked up a handful of sand and grain, carried it to the water, and threw it in. The sand sank and the food floated, enabling her to scoop it off the water. This new, efficient method of separating the sand from the grain was quickly learned by other members of the troop and continues to be passed on to succeeding generations. Yet, as Fausto-Sterling noted, an outside observer, unaware of the history of the behavior, might guess from its apparent universality that it was genetically based.

Indeed, many researchers have now concluded that a wide variety of behaviors in primates are culturally (rather than genetically) transmitted. An article by several top field researchers lists 39 different behavior patterns, including types of tool usage, grooming, and courtship behaviors, that are present in some chimpanzee groups but absent in other genetically identical (and often geographically nearby) groups. Furthermore, these experts noted that there is tremendous variation in these behaviors even within chimpanzee communities—another argument that the behaviors are culturally transmitted (Whiten et al., 1999). These findings illustrate that it may be unwise to assume that variations in social behavior, even among our primate cousins, are necessarily due to evolutionary pressures.

Animal data do not always support the thesis that males are "programmed" for promiscuity and females are instinctively more selective. Examples of the variety of behavior among animal species are provided by Sarah

Hrdy (1981, 1999), whose extensive descriptions of relations between the sexes among different groups of primates illustrated that a pattern of male–female differences involving male promiscuity and female sexual selectivity and male dominance and competitiveness and female subordination is neither "natural" nor universal among these, our closest animal relatives. Indeed, even if females are seeking reproductive success, they are not necessarily "programmed" to attain it by choosing and remaining with a single mate. In some primate species, such as chimpanzees, bonobos, and langurs, females solicit and copulate with many partners many times (Hrdy, 1999). By manipulating information about paternity, the mother's "sexual promiscuity" protects infants. Because it is difficult for any male to be certain that he is or is not the father of a particular infant, he may refrain from attacking and killing it.

In some human societies, too, women enhance their reproductive success by having sex with several men. Among some traditional forager societies in South America, such as the Ache of Paraguay and the Bari of Venezuela, people believe that a child has multiple fathers—and so married women take several lovers during pregnancy. All of the lovers are considered fathers to the baby and have some responsibility to feed and protect it (Angier, 1999).

Other evolutionary perspectives have been developed to explain the wide range of behaviors observed among human beings. For example, Joan Roughgarden (2004) proposed that the evolution of many traits can be traced to a process of social selection: the selection of physical and behavioral traits that confer an advantage in terms of social acceptance by the group (she calls such traits "social-inclusionary traits"). Group acceptance is necessary for survival and successful reproduction, so traits that enhance it ought to be passed down through generations. When animals within a species seek each other out, she argued that they are not necessarily seeking each other's genes but rather access to the resources controlled by the other. To share such resources, the individual must be accepted; hence, the importance of possessing social-inclusionary traits. Roughgarden noted that many behaviors that make little sense in terms of traditional sexual selection theory do make sense in terms of social selection. For example, female–female courtship pairings occur regularly among Japanese macaques, even when males are present. Why would a female monkey waste her time copulating with another female if her main purpose is to find a mate with good genes to ensure the survival of her offspring? The female needs allies to ensure her place in the dominance hierarchy, and a female macaque's ability to form strong same-sex bonds is, according to this perspective, a social inclusionary trait that is adaptive.

Another approach to evolutionary theory is "biological exuberance"—the idea that biological systems are extravagant and abundant, naturally producing a diverse range of traits even if all such traits do not serve a specific function (Bagemihl, 1999). This perspective denies that all evolution is driven by competition and geared toward the narrow purpose of reproducing individuals' genes, arguing instead that nature tends to express a wide range of developmental possibilities. The notion of biological exuberance rests on studies of the diversity of social/sexual behavior in nature, including same-sex pair bonds and the presence of nonreproducing relatives who help with offspring.

So, the notion that gender differences in behavior stem from different genetically based strategies evolved by females and males to maximize their reproductive fitness, while intriguing, has not been proven. If a genetic basis should be established for some of the behaviors in question, to date scientists have no way of knowing whether their persistence is the result of random genetic events or (as sociobiologists argue) of adaptations for fitness maximization (Fausto-Sterling, 1992). And, as seen in the previous examples, if humans *have* evolved behavioral tendencies to maximize reproductive success, these tendencies probably cannot be summed up in such simple terms as "men compete and women choose" or "men are promiscuous and women are selective." This is not to say that there is no merit in an evolutionary approach to understanding human behavior; in fact, many researchers are amassing data to explore various possibilities of genetic components to human behavior. In many respects, however, the approach remains controversial, and claims for or against the evolutionary basis of female–male differences are more reflective of the claimant's preference for a particular explanation than of any conclusive evidence for that explanation.

BIOSOCIAL MODEL

The biosocial model of female–male differences and similarities blends the idea of "built-in" sex differences from evolutionary theories with the idea of "socially constructed" differences and similarities that provides the basis for social structural theories. **Biosocial theory** "focuses on the interactive relations between the physical attributes of men and women and the social contexts in which they live" (Wood & Eagly, 2002, p. 701). The theory posits that male–female differences arise from the way women and men are distributed in social roles in any given society. However, it does not assume that only social expectations guide this distribution. Rather, the theory suggests that biological processes, such as changes in hormone levels, work together with psychological processes, such as sex-typed social expectations, to "orient men and women toward certain social roles and to facilitate their performance of these roles" (p. 702).

For example, biosocial theory might explain men's attraction to and engagement with competitive roles by noting *both* the social expectation that men will be competitive *and* the tendency for men's testosterone levels to rise when they are expecting to be in competitive situations. Similarly, the theory might explain women's attraction to and involvement in the mothering role by noting *both* the cultural pressures toward motherhood for women *and* the hormonal changes that accompany childbirth and seem to stimulate nurturing behavior (Wood & Eagly, 2002).

But what causes societies to foster different expectations for women and men and to try to channel women and men into different roles in the first place? Wood and Eagly argued that the underlying causes for psychological sex differences are twofold: (1) the physical differences between women and men, especially women's ability to bear infants and nurse them, and men's greater size, speed, and upper body strength; and (2) the kind of society, in terms of social, economic, technological, and ecological forces, in which people live. Under certain conditions, they argued, it can be easier and more efficient for one sex than the other to accomplish certain activities, so the roles are divided to reflect that. For example, in an environment in which food must be obtained by hunting over long distances using bursts of speed, it might make sense for a society to assign the task of obtaining food to men. In an environment where parents must have many babies in order that even one or two will live to adulthood and the only way to ensure an infant's survival is to nurse it for at least the first year of life, it might make sense for a society to assign infant care to women. Thus women's and men's "built-in" strengths are utilized to full advantage, and women and men work together in a division of labor that benefits both. Note, however, that the particular division of labor specified in these examples makes sense only under certain social conditions. If the best way to obtain food in a particular environment is to grow a garden in the backyard or to go to an office and spend all day at a computer to earn money to go the grocery store, there is no special advantage to assigning "food-getting" to men—even though they *are* bigger, stronger, and faster. In a society in which most couples have only one or two children and there are many supports for their survival, it would not be particularly efficient to assign women to spend their lives nurturing children.

Biosocial theory predicts that there would be most consistency in gender roles across societies in which such roles are most clearly tied to sex differences in physical attributes: male size and strength and female capacity for pregnancy and lactation. It also predicts that sex differences will vary systematically among societies according to the conditions that affect the impact of pregnancy, childbirth, and nursing on women's activities or the impact of size and strength on men's activities. For example, in a society where most men's work does not demand strength and where it is common practice *not* to rely exclusively on breast-feeding to nourish infants, there should be fewer pressures toward sex-differentiated behaviors than in a society where men must be physically strong to succeed and women must breast-feed their infants for a long time. The theory also predicts that patriarchal social structures (structures that enshrine male dominance over women) are most likely to occur in societies where women's reproductive activities conflict with the opportunity to perform behaviors that produce power and status in that society. Finally, to guarantee a socially efficient division of labor, the theory predicts that there will be strong socialization pressures for girls and boys to develop different, gender-appropriate kinds of behavior.

General support has been found for the predictions of biosocial theory. Cross-cultural evidence reveals a consistent tendency for societies to be organized to enable mothers to bear and care for children and to take advantage of men's strength and speed (Wood & Eagly, 2002). However, the specific tasks assigned to women and men vary according to the environmental conditions (e.g., if hunting can be done without long absences from home, so that it does not interfere with child care, women hunt). Cross-cultural comparisons also

Reflections : An Evolutionary Basis for Sex Differences in Jealousy?

Which of the following scenarios would cause you more distress: (a) finding out that your partner had passionate sexual intercourse with another person, or (b) finding out that your partner had formed a deep emotional attachment with another person? Some proponents of evolutionary theory predict that women and men will answer this question differently: men will be more upset by sexual infidelity; women will be more distressed by emotional infidelity.

On what basis is this prediction made? Evolutionary theorists suggest that men's reproductive fitness is more threatened by the first scenario. If a man's female partner has sexual intercourse with another man, how does the first man know whether or not he is the father of her child? He may be devoting resources to raising a child that does not carry his genes. On the other hand, women's reproductive fitness may be more threatened by the second scenario. If a woman is pregnant, she knows the child is hers; however, she also knows that her chances of raising the child successfully to adulthood will be better if the father stays around to invest his resources in the child rather than forming a new relationship with another woman. So sexual jealousy may have been more adaptive for men, and emotional jealousy may have been more adaptive for women, and each sex may have evolved automatic mental processes that trigger jealousy in response to different events.

Researchers who have tested this question have found support for the predictions of evolutionary psychologists (e.g., Buss, Larsen, Western, & Semmelroth, 1992). However, you may have found yourself stymied by the question about which scenario would bother you more, and feel that *both* situations would distress you, albeit in different ways. Is there something about the way this question was asked that makes it difficult to answer? Could the question be asked in ways that might produce different results?

The question is asked in a way that makes sense within evolutionary theory, for at least some versions of the theory predict male–female differences on the dimensions of sexual emotional jealousy. But some researchers have asked the question in a different way. Instead of forcing people to make a choice between the two scenarios, they presented respondents with each of the two scenarios one at a time and asked them to rate their reactions to each one in terms of how angry, jealous, calm, relieved, threatened, and hurt they would be (DeSteno, Bartlett, Braverman, & Salovey, 2002). When the scenarios were presented this way, there were no male–female differences in whether sexual or emotional infidelity generated more distress; rather, women were somewhat more distressed than men by both scenarios.

Why do the different ways of asking this question produce different findings with respect to female–male differences? Can these more recent findings be explained by evolutionary theory? Can they be explained by one of the other theoretical approaches to gender?

reveal that patriarchy "emerged in part from the difficulties women experienced in efficiently combining their reproductive activities with skilled tasks of production, which maximally contributed to power and status in more complex societies" (Wood & Eagly, 2002, p. 218). Bearing and rearing children takes time and energy, making it difficult for women to engage in the kind of training and skill development they might need for higher-status roles. Finally, there is considerable evidence that caregivers socialize children to learn a gendered division of labor appropriate for their society.

The biosocial model represents an ambitious and intriguing combination of biological and social approaches to understanding why the sexes differ in their behavior, yet it leaves some questions unanswered. Just how built-in is the relationship between biological sex differences and behavioral sex differences? How did activities that require extensive training and skill emerge as higher in power and status than the ability to bear and nurse children? The developers of this model say they do not view psychological sex differences, even universal ones, as necessarily hard-wired. Rather, they say, "our biosocial model treats behavioral sex differences as repeatedly constructed or emergent given the evolved attributes of the human species, the developmental experiences of the sexes, and the social and ecological structures affecting men and women within a society" (Wood & Eagly, 2002, p. 718).

The four theoretical approaches discussed to this point have all focused on the reasons for gender differences. Psychoanalytic/identification theories locate the origins of the differences in anatomy and examine the early development of parent-child relationships. Social structure/cultural theories pinpoint culturally based power and status differences between females and males as the reason for gender differences in behavior. Evolutionary theories point to genes as the cause for male–female differences. Let us turn now to three theoretical approaches that focus on the "how" rather than the "why" of gender differences and similarities: social learning, cognitive developmental, and social interaction process theories.

SOCIAL LEARNING THEORY/ SOCIAL COGNITIVE THEORY

Social learning theory (Bandura, 1977) suggests that the child develops both gender identity and gender role through a learning process that involves modeling, imitation, and reinforcement. The theory rests on the assumption that boys learn to be masculine and girls to be feminine because gender-role-appropriate behavior is rewarded and gender-role-inappropriate behavior is punished or ignored. Children learn which behaviors are gender-role appropriate by observing and imitating adult and peer models, as well as through trial and error in their own behavior. Social learning theory suggests that a child is most likely to imitate a model who is readily available and perceived as powerful, nurturant, and similar to the self (Mischel, 1970). According to this viewpoint, parental models, particularly a same-sex parent, are the most effective in influencing the child's behavior. The theory suggests that parents and other socializing agents map out gender roles for the child, and then the child is differentially reinforced for following the appropriate one. Children begin to be aware of the two gender roles as early as the first year of life (M. Lewis & Weinraub, 1979; Poulin-Dubois, Serbin, Kenyon, & Derbyshire, 1994), and as early as age 3 children imitate same-sex models more than other-sex models (Bussey & Bandura, 1984).

As the child is repeatedly reminded that he is a boy or she is a girl and differentially reinforced for doing boy things or girl things, it gradually becomes rewarding for him to think of himself as a boy and for her to think of herself as a girl. Thus, through observation, imitation, and reinforcement, the formation of an appropriate gender role precedes and lays the groundwork for establishing gender identity.

Boys are subject to more intense gender socialization pressure from parents than girls are (Lytton & Romney, 1991; Maccoby & Jacklin, 1974; C. L. Martin, 1990), and they also exert this type of pressure on one another. Even among toddlers, boys are more likely than girls to be scolded by their same-sex peers for participating in other-sex activities (Fagot, 1985). Boys are more likely than girls to attend to and imitate same-sex models and to reject behaviors and objects associated with the other sex (Bussey & Bandura, 1984; Bussey & Perry, 1982). In fact, whereas both boys and girls look longer at stimuli linked to their own gender, by the age of 23 months this preference for looking at gender-appropriate toys is stronger among boys than girls (Serbin, Poulin-Dubois, Colburne, Sen, & Eichstedt, 2001). According to social learning theorists, the stronger preference by boys for gender-appropriate activities is caused by parents' greater emphasis on gender differentiation for sons than for daughters (Bandura & Bussey, 2004).

Social learning theory may appear, at first glance, to treat the child as a relatively passive learner, but the socialization process is much more complex, cognitively mediated, and interactive than such a view implies. Children's influence on their parents' behavior may be just as strong as the reverse (Maccoby, 1992). For instance, an initially small difference between a female and male infant in response to comforting may gradually be magnified because it produces, through differential reinforcement of the parents for comforting behavior, differences in the degree of comforting the parents will provide the two infants. The different levels of comforting behavior directed toward the two infants will then cause greater differences between them, which will in turn cause the parents to treat the two even more differently, and so on. Some theorists have suggested that many aspects of gender roles may be learned through reciprocal role learning: learning one gender role through interacting with a person (e.g., a parent) playing the complementary one (Lamb, Owen, & Chase-Lansdale, 1979). The process works through subtle reinforcement: "Interaction proceeds most smoothly (i.e., positive reinforcement occurs) when the behavior of the daughter meshes smoothly with the masculine behavior of the father. This is most likely to occur when she behaves in a feminine manner" (p. 94).

On the whole, there is a great deal of evidence that social learning plays a part in acquiring gender roles. For example, knowledge about gender stereotypes increases and becomes more complex with age from preschool to college (Leahy & Shirk, 1984; C. L. Martin, 1993; C. L. Martin, Wood, & Little, 1990), and the trend toward same-sex modeling increases during the same period (Bussey & Bandura, 1984). Children whose mothers model nontraditional (for women) activities in the home are less likely than other children to show preferences for gender-typed activities, whereas children whose fathers adhere to traditional gender roles display more knowledge of what activities and occupations are generally associated with each gender (Serbin, Powlishta, & Gulko, 1993).

It is clear that the learning of gender roles and gender identity is not directed solely by reinforcement but has a strong cognitive element. Children attach meanings to their observations of others, and to rewards and punishment directed at themselves or others. In the first place, direct reinforcement does not play as strong a part as one might think. For example, parents do not treat their male and female children differently enough to account for gender-role differences (Lytton & Romney, 1991; Maccoby & Jacklin, 1974). Also, young children are apparently impervious to reinforcement from certain sources, with boys responding more to male peers and females responding more to teachers and female peers (Fagot, 1985). In the second place, the importance of imitation in learning gender roles is not as clear-cut as the theory predicts. Children do not always select same-sex models to imitate (Maccoby & Jacklin, 1974; Raskin & Israel, 1981), and the imitation process may be more complex than simply choosing a single model in a given situation. Research by D. G. Perry and Bussey (1979) indicates that children may observe the different frequencies with which males and females, in general, perform certain behaviors in given situations and may then use these observations to construct abstract models of female-appropriate and male-appropriate behavior. Once a child has constructed these abstract models, he or she is more likely to imitate a particular same-sex person if that person usually behaves in ways that fit the child's model for sex-appropriate behavior. Thus a girl might not imitate the behavior of a mother whom she sees as an atypical female, and a boy might imitate his father only when the father behaves in ways the boy sees as representative of males in general.

The modification of social learning theory presented by Perry and Bussey incorporates a view of the child as an active participant in the socialization process and implies that cognitive abilities are important in this process. A similar view was elaborated by Albert Bandura (1986), who renamed his version of social learning theory **social cognitive theory.** This theory, which was applied to gender development by Bussey and Bandura (1999), suggests that, although children may initially learn gender roles through external rewards and punishments, as they mature they begin to regulate their own actions through internal rewards and punishments. Research shows that children learn at a very young age to discriminate between conduct that is appropriate for girls and conduct that is appropriate for boys and then begin to evaluate and regulate their own behavior based on this knowledge (Bussey & Bandura, 1992). For example, 4-year-old boys anticipated that they would feel good about themselves if they played with a truck and bad about themselves if they played with a doll. These anticipated feelings apparently guided their behavior when they were presented with these toys. Boys presented with "feminine" toys used a variety of strategies to avoid playing with them: objected to the experimenter that they did not like dolls, tried to have the dolls removed from the room, or used the beaters in a cooking set as guns or drills. One 7-year-old boy who was induced to change diapers on a baby doll for the filming of a videotape later commented, "It's the most awful thing I have ever done" (p. 1247).

Although much of the relevant research has been done with children, social cognitive theory is not restricted in its focus to childhood socialization. Rather, its proponents argue that, "as different periods of life present new demands for self-renewal, adaptation, and change," individuals reflect on their behavior and organize it to fit what they see as the requirements of their roles (Bussey & Bandura, 2004, p. 93).

The external approval and disapproval children use to shape their personal internal standards of behavior do not come just from parents or other specific, important adults but from peers. According to one recent theory of **group socialization** (J. R. Harris, 1995), peers are the mediators and interpreters of cultural views of gender. This theory postulates that children become socialized primarily by identifying with their peer group and taking on that group's norms for attitudes and behavior. According to this theory, cultural knowledge and behavior are transmitted not directly from parents to their children but from the parents' peer group and other cultural sources to the children's peer group. The peer groups filter cultural transmissions. For example, children quickly learn what behaviors from their home context are acceptable to their peer group. They do not transfer behavior learned at home to the peer group unless it is shared and approved by most of the other children. If children come from atypical homes, they censor their home-learned behavior, and it tends not to get transferred to the group.

Thus sophisticated approaches to the social learning process emphasize cognition and the meanings that the child learns to attach to gender-linked behavior. The theoretical approach described next emphasizes cognition as the main issue in the development of gender-consistent behavior.

COGNITIVE THEORIES

Cognitive Developmental Theory

Cognitive developmental theory (Kohlberg, 1966; Kohlberg & Ullian, 1974) proposes that gender, like other concepts, cannot be learned until a child reaches a particular stage of intellectual development. Between the ages of 3 and 5, a child acquires **gender constancy**—an understanding that a person's gender is fixed and cannot be altered by a change in hairstyle, dress, or name. Before that age, according to Kohlberg, although a child may have learned that people can be categorized as either male or female, she or he may sometimes make errors in classifying the self or others and think that arbitrary changes in classification can occur (e.g., a little girl may say, "When I used to be a boy . . ."). Slaby and Frey (1975) describe the formation of gender constancy and of belonging to one gender as having three stages: (1) an awareness that two sexes exist and of belonging to one of them (attained around age 3), followed by (2) an understanding that gender does not change over time (stability), followed in turn by (3) an awareness that gender remains unchanged across situations and behaviors (constancy). The idea that children do not understand the permanence of gender categories until achieving a certain stage of cognitive development is rooted in Jean Piaget's (1954) theory that children's cognitive development occurs in stages. Piaget argued that children do not have an understanding of physical constancy (e.g., constancy of mass or volume) before approximately ages 4 to 7.

According to the cognitive developmental approach, once the child has categorized her- or himself with some certainty as female or male, it becomes an important, self-defining category (Martin, Ruble, & Szkrybalo, 2002). She or he will use this self-categorization as an organizing focus for attaching value to behaviors. The child will attach higher value to gender-appropriate behaviors and will find the performance of gender-appropriate behaviors more reinforcing than gender-inappropriate behaviors. In other words, gender-appropriate behaviors acquire a meaning that makes them self-reinforcing for the child, whereas gender-inappropriate behaviors acquire negative connotations and are avoided. The little girl embraces "feminine" values; the little boy adopts "masculine" ones. At this stage, the child may identify with a same-sex parent, using the parent as one of many guides for establishing correct behavior for her or his gender category. Other models, such as peers, television, and stories, will also be used, and rewards and punishment meted out to the child will be used by the child as additional cues to appropriate behavior.

Cognitive developmental theory portrays the child as actively searching for cues as to how to behave competently and correctly rather than as being passively shaped by environmental forces. In the process of seeking out the correct way to behave, the child passes through a stage of great rigidity with respect to gender roles. Children ages 6 to 7 often have oversimplified, inflexible views of the two gender roles and adhere tenaciously to gender stereotypes. At this age, for example, a child may refuse to believe that women can be physicians or carpenters, even if the child's own mother holds one of these positions. It is as if the child at this stage is trying to solidify a sense of gender identity by renouncing any form of ambiguity. At a later age, secure in a gender identity, the child becomes less uncomfortable about occasional deviations from the "appropriate" gender role and less rigid about gender stereotypes.

Cognitive developmental theory receives support from studies that show that children's basic gender identity guides their behavior. For example, some studies have found that young children who can successfully label the two sexes or who can identify and label their own sex behave in more gender-stereotypic ways: They spend more time with same-sex playmates and tend to choose gender-typed toys (Fagot, 1985; C. L. Martin & Little, 1990). Children who begin successfully labeling gender at an early age show increasingly gender-typed behavior over time (Fagot & Leinbach, 1993). Research also shows that children value their own gender group more highly than the other group (C. L. Martin, 1989; Powlishta, 1990). Moreover, between the ages of 3 and 8, children show a progression in their views of gender stereotypes that is re-lated to other measures of cognitive flexibility (Coker, 1984; Leahy & Shirk, 1984); this same progression has also been found in other cultures (Munroe, Shimmin, & Munroe, 1984).

Cognitive developmental theory indicates that the adoption of gender roles occurs as a result of identifying with a gender category, but much gender-typing occurs *before* the age of gender constancy. For example, by the age of 6 to 8 months, babies seem to be able to discriminate female from male voices (C. L. Miller, 1983). By 9 to 11 months they not only can tell male and female faces apart (Leinbach & Fagot, 1993) but can detect relationships between faces of women and men and gender-related objects (Levy & Haaf, 1994). How can children make these distinctions before they have reached the level of cogni-tive development that allows them to understand gender as a category? One explanation, based on a comprehensive study of children ages 5 to 12, is that cognitive development and social learning are associated with different as-pects of the process of adopting gender roles (Serbin, Powlishta, & Gulko, 1993). According to this research, cognitive development is most strongly as-sociated with *cognitive* aspects of gender-typing such as knowledge of stereo-types and flexibility in applying them; social learning is most strongly linked to *affective* aspects of gender-typing such as preferences for gender-appropriate activities, occupations, and peers. Other psychologists have suggested that early differentiation in gender-related behavior may be due to biological in-fluences or parental reinforcement—or that perhaps, since it is so difficult to measure cognitions in infants and very young children, researchers are wrong about the ages when gender identity and labeling begin to occur (C. L. Martin et al., 2002). These authors argued that children's development of categories and cognitions relevant to gender begins earlier than previously thought, and they suggested that much more research on very young children is required be-fore we can understand the roles played by cognition and social/observational learning in gender development. However, they asserted that the crucial as-pect is not the age at which children achieve gender constancy but "children's recognition of the categorical importance of gender, which in turn motivates them to comply with gender norms at a particular point in development. This process is cognitive-developmental whether it occurs at 3–5 years or 5–7 years of age or whether it occurs in relation to understanding the stability rather than the consistency of gender identity" (p. 910).

Gender Schema Theory

A **schema** is a cognitive structure (a network of associations or set of interre-lated ideas) that guides and organizes the way an individual processes and makes sense of information. A person holds a variety of schemas, each one helping to structure information into categories that are important to him or her. A person might (or might not) have schemas with respect to age, to eth-nicity, to gender, to particular occupations, and to proper versus rude behav-ior. These schemas are used in evaluating and assimilating new information.

Information that is relevant to a person and fits a schema held by that person is attended to and processed quickly, whereas information that does not relate to an existing schema is ignored. Thus a person who is **gender schematic** (one with a strong gender schema) would spontaneously sort people, characteristics, and behaviors into masculine and feminine categories, regardless of their differences on other dimensions unrelated to gender. He or she would, for example, be more likely to remember things relevant to gender than things relevant to nationality and to make faster, easier, and more confident decisions about the applicability to the self or others of gender-related than nationality-related traits. An individual who is **gender aschematic** (one with a very weak gender schema) would be unlikely to categorize ideas, behaviors, and characteristics according to gender. It has been argued that when interacting with and forming initial impressions of others, people activate their gender schemas more quickly than schemas based on less easily observable attributes. The easy activation of such schemas can both stem from and reinforce gender stereotypes (Deaux & Major, 1987).

People who hold themselves to rigid standards of femininity and masculinity may be strongly gender schematic. As Bem (1985) suggested, highly masculine or feminine individuals may differ from others "not in their *ability* to organize information on the basis of gender but in their *threshold* for doing so spontaneously" (p. 197). Bem's own research and that of others (Signorella, Bigler, & Liben, 1993) provided some support for this idea. However, research shows that a person need not adhere to gender stereotypes to be gender schematic. For example, a woman who does not describe herself in stereotypically feminine ways may still process information readily in terms of gender, perhaps because she is interested in gender for academic or political reasons (Freedman & Lips, 1996).

Two cultural conditions explain the widespread reliance on gender schema for organizing information. First, social ideology and customs construct a large number of associations between gender and other qualities, behaviors, concepts, and categories (e.g., there is a long list of behaviors considered feminine or masculine). Second, society assigns great functional importance to gender distinction, using gender as a basis for many norms, taboos, group membership, and institutional arrangements (Bem, 1985). Thus "gender has come to have cognitive primacy over many other social categories because the culture has made it so" (p. 212). Children are taught not only a large network of sex-related associations that can form the basis for a gender schema but also the message that "the dichotomy between male and female has intensive and extensive relevance to virtually every domain of human experience" (p. 212).

There is a great deal of evidence that, even by very early ages, children have begun to develop networks of associations with respect to gender. For instance, researchers conducted one study in which they showed infants a toy, such as a doll, while simultaneously having them listen to the question, "Where is my toy?" Then they showed the infants pictures of a girl and a boy and measured the amount of time they spent looking at each face. There was a reliable tendency (evident in girls by age 18 months and in boys by 24 months) to look longer at the face that was "gender appropriate" for the toy being shown (Serbin, Poulin-Dubois, Colburne, Sen, & Eichstedt, 2001). In another study, 2-year-old children's surprise at gender-incongruous behaviors was measured by testing whether they would look longer at photographs depicting unusual pairings of gender and behavior (Serbin, Poulin-Dubois, & Eichstedt, 2002). They found that these toddlers looked longer at a picture of a man putting on lipstick than of a woman putting on lipstick—suggesting that they had formed associations between certain activities and gender groups. Researchers have also found that, at 24 months of age, girls tend to choose a male doll to illustrate a masculine activity such as fixing a car or shaving and a female doll to illustrate a feminine activity such as rocking a baby or vacuuming (Poulin-Dubois, Serbin, Eichstedt, Sen, & Beissel, 2002).

Every association that makes up the network of associations that we call a gender schema need not be taught directly to a child. Instead, children may construct distinctions based on dimensions of meaning that emerge as part of their experience. Beverly Fagot and Mary Leinbach (1993) speculated that a young child's abstract generalizations about women and men "may have their roots in the infant's different sensory experience of men and women—their shape and texture, the sounds they make, their movement patterns" (p. 220). They noted research demonstrating that 4-year-old children

> assign bears, fire, and something rough to boys and men, while butterflies, hearts, and flowers are for women and girls. We strongly doubt that such notions are taught directly. True, children may observe women, more often than men, with or wearing flowers, but do they see men in the company of bears or women with butterflies? It is at least plausible that these youngsters have begun to associate qualities such as strength or dangerousness with males, and gentler qualities with females, whether or not they can name the attributes involved. (p. 220)

Such metaphorical associations may help children build gender schemas by allowing the children to construct schemas around broad themes or dimensions (such as associating women with softness and roundness and men with hardness) rather than with specific objects (Leinbach, Hort, & Fagot, 1997). Research suggests that, even as early as 18 months of age, toddlers have begun to form both metaphorical and more specific associations with masculinity, linking such items as firefighter hats, hammers, fir trees, and bears with males (Eichstedt, Serbin, Poulin-Dubois, & Sen, 2002).

Bem (1981, 1985) suggested that people differ in the degree to which they use the gender schema to process information about themselves and others, and she argued that strongly gender-typed individuals are those who have a strong tendency toward gender-schematic processing. **Gender schema theory** states that individual differences in reliance on the gender schema stem from differences in the degree to which the gender dichotomy is emphasized during socialization. Direct research support for this aspect of the theory is not yet available; however, Bem (1985) has speculated on her theory's implications for parents trying to raise gender-aschematic children in a gender-schematic society. She suggested first that parents teach children about sex differences in a way that emphasizes the biological aspects and de-emphasizes the cultural correlates of maleness and femaleness, thus providing the child with a much narrower and more precise network of associations on which to construct a gender schema. She argued that children should be taught that genitalia are the definitive attributes for distinguishing females from males and that other attributes such as dress, occupation, or behavior are irrelevant. Second, she suggested that parents provide alternative schemas for their children to use in interpreting the wider culture's large set of sex-related associations. In particular, she proposed that children be provided with an "individual differences schema" (a great deal more variability exists between individual members of a group than between most groups), a "cultural relativism schema" (different people believe different things), and, finally, when children are able to understand it, a "sexism schema" (an understanding of the history and process of sex discrimination). All of these alternative schemas should help the child organize information about the cultural correlates of maleness and femaleness without incorporating them into a gender schema.

Bem (1985) provided an example of an outcome of her first suggestion:

> The liberation that comes from having an unambiguous genital definition of sex and the imprisonment that comes from not having such a definition are nicely illustrated by the story of what happened to our son Jeremy, then age four, the day he decided to wear barrettes to nursery school. Several times that day, another little boy told Jeremy that he, Jeremy, must be a girl because "only girls wear barrettes." After trying to explain to this child that "wearing barrettes doesn't matter" and that "being a boy means having a penis and testicles," Jeremy finally pulled down his pants as a way of making his point more convincingly. The other child was not impressed. He simply said, "Everybody has a penis; only girls wear barrettes." (p. 216)

Gender schema theory needs and will inspire more research. It builds on both cognitive developmental and social cognitive theories in that it portrays the child as both actively constructing gender categories and responding to environmental cues, and it provides an interesting perspective on how the sociocultural context influences the acquisition of gender roles.

SOCIAL INTERACTION PROCESS THEORIES

Both social learning/social cognitive and cognitive developmental theories are "process" theories that focus on the mechanisms through which gender roles are acquired. They also tend to emphasize learning behavior during childhood as a basis for lifelong gender roles. But is childhood learning the whole story when it comes to behaving "like a woman" or "like a man" in later life? Does a woman act feminine mainly because she was rewarded in childhood for doing girl things and she internalized feminine values? Or does the process continue beyond early learning of gender roles to encompass her choices and her interactions with others throughout her life? Some theoretical models of gender-related behavior have highlighted the processes that maintain continuity in behavior once it is learned and that elicit such behavior in particular social contexts.

Continuities in Interactional Styles

Will an ill-tempered child grow up to be a grouchy adult? What determines whether a dependent child matures into a dependent adult? Does the gender of the child make a difference? Two aspects of the way an individual interacts with the social environment provide keys to answering these questions: cumulative continuity and interactional continuity (Caspi, 2000; Caspi, Bem, & Elder, 1989).

Cumulative continuity is the process through which an individual, beginning in childhood, selects and creates environments that fit her or his preferred forms of behavior—and these selected environments, in turn, reinforce and sustain that behavior. A shy child, for example, may select environments in which little social contact is required. Such environments will not push the child in the direction of becoming more gregarious; rather, they will sustain the child's shyness. The older the child gets and the more independent from parentally chosen environments, the more influential is this tendency to select environments that feel comfortable and that reinforce already-existing behavior patterns (Scarr, 1988). This process is truly cumulative in that, over time, the choices have a snowball effect, reinforcing more and more strongly the original behavioral preferences.

Interactional continuity refers to the two-way transactions between the person and the social environment. The person's behavior elicits reactions from others, and those reactions promote continuity in the original behavior through reinforcement, confirmation of expectations, and confirmation of the person's self-concept. For example, an aggressive child expects others to be hostile and so behaves in ways that trigger hostile reactions in others—confirming the child's expectations and making aggressive behavior still more likely in the future.

If small initial temperamental differences exist between females and males, continuity theory suggests that such differences might well be solidified and even magnified over the life course as individuals choose compatible environments and elicit reactions from others. Some researchers have suggested that male and female infants differ on such dimensions as activity level and amount of crying. It is difficult to be certain that such differences exist at birth, however, because reactions to females and males differ from the first moments of the infant's encounter with the world. Continuity theory implies, however, that differences that exist for *any* reason can be maintained and amplified through interactional and cumulative continuity.

A particularly interesting aspect of this analysis for understanding gender-related behavior is that the outcomes of these continuity-oriented processes depend on the degree to which the individual's preferred behavior fits the social expectations for females and males. For example, one study of individuals who reached adulthood during the 1940s shows that boys who were shy grew up to be men who were described as aloof, lacking social poise, and showing a reluctance to act. These men, compared to other men, were delayed in marrying, becoming fathers, and establishing stable careers—acting out, in general, a reluctance to enter new and unfamiliar social settings and role transitions (Caspi et al., 1989). An examination of the life course of the shy men shows the snowball effect of early shyness: They tended to delay entering a stable career, which in turn lowered their overall achievement, which in turn decreased their occupational stability. The researchers suggested that these men's shyness slowed them down precisely because it did not fit with the role requirements for American men: taking the initiative during courtship and being assertive at work.

In contrast to males, shy girls did not grow up to be adults who delayed marriage and parenthood. Although their shy interactional style seemed to endure, the descriptions of them were less negatively tinged than those of the shy men. The shy women were described as quietly independent, intellectual, and inner directed. It appears that shyness in females, being more expected than in males, elicits more positive reactions from others and thus does not inhibit females' social relationships in the same way it inhibits males'. Similarly, shyness did not affect the timing of marriage and parenthood for women because they did not have to take the initiative in courtship. Shyness did seem to affect women's working life, however. Shy women were much more likely than other women to have no employment history or to have left employment as soon as they were married or had a child. Shyness is obviously more compatible with the traditional expectations for females than with those for males. The importance of social context and of role expectations, even in the expression and life consequences of early personality dispositions, is clear here. Early shyness meant different things for the lives of the women than for the lives of the men. Had these individuals grown up in a time and place in which shyness was acceptable for men and not for women, the results would have been very different.

An Interactive Model of Gender-Related Behavior

The models of gender differences that we have considered so far focus on how people acquire gender roles. They begin with childhood and show how various forces encourage some behavior and discourage others, eventually solidifying a repertoire of behaviors that fit expectations for a person's gender. The interactive model proposed by Kay Deaux and Brenda Major (1987) does not look at long-term causes of gender-related behavior. Rather, it zeros in on aspects of the immediate social situation that promote or inhibit behavior that is congruent with femininity or masculinity. In other words, its focus is on the *display* of gender-related behaviors rather than on their *acquisition.*

The **interactive model of gender-related behavior** is built on the idea that an individual's gender-related behaviors in a social interaction are influenced by what others expect, what the individual believes about her- or himself, and situational cues. The processes involved in this influence are expectation confirmation (both "seeing" only what one expects to see and self-fulfilling prophecy) and the individual's strategies to both confirm her or his self-view and present an acceptable image to others. A key concept in the model is the **gender belief system,** described by Kay Deaux and Marianne LaFrance (1998) as "a multifaceted, all-encompassing set of ideas that people have about gender

. . . [including] . . . stereotypes that people have about the characteristics of women and men; the attitudes that they hold about the social roles occupied by women and men; and the views men and women themselves have about their own gender identity" (p. 793).

In the abstract, the model works as follows: Two people, a perceiver and a target, approach an interaction, each with a set of beliefs *about the target*. The perceiver's beliefs about the target are based on the gender category (female or male) of the target as well as on personal experience with that individual. Beliefs related to the gender category of the target can be activated or made especially salient by certain occurrences or environmental conditions. These beliefs influence the perceiver's actions toward the target. The target enters the situation with a set of beliefs about the self, particular aspects of which may be emphasized by the situation or by recent occurrences. The target interprets the actions of the perceiver, weighs possible alternatives, then takes actions that may either confirm or disconfirm the expectations of the perceiver. The course of the entire interaction is affected by certain modifying conditions: the social desirability of the behavior the perceiver expects from the target, the certainty with which that expectation is held and communicated, and the relative balance between the target's concerns with sustaining her or his self-concept and presenting a positive image.

The model diagrammed in Figure 2.2 can be illustrated by the following example (Deaux & Major, 1987). In this example, the perceiver is Manager X, who supervises two entry-level managers, Joan and John. The situation is a performance appraisal exercise involving leadership of a small group.

> We begin by summarizing an interaction sequence that should maximize the likelihood that sex differences in leadership style will emerge. Manager X firmly believes that men and women have quite different characteristics, particularly in the area of leadership style (Box A). These beliefs are not only chronically accessible for Manager X but have been recently activated by an incident at work that highlighted differences between women and men (Box B). These beliefs prompt Manager X to convey quite different messages to Joan and John as to what is expected in the exercise (Box C). For example, Manager X hints to John that the group session is an opportunity for him to show his ability to take charge, but Manager X emphasizes the cooperative aspects of the group situation when talking to Joan.
>
> To continue our maximal sex differences example, assume that Joan and John have quite different histories of leadership experience and quite different self-images as to their leadership abilities and preferred styles (Box D). Furthermore, the group context, because of past associations, activates different issues for the two managers, differences that are accentuated by the expectancy the manager has conveyed (Box E). Not surprisingly, John interprets the situation as an opportunity to show how well he can take charge, whereas Joan interprets the situation as an opportunity to show her cooperative talents (Box F). Joan and John then act quite differently in the group setting (Box G). This observable sex difference in behavior then feeds back to confirm the initial beliefs of Manager X (Box I) as well as the initial self-assessments of John and Joan (Box J). (p. 372)

The same basic scenario would produce few male–female differences if Manager X did not view male and female leadership styles differently, Joan and John had equivalent beliefs about their own leadership styles and abilities,

Figure 2.2   A model of social interaction for gender-related behavior.

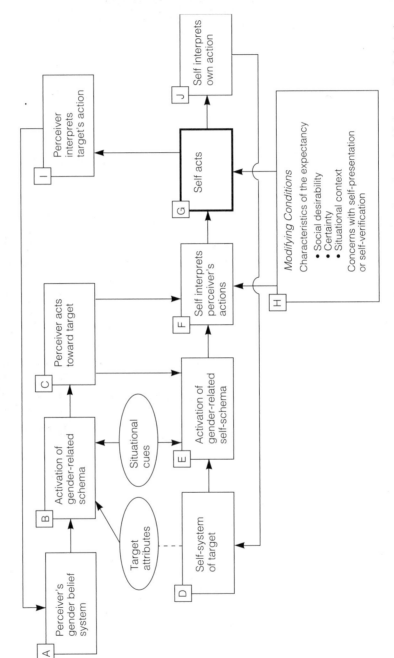

Source: From K. Deaux and B. Major (1987). Putting gender into context: An interactive model of gender-related behavior. *Psychological Review, 94*(3), 372.

Overview — Theories of the gendering of identity and behavior

Theory	The *Why* of Gender Differences	The *How* of Gender Differences
Psychoanalytic/identification	Early theories emphasized anatomical differences between the sexes. Later theories emphasized the different cultural values attached to girls and boys.	Children identify with a same-sex parent.
Social structural/cultural	Power and status differences exist between women and men in many societies. There is a gendered division of labor that is self-perpetuating.	Social arrangements and structures in societies support and maintain differing behaviors for females and males.
Evolutionary	Humans and other organisms have a drive for reproductive success: to pass along their own genetic heritage.	Different behaviors may be linked to reproductive success for females and males. When this is the case, females and males may have evolved with differing behavioral tendencies.
Biosocial	Human societies self-organize to maximize the efficiency with which the tasks involved in surviving and thriving are carried out. Individuals are motivated to fit in with the social expectations promoted by their societies.	Cultures build on the physical differences between women and men by socializing the two sexes toward a division of labor that is efficient under the particular environmental conditions they face. Individuals respond to these social expectations and to their own biological processes and constraints by adopting gendered roles.
Social learning/social cognitive	Children want to receive rewards from others and to achieve a sense of competence and self-efficacy.	Modeling, imitation, and reinforcement, including self-reinforcement, are the means through which children acquire their gender identity and gendered behavior.

Overview Theories of the gendering of identity and behavior *(concluded)*

Theory	The **Why** of Gender Differences	The **How** of Gender Differences
Cognitive developmental	Children are motivated to learn the correct ways to categorize and fit into their social world.	As children become cognitively mature enough to grasp gender categories, they place themselves in a category and try to behave in ways they see as a good fit to that category.
Gender schema	Children are motivated to learn the correct ways to categorize and fit into their social world.	Children begin at an early age to develop networks of associations with gender. These schemas guide their interpretation of events and of their own and others' actions, and they also guide their behavioral choices.
Continuity	People may direct different treatment and expectations toward girls and boys, starting in early childhood.	Small initial differences in treatment or temperament are magnified over time through the processes of interactive and cumulative continuity.
Interactive	In social situations, people adjust to the expectations of others. These expectations often are related to the gender belief system.	In any social situation, people's behavior is influenced by a combination of what they think others expect and their own inclinations. In situations in which either or both of these factors are influenced by components of the gender belief system, gender differences in behavior will occur.

and nothing happened to trigger gender-related expectations in either party. However, the situation would become more complicated if the manager's expectations were inconsistent with those of Joan and John—for instance, if Manager X believed that women and men manage very differently, but Joan and John had very similar self-concepts and behavioral tendencies. In such cases, the modifying conditions in Box H must be considered. For instance, Joan and John would be more likely to behave differently, despite their similarity in self-concepts and behavioral dispositions, if the manager had a great deal of power and conveyed the expectations very clearly and if their concern with presenting themselves in a positive light was stronger than their concern with behaving in a way consistent with their self-concepts.

The models discussed earlier in the chapter postulate explanations for the stability of and differences in the behavior of women and men. The interactive model presented by Deaux and Major provides a possible explanation for the flexibility and variability of gender-related behavior: why, even if they have learned well how to be "feminine," women do not always act that way and why, when the conditions are arranged a certain way, even the most pre-dictably "macho" man will be unassertive and compliant. Both types of mod-els are necessary for an understanding of gender-related behavior.

PERSPECTIVES ON DIFFERENCE

This book, and much of the psychological research on gender, centers on three basic questions: What do we know about the similarities and differences be-tween women and men? Where does that knowledge come from? How is that knowledge shaped and limited by cultural perceptions of femininity and mas-culinity? Each of the theories discussed in this chapter provides a framework for investigating gender similarities and differences, and each of the frame-works shapes and limits what we notice. The theories address the issue of how and why female and male human beings might come to be different. Some of the theories, such as Freudian psychoanalytic theory and evolutionary theo-ries, take female–male difference as a given and attempt to explain why it is in-evitable. Others, such as social learning and social interaction process theories, emphasize the flexibility of cultural processes that produce differences and show how different social environments might produce alternative patterns of male–female difference.

But should we be focusing so strongly on differences? Or should we accept that gender differences, however produced, are minor and search instead for the similarities between women and men? Perspectives on gender differences have shifted dramatically over the centuries between a hierarchical one that looks at women and men as essentially similar though differently developed and one that looks on the sexes as opposites. Missing, of course, is a perspec-tive that views women and men as very similar and *equally* well developed.

Both the hierarchical and the opposites views of gender differences have been used as "explanations" for female inferiority, and a generation of feminist-oriented psychologists, beginning in the 1970s, rejected this emphasis on female–male difference and focused instead on demonstrating that men and women are similar in their abilities, in their traits, and in their reactions to many situations. However, tension has developed between this approach and another that reemphasizes the study of differences—this time from the viewpoint that the qualities distinguishing women from men are positive ones, not sources of inferiority. The latter approach emphasizes the differences in females' and males' experiences and women's role in reproduction. Rachel Hare-Mustin and Jeanne Maracek (1990) offered the labels *alpha bias* and *beta bias* for these two approaches. **Alpha bias** is a tendency toward exaggerating dif-ferences. **Beta bias** is an inclination to ignore or minimize differences. They noted that each approach is problematic. Alpha bias can support the boundaries between females and males and the marginalization of women. It can also be used to uphold the status quo by arguing that the social environment has been constructed to accommodate gender differences rather than create or perpetuate status inequalities. Beta bias "draws attention away from . . . differences in power and resources between women and men" (p. 44) and ignores special needs of women and men.

Which is the best approach? Neither. Both. If we focus on similarities at the expense of differences, we risk failing to understand the ways women and men experience the world differently. If we focus on differences at the expense of similarities, we risk perpetuating the notions of inferiority that a "male as norm" tradition has foisted on women. The tension between the two approaches may be necessary. Kimball (1995) argued that we should practice "double visions," refusing to choose either the emphasis on similarities or the emphasis on differences as more true than the other. If we deliberately engage the tension between the two approaches when we compare people across genders (and other categories that are socially constructed), we will be more aware of the complexities of our social world. Moreover, as Elizabeth Percival (1991) noted, that tension may help us to be conscious of both the similarities and the differences among women and among men of different races, classes, ages, and sexual orientations. For example, just as women and men share many qualities and experiences that cut across gender lines but also are likely to have differing experiences, so women of different races or men of different races are also likely to share many qualities and experiences that cut across racial lines but also to have differing experiences. Although the pull to choose between emphasizing similarities or emphasizing differences is compelling, ignoring either approach is the most dangerous choice of all.

SUMMARY

Seven general types of theories address the origins, development, and maintenance of behavioral and personality differences and similarities between human males and females. Psychoanalytic/identification theories emphasize individual personality development, ascribing particular importance to early parent-child relationships. Another set of theories focuses on social structure and culture, emphasizing the role of social arrangements on the maintenance of gender roles and stereotypes. Power and status differences between women and men and the division of labor by sex have been pinpointed within this theoretical context as important factors in maintaining gender differences in behavior. A third set of theories proposes an evolutionary framework to explain differences between human females and males, arguing that observed differences between the sexes have a genetic basis and have arisen through adaptation. A fourth approach, biosocial theory, posits that female–male behavioral differences arise from the interaction between biological sex differences and social expectations that are rooted in particular environmental contexts. The social learning and cognitive approaches place strong emphasis on the processes governing the development of gender identity and gender roles. Both theories focus on the role of the wider social environment and the child's understanding of it in developing gender identity, roles, attitudes, and stereotypes. Social learning theory emphasizes observation, imitation, and reinforcement and conceptualizes the child as someone who acts in ways most likely to result in social reinforcement. Cognitive developmental theory stresses the child's active attempt to understand social rules and to be socially competent. Another cognitive theory, gender schema theory, emphasizes the associations children learn to make with gender. The social interaction process approach continues to focus on process but extends to an explanation of behavior over the life course. Within this approach, Deaux and Major's (1987) interaction process model focuses not on distant or long-term factors but on the specific conditions of particular social interactions that promote gender-differentiated or gender-similar behavior. Their model helps us understand why gender-related behavior is flexible and variable and why, in the face of fairly consistent socialization pressures to be different, women and men still frequently behave similarly.

No theory discussed in this chapter has emerged as adequate to explain all aspects of gender, although some, based on the evidence, seem to be more adequate than others. All are useful, however, in that their presence gives rise to questions that can be investigated and to ideas that can be debated. They provide, at least, a place to begin the analysis.

Much of the research described in the remainder of this book is based on these theories; if you read carefully, you will find both support and contradiction for the various theoretical approaches. You will also find instances in which the adoption of a different theory would have led the researcher to frame questions differently and to measure different things. The message is that in research, as in the rest of life, the answers one gets depend partly on the questions one asks—so it is important to understand where the questions come from! Of course, the answers a researcher gets also depend on *how* the questions are asked, a subject to which we turn in the next chapter.

KEY TERMS

theory	anal stage	gynocentric
psychoanalytic theory	phallic stage	devaluation
consciousness	latency phase	sexualization
unconscious	genital stage	gender-role strain
id	Oedipus complex	gender identity
ego	penis envy	gender role
superego	Electra complex	sexual orientation
oral stage	phallocentric	social structure theories

social dominance
   theory
social role theory
evolutionary theories
sociobiology
evolutionary
   psychology
biosocial theory
social learning theory

social cognitive theory
group socialization
   theory
cognitive developmental
   theory
gender constancy
schema
gender schematic
gender aschematic

gender schema theory
cumulative continuity
interactional continuity
interactive model of
   gender-related
   behavior
gender belief system
alpha bias
beta bias

Researching Sex and Gender
Exploring the Whys and Hows

At the beginning of the 20th century, Helen Thompson, a graduate student at the University of Chicago, embarked on an ambitious thesis project. She wanted to "obtain a complete and systematic statement of the psychological likenesses and differences of the sexes by the experimental method" (Thompson [Woolley], 1903). Thompson used 50 Chicago undergraduates, half of them male and half female, of the same age and background. She tested various motor skills and sensory abilities that at the time were thought to reflect mental ability: auditory and visual reaction times, ability to hit a target, rapidity of finger movement, pain threshold, and ability to discriminate heat and cold. It was the first time anyone had systematically compared men and women on a wide variety of abilities measured in a controlled, laboratory setting.

Thompson found a striking *lack of evidence* for sex differences in mental abilities. Men and women performed differently on some tests, but it was the similarities rather than the differences between the sexes that were most impressive. These similarities could be readily seen when Thompson graphed her data. The distribution curve of scores on any particular test for the women in her sample overlapped almost completely with the distribution curve of the same scores for the men. This research provided the first empirical basis for questioning the popular assumption, shared and promulgated by many scientists, that women's and men's different mental abilities fitted them for different social roles.

Helen Thompson's approach to the question of female–male differences in ability is a classic illustration of scientific psychology: the attempt to test ideas about human behavior against observable reality. Psychologists, like other scientists, are trained to be skeptical—to withhold acceptance of theories or ideas until provided with evidence that the theories are correct. Although we enjoy spinning an elegant theory, we are taught that theory construction is only the first step in the scientific process; theories should be tested to see how well they fit the facts as we know them.

In this chapter we examine how facts about gender are known and how theories about gender can be tested. In particular, we consider these questions:

- Can science tell us the truth about gender?
- How can we test ideas about gender differences and similarities?
- How can we test ideas about why gender differences exist?
- What are the key sources of bias in research on sex and gender?
- Is psychology androcentric?

....

ASKING QUESTIONS ABOUT GENDER: SCIENCE AND THE SEARCH FOR TRUTH

Much effort is devoted to finding the right ways of testing theories against real-world data—in other words, the right research methods. Even when we have used the most careful methods and theories *seem* to fit the facts, however, we must still be cautious, asking three questions:

1. How well have we been able to measure reality? For example, if we do not notice a change in a person's attitude, does that mean that no change has occurred, or that our way of assessing change is not sensitive enough? In 2002, before the United States declared war on Iraq, Secretary of Defense Donald Rumsfeld famously argued, "Absence of evidence is not evidence of absence." Although a prolonged search for evidence that never turns up any results may lead us to conclude that, to the best of our knowledge, there is nothing to find, it is still possible that the search was simply not good enough. Absence of evidence does not prove that evidence does not exist.

2. How may we have altered or even produced the "facts" by studying them? For example, if a middle-class researcher finds working-class men to be hostile, is that hostility characteristic of working-class men, or is the hostility being

elicited by the presence of the researcher? Like the investigators on television's *CSI* series, who always have to have their gloves and little plastic bags handy, researchers must be aware that their presence can "contaminate the scene."

3.   How are our own backgrounds and biases influencing what we notice and do not notice and how we "construct" reality? For example, in 17th-century Europe, the prevailing medical opinion was that a woman could not become pregnant unless she experienced an orgasm, and counterexamples to this belief were simply not noticed or were explained away. Anyone who has watched an important game with sports fans rooting for opposing teams is probably familiar with the influence of bias on the reality we perceive.

The need to ask these questions does not mean that the research enterprise is useless; it does mean that constant tension exists between the search for unequivocal proof and the awareness that total certainty is simply not possible. This tension is exemplified by two approaches to knowledge, labeled *logical positivism* and *social constructionism.*

Logical positivism assumes that reality is independent of the knower and can be discerned "objectively" under the proper conditions. According to this approach, if scientific evidence is gathered rigorously, under the right conditions, a researcher can arrive at pure, unbiased truth.

In contrast, **social constructionism** holds that it is impossible to discover pure truth because there is no such thing. Rather, all of our so-called facts are really only educated guesses. Researchers hold expectations and implicit beliefs that affect the way they search for knowledge. Those expectations and beliefs, which are not only individual but are also shaped by cultural consensus, color their perceptions of reality. In short, according to social constructionism, researchers do not discover independently existing facts through objective observation; rather, they construct knowledge that is influenced by the social context of their inquiry. "What is produced by such knowledge-seeking . . . is not a free-standing and revealed truth, but a best guess, based on selective vision, using limited tools, shaped by the contextual forces surrounding the search. It is not Truth; it is a historically and contextually situated understanding, a social construction" (Bohan, 1992, p. 8).

If you take the social constructionist approach, must you give up on science? Even if we favor a cautious, social constructionist approach to knowledge, we need not turn away from scientific research. Rather, we must remain conscious of the ways in which the research process and its results are shaped and limited by social context.

Given the limitations of research, what constitutes acceptable evidence in favor of or against a theory? In the realm of sex and gender, this question has been crucial. The ease with which particular theories about sex and gender are accepted depends to a large extent on how well they fit with popular notions held about women and men by the culture. A theory that seems to challenge these notions will be subjected to more intense scrutiny and to higher standards of evidence than will one that seems to fit in with and justify them. And even research evidence that is conceded to be ironclad can be conveniently forgotten or over-

$\mathcal{O}verview$	Approaches to knowledge	
Approach	**View of Reality**	**View of Science**
Logical positivism	Reality exists independent of the knower and can be perceived objectively.	Science can uncover unbiased truth.
Social constructionism	There is no independent, pure truth, and the knower's perception of the world is always shaped by the social context.	Science does not so much discover truth as construct knowledge.

looked when it goes against favored assumptions. For example, Leta Hollingworth (1914) accused her male colleagues in psychology of adopting a double standard of scientific proof, refusing to subject their assumptions about male–female differences to the same careful criticism they devoted to other assumptions. Imagine her exasperation when her own adviser, Edward Thorndike, held fast, in the absence of data, to the notion of a "maternal instinct" in women long after he had abandoned other instincts as too vague and mentalistic. The problem noted by Hollingworth has not disappeared. The impact of biases about sex and gender on the design, conduct, interpretation, and acceptance of research continues to be felt.

Most of this chapter deals with the methods and issues that must be addressed by anyone trying to do good research on sex and gender—even though we believe that no amount of rigor in the research process will produce a "pure" truth about sex and gender. Research on sex and gender tends to focus on two basic questions: (1) *What* differences and similarities exist between women and men? and (2) *Why* do particular differences exist? It makes little sense to pursue the *why* question until we answer the *what* question, establishing the existence of a gender difference.

WHAT DIFFERENCES AND SIMILARITIES EXIST: METHODS FOR COMPARING THE SEXES

How do we know whether a particular gender difference exists? Researchers who want to collect evidence of differences or similarities between males and females can use any of several approaches. For example, they can use a *descriptive* method of research, aiming to describe behavior as accurately as possible while affecting behavior as little as possible. Or researchers can use an *experimental* method, in which they deliberately manipulate behavior to see how the behavior changes.

Many research methods look at a limited and to some extent isolated piece of behavior. They focus on an aspect of behavior that has had its context stripped away, so that researchers obtain control and precision, although they may lose the opportunity for depth and breadth of understanding as a result. Helen Thompson's experiment, described at the beginning of the chapter, is one example. It yielded quantitative data about how the participants performed isolated, specific motor and sensory tasks in a laboratory. But the study could not provide qualitative information about how the participants used their abilities in the real world.

In the quest for control, precision, and detachment, researchers may miss the connections linking experience and behavior to social and material conditions (Morawski, 1994). These limitations of traditional forms of research have increasingly frustrated feminist researchers, provoking the rise in popularity of qualitative methods such as narrative research, phenomenological approaches, and discourse analysis, which are discussed in the following section.

Descriptive Methods

A researcher may choose to study a few individuals in depth, using a case history or narrative approach. The **case history method,** sometimes used in clinical research, involves gathering many details about one or several individuals, usually through interviews. This allows the researcher to gather a lot of information and to delve deeply into complex issues that may be difficult to measure in large samples or with less attention to particular individuals. The information gathered is then used to support, develop, or refine a particular explanation of behavior. Freud, Horney, and other psychoanalysts relied on the case history approach to construct their theories. The case history provides a richness of detail that can suggest ways of understanding very complex processes. However, the method offers little protection against the influence of researcher bias—a real disadvantage in the realm of sex and gender research in which biases are often strong and unacknowledged.

The **narrative approach** also involves gathering a lot of information from a single individual, but, unlike the case history approach, it gives the research participant the opportunity to react to the researcher's interpretation of the participant's life story. The participant's interpretations of her or his own experiences are reported and given at least equal weight to the interpretations gleaned by the researcher. For example, Rosario Ceballo (1999), who interviewed an African American social worker named Mary, describes how Mary's own interpretation of her life differed from that of Ceballo's:

> In the second round of interview, I asked Mary if she had always been a determined and strong-willed woman, a question obviously based on my own overall assessment of her identity. To my surprise, Mary replied:
>
>   No, I don't think I'm that way. . . . When I think of strong-willed, I think of people who go out there and tackle it and get the job done and come what might, and fight all the battles, and overcome all the struggles, and knock anybody down that gets in your way, and that's not me. (p. 316)

Ceballo used Mary's comments to shape her own understanding of the issues she was studying, thus illustrating a key aspect of narrative research: the inclusion of the research participant as someone who guides and shapes the research.

The **phenomenological method,** another qualitative approach, is oriented toward understanding behavior from the perspective of the person being studied. Like the case history and narrative methods, it is based on in-depth, subjective information collected in interviews. This method, however, demands that the researcher be free of theoretical preconceptions before constructing a theory based on the information provided by the individuals being studied (e.g., see Daniluk, 1993). In addition, the analysis is supposed to be precise enough, based on specific words and phrases in interview transcripts, that two independent researchers trained in the phenomenological method will reach the same interpretation when analyzing a particular interview. This ideal is difficult to achieve, and the approach shares a problem with the case history method: When only a small number of people are studied, they may not be representative of the population to whom the researcher wishes to generalize.

A newer, fairly influential method in the social sciences is **discourse analysis,** the analysis of the language in texts, such as interview responses, discussions, and essays. In discourse analysis, words and phrases are not taken at face value, and language is not treated as simply a way of communicating information. Rather, the researcher tries to "deconstruct" or interpret ways of talking and writing. For example, New Zealand researchers Nicola Gavey and Kathryn McPhillips (1999) used discourse analysis to explore the reasons young women who had made a rational decision to insist on condom use in heterosexual intercourse actually failed to do so when confronted with a real situation. In interviewing these women, Gavey and McPhillips found that they talked about their heterosexual encounters as romances, in which the men took the initiative and the women were relatively passive. Through this way of talking and thinking about heterosexual intimacy, argued the researchers, the young women constructed expectations for themselves that they found difficult or impossible to violate without threatening their own sexual identity.

Evidence may also be collected through **naturalistic observation.** For example, a researcher interested in comparing girls and boys on aggression might spend hours watching nursery school children at play, keeping track of the number and type of aggressive behaviors displayed by boys and girls. However, it may be difficult to know how much the setting or the sample is responsible for the patterns observed. If boys are more aggressive than girls, how much is this difference a function of the particular nursery school environment or the particular group of children who attend that school?

The problem of researcher bias also comes up in naturalistic observation. Several studies have shown, for example, that observers rate behavior of a child differently, depending on whether they think the child is female or male (Condry & Condry, 1976; Condry & Ross, 1985; Gurwitz & Dodge, 1975). Condry and Condry (1976) showed participants a videotape of an infant responding to emotionally arousing stimuli. Participants who thought the child was a boy rated an ambiguous negative reaction to one stimulus as anger, whereas those who thought the child was a girl rated the same response as fear. Such findings cast doubt on the ability of researchers to be unaffected by their own gender stereotypes.

Survey methods of data collection use a standardized questionnaire or interview to collect information from a large number of people. This type of investigation, if based on a large representative sample of respondents, may allow a researcher to make some general statements about female–male differences in responding to certain types of questions. However, interpretation is still difficult; questionnaire and interview responses may be influenced heavily by respondents' desires to look good or to please the researcher and by memory biases. Thus, for example, on a survey asking subjects to rate the relative importance in their lives of marriage and career, a male–female difference in responding may reflect women's knowledge that they are expected to place more value on marriage and men's knowledge that they are expected to place more value on career.

Survey research also has the limitation that the results are **correlational.** In other words, the method is capable of showing that two things are related to each other, or go together, but cannot show that either one caused the other. Thus, in the preceding example, the finding that females were more likely than males to rate marriage as more important than career would simply mean that, for the sample studied, being female was associated with a greater likelihood of making that response. The researcher could not assume that being biologically female or male *caused* the difference in responding. Sex might be related to some other, unmeasured variable that was the real cause of the difference. For instance, maybe the underlying reason for differences in the perceived importance of career is whether one's same-sex parent has had a satisfying career, and men's fathers may be more likely than women's mothers to have done so.

Experimental Methods

The most controlled way to test the tenets of a theory is an **experiment.** In this methodology, the researcher directly manipulates (that is, sets at different levels) one variable, called the **independent variable,** while measuring its effects on another variable, the **dependent variable.** The researcher must control all other factors that might influence the dependent variable, so that the experimental conditions differ only in the level of the independent variable. This entails assigning research participants to experimental conditions randomly, so there are no systematic differences at the outset in the kinds of people assigned to each condition. It also entails manipulating the independent variable and measuring the dependent variable under identical circumstances for each level of the independent variable. If all these conditions are met, it should be possible to draw conclusions about a cause-and-effect relationship between the independent and dependent variables—to conclude that changes in the level of the independent variable *caused* changes in the dependent variable.

As an example, suppose a researcher wanted to test the hypothesis that women who exercise during pregnancy experience fewer physical complaints than do women who do not exercise. Exercise during pregnancy is the independent variable in this experiment. The dependent variables are indicators of physical complaints such as reports of symptoms such as backache and fatigue or specific physiological measures such as blood pressure. The researcher might screen a group of women for health risks early in pregnancy, then randomly assign each of them to either an exercise group or a control group. The two groups would be handled identically except for the amount of exercise. For instance, both would receive the same amount of attention, would be under the same constraints to report to the researcher, and would be given similar expectations about the impact on their pregnancy of participation in the project. Dependent variables, such as symptom reports and physiological measures, would be assessed, and the two groups would be compared on their scores. If the two groups differed significantly, it would be possible to conclude that the amount of exercise had caused the difference. This example is diagrammed in Figure 3.1.

In practice, however, it is often extremely difficult or impractical to control all the necessary variables in an experiment. For example, how would researchers

Figure 3.1   The experimental method. The experiment is designed to test the effect of exercise during pregnancy on physical problems and complaints.

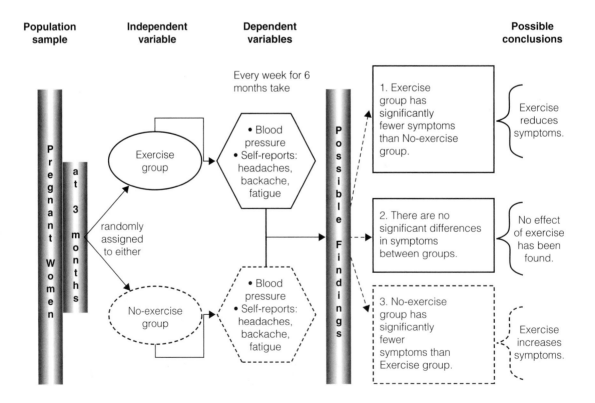

give the same amount of attention to each group, given that one group is participating in the exercise program and one is not? In addition, researchers sometimes inadvertently ignore crucial variables. For instance, what if the important variable was not the exercise itself but the camaraderie enjoyed by a group of women exercising together? If the researchers did not think about this variable when designing the exercise program, they would miss any clue to its importance. Although the experimental method provides the most potential for controlled examination of the effects of particular variables, in any given study such control may be illusory.

Not only must researchers be careful as they design the manipulation of the independent variable, they must also be concerned about whether they are measuring the dependent variable accurately and appropriately. This sounds fairly easy with a dependent variable such as blood pressure, but what about more "slippery" variables such as self-esteem or self-concept? For example, researchers can measure the latter two variables using methods that tap either "explicit" or "implicit" attitudes. *Explicit* measures include questionnaires, interviews, and other self-report procedures in which the respondent knows he or she is being asked about attitudes. Thus, if someone asks you up front to rate how feminine you think you are, that researcher is measuring your explicit self-concept with respect to femininity. If the researcher wants to assess your *implicit* self-concept with respect to femininity, he or she would use a procedure that is more sneaky: perhaps asking you to sit at a computer and respond as quickly as possible to questions about whether you would pair the terms "me" or "not me" with a sequence of feminine adjectives, such as "dainty," "gentle," and "nurturing." The researcher would measure your implicit self-concept of femininity by how quickly and consistently you paired yourself with the feminine adjective—but you might never be aware of what the procedure was measuring.

Researchers have found some intriguing differences between explicit and implicit measures of self-related attitudes. For example, the relationship between explicit and implicit measures of self-esteem has been found to be stronger for White men than for White women or Asian men or women (Greenwald & Farnham, 2000). These researchers also found that, when measuring masculine and feminine self-concepts, implicit measures showed much greater differences between men and women than did the explicit self-report measures. In other words, men seemed to have more masculine self-concepts and women more feminine self-concepts when these self-concepts were measured implicitly rather than explicitly.

If a researcher wanted to measure self-esteem or self-concept as dependent variables in an experiment, would it be better to measure them implicitly or explicitly? We don't know the answer to that question. What we do know is that, in this example as in many others, the method chosen may well make a difference to the results.

Even with the experimental method, researchers cannot use sex as an independent variable and prove that biological sex differences are the cause of differences in dependent variables. Why? First, it is impossible to manipulate sex—to randomly assign people to be females or males. Second, it is a hopeless task to disentangle biological sex from the many other variables (e.g., training, expectations) associated with it. Thus two of the conditions for inferring cause and effect through the experimental method are not met: manipulation of the independent variable and control of extraneous variables. All data on sex differences, no matter what research method is used, are *correlational* data, and in that sense it is more accurate to speak of "sex-related" differences than of sex differences.

"Heavy-Duty" Strategies: Longitudinal Studies and Meta-Analysis

Researchers use two more techniques to add to the power of the methods we have just considered. The first, the **longitudinal study,** involves following the same research participants over an extended period of time, usually years, and obtaining data from them repeatedly during that time. The second technique, **meta-analysis,** involves using statistical methods to combine the findings of many different studies of the same behavior in order to evaluate the overall pattern of findings.

LONGITUDINAL STUDIES   Longitudinal studies enable us to find out the ages at which particular gender differences appear and disappear. They can also identify variables that predict later differences in behavior—perhaps differentially for females and males.

Perhaps the most famous longitudinal study in psychology was Lewis Terman's (1925) "gifted children" research. Beginning in 1922, Terman selected over 1,000 preschool and elementary school children and 300 high school students, all of whom had intelligence test scores (IQs) of 140 or more. For more than half a century, Terman and, after his death, other psychologists maintained contact with these people and monitored their achievements (Friedman et al., 1995; Oden, 1968; Terman & Oden, 1947, 1959). It was a gigantic undertaking, and one that provided a wealth of information about the extent to which high tested intelligence in schoolchildren predicts achievement across the life span. Although the project was not conceived with the idea of examining gender differences, its findings in this area have been very telling: High IQ was a much better predictor of achievement for males than for females. Very bright boys were likely to go on to chalk up accomplishments in the arts, science, literature, business, or public affairs as adults; very bright girls were considerably less likely to do so. More than two-thirds of the girls with IQs of 170 or more became housewives or office workers in adulthood. Follow-up studies show that many of them devoted their lives to supporting their husbands' careers or to child rearing (Tomlinson-Keasey, 1990).

Many of the questionnaire responses of some of these high-IQ women in later life reflect a sense of failure or lack of confidence in their abilities:

> You might be interested to know that if I ever had a good mind, it has been lost in the shuffle. I seem to have stagnated and I am aware that I'm not using any capacity that I have to the fullest; however, don't give up hope, maybe I'll make you proud yet.

> As I grow older, I am more and more surprised at the thought that I was ever considered a gifted child. I realize that I am slightly more intelligent than the average, but only slightly.

> I have not used my gifts and regret this very much. Also I believe IQs change and mine dropped considerably. I'm no longer very competent in any area. My children all turned out well but not due to me, rather to a strict father who allowed no nonsense. (quoted in Tomlinson-Keasey, 1990, pp. 229–230)

Being male or female, then, was a far better predictor of recognized achievement in adulthood than was having high intelligence. Furthermore, opportunities for achievement in adulthood (opportunities that were disproportionately available to men) helped to maintain a high IQ. Those women who were able to transcend gender-role expectations in their educational and occupational pursuits maintained intellectual levels similar to those of the men. Occupation, not gender, accounted best for IQ changes over the life span (Bayley & Oden, 1955).

The study does not explain the gender difference in adult achievement, but it serves a crucial function by demonstrating two points: (1) The gender difference in adult achievement is clearly not due to an earlier difference in intelligence and (2) gender is eclipsed by occupation as an explanatory variable for adult changes in IQ.

The Terman study was designed to link variables measured during childhood with other variables measured in adulthood. A longitudinal study that examined a shorter time period is the Stanford Longitudinal Study (e.g., Maccoby, Snow, & Jacklin, 1984; Martin, Maccoby, & Jacklin, 1981; Snow, Jacklin, & Maccoby, 1981). This study followed three cohorts of children from birth through the preschool years, gathering data at frequent intervals on a long list of child behaviors and aspects of parent-child interaction. The researchers began by collecting information about hormone levels at birth for each child, then went on to measure such things as tactile sensitivity, muscle strength, sociability, timidity, and parental responsiveness. Among the most interesting findings is that, for many variables, birth order accounted for as much or more variability as sex (e.g., Snow et al., 1981). Also intriguing are findings that support the idea that similar socialization practices may have different effects for girls and boys. The Stanford researchers examined the relationship between the mother's responsiveness to a child at 9 months of age and the child's willingness, 9 months later, to interrupt the mother's conversation with another adult (Martin et al., 1981). They found that mothers' nonintrusiveness (their tendency to avoid interrupting the child when she or he was playing successfully alone) had different correlates for girls and boys. Boys whose mothers were nonintrusive at 9 months tended to play independently at 18 months; however, girls whose mothers were nonintrusive were more likely than other girls to seek proximity and attention from their mothers when observed 9 months later. Parenting style apparently interacts with other variables—environmental, biological, or both—to produce different outcomes for the two sexes.

Another reason for doing longitudinal research is to examine the historical context of gender differences. For example, Abigail Stewart and Joan Ostrove (1998) examined data obtained from two groups of women at the age of 24. Women in the first group were 24 in 1967; those in the second group were 24 in 1978. In the first group, nearly two-thirds of the women were married, and 16% were mothers at the age of 24. In the second group, whose members reached the age of 24 eleven years later, only 13% were married, and none were mothers at that age. Thus the experience of early adulthood was clearly different for these two cohorts of college-educated American women—and a longitudinal study that followed only one of these cohorts would have risked making inappropriate generalizations related to women's life course.

META-ANALYSIS   To draw conclusions about whether there are gender differences in a particular behavior, we must examine the results of many studies of that behavior. If someone wanted to determine whether there were gender differences in nurturance, for example, he or she would gather all the studies that compared nurturing behavior in males and females and would look at the overall pattern of results. Suppose 70% of the studies showed that females behaved in a more nurturing way than males, 10% showed males to be more nurturing, and the remaining 20% showed no gender differences. The researcher might well conclude that gender differences in nurturance were fairly well established and that females were, in general, more nurturing than males.

This approach has some serious limitations. Although the studies included in a review may vary greatly in quality and on dimensions such as the variability in the sample and the size of the difference found, in this approach all are simply tabulated together and given equal weight. Meta-analysis, on the other hand, facilitates a more sophisticated appraisal of the overall picture.

To conduct a meta-analysis, the researcher first makes a concerted attempt to gather a well-defined, complete set of studies of the behavior in question. She or he must be careful to find and include well-done but unpublished studies, such as theses. Then, using the means and standard deviations for males and females reported in each article, the researcher calculates the **effect size** (the amount of variation in the results that is attributable to gender) for each study.

There are two commonly used measures of effect size: (1) the proportion of variation in the mixed (male plus female) population that can be accounted for by gender differences and (2) the distance, in standard deviation units, between the means for males and females. Once the researcher has determined the effect size for each study in the collection, she or he can calculate the average effect size across all the studies in order to draw conclusions about whether there is a gender difference and, if so, how large and important it is.

A good illustration of the kind of information meta-analysis can yield comes from Warren Eaton and Leslie Enns (1986). They gathered 127 studies of male–female differences in human motor activity level (defined as the individual's customary level of energy expenditure through movement). Although there had been a widespread belief that males have a higher motor activity level than females, reviewers of the literature had found the results too mixed to be conclusive. If females and males do differ in activity level, the difference might have some interesting implications: for example, more active infants receive more attention from their caretakers; so if males are generally more active, they may be eliciting different kinds of caretaker behavior than females. Such a difference in caretaker behavior might be the basis for other behavioral differences between female and male infants. Thus Eaton and Enns used meta-analysis to try to determine whether and to what extent a gender difference in human motor activity level exists.

When Eaton and Enns calculated the effect size for the gender differences reported in the 127 studies, they found that the average difference between the male and female mean activity level scores was just under one-half of a standard deviation. Furthermore, the proportion of total population variance in activity level that could be accounted for by gender was about 5%. That means 95% of the variability in activity level could be attributed either to variation *within* gender groups or to experimental error (random fluctuations, measurement error).

Only 5% of the variance in the activity level of mixed-sex populations could be explained by gender differences? This result may seem to indicate that male–female differences in activity level are too small to be important. However, many of the group differences or experimental effects reported in psychological research are of this size (Eagly & Wood, 1991). Besides, as Eaton and Enns note, small differences in means can translate into large differences in the proportions of males and females at the extremes of a given behavior.

Why would that matter? Suppose there are more males than females at the upper extremes of activity level. Then casual observers are more likely to see a boy than a girl who is extremely active, perhaps even "hyperactive." Although only a few children of either sex reach this top level of activity, observers will tend to notice the difference in the proportions of males and females at this extremely high activity level. They will use this information to define or reinforce their gender stereotypes. Thus a teacher who has, over several years of working with children, encountered four boys and one girl who could be characterized as "hyperactive" may find it easy to subscribe to the belief that boys are more active than girls, even though, among the hundreds of normally active other children the teacher has taught, no striking gender differences in activity level appear. In this way, a gender difference that is noticeable only at the extremes of a behavioral distribution can form the basis for a much broader gender stereotype.

Meta-analysis is the most useful tool researchers have found for combining the results of many studies of a particular male–female difference. It can provide information about the average strength of the relationship between gender and a particular behavior and can tell the researcher what other variables, such as age or situational effects, may be affecting that relationship. Yet the results of a meta-analysis are only as good as its sample of studies. If a complete sample of studies is not included or if the studies included have inaccurate results due to bias or sloppy data collection, the meta-analysis can tell us little of value. Also, if the sample of studies used is overrepresentative of biased situations (e.g., if most of the experimenters in the sample are male or if most of the measures used are biased in favor of females), the results of the meta-analysis will reflect the same bias (Eagly & Carli, 1981). Finally, like other researchers, the person conducting a meta-analysis will have to interpret the results to examine the way the scores are distributed, as discussed next.

Differences and Distributions

Whenever a researcher collects quantitative data to compare two or more groups of individuals, he or she is faced with the problem of interpreting that data—deciding whether the data reflect a real difference between the groups. Suppose, for example, a researcher asked a sample of girls and a sample of boys to complete a jigsaw puzzle and measured the time it took each child to complete the task. How would the researcher use the data to determine whether girls and boys differ in their ability to complete such a puzzle quickly?

One fairly simple way to compare the girls' and boys' performance would be to compare the average times taken by children in each group to complete the puzzle. If the boys took an average of 340 seconds and the girls an average of 260 seconds, it would be tempting to conclude that girls were faster than boys at this kind of task. Such a conclusion would be premature, however, until the researcher had taken into account two important issues: (1) the distributions of the boys' and girls' time scores and (2) the statistical significance of the difference in mean scores.

EXAMINING DISTRIBUTIONS   A **distribution** is the frequency with which certain responses or scores are obtained when a group is studied. If the researcher in our hypothetical puzzle experiment draws a graph showing the number of children with each particular time score, the distribution of scores will probably look like a "normal" or bell-shaped curve, as shown in Figure 3.2. The highest part of the curve shows the scores most often attained and represents the average score for the group. Children whose scores fall to the right of the highest point have performed above the average time, and those whose scores fall to the left have performed below the average time.

Now suppose the researcher graphs the boys' and girls' scores in the puzzle experiment separately, as shown in Figure 3.3. The researcher can learn a great deal about how to interpret the 80-second average time difference between the boys and girls by examining the degree and pattern of overlap between the two distributions. The more the two distributions overlap, the greater the indication that the average boy and the average girl perform at similar levels. The amount of overlap shown in Figure 3.3 shows that, even though the boys as a group averaged 80 seconds slower than the girls, some boys still solved the puzzle faster than the average time for the girls.

Figure 3.2 The normal curve.

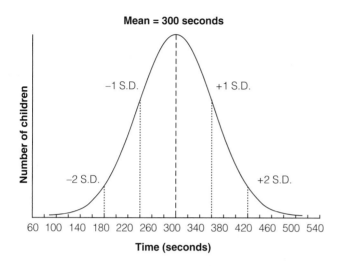

Figure 3.3 Distribution of puzzle solution time, graphed separately for girls and boys, showing overlap between the distributions.

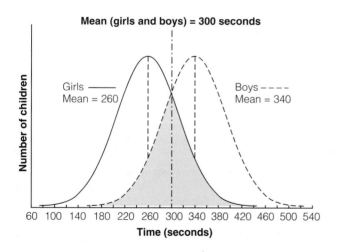

In fact, even if no difference in average scores had been observed between the two groups, it would be useful to examine the distributions. Why? The two groups could achieve identical averages in very different ways, and a difference in their amount of variability can be just as interesting as a difference in their means. Figure 3.4 illustrates some of the possibilities.

𝓕𝒾𝑔𝓊𝓇𝑒 3.4 Examples of different ways in which boys and girls could achieve identical averages in puzzle solution times.

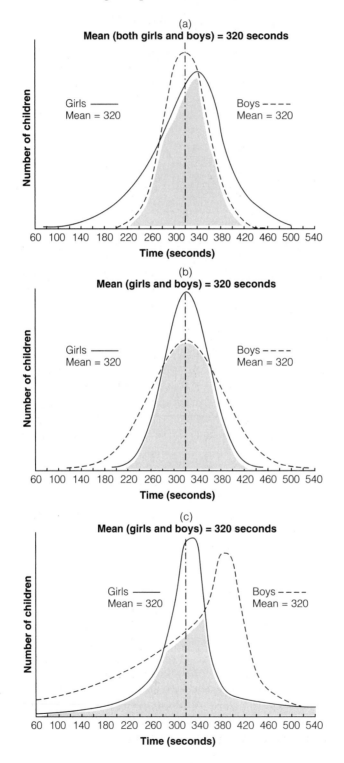

In Figure 3.4a, the two groups have the same mean, but the shapes of the distributions are different. In this case, the boys' time scores fall into a narrow range around the mean, but the girls' scores are more spread out, particularly toward the very low (i.e., fast) end of the distribution. A few girls obviously solved the puzzle extremely quickly; a number of girls solved the puzzle faster than even the fastest boy, and some were slower than the slowest boys. In Figure 3.4b, the girls' scores fall into a narrow range around the mean, and those of the boys are more spread out. However, in this case, the spread is evenly balanced: Boys are showing more variability than girls in their performance, but there are just as many boys who solve the puzzle more slowly than girls do as there are boys who do it faster than girls. In Figure 3.4c, the two distributions overlap; however, whereas most boys score slower than the average time for girls, there are more boys than girls who complete the puzzle in the very fastest times.

In many cases, reporting mean differences between groups without paying attention to the distribution of scores is misleading and encourages stereotyping. For instance, in our puzzle example, the distribution of the scores might indicate that the average time is identical for boys and girls, so the average boy was not slower than the average girl. Rather, as depicted in Figure 3.4a, there might be a subgroup of girls who were faster than both the average boy *and* the average girl.

Olga Favreau (1993) provided an excellent example of the difference that focusing on averages or distributions produces. When considering the perception of color, we could, based on averages, make the statement that women perceive color better than men do. However, more accurate information is provided by the statement that more men than women are color-blind. Thus it is good practice for researchers to report on distribution overlap and variability as well as average differences.

STATISTICAL SIGNIFICANCE   When interpreting data, the researcher must also deal with the possibility that a particular finding can occur by accident. The 80-second average difference between the male and female samples in our hypothetical example may be nothing more than a fluke. Maybe this sample of girls is especially quick for some reason or the boys are a slower than usual bunch.

To calculate the probability that a particular result could occur by chance alone, scientists use statistical tests that take into account sample size and variability. By convention, if the probability of the result occurring by chance alone is less than 5%, the finding is accepted as **statistically significant.** Even when a result is statistically significant, however, some caution is in order. Not all statistically significant differences are socially significant or even meaningful. As Petersen and Wittig (1979) noted, because the calculation of statistical significance is based partly on sample size, extremely large samples may reveal statistically significant results that are essentially meaningless. In a sample of 100,000 males and 100,000 females, an IQ difference of 0.02 point would be statistically significant despite the fact that the difference is too small to be reliably measured by an IQ test in the first place and too tiny to have any practical implications.

Overview
....

Research methods

Method	Description
Case history	A qualitative method in which the researcher examines one or several individuals in depth, usually through interviews
Narrative approach	A qualitative method in which the researcher examines an individual in depth, usually through interviews, and gives the individual the opportunity to react to the researcher's interpretations
Phenomenological method	A qualitative method that aims to understand behavior from the perspective of the person being studied, often based on interviews
Discourse analysis	A qualitative method that analyzes the language in texts such as interview responses, discussions, and essays
Naturalistic observation	A method in which the researcher carefully watches individuals in their normal setting, keeping track of the number and type of certain kinds of behaviors
Survey	A quantitative method in which the researcher uses a standardized questionnaire or interview form to collect information from a large number of people
Experiment	A quantitative method in which the researcher manipulates one variable while measuring the effect on another variable
Longitudinal study	A study, using one of the already mentioned data-gathering approaches, that collects data repeatedly from the same respondents over a period of time
Meta-analysis	A statistical method for combining the results of many different studies of the same behavior

Knowledge as Self-Reflexive

No matter what methods social scientists use to discover whether particular gender differences exist, their findings tend to transform the situation under study. When researchers publish a finding such as "in dual-career couples wives spend a lot more time doing housework than husbands do," the very dissemination of that information may eventually change the situation. Individual women, finding out that their situation is not unique, may become angry enough to insist that their partners take on more of the domestic duties. Individual men, seeing the documentation of the unequal distribution of household tasks, may change their own behavior out of a sense of fairness. Other men and women may respond differently, seeing the findings as confirmation that they are in step with the majority and becoming more committed to an uneven distribution of household labor. In either case, the knowledge gained by researchers who study human behavior is not independent of that behavior. It has an impact on it. By finding and reporting a gender difference, researchers can contribute to the magnitude and perceived importance of that difference.

WHY GENDER DIFFERENCES EXIST: NATURE, NURTURE, AND THE INTERACTIONIST POSITION

By now it should be clear that attempts to establish the existence of particular differences or similarities between the sexes are complicated by a number of factors. The issues become even more complex when researchers confront the second of our two questions: *Why* do differences exist?

Is human behavior determined more by environment or heredity? This question has obsessed the field of psychology for decades, and no introductory psychology student escapes exposure to it. In the realm of sex and gender, the question becomes "Are female–male differences part of our human inheritance, or do we learn to be feminine and masculine by interacting with the environment?"

Emphasizing either "nature" or "nurture" brings dangers. There is little doubt that heredity plays a role in the distribution of some abilities and personality traits. Researchers have demonstrated, for instance, that the correlation between intelligence levels of identical twins (who share the same genes) is stronger than that between fraternal twins and other siblings (Bouchard, Lykken, McGue, Segal, & Tellegen, 1990) and that, within normal-functioning families, mothers' IQ levels are better predictors of their children's IQ levels than are parenting styles and certain other environmental variables (Scarr, 1991). Yet the implications of such findings for gender differences are far from clear. For example, there is no solid evidence that particular abilities are more likely to be passed on genetically from parents to sons than to daughters (or vice versa). Furthermore, different opportunities and pressures affect what boys and girls do with their abilities.

A one-sided emphasis on heredity can mean that a researcher will not look for socioenvironmental explanations for behavior; a rigid emphasis on environment may blind a researcher to biological underpinnings of behavior. Neither nature nor nurture by itself can explain the development of particular human behaviors or traits. For example, even if doctors know that a person carries the specific genetic defect for sickle-cell anemia, they cannot accurately predict what symptoms will develop and with what severity and timing (Fausto-Sterling, 1992). The course of the disease is influenced not only by the genetic defect but also by the individual's environment.

Another example of the complex relationship between heredity and environmental factors comes from studies of the brain. A growing body of research indicates that the physical structure of the adult brain is established through the interaction of the maturing child with his or her environment. As an infant matures, nerve cells in the developing brain compete to form connections with other cells. Nerve cells that do not form such connections do not survive, and only pathways between cells that are used (through stimulation from the environment) become established. Thus the child's environment has a direct physical effect on brain development. Similarly, the child's brain affects the way she or he experiences the environment by limiting the ability to perceive certain things, such as colors, and the ability to make sense of information (Lerner, 1998).

The Interactionist View

In fact, many scientists argue that it is meaningless to consider either heredity or environment in the absence of the other or to treat their relationship as a simple additive one. Both are always important. Anne Anastasi (1958b) contended that the question to which researchers should address themselves is not *how much* of an individual's behavior is determined by heredity and *how much* by environment but *how*—in what ways—genetics and environment work together to produce behavioral outcomes. This question implies that the presence of particular genetic or environmental components merely increases or decreases the probability of specified behavioral results. Neither one is more or less important. Both heredity and environment are always present and interacting with each other. Biologist Anne Fausto-Sterling (1992) argued for an analysis "in which an individual's capacities emerge from a web of interactions between the biological being and the social environment. Within this web, connecting threads move in both directions. Biology may in some manner condition behavior, but behavior in turn can alter one's physiology" (p. 8).

A clear example of such a reciprocal relationship between behavior and physiology is provided by Miriam Lowe (1983) in her analysis of male–female differences in strength and physical performance. She noted that the assumption that men are strong and women are weak has powerful consequences for the way men and women both view their bodies and try to shape them according to different standards of health and beauty. Even in infancy, parents exercise boys more than girls, and, as children develop, girls are channeled into more sedentary kinds of play than boys are, a pattern that continues into adulthood. Studies show, however, that when women break out of the "weak" stereotype, their bodies can change dramatically: When women and men begin training with weights, women increase their strength faster than men do, and the physical performance of American women athletes differs from that of their nonathletic female counterparts much more than men athletes' performance differs from that of nonathletic men (Bishop, Cureton, Conerly, & Collins, 1989; O'Hagan, Sale, MacDougall, & Garner, 1995). When women become more active physically, not only their strength but also other physical attributes change. Percentage of body fat decreases, and bones become stronger and more dense. All of these findings lend support to the idea that social stereotypes can influence physical attributes by influencing behavior—an example of the interactionist position that how an individual turns out is a function of the joint effects of heredity and environment. Figure 3.5 illustrates this process.

Biologist Ruth Hubbard (1990) coined the term **transformationism** to describe the way biology and environment work together, with neither being more fundamental than the other to an organism's development. She argued,

Figure 3.5   An example of the interaction of nature and nurture.

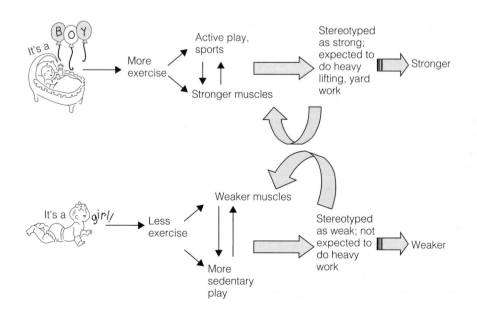

in concert with other scientists, that neither biology nor environment can be said to "determine" reactions to the other. Rather, at every level of development, the combination of biological and environmental factors transforms the organism so that it responds differently to other concurrent or subsequent biological or environmental influences:

> If a society puts half its children in dresses and skirts but warns them not to move in ways that reveal their underpants, while putting the other half in jeans and overalls and encouraging them to climb trees and play ball and other outdoor games; if later, during adolescence, the half that has worn trousers is exhorted to "eat like a growing boy," while the half in skirts is warned to watch its weight and not get fat; if the half in jeans trots around in sneakers or boots, while the half in skirts totters about on spike heels, then these two groups of people will be biologically as well as socially different. Their muscles will be different, as will their reflexes, posture, arms, legs and feet, hand–eye coordination, spatial perception, and so on. . . . There is no way to sort out the biological and social components that produce these differences, therefore no way to sort nature from nurture. (pp. 115–116)

Cross-Cultural Research

In the quest to understand just how heredity and environment work together to influence such things as ability, behavior, personality, and appearance, researchers have often turned to cross-cultural comparisons. Examining other cultures helps to jolt us out of the assumption that the social and behavioral patterns of our own culture are somehow completely "natural" or that they represent the only normal kind of human organization.

In the realm of sex and gender, the pioneer of cross-cultural research was anthropologist Margaret Mead (1935). Mead noted that most human societies used the conspicuous categories of age and sex to structure expectations about people, "whether it be the convention of one Philippine tribe that no man can keep a secret, the Manus assumption that only men enjoy playing with babies, the Toda prescription of almost all domestic work as too sacred for women, or the Arapesh insistence that women's heads are stronger than men's" (p. xi). Mead contrasted the Arapesh, a tribe in which both women and men were expected to be gentle, responsible, and nurturant, with the Mundugumor, in which men and women both were individualistic, ruthless, aggressive, and nonnurturant, and the Tchambuli, a group wherein the women were raised to be dominant, impersonal, and in charge and the men were less responsible and emotionally dependent. She concluded the following:

> If those temperamental attitudes which we have traditionally regarded as feminine—such as passivity, responsiveness, and a willingness to cherish children—can so easily be set up as the masculine pattern in one tribe, and in another be outlawed for the majority of women as well as for the majority of men, we no longer have any basis for regarding such aspects of behavior as sex-linked. (pp. 279–280)

Anthropologists continue to debate Mead's specific conclusions about cross-cultural differences in gender roles. But her work and that of her successors alert us to a wide variety of human behaviors that can vary as a result of different combinations of heredity and environment.

Animal Research

Research with nonhuman animals is another strategy that has been used to try to understand how biology and environment interact to produce certain behavioral outcomes. Because it is easier and more acceptable to control both the genetics (through breeding) and the environment of individual animals in a laboratory situation than it ever is to control such factors for humans, laboratory research with animals can investigate questions that are difficult or impossible to approach with humans. For example, it would be out of the question to inject pregnant humans with cross-sex hormones to observe effects on the behavior of their offspring, but such research is done with animals. Similarly, we may not isolate human infants at birth to observe the effects of a lack of socialization on sex-differentiated behaviors, but such a technique is sometimes used with animals.

Animal research helps generate ideas about what may be happening in human development to produce sex-related differences in behavior. However, there are many differences between humans and even our closest animal relatives, the primates, and it is dangerous to make direct generalizations from animal research to human behavior. For example, although psychologists have been somewhat successful in teaching rudimentary language to certain primates, these animals do not seem to have the sophisticated linguistic abilities demonstrated by humans. Obviously, primates do communicate with one another, and their communications may often be "gendered," in the sense that they are related to female–male relationships. However, because human capacity for language is very different from that of other primates, we would not want to base conclusions about human male–female communication solely on information gleaned from chimpanzees or gorillas.

Even with animals, distinguishing biological from environmental influences on behavior is not a simple matter. We do not, for instance, know what cues are used by other animals to differentiate between males and females and what steps they take to socialize their young and their peers into sex-appropriate behavior (Fedigan, 1982). It may be, for instance, that smell is a very important component in an animal's ability to differentiate between its male and female peers. If so, attempts to study the impact of sex hormones per se on animal behavior may be doomed to failure. Sex hormone treatments may disturb the "sex smell" sufficiently that animals that have received sex hormone treatments will be treated very differently by their peers than will those that have not received hormone injections. Thus the impact of the sex hormones on behavior would be confounded with the impact of differential treatment.

Method	Description
Cross-cultural research	An examination of a phenomenon in several cultures: This approach enables the researcher to compare cultures, to test the universality of particular behaviors, and to sample the variability of human behavior.
Animal research	An examination of nonhuman species: Because selective breeding permits easier control of the genetics of nonhuman animals and because humans' ethical standards against manipulation of the environment are lower for nonhuman species, researchers may conduct experiments with nonhuman species that may not be carried out with people. The results can illuminate the interaction of heredity and environment, but generalizing from nonhumans to humans is problematic.

In addition, the use of animals as research subjects does not free researchers from ethical concerns. Rather, animal research raises a new series of ethical issues. For all of these reasons, animal research does not provide any easy answers in the nature–nurture debate.

In short, whether studying human beings or other animals, researchers must be mindful of the interaction between nature and nurture, between heredity and environment. The meaningful question is, as Anastasi (1958b) argued, not "Which one?" or "How much?" but "How?"—in what ways do our genetic heritages interact with the worlds in which we live to produce the complex packages we know as females and males?

BIASES AND PITFALLS: PROBLEMS ENCOUNTERED IN THE STUDY OF SEX AND GENDER

The idealistic view of science is that it is an objective search for truth conducted by unbiased researchers, but the reality seldom approaches the ideal. The research process cannot be completely objective or separate from the social context in which it occurs. The existence of a "value-free science" is now commonly recognized as a myth. A scientist cannot avoid being influenced by the assumptions and agendas of the surrounding culture. Even chemists and

Reflections : Bias and Science

For years, American women were urged and cajoled to avoid the discomforts of menopause and even the effects of aging by taking hormone replacement therapy. Even if they were not suffering any severe problems, they were told that hormone replacement therapy was safe and that it would bring many benefits to their health. Famous actresses beamed from the television screen as they described the advantages of the drug. Doctors and other medical professionals for the most part were no less enthusiastic.

Then in 2002 the medical establishment reversed course. Hormone replacement therapy, it turns out, apparently does not reduce the risks of heart disease and stroke as once proclaimed. In fact, for some women, hormone replacement therapy might increase the risk of contracting these problems. What went wrong?

In part, the answer is a very crude form of bias. The predecessor of hormone replacement therapy was estrogen therapy. Its use to treat the symptoms of menopause was popularized by Dr. Robert Wilson in 1966. Wilson wrote a book, gave speeches, and toured the country promoting estrogen therapy. But Wilson had not come to his belief in the drug only as a result of research; he was paid to write the book and promote the drug by its manufacturer.

The most interesting and dangerous forms of bias in science, however, are more subtle than the bias in this case. In fact, the history of hormone replacement therapy may illustrate these other forms of bias as well. Two recent large-scale studies of hormone replacement therapy came up with very different conclusions about the drug.

In one study, conducted by the Women's Health Initiative, volunteers were randomly assigned either to take hormone replacement therapy or to take a placebo. This is the study that found that hormone replacement therapy increases the risk of heart disease. It contradicted the findings of another study, the Nurses' Health Study, in which thousands of nurses reported to researchers for years about their habits, their health, and the drugs they were taking. The Nurses' Health Study found that hormone replacement therapy is linked to a decreased risk of heart disease.

As Gina Kolata reported in the *New York Times* (2003, pp. D1, D6), "Doctors and researchers have been struggling with an intractable problem: How could two large high-quality studies come to diametrically different conclusions about menopause, hormone therapy, and heart disease?" She quoted one doctor who asked, "Is there an intrinsic flaw in either of these approaches?"

No research is perfect, but this example of getting different results when using different methods is quite dramatic—and the puzzle it poses is very personal for many women. What do you think explains the different findings?

physicists may overlook observations that seem incongruent with accepted theory. Objectivity may be an even more remote possibility in the social sciences, in which the processes under study are directly and personally significant to the researcher. The study of gender, which is basic to self-perception and social relationships, is virtually impossible to approach in a completely unbiased way.

Differences in the values researchers hold with respect to knowledge and the research process can be large. For example, Mary Ricketts (1989) found that

North American feminist psychologists tended to place more emphasis on external or social determinants of human behavior than on biological determinants and more on persons' subjective experience than on their behavior. Among feminist psychologists, lesbians favored an emphasis on subjective experience and on social determinants more than heterosexuals did.

Researchers may also differ in their orientation toward the potential uses of their research findings. Feminist researchers often urge that research findings be communicated back to the community of participants (G. M. Russell & Bohan, 1999). This principle probably affects what aspects of the research receive most attention from the researchers and are communicated most quickly. For example, compared with quantitative findings, responses to open-ended questions may provide material for more interesting and dramatic feedback to the community of participants. When Glenda Russell surveyed reactions to passage of an amendment to Colorado's constitution that removed legal recourse for lesbians and gays who encountered discrimination, the words and experiences of participants became the basis for an oratorio and a documentary video. Thus the "experiences of research participants were reflected back to them and to the community as a whole in song and on film—individual and collective voices made available to the public through psychological research" (G. M. Russell & Bohan, 1999, pp. 409–410).

Although all researchers are bound to be influenced by personal and cultural values, they must *try* to be aware of their biases, to acknowledge them, and to eliminate the blind spots they engender. Most of the problems stem from biases that are not merely personal but cultural. Researchers must look not only to their own blind spots but to those of the entire scientific enterprise. The following section, which draws on several thorough examinations of sexism in research (Eichler, 1983; Favreau, 1977; McHugh, Koeske, & Frieze, 1986; Stark-Adamec & Kimball, 1984), details some of the aspects of the research process in which bias can be expressed.

Choosing a Research Topic

Laboring under the inevitable constraints of time, energy, and motivation, a scientist can do only so much research during her or his career. How does a scientist choose what questions to study and what to set aside?

The decision is based not only on the researcher's interest but also on what topics are considered important by the researcher's employers, professional colleagues, and funding agencies. All of these factors are susceptible to bias. A researcher will not think to study the underlying causes of sexual harassment, for instance, if he or she is oblivious to its prevalence or shares cultural assumptions that such behavior is merely an inevitable manifestation of sexual attraction between men and women who work together. Or a researcher may wish to study sexual harassment but may find that employers and colleagues dismiss it as a frivolous topic and that funding agencies are unwilling to provide support.

In recent years, there has been a veritable explosion of research on topics relevant to sex and gender to women's experience, and, to a lesser extent, to men's experiences as universities, professional associations, and granting agencies have bowed to pressure to legitimize such topics.

Formulating the Research Question

The way a question is articulated may have built-in biases that keep investigators from finding results that cast doubt on their assumptions. If the investigator has not considered the possibility that males and females experience a particular situation (e.g., acting aggressively toward another person) differently, the hypothesis she or he formulates may reflect this lack of awareness of gender as an important variable.

The reverse is also true: Researchers may perpetuate sexist biases by using different concepts to describe the same activities for women and men. For example, the term *maternal deprivation* is used in discussion of the children of employed mothers, but the parallel term, *paternal deprivation,* is never used when discussing children of employed fathers (Eichler & Lapointe, 1985). Someone who frames a hypothesis about the impact of maternal deprivation on preschool children will not interpret anything he or she observes as being due to *paternal* deprivation, even though the children being studied may actually be more "deprived" of their fathers' than of their mothers' presence.

Within the field of the psychology of gender, a prevailing bias that has shaped many research questions has been the tendency to focus on personality and individual differences rather than on social conditions that differ for males and females. For example, to explain why women appear to achieve less than men, researchers studying women's achievement have tended to search for personality differences between women and men, such as a lack of achievement motivation or fear of success among women. This focus perpetuates the stereotype that women are not achievement oriented (Kahn & Yoder, 1989). An approach emphasizing social forces rather than personality characteristics might focus instead on the "glass ceiling" that many women report encountering in their attempts to move up in their organizations and on the "glass escalator" that men in female-dominated jobs sometimes encounter. Clearly, researchers taking these two approaches would find very different reasons for women's lack of achievement relative to men.

Research Design

The design of a research study offers many potential pitfalls. The research may be biased as a result of a variety of factors, from the interaction between the researcher and the participants to the way in which variables are measured.

THE SOCIAL PSYCHOLOGY OF THE PSYCHOLOGICAL EXPERIMENT
Many years ago, Saul Rosenweig (1933), in a pioneering paper on the social psychology of the psychological experiment, mentioned sex as a "personal quality" of the experimenter that could introduce "errors of personality influence" into the laboratory. In other words, whether the experimenter was female or male might influence the results simply because people react differently to men and women. **Sex-of-experimenter effects**—results produced by the gender of the researcher—have been found in virtually every area of psychological research (Jemelka & Downs, 1991; Littig & Branch, 1993; S. W. Williams, Ogletree, Woodburn, & Raffeld, 1993).

Other aspects of the experiment can also interact with gender, causing artifactual findings. It has been found, for instance, that female participants are more likely than males to comply with the demand characteristics of an experimental situation (Rosenthal, 1966). Thus a male–female difference in a laboratory study may reflect nothing more than the fact that women are more likely than men to act as they think the experimenter wants them to.

Research on human behavior is a social endeavor taking place in a particular social context. It would be unrealistic to expect the interactions between researcher and participant to be uncontaminated by the gender stereotypes and gender-related habits of the surrounding culture. Psychologists studying female–male similarities and differences have gradually acknowledged this problem and taken measures to deal with it: by specifying and counterbalancing when appropriate the sex of the experimenters and the participants; by minimizing demand characteristics; and by being aware of potential artifacts that would make gender differences appear to exist when they are not really present. Such precautions can move the interpretation of research in the direction of greater accuracy, but they cannot eliminate the difficulties completely.

THE RESEARCH CONTEXT   Researchers must be sure that the research context is similar for male and female participants so that gender differences do not emerge as artifacts of the research situation. For instance, suppose a researcher wants to study whether men and women are equally likely to conform when they are pressured to agree with a particular opinion. In the experiment, a male confederate of the experimenter makes persuasive statements, and the reactions of male and female subjects are compared. Notice that males are being pressured by a same-sex peer, whereas females are being pressured by an other-sex peer. If the experiment reveals gender differences, confident conclusions cannot be drawn because male and female subjects are operating under different conditions.

Similarly, a researcher attempting to compare the on-the-job behavior of female and male secretaries could not safely draw conclusions about gender differences because the females would be occupying a traditional role in which women form the majority, whereas the males would be holding a job considered unusual for their sex. Female and male secretaries, then, would be working under different kinds of social pressures. To compare their behavior without taking these differences into consideration would be to invite inaccurate conclusions.

SELECTING PARTICIPANTS   Another important aspect of research design is the choice of participants or respondents. Who should be studied and with whom should they be compared? The people to be studied should be representative of those about whom the researcher wishes to draw conclusions. Obvious though this point may seem, it used to be common practice for researchers to study only one sex (usually males) while drawing conclusions about people in general.

To put information about a particular group into perspective, it is necessary to make comparisons with other groups. For instance, the finding that 24% of a sample of pregnant women agreed with the statement "I sometimes feel as if I am going to have a nervous breakdown" might be taken as supporting the stereotype that pregnancy is a time of emotional stability—unless, as was the case in the study in question, it was balanced by the finding that 57% of the comparison group (female college students) agreed with the same item (Barclay & Barclay, 1976). When the symptoms reported by pregnant women are compared with those reported by their husbands, nonpregnant women, and husbands of nonpregnant women, the myth that pregnancy is a time of emotional instability receives little support (Lips, 1982a, 1985a). In a similar vein, it would not be appropriate to form generalizations about the impact on men of being fired from a job by studying only men who sought help for distress after such an event. These men ought to be compared with men who had not been fired—and, if possible, with men who had been fired and not sought help. Likewise, it would be inappropriate to draw conclusions about men in general from a study of male athletes, male prisoners, male political leaders, or any other special group of men without putting such a group in the context of a broader population of men.

Not only must researchers use comparison or contrast groups, they must choose such groups and examine the assumptions governing their choices with care. For example, when comparing males and females, it may not always be appropriate to equate the two groups for age because the order of some activities across the life span differs for women and men (McHugh et al., 1986). For example, if you were to compare the career achievements of 40-year-old male and female scientists, you might find that the men had published more papers and received more promotions and awards than the women. This finding might cause you to conclude that the men were better scientists or more adept at and interested in their research than were the women. But a 40-year-old man may have had more years to concentrate on his career than a 40-year-old woman. The women may have taken some time away from work to care for children or simply been torn in more directions because of family responsibilities. The difference in achievement, then, would not mean anything about scientific ability, interest, or motivation.

CHOOSING AND MEASURING DEPENDENT VARIABLES   A crucial part of the research design is the choice of dependent variables or measures. If a study is concerned with marital satisfaction, for instance, how will that satisfaction be defined and measured? Will both members of the couple be asked to rate their happiness on a scale from 1 to 10? Will they be watched to see how many arguments they have? Will mood ratings be taken? Obviously, the measure of marital happiness chosen can affect the results of the study.

In comparing females and males on any variable, care must be taken that the measure used to chart that variable is truly equivalent for the two groups. For instance, early research on achievement motivation used a test that featured all-male illustrations (McClelland, Atkinson, Clark, & Lowell, 1953). If women and men behaved differently, was it because they differed in their basic approaches to achievement or simply because the male illustrations had different effects on women and men?

Another example of bias built into dependent measures comes from conformity research (Weyant, 1979). Early studies tended to support the notion that women were more likely than men to conform to group judgments. However, when researchers are careful to use topics that are equally familiar to women and men, the gender differences in conformity weaken or disappear (Karabenick, 1983). Early investigators who ignored the familiarity issue were inadvertently using measures of conformity that were not equivalent for their female and male respondents; thus, in retrospect, their findings of apparent gender differences are not surprising.

Research Design and Cultural Diversity

Questions concerning the selection of samples, comparison groups, and measures become even more complex when we acknowledge that gender interacts with ethnicity, race, class, and other variables. Most psychological research on gender has focused on middle-class White women and men. Moreover, all too often "studies of gender differences and socialization based solely on European American women and men are regarded as revealing generalizable facts about gender per se—facts about people; but similar studies based solely on African American women and men are regarded as revealing nongeneralizable facts about African Americans alone" (Landrine, Klonoff, & Brown-Collins, 1995, p. 57).

Although feminist psychologists are increasingly conscious of the diversity among women, most research still omits the perspectives of poor women (Reid, 1993; Saris & Johnston-Robledo, 2000) and women of color (Landrine, Klonoff, & Brown-Collins, 1995). This happens either because members of these groups are simply not included in studies (perhaps because of the effort required to include them) or because when they are included their responses are interpreted from a White middle-class cultural perspective.

Hope Landrine and her colleagues (Landrine, Klonoff, & Brown-Collins, 1995) argued that it is critically important to design research that encompasses an awareness of the differing ways members of various groups may be interpreting the same questions, words, or behaviors:

> Do African American and European American women who raise their voices in an experiment engage in "the same" behavior? If so, what behavior is it— how do we label and interpret it—as anger or as enthusiasm? Are Japanese American, Chinese American, African American, and European American women who sit quietly and do not voice an opinion in a situation engaging in "the same" behavior? If so, what should the researcher call that behavior? Were they conforming to the Japanese norm of *enryo* or to the Chinese norm of *jang;* were they being passive and nonassertive or simply nonchalant and "chilled"? How does the researcher decide what has been "observed," and what do we do if the label used to tally and report on participants' behavior does not match the label that research participants choose? (p. 60)

Landrine and her colleagues suggested that researchers collect information about how participants are interpreting the questions and the research situation. In a simple demonstration of their point, they asked White women and women of color to rate themselves on various adjectives and then to indicate the meaning of the adjectives. They found that White women and women of color did not differ on their self-ratings on the adjectives; however, they did differ quite significantly on the meanings they chose to explain those adjectives. In a similar vein, researchers studying men's perceptions of masculinity found that men in different ethnic groups may differ in their interpretation of the masculine role. In one study, Latino men were the strongest endorsers of items on a scale developed to measure "traditional" male ideology, followed by European Americans and African Americans. Furthermore, for each group, ethnic belonging (the sense of attachment to one's own ethnic group and culture) was positively related to the endorsement of the male ideology items, suggesting differences within as well as between ethnic groups in meanings and importance assigned to items that are supposed to measure masculinity (Abreu, Goodyear, Campos, & Newcomb, 2000). A failure to be sensitive to such possible differences of meaning in designing research could strongly distort the interpretation of findings.

Data Analysis

Research on sex and gender is strongly oriented toward examining the differences between groups. As discussed in Chapter 2, this orientation is known as an *alpha bias.* Differences between males and females are used as springboards for understanding the way gender works. The problem with such a strong orientation toward differences, however, is that it leads researchers to look for evidence of differences and to ignore similarities. In analyzing data, researchers may focus on testing the difference between the mean scores of males and females while overlooking the pattern of overlap between them or the shapes of the score distributions. In reporting results, they may stress the areas in which differences were observed and give only passing mention or no mention to areas in which the two groups appeared to be similar.

In addition, the publication policies of scholarly journals encourage the alpha bias. A finding of "no difference" is often considered uninformative and rejected for publication because statistical tests cannot show definitively that there is no difference between populations. The failure to find a significant difference between two groups is not evidence that the two populations from which the groups came are identical; it may mean that the differences are small or that the method of testing for them was inappropriate. Thus journal editors have more confidence in findings of difference than no difference, and there are strong pressures to find and report gender differences. Readers of the psychological literature must be mindful of the possibility that for every study that reports male–female differences there may be a comparable study in which no differences were found gathering dust in a file cabinet.

Data Interpretation

Some would argue that the largest scope for the expression of bias lies in the *interpretation* of findings. A prime pitfall here is making generalizations that are too broad: drawing conclusions about human beings from the study of other animals, about all human beings from the study of one sex, or about adult gender differences from the study of children.

A similar problem occurs when researchers study people who are having difficulties with a normal process (such as menopause or the menstrual cycle) and then generalize their conclusions to all people who are experiencing that process. Information gathered about a female patient may be generalized unthinkingly to females in general, and information about male homosexual patients may be wrongly assumed to characterize gay men (Stark-Adamec & Kimball, 1984). This type of overgeneralization is most likely to occur when the observations of patients conform to stereotypes about the group.

Many other problems in interpreting data are less easily recognized, including the differential evaluation of the behaviors of males and females, use of male-centered norms to evaluate female behavior, use of the assumptions of one's own culture to explain behaviors observed among members of other cultures, viewing human behavior "through the lens of heterosexual experience" (L. S. Brown, 1989, p. 447), using human-focused language to describe animal behavior, and assuming that observed gender differences have biological causes. Let us take a closer look at each of these potential sources of bias.

LABELS   Similar behavior by male and female participants may be labeled and evaluated differently by researchers—a situation that often originates in and perpetuates social stereotypes of the two sexes. The sexually active behavior of a female adolescent may be labeled "promiscuous," whereas that of a male adolescent may be called "experimental" (Eichler & Lapointe, 1985).

When males and females show differences on a particular trait or skill, sexist biases may be reflected and perpetuated by the way the characteristic is labeled. For example, some psychologists have demonstrated gender differences in the ability to recognize a pattern or shape embedded or hidden in a larger field and in the ability to focus on the overall field. The first of these abilities, long thought to be more common in males, has been labeled "field independence," and the second, often cited as more common in females, has been called "field dependence." As Dale Spender (1980) noted, these labels tend to make the female-linked ability sound negative—women are "dependent" on the context, but men can transcend it. If the concepts had been labeled "context blindness" and "context awareness," however, the male-linked ability would have a negative connotation, and the female-linked one would sound more positive. In a similar vein, feminine-stereotyped behavior, such as a sympathetic response to an incompetent worker, may be labeled "compassionate" when a woman performs it but "weak" when a man does it. Ideally, of course, the characteristics associated with either sex should not be arbitrarily devalued through the labeling process.

ANDROCENTRIC NORMS   In the interpretation of findings of gender differences, there is a tendency to use **androcentric norms**—to apply male behavior as the norm against which to measure females. If women are found to be less ready than men to do "whatever it takes" to succeed in a career, a researcher may discuss the finding in terms of women's relative lack of ambition. If men are found to be less ready than women to do "whatever it takes" to have time to spend with their children, it is less likely that researchers will discuss the finding in terms of men's relative lack of caring and responsibility. Even the terms for some desirable qualities and behaviors may be defined in ways that make masculine behavior normative: *achievement* is success outside the home, not within it; *responsibility* is taking charge of others, not taking care of them; *bravery* is facing battle, not facing childbirth.

ETHNOCENTRISM   The interpretation of findings may also be biased by **ethnocentrism,** which is the tendency to apply the assumptions and terms of one's own culture to other cultures. For example, anthropologists long assumed that, in societies where menstruating women are secluded, this seclusion is a restriction imposed by men and is experienced by women as an *exclusion.* More careful research suggested that, at least in some societies, women see their menstrual seclusion as a positive time—a holiday from their normal duties (P. G. Allen, 1986). Studying the customs of other cultures can open our eyes to the possibilities for female–male relationships only if the data are not interpreted to fit our cultural preconceptions.

HETEROSEXISM   People with a homosexual orientation—lesbians and gay men—form a significant minority. However, their experiences are often made invisible by **heterosexism,** which is the use of heterosexual relationships as the norm for evaluating all relationships. Researchers may mean only heterosexual couples when they speak of "couples" and only two-heterosexual-parent families when they speak of "families" (L. S. Brown, 1989). Heterosexual relationships are often used as the norm against which lesbian or gay male relationships are evaluated. Yet the study of both same-gender and mixed-gender relationships is a source of clues about what works in intimate relationships in general, and examining the experience of lesbians and gay men is likely to help researchers get a clearer view of the construction of gender by providing a different perspective.

ANTHROPOMORPHISM   Although research with other animals can provide clues about human behavior, animal behavior may be misinterpreted as a result of **anthropomorphism,** which is the tendency to interpret animal behavior in human terms. Anthropomorphism is often perpetuated by the use of anthropomorphic language (language that refers to human traits or behaviors) to describe animal data. This practice is common in some sociobiological writing, and it can make the researcher's understanding of an animal's motivation and behavior appear more complete than is actually the case.

For example, Barash (1979) used the term *rape* to describe what appears to be a male's forcing of sexual advances on an unwilling female among a variety of species, including mallard ducks and even plants! Although the use of the word *rape* creates an attention-getting description, it does little to clarify what is going on. How, for instance, does the researcher establish that a female flower or a female duck is "unwilling"? More seriously, is this use of the word meant to imply that because rape supposedly occurs in nonhuman species it is a biological and "natural" phenomenon? How would such trivialization of the notion of rape affect the view of rape among humans?

Another example of anthropomorphic, biased language used to describe animal behavior is the use of the word *harem* to describe primate groups comprising a single male and many females (Bleier, 1984). In human terms, a *harem* refers to a group of women who are virtually owned by a powerful male and who are economically and sexually dependent on him. The word carries these same connotations when used with primates, but careful observation shows this to be inaccurate in many cases. For many primate species, the solitary male member of the group holds a peripheral rather than central position and is tolerated by the females mainly for his sexual function (Fedigan, 1982; Hrdy, 1999). Once again, the use of a term that has particular meanings in the human context creates confusion when applied to animal behavior and lends unwarranted support to the notion that a particular social arrangement among humans has a biological basis.

RELIANCE ON BIOLOGICAL EXPLANATIONS TO FILL GAPS   A distressing tendency among researchers of sex and gender is to postulate biological bases for observed gender differences whenever other explanations are not obvious, even when the biological mechanisms that might be involved are not apparent. This hasty falling back on biological explanations just because no other explanation has been found is something like attributing our observations to magic—"We don't know how it happens, so it must be magic (or hormones)."

One example of this type of reasoning comes in the interpretation of gender differences in mathematics achievement. After careful research on mathematically talented children had shown that the girls in these samples performed somewhat less well than the boys, Camilla Benbow and Julian Stanley (1980) concluded that the performance differences were due to superior male math ability. Benbow later suggested that exposure in the womb to high levels of the male hormone testosterone, rather than gender differences in upbringing, were the key to males' better performance (Benbow, 1988). Her suggestion is based on the finding that extremely mathematically gifted youngsters are much more likely than their less gifted counterparts to be left-handed and on research that indicates a possible connection between left-handedness and prenatal exposure to testosterone. (The issue of gender differences in mathematics achievement will be discussed at length in Chapter 6.)

The apparent assumption here is that researchers know all there is to know about social–environmental influences on the behavior in question and exhausted these possibilities before finally putting their faith in biology as the cause of differences. However, although researchers have tested some socialization explanations, psychologists are still a long way from a complete understanding of all the subtle mechanisms of social–environmental influence. It is extremely unlikely that all such possibilities have been ruled out. Also, as discussed earlier in the chapter, biology and environment work so closely together that it is virtually impossible to rule out one or the other altogether in the explanation of behavior. Although researchers may eventually understand the ways that biology interacts with environment to influence the gender–mathematics relationship, it is probably premature to attribute the differences with any certainty to hormonal influences.

An overreliance on biological explanations can also be seen in faulty evolutionary theorizing. Researchers may be too quick to conclude that observed gender differences exist because they are adaptive for survival. It is probably safe to assume that if there is a genetic basis for a particular difference, it is at least not maladaptive enough to have been selected out (Stark-Adamec & Kimball, 1984). However, it is important to consider all the possible reasons for an apparently stable difference, including environmental and social learning factors.

One strategy sometimes used to support an evolutionary interpretation of behavior is what Ruth Bleier (1984) called "validation by prediction." Proponents of this approach use evolutionary theory to "predict" an already established fact; then, having supposedly demonstrated the validity of the theory by the correctness of the prediction, they freely apply the theory to interpret other observations.

Bleier noted, however, that a variety of logical predictions may follow from a set of premises. For example, the premise that women have a great biological investment in each pregnancy by virtue of their need to ensure the survival of their genes might lead logically to the following predictions: a low incidence of postpartum depression in women because depression interferes with optimum infant care; a high incidence of postpartum depression in fathers due to deprivation of the spouse's attention; and a low incidence of depression among

Overview — Biases and pitfalls in research on gender

Research Step	Key Potential Biases
Choose a topic	Employers, colleagues, and funding agencies may discourage the study of certain topics.
Formulate the research question	Possible gender differences may be either overlooked or assumed. Personality characteristics or other individual differences are more likely than social forces to be considered potential influences on gender differences.
Design the research	Sex-of-experimenter effects and variations in the way the research context influences males and females may skew results. The choice of participants may reflect sexist assumptions, and the absence of appropriate comparison groups may limit the usefulness of the research. Dependent variables and methods for measuring them must be chosen with care to ensure that they are equivalent for males and females.
Analyze the data	The orientation toward differences, or alpha bias, may lead the researcher to ignore similarities. Inadequate analysis may result from the tendencies to focus on differences in average scores and to overlook the overlap between males and females and the pattern of the distribution of results and their variability.
Interpret the data	Faulty generalizations may result from drawing conclusions about human beings from the study of animals, about all people from the study of one sex, and about adult differences from the study of children. Androcentric norms, ethnocentrism, heterosexism, anthropomorphism, and the tendency to assume that biology can explain unexplained gender differences all lead to faulty interpretations.
Publish the findings	The publication policies of scholarly journals may lead to the rejection of studies that find no gender difference or that focus on gender similarities. The popular media are likely to oversimplify and dramatize conclusions, and they are most likely to publicize findings either that can be sensationalized or that match their biases.

women in general because most of them are following their biological urge to produce children. All of these predictions follow logically from the sociobiological premise—but none are correct.

Publication of Findings

If the interpretation of data by researchers can be influenced by bias, the popularization of these interpretations tends to magnify the bias by oversimplifying the conclusions. In the example of gender differences in mathematics achievement discussed in the preceding section, media coverage made the attribution of gender differences to biology sound even more conclusive than the researchers probably intended. "Do Males Have a Math Gene?" asked a *Newsweek* headline (D. A. Williams & King, 1980); with more assurance, a Canadian paper headlined an article "Male Hormones Key to Math, Study Says" (*Winnipeg Free Press,* 1986).

The biases in media coverage of scientific results are partly due to the media's habit of distilling simple statements from complex facts. However, they often also reflect the biases of the writer or publication that provides the coverage. An obvious example is the headline given by *Playboy* magazine to an article on sociobiology: "Do Men Need to Cheat on Their Women? A New Science Says Yes" (S. Morris, 1978).

Although scientists cannot always be held responsible for how media distort their work, they should at least exercise care when making statements. Readers should keep in mind that only the most sensational-sounding findings are likely to be reported and that coverage may reflect editorial bias, the distillation of the most dramatic conclusions from a more complex set of findings, and the stripping away of hedges and qualifications provided by the scientist.

SCIENCE AND ANDROCENTRISM

Some authors suggest that science has helped to promote and maintain male dominance over women and has been a male-centered institution (Bleier, 1984; E. F. Keller, 1985; Morawski, 1994). Some scientific theories about women have even seemed to be shaped by an attitude of dislike and distrust of women, known as **misogyny.** Science has influenced women's lives without allowing women a voice in the process. Its findings have often ignored or distorted women's experience. The science of psychology specifically has been accused of supporting stereotypes about women and men that, in turn, have buttressed political, legal, and economic inequalities between the sexes (Morawski, 1994).

Could it be that science as an institution has been so shaped by men that it can never shed an androcentric bias? Many feminist scientists would answer "No," yet there is a growing realization that science as an institution will not easily be overhauled by egalitarian or feminist concerns. The scientific enterprise—

its accepted way of doing things, its values, its areas of focus—has been shaped by generations of men, and its rewards are still reserved mainly for men.

Values

Science revolves around values of objectivity, prediction, and control. Several writers have highlighted the separation and control-oriented themes in the scientific endeavor: The ultimate object is the conquest of and control over nature (E. F. Keller, 1985). "Man" is considered to be separate from the natural world and destined to dominate it. The term *man* rather than *humanity* is probably the more accurate term in this context both because nature is characterized as feminine (e.g., Mother Nature) and because women historically have been excluded from participation in science. Even in the social sciences, women have often been treated as somehow separate from the mainstream of human activity, as deviants from the male norm. From Aristotle's notion of "woman as defective man" through the current definition of *work* as paid employment, social science has revealed a consistent proclivity to use men as the norm and to define women as "different."

Participants

Science has traditionally been a male activity and, except for life sciences and psychology, it continues to be as Figure 3.6 shows. Women make up about 13.8% of the engineering workforce, 27% of employed mathematical and computer scientists, and 29.9% of employed natural scientists (U.S. Census Bureau, 2006a). African American and Hispanic women, showing the double disadvantage of being both female and members of racial minorities, are underrepresented in scientific and technical fields relative to African American and Hispanic men, who are already underrepresented relative to European American men.

Women are moving into the social sciences in larger numbers. More than 77% of recently graduated U.S. psychology majors are women (National Science Foundation, 2004b). Women make up about 66% of the students graduating with doctoral degrees in psychology, but they make up only 45.4% of assistant professors in psychology at the top 50 U.S. educational institutions. Moreover, women are less likely than men to receive tenure, and they wait longer for tenure and promotion (National Academy of Sciences, 2006b).

Relatively few women have risen to prominence or have become influential policymakers within the realm of science. Women are also underrepresented in the National Academy of Sciences. They make up only 19.7% of Academy members in the field of psychology (National Academy of Sciences, 2006a). As Figure 3.7 shows, few women have been awarded a Nobel prize in science.

The image of the research scientist continues to be a masculine one, albeit not always particularly complimentary (Thomas, Henley, & Snell, 2006). In this study of college students' drawings of scientists, the typical portrayal was a bespectacled man in a lab coat, with wild hair, standing over an apparatus that was issuing smoke. Media portrayals may be even more stereotypic: male scientists

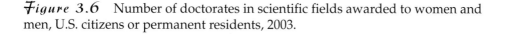

Figure 3.6 Number of doctorates in scientific fields awarded to women and men, U.S. citizens or permanent residents, 2003.

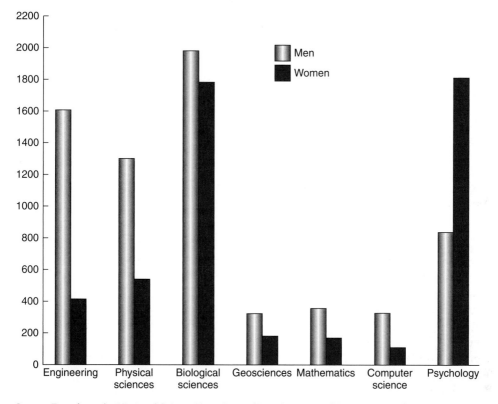

Source: Data from the National Science Foundation (2004a). Retrieved June 20, 2006, from www.nsf.gov/statistics/nsf05300/dst.htm, tables 6 and 7.

may be portrayed fictionally as cold, dominance-oriented, and uninterested in people whereas female scientists are portrayed as marginal and sexualized (Flicker, 2003; Keller, 1985). Such images reflect the meshing of stereotypes about gender with stereotypes about science. Science is for rational, intellectual men, not for irrational, emotional women. Small wonder that women have difficulty seeing themselves as scientists.

Psychology as a field has come some distance from the era in which eminent research psychologists such as Helen Thompson Woolley faced extraordinary difficulty obtaining a professional position simply because they were women. But some of the apparent progress in accommodating women is due to the "hard" and "soft" divisions within psychology. The "hard-soft" distinction is often interpreted as "masculine-feminine." Women are more likely to end up

Figure 3.7 Percentage of Nobel laureates in science fields by gender, 1901–2005.

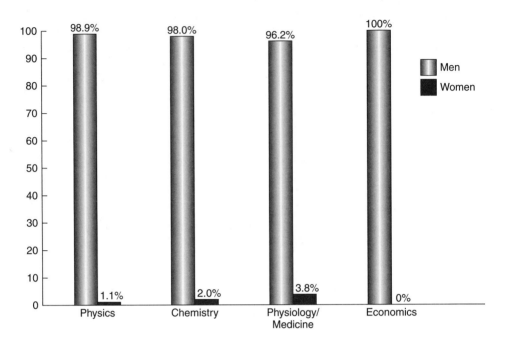

Source: Based on data from the Nobel Foundation (2006). Retrieved June 21, 2006, from http://nobelprize.org/nobel-prizes/

in the "soft" areas of psychology, such as developmental and clinical, whereas men are more likely to be in the "hard" areas of quantitative and cognitive psychology (National Opinion Research Center, 2005). This hard-soft distinction is basically meaningless; the intellectual effort and rigor required to understand and do good research are no less demanding in the soft than in the hard areas. The distinction perpetuates an implicit bias in favor of the importance of the hard branches of science and serves as a subtle reminder that such branches are masculine (Keller, 1985).

The claim is sometimes made that if there were more women in science, science itself would be different, perhaps fundamentally so (Keller, 1985). As long as the women in a particular scientific field remain a small minority, however, the likelihood is that it is they rather than science that will be changed by their participation. Women entering the fields of science and technology have been compared to immigrants in a new country; after working so hard to gain admission and establish themselves, it is unlikely that they will be severely critical of their new milieu (U. M. Franklin, 1985). But if women enter a field in large numbers, they can have a noticeable impact on the discipline.

In psychology, a field that relatively large numbers of women have entered, the effect of women's increasing participation has been dramatic on at least one dimension: the topics addressed by psychological research. Major psychological journals now carry significantly more articles dealing with gender and with issues specifically related to women. Prior to 1960, there were proportionally more references to men than to women in the psychological literature. That balance began to shift during the 1960s, and from 1974 to 1997 about 65% of the references were to women (Moon & Hoffman, 2000). Guidelines for the conduct of nonsexist research have been published by both the American and the Canadian Psychological Associations (McHugh et al., 1986; Stark-Adamec & Kimball, 1984), and conscious efforts are made to include women on editorial boards.

Yet problems remain. There is still a tendency to "ghettoize" research on women and on gender, as if such topics could be split off into a subdiscipline, and debates rage about the appropriateness of taking a feminist approach—one explicitly oriented to understanding and improving the situation of women—to the study of human behavior. Women and men trying to do nonsexist psychological research or practice or to work from an explicitly feminist perspective must still confront the question of how to help develop a psychology that has shed completely its old androcentric bias.

A TRANSFORMATIONAL PSYCHOLOGY OF GENDER?

Michele Wittig (1985) and others (Bohan, 1992; Morawski, 1994) have argued that the field of psychology as a whole needs to shift perspectives away from the old notion that behavior and our understanding of it can be separated from each other and from their social context. Rather, psychologists must acknowledge that their research methods, theories, and judgments about the validity of their theories are influenced by their historical, personal, social, and cultural milieu. This acknowledgment inevitably brings those engaged in the research enterprise face to face with the tension between trying to be sensitive to the effects of the social context and trying to transcend them. In studying the psychology of gender, this awareness of the influence of their personal values and social milieu should not paralyze researchers, but it should force them to use methods that include an examination of the context of behavior, that allow multiple causes of behavior to emerge, and that allow for the possibility that the attempt to study a behavior may change it.

If researchers of the psychology of gender reject the idea that they are separate from the process they are trying to study, Wittig (1985) argued, they can resolve some of the dilemmas facing the psychology of gender. For example, she suggested that a psychology of gender can be change oriented and emancipatory without becoming trapped in ideology: "Constructing what could be requires knowledge of what is . . . propositions in the psychology of gender are both an attempt to understand the functioning of gender in the world as it is and an articulation of what could be" (p. 804). Careful scholarship need not preclude advocacy; rather, advocacy can contribute to scholarship by influencing the content of theory and the choices of topics and methods of study while scholarship acts as a check on the claims made by advocacy. Wittig argued that a "transformational psychology of gender" is oriented not only toward change in the world beyond the field of psychology but also toward a transformation of the discipline itself from within—into a nonsexist psychology. Such a psychology is not yet a reality, but the self-critical processes necessary to the transformation are being vigorously undertaken.

SUMMARY

We are concerned in this book with the questions of what is known about gender similarities and differences, where that knowledge comes from, and how the knowledge is shaped by culture. This chapter has focused heavily on the second question: Where does our knowledge of gender come from? What we have seen is that no pure and uncontaminated sources of such knowledge exist.

There are a variety of research methods for gathering information about sex- and gender-related aspects of human behavior, yet no one method is adequate to the task. Narrative, phenomenological, discourse analytic, observational, survey, and experimental methods can all shed some light on the links among sex, gender, and behavior, but none of them allows the researcher to conclude with certainty that biological sex differences cause behavioral differences. Because biological sex cannot be manipulated and because it is always confounded with a variety of social–environmental variables, sex difference research is always correlational. Therefore, it is more accurate to speak of sex-related differences than of sex differences. Moreover, it is becoming clear that biological and environmental factors ("nature" and "nurture") have such closely linked, reciprocal roles in human development that it is usually meaningless to try to isolate either biology or the environment as the sole cause of an observed female–male difference.

Problems of bias abound in the research on sex and gender. Cultural stereotypes about masculinity and femininity influence the research at many levels and stages, from the choice of the research topic to the research instruments, to the behavior of the experimenter, to the language and concepts used in the interpretation of findings. There is a pervasive tendency to look for differences rather than similarities between females and males, not only because of the stereotyped preconceptions of the researchers but also because findings of differences are more likely to be published than are findings of similarities.

The entire enterprise of scientific research, as currently constructed, still has echoes of an androcentric approach. It has been developed in a culture dominated by masculine values, and most of the participants in the scientific enterprise have been men. A transformation is under way, however, fueled by feminist concerns and by the entry of increasing numbers of women into the scientific professions. This change is being felt in the field of psychology, in which increasing attention is being paid to research on gender and on topics of special concern to women and in which many traditional assumptions about the research process are being critiqued. Although we do not yet have a psychology free of sexism, we are more conscious of the potential pitfalls in researching sex and gender. We are moving away from a psychology that unwittingly helps perpetuate masculine and feminine stereotypes and the power imbalances between women and men.

KEY TERMS

logical positivism

social constructionism

case history method

narrative approach

phenomenological method

discourse analysis

naturalistic observation

survey methods

correlational methods

experiment

independent variable

dependent variable

longitudinal study

meta-analysis

effect size

distribution

statistically significant

transformationism

sex-of-experimenter effects

androcentric norms

ethnocentrism

heterosexism

anthropomorphism

misogyny

Worlds Apart?
Gender Differences in Social Behavior and Experience

*J*n May 1995 Alison Hargreaves became the second person to complete a solo ascent of Mount Everest without supplementary oxygen. Three months later, she fell to her death after reaching the summit of K2. Many press reports focused more on her status as a "mother of two" than on her elite climbing accomplishments. On March 14, 1990, Susan Butcher stormed into Nome, Alaska, recording her fourth victory in 5 years in the 1,158-mile Iditarod Trail Dog Sled Race. As in previous years, people made much of the fact that she was female; her victory was somehow more surprising because of her sex. Automobile racer Sarah Fisher was voted the most popular driver in the Indy Racing League in 2002, yet she had enormous difficulty finding a sponsor because she was a woman. Similarly, when Manon Rheaume began to play hockey for Tampa in 1992, more attention was paid to the fact that she was the first *woman* to play professional hockey than to her record.

A man who changed careers from coal mining to nursing reported that his friends thought "there's got to be something slightly wrong with the man if he wants to go into training to be a nurse" (Cross & Bagilhole, 2002, p. 213). In a similar vein, a male community care worker noted that some men thought he must be gay because a man should not want to do this kind of work, and a man who switched from being a car mechanic to working as a cleaner reported that he could not tell his friends what he does for a living because they would make fun of him for doing a woman's job (Cross & Bagilhole, 2002). The founder of an Italian association for househusbands asserted that many men who stay at home to do domestic work while their wives are employed outside the home feel ashamed of their role: "Lots of men come to me in secret and admit they are househusbands. . . . It's as if they have committed a sin, and with us they can confess. You should see how relieved they are" (Arie, 2004).

Expectations for women and men are still so different in some domains that observers are surprised, even shocked, when an individual woman or man "crosses the line" to behave in a way that is normative for the other group. Women and men are even described as "opposite sexes." How different are we really? In terms of how we spend our time, women and men are very different indeed: Women do most of the housework, men play most of the football, women do most of the typing, men run most of the corporations, women do most of the child care, men commit most of the violent crimes. Small wonder if people conclude that human males and females differ dramatically in abilities, motivation, and temperament.

However, as we have seen, gender difference in behavior can result from a complex interaction between characteristics of the individuals and characteristics of the social environment. The observation that men commit more violent crimes than women cannot be interpreted as proof that males are always more aggressive than females. The fact that women do most of the child care does not itself prove that women are generally more nurturing than men. This chapter surveys the research evidence for the existence of gender differences in several areas of social behavior.

In this chapter, we consider the following questions:

- How important is context in producing gender differences?
- Are men really more aggressive than women?
- Is one sex more susceptible to influence than the other?
- Do women and men differ in dominance?
- Are women more nurturing than males?
- Is there a male–female difference in the tendency toward empathy?

- Who is more altruistic: women or men?
- How do role expectations, status, the focus on studying particular kinds of behavior, and observer bias contribute to our conclusions about how females and males differ?

NOW YOU SEE IT, NOW YOU DON'T: GENDER DIFFERENCES IN CONTEXT

Gender differences appear in some contexts but not others, leading to the suspicion that many behavioral differences between women and men and girls and boys are not "built in" or "set," either by biology or early learning. Instead, they are a product of—or at least amplified by—circumstance. For example, teachers are fond of saying that girls have a "civilizing" effect on boys: that boys do not act up as much when girls are around as when they are in all-boy groups. What they are saying, really, is that the boys' behavior changes with the social context and that gender differences in behavior are less extreme in some situations than others.

The idea that gender differences in behavior stem from qualities that are resident in or possessed by women and men is sometimes labeled **essentialism** in feminist theory. This approach can be contrasted with social constructionism, first described in Chapter 3. Social constructionism is the idea that gender is something that is not composed of traits possessed by individuals but rather something that occurs in interactions among persons. That is, there is a social agreement that certain behaviors are appropriate for women and men (or girls and boys) in certain situations. The difference between the two approaches is illustrated by Janice Bohan (1997):

> By way of analogy, consider the difference between describing an individual as friendly and describing a conversation as friendly. In the former case, "friendly" is constructed as a trait of the person, an "essential" component to her or his personality. In the latter, "friendly" describes the nature of the interaction occurring between or among people. Friendly here has a particular meaning that is agreed upon by the participants, that is compatible with its meaning to their social reference groups, and that is reaffirmed by the process of engaging in this interaction. Although the essentialist view of gender sees it as analogous to the friendly person, the constructionist sees gender as analogous to the friendly conversation. (p. 33)

Theorists disagree over whether the essentialist or the social constructionist approach is most useful or correct. It is important to keep in mind, however, that much of the psychological research on gender is grounded in essentialist assumptions.

GENDER DIFFERENCES IN SOCIAL BEHAVIOR: A SAMPLING OF CURRENT FINDINGS

In the previous chapter, we explored the techniques available for determining the presence of gender differences. Let us turn to an examination of what these techniques have found in the realm of social behavior. For each of several kinds of social behavior, we will examine the evidence for the reliable presence and magnitude of female–male differences. Where differences are found to exist, we will review evidence concerning the reasons for these differences. Similar examinations of evidence for gender differences and similarities in other domains, such as intellectual abilities, achievement, communication, intimacy, sexuality, and morality, will be presented in later chapters.

Aggression

In the fall of 2002 residents of the Washington, D.C., area were terrorized by a series of sniper attacks. The two men who were eventually arrested were linked by police to 20 shootings that left 13 people dead and 5 injured. In the same year, in Erfurt, Germany, 19-year-old Robert Steinhaeuser killed 13 teachers and two students before shooting himself. In 1999, at Columbine High School in Littleton, Colorado, two young men killed 12 fellow students and one teacher and wounded 23 others before turning their guns on themselves. In 2003 current and former female students at the U.S. Air Force Academy came forward to report a pattern of sexual assaults and rapes by male students that had apparently gone unchecked for years. It is difficult to imagine these situations with women as the aggressors. Is that because males really are more aggressive than females, or do they simply commit more "spectacular" acts of aggression? Do males have stronger aggressive drives than females do, or have they simply not been taught as carefully as females that they must control those drives?

Psychologists often measure aggression in laboratory situations. In one typical study, undergraduate student volunteers came to the lab to participate in a reaction time competition (Zeichner, Parrott, & Frey, 2003). During the competition, they were provoked by receiving electric shocks from a confederate. They could either retaliate against the person by using similar shocks or choose to refrain from retaliation. The young women and men in this study did not react in exactly the same way. The men administered more shocks, chose more intense shocks, and were more likely than the women to choose the highest intensity shock available. The women took longer to become aggressive and started out with lower levels of shock. Such findings are fairly typical of laboratory studies of aggression.

Maccoby and Jacklin (1974) concluded from their extensive review of studies that greater male than female aggressiveness was well-established. The difference occurred for both physical and verbal aggression and across a variety of cultures. It appeared between ages 2 and 3 and continued through the college years, after which there was little information available.

A decade later, Janet Hyde (1984b) used meta-analysis to evaluate the size of the gender difference and to examine its developmental aspects. She found that gender differences accounted for an average of 5% of the variance in aggression in the 75 studies in her sample. The male mean was about one-half a standard deviation higher than that of the females. Thus, within-gender variation in aggression appears to be much larger than between-gender variation.

The gender difference tended to be larger for younger than for older people: For children under the age of 6, gender accounted for 7% of the variance in aggression, whereas for college students, gender accounted for only 1%. However, aggression was generally measured differently for preschool children and college students. For preschoolers, physical or verbal aggressive behaviors were often measured, whereas for college students, aggression tended to be measured by willingness to administer an electric shock to another individual. Hyde also found that gender differences tended to be larger for physical than verbal aggression; in naturalistic, correlational studies than in experimental studies; and in earlier (1966–1973) than later (1978–1981) studies. The smaller differences in later studies may stem from changes in gender socialization patterns, changes in perceptions by observers, or an increased likelihood of publication of "no difference" findings after Maccoby and Jacklin's (1974) review. In a recent review of major meta-analyses on gender and aggression over two decades, Hyde (2005) concluded that evidence for male–female differences in physical aggression is particularly robust and that differences in verbal aggression tend to be smaller. She noted as well, however, that contextual factors appear to be very important in the size of gender differences in aggression.

It is difficult to know how much a researcher's or observer's expectations may affect reports of male–female differences in aggression. John Condry and David Ross (1985) showed college students a videotape of two children playing roughly in the snow. The children were disguised by their snowsuits, and the researchers varied the gender labels for each child. Observers who thought they were watching a boy acting aggressively against another boy rated the behavior as significantly less aggressive than those who thought they were watching a boy acting aggressively against a girl or a girl acting aggressively against either a boy or a girl.

Apparently, the observers tended to discount the aggressiveness of an interaction between two boys and to inflate the aggressiveness of the same interaction when it involved a girl. If researchers tend to see aggression as something masculine, might they overlook types of aggression that girls and women use frequently? Males seem more likely to engage in **overt aggression** (aggression that physically hurts or threatens another person), but females may favor **relational aggression** (aggression that hurts or threatens another person by damaging his or her relationships; sometimes called indirect or social aggression). For instance, they may spread negative information about a person or intentionally exclude a person from a group. Hyde's (2005) review concluded that there is still not enough evidence to know whether girls engage in more relational aggression than boys do: gender differences appear largest when measured by direct observation, but much smaller when measured by peer ratings, self-reports, or teacher ratings. Archer and Coyne (2005) also concluded that studies do not always show that girls are more relationally aggressive than boys; however, they noted that studies consistently show that girls engage in more relational than physical aggression, whereas the reverse is true of boys. To make the issue more complicated, patterns of gender differences in relational aggression seem to vary by age: few male–female differences in relational aggression appear among very young children, but differences appear larger in late childhood and possibly peak during adolescence, and wane again among adults—perhaps because young men's relational aggression increases to match women's levels (Archer & Coyne, 2005).

Why should girls emphasize relational rather than overt physical aggression? One obvious reason is that such forms of aggression do not violate notions of femininity and are more socially acceptable for them. Social norms and expectations do influence the expression of aggression: Female–male differences in aggression are largest when expectations for women and men differ most strongly (Eagly & Steffen, 1986).

Eagley and Steffen asked college students to imagine the aggressive behavior detailed in each of the studies included in the meta-analysis and to rate the harmful consequences of the act, the anxiety or guilt they themselves would feel in performing it, how much danger they would face in performing the act, and the likelihood that the average man or woman would perform the act. Women were more likely than men to rate the aggressive acts as harmful, potentially guilt inducing, and dangerous to the performer. Raters also said the average man was more likely than the average woman to perform these aggressive acts.

Besides these gender differences, there was another interesting finding. The respondents did not know the outcomes of any of the studies for which they provided ratings of the aggressive behavior used as dependent variables. However, the more males and females differed in their ratings of particular aggressive behaviors, the larger was the male–female difference in studies using those behaviors. Studies of aggression that used behaviors for which expectations and norms were most different according to the raters found the largest gender differences in aggression.

Eleanor Maccoby (1998), who has spent most of her career observing children's behavior, noted that "most boys are *not* aggressive, in the sense of possessing a consistent personality disposition that involves frequent fighting and getting into trouble with adults and peers through fighting" (p. 36). Rather, she said, boys' rough play often seems to indicate high spirits rather than aggression.

Maccoby pointed out that we are used to thinking of boys' aggressiveness as a personality trait, but it may be more accurate to think of it as a product of particular situations: "a characteristic of male-male play—better seen as a property of male dyads or groups than of individuals" (p. 37). She observed that boys are not equally aggressive under all conditions but are especially likely to aggress when interacting with other boys. Boys, she said, almost always choose other boys as targets for their aggression, and they are less likely to respond aggressively when *girls* direct aggressive or assertive actions against them than when boys do.

Maccoby's observations recall the distinction between the essentialist and social constructionist modes of thinking about gender, discussed earlier in the chapter. Aggression is not necessarily an essential trait more likely to be possessed by individual males than by individual females. Rather, particular situations permit and encourage more aggressive behaviors among males than among females or between males and females. A key situational factor in whether a boy will behave aggressively appears to be the gender of the other people in the situation. As Maccoby said, "the gendered aspect of an individual's behavior is brought into play by the gender of others" (p. 9).

Should the research findings on gender differences in aggression be interpreted to mean that women tend to behave nonaggressively? Probably not. As Jacquelyn White and Robin Kowalski (1994) noted, there is ample evidence of aggressive behavior by women, and it is likely that women have as much potential as men do to be aggressive—under the right conditions. For instance, national surveys have found no difference between women and men in their rates of physically aggressive acts against a spouse (Archer, 2000; Straus, 1999) or of physical child abuse (Wauchope & Straus, 1990). However, women face more social restrictions in their expression of aggression than men do; thus, men's aggression may be more public and physical, whereas women's may be more private and indirect.

Early studies showed that girls and boys were equally aggressive when offered equal rewards for aggressive behaviors (Bandura, 1973). Equal rewards are rarely present, however, given the differing norms for behavior learned by girls and boys. Boys approve of and expect more rewards and fewer punishments for aggression than girls do (Huesmann, Guerra, Zelli, & Miller, 1992; Perry, Perry, & Weiss, 1989). Thus, unless especially angered or provoked, females may be either more inhibited about expressing aggressive feelings or more in control of their aggressive reactions than males are (Frodi, Macaulay, & Thome, 1977). Researchers have shown, however, that if the salience of social norms is removed so that men and women have no reason to expect different levels of approval for aggressive actions, the gender difference in aggression can evaporate. In one lab study, some participants were made to wear name tags, sit close to the experimenter, and reveal personal information, whereas others were allowed to be anonymous. All participants played interactive video games in which they "bombed" other players. Among participants who had to identify themselves, the expected gender difference appeared: men dropped more bombs on their opponents. Among "anonymous" participants, however, there were no significant gender differences (Lightdale & Prentice, 1994).

Some researchers think emotional arousal is a key to understanding gender differences in aggression. Perhaps males are more easily aroused by aggression-related stimuli, or maybe they have more trouble regulating their emotional reactions than females do. If these notions were correct, we would expect women and men to differ little in their aggression levels when they are not particularly emotional (because then there is no need to control emotions) or when they are very emotionally aroused (at high levels, women's ability to regulate their own reactions may break down). We would expect a larger gender difference in situations that generate a moderately high amount of emotional arousal. In support of this idea, one meta-analysis found gender differences in aggression were smallest in studies that produced either very low or very high levels of emotional arousal and largest in studies that evoked intermediate levels of arousal (Knight, Guthrie, Page, & Fabes, 2002).

Women have more anxiety about aggressive feelings and feel more anxious after being aggressive than men do (Frodi et al., 1977). Women are also more likely than men to make self-critical statements about their own aggression to avoid disapproval (A. Campbell & Muncer, 1987). Perhaps this is because women and men explain their aggression differently. Women tend to describe their aggression as a loss of self-control, whereas men describe it as a way of imposing control over others (Astin, Redston, & A. Campbell, 2003). But if women are anxious about their aggression because they view it as losing control, they also seem more likely than men to feel that their own aggression is justified—that they were simply pushed beyond the limits of their endurance. Sarah Astin and her colleagues (2003) found that, when describing episodes of their aggression in their own lives, women described their aggressive actions as more morally acceptable than men did.

If aggression anxiety is reduced, either through strong justification for the aggression or confidence that aggression will be an effective strategy, women's likelihood of aggression may rise. For instance, Jack Hokanson and his colleagues (Hokanson & Edelman, 1966; Hokanson, Willers, & Koropsak, 1968) found that males' physiological arousal decreased dramatically after they were allowed to give electric shocks to someone who had insulted them. Females showed no such "relief response" following aggression; in fact, their arousal decreased following a friendly response toward their insulter. However, the researchers were able to teach the relief response for aggression to women simply by changing their reinforcement history: rewarding aggressive responses with nonshock trials and shocking subjects if they made a friendly response.

Do females and males follow similar paths toward becoming violent? Relatively little is known about whether different factors predispose females and males toward aggressive behavior. However, physical or sexual abuse in childhood seems to be more strongly related to later violent behavior among women than men (Greenfeld & Snell, 1999). Also, women who engage in antisocial violence are more likely than their male counterparts to have relatives who are socially deviant. These findings hint at possible differences in the ways that men and women become aggressive and in the kinds of interventions that might be effective (Loeber & Stouthamer-Loeber, 1998).

There are some serious limitations to the psychological literature on gender differences in aggression. Most of the studies have been carried out on populations that are the most easily accessible to researchers: preschool and schoolchildren and college students. There are practically no laboratory studies of adults older than college age. Moreover, the measures of aggression used in controlled studies have, of necessity, been artificial and limited. In real life, the pattern of greater male than female aggression appears more clear-cut. As shown in Figure 4.1, men commit far more homicides than women do, and men are also more frequently victims of such crimes. Also, crime statistics show that females account for 75.6% of victims of fatal violence and 84.7% of victims of nonfatal violence within families (U. S. Bureau of Justice Statistics, 2004). Women account for only 14% of violent offenders reported to the criminal justice system and only 8% of convicted violent felons (U.S. Bureau of Justice Statistics, 2005). These statistics suggest that men are much more likely than women to engage in very physically violent behavior.

Why would gender differences in physical aggression exist? Perhaps because boys are directly taught more aggressive behaviors than girls are, or perhaps boys are rewarded more for expressing aggression and girls are rewarded more for inhibiting it. Certainly, boys are surrounded with models of male aggression in sports and the popular media. From male political leaders

Figure 4.1   Number of homicide offenders in the United States by gender, 1976–2002.

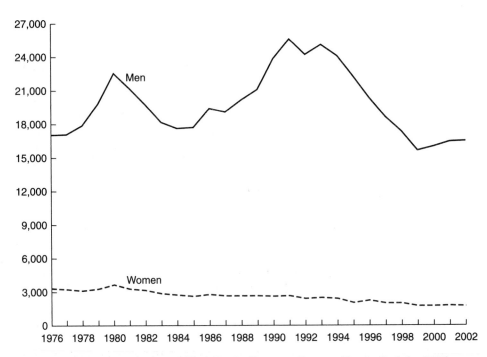

Source: U.S. Department of Justice, Office of Justice Programs, Bureau of Justice Statistics (2004).
Homicide trends in the United States: Trends by gender. Retrieved June 23, 2006, from
www.oip.usdoj.gov/bjs/homicide/tables/osextab.htm

making threats and talking tough about war and terror to the Terminator (a machine, but still, somehow, male) cutting a swath of destruction to carry out his programmed mission, male images of aggression are almost inescapable. Female aggression, despite the upsurge of films such as *Girlfight* and *Kill Bill* (and despite the portrayal of the villain in *Terminator 3* as a female machine), is not seen as often in popular or news media.

Males are more rewarded by their peers than females are for overtly aggressive behavior (Fagot & Hagan, 1985), and overt aggression by females tends to meet with disapproval, even in children. Parents do not consistently encourage aggression in sons and discourage it in daughters (Lytton & Romney, 1991); however, mothers and father may well model aggression differently.

Gender differences in aggression do not reflect a straightforward personality difference between women and men. Rather, these differences reflect a more complicated interplay among social expectations, predispositions, and particular circumstances. One more issue to consider is power. In a context of social power in which males are more likely than females to learn that it is acceptable and that they have a *right* to get their way through overt aggression, males are more likely than females to engage in such aggression.

To the extent that males are bigger, stronger, and better trained in aggressive techniques than females are, overt aggression is more likely to be an effective strategy for them. Furthermore, in situations in which women are economically dependent on men—situations that are frequent in societies in which men are given preferred access to resources such as education, employment, and income—men may find physical aggression a less risky strategy than women do and so employ it more. Cross-cultural studies show that societies differ in the degree to which they encourage male aggression, and gender-related differences in aggression reflect these cultural norms (e.g., Block, 1973; Mead, 1935). Societies in which there is a great deal of emphasis on warfare, aggressiveness, and bravery tend to foster conditions in which women become property to be conquered or prizes to be won by male warriors. In contrast, in certain forager societies aggression and violence of all kinds are frowned upon. In such societies, gender differences in aggression appear to be minimal (O'Kelly & Carney, 1986). Male aggression that is specifically directed against women is greater in cultures in which women have little economic or political power or authority (Sanday, 1981a). Women's use of aggression is probably also related to power. When researchers interviewed adolescent girls about their use of relational aggression, these girls reported that such aggressive behavior increased their status: girls who spread rumors or excluded other girls from their social group were viewed as holding more power (Owens, Shute, & Slee, 2000). These power-related issues are discussed further in Chapters 11 and 12.

Some of the biological factors postulated as causes for the gender difference in aggression will be examined in the following chapter in the discussion of sexual differentiation. It is possible but unproven that one or more of these biological factors contributes to a predisposition for males to behave in a more physically aggressive way than females, perhaps by building in a sensitivity to

Overview   Gender differences in aggression

Issue	Summary of Findings
Physical vs. verbal aggression	Gender differences appear larger for physical than verbal aggression.
Overt vs. relational aggression	Males are more likely than females to display overt aggression; females are more likely than males to display relational aggression.
Spontaneous vs. provoked aggression	Males are more likely than females to be spontaneously aggressive, but females and males are equally likely to be aggressive when provoked through insults or other means.
The impact of norms and expectations	Gender differences in aggressive behavior are largest for behaviors and situations in which the norms with respect to aggression are most different for males and females.

certain kinds of stimuli or by making certain aggression-related responses more rewarding. However, the existence of such a predisposition would not lead inevitably to male–female differences in aggressive behavior; biological and social influences on behavior work in combination.

Influenceability

There is a stereotype that women are more easily influenced or more compliant than men. However, little evidence supports such a sweeping generalization (Eagly & Wood, 1985; Maccoby & Jacklin, 1974). When gender differences are found, they usually do show greater female conformity (e.g., Collin, Di Sano, & Malik, 1994); however, a meta-analysis of social influence studies indicated that the gender difference is quite small, with male and female means about one-quarter of a standard deviation apart (Eagly & Carli, 1981).

In some conflict situations, men negotiate more favorable outcomes for themselves than women do (Stuhlmacher & Walters, 1999). However, this is not necessarily because women are more easily influenced or persuaded. It may be due to lower initial expectations by women (Kaman & Hartel, 1994) or because other motives, such as relationship concerns, affect their behavior.

Gender differences in conformity tend to be associated with particular situational variables (Eagly & Carli, 1981). For example, status differences between women and men provide a possible explanation for gender differences in influenceability (Eagly, 1983; Eagly & Wood, 1982; Hopcroft, 2002). The difference is larger in laboratory studies when participants are confronted with group pressure and in studies in which subjects know they are under observation. Male researchers have been more likely than female researchers to find gender differences in influenceability. Also, race or ethnicity may be an important variable. In the United States, African American females tend to be less easily influenced than their African American male or European American female counterparts (K. A. Adams, 1980, 1983).

Both sexes show less conformity when dealing with a topic or task that is familiar or gender appropriate (Karabenick, 1983; Sistrunk & McDavid, 1971). But even though gender-biased topics may contribute to findings of gender differences in particular studies, there is no evidence that the research in this area has an overall masculine content bias (Eagly & Carli, 1981). Thus the general finding of modestly greater female than male influenceability in certain situations cannot be attributed solely to this bias.

At least some of the observed differences may occur not because women conform more but because men conform less when they are subjected to group pressure (Eagly, Wood, & Fishbaugh, 1981). It has usually been assumed that women more often than men change their opinions to coincide with those of a group in the interest of group harmony. However, these researchers showed that women's opinions tended to remain unchanged when confronted with a group. Rather, it was the men's opinions that changed—in the direction of greater nonconformity.

Eagly and her colleagues suggest that the sometimes observed gender difference in who can be influenced may stem not from greater female compliance but from male concern with not *appearing* influenceable. Males may tend to think of nonconformity or independence as "masculine" and tailor their behavior in that direction. Men are automatically ascribed higher status than women under many circumstances; they also tend to hold higher-status positions (Lockheed, 1985; Lockheed & Hall, 1976). With higher status come expectations for greater influence, and these expectations may become self-fulfilling prophecies. Men are expected to exert more influence because of their higher status; thus they act in influencing ways, whereas women, who are not expected to exert as much influence, act in conforming ways. The result is a status difference disguised as a gender difference.

The impact of status is particularly evident when we look at influence in female–male interactions. As we would expect if females are ascribed lower status than males, women and girls are more likely to successfully influence other females than to influence males. Men tend to resist influence by women, particularly when the women use influence strategies that are competent and direct (Carli, 2001). In neutral task situations in the laboratory, males reject influence from females more than females reject influence from males (Hopcroft, 2002).

Social context also makes a difference in the way women and men respond to interpersonal influence. Women seem to be more persuaded by arguments that are delivered face-to-face rather than via e-mail; men respond similarly to both types of communication (Guadagno & Cialdini, 2002). On the whole, these researchers found that the less social interaction involved in a persuasion attempt, the less persuaded women were.

Important to the evaluation of this body of research (and other research on gender) is Alice Eagly and Linda Carli's (1981) finding that greater female influenceability is significantly more likely to be found by male researchers. The finding cannot easily be explained as an effect of higher-status male experimenters or influencing agents: Group pressure studies commonly use same-sex groups, and many conformity studies do not identify the influencing agent by sex. Rather, Eagly and Carli suggested that bias related to the gender of the researcher may enter the design in a number of ways. Researchers may choose topics that favor the interests and expertise of their own gender, or they may unwittingly design settings and procedures that make participants of their own gender more comfortable and self-confident and therefore less easily influenced.

To find out about the generality of the tendency for male researchers to report more gender differences, Eagly and Carli compared their findings to those in a sample of studies collected by Hall (1978) on interpreting nonverbal communication. Where gender differences are found in the accuracy of interpreting nonverbal communication, they tend to favor females; however, the male researchers in Hall's sample were *less* likely than female researchers to find such gender differences. Eagly and Carli suggested, then, that there is no overall tendency for male researchers to find more gender differences; rather, both male and female researchers introduce bias in ways that make the portrayal of their own gender more favorable.

Dominance

Dominance encompasses a wide range of behaviors that have to do with imposing one's will on others and controlling and influencing others' behavior. In our culture, males are stereotypically viewed as more dominant than females, and there is some truth to that stereotype, at least in certain situations. However, as is the case with aggression and conformity, it is difficult to disentangle the effects of gender on dominance behavior from the effects of status.

Studies of African American, European American, and Hispanic undergraduate students showed a stronger orientation toward social dominance among men than women across all three groups (Sidanius, Pratto, & Rabinowitz, 1994), and males scored higher than females on personality measures of dominance (Feingold, 1994a). In mixed-sex groups or pairs, men tended to dominate the conversation, talking more than women, interrupting or ignoring women, and failing to pick up conversational topics raised by women (Eakins & Eakins, 1978; Krupnick, 1985; Lockheed & Hall, 1976; Spender, 1980; Zimmerman & West, 1975). Research on the speaking patterns of Japanese couples revealed that men and women did not differ so much on the *number* of interruptions but rather on the nature of those interruptions (Itakura & Tsui, 2004). These researchers characterized the men's speaking patterns as "self-oriented" and the women's as "other-oriented." Men's interruptions appeared aimed toward gaining center stage and controlling the conversation; women's interruptions seemed focused on supporting the men's storytelling by showing interest and creating opportunities for them to demonstrate their knowledge. Women speak more tentatively than men do when they are in mixed-sex pairs, and this strategy has a mixed payoff. Women who speak tentatively are more influential with men but less influential with women in such groups (Carli, 1990).

In initially leaderless groups of women and men, men are more likely than women to emerge as leaders, particularly if the groups are short-term or working on tasks that do not require much social interaction. However, women are slightly more likely than men to become social leaders (Eagly & Karau, 1991).

When college women and men whose dominance has been measured with a personality test are placed in same-gender pairs, the high-dominant individual assumes leadership most of the time. However, in female-male pairs, the male partner is more likely to assume leadership, regardless of dominance score (Carbonell, 1984; Davis & Gilbert, 1989; Lips & Keener, in press; Megargee, 1969; Nyquist & Spence, 1986; Ritter & Yoder, 2004). When women and men are interacting together, then, men often act in more dominant ways than women do. This pattern provides another example of Maccoby's (1998) contention that, to a large extent, gendered behavior is prompted by the gender of others in the interaction.

In same-sex groups, there are more differences in verbal assertiveness in male than in female groups (Kimble, Yoshikawa, & Zehr, 1981). Elizabeth Aries (1976) found that all-male groups established a more stable dominance order over time and showed more instances of one member addressing the group as a whole than did all-female groups. Comparing all-male and all-female groups, researchers find more emphasis on clear dominance hierarchies in the male groups (Baumeister & Sommer, 1997; Low, 2000).

Some researchers have argued that gender differences in dominance are linked to gender differences in aggression. However, many forms of dominance in human society do not involve aggression. Successful dominance in some situations may even involve an inhibition of aggression. It is more likely that status and role expectations govern dominance behavior. For instance, the more competent a person is seen as being in a particular situation, the more leadership she or he will be able to assume.

Postulating that men take on group leadership roles because they get more automatic respect and deference from the group from the beginning, Marlaine Lockheed and Katherine Hall (1976) devised a way to reduce the impact of these initial status differences. They provided women with task experience to build task-specific expectations of competence before putting them into mixed-sex groups to work on the task. This strategy had a marked impact. In mixed-sex groups, men were 4 to 7 times more likely than women to emerge as leaders *unless* the women in the group had been given the opportunity to develop competence on the task ahead of time, in which case female ranking improved fairly dramatically. In groups in which the female participants had been given, through experience, task-specific expectations of competence, women were more active than in other groups, and a woman was ranked either first or second in leadership-related behaviors in all groups.

Another example of the impact of perceived competence on dominance can be found in the relationship between leadership and the gender stereotyping of the group task. One study (Wentworth & Anderson, 1984) found that male undergraduates were more likely than their female counterparts to emerge as leaders when the group was working on a "masculine" (how to invest $10,000) or neutral (how to spend $10,000 on entertainment items) task; however, females took the leadership role for the "feminine" task (how a young woman should spend $10,000 on her wedding).

How does perceived competence or status translate into leadership or the ability to dominate a group? Apparently, group members behave quite differently toward those whom they view as having high or low status. Butler and Geis (1990), for instance, found that male leaders received more smiles and fewer frowns than female leaders when making equivalent contributions to group discussions. In fact, the more a female leader talked, the more unfavorable were the facial expressions directed toward her by other members of the group—male and female alike. The researchers attributed the differing reactions to group members' perception that women were violating role and status expectations by trying to lead. Given the differing nonverbal reactions to female and male leadership attempts, it is likely that males find it easier than females to dominate or lead a group. However, this may have little to do with gender differences in predisposition toward dominance.

The complexity of the relationship among status, social expectations, and dominance behavior is illustrated by research on how gender and race interact in helping to determine dominance behavior. Race, like sex, is considered by researchers to be a status characteristic—a characteristic that automatically influences the status ascribed to a person. Although an individual's overall status is thought to be made up of a combination of all the status characteristics relevant to the person judging it, it seems to be more complex than a simple average (Adams, 1983). American research indicated that being Black is associated with a lower status than being White, just as being female is associated with a lower status than being male. African American women, then, might be expected to have the lowest perceived status of the four possible sex-race combinations. This prediction is not supported, however. Black women have been found more likely than White women to assume leadership positions in all-female groups (Fenelon & Megargee, 1971), and a study of influence in dyads showed that Black females were better than Black males and White females at resisting challenges to their preferences (Adams, 1980). Black males sustained fewer challenges from White than from Black partners.

More recent research on conversations within mixed-gender, same-race groups suggests that African American women work more assertively at conversational control in mixed-gender groups than European American women do (Filardo, 1996). In European American groups, a significantly higher percentage of the women's than of the men's utterances were interrupted and never completed—but this was not true in the African American groups. In the African American groups, the men had a high percentage of speech that expressed commands, dominance, or a lack of consideration for the viewpoint of others (e.g., "That's stupid," or "*This* way!"), but the women in these groups still managed to say what they wanted to say. Thus African American women's tendency to complete what they wanted to say was apparently based on their own assertive and active behavior rather than on any particular accommodating behavior on the part of African American men.

Clearly, it is too simple to think of status as something that is unchanging across social contexts. The status accorded to gender, race, or other attributes may vary according to the norms of the situation and the status characteristics of the person with whom the individual is interacting (Adams, 1983). The interaction between gender and race in dominance situations suggests that gender differences in dominance may be largely socially produced and vulnerable to situational change. This research also illustrates the dangers of trying to understand gender differences by studying only members of a particular racial or cultural group.

The research we have been looking at has been done in the United States. What results would we find if we examined gender and dominance in other cultures? Leadership and dominance are often encouraged in American society, but cultures such as the Arapesh (Mead, 1935) and the Mbuti (Sanday, 1981a) favor equality and discourage leadership and dominance hierarchies. In such groups, there tends to be more equality of power and less role differentiation between women and men. Among the Mbuti, for example, diversity of opinion may be expressed through discussion, and participation in such discussions is evenly divided between males and females of all adult age levels. However, prolonged disagreement is labeled "noise" and is discouraged because it is considered offensive to the forest.

In still other societies, certain aspects of leadership and status are or have been assigned to women. For example, the Constitution of the Iroquois, the North American Indian confederacy of six nations that was formed in the mid–15th century, declared that women were the progenitors of the Nation, that descent of the people would run in the female line, and that the women would own the land and the soil (Sanday, 1981a). This principle acknowledged significant power for the women. Women of the Seneca, one of the six nations, controlled all cultivated tribal land, had the final say over the distribution of surplus food, and exercised strong influence, through their councils, over tribal decisions with respect to warfare and peace negotiations (Jensen, 1990).

Other North American Indian groups, such as the Hopi and the Navajo, also have strong traditions of female power (Katz, 1977; O'Kelly & Carney, 1986). Part of the process of the colonization of Native Americans by invading Europeans was the undermining of this female power. Native Americans were increasingly pressured by missionaries and government officials to adopt the European values and practices of female subordination (Jensen, 1990). Research

Overview — Gender differences and similarities in influenceability and dominance

Influenceability	Researchers have found a small tendency for women to be more easily influenced than men. However, this effect does not always occur; it is linked to particular situations and is likely explained by differences in expertise, status, or norms for masculinity and femininity. Men resist influence from women more than women do; this pattern suggests that the relative status of the would-be influencer is important.
Dominance	Men tend to show stronger orientation to social dominance than women do; in laboratory studies, all-male groups exhibit more concern with dominance than do all-female groups. In mixed-sex groups and pairs, men are more likely than women to emerge as leaders. This pattern may be largely explained by our learned tendency to ascribe more status to men than to women.

on gender differences in dominance might have produced quite different results in certain Native American and European American groups at this time.

Nurturance

Women score higher than men do on personality measures of nurturance (Feingold, 1994a), and cross-cultural research illustrates that, in middle childhood, girls in many different cultures are more likely than boys to be involved with nurturing infants (Edwards, 2002). Women are so often seen in nurturing roles, not only as mothers caring for small children but as nurses, child-care workers, and social workers, that it is easy to accept a stereotype of women as the more nurturing sex. This stereotype permeates the writings of professionals about women and about motherhood (Ruddick, 1989), and in North America it is applied to European American middle-class women (Rich, 1976), poor women (Belle, 1984), Latina women (Mirandé & Enriquez, 1979), and African American women (McCray, 1980). In fact, as seen in earlier chapters, the idea that women had a maternal instinct, a built-in tendency to care for small children, was popular in psychology for a time.

It is now understood, however, that greater female than male participation in nurturing activities cannot by itself be taken as an indication that women are "naturally" more nurturant than men; rather, the participation rates may reflect social pressure, gender identification, and the nature of the choices available to women and men.

Nurturance involves caring for and promoting the welfare of others. Many activities fall under this definition, from comforting a sick child to soothing the

Reflections : Gender Differences in Responses to Terrorism and Military Conflict?

To many people war is seen as something masculine and peace as feminine. In fact both men and women need to work together to build genuine peace.

—the Dalai Lama, quoted on the website of Women Building Peace, http://www .international-alert.org/women/

Women and men are often perceived as different in terms of aggression and dominance, and some people have speculated that the world would be a more peaceful place if women were in charge. Thane Peterson (2003), writing in *Business Week*, mused, "Wouldn't we be a lot better off if women were in charge, given all the violence and atrocities perpetrated by men and male-run governments in places like Bosnia, Rwanda, and Iraq?"

Researchers Lyle Bourne, Alice Healey, and Francis Beer (2003) investigated gender differences in responses to military conflict and terrorism by exposing students to hypothetical attack scenarios and asking them to choose the best response to such attacks. For instance, students would read about Bagumba, a fictional Middle-Eastern nation, directing artillery fire at military outposts of Afslandia, a fictional Middle-Eastern ally of the United States. What should the United States do in response to this aggression by Bagumba? The students had to choose from a list of many options, such as denouncing Bagumba's hostile actions, mining several of Bagumba's bridges and industrial plants, and using battlefield nuclear weapons against key command sites in Bagumba.

Both women and men started out by recommending a measured reaction to an initial attack. However, if the attacks persisted, both groups gradually increased their chosen reaction until they reached or exceeded the level of the attack itself. And there *was* a difference between women's and men's responses—but not a simple one.

Women and men did not usually differ in their overall levels of conflict; however, the presence of a peace treaty affected their responses in very different ways. If the attack involved the violation of an existing peace treaty, men gave harsher, more vindictive responses than if no peace treaty was present. However, women gave milder responses to attacks when a peace treaty was in place than when it was not.

The researchers speculated that the peace treaty signified a relationship—and that women were more concerned than men with preserving and protecting that existing relationship. They noted that "when a relationship, signified by a peace agreement, exists between the two sides, men seem more likely than women to act defiantly in the face of any active transgression" (pp. 193–194).

Is this explanation convincing? Do these findings have any practical implications for gender, leadership, aggression, and real-world war and peace?

ruffled feathers of a tired, grumpy spouse to mending a leaky roof so that one's family will be warm and dry. There is no evidence of a gender difference in nurturance that holds across all such activities. Even for responses to babies, for which, stereotypically, one might expect the most clear-cut gender difference to favor women, the research reveals a cloudy picture. The sexes do not differ in their physiological responses (heart rate, blood pressure, skin conductance) to an infant's cry, although females are more likely to report that the crying bothers them (Frodi & Lamb, 1978). Men can be as good as women at feeding infants and at correctly identifying the meaning of a baby's cry. College males and females have been found to be equally good at discriminating among different kinds of baby cries (Parke, 1981), and fathers are as good as mothers at using infants' cues to guide their own caregiving behavior (Parke & Sawin, 1976). In fact, observations of more than 55,000 adult-child pairs in 23 cultures provides evidence that there is a unique affiliative bond between men and their children: Men reliably choose to associate with and act in nurturing ways toward children even when not in their homes or with women (Mackey, 2001).

In the hospital, just after their babies' birth and later at home, fathers observed by Parke and Sawin were as likely as mothers to hold, rock, talk to, and smile at their babies; during bottle feeding, babies took just as much milk from their fathers as from their mothers. However, some studies show that boys are less responsive than girls to an unfamiliar infant in a waiting-room situation (Blakemore, 1998; Feldman, Nash, & Cutrona, 1977) and that new mothers paid more attention than other adults to a baby who was not their own (Feldman & Nash, 1978). In the latter case, however, more than a simple gender difference was observed: The new mothers were more responsive not only than men but also than women who did not have children and women who were pregnant.

Expectations in the area of nurturance differ for women and men. Children perceive their mothers as more nurturing than their fathers (Carunungan-Robles, 1986; Hopkins & Klein, 1993). This perception may be based partially on the different ways mothers and fathers express their care and support. Furthermore, the feminine stereotype of emotional expressiveness and nurturance seems to make it easier for women than for men both to provide and to obtain social support from close relations (Barbee, Cunningham, Winstead, Derlega, et al., 1993).

Gender differences in nurturant behavior, when they are found, can be traced to social context, stereotyping, and social pressure. Cross-cultural research shows that girls and boys differ more in nurturance in those societies in which girls are directly socialized more toward nurturance than boys are. In cultures in which these differential socialization pressures are minimal—in which, for instance, both girls and boys are expected to help with infant care— gender differences in nurturance are minimal as well (Whiting & Edwards, 1973).

In North America, differences in reactions to infants are more likely to show up in self-reports or in situations in which participants know they are being observed and evaluated than in other situations (Berman, 1976, 1980). Also, it is masculine sex typing, rather than being male, that seems to interfere with nurturant behavior. In one study, androgynous men were as responsive to a baby and to a kitten as women were, but masculine men were less responsive (Bem, Martyna, & Watson, 1976). In another, Judith Blakemore (1998) found that parents who said they were tolerant of "girl-like" behavior in their sons tended to have sons who showed a lot of interest in babies and were very nurturing toward them.

Although there is strong evidence that gender stereotypes and expectations have a large impact on nurturant behavior, researchers continue to investigate the possibility that biology plays a role in the development of some gender differences in nurturance. This research will be discussed in Chapter 5. Whatever potential differences may be provided for by biological factors would have to develop through the individual's interaction with her or his social and physical environment. Despite some interesting changes that have begun to take place in that environment, it is still less supportive of male than female nurturance.

Empathy

Empathy, the quality of being sensitive and responsive to the feelings of others, is often cited as a feminine characteristic. Women are said to have "woman's intuition," to be good at listening to people's problems, and to be swayed more easily than men by emotional appeals. This stereotype has been echoed in decades of social and psychological theory about women, from Freud's notion of women's weak superego to Parsons and Bales's instrumental-expressive distinction between male and female roles (Eisenberg & Lennon, 1983). When the evidence is examined, however, this particular stereotype does not hold up very well.

A meta-analysis of empathy research showed that when gender differences in empathy exist they tend to favor females (Eisenberg & Lennon, 1983). However, such differences were found inconsistently and seemed to depend on the method used to measure empathy.

When the measure used was self-report—responses to questionnaire items such as "I tend to get emotionally involved with a friend's problems"—females scored much higher than males on empathy. Every study in the sample showed a statistically significant difference, and the mean empathy score of the females was, on average, almost a full standard deviation above that of the males. For other measures, however, the gender difference was considerably less clear-cut. When measuring responses to emotional situations simulated in the lab or on videotape, most studies found no gender difference in reports of sympathy or concern or of feeling the same emotion as the situation's protagonist. Measures of physiological response to another person's emotional distress also yielded no evidence of greater female than male sensitivity to others' feelings. When children's reactions to others' distress were observed unobtrusively, gender differences were not found. However, when children were explicitly questioned about their reactions, girls showed more nonverbal signs of empathy than boys did.

On the whole, the gender difference in empathy is most evident in studies in which it is most obvious to the participants that their empathy is being measured (Eisenberg, Fabes, & Shea, 1989; Garner & Estep, 2001). This may occur because of demand characteristics of the research situation—that is, cues to the participants about how to behave (Eisenberg & Lennon, 1983). Why should demand characteristics produce a gender difference instead of across-the-board increases in empathic responses? Females and males are quite likely to differ in how empathetic they would like to appear to others. Because empathy is a stereotypically feminine trait, it is not surprising that when they know empathy is being measured, as in the case of the self-report studies, females produce more empathy responses than males do.

Further support for the influence of gender stereotypes on the gender difference in empathy can be found in research linking empathy to gender-typing. Self-reports of empathy are correlated positively with self-ratings of femininity and negatively with self-rated masculinity (Foushee, Davis, & Archer, 1979), and people who are gender-typed as masculine show fewer empathetic behaviors than androgynous or feminine individuals when listening to someone describing personal problems (Bem et al., 1976).

One measure of empathy for which there is a fairly consistent finding of higher levels for females is sensitivity to nonverbal cues. Researchers have reported that females seem to be moderately better than males at all ages at interpreting the meaning of auditory cues (such as tone of voice), and among adults women are better than men at decoding visual cues such as facial expression, particularly when the nonverbal message is intentional (Eisenberg & Lennon, 1983; Hall, 1978, 1984; Rosenthal & DePaulo, 1979). Some investigators feel that women learn to refrain from "eavesdropping" on nonverbal cues that the sender cannot control. This pattern appears to strengthen from childhood to adulthood—a clue that it may be shaped through social learning.

Empathy for others' feelings in general and sensitivity to nonverbal emotional cues in particular probably relate to situational factors such as status and role. Rosenthal and his colleagues (Rosenthal, Archer, DiMatteo, Kowumaki, & Rogers, 1974) found that men who were training for or working in occupations that required nurturance or sensitivity were as good as women at decoding nonverbally expressed emotions. Whether this finding can be attributed to the effects of practice or to the self-selection of unusually sensitive men for such occupations is difficult to know.

Women's greater sensitivity may be due to their lower status in many situations. People with subordinate status may have to develop more sensitivity to others' feelings than high-status people do, as a matter of survival (Snodgrass, 1985). Lipman-Blumen (1984) has argued that "woman's intuition" is a skill developed by women to help them predict and thus control or at least cope with the moods and behaviors of the more powerful men with whom they must interact. However, the tendency for subordinates to accurately read the nonverbal messages sent by the powerful may be due not so much to greater sensitivity by subordinates but to greater expressivity by the powerful. In other words, people with power may be especially expressive of what they think of their subordinates even while being careful not to express much information about themselves (Snodgrass, Hecht, & Ploutz-Snyder, 1998).

Altruism

Consistent with the stereotype that women are more nurturant and empathetic is the notion that they have a stronger tendency than men to do things for others, to be helpful to people in need. This assumed gender difference has been widely studied, but results have proved inconsistent. Girls clearly have more of a reputation for altruistic behavior than boys do (Zarbatany, Hartmann, Gelfand, & Vinciguerra, 1985). However, when actual helping behavior is measured, females do not consistently come out ahead. In fact, differences are found more often in the direction of greater male than greater female helpfulness (Eagly & Crowley, 1986; Piliavin & Unger, 1985).

Researchers trying to make sense of apparently contradictory findings in this area have focused on the situational variables that distinguish settings in which males tend to be more helpful from those in which females do (Eagly & Crowley, 1986). In general, they have found that men are more likely than women to help in potentially dangerous situations or when some kind of active intervention is required, such as when a victim has apparently collapsed on the subway (Hamilton, 2001). The presence of an audience also accentuates the tendency for men, more than women, to be helpful to strangers (Wollman, Griggs, & Stouder, 1990), probably because an audience is a reminder of the norm that men are supposed to be chivalrous.

The kind of activity required of the helper also makes a difference: Each sex, but especially males, is more likely to help when the activity required is gender-role appropriate. There is also evidence that characteristics of the person who needs help can be important. Some research has found that males are more likely to help females and females to help males, at least in nonthreatening situations (Bickman, 1974). Another investigation suggested that this pattern is magnified by how dependent the potential recipient appears to be (Wolfson, 1981). The latter pattern may hold only in relatively nonthreatening laboratory-type situations, however. In real-world situations, such as hitchhiking or stopping a stranger on the street at night, women may receive more help from both sexes, both because women are presumed to be frailer and more dependent than men and because both males and females may feel more suspicious and threatened when approached by a male than a female for help.

In summary, gender differences in helping behavior seem to be largely determined by situational and gender-role-related factors.

WHAT HAPPENED TO THE DIFFERENCES?

Gender differences in various aspects of social behavior generally range in size from small to moderate and are often sensitive to situational factors. In a recent review of meta-analyses on gender differences in cognitive, social and personality, and other variables, Hyde (2005) concluded that 78% of the gender differences found could be classified as either small or close to zero. This result was particularly striking, she argued, because the analyses tended to address behavioral and cognitive realms in which gender differences were expected to be significant. Criteria for labeling a difference "small" or "large" can be controversial (Eagly, 1995; Hyde & Ashby Plant, 1995), and differences that seem inconsequential at first blush may have important consequences (Rosenthal, 1990). Yet the gender differences in social behavior and personality discussed in this chapter seem minor when contrasted with some of the

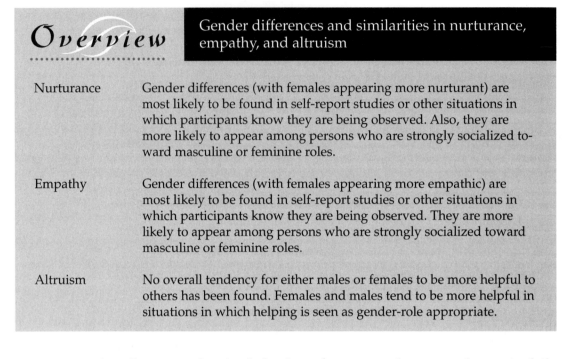

Overview — Gender differences and similarities in nurturance, empathy, and altruism

Nurturance	Gender differences (with females appearing more nurturant) are most likely to be found in self-report studies or other situations in which participants know they are being observed. Also, they are more likely to appear among persons who are strongly socialized toward masculine or feminine roles.
Empathy	Gender differences (with females appearing more empathic) are most likely to be found in self-report studies or other situations in which participants know they are being observed. They are more likely to appear among persons who are strongly socialized toward masculine or feminine roles.
Altruism	No overall tendency for either males or females to be more helpful to others has been found. Females and males tend to be more helpful in situations in which helping is seen as gender-role appropriate.

virtually nonoverlapping behaviors of women and men we observe in daily life. If gender differences in the lab are not striking and dramatic, how is it that women and men end up leading such different lives? How is it that most bank managers are men and most tellers are women? That most single parents are women? That most of the world's nations have never had a female head of state? That so many more men than women play hockey and football? We are faced with the task of reconciling research findings of frequently unremarkable behavioral differences between the sexes with our observations that in daily life women and men often seem to differ dramatically in their concerns, their accomplishments, and the way they spend their time.

Several factors can work to maximize the apparent disparity between the findings of carefully controlled research in laboratory or classroom situations and casual observations in everyday life. Psychologists have designed their research to determine whether, all things being equal, females and males will differ in the way they respond to certain situations. They have tried, although not always with success, to ensure that conditions in their studies are equivalent for males and females. But outside the laboratory, all things are seldom equal for males and females. Men and women face different expectations, different pressures, and different constraints.

Psychological research has demonstrated that, for instance, women *can* be as aggressive as men and men *can* be as nurturant as women, but it does not follow that, given current social conditions, they *will* be. One reason for the apparent discrepancy between some of the research findings and everyday life is the difference between potential and actual behavior. Psychologists have often tried to control or minimize the impact of social context on the behavior they are studying. To the extent that they succeed in doing this, they may see gender differences that are smaller than those we observe in everyday life. In everyday life, however, two aspects of the social context are often confounded with being female or male: role expectations and status.

Role Expectations

We have seen that some of the largest gender differences appear in situations in which people know they are being observed and that self-reported behaviors often differ more than unobtrusively observed behaviors for women and men. According to a gender-role perspective, female–male differences in social behavior occur partly because people are responding to social norms about how women and men should behave and partly because, by playing their expected roles, women and men tend to develop different attitudes and skills. This perspective is articulated in social roles theory (Eagly, 1987), discussed in Chapter 2.

Clearly, gender-related behavior is influenced by people's ideas about how others want and expect them to behave. Aggression and dominance are prescribed behaviors for the masculine role; compliance, nurturance, and empathy are for the feminine role. And role expectations extend beyond the general concepts of masculinity and femininity, to the specific roles occupied with differential frequency by women and men: secretary, company president, wife, husband, mother, father, scientist, cab driver, and so on. Company presidents, more often than secretaries, are put in situations in which they are expected to be dominant. The fact that most company presidents are men is both a result of and a perpetuation of the expectation that men are more dominant than women. Men are more likely than women to be promoted to this position because they are seen as having the capacity to be appropriately dominant; once in the position, a man confronts many situations in which dominance is expected, so his behavior becomes more dominant. Thus the demands of the roles in which women and men find themselves because of their gender act to reinforce gender-related behavior and gender stereotypes. When women and men are in similar occupational roles, however, as in studies of female and male managers, they respond to similar role pressures and their behavior tends to be similar (Eagly & Johnson, 1990).

It is noteworthy that most of the studies comparing females and males on social behavior have been done with children or college students—people who, although certainly subject to gender-role expectations, have not yet become heavily involved in the occupational or parental roles that reinforce these gender expectations.

Status

It is all but impossible for researchers to disentangle gender and status. In most situations, males are ascribed higher status than females, so when behavioral differences between the sexes are observed, it is difficult to know whether to attribute them to gender or status. High-status people may find it easier and more appropriate than low-status people to act aggressively and dominantly; low-status people are more likely than high-status people to find themselves in situations in which conformity and sensitivity are required (Aries, 2002).

Researchers have often been at great pains to be aware of the effect of status in research on gender, to measure it, and to control for it, if possible. The latter is not always easy. For instance, in trying to construct stimuli in which a male and a female are each portrayed in role-appropriate but equally high-status jobs, researchers have been stymied by the impossibility of finding a really high-status job that is typically considered female appropriate. To make the issue even more complicated, the status ascribed to gender may be inconsistent with the status achieved in a particular occupation. A woman who holds a high-status position such as physician is likely to be pegged as a nurse by people who do not know her. Similarly, male nurses are often mistakenly taken as physicians. Such situations of status inconsistency add to the difficulty of investigating the relationship between gender and status.

To the extent that status differences between males and females are successfully controlled in research, the researcher may observe few gender differences. For example, the use of a speaking style that is filled with intensifiers, hedges, hesitations, and questioning intonations—often considered a "feminine" speaking style—is linked much more strongly to social power and status than to gender. Both females and males, when in low-status positions, are more likely than high-status individuals to use this speaking style (C. Johnson, 1994). Similarly, when researchers manipulate the amount of power or expertise held by partners in mixed-sex interactions, persons high in power—whether they are women or men—display high visual dominance (Dovidio, Ellyson, Keating, Heltman, & Brown, 1988). When power and expertise are *not* manipulated by the researcher, however, gender-related expectations about status apparently take over. Men display high visual dominance (looking at the other person more when speaking than when listening), and women show low visual dominance (looking more when listening than when speaking).

A study by Jean Twenge (2001) shows that women's self-reported assertiveness and dominance has changed over the years in tandem with women's status. She examined the changes in women's status between 1931 and 1993, as indicated by their educational attainment and work roles. Then she looked at how self-report measures of young women's assertiveness and dominance varied over the same time frame. She discovered a positive correlation between the two sets of measures: Women's assertiveness and dominance rose as women's status rose and dropped when their status fell. Twenge did not examine men's status and assertiveness, but it seems reasonable to conclude that gender differences in assertiveness and dominance would be smaller in social environments in which there was little difference in women's and men's status.

Because researchers generally try to control for status when comparing females and males, they probably observe smaller gender differences in the laboratory than others see in the outside world. A research participant coming into a psychologist's lab is removed from her or his normal social context, with all its expectations. The researcher is careful to treat female and male participants exactly the same way and to have them respond to identical stimuli. In the outside world, however, there are many dimensions on which males and females are probably *not* treated the same way.

For example, a study of influence might expose males and females to a series of identical challenges to their opinions, to see whether one gender is more persuasible than the other. Using this method, the researcher may find minimal gender differences in persuasibility. Outside the lab, however, it is unlikely that people use exactly the same tactics to challenge the opinions of women and men. Instead, the status and role expectations associated with femininity and masculinity will produce, in many situations, different approaches to influencing women and men and more noticeable gender differences in susceptibility to influence.

Choosing Behaviors to Study

Researchers find it most practical to study behaviors that can be defined clearly and measured precisely. This predilection usually leads them to focus on isolated behaviors rather than on complex processes or the expression of a behavioral disposition across a wide range of situations.

For example, researchers studying nurturance may focus on parental reactions to a new infant during the first few weeks after birth. They may define *nurturance* as the amount of time the parent spends holding, touching, smiling at, or talking to the baby during the hours of observation. Yet nurturance is potentially a much broader concept. It could be thought of as including awareness of the infant's needs, the amount of one's attention focused on the child even when not interacting with him or her, the proportion of one's daily decisions and choices that are made with the child in mind, and so on. These aspects of nurturance would be much harder to measure than holding, touching, and smiling. If they could be measured, perhaps conclusions about gender differences in nurturance would be very different.

Researchers' conclusions about sweeping categories of behavior such as nurturance and aggression are based on analyzing isolated, easily measurable behaviors. This focus on easily measurable behaviors may be another factor responsible for the difference between research findings of small gender differences and casual observation of apparently larger differences on certain dimensions.

The Observer Bias Problem—Exaggeration of Small Differences

A final important reason for the apparent discrepancy between research findings and casual observation is the bias built into casual observation. As discussed in earlier chapters, people are strongly influenced in what they notice and remember by their stereotypes and schemas. Observations that fit into preexisting cognitive categories tend to be incorporated more easily than those that do not. Thus someone who believes the general stereotype that women are more altruistic than men will tend to notice and remember instances of women being helpful as confirmation of the stereotype but discount instances of selfish behavior by women and unselfish behavior by men as exceptions to the general rule.

Here is an example of the way gender stereotypes can influence observations of behavior. Patricia Bradley (1981) had male and female college students observe discussion groups in which either a male or female confederate argued a position contrary to that of the other group members. Half of the confederates argued their position without providing any evidence; the other half provided data to back up their arguments. Within these conditions, half of the confederates used tag questions (such as "Don't you think?") and disclaimers (such as "I may be wrong, but"), and the other half did not.

Bradley found that female and male confederates who behaved identically were evaluated differently. When women argued a position without evidence, they were rated as less intelligent, knowledgeable, and influential than men who made the *same* arguments without evidence. Women who used tag questions and disclaimers were rated as less intelligent and knowledgeable than men who spoke in the same way.

It is likely that the different ratings of the similarly behaving male and female confederates were due to stereotype-skewed perceptions of their behavior. In another study, participants listened to tape recordings of conversations between female and male speakers. Both speakers used tag questions and qualifiers equally, but listeners reported that the women used them more often than the men (Newcombe & Arnkoff, 1979). These results suggest that we cannot always trust our own observations when assessing gender differences in behavior.

As noted in the discussion of meta-analysis, the frequency of extreme levels of behavior can make a strong impression on people. If we see women and men differing in the frequency with which they engage in extreme levels of a particular behavior, this observation can contribute dramatically to gender stereotypes. For example, it is likely that most of us have heard of many more instances of extreme violence perpetrated by men than by women, and thus it is easy for us to believe that men are much more aggressive than women. At most levels of aggression, however, the gender difference is probably much less dramatic; the behavior of a relatively small number of very violent individuals has a disproportionate impact on our beliefs about women and men in general.

In weighing the results of research against our own observations, then, we cannot take either the research or our own observations entirely at face value. Apparent gender differences often reflect differences in situational role expectations and status. When researchers successfully control for these factors, they find smaller gender differences. Such findings say much about what the social world might be like if differential role and status expectations about women and men were abolished; they say less about the social world as it is.

The control and precise measurement required to carry out research often preclude the study of aspects of behavior that are less tangible or not as easily observed, in favor of the obvious and easily quantifiable. Many of the more

$\mathcal{O}$*verview*	Why gender differences may look smaller in the lab than outside it
Role expectations	When researchers bring participants into the lab, they do their best to remove different role expectations for women and men. In the world outside the lab, gendered role expectations often have a strong presence and affect behavior.
Status	Men are ascribed higher status than women as a general rule. Within the lab, researchers do their best to minimize these status differences. In the outside world, the status differences may contribute in important ways to gender differences.
Which behaviors are studied	Researchers define the qualities they wish to measure (such as aggression or nurturance) in particular ways that allow them to be measured easily. Broader definitions might produce different results.
Observer bias	We perceive women's and men's behavior through the "lens" of gender expectations and stereotypes. Thus gender differences that we observe in the outside world may be magnified by stereotypes.

complex and subtle aspects of behavioral gender differences may thus be over-looked by research, although they may be apprehended in a qualitative way by observers. It is dangerous to rely too heavily on one's casual observations, however, because they too are heavily prone to bias.

SUMMARY

What do we know about the differences and similarities between women and men? The research provides us with limited answers. Despite the popular habit of referring to women and men as "opposite sexes," psychological research finds little evidence for such dramatic distinctions in many areas of social behavior. Men are found to be more often physically aggressive and dominant than women, but women are aggressive and dominant too under certain circumstances. Women show a small but reliable tendency to be more easily influenced than men; this difference appears in some situations but not others. Women self-report more nurturance and empathy than men do; no across-the-board differences in behavior are found, but the range of behaviors studied has been small. Gender differences in altruism seem to depend on the circumstances.

Much of our research-based knowledge about gender similarities and differences comes from studies that focus on behavior in the absence of its social context. Yet for all the social behaviors discussed here, status and role expectations seem to be important mediators of gender differences. The influence of role expectations is seen in the tendency for larger gender differences to appear when research participants are reporting their own feelings or are aware of being observed. The influence of status is seen in the tendency to find smaller gender differences under conditions in which an effort has been made to equalize the status of male and female participants. It is reasonable to expect, then, that the overall picture of gender differences in behavior will be different across cultural and historical situations in which role and status expectations for males and females vary.

The literature on gender differences in social behavior has many limitations. Behavior tends to be studied apart from its social context to achieve careful control of variables confounded with gender; thus results are sometimes uninformative about the processes through which the social environment supports or discourages gender differences in behavior. Behaviors that are chosen for study tend to be ones that are most easily measured; many subtle, complex aspects of the relationship between gender and behavior may be lost. Despite its limitations, however, research on gender and social behavior provides an important corrective to the biases of the casual observer.

KEY TERMS

essentialism   overt aggression   relational aggression

Biology and Environment
The Process of Becoming Female or Male

At the 1985 World University Games in Kobe, Japan, a young Spanish track and field athlete was quietly summoned by officials and ordered to withdraw from a scheduled race. Heartsick and shaken, Maria Patino faked an injury during warm-up and did not run because the officials had warned that the alternative was to make public a devastating discovery: She had "failed" the sex test. According to the results of the buccal smear, a test of the sex chromosome pattern in cells scraped from inside her cheek, Patino was not a normal female. Instead, her chromosome pattern was that of a male. The discovery made her an unwilling member of a small sorority: About a dozen women have been banned from Olympic competition for not being sufficiently female (Carlson, 1991).

Patino had never for an instant doubted her own femaleness. Months of subsequent medical examinations revealed that hers was a case of androgen insensitivity: a male chromosomal pattern that had not resulted in the development of a male body because of complete and permanent inability to respond to testosterone. She had no uterus, but she had female genitals, female body proportions, female secondary sex characteristics, and normal sexual response.

Femininity testing was introduced by the International Amateur Athletic Federation (IAAF) in the late 1960s after reports that men had been masquerading as women in female sports. Maria Patino became the first woman publicly to challenge her disqualification. During her struggle for reinstatement, she lost her scholarship and her access to her coach. Her records and titles were stricken from the books. Her boyfriend and many of her friends abandoned her. Finally, 3 years later, acknowledging that her body did not, in fact, give her any unfair advantage with respect to other female athletes, the International Olympic Committee officially requalified her. Furthermore, her case helped convince the IAAF that the system of testing should be changed.

If Maria Patino's story sounds complicated, consider this story. Decades ago a research team, working first in the Dominican Republic and then in New Guinea, reported on an unusual phenomenon. A small number of children raised as girls developed male secondary sex characteristics at puberty. Their voices deepened, they grew beards, and they developed adult-size penises and scrotums. Almost all of these "girls" made successful transitions to being male, married, and fathered children (Imperato-McGinley, Guerrero, Gautier, & Peterson, 1974; Imperato-McGinley, Miller, et al., 1991; Imperato-McGinley, Peterson, Gautier, & Sturla, 1979).

What is going on here? Despite cautious talk about overlapping distributions of behavior for women and men, can we not safely hold to the belief that, at least in biological terms, the categories "female" and "male" are discrete, nonoverlapping, and unambiguously separate? No. The preceding examples are only two of many cases in which sex—biological maleness or femaleness—has turned out to be a fuzzier category than it first appeared.

This chapter examines what makes an individual female or male. In particular, we consider these questions:

- What are the biological processes that result in the differentiation of humans into male and female?
- To what extent do physical sex differences, such as hormonal concentrations, have implications for gendered behavior?
- What happens when one or more of the biological processes of sexual differentiation is disrupted?
- What can studies of mixed-sex individuals tell us about the link between biology and gender-role behavior?
- What can studies of these individuals tell us about gender identity?
- What do we know about the reasons for different sexual orientations?

- Are within-sex variations in hormone levels linked to variations in behavior such as aggression?

....

THE BIOLOGICAL PROCESS OF SEXUAL DIFFERENTIATION

Sexual differentiation is a complex process and one that differs considerably across species. Among reptiles such as crocodiles and turtles, eggs are laid with the potential to hatch into either females or males. The temperature in their environment determines their sex: A colder temperature produces more males, and a warmer one results in more females (Angier, 1999). Among many species of tropical fish, it is common for individuals to change sex during their development. All members of the sand tile species are born female—and then a few of them change into males in adulthood as required for sexual reproduction. In a rarer pattern, all clown fish are born male, and they all change into females upon reaching later adulthood (Rabin, 1998). At any rate, there is no species that has no females. There are a few species that breed asexually, through self-replication, and these species have no males. It has been argued that females are the "ancestral" sex among animals, with males evolving later in response to pressures for sexual reproduction (Crews, 1993).

The process of human sexual differentiation is accomplished in several steps. First, the individual's sex is genetically determined at conception. Then, as the embryo develops, the "indifferent gonad" develops into male or female sex glands. In turn, these glands begin to secrete the appropriate male or female sex hormones, which circulate throughout the bloodstream and are responsible for the sexual differentiation of other bodily organs: the internal reproductive tract, the external genitalia, and, to a disputed extent, areas of the brain. At each step of this process, the basic tendency is for development to proceed in the direction of producing a female unless this pattern is disrupted by the presence of the Y chromosome or male hormones.

Genetic Determination of Sex

Every normal human cell contains 46 chromosomes, arranged in 23 pairs. One chromosome of each pair is contributed by the mother of the individual and one by the father. Twenty-two of the chromosome pairs carry genes that determine hereditary characteristics of the person. The 23rd pair, called the **sex chromosomes,** differs for women and men. If the individual is female, the sex chromosomes are represented as XX; if male, the pair is designated XY. The two types of sex chromosomes are illustrated in Figure 5.1.

Only males carry a Y chromosome, which is very small (about one-sixth the size of the X) and contains little genetic material. However, it does apparently carry a gene that acts as a "switch" for maleness: the sex-determining region

Figure 5.1   The 23 pairs of chromosomes in the normal male and normal female person. The sex chromosomes are the 23rd pair.

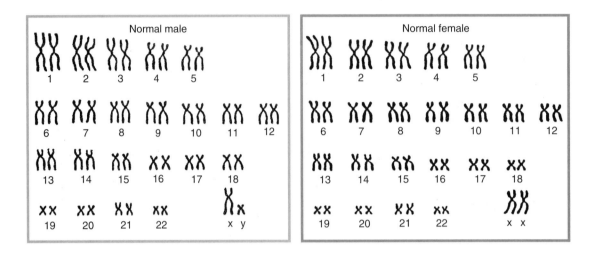

(SRY) (Sloane, 2002). Thus a person's genetic sex is determined by his or her father. If the sperm cell that happens to fertilize the egg at conception carries an X chromosome, the individual will be female; if it carries a Y chromosome, the individual will be male. Because the Y chromosome has no "matching partner," but is normally paired with an X chromosome, little of its DNA mingles with that of any other chromosome. That means the Y is passed along from father to son for generations with only minor mutations. Some population geneticists argue that the Y chromosome in every man now alive is more than 99.99% the same as the Y chromosome of a common ancestor who lived more than 50,000 years ago (Kunzig, 2004). Such researchers study the very small differences among Y chromosomes to document the spread of humans across the earth—and they sometimes come up with startling and controversial conclusions. For example, one research team recently reported the presence of a particular DNA variable in the Y chromosome in about 8% of the men sampled in regions of Central Asia—and the distribution of this variable matched the historical records of the empire of Genghis Kahn. They used these findings to argue that this 12th-century conqueror made a huge contribution to the gene pool of Central Asia (Zerjal et al., 2003).

Sons inherit more characteristics from their mother than daughters do: the genetic material carried on the son's X chromosome, always contributed by the mother, is active in every cell of his body. However, for the daughter, who has two X chromosomes, one contributed by each parent, each cell "decides" (apparently randomly) whether to keep the genes on the maternal or paternal X chromosome active—the other X chromosome is inactivated. Thus, in some cells of the daughter's body, the genes on the X chromosome contributed by her mother are active, and in other cells of her body, the genes on the X chromosome contributed by the father are active. She becomes a "mosaic" of the traits carried on her two parents'

X chromosomes (Angier, 1999). Recent research has unraveled some of the mystery of how this happens. Some sequences of what has sometimes been called "junk" DNA, previously thought to be useless, are apparently relevant to the inactivation process (Carrel & Willard, 2005). These researchers also discovered that about 15 to 25% of the genes on the inactivated X chromosomes in women actually remain partially active, so that some genes are expressed from both the active and the inactive chromosome. This means that some genes are expressed at twice the level in women as in men—something that may have implications (not yet understood) for both sex differences and variability among women.

The Human Genome Project has now analyzed virtually all of the genetic code of the X chromosome (Weiss, 2005). The findings are somewhat startling. For example, although the Y chromosome "turns on" maleness, many of the genes on the X chromosome are also crucial to male development. About 100 X genes are involved in sperm production, for instance, and some allow the body to respond to male hormones (Ross et al., 2005). But perhaps this should not be so surprising. After all, X chromosomes are not just for women; every man has X chromosomes in every cell of his body.

SEX-LINKED CHARACTERISTICS   When the genes for a particular trait are carried partially or totally on one of the sex chromosomes, the trait is said to be **sex linked.** Almost all of the relatively few traits identified as sex linked are associated with genes carried on the X chromosome, and these traits are typically pathological.

The presence of such X-linked genes accounts for the greater male than female susceptibility to certain genetic disorders. In fact, 307 hereditary diseases (more than 10% of known hereditary diseases), including muscular dystrophy, hemophilia, and colorblindness, have been linked to genes carried on the X chromosome (Weiss, 2005). The gene for hemophilia is sex linked and recessive. A father carrying this gene cannot transmit it to his son because he contributes only a Y chromosome to his son, and the gene is carried on the X chromosome. He can, however, transmit the gene to his daughter, to whom he contributes an X chromosome. His daughter will not express any symptoms of hemophilia unless she has also inherited a hemophilia gene on the X chromosome contributed by her mother. If, as is normally the case, the genetic material on the X chromosome from at least one of the parents is programmed for the development of a healthy blood-clotting mechanism, the daughter will not develop hemophilia. Because the trait of hemophilia is recessive, it will be masked by the presence of a normal blood-clotting gene on the other X chromosome. The daughter continues to carry the gene, of course, and may transmit it to her sons or daughters. If she does transmit to her son, the hemophilia will be expressed because the son has no other X chromosome (only a Y chromosome) carrying a normal dominant gene that would mask the recessive trait.

SEX-LIMITED CHARACTERISTICS   Some traits are **sex limited** rather than sex linked. These traits are carried on genes that are not on either of the sex chromosomes but are, nonetheless, generally manifest in only one sex. In this case, the trait requires the presence of male or female sex hormones to appear. Baldness, for example, is a trait that is carried genetically but that requires the presence of a certain level of male sex hormones to be expressed.

ABNORMALITIES   Occasionally, through errors in cell division, an individual is conceived who has some chromosomal abnormality—extra or missing chromosomes. Such abnormalities are sometimes present in the sex chromosomes. For example, an individual may be born with a single X chromosome (XO), an extra X chromosome (XXX), an extra Y chromosome (XYY), or patterns such as XXY (Klinefelter's syndrome) or even XXXY.

In these rare instances, unless there is at least one Y chromosome present, the body type will tend to develop as female unless something later interferes. The basic pattern of mammalian development is female, and every fertilized egg will tend to develop into a female unless the pattern of development is altered by the presence of a Y chromosome, which stimulates testosterone production, or the addition of testosterone from another source (Sloane, 2002). It is thought that an individual with only a single Y chromosome cannot survive, and no person with this chromosome pattern has ever been found (Money & Ehrhardt, 1972).

Various behavioral, personality, and intellectual difficulties have been ascribed to the presence of chromosomal anomalies, but the rarity of the conditions and the fact that in some cases they are noticed only when the individual gets into trouble or seeks help for a problem makes the evidence difficult to evaluate.

Some attempts have been made to demonstrate that particular abilities or behavioral tendencies are linked to the sex chromosomes. For example, there has been speculation that aggression might be linked partially to the Y chromosome. Some studies show that XYY males (men with an extra Y chromosome) are found in higher rates in prisons and institutions for the criminally insane. However, careful examination of the findings indicates that these men are no more likely and indeed are less likely to commit *violent* crimes than normal males are (Price & Whatmore, 1967a, 1967b), so there is no basis for the belief in a link between aggression and the extra Y chromosome. Researchers now believe that most XYY men live normal, productive lives (Ike, 2000).

Gonadal Development

For the first 7 weeks, the anatomical development of XX and XY embryos seems to be identical. Each develops a "neutral" gonad or sex gland and begins to form two sets of internal reproductive structures: female **Müllerian ducts** *and* male **Wolffian ducts.** Until the 8th week of development, then, all embryos have the potential to develop in either a male or female direction. Whatever genes are involved up until this point must be present in both sexes.

The influence of chromosomes on sexual differentiation appears to be most important during the 8th week of development, when the indifferent gonad begins the process of either male or female organization. At this point, if a Y chromosome is present, it promotes the synthesis of a protein called the H-Y antigen, which, among other things, helps the gonad differentiate into an embryonic testis—the male sex gland.

If no Y chromosome is present, the gonadal tissue begins, in later weeks, to differentiate into an ovary, the second step in female development. Once again, the basic pattern of development is female, unless that pattern is changed by the presence of a Y chromosome. Scientists are still trying to discern the location of an "ovarian initiator," a genetic signal that acts, in concert with the absence of the Y chromosome, to trigger this next phase of female development (Sloane, 2002).

Hormones

Once the gonads are formed, they begin to secrete the sex hormones. The rest of the process of sexual differentiation is directed by these hormones, chemical substances secreted into the bloodstream and carried to every cell of the body.

In the developing male embryo, the testis synthesizes testosterone, part of a group of chemically similar male hormones called *androgens.* Testosterone influences the male reproductive tract, the Wolffian duct system, to begin developing. At the same time, the testis secretes a hormone called the Müllerian Inhibiting Substance (MIS), which causes the female duct system to degenerate and disappear (Yahr, 1988).

In the developing female embryo, the ovary begins to secrete the hormones estrogen and progesterone. The male duct system degenerates, and the female system develops to form the internal organs of the female reproductive system. Scientists traditionally believed the absence of testosterone rather than the presence of estrogens accounts for female differentiation at this stage, but more attention is now focused on the role of the ovarian hormones (Collaer & Hines, 1995; Fausto-Sterling, 1992). Some scientists have argued that there must be, in females, a "Wolffian inhibiting factor" (comparable to the MIS in males) that causes the Wolffian duct system to self-destruct; however, such a substance has not been found (Angier, 1999). In any case, from about the 8th week to the 24th week of the gestation period, fetuses with XY (male) chromosomes have higher levels of testosterone than fetuses with XX chromosomes. After 24 weeks, gonadal hormones are low for both sexes until birth, after which there is another surge of testosterone and male levels are again higher than female levels for about 6 months (Hines, 2004).

Although the androgens are often called *male hormones* and the estrogens and progesterone are called *female hormones,* individuals of both sexes synthesize these hormones. All three hormones can be produced in the ovaries, testes, or adrenal glands. Researchers who assayed the concentrations of two androgens, two estrogens, and progesterone from the umbilical cord blood of infants at birth found that the concentration of only one of these hormones, testosterone, differs for female and male infants. The level of the estrogens and progesterone actually vary more according to birth order than sex: Firstborns of both sexes had higher levels of all three than later-borns did (Maccoby, Doering, Jacklin, & Kraemer, 1979).

At puberty, the sex hormones prompt the development of secondary sex characteristics such as breasts for females and beard growth and more muscles for males. The fact that testosterone enhances muscle growth motivates athletes—both male and female—to take steroids (which are similar to this hormone in structure and action) despite their negative side effects.

In fact, the complexities of taking steroids are very little understood; they sometimes seem to have unexpected effects and different effects on women and men. For instance, baseball hero Mark McGwire was criticized for his use of the steroid androstenedione, a substance that is produced naturally in the body and used to make testosterone. However, a recent study found that men who took supplemental androstenedione did not get any advantage in strength over a control group of men and that the steroid had no apparent effect on testosterone levels in their blood. What the steroid takers did get was an increase in blood levels of the female hormone estrogen and a significant decline in levels of the "good" cholesterol that helps to prevent heart disease. Interestingly, it is reported that women who took androstenedione did experience an increase in blood levels of testosterone (B. G. Coleman, 1999).

Internal Reproductive Tract

In males, the androgens secreted by the embryonic testis organize the internal ducts into the male reproductive tract: vas deferens, epididymis, seminal vesicles, urethra, and prostate. Meanwhile, the MIS causes the still-present female ducts to atrophy. In females, the male ducts atrophy, and a female reproductive tract—fallopian tubes, uterus, and vagina—develops from the female ducts.

External Genitalia

The external genitals of the male and female differentiate from the same basic structure, as shown in Figure 5.2. Until the 8th week of fetal life, the external genital appearance of both sexes is identical, and the genitals can differentiate in either direction. In males, under the influence of testosterone, the genital tubercle develops into a penis, and the labioscrotal swelling becomes a scrotum. In females, by the 12th week, the genital tubercle has turned into a clitoris, and the labioscrotal swelling has become the labia. Female development at this stage has been attributed to the absence of testosterone, but the possible role of the estrogens or progesterone in the development of the genitals has not been explored.

Brain

"How Female Is Your Brain?" asks the headline of a *Washington Post* article (Moir & Jessel, 1991). The article includes a 10-item test that asks, among other things, how well you can remember a song you have recently heard, how likely it is that you would detect a clandestine affair between two of your friends, and how likely you would be to try to back your car into a tight parking space.

Can the answers to such questions really tell us anything about the femaleness of our brains? According to the questionnaire authors, the answer is yes—female and male brains are better at different things because of the way they are organized, and that organization is the direct result of the early process of sexual differentiation: "What gives us a male or a female brain is the degree to which our embryonic brains are exposed to male hormone. The die

Figure 5.2   Three stages of external genital differentiation in the human fetus.

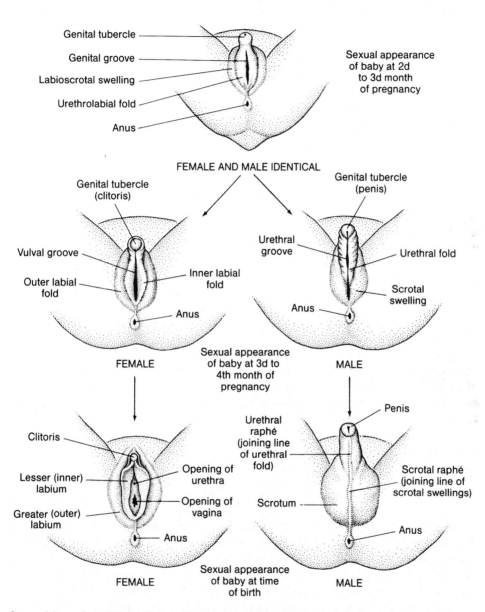

Source: Money, J., and Ehrhardt A. A. (1972). *Man and woman, boy and girl* (p. 44). Baltimore: The Johns Hopkins University Press. © 1972 by the Johns Hopkins University Press. All rights reserved. Reprinted by permission of the publisher.

is cast *in utero;* after that, the luggage of our bodies, and society's expectations of us, merely supplement this biological fact of life" (p. K3).

Is it really true that hormone levels *in utero* somehow fix the brain in a male or female organization in the same way they determine the development of the genitals as male or female? Genital differences between females and males are obvious; brain differences are far less so. In light of the transactional perspective on the biology–environment relationship discussed in Chapter 3, the notion that everything that comes after a critical exposure to hormones before birth is merely "supplemental" to an essential biological fact is absurdly simplistic.

Animal studies indicate, however, that in some species sex hormone levels present at a critical prenatal or postnatal period *do* influence the development of the brain. In rats, exposure to testosterone at a critical period just after birth results in a subsequent sensitivity of the brain to male hormones and an insensitivity to female ones (Levine, 1966). This differential sensitivity is demonstrated in the response of the mature animal to hormone injections. For example, if testosterone is injected into a newborn female rat, the rat's normal female sexual receptivity behavior seems to be lost permanently. In adulthood, she fails to show the usual female response even when given large replacement injections of female hormones. Moreover, she tends to show extremes of *male* sexual behavior, including the motions associated with ejaculation, when injected with testosterone.

Early hormonal exposure affects the hypothalamus, the part of the brain that controls the pattern of release of gonadotropins by the pituitary gland (Levine, 1966). The gonadotropins, in turn, control the secretion of the sex hormones by the gonads. The presence of testosterone during a critical period causes a noncyclic pattern of hormone release to develop, whereas the absence of testosterone causes the development of the characteristically female pattern of cyclic release of hormones and the occurrence of ovulation at regular, fairly predictable intervals.

More recent research challenges the notion that only the presence or absence of androgens affects brain development: Estrogens may also play a role (Fitch & Denenberg, 1998). In female rats, removal of the ovaries during a critical period results in changes to the brain structure. The critical period for the "feminizing" effects of estrogens is longer than the critical period for the "masculinizing" effects of androgens, and the mechanisms may be different. Clearly, there is much to learn about the impact of early hormone exposure on sexual differentiation of the brain, but at least some research suggests that there are two parallel processes taking place during this differentiation, one influenced by androgens and another influenced by estrogens.

Might the human brain too be affected by sex hormone levels at critical periods? The relevance of the animal literature to humans is limited in this area because human behavior is, in general, more subject to learning and the social environment and less governed by hormones than is that of animals lower on the phylogenetic scale (Collaer & Hines, 1995). Thus far, the impact of prenatal and early postnatal hormone levels on the developing human brain remains an area of research and controversy. For example, it has not been demonstrated that early exposure to androgens is critical in establishing the

Overview   The process of normal sexual differentiation

Step	*Timing*	*Male Differentiation*	*Female Differentiation*
Chromosomes	At conception	XY	XX
Gonads	8th week after fertilization	H-Y antigen influences the gonadal tissue to organize into an embryonic testis.	If male differentiation did not occur, about 2 weeks later the gonadal tissue is organized into an ovary.
Hormones	After differentiation of gonads	Testis secretes testosterone and MIS.	Ovary secretes estrogen.
Internal reproductive tract	8th–12th week	Androgens organize the internal ducts into vas deferens, epididymis, seminal vesicles, urethra, and prostate. MIS causes female ducts to atrophy.	In the absence of androgens, internal ducts are organized into fallopian tubes, uterus, and inner vagina.
External genitalia	Completed by the 12th week after fertilization	Genital tubercle develops into a penis, and labioscrotal swelling becomes a scrotum.	Genital tubercle becomes the clitoris, and labioscrotal swelling becomes the labia.
Brain/ nervous system	Perhaps at a number of different stages	Brain and nervous system may become "masculinized" and "defeminized" in certain ways through the degree of exposure to hormones. Timing and mechanisms are unknown.	Brain and nervous system may become "feminized" and "demasculinized" in certain ways through the degree of exposure to hormones. Timing and mechanisms are unknown.
Rearing/ socialization	After birth	Child is labeled a boy and socialized to be masculine.	Child is labeled a girl and socialized to be feminine.

pattern of hormone release in humans. In fact, if adult male primates are, via transplant, given ovaries, they can ovulate and have menstrual cycles (Norman & Spies, 1986).

On the other hand, researchers have identified some small structural differences in the brains of human females and males. The sexually dimorphic nucleus (SDN) is a part of the preoptic area (POA) of the hypothalamus; some researchers have reported that it becomes noticeably different in males and females between 2 and 4 years of age and that it is more than twice as large in adult men than it is in adult women (Breathnach, 1990; Hofman & Swaab, 1989; Swaab & Hofman, 1988). The function of the SDN-POA is not known, but it lies within an area of the brain, the anterior hypothalamic preoptic area, that is implicated in sexual and maternal behavior and in the regulation of gonadal hormones (Hines, 2004). What causes the male–female difference in the size of the SDN-POA? Is it an outcome of hormone exposure at some critical period? And what implications does it have for women's and men's behavior or experience? The answers are not yet clear.

DO PHYSICAL SEX DIFFERENCES HAVE IMPLICATIONS FOR BEHAVIOR?

Researchers have been intrigued with the possibility that the presence of testosterone at critical periods of human sexual differentiation might "masculinize" or "defeminize" the central nervous system. What might it mean for the nervous system to be masculinized? Perhaps the brain would be organized so that the individual would be more predisposed or prepared to learn specifically masculine behaviors. In a similar vein, some researchers think the presence of estrogen during critical periods may have a "feminizing" or "demasculinizing" effect. Both sets of changes might occur through the impact of the hormones on cell growth, electrical activity, or biochemistry, but no one is sure.

Although scientists do not know *how* the masculinization or feminization may occur, and although the overlapping behaviors of human males and females make the hypothesis difficult to test, they have spent a lot of time investigating the possibility that physical sex differences have implications for behavior. Their investigations have focused on both animals and humans.

Animal Studies

If the presence of testosterone at a critical differentiation period "masculinizes" the central nervous system so that the individual is predisposed to learn certain particularly masculine behaviors, then an animal injected with testosterone during the critical period should later show more "masculine" behaviors than one that was not. Some animal studies using this method have provided support for a link between critical-period testosterone administration or removal and nonsexual behaviors such as rough-and-tumble play and threat.

A group of researchers (Goy, 1968, 1970; Phoenix, Goy, & Resko, 1968) found that young female rhesus monkeys whose mothers had been injected with testosterone during pregnancy showed more play initiation, rough-and-tumble play, threats, and chasing behavior than normal females did. These findings suggest that hormones, through action on the developing brain, influence behavior. However, the extent of the testosterone effect is difficult to assess for two reasons. First, behavioral differences are ascertained through direct observation of the animals by investigators who cannot but be aware of each animal's condition. Although this procedure probably has no serious effect on the measurement of gross and dramatic behavior differences, it may have a biasing effect on the interpretation of more subtle behaviors. Second, animals castrated or treated with testosterone during early development may differ in appearance and even in smell from their normal same-sex peers. Goy's androgenized female monkeys, for example, although genetically female, had a scrotum and a penis. It is possible that their difference in appearance affected their treatment by their cohorts—accounting, perhaps, for at least some of their deviation from expected female behavior.

Animal research also makes it clear that environmental variables can influence the physiological processes that produce sex differences in the brain and behavior.

Kim Wallen's (1996) review of 30 years of research on rhesus monkeys illustrates that certain behavioral sex differences are more responsive than others to hormones. For aggressive and submissive behaviors, sex differences were affected more by the social than the hormonal environment. For example, monkeys who were reared in cages, reared without mothers, and allowed only brief periods of interaction with peers every day showed higher levels of male aggression and female submission.

On the other hand, male–female differences in rough-and-tumble play occurred in all rearing environments. However, the differences were larger in some environments than others, mostly because the males were responsive to the environment. No social environment raised the frequency of female monkeys' rough-and-tumble play, but prenatal administration of androgens did. Wallen concluded that the behavioral sex differences that show the least variability across social contexts are the most strongly affected by the prenatal hormonal environment. Whereas hormones produce predispositions toward behavioral sex differences, she argued, nature needs nurture: The expression of the predispositions is shaped by the social environment in which the monkey is raised.

Environmental influences do not have to occur prenatally. For instance, among rodents a group of neurons called the *spinal nucleus of the bulbocavernosus* (SNB), which helps to control erection and ejaculation, grows and shrinks in males according to the season. It shrinks in the winter, which is not a good time to have young, and swells in the summer. However, when male hamsters that have been in winterlike conditions are placed in a cage with a receptive female hamster, their SNB increases in size, testes enlarge, and hormone levels rise. Thus the nervous system responds to the environment and to experience (Breedlove, as cited in Azar, 1998).

Human Studies

We humans depend greatly on learning to develop behavior patterns. Our behavior is largely mediated by cognitive factors: our thoughts about the meanings of objects and actions. Also, human social organization is complex. These factors make physiological influences on human behavior difficult to isolate and interpret. The presence of strong social-environmental pressures toward behavioral gender differences is always a confounding factor in the assessment of physiological effects. Also, for ethical reasons, researchers cannot experiment with the hormone balance in human fetuses. Attempts to address the question of the behavioral implications of physical sexual differentiation in humans have thus been, of necessity, limited and not entirely conclusive.

Three major hypotheses, based on the early evidence, guided research on the behavioral impact of biological sex differences for many years (S. W. Baker, 1980):

1. *Gender-role behavior* is influenced, in some respects, by the prenatal hormonal environment.
2. *Gender identity* is determined not by chromosomes or hormonal influence but by rearing. Furthermore, there is a critical period, between 18 and 24 months of age, after which it is very difficult or impossible to reassign a child successfully to the other gender.
3. *Sexual orientation* is determined more by rearing than by chromosomal, gonadal, or hormonal factors.

These hypotheses have been modified somewhat over the years, with researchers now tending to lump all three dimensions—gendered behavior, gender identity, and sexual orientation—together under the heading of *behavioral sex differences* (i.e., behavior for which there is a disparity between the average female and the average male, although there may be a large overlap for the two sexes) (Collaer & Hines, 1995; Fitch & Denenberg, 1998).

Researchers have sought evidence that prenatal levels of androgens, estrogens, and progestins affect the probability that an individual will demonstrate behaviors that are closer to the norm for one sex or the other. The most popular model guiding this search is the idea that prenatal androgens tend to masculinize or defeminize behavior (i.e., make it more likely that the individual's behavior will be more like that of the average male and less like that of the average female). There are also suggestions that prenatal estrogens may masculinize or defeminize behavior or that they may have a feminizing or demasculinizing effect (Collaer & Hines, 1995). In reading about this research, it is important to notice that the findings represent *correlations* between various kinds of exposure to hormones in the womb and various patterns of later behavior and that they tell us virtually nothing about how those effects may have come about.

GENDER ROLES: INTERSEXED INDIVIDUALS   Most data on the effects of prenatal hormones on human development and behavior have come from the study of people whose sexual differentiation was disrupted *in utero* by hormonal imbalance. Such individuals, known as **intersexed** individuals, form between 1% and 4% of the population. They have been extensively studied over the past four decades. The hormonal imbalance can be the result of drugs administered to the pregnant mother, stress experienced by her, or a glandular malfunction of genetic origin. As a result of the prenatal hormonal disruption, the individual is born with the sexual anatomy incompletely differentiated. For instance, an intersexed baby may be born with ambiguous external genitalia or with genitalia incongruous with internal reproductive structures. By studying the behavioral and personality concomitants of various forms of intersexuality, investigators have hoped to discover the connection between specific aspects of physiological sex and behavior.

What happens to an infant whose sex at birth is ambiguous? In our society, an individual's sex is not allowed to remain ambiguous. It is thought crucial to assign the child a male or female identity as quickly as possible—even if that assignment is fairly arbitrary—and to provide treatment (drugs or surgery) that will help the child's body fit the assigned identity. To help make the assignment of identity as definite as possible, doctors routinely tell parents that an infant whose sex appears indeterminate is "really" male or female and simply needs treatment to bring all bodily features in line with the "correct" sex (Kessler, 1990).

The determination of sex assignment is not based on discovering the child's "true" sex (because the child possesses a mixture of sexual characteristics and is thus truly intersexual). Rather, it is based on an assessment of how well, given the physical characteristics present at birth and the possibilities for treatment, the child will be able to function as a female or male in later life. This assessment is necessarily based on sociocultural assumptions surrounding gender. For instance, in the late 19th century, women's ability to bear children was viewed as their essential characteristic. In that period, the presence or absence of ovaries was often the determining factor in assigning gender to intersexed individuals. Current thinking appears to favor the importance of external genital anatomy over that of internal reproductive organs. An infant with a normal-appearing penis would likely be reared as a male, even if normal female internal reproductive structures were present (Kessler, 1990), because the alternative of surgically removing the penis is disturbing to physicians and parents.

We have little information, then, about what would happen to intersexed children if they were left to grow up in our society with ambiguous sex assignment. Most of the research discussed in the following sections deals with individuals who did receive some form of treatment or intervention because of their ambiguous sex. However, consider the strong cultural bias that is implied in such procedures. Culture and medical practice work very hard to maintain clear distinctions between the sexes and to make sure that everyone can fit into a two-sexed society, despite long-standing scientific knowledge that a significant number of individuals simply do not fit this binary distinction. What would happen if scientific knowledge were directed at helping intersexed individuals live happily and healthily as intersexuals and helping the wider society acknowledge and accept their presence?

ELEVATED PRENATAL ANDROGENS   Studies of intersexed individuals have covered a wide range of disorders, and if you are interested see reviews by S. W. Baker (1980), Collaer and Hines (1995), and Berenbaum (1998), and an important summary work by two pioneers in the field, John Money and Anke Ehrhardt (1972). Most of the evidence comes from girls with **congential adrenal hyperplasia (CAH).** This genetically transmitted syndrome causes the adrenal glands of the fetus to malfunction, resulting in a release of excess androgens from the prenatal period onward. Girls with CAH are born with masculinized genitalia, but their internal reproductive organs are female. If the syndrome is diagnosed at birth, these girls receive surgery to feminize their genitals and are placed on lifelong cortisone therapy to compensate for the continuing adrenal malfunction. These individuals, then, are in some respects comparable to the genetically female animals who were exposed experimentally to androgens during the early critical period of central nervous system differentiation. Boys with CAH are born with a normal masculine appearance. However, they too must be treated with cortisone, or the extra output of androgen will cause their puberty to occur years early.

If the presence of significant amounts of androgens during a prenatal critical period causes the brain and central nervous system to differentiate in a masculine direction, children with CAH should show evidence of this effect. Two early studies examined children born with this syndrome for signs of masculinization of behavior and personality. In both cases, the sample is small and covers an age range of young children to middle adolescence, so the reliability of the findings is difficult to assess. Nonetheless, the results of the two studies are quite consistent, and they provide us with some clues about possible effects of prenatal androgenization on humans.

The first study (Ehrhardt & Money, 1967, described in Money & Ehrhardt, 1972) compared 25 fetally androgenized girls (15 with CAH and 10 who had been androgenized by progesterone taken by their mothers during pregnancy) with a control group of 25 normal girls, matched on the basis of age, IQ, socioeconomic background, and race. Data were collected by interviewing each girl and her mother, using a standard format.

On the basis of the interviews, several significant differences were found between the two groups. The fetally androgenized girls were more likely to regard themselves as tomboys, tended to have a higher preference for athletic activity and for joining boys in energetic play, preferred practical rather than pretty clothes, showed less interest in dolls, and showed relatively more interest in a career and less in marriage than the control girls did. No differences were found on several other dimensions such as aggression, sexual orientation, enjoyment of personal adornment such as jewelry and perfume, and observable amount of sexual play or interest.

These interesting findings cannot be accepted uncritically, however. Data were collected by interview, and the interviewers apparently were not blind to the diagnostic category (androgenized vs. nonandrogenized) of the girls they were questioning. Thus the possibility of unintentional researcher bias cannot be excluded. Furthermore, no observational data were collected, so the conclusions rest heavily on self-report. Some critics have also noted that many variables are confounded with exposure to excess prenatal androgens in the CAH children. The social environments of the two groups may have been different. The families of the androgenized girls may have been affected by the birth of an "abnormal" child, and the girls may have received special treatment because of parental guilt over their condition or expectation of a tendency toward masculinity. Also, these children must take regular doses of cortisone to counteract the effects of the excess androgens. In adults, cortisone treatment can cause mood elevation and hyperactivity, so maybe the differences between CAH children and controls were caused by the cortisone rather than the prenatal androgen exposure (Fausto-Sterling, 1992). Finally, the girls themselves, who were aware of their condition, may have felt they had more excuse than their counterparts to behave in a masculine way.

A second study (Ehrhardt & Baker, 1974) was designed to take some of these criticisms into account. In this investigation, 17 females and 10 males with CAH were compared with their unaffected same-sex siblings and parents. Thus the possibility of general family differences between androgenized and control children was removed. Also, the inclusion of males in the study allowed for a broader examination of early androgen effects. Data were still collected through interviews, however, with interviewers aware of the diagnostic category of the children.

This study found several differences between androgenized girls and their unaffected sisters and mothers. The androgenized girls were more often described by themselves and their families as having a high level of intense physical energy expenditure and showing a preference for boys over girls as playmates. Girls with CAH were less likely to show an interest in dolls or infants or to daydream about or role-play marriage or motherhood than were their sisters or their mothers during childhood. No differences between the groups were found on career interest. Significantly more of the CAH girls identified themselves as having been tomboys during all of their childhood, preferred functional clothing over clothing considered attractive for girls at that time, and showed low interest in jewelry, makeup, and hairstyles.

Despite these differences from their sisters and mothers, the androgenized girls were clearly identified in the female role and were not unhappy with being girls. Their behavior was not considered abnormal by themselves or their families but followed a pattern of tomboyism that is quite acceptable for girls in this culture. Interestingly, a follow-up of this sample of girls when their mean age was 16 showed that about half of them had become much more interested in their appearance, in grooming, and in dressing in a way considered attractive for girls (Ehrhardt & Baker, 1976).

For the males in this study, only one difference was found. Boys with CAH were more often reported as showing a long-term high level of energy expenditure in sports and rough outdoor activities than their brothers were.

In this study, the investigators intensively interviewed parents to determine whether they had any ambivalence or anxiety about their CAH offspring's sexuality—anxiety that might be manifested in differential treatment. They were able to uncover none. Similarly, their interviews with the girls themselves revealed no significant, persistent concern with being "born different."

The studies show results that are reasonably consistent: Girls in the CAH groups more often than control girls were described as showing high energy expenditure, tomboyism, preference for functional over attractive clothing, and low interest in and rehearsal for marriage and motherhood roles. Because normal boys and girls are thought to differ on these behaviors, the tentative conclusion was drawn that prenatal androgenization, through action on the developing brain, masculinizes behavior.

But "masculinizes" may not be the most appropriate word. Alexandra Kaplan (1980) noted that the behavior of the CAH girls seems more androgynous—a combination of femininity and masculinity—than masculine. More problematic than the terminology used, though, is the confounding of the effects of prenatal androgenization with a number of other variables: cortisone treatment, knowledge of being different, and parental attitudes and behavior.

Further studies of CAH children have tried to remove some of the confounding variables. For example, some researchers have found that there appears to be little relationship between the degree of genital virilization (the extent to which the girl's genitals look male) and the degree of male-typical play—suggesting that the latter is not simply the result of looking or feeling "different" or of the amount of medical attention required (Berenbaum & Hines, 1992). Though none of the studies can rule out all possible confounding variables, some reviewers argue that we can discern a pattern by looking at the findings of a large number of studies (Collaer & Hines, 1995; Hines, 2004). In general, these reviewers reported that the most consistent finding for CAH girls is a higher probability of male-typical "rough" play. These girls also tended to report stronger preference for "boys' toys" and for male playmates than did their unaffected sisters or than other girls matched for demographic background (Hines, 2004).

If there *are* differences between CAH girls and their peers, do these differences last into adolescence and adulthood, or are they gradually eroded by the similar socialization pressures faced by both groups? This is an interesting question because the answer can tell us something about how biology and environment work together to affect a girl's adherence to feminine gender expectations.

As a girl matures, her circle of friends and acquaintances expands outward; she becomes less dependent on her family and more dependent on her peers, teachers, the media, and other sources for information about how to behave. We might expect that the difference between CAH girls and other girls would diminish as this happens. Most nonfamily socializing agents have no idea that the CAH girls are different from other girls, so they would socialize them in the same ways—toward feminine gender-role expectations.

Few studies have addressed this question. An early study by John Money and Dana Mathews (1982) followed up 12 women who had been exposed prenatally to high levels of masculinizing hormones (though they were not CAH girls). They found that, although they had been characterized as tomboys and had been avidly interested in sports in high school, none of these women had maintained an active participation in sports, either as a career or a pastime.

More recently, Sheri Berenbaum (1999) collected data from 24 adolescent girls and 18 boys with CAH, along with 16 unaffected sisters and 24 unaffected brothers. Participants and their parents reported on the frequency with which the children participated in the list of female-typical and male-typical adolescent activities shown in Table 5.1. Each adolescent also indicated whether he or she was interested in each of a list of male-typical and female-typical careers. Male-typical careers (chosen on the basis of census data on proportions of women and men in particular occupations) included engineer, architect, and airline pilot. Female-typical careers included professional ice-skater, X-ray technician, and beautician.

Berenbaum found large and significant female–male differences on all the measures of activities and career interests. When she compared the CAH girls with the unaffected girls, the only measure that did not show a significant difference was their self-report of female-typical activities. She concluded from these findings that early androgen exposure has effects that last into adolescence, increasing male-typical and reducing female-typical interests.

More research is needed to verify Berenbaum's conclusion. But think for a moment about what these findings might imply. Could prenatal hormone levels really affect preferences for activities as specific as fishing? Thinking about becoming a car mechanic? Going to slumber parties? Reading fashion magazines? Aspiring to be a professional ice-skater?

Table 5.1   Sex-typed adolescent activities used in Berenbaum (1999).

Male-Typical Activities	Female-Typical Activities
Working with engines and electronics	Thinking about becoming a secretary or typist
Playing football	Doing needlepoint, embroidery, macramé
Thinking about becoming a car mechanic	Going to slumber parties
Riding motorcycles	Collecting dolls
Building models	Trying out for cheerleading
Hunting	Writing in a diary
Doing yard work or taking out the garbage	Reading teen magazines
Playing baseball	Playing with makeup
Washing or waxing the car	Reading glamour or fashion magazines
Reading sports magazines	Sewing or knitting
Playing sports games	Reading romantic novels
Fishing	Making jewelry
Playing basketball	Playing dress-up

Berenbaum argued that the effect of androgens is not necessarily direct. In other words, exposure to a high level of androgens would not necessarily predispose an individual toward fishing or hunting. Rather, they would have an indirect effect, maybe by influencing the ability to develop mechanical skills or preferences for certain kinds of sensory environments. Social experiences might then build on these differences in abilities and preferences. For example, "Because of their interest in certain activities, females with CAH may differ from typical girls by seeking out different environments (e.g., organized sports) and by responding differently to environments provided to them (e.g., a home computer). These environments might act, in turn, to reinforce the initial interests and facilitate the development of specific skills."

Once again, we see that nature and nurture work together: Biology and social environment interact to influence an individual's behaviors, choices, and experiences. Behavior is not mechanically predetermined by hormones.

ANDROGEN INSENSITIVITY   Some individuals who are genetically male have a genetically transmitted disorder that makes their cells partially or completely unable to respond to their high prenatal levels of androgens. This is called **androgen insensitivity syndrome (AIS).** They may be born with female or ambiguous external genitalia—labia, clitoris, and a short vaginal opening. They do not have internal female reproductive organs such as fallopian tubes and a uterus. They are usually reared as females because there is nothing obviously masculine about their appearance, and sometimes their condition is not diagnosed until they fail to menstruate during adolescence. At maturity, these women look feminine in body shape, with generous-sized breasts, thick hair, and clear, attractive skin. Their gender-role behaviors are consistent with their sex of rearing (Masica, Money, & Ehrhardt, 1971; Money & Ogunro, 1974). When reared as females, these individuals, though genetically male, reportedly show no sign of the "masculinized" behavior patterns reported for the CAH girls. In fact, they do not think of themselves as males at all but as females. The case of Maria Patino, described in the opening paragraphs of this chapter, fits into this category.

Women with androgen insensitivity provide an interesting counterpoint to some myths about testosterone: the notion, for example, that testosterone is the key element of libido, that without testosterone there can be no sex drive. Women with AIS, who cannot respond to testosterone, should therefore have no sex drive. However, these women report that they certainly *do* have sexual feelings, erotic fantasies, and orgasms (Angier, 1999). The notion that testosterone is the hormone of aggression is also brought into question by this group of women—women who should be mild mannered and passive according to this belief but who can be as aggressive as anyone else. As one AIS woman is quoted as saying: "I'm just like my mother, an aggressive, obnoxious human being. . . . I'm the daughter my mother created. I'm the woman I was meant to be" (as quoted in Angier, 1999, p. 35).

GENDER ROLES:
VARIATIONS IN NORMAL DEVELOPMENT

All males are not hormonally identical, and neither are all females. Within each sex there is a lot of variation in the relative proportions of male and female hormones present in the body at any developmental stage. These within-sex differences in hormone levels can sometimes be as important as sex differences in predicting what children will be like.

Here is one example: Researchers measured sex hormone levels in umbilical cord blood at birth and then measured timidity when these children were 6 to 18 months old (Jacklin, Maccoby, & Doering, 1983). They found girls were slightly more timid than boys. But what they were particularly interested in was the relationship between neonatal hormone levels and later timidity. For boys, neonatal hormone levels were clearly linked to timidity. The higher their levels of progesterone and testosterone had been at birth, the lower their timidity was later on. On the other hand, the higher their estrogen levels at birth, the higher their later timidity. For girls, there was no relationship between hormone levels and timidity.

These results are correlational: They do not prove that neonatal hormone levels *caused* later differences in timidity. However, researchers intrigued by the theory that hormones have an organizing effect on the developing brain have continued to compile evidence for hormone-behavior links.

Melissa Hines and her colleagues recently examined the correlation between hormone levels in pregnant women and the gender-role behavior of the children of these pregnancies at the age of 3.5 years (Hines, Golombok, Rust, Johnston, & Golding, 2002). In the pregnant women, they measured both testosterone and sex hormone-binding globulin (SHBG), a large protein molecule that binds testosterone, transports it in the bloodstream, and prevents it from binding to testosterone receptors in the brain. (High levels of SHBG should mean that less testosterone has an opportunity to affect the brain.) They measured gender-role behavior using the Pre-School Activities Inventory, a measure on which parents rate the child's participation in sex-typical activities.

These researchers found a relationship between prenatal hormone levels and gender-role behavior for the preschool girls in their sample but none for the boys. For girls, higher levels of prenatal testosterone predicted higher levels of male-typical behavior. Maternal testosterone levels during pregnancy accounted for about 2% of the variance of gender-role behavior of these preschool girls. This relationship could not be explained by other factors they measured, such as the presence of older siblings in the home or the parents' adherence to traditional gender roles. Hines and her colleagues interpret these results as supporting the idea that normal variability in prenatal testosterone levels may contribute to individual differences in girls' gender-role behavior.

Richard Udry (2000) investigated the notion that levels of prenatal hormones might be linked to gender-role behavior of women even in adulthood and that hormone levels might limit the impact of feminine role socialization.

He studied 163 female adults, 27 to 30 years old, whose mothers had provided blood samples during the second semester of pregnancy (thought to be a critical period for the impact of testosterone on the developing brain). He measured how feminine the women's adult behavior was by assessing their interests, the importance they placed on home and family, their job status, and their scores on psychological scales of masculinity and femininity. Table 5.2 lists some of the items included in these measures.

Udry found a correlation between a mother's hormone levels during pregnancy and her daughter's gender-related behavior 30 years later. The higher the SHBG level in the mother (and thus the lower level of testosterone available to the fetus), the more feminine the daughter scored on the indicators of gender-role behavior.

Udry also asked the women to recall how much their mothers had socialized them during childhood to be feminine or masculine. The women indicated whether their mothers had encouraged them to do each of a list of 26 activities. Sample feminine items on this list were "encouraged you to wear jewelry," "to take dancing lessons," and "to plan to have children." Sample masculine items were "encouraged you to defend yourself physically," "to be athletic," and "to have an interest in math." To obtain an estimate of feminine gender-role socialization, Udry subtracted the number of feminine items endorsed from the number of masculine items, thus implicitly accepting a bipolar conceptual model of femininity-masculinity. As discussed in Chapter 1, this model has been controversial among gender researchers, many of whom do not accept the notion that masculinity and femininity are opposite poles of a single dimension. As Urdy noted, the significant correlations found between the impact of gender-role socialization and androgen exposure in utero depend on the use of this bipolar model.

Udry reasoned that high prenatal exposure to androgens would make women less responsive to their mothers' efforts to socialize them toward femininity. His findings supported his hypothesis, at least in part. As shown in Figure 5.3, the impact of feminine socialization appears highest for women with low exposure to androgens *in utero* and lowest for women with high exposure.

Udry takes these findings as support for his hypothesis that biology constrains the effects of gender-role socialization. His data are a good fit to this idea; however, because the research is correlational, other interpretations may be possible. Perhaps, for example, it was a tendency toward compliance and/or a tendency toward low self-esteem, rather than such gender-specific qualities as desire for children, that were affected by hormone levels. Then the girls with the lowest androgen exposure would be most compliant with their mothers' attempts to socialize them toward femininity and so would display more feminine role behavior as adults.

Another issue we must consider in interpreting this and all research on the link between hormones and femininity or masculinity is the way *femininity* and *masculinity* are defined. Do the qualities listed in Table 5.2 form an adequate definition of feminine behavior, and does the bipolar model of masculinity-femininity on which these findings depend offer an adequate picture of gender role behavior?

Table 5.2 Measures of adult gendered behavior used by Udry (2000)[1].

Assessment Categories	Assessment Items within Categories	Feminine Response to Assessment Items
Importance of home	1. Ever married to a man 2. Number of live births 3. Index of sex-role orientation 4. Importance of career 5. Importance of children 6. Domestic division of labor in most recent relationship (e.g., cooking, child care, car repair) 7. Sex-typed activities in most recent relationship (e.g., who drove, who paid, who decided)	1. *Yes* is feminine. 2. High number is feminine. 3. *Traditional* is feminine. 4. *Not important* is feminine. 5. *Important* is feminine. 6. *Cooking* and *child care* are feminine. 7. *Male pays, decides, drives* is feminine.
Feminine interests	1. Importance of marriage 2. Feminine appearance 3. Strong Vocational Interest Inventory (are the respondent's occupational interests like those of other women?) 4. Likes baby care	1. *Important* is feminine. 2. Feminine demeanor, facial attractiveness, use of jewelry, and use of cosmetics are rated by interviewer. 3. Occupational interests like those of other women are feminine. 4. Agreement is feminine.
Job status	1. Proportion of females in current or most recent occupation 2. Socioeconomic status of current or most recent occupation 3. Proportion of females in work unit on last job	1. Higher proportion of females is feminine. 2. Lower socioeconomic status of occupation is feminine. 3. High proportion of females in work unit is feminine.
Masculinity-femininity	1. Bem Sex Role Inventory 2. Adjective checklist 3. Personality research form	1. High femininity and low masculinity are feminine. 2. Low percentage of masculine items checked is feminine. 3. Femininity and masculinity scores are assigned.

[1]A combination of the measures within each of the categories was used to determine how much the 163 women in this study adhered to feminine gender roles. The study showed a correlation between the level of androgens these women were exposed to before birth and how feminine their behavior was in adulthood.

The difficulties in determining the biological correlates of behavioral "feminization" and "masculinization" suggest that it is too simplistic to think of general feminizing or masculinizing effects of gonadal hormones. Collaer and

Figure 5.3 Possible prenatal influences on adult women's gendered behavior. The five lines show the relationship between a mother's encouragement of femininity and adult feminine behavior for women with different levels of prenatal androgen exposure. It appears that, for women with high exposure, there is little relationship between a mother's encouragement to be feminine and a daughter's feminine behavior as an adult. For women with low androgen exposure, however, the relationship between early socialization and later feminine behavior (as defined by Udry, 2000) is much stronger.

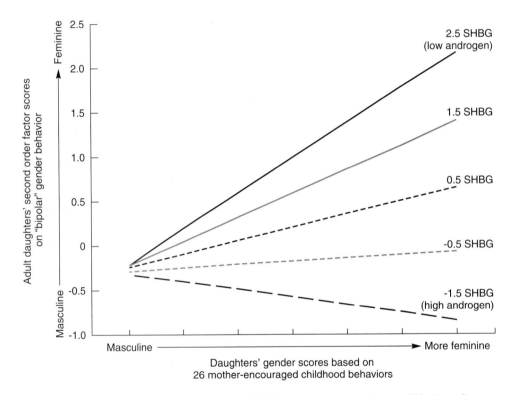

Note: This is a reconstruction based on Udry's (2000) figure 1 and supporting text. Udry's results, as he noted, depend on the treatment and assessment of femininity as the opposite pole of masculinity.

Hines (1995) speculated that "a comprehensive theoretical model of sexual differentiation will require expanding the concepts of a separate dimension of masculinization and feminization to posit a separate dimension for each sexually differentiated characteristic." Each behavioral characteristic that shows gender differences, they argued, is "regulated by different neural circuitry and might be expected to have somewhat different critical periods and hormone sensitivities" (p. 90). A newer, more complex model of the influence of prenatal hormones on sexual differentiation would be required to explain findings that, for example, high prenatal testosterone is sometimes associated with no change in some female-stereotypical behaviors, an increase in others, and a reduction in still others. Researchers who want to explore hormone–behavior connections without using the fuzzy concepts of femininity and masculinity have focused instead on specific categories of behaviors. We turn now to one of these categories: aggression.

Aggression

Aggression is easier to define than *femininity* and *masculinity,* but its meaning is still not unambiguous. Most psychologists define *aggression* as behavior that is intended to injure someone, rather than behavior that is simply competitive, energetic, or assertive. One difficulty with trying to link hormone levels to aggression is that researchers do not always agree on what behaviors should be classified as aggressive.

Many studies on animals (Wallen, 1996) and humans (Collaer & Hines, 1995) show a link between exposure to excess androgens prenatally and later levels of rough-and-tumble play. It may be tempting to connect rough-and-tumble play to aggression; however, many years ago Robin DePietro (1981) argued convincingly that there is a clear distinction between the two behaviors. She observed that children had very little trouble distinguishing between playful mock fighting, which requires a lot of cooperation, and real aggression. Rough-and-tumble play can lead to aggression through accidental injury or because some children who engage in it become extrasensitive to threatening stimuli.

So what kinds of evidence *do* link hormones to aggression? There are two kinds of studies: those that examine correlations between prenatal exposure to testosterone and later aggressive behavior and those that examine correlations between circulating levels of testosterone in the bloodstream and measures of aggression. Studies of the first type are based on the idea that early exposure to testosterone *organizes* the brain in a way that predisposes the individual to learn and act out aggressive behaviors. Those of the second type are based on the idea that circulating testosterone at a given time *activates* aggressive tendencies (built in by organized predispositions), affecting the likelihood that aggressive behaviors will be performed.

The assessment of a link between prenatal testosterone exposure and aggression relies largely on studies of children, such as the CAH girls, who happened to be exposed to extra doses of testosterone while their mothers were pregnant. Most of these studies do not link androgens specifically to aggression (Collaer & Hines, 1995). And the studies that do show this correlation can be difficult to interpret. For example, in one study, Sheri Berenbaum and Susan Resnick (1997) compared CAH individuals aged 3 to 35 years with controls on paper-and-pencil measures of aggression. On these measures, respondents indicated how likely they were to respond aggressively to a variety of situations. For the youngest respondents, parents rated their children's tendency toward aggression. Females with CAH scored higher on these aggression measures than control females, but the difference was significant only in adolescents and adults.

These results are difficult to interpret, not only because the aggression–hormone correlation was demonstrated only for the older respondents, but also because of the way aggression was measured. Scores on paper-and-pencil measures of aggression are not always related to actual aggressive acts; they may not be a good indicator of real-life aggression (Mazur & Booth, 1998).

There are many more studies examining the correlation between circulating testosterone and aggression in adulthood. Such studies have become more frequent since the 1970s, when researchers developed techniques for determining testosterone levels from saliva samples. Some of the studies show little evidence of a correlation between testosterone levels and aggression (Doering, Brodie, Kraemer, Becker, & Hamburg, 1974; Moyer, 1974). However, some indications of an aggression–testosterone link have been found.

Studies on male prisoners have reported a positive relationship between testosterone levels and history of arrests or aggressive behavior in prison (Kreuz & Rose, 1972) and history of violent crimes (Dabbs, Carr, Frady, & Riad, 1995; Dabbs, Frady, Carr, & Besch, 1987). One study showed that, among male prison inmates who had committed homicide, those high in testosterone were more likely than others to have known their victims and to have planned their crimes in advance—although this difference does not necessarily mean they were more aggressive (Dabbs, Riad, & Chance, 2001).

When groups other than prisoners are studied, correlations are sometimes found between testosterone levels and various behaviors that may be interpreted as aggressive. Hockey players' testosterone levels were strongly correlated with response to threat when facing an aggressive situation in a game or practice (Scamarella & Brown, 1978). Men producing high levels of testosterone were less likely to marry, more likely to divorce, and more likely to leave marriages because of troubled relationships, extramarital affairs, and throwing things at or hitting their spouses (Booth & Dabbs, 1993). A study of nearly 4,500 U.S. military veterans found that testosterone levels were correlated with a variety of antisocial behaviors: delinquency, drug use, alcohol abuse, and being AWOL (Dabbs & Morris, 1990). The relationship between testosterone and these behaviors was much stronger in low- than in high-socioeconomic status men, indicating that environment moderates the relationship between hormones and behavior. Furthermore, the size of the effect is small; it becomes noticeable mainly at extreme levels of testosterone.

A series of studies using small samples of men in different occupations found that actors had higher testosterone levels than ministers (Dabbs, de La Rue, & Williams, 1990). This finding proves nothing about aggression, but its authors suggest that the two occupations differ in the amount of dominance and antisocial behavior they require. However, the small sample sizes and such inconsistencies as the fact that football players did not differ significantly from physicians or professors in their testosterone levels cast some doubt on this interpretation. A more recent study of firefighters' performance in fighting fires and providing emergency medical service suggests that testosterone levels had no direct link to the men's performance or preference for either activity. Rather, testosterone may have interacted with personality traits to intensify preference and performance in directions the men were already inclined to take (Fannin & Dabbs, 2003).

Any link that may exist between circulating testosterone and aggression seems to be stronger in men than women. Testosterone levels are higher among trial lawyers than among tax lawyers—if they are male but not if they are female (Dabbs, Alford, & Fielden, 1998). Female prison inmates who had high testosterone levels displayed more domineering and intimidating behavior than other women. But this correlation is muddied by the fact that the high-testosterone women were also younger and thus perhaps stronger and less vulnerable (Dabbs & Hargrove, 1997). In lesbian couples, low-testosterone women report more use of rough tactics to deal with conflict resolution when they have been drinking, but high-testosterone women report using rough tactics equally when drinking or not drinking. However, there appears to be no overall tendency for high-testosterone women to use more rough tactics (Baker, Pearcey, & Dabbs, 2002).

A difficulty with all of these studies is that they are correlational. They cannot prove testosterone levels cause behavioral differences but only that a relationship exists between the two variables. A few studies have recently taken an experimental approach, actually administering testosterone to men and measuring specific behaviors. One double-blind placebo-controlled experiment found that testosterone administered via a gel on the skin resulted in increased self-reported feelings of arousal and hostility among both men and women, with stronger effects for women (Dabb, Karpas, Dyomina, Juechter, & Roberts, 2002). However, no behavioral aggression was measured. In another study, researchers administered testosterone to men and monitored changes in their self- and partner-reported aggression. They found no effect of the extra testosterone on aggression (O'Connor, Archer, Hair, & Wu, 2002).

One of the most common methods of exposure to externally administered hormones is through the use of anabolic steroids. Such usage is fairly frequent among athletes: Researchers who administered an anonymous questionnaire to more than 500 men and women entering five different gymnasiums found that 18% of the men and 3% of the women reported using the adrenal hormone androstenedione, and 5% of the men said they had used anabolic steroids within the past 3 years (Kanayama, Gruber, Pope, Borowiecki, & Hudson, 2001). At doses typically taken by bodybuilders, anabolic steroids have been linked to aggression. Harrison Pope and his colleagues carried out a double-blind, placebo-controlled study in which they administered 600 mg per week of testosterone cypionate or a placebo to 56 normal male volunteers (Pope, Kouri, & Hudson, 2000). The men receiving the testosterone—but not those receiving the placebo—showed significant increases on several measures of aggression. These researchers stated that the high doses of hormones associated with bodybuilding are likely to affect aggressive behavior in at least some of the men who take it.

Research with animals suggested that administration of anabolic steroids during adolescence affects aggression by changing the way the hypothalamus develops and acts in the control of aggression. These effects may disappear if steroid use is discontinued. One study examined adult hamsters that had been given anabolic steroids as adolescents. These hamsters were tested for aggression at 1, 4, 11, 18, or 25 days after withdrawal of the drug. Until the 12th day after withdrawal, the animals who had received the steroids were more aggressive than the control animals; after that the aggressive behavior of the two groups was the same (Grimes, Ricci, & Melloni, 2006).

One reason it is so difficult to discern an impact of testosterone on behavior is that testosterone levels are not constant. Not only do they change throughout the day, but they also change in response to circumstances. For example, men's level of testosterone sometimes rises when they anticipate competition (Booth, Shelley, Mazur, Thapr, & Kittok, 1989; Mazur, Booth, & Dabbs, 1992) and when they have been insulted (and are presumably preparing for retaliatory aggression) (Cohen, Nisbett, Bowdle, & Schwartz, 1996).

Men's testosterone levels also change in response to victory or defeat in competition. Testosterone levels stayed high longer among winners than losers of a tennis match; no such difference occurred between winners and losers of a lottery (Mazur & Lamb, 1980). Among wrestlers, testosterone levels declined more quickly among losers than winners (Elias, 1981). Winners of competitive reaction-time tasks showed higher postcompetition testosterone levels and a slower decline of these levels than losers did (Gladue, Boechler, & McCaul, 1989). Even winners of chess competitions showed higher levels of testosterone than their losing counterparts did (Mazur et al., 1992). The same effect has been observed among men who observe, rather than participate in, competition. After the 1994 World Cup soccer tournament, in which Brazil defeated Italy, testosterone increased among Brazilian fans and decreased among Italian fans who had watched the match on television (Fielden, Lutter, & Dabbs, 1994).

Clearly, the search for a simple one-way cause-and-effect model of testosterone's influence on aggression is misguided. Research on circulating testosterone implicates it as both a cause *and* an effect of social behavior (Dabbs, 1992). Furthermore, testosterone is only one of many hormones in the human body that may vary simultaneously and interact with one another in ways as yet unknown.

In the face of such complexity, can we draw conclusions about the impact of testosterone on aggressive behavior? Why has there been so much research focused on the relatively narrow issue of demonstrating a causal link between testosterone and aggression? Melissa Hines (1998) suggested that sometimes we focus on this type of relationship because it fits neatly with our existing schemas—our ways of thinking about the world. For example, if we think of men as more aggressive than women and we know that men have a lot more testosterone than women, we may link these two ideas in our schemas about gender. Then, we are likely to notice and remember information that seems to support this notion and to misremember or distort information that does not support it. When this happens, she noted, "it is easy for erroneous conclusions to seem obvious based on limited data" (p. 378).

The bottom line is that nature needs nurture. In much of the research cited, the most basic difficulty in determining physiological influences on human

Overview   Sex hormones and human behavioral differences

Behavior	Hypothesis	What the Research Says
Rough-and-tumble play	Elevated prenatal androgens influence the central nervous system to differentiate in such a way that the individual is more predisposed toward high-energy active play.	CAH girls are more often described as tomboys, having more high-energy expenditure and being more interested in sports. It is not clear whether this pattern persists into adulthood.
Aggression	• Elevated prenatal androgens influence the central nervous system to differentiate in such a way that the individual is more predisposed to learn and perform aggressive behavior.	• Research on CAH girls has not provided compelling evidence for a link between elevated prenatal androgens and aggressive behavior.
	• Elevated levels of circulating androgens make an individual more likely to engage in aggressive behavior.	• Correlations have been found between men's levels of circulating testosterone and some measures of aggression. However, it is not clear whether the hormone levels cause the aggression or the aggressive situation or behavior causes a change in hormone levels. A small amount of experimental research on humans shows that anabolic steroids administered in high doses increase the likelihood of aggression, and animal research suggests a mechanism through which this effect can occur.
Gender-typical activities	Elevated prenatal androgens predispose individuals to learn skills and perform activities that are male typical.	Some studies of CAH girls report they are more likely than other girls to have male-typical interests and less likely to have female-typical interests. Studies of normal girls, but not boys, show a correlation between prenatal testosterone and male-typical behavior. This kind of correlation has been found among adult women too.

gender-role behavior is that there are simply no clear, agreed-upon criteria concerning which behaviors are male and which are female. In most areas, there is an enormous degree of overlap between the behavior of the two sexes. Indeed, the range of male sexual behavior patterns that we would call both "masculine" and "normal" is wide enough that a change brought about by hormones would have to be very dramatic to capture our attention. Similarly, the tomboyish behavior of the CAH females in the foregoing studies would almost certainly have gone unnoticed had it not been specifically sought because it falls well within the range of normal female behavior in this culture. In fact, the majority of girls and women report themselves to have been tomboys at some time during childhood (Hyde, Rosenberg, & Behrman, 1974; Morgan, 1998).

If sex hormones, through their influence on the fetal brain or some other mechanism, do produce the substrata for gender-role behavioral differences, these substrata merely provide basic predispositions that interact with environmental forces. Such interactions can produce a variety of behavioral outcomes. For instance, Ehrhardt (1985) noted that, although higher androgen levels may affect the brain, predisposing boys to exhibit more physically active play, the socialization process widens this gap. Being reinforced for physically active play, as boys more often are than girls, may encourage competition in active sports, which may in turn foster a competitive orientation, assertiveness, leadership skills, and dominance. The sex hormone difference may affect a specific, limited aspect of behavior, such as the threshold for expression of physically energetic play; however, this difference may be amplified and made more important by a variety of other factors.

GENDER IDENTITY

Gender identity is the individual's private experience of his or her gender: the concept of the self as male or female. This is such a powerful and important part of a person's self-image that in most adults it is virtually impossible to change it. (If you do not believe this, try for a moment to think of yourself as still "you" but as the other sex.) Are we born with a gender identity, or does it develop after birth?

There was a famous case in which a 7-month-old boy was the victim of a surgical accident that destroyed his penis. The boy had been normal in every respect, but the loss of the penis resulted in a decision by his parents to reassign his sex as female and to rear him as a girl. At the age of 17 months, the child's name, clothing, and hairstyle were changed to fit feminine norms, and surgery to feminize the genitals was undertaken shortly thereafter (Money & Ehrhardt, 1972). Because the child, referred to in the scientific literature as "John/Joan," had an identical twin brother, it became possible to compare the way two children with exactly the same genetic and prenatal background developed when one was reared as a boy and the other reassigned and reared as a girl.

According to Money and Ehrhardt, the child who was reassigned as a girl quickly developed typical feminine interests and behavior, whereas the other child maintained his masculine patterns. Moreover, they said, the girl clearly thought of herself as a girl, whereas the boy's self-concept was unambiguously masculine. Thus, they reported, the gender identity of each child was apparently shaped by the sex of assignment and rearing more than by genetic or other physiological determinants.

Money and Ehrhardt's conclusions were premature, however. A follow-up of the sex-reassigned individual as an adult revealed that he had reclaimed a masculine gender identity during his teens and that he remembered always feeling uncomfortable and "not right" as a girl—even though he had no idea about the accident and the drastic solution (Colapino, 1997; Diamond & Sigmundson, 1997). In her mid-teens, almost immediately after being told what had happened, the individual adopted a male name and demanded male hormone treatments and surgery to change herself back into a male. He had his breasts surgically removed and a rudimentary penis constructed just prior to his 16th birthday. At age 21, he underwent surgery for the construction of improved male-looking genitalia. At the age of 25, he married and became a stepfather to his wife's three children. Thereafter, he lived an apparently well-adjusted life as a man for more than a decade. However, in his late 30s his life began to unravel. His twin brother died, he lost his job, and he separated from his wife. At the age of 38, he committed suicide (Canadian Press, 2004).

The sad outcome of the John/Joan case, once used as critical evidence for the malleability of gender identity, is now sometimes cited as proof that gender identity is immutably fixed by chromosomes and hormones. But this conclusion, like Money and Ehrhardt's earlier optimistic conclusions about the success of the John/Joan case, is probably unwarranted. In at least one other case of accidental destruction of a baby's penis and subsequent reassignment of that baby as a girl, the outcome was apparently very different. In the latter case, the surgical accident occurred when the child was 2 months old, and the decision to rear the child as a girl was made before the child was 7 months old. That individual was followed up at age 16 and again at 26 years of age. She reported that she was living as a woman and was firm in her identity as female. The team reporting on this case speculated that the successful assignment of a female gender identity may be traceable to the fact that the reassignment as female occurred much earlier (before 7 months) in this case than in the John/Joan case (17 months) (Bradley, Oliver, Chernick, & Zucker, 1998).

Other studies have compared the gender identities of intersexed individuals who had the same physiological indicators of sex; some were assigned and reared as females and others as males. In most cases, core gender identity developed consistent with the sex of assignment and rearing, as long as the assignment was made between the child's 18th and 24th month of life and the parents communicated no ambiguity or doubt about the child's sex. The CAH girls discussed in the preceding section all formed female gender identities. In cases of CAH in which genetically female individuals were reared as males, however, they formed a male gender identity (Money & Daley, 1977). Similarly, of the respondents with a history of androgen insensitivity, almost all formed a gender identity concordant with their sex of rearing. In the same vein, the males with a history of prenatal exposure to progesterone had no difficulty maintaining a male gender identity.

On the whole, the evidence suggests that people form their gender identities according to whether, from an early age, they are labeled and treated as males or females. There is no clear, consistent evidence that early exposure to sex hormones influences the development of core gender identity (Collaer & Hines, 1995; Hines, 2004). However, the outcome of the famous twin case as well as scattered findings that girls and women who have been exposed to excessive androgens prenatally may sometimes be less content with female gender identity (see Collaer & Hines for a review) suggest that hormonal influences should not be completely ruled out. As in other areas of female–male differences, core gender identity must be a product of a continuing interplay between genetic potential and environment.

Once formed, how resistant to change is a person's gender identity? Early research showed fairly consistently that gender identity is "set" very early in life and thereafter usually cannot be altered successfully. Some of the most dramatic findings in this respect were reported by Hampson and Hampson (1961), who studied 31 CAH females. In these patients, the syndrome had not been treated at birth, and they continued to be exposed to excess androgens postnatally. Thus they had grown from childhood with masculine-appearing genitalia and had a tendency to develop male secondary sex characteristics at puberty. They had been raised as girls, however, by parents who had been told their daughters were genetically female. Despite the problems these girls must have had in coping with their paradoxical appearance, all but five of them established an unambivalently female gender identity. This identity did not change even when male secondary sex characteristics began to develop at puberty.

The Dominican Republic study cited at the beginning of this chapter challenged the conclusion that gender identity, once formed, is virtually irreversible in later life (Imperato-McGinley, Guerrero, et al., 1974; Imperato-McGinley, Peterson, et al., 1979). Julianne Imperato-McGinley and her coworkers identified a group of intersexed males with a genetically transmitted enzyme defect that interfered with the body's ability to use testosterone for sexual differentiation. This syndrome, 5-alpha-reductase deficiency, occurs in approximately 1 of 90 males in one isolated area of the Dominican Republic. These genetic males were born with ambiguous genitalia—a clitorislike phallus and an incompletely developed scrotum—and many of them had been reared as girls. Of 18 males who had been reared as females, 17 had changed to a male gender identity at adolescence. These individuals recalled feeling different from other girls as they approached adolescence, usually because of physical differences. Their change in gender identity occurred gradually, paralleling to some extent the development of male secondary sex characteristics. Most of these males also successfully adopted the male gender role and developed sexual relationships with women.

The findings of the Imperato-McGinley team were startling because they appeared to fly in the face of the notion that gender identity was set in the second to third year of life. A closer look at the research reveals, however, that the individuals studied by these researchers probably had not consolidated a female gender identity during childhood because they had not been unambiguously reared as females. In the first place, these children cannot have been regarded by their parents as proper girls because they did not possess a vagina and were thus incapable of intercourse and childbearing. In their village societies, where the feminine role was strongly focused around marriage and bearing and rearing children, these "girls" would have great difficulty finding a satisfactory niche. In the second place, the genetic disorder affecting these children was common enough in this small society to have acquired a name. Affected children were labeled *guevote* (penis at 12) or *machihembra* (first woman, then man). Such labels reflect an expectation that gender will change, and this expectation may have been incorporated into the developing child's sense of gender identity. It is unlikely, then, that the individuals met the criterion of unambiguous rearing as girls that would have promoted a solid female gender identity in early childhood.

Imperato-McGinley and her colleagues argued that the change to a male gender identity reflected biological predispositions based on prenatal androgen influences on the brain. In other words, these individuals had "masculinized" brains because of their exposure to male hormones *in utero* and, when their social environment allowed it, their brains were "activated" by the upsurge of testosterone at puberty into a readiness to adopt a male gender identity. Thus these researchers used their findings to argue that gender identity is biologically determined. However, the environmental and biological factors leading up to the observed shift in gender identity are so confounded with each other that there are no grounds for accepting this conclusion.

Appearance and behavior are susceptible to hormonal influence, but identity seems more likely to be constructed socially—though it might well be affected by appearance and behavior and by the masculine or feminine labels applied to them. As discussed in earlier chapters, the very categories *female* and *male* are social constructions, agreed-upon classifications with characteristics assigned, to some extent, by social consensus. Some groups, such as the Mandaya of the Philippines, have languages that do not use gender distinctions and use occupation or status rather than gender as ways of classifying people or activities (Yengoyan, 1982). It is difficult to believe that brain organization directly predisposes an individual to adopt one or the other of these socially constructed gender identities. Yet the findings of this study are challenging and provocative. They suggest that gender identity may be more fluid than once thought, evolving and becoming reintegrated as the individual develops. They raise more questions about the conceivable role of prenatal or postnatal hormones in affecting the brain's possible "predisposition" toward maleness or femaleness (S. W. Baker, 1980).

Gender Dysphoria and Transgendered Individuals

A small but significant number of persons find it difficult or impossible to reconcile themselves to the sexual or gender identity they have been assigned. These individuals are deeply dissatisfied and unhappy with their assigned label of *female* or *male*. This dissatisfaction is sometimes labeled **gender dysphoria.** Part of the feeling is summed up by Kate Bornstein (1994):

> I know I'm not a man—about that much I'm very clear, and I've come to the conclusion that I'm probably not a woman either, at least not according to a lot of people's rules on that sort of thing. The trouble is, we're living in a world that insists we be one or the other—a world that doesn't bother to tell us exactly what one or the other is. (p. 8)

In a similar vein, Holly Boswell (1997) stated, "I have [n]ever understood what it is to be a man or a woman. . . . I seem to be neither, or maybe both, yet ultimately only myself" (p. 54).

This sense of discomfort with gender identity has led a number of people to question gender categories in general. Why must there be only two genders? Who makes the "rules" about what women and men should be like? There is an active **transgendered community** made up of people who, in various ways, are transgressing gender boundaries. This group includes pre- and postoperative **transsexuals** (people who have had or want to have surgery to change their bodies to match those of the other sex), **transvestites** (also called *cross-dressers,* who enjoy dressing in the clothing of the other sex), as well as individuals sometimes called **transgenders** (people who live all or part of the time in the identity of the other sex but have no intention of having surgery to change their bodies). According to the National Center for Transgender Equality, there are as many as 3 million transgendered Americans (Associated Press, 2006).

Transgender activists argue that the binary system of gender is a social construction: something that is agreed to by society because it is convenient and not because it is based on "natural" distinctions. They argue for the freedom to transcend this binary system:

> I started out thinking that a theory of gender would bridge the long-standing gap between the two major genders, male and female. I'm no longer trying to do that. Some people think I want a world without gender, something bland and colorless: that's so far from how I live! I love playing with genders, and I love watching other people play with all the shades and flavors that gender can come in. I just want to question what we've been holding on to for such an awfully long time. I want to question the existence of gender, and I want to enter that question firmly into the fabric of this culture. (K. Bornstein, 1994, p. 58)

> So the word "transgender" describes much more than crossing between the poles of masculinity and femininity. It more aptly refers to the transgressing of gender norms, or being freely gendered, or transcending gender altogether in order to become more fully human. Transgender has to do with reinventing and realizing oneself more fully outside of the current system of gender. (H. Boswell, 1997, p. 54)

Much of the time, the transgender community is fairly invisible. To society at large, the most obvious reminder that gender is not a simple "two sizes fit all" matter has come from highly publicized stories of a few transsexuals.

TRANSSEXUALISM   Over the last three decades, several individuals in the public eye have made headlines by undergoing surgical procedures to change their sex assignment. James Morris, a well-known writer and reporter, chose to become Jan Morris and told the story of the transition from male to female in a best-seller called *Conundrum* (1974). Renee Richards, playing on the female professional tennis circuit, raised criticism and protest because she had previously been a man playing on the male circuit. What mysterious process, many people asked, would cause an adult with an outwardly settled, stable life to want to change his or her sex?

A transsexual is a person—male or female—who firmly believes he or she was born with the body of the wrong sex. This conviction dates from early childhood, usually as far back as the person can remember. It is usually not amenable to change through life experiences, rewards for "normal" behavior, or therapy (R. Green, 1974). The transsexual may well believe that he or she can be helped only by changing, in terms of both identity and body, to the other gender and sex—because modern Western culture does not easily allow an individual to claim a gender or sexual identity other than female or male. If a person is deeply unhappy with his or her given gender/sex, the only way out seems to be to switch to the other gender/sex.

Transsexualism is an extreme form of gender dysphoria. It is a rare experience, estimated to occur once among every 20,000 to 30,000 genetic males and once among every 50,000 to 100,000 genetic females (American Psychiatric Association, 1994; Gooren, 1990). To all appearances, a transsexual has acquired the *wrong* gender identity, and, once acquired, this identity seems to be virtually unchangeable. Such individuals may lead lives that are outwardly congruent with their anatomical sex, but their conviction that their body is wrong for them is often strong enough to cause them to seek surgery to change it. A male-to-female transsexual may achieve a body congruent with a feminine self-image by taking regular doses of estrogen to acquire female secondary sex characteristics and having a vagina surgically constructed from the penile tissue. A female-to-male transsexual may take male hormone treatments and have surgery to construct a makeshift penis. In neither case is chromosomal sex changed; the individual remains genetically male or female despite surgically and hormonally wrought changes in appearance.

A transsexual who is seeking surgery must convince doctors that she or he is reasonably emotionally stable. Then, before any surgery is performed, the transsexual is required to spend a significant period living the life of the other gender, adopting the appearance and mannerisms associated with that gender. The rationale for this requirement is to ensure that the individual will be comfortable in the new identity. He or she is not generally encouraged to become comfortable with a transsexual identity but rather to choose to be either male or female and to "play that part" for the world at large. Kate Bornstein (1994) recalls,

> I was told by several counselors and a number of transgendered peers that I would need to invent a past for myself as a little girl, that I'd have to make up incidents of my girl childhood; that I'd have to say things like "When I was a little

girl. . . ." I never was a little girl; I'd lied all my life trying to be the boy, the man that I'd known myself *not* to be. Here I was, taking a giant step toward personal integrity by entering therapy with the truth and self-acknowledgment that I was a transsexual, and I was told, "Don't *tell* anyone you're transsexual." (p. 62)

During the 1- to 2-year trial period, preoperative transsexuals receive hormones to begin changing their bodies. A male is treated with estrogen to stimulate breast development, smoother skin, and reduced muscularity. A female takes testosterone to suppress menstruation and cause the growth of facial and body hair. After the trial period, if surgery is judged appropriate, a male-to-female transsexual has the penis and testicles removed and external female genitals constructed. The female-to-male transsexual has the breasts removed, and a penis is constructed from abdominal skin. Depending on the surgical method used, this penis may be semierect and may or may not be sexually sensitive.

There is much controversy over the benefits of sex-reassignment surgery. Some studies of postoperative transsexuals have found high levels of satisfaction with the surgery and the new life (Blanchard, Steiner, & Clemmensen, 1985; Pauly, 1968). Critics have charged, however, that such an outcome is comparable to the satisfaction neurotics feel when allowed to carry out their obsessive behavior or that addicts feel when allowed access to their drug; it does not justify such drastic surgery. Defenders of the treatment argue that, within a medical framework, no other methods have been found effective for reducing the distress transsexuals experience (Blanchard et al., 1985). One interesting outcome of sex reassignment may be a change in economic status. Blanchard (1985) found evidence that taking on the male role was correlated with improved economic status for females, whereas reorientation as a female was associated with lowered economic status for males. Being male, no matter how it is achieved, is apparently associated with a higher income.

The origin of the transsexual's conviction of not fitting his or her assigned sex or of the transgendered person's discomfort with gender boundaries remains a mystery. As Holly Boswell (1997) muses, "So, is transgender simply a result of being more honest with oneself and resistant to socialization, or is it chromosomally or hormonally induced, or better described as spirit taking precedence over form? All I know is that I could no longer live any other way, and have since found many others who share this experience" (p. 54). Suggestions that such feelings have a physiological basis have so far received no support because these individuals appear to be normally sexually differentiated and not intersexual in any sense.

Some writers have speculated that transsexualism is an outcome of the social definition and construction of gender roles. Janice Raymond (1979), for example, noted that male-to-female transsexuals frequently adopt an exaggerated version of feminine role behavior, becoming more stereotypically feminine than most women. This tendency may be based on an extremely rigid view of masculine and feminine gender roles. Perhaps, Raymond suggested, if each sex were allowed greater latitude in terms of what behavior was considered appropriate for their gender role, individuals would not feel the need to change their bodies to match their behavioral preferences.

There is, in fact, some evidence that in societies that allow for more than two gender-role categories individuals can sometimes live outside the limits of strict masculinity or femininity without feeling dissatisfied with their bodies. For example, Unni Wikan (1977) described a "third gender" in the Arab state of Oman, the *xanith*. The *xanith* are biologically men, but they do not adopt the traditional male role. They work as homosexual prostitutes and as skilled domestic servants. They have male names, adopt dress and hairstyles that are distinct from those of both men and women, and can, with impunity, violate the restrictions of purdah, the cultural system of female seclusion. Thus they may speak with women on the street and see a woman's unveiled face. In addition, Wikan reported, the *xanith* are not irrevocably stuck in their role; they can adopt the male role simply by getting married and proving themselves able to perform heterosexual intercourse. Perhaps the existence of this third gender-role option undercuts the development in some men of an urgent sense that their bodies are wrong and must be changed.

Overview Gender identity and gender dysphoria

	What	**When**	**Why**
Gender identity	An individual's sense of belonging to a particular gender category	Researchers believe it is usually formed before the age of 2 and is difficult to change after that.	Scientists are not completely sure what accounts for gender identity formation. Whereas some argue that there is a biological basis, many others attribute it to the processes of learning and cognitive development.
Gender dysphoria	A sense of discomfort or unhappiness with the gender category in which one is placed.	Many people report that this dissatisfaction began at an early age and never diminished.	Since scientists do not know exactly what controls gender identity, they are not sure why some people do not form a comfortable gender identity that matches the category in which they are placed by society.

Reflections   When Gender Identity and Gender Category Do Not Match

How important is it to be in the gender category that matches one's gender identity? It is important enough that it affects one's life in countless ways. Take the case of Luciana Buonocore. Born a male in Italy 29 years ago, he was mistakenly registered as female on his birth certificate and given the feminine name Luciana instead of the masculine form, Luciano. It was a simple bureaucratic error, but one from which it proved remarkably difficult to recover (Williams, 2002).

When Luciana applied for a national identity card at the age of 14, he was refused because his obvious maleness did not match the sex on his birth certificate. When, at 18, he tried to join the army, they rejected him because no women were allowed. He could not get a driver's license either, because officials would not issue a license marked "M" to someone whose birth certificate read "F."

Things came to a head when he wanted to get married. Officially, he would be a woman marrying another woman—a union not recognized as legal under Italian law. In desperation, he went to court to have his sexual identity changed under an Italian law that allows people who have had a sex change operation to change their legal identity to match their new sex. Although he has never had a sex change, it was the only way legally to change his name and the sex on his birth certificate. After an examination, the court agreed that he was male—and he became Luciano.

Luciano had a gender identity that matched his body, but he could not easily escape the problems that come from being forced into a gender category that one does not fit. Even more complicated are the lives of those whose gender identity does *not* match their body.

At the age of 18, Parinya Kiatbusaba, a Thai kickboxer, had won all but 3 of his more than 30 fights. Known as a fierce fighter in a sport that is Thailand's symbol of masculinity, he had a powerful sideways kick that aimed above an opponent's neck, then hooked downward. But Parinya, known as "Nong Toom" in the kickboxing world, would come to the ring wearing lipstick, eyeliner, and nail polish and was once quoted as saying, "It is hard to fight beautiful men. . . . I can easily knock them out. On the other hand, I want to hug and kiss them" (Kahn, 1998).

Parinya was proud to have the body and skill of a great fighter but sad that in his heart he was a woman. When he decided to use the money he had made as a kickboxer to finance a sex-change operation, he felt he was finally becoming himself. But when Parinya left a Bangkok hospital as a woman, she faced a very different set of career options. She wanted to continue to box, but in Thailand women are not allowed in the ring lest they anger the spirits. She was in demand as a model and for television talk shows. She pondered the notion of founding her own boxing camp. Eventually, she served as a consultant and minor player in a Thai film about her life, appropriately titled *Beautiful Boxer*.

When individuals change their gender category to match their identity, do they change everything about themselves? Clearly not, if these two stories are representative. But what does change is the set of social opportunities and rules that define their lives.

The unanswered questions surrounding transsexualism illustrate the extent of our ignorance about how gender identity develops. Although on one hand individuals with ambiguous sexual differentiation often hold firmly to the gender identity consonant with their assigned sex despite contradictory signals from their body, on the other hand transsexuals refuse the gender to which they were assigned, even though it matches their body.

SEXUAL ORIENTATION

Sexual orientation, the degree of erotic and affectional responsiveness to the other sex (heterosexuality) or to one's own sex (homosexuality), is a third aspect of behavior in which the sexes differ, on average. Researchers have tried for years to discover a clear link between sexual orientation and biological factors such as early hormone exposure. However, the link appears to be complex. Indeed, the more scientists investigate, the less it appears that there is any simple biological "cause" for sexual orientation. Increasingly, researchers are focusing on complex and subtle biological–environmental interactions among genetics, the early hormonal environment, the development of the brain, socialization, and other social-contextual factors (Rabin, 2006).

To illustrate the limitations of a single-variable approach in which one biological variable is investigated as a cause of sexual orientation, let us examine the research attempting to link prenatal hormonal exposure to sexual orientation.

Whereas early hormone exposure may play a role, such exposure does not guarantee a particular sexual orientation. Most prenatally androgenized CAH girls develop a heterosexual orientation (Berenbaum & Snyder, 1995; Ehrhardt & Baker, 1976; Money & Schwartz, 1977). However, a somewhat larger proportion than might be expected report a homosexual or bisexual orientation (Money, Schwartz, & Lewis, 1984). A study of women whose mothers were exposed to DES (a synthetic estrogen) during pregnancy indicated that these women were more likely than other women to give responses consistent with homosexuality or bisexuality on measures such as sexual fantasy, sexual responsiveness, and sexual relations (Meyer-Bahlburg, Ehrhardt, Rosen, Gruen, Veridiano, Vann, & Neuwalder, 1995). Again, though, the differences between the DES-exposed women and other women were modest. Of 60 DES-exposed women, only 4 listed a lifelong predominantly homosexual orientation, as compared to none in the control group. Also, "Most of the differences between DES and control women were limited to degrees of bisexuality, and for many of the women, the bisexuality was confined to imagery and was not expressed in actual sex with partners" (p. 19).

Second, researchers have been unable to make a clear and compelling cause-and-effect link among early hormone exposure, childhood sex-typed activities, and sexual orientation. Studies that have identified boys with cross-sex-typed behavior and followed them to manhood show that such behavior is a fairly strong predictor of homosexual orientation. However, similar research has not been done with girls (Bailey & Zucker, 1995). Studies in which adults are asked to remember their childhood activities show, for both women and men, that individuals who report a homosexual orientation remember significantly more cross-sex-typed behavior in their childhood than do individuals who report a heterosexual orientation. Bailey and Zucker note that, in these studies, cross-gender behavior in childhood is more predictive of adult homosexuality for males than for females.

So research has demonstrated, for girls but not for boys, that early exposure to androgens is linked to more masculine-typed activity and toy choices (Berenbaum & Snyder, 1995). For both men and women, but more convincingly for men, cross-gender behavior in childhood may predict homosexual orientation in adulthood (Bailey & Zucker, 1995). Some researchers would like to put these findings together into a model that says the impact of prenatal hormones on sexual orientation is demonstrated by their link to sex-typed activities. However, many people who report a homosexual orientation behave in gender-typical ways. Perhaps this means that psychosocial factors are more important for some people than others in influencing sexual orientation (Bailey & Zucker, 1995). As we have seen repeatedly in this chapter, early exposure to hormones may help to *predispose* individuals to behave in particular ways, but such exposure does not, in and of itself, cause particular behaviors or experiences. Rather, an outcome such as sexual attraction to women, men, or both must depend on a complicated dance between biology and social environment. If prenatal hormone exposure does influence sexual orientation, it is one part of a complex interaction of nature and nurture.

Some researchers have argued that there is a genetic component to male homosexuality, citing the finding that brothers of gay males are 4 to 5 times more likely than those of heterosexual males to be homosexual or bisexual and that identical twins usually show the same sexual orientation (Pillard & Weinrich, 1986). One study showed that 48% of identical twin sisters of lesbians also were lesbians, compared with only 16% of fraternal twins and 6% of genetically unrelated adopted sisters (Bailey, Pillard, Neale, & Agyei, 1993). A similar pattern was found for gay men (Pillard & Bailey, 1991). However, some identical twins show different sexual orientations, indicating that there is not a simple cause-and-effect relationship between particular genes and particular sexual orientations. Any genetic predisposition must work together with other factors to influence sexual orientation. Such a conclusion should not be surprising. It is not unusual for a genetic predisposition to work in concert with other variables; in fact, it is quite normal. Researchers who study animals have even found some clear cases in which specific genes are triggered or "turned on" by environmental stimuli—such as a change in the social dominance hierarchy in which the individual is living (Rabin, 2006).

The findings of one study have been used to suggest that male homosexuality is correlated with specific aspects of brain organization. Using brain tissue from autopsies of 41 individuals (19 men identified as homosexual, 16 men identified as heterosexual, and 6 women identified as heterosexual), Simon LeVay (1991) found that one node of the hypothalamus was, on average, significantly smaller (similar to the average size for the women) in the homosexual than in the heterosexual men. The sample is small, and the correct interpretation of the correlational findings is impossible to determine with certainty, especially since the members of the three groups died from different causes. The brain difference, if found to be reliable, could be an effect rather than a cause of sexual orientation, or it could be an anatomical feature that happens to be correlated with homosexuality but does not contribute to it. Despite the headlines that greeted these findings—"Brain May Dictate Sexuality: Differences Found in Critical Region" (Suplee, 1991)—researchers are a long way from identifying the precise ways biological factors may contribute to male homosexuality.

As for female homosexuality, its determinants seem even more complex. Some lesbians report they recognized their lesbian identity by age 12, more than half say they recognized it by the time they reached the age of 21, and about 58% say they did not feel as if they had any choice about their sexual orientation (Rabin & Slater, 2004). Others describe lesbian identity as a choice, often made later in life after considerable heterosexual experience (Golden, 1987). For the latter group, sexual orientation seems to be experienced as more fluid than popular notions of homosexuality-heterosexuality have described. Such findings, which are relatively recent despite decades of research on sexual orientation, remind us that researchers' assumptions often preclude the investigation of certain questions. It has taken psychologists a long time to examine the variations in lesbian experience. Some of the newer findings and theories bring us face-to-face with the notion that people may not always be classified so easily as homosexual, heterosexual, or bisexual. They suggest, as well, the necessity to consider a social constructionist view of sexual identity along with the traditional essentialist view that sexual orientation is a quality or characteristic of an individual (Bohan, 1996). Finally, they remind us of the gaps that remain in scientists' understanding of sexual orientation.

SUMMARY

The biological categories *female* and *male*, often thought of as completely discrete, have been shown to have some potential for overlap. Physiological differentiation of the sexes begins at conception with the genetic determination of sex and continues through several stages of fetal development: the differentiation of the gonads, their secretion of sex hormones, and the resulting differentiation of the internal reproductive organs and the external genitalia. In addition, sex hormones may have an impact on the developing brain, differentiating it in some respects for males and females. The extent, mechanism, timing, and implications of sexual differentiation of the human brain remain controversial.

Under normal circumstances, the differentiation proceeds in the same direction at every stage, producing an individual who is unambiguously either female or male at birth. However, on rare occasions the process is disrupted and the individual differentiates as male at some stages and as female at others. Such individuals, called *intersexuals,* provide valuable information about the relationship between the physiological and psychological aspects of sex and gender.

Many questions have been raised about the biological bases of sex dimorphic behavior—behavior on which groups of females and males tend to differ. Research using intersexed individuals has focused on three types of behavior: gender-role behavior, gender identity, and sexual orientation. The evidence linking sexual orientation to sexual differentiation is suggestive but inconclusive. For gender identity, most of the research suggests that children usually adopt an identity that is congruent with their sex of assignment and rearing, regardless of biological abnormalities that may tend to contradict it. For the latter pattern to hold, researchers believe sex assignment must be done before the third year of life, and the individual must be reared unambiguously according to the gender to which she or he was assigned. There is more for scientists to learn about gender identity, though, as illustrated by the outcome of the famous John/Joan case, the Imperato-McGinley findings of gender identity shifts in adolescence among one group of male intersexuals, and by some individuals' experience of gender dysphoria and transsexualism. For gender-role behavior, some evidence suggests a connection between prenatal exposure to androgens and such "masculine" behaviors as rough-and-tumble play. However, early hormonal exposure is usually confounded with other variables, such as continuing cortisone treatments, the awareness of having been born different, and perhaps parental anxiety, and the evidence remains equivocal.

Even among normal individuals, both male and female hormones are synthesized by both sexes, and there are wide individual variations in the levels of circulating sex hormones. These variations affect the development of secondary sex characteristics at puberty and so may affect gender-related behavior indirectly by helping to create a more or less stereotypically masculine or feminine body build and appearance. Studies on muscle strength and timidity in young children suggest that within-sex individual differences in hormone levels at birth may be as important as sex in predicting these qualities. Attempts have been made to relate within-sex differences in male hormone levels to aggression; however, the evidence on this point remains weak. Scientists still have much to learn about biological influences on human behavior in general and on human sex and gender in particular. Nothing that has been uncovered so far, however, points to chromosomes, hormones, or anatomy as direct, unilateral determining factors in gender-role behavior, gender identity, or sexual orientation. Rather, research points to the importance of interactions between biological and environmental factors.

KEY TERMS

sex chromosomes
sex-linked traits
sex-limited traits
Müllerian ducts
Wolffian ducts
intersexed

congenital adrenal
  hyperplasia (CAH)
androgen insensitivity
  syndrome (AIS)
gender dysphoria

transgendered
  community
transsexuals
transvestites
transgenders

Perceptual and Cognitive Abilities
Gender Similarities and Differences

In 1903 James McKeen Cattell, an influential professor of psychology at Columbia University, published a study of 1,000 eminent persons. In title and content it was, in fact, a study of eminent *men;* only 32 women were included in Cattell's list. Cattell himself made no apologies for the dearth of female representation in his catalog of eminence, noting that it was well-known that women were much less likely than men to depart from average levels of ability (Cattell, 1903).

Cattell's argument was completely in step with his times. Only a few years earlier, the renowned Francis Galton, after testing 9,337 persons in his Anthropometric Laboratory in England, had declared that women were inferior to men in all their capacities (Boring, 1929). And in 1879 Gustave Le Bon, one of the founders of social psychology, had noted that "all psychologists who have studied the intelligence of women . . . recognize today that they represent the most inferior forms of human evolution and that they are closer to children and savages than to an adult, civilized male" (as quoted in Gould, 1981, p. 104). Indeed, many of the research efforts of the new discipline of psychology in the early part of the 20th century were devoted to demonstrating the assumed biological inferiority of women (Shields, 1975) and non-Caucasian racial groups (Guthrie, 1976).

*Clearly, the belief that women and men differ in their perceptual and cognitive abil-
ities has a long history. But what does contemporary research have to say on this
topic? Do women and men differ on these dimensions and, if so, why? These issues
are the focus of this chapter. In particular, we explore these questions:*

- Is one sex more variable than the other with respect to cognitive abilities?
- Are there male–female differences in general intelligence?
- Do women and men differ in aspects of sensation, perception, or attention?
- Is one sex better than the other at learning and memory?
- How do women and men compare in their verbal performance?
- What about mathematics and quantitative performance?
- Do the sexes differ in their visual-spatial performance?
- How can we explain the differences that *have* been observed?

THE GREATER MALE VARIABILITY HYPOTHESIS

Many psychologists and educators of Cattell's generation held firmly to the belief that men, as a group, were more variable than women—that men were more
likely than women to be found at the high and low extremes of intelligence.
Men were more likely than women to be geniuses; they were also more likely
than women to be mentally subnormal. Women were most likely to be of average
intelligence.

The belief in greater male variability was congenial to those who were interested in maintaining the status quo between the sexes. In the first place, the
greater variability claimed for the male sex was considered a positive quality—
a progressive force in the evolution of the human species. Greater variability was
one more plank in the platform of male superiority, as was the idea that the
greater male variability meant most geniuses would be male. It was an idea that
provided ammunition to those who wished to exclude women from graduate
and professional schools and to channel educated women into low-paying, low-
status jobs.

The idea that males varied more in intelligence than females was probably
accepted as a truism by many early–20th-century observers. Most areas in
which eminence could be achieved were clearly dominated by men; males also
tended to outnumber females in institutions for the mentally retarded. The notion that these male–female differences might be explained by causes other than
sex differences in the distribution of intelligence received little consideration. In
the end, it was a female psychologist, Leta Hollingworth, who most successfully cast doubt on the greater-male-variability hypothesis (Silverman, 1989).

Hollingworth knew from bitter personal experience that the road to eminence for a woman had as much to do with social custom and prejudice as with her degree of intelligence. Her graduate education in psychology occurred in a climate in which graduate scholarships were not open to women, and most faculty members had never worked professionally with women or taught female students. The chairman of her department was an active campaigner against higher education for women, and the dean of her faculty stated publicly that few women were capable of truly advanced, original work (R. Rosenberg, 1982). Her own major adviser, Edward L. Thorndike, a believer in the variability hypothesis, argued that "in particular, if men differ in intelligence and energy by wider degrees than do women, eminence in and leadership of the world's affairs of whatever sort will inevitably belong oftener to men. They will oftener deserve it" (Thorndike, 1910, p. 35).

It was while working at her first job, as a tester at New York City's Clearing House for Mental Defectives, that Hollingworth began to focus her attention on the variability hypothesis. Although most of the retarded children referred to her for testing were boys, a situation predicted by the variability hypothesis, she noted that the disproportionate number of males was due primarily to the large number of boys under the age of 16. Her observations led her to believe boys of below-average intelligence were likely to come to the attention of the law at a much earlier age than their female counterparts were. Boys were less restricted and so were more likely to get into trouble; moreover, the undemanding social expectations for girls—that they be passive and dependent—made it less likely that low intelligence would be noticed. In adulthood, a low-intelligence female sometimes found a niche as a housewife, domestic worker, or prostitute and came to a mental institution only when illness or the death of the man on whom she was depending intervened. A low-intelligence male had fewer options and was likely to end up in a mental institution much sooner (Hollingworth, 1922). Social factors rather than differences in the variability of intelligence, then, could explain the preponderance of males in institutions for the mentally retarded.

Hollingworth believed the apparent underrepresentation of women at the top end of the distribution of intelligence could also be explained by social factors. After reviewing measurements made on 20,000 infants at birth, she concluded that there was no difference in variability between females and males. She went on to chastise psychologists for failing to consider the impact of domestic and child-rearing tasks—"a field where eminence is impossible"—on women's capacity to achieve the distinction associated with genius (Hollingworth & Montague, 1914). Only when the latter explanation had been ruled out, she argued, should psychologists consider differences in intelligence or variability as an explanation for sex differences in the attainment of eminence.

After Hollingworth's articles on sex differences in mental traits appeared in the prestigious *Psychological Bulletin* (Hollingworth, 1916, 1918), the greater-male-variability hypothesis was discredited. New discoveries about how the X chromosomes function in females, as discussed in Chapter 5, suggest, in fact, that women as a group are more variable than men (Carrel & Willard, 2005). Arguments have continued to rage, however, about whether the sexes differ in intellectual abilities or in cognitive style; that is, in the way we think and approach problems.

GENDER DIFFERENCES IN INTELLECTUAL PERFORMANCE

Many of the popular stereotypes of women and men are based on the assumption that the two sexes approach the task of thinking in very different ways. It is widely held, for instance, that men are logical and women are intuitive, that it is a rare woman who has a "head for figures," and that men are more quickly frustrated and bored than women when performing simple repetitive tasks. Is there any basis to the idea that males are better suited to the task of calculating formulas or that females are better at spelling and typing? Researchers in this area have found a few gender differences in performance, but they tend to be smaller than the stereotypes would lead us to expect.

General Intelligence

There are no meaningful differences between males and females in general intelligence, either in childhood (Rojahn & Naglieri, 2006) or adulthood (van der Sluis, Posthuma, Dolan, de Geus, Colom, & Boomsma, 2006), although there are some male–female differences in performance on particular subtests of the tests designed to measure general intelligence and some differences in the rate at which certain abilities develop in girls and boys. This finding is not surprising: Early versions of the Stanford-Binet intelligence test showed a slight tendency for women to score higher than men, but items that contributed to this difference were subsequently eliminated. Later IQ tests were constructed by including various subscales, on some of which females tended to score better and on some of which males tended to score better, thus effectively eliminating gender differences in overall scores.

Sensation, Perception, and Attention

From the age of 4 onward, girls tend to outscore boys on tests of perceptual speed and accuracy (Antill & Cunningham, 1982; Fairweather, 1976; Feingold, 1988; Hedges & Nowell, 1995). Boys over the age of about 9 show faster reaction times than their female counterparts. However, when semantic or symbolic information must be processed to choose a response, females react faster than males, and the female advantage increases as the amount of information to be processed increases (Fairweather & Hutt, 1972).

Women have better high-frequency hearing than men do (McGuinness, 1972). Evidence also suggests that females react more strongly than males to sound intensity. Females are more intolerant than males of loud sounds; by about the level of 85 decibels, females may hear a sound as twice as loud as males do (McGuinness, 1972). Perhaps for this reason, young adult males are comfortable with higher levels of background noise than females are (Rogers, Harkrider, Burchfield, & Nabelek, 2003). In the visual mode, men seem to be more sensitive than women to intensity changes; in dark conditions, however, women adapt more rapidly than men to lower light levels and show more sensitivity at these levels (McGuinness, 1976, 1985).

When males and females are asked to tell, by listening to a list of words, where a particular sound or letter occurs in each word, males perform much more poorly than females (McGuinness & Courtney, 1983). These researchers conclude that males have more trouble than females in forming a visual image of a word while operating in an auditory, or listening, mode. They suggest that this difficulty may be a factor underlying some gender differences in linguistic performance.

There is some controversy about whether male and female infants differ in the kinds of visual stimuli to which they pay most attention. A study in which 1-year-old infants were presented with a video of either cars moving or a face moving showed that the females paid more attention to the face, and the males paid more attention to the cars (Lutchmaya & Baron-Cohen, 2002). The authors interpreted this result as support for the idea that males' attention is drawn more to mechanical motion and females' attention is drawn more to biological motion. In another widely cited study, infants were exposed to an active, expressive person and a similar-sized inanimate object (Connellan, Baron-Cohen, Wheelwright, Batki, & Ahluwalia, 2000). Female infants looked longer at the person, whereas males spent more time looking at the object. Such findings fit neatly with the stereotype that females are more socially oriented and males are more object oriented. Indeed, because males focus so strongly on objects, one of these researchers (Baron-Cohen, 2003) argued that males grow up to be *systematizers*, who enjoy the mechanical world and abstract systems and like to figure out how systems work. Females, on the other hand, become *empathizers*, who are good at recognizing and responding to others' feelings. Such sweeping conclusions are the subject of intense debate, however. In a critical review of research on infants' processing of objects, Elizabeth Spelke (2005) noted that numerous studies over the past several decades provide no consistent evidence that male infants are more focused on objects and females on people.

Spelke (2005) also argued that if "newborn males are predisposed to learn about mechanical objects, then we should expect older male infants to show superior knowledge of objects and their behavior" (p. 952). Yet despite decades of systematic research on male and female infants' performance on tests of object perception and mechanical reasoning, thousands of studies "provide no evidence for a male advantage in perceiving, learning, or reasoning about objects, their motions, and their mechanical interactions" (p. 952). Rather, she concluded, infants of both sexes perceive and learn about objects in much the same ways.

What about adults' attention to objects? In an interesting experiment with adults, Diane McGuinness and John Symonds (1977) presented pairs of photographs to subjects stereoscopically (that is, one photograph is presented to one eye while the other photograph is simultaneously presented to the other eye). In this situation, the two stimuli compete to be "seen," and the person sees either one of them at a time or an image that combines them in some way. Each pair of photographs contained one picture of an object and one picture of a person. Male subjects reported seeing objects more than people, but females reported the reverse. This phenomenon was tested again, this time using a simple measure of time spent looking at each of two pictures (Jobson & Watson, 1984). These researchers found a gender difference in the attention paid to objects versus persons but only for younger respondents. For those older than 35, there was no gender difference: Both females and males spent more time looking at pictures of persons. Some research with adults showed that women are faster than men at recognizing male faces, whereas men are faster than women at recognizing female faces (Hofmann, Suvak, & Litz, 2006).

Learning and Memory

A review of the literature by Maccoby and Jacklin (1974) indicated no gender differences in learning and memory. The stereotype that females are better at rote learning and males are better at learning complex tasks receives no support. Some research shows that women may process information more rapidly than men do (McGuinness & Pribram, 1979). Many studies show no female–male differences on tests of memory (e.g., Joseph, McKay, & Joseph, 1982; Savage & Gouvier, 1992). However, others have found a female advantage on tests of verbal memory (Kimura & Clarke, 2002; Trahan & Quintana, 1990). Some apparent gender differences in the recall of visual material have been attributed to gender differences in verbal fluency: Females may simply be better than males at describing what they remember rather than at remembering itself (McGuinness & McLaughlin, 1982). Where gender differences in learning or memory are found, they can usually be traced to gender differences in familiarity with or interest in the topic at hand (Herrmann, Crawford, & Holdsworth, 1992). These authors found that women were better than men at memorizing a shopping list, but men performed better than women when asked to memorize directions to a particular place. In another study, researchers labeled an ambiguous shopping list as either a grocery or hardware list and told some participants that men were good at recalling such lists and some that women were good at recalling them (Colley, Ball, Kirby, Harvey, & Vingelen, 2002). Women showed the best memory performance when the list was labeled *grocery* and when they were told women were good at the task; similarly, men showed the best memory when the list was labeled *hardware* and when they were told men were good at the task.

Women may remember emotionally intense stimuli better than men do. In one study, researchers showed emotionally arousing and disturbing pictures to women and men and then asked them to recognize them 3 weeks later (Canli, Desmond, Zhao, & Gabrieli, 2002). Women recognized about 75% of the pictures, and men recognized about 60% of them. In addition, MRI scans showed that, while initially viewing the pictures and while remembering them, women and men activated different brain structures. These researchers speculated that women have more overlap than men do in the brain regions they use to process emotions and to remember stimuli. This idea remains to be explored further.

The tendency to learn and remember gender-related information better than gender-unrelated information seems to be strongest among individuals who are highly gender-typed (Cann & Garnett, 1984; Hepburn, 1985). This finding is perhaps best explained by gender schema theory—the notion that individuals who are gender-typed have learned to perceive and process information in terms of gender categories (Bem, 1985).

Verbal Performance

For years it was consistently reported in the psychological literature that females outperform males on verbal tasks (Anastasi, 1937/1958a; Hyde, 1981; Maccoby & Jacklin, 1974; McGuinness & Pribram, 1979; Tyler, 1947/1965). Although the gender difference in verbal performance appeared consistent, its size was very small. A meta-analysis by Hyde (1981) showed that gender accounted for an average of only 1% of the variance in verbal performance scores, leaving the other 99% of variation in verbal performance to be explained by other factors.

Comparing test performances of samples of children and adolescents between 1947 and 1983 showed that gender differences in verbal performance, as well as in other cognitive skill areas, declined drastically over those years—at least among adolescents (Feingold, 1988). However, a review of data collected between 1960 and 1992 in six studies that used national probability samples of adolescents and young adults revealed no clear change in the magnitude of gender differences in performance on tests of reading and writing (Hedges & Nowell, 1995). Gender differences favoring females were consistently small in reading tests and moderate in writing tests. A meta-analysis using 165 studies found no gender differences in verbal performance, either across all types of verbal tests or within specific tests such as vocabulary, reading comprehension, and essay writing (Hyde & Linn, 1988). However, these reviewers did find small gender differences favoring females in anagrams and general/mixed verbal abilities, a small difference favoring males in analogies, and a moderate difference favoring females in speech production. It appears that there are consistent gender differences on some types of verbal performance, but many types of verbal tasks show no differences.

Researchers continue to report gender differences in some aspects of verbal performance. For example, Hines (1990) reported a large female advantage of more than one standard deviation on tests of associational fluency (generating synonyms). Some differences in the frequencies of particular verbal difficulties are striking: Boys are 3 to 4 times more likely than girls to be stutterers (Skinner & Shelton, 1985) and 5 to 10 times more likely than girls to be dyslexic (Vandenberg, 1987).

Gender differences in aspects of verbal performance such as reading, spelling, and grammar are reported most consistently among children; girls perform better than boys in many samples (Feingold, 1993). However, studies of adolescents also show some differences in verbal performance. A study of high school students in Japan and the United States showed that in both countries girls averaged significantly higher than boys on word fluency (Mann, Sasanuma, Sakuma, & Masaki, 1990). The Program for International Student Assessment (PISA), which measured the performance of 15 year olds in 43 countries, found that girls generally outperform boys in reading and literacy in all countries (OECD/UNESCO, 2003). A study of cognitive performance among Chinese high school students showed girls performing at higher levels than boys on word knowledge (Huang, 1993). However, males have scored higher than females on the verbal portion of the Scholastic Assessment Test (SAT) since the early 1970s. This may be because low-ability males do not take the test and because SAT-Verbal has been weighted heavily with analogies—the only verbal test on which males tend to outscore females (Halpern, 1992). Analogy items recently have been removed from the SAT-Verbal (Pringle, 2003).

Quantitative Performance

Meta-analyses done more than a decade ago showed a tendency for males to outperform females on mathematical tests; however, only between 1 and 5% of the variance in mathematics performance could be explained by gender (Hyde, 1981; Rossi, 1983). Meta-analyses that include more recent studies indicate that the gender gap in average level of mathematics performance may be slowly decreasing (L. Friedman, 1989; Hyde, Fennema, & Lamon, 1990; Nowell & Hedges, 1998) and is often negligible. Figure 6.1 shows two overlapping

Figure 6.1 Two normal distributions that are 0.15 standard deviations apart (i.e., $d = 0.15$, the approximate magnitude of the gender differences in mathematics performance, averaging over all samples).

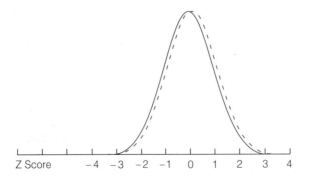

distributions that approximate the size of the gender difference in mathematics performance, averaging over the more than 100 samples (representing almost 4 million subjects) used in the Hyde, Fennema, and Lamon meta-analysis.

In this meta-analysis, gender differences in mathematics performance were found to be greater for White Americans than for African, Hispanic, or Asian Americans or for Canadian or Australian samples. A similar pattern of larger gender differences in samples of White American students than in samples of minority students emerged in the L. Friedman (1989) meta-analysis. Cross-cultural studies often do not show the same pattern of males outperforming females in mathematics that is found in the United States (Feingold, 1994b; Huang, 1993; Skaalvik & Rankin, 1994). However, the PISA study found that, in 42 of the 43 countries studied, boys scored higher than girls overall in mathematics (OECD/UNESCO, 2003).

Research in cognitive psychology and neuroscience reveals that several different cognitive abilities must develop in order for humans to think mathematically (Spelke, 2005). These include the ability to think of small, exact numbers (e.g., to know the difference between two objects and three objects), the capacity to think of large, approximate numbers (e.g., to know 75 is greater than 50), fluency in the use of verbal counting words and quantifiers, and the ability to think in terms of environmental geometry (space) and landmarks. All of these abilities must work together for us to engage in mathematical reasoning; they develop sequentially and become integrated during childhood. Researchers have not found any female–male differences in the development and emergence of these primary mathematical abilities during childhood (Spelke, 2005). There is little support, then, for the notion that males and females differ in the basic "building block" abilities that underlie mathematical thinking.

Some differences do emerge on more complex mathematical tasks, beginning as early as elementary school and increasing with age. Girls show a slight advantage in arithmetic computation in elementary and middle school (Feingold, 1993). Some studies found that boys do better than girls on one particular type of quantitative performance, mathematical problem solving, as early as the first grade (Lummis & Stevenson, 1990). In the Lummis and Stevenson study, first-grade males outperformed females in problem solving by equivalent amounts across samples in three countries: the United States, Japan, and Taiwan. Although Japanese girls achieved higher average scores on problem solving than American boys did, the gap in problem-solving performance between Japanese boys and Japanese girls was as great as that between American boys and American girls. This difference occurred despite girls' and boys' apparently equivalent adeptness at computation and understanding the mathematical operations needed to solve the problems.

The majority of studies show no gender differences in performance on general mathematics achievement tests until early adolescence—a finding that holds across a variety of cultures (Lummis & Stevenson, 1990). Gender differences favoring males in mathematical problem solving appear most reliably in high school and are maintained or increased in college. The estimated size of the gender difference is such that about 43% of high school females and 57% of high school males will score above the average score for the whole high school sample (Hyde, Fennema, & Lamon, 1990). Problem solving, then, appears to be the only area of mathematics achievement in which the gender difference may be a cause for concern. As Hyde and her colleagues note, problem-solving skill is critical for success in such fields as engineering and physics.

On the whole, gender differences seem to be smallest and may favor females when the samples studied are from the general population. The differences are larger with more selective samples and appear largest for samples of highly precocious persons (Hyde, Fennema, & Lamon, 1990). Smaller gender differences in performance are found in samples from lower than from higher socioeconomic groups (Fischbein, 1990).

Although high school boys tend to outperform girls on standardized tests of mathematical problem solving, girls often obtain higher grades in mathematics than boys do (Kimball, 1989). This anomalous finding has been shrugged off by researchers who are convinced of male quantitative superiority as being due to girls' better behavior in school (Benbow & Stanley, 1982). It may, however, reflect differences between the two types of testing situations: Boys are advantaged in the standardized testing situation and girls are advantaged in the classroom testing situation. Such differences could involve issues such as test anxiety (Crocker, Schmitt, & Tang, 1988) or content of items included on the tests.

Considerable interest in gender differences in mathematical ability was aroused by the work of Benbow and Stanley (1980, 1982, 1983; Benbow, 1988). These researchers examined scores on the SAT-M (a standardized test of mathematical reasoning) for about 50,000 seventh- and eighth-grade children identified by the Johns Hopkins National Talent Search. To be included in the sample, a child had to score in the top 3% nationally on a standardized achievement test. Among these high-ability children, Benbow and Stanley found a mean difference in performance of 30 points favoring boys. Although this difference is statistically significant, it represents only about three-eighths of the size of the combined standard deviations for males and females in the sample. Benbow and Stanley's most striking finding, however, was the ratio of boys to girls among the highest scorers. In the upper reaches of the distribution, the higher the score, the greater the ratio of males to females who attained it. Among children who scored above 500, the ratio of boys to girls was 2.1 to 1; among those scoring above 600, the ratio of boys to girls was 4.1 to 1; among those scoring over 700, boys outnumbered girls 13 to 1 (Benbow & Stanley, 1983).

Although the research carried out by Benbow and Stanley has provided a wealth of useful information about gifted children, it is easy to make too much of these dramatic-sounding results. In the first place, they are based on a comparison of two sample groups (high-performing females and males) that do not necessarily represent a common population (Nesselroade & Thompson, 1995). In other words, the "high-ability population" from which the children in this study were picked may actually be different in a variety of ways for girls and boys. For example, perhaps for various reasons unrelated to ability, more boys than girls participated in the Talent Search.

In the second place, they are based on a sample of girls and boys who are much more mathematically talented than average. Furthermore, these children, as voluntary participants in the Talent Search, were to some extent self-selected for motivation and interest. As noted earlier, gender differences in mathematics performance are found to be greatest in the most select samples. Benbow and Stanley's research provides no information about gender differences in mathematical performance among average males and females.

In the third place, the focus on male–female ratios among extremely high scorers makes gender differences in mathematics performance appear more important than they are (J. D. Rossi, 1983). For example, in their sample, which already represents only the top 3% of intellectually talented children, only about 7 of every 1,000 boys and 5 of every 10,000 girls scored over 700. At this rarefied level, so few individuals are actually affected that even a large difference in the proportions of males and females has little practical significance. Benbow (1988) reported that follow-up data on the mathematically gifted children in her sample show that, of the 47% who went to graduate school, 42% of the men and 22% of the women chose scientific or mathematical fields—statistics that show, by implication, that the majority of even this highly gifted sample did *not* take up science or mathematics as a career. A report on the status of Benbow and Stanley's participants at the age of 33—20 years after their participation in the study—indicated that the males were far more likely than the females to become mathematicians, computer scientists, or engineers and that the females were far more likely than the males to become homemakers or health care workers (Benbow, Lubinski, Shea, & Eftekhari-Sanjani, 2000). Since both the males and females were very high in math ability, it is clear that ability is only one of several factors that influence the career paths students take.

In the fourth place, the gender differences occurred specifically on the SAT-M, a test that seems, perhaps because of its content or administration, to produce larger gender differences in performance than other tests (Hyde, Fennema, & Lamon, 1990). Moreover, the SAT-M seems to underpredict later mathematics performance for women relative to men: Girls and boys with the same scores on the SAT-M go on to perform differently in college mathematics classes (the girls get better grades) (Royer & Garofoli, 2005). This finding calls into question the use of the SAT-M as the sole criterion to define who is mathematically talented.

Finally, some critics have noted that there was a great deal of variability in males' performance at the top levels; in fact, variability among the males was consistently greater than among the females (Becker & Hedges, 1988). For example, in one year, 19% of the boys outperformed the highest-scoring girl in the sample, but in another year, the highest-scoring girl did better than all but 0.1% of the boys (Tobias, 1982). Thus the significance of gender differences in mathematical performance remains a matter of debate.

Visual-Spatial Performance

Visual-spatial abilities are those that enable us visually to perceive and locate objects and their interrelationships. This broad class of abilities includes, among other things, the capacity to rearrange mentally and rotate objects or figures and to pick out or "disembed" a simple figure or shape from its background.

Gender differences in visual-spatial performance favoring males have been reported more consistently than any other cognitive differences (D. Cohen & Wilkie, 1979; Connor & Serbin, 1985; Halpern, 1992; Maccoby & Jacklin, 1974; Willis & Schaie, 1988). Hyde (1981) reported that across all the studies she reviewed, gender accounted for less than 5% of the variability on visual-spatial tests. Gender accounts for substantially more of the variance in some types of visual-spatial performance than in others (Linn & Petersen, 1985; Voyer, Voyer, & Bryden, 1995). There are some indications that gender differences are decreasing (Feingold, 1988; Rosenthal & Rubin, 1982; Voyer et al., 1995) and that, like the gender differences in mathematical performance, they appear largest in the highly select samples (Becker & Hedges, 1984). Gender differences often involve speed of responding rather than accuracy (Blough & Slavin, 1987).

Critics argue that visual-spatial ability has not been defined precisely or separated from spatial abilities in general and that different measures of visual-spatial ability actually assess different abilities (Caplan, MacPherson, & Tobin, 1985; Linn & Petersen, 1985; Voyer et al., 1995). Marcia Linn and Anne Petersen (1985) concluded that there are at least three different types of spatial ability: spatial visualization, spatial perception, and mental rotation.

Spatial visualization, most often measured using the embedded figures test (see Figure 6.2 for an example), involves complicated, multistep mental

Figure 6.2 Examples of drawings used in the embedded figures test.

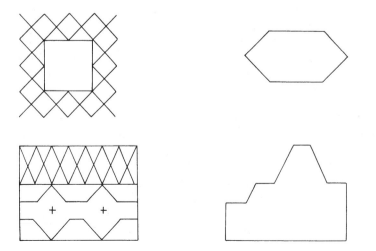

manipulations of spatial information. Participants may be asked to "disembed" a simple figure from a complex background or to imagine how a piece of paper would look when folded a certain way. This type of task, which seems to require analytic ability, shows no reliable gender differences at any point in the life span, according to Linn and Petersen's meta-analysis.

The second type of ability, **spatial perception,** involves determining spatial relationships with respect to one's own body orientation, in spite of distracting information. It is often measured by the rod-and-frame test, in which a person must adjust a tilted rod inside a tilted frame to true vertical, in the absence of visual context clues. This ability is a spatial but not necessarily visual one. Good performance requires the use of kinesthetic cues (cues relating to body motion, position, and gravity). Linn and Petersen found that beginning at age 8 males show a small advantage over females on this type of task, and the size of the gender difference is larger (two-thirds of a standard deviation) for samples in which participants are older than 18.

The third type of spatial ability, **mental rotation** of figures, is the only one for which Linn and Petersen concluded that strong gender differences exist. Performance in this category is measured by showing the person a picture or object and asking questions about it that require the visualization of that picture or object from another angle. Scores are based on speed rather than accuracy of rotation (accuracy tends to be very high). Gender differences favoring males were detected across all ages on this type of task, although the size of the effect varied from one-quarter of a standard deviation to an entire standard deviation, according to the specific test used. The reason for better male performance on this type of task is not yet clear. It may reflect the acquisition or use of different cognitive strategies for finding a solution that could, in turn, be related to differences in males' and females' experiences with this type of task.

A more recent replication and extension of Linn and Petersen's analysis provides support for their finding that the gender differences in mental rotation are the most robust (Voyer et al., 1995). These researchers also noted that some tests are more likely than others to show gender differences and that the administration procedures used can affect the magnitude of the female–male difference obtained. They concluded on the basis of a meta-analysis of 286 comparisons of female and male performance that gender differences are clearly established in some areas of spatial abilities.

A fourth type of spatial ability, **spatiotemporal ability,** involves judgments about moving visual displays, such as predicting when a moving object will reach a particular spot. Some researchers have found that females are less accurate than males in such judgments (Halpern, 1992). However, prior experience affects performance on this type of task, and feedback improves the performance of both women and men (Law, Pellegrino, & Hunt, 1993). It is possible, therefore, that men and boys perform better on this type of task simply because they have more experience with similar tasks.

What are the implications of gender differences in certain visual-spatial abilities? Are they important to scholastic success or career choice? It may be tempting to attribute more importance to these differences than they deserve. For example, Paula Caplan and her colleagues (1985) noted the frequency with which anecdotal examples of female inferiority in spatial ability are cited (e.g., the shortage of female chess masters) in contrast to equally valid examples of female spatial competence:

> the buying of furniture with a view toward how it can be rotated and fitted within a particular space; learning to type without watching the keyboard . . . and the designing and using of clothing patterns that must be turned, flipped, and inverted, and then worked on while the user visualizes how they will look when re-turned, reinverted, and reflipped. (p. 789)

Can the differences between the sexes in visual-spatial ability account for the shortage of women in professions that require this ability, such as architecture and engineering? The answer is no. Hyde (1981), making the initial assumption that a person would have to be in the top 5% of the range of spatial abilities to be qualified for a profession such as engineering, calculated that if spatial ability were the only determining factor the ratio of males to females in such professions would be 2 to 1. In actual fact, the proportion of women in the engineering fields has been less than 10% for many years, and women in the United States still earn fewer than 19% of undergraduate engineering degrees (National Center for Education Statistics, 2005). Gender differences in spatial ability potentially could explain only a small part of this male dominance in the engineering profession.

This conclusion is reinforced by a recent computer simulation study in which researchers created a virtual organization in which promotion through eight levels of seniority was based *solely* on ability. They then plugged in equal numbers of imaginary female and male entry-level employees, along with the assumption that the women had less ability than the men by either 1% or 5%. When there was assumed to be a 1% difference in ability levels, women ended up with 35% of the top-level jobs, and when the women's ability deficit was assumed to be 5%, they received 29% of the top jobs (Martel, Lane, & Emrich, 1996). In most scientific and technical organizations, women do not hold anything like such high percentages of the top jobs—suggesting that many other factors besides ability differences come into play in keeping women out of such positions.

EXPLAINING THE DIFFERENCES

Despite the relatively small size and limited nature of the observed gender differences in performance on some cognitive tasks, psychologists have invested a great deal of energy in trying to explain these differences. The result is an often bewildering array of possible explanations for the existence of differences that may or may not be important.

Area of Intellectual Performance	Research Findings on Differences/Similarities
General intelligence	• There are no differences between females and males.
Sensation and perception	• Starting in childhood, females do better on tests that require fast, accurate processing of information. • Women may be more sensitive than men to some sounds. • Men are more visually sensitive than women are to changes in light intensity. • Males may have more trouble than females do forming a visual image when listening. • There is an ongoing controversy about whether males and females differ in the kinds of stimuli (objects vs. people) to which they pay most attention.
Learning and memory	• Some research finds that women are better than men at verbal memory; however, this may be because women are better than men at describing what they remember. • Both women and men learn and remember "gender-appropriate" information better than "gender-inappropriate" information.
Verbal	• Overall, gender differences are small and, when they appear, favor females. • Female–male differences in particular verbal skills may be larger. For example, women perform significantly better than men on tests of verbal fluency, and boys are much more likely than girls to be stutterers.
Quantitative	• Researchers report a small and perhaps decreasing tendency for males to outperform females on some tests, such as mathematical word problems. • Differences are largest in the most select samples.
Visual-spatial	• Gender accounts for more performance differences in some types of visual-spatial ability than others. • There are no reliable gender differences in spatial visualization. • Beginning at age 8, males show a small advantage over females in spatial perception. This difference is greater in older respondents. • Large gender differences favoring males are found in speed of mental rotation. • There are some reports of superior male performance on tests of spatiotemporal ability.

Reflections : Chess Queens and Kings

World chess champion Gary Kasparov was quoted in a *London Times* interview as saying that chess is "a mixture of sport, psychological warfare, science, and art. When you look at all these components, man dominates. Every single component of chess belongs to the areas of male domination" (quoted in Hoffman, 2003, p. 76).

Indeed, the notion of two players hunched over a chess board planning strategy and contemplating future moves conjures up a vision of two men, not two women. With good reason. There are about 1,200 "national masters" in the United States Chess Federation, and only 14 of them are women. Of the 100 acknowledged best players in the world, only one—tenth-ranked Judith Polgar of Hungary—is female (Hoffman, 2003).

Could female–male differences in visual-spatial ability form the basis for this lopsided distribution of chess masters? Could it be that chess "queens" are destined to be a rare species? Before leaping to the conclusion that women are at an ability disadvantage in the realm of chess, it is instructive to look at the social factors that have discouraged female participation. Women were not allowed in most chess clubs until the

19th century. In 1897, the first female participants in an international tournament were met with the fear that they "would come under great strain lifting the leaded, wooden chess sets" (Hoffman, 2003, p. 75).

These days, there are at least some forces encouraging girls to take up chess. Female chess champions lead workshops for schoolgirls in which they teach the chess strategies employed by great women players. The instructors urge their charges to "play like girls" and try to present themselves as role models who not only play championship chess but also "have a life." Jennifer Shahade, the 2002 U.S. women's chess champion, experiments with her public image to convey the idea that chess is "cool" and to counter any notion it is in any sense unfeminine. In a series of photographic self-portraits, she wears a pink wig, a slinky dress, and pink fuzzy gloves and is shown reading one of the most serious books about chess. The idea she hopes to promote is that a woman can be both sexy and intellectual, both frivolous and serious, both fun loving and a wickedly competent chess queen.

Biological Explanations

If performance differences are partially based in biology, does that mean they are inevitable and immutable? No. As seen in earlier chapters, biology and environment interact so closely that a biologically based predisposition in the direction of a particular behavior or ability is usually only one of many determining factors in the development of gender differences.

HORMONES   There are at least two ways hormones can potentially influence ability and performance: The actual level of hormones circulating in the bloodstream might have a direct effect, or there might be an indirect effect of prenatal hormones through their action on the developing brain. In this section, we examine research that deals with the first possibility: an impact of circulating hormones. The next section, on brain lateralization, includes a discussion of the second possibility.

Researchers have long speculated that hormones circulating in the bloodstream may affect cognitive performance. However, because there are so many hormones and because their levels can fluctuate in response to daily or longer rhythms or to certain kinds of events, it is difficult to discern clear hormone-cognition relationships. One study examined the links between circulating levels of several sex hormones and several measures of cognitive performance in a group of elderly women (Buckwalter & Galen, 2000). They found that high estradiol (a kind of estrogen) levels were associated with better scores on certain tests of verbal memory but with worse scores on certain tests of visual memory. Also, higher testosterone levels were linked to higher performance on verbal fluency tests but not on other tests of cognitive performance. It was not possible to draw a simple conclusion that higher levels of hormones relate to better cognitive performance.

Also, women's and men's performance may be differentially associated with particular hormone levels. For example, researchers have found that women with high testosterone levels obtain higher spatial scores, but men with high testosterone levels score lower on some spatial tests (Gouchie & Kimura, 1991; Shute, Pellegrino, Hubert, & Reynolds, 1983). This pattern of findings suggests that, for spatial ability at least, there is an optimal androgen/estrogen balance that is slightly below that of the average man and above that of the average woman (Kimura, 1987).

Some researchers interested in the relationship between circulating hormone levels and cognitive performance have studied women's performance at various phases of the menstrual cycle, when levels of circulating estrogen are high or low (Hampson & Moffat, 2004; Kimura & Hampson, 1994). They found that women perform somewhat better on verbal articulation tasks (e.g., saying, "A box of mixed biscuits in a biscuit mixer" five times in a row as quickly as possible) and fine-motor-skill tasks at times in their cycle when estrogen levels are high rather than when they are low and somewhat better on certain spatial tasks, such as the rod-and-frame task, at times when estrogen levels are low rather than when they are high (Hampson, 1990a, 1990b). However, the differences related to menstrual-cycle phase were small in comparison to individual differences among the women. Verbal fluency has also been shown to increase in young women when estrogen levels are higher (Maki, Rich, & Rosenbaum, 2002).

Fluctuating hormone levels in men, such as the drop in testosterone between morning and evening, might also show some small relationship to cognitive performance. Doreen Kimura (2002) reported that she has observed seasonal fluctuations in men's spatial performance: They perform better in the spring, when testosterone levels are low. Researchers studying men have also found a negative relationship between levels of FSH (follicle-stimulating hormone) and tests of some forms of visual-spatial functioning (Gordon & Lee, 1986).

This line of research, then, provides some evidence for a link between circulating hormone levels and cognitive-perceptual performance, but the effects are small and may be of little practical significance. However, one insight from this research is that sex differences (and individual differences) in various aspects of cognitive performance may be dynamic and responsive to particular conditions. Menstrual and other hormonal cycles are discussed in more detail in Chapter 8.

BRAIN ORGANIZATION   The notion that sex-related cognitive differences are caused by sex differences in brain organization has received a good deal of press: "Women's Intuition Linked to Thicker Nerves in Brain," proclaimed a newspaper headline (*Winnipeg Free Press,* 1986); "Male Brain, Female Brain: The Hidden Difference," announced *Psychology Today* (Kimura, 1985); "Men don't seem to listen? Well, they only use half a brain" (Enman, 2000), asserted one newspaper headline.

The idea that male and female brains are different has a long history. At one time, the explanation for women's "obvious" intellectual inferiority was their smaller brains—an idea that was quickly dropped when it was demonstrated that, relative to body weight, women's brains were proportionally larger than men's (Shields, 1975). The current focus, however, is not on brain size but on the organization of functions within the brain.

Although the human body appears relatively symmetrical—the left side looking more or less like a mirror image of the right—we are not symmetrical in terms of our competence at different activities. A person is better at writing with one hand than with the other, kicks a football better with one foot than the other, prefers one ear over the other when listening closely. The majority of people are right-handed; handedness may or may not be consistent with foot or ear preferences. The tendency for individuals to be better at certain activities using one side of their body than the other has been taken as evidence for the way functions are organized in the brain.

The outermost part of the human brain, the **cerebral cortex,** is divided into left and right halves, or hemispheres, connected by a mass of nerve fibers called the **corpus callosum** (see Figure 6.3). Each hemisphere of the brain's cerebral cortex governs the activities of the opposite side of the body (that is, the left side of the brain controls the right hand, the right ear, the right leg, and the right visual field). Scientists also believe that the two hemispheres of the brain are the locations for different abilities. In normal right-handed people, the capacities for language and for analytical, mathematical, and sequential information processing tend to be located in the left hemisphere. The right hemisphere is the site for more holistic and nonverbal information-processing skills, musical ability, and certain types of spatial skills. These generalizations do not hold for left-handed individuals; nor is it the case that the locations of various abilities are simply reversed for left-handers (Springer & Deutsch, 1998).

Because verbal and certain spatial skills seem to be located on different sides of the brain, researchers have found it tempting to speculate that female superiority on verbal tasks and male superiority on some spatial tasks might

Figure 6.3 Sensory inputs to and functions of the two brain hemispheres for the normal right-handed person.

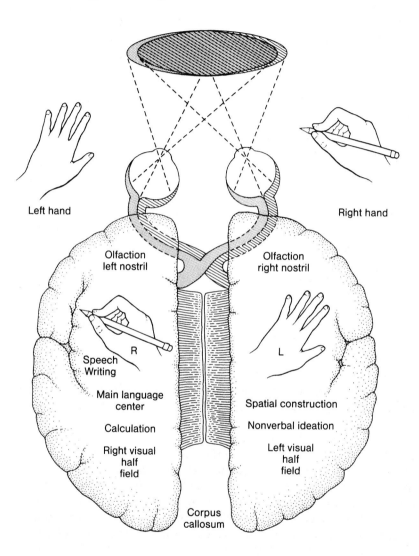

be related to sex differences in the development of the left and right hemispheres. Could it be that females have a better-developed left hemisphere (to explain the female advantage—albeit a rapidly disappearing one—in verbal skills) and males have a better-developed right hemisphere (to explain the male advantage in some spatial skills)? At first blush, the explanation sounds seductively simple. But wait. In addition to verbal skills, the left hemisphere also seems to be the location for analytic and sequential skills, in which the sexes do not differ. If earlier or stronger left-hemisphere development explains female superiority on verbal tasks, might it not also be reasonable to expect that the same process would guarantee female superiority in mathematical performance? If brain organization does relate to gender differences in cognitive performance, the relationship must be more complex than each sex simply being better developed on different sides of the brain.

Much research has focused on possible sex differences in the degree to which particular functions are localized in one side of the brain—that is, the degree of hemispheric **lateralization** or specialization. Levy (1972) proposed that greater hemispheric lateralization for spatial ability enhances performance for that ability and that male superiority on spatial tasks is due to greater lateralization of spatial skills among men than among women. Her proposal laid the groundwork for a dizzying flurry of research in which males and females were compared for their lateralization of verbal and spatial abilities.

Three sorts of evidence have been used to gauge lateralization in women and men: clinical studies of brain-damaged patients, behavioral tests of normal individuals, and studies of brain activity and anatomy. Many of these studies have been reviewed by Merrill Hiscock and colleagues (Hiscock, Inch, Jacek, Hiscock-Kalil, & Kalil, 1994; Hiscock, Israelian, Inch, Jacek, & Hiscock-Kalil, 1995) and by Springer and Deutsch (1998). In general, clinical studies of brain-damaged individuals have found that, for men, damage to the left hemisphere is associated with more impairment of verbal than nonverbal performance, whereas damage to the right side of the brain is associated with greater impairment of nonverbal than verbal performance. For women, however, verbal and nonverbal performance do not seem to be affected differentially by the side of the damage, suggesting that verbal and nonverbal abilities are distributed across both hemispheres. Several studies have failed to confirm this pattern, however, finding no differences between males and females in the effects of damage to the left or right hemispheres (R. A. Bornstein, 1984; Herring & Reitan, 1984; Snow & Sheese, 1985).

The earlier work has been criticized on a number of grounds, including the lack of similarity to the general population of the samples used and the confounding of sex with other variables. Research with brain-damaged patients by Doreen Kimura and her colleagues indicated that no single rule about sex differences in brain organization holds across all aspects of thinking (Kimura, 1985, 1987, 1993, 2002). They are finding that for producing speech and making hand movements that contribute to motor skill, women's brains seem to be more focally organized than men's (that is, these abilities seem to be localized in a more restricted area of the brain for women than for men). Basic speech function appears to be more dependent on the anterior (front) than the posterior (back) region of the brain for women and more equally distributed between the two regions for men. However, for tasks such as defining words, the sex difference appears to go in the opposite direction: Women's brains are organized more diffusely than men's. Finally, for a variety of other verbal tests, there is no obvious sex difference in brain organization. Clinical research, then, does not support the simple view that men's brains are more lateralized, in general, than women's brains.

Kimura (1987) argued that her research with brain-damaged persons demonstrates differences in brain organization between human females and males. She noted, however, that there are wide individual variations within each sex, that sex is only one of several individual-difference variables that are correlated with brain organization, and that "the population differences in abilities that we see between men and women do not have a high predictive value for individuals. As a means of screening for admission to occupations or life activities, genital sex is a very poor instrument" (p. 146).

Behavioral tests with normal participants use tasks in which two different stimuli are presented simultaneously to the different sides of the brain, with participants tested later to determine which inputs are best recalled. Perhaps the most common of such tests is the dichotic listening test, in which different lists of numbers or spoken syllables are simultaneously presented through earphones to the participant's left and right ears. If the participant later shows a tendency to remember the stimuli presented to one ear better than those presented to the other, the result is taken as evidence that the person's verbal abilities are more strongly lateralized in the brain hemisphere corresponding to that ear. If males are more strongly lateralized than females for verbal abilities, we would expect men to show a greater right-ear (left-hemisphere) advantage than women on this test.

After an exhaustive review of auditory and visual laterality studies, Hiscock and colleagues (Hiscock et al., 1994; Hiscock et al., 1995) came to the conclusion that female–male differences in lateralization are small, with sex accounting for only 1 to 2% of differences in lateralization. Similarly, Voyer (1996) concluded that sex differences in language lateralization are extremely small. The sexes do seem to differ reliably in manual asymmetry—the degree to which one hand is dominant—but in this case it is the women who show more "handedness," and thus, presumably, greater lateralization (L. J. Harris, 1992). On the whole, the results of behavioral studies, like those of the clinical studies discussed earlier, do not provide overwhelming support for the idea of an important difference in brain lateralization between women and men.

Studies of brain anatomy have reported some evidence of small differences between male and female brains, which have been interpreted as implying more lateralization for males than females (de Lacoste-Utamsing & Holloway, 1982; Wada, Clark, & Hamm, 1975). In particular, researchers have focused on the corpus callosum, the "bridge" between the left and right hemispheres. If that bridge is more developed in one sex than the other, would that mean transmission between the two hemispheres is more efficient for that sex?

Some research on brains examined at autopsy showed that the corpus callosum is larger, at least in the posterior of the brain, in women than in men (Kimura, 1987). Two studies of the brains of living human beings, using magnetic resonance imaging, contribute to the controversy by providing contradictory results. In one of these studies, no male–female difference in the size or surface area of the corpus callosum was found. However, a striking difference in the *shape* was observed. The posterior region of the corpus callosum (the splenium) was more bulbous in females and more tubular in males (L. S. Allen, Richey, Chai, & Gorski, 1991). This difference was not evident in children younger than age 16. Another study did not find sex differences in the posterior region (Byne, Bleier, & Houston, 1988). According to the latter group of researchers, the most striking finding was the large variation in the size and shape of the corpus callosum, irrespective of gender or age. Clearly, research in this area is not yet at the stage at which it can be cited with confidence to prove or disprove the hypothesis of greater male than female lateralization. To further complicate the issue, researchers are increasingly convinced that sex differences in brain anatomy may vary across the life span, indicating that whatever sex differences in brain organization exist may be dynamic rather than static, present at some periods of life but not at others (Kimura, 1985).

On the whole, then, there is no overwhelming evidence that males are more lateralized in general than females. However, at least for some particular abilities, the brains of the two sexes may differ in their organization. Suspending all doubts for a moment and accepting the hypothesis as true, we would still be left with two basic questions: Does brain organization really make a difference to cognitive performance and, if so, how?

Many of the theories about the relationship between brain organization and performance focus specifically on lateralization. We have already seen, however, that whatever sex differences in lateralization exist are more likely to be specific to particular types of abilities, such as speech production or vocabulary, than to encompass broad categories such as "verbal abilities" or "spatial abilities." Yet most of the research designed to explore the relationship between brain organization and performance in women and men has been aimed at showing a relationship between gross measures of lateralization (that is, is one sex more lateralized than the other?) and broad categories of abilities. The studies are ingenious, but they cannot provide completely useful answers because they are focusing on the wrong questions.

The idea that prenatal hormone levels may indirectly affect cognitive abilities by influencing the developing brain is a popular one that has received support from animal research and forms the basis for some theories about male–female differences in cognitive abilities among humans (e.g., Kimura, 1987; Nyborg, 1983). Kimura (2002) suggests, for example, that "the effects of sex hormones on brain organization occur so early in life that from the start the environment is acting on differently wired brains in boys and girls. Such effects make evaluating the role of experience, independent of physiological predispositions, a difficult if not dubious task" (p. 32).

Early research by Melissa Hines and Carl Shipley (1984) provided one of the few direct tests with humans of these proposed prenatal hormone–brain organization–cognitive performance links. They compared women who had been exposed prenatally to DES, a synthetic estrogen, to their nonexposed sisters, hypothesizing that the DES-exposed women would show greater hemispheric lateralization and a more masculine pattern of cognitive performance (that is, better visual spatial performance and poorer verbal performance) than their sisters. (Although DES is an estrogen, it is now thought by researchers to have a masculinizing effect because it is now known that testosterone converts to estrogen.) They found, in fact, that the DES-exposed women did seem to be more lateralized, at least as measured by their performance on a dichotic listening task. It is possible that prenatal hormone levels affected brain lateralization. However, they found *no* relationship between lateralization and cognitive performance. The DES women did not differ from their sisters on verbal or visual-spatial measures. Although this one study does not rule out the possibility that lateralization is related to cognitive abilities, it certainly indicates that the relationship is too weak or too complex to be measured in a small sample of women. Indeed, the potential complexity of lateralization-ability relationships is illustrated by findings that the degree of lateralization can show *opposite* relationships with spatial performance in the two sexes: Greater left-right differences in electrical brain activity are sometimes associated with higher spatial scores for males and lower spatial scores for females (Hoyenga & Hoyenga, 1993). Thus there is as yet no clear evidence of how lateralization differences are linked to specific cognitive abilities.

It is worthy of note at this point that sex differences in brain asymmetry, if they exist, could be the result of environmental as well as genetic or hormonal factors. For example, some studies suggest that children's lateralization of verbal skills is affected by the quality and quantity of their exposure to language (Borowy & Goebel, 1976; Geffner & Hochberg, 1971). And a growing accumulation of research on neuroplasticity shows that sensory input can change the brain (Schwartz & Begley, 2002). For example, among blind persons who read Braille, the area of the somatosensory cortex (the part of the brain that processes information derived from the sense of touch) devoted to the "reading finger" is much larger than it is among either sighted persons or blind persons who do not read Braille. Such research suggests that if the sexes do differ in the way their brain is organized to process information, the difference could be, at least in part, a function of such environmental factors as the amount of talking parents do to their male and female infants.

Before leaving the topic of brain organization, a final comment is in order. Understanding of the organization and functioning of the human brain is still far from complete. Furthermore, the emphasis on lateralization as the most crucial feature of brain organization has diminished (Efron, 1990). The network of connections in individual human brains may be so unique as to make the individuality "of fingerprints or facial features gross and simple by comparison" (Sperry, 1982, p. 1223). Divisions of the brain other than left-right (e.g., up-down, front-back) might yet prove to be important; moreover, scientists are still trying to understand the way the brain functions as a coherent whole. One commentator compares our understanding of the brain with that which might be achieved by someone totally unfamiliar with cars if he experimented by removing parts of the car:

> He removes different parts of the car, observing that the removal of a wheel makes the ride bumpy, draining the brake fluid makes it difficult to stop, and removal of the battery or engine prevents forward motion altogether . . . he thus localizes some functions . . . [but] . . . uncovers little information about their mechanisms. (Fausto-Sterling, 1992, p. 48)

Fausto-Sterling may be too harsh in her evaluation of the current state of neu-ropsychology. Nevertheless, given the contradictory evidence and the large gaps in our knowledge about the brain, we should be extremely cautious about jumping to conclusions about links between brain organization and gender differences in cognitive performance.

We probably should also be cautious about the practical significance of some of the findings relating hormones or brain organization to performance. Scientists have, for example, found some evidence for relationships among handedness, testosterone, allergies, myopia (nearsightedness), and mathemat-ical performance (Benbow, 1986, 1988; Geschwind & Behan, 1982). Interesting theories have been developed to explain these correlations (e.g., Geschwind & Galaburda, 1985). They are fascinating because they suggest connections among such diverse findings as the higher frequency of left-handedness and speech disorders in males, females' greater resistance to viral and bacterial dis-eases, and the greater female susceptibility to autoimmune disorders such as lupus, arthritis, and allergies. The theories may have little practical significance for the issue of gender-related differences or similarities in particular abilities, however. And how useful is it to confirm such interrelationships? If we could say for certain that left-handed myopic males with many allergies make the best mathematicians, would we give up on everyone else? And, as McGuinness (1988) asked, how would such a finding help us understand the majority of mathematically talented people, who simply do not fit such a category?

Social/Affective Explanations

Anyone who has ever taken a test knows there is more to success or failure than intellectual competence. There are matters of long-term training and immedi-ate preparation, mood, fatigue, confidence, and motivation—all of which may, in turn, be influenced by the expectations of others, the cultural or institutional climate, and immediate situational factors.

How might the kinds of emotional and social factors just listed systemati-cally differ for the two sexes and thus help to explain differences in their perfor-mance on certain kinds of tasks? We will look briefly at the possible roles of direct training, gender-role socialization with respect to the development of particular skills, and gender-related differences in self-confidence and motivation as causes of some of the observed gender differences in cognitive performance.

TRAINING AND EXPERIENCE   Even in cases in which the level of a par-ticular ability is partially determined by physiological factors, the ability is usu-ally susceptible to training. For example, some of us may have more potential than others to become great athletes, but all of us can improve our athletic skills to some extent through instruction and practice. It is quite clear, likewise, that spatial, verbal, and mathematical skills can all be increased through training.

Both sexes show a positive relationship between experience and practice on visual-spatial tasks; the more a person has participated in visual-spatial activities, the better she or he is likely to score on tests of visual-spatial abil-ity (Baenninger & Newcombe, 1989; Connor & Serbin, 1985; Newcombe,

Overview   Biological explanations for cognitive differences

Possible Cause	Hypothesis	Research Support
Circulating hormones	Level of sex hormones (such as testosterone or estrogen) circulating in the bloodstream affects cognitive performance.	• Some research finds differences in women's performance on certain cognitive tasks during different parts of the menstrual cycle. • Some research finds correlations between levels of certain sex hormones and performance on cognitive tasks among elderly women. • Seasonal fluctuations in performance on some spatial tasks have been observed in men.
Brain organization	Prenatal exposure to different levels of sex hormones causes sex differences in brain organization (e.g., differences in hemispheric specialization). Some researchers have zeroed in on the idea that men's brains are more lateralized than women's brains. Such differences in organization are hypothesized to lead to female–male differences in cognitive performance.	• Research on brain-damaged patients does not provide strong support for the idea that men's brains are more lateralized than women's brains. • Some research with brain-damaged patients indicates that, for certain specific abilities, there may be sex differences in how focused or diffuse the abilities are in the brain. • Studies of auditory and visual laterality conclude that men are, to a small degree, more lateralized than women. • Studies of "handedness" suggest that women are more lateralized than men on this dimension. • There is conflicting evidence about whether the corpus callosum is larger in women than in men.

Bandura, & Taylor, 1983; Voyer & Voyer, 2001). Traditionally, masculine toys and activities involve more visual-spatial skills than feminine ones do, so perhaps male–female differences in performance on visual-spatial tasks reflect differences in their spatial experience. One study found that 37% of the male–female differences in elementary schoolchildren's block design (a spatial test) scores could be accounted for by the difference in the availability of "masculine" toys in their home environment (Serbin, Zelkowitz, Doyle, Gold, & Wheaton, 1990). However, these correlational findings may imply only that people who are good at spatial activities seek them out. A stronger argument for the effect of experience on performance comes from experimental studies of training in spatial skills. A meta-analysis of such studies showed that both females and males benefit, apparently equally, from direct training (Baenninger & Newcombe, 1989).

Gender difference in mathematics performance can also be partially explained by the fact that females simply take fewer math courses than males (Benbow & Stanley, 1982; Fox, 1981). When the number of courses taken is held constant, gender differences in mathematics achievement are greatly reduced, although not always eliminated (De Wolf, 1981; Ethington & Wolfle, 1984; Fennema & Sherman, 1977; Kimball, 1989).

Even when males and females take the same courses in mathematics, however, they do not necessarily receive the same training. In the first place, mathematically gifted males are more likely than gifted females to engage in extracurricular study and activities related to mathematics (Kimball, 1989) and are more likely to receive parental encouragement for mathematics achievement (Fox, 1981; Yee & Eccles, 1988). For example, parents buy more math- and science-related items for their sons than their daughters across all grade levels (Bleeker, 2003). Such differences in parental encouragement and expectations have been linked clearly to children's expectations and performance in mathematics (Fredricks & Eccles, 2002). Fathers who report stronger traditional gender stereotypes with respect to mathematics have sons who report more interest in math and daughters who report less interest (Bleeker, 2003).

Even within the same mathematics classroom, boys and girls may not be getting the same education (Sadker & Sadker, 1994). In high school mathematics classes, boys are consistently spoken to and called on more and receive more social interaction, individual instruction, feedback, and encouragement (Eccles, 1989; Leder, 1990; Stallings, 1985). Researchers have also shown that, when working in small groups in mathematics classes, girls receive less information from their peers than boys do (Webb & Kenderski, 1985; Wilkinson, Lindow, & Chiang, 1985).

One observer reported that, in seventh-grade, lower-track math and science classrooms, boys received more attention than girls in the form of simple interactions with teachers (Martin, 2001). Girls received more complex interactions (interactions that involved lengthy explanations or substantial conversation) than boys, but it was the boys who dominated teachers' time and attention. She noted, for example, that in one class the teacher made consistent eye contact with the all-boy second row, while frequently turning his back on the all-girl first row and called on boys first when hands were raised. Boys were warned repeatedly before being punished when they broke the rules or disrupted the class; girls were ignored or spoken to quietly for similar behavior.

Further evidence of the importance of training and practice on mathematics achievement comes from findings showing that the international gap in math achievement between the United States and China and Japan is far greater than the average male–female gap observed within countries. Researchers who tested kindergarten, first-grade, and fifth-grade children in these three countries found no differences in reading or general intelligence, but they did find increasing international differences in mathematics performance with increasing age. (No significant male–female differences in mathematics performance were found for any of the grade levels.) American first graders were surpassed by those in China and Japan by an average of 10% on a standard math test. By the fifth grade, the top American class scored on average below the lowest Japanese class and the second-lowest Chinese class. Of the 100 highest-scoring fifth graders, only one was American (Stevenson, Lee, & Stigler, 1986).

Rather than looking for biological explanations, as they might have done had they been reporting gender differences, these researchers sought social explanations for these vast international differences. What they discovered is that Chinese and Japanese students receive more formal school training in mathematics than their American counterparts: They spend 240 days a year in school compared to the Americans' 180. Also, Japanese and Chinese parents give their children more help with math homework than U.S. parents give theirs. The basis for the difference in parental actions can be found in their beliefs about the reasons for academic success: American parents attribute success more often to ability; Chinese and Japanese parents attribute it to effort.

Spatial performance too appears to be affected by relevant experience. A study of college undergraduates revealed that, for women, performance on the Mental Rotation Test was significantly positively correlated with previous participation in spatial activities and computer experience (Quaiser-Pohl & Lehmann, 2002).

For verbal skills as well, evidence points to the impact of specific training. Starting in infancy, females are vocalized to more often than males, which may, in turn, lead to increased vocalization by female infants (Bee, Mitchell, Barnard, Eyres, & Hammond, 1984; Maccoby & Jacklin, 1974). Regardless of the reason for the original difference, the two processes probably act in an ever-strengthening feedback loop to increase females' experience and practice with speech production skills at an early age.

This pattern does not seem to hold across cultures, however. In Greece, where there is strong cultural preference for male over female infants, mothers speak more affectionately to male than female infants, and home-reared male infants seem to be more vocally responsive and interactive with their mothers than females do—a finding researchers have speculatively linked to other studies showing that Greek males tend to outperform females in cognitive tasks, even verbal ones (Roe, Drivas, Karagellis, & Roe, 1985). Even in North America, some research shows that, by the time children are toddlers, mothers' speech to boys and girls differs significantly on dimensions thought to stimulate cognitive development. Mothers' communication to their sons includes more questions, more numbers, more verbal teaching, and more action verbs than their communication to their daughters does (Weitzman, Birns, & Friend, 1985), and parents discuss emotions more with daughters than with sons (Adams, Kuebli, Boyle, & Fivush, 1995). It is becoming increasingly clear that early parent–child interactions have an impact on a child's cognitive development and that these interactions may differ in many subtle ways for girls and boys. Much more research is needed to understand just how this process works.

GENDER-ROLE SOCIALIZATION   In North America, feminine and masculine gender roles fit neatly into the observed pattern of performance differences between women and men. Even among children and adolescents, mathematics and technical and mechanical pursuits based on spatial ability are thought to be masculine domains, whereas verbal and artistic skills are considered feminine (S. L. Boswell, 1985). A study of elementary school students in Taiwan, Japan, and the United States found that as early as first grade children and their mothers in all three countries believe boys are better at mathematics and girls are better at reading (Lummis & Stevenson, 1990). Teachers also stereotype mathematics as a male domain (Keller, 2001).

From preschool onward, children set very gender-stereotypic occupational goals and are encouraged in gender-stereotyped interests (Archer, 1984; Franken, 1983; Koeller, Baumert, & Schnable, 2001). An examination of children's school-subject preferences in the United States, Japan, and Taiwan showed that in all three cultures boys prefer math, science, and sports, whereas girls prefer music, art, and language arts (Evans, Schweingruber, & Stevenson, 2002). These preferences play a role in achievement: The more interested children are in a subject, the better their test performance. Variations in the size of the gender difference in preferences across the three cultures led the researchers to conclude that "cultural variations in socialization and schooling practices can minimize or exaggerate gender differences in interests and achievement scores" (p. 166). These findings are not surprising given that the activities and toys encouraged for boys and girls are so different.

Boys are given more mechanical toys such as models and tools; not only do such toys encourage the development of spatial ability but their definition as "boys' toys" encourages the attitude that this type of ability is a masculine one. In one study of sixth-grade students, boys reported more experience with a wide variety of tools such as batteries, electric toys, fuses, microscopes, and pulleys, and girls said they had more experience with activities such as bread making, knitting, sewing, and planting seeds (Jones, Howe, & Rua, 2000). When asked about their interests, the boys were more likely to list atomic bombs, atoms, cars, computers, X rays, and technology; the girls were more likely to list animal communication, rainbows, healthy eating, weather, and AIDS. It has also been found that fathers and mothers tend to encourage gender-stereotypic play and choice of toys with their sons and daughters—a pattern that is bound to result in girls' having fewer opportunities than boys to engage in play that involves mechanical and spatial skills (Caldera, Huston, & O'Brien, 1989).

The fact that children learn to label various tasks as *masculine* or *feminine* is clearly relevant to their performance on these tasks. Children perform better, work longer and harder, and evaluate the appeal of the same task as greater when it is labeled appropriate to their own gender than when it is labeled appropriate to the other gender (Davies, 1989/90; Hargreaves, Bates, & Foot, 1985), although some researchers have found the effect of gender-typed labeling to be stronger for boys than girls. For both sexes, mathematics achievement in elementary and junior high school is positively correlated with the belief that mathematics is gender-role appropriate (Paulsen & Johnson, 1983). The impact of gender labeling of tasks can be seen even more clearly when cultures are compared. In cultures that label reading a masculine-appropriate skill, for example, males' performance on reading and vocabulary tests equals or exceeds that of females (Finn, 1980).

The gender appropriateness of particular academic subjects may be conveyed through the gender of the teacher. Because beginning in junior high school more mathematics teachers are male and more English teachers are female, the notion that math is for boys and English is for girls may be reinforced. Certainly, by the time students reach the college level, courses in mathematics, the physical sciences, and engineering are far more likely to be taught by male than by female professors and to be dominated by male students. Female students often report that they feel excluded and out of place in such courses (Seymour, 1995).

The impact of gender labeling of academic subjects has potentially serious implications beyond immediate academic performance because it can affect children's course choices and thus, eventually, their career paths. The avoidance of mathematics courses in high school closes a number of college study options for women, thus helping to perpetuate male–female segregation into different careers. Actually, males are more likely than females to stereotype mathematics as a male domain (Hyde, Fennema, Ryan, Frost, & Hopp, 1990). It is likely that, especially during adolescence, females are sensitive to these male stereotypes and may avoid mathematics and technical subjects in response to them (Lips & Temple, 1990).

SELF-CONFIDENCE   Some of the effects of gender-role socialization on cognitive performance may have their impact through gender differences in self-confidence. Simply labeling a task "for girls" or "for boys" raises the expectations of the "appropriate" group for success on that task. Males are more likely to expect to do well on masculine tasks and in masculine intellectual areas (Crandall, 1969; Deaux & Emswiller, 1974). Females are more confident of success on feminine-typed tests, such as verbal ones, and less confident on masculine-typed tests, such as spatial ones (Lenney, 1977).

In high school and college, males have more self-confidence than females do in their mathematical, scientific, and technical abilities (J. R. Campbell, 1991; Hyde, Fennema, Ryan, et al., 1990; Lips, 2002; Seymour, 1995). Even when girls are doing well in mathematics, they do not feel competent, perhaps because they are so often surrounded, in academic settings, with people who do not think females can do well in mathematics and technical areas. For example, one study of Canadian elementary school students revealed that the girls and boys performed equally well on tests of mathematics achievement, but the girls were more likely than the boys to express less confidence relative to their actual achievement (Lloyd, Walsh, & Yailagh, 2005). A recent study of U.S. high school students found that, despite only small gender gaps in a few areas of mathematics achievement, female students had more negative attitudes and self-concepts with respect to mathematics than males did (McGraw, Lubienski, & Strutchens, 2006). In one study of male and female engineering students, the women rated themselves as currently stronger in mathematics and science than the men did; however, the women rated the possibility of a future for themselves in math and science areas lower than the men did (Lips, 2000b).

Male students tend to believe females are not talented in mathematics and science (Seymour, 1995), and teachers have generally lower expectations of female than male students in these fields (Fennema, Peterson, Carpenter, & Lubinski, 1990; Seymour, 1995). In fact, when teachers are asked to nominate their most successful math students, they tend to choose males disproportionately and inaccurately—overestimating how well male students will perform (Fennema et al., 1990; Walkerdine, 1989) and underestimating how well females will perform (Kissane, 1986).

All of these factors may contribute to girls' and women's experience of stereotype threat (Steele, 1997), a tendency to perform poorly in situations in which individuals fear they will be judged by or are at risk of confirming a negative stereotype about their gender (discussed at length in Chapter 1). Many studies of high school and university students now show that in testing situations in which the stereotype that "girls/women aren't good at math" is relevant, girls' and women's performance suffers. If the stereotype is made especially salient, such as by telling participants that the test has shown gender differences in the past, females perform poorly and may even protect their self-esteem by attributing their poor performance to stress or to a "tricky" or unfair test (Keller, 2002). However, in the case of a well-known stereotype such as this one, there need not be an explicit reminder of the stereotype in order for it to affect performance. In fact, the only effective way to counteract the effects of stereotype threat seems to be to "nullify" the stereotype: to state explicitly that it does not hold in this situation. When respondents were told explicitly that no gender differences had been found on the mathematics test they were about to take, the females performed significantly better than they did under other conditions (Smith & White, 2002).

Where do gender differences in mathematics self-confidence come from? Research suggests these differences come from parents, teachers, and peers. For example, parents seem to expect more from their children in gender-stereotypic areas. Thus, for instance, parents expect higher achievement from sons than from daughters in mathematics and credit sons with more talent than daughters for successful mathematics performance (Yee & Eccles, 1988). Particularly in the realm of mathematics achievement, research shows that parents' differential expectations for their sons and daughters are communicated to their children at a young age (Entwisle & Baker, 1983). After tracking 1,100 children semester by semester over the first three grades, these researchers noted that, despite the fact that the boys' arithmetic marks or general aptitude did not exceed girls' in first grade, boys developed higher expectations for their performance in mathematics than girls did. These higher expectations do not seem to be based on past performance or teachers' evaluations but rather on parents' expectations for their children's performance. Other research also shows that parents' beliefs about their children's math aptitude may be better predictors of the children's attitudes toward math than measures of past performance are (Eccles, 1993; Jacobs & Weisz, 1994; Fredricks & Eccles, 2002) and that parental expectations are a significant predictor of high school students' decisions to participate in advanced mathematics classes (Ma, 2001).

Confidence may also be sapped by a steady drip of messages in educational or professional settings that one is not expected to be competent or to perform well. Women who have "made it" in scientific careers often remember that it was not a single dramatic incident that hampered their self-confidence but a series of smaller events. For instance, Meg Urry (2005), now a professor of physics and director of the Yale Center for Astronomy and Astrophysics, wrote recently of her experiences as a student of physics. She remembered professors having conversations in her presence about "inferior" women scientists hired because of affirmative action, a professor illustrating his lectures about optical imaging with a photograph of a seminude woman, of being told she was feeling alienated because of her "difficult personality." Any one of these and other events could have been shrugged off, she commented, but the accumulation became dampening for her self-confidence. "Discrimination isn't a thunderbolt," she wrote, "it isn't an abrupt slap in the face. It's the slow drumbeat of being underappreciated, feeling uncomfortable and encountering roadblocks along the path to success . . . [that] . . . make women feel out of place" (p. B4). Urry is now a confident, successful scientist at a top institution—but how many women have been deterred from a scientific career by the kinds of subtle discrimination she describes?

MOTIVATION   A potentially useful framework for understanding gender differences in achievement choices is the expectancy/value model developed by Jacquelynn Eccles and her colleagues (Eccles, 1985; Eccles [Parsons] et al., 1983). The model proposes that the decision to pursue achievement in a particular area is most directly linked to expectation for success and to the importance or value an individual attaches to achievement in that area. See Figure 6.4. We have already seen that male and female expectations for success may differ for mathematical, verbal, and spatial tasks. Do the sexes also differ in the value they attach to success in these areas?

There is some evidence from studies of achievement in mathematics and science that males and females do differ in the way they attach values to various achievement activities. As early as the seventh grade, boys see mathematics as more useful than girls do (Eccles, Wigfield, Harold, & Blumenfeld, 1993; Fennema & Sherman, 1977; Marsh & Yeung, 1998), and in college, women have difficulty imagining themselves in science careers (Lips & Asquith, 1995).

Reflections

Gender and Science: A View From Both Sides

If you ask Dr. Ben Barres of the Stanford University School of Medicine whether discrimination against women exists in science fields, he will answer with an unhesitating "Yes." He will go on to cite statistics about peer reviewers awarding lower competence scores to female than to similarly qualified male scientists and about the ways competitive selection processes in science have been dominated by male judges. In fact, he has done just this in a 2006 article in the prestigious science journal *Nature*. Yet more than most men, Dr. Barres is in a position to understand the ways in which discrimination—rather than an absence of ability—may explain why fewer women than men have achieved scientific eminence. Dr. Barres is a transgendered person who started university as a young woman and now has changed sex, so he has literally experienced the issue from both sides.

As an undergraduate, when Barres (then she) was the only student in a large class of mainly men to solve a difficult problem, he remembers the professor's reaction: "Your boyfriend must have solved it for you." He remembers, as a female, losing a prestigious graduate fellowship to a male student even though, according to the Harvard dean who read both proposals, Barres had a much stronger application. And he recalls that, just after he had made the transition from female to male, he overheard one faculty member comment that "Ben Barres gave a great seminar today, but then his work is much better than his sister's" (p. 134).

Barres was motivated to write his commentary on gender discrimination in science by the furor over a controversial speech by Harvard President Lawrence Summers (2005). Summers, addressing an audience of academics, opined that there were fewer women than men in science fields for three reasons: (1) women are less willing than men to make the sacrifices of family and leisure time necessary for a top-level scientific career; (2) more men than women are innately very high in the abilities relevant to high-level scientific work; and (3) there is some discrimination against women in science. Many female scientists responded with fury to the notion that discrimination was a third and more controversial explanation for the problem than biological differences and lack of commitment. Barres's perspective, however, is unique.

As a transgendered person, Barres notes that he has tremendous respect for the impact of biology on male–female differences. He believes that his transgendered identity was prompted by fetal exposure to high doses of a testosteronelike drug. He noted that his own spatial abilities improved when he began taking testosterone treatment as part of his female-to-male transition. Yet, he comments, "By far, the main difference that I have noticed is that people who don't know I am transgendered treat me with much more respect. I can even complete a whole sentence without being interrupted by a man" (p. 135). Barres, like many of his female colleagues, argues that, although there are certainly biological differences between women and men—maybe even some that are relevant to cognitive abilities—the most important reason for the discrepancy between women's and men's participation in science is that women and men have been treated differently.

Figure 6.4 Theory of subjective task value and achievement (adapted from Wigfield & Eccles, 1992). According to subjective task value theory, four aspects of task value contribute to the likelihood that an individual will engage in a particular task. People tend to engage in tasks they positively value and avoid tasks they negatively value.

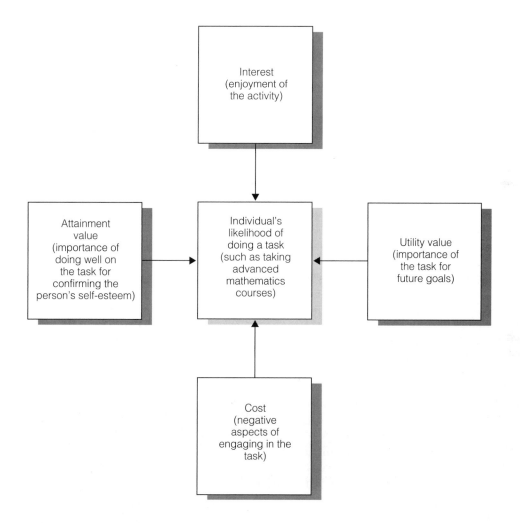

Among high school students, the value males attach to mathematics achievement is strongly related to their performance history: The better they have done in the past, the more highly they value mathematics achievement (Eccles, 1985). For females, the value placed on mathematics achievement is much more independent of their past performance. College women's enrollment in mathematics and science courses is strongly predicted by their reported enjoyment of learning science and mathematics and by positive experiences in such courses (Lips, 1996). Eccles (1987) suggested that gender roles influence achievement patterns mainly through their effect on the value that females and males attach to different achievement options.

Other research supports the idea that task value is an important determinant of achievement behavior and that males and females differ in the factors that influence these values. One study of mathematics and science participation among female college students found that the reason given most often for avoidance of math and science was a lack of interest in and enjoyment of these academic subjects (that is, low intrinsic value)—a reason that was cited far more often than perceived difficulty or lack of career relevance (Lips, 1984). Female students may not enjoy their classes in mathematical and scientific fields because they feel their approaches to learning and problem solving are not welcomed or valued in these classes. For example, Turkle and Papert (1990) examined the reactions of first-year Harvard University students as they negotiated their first computer programming course. The students were instructed to adopt a formal approach to programming that required breaking the problem into parts. This approach felt alien to many students, particularly the women. They were discouraged from adopting a more holistic approach, even though that would have been equally effective. Consequently, they became alienated from their work and did not enjoy the class.

In a study of computer-related attitudes among college students, women's intentions to major in computer science were related more strongly to interest in and enjoyment of computers than to a more pragmatic desire to find a high-paying, advancement-oriented job, but the reverse pattern was true for men (Lips & Temple, 1990). Research shows, as well, that one reason for college males' greater tendency to choose courses and career goals in mathematics and science is their concern with status and success. College men and women see science careers as equally difficult and demanding, but men seem to see that demandingness as a more positive feature than women do (Lips, 1992). Thus females and males, at least in high school and college, may be motivated by different factors in their pursuit of achievement in mathematical, scientific, and technical fields. The precise origin of these differences, how they affect performance, whether they extend to other areas, and how early they begin to appear are all matters that await further investigation.

The four social/affective factors discussed in this section—training, gender-role socialization, self-confidence, and motivation—work in interlocking ways to help produce small performance differences between males and females in certain verbal, mathematical, and visual-spatial tasks. Girls and boys are taught, implicitly and explicitly, that mathematical and visual-spatial tasks are masculine and that verbal tasks are feminine. In concert with this differential labeling goes differential training, starting with parental vocalization to infants and toddlers and continuing with gender-typed toys and activities and different amounts of teaching in school. The labeling also produces gender differences, both in self-confidence on these tasks and in the value attached to achievement in these areas, which, in turn, relate to decisions about trying to achieve and to performance itself.

Social-environmental factors clearly overshadow ability differences between women and men in determining achievement in various fields. One way to get a feel for this is to examine the distribution of prestigious awards such as the Nobel prizes in science and literature. Males have dominated these awards in the areas of science, in which women have won just over 2% of the total number of prizes in physics, chemistry, and physiology and medicine since the awards began in 1901—a male-to-female ratio greater than 43 to 1. Some might argue that this distribution reflects male superiority in quantitative and spatial abilities, but these ability differences are far less dramatic than

Overview — Social-affective explanations for gender differences in cognitive performance

Social-Affective Factor	*Impact*
Training and experience	• For both sexes, there is a positive relationship between experience and performance on visual-spatial, verbal, and quantitative tasks. • It is important to remember that, even when males and females are in the same classroom, they do not necessarily receive the same training.
Gender-role socialization	• Parents, teachers, and peers often reinforce stereotypes about male–female differences in cognitive abilities, and children learn early to label certain tasks *feminine* and certain tasks *masculine*. • A great deal of research shows that students express more interest in and perform better in realms that they have learned are "appropriate" for their gender.
Self-confidence	• Both males and females display more confidence and better performance on tests on which they think their own gender group usually does better. • Stereotype threat can affect performance whenever there is a well-known stereotype, even when that stereotype is not made explicit.
Motivation	• Both females and males are more motivated to perform well in areas to which they attach value (e.g., areas they like or that are important for future goals). • The two groups have sometimes learned to attach different values to achievement in particular areas, such as mathematics.

the ratio of male to female prize-winners. However, in literature—a field based on verbal abilities, which are not claimed to be superior in men—women won fewer than 17% of the Nobel prizes awarded over the last century, which is a ratio greater than 9.5 to 1 in favor of men (Lips, 1999). Men's domination of both sets of awards is so striking that it is impossible to attribute it only to gender differences in cognitive abilities—particularly in the case of literature, in which there is no indication at all of superior male ability.

SUMMARY

Despite psychology's long history of searching for intellectual differences between the sexes, such differences have, for the most part, proved relatively modest and elusive. There is some evidence for male–female differences in sensation and perception: Females outscore males on tests of perceptual speed and accuracy and are more sensitive than males to changes in sound intensity. Under lighted conditions, males seem to be more sensitive than females to changes in the intensity of visual stimuli.

Most of the recent research attention has, however, concentrated on cognitive rather than perceptual performance differences. Traditionally, males and females have been thought to differ in their performance on verbal, quantitative, and visual-spatial tasks. Generally speaking, research now shows a tendency for females to outscore males on tasks that require certain verbal skills and small differences favoring males on mathematical problem-solving tasks and tasks requiring spatial perception. A somewhat larger difference favoring males is found for visual-spatial tasks that require rapid mental rotation of pictures or objects. For these broad areas of cognitive performance—verbal, quantitative, and visual-spatial—the presence and magnitude of a gender difference depends on the specific aspect of performance being tested and the specific population being studied. Given the current state of the research, it is no longer appropriate to make general statements about one gender outperforming the other in one of these three broad areas. As for the specific differences that have been observed, none are anywhere near large enough to explain the disproportionate number of males as compared to females in the scientific and technical professions.

Psychologists have spent a great deal of energy trying to explain gender differences in certain aspects of verbal, mathematical, and visual-spatial performance. A number of biological mechanisms have been postulated as causal factors: direct action of circulating sex hormones, sensitizing effects of prenatal hormones on the developing brain, and the degree of lateralization of specific functions in the left and right hemispheres of the brain. At present, new evidence is emerging in support of some aspects of the circulating-hormones hypothesis, and, under the glare of a great deal of research attention, the hypothesis linking cognitive performance differences to greater lateralization of functions in the male than in the female brain has begun to look overly simplistic. Some evidence suggests, however, that particular abilities may be organized differently—some more diffusely and some more focally—in female and male brains.

Several social/affective factors appear to play interlocking roles in helping produce gender differences in cognitive performance. Some verbal tasks are gender-typed as feminine, whereas mathematical and certain visual-spatial tasks are labeled masculine. As a consequence of this labeling, boys and girls receive different amounts of direct training and parental encouragement for achievement in these areas. The labeling, training, and parental support all influence children's self-confidence and the value they attach to success on particular tasks, which, in turn, influence performance. These social/affective factors, in interaction with whatever biological predispositions toward gender differences exist, help increase gender differences in performance. Yet despite all these pressures in the direction of differences, the result is only a small to moderate gender gap on a few cognitive tests. For tasks in all three cognitive areas, the gap is most noticeable at the top extreme of the performance distribution on certain kinds of tests or tasks. Sizable gender differences continue to be observed in curricular and career choices; however, it appears that these differences have little to do with cognitive abilities and much to do with gender-related expectations and cultural barriers to participation.

None of the research discussed in this chapter provides any justification whatsoever for sex discrimination in education, employment, the law, or any of our social institutions or for the segregation of jobs according to gender. The finding that gender differences in abilities are so few in number and so small in size indicates clearly that individual differences rather than gender differences are the ones to be kept in mind when deciding what educational programs are best suited to various people, what roles each spouse should play in a marital relationship, or who is the best person for a particular type of job. As a favorite women's movement slogan puts it, "The best man for the job is often a woman," and we might add, "The best woman for the job is often a man."

KEY TERMS

spatial visualization	spatiotemporal ability	corpus callosum
spatial perception	cerebral cortex	lateralization
mental rotation		

7

Sexual Lives and Orientations

*W*omen need a reason to have sex," muses Billy Crystal's character, Mitch, in the movie *City Slickers*. "Men just need a place." This comment reflects something of the popular opinion about gender differences in a realm in which such differences may seem especially relevant: the realm of sexuality.

Two of the best-known sexual stereotypes, particularly in the context of heterosexuality, are the reluctant, uninterested female and the male who is always ready. Such beliefs in fundamental male–female differences in sexual response, drive, and desires have served as a justification for practices and institutions as diverse as prostitution, stag parties, "men's magazines," romance novels, men-only clubs, and the custom of veiling women from head to toe in certain cultures. Basic to the gender stereotypes about sexuality has been the notion that men have a much stronger sex drive than women do. Conveniently paired with this belief has been the idea that there are two kinds of women: the promiscuous, seductive ones, who tempt men away from their more important pursuits and who fill the roles of prostitutes and performers in pornographic films, and the virtuous ones, who are restrained and selective in their sexual behavior. Although such stereotypes have begun to fade in some quarters, there are many indications that people expect women and men to differ in their approach to sexuality.

How do these expectations relate to the research findings about male and female sexuality? This chapter presents some answers by examining the following:

- Is there a "double standard" used to judge sexual behavior?
- How does the physiology of sexual response differ for women and men?
- What does research say about frequency and type of sexual activity?
- Do women and men differ in sexual motives, values, and attitudes?
- How can we understand sexual orientation?
- How can we explain behaviors including pornography, rape, and sexual abuse that link sexuality to destructive power?

THE DOUBLE STANDARD

The **double standard** refers to just that: two different standards of sexual behavior, one for women and one for men. It is based on the assumption that males have a greater desire and need for sexual activity than females do. This supposed difference in males' and females' need for sex makes it seem appropriate, in a heterosexual context, for men to be the sexual aggressors and pursuers and for women to be the sexual gatekeepers, making sure things do not get out of hand. Believers in the double standard do not hold a man responsible for pushing an unwilling woman to engage in sexual activity; rather, they maintain it is the woman's responsibility to set limits. *He* supposedly cannot help himself; *she*, with her supposedly weaker sex drive, can.

This set of assumptions carries enormous implications for the sexual behavior and experience of women and men and for the power relationship between them. It trivializes women's sexual feelings, refusing to allow for the possibility that female sexual desire is important in its own right. It trivializes men's capacity for self-control, suggesting that men are helpless before their sexual impulses. It means that women more than men risk ruined reputations by becoming known as sexually active, that men more than women risk ruined reputations by becoming known as sexually inactive, and that women who have been sexually assaulted, harassed, or raped are often blamed for their own victimization. Fallout from the double standard may include men's failure to learn to take responsibility for controlling their sexual behavior, women's failure to learn about their own capacity for sexual pleasure, and a reluctance of sexual partners to communicate with each other about their feelings.

Despite its long history, the double standard is not rooted in fact. Women and men are very similar in the physiology of sexual response, and women have an enormous capacity for sexual pleasure. It may be, in fact, that the gender differences we observe in sexual behavior are a result of the different ways social disapproval is dished out to women and men because of the double standard and of women's awareness that if sexual activity results in pregnancy, their lives will be the ones most dramatically affected.

THE PHYSIOLOGY OF SEXUAL RESPONSE

Until the 1960s most people's knowledge about the body's response to sexual arousal was limited to their own (and what they could tell about their partners') experience. Because sexuality was considered an extremely private matter, the idea that researchers could actually observe and measure people engaged in sexual activity in the laboratory was unthinkable. However, in 1966, the pioneers of this type of research, William Masters and Virginia Johnson, published data on 382 women and 312 men whom they had observed in thousands of cycles of sexual arousal and orgasm (Masters & Johnson, 1966).

Sexual Response: Four Phases

One thing Masters and Johnson did not find was a fundamental difference between women and men in their physiological patterns of sexual arousal and orgasm. For both sexes, the physical response to sexual stimulation was described as four phases: excitement, plateau, orgasm, and resolution. The two basic physiological processes involved in these phases are **vasocongestion** (the accumulation of blood in the blood vessels of a particular region) and **myotonia** (muscle contraction). The four phases identified by Masters and Johnson, described in the following sections, are diagrammed for females and males in Figures 7.1 and 7.2.

EXCITEMENT   The initial **excitement phase** can be triggered by any of a variety of sexually arousing stimuli. Vasocongestion of the genital organs begins to occur. In males, this increased blood flow to the genitals causes the penis to become erect, a reaction that tends to occur within a few seconds of the stimulation. In females, the increased blood flow causes fluids to seep through the membranes of the vaginal walls, producing lubrication. This lubrication, which signals the beginning of arousal, begins within 30 seconds after the arousing stimuli. The glands of the clitoris also swell as a result of vasocongestion. In both sexes, the nipples may harden and become erect as a result of contraction in muscle fibers.

During the excitement phase, the labia swell and the upper two-thirds of the vagina expands. In males, the scrotum is pulled closer to the body and the testes begin to be elevated. In both males and females, there is an increase in heart rate and blood pressure. Although this phase is governed by the same physiological processes for males and females—vasocongestion and myotonia—the different anatomies of the two sexes dictate different physical and social consequences. The erect penis cannot be ignored as easily as the moist vagina.

Figure 7.1 The stages of sexual response in human females.

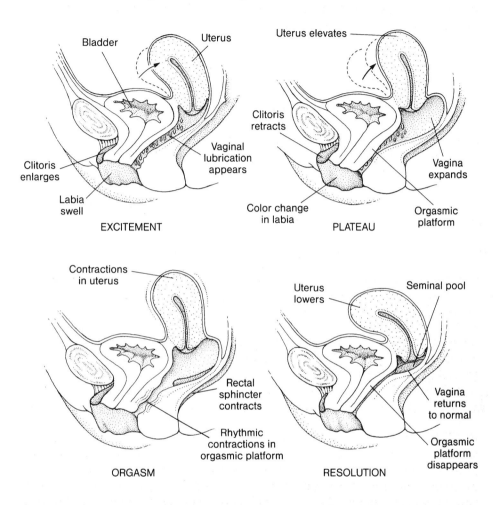

PLATEAU   If sexual stimulation continues with sufficient intensity, a peak level of vasocongestion is reached in the **plateau phase.** Rate of breathing, pulse rate, and blood pressure increase further. A male's penis becomes fully erect, and the testes swell and are further elevated. In females, the clitoris retracts, the labia deepen in color, and the tissues surrounding the outer third of the vagina swell to form the "orgasmic platform"—a change that has the effect of narrowing the opening to the vagina. As stimulation continues, both vasocongestion and myotonia continue to build toward the tension required for orgasm. If stimulation is withdrawn before orgasm, the person enters directly into the resolution phase. However, without the discharge of tension that occurs in orgasm, the resolution phase progresses slowly and can be quite uncomfortable. Men

Figure 7.2   The stages of sexual response in human males.

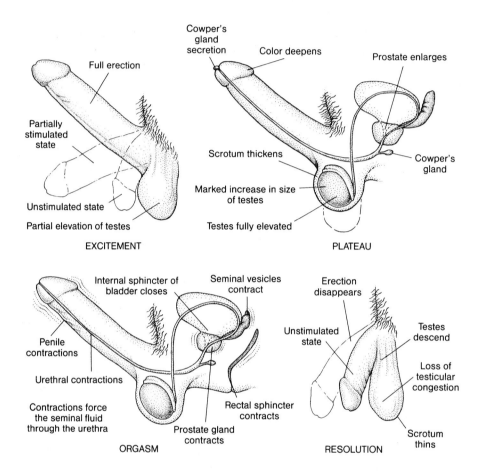

call this condition "blue balls"; women do not seem to have an equivalent phrase, despite the fact that, as will be discussed later in the chapter, not reaching orgasm is a more common experience for them than for men.

ORGASM   In both sexes, when arousal reaches a critical point, it triggers **orgasm,** a series of involuntary rhythmic contractions of the pelvic organs. For males, the first part of orgasm involves the contraction of the vas, seminal vesicles, and prostate to force the semen into position in a bulb at the base of the urethra. Once this has happened, ejaculation is inevitable. Next, the bulb and the penis begin rhythmic contractions, causing the ejaculation of the semen.

For females, orgasm is a series of contractions of the orgasmic platform and the uterus. Surrounding muscles may also contract. In both sexes, pulse rate, blood pressure, and breathing increase sharply, and muscles throughout the body, such as of legs, thighs, and back, may contract. The whole process lasts only a few seconds. Some research suggested that some women also ejaculate during orgasm (Perry & Whipple, 1981). These researchers discovered a fluid that is chemically similar to seminal fluid spurting from the urethra during orgasm in a few women. Female ejaculation has been speculatively linked to an area called the **G-spot** (in honor of a physician named Grafenburg, who first raised the possibility that this area was an especially sensitive one), located on the top side of the vagina halfway between the back of the pubic bone and the cervix. The whole notion of female ejaculation is still very controversial, however. The G-spot cannot be located for all women, and even among those for whom it can be, there is not always evidence of ejaculation. In some studies, chemical analysis of the fluid ejaculated by women found it to be similar to urine (Alzate & Hoch, 1986; Goldberg et al., 1983). However, several other studies have found the fluid to be different from urine (Whipple, 2000). Questions about ejaculation aside, some sex researchers continue to be intrigued by the possibility that, at least for some women, stimulation of the anterior wall of the vagina is an important aspect of sexual arousal (McCormick, 1994).

Whether or not the sexual partners experience simultaneous orgasm and whether there is a partner at all, orgasm is the same physiological process. For females, however, there is greater individual variation in duration and intensity of orgasm than there is for males. Also, for women, orgasm achieved through masturbation appears to be more intense than orgasm from intercourse, probably because a woman has better control over the type and intensity of stimulation during masturbation.

People would not go to so much trouble to have orgasms if they were simply a set of muscular contractions. The sensations of orgasm are very intense and pleasurable, and the release of sexual tension leaves the individual feeling satisfied and relaxed. These feelings are much the same for women and men. In one study, male and female college students gave written descriptions of what an orgasm felt like. A panel of experts (doctors and psychologists) who read the descriptions could not reliably distinguish between those that had been written by women and those that had been written by men (Vance & Wagner, 1976).

RESOLUTION   Following orgasm, the body enters the **resolution phase.** The processes that led up to orgasm—vasocongestion and myotonia—are reversed. Muscular tension is relaxed, and blood is released from the engorged blood vessels. In women, the clitoris shrinks to its normal size, the orgasmic platform relaxes, and the vagina and uterus return to normal. In men, the erection of the penis is lost, and the scrotum and testes return to normal. In both sexes, pulse rate, breathing, and blood pressure gradually return to unaroused levels.

Resolution usually takes 15 to 30 minutes after orgasm. However, when orgasm has not occurred, it can take up to an hour. Among women who frequently experience sexual arousal without orgasm, the buildup of vasocongestion without discharge by orgasm can produce a great deal of discomfort.

One notable sex difference in response occurs in the resolution phase: Men experience a **refractory period,** lasting from a few minutes to 24 hours, during which they typically cannot be restimulated to erection and orgasm. No such refractory period occurs for women, making it possible for them to experience multiple orgasms.

LIMITATIONS OF MASTERS AND JOHNSON'S RESEARCH   The   four phases of sexual response Masters and Johnson described are commonly spoken of as "the human sexual response cycle." The physiological responses they identify are undoubtedly characteristic of many instances of sexual arousal, but there are many reasons to doubt their vision of this cycle as universal.

Leonore Tiefer (1995) noted a number of biases in the way participants were selected for this research. First, to be accepted as a research participant, a person had to have a history of achieving orgasm through masturbation and sexual intercourse. Thus anyone who did not masturbate or who did not regularly have orgasms from intercourse was excluded from the study. Second, the researchers deliberately sought a sample of participants who were above average in intelligence, education, and socioeconomic status. Third, volunteers for the study were characterized by a strong interest in effective sexual performance and a willingness to have that performance observed and analyzed, probably making them different from the general population. All of these selection biases make it difficult to be sure that the sexual responses observed by Masters and Johnson are characteristic of human beings in general rather than of a particular population. Of particular concern, according to Tiefer, is the probability that the women who participated were less representative of women in general than the male participants were of men in general. Why? Because, as we will see later in this chapter, women are less likely to masturbate and are less consistent in experiencing orgasm—both requirements for inclusion in the study—than men are.

There are other problems as well. Participants who did not experience orgasm in the laboratory were reassured and coached to help "improve" their future performance. Participants were clearly exposed to a strong message that only certain sexual responses were adequate and that effective sexual stimulation was stimulation that led to those responses. In general, the research seems oriented toward confirming a particular model of human sexual response rather than exploring the potential diversity of such response.

Critics have also assailed the assumptions implicit in the Masters and Johnson model, particularly the reduction of sexual activity to physiological responses and the omission of sexual desire, attraction, and emotions. Tiefer (1995) argued that the seemingly gender-neutral model actually favors a male approach to sexuality by focusing on the physical aspects of sexuality and leaving out the emotional and intimacy aspects that women are trained to value.

The Masters and Johnson model, she noted, "assumes that men and women have and want the same kind of sexuality since physiological research suggests that, in some ways and under selected test conditions, we are built the same. Yet our social realities dictate that we are not all the same sexually—not in our socially shaped wishes, in our sexual self-development, or in our interpersonal sexual meanings" (p. 56).

Sexual Response: Issues

THE MYTH OF THE VAGINAL ORGASM   One of the most popular misconceptions about orgasm, arising from Freudian theory, was that women can experience two distinct kinds of orgasm: one kind resulting from clitoral stimulation and a different (better) kind resulting from stimulation of the vagina by the penis during intercourse. As mentioned in Chapter 2, Freud believed that part of the psychological maturation process for women involved abandoning the attainment of orgasm through clitoral stimulation and shifting to a preference for orgasm attained through heterosexual intercourse. Indeed, his theory characterized the clitoral orgasm as "infantile," and many women seeking to avoid this label spent hours (and fortunes!) in psychiatrists' offices trying to figure out what unconscious fixation was blocking them from reaching orgasm with their partners without clitoral stimulation.

Masters and Johnson's research undercut the distinction between the clitoral and vaginal orgasm by showing that there is no physiological difference between orgasms that occur during intercourse and those that occur as a result of manual or oral stimulation of the clitoris. In fact, almost all orgasms involve stimulation of the clitoris. The vagina is a relatively insensitive organ—a useful feature given that one of its main functions is to serve as the route through which childbirth occurs. It is, however, sensitive to pressure, and it is this sensitivity that makes insertion of the penis pleasurable. As well, the G-spot may be responsible for vaginal-based arousal or even orgasm (Whipple, 2000). The clitoris, which grows from the same fetal structure as the penis (see Chapter 5), is an exquisitely sensitive organ—so sensitive, in fact, that direct contact can be painful. Vaginal intercourse can indirectly stimulate the clitoris by pulling on the inner labia, which in turn causes the clitoral hood to move back and forth against the clitoris. Thus clitoral stimulation is usually what triggers orgasm, and the distinction between the clitoral and vaginal orgasm does not make sense.

Perhaps one of the reasons people have been confused about the roles of the vagina and clitoris in producing orgasm is that most of the clitoris is so well hidden. It was less than a decade ago that a team of researchers, led by Australian surgeon Helen O'Connell, discovered that the clitoris is much more than the small mound of flesh that can be seen when a woman's vulva is examined (O'Connell, Hutson, Anderson, & Plenter, 1998). In fact, the clitoris is 10 times larger than it looks: Under the visible tip of the clitoris, hidden behind the pubic bone and a layer of flesh, is a much larger mass of erectile tissue that contains blood vessels and nerves—all part of the clitoris.

Why has it taken so long for the true size of the clitoris to be discovered? One possibility is that earlier research was done by examining the cadavers of older women, in whom the erectile tissue had shrunk. Another is that, until the recent increase in the number of women doing medical research, no one was curious enough about female sexuality to investigate carefully.

MULTIPLE ORGASM   In the sample studied by Masters and Johnson, women did not enter a refractory period after orgasm, and many women were capable of having a series of orgasms within a short period of time. During the resolution phase, if a woman is stimulated again she can often be aroused, return to the excitement or plateau phase, and have another orgasm. Much less stimulation is required for these subsequent orgasms although they can be just as intense as the first, and the cycle can be repeated several times. Masters and Johnson found that, using masturbation, some women could have 5 to 20 orgasms—up to 50 using a vibrator.

Not all women experience multiple orgasms, and even those who do can often feel satisfied with just one. Some men may be capable of multiple orgasms too, although data supporting this are scant (Robbins & Jensen, 1977; Zilbergeld, 1978).

All this variability in the experience of orgasms has led some scientists to ask: Why do we have orgasms anyway? For men, the answer, according to evolutionary theorists, is easy: Male orgasm distributes sperm, so males who have more orgasms are likely to have more offspring. Thus the capacity for orgasm ought to be adaptive in males—a characteristic promoted through natural selection.

But what about women? Orgasm is not necessary for successful sexual intercourse or for conception, so why would women have evolved with the capacity for orgasm? This question has been tackled by many evolutionary theorists. Their arguments range from the possibility that women are more likely to experience orgasm with men they unconsciously view as the "fittest" potential fathers, to the idea that the uterine contractions during orgasm effectively act to retain more sperm during intercourse. Primatologist Sarah Hrdy (1981) suggested that orgasms evolved in female primates as a way to protect offspring. She noted that, among some primates, females mate with one male after another until they have an orgasm. When pregnancy results, many males are potential fathers of the infant, which often means that none of the potential fathers will harm the infant. Biologist Elizabeth Lloyd (2005), however, argued that female orgasm is not adaptive in humans. Rather, it serves no evolutionary function but is left over from the parallel developmental process of female and male embryos during the first 8 weeks after conception. In other words, females get the nerve pathways necessary for orgasm simply because they started out with the same basic body as males. Like nipples in men, Lloyd argued, orgasm in women is an artifact that serves no useful purpose. For women, she asserted (against a background of much criticism from other theorists), orgasm is not adaptive, just fun.

AROUSAL   Are there male–female differences in patterns of sexual arousal? For years researchers reported that women were less likely than men to recognize their own physiological sexual arousal (Heiman, 1977; Laan & Everaerd, 1995). According to some studies, women's self-reports of sexual arousal did not match up particularly well with physiological measures: Women with vaginas that were moist and engorged reported that they were not sexually aroused. Men, on the other hand, rarely showed such a lack of synchrony between subjective and physiological measures of sexual arousal. Many explanations for this difference were suggested, including the idea that women had been so well trained to ignore or repress their sexual feelings that they did not learn to recognize them properly. More recent research, however, suggests that the observed discrepancy between subjective and physiological arousal for women may be an artifact of the way the research was done. When the two types of sexual arousal measures (subjective and physiological) are assessed continuously during exposure to erotic films and statistical techniques able to take wide individual variations into account are used, researchers now find a strong relationship between the two measures (Rellini, McCall, Randall, & Meston, 2005). So perhaps women and men are not so different when it comes to recognizing their own sexual arousal.

Another possible female–male difference in sexual arousal has recently caught investigators' attention, however: the category specificity of arousal. Researchers measured the genital and subjective arousal of women and men who identified themselves as heterosexual or homosexual as they viewed erotic films of male-male, female-male, or female-female sexual activity (Chivers, Rieger, Latty, & Bailey, 2004). They found that men tended to be significantly more aroused, both subjectively and genitally, by sexual films depicting the category of person to whom they were attracted than to films depicting the category of person to whom they were not attracted. In other words, heterosexual men were much more strongly aroused to erotic films depicting women, and homosexual men were much more strongly aroused to erotic films depicting men. For women, though, the pattern was different. Regardless of their sexual orientation, women's genital arousal was about the same whether they were watching sexual films of two women, two men, or a man and a woman. The relation between women's sexual orientation and their subjective arousal to the films was also somewhat weaker than men's.

These researchers argued that women's sexual arousal is less category specific than men's—that women can be aroused by sexual stimuli even if those stimuli do not match their sexual orientation. Arousal, they speculate, may play a very different role in female and male sexuality. It is not yet clear whether these intriguing conclusions are correct or what implications they may have. However, long-held conclusions about women's ability to recognize their own arousal have now been challenged as artifacts of the way arousal was measured. In the realm of sexuality in which measurement is notoriously difficult, it is probably wise to treat dramatic-sounding new findings with caution.

SEXUAL DYSFUNCTION   Difficulties with sexual functioning, such as the inability to get an erection in men and the inability to have an orgasm in women or men, are common problems that cause a great deal of anxiety to the individuals experiencing them. Besides the obvious fact that they interfere with sexual pleasure, there are other reasons these problems are sources of so much distress: People feel they cannot discuss them with others, and the cultural labels attached to the problems (e.g., "impotence" and "frigidity") are very negative. Masters and Johnson's research dispelled a lot of the secrecy surrounding sexual dysfunction and fostered a behavioral approach to treatment (Masters & Johnson, 1970).

Both males and females can experience difficulty with arousal and orgasm, painful intercourse, and low sexual desire. However, there are differences in the frequencies with which these problems occur for women and men. Women are considerably more likely than men to report difficulty achieving orgasm. Men are much more likely than women to have a problem with their orgasm happening too quickly (premature ejaculation).

It is estimated that about 40% of men experience occasional difficulty in getting an erection (Lawson, 2003). Such difficulties can affect men at any age. In recent years, it has become easier to admit this problem. The availability of Viagra and the huge advertising campaign that accompanied it have made erectile problems almost trendy. Young virile-looking men appear in ad campaigns discussing ED (erectile dysfunction), helping the TV audience to draw the conclusion that all such problems can be solved with the appropriate drug. These ads may soon be joined by parallel ones in which young beautiful women discuss FSD (female sexual dysfunction) as something that can also be cured with just the right pill. Drug companies are hot on the trail of a drug that will be the equivalent of Viagra for women, but some doctors and psychologists counsel caution (D. Smith, 2003). Perhaps a lack of sexual desire or of orgasm is not always a problem. When it is a problem, perhaps it can best be addressed through social or relationship changes rather than by taking a drug.

Early sex surveys found that about 30% of women reported never or only occasionally having orgasms during intercourse (Kinsey, Pomeroy, Martin, & Gebhard, 1953; Terman, 1951), but later surveys show only about 10 to 15% of women saying they seldom or never have orgasm (Hunt, 1974). The latter study also uncovered some evidence for orgasm inconsistency in men, particularly for those under the age of 25. A more recent survey in the United States found that 75% of men report *always* reaching orgasm during sexual activity, but only 29% of women do (Michael, Gagnon, Laumann, & Kolata, 1994). The discrepancy between the early and later surveys may partly reflect a difference in the populations sampled.

One of the difficulties with sex surveys is that the people who choose to respond to them may not be representative of the "average" population. Alfred Kinsey's research took place at a time when sexuality was a taboo topic. Thus, not only may he have had trouble obtaining honest responses, but his respondents, by agreeing to discuss their sexual habits with him, showed themselves to be a rather daring segment of North American society in the late 1940s. Morton Hunt tried hard to obtain an unbiased sample of the U.S. population but did not succeed completely. The Kinsey and Hunt samples are not fully comparable in terms of the age, race, marital status, and socioeconomic status of the respondents. Another possible problem with the comparability of the two surveys is that it may have been more acceptable in the 1940s for women to admit to difficulties with orgasm. Now, in the age of the multiple orgasm for women, it may simply be harder for women to admit orgasm inconsistency, even on an anonymous questionnaire.

The finding that women report more difficulty with orgasm than men do may be largely a function of ineffective stimulation of the woman. Women can masturbate to orgasm about as quickly as men can; it is during intercourse that they tend to experience difficulty or slowness in responding.

$\mathcal{O}verview$ Are there sex differences in sexual response?

Issue	Sex Difference?
Physiological phases of sexual response	Masters and Johnson found that both women and men in their lab went through four stages of physiological response: excitement, plateau, orgasm, and resolution.
Multiple orgasm	Women are more likely than men to be capable of being restimulated to orgasm during the resolution phase.
Arousal	Some evidence suggests women may be less category specific than men in their arousal to sexual stimuli.
Sexual dysfunction	Both sexes can experience difficulties with sexual desire, arousal, orgasm, and painful intercourse. In the context of heterosexual intercourse, women are more likely than men to have difficulty reaching orgasm; men are more likely than women to reach orgasm too quickly.

Female–Male Differences in the Experience and Meaning of Sexuality

Women and men may have similar patterns of physiological sexual response, but does this mean they experience sexuality in the same way? Researchers argue that the answer to this question is "No." Social psychologist Anne Peplau (2003) recently outlined four broad differences in women's and men's sexuality that she says are supported by research:

- On many measures, men show greater sexual desire than women do.
- Women place more emphasis than men do on committed relationships as a context for sexuality.
- Aggression is more strongly linked to sexuality for men than for women.
- Women's sexuality tends to be more fluid and capable of changing over time.

According to Peplau, these male–female differences characterize not only heterosexuals, but also lesbians and gay men. Let us look at each of these issues in turn.

SEXUAL DESIRE   In 1978 and again in 1982, researchers conducted studies in which college students were approached by attractive members of the other sex and asked one of the following questions: "Would you go out tonight?" "Will you come over to my apartment?" or "Would you go to bed with me?" (R. Clark & Hatfield, 1989). Not surprising to those of us familiar with sexual norms for women and men, men were more willing than women to accede to sexual invitations from potential partners. The great majority of men were willing to have a sexual encounter with the woman who approached them; however, not one woman agreed to such an encounter with a man.

Do these findings mean that women are less interested in sex than men are? Not necessarily. The double standard of expectations for females and males affects the way female-to-male and male-to-female propositions are interpreted. The women might have been worried about what the attractive man would think of them if they agreed to have sex with him so casually. The men who were propositioned would have few such worries. Beyond the double standard, another consideration might well have inhibited women from accepting the man's invitation: fear. Women have good reason to fear sexual violence, and women may well be cautious about making themselves vulnerable.

Despite such possible explanations for women's "lack of interest," a traditional stereotype has held that women simply have less desire for intercourse than men do. Kinsey and his colleagues noted that wives wanted intercourse less often than their husbands did. However, according to the Hunt survey, fewer than 5% of the wives wanted intercourse less often than their husbands did, and in a survey conducted by *Redbook*, one-third of the wives reported a wish for more frequent intercourse (Levin & Levin, 1975). It is difficult to infer a trend here because the samples may be very different. The more recent findings do indicate, however, that many women are interested in intercourse and that interest is not limited to married adults. A *Seventeen* magazine survey of a national sample of single females and males between the ages of 14 and 21 found that, of those who were sexually active, 99% of the males and 91% of the females reported that they enjoyed intercourse (Pesmen, 1991).

It is hard to know how much to believe such findings. Do people who respond to magazine surveys about sex represent the population? Are their answers influenced at all by what they think they *should* be feeling? And what exactly is sexual desire anyway? Is it the same thing as enjoyment of sex? Capacity for sexual pleasure?

Roy Baumeister and his colleagues (Baumeister, Catanese, & Vohs, 2001) reviewed a great deal of research and concluded that men's **sex drive** (sexual motivation or desire for sex) is stronger than women's. They noted, however, that this is not the same thing as saying that men enjoy sex more than women do. They found that men thought more about sex, had more sexual fantasies, masturbated more often, were more willing to initiate sex, were more willing to make sacrifices for sex, and were less willing to give up sex.

Women may like sex, but they do not spend a lot of time thinking about it. In one national survey of women aged 20 to 65, only 14% of respondents said they thought about sex "with interest or desire" every day, and only 26% said they thought about it several times per week (Bancroft, Loftus, & Long, 2003). In another national survey, more than half the male respondents said they thought about sex every day or several times a day, but only 19% of the women said this (Laumann, Michael, Gagnon, & Michaels, 1994).

These data seem convincing, but perhaps we should be cautious in accepting wholesale the conclusion that men are more interested in sex than women are. Could women's relative lack of interest be directed mainly at sex as defined by men?

Perhaps, in the attempt to study sexual desire, it is inappropriate to focus on the desire for intercourse. We have already seen that intercourse may not be the most satisfying form of sexual activity for women. If middle-class wives prefer, as one study found, to read a book than engage in sexual activity with their husbands (Mancini & Orthner, 1978), that preference may reflect not a lack of sexual desire but a lack of sexual satisfaction through intercourse.

When it comes to sexual activity, women and men may differ not so much in the frequency with which they desire the activity but in the kinds of activities they desire. Research with college students and newly married couples showed that women desire more activities in sex that demonstrate love and intimacy, whereas men wanted more activities that are sexually arousing (Hatfield, Sprecher, Pillemer, & Greenberger, 1988). Another study focused on sexual urges and fantasies outside of heterosexual activity (Jones & Barlow, 1990). Male and female undergraduate students self-monitored their sexual fantasies (internally generated sexual thoughts), urges (externally provoked sexual thoughts), and masturbatory fantasies for 7 consecutive days. Women and men did not differ in the frequency of their sexual fantasies. However, men reported more urges and masturbatory fantasies than women did.

Despite stereotypes that women experience less physical sexual desire than men do, there is evidence that women do indeed "embody" their feelings of sexual desire; they do not simply desire a disembodied emotional experience of sexual connection. Researchers who interviewed adolescent women about their experiences of sexual desire found that the women associated sexuality with strong feelings of physical pleasure and with self-knowledge:

> Both sexual desire and sexual pleasure are known to them as profoundly physical experiences—as feelings that they perceive in their own bodies. They are able to describe these experiences in specific terms, reflecting their clear acquaintance with these feelings: Zoe called it a "tingling or shivering," Eugenia explained that it is "a burn, a throbbing down there, in between my legs . . . sometimes I get wet . . . it was just like my body wanted to just be like touched and explored." (Tolman & Szalacha, 1999, p. 29)

These researchers noted, however, that experiences of sexual violation or living in a social context in which sexual violence was prevalent appeared to dampen young women's emphasis on pleasure and increase their emphasis on vulnerability in connection with sexuality. Girls who had not had to negotiate much sexual violence in their personal lives, relationships, or social landscapes spoke "about having feeling bodies and about knowing that their bodies and sexuality can be a source of physical, emotional, and relational pleasure and even strength" (p. 30). However, girls who had experienced sexual violation personally or close to them in their social environment spoke of their sexual feelings with a sense of dissociation and disconnection from their bodies. For example, one young women from this group said, "It's all in my head, I think about it, but my body has nothing to do with it. You know, sure my body feels desire if someone touches me or feels pleasure, but pretty much it's in what you're thinking about" (p. 31).

Some writers have suggested that women's sexual desire may fluctuate with the menstrual cycle. A peak in desire may occur at the ovulation phase for some women and at the premenstrual, menstrual, or postmenstrual phase for others (A. R. Gold & Adams, 1981; Kinsey et al., 1953; Van Goozen et al., 1997). Although such correspondence between the menstrual cycle and sexual desire may be experienced by individual women, there is, as yet, no evidence that women as a group show any regular pattern of cyclic fluctuation in sex drive (Morrell, Dixen, Carter, & Davidson, 1984).

Clearly, the matter is complex: The last word on whether women and men differ in the strength of their sexual desire is yet to be written. If women are more restrictive in when and with whom they have sex, it does not necessarily signify a lack of interest in sex or that sex is less important to them than it is to men. It might mean that their level of interest fluctuates with their bodily rhythms. It might mean they have learned (or evolved?) to focus their sex drive more narrowly and carefully on partners with whom its expression will be safe and useful for relationships. As one group of researchers noted, "a variety of data suggests that sex matters quite a lot to women. For example, . . . [S]ex matters enough to women that they restrict the number of partners with whom they have sex and are more selective than men about the sexual partners they choose." (Andersen, Cyranowski, & Aarestad, 2000, p. 384)

RELATIONSHIP CONTEXT OF SEXUALITY   North American women spend a great deal of money and time on romance novels. Indeed, in 2001, $1.52 billion dollars was spent on romance novels, such novels accounted for more than half of all paperback fiction sales in the United States, and most of those spending this money were women (Romance Writers of America, 2002). Men, on the other hand, rarely seem to read romance novels, but as a group they do spend a lot of money on pornography. Romance novels and pornography both contain a lot of sex, but they take very different approaches to it. In romance novels, the sex is the consummation of a passionate attraction to a particular person; in pornography, the sex is often anonymous, has no implications at all for a relationship, or involves multiple partners.

Might the differences in women's and men's reading preferences mirror differences in their feelings about sexuality? Anne Peplau (2003) would argue "Yes": Women are more likely than men to emphasize committed relationships as a context for sexuality. To support this conclusion, she cited studies showing that women have more tendency than men to "romanticize" sexual desire; that women's sexual fantasies are more likely than men's to involve a familiar partner, affection, and commitment; and that both heterosexual women and lesbians have less permissive attitudes toward casual sex than men do. In further support of this idea is a finding reported by Lisa Diamond and Ritch Savin-Williams (2000): Among the sexual-minority adolescents they surveyed, 70% of the women but only 5% of the men reported having their first same-sex sexual contact within an established romantic relationship.

Surveys in North America show that women have much more negative attitudes than men do about casual premarital or extramarital sex (Laumann et al., 1994; Oliver & Hyde, 1993). Women and men, at least during the college years, respond differently to the question, "What are your motives for having sexual intercourse?" Women tend to stress love and commitment to their partner (e.g., "emotional feelings that we shared"), whereas men are more likely to emphasize physical needs and pleasure (e.g., "need it," "to gratify myself") (Carroll, Volk, & Hyde, 1985). The same researchers found that 45% of college women but only 8% of college men answered, "Always" to the question, "For you, is emotional involvement a prerequisite for participating in sexual intercourse?" In one survey, twice as many male as female teenagers said they would have sex on a date simply because they were sexually attracted (Pesman, 1991).

The research does not, however, imply that men are uninterested in relationships. Men may be more romantic than women in some ways: They are more likely to fall in love quickly, view their couple relationship in romantic terms, and suffer terribly when the relationship ends (Hill, Rubin, & Peplau, 1976; Rubin, Peplau, & Hill, 1981). Also, a study examining the relationship values of college students found that women and men did not differ in the values they placed on attachment and were equally concerned with having a secure, committed, sexually exclusive relationship (Cochran & Peplau, 1985).

AGGRESSION AND SEXUALITY   Men but not women seem to think of their sexual selves along a dimension of aggression. When describing their own sexuality, men vary in the extent to which they see themselves as aggressive, powerful, experienced, domineering, and individualistic; however, this dimension seems to be irrelevant to women's descriptions of their sexual selves (Anderson, Cyranowski, & Espindle, 1999). By contrast, women use a dimension to describe sexuality that it not used by men: embarrassment, conservatism, and self-consciousness. Men also are more likely than women to be assertive in sexual interactions: making the first move, taking the lead, setting the pace (Impett & Peplau, 2003). These findings suggest a stronger link between sexuality and aggression for men than for women. Table 7.1 illustrates the differences in the ways men and women describe themselves as sexual persons.

An even more obvious argument for a sexuality-aggression link for men is the prevalence of rape—which is rarely perpetrated by women and often perpetrated by men. We will look more closely at rape in the section on coercive sexuality toward the end of the chapter.

FLUIDITY AND CHANGEABILITY OF SEXUALITY   Is women's sexuality more malleable than men's in response to situational, cultural, or social factors? Some evidence suggests the answer may be "Yes." Roy Baumeister (2000) reviewed many studies showing that, for example, women vary more than men in the frequency of their sexual activity. A woman may have sex frequently while in a relationship, then none at all for months if the relationship ends. Men are more likely to maintain a level of sexual activity through the ups and downs of relationships, even if that means the substitution of masturbation for partnered sex.

Baumeister also showed that women's sexuality may be more strongly influenced than men's by changes in their social or cultural environments. For example, both women's and men's propensity to identify with a same-sex sexual orientation increases as their level of education increases, but this association appears much stronger for women than men. And living in same-sex institutions is linked to increased likelihood of same-sex erotic relationships between women (Peplau & Garnets, 2000).

Table 7.1 Dimensions that characterize men's and women's sexual self-schemas.

Men and women who describe themselves as sexual also endorse a variety of other adjectives to describe themselves. The column for each dimension contains the adjectives that were grouped into that dimension by the data analysis.[1] Note that, although both women and men apparently think of their sexual selves as passionate, they endorse a somewhat different pattern of adjective to describe that dimension. Also note that only men endorse a pattern of adjectives that can be labeled "powerful-aggressive," and only women produce a dimension that can be labeled "embarrassed-conservative."

Factor					
Passionate-Loving (Men)	*Passionate-Romantic (Women)*	*Powerful-Aggressive (Men Only)*	*Open-Minded-Liberal (Men)*	*Open-Direct (Women)*	*Embarrassed-Conservative (Women Only)*
Compassionate	Romantic	Aggressive	Liberal	Direct	Embarrassed
Warm-hearted	Passionate	Powerful	Open-minded	Straightforward	Conservative
Passionate	Warm	Outspoken	Broad-minded	Frank	Cautious
Loving	Loving	Experienced		Outspoken	Self-conscious
Sensitive	Feeling	Exciting		Broad-minded	Timid
Feeling	Sympathetic	Domineering		Experienced	Inexperienced
Romantic	Arousable	Direct		Casual	
Soft-hearted	Stimulating	Spontaneous		Open-minded	
				Uninhibited	

[1]Source: Data are from Andersen, Cyranowski, & Espindle (1999) and Andersen & Cyranowski (1994).

Finally, Baumeister showed that attitude-behavior consistency in the realm of sexuality is lower for women than for men. For example, women are more likely than men to have sex when they do not feel like it or to not have sex when they do feel like it. And women seem more likely than men to have inconsistencies in their reports of sexual feelings, identifications, and actions (Peplau & Garnets, 2000). For example, a woman may report that she is attracted to other women but has not had sex with a woman; such an "inconsistency" is less likely to be reported by a man (Laumann et al., 1994).

There is another line of evidence for women's greater sexual malleability or "erotic plasticity": changes in sexual orientation. Lisa Diamond (2003) studied 18- to 25-year-old women who identified as lesbian or bisexual. She found that more than 25% of these young women changed their sexual identity over a period of 5 years. Other researchers have also documented changes in women's sexual identity, from a heterosexual to a lesbian identity (e.g, Kitzinger & Wilkinson, 1995) and from a lesbian to a heterosexual or bisexual identity (e.g., Bart, 1993; Rust, 1992). Such changes appear to be less common in men.

IMPLICATIONS FOR UNDERSTANDING GENDER AND SEXUALITY

The four sets of gender differences listed by Peplau (2003) suggest that there may not be one single model that explains both male and female sexuality. Or, if there is a single model, perhaps it needs to be shifted away from traditional concepts based largely on male sexuality and to be expanded and repositioned in a way that takes better account of female sexuality. For example, instead of concluding that "men are interested in sex, but women are interested in relationships," perhaps we should be rethinking our definition of *sexuality* so that it includes the wide variety of attractions and connections that are possible in erotic/romantic relationships. Should we, as Anne Peplau and Linda Garnets (2000) suggested in their call for a new paradigm for understanding women's sexuality, be using the term "relational orientation" instead of "sexual orientation"? Should we acknowledge and study the multiple pathways through which sexual identities, feelings, and behavior can develop? It appears that there are many questions left to answer.

SEXUAL ACTIVITY

In 1995 researchers conducted interviews about sexuality with a nationally representative sample of more than 20,000 students in grades 7 through 12. When they interviewed a subset of these students again one year later, they discovered some interesting discrepancies between students' responses in the first and second interviews (Rosenbaum, 2006). In the first interview, about 13% of the respondents said they had taken a virginity pledge: a pledge to delay sexual activity until marriage. In the second interview, about half of those students denied having taken such a pledge. These respondents who "retracted" their virginity pledge were likely to have had sexual experience since the first interview, and perhaps it was more comfortable to deny that they had ever pledged to delay sex than to admit they had broken their pledge. In a similar vein, about a third of the respondents reported in the first interview that they had had sexual intercourse; however almost 11% of these students denied having ever had sexual intercourse when they were interviewed again a year later. These "deniers" who, according to their statements in the first interview had had an average of 2.22 sexual partners, were likely to have taken a virginity pledge in the interval between the first and second interviews. Perhaps they were able to convince themselves that they had regained their virginity by taking the pledge!

These findings point to the difficulties inherent in trying to study sexual activity through the use of self-report surveys and interviews. Respondents may distort reality by exaggerating or denying their sexual activity, they may be unable to remember accurately events that are long past, and they may have difficulty estimating frequencies and time spent in certain activities. In one study that asked students how honestly they had answered survey questions about their sexual experiences, 25% of male and 15% of female middle school students and 10% of high school students reported they had overestimated their sexual experience (Siegel, Aten, & Roghmann, 1998).

Yet, information about the type and extent of people's sexual activity generally comes from self-reports elicited through surveys (e.g., A. P. Bell, Weinberg, & Hammersmith, 1981; Hite, 1976, 1981; Kinsey, Pomeroy, & Martin, 1948; Kinsey et al., 1953; Michael et al., 1994; Pesmen, 1991). And although such surveys have proven invaluable in providing knowledge about sexual activity, there are additional reasons to be skeptical about the degree to which the survey results reflect the sexual behavior of the general population. Volunteer participants in sex research tend to be more experienced and less inhibited in their sex lives than most people (Kaats & Davis, 1971; Maslow & Sakoda, 1952), so they are not an unbiased sample of the population. Making the sample still more biased may be the deliberate exclusion of particular groups. For example, the Kinsey report did not include Black respondents, and Hunt, in an effort to make his sample comparable with Kinsey's, dropped Black respondents when comparing his results with the Kinsey report. One representative survey of 3,432 adults was limited to respondents over the age of 18 (Michael et al., 1994). Given these drawbacks, it might be more appropriate to take the data provided by these surveys as rough approximations of the experience of the general population than as completely accurate representations of it.

A few years ago, two researchers gathered the existing studies of male–female differences in sexual attitudes and behaviors and performed a meta-analysis (Oliver & Hyde, 1993). Table 7.2 shows the differences they found, grouped into categories according to the size of the difference. In many areas the differences are small or negligible. There are only two areas in which women and men were found to differ to a really striking degree: the amount of casual sexual intercourse and the incidence of masturbation. These findings fit well with our discussion of the ways women and men appear to differ in their experience of and meaning attached to sexuality.

Heterosexual Intercourse

Kinsey's data, collected in the 1940s, indicated that 33% of women and 71% of men had had premarital sexual intercourse by the age of 25. The Hunt report indicated that by the 1970s, the comparable percentages were 67% for women and 97% for men. A recently released report from the National Center for Health Statistics indicates that, by age 24, 89% of men and 92% of women report they have had heterosexual intercourse, and an additional 3% of each group say they have had oral sex, but not intercourse, with an opposite-sex partner (Mosher, Anjani, & Jones, 2005). This survey also found that more than half of teens aged 15 to 19 had engaged in oral sex, including almost a quarter of those who had never had sexual intercourse. Other surveys show a similar increase in premarital sexual activity among adolescents and young adults, with a larger increase evident for women than for men and a trend toward first intercourse occurring at earlier ages. All over the developed world, most young women and men now become sexually active as teenagers: Three-quarters of young women have had intercourse by the age of 20 (Alan Guttmacher

Table 7.2   Gender differences in similarities in sexual behaviors and attitudes.[2] The characterization of differences as small, moderate, or large is based on statistical criteria.

Nonexistent or trivial gender difference

- Attitudes toward homosexuality
- Attitudes toward civil liberties for gays and lesbians
- Incidence of kissing
- Attitudes toward masturbation
- Incidence of oral sex
- Incidence of petting

Small gender difference

- Number of sexual partners
- Acceptance of double standard
- Attitudes toward extramarital sex
- Frequency of intercourse
- Incidence of homosexuality
- Anxiety, fear, guilt
- Attitudes toward premarital sex
- Age at first intercourse
- Intercourse with fiancé(e)

Moderate gender difference

- Intercourse in a committed relationship
- Sexual permissiveness

Large gender difference

- Intercourse in casual relationships
- Incidence of masturbation

[2]Source: This table is based on information in Oliver & Hyde (1993) and Andersen, Cyranowski, & Aarestad (2000).

Institute, 2003a). In the United States about 25% of adolescents have had intercourse by age 15 (Mosher et al., 2005).

Young women's sexual attitudes and behaviors have changed more than young men's over time. A recent meta-analysis of 530 studies comprising almost 270,000 participants revealed that between 1943 and 1999, both women and men became more sexually active and more approving of sexual activity, but changes were more striking among women (Wells & Twenge, 2005). Before 1970, the average age at first intercourse was reported as 19 for women and 18 for men; this dropped to 15 for both genders by the late 1990s. During the 1950s, 13% of teenaged girls and young women said they were sexually active; by the late 1990s, 47% reported sexual activity. During the same time period, teenaged boys' and young men's reports of sexual activity actually dropped from over 60% in the early 1950s to just under 50% in the late 1990s. Before 1970, 49% of young males and 44% of young females reported they had engaged in oral sex; after 1990, 70% of young males and 69% of young females said they had done so. Young women's approval of premarital sex went from 12% in the late 1950s to 73% in the 1980s. During the same period, young men's approval of premarital sex rose from 40% to 79%.

There is little evidence that the average young adult has a great deal of variety in sexual partners before marriage. Surveys taken in the early 1970s suggested, for example, that more than half the women who engaged in premarital intercourse had only 1 partner, often their fiancé (Hunt, 1974; Kantner & Zelnick, 1972) and that married men had typically had about 6 premarital partners. About 20% of sexually experienced men have had only 1 partner by their late teens; 30% have had 6 or more partners by that age (Alan Guttmacher Institute, 2003b). Respondents to a national survey of over 10,000 college students indicated that most (69% of women and 56% of men) had engaged in sex with only 1 partner over the previous 30 days, and only a few (6% of women and 9% of men) had engaged in sex with 2 or more partners during the previous 30 days (Eisenberg, 2001). According to a National Center for Health Statistics survey, men aged 30 to 44 have had an average of 6 to 8 female sexual partners in their lifetime, and women in the same age group have had an average of 4 male partners (Mosher et al., 2005).

Some people do have a large number of sexual partners. Apparently, however, such people are in the minority. A representative survey of American adults found that 26% of Americans reported having had only 1 sexual partner, and only 9% said they had had 21 or more (Laumann et al., 1994). More recent data indicated that, among women ages 15 to 44, 4% of Latina women, 10% of European American women, and 9% of African American women have had 15 or more male partners in their lifetime. Among men in the same age range, 18% of Latino men, 22% of European American men, and 34% of African American men have had 15 or more female sexual partners in their lifetime (Mosher et al., 2005).

Sexual activity is affected by a variety of factors. Currently, the AIDS epidemic as well as the prevalence of other sexually transmitted diseases may be a factor in people's decisions with respect to whether and with whom to be sexually active. These issues are discussed in later sections.

First intercourse may be greeted with different reactions by females and males. Among the adolescents studied by Sorenson (1973), males were more likely to report feeling positive: excited, joyful, and mature. Females were more likely to say they felt negative emotions: guilt, sorrow, and disappointment. Disappointment may be a common reaction for women. One sample of college women, rating their experience of first intercourse on a 1 to 7 scale (1 = didn't experience pleasure at all, 7 = strongly experienced pleasure), gave it an average rating of only 3.9 (Weis, 1983). About 90% of men and 70% of women reported in a more recent survey that they wanted to have intercourse the first time they did it (Michael et al., 1994). The reasons for doing so differed for the two genders: Nearly half the women but only a quarter of the men said they had intercourse out of affection for their partner. More than half the men but only a quarter of the women cited curiosity

Figure 7.3   Feelings about first intercourse by males and females whose first sex was before 20 years of age. Of the 18- to 24-year-old females who had first intercourse before age 20, 9.6% indicated that it was *not voluntary.*

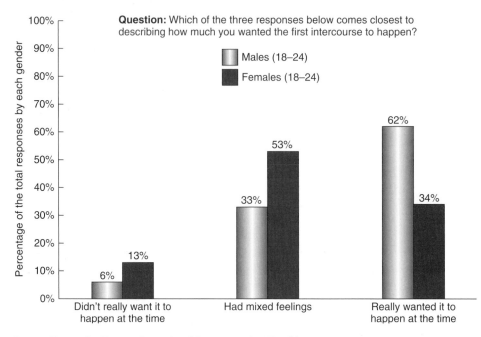

Source: Centers for Disease Control and Prevention (2005), table 8.

as their main motivation. Figure 7.3 illustrates some other gender differences in reaction to first intercourse.

Among married couples, there is a great deal of variability in the frequency of coitus. According to one survey, the average couple in their mid-20s has intercourse between two and three times a week, with the frequency declining gradually over the years (Michael et al., 1994). Women report slightly less satisfaction with marital sex than men do, but both women and men express relatively high levels of satisfaction. On surveys, men are more likely than women to say they have engaged in extramarital sex, with about half the men and one-quarter of the women engaging in it at least once. The incidence of extramarital sex for women seems to have increased since the 1960s (A. P. Thompson, 1983), but, in general, the affairs do not seem to be casual ones. Many of the women who have had extramarital sex have done so with only one partner (Blumstein & Schwartz, 1983). One large-scale survey indicated that more than 80% of women and 65 to 85% of men of all ages report having no extramarital affairs (Laumann et al., 1994).

Homosexual Activity

The Kinsey surveys indicated that 37% of men and 13% of women had at least one homosexual experience leading to orgasm during adulthood (Kinsey et al., 1948, 1953). However, only 4% of males and 2% of females reported that they were exclusively homosexual. Hunt's (1974) data revealed a somewhat similar frequency of homosexual experience: 20 to 25% for men, 10% for married women, and 20% for unmarried women. The numbers are lower in more recent surveys. A large University of Chicago survey found that only 4% of women reported having had sex with another woman after the age of 18, and fewer than 2% had had sex with another woman in the past year (Laumann et al., 1994). In the same survey, 9% of men said they had engaged in sex with another male since puberty, just over 5% had had sex with a man since turning 18, and only 2% had had sex with a man in the past year. A more recent representative survey found that, among men aged 15 to 44, 6% reported having oral or anal sex with another man in their lifetime, and 2.9% said they had had a male sexual partner in the last 12 months (Mosher et al., 2005). Among women in the same age range, 11% answered "Yes" when asked if they had ever had any sexual experience of any kind with another woman, and 4.4% said they had done so within the last 12 months. About 1% of men and 3% of women reported having both male and female sexual partners within the last 12 months. A national survey of over 10,000 college students found that 2% of female and 3% of male respondents said that they engaged in sex only with same-sex partners; 4% of female and 2% of male respondents said they had both same-sex and opposite-sex partners (Eisenberg, 2001).

Some of the reported gender differences in homosexual behavior seem to parallel those reported for heterosexual activity. Males report more sexual activity with more partners than females do, and females are more likely to want and to be involved in long-term, emotionally close relationships (Bell & Weinberg, 1978; Hunt, 1974; Meredith, 1984; Peplau, 1981). Women in our culture are socialized more strongly than men are to value close relationships, so this finding is not surprising. However, a large proportion of both lesbians and gay men live with a partner in a committed relationship (Patterson, 1998).

Within same-gender relationships, the amount of sexual activity varies widely, just as it does in mixed-gender relationships. This variation can be seen in the conflicting results obtained by researchers studying lesbian sexuality. One review of the literature led to the conclusion that lesbian women and heterosexual women are similar in the frequency with which they have sex (Peplau & Amaro, 1982); by contrast, however, a large-scale survey indicated that lesbian couples have sex much less frequently than any other type of couple (Blumstein & Schwartz, 1983). Some research suggested that the frequency of genital sex often declines dramatically between lesbians in long-term, committed relationships (McCormick, 1994; Nichols, 1990).

Like heterosexual activity, homosexual activity is responsive to the norms of the surrounding culture. For example, studies of the history of lesbian relationships show that, under some conditions, lesbian couples of the 1940s and

1950s adopted the sexual roles of "stone butch" and "femme" (M. D. Davis & Kennedy, 1990; E. Newton, 1984). The butch was the sexual initiator or doer, and the femme was the more passive partner. Although, at first glance these roles may seem to echo traditional male–female heterosexual roles, they were actually quite different. The ideal of the "stone butch" was to be untouchable: to gain sexual pleasure from giving pleasure and not to allow her partner to reciprocate. The active, butch partner's fulfillment came from satisfying her partner. The femme, being more passive, was able to acknowledge and focus on her own sexual responses, to demand and receive sexual pleasure. These roles were socially constructed as ways of expressing lesbian cultural identity and female-female sexual love, and they were enforced by the norms of the lesbian community of the times (M. D. Davis & Kennedy, 1990). Currently, the emphasis on these roles has greatly diminished, as lesbian communities have found other ways to express their distinct identity:

> In the late sixties in Buffalo, with the development of the political activities of gay liberation, explicitly political organizations and tactics replaced butch-fem roles in leading the resistance to gay oppression. Because butch-fem roles were no longer the primary means for organizing the community's stance toward the straight world, the community no longer needed to enforce role-appropriate behavior. (M. D. Davis & Kennedy, 1990, p. 397)

Masturbation

Both the Kinsey and Hunt surveys indicated a large gender difference in the proportion of respondents who reported having masturbated to orgasm. Almost all males but only about two-thirds of females reported having masturbated. Furthermore, males reported having begun masturbating at an earlier age than females. Other data support these findings (J. K. Davidson & Moore, 1994; Leitenberg, Detzer, & Srebnik, 1993; Oliver & Hyde, 1993). Part of the gender difference may be attributable to males' greater willingness than females' to report masturbation, but it is interesting to note that females *do* report more of some kinds of sexual activity in recent surveys than they did in earlier ones, suggesting that they now feel freer to admit sexual activity than they did in Kinsey's day. However, the percentage of women reporting that they masturbate has remained relatively constant.

Some experts feel that there is a connection between the finding that a large proportion of women do not masturbate and the finding that many women have difficulty reaching orgasm. Women who have not masturbated may be unaware of the kind of stimulation that gives them the most pleasure and may not learn to be comfortable with their own body and sexual responses. Kinsey's data did, in fact, suggest that women who masturbate to orgasm before marriage are more likely to experience orgasm during sex with their husbands (Kinsey et al., 1953). At least one writer has argued that sex, like any other skill, must be learned and practiced; learning about one's own body through masturbation can build a sense of independence and pleasure (Dodson, 1974).

Contraception

Despite the emphasis on sexuality in our culture, there is a curious reluctance to connect sexuality with pregnancy. Media depictions of sexual encounters have increased in number and explicitness in the last two decades (Brown, Childers, & Waszak, 1990). However, these depictions often ignore the reproductive potential of sexual intercourse: Rarely does the heroine of a romance novel stop to demand condom use before she allows herself to be seduced by the hero, and even the most sensitive of movie heroes are not seen to use contraception themselves or to inquire of their sex partners whether they are using birth control before jumping into bed. One recent report indicated that the amount of sexual content on television is increasing steadily: in 2005, 77% of prime-time programs sampled had sexual content, as compared to 67% in 1998 (Kaiser Family Foundation, 2005). That same report found references to safe sex in only 14% of all shows with sexual content.

One of the sources of the fear of pregnancy has traditionally been the disgrace associated with unwed motherhood. That stigma has lessened somewhat. A report by Rutgers University's National Marriage Project in the summer of 1999 revealed that the percentage of teenage girls who said having a baby out of wedlock can be a "worthwhile lifestyle" rose from 33% to 53% over the two previous decades (Popenow & Whitehead, 1999). In the United States, more than one-third of births were to unmarried mothers in 2003 (National Center for Health Statistics, 2005).

The fear of pregnancy, while still real enough, is less salient to present-day North American women than it was to women in the first half of the last century. The provision of birth control information to women was technically illegal in the United States until 1918, when the law was changed as a result of the energetic efforts of Margaret Sanger and her colleagues in the National Birth Control League. Sanger, who started her career as a nurse, was moved to tears and anger by her repeated exposure to the plight of poor women worn out from a continuous series of pregnancies that they could not prevent. These women begged her for the facts about how to prevent pregnancy; however, even her nurse's training had not included that information.

A turning point came for Sanger after a woman whose life she had helped save in the aftermath of an abortion pleaded with the doctor to tell her how she could avoid becoming pregnant again. The doctor laughed and told the woman to get her husband to sleep on the roof. Three months later, the woman died from another abortion, and Sanger left her nursing career behind to devote herself full-time to making birth control available to women. During the struggle, she was publicly reviled, jailed, and frequently subjected to frustration and humiliation. In the end, however, she and the organization she founded prevailed: It became legal for doctors to give contraceptive information to women, and a network of birth control clinics was eventually established (Sanger, 1938). In Canada, too, the birth control movement, under the guidance of women such as Mary Elizabeth Hawkins and Dr. Elizabeth Bagshaw, made contraception more available for women—although as late as the mid-1930s an Ottawa social worker was charged with criminal activity for distributing family planning information (Van Preagh, 1982).

Despite the current availability of effective methods of birth control, not all sexually active adolescents use them consistently. Teenage women's reported use of contraception at first intercourse rose from 43% in the 1970s to 79% in 1999–2000 (Alan Guttmacher Institute, 2005). However, 31% of adolescents surveyed in one recent study reported using no contraceptive method during their first sexual intercourse (Manning, Longmore, & Giordano, 2000).

After years of alarming rises, recent years have seen a decrease in teen pregnancy rates in the United States. In 2003, teen birth rates were down 3% from the previous year; this represents a 33% decline since 1991 (Hamilton, Martin, & Sutton, 2004). Nonetheless, there are more than 850,000 adolescent pregnancies per year in the United States, and in 2001 there were 453,725 births to women under the age of 20 (Henshaw, 2003). Almost 1 of every 11 females under the age of 20 gets pregnant, and more than 34% of these pregnancies occur in girls who are 17 years old or younger. Nearly 3 in 10 teen pregnancies end in abortion. Teen pregnancy is more common in some racial/ethnic groups than others: Among 15- to 19-year-old women in 2003, there were 17.6 births per 1,000 Asian or Pacific Islander women, 27.5 births per 1,000 non-Hispanic White women, 64.8 births per 1,000 Black women, and 82.2 births per 1,000 Hispanic women (Hamilton et al. 2004).

The United States has one of the highest teen birth rates in the developed world: just over 46 births per 1,000 teenagers (Henshaw, 2003). Figure 7.4 shows how U.S teen birth rates compare to those in other countries. American teenagers do not show different patterns of sexual activity than teens in these other countries; however, they seem to use contraception less consistently. The causes may lie partly in a lack of information about or easy access to birth control techniques; other Western countries have for years made contraceptives and birth control information more easily accessible to adolescents. However, attitudes toward sexual activity, some of them based on our old friend the double standard, also seem to contribute to the problem. The gender-role norms that say women do not take the initiative in sex may make it especially difficult for a young woman to prepare actively for the possibility of intercourse (Hynie & Lydon, 1995).

The attitude that women should be the gatekeepers of sexuality means the responsibility for preventing pregnancy is usually placed squarely on their shoulders, making men less likely to take responsibility for contraception. But what happens when a man *does* take such responsibility? In one study, college students were shown a videotape of the development of a first sexual encounter between a young man and young woman (Bryan, Aiken, & West, 1999). In three different versions of the video, the man either

Figure 7.4   Rates of teen pregnancy in 30 selected countries, 2000 to 2005.

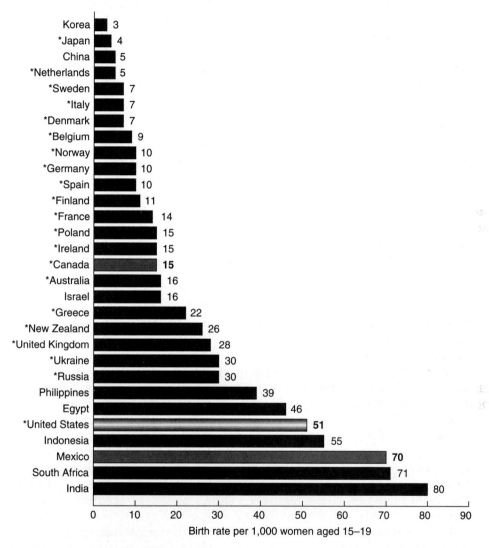

Note: *Indicates more developed

Source: United Nations Statistics Division (2005), table A6.

did not say or do anything about using contraception, verbally proposed using a condom, or nonverbally introduced the condom into the encounter. Students viewing the video were asked to rate the man on several characteristics.

The researchers found that, when the man proposed using a condom, he was viewed as nicer and more mature but less romantic and exciting than when he did not suggest condom use. Women seemed more favorably impressed when the condom was introduced verbally rather than nonverbally. Interestingly, men who viewed the videos estimated that suggesting condom use diminished the chance that sexual intercourse would take place—but the women made no such prediction. It appears that young women are quite willing to share the responsibility for condom use with their sexual partners.

If adolescents do become pregnant, the consequences can be serious for both the female and the male involved. Women who become mothers and men who become fathers during their teenage years are less likely than their counterparts to graduate from high school, and teenaged mothers trying to juggle the development of their own identities with the conflicting demands of parenthood may experience distress and depression (Coley & Chase-Lansdale, 1998). Adolescent males involved in a pregnancy show more psychological distress as young adults than do their counterparts whose girlfriends did not become pregnant. This is true whether the pregnancy ends in abortion, in the assumption of fathering responsibility, or in the abdication of parenting responsibilities to the girlfriend (Buchanan & Robbins, 1990).

Throughout the adult years of fertility, women are far more likely than men to take the responsibility for preventing pregnancy. When college students submit anonymous written questions about sexuality, the women ask twice as many questions about contraception and pregnancy as the men do (Valois & Waring, 1991). The most frequently used methods of birth control among American women are those that do not require male cooperation: sterilization and the birth control pill. Considerably less common are the diaphragm, implants, injectables, vaginal spermicides, and the intrauterine device (IUD). (Alan Guttmacher Institute, 2005).

Women's choices about contraception vary by age: Younger women are more likely to rely on the birth control pill and condoms; women 35 and older are more likely to choose female or male sterilization (National Center for Health Statistics, 2005). Figure 7.5 shows how contraceptive use shifts with age.

Experts now urge sexually active persons to use condoms, not just for the prevention of pregnancy but for protection from sexually transmitted diseases such as herpes and HIV. This emphasis on the importance of condoms, in combination with the greater visibility of condom advertising, has apparently led to an upsurge in their use. Among teenagers at least, condoms are a popular method of contraception, relied upon by 44.6% of those women who regularly use contraception. This method is slightly exceeded in popularity by the birth control pill (53.8%) (National Center for Health Statistics, 2005).

Figure 7.5   Women's contraceptive use in 2002 in the United States, according to age.

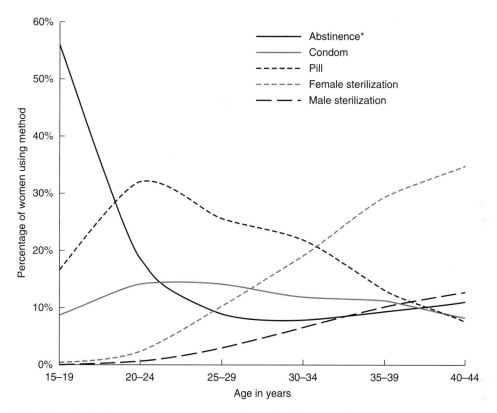

Note: *Never had intercourse or no intercourse in 3 months before interview.

Source: Centers for Disease Control and Prevention (2004b), table 6.

Sexually Transmitted Infections

Americans were stunned in November 1991 when basketball superstar Magic Johnson called a news conference to announce that he was retiring from the game because he had become infected with the **human immunodeficiency virus (HIV)** that causes **acquired immunodeficiency syndrome (AIDS)**. In that news conference, Johnson urged young people to heed his message that "safe sex is the way to go." Johnson's high profile and popularity brought new attention to bear on the issues of safe sex and AIDS—attention that may have caused at least some people to take more seriously the risks associated with sexually transmitted diseases.

A host of potentially serious diseases can be transmitted through sexual contact: HIV, herpes, chlamydia, syphilis, and gonorrhea. There were nearly 19 million new cases of sexually transmitted diseases in the United States in 2000, almost half of which were among young people ages 15 to 24 (Weinstock, Berman, & Cates, 2004). Figure 7.6 provides an overview of the impact of HIV/AIDS in the United States. It is estimated that in a single act of unprotected sex with an infected partner, a teenage woman has a 1% risk of contracting HIV, a 30% risk of acquiring genital herpes, and a 50% chance of contracting gonorrhea (Alan Guttmacher Institute, 1999).

Fear of sexually transmitted infections does not seem to deter adolescents from becoming sexually active or ensure that they protect themselves from risk. In one study of sexually active urban, minority, young people, about a

Figure 7.6   People in the United States living with HIV and AIDS infections, by gender, 1998–2004.

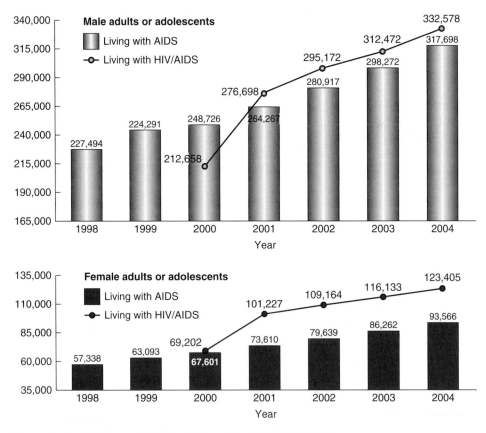

Source: Centers for Disease Control and Prevention (2002, 2003, 2004a).

third of younger teens and a quarter of older teens said they used condoms in no more than half of their sexual encounters (O'Donnell, O'Donnell, & Stueve, 2001). One-quarter of college students say they never use condoms, and almost a third say they use them inconsistently (Eisenberg, 2001). The use of alcohol seems to make little difference in such behavior. One study of adolescents found that sexual events preceded by drinking were no less likely to involve condom use than sexual events that were not preceded by drinking (Morrison, Gillmore, Hoppe, Gaylord, Leigh, & Rainey, 2003).

Findings from the Youth Risk Behavior Survey, conducted by the U.S. Department of Health and Human Services, also suggested that sexually risky behavior by adolescents is decreasing. Results from the survey showed that, from 1999 to 2005, the prevalence of sexual experience (defined, for purposes of the survey, as "having ever had sexual intercourse") declined among male high school students from 54.1% to 46.8%, and the prevalence of multiple sex partners declined from 18.7% to 14.3%. Among sexually active students, condom use increased from 46.2% to 62.8% over the same time period. However, in 2005 only 70% of male students and 55.9% of female students reported that they used condoms the last time they had sexual intercourse (Centers for Disease Control and Prevention, 2006).

The source of the most serious concern about sexually transmitted disease has been AIDS, which is caused by HIV, a slow-acting retrovirus. An individual who tests positive for the presence in the blood of antibodies to this virus (that is, an individual who is HIV-positive) does not necessarily have AIDS. However, current thinking in the scientific community is that 40% of persons with HIV will develop AIDS within 5 to 10 years. The virus attacks the immune system, the body's natural system for fighting off disease, allowing other diseases, such as rare cancers and infections, to go unchecked. Although there are now many long-term survivors of the disease and increasingly effective treatments have been developed in recent years, most victims have a short life expectancy.

The virus is transmitted through bodily fluids—blood, semen, or the milk of nursing mothers—often by carriers who have no symptoms themselves. It is known to be passed from person to person through sexual contact, blood transfusions, and the use of contaminated hypodermic needles (e.g., among intravenous drug users) and from an infected mother to the fetus in her womb or to her nursing child through breast milk. During heterosexual contact, the disease is up to 17 times more likely to be passed from a man to a woman than vice versa (Padian, Shiboski, & Jewell, 1991).

From a global viewpoint, AIDS is a crisis that has outstripped even the most dire predictions of a decade ago. The Joint United Nations Program on HIV/AIDS estimates that, at the end of 2005, 38.6 million people were living with HIV/AIDS—44.8% of them women and 5.9% of them children—and 2.8 million people died in 2005 alone (UNAIDS, 2006a). In the United States, some 1.2 million people were living with this infection in 2005, and about 25% of the infected adults were women (UNAIDS, 2006b). Women comprise a high proportion of people with HIV/AIDS, both in North America and in other parts of the world, as shown in Figure 7.7.

Figure 7.7   Estimated number of people living with HIV worldwide, 2003 and 2005.

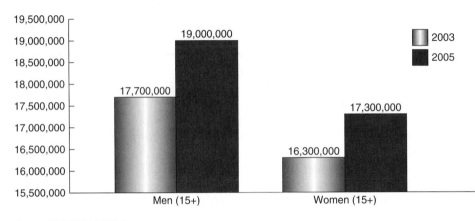

Source: UNAIDS (2006a).

The risk factors for AIDS are frequency of sexual contact and exposure to contaminated blood. In the United States, about half of HIV infections diagnosed in 2004 were among men who have sex with men; in Canada, this category accounted for 43% of diagnoses. For women in these (and many other) countries, a major risk factor is the behavior of their male partners; some research shows that about two-thirds of men who have ever had sex with men also have had sex with women (UNAIDS, 2006a). Many HIV infections come from the exposure to contaminated blood that is associated with injecting drugs. About 20% of new HIV infections in the United States are attributable to this risk factor.

There are significant racial/ethnic disparities in HIV and AIDS in the United States and Canada. African Americans, who make up about 12% of the U.S. population, account for 50% of new HIV diagnoses in areas with long-term confidential reporting. Hispanics, who make up 14% of the population, comprise 18% of new diagnoses (UNAIDS, 2006a). The death rate from AIDS in 2003 was 7 times higher in African American than European American men and 14 times higher in African American than European American women (National Center for Health Statistics, 2005). Aboriginal persons form 3% of Canada's population, but 5 to 8% of people living with HIV and 6 to 12% of new HIV infections (UNAIDS, 2006a).

For women, the disease is complicated by its relationship to reproduction. Without intervention, an HIV-infected pregnant woman has a 15 to 30% chance of having an infected baby. Transmission of the virus from an infected pregnant mother to her fetus accounts for 92% of all AIDS cases reported in children (S. F. Davis et al., 1995). Developments in drug treatments for and monitoring of pregnant women have led to a dramatic drop in AIDS cases among children in the United States, leading to the hope that perinatal transmission of HIV could be eliminated in this country (Centers for Disease Control and Prevention, 1998b). However, many countries do not have the resources to test pregnant women for HIV or to provide the drugs and alternatives to breast milk necessary to prevent mother-child transmission.

To reduce the risk of AIDS, it is critical that all sexually active individuals practice safer sex: decrease the number of sexual partners, learn more about the backgrounds of their partners, and use latex condoms with spermicide. A new line of defense is soon to become available: microbicides. Microbicides are creams or gels that can be inserted into the vagina before intercourse to reduce the risk of HIV transmission (UNAIDS, 2006a). Many such substances are currently being tested; their development will give women more control over their exposure to the risks inherent in unprotected sex. These cautions apply equally to heterosexual and homosexual activity. Some years ago, as the magnitude of the problem became clear, there was a shift away from casual sex in gay communities (Lyons, 1983). Condom use increased, and more gay men than heterosexual men began to use condoms (Treffke, Tiggemann, & Ross, 1992). However, there may be a resurgence of risky sexual behavior among this group. The number of cases of HIV infection among men who have sex with men has shown a recent rise, even as cases among other categories of individuals (injection drug users, heterosexual adults, and adolescents) have decreased (Centers for Disease Control and Prevention, 2004).

Life-Span Issues

Sexuality changes across the life span, and the patterns of change seem to be different for females and males. For one thing, women often find themselves much more able to enjoy sexual activity in middle age than they did when they were younger. Women are more likely than men to report increases from young adulthood to old age in measures such as frequency of orgasm, subjective pleasure in sexual activity, and satisfaction with sex life (Adams & Turner, 1985). Kinsey's survey indicated that women had orgasms more consistently at age 40 than they did as young adults, and the University of Chicago survey of American adults found that more women in their 50s reported that they "usually" had orgasm during sex with their partners than did women in the earlier decades of life (Michael et al., 1994).

Men are more likely to enjoy sexual activity from adolescence onward. One analysis (H. S. Kaplan & Sager, 1971) suggested that teenage males in our culture have an intense genitally focused sexuality. With the passing years, male sexual desire becomes somewhat less urgent, so that by age 30 a man is satisfied with less frequent orgasms. The adult man expands his sexuality from a narrow focus on genital pleasure to include the broader sensual and emotional aspects of sexuality. In women, there is an early appreciation of the sensual and emotional aspects of sexuality, but the genital response is often limited and inconsistent in adolescence and young adulthood. Often it is only in later adulthood that women develop a capacity for intense genital pleasure.

But the pattern just described is not necessarily "natural." In different cultures, the male and female patterns of sexuality can vary widely. For example, researchers described the sexual practices in two contrasting societies: a small Irish community on the island of Inis Beag (Messenger, 1971) and a South Pacific island called Mangaia (D. S. Marshall, 1971). On Inis Beag, where there was an attitude of secrecy and fear about sex, premarital sex was all but unknown, intercourse was something that happened infrequently and quickly, and many people could not imagine that female orgasm existed. On Mangaia, by contrast, both boys and girls received sexual instruction from adults and were encouraged to have sexual experience with several partners before marriage, and all the women apparently learned at a young age to have orgasms.

These two cases are not isolated instances of variation in human sexual customs and expectations. Anthropologists have uncovered a wide variety of rules governing sexuality in different cultures. For example, among the Truk of the Caroline Islands in the western Pacific Ocean, a man may sleep with the wives of any of his wife's brothers, and a woman may sleep with her sisters' husbands; also, men but not women can demand a divorce on grounds of adultery. In many foraging societies, there is little or no sexual double standard, and virginity is not an important issue. Among the Hagen of New Guinea, conversely, virginity has traditionally been highly prized in brides, and wives are supposed to be chaste. However, sex is thought to be unclean and dangerous for both men and women, and hence the value placed on abstinence is almost as great for males as it is for females (O'Kelly & Carney, 1986). Clearly, sexuality can vary dramatically with cultural context.

The influence of culture on sexuality is particularly striking in the way our society regards sexuality and aging. Elderly people are often considered asexual (Daniluk, 1998), and, as people age, they commonly fear the loss of sexual interest and ability. Also, sexuality among the aged is sometimes thought of with disgust or amusement in our youth-oriented culture—the same behavior that might be taken as evidence of "virility" at 25 is called "lechery" at 65. North America is not the only part of the world where such myths flourish. Japanese researchers, for instance, have found that a decline in sexual activity among the elderly is partly attributable to cultural expectations (Mamiya, 1984).

The myths about aging and sex affect women and men somewhat differently, both because of gender roles and because of the difference in male and female life spans. The performance-oriented male sexual role is threatened when erections start to occur more slowly or infrequently, and the female sexual role as an attractive object is threatened when her appearance no longer conforms to the youthful stereotype that is synonymous with beauty in our culture. Physiological changes that occur with age can slow down sexual response: Men may have slower erections with more need for direct genital stimulation, and women may lose fatty tissue around the vagina, making intercourse uncomfortable without added lubrication. However, good health and regular sexual activity can promote men's and women's sexual functioning into their 70s and 80s if they do not fall victim to the myth that "old" means "sexless" (Butler & Lewis, 2002).

A particular difficulty for women in heterosexual relationships is that they are extremely likely to outlive their mates. Because there is a shortage of men in the over-65 age group, and because women in our culture tend not to seek out younger partners, widowhood often implies forced celibacy for women whose orientation is exclusively heterosexual. In fact, while only one-third of men in their 70s report that they are not having partnered sex, 70% of women in this age group report that they did not have sex with a partner over the past year (Michael et al., 1994).

EXPLAINING GENDER DIFFERENCES IN SEXUALITY

Physiology and Anatomy

Male–female differences in sexual anatomy have been postulated as a source of gender differences in sexual behavior. As noted earlier in the chapter, males can easily see their sexual organs and their arousal has obvious, visible signs. Females, however, can visually examine their own genitals only by using a mirror, and their arousal response is not as obvious and unmistakable as the male's erection. This difference may lead males to discover masturbation earlier and to feel more comfortable with their sexual anatomy and responses than females do. This explanation may provide part of the reason for the gender differences in masturbation and other sexual activity.

Some animal research links testosterone to sexual behavior, and there has been some speculation that, in humans, men's higher levels of sexual activity are due to their having higher levels of testosterone than women have. However, women's bodies are likely more sensitive to testosterone than men's are (Sherfey, 1966; Sherwin, 1988). Some research does link androgen secretion to sexual arousability in humans (Knussman, Christiansen, & Couwenbergs, 1986; Sherwin, 1988), but social factors and past experience apparently outweigh the hormonal effects (Barfield, 1976).

Evolutionary Theories

The evolutionary approach to behavior (see Chapter 2) postulates that much of our social behavior has evolved as strategies to ensure reproductive success—to produce as many healthy offspring as possible. In the framework of sexual selection theory, reproduction is the main function of sex, and the differences in male and female sexual behavior stem from the different conditions that favor reproductive success for the two sexes (e.g., Buss, 1994; Symons, 1979).

According to this approach, because males can produce millions of sperm, the best way for them to ensure that their genes will be reproduced is to impregnate as many women as possible; hence, the tendency to greater promiscuity among males. Because females can produce only one egg per month, their best reproductive strategy is to be very selective about whom they mate with, choosing someone who is healthy and likely to sire healthy children and perhaps who will provide safety and security for those children. Although sexual selection may be one of several influences that has shaped gender differences in sexuality, the explanations of these differences offered by this approach are still speculative. Indeed, many aspects of sexual selection theory have been challenged by evolutionary biologists (see Roughgarden, 2004, for a detailed explication of such arguments). For example, many species provide exceptions to the idea that males always compete for mates and females always choose on the basis of "best" genes. Also, there are numerous examples (among nonhuman primates as well as humans) in which sexual behavior is clearly linked more to pleasure and to cementing relationships than to procreation—and much more mating takes place than is necessary simply to ensure procreation. There are also many examples in which males exercise choice and refuse the sexual overtures of females—something they should not do if they are simply trying to spread their sperm as far and wide as possible. Gender differences in promiscuity can be explained as easily by gender differences in sexual socialization or in women's fear of sexual violence as by sexual selection. Convincing evidence for an evolutionary explanation of this difference would involve demonstrating both that the behavior in question has a genetic basis and that it is adaptive for reproductive fitness.

Sociocultural Influences

The double standard has long dictated that women restrict and are restricted in their sexuality more than men do and are. This difference in what males and females are implicitly given permission to do may well influence the sexual expression and experiences of both. Women, more often watched and warned about sexuality than men and encouraged to play a "gatekeeper" role, may learn to inhibit their sexual responses. Once in a committed sexual relationship, when they have no reason for inhibition, they may find they have learned the lesson too well: They find it difficult to let go. Men, who are allowed more leeway in terms of masturbation, exposure to erotica, and heterosexual activity and who may even learn to view sex as a way to "prove" their masculinity, may learn early on to treat sex as a goal-oriented activity—the goal being to produce an orgasm or to "score." This narrow focus may cause them to miss out on some of the pleasure of sexual experience.

The "sexual scripts" that lead women to associate being "good" with avoiding sex and lead men to associate sex not with intimacy but with achievement and conquest tend to limit the sexuality of both women and men. They are also the source of a good deal of grief, especially in adolescence and young adulthood, as the two genders find themselves working at cross-purposes in their attempts to develop satisfying sexual relationships.

The double standard itself is based on the notion that male sexual needs are stronger and therefore more important than female sexual needs. This notion is one more reflection of the greater power and status accorded to men than women in our culture. Perhaps we have not come so far from the time when Freudian theory could describe the whole process of psychosexual development as revolving around male anatomy. Despite the vast increase in technical knowledge about sex since Freud's day, some of the assumptions remain unchanged. Sex is still often defined in terms of the penis (Rotkin, 1972). "Real" sex involves male ejaculation into the female vagina. The terms *foreplay* and *afterplay* underline this point. Anything that occurs before or after intercourse is somewhat beside the point, even if it includes female orgasm.

Children are still sometimes taught that the female sexual organ is the vagina, when in fact the clitoris is the center for female sexual gratification. Men are still made to feel inadequate if they cannot bring a woman to orgasm during intercourse, despite the research showing that the thrusting of the penis in the vagina is not a particularly effective way to stimulate a woman to orgasm. When the aim of sexual activity is reproduction, intercourse is, of course, necessary. However, when the aim is sexual pleasure and intimacy, intercourse is not necessary, as many gay and lesbian couples will attest.

It is quite likely that both women and men would be happier in their sexual relationships if sexual intercourse were defined as just one of the possible expressions of sexuality rather than the most important one. A redefined sexuality that places as much emphasis on the clitoris as the penis and that removes the performance-in-intercourse orientation for males may help to make sex not one more expression of the status difference between women and men but rather a source of pleasure, self-esteem, and empowerment for both.

SEXUAL ORIENTATION

In May 1991, Heidi Leiter, a 17-year-old high school senior, broke new ground at her high school prom: The date she brought was a woman. The pair became the first openly lesbian couple to attend a high school prom in their region (B. A. Masters, 1991). Reaction of Heidi's classmates was generally unenthusiastic, and her choices apparently isolated her from other students. However, the fact that she was able to be open about her sexual orientation at all is one indication of change in public attitudes about homosexuality that was beginning to take hold in the early 1990s. Since that time, North America has seen some dramatic changes in recognition of same-gender relationships. The U.S. Census Bureau now counts same-sex couples, and according to the 2000 Census, there are 594,391 such couples living together in the United States (Cherrin, 2003). Same-sex "civil unions" have become legal in Vermont, and Massachusetts legalized gay marriage. Canada has also legalized same-sex marriage, and the legal rights of same-gender couples have expanded in a variety of ways in many parts of the United States and elsewhere in the world. In spite of this growing openness, however, there is also strong resistance to the expansion of rights for gay and lesbian couples. For example, 37 states have passed legislation that restricts legal marriage to heterosexual couples and seven states are preparing to vote on constitutional amendments to restrict legal marriage to unions between a man and a woman. Also, many people are still confused about the meaning of sexual orientation.

Heterosexuality, Homosexuality, and Bisexuality

Sexual orientation refers to a person's attraction to and preference for sexual partners of the same or other sex. **Heterosexual** is the label used for a person who prefers partners of the other sex, **homosexual** is the label applied to a person who prefers partners of the same sex, and **bisexual** is the term used to describe a person who can be attracted to partners of either sex. The terms **gay** and **straight** are often used to refer to homosexually oriented and heterosexually oriented persons and their communities, respectively, and women who are sexually and affectionally attracted to other women (i.e., whose sexual orientation is homosexual) are called **lesbians,** after the island of Lesbos. In ancient Greece, Lesbos was the home of the poet Sappho, famous for her love poetry to women.

It is difficult to say how many people practice heterosexuality, homosexuality, or bisexuality because these orientations seem to be points on a continuum rather than completely discrete categories. The data do seem to indicate, however, that more males than females have homosexual experiences and that males are more likely than females to practice exclusively homosexual lifestyles (Hunt, 1974; Kinsey et al., 1948, 1953; Michael et al., 1994). A study that investigated sexual orientation in one sample of adults, based on reported percentage of sexual fantasies and sexual experiences with women and men, found that one-third of both females and males reported at least occasionally fantasizing about sexual encounters with same-sex partners. In addition, one-third of the males also reported having at least one intimate sexual experience with another man; only 10% of females reported an intimate homosexual experience (Ellis, Burke, & Ames, 1987).

As discussed earlier in the chapter, people can have homosexual experiences without labeling themselves homosexual, and many people who think of themselves as gay still relate sexually to other-sex partners. Kinsey's conceptualization of heterosexuality-homosexuality as a continuum with many points in between was an important breakthrough in understanding sexual orientation. More recently, Storms (1980) offered a model of sexual orientation based on two independent dimensions—homoeroticism and heteroeroticism—instead of a single continuum. In this model, a person who is high only in heteroeroticism (sexual attraction and arousal to members of the other gender) tends to be involved only in heterosexual sexual relationships; a person high only in homoeroticism (sexual attraction and arousal to members of his or her own gender) tends to be involved only in homosexual sexual relationships; and a person high in both tends to be involved in both. This scheme allows us to think of homoeroticism and heteroeroticism as different dimensions rather than opposites: Being high on one does not automatically mean being low on the other. Some researchers also suggest that we can also think of bisexuality, not just as a combination of the two dimensions of homoeroticism and heteroeroticism but as a third dimension that can vary independently of the other two (e.g., Gonsiorek, Sell, & Weinrich, 1995). Paula Rust (2000) argued that the categories we use for sexual orientation are simply too limited:

> First, women and men are not opposites: The genders share many human traits, and coexisting attractions to women and men are, therefore, no more inherently contradictory than coexisting attractions to blue and brown eyes. Second, some people do not fall neatly into culturally constructed categories of womanhood and manhood (e.g., cross-dressers, gender blenders, and transgenderists) or biological sex (intersexed individuals), and not all men are male and not all women are female (e.g., transgenderists and preoperative transsexuals). Given that gender is not dichotomous and not related simply to biological sex, a sexual classification system based on a simplistic dichotomous distinction between male men and female women is not viable. . . . (pp. 208–209)

But even when observers agree on which categories to use, it is difficult to decide which people to place in those categories. Researchers do not agree on the operational and conceptual definitions of sexual orientation.

One survey of 228 research articles found that only 28 of them provided a conceptual definition of sexual orientation. These definitions varied from study to study, including or excluding such elements as physical sexual activity; affectional attachment; erotic fantasies; arousal; self-identification as bisexual, heterosexual, or homosexual; and awareness of attraction to one sex (Shively, Jones, & De Cecco, 1983/84). There is confusion even among researchers, then, about the exact meaning of sexual orientation. Indeed, some researchers have called for an abandonment of such categorical labels as heterosexual, bisexual, and homosexual, arguing that vast individual differences within each category make the distinctions artificial (Paul, 1985). Others have called upon researchers to stop imposing identities and labels on people and to focus instead on articulating a descriptive language of relationships (De Cecco & Shively, 1983/84).

Researchers' struggle to come to grips with the meaning of sexual orientation may eventually lead to a major reevaluation of our understanding of sexual desire and sexual relationships. One source of movement in this direction is the attempt to reevaluate sexual orientation from a social constructionist perspective. Janice Bohan (1996) noted that psychology has approached sexual orientation from "the essentialist assumption that sexual orientation is a primary, nuclear quality of self with which each individual must come to terms" as opposed to "a socially constructed meaning imposed on experiences that could equally well accommodate myriad other meanings" (p. 9). In other words, if, as a culture, we had learned to put different interpretations and labels on the experiences associated with sexual attraction, we might think very differently about sexual orientation. However, collectively we have learned a particular set of conceptual categories and terms about sexual orientation: "the culture we live in constructs sexual orientation as a core, nuclear, essential defining attribute of identity, which can be defined by membership in one of two (or at best three) categories. Hence, individuals living in this culture . . . experience their own and others' sexual orientation in these terms" (p. 9). So, in our culture, if a person feels attraction to members of her or his own sex, she or he is likely to accept, or at least consider strongly, a lesbian or gay identity—because that is what such feelings are interpreted to mean.

As Bohan (1996) pointed out, most research on sexual orientation has been carried out in an essentialist framework, treating sexual orientation as a core quality of an individual, the cause and correlates of which can be discovered. Using this approach, scientists have been only moderately successful; they do not agree on what causes people to develop different sexual orientations. There is a fair amount of negative evidence—that is, studies failing to find relationships between various factors and particular sexual orientations. As discussed in Chapter 5, for example, there is suggestive but still insufficient evidence for various biological bases for homosexuality. Evidence for various environmental causes is just as weak. One very comprehensive study of homosexuality found no evidence that homosexuality could be traced to disturbed parental relationships, being labeled by others as homosexual, unpleasant early heterosexual experiences, or being seduced at a young age by an older person of one's own sex (A. P. Bell et al., 1981). A study that set out to investigate the idea that women's traumatic sexual experiences with men might be a significant factor in the development of a lesbian identity found no support for this notion (Brannock & Chapman, 1990). The only significant difference found between lesbians and heterosexual women was that heterosexual women reported more categories of traumatic heterosexual experiences than lesbians did.

Why has it been so difficult to uncover the antecedents of sexual orientation? Perhaps because researchers have allowed their assumptions about sexuality to narrow their approach to the question. First, despite increasing evidence that there are many kinds of homosexual and bisexual preferences, just as there are many kinds of heterosexual preferences, researchers have tended to treat each category as discrete rather than fuzzy and to look for a single cause to explain each sexual orientation. Probably there are many different causes and combinations of causes that lead to many different shades of sexual orientation and experience. Even sexual attraction and emotional attachment may sometimes pull a person in different directions. One recent theory suggested that love and sexual desire are not necessarily aligned in sexual orientation—that individuals may sometimes experience sexual desire for same-sex individuals but still fall in love with someone of the other sex, or vice versa (Diamond, 2003).

Second, researchers have often been guided by theories that suggest sexual orientation is always "set" very early in life. In fact, sexual identity and orientation can evolve and change across the life span; this seems especially true of women. For example, many bisexual women do not have their first sexual experience with another woman until middle age (Blumstein & Schwartz, 1976), many women make the transition from heterosexuality to a lesbian identity in adulthood (Kitzinger & Wilkinson, 1995), and some lesbian women also adopt a heterosexual identity in later life (Bart, 1993).

Ann Peplau and her colleagues proposed that the development of women's sexual orientation be thought of as an **intimate career**—the sequence and patterns of a person's intimate relationships across the life span (Peplau, Spalding, Conley, & Veniegas, 1999). This model acknowledges that there are multiple paths that might lead one woman to identify as heterosexual and another to identify as bisexual or lesbian—just as there are multiple pathways toward a career as a Web designer or a personal trainer. They argue also that the factors shaping a woman's attractions and relationships—the availability of partners, the importance of passion, other family relationships, and so forth—change as she moves through life, and so a woman may change her sexual identity to adapt to these shifts in her internal and external environments. In light of new approaches that suggest women's sexuality tends to be more fluid than men's, this model might help researchers think of women's sexual orientation in new and useful ways.

Finally, perhaps researchers have had so much trouble understanding sexual orientation because they have focused most of their efforts on trying to explain the occurrence of the "deviant" orientations of homosexuality and bisexuality. Only recently have researchers begun to study the underpinnings of heterosexual identity instead of taking it for granted as something that unfolds

$\mathcal{O}$*verview*	Issues in understanding sexual orientation/identity
Definition	• Researchers do not agree on how to categorize individuals in terms of sexual orientation.
Social constructionist vs. essentialist framework	• Is sexual orientation a core, defining, "built-in" aspect of an individual? (essentialist perspective) • Or is sexual orientation an identity that individuals accept because their culture encourages them to interpret their own feelings in a particular way? (social constructionist perspective)
Gender differences	• The pathways to particular sexual identities seem to be different for women and men. Women may experience more fluidity in their sexual identities.

"naturally" (Eliason, 1995; Freedman & Lips, 2002). An alternative approach might be more fruitful. For example, what if bisexuality were considered the natural state? Then the important questions would concern not what errors in development and upbringing lead to homosexuality but rather what leads people to reject half the population as potential sex partners in order to become exclusively heterosexual or exclusively homosexual. Or what if no particular object choice but only the existence of sexual desire were considered natural? Then research would focus on the combinations of factors leading to different possible foci of that sexual desire.

Attitudes Toward Homosexuality

Homosexuality has been considered a stigma in our culture, so much so that Weinberg (1972) coined the term *homophobia* to describe the widespread irrational fear and intolerance of homosexuality. Greg Herek (2000) has argued that the term *homophobia* should be replaced by **sexual prejudice.** *Homophobia,* he said, is too limited a term because it makes prejudice against gays and lesbians sound too much like an illness and based only on fear. Gay men and lesbians risk discrimination in employment and housing, and "coming out" as gay can precipitate the loss of support of friends and family.

Discrimination on the basis of sexual orientation, not prohibited by the Civil Rights Act of 1964, is legal in most workplaces in the United States, although some states, cities, and counties have adopted antidiscrimination ordinances. And although American adults have shown increased support for basic civil liberties of lesbians and gay men, they still express negative attitudes—moral condemnation and personal discomfort—toward homosexuality (Herek, 2000b; Sherrill & Yang, 2000). Even private, intimate sexual practices between consenting adults of the same sex were illegal in some states until a 2003 U.S. Supreme Court ruling, which affirmed that individuals have a right to privacy and that the state has no right to interfere in such situations (Keller & Taylor, 2003). Research on university campuses in the United States indicates that at least two-thirds of lesbian and gay students report that they have been verbally insulted, one-quarter have been threatened with physical violence because of their orientation, and nearly all have overheard derogatory comments about gays and lesbians (Herek, 1993).

Homosexuality is more negatively sanctioned in males than in females, particularly by men (Haslam & Levy, 2006; Herek, 2000b; Whitley & Kite, 1995). Perhaps as members of the higher status sex, males can be forgiven less easily for deviating from their assigned role than females can. Homosexuality also receives more disapproval from male than female college students, but there are no gender differences in attitudes in general adult samples. The bias against homosexuality is apparent in the evaluation of lesbian and gay love relationships. In one study, heterosexual undergraduates presented with identical information about a hypothetical couple described that couple as "less in love" and "less satisfied with their relationship" when the couple was portrayed as gay or lesbian than when it was portrayed as heterosexual (Testa, Kinder, & Ironson, 1987).

These negative attitudes have made it difficult to study lesbian and gay populations. The gay and lesbian population has been difficult for researchers to identify, a situation that may result in the use of biased samples to draw conclusions about these groups. In addition, these attitudes have a direct impact on the feelings of gays and lesbians, making it difficult, for instance, for researchers to unravel the correlates of identifying oneself as gay or lesbian or of incorporating same-gender sexual relationships from being labeled deviant or from being a victim or potential victim of discrimination. These concerns were especially pronounced when Evelyn Hooker, the first psychologist to study a sample of normal gay men at a time when homosexuality was triply stigmatized as "a sin, a crime, and a disease," began her work in 1953. It was the McCarthy era, and the consequences of being labeled homosexual could be disastrous. Thus Hooker (1993) gave the highest priority to developing a sense of confidentiality and trust:

> The first absolute condition was secrecy and confidentiality. By great good fortune, our home was a very spacious estate of an acre of ground with a garden study separate from the house. It was there that the research was conducted. Once a person opened the garden gate, he was invisible to the neighbors. Without this superb place in which to conduct the research, I would never have attempted it. (pp. 450–451)

The words of Joseph Beam, a gay African American writer who died of AIDS at the age of 33, capture some of the feeling of isolation that can accompany the acceptance of this identity in a nonsupportive environment:

> In the winter of '79, in grad school, in the hinterlands of Iowa, I thought I was the first black gay man to have ever lived. . . . I lived a guarded existence: I watched how I crossed my legs, held my cigarettes, the brightness of the colors I wore. I was sure that some effeminate action would alert the world to my homosexuality. . . . Several years passed before I realized that my burden of shame could be a source of strength. (as quoted in Trescott, 1991, p. C5)

Both university and community environments are far more likely now than in 1979 to be supportive of individuals who identify as gay, lesbian, or bisexual. Yet hate crimes against such individuals—the murder of Matthew Shepard stands out as a tragic example—are a reminder that sexual prejudice is still a significant aspect of our cultural environment.

SEXUALITY AND POWER: EROTICA, PORNOGRAPHY, AND COERCIVE SEXUALITY

Part of the stereotype that men have a stronger sex drive than women is a belief that men are more frequently and more easily sexually aroused by erotic material. The consequences of this belief for women's and men's feelings about their own sexuality and for the sexual power relationship between the sexes are enormous. Most material that is meant to be sexually arousing is produced for a male audience. Perhaps because it is explicitly geared to men rather than to both sexes, this material tends to present a view of women that is simultaneously idealized (in terms of physical beauty) and belittling (women are portrayed as passive objects of sexual desire, as bodies rather than people). Not surprisingly, women have never been encouraged to view this type of material; its very presence sometimes renders a store, a bar, or an entire section of a city virtually off limits for women. One impact of the presence of large amounts of male-oriented erotic material, then, is to make real live women feel unwelcome and out of place in the areas where images and fantasies of sexuality are sold.

Such a situation is highly unlikely to foster in women a sense of empowerment and joy in their own sexuality. To make matters even more difficult, there is an increasing trend toward the portrayal of brutalization and degradation of women in sexually oriented materials, a development that makes such materials even less palatable to women and that reinforces myths of male sexual dominance and female sexual powerlessness and passivity. The development of an entire industry dedicated to producing and marketing sexually arousing materials specifically for a male audience obviously makes at least good economic sense: The pornography industry makes millions of dollars per year in sales to men. But does it make sense on any other dimension? Are women really not interested in erotic materials? What impact does the consumption of existing erotica and pornography have on men? And how does pornography fit into the larger problem of coercive sexuality?

Responses to Erotica

The women in the early Kinsey surveys reported less responsiveness than the men to most types of erotic materials. However, later studies suggested that women and men are not very different in their arousal response to erotic stories, pictures, and films. In general, it appears that women can be as physically aroused as men by the typically available X-rated films and videos (Griffitt, 1987), and women and men can masturbate to orgasm equally quickly when viewing these materials (Fisher, Pollack, & Malatesta, 1986). Yet women are less likely than men to seek out these materials. This fits with the commonly reported finding that women engage in sexual fantasy less than men do (Leitenberg & Henning, 1995). However, the latter authors also speculate that most commercial pornography is aimed at, and fits better with, the sexual fantasies of men than those of women:

> If one examines the typical X-rated movie, one immediately sees naked bodies engaged in sexual activity without much story line, gradual buildup, affection, emotional ties, and so forth. The fantasy being portrayed is primarily the male fantasy of multiple female sexual partners ever ready for sexual activity of any kind without any chance of the man being rejected. On the other hand, the primary fantasy of the typical romance novel is a woman who inflames the passion and lifelong love of a desirable man under difficult circumstances. The strong, dominant man is overcome by feelings of love and sweeps the heroine away. (p. 484)

Impact of Erotica and Pornography on Behavior

How might viewing or listening to sexually arousing material affect someone? Might it affect the person's level of sexual interest, performance of particular sexual acts, perception of his or her sexual partner, or satisfaction with her or his sexual relationships? Most of the research shows short-term effects. For instance, one study of male exposure to sexually explicit slides found that in the week following there was no increase in sexual activity although there was a significant increase in masturbation on the day of exposure (M. Brown, Amoroso, & Ware, 1976).

Exposure to erotic material may affect a man's evaluation of his mate. Men, but not women, who saw a series of nude photographs from *Playboy*, *Penthouse*, and *Playgirl* magazines later rated their mates as less sexually attractive than did their counterparts, who were exposed instead to pictures of abstract art (Gutierres, Kenrick, & Goldberg, 1983). Research also shows that even nonviolent pornography may reduce male sensitivity to female victims of sexual assault by making women appear sexually promiscuous—in other words, by suggesting that women are "asking" to be raped (Zillman & Weaver, 1989). However, other researchers have failed to find any link between exposure to nonviolent pornography and attitudes toward women or rape (Padgett, Brislin-Slutz, & Neal, 1989). Research does not appear to have addressed the question of how exposure to erotica and pornography affects women's and men's own self-perceptions and body image. One might, for example, predict that exposure to the photographs of apparently flawlessly beautiful women in magazines such as *Playboy* could shake a normal-looking woman's self-confidence in her own attractiveness, particularly if her male partner seems impressed.

Because so much of the sexually arousing material that is produced for men tends to portray women more as objects than as human beings, it is not surprising that there has been a trend toward increasing portrayals of violence against women in such material. When explicit violence is added to sexually arousing material, the issues of impact become even more complex. Might a viewer who learns to associate sexual arousal with depictions of rape scenes, for example, be tempted to try rape in real life? Moreover, in pornography, a woman who is raped, humiliated, or brutalized is usually shown to resist initially but eventually to become sexually aroused by the way she is treated. Exposure to this type of fantasy may encourage men to behave in sexually coercive ways in the mistaken belief that the experience will not ultimately be a bad one for the woman.

Exposure to sexually violent pornography can increase men's acceptance of interpersonal violence against women and of rape myths such as "Every woman secretly wants to be raped" (Demaré, Briere, & Lips, 1988; Malamuth & Check, 1981). Repeated exposure to violent pornography also results in decreased sensitivity to female victims of violence in nonsexual contexts (Linz, Donnerstein, & Penrod, 1984). Furthermore, laboratory studies in which males are exposed to aggressive or nonaggressive pornography and then given the opportunity to behave aggressively against another person by delivering electric shocks show that exposure to aggressive but not nonaggressive pornography increases the aggressive behavior of male participants against females but not against males (Donnerstein, 1980, 1983; Malamuth, 1984). Exposure to aggressive pornography is strongly related to arousability to rape scenes, acceptance of rape myths, and self-reported likelihood of committing rape (Briere, Corne, Runta, & Malamuth, 1984). Finally, a survey of college males indicated that self-reported use of sexually violent but not nonviolent pornography plays a significant role in predicting self-reported likelihood of using sexual force or rape against women and of self-reported use of actual sexual coercion or force (Demaré et al., 1988; Demaré, Lips, & Briere, 1993).

In summary, although exposure to pornography does not seem to have a major, lasting impact on sexual behavior, there is evidence that violent pornography can have an impact on men's aggressive behavior against women as well as on their attitudes toward violence against women and toward female victims. However, the correlational research is equally suggestive of the possibility that men who are predisposed to sexual violence and who already hold disparaging attitudes toward women are more likely than other men to use violent pornography. The sexual socialization of males provides the market for such material, and the material reinforces the way many men have been taught to view women.

Little research has addressed the impact of exposure to violent pornography on women, probably because men are the main consumers of pornography. However, since violent pornography is now a fairly visible feature of the media environment, it may well be having an impact even on those who are not its intended audience. Individual women often report that they feel humiliated and angry when forced to stand next to a rack of pornographic magazines at the checkout counter of their local store; such feelings are compounded when women have their children with them. Women speak of feeling violated and hurt when confronted with the violent antiwoman images in pornography, particularly when they discover that their male partners are consumers of such images. And one South African study shows that viewing images of sexual violence—or other violence—against women can cause women to feel disempowered (Reid & Finchilescu, 1995). There seems little doubt that exposure to pornography affects women's feelings about themselves and their attitudes toward men, although these relationships have not been extensively researched.

Coercive Sexuality

Relating sexually to another person implies exposing oneself to that person, at least physically and often emotionally. That exposure gives the partners some power over each other. In addition, knowing that one is desirable and desired sexually can confer a sense of power and secure self-esteem. Thus sexuality almost always involves issues of vulnerability and power. Perhaps it should not be surprising, then, to find that power and dominance can sometimes overwhelm the relationship aspects and even the physical pleasure aspects of sexuality—that sex can become an expression of dominance rather than of love or lust. There is a very noticeable gender difference here: Sexual coercion or violence is much more likely to be used by men than women. In a social context that tends to accept and encourage male dominance in so many situations, such a gender difference is almost inevitable.

RAPE   Forcing sexual relations on someone against that person's choice is a common crime of sexual violence. In fact, most people would argue that there is nothing sexual about this violent act—so what is it doing in a chapter on sexuality? **Rape** is discussed here because so many people, perhaps particularly men, include rape in their understanding of sexuality. Something that starts out construed by the participants as a sexual encounter can become a violent one instead.

Interviews with a random sample of San Francisco women led researchers to conclude that a woman faces a 26% chance of being raped during her lifetime (D. E. H. Russell & Howell, 1983). One reviewer found that most estimates of the prevalence of rape or sexual assault among adult women range from 14% to 25% (Koss, 1993). This figure is much higher than police reports of rape; it is widely acknowledged that rape is one of the most underreported crimes (Koss, Heise, & Russo, 1994). Men have less reason to fear rape than women do, unless they are in prison, where the rape of men by other men is common (Lockwood, 1980). However, there are rare instances in which men are raped by women (Sarrel & Masters, 1982). Although the latter occurrence might seem physically impossible, it is not; penile erection is not under strict conscious control and may occur in response to such emotions as anger or fear.

The Bureau of Justice Statistics reports that, in 2004, women were the targets of 209,880 rapes or sexual assaults—about 67% of them perpetrated by people they knew (Catalano, 2005). By contrast, men were the targets of 6,200 rapes or sexual assault—all by strangers.

Women on college campuses are at higher risk of rape and sexual assault than some other groups of women: Survey data indicated that, on a campus of 10,000 students, there are about 350 rapes every year (Fisher, Cullen, & Turner, 2000). A troubling feature of this finding is that many of the women surveyed did not characterize their experience of forced sex as rape. Their reluctance to name the experience apparently stemmed from embarrassment, blaming themselves, not understanding the definition of *rape*, or not wanting to label an acquaintance a rapist.

Women who have been raped are not always given the help they need when seeking medical treatment. A study of a nationally representative sample of rape survivors found that 42% were not tested for sexually transmitted diseases when they sought emergency room care (Amey & Bishai, 2002). Furthermore, only 20% were given emergency contraception to prevent pregnancy from the rape.

College students estimated that 45% of men would commit rape if they could be sure they would not be caught and that 32% of women would enjoy being raped if no one would know about it. When these same students were asked to report their own likelihood, 51% of the men reported at least some likelihood that they would commit rape if they would not be caught, but only 2% of the women reported any likelihood at all that they would enjoy being raped (Malamuth, Haber, & Feshbach, 1980). The average number of college males indicating some possibility that they would rape a woman under certain conditions has been estimated to be about 35% (Malamuth, 1981), although in different samples it can be as high as nearly 60% (Briere & Malamuth, 1983) or as low as 17% (Demaré et al., 1988). The self-reported likelihood of rape is correlated with acceptance of rape myths, fantasies about forced sex, and sexual arousal in response to rape depictions.

There is some evidence that men may be reluctant to recognize their own sexual aggression. In one survey, 54% of women said they had been sexually victimized or coerced in some way, but only 25% of men said that they had engaged in any sexual aggression (Koss, Gidycz, & Wisniewski, 1987). The large discrepancy suggests that men do not recognize or acknowledge their behavior as sexually coercive. And who is most likely to be sexually coercive? One model suggests that the men who are most likely to be sexually coercive against women are those who engage in a lot of casual, impersonal sex and who are high in hostility toward and desire to dominate women (Malamuth, 1996).

Attitudes about the acceptability of force in sexual interactions may have an early start. When Zellman and Goodchilds (1983) questioned a broad spectrum of Los Angeles teenagers, they found that only 21% of them replied that, under each of nine specific conditions, it was definitely not all right for "a guy to hold a girl down and force her to have sexual intercourse." Force was viewed as most acceptable in cases in which the girl had led the boy on or made him sexually excited or when the couple had been dating for a long time. Both male and female teenagers were reluctant to define forced sex as rape, particularly when the couple involved was portrayed as dating steadily, and they tended to assign some of the blame for forced sex to the female. Similar results were found in a more recent study of Israeli high school students' attitudes toward date rape. These students, particularly the males, often minimized the seriousness of sexual coercion and attributed it to characteristics or behavior of the victim (Geiger, Fischer, & Eshet, 2004). These findings reflect the presence of the traditional double standard in teenagers' attitudes, particularly in the stereotype that it is the girl's responsibility to control sexual behavior. Against such a background, it is perhaps not surprising that a significant number of college males say there is some possibility that they would commit rape.

College students' self-reported attitudes about rape may stem in part from the prevalence of rape on college campuses. As many as 27.5% of college women in the United States and 23.3% of college women in Canada have experienced rape or attempted rape (Koss et al., 1994), and a Department of Justice

Reflections

Rape and Threats of Rape: A Way to Intimidate Women and Keep Them Off Male Turf?

In 2003 a scandal rocked the U.S. Air Force Academy: A total of 56 female cadets charged that they had been sexually assaulted at the school over the previous 10 years. Many people were stunned. In an environment that is supposed to embody discipline and honor, how could such a pattern of sexual violence against women occur? And how could it have been kept secret for so long?

When reporters went looking for answers, one thing they found is that the Air Force Academy situation was far from isolated. Indeed, women throughout the armed forces have apparently been targets of sexual assault and harassment for decades, but few measures have been taken to protect them (*USA Today*, 2003).

A survey of military women who served in the 1991 Persian Gulf War found that they were stressed by more than combat exposure: More than 8 percent of them had been raped, and more than 32 percent had been "physically sexually harassed" (Wolfe, Sharkansky, Read, Dawson, Martin, & Ouimette, 1998). In the same era, the Navy found itself dealing with the "Tailhook" scandal: At a convention of navy aviators, some 100 military and civilian women were sexually assaulted (O'Neill, 1998). Some years later, several male soldiers at the Army's Aberdeen Proving Ground were charged with the rape and sexual abuse of a number of young female soldiers who had just completed basic training (O'Neill, 1998). And a survey of a nationally representative sample of over 3,500 female veterans revealed that more than half had been sexually harassed while in the military, and almost one-quarter (23%) had been sexually assaulted (Skinner, Kressin, Frayne, Tripp, Hankin, Miller, & Sullivan, 2000).

The rates of sexual assault show few signs of diminishing. In one survey of 558 women veterans who had served in Vietnam or after, 28% reported they had been raped. The rate of reported rape did not differ across eras of service (Sadler, Booth, Cook, & Doebbeling, 2003). The Pentagon recently released a report showing that reported sexual assaults had increased by 40% in 2005—an increase that is attributed to new confidential reporting policies that make it easier for women to report rapes (Department of Defense, 2006).

Clearly, women in the military face a greater risk of rape than do women in other workplaces—and their greatest risk of such victimization is not from enemy soldiers but from their own colleagues. What could cause such a pattern?

Analysts point to a lack of accountability to civilian law enforcement agencies, outdated military statutes, and a tendency to tell victims they should keep silent to protect their unit or their branch of the military (*USA Today*, 2003). It is likely that all these factors are important. Yet underlying them may be a more basic issue: Until very recently, and perhaps even now, women in the military have been viewed as interlopers. Military service, particularly with respect to combat, has been a quintessentially masculine endeavor. Such a viewpoint makes women targets of hostility and undercuts the idea that their welfare should be taken seriously. Could it be this hostility, rather than the sexual tension that can occur when women and men work in close quarters, that produces the high rates of sexual assault among military women and the failure to design adequate remedies?

survey indicated that a woman has between a 1 in 4 and 1 in 5 chance of being raped while in college (Fisher, Cullen, & Turner, 2000). A large proportion of rapes of college women occur when the victim is intoxicated (Abbey, 2002; Mohler-Kuo, Dowdall, Koss, & Wechsler, 2004). The danger of rape on campuses has become even more serious in recent years with the availability of "date rape" drugs, such as Rohypnol, which can be slipped into a drink, quickly rendering a woman unconscious and unable to resist. Few women report their experiences of rape or sexual assault, perhaps because until a few years ago campus administrations treated rape as a prank that got out of hand rather than as a crime. The consequences of academic institutions' silence in the face of rape are very negative for female students: Victims may drop out of classes or even leave school, and a ripple effect through the female student population may diminish confidence levels and assertiveness (Hirsch, 1990). The words of one young college graduate, several years after being gang-raped at a fraternity party during her junior year, provide some sense of the pervasive, lasting effects of such an experience: "I'm a lot more hesitant about things, more cautious. I'm much more comfortable with things I'm used to. I think I'm probably more scared. Like, I'm much more comfortable just being home" (as quoted in Hirsch, 1990, p. 56).

WHY IS SEXUAL ASSAULT SO COMMON?   The finding that many ordinary men say there is some likelihood they would commit rape lends support to the argument, often made by feminists (e.g., Brownmiller, 1975; D. E. H. Russell, 1984), that a tendency toward sexual aggression against women is part of the traditional masculine gender role. Males are socialized to be dominant and aggressive, and there are many messages, including those contained in violent pornography, that it is appropriate to express these tendencies in a sexual context. Clearly, rape is not simply a result of a sexually frustrated male's need for an outlet: Self-reported adequacy and importance of his sex life are not related to a man's self-reported likelihood of rape (Briere & Malamuth, 1983). The high incidence of gang rape (a rape committed by more than one assailant) also points to the conclusion that rape is a way of proving masculinity and dominance rather than achieving sexual release.

The feminine gender role may also contribute to rape, in that females are socialized to be passive, weak, and fearful—prime qualities for the construction of vulnerable victims. In fact, research on the avoidance of rape shows that women whose socialization does not reflect the traditional feminine image are more successful at avoiding attempted rape (Bart, 1980). Bart found that background differences involving women's autonomy, competence, and self-reliance are related to the ability to avoid rape—for example, size and weight, never having been married, regular sports involvement, knowledge of first aid and self-defense, and assertiveness training. Moreover, in an actual attempted rape situation, women who use the most strategies to avoid rape are the most successful; the likelihood of being raped increases when a woman relies on only one strategy to avoid it. These data suggest that women should be prepared to use many methods of avoiding rape and that reliance on such "feminine" modes of influence as pleading and reasoning with the rapist is ineffective.

A set of social norms, based on the double standard, that suggest only "virtuous" women deserve full protection from sexual assault also contributes to the prevalence of rape. In certain Latin American countries—Costa Rica, Ecuador, and Guatemala—the law does not recognize forced sexual intercourse as rape unless the woman is chaste and honest (Heise, Pitanguy, & Germain, 1993), and in the courts of Pakistan, the Hudood Ordinance, introduced in 1979 and currently the subject of fierce debate, requires that a woman must have four male witnesses to prove she was raped. Otherwise, the victimized woman is assumed to have committed adultery and can be imprisoned as a criminal ("TV Debates," 2006). The rape of a prostitute is thought by some to be a contradiction in terms. One Australian judge, for instance, noted during sentencing of a man who had raped a prostitute at knifepoint that rape was less traumatizing for prostitutes than for other women because prostitutes were involved in sex as a business (Magazanik, 1991).

A man's rape of his wife has also been thought, until recently, to be a contradiction in terms. The thinking was that marriage gave a man full sexual access to his wife, so there could be no such thing as rape in the marriage relationship. The wife's willingness to engage in sex on any particular occasion was not relevant. In 1977, Oregon became the first U.S. state to make marital rape illegal, and since then all other states have followed suit (Neft & Levine, 1997). Until 1983, Canadian law said that a man who raped his wife, even if the couple were separated, could be charged with assault only if there were injuries.

INCEST   Incest, defined as sexual relations between relatives, is often coercive and exploitative because in many cases it involves an older powerful relative forcing sex on a younger, inexperienced one. Studies show that female children tend to be sexually victimized by adult males more often than male children are victimized by males or females. Between 4% and 12% of all women surveyed report a childhood sexual encounter with an adult male relative, and for 1 woman in 100 that adult male relative is her father (Herman, 1981). In a 1991 study in three states—Alabama, North Dakota, and South Carolina—20% of female rape victims under the age of 12 had been raped by their fathers, and 46% had been raped by other family members (U.S. Department of Justice, 1994).

Fewer men report having been victimized sexually by an adult during childhood; among those who do, the adult is far more likely to have been male than female. It appears that men are far more likely than women to take sexual liberties with children. This may be because men tend to hold more power in the family situation than women do, giving them a sense that they have a right to impose their will on other family members and making it unlikely that others will interfere. It may also be due partly to our culture's sexual socialization of men and women. Men are conditioned to be attracted to sexual partners who are young, delicate, and naive—the qualities of children—whereas women do not learn to associate these characteristics with sexual desirability.

SUMMARY

Research on gender and sexuality has occurred in the context of a double standard of behavior for women and men. Men, thought to have the stronger sex drive, have implicitly been given more permission to engage in sexual activity. Men do seem to report more interest in sex; for instance, they think about it more often than women do. However, research indicates that, physiologically, there are strong similarities between males and females in their response to sexual stimulation. The main difference is that females are capable of multiple orgasms whereas most males are not. Women, however, are more likely than men to report difficulty in achieving orgasm, at least during intercourse. Both sexes can masturbate to orgasm quickly and easily; however, women are considerably less likely than men to masturbate. Women who do masturbate are less likely to have trouble reaching orgasm during sexual activity with a partner.

Women and men may differ in the ways they experience and assign meaning to sexual relationships. Men may have more motivation than women do to have sex, regardless of the surrounding relationship; women seem to place more emphasis on the relationship when making sexual decisions. In line with this pattern, women's sexuality may be more malleable and fluid than men's—changing more easily in response to relational and cultural context. And men seem to have a stronger association than women do between sex and power or aggression.

Frequency of premarital intercourse has increased over the years, especially among women, leading to a reduction in the gap between men and women in the extent of such activity. Men still tend to have more sexual partners before marriage than women do and are more likely than women to feel positive about their first experience of intercourse. Men are more likely than women to report engaging in extramarital sex. Among heterosexuals, the possibility of pregnancy has a greater effect on female than on male sexuality: Women are more likely than men to report that fear of pregnancy interferes with the free expression of their sexuality, and women are more likely than men to take responsibility for birth control.

The AIDS epidemic appears to be having some impact on sexual attitudes and behavior. Sexually active teenagers of both sexes worry about contracting the disease although they often fail to use condoms, which reduce the risk.

No single explanation seems to account for gender differences in sexual behavior. Differences in anatomy may provide some of the basis for the differences in the way males and females explore their feelings and are socialized, by both parents and peers, with respect to sexuality. Different cultural standards of sexual behavior for women and men contribute to the development of different value orientations, attitudes, and behavior. The cultural tendency to define sexuality in terms of male anatomy and needs leads to coercive sexual behavior by males and often to frustration and dissatisfaction for both females and males in heterosexual relationships. Yet, despite all this, a reasonable number of people achieve happy, satisfying heterosexual relationships. Apparently males and females are not so different that their shared humanity and concern for relationships cannot transcend the difficulties wrought by anatomy, gender-role socialization, and the cultural ideology of male dominance—at least some of the time!

Men are more likely than women to report engaging in homosexual activity and to define themselves as exclusively homosexual. Homosexuality is more negatively sanctioned in men than women in our culture, and men also express more disapproval of homosexuality than women do. On the positive side, individuals in gay and lesbian relationships do not have to accommodate the gender-role expectations that have such a powerful impact on heterosexual relationships.

Both men and women can be aroused easily by erotic material or fantasies. However, most commercially produced erotic material is aimed at heterosexual males. Much of that material depicts sexual violence against women as sexually arousing. Research shows a link between men's consumption of such sexually violent material and tendencies to accept violence against women, to actually behave aggressively toward women in laboratory situations, to report some likelihood of raping a woman if given a clear opportunity, and to report having achieved intercourse with a woman through coercion or physical force. The availability of violent pornography is only one source of the message to males in our culture that the use of aggression and power in a sexual context is often permitted and approved. The high incidence of rape and incest seems to result not from uncontrollable male sexual desire but from masculine socialization toward sexual dominance and an ideology that allows males to feel they have a right to impose their will on females. Rape has much more to do with power than with sexuality. The high prevalence of this crime is a strong signal that social power differences are built into gender differences. If we imagine a society in which rape is an extremely rare occurrence, we are probably imagining one in which women and men hold equal status.

KEY TERMS

double standard

vasocongestion

myotonia

excitement phase

plateau phase

orgasm

G-spot

resolution phase

refractory period

sex drive

human immunodeficiency virus (HIV)

acquired immunodeficiency syndrome (AIDS)

heterosexual

homosexual

bisexual

gay

straight

lesbians

sexual orientation

intimate career

sexual prejudice

rape

Hormonal and Reproductive Connections

*J*n England, during the past two decades, several women have been given reduced sentences or probation for murder because they committed the crimes during the week before the onset of their menstrual cycle—and each used the defense that she suffered from severe premenstrual syndrome (PMS) (Sommer, 1984). PMS was cited as a source of diminished responsibility, making the women prone to uncontrollable acts of violence during the premenstrual period. A Virginia physician, arrested for driving under the influence of alcohol, successfully used PMS as her defense (*Washington Post,* 1991).

There are numerous other anecdotes of women's hormonal or reproductive physiology being labeled a source of instability. Several years ago, a Canadian judge disallowed the evidence given by a woman in her 50s because, he said, women at that stage of life (presumably referring to menopause) were known to imagine things. And once, during an interview about my research on the psychology of pregnancy, a reporter greeted my finding that most pregnant women did not report unusual emotional difficulties with open astonishment and disbelief: "Everyone knows," she sputtered, "that women go a little crazy for 9 months when they're pregnant"! "Everyone knows," indeed, that the hormonal changes involved in female reproductive processes—menstruation, pregnancy, childbirth, postpartum adjustment, breastfeeding, menopause—render women less emotionally stable than men. But is "everyone" correct? Are the physiological processes involved in reproduction really debilitating to women?

And what about men? Researchers have suggested, for instance, that high testosterone is related to antisocial behavior (Dabbs, 1992), but they have focused on one-time measurements of testosterone rather than on examination of changing levels. Could men's moods be affected by hormonal cycles? Is there such a thing as "male menopause"? Are there cycles besides the menstrual cycle that might be linked to emotions or behavior in both women and men? To answer these questions, it is necessary to move beyond the stereotypes to the research.

In this chapter, we will do just that. We will examine research that asks these questions:

- What hormonal changes take place during the menstrual cycle?
- Are these hormonal changes related to changes in a woman's emotions? Behavior? Sensory processes? Cognitive performance?
- What is PMS and how many women does it affect?
- What influence does our culture have on the experience of the menstrual cycle?
- Do men have hormonal cycles too?
- How does pregnancy affect women physically and emotionally, and are these effects shaped by a woman's culture?
- Do expectant fathers have emotional symptoms?
- How does the experience of childbirth affect women and their partners?
- Does postpartum depression exist?
- What is the psychological impact of abortion?
- What hormonal changes happen during menopause, and what kinds of physical and psychological changes occur at the same time?
- What is "male menopause"?

By the end of the chapter, it will be clear that questions about hormones and behavior are quite complex and that, once again, the interplay between biology and culture cannot be ignored when trying to understand the impact of physiological processes.

THE MENSTRUAL CYCLE

For centuries, the existence of the menstrual cycle has been used to characterize women as unstable and therefore unfit for certain responsible social and economic positions. This is, of course, in contrast to men, whose physiological state has been thought to be relatively constant. (As will be noted later in the chapter, however, male hormone levels are *not* particularly constant.) In fact, women's reproductive anatomy and physiology have long been considered a source of danger to both physical and emotional health.

At the beginning of the 20th century, some educators took strong stands against coeducation in adolescence on the basis that daily association with boys would interfere with the "normalization" of a girl's menstrual period; the suggestion was also made that if girls were forced to exercise their brains at puberty they would use up the blood needed later for menstruation (see Shields, 1975). In fact, well into the 20th century, doctors viewed women as always having the potential to be made sick by virtue of the mere possession of a uterus and ovaries; menstruation, pregnancy, and menopause were seen as physical diseases and intellectual handicaps (Ehrenreich & English, 1979). In addition, even dry scientific texts have tended to wax lyrical when discussing menstruation, sometimes describing it as a sign that a woman's body *wants* to have children! For example, Ganong's 1977 *Review of Medical Physiology* unabashedly noted that "Menstruation is the uterus crying for the lack of a baby" (as quoted in Laqueur, 1990). The echoes of these beliefs still haunt our culture's approach to women and to reproduction.

Hormonal Rhythms

In women, the cyclic pattern of sex hormone levels is maintained through a negative feedback system involving the hypothalamus, the pituitary gland, and the ovaries. The ovaries, which produce the sex hormones estrogen and progesterone, are regulated by the pituitary gland, which in turn is regulated by the hypothalamus, which responds to the levels of estrogen and progesterone produced by the ovaries. The **menstrual cycle,** which lasts 28 days on average but may vary a great deal among individuals and even within the same individual, happens in four phases:

1. In the **follicular phase,** the pituitary secretes follicle-stimulating hormone (FSH), stimulating a follicle in one of the ovaries to secrete estrogen and to bring an egg to maturity.

2. In **ovulation,** the follicle ruptures to release the mature egg. At this point, the estrogen level is high—a condition that stimulates the hypothalamus to produce LH-releaser, which in turn causes the pituitary to produce LH (luteinizing hormone). The high estrogen level also inhibits production of FSH. In the uterus, the high levels of estrogen stimulate the lining to thicken and form glands that will secrete substances to nourish the embryo if conception occurs.

3. In the **luteal phase,** the LH stimulates the follicle to turn into a glandular mass of cells called the *corpus luteum,* which in turn manufactures progesterone. As the progesterone levels rise, they stimulate the glands of the endometrium, or uterine lining, to secrete nourishing substances. They also inhibit the pituitary's production of LH, eventually causing the corpus luteum to degenerate and the levels of both progesterone and estrogen to drop sharply after 10 to 12 days. However, if the egg has been fertilized and implanted in the womb, the hormone levels will not drop, and the next phase will not occur.

4. The final phase, **menstruation,** involves shedding the inner uterine lining, the endometrium, which flows out through the cervix and the vagina. Levels of progesterone and estrogen are low, and FSH levels begin to rise again in preparation for the beginning of another cycle.

Although menstruation is technically the end of the cycle, the first day of menstruation is counted as day 1 of the cycle because it is the easiest to identify. The changes in the levels of ovarian and pituitary hormone levels across the cycle are shown in Figure 8.1.

Given the dramatic shifts in the levels of estrogen and progesterone over the 28-day cycle, we should not be surprised by the suggestion that the cycle variation affects moods, feelings, performance, and behavior. In fact, many women do report symptoms such as periodic shifts in mood that seem to correlate with their menstrual cycle. Some women report that they become depressed and irritable just before or during their menstrual period. Others report physical symptoms such as cramps or headaches at this time of the month. There is a lack of universal agreement on what symptoms occur when, but because a significant number of women report *some* symptoms that seem to vary with the phase of their menstrual cycle, it seems worthwhile to pursue the issue of what might cause such symptoms.

While examining these issues, it is important to remember that the fact that certain symptoms may correlate (that is, occur together) with certain phases of the menstrual cycle does not necessarily imply that they are *caused* by the hormonal changes that characterize that part of the cycle. It is very difficult, in fact, to ascertain whether these reported symptoms are due to physiological changes in a woman's body or to her learned expectations of menstrual effects. Research (e.g., Schacter & Singer, 1962; Walster, 1974) indicates that people actually tend to label their moods according to their expectations about how they should feel in certain situations.

Emotional, Behavioral, Sensory, and Cognitive Correlates of the Menstrual Cycle

MOOD   For decades, psychologists have referred to a **premenstrual syndrome** of high tension, depression, irritability, and assorted physical symptoms, said to occur during the days immediately preceding the onset of menstruation (K. Dalton, 1964; R. T. Frank, 1931). Some research has found that

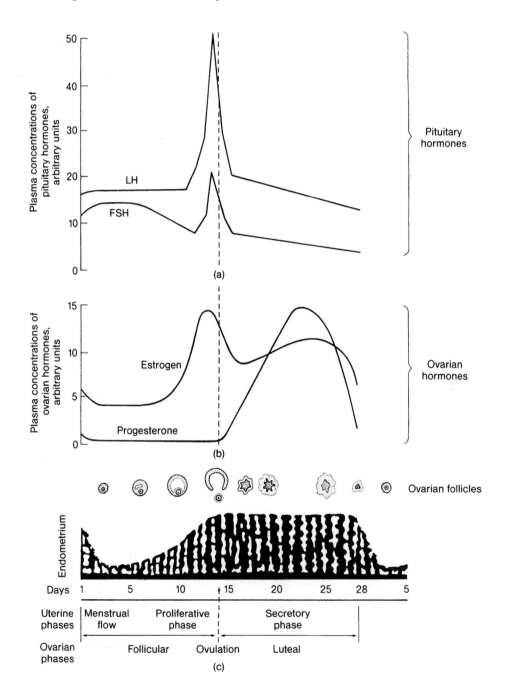

Figure 8.1 Changes in hormone levels across the menstrual cycle. (a) Levels of hormones produced by the pituitary. (b) Hormones produced by the ovaries. (c) Changes in follicles in the ovary and the endometrium of the uterus.

women report more anxiety, hostility, or depression during the premenstrual and menstrual phases than at other times (e.g., Golub, 1976; Hamilton, Gallant, & Lloyd, 1989; Paige, 1971). However, other studies have found no relationship between mood and the menstrual cycle (e.g., Laessle, Tuschl, Schweiger, & Pirke, 1990; Mansfield, Hood, & Henderson, 1989), and some have reported findings contradictory to those expected (e.g., McFarlane, Martin, & Williams, 1988; Parlee, 1982).

Some support for a hormonal cause of mood fluctuations comes from the finding that women taking oral contraceptives (and thus not experiencing normal cyclic variations in hormone levels) report fewer cyclic mood changes (Paige, 1971; Rossi & Rossi, 1977). However, there is another possible explanation for the absence of mood fluctuations in women taking oral contraceptives: Oral contraceptives reduce the monthly menstrual flow and make it more predictable—and negative moods may be due to anticipated flow and the bother that goes with it rather than to hormone levels (Paige, 1971; Parlee, 1982).

When women are asked to keep daily records of their moods and symptoms over several months, the results generally indicate a great deal of variability in individual women's patterns, with individual records showing very little evidence of rhythm. However, when the records of many individual women are combined, some studies show regular cyclic changes in such things as fatigue, abdominal pain, breast tenderness, appetite, headaches, and irritability (Laessle et al., 1990; Parlee, 1973). Different studies tend to show cyclic changes in different patterns, and these inconsistencies remain unexplained.

Accurate estimates of the proportion of women who experience mood fluctuations across the menstrual cycle are unavailable; different studies provide substantially different numbers. One reviewer estimates that 50% to 75% of women show some mood fluctuation, but at least 25% show none at all (Hyde, 1986). Moreover, despite the menstrual cycle, the variability in women's moods does not seem to differ appreciably from the variability of men's moods, as shown by a study in which husbands and wives charted their daily moods for 2 months (Dan, 1976). Finally, the influence of the menstrual cycle on mood seems to pale in comparison to that of other variables. Studies show, for instance, that environmental and social variables account for more variability in mood than cycle phase does (Good & Smith, 1980; Mansfield et al., 1989).

Frequently, reports of current symptoms do not match retrospective reports (based on memory) from the same women (McFarlane & Williams, 1990, 1994). The situation looks even more complex when researchers include men in their samples and when they broaden their focus to include the possibilities of other cycles, such as lunar and day-of-week. Jessica McFarlane and Tannis Williams (1994) followed 60 women and 10 men for 12 to 18 weeks, obtaining daily mood data. Mood ratings were later matched against information about menstrual cycles, lunar cycles, and days of the week. They found that two-thirds of both the women and the men showed cycles in their moods. Thus it might be viewed as "normal" for a person to have a regular pattern of emotional ups and downs. However, these mood cycles were very different for each individual, and few of them matched such expected patterns as premenstrual blues or weekend highs. The data showed that more of the women had a negative mood phase at some other point in their menstrual cycle than premenstrually and that 55% had no mood changes that correlated with the menstrual cycle.

Even in cases in which relationship between the menstrual cycle and mood has been demonstrated, interpretation is difficult. Most people assume that hormonal changes associated with the cycle cause the mood change. However, the direction of causality in some cases may be precisely the reverse, as it has long been known that psychological stress can delay menstruation or cause it to begin ahead of schedule (Parlee, 1973). In fact, women's experience of moods seem to be related to complex interactions among menstrual cycle phase, stress hormone levels, and occupational stress (Davydov, Shapiro, Goldstein, & Chicz-DeMet, 2005).

Another problem is that the focus of investigation has often been on negative symptoms, the assumption being that women experience more negative moods than "normal" during the premenstrual and menstrual phases. However, when researchers look for positive changes in the premenstrual phase, they can find those as well. In one study, 66 women of a sample of 100 reported at least one positive change associated with premenstruation. In all, seven different positive changes were reported: increased sexual interest, tendency to clean or tidy, increased sexual enjoyment, tendency to get things done, more attractive breasts, more energy, and more creative ideas (D. E. Stewart, 1989).

One group of researchers developed the "Menstrual Joy Questionnaire," which asked respondents about their experience of high spirits, increased sexual desire, vibrant activity, revolutionary zeal, intense concentration, and feelings of affection, self-confidence, euphoria, creativity, and power during their menstrual cycle (Delaney, Lupton, & Toth, 1987). When another group later administered the questionnaire to female college students, they found that it seemed to "prime" the respondents to include more positive responses in later, broader measures of attitudes toward menstruation (Chrisler, Johnston, Champagne, & Preston, 1994). Clearly, the questions asked by researchers shape what we "know" about menstruation.

Others have looked for positive symptoms at midcycle. Perhaps women feel "normal" most of the time, except for feeling especially positive at midcycle, a pattern that would be impossible to detect using only negative symptom measures. Barbara Sommer (1975) had participants complete daily checklists of positive and negative moods for 4½ weeks. When the results were analyzed, the only statistically significant finding was an increase in positive affect at midcycle. How might attitudes toward the menstrual cycle change if women began to think of the midcycle as a high point rather than focusing on the premenstrual and menstrual phases as low points?

BEHAVIOR, PERFORMANCE, AND COGNITION   Some investigators have looked for correlations between phases of the menstrual cycle and the occurrence of specific behaviors. Cyclic changes have been reported in behaviors such as volunteering to be a participant in a study (Doty & Silverthorne, 1975), consumption of sweet food (Bowen & Grunberg, 1990), deciding to seek psychological services (Surrey, Scott, & Phillips, 1975), alcohol consumption (Dumas, Calliet, Tumblin, & King, 1984), and maternal response to a child's illness (Tuck, 1975).

Mary Parlee (1973) noted that investigators tended to report that abnormal behaviors are most likely to occur in women during the premenstrual or menstrual phase of their cycle. The alleged link between these behaviors, which include commission of violent crimes, loss of control of an aircraft, suicide, and admission to hospital with acute psychiatric illness, might seem at first glance to imply that women are a menace to themselves and others for a few days every month. However, as Parlee's careful critique shows, such a general conclusion is unwarranted. Some of the reports are based on extremely small samples of women, and many have used methods such as retrospective reports of cycle phase, the accuracy of which is highly suspect. Moreover, she cautions, correlational data from special groups of women (e.g., female criminals) should not be used to make general statements about all women or about other special groups of women (e.g., female artists). Even supposing that women disposed to commit violent crime are more likely to commit it premenstrually, we cannot assume that women with strong inhibitions about violent behavior will be significantly more likely to commit violent acts at a particular point in the menstrual cycle. One group of reviewers concluded that, among women who are potential committers of pathological acts, the period surrounding the beginning of menstruation is a likely time for such acts to occur (Friedman, Hurt, Arnoff, & Clarkin, 1980). However, others have concluded that there is no acceptable evidence linking the menstrual cycle to criminal behavior and that the lack of scientific knowledge is so glaring that evidence about menstruation and crime should not be admissible in criminal trials (Harry & Balcer, 1987).

Popular opinion holds that women perform tasks more poorly during the premenstrual phase of the cycle. When the heroine of the popular movie *Clueless* offered the excuse that she was "surfing the crimson tide" for her inability to attend class and complete the required assignments, she was using a time-honored strategy. Female high school and college students have long used (and abused) the stereotype that menstruation impairs performance. Most objective measures do not show any general impairment in cognitive tasks, work and academic performance, or perceptual-motor performance associated with the menstrual cycle (Sommer, 1973, 1983, 1992). Studies using standard cognitive tests, academic examinations, reaction-time measures, quantity and quality of factory production, typing, and keypunching all fail to show menstrual cycle-related changes in performance. However, studies do show that women *believe* their performance is lower during the premenstrual and menstrual phases.

Female college students say they believe their academic performance is impaired by premenstrual symptoms. However, their performance, when measured objectively by tests and examination scores, does not show cyclic variation (Richardson, 1989). One study examined the performance of female professional typists throughout the menstrual cycle (Black & Koulis-Chitwood, 1990). This study found no evidence of any variation in typing performance (errors or speed) as a function of the cycle. A study of hand steadiness, conducted by military researchers to assess individual differences in the skills necessary to perform such tasks as holding and firing a handgun, did show that women with normal menstrual cycles experience a drop in hand steadiness during the premenstrual phase. On the whole, however, normally cycling women showed more steadiness than a comparison group of men did (Hudgens, Fatkin, Billingsley, & Mazurczak, 1988). Researchers have also studied female pilots to see whether their performance on a flight simulator would change with the menstrual cycle. It turns out that, even though hormone levels (both estrogen and progesterone) showed significant changes across the cycle in the women studied, their flight simulator performance showed no parallel changes (Mumenthaler, O'Hara, Taylor, Friedman, & Yesavage, 2001).

As noted in Chapter 6, one research lab has found evidence for cyclic changes in the performance of selected cognitive tasks (Hampson & Moffat, 2004; Kimura & Hampson, 1994). These researchers have found that women perform somewhat better on verbal articulation and fine motor-skill tasks at times during the cycle when estrogen levels are high (midcycle) and are better at certain visual-spatial tasks at times when estrogen levels are low. However, the differences related to menstrual-cycle phase were small in comparison to differences among women. Other researchers too have found changes in spatial and other kinds of cognitive performance across the menstrual cycle. For example, some studies suggest that women's performance is less lateralized in the late luteal phase (the week before menstruation) when progesterone levels are relatively high: During this phase women showed less right-ear advantage in dichotic listening and less asymmetry in visual recognition tasks using visual half-field techniques (Alexander, Altemus, Peterson, & Wexler, 2002; Hausmann, Becker, Gather, & Guentuerkuen, 2002). One type of implicit memory—the ability to generate examples of a category—has been found to be better at the midluteal than the follicular phase (Maki, Rich, & Rosenbaum, 2002). These findings suggest that any effect of menstrual cycle phase on cognitive performance is more complicated than a general increase in performance at midcycle and a decrease during the premenstrual phase.

Researchers in sports medicine have tried to determine whether there are links between the menstrual cycle and performance of female athletes. The results are mixed. One recent study of female athletes found no difference between the early follicular phase (the phase between menstruation and ovulation) and the midluteal phase (the phase between ovulation and menstruation) on variables such as muscle strength, anaerobic performance, aerobic endurance performance, maximum heart rate, and body composition (Lebrun, McKenzie, Prior, & Taunton, 1995). They did, however, find a slight tendency for aerobic capacity to decrease during the luteal phase. Although the magnitude of the effect varied a great deal among participants, it was large enough in some individuals to make it worthy of consideration. Another group of researchers demonstrated with a small sample of women that adapting a weight-training regimen to the phases of the menstrual cycle may be beneficial for building muscle strength. They compared a training routine in which women trained every third day throughout their cycle (regular training) with one in which they trained every second day during the follicular phase and about once a week during the luteal phase (menstrual-cycle-triggered training). The differences in resulting muscle strength were noteworthy: All participants showed better gains in muscle strength using the routine that was adapted to the menstrual cycle (Reis, Frick, & Schmidtbleicher, 1995). Why? The researchers postulate that the high levels of estradiol during the follicular phase have an anabolic (muscle-building) effect, which works in synergy with the training.

SENSATION AND PERCEPTION   A number of studies have examined sensory responsiveness across the menstrual cycle. Visual, auditory, olfactory, taste, and touch sensitivity have all been studied in relation to the cycle, along with skin conductance and brain wave activity. Some studies have found changes in sensitivity to such stimuli as tactile vibrations and auditory thresholds. Others have examined heart rate and blood pressure reactivity to stressors, some finding a correlation between reactivity and cycle phase (Tersman, Collins, & Eneroth, 1991) and others finding no such correlation (Weidner & Helmig, 1990). One group of researchers even reported that women are more sexually aroused in response to male fragrance during the preovulatory than during the follicular phase of the cycle (Graham, Janssen, & Sanders, 2000).

The early research was reviewed by Parlee (1983) and Sommer (1983). There is a great deal of variation in the findings: Some studies report cyclic fluctuations in sensitivity, but others do not. The studies that do report variation, particularly for visual and olfactory thresholds, tend to find increased sensitivity or responsiveness in the middle of the cycle and reduced sensitivity around menstruation. Pain thresholds seem to be lower in the premenstrual phase. However, conclusions are hampered by a number of problems: (1) Much of the research was designed to uncover the reasons for cognitive impairment associated with the menstrual cycle—impairment for which there seems to be little evidence. (2) Many of the findings have never been replicated. (3) In many studies, measures were not taken often enough during the cycle to provide an accurate and complete picture of the pattern of fluctuations in sensitivity. (4) There is a wide variation in the way cycle phases were defined. Menstrual-cycle effects on sensory processes are probably very small, and it may be too early to try to explain them given the large discrepancies that exist in the findings. However, it is important for researchers to be aware of the possibility that changes in the action of the central nervous system may accompany the cyclic changes of the menstrual (or, indeed, any other) cycle.

Overview	Psychological correlates of the menstrual cycle
Mood	• Some studies find mood fluctuations across the menstrual cycle, but there is a lot of individual variation among women (and among studies). • Women's moods are not more variable than men's. • Environmental and social variables account for more variability in mood than does menstrual cycle phase.
Behavior/performance	• Women believe menstrual symptoms interfere with their performance. • Most studies show no impairment of performance associated with particular menstrual cycle phases. • Some researchers have found small variations in verbal articulation and visual-spatial and fine motor skills tasks across the menstrual cycle. These variations are small in comparison to individual variations among women.
Sensation and perception	• Some researchers have found cyclic fluctuations in sensitivity to certain visual, olfactory, and pain stimuli. • Conclusions are hampered by a variety of methodological issues.

PMS and Other Problems

PMS   In recent years, most women's magazines have devoted considerable space to the topic of the premenstrual syndrome (PMS). The articles tend to be negative in tone, emphasize negative aspects of the menstrual cycle, and support the stereotype of women as maladjusted by virtue of their normal reproductive processes (Chrisler & Levy, 1990).

Treatment groups for PMS have sprung up at women's health clinics around the continent, and the shelves of health food stores display a variety of products supposedly geared to the relief of this syndrome. The advertisements for such products are calculated to heighten women's anxiety about the possible debilitating side effects of menstruation, and their widespread visibility encourages the assumption that the majority of women suffer from severe menstrual problems. Clearly, popular interest in PMS is high.

The publicity and interest surrounding PMS are fascinating, given that it is a poorly defined cluster of severe premenstrual symptoms that appears in a very small proportion of the female population. The number and type of symptoms said to characterize PMS vary from study to study. However, there seems to be agreement that the syndrome can include emotional problems (e.g., tension, anxiety, depression, irritability, and hostility), physical problems (e.g., abdominal bloating, swelling, breast tenderness, headache, and backache), and behavioral problems (e.g., avoidance of social contact, change in work habits, increased tendency to pick fights, and crying spells) (Abplanalp, 1983). As all of these are common symptoms that may be experienced in varying degrees of severity by almost anyone at any time of the month, some caution is indicated in labeling women as sufferers of PMS. In general, PMS should involve, on a regular basis, a significant increase in moderate to severe physical *and* psychological symptoms during the premenstrual phase, with marked relief associated with onset of menstruation. When stringent criteria are used to define PMS, it is difficult to find enough women from a large unselected sample to study it; severe, disabling premenstrual symptoms are reported by relatively few women (Abplanalp, 1983).

Despite the difficulties in diagnosing PMS, a formal psychiatric diagnosis, **premenstrual dysphoric disorder (PMDD),** has been included in an appendix (as a disorder requiring further study) of the latest revision of the American Psychiatric Association's catalog of psychiatric disorders, the DSM-IV. Many believe much more research is needed before such a diagnostic category can be used with confidence, and it is dangerous to women to assume that the physical symptoms some women experience premenstrually are signs of mental illness (Caplan, 1993; Hamilton & Gallant, 1990). In one study of 276 women who met the criteria for PMDD, researchers charted their symptom reports across two menstrual cycles. The most frequent symptoms (moderate-to-severe for up to 3 days) were anger/irritability (76%), anxiety/tension (71%), tired/lethargic (58%), and mood swings (58%). However, there was a great deal of variability among the women and even between cycles for individual women (Pearlstein, Yonkers, & Fayyad, 2005).

The label PMS (or PMDD) seems to be applied easily by women to their own symptoms, perhaps because of the publicity surrounding the term. However, when women who label themselves PMS sufferers are compared to other women on daily prospective symptom reports, researchers find few or no differences between the two groups (McFarlane & Williams, 1994). A more recent study revealed that 86% of the women in one study reported they had some degree of PMS, but their self-reported moods bore no significant relationship to menstrual cycle phase (Reilly & Kremer, 2001). Shirley Lee (2002), interviewing women in Winnipeg, Canada, about their experience of menstruation, found that most of the women accepted the label PMS for their symptoms and considered their cyclic changes in an illness framework. However, a small subgroup of women labeled their menstrual changes positive and healthy, and they resisted the idea that premenstrual changes, even uncomfortable ones, were a "sickness." Table 8.1 lists some of the comments made by women in this positive group compared to some made by the larger group.

Table 8.1   Excerpts from narratives of women labeled "positive" and "negative" with regard to menstruation in Lee (2002, pp. 25, 30).

"Positive" Women	*"Negative" Women*
I love it. I just love it because I feel it's like a cleansing. (p. 25)	I hate it. I hate it. It's still embarrassing for me. (p. 25)
It's very special to be able to have that cycle. . . . it's all part of fertility and what it means to be a woman. (p. 25)	I think of a really bad experience . . . pain would be one of the things that comes to mind. . . . I don't find it the least bit pleasant or in any way healthy. It's just sort of a big bad part of the month. (p. 25)
It's pretty cool that we can do that, like we can bleed without hurting and without it challenging our health. . . . it's a pretty cool process what our bodies can do. . . . I feel more creative and more in touch with myself. . . . it's like a reaffirmation of my womanhood. (p. 30)	I see it only as an inconvenience and an expense. I mean, let's face it, it's dirty, it's smelly. (p. 30)

Various treatments for PMS have been heralded at different times by the press. So far, there is no good evidence that any of them work. Most of the studies allow for the contamination of treatment effects with the effects of expectations because women who are given the treatment are told they are getting something that will cure their problem. A high proportion of women with PMS report benefiting from treatment, no matter what is used; in other words, they show a placebo effect—an effect apparently caused by the *expectation* that the treatment will help rather than by the treatment itself (Elsner, Buster, Schindler, Nessim, & Abraham, 1980). When double-blind, controlled studies are conducted (that is, studies in which neither the researcher nor the participant knows until the study is over which women have been given the treatment drug and which have been given an ineffective placebo), none of the treatments turn out to be any more effective than the placebo. This conclusion holds even for progesterone therapy, the most widely acclaimed treatment for PMS, now shown to be ineffective (Freeman, Rickels, Sondheimer, & Polansky, 1990; Robinson & Garfinkel, 1990). Research shows that the most effective management of PMS involves simple stress control and sensible levels of diet and exercise (Robinson & Garfinkel, 1990).

Perhaps one of the reasons so many women have been quick to accept the media-backed notion that PMS is a widespread disease is that the syndrome provides a "valid" label for menstrual-related discomfort and represents that menstrual complaints have for the first time been taken seriously by doctors. However, the level of discomfort experienced by most women is not severe or disabling enough to qualify as PMS or PMDD, and it is dangerous to women to foster the idea that large numbers of them experience the normal fluctuations of the menstrual cycle as a disease. There is no reason to return to the era when women's "raging hormonal influences" were thought to disqualify them from important jobs, for example. This is not to say that the severe premenstrual problems experienced by a few women are not real or important, but PMS should be acknowledged for what the evidence shows it to be—a rare disorder and one that is as yet poorly understood.

DYSMENORRHEA   **Dysmenorrhea,** or painful menstruation, is the most common menstrual problem, reported by 31 to 92% of women (Friederich, 1983; Wildman & White, 1986). The frequency and severity of discomfort vary widely among women and even in the same woman over time, and dysmenorrhea often occurs together with other chronic, painful conditions such as bladder infections and irritable bowel syndrome (Berkley, 2005). Under normal conditions, the cause of the problem is now thought to be the release of **prostaglandins** (hormonelike substances) from the lining of the uterus (Budoff, 1980). These chemicals cause excessive contractions in the uterine muscles, decreased blood flow, and increased sensitivity to pain, all of which contribute to menstrual cramps. Women reporting severe menstrual pain have been found to have unusually high levels of prostaglandins. Various prescription antiprostaglandin drugs are used to treat menstrual pain, and studies show that about 80% of women are helped by these drugs (Friederich, 1983). Aspirin, which is a mild antiprostaglandin, is also effective for some women. In addition, strategies to increase blood flow and release congestion are helpful. Thus, physical exercise may be a good idea, and many women report that orgasm, whether achieved through masturbation or sex with a partner, works very well to relieve menstrual cramps.

Sometimes dysmenorrheal is caused by **endometriosis,** a condition in which endometrial tissue (the type of tissue that normally lines the uterus) grows outside the lining of the uterus. This common problem affects about 20% of women and is particularly common among 30- to 40-year-old women (Hawkins & Hart, 2003). A large proportion of women affected by endometriosis experience significant pain, and the problem is not eradicated by menopause or by hysterectomy. Pain relievers and hormone treatments are effective for some women, and recent research suggests that thermal biofeedback also may be useful (Hawkins & Hart, 2003).

Social and Cultural Influences on the Menstrual Experience

According to historical and anthropological evidence, menstruation has never been merely a physiological event. The menstruating woman has often been regarded as a participant in a strange and dangerous process, as someone who is unclean, or as someone who is especially powerful. In many cultures, she was secluded during her period and forbidden to prepare food or to have any contact with men. According to first-century Roman historian Pliny, the touch of a menstruating woman would cause new wine to turn sour, razors to become blunt, and boiled linen to turn black. In some societies, a menstruating woman is viewed as polluting anything she contacts, and sometimes, as among the Arapesh of New Guinea, women are secluded in menstrual huts during their periods to protect others from their dangerous powers. In other cultures, there are positive—albeit less powerful—images for menstruation. According to Japanese tradition, a girl's first menstruation is "the year of the cleavage of the melon." One Indian phrase for menstruation is the "flower growing in the house of the god of love" (Delaney, Lupton, & Toth, 1987).

Even today in our culture, menstruation is sometimes referred to as "the curse," some religions regard menstruating women as unclean, and some people hold a taboo against sexual relations during the menstrual period. Some have argued that cultural reactions to menstruation reflect attitudes toward women. Gloria Steinem (1983), for instance, fantasized that if men could menstruate, cyclic fluctuations would be viewed as an advantage rather than a liability. At any rate, as many observers have noted, societal concerns about the possible debilitating effects of menstruation seem to have resurfaced with every new push for gender equality.

It would be surprising if the cultural meanings attached to menstruation did not have an influence on how women experience it. Indeed, it is probable that the biological influences of the menstrual cycle on women's experience are magnified many times by the cultural influences. We will examine research on cultural attitudes toward menstruation and the impact of these attitudes on women's experience in the following sections.

MENARCHE   The first onset of menstruation is called **menarche,** and it represents an important developmental milestone in women's lives. One study of 137 women ages 18 to 45 found that every one of them remembered their first menstruation and most could describe the associated events in detail (Golub & Catalano, 1983). Yet such is the air of embarrassment surrounding menstruation in our culture that menarche usually occurs not only without fanfare but often in relative secrecy.

Typically, across a variety of cultures, mothers are the main sources of information for daughters at menarche (Chrisler & Zitell, 1998). What kinds of information and attitudes about the menstrual cycle do these mothers convey to their daughters? According to one interview study of 138 women, the preponderance of the messages is negative, and mothers share little of their own experience with their daughters (Costos, Ackerman, & Paradis, 2002). These authors found that many mothers did not discuss menstruation with their daughters at all or simply gave them instructions on how to manage it (e.g., how to use a menstrual pad or tampon) without any other discussion. Furthermore, they sometimes expressed sorrow that their daughter was "growing up" and worry that she could get pregnant. As one respondent described it,

> I just remember noticing a brownish/reddish mark on my underwear and I showed it to my mother and she said, "Oh, my poor little girl isn't a little girl any more! Oh no! Do you realize that from now on you'll always have to take a handbag wherever you go and make sure you always carry sanitary napkins with you and never go anywhere without them EVER again!" And she almost cried because I wasn't a little girl anymore. And reminded me that I would get pregnant. (p. 54)

One study of 9- to 12-year-old girls found that most of them equated menstruation with growing up and being normal, but almost a third of them believed menstruation to be embarrassing, a nuisance, or disgusting, and many of them believed menstruating women should not swim or be active in sports (L. R. Williams, 1983). Eighty-five percent of these girls thought that a girl should not talk about menstruation to boys; 40% thought she should not discuss it even with her father. It appears, then, that negative attitudes toward and expectations about menstruation have been part of the anticipation of menarche for many girls.

Advertisements for tampons and sanitary napkins may well contribute to these negative attitudes. Such advertisements tend to suggest that their product will help get the menstruating woman through a difficult and embarrassing time, that its use will make the woman able to carry on "almost as if she were her normal self." A content analysis of the educational booklets published by the manufacturers of menstrual hygiene products found that, although the more recent booklets contain more accurate and positive information than the earlier booklets, they still tend to promote secrecy about menstruation (Erchull, Chrisler, Gorman, & Johnston-Robledo, 2002). An analysis of depictions of menstruation in film and television indicates that menstruation is portrayed as a symbol of difference between women and men—a sign that the two groups are inexorably different (Kissling, 2002). Clearly, media messages about menstruation are ambivalent at best and negative at worst.

Some researchers have wondered whether the social events and emotional experiences surrounding menarche may set the stage for how a woman will experience menstruation in subsequent years. One group has suggested that to overcome some of the negative meanings associated with menarche a positive new tradition or ritual should be developed (Logan, Calder, & Cohen 1980, as cited in Golub, 1983). These researchers wrote five brief stories describing possible responses to a girl's first period. They gave the stories to girls between the ages of 8 and 17, mothers of girls in this age range, and women psychologists. The mothers and daughters chose "Congratulations, our little girl is growing up" as the best response to being told about the beginning of menstruation, and the psychologists preferred "Something special has happened." What symbolic gesture might be appropriate? Mothers favored a special toast to the girl from both parents or a meal in her honor. However, the girls themselves, shying away from a situation in which they would be the center of attention, thought that the best gesture would be a hug or kiss and a gift to mark the occasion. It is difficult to be sure what effect such a positive celebration of menarche would have on women's later menstrual experience, but it should certainly help to counteract the negative expectations and attitudes with which many girls approach menstruation.

ATTITUDES, EXPECTATIONS, AND THEIR IMPACT ON MENSTRUAL SYMPTOMS   About two decades ago, a survey of 1,034 Americans, a representative sample over the age of 14, indicated that a significant minority of people associated menstruation with some degree of impairment: 35% believed menstruation affects a woman's ability to think, 26% believed women cannot function as well at work when menstruating, and 30% believed women need to restrict their physical activities during menstruation (*The Tampax Report,* 1981). Eighty-seven percent of the respondents agreed that women are more emotional when menstruating, although when asked about their or their partner's most recent menstrual period, 42% and 58%, respectively, reported no mood or personality changes either menstrually or premenstrually. Attitudes may have changed somewhat since that survey. Even among well-educated women, knowledge of the menstrual cycle can be incorrect and negatively biased (Koff, Rierdan, & Stubbs, 1990). However, attitudes about menstruation appear to be gradually changing. Although young women may still consider it an annoyance, they are less likely than middle-aged women to view it as disabling—and both younger and middle-aged women are willing to endorse some positive aspects of menstruation (Marván, Cortés-Iniestra, & González, 2005).

Widespread cultural stereotypes exist about menstruation (E. Martin, 1987). Koeske and Koeske (1975) used a questionnaire to measure participants' reactions to a written excerpt from a hypothetical student's interview with a college counselor. They examined the effect of information about the student's menstrual cycle phase, mood, and environment on the participants' formation of attributions about the student. Results showed that participants displayed a clear-cut attributional pattern in which they linked the negative moods of depression and irritability to the occurrence of the premenstrual phase of the student's cycle. It appears that our culture provides an emotional label of "premenstrual tension" to any negative moods that may occur at this point in a woman's cycle. The researchers noted that this attribution pattern presents a number of dangers. It obscures the very wide individual variation among women in menstrual and premenstrual symptoms. It uses women's biology to explain negative but not positive moods, and it may result in the exaggeration of the likelihood or recall of negative moods. If a woman accepts this attribution for her own emotions, it might even reduce the likelihood of her taking action to alter an upsetting external situation. She might believe premenstrual tension, not the external situation, is the source of the upset.

Attitudes toward menstruation may be influenced by a broader set of cultural attitudes called **sexual objectification.** Such attitudes define female bodies in terms of ideals of beauty and sexual attractiveness, and they require that "messy" biological functions be concealed in order to support these sanitized ideals. When people are reminded of biological functions, their attitudes toward individual women and women in general may be more negative. One researcher tested this theory by having participants interact with a confederate who "accidentally" dropped either a hair clip or a tampon out of her purse. In all other ways, the confederate's behavior and appearance was identical; however, participants responded more negatively to her when she dropped the tampon. Dropping the tampon led to decreased liking for the confederate and lower evaluations of her competence (Roberts, Goldenberg, Power, & Pyszczynski, 2002). Sexual objectification seems to affect women's self-views too: Women who accept and internalize these sexually objectified ideals for themselves tend to have more negative attitudes and emotions about their menstrual cycle (Roberts, 2004).

Do women accept the stereotypic beliefs about menstruation with respect to their own experience or only for "women in general"? In one study (Brooks, Ruble, & Clarke, 1977), college women were asked to respond to a symptom questionnaire *as if* they were premenstrual or at midcycle. Their responses indicated that they expected to experience more severe symptoms in the premenstrual than in the intermenstrual phase, a result that parallels the stereotypic expectations for women in general found in previous studies.

If cultural expectations about menstrual symptoms are so prevalent, might they not influence the self-reports or even the actual experience of menstrual symptoms? Probably. When women are told that the menstrual cycle is the focus of a daily symptom-reporting study, they report significantly more negative psychological and physical symptoms at premenstrual and menstrual cycle phases than do women who are given a different rationale for the study (Aubuchon & Calhoun, 1985).

In one study, women completed daily questionnaires in which they reported their physical and emotional symptoms. Later, some of these women were asked to recall the ratings they had made on a day when they were menstruating; others recalled a day when they were not menstruating. Finally, the women completed a questionnaire about how they thought they were "typically" affected by menstruation. The women who thought that menstruation was typically associated with distress tended to remember their menstrual days as distressing—more distressing, in fact, than they had reported at the time. The more a woman believed in the phenomenon of menstrual distress, the more exaggerated were her recollections of her negative menstrual symptoms (McFarland, Ross, & DeCourville, 1989).

When obtaining symptom reports from women, how do researchers know how much of the symptomatology is caused by the biological changes associated with the menstrual cycle and how much is caused by expectations and stereotypic beliefs? Diane Ruble (1977) used a creative approach to separate the effects of expectations from the effects of biology. She told 44 undergraduate students that new scientific techniques made it possible to predict the expected date of menstruation. Then, after using this bogus technique on each woman (hooking her up to an EEG machine), she informed her, according to the group to which the student had been randomly assigned, that (1) her period was due in 1 or 2 days (premenstrual group); (2) her period was not expected for 7 to 10 days (intermenstrual group); or (3) no information was available about cycle phase (control group). These women were given supposedly accurate information about their cycle phase, but the information each was given was, in reality, randomly determined and independent of her actual cycle phase. After being given this information, each woman went to a second room where another experimenter, unaware of the group to which the woman had been assigned, asked her to rate her experience of a set of supposedly menstruation-related symptoms. All of the women were really in the 21st or 22nd day of their cycles, and their testing had been scheduled on the basis of a menstrual history taken earlier. However, regardless of their actual cycle phase, women who believed they were premenstrual reported more premenstrual symptoms than did those who believed they were intermenstrual. These findings suggest that expectations can and do influence women's self-reports of menstruation-related symptoms and indicate caution in the interpretation of such studies.

Although there is reason to believe that hormonal changes during the menstrual cycle affect mood and behavior, the research indicates that sociocultural factors play a major role, perhaps the most significant role, in determining these effects. There are still many unanswered questions, however. For instance, we know little about the specific reasons for the wide individual variations among women (or even in the same woman over time) in the level of menstrual and premenstrual symptoms. Issues such as diet, stress, and fatigue may well be important, but they remain to be investigated. Also, it is clear that most women must continue to perform their jobs in the workplace or home despite any menstrual symptoms they may experience. It would be interesting and practical to study the strategies used by the women who cope most successfully with recurring menstrual symptoms.

Overview   Social expectations and the menstrual cycle

- Mothers are the main source of information for girls at menarche, and much of that information is negative.

- Western cultural stereotypes of menstruation as a time of negative emotionality are widely held by both women and men.

- Expectations affect women's symptoms. For example, women who are tricked into believing they are premenstrual report more "typical" premenstrual symptoms.

- A woman's belief in the phenomenon of menstrual distress is related to her likelihood of experiencing such distress; women who say they usually experience menstrual distress remember their last menstrual period as more distressing than they reported at the time.

HORMONES AND THE MALE EXPERIENCE

Male Puberty

The onset of puberty occurs about 2 years later for boys than for girls. In both sexes, the physical changes of adolescence are triggered when the hypothalamus increases secretions that cause the pituitary gland to release gonadotropins in large amounts. **Gonadotropins,** hormones that stimulate the gonads to activity, are chemically the same in males as in females, but their presence produces different results in the two sexes because the gonads they act upon are different. In males, they stimulate the testes to increase testosterone production; in females, they cause the ovaries to produce estrogen.

Under the influence of increased hormone levels, both sexes experience a growth spurt and develop secondary sex characteristics. Internal reproductive organs also undergo further development. In girls, this development has a dramatic manifestation in menarche. In boys, the penis and testes increase in size, as do the prostate gland and seminal vesicles. When the prostate and seminal vesicles begin functioning under the influence of increasing testosterone levels, ejaculation becomes possible. **Spermarche,** or the first ejaculation, usually occurs about a year after the growth spurt has begun, often at age 13 or 14, but the timing can vary widely among individuals. Early ejaculations may or may not contain viable sperm, as the timing of sperm production also varies. Sperm production is necessary for fertility.

Just as girls may be shocked and upset by menstruation when they are unprepared, boys may be frightened by their first experience of ejaculation. Although boys are typically used to masturbating before puberty and have experienced orgasms, they are often taken by surprise the first time masturbation leads to ejaculation. As one man, looking back on his first ejaculation during masturbation, commented to a researcher, "[I] couldn't believe it when something shot out of my penis" (Crooks & Bauer, 1987, p. 460). A major worry, he went on to say, was that God was punishing him for his sinful behavior.

One study shows that boys are often unprepared for their first experience of ejaculation but that the lack of preparation is not necessarily associated with a negative reaction to the event (Gaddis & Brooks-Gunn, 1985). Only 3 of 13 adolescent boys interviewed had had ejaculation explained to them, in all cases by an adult male; most had obtained their information from reading. Furthermore, only 4 had discussed their first ejaculation after the experience. The majority of the boys reported that they had experienced strong positive feelings at spermarche. No one was upset or strongly ashamed; however, 1 was very embarrassed, and 2 were very frightened. It is clear, however, that most boys are left to form their own impressions of their first ejaculation experience because parents rarely communicate with their sons about this issue. In one interview study, when parents of adolescent sons were asked if they had future plans to talk with their sons about first ejaculation, most (54%) responded "I've never thought about it" (Frankel, 2002).

Male Cycles

If the menstrual cycle is associated with some changes in mood and behavior for a certain proportion of women, one possible implication is that women are, on average, more variable in mood and behavior than men are. This suggestion is based, of course, on the assumption that men are not subject to any cycles of their own. Investigation of this assumption dates back to Leta Hollingworth (1914) who painstakingly followed 6 women and 2 men with daily tests of cognitive performance over 4 months. She found no female–male differences in performance variability or patterns of performance change. More recently, Alice Dan (1976) followed 24 married couples for 2 months, using tests of mood and problem-solving performance. She also found no differences in variability between women and men.

If the menstrual cycle contributes to variability in women, and women on the whole are not more variable than men, men must have their own sources of variability. It is of interest, then, to look briefly at the issue of male cycles, an issue that has been virtually ignored by researchers. Is it possible that men experience physiological cycles that create as much variability and vulnerability as the female menstrual cycle does but that these cycles have been overlooked by the culture and, hence, not magnified in their effects by social expectations? Indeed, it is. Researchers studying biological rhythms in males have identified monthly cycles of efficiency and irritability (J. C. Hoffman, 1982).

Cycles are a universal aspect of life. Both men and women experience daily rhythms on physiological dimensions such as body temperature, blood sugar levels, and sleeping/waking. Such cycles can affect alertness, mood, and performance (Laberge et al., 2000; Monk, Moline, Fookson, & Peetz, 1989). There may also be seasonal cycles. One Italian study of suicide records over 12 years identified different seasonal variation cycles in suicide for women and men (Micciolo, Zimmerman-Tansella, Williams, & Tansella, 1989). Estelle Ramey (1972) reviewed limited evidence that men show cyclic mood variations ranging in periodicity from 4 to 9 weeks. These studies showed that there may be a great deal of variability among individual men in the cyclic patterns of their moods and physical symptoms, just as there are large individual differences among women. McFarlane and Williams (1994), who found evidence for mood cycles among both women and men, also found that there was a great deal of individual variability in both sexes. Furthermore, the mood cycles did not necessarily conform to the menstrual cycle for women or to such obvious social markers as weekends for either men or women. Thus the female menstrual cycle may be only one of a number of human biological cycles that have a potential impact on mood or behavior.

Ramey (1972) cited one study, carried out in Denmark, in which fluctuations of testosterone levels in male urine were followed for 16 years. A 30-day rhythmic cycle of hormone levels was found. Another study cited by Ramey involved male managers and workers in a factory. The investigator in this case measured not hormones but mood and found an emotional cycle of 4 to 6 weeks in which low periods were characterized by apathy, indifference, and overreactions to minor problems and high periods by feelings of well-being, energy, lower body weight, and a decreased need for sleep. These cycles can be altered by shift work (Ohira et al., 2000). A study by Doering, Brodie, Kraemer, Becker, and Hamburg (1974) measured both hormonal fluctuations and moods in 20 men for 2 months and found evidence supporting a link between the two. They reported a significant positive correlation between levels of self-reported depression and concentration of plasma testosterone in the blood. Their data, however, showed only weak evidence for rhythmic changes in testosterone levels.

We have seen that women's responses to the biological changes of the menstrual cycle are subject to sociocultural influences. It is logical to suppose, as well, that men's mood fluctuations are sensitive to social forces. One demonstration of this phenomenon is reported by Rossi and Rossi (1977), who found that the "social time" of the 7-day week may be as important as the "body time" of the menstrual cycle. These researchers had 67 female and 15 male college students complete daily mood-adjective checklists for 40 days. Many of the women showed menstrual cycle-related variations in mood, but the day-of-the-week effect was more pronounced for males, making overall mood variability the same for both sexes. A similar study of couples ages 25 to 45 found that, even for women, day of the week accounted for more mood variability than menstrual cycle phase did: For females and males, negative moods and arousal levels decreased on weekends (Mansfield et al., 1989). A third study also showed more fluctuation in women's moods over the days of the week than over the menstrual cycle (McFarlane et al., 1988). It appears that "social time" creates important cycles for both women and men.

Another possible source of variability in males is the influence of their female partners' menstrual cycles (Dan, 1979). Such an effect could have both social and biological components. In one study, after 90 days of daily mood reporting, the only significant effect associated with the menstrual cycle was that *men's* arousal scores were higher during their wives' menstrual phase than during their follicular phase (Mansfield et al., 1989).

Much more research remains to be done before male hormonal cycles are understood. Other cycles do not have the clear marker of menstruation to help researchers determine cycle phase, making the discovery of fluctuations more difficult. The lack of an obvious marker also makes it difficult for the individual man to be aware of any regular fluctuations he may be experiencing in mood or performance.

What impact might it have on men to know or not know about their own cycles? It may be that men, lacking a knowledge of their own cycles, are more disadvantaged by them than women are by the menstrual cycle. When a man experiences a "low" time, he may be unaware of any cycle-based reason for it and so may wrongly attribute difficulties to his own incompetence, dislike of his work, or unreasonable coworkers. However, knowledge of an upcoming "low point" in his emotional cycle might, through a self-fulfilling negative expectation, cause a man to be more depressed or to perform more poorly during this time than he would have if he had not been given this information about his cycle (as suggested for women in Ruble's 1977 research). As researchers begin to attend to the issue of male cycles, we begin to see that the menstrual cycle in women is not unique among human cycles in the magnitude of its effects. We are also beginning to understand how effects on female and male mood and performance are produced by awareness of and learned expectations about cyclic physiological changes.

PREGNANCY AND CHILDBIRTH

Physical and Emotional Aspects of Pregnancy

When a woman becomes pregnant, her normal monthly hormonal cycle is interrupted, and she experiences a state in which both estrogen and progesterone levels are more or less constantly high. Hormonally, pregnancy is most similar to the phase of the menstrual cycle that occurs just after ovulation and that has been characterized by some researchers as one of generally positive moods. In our culture, it is not unusual to hear pregnant women described as happy, content, fulfilled, and glowing. Could it be that a sense of well-being associated with pregnancy is produced by high hormone levels?

Conversely, there is much to suggest that pregnancy, far from being viewed as a time of particularly positive feelings, is seen by many as a disability. Medical research on pregnancy often seems based on the notion that the pregnant woman is to some extent disabled and tends to focus on negative symptoms. So pervasive is this focus that it is difficult to find a pregnant woman described as healthy or normal in the medical literature. As Rothman (1982) noted, healthy pregnant women are classified simply as "low risk." Social scientists, too, have been influenced by the notion of pregnancy as a time of special difficulty and vulnerability for women. Psychological research on pregnancy was dominated for years by the psychoanalytic idea that pregnancy brings up a host of unconscious conflicts about femininity, sexuality, and the woman's relationship to her own mother (see, for example, Bibring, 1959; Deutsch, 1945). Thus, there has been a tendency, in both medical and psychological research, to focus on the problems of pregnancy, and only recently have researchers begun to examine the normative aspects of the experience.

PHYSICAL SYMPTOMS OF PREGNANCY   Research on the pregnancy experience of normal women indicates that a group of physical symptoms is commonly reported during pregnancy, but the variation among women is tremendous (Lips, 1982a, 1985b). Perhaps the symptom most commonly linked to pregnancy in the popular consciousness is morning sickness—a tendency toward nausea and vomiting shortly after rising. It has been difficult to get an accurate estimate of the proportion of women who suffer from morning sickness during their pregnancies, and women who have been pregnant several times often report that each pregnancy was different with respect to this symptom. In one group of women studied recently, 80% reported retrospectively that they had experienced nausea during pregnancy, and 56% reported vomiting. Many had also experienced food cravings (61%) and aversions (54%) (Bayley, Dye, Jones, DeBono, & Hill, 2002). A lower frequency of nausea was found in a study of 108 normal, healthy women questioned during the third to fifth month of their pregnancy: 24% reported moderate to high levels of nausea and vomiting. That this rate of nausea is linked to pregnancy can be seen by the rate at which it was reported by three comparison groups: 3% for expectant fathers, 5% for nonpregnant women, and 3% for husbands of nonpregnant women (Lips, 1982a).

Physicians and researchers influenced by psychoanalytic theory traditionally postulated that women who experience nausea and vomiting during pregnancy are denying their femininity (Deutsch, 1945), are unconsciously rejecting or expressing ambivalence toward their unborn child (Chertok, 1969), or are just plain neurotic (Pajntar, 1972). These explanations seem to reflect a view of women that is uncomplimentary, to say the least. It is a view that sees women teetering precariously on the brink of neuroticism, requiring only the normal changes of pregnancy to push them over. A review of the research on pregnancy nausea provides little support for any of these explanations; researchers do not know why some women experience these symptoms and some do not (Macy, 1986).

Responses to a 55-item list of symptoms showed that pregnant women could be distinguished from comparison groups by a small cluster of physical symptoms (Lips, 1982a, 1985a). In the first half of pregnancy, this cluster included nausea and vomiting, a desire to take naps and stay in bed, dizziness or fainting, and a definite lack of bursts of energy and activity. In the 6th to 8th months of pregnancy, it included feelings of heaviness and excessive weight gain. In the 9th month, it included feelings of awkwardness, discomfort, heaviness, swelling, general aches and pains, and backache. However, although more pregnant women than other people reported these symptoms on the average, many pregnant women did not.

EMOTIONAL SYMPTOMS OF PREGNANCY   Our cultural "script" for pregnancy includes a variety of emotional dimensions. We allow pregnant women to act a little unreasonable and are tolerant of emotional outbursts and strange requests. Conversely, as noted earlier, there is an expectation that the pregnant woman will "glow." The self-reports of pregnant women provide little support for these generalizations. Pregnant women do not differ from other women in the tendency to describe themselves as beautiful, attractive, and radiant—the "glow" factor—and a group of adjectives describing negative emotionality (irritability, mood swings, tension, depression, anxiety, and upset) failed to distinguish pregnant women from comparison groups at any stage of pregnancy (Lips, 1985b).

Some studies have, however, found higher rates of depression among pregnant than nonpregnant women (Lips, 1985b) and increased rates of depression as pregnancy progresses (Gjerdingen, Froberg, & Kochevar, 1991). In addition, pregnancy does not seem to be associated with increased psychological well-being for most people. According to one study, fewer than 15% of women and 10% of men report increased psychological well-being during pregnancy (Condon, 1987).

Physical and emotional symptoms may go together in pregnancy. One study of 186 women receiving prenatal care found that 23% of the women met screening criteria for anxiety or depression and that these women were more likely than other women to report physical symptoms (Kelly, Russo, & Katon, 2001). This study did not compare pregnant women to anyone else, so it does not show that pregnancy is associated with anxiety or depression; it does show that depressed or anxious women who are pregnant tend to have physical problems as well.

Hormone levels may tend to predispose pregnant women toward positive moods, at least during some stages of pregnancy. However, if this tendency exists, the mixed evidence about the types of emotions actually experienced by pregnant women suggests that it can be overwhelmed by other factors. These factors might include the fatigue and other physical discomforts sometimes associated with pregnancy, changes in body image, anxiety about new responsibilities, or resentment of an unwanted pregnancy (Lips, 1982c). Even the positive moods associated with pregnancy are undoubtedly not totally explainable by hormone levels. Pleasure and excitement about having a child could certainly produce a positive mood shift during pregnancy. Furthermore, in a culture that still emphasizes childbearing as the route to fulfillment for women, women are actually socialized to "glow" when pregnant, and pregnant women sometimes comment that they feel guilty or inadequate if they display negative emotions.

Social and Cultural Influences on the Pregnancy Experience

Besides being a biological state, pregnancy is also part of a social role. Pregnancy is a social stimulus, eliciting particular responses from people with whom the pregnant woman interacts. Two researchers did an experiment in which a woman made up to look pregnant rode a busy elevator in a high-rise building (Taylor & Langer, 1977). She stood in one back corner of the elevator, and another woman, carrying a parcel so that she would take up as much space as the "pregnant" woman, stood in the other back corner. The reactions of people, particularly men, boarding the elevator were striking: They studiously avoided crowding the "pregnant" woman, sometimes almost trampling on the other woman in the process. Moreover, they did a lot of staring at the "pregnant" woman—a reaction people often display to someone with an obvious physical handicap or stigma. It is no wonder that pregnant women sometimes feel self-conscious about their appearance or notice that people seem to be treating them differently. They are reacting to a real change in their social environment.

Other research indicated that people think of pregnant women as emotional, irritable, and suffering from various physical symptoms. In one study, college students were given a description of a day in the life of a young woman and were asked to rate her mood as well as various factors on their importance in determining the woman's mood (Lips, 1980). In half the descriptions, the woman was said to be 5 months pregnant, and in the other half, no mention of pregnancy was made. The students generally rated the woman's mood as more positive when she was described as pregnant. However, when trying to give reasons for the woman's mood, they used pregnancy more often as an explanation for negative than for positive moods. Moreover, pregnancy was, almost without exception, described as a source of stress by students who mentioned it spontaneously. Clearly, these students, most of whom had never been pregnant, had learned the social stereotypes about pregnancy. They are not alone. Another group of college students was asked to complete a symptom checklist "as if they were a woman who was 5 months pregnant" (Lips, 1980). In general, their answers indicated that they thought pregnancy was characterized by a variety of physical symptoms, notably nausea, feeling overweight, and fatigue. For pregnancy, as for menstruation, there is apparently a well-known set of cultural expectations.

In trying to determine the links among physiological changes, expectations, and emotions, it cannot always be assumed that causality works in a particular direction, from physiological to emotional change. A case in which emotional changes apparently have physiological consequences is **pseudocyesis,** or pseudopregnancy. The physical symptoms that characterize pseudocyesis are similar to those associated with pregnancy: menstrual disturbance, abdominal enlargement, swelling and tenderness of the breasts, softening of the cervix, enlargement of the uterus, nausea and vomiting, and weight gain. Pseudocyesis patients have even reported that they can feel fetal movements. The symptoms of pseudocyesis, although not common, are not extremely rare, appear most frequently in women who are sterile, and can appear occasionally even in men. Key causal factors are thought to be a fear of, or wish for, pregnancy (Barglow & Brown, 1972; Whelan & Stewart, 1990).

Another instance in which emotions appear to lead to the physiological reactions of pregnancy rather than vice versa is the **couvade syndrome** (Trethowan, 1972), in which expectant fathers suffer from physical symptoms during their wives' pregnancy or labor. These symptoms are sometimes, but not always, similar to those experienced by the pregnant woman: nausea and vomiting, alterations of appetite, abdominal pain, swelling, and spurious labor pains. In one study, expectant fathers reported significantly more backaches, colds, and headaches than a comparison group of men. In addition, the expectant fathers showed unintentional weight gain, particularly during the third trimester (Clinton, 1987). There is speculation that the symptoms are caused by the man's high anxiety about his wife's pregnancy. Trethowan, who suggests that the expectant father is not usually aware of the connection between his symptoms and his wife's pregnancy, estimated that 1 of every 4 or 5 expectant fathers experiences this syndrome. However, other research shows that the syndrome is much less common than this (Lips, 1982b).

The couvade syndrome takes its name from a set of customs in various cultures that anthropologists have named **couvade** (from the French verb *couver*—to brood or hatch). Couvade rituals are expressions of father involvement in the birth process. One form that such rituals may take is that of the father-to-be, simultaneously with his wife's confinement taking to his bed, simulating labor and delivery, and receiving attention comparable to that received by the laboring mother. The practice may be carried out to protect the mother and infant by decoying evil spirits away from them during the vulnerable time of childbirth, to help the woman in her efforts, or to announce in a powerful nonverbal way that a particular man is the father of the child. The couvade syndrome when observed in our industrialized society is not part of such a ritual, yet it may, in a sense, reflect some of these same motives.

The existence of pseudocyesis and the couvade syndrome, despite their relative rarity, underlines the complexity of the interaction that can occur between hormones and social and emotional factors in the production of physical symptoms. The finding that nonpregnant women and even men sometimes experience symptoms that simulate those of pregnancy lends weight to the notion that our culture teaches us how a pregnant woman is supposed to feel and act. If most members of the culture acquire this information through a process of social learning, those who eventually find themselves pregnant may develop the symptoms they (and others) have learned to expect. It is difficult to determine the extent to which expectations or hormones are responsible for this development.

PREGNANCY AND REPRODUCTIVE TECHNOLOGIES   Technologies such as artificial insemination, in vitro fertilization, fetal monitoring, ultrasound, embryo transplants, and surrogate motherhood have expanded some people's choices in the area of childbearing and have implications for the psychology of childbearing. The psychological, not to mention political and ethical implications of some of these technologies have not been adequately explored. For instance, little is known about what a surrogate mother—a woman who agrees, or contracts, to carry a pregnancy to term and then to turn the baby over to someone else—can expect to experience and what factors might shape that experience. Questionnaire and interview studies of small samples of surrogate mothers suggest that many of them feel very positive about the experience of surrogacy (Kleinpeter & Hohman, 2000; Van Den Akker, 2003) and that the key factor in their satisfaction is their relationship with the couple for whom they are bearing the child (Hohman & Hagan, 2001). Researchers are only beginning to explore how these women deal with their emotions toward the developing fetus; however, one model suggested that surrogate mothers sometimes distance themselves from the developing fetus and prepare themselves to give up the baby by focusing on the "business" understanding that they are providing a service for which they are being paid (Baslington, 2002).

One issue that has been studied to some extent is the effect on expectant parents of knowing the sex of the fetus. Yet the findings here are mixed. For instance, one study found that parents' reactions to their infants were unaffected by knowledge of fetal sex before birth (Sweeney & Bradbard, 1988), whereas another found that parents who knew the sex of the fetus scored lower on attachment to the fetus than did parents who did not know the sex (Wu & Eichmann, 1988).

Knowledge of fetal sex can and has been used by some parents to select the sex of their children (by aborting fetuses not of the desired sex). There is a long tradition in many cultures of preference for male children, especially for male firstborns, and this preference may be reflected in the way so-called sex selection technology is used. One study of American undergraduate students found preference for a male firstborn. In this sample, of those who indicated a willingness to use sex selection, 73% preferred sons—a finding that held across race, religion, age, and income levels (Steinbacher & Gilroy, 1990). A more recent study of U.S. college students revealed that the tendency to prefer sons has not disappeared. Researchers found a significant overall preference for firstborn males—a tendency that was particularly notable among students who said they would be willing to use sex selection technology (Swetkis, Gilroy, & Steinbacher, 2002).

Expectant Fatherhood

Expectant fathers do not experience the dramatic physiological changes of pregnancy—or do they? One study measured blood levels of hormones of couples attending hospital prenatal classes both before and after the birth of their infants. After the first blood sample was taken, participants were exposed to the sounds, sights, and smells of newborn infants, and then a second sample was taken. Both women *and* men showed changes in hormone levels that were specific to pregnancy stage: higher levels of some hormones (prolactin and cortisol) in the late prenatal period and lower levels of others (testosterone and estradiol) in the postnatal period. And both expectant mothers *and* fathers showed physiological changes after exposure to the infant-related stimuli (Storey, Walsh, Quinton, & Wynne-Edwards, 2000). The fathers who showed the greatest reactivity to the infant stimuli were those who had the highest levels of prolactin and the greatest postnatal reductions in testosterone. So perhaps hormones do play a role in preparing men to take on fathering behaviors.

Whereas there is disagreement over the extent to which hormones are important to fathering, it is very clear that social customs play an important part in defining the paternal role. For example, the father's role in pregnancy and childbirth changed quite dramatically in North America during the 1970s. The father-to-be now takes an active role in pregnancy: attending childbirth preparation classes with his spouse, working with her on prenatal exercises, and being present during childbirth to provide support. In 1972, one survey showed that fathers were permitted in the delivery room in only 27% of American hospitals; by 1980, this number had increased to 80% (Parke, 1981).

Some expectant fathers say they feel caught in a double bind: encouraged to participate in pregnancy and birth but simultaneously excluded from the childbearing experience, with few good models to point the way to active, involved fatherhood (P. L. Jordan, 1990). They may have a number of concerns, such as queasiness, increased responsibility, uncertain paternity, and worry about losing their spouse; however, men often keep these concerns to themselves (Shapiro, 1987). Despite the adjustment they are making and the possibility of couvade symptomatology, expectant fathers show a lower rate of health care seeking during their wife's pregnancy than before conception or after delivery (Quill, Lipkin, & Lamb, 1984).

Psychological theories about expectant fatherhood, like those concerning expectant motherhood, used to emphasize a psychoanalytic approach. His partner's pregnancy was thought to stir up a man's underlying conflicts about his own masculinity and femininity, his relationship to his father, and his needs to be dependent and nurtured (A. Coleman & Coleman, 1971; Lacoursiere, 1972). If such feelings are experienced, some of them may be directly attributable to the social norms regarding the father's role in pregnancy and childbirth. It is not surprising to find that a man may feel anxious and dependent at a time when his partner is involved in a life-changing experience from which he is excluded.

In the social climate of father participation in pregnancy and childbirth, however, expectant fatherhood is experienced positively by many men (Grossman, Eichler, & Winickoff, 1980; Lips, 1982c). In one study of middle-class couples expecting a child, the themes mentioned most frequently by the men in response to an open-ended question about how their lives had changed since the beginning of the pregnancy were a new emphasis on planning for the future, concern with finances, and an increased necessity to help with the housework (Lips, 1982c). What expectant fathers said they liked most about the pregnancy was the anticipation of the baby and their wives' happiness; what they liked least was their wives' discomfort and fatigue. A positive aspect of pregnancy, especially first pregnancy, for many fathers is that the shared experience draws them closer to their spouse (Lips & Morrison, 1986). Men who have made a conscious decision to become fathers tend to participate actively in decisions with respect to pregnancy and childbirth and to become emotionally invested in the process (Peterson & Jenni, 2003). Expectant fathers prepare actively for parenthood by seeking information on how to be a good father and by trying to adjust to the expectations of their new role (Gage & Kirk, 2002). Contrary to what many pregnant women think, men do not necessarily count the woman's pregnant body as a disadvantage of pregnancy. Men frequently report finding their pregnant wives attractive, and they complain about a diminished frequency of sexual activity (W. E. Miller & Friedman, 1988).

When a planned and desired pregnancy is ended by miscarriage, fathers suffer deeply along with mothers; however, fathers' suffering is often ignored or discounted (McCreight, 2004). Men are expected to be emotionally strong and to support their partner in such a loss—and few of the normal supports for bereaved persons are available to them. In this situation, fathers report feelings of self-blame, loss of identity, and the necessity to hide feelings of grief and anger.

For years, research on expectant fatherhood lagged behind that on pregnancy, probably because the father's inclusion in the preparation for and experience of childbirth has been relatively recent and because the father experiences no obvious physiological changes comparable to those of pregnancy. Research is still particularly lacking on certain issues that are unique to fathers and prospective fathers. Little is known, for example, about the psychological aspects of fatherhood achieved by proxy—through the woman's artificial insemination with another man's sperm. Still less is known about men's reactions to the loss of a potential child through women's decisions to abort a pregnancy, to give up a baby for adoption, or to refuse to acknowledge a man's paternity.

Childbirth and the Postpartum Experience

Childbirth, which used to be a female domain from which men were largely excluded, has changed dramatically in our culture during the past century. Two changes in particular stand out: (1) The process of childbirth is now largely governed by medical procedures, and (2) fathers are frequently present at the birth of their children. During the transition, women have lost considerable control over childbirth. Midwives and female relatives have been replaced by doctors and husbands, and although such changes may have positive aspects, they also have negative ones.

The management of birth is now considered a medical specialty; birth is treated as a physical-mechanical process rather than a spiritual or social one. In our society, the doctor, not the woman, is said to deliver the baby. The husband may be present to support and "coach" his spouse, but the real control is in the hands of the physician. In this context, it is easy for a woman to feel powerless and vulnerable during labor and delivery—feelings that no doubt color her experience of childbirth and its aftermath. However, the woman experiencing childbirth in a modern medical context need worry considerably less than her 19th-century counterpart or than women in developing countries that she will die in childbirth, a factor that must also influence the way she approaches and experiences the birth.

The experience of labor and delivery in our North American context is a dramatic, emotional, and physically draining experience for the mother and often for the father as well. Both women and men often report that it was a "peak" experience (Lips & Morrison, 1986), although, if difficulties or complications arise, it can be frightening and very painful. Both partners can share the experience up to a point, but only the mother's body goes through the physical trauma of childbirth. During labor, the woman experiences increasingly strong and frequent contractions of the uterus as the baby moves into and down the birth canal. These contractions, although painful, can often be made tolerable by the woman's use of special breathing techniques and by the partner's use of massage and focusing exercises. After the delivery, the woman is likely to be exhausted, but this fatigue is not the only physical change she experiences. Some researchers have estimated that during labor a woman's progesterone level drops so rapidly as to represent the greatest change in concentration of this hormone she experiences in her lifetime, compressed into a few hours (Hamburg, Moos, & Yalom, 1968).

One researcher has argued that both childbirth and breast-feeding have a sexual pleasure component for women that has been ignored (Newton, 1971). Childbirth in particular, she noted, shares some physical and psychological similarities with orgasm. Breathing patterns, facial expression, uterine and abdominal contractions, clitoral engorgement, lowered inhibitions, increased physical strength, greater flexibility, and decreased sensitivity to external stimuli are similar in childbirth and orgasm; in fact, some women experience orgasm during childbirth. (This does not mean that the pain of childbirth is pleasurable for women. It is the combination of pressure and vasocongestion that may trigger orgasm.) Immediately after childbirth, as after orgasm, there is typically a sudden return of sensory acuity and feelings of joy and well-being. The possibility of a woman's experiencing sexual pleasure in childbirth is rarely mentioned, probably because our culture views any sexual connotations of this event as inappropriate.

The tragic 2001 case of Andrea Yates, the Texas woman who drowned her five young children in the bathtub while in the grip of delusions caused by severe postpartum depression, serves as a stark reminder that, under certain conditions, childbirth and its aftermath can trigger serious psychological symptoms. A reaction as severe as that experienced by Yates is very rare, yet for many women physiological and social factors conspire to make the period following the birth of a child (the postpartum period) stressful. Many new mothers experience some negative emotions in the days, weeks, or months after childbirth. Clinicians and researchers have labeled these negative feelings **postpartum depression,** a label that may be misleading because it is used to refer to several different types of experience. Experts now acknowledge three kinds of postpartum depression: (1) the "blues," characterized by emotionality and readiness to cry, which lasts for the first few days after delivery; (2) "neurotic" postpartum depression, characterized by depressed feelings and symptoms such as loss of appetite and insomnia, which lasts at least 2 weeks and occurs within the first few postpartum months; and (3) postpartum psychosis, a serious breakdown in the ability to cope, often including delusions and suicidal and infanticidal thoughts and requiring psychiatric care. Indications from the research literature are that the blues occur in 50 to 80% of women (Harding, 1989; Hopkins, Marcues, & Campbell, 1984), whereas postpartum psychosis occurs in less than 1% (Herzog & Detre, 1976; Kaij & Nilsson, 1972). For the intermediate category of neurotic depression, frequency estimates range from 10 to 30% (Bledsoe & Grote, 2006; Cutrona, 1982; Hopkins et al., 1984; O'Hara & Swain, 1996). These rates may be higher among adolescent mothers: one recent study revealed that 57% of a sample of adolescent women reported moderate to severe depressive symptoms in the 4 years after delivery (Schmidt, Wiemann, Rickert, & Smith, 2006). Rates may also vary widely across cultures: one review indicated the reported prevalence of postpartum depression across 40 different countries ranged from near zero to almost 60% (Halbreich & Karkun, 2006). And the effects of such depression reach beyond the mother and baby: Fathers whose partners experience postpartum depression have a higher risk of psychological symptoms (Roberts, Bushnell, Collings, & Purdie, 2006).

Some researchers have theorized that the large drop in the woman's progesterone level at delivery and the dramatic drop in estrogen levels during the first postpartum week are responsible for postpartum depression. However, a causal link between the hormonal change and the emotional change has not been demonstrated (O'Hara, 1997).

Studies in which hormone levels are measured during pregnancy and the postpartum period have found no consistent differences in these levels between those women who develop postpartum depression and those who do not (Cutrona, 1982). However, since some studies find that women who experience severe menstrual problems are more likely to experience postpartum depression, Cutrona speculated that there may be a small group of women whose depression is due to an unusual sensitivity to hormonal changes. And hormones may not be the only physiological factors relevant to postpartum depression. One researcher found that, across 22 countries, higher DHA (docosahexaenoic acid) content of new mothers' milk and higher seafood consumption rates both predicted lower prevalence of postpartum depression (Hibblen, 2002). He argued that DHA levels are kept from being depleted when mothers consume an adequate diet, and that depleted levels of DHA predispose mothers to depressive symptoms.

The hormonal changes associated with childbirth and the postpartum period are real enough, but culture affects the way physical changes and symptoms are interpreted. Social expectations are likely to contribute to a woman's labeling of her feelings as postpartum depression—especially since some of the physical changes associated with late pregnancy and the early postpartum period (such as sleep difficulties) often characterize depression in other circumstances (B. J. Kaplan, 1986). Furthermore, the social context can affect a woman's experience of and labeling of symptoms.

Researchers have investigated a number of psychological and cultural-environmental correlates of postpartum depression. Their findings suggest that stressful life events, delivery-related stress, poor marital relationship, lack of social support from others, and prior history of psychiatric symptoms are all factors that may be important in predisposing a woman to postpartum depression (Cutrona, 1982; O'Hara & Swain, 1996). One meta-analysis found 13 variables that were significantly predictive of postpartum depression: prenatal depression, low self-esteem, child-care stress, prenatal anxiety, life stress, lack of social support, troubled marital relationships, depression history, difficult infant temperament, maternity blues, lack of marital status, low socioeconomic status, and unplanned or unwanted pregnancy (Beck, 2001). Social support from the spouse and parents seems to be particularly important in protecting women from postpartum depression (Besser, Priel, & Wiznitzer, 2002; Haslam

Pakenham, & Smith, 2006). In the postpartum period, as with pregnancy and the menstrual cycle, the relationships that may exist between hormone levels on one hand and feelings and behavior on the other are complicated by the presence of many social and environmental factors.

Researchers who have examined women's accounts of their own experience of postpartum depression have found that women attribute their depression to various causes: hormones, role changes, negative breast-feeding experience, difficult birth experiences, lack of sleep, and loneliness. Regardless of the ascribed cause, however, the women report similar experiences of depression: uncontrollable crying, a sense of being overwhelmed, shock, shame, guilt, eating problems, and fear that they will lose control of their emotions (Ugarriza, 2002).

There is a great deal of variation in women's responses to childbirth, and much of that variation seems linked to the reactions of others in their social environment. Natasha Mauthner (1999), who interviewed 40 new mothers, concluded that postpartum depression was most likely to occur when women did not have a supportive, nonjudgmental social-cultural environment in which to experience and express their feelings and needs. In a similar vein, Paula Nicolson (1999), who interviewed 25 women periodically as they progressed through pregnancy and the postpartum period, found that new mothers were bothered by the assumptions of those around them that their feelings of depression were inappropriate responses to a happy event. Women in her study noted that they were happy to be mothers but unhappy at the losses that accompany the early stages of motherhood: loss of autonomy and time to themselves and changes in appearance, sexuality, and occupational identity. Nicolson argued that "if these losses were taken seriously and the women encouraged to grieve . . . postpartum depression would be seen by the women and their partners, family, and friends as a potentially healthy process towards psychological re-integration and personal growth" (p. 162).

Of course, there is more to the postpartum period than depression. Attachment to the baby develops gradually in both parents over the first several months (Feeney, Hohaus, Noller, & Alexander, 2001). This process of attachment can be influenced by a number of variables. Fathers present at the birth of their infants show more intense attachment to their babies (G. H. Peterson, Mehl, & Leiderman, 1979). Mothers who have experienced marital problems and ambivalence about the pregnancy are more likely to be depressed and to have difficulties interacting with the baby (Field et al., 1985). Conversely, despite popular concern about the psychological impact of birth technology, interventions such as cesarean section have not been shown to increase the likelihood of postpartum depression (Carter, Frampton, & Mulder, 2006) or to have an adverse effect on the mother-infant relationship (Bradley, 1983). On the whole, it is clear that both parents have the capacity to develop an intense attachment to the new baby, given the close contact necessary to do so.

Reflections : Breast-Feeding, Motherhood, and Culture

One of the decisions new mothers must make is whether and how long to breast-feed their babies. Although you might think such a decision would be based on some combination of the baby's welfare and the mother's inclination to breast-feed, there is another important factor: culture. If a culture frowns on breast-feeding in public, it becomes difficult and impractical for a mother who is not at home all the time to nurse her baby. If a culture tells women that infant formula is better or simply an acceptable alternative for babies, a major incentive to breast-feed is undermined. Breast-feeding is a biological process, but as in so many other areas of gendered activities, relationships, and families, it is profoundly affected by the social environment.

Perhaps the most breast-feeding-friendly nation in the world is Norway. In that country, 99% of mothers breast-feed their newborns from the start—as compared to 70% in the United States, 72% in Canada, and 50% in France (Alvarez, 2003). How does this high percentage come about? Norwegian society has endorsed the idea that mothers should breast-feed, and it provides a wealth of support for women who are doing it.

In Norway, mothers may nurse their babies without fear of disapproval in virtually any setting: on buses, in restaurants, in public parks, at the office. In fact, employed mothers may take 2 hours off per day to breast-feed—either at work or at home. In the United States, women's hectic schedules and the lack of accommodation for breast-feeding in most workplaces makes it a difficult choice.

In the United States, new mothers often receive samples of infant formula as they leave the hospital. In Norway, infant formula is nowhere to be seen in hospitals, and advertising it is forbidden. Furthermore, Norway has instituted a variety of support mechanisms for nursing mothers: breast-feeding instruction for new mothers, baby-friendly hospitals in which new babies are housed in the same room as their mothers and can be fed on demand, and support groups. So strong is the support (and pressure) to breast-feed that women feel it is virtually a requirement of motherhood. As one woman commented to a reporter, "They feel like failures if they cannot breast-feed" (quoted in Alvarez, 2003, p. A3).

But perhaps the most important difference between the two countries is Norway's long maternity leave. New mothers receive 10-month maternity leaves at full pay or 12 months at 80% pay. This long adjustment period makes it practical to breast-feed. By contrast, new mothers in the United States often get only a few weeks of maternity leave—for some, not enough time to get comfortable with breast-feeding and pumping milk before going back to work.

What does Norway's policy communicate about the importance of motherhood? Is the emphasis on and support for breast-feeding a positive thing for women? How does it shape the experience of being a mother?

Abortion

Every year, more than one and a quarter million women in North America end their pregnancies through abortion. Almost 21 of every 1,000 U.S. women ages 15 to 44 had an abortion in 2002 (Figure 8.2), and almost 24% of pregnancies

Figure 8.2   Induced abortions per 1,000 women ages 15 to 44 by race or ethnicity, United States, 2002.

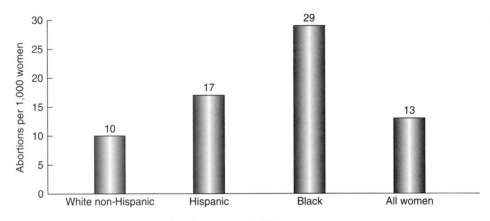

Source: Centers for Disease Control and Prevention (2005).

were terminated by abortion (Finer & Henshaw, 2006). The decision to terminate a pregnancy is a difficult one for many women, often made more problematic by the raging political controversy that surrounds the issue.

Women who obtain abortions come from a wide variety of backgrounds. At current rates, more than one-third of U.S. women will have had an abortion by the age of 45. More than half of abortions are performed on women in their 20s, and two-thirds are on never-married women. More than 60% of abortions are on women who have already had one or more children. Women who are poor and women who are Black are more likely than other women to have abortions (Boonstra, Gold, Richards, & Finer, 2006). One study found that 12% of the mothers seeking abortions had a youngest child less than 1 year old, and 25% had a child younger than 2 (Russo, Horn, & Schwartz, 1992). Women usually have several reasons for choosing abortion. Commonly cited are external reasons such as the inability to afford a child, responsibilities to existing children, education and job responsibilities, social disapproval, and partner's unwillingness to have a child and internal reasons such as a lack of maturity (Figure 8.3) and personal health concerns (Russo et al., 1992).

The most careful studies that have been done suggest that abortion is not linked to severe psychological trauma; women may feel some guilt and regret, but they also feel relief and happiness after the termination of an unwanted pregnancy (Adler, 1975; Adler, David, & Major, 1992; Boonstra et al., 2006; Shusterman, 1976; Turell, Armsworth, & Gaa, 1990). In most cases it appears that abortion is no more likely to cause psychological problems than giving birth (Wilmoth, de Alteriis, & Bussell, 1992). A study that followed 442 abortion patients for 2 years after the abortion found no elevation in the rates of disorders

Figure 8.3   Teenage live birth and abortion rates per 1,000 women, United States, 2002.

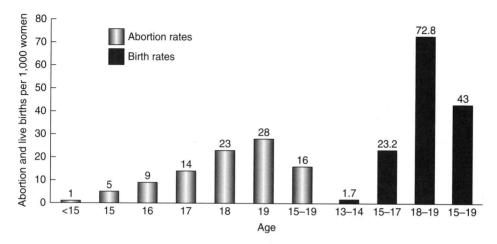

Source: Centers for Disease Control and Prevention (2005), tables 4 and 5.

such as depression and posttraumatic stress disorder (PTSD); indeed, the rates of PTSD were lower in postabortion patients than in the general population (Major, Cozzarelli, Cooper, Zubek, Richards, Wilhite, & Gramzow, 2000). Studies that have focused specifically on adolescents who had abortions have also found little evidence of psychological harm (Adler, Ozer, & Tschann, 2003). However, certain factors may predispose women to experience negative consequences: being pressured into abortion (Greenglass, 1976), lack of support from significant others (Major & Cozzarelli, 1992; Turell et al., 1990), younger age, having no other children, abortion during the second trimester of pregnancy, strong religiosity (Turell et al., 1990), and blaming the pregnancy on one's character (Major & Cozzarelli, 1992). In terms of physical harm, there is no evidence that abortion during the first trimester produces any long-term risk of infertility, miscarriage, or other pregnancy-related problems. Also, despite claims found on some Internet sources, careful review of the evidence conducted in both the United States and Britain show no link between abortion and breast cancer or any other type of cancer (Boonstra et al., 2006).

Regardless of the ultimate decision, confronting the choice to have or not to have an abortion can force a woman to grapple with the balance between her own needs and those of others (Gilligan, 1982). Counseling during the decision period can be very important. Yet sometimes abortion counseling is inadequate to help women explore their feelings surrounding the issue, taking instead the narrow emphasis of handing out contraceptive information and warning women not to become pregnant again (McDonnell, 1984). Although this emphasis is prompted by social concern over the large number of repeat abortions, it is possible that the problem would be better addressed by helping women to work through feelings about their pregnancy and abortion.

In men, one reaction to abortion may be a sense of helplessness and loss of control. Others may feel ambivalent (Flugstad, 2002). Anecdotal reports suggest that men may also feel isolated, angry at themselves and their partners, and worried about emotional and physical damage to the woman. Among men who are supportive of their partner, many focus on concern for her and hide or deny their own feelings (Wade, 1978). They may keep silent about the decision in an attempt to allow the woman to make her own choice, but some women may experience this silence as an abdication of responsibility. And some men truly do abdicate their responsibility in this situation, leaving the woman to cope on her own with whatever decision she makes.

Some research has examined the values, belief systems, and characteristics of the people who take active stands either against abortion or in favor of choice with respect to abortion. Sociologist Lorna Erwin studied members of Canadian groups who identify themselves as "pro-life" and "pro-family" (Rauhala, 1987). She found that religion was the single most important factor distinguishing these people from the general public in Canada. They were far more likely than the average Canadian to say that religion was important to them and to attend church more than once a week. More than 85% of them were concerned about feminism and about homosexuality as threats to the family, and a majority disapproved of the mothers of preschoolers working outside the home. Kristin Luker (1984), who studied American pro-choice and antiabortion activists, found that more than 80% of the highly involved persons on both sides of the issue were women and that these two groups of women differed in many ways besides their views on abortion. The typical pro-choice activist had one or two children, was married to a professional man, had some professional training herself, was employed, and had a relatively high family income. Religion was not an important part of her life, and she rarely attended church. By contrast, the typical antiabortion activist had three or more children, was a high school graduate, was married to a man who ran a small business, and enjoyed a family income that was about $20,000 a year less than that of her pro-choice counterpart. Religion was very important to her, and she attended church at least weekly.

The pro-choice activists tended to believe that men and women have equal rights and responsibilities, that parenthood is not a "natural" role for women but one that should be chosen freely, and that sex is for pleasure and enhancing intimacy rather than only for procreation. By contrast, the antiabortion women tended to believe that women are naturally more suited than men to fill nurturing family roles, that men are more suited for work in the public sphere outside the home, and that the main purpose of sex is procreation. Thus the two groups of women differed sharply in their values and life choices, and Luker argued that their stances on abortion act to rationalize and justify these personal commitments. Women who have made traditional motherhood and family roles central to their lives may well feel threatened and devalued by a movement that would give women the power to restrict their involvement in such roles. Women who have defined themselves not just as mothers but also as workers outside the family circle are profoundly uncomfortable with an ideology that enshrines motherhood as the primary role for most women. Abortion is the issue over which these two groups of women have come into obvious conflict, but Luker argued that the conflict actually encompasses a struggle between two very different ways of life.

The "values divide" between holders of pro-choice and pro-life attitudes may not be as great among people who do not characterize themselves as activists on these issues. Many people feel ambivalent about abortion rights: They hold both positive and negative views about this issue (Craig, Kane, & Martinez, 2002). Researchers who examined General Social Survey data from 1973 to 2000 found that, whereas women homemakers tended to express more pro-life attitudes than either employed women or men, the abortion-related attitudes of all three groups were correlated with similar things and showed similar changes over time (Jelen, Damore, & Lamatsch, 2002). For all three groups, church attendance was associated with antiabortion attitudes. Also, disapproval of euthanasia and of premarital sex predicted disapproval of abortion. Measures of personal ideology, public or private feminism, and opinions about the ideal number of children were less important in predicting attitudes toward abortion.

Among college students, there seems to be a normal distribution of abortion attitudes, and women do not differ from men in favorability toward abortion (Carlton, Nelson, & Coleman, 2000). In this population, individuals with direct abortion experience reported significantly more pro-choice attitudes than did those without such experience.

Can common ground between these two groups be discovered? Yes, according to anthropologist Faye Ginsburg, who has studied abortion activism in the United States. She described the brief emergence during the 1980s of a group called Pro-Dialogue in North Dakota, which enabled people on both sides of the abortion debate to agree on a policy that stressed positive alternatives to abortion: effective sex education, research on safer means of contraception, improved adoption services, and economic support programs for parents. Later, an organization called the Common Ground Network for Life and Choice began to provide a framework for activists from both camps to work together on issues such as teen pregnancy and the provision of resources for impoverished mothers and their children (Ginsburg, 1996). The flowering of this group demonstrates that shared values can sometimes be found between pro-choice and antiabortion activists if they are willing to examine together the context in which childbearing takes place.

MENOPAUSE

Around age 40, a woman's ovaries begin to stop responding to stimulation by pituitary hormones to produce estrogen and progesterone. Over the next 10 to 15 years, menstrual periods become increasingly irregular. During this time, sometimes called *perimenopause,* a woman may experience some changes such as very heavy menstrual flow, vaginal dryness, and sleep difficulties. Eventually, the menstrual periods stop. When a woman has had no menstrual periods for 1 year, she is said to have reached **menopause** (Voda & Eliasson, 1983).

As estrogen levels fall, the woman may experience a number of physical changes. It is not known whether the drop in estrogen causes all of these changes, and there is some debate about the proportion of women who experience them. For example, in one study of 40- to 60-year-old women, those going through menopause reported no greater frequency of physical symptoms than pre- or postmenopausal women (Frey, 1981). The most common symptoms attributed to menopause are hot flashes, vaginal dryness, urinary problems, and bone thinning (osteoporosis). In North America, hot flashes are perhaps the best known of menopausal symptoms, although their cause is not well understood. During a hot flash, the blood vessels in the woman's skin dilate and her skin conductance increases—and she feels extremely hot (Swartzman, Edelberg, & Kemmann, 1990; Weir, 2004). However, there is great cultural variation in the prevalence of this symptom. It is so uncommon among Japanese women, for instance, that there is no specific term for it (Lock, 1993).

Women's reactions to menopause are complicated by a barrage of sometimes frightening and conflicting information from medical sources. Some physicians regard menopause as a *disease* of estrogen deficiency that must be "managed" by the medical profession until a woman's death. One medical expert draws an analogy between diabetes, a disease of insulin deficiency, and menopause, arguing that it is just as natural to give estrogen to menopausal and postmenopausal women as to give insulin to diabetics (Rauramo, 1986). This medical model of menopause focuses on debilitating physical symptoms and implies that the only ways for women to prevent the inevitable downhill slide are estrogen replacement therapy (ERT) or other medical interventions.

By contrast, a nonmedical, "life transition" model of menopause implies that menopause is

> a natural development process that signals a life transition in much the same way as puberty does. Puberty may be associated with skin problems and emotional distress, but these problems are not viewed as symptoms of an underlying "clinical disorder" nor are attempts made to prevent puberty by suppressing hormone production. Similarly, according to this model, menopause may be accompanied by hot flashes and the emotional turmoil associated with identity and role issues, but these are dealt with as problems associated with a normal and expected transition rather than as indicative of a disease process. The focus is

not on "deficiency" and artificially maintaining a particular hormonal state but rather on viewing menopause as an inevitable life stage associated with new challenges and freedoms. (Gannon & Ekstrom, 1993, p. 277)

The sociocultural context that is prevalent with respect to menopause may well affect a woman's attitudes toward this change in her life. Suggestive evidence for this conclusion is provided by two researchers who asked a large sample of adults to express their attitudes toward menopause in one of three contexts (Gannon & Ekstrom, 1993). One group gave their attitudes toward three medical problems, including menopause; a second group described attitudes toward three life transitions, including menopause; and a third group responded to three symbols of aging, including menopause. They found that the medical context elicited the most negative and least positive attitudes from respondents. Older respondents and those who had experienced menopause also showed more positive attitudes.

Attitudes toward menopause are important because they may mediate a woman's experience and behavior. Negative attitudes, beliefs, and expectations among premenopausal women have been found to predict reported distress at the time of menopause (Avis & McKinlay, 1991; Hunter, 1990).

The lowered levels of estrogen that begin at menopause do reduce a protective effect that younger women enjoy against heart disease (Stuenkel, 1989; Voda & Eliason, 1983) and against the thinning bones of osteoporosis (Ziegler, Scheidt-Nave, & Scharla, 1995). Each of these diseases is a serious health hazard for older women, so women used to be pressured to begin ERT at menopause and continue for the rest of their lives. However, recent research shows that estrogen replacement does not protect women from heart disease and that it is linked to an increased risk of breast, endometrial, and ovarian cancer (Grodstein, Manson, & Stampfer, 2001; Mayo Clinic, 2001). Thus many women are now choosing to forego supplemental estrogen during the menopausal transition. For example, one Swedish study of 53- to 54-year-old women showed that the women perceived hormone replacement therapy as more risky and less beneficial in 2003 than in 1999 and that the proportion of women using hormones had dropped from 40.5% to 25.3% (Hoffmann, Hammar, Kjellgren, Lindh-Åstrand, & Brynhildsen, 2005). Studies show that whether women think of menopause as a medical problem bears more weight on their decision to use ERT than does their perception of risk from osteoporosis and heart disease (Logothetis, 1991) and that women are more likely to be concerned about the relief of short-term problems such as hot flashes than longer-term problems such as osteoporosis (Rothert et al., 1990).

In making decisions about ERT, women must weigh their own medical history and susceptibility to particular health problems. However, there is a set of non-controversial recommendations to improve the odds against osteoporosis: adequate dietary intake of calcium and vitamin D, a daily program of weight-bearing exercise including a 30-minute walk, and no smoking (Pearson, Burkhart, Pifalo, Palaggo-Toy, & Krohn, 2005). Some of these behaviors have a beneficial effect on other menopausal symptoms; for instance, women who are physically active experience fewer symptoms (Wilbur, Dan, Hedricks, & Holm, 1990).

Some women report increased depression and irritability around the time of menopause. To put these reports in perspective, consider the findings of Neugarten and Kraines (1965), who studied "menopausal" symptoms among women of different ages. They found the highest levels of symptoms in menopausal women and adolescents and the lowest level among postmenopausal women. Adolescents reported more psychological symptoms; menopausal women noted more physical ones. Thus, psychologically, adolescence may be a more difficult time for women than menopause. At any rate, there is no evidence for a general increase in depression at menopause (Lennon, 1987).

The emotional changes that some women experience around menopause may well be linked to social-environmental variables. A woman at this stage is losing her ability to bear children—an ability that our culture tends to emphasize as crucial to the feminine role. If she had children during her 20s, they are growing up and moving away and are no longer dependent on her, a change she may experience as either positive or negative. She may also be conscious of "losing her looks" as she ages and may feel that this change in appearance jeopardizes her relationship with her husband or partner. There are reasons here for a woman to reappraise her life and her priorities and possibly to become depressed if she decides that she is losing everything that is worthwhile.

One study of middle-aged women indicated that depression at menopause is strongly related to the degree of role loss a woman is experiencing and linked menopausal depression to the "empty nest" (Bart, 1971). This researcher also found that in cultures in which a woman is still gaining rather than losing status as she ages, negative emotional reactions at menopause are rare. Other research has found that many women are, in fact, overjoyed to have an empty nest again—to be free of the responsibilities of parenthood so that they can reorganize their lives and try something new (Rubin, 1979). Another study has shown that the most marked increases in depression among postmenopausal women are associated with multiple causes of worry and stress, including adolescent children, ailing husbands, and aging parents (McKinlay, McKinlay, & Brambilla, 1987). These findings indicate once more that cultural-environmental factors can modify strongly a person's reaction to physiological changes.

"Male Menopause"

In men there is no sudden change in hormonal level at a particular age. Rather, a man's level of testosterone and sperm production decreases very gradually from the age of about 25 onward (Charlton, 2004). In their 70s and 80s, in a transition sometimes labeled **andropause,** men experience a thinning of the ejaculate, a reduction of ejaculatory pressure, and a decrease in the levels of FSH and LH. One physical change that is quite common for men over the age of 40 is enlargement of the prostate gland. This enlargement, which is thought to be related to changes in hormone levels, causes urinary problems; it can be remedied by surgery or drugs. Another change is a gradual drop in libido (Davidson, 1989). As for menopause, physicians have experimented with hormone replacement therapy to treat the symptoms associated with andropause. Testosterone patches have been shown to have positive short-term effects on aging men's lean body mass, cognitive function, sexual interest, and erectile functioning; however, the long-term risks of this hormone therapy for the cardiovascular system and other potential problems are unknown (Charlton, 2004).

Although the physical changes are very gradual, some men seem to experience a psychological crisis at middle age—a crisis that has sometimes been dubbed "male menopause." Research shows that men in their 40s show higher depression scores and more alcohol and drug use than other adult men; however, they do not differ from other men in anxiety, life satisfaction, or happiness (Tamir, 1982). The problems that men in this age range experience might be due not to their changing hormone levels but to psychosocial factors. For example, David Gutmann (1972) referred to the male midlife crisis as a "loss of the future." He claims that by about the age of 50 many achievement-oriented men begin to feel that they are not going to become any more successful or move any closer to their goals. Gutmann's interviews with men in this age group in several different cultures offered some support for this concept. His research suggested that a man may greet the realization that he cannot improve his future either with a relieved sense of letting go and a moving out of the rat race or with an inner crisis in which he struggles with the fact that he has not achieved his goals to his own satisfaction. This theme of an aspiration-achievement gap for middle-aged men was echoed by D. J. Levinson (1978). Aging men may also experience a midlife crisis because the physical changes they experience, such as increasing vulnerability to illness and fatigue, make it more difficult for them to live up to the masculinity ideal of strength and dominance. Such perceived threats to masculinity may lead to depression or to an enhanced need to "prove" their masculinity (Gray, 1997).

Another explanation that is offered for a male midlife crisis is the change in family relationships that occurs at this time. Children are moving away from home, leaving their parents alone together for the first time in many years. Women, freed from their parental roles, may return to work or school, developing new interests and responsibilities and forcing a renegotiation of the couple's relationship. These changes may be experienced as threatening by the man; conversely, they may be viewed as opportunities to explore new directions.

It is clear that both women and men can experience negative emotional reactions to the important changes in role that occur at midlife. Women, however, have been taught to expect these changes and to label them *menopausal*. These expectations probably contribute to the strength of the symptoms they experience and to their coping strategies. Although some midlife symptoms are related to the physical aspects of aging, it seems reasonable to expect that both women and men may react negatively when they find themselves no longer able to fulfill some aspects of the roles that society has defined as central for them: child rearing for women and successful career achievement for men. As feminine and masculine gender roles become more flexible, perhaps midlife will be regarded increasingly by both women and men as a welcome opportunity to shift gears and try something different.

Overview   The menopausal transition

- The physical changes of menopause for women are associated with the gradual drop in the ovaries' production of estrogen and progesterone after age 40 and the eventual cessation of menstrual periods.

- Symptoms vary across cultures. In North America, the most well-known symptom is hot flashes.

- Women's reactions to these changes are influenced by whether they view menopause as a medical problem or a life transition.

- Men experience a more gradual change in hormone production from age 30 onward.

- For both women and men, the physical changes associated with midlife can occur in tandem with the loss of important roles.

SUMMARY

Women's menstrual cycle makes it obvious that they are experiencing cyclic fluctuations of hormone levels, whereas men display no easily discernible signs that their physiology is not completely stable. However, research shows that both women and men are subject to a variety of biologically and socially induced cycles that relate to mood and behavior, and women are no more variable than men in mood and performance. There is also strong evidence that relationships between biological cycles and such correlates as symptoms, moods, or performance can be modified dramatically by factors in a person's environment. Furthermore, although women are subject to the processes of pregnancy, childbirth, and menopause that involve both large hormonal changes and culturally recognized sets of physical and emotional symptoms, men are not unaffected by the drastic life changes that go along with having a child or losing an important role. Thus, even with regard to the particular experiences of pregnancy and menopause, causality of symptoms cannot be attributed simply to hormonal changes but must be considered a blend of biological and social factors.

In general, research on hormonal and reproductive issues seems to have been guided by the assumption that they are "women's problems" and has focused on trying to understand them by reference to hormone levels. Accordingly, research on male reactions to these events has been scanty. Much more research on both women and men is needed before the myths about "raging hormones," pregnancy, postpartum depression, and menopause can be replaced with facts.

KEY TERMS

menstrual cycle
follicular phase
ovulation
luteal phase
menstruation
premenstrual syndrome
premenstrual dysphoric
   disorder (PMDD)

dysmenorrhea
prostaglandins
endometriosis
menarche
sexual objectification
gonadotropins
spermarche

pseudocyesis
couvade syndrome
couvade
postpartum depression
menopause
andropause

9

Mental and Physical Health
Stress, Change, and Adaptations*

Traditionally held gender roles tend to associate femininity with weakness, delicacy, and vulnerability. Masculinity, in contrast, is associated with strength, toughness, and invulnerability. It is perhaps not surprising, then, that women's physical and mental health has been considered fragile in comparison to men's and that the history of professionalized health care has, at least until recently, been largely one of male doctors giving advice to female patients (Ehrenreich & English, 1979). Women's vulnerability to both physical and mental ailments was once believed to be traceable in large measure to their reproductive physiology and anatomy: The mere possession of a uterus rendered a woman susceptible to a variety of disorders. During the 19th century, doctors argued that normal feminine functions put all women at risk. As one physician put it, those women who were not "crippled on the breakers of puberty" might be "dashed to pieces on the rock of childbirth" or "ground on the ever-recurring shallows of menstruation, and . . . the final bar of menopause" (Engelmann, 1900, as quoted in Ehrenreich & English, 1979, p. 110). Furthermore, doctors asserted that in women diseases of the stomach, liver, heart, lungs, and other organs were usually no more than sympathetic reactions to disorders of the uterus. Even tuberculosis, which was attributed to environmental causes when contracted by males, was believed to be a result of menstrual malfunction when it occurred in females

---

*With assistance from Martha Wilson

(Ehrenreich & English, 1979). Most famous of all female disorders, however, was **hysteria**—from the Greek word meaning *uterus*—a mysterious disease marked by fainting or fits and a variety of symptoms such as loss of voice or partial paralysis, with no apparent physical cause. It was considered a disease of the uterus, despite the lack of evidence that the symptoms had any organic basis whatsoever. Sigmund Freud eventually redefined *hysteria* as a mental rather than physical disorder; nevertheless, it was still considered a feminine disease. In retrospect, modern commentators have explained it as a result of the stifling restrictions attached to the role of the upper-class woman during the 19th and early 20th centuries.

In this chapter, we examine ways in which gender roles interact with physical and mental health. In particular, we ask these questions:

- Is it really true that women are the "weaker sex"?
- How do women and men differ with respect to general health and fitness?
- Do men's and women's roles expose them to different health-related occupational, socioeconomic, or behavioral risk factors?
- To what extent are systems of health care and health research affected by gender roles and stereotypes?
- Do women and men differ in their patterns of mental illness?
- How have gender stereotypes influenced diagnostic categories for mental illness?
- Do gender stereotypes influence judgments about whether a person is mentally healthy?
- Are men and women differentially vulnerable to stresses that can interfere with mental health?
- How can ideas about gender influence the treatment of emotional problems through psychotherapy or prescription drugs?

VULNERABILITY AND STRENGTH

The idea that women are the weaker, more vulnerable sex and men are stronger and better able to withstand the rigors of life and work both stems from and provides a convenient justification for the social arrangements of the cultures in which it prevails. In fact, however, the evidence provides a rather mixed picture of male–female differences in vulnerability and strength. In brief, although some studies show that women report more minor physical symptoms and seek medical help more often than men do, men are more vulnerable than women to serious illnesses at every stage of life, and the male's life span is shorter than the female's. Women and men each report higher rates of certain mental illness symptoms. In terms of muscular strength, men generally outperform women, but the gap is not necessarily as large as the "tough man–fragile woman" stereotype would suggest.

Physical Vulnerability and Mortality

Males are more likely than females to suffer injury or death prenatally or during the birth process and to be victims of childhood diseases. Although 108 to 140 males are conceived for every 100 females, by the time of birth the ratio of males to females has dropped to between 103 and 106 to 100 in the United States. Miscarriage, stillbirth, and death from birth-related injuries are more likely to affect males than females. Male infants are more likely than females to suffer from congenital malformations and from a wide variety of genetically linked diseases and to die during the first year of life. During the teenage years, males are more likely than females to die in accidents. The survival rate of women from such conditions as starvation, exposure, fatigue, and shock is better than that of men. In the United States, females outnumber males by the early 20s; by the age of 65 there are about 3 women for every 2 men; and among those who live to be 100 the ratio of women to men is 4 to 1. The sex differential in longevity has traditionally been smaller among African Americans and Hispanic Americans, whose life expectancy at birth is 6 to 7 years shorter than that of European Americans. This effect is likely due to low income which tends to be correlated with race (Go, Brustrom, Lynch, & Aldwin, 1995; Markides, 1989). Interestingly, the life expectancy for African American women has increased and is currently higher than the life expectancy for White men in the United States. However, people from households with annual incomes of less than $10,000 live an average of 3 to 7 years less, depending on gender and race, than do people from households with an annual income of at least $25,000 (U.S. Department of Health and Human Services, 2000). Around the world, poverty is related to shorter life expectancies for both genders (World Resources Institute, 2005).

In developing countries, where poverty and malnutrition are more prevalent, sex differences in life expectancy are narrower: closer to 2 years than to the 7 years found in developed countries. In Nepal, men's life expectancy actually exceeds that of women (United Nations Development Program, 2005). This higher female mortality has been linked to the low cultural value placed on females relative to males. Boys are given better care, including better nutrition and access to medical treatment, than girls, who are more likely to be neglected.

Although the possession of a uterus does not endanger a woman's health in the way 19th-century doctors claimed, it does present one potentially serious risk to women's health and survival: childbearing. The World Health Organization has estimated that in developing countries deaths from maternal causes (pregnancy and childbirth) are among the five major causes of death for women aged 15 to 44; in one-third of the countries, these causes rank first or second in overall death rates. In the United States, complications of pregnancy and delivery account for less than 1% of the deaths of women between 15 and 49, but in developing countries, these causes may account for up to one-quarter of such deaths. And within the United States, maternal death rates vary dramatically among ethnic/racial groups, most likely due to differences among these groups in socioeconomic status and access to health care. During the 1990s, whereas for non-Hispanic White women the maternal death rate was about 6 in every 100,000 births, the death rate for Hispanic women was 10 per 100,000, and for African American women it was a sobering 25 per 100,000 (L. Bell, 1999). Data for 2003, the most recent year available, show that these statistics have changed little: age-adjusted maternal mortality rates per 100,000 people stand at 6.3 for non-Hispanic White women, 8.6 for Latina women, and 25.5 for African American women (National Center for Health Statistics, 2005).

Even when it does not directly lead to the mother's death, pregnancy is a serious drain on women's health in countries where women do not have access to enough food to meet their increased caloric and nutritional requirements. Countries with the lowest life expectancy for females also tend to have the highest fertility rates (World Health Organization, 2006).

Illness Rates

Men are more likely than women to die from heart disease, cancer, lung disease, pneumonia and flu, and liver disease. Women are more likely than men to die from strokes, diabetes, and kidney disease, and they account for almost all the deaths from breast cancer. Men's death rate from prostate cancer is about the same as women's from breast cancer (National Center for Health Statistics, 2005). The rates of death due to suicide and homicide are strikingly higher for men than for women. Men use and abuse alcohol and illegal drugs more than women do; however, women are much more likely than men to be treated with prescription medications for their mental and physical problems (National Center for Health Statistics, 2005).

These statistics can be somewhat misleading. An emphasis on the differences between women and men obscures the fact that, depending on a variety of conditions, both sexes can be threatened by such serious illness as heart disease and cancer. The two leading causes of death for both women and men are heart disease and cancer (National Center for Health Statistics, 2005). Although more young men than young women die of heart disease, heart disease is the leading killer of American women, and a woman's first heart attack is more likely than a man's to be fatal. The overall death rate 2 years after hospital discharge following a heart attack was found to be 28.9% for women as compared to 19.6% for men in one U.S. study (Vaccarino, Krumholz, Yarzebski, Gore, & Goldberg, 2001). Women's higher mortality levels hold only among patients younger than age 60, however. Among older patients, women are apparently not at greater risk than men. Women who both smoke and use oral contraceptives are at substantially increased risk for heart attacks.

Fatalities from breast cancer, another disease that threatens many women, vary across racial/ethnic groups. African American women have a higher fatality rate from breast cancer than do European American women. In 2003 the age-adjusted death rate from breast cancer was 34 of every 100,000 African American women and 24.7 of every 100,000 European American women (National Center for Health Statistics, 2005). See Figure 9.1 for a comparison of death rates from breast cancer.

Across all ages, women report more physical illness symptoms than men do, take more prescribed and over-the-counter medication, and visit the doctor more often (National Center for Health Statistics, 2005). The dramatic differences

Figure 9.1   Women's death rates from breast cancer by race, ethnicity, and age, 2003.

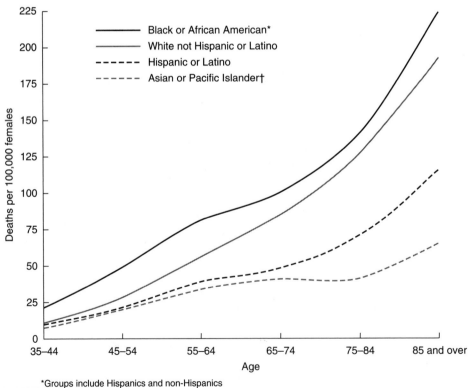

*Groups include Hispanics and non-Hispanics
†Death rates known to be underestimated

Source: National Center for Health Statistics (2005), table 40. Retrieved from http://www.cdc.gov/nchs/data/hus/hus05.pdf#040

between women and men in their interactions with the health care system are shown in Figure 9.2. The types of symptoms reported by women and men also differ: Women report more headaches, urinary problems, abdominal pain, and weight problems, whereas men report more ulcers, asthma, and eye problems (Kane, 1991).

When the definition of *mental illness* is restricted to diagnoses involving mental disorganization (e.g., confusion, disorientation) or interpersonal distress (e.g., anxiety, depression), women are considerably more likely than men to be diagnosed and treated for mental illness (Kane, 1991). This finding holds across all ethnic groups but not across all types of marital status. In fact, it is only among the married population that women are more likely than men to

Figure 9.2 Interactions of women and men in the United States with the health care system during 2004. As these data show, women utilize the health care system more frequently than men do.

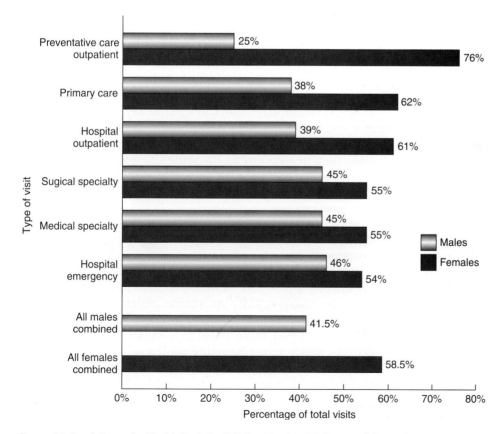

Source: National Center for Health Statistics (2004), tables 1 and 2. Retrieved September 21, 2006, from http://www.cdc.gov/nchs/products/pubs/pubd/hestats/estimates2004/estimates04.htm

receive psychiatric treatment. When particular categories of mental disorders and treatments are examined, the pattern of observed gender differences is mixed. Men have higher rates of treatment for alcohol and drug use disorders, but women far outnumber men in diagnoses of depression, and the sexes are diagnosed and treated for schizophrenia with about equal frequency. Women are far more likely than men to be diagnosed with the eating disorders anorexia and bulimia. Many potential biases are built into these diagnostic patterns, however, which we will explore later in the chapter (Hartung & Widiger, 1998).

Fitness and Strength

As a group, women are shorter, lighter, and less muscular than men and are regarded in our society as generally unable to perform heavy manual work. Research has demonstrated, however, that young women (college students without special training) are able to do strenuous work, expending 2,369 kilocalories for $8\frac{1}{2}$ hours (Wardle, 1976). This expenditure of energy is approximately equal to that required in unmechanized coal mining—usually considered one of the most demanding occupations. Thus, although women have, on average, less muscular strength than men do, it would be a mistake to characterize them as weak. This conclusion is affirmed by a look at women in other cultures. For example, researchers working in a University of Nairobi laboratory found that an African woman who is accustomed to the task can easily carry on her head a load that is equal to two-thirds of her body weight—and do so while expending far less energy than a male U.S. Army trooper hauling an equivalent load (Maloiy, Heglund, Prager, Cavagna, & Taylor, 1986). Women become both stronger and more muscular with training. Research on the responses of young women and men to resistance training (training with weights) makes it clear that, in response to the same short-term training program, women and men achieve similar increases in muscle size and that women make *greater* relative gains in strength (O'Hagan et al., 1995). In addition, weight training lowers cholesterol levels in both women and men (Vergano, 1999).

Men's advantage in muscular strength has been amply demonstrated by their performance in athletic competition. In Olympic events in which both sexes participate, men consistently obtain better performance records. However, the differences between men's and women's records in track, field, and swimming events are decreasing rapidly as female athletes receive proper training. For instance, during the 12 years between 1972 and 1984, the women's record for the marathon dropped more than 23 minutes while the men's dropped only 22 seconds. When Paula Radcliffe set the world record for the marathon in 2003, she sliced the male–female difference in world record times to just $10\frac{1}{2}$ minutes. The world swimming record set by Janet Evans in the 400-meter freestyle in the 1988 Olympics was 2 seconds *faster* than Mark Spitz's 1968 world record in the same event (Swardson, 1991). Florence Griffith Joyner's 1988 world-record time in the 100-meter run was faster than the

Olympic gold medal times of male runners up until the 1930s. And speed skater Bonnie Blair's winning time for the 500-meter Olympic gold medal in 1994 was faster than the times of all male gold medal winners in the same event up until 1976 (Funk and Wagnalls Corporation, 1994). In events that require endurance as well as speed, such as the ultramarathon, women can outcompete men. Women hold the speed record for swimming the English Channel in both directions, and in 1995 Allison Streeter set a new world record for the number of crossings when she swam the Channel for the 32nd time. In 1988, Paula Newby-Fraser won the women's division of the famous Ironman Triathlon—with a time that placed her ahead of all but 10 of the hundreds of male contestants. In 1988, Susan Butcher became the first person to win a third consecutive Iditarod, a grueling long-distance sled dog race. Ann Trason, a 7 time women's winner of the 100-mile Western States Endurance Run—a course that covers dirt trails through the Sierra Nevada mountains—has on two occasions been beaten by only one male competitor.

Among nonathletes, men generally are stronger than women (Musselman & Brouwer, 2005) and participate in more physical activity than women do (National Center for Health Statistics, 2005). On average, women have lower levels of cardiovascular fitness than men do at all age levels, although in North America neither men nor women meet the standards for cardiovascular fitness set by health organizations (Adams, Johnson, Cole, Matthiasson, et al., 1990; Shephard, 2000). For both sexes, fitness levels improve markedly with regular physical exercise.

Overview — Women's and men's physical vulnerability, fitness, and strength

- Men have shorter life expectancies than women do; this difference is largest in developed countries.

- Pregnancy and childbirth are significant causes of death for women in developing countries but not in developed countries.

- Men are more likely than women to die from suicide or homicide.

- Across all age groups, women report more physical illness symptoms, take more medication, and visit the doctor more than men do.

- On average, women are shorter, lighter, and less muscular than men; however, women develop strength quite rapidly under training conditions.

- Women can outperform men on physical tasks that demand endurance.

Examining these three lines of evidence—vulnerability and survival rates, illness rates, and measures of fitness and strength—the reliability of the strong man–weak woman stereotype is far from clear-cut. Let us turn next to an examination of gender-related patterns in specific areas of physical and mental health and their underlying causes. Physical and mental health are discussed under separate headings, but it will soon become clear that they are strongly interrelated, each one dynamically interacting with the other.

GENDER AND PHYSICAL HEALTH

General Health and Fitness

Men have a shorter life expectancy than women do, and males are more likely than females to succumb to a variety of serious diseases. Part of the explanation for these differences is genetic. Males, as seen in Chapter 5, are more likely than females to inherit a variety of sex-linked disorders. Other biological explanations have been offered for some of the gender differences. Women's relatively high estrogen levels may offer them at least temporary protection against heart disease (Hazzard, 1986); heart attacks increase for women as their estrogen decreases. Another suggestion is that women's lower metabolic rate and relatively greater percentage of body fat than men's contributes to their survival in difficult conditions. Support for the biological vulnerability explanations of gender differences in health comes from studies in which populations of males and females living very similar lifestyles are still found to differ in life expectancy. For example, a study of 40,000 American monks and nuns, all of whom were, of course, unmarried, did not smoke or drink alcohol, had similar diets, and were teachers, found that despite the similarity in lifestyle the women had a life expectancy advantage of more than 5 years by the age of 45 (as cited in Nicholson, 1984). Other research, however, has shown that there is a tendency for males and females to die at equal rates from specific diseases when their environment and lifestyle are similar. For example, among male and female long-term psychiatric patients, the death rate from heart disease is similar for the two sexes, whereas in the general population men are 4 times more likely than women to die of heart attacks (Craig & Lin, 1984).

Several writers have argued that gender roles make an important contribution to gender differences in health. One way in which this might happen is that the masculine role prompts men to behave in ways that are dangerous to their health (Harrison, 1978). Brannon (1976), for example, argued that the stereotyped masculine role contains four elements: the avoidance of femininity, the need to be superior to others, the need to be self-reliant and independent, and the need to be more powerful than others. The attempt to live up to such a role may cause a great deal of anxiety. The stress of not meeting his achievement aspirations, for instance, may be difficult for a man to handle, and a man trying to live up to the "self-reliant" part of the masculine role has another potential handicap: He cannot allow himself to relieve his anxiety by talking about his problems. The physical effects of stress generated by a competitive orientation may be worsened by the man's attempts to relieve that stress through drinking, smoking, or other drug use. Furthermore, the desire to appear powerful may lead a man to engage in risky behaviors, such as driving dangerously or fighting (Iacuone, 2005). Young men, particularly young African American men, are far more likely than young women to be the victims of homicide (National Center for Health Statistics, 2005). All of these factors, each one stemming in some way from the masculine role, contribute to the likelihood of an earlier death for men than for women.

Eisler (Eisler & Skidmore, 1987) developed a scale to assess masculine gender role stress (MGRSS). This is distinguished from purely sex-typed masculinity in that not all compliance with masculine norms is necessarily stress producing. For instance, socially desirable masculine traits that are assessed by many measures of sex-typed masculinity include assertiveness, self-confidence, and autonomy—traits that do not necessarily negatively affect one's health. The MGRSS was found to be conceptually and operationally distinct from sex-typed masculinity. Interestingly, though, the research suggested that those who score high on the MGRSS are more likely to participate in high-risk health behaviors than those who score high in socially acceptable masculine traits. In fact, these participants may not be at especially high risk for health problems.

Factor analysis of the MGRSS revealed five underlying factors:

- Physical inadequacy: fear of an inability to meet masculine standards of physical fitness (in sports or sexual prowess);
- Emotional inexpressiveness: fear of vulnerability in expressing one's emotions (love, weakness, hurt feelings) and fear of dealing with others' vulnerable feelings;
- Subordination to women: fear of being outperformed by women in activities at which men traditionally are expected to excel (work or sports events);
- Intellectual inferiority: fear of appraisal as unable to think rationally or be decisive (not smart enough to handle particular situations); and
- Performance failure: fear of failure to meet masculine standards in the arenas of work and sexual adequacy.

Both men and women with high MGRSS scores were moderately linked with Type A coronary-prone behavior, hostility, and elevated blood pressure. They also reported less life satisfaction than their low-scoring MGRSS counterparts. Also, men with high MGRSS scores may have more difficulty with stress, hostility, anxiety, and high-risk health behaviors than do men who endorse socially acceptable masculine traits (Eisler & Skidmore, 1987).

The feminine gender role may also contribute to gender differences in health patterns. The feminine ideals of expressiveness and intimacy may help

Title IX, a 1972 law that bars sex discrimination in educational programs receiving federal government financial assistance, has dramatically increased young women's participation in sports and the likelihood that they will aim for college athletic scholarships. © Jill Braaten, Photographer, The McGraw-Hill Companies

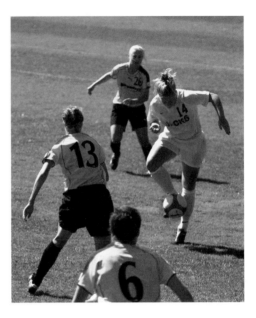

women avoid the stress-generating patterns of competitiveness and suffering in stoical silence that are encouraged by the masculine role. In addition, the lack of necessity to show off strength or power may keep women out of risky situations. There is a potential trade-off here, of course: Men die during their risky undertakings, but women may die of boredom! In fact, boredom, the lack of a sense of purpose, and the absence of intellectually challenging work has been cited as a source of ill health for women caught in restrictive roles—from the affluent "hysterical" women of the early part of the last century to the middle-class housewives experiencing the numbing malaise that Betty Friedan in *The Feminine Mystique* (1963) characterized as "the problem that has no name."

A direct and obvious contribution of the feminine role to women's lower levels of fitness has been the notion that strength is unfeminine and that athletic activity is primarily for men. In recent years, there has been an increased media focus on female athletic activity in the United States, due largely to the equality of access to athletic training and facilities in schools and colleges legislated by Title IX and to corporate sponsorship of "big-time" sports events for women. The World Cup soccer win by the U.S. women's team in 1999 led to unprecedented public awareness of women's sports. However, the attitude that muscles and sweat are not ladylike may still hold for many people. Not until the 1984 Olympics in Los Angeles was a woman's marathon considered an appropriate event; little girls are still sometimes taught to do special "girls' push-ups," to throw a softball underhand, to play certain sports less intensively than boys, and to rule out participation in other sports altogether. This young population also experiences homophobia: Some girls may avoid participating in athletics for fear of being labeled a "sports dyke."

Females participate less regularly in physical exercise than males do, and studies show that a variety of sports activities continue to be perceived as essentially masculine. Between 1985 and 1990, participation in sports and fitness activities declined 12% among the American public—and the declines were greater among women than men (Robinson & Godbey, 1993). That decline appears to have been reversed. Between 1998 and 2003, both men and women increased their reported levels of regular leisure-time physical activity in all age groups, although women's levels are still lower than men's (National Center for Health Statistics, 2005). Despite a continuing tendency for the media to focus more on male than female sports, athletes such as tennis champions Kim Clijsers, Justine Henin-Hardenne, and Serena Williams, Canadian hockey team captain Cassie Campbell, sailing great Paige Railey, and Olympic gymnast Carly Patterson are visible as role models for young women. Girls and women with disabilities are also presented with athletic role models, such as Jean Driscoll, who has set five world records in the wheelchair division of the Boston Marathon, Louise Sauvage, who has also won the Boston Marathon and is a gold and silver medalist at the 1996 Paralympic Games, and Candace Cable, a marathon winner who also competes in cross-country skiing in the Winter Paralympics. The visibility accorded such women may gradually erode the stereotype that women are, or should be, weak and fragile; however, it has not, as yet, encouraged the majority of girls and young women to become regular participants in sports and exercise.

The evidence is clear that exercise is important to women's health. Among young women, exercise appears to be of critical importance in building the bone density needed to help stave off osteoporosis in later years (Klohn & Rogers, 1991). Regular exercise is also associated in women with a reduced risk of breast cancer (Bernstein, Henderson, Hanisch, Sullivan-Halley, & Ross, 1994), improved cardiovascular fitness and blood levels of "good" (HDL) cholesterol (Hardman & Hudson, 1994), and increased strength and lowered levels of body fat (Marks, Ward, Morris, Castellani, & Rippe, 1995). Exercise has also been found to promote increased feelings of self-efficacy in both women and men—with a more dramatic effect for women (McAuley, Courneya, & Lettunich, 1991).

A particular source of concern about physical exercise for women has been the relationship between exercise and reproduction. Some women who follow a very demanding exercise schedule experience a temporary disruption or cessation of their menstrual cycle. This is most likely to occur in women with a history of irregular menstruation, although menstrual periods tend to return when the athlete reduces the intensity of her training regimen. If a female athlete maintains her normal body weight, the menstrual cycle change may simply be a temporary way for the body to conserve energy under stress—a normal, adaptive, and transient body phenomenon (Bonen, 1994). However, if an athlete participates in very high levels of aerobic exercise and consumes an inadequate supply of calories, she may experience a rapid loss of body weight in concert with the cessation of menstruation. In this case, the missing menstrual periods may signal lowered estrogen levels and the loss of calcium from bone tissue, setting the stage for the development of early osteoporosis (Aulin, 1995). Thus it can be extremely dangerous for female athletes to set unrealistic goals for weight loss.

Occupational Health and Safety

Because women and men often do different kinds of work, they are vulnerable to different kinds of job-related injuries and illnesses (Doyal, 1995). Exposure to toxic chemicals is common for women in such female-dominated occupations as lab technology, computer chip manufacturing, laundry and textile work, and cosmetology. Exposure to radiation may be a problem for dental hygienists, X-ray technicians, and some nurses. The necessity to sit or stand for long periods of time places workers such as secretaries, telephone operators, waitresses, and sales clerks at risk for circulatory diseases and back problems. The female-dominated jobs of teaching, child care, social work, and health care all carry a high risk of infection. The male-dominated jobs in trades and construction make their occupants vulnerable to accidental injury, as do certain factory jobs. Police and military work, also male-dominated, carry risks of death and injury through accidents and violence.

Some occupational hazards, such as radiation and toxic chemicals, may be especially problematic for women of childbearing age, as they may affect a developing fetus. Thus some companies tried to exclude fertile women from jobs that involve this kind of dangerous exposure. The economic implications for women of such restrictions can be enormous; some women chose sterilization in preference to losing a high-paying job. However, some analysts argued that the focus on pregnancy risks obscured the issue that exposure to toxic chemicals or radiation is not good for anyone and that, rather than excluding fertile women from certain jobs, companies should find ways to reduce dangerous exposure for *all* workers (Win-O'Brien, 1980). This argument gleaned support from findings that not only the female reproductive system is at risk from toxins; occupational exposure of male workers to certain chemicals can damage their reproductive abilities as well. For instance, exposure to lead can result in reduced sexual drive, decreased ability to produce normal sperm, and sterility in males (Gold, 1981). In 1991 the Supreme Court agreed with this argument in a ruling on the employment practices of Johnson Controls, a leading manufacturer of automobile batteries. The company had refused to employ women in departments in which lead was used because lead exposure could pose a risk to a woman's fetus. No similar restriction on men's lead exposure existed, although lead exposure can cause cardiovascular problems and infertility in both sexes. The Supreme Court ruled that the company's policy was discriminatory and that concerns about fetal risk could not legally be used to keep women out of jobs they could perform satisfactorily (Dabrow & Ameci, 1991).

Employment in general, though, does not make women or men more vulnerable to health problems. For both women and men, multiple roles are beneficial to both physical and mental health. Women who combine employment and family are healthier than nonemployed women; men who are employees, spouses, and fathers are healthier than men who occupy fewer roles (Barnett & Hyde, 2001).

Socioeconomic Risk Factors

In general, the poor are more vulnerable to illness and disabilities than are upper- and middle-income groups (Doyal, 1995; Gladwell, 1990). For instance, people who are classified as "poor" in the United States are more than 3 times more likely than people who are not poor to report that their health is only fair or poor, and poor people are more than $2\frac{1}{2}$ times more likely than people who are not poor to suffer from limitations of activity caused by chronic health conditions (National Center for Health Statistics, 2005).

Poverty is becoming increasingly "feminized" all over the world. In the United States, 11.8% of men and 14.8% of women live below the poverty line (U.S. Census Bureau, 2005). When male–female comparisons are made within racial groups, African American women appear particularly likely to be poorer than their male counterparts: African American females make up 58.7% of the total population of African Americans for whom poverty status can be determined (U.S. Census Bureau, 2005). Thus women, particularly African American women, are at higher risk than men for health problems associated with low socioeconomic status. The risk of death from heart disease is greater for African American women than for any other group of U.S. women, and, in a difference from the pattern for the European American population, hypertension is about as great a problem for African American women as for African American men (National Center for Health Statistics, 2005). Low-income women of color are more likely than other women to die from complications of pregnancies and abortions. Stress levels associated with being poor, belonging to a marginalized group, living in unsafe conditions, and being unable to secure adequate health care insurance are potential contributors to health problems. Ratings of stress have been found to be higher among female immigrants from Central America than among Mexican Americans or Anglo Americans (Selgado de Snyder, Cervantes, & Padilla, 1990).

Among men, African Americans are more likely than European Americans to have hypertension or to die from injuries suffered at work, and they have higher death rates from cerebrovascular diseases, cirrhosis of the liver, tuberculosis, diabetes, and homicide (National Center for Health Statistics, 2005).

Health and Illness Behaviors

There is evidence that women and men differ in some of the behaviors that are related to maintaining health, responding to symptoms of illness, and treating health problems. These differences, which frequently seem to reflect gender-role expectations, may well explain some of the differences in illness rates and life span between the sexes.

Maintaining health involves proper nutrition, rest, exercise, and cleanliness; the avoidance of self-destructive activities such as smoking, overindulgence in alcohol and other dangerous drugs, and overexposure to the sun; and preventive health care such as medical and dental checkups and self-examination for signs of cancer and other problems. Women seem to engage in such health-oriented behavior more than men do. Women are more knowledgeable about and interested in health than men are (Beier & Ackerman, 2003), have more dental and medical checkups, and engage in fewer behaviors that are a direct risk to health (National Center for Health Statistics, 2005). Women's greater use of preventive health care services may help account for both their higher illness rates and their lower mortality rates; women tend to be diagnosed and treated earlier for certain diseases that cause death in men. However, despite their tendency to use health services more than men do, American women still make less than optimum use of preventive health care. Among women age 50 and over of all education levels, the use of mammograms to screen for breast cancer more than doubled from 1987 to 2000. However, screening levels had dropped slightly by 2003, and the screening rates for women who are poor or have low educational levels continue to lag well behind those of more privileged women (National Center for Health Statistics, 2005). Over 80% of women aged 18 to 64 have a yearly Pap smear—a test that is critical for the early detection of cervical cancer. African American women are slightly more likely than European American women to have regular Pap tests and mammograms. Women may forgo medical tests because of a lack of health insurance, which, in the United States, is almost exclusively tied to full-time employment. Women's self-reported incidence of Pap smears, mammograms, and regular care by doctors is strongly correlated with their income levels (National Center for Health Statistics, 2005).

One difference in men's and women's behavior that can be linked to their different mortality rates is smoking. Years ago, in a rare and dramatic example of gender-role stereotypes exerting a genuinely protective effect on women, it was considered unladylike to smoke. Tobacco companies have done all they can to reverse this stereotype. Advertising campaigns reminding women that they have "come a long way" were designed to link smoking with women's liberation, and smoking increased among teenage girls and older women during the 1970s and 1980s. Smoking rates among high school students rose by almost a third between 1991 and 1997 (Schwartz, 1998). The Centers for Disease Control reported that 23% of female and 22.9% of male high school students smoke and that 9% of girls and 8% of boys in middle school smoke (Tobacco Information and Prevention Source, 2006). Among persons aged 18 to 24, 26.3% of men and 21.5% of women are smokers (National Center for Health Statistics, 2005c). The age-adjusted incidence rate for lung cancer has decreased by 9% among men, whereas the rate has increased by 143% among women over the past 30 years. Compared to rates for American men, which are relatively steady, tobacco-related deaths among American women under age 70 have been rising steadily since 1965. In 1979 women accounted for 26% of lung cancer deaths; by 2002 that number had risen to 42.8% (American Lung Association,

2005). Women aged 35 or older who smoke are about 12 times more likely to die of lung cancer than women who do not smoke, 10.5 times more likely to die of chronic obstructive pulmonary disease, and twice as likely to develop heart disease (American Lung Association, 2006).

When illness symptoms do arise, women are more likely than men to try to do something about them, by treating them or by seeking medical help. Part of the explanation for this gender difference may be that women are more attentive than men to their internal state (Pennebaker, 1982). In addition, admitting weakness and seeking help are acceptable parts of the feminine but not the masculine role, making it easier for women than men to report illness (Addis & Mahalik, 2003). Using this masculine gender socialization framework, individual differences among men in help-seeking can be explained by differences in the types of masculine ideology they endorse. Another possible framework for understanding men's help-seeking is a social-constuctionist one: Men may actively construct meanings of masculinity within certain potential help-seeking situations (Addis & Mahalik, 2003). The latter approach would be useful for explaining why men might seek help in certain situations but not others. For example, a man might seek help if he sees his problem as a "normal" one for men in that context but avoid seeking help if he views the problem as something that normal, masculine men do not have.

Another reason women are more likely to seek help and treatment is that women are more likely than men to be socialized to pay attention to and deal directly with symptoms of illness because mothers have traditionally taken primary responsibility for health care in families. However, lack of information or money may keep women from seeking medical help in certain situations. For example, women delay much longer than men in seeking treatment for heart attack symptoms, possibly because, unlike men, they do not expect to be at risk for heart attacks, and they may feel they cannot afford a visit to the doctor (Moser & Dracup, 1993). Also, women are less likely than men to experience a crushing chest pain when they have a heart attack. Women may have more ambiguous symptoms associated with heart attack such as shortness of breath or pain in the neck or jaw.

Health Care

Although women use the health care system more than men do, it frequently does not meet their needs. Medicine is still dominated by men, despite the influx of women into medical schools and the fact that women fill most of the support roles in health care. About 70% of physicians and 78% of dentists in the United States are men; 92.2% of registered nurses and 67.3% of physician's assistants are women (U.S. Census Bureau, 2006a). Gender stereotypes used to abound in what medical students were taught. Disorders specific to women were often trivialized or described as psychological in origin, whereas men's symptoms were more likely to be seen as physically rather than emotionally based (P. Long, 1991; Wallston, DeVellis, & Wallston, 1983). A clear illustration of this tendency was found by two researchers who examined standard medical texts for discussions of dysmenorrhea, nausea of pregnancy, pain in labor, and infant behavior disorder (Lennane & Lennane, 1973). They found that each of these problems was routinely attributed to the women's mental or emotional state, despite the lack of any evidence that these problems are psychological in origin and a great deal of evidence in the other direction. The textbooks slowly began to change in recent decades; however, physicians, especially male physicians, may still tend to attribute women's symptoms to emotional causes. Studies show that female patients are more likely to have tests ordered for them by female than by male doctors (Lurie, Slater, McGovern, Ekstrum, et al., 1993; Muller, 1990) and less likely to have certain tests ordered at all (Hochleitner, 2000).

If women do feel better about care they receive from a female physician, they are still unlikely to find one in certain specialties. For example, only a small percent of all board-certified plastic surgeons in the United States are women, but the vast majority of cosmetic surgery patients are women. Women are most often found in specialties such as internal medicine, pediatrics, family practice, and obstetrics/gynecology; they are still scarce in most surgical specialties. Women now make up one-half of assistant professor positions in medical schools, but women senior administrators in such institutions remain extremely rare (American Medical Association, 2006).

There is some evidence that doctor–patient interactions may differ for male and female patients. In an early study that included male physicians only, researchers analyzed more than 300 taped interactions between doctors and patients, looking for patterns of seeking and offering information (Wallen, Waitzkin, & Stoeckle, 1979). Doctors spontaneously offered information equally often to men and women, but women asked more questions than men and so received more informative statements. However, when total time spent explaining rather than number of explanations was measured, there were no differences between male and female patients—a finding that suggests that men received fuller explanations without asking as many questions. There was also a tendency for the doctors to "talk down" to the female patients. In a more recent study, male and female patients recovering from heart attacks expressed different reactions to their level of communication with the health care system. Men reported receiving more information than women did and were more satisfied than women were with the way health care providers had met their need for information. In particular, men reported receiving more information about test results, treatments, the role played by each different doctor, and ways their families could support them in changing their lifestyle. However, both men and women wanted more information about certain issues: women wanted more information about angina and high blood pressure, and men wanted more information about sexual function (Stewart, Abbey, Schnek, Irvine, & Grace, 2004). Concerns about information are far from frivolous: In this study, patients who said they had received more information also reported less depression, more self-efficacy, and more preventive health behaviors.

Do doctors treat male and female patients with similar symptoms differently? In one study (Armitage, Schneiderman, & Bass, 1979) male patients were given more extensive lab tests and other forms of attention—a finding that led the researchers to conclude that women were given less medical attention than men were for the same problem. We have already seen that there may be gender biases in the ways doctors diagnose and treat patients with heart disease (Hochleitner, 2000), and researchers continue to report that coronary heart disease is underdiagnosed in women (Mieres et al., 2005). Researchers also reported that physicians behave differently toward male and female problem drinkers, being less likely to identify the problem in women (Wilson, Kahan, Liu, Brewster, Sobell, & Sobell, 2002). On the other hand, although past research suggested that doctors treat pain less aggressively in women than men, more recent research does not support this conclusion (Weisse, Sorum, & Dominguez, 2003). There is also little documented gender bias in doctors' management of depression in women and men (Frayne, Skinner, Lin, Asch, & Freund, 2004). Interestingly, some research suggests that female and male primary care doctors both use fewer referrals and tests when treating genital-specific conditions of patients of their own sex. Female physicians in this study were more likely than males to refer men with prostate problems to a specialist; male physicians were more likely than females to recommend an office visit to women with vaginal discharge and itching (Boulis & Long, 2004).

Gender bias in the physician–patient relationship is not a one-way street; people make judgments about doctors on the basis of their gender. Researchers in one study showed respondents photos of doctors and asked them to predict the doctors' behavior. The female doctor was expected to have a better personal manner, better technical and explanatory skills, and to be more likely to explore emotional aspects of health and empower the patient—and respondents said they would be more likely to have faith in her diagnoses and to comply with her treatment (Shah & Ogden, 2006). Such gender stereotypes are extended by physicians to one another too. Physicians who were asked to judge the scientific quality of medical articles written by other physicians judged them differently when they were attributed to a male or female author. When the article was based on quantitative research, it was judged the same whether the respondents believed it was written by a man or a woman. However, when the article was based on qualitative research, it was rated as more accurate, trustworthy, relevant, and interesting when respondents believed it to be written by a woman than when they believed it to be written by a man (Johansson, Risberg, Hamberg, & Westman, 2002).

A women's health movement emerged in recent decades as women began to try to reduce their dependence on the medical system and assume an active role in their own health care. The focus has been on education and empowerment in the area of health, encouraging women to obtain full information, become aware of treatment consequences, exercise the option to refuse treatment when appropriate, and seek complete access to their medical records. The approach is one that puts as much knowledge and power as possible in the hands of the patient, rather than treating the patient as a passive recipient of physician recommendations. Although the movement arose among women because they were dissatisfied with the male-dominated medical system, such an approach could also be empowering for male patients.

The Politics of Health Research

A 1984 report by the National Institutes of Health titled *Normal Human Aging* was based entirely on data obtained from men (Horwitz, 1990). A prestigious large-scale study of the relationship between coffee consumption and heart attacks used 45,589 participants—all of them male. A study testing the efficacy of low daily doses of aspirin against migraine headaches included 22,071 male participants and no females (Adler, 1990). These examples are illustrative of a general pattern in the way health research dollars have been spent in the United States. Until fairly recently, most research has studied the health of men.

Why the omission of women from health research? Until 1985, studies funded by NIH and other agencies routinely excluded females (even female mice or rats) because their menstrual cycles complicated the findings. The idea that such "complications" should be studied because of their very relevance to women's health appears to have been overlooked. Not until pressure from women brought these patterns to light did official NIH and Alcohol, Drug Abuse, and Mental Health Administration policy change to include females in clinical research.

Because research on women's health has been neglected for so long, the extent to which many health issues are gender related has not been well explored. Attempts to remedy the situation include the Women's Health Equity Act passed in 1991. This act included bills to establish an NIH Office of Research on Women's Health and a women's research office in the Alcohol, Drug Abuse, and Mental Health Administration as well as provisions to include more women as participants in publicly funded research. The new NIH office has coordinated a 14-year women's health initiative, studying 15,000 women across the United States to discover ways of reducing women's rates of cardiovascular disease, cancer, and osteoporosis. This study includes a representative mix of women from various social classes and races, and new guidelines now mandate gender and other forms of equity in all government-funded health research projects. All applicants for funding must show that any gender, racial, or other bias in their research sample is necessary to answer the particular research question (U.S. National Institutes of Health, 1992). This initiative has already yielded important information about the effects of hormone replacement therapy, and the women who participated in the studies will continue to be followed until 2010 (National Institutes of Health, 2006). It has also helped to launch an area of research known as **gender-specific medicine,** in which the focus is on how diseases and treatment may progress differently for women and men. This field now boasts its own journal and international congresses, which provide opportunities for advancing knowledge whether and when the sex of the patient is important in treating diseases as diverse as lung cancer and AIDS.

More recently still has come a realization that the health needs of lesbians have been ignored by the research community. A study released in 1999 by the Institute of Medicine showed that "gay women's medical needs are largely a mystery to their doctors" (Herscher, 1999, p. A2). The study concluded that additional data are needed to establish whether the health risks faced by lesbians are different from those faced by heterosexual women and called for research that would address these issues. Research has now begun to do this, examining issues from lesbians' experience of childbirth (McManus, Hunter, & Renn, 2006) to the provision of services to lesbian clients by domestic violence agencies (Helfrich & Simpson, 2006). Health needs of gay men have also begun to receive more attention from researchers. In the past researchers focused narrowly on sexuality and sexually transmitted disease with this population, but they are now beginning to investigate other issues such as perceptions of discrimination in retirement care facilities (Johnsons, Jackson, Arnette, & Koffman, 2005) and the problems associated with aging (Brotman, Ryan, & Cormier, 2003).

Gender and Health Among the Elderly

Proportionately more women than men live to an advanced age, and the gap between the number of women and the number of men widens with increasing age. More women than men live alone in later life; elderly women are also

$\mathcal{O}$*verview*   Women, men, and physical health

- Gender roles have an impact on physical health through the behaviors they prohibit or encourage.

- Men engage in more physically risky behaviors, perhaps because they are trying to live up to the "tough" stereotype of masculinity; women sometimes avoid strenuous physical exercise because it is not expected of them.

- Women and men are vulnerable to different kinds of job-related illnesses and injuries because they do different kinds of work.

- Women are more likely than men to be poor; poor people are more vulnerable to illness.

- Women engage in more health-oriented behaviors (such as doctor visits and self-examination) than men do.

- Women and men may be treated differently by health care systems.

- In the past, health research has often overlooked and omitted women; corrective measures to remedy this pattern of neglect are now being taken.

considerably more likely than elderly men to live in poverty (Dodge, 1995; National Center for Health Statistics, 2005). Partly as a consequence of being alone, elderly women are more likely than men to live in nursing homes.

Elderly women and men do not differ in their self-reported health status. However, their health status does differ according to a number of other measures. Elderly women are more likely than men to need eyeglasses and to have cataracts; elderly men are more likely than women to have hearing difficulties. Older women have higher rates of unintentional injuries than older men; they also report more disabilities in work-related activities and more trouble with such daily living activities as bathing, dressing, shopping, and housework (National Center for Health Statistics, 2005). Although women report more difficulties, they are less likely than men to receive help with activities such as preparing meals and doing housework (Doyal, 1995).

Elderly women make more visits to doctors than elderly men do. When they do see a doctor, they are more likely than their male counterparts to be prescribed drugs (National Center for Health Statistics, 2005).

Cultural gender roles as well as sex differences in longevity contribute to the different health issues that women and men face as they age. The tradition that women marry men older than themselves means that more women than men are widowed during old age. Women's traditional assignment to low-paid or unpaid work means they have less economic security with which to face their old age—a factor that is intensified for poor women and women whose economic opportunities have been further hindered by racism. But women's traditional task of maintaining family and friendship connections can translate into more social and emotional support as they age; elderly women report more contact with friends and family than men do (Canetto, 2001). The health issues of aging are difficult for both women and men. Women face more physical impairment and have fewer financial resources with which to compensate, but a lifetime of adhering to masculine role expectations poorly prepares men to cope with disabilities, living alone, or taking on the care of a disabled spouse.

WOMEN, MEN, AND MENTAL ILLNESS

Patterns of diagnosis and treatment for mental illness are very different for women and men. Responses to the National Health Interview Survey indicate that women are more likely than men to report symptoms associated with severe psychological distress (National Center for Health Statistics, 2005). The extent to which this result reflects a greater willingness on the part of women than men to admit symptoms is not clear. Findings from the National Co-Morbidity Study (Kessler, McGonagle, Zhao, & Nelson, 1994) suggested that there are no gender differences in the overall prevalence of mental disorders but that women and men differ in specific types of disorders. According to the Diagnostic and Statistical Manual (DSM-IV) of the American Psychiatric Association (1994), male–female differences in the prevalence of diagnoses occur in a number of mental disorders. For instance, women are more likely than men to be diagnosed with major depression, panic disorders, anxiety disorders, and eating disorders; men are more likely than women to be diagnosed with a variety of substance abuse disorders, pathological gambling disorder, and narcissistic, antisocial, and compulsive personality disorders. However, even a source as authoritative as the DSM-IV may not portray gender differences in patterns of mental illness with complete accuracy. In some cases, the observed differences may reflect biases in sampling and biases within diagnostic categories (Hartung & Widiger, 1998). We should remember, too, that feminine and masculine roles may predispose women and men to express their distress in different ways and to seek help with different frequencies, thus laying the groundwork for these gender-differentiated patterns of symptoms. It is also possible that gender stereotypes affect how others respond to symptoms and how illnesses are diagnosed. It is important, however, not to view mental illness as some sort of personal flaw; to do this would be analogous to viewing diabetes as a personal flaw.

The impact of gender roles on patterns of mental illness is illustrated by the finding that women are more likely than men to talk about and seek treatment for their symptoms (see Figure 9.3) (Muller, 1990; National Center for Health Statistics, 2005). Prescribed gender roles make it acceptable for women to acknowledge weakness and to seek help; the masculine role encourages men to "tough it out" when they experience problems and to frame their decisions about help-seeking with reference to the masculinity norms that apply in a given context (Addis & Mahalik, 2003). The extremes of both styles are problematic. The drawbacks of the masculine role can be seen in the findings that men are more likely to deal with depression by turning to drugs or alcohol (J. B. Williams & Spitzer, 1983) than by seeking treatment. Conversely, the disadvantage of the feminine help-seeking approach is that it can indirectly encourage dependence and low self-esteem. Such dependency may reinforce the very feelings of overwhelming helplessness that produced the symptoms in the first place and contribute to exacerbation of the illness. A potentially serious outcome of turning to medical treatment to solve certain emotional problems is an addiction to mood-altering prescription drugs. The majority of the prescriptions for mood-altering drugs are written for women, and women are the major abusers of these drugs (National Center on Addiction and Substance Abuse, 2006).

The masculine and feminine role differences in the acceptability of seeking medical help and the gender stereotypes that affect how the symptoms are responded to and diagnosed by health professionals point to the impact of gender roles on the patterns of mental illness in women and men. Their influence is most obvious in certain specific diagnostic categories. We turn briefly now to an examination of five particular types of mental illness for which gender differences have been found: depression, alcoholism, eating disorders, agoraphobia, and antisocial personality.

Figure 9.3   Interactions of U.S. females and males with the mental health care system, 2004. Women may seek help for mental illness more often than men do; women and men seek help for different kinds of problems.

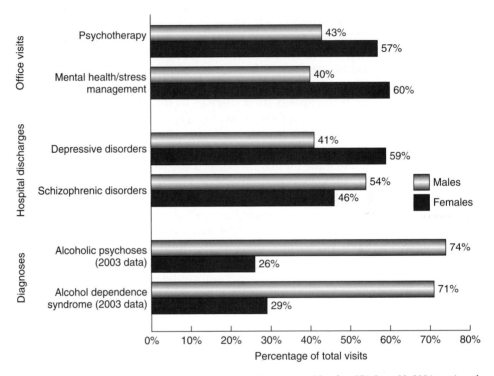

Sources: National ambulatory medical care survey: 2004 summary, Number 374, June 23, 2006, retrieved October 5, 2006, from http://www.cdc.gov/nchs/data/ad/ad374.pdf; National hospital discharge survey: 2004 summary, Number 371, May 4, 2006, retrieved October 5, 2006, from http://www.cdc.gov/nchs/data/ad/ad371.pdf; and Surveillance report Number 72, Trends in alcohol-related morbidity among short stay community hospital discharges, United States, 1979–2003, National Institute on Alcohol Abuse and Alcoholism, August 2005, retrieved from http://pubs.niaaa.nih.gov/publications/surveillance72/HDS03.pdf

Depression

A major depressive episode is characterized by either a depressed mood (e.g., decreased energy, feelings of worthlessness or guilt, difficulty concentrating or making decisions, recurrent thoughts of death or suicidal ideation, plans, or attempts) or a loss of interest or pleasure in almost all activities. Women are twice as likely as men to experience a major depressive episode and to be diagnosed and treated for other, less acute types of **depression** (American Psychiatric Association, 1994). Gender differences first become noticeable in adolescence, when girls begin to show significantly more depressive symptoms than boys do (Cicchetti & Toth, 1998).

The relationship between depression and gender may vary according to ethnicity, but the research is unclear on this point. Greater female than male rates of depression have been found among European Americans (Radloff, 1980), Native Americans (Lafromboise, Berman, & Sohi, 1994), Cuban Americans (Narrow, Rae, Moscicki, Locke, & Regier, 1990), and other Hispanic American groups (Russo, Amaro, & Winter, 1987), but some studies show no gender difference in depression for African Americans (Markush & Favero, 1974). However, it is difficult to evaluate differences among ethnocultural groups using instruments (such as the scales or symptom categories psychologists use to measure depression) that were designed primarily for European Americans. With respect to depression, European Americans may be more likely to express sadness and guilt, whereas African Americans may be more likely to express similar feelings through somatic symptoms, irritability, or suspiciousness (Jacobsen, 1994). Furthermore, it is difficult to compare depression across groups without taking into account a variety of other variables. For example, one study showed that what appeared to be ethnocultural group differences in depression were explained largely by the differing socioeconomic circumstances of the various groups. When socioeconomic status and substance abuse were controlled, African American, Irish American, and Dominican and Puerto Rican women showed similar scores on depression, negative affect, and somatic complaints (H. L. Johnson, Johnson, Nusbaum, Glassman, Bejarano, & Rosen, 1999).

Female–male differences in depression rates may sometimes be explained by the presence of a few women who score very high on measures of depression (Golding, 1988). In addition, the gender effect, like the effect of ethnicity, may be an indirect reflection of other factors such as employment, low socioeconomic status, and stress. For example, one study of depression in an employment setting showed that, after controlling for the effects of salary, age, education, and job classification, no gender differences in depression remained (Maffeo, Ford, & Lavin, 1990).

Theories that have been proposed to account for the gender differences in depression include (1) the notion that the feminine role predisposes women to depression by encouraging them to feel and act helpless, (2) the idea that women face more stress than men do and so are more likely really to be helpless or powerless, (3) the possibility that women are particularly sensitive to stressors that are related to the disruption of interpersonal relationships, (4) the hypothesis that the differences in depression are biologically based, and (5) a developmental model suggesting that particular feminine qualities that develop in childhood interact with environmental challenges that occur in adolescence to produce a greater incidence of female depression. No general agreement among researchers has been reached about which explanation is best; it is quite likely that each of these theories captures a portion of the truth.

Following is a summary of these theories and how they propose to account for gender differences in depression:

1. The *feminine role* predisposes women to depression by encouraging them to feel and act helpless.

    *   It teaches them to respond to stress in powerless, helpless ways (Radloff, 1980; Ruble, Greulich, Pomerantz, & Gochberg, 1993).
    *   It conveys and reinforces a sense of "learned helplessness" that one's actions have no effect on one's situation.
    *   It rewards and punishes males more than females for their actions, conveying from an early age that men's responses mean more and that men have more control over their rewards and punishments through their actions.

2. Women face more *stress* than men and so are more likely really to be helpless or powerless.

    *   Women are more likely than men to have low status and to live under a variety of chronically stressful life conditions (experiencing, for example, rape, other forms of sexual abuse, domestic violence, and sexual harassment).
    *   Women in Wales and Ghana reported three key issues of distress: money problems, relationships with men, and motherhood (Walters, Avotri, & Charles, 1999).
    *   Stressors that emerged as threatening women's mental health in the Beijing Platform for Action, adopted at the 1995 Fourth World Conference on Women, included disproportionate responsibilities of women, poverty and economic dependence, violence, negative attitudes toward women and girls, racial and other forms of discrimination, marginalization, powerlessness, and overwork (Okorodudu, 1999).

3. Women are particularly sensitive to stressors that are related to the *disruption of interpersonal relationships.*

    *   Researchers have found that women are more concerned than men about rejection and abandonment (Pidano & Tennen, 1985).
    *   However, there is evidence that men are more devastated than women by breakups of intimate relationships (see Chapter 7).
    *   Relationship loss is an important precursor of depression for both women and men; it remains to be seen whether women are more affected by it than men.

4. The differences in depression are *biologically based.*

    *   Depression may be linked to the hormonal changes associated with women's reproductive processes (menstruation, postpartum period, menopause).
    *   However, research has not been able to demonstrate a clear link between depression and onset of puberty but only with age (Angold & Rutter, 1992); further, menopause is not associated with an increase in depression,

and research linking depressed mood to the menstrual cycle and to the postpartum period has not demonstrated any hormonal basis.

- Some researchers suggested that hormone levels or changes alone cannot account for the large differences in depression between males and females that have been observed (Klerman & Weissman, 1980).

5. Men and women show different patterns of responding to their own feelings of depression.

- In general, men tend to react to depression by engaging in activities to distract themselves from their feelings; women, conversely, tend to reflect on their depression and think about its possible causes and implications.
- Nolen-Hoeksema (1987) argued that a ruminative, inactive response set for depression might amplify and prolong a depressive episode, whereas an active response set might dampen and shorten it.
- A ruminative, inactive response set may lead someone to focus solely on her depression, which may strengthen the depressed mood and reinforce negative cognitions, thus increasing the depression further; the other extreme, however, may be just as counterproductive—even though one may lead to a more severe depressive episode.

6. Particular feminine qualities that occur in adolescence may produce a greater incidence of female depression.

- Even before adolescence, girls and boys tend to differ on qualities that are risk factors for depression; these early differences then interact with the challenges posed by adolescence to produce gender differences in depression (Nolen-Hoeksema & Girgus, 1994).
- One of these risk factors is the ruminative, self-focused response to depression, which appears to be greater in girls. Another is an interactive style of cooperation and maintenance of positive relationships, which also appears to be greater in girls. Boys tend to interact in a more dominant and competitive style. Also, boys tend to be more aggressive, particularly physically aggressive, than girls.
- These risk factors, coupled with the challenges that can accompany female adolescence (e.g., greater restriction on their activities by parents, greater peer pressures to narrow their activities to fit feminine gender-role expectations, and a dramatic increase in the risk of sexual abuse and harassment) tend to put girls at more risk than boys for difficulties with depression.

In a study that examined the relationship among femininity, masculinity, and gender in young men and women, Sanfilipo (1994) found that, compared with gender-role features, gender alone was weakly or not related to various depressive experiences. In fact, Sanfilipo's results suggested that culturally prescribed gender-role characteristics may be more crucial than gender with regard to various features of depressive experiences in young adults.

Is there a biological basis for the greater incidence of depression in women? Are women socially and culturally predisposed to depression by a feminine role that encourages them to act and feel helpless? Do women experience more stress than men, and is this excess stress to blame for the higher rates of depression? Is gender less important than gender role in the way depressive experiences are managed? Are health care professionals still more inclined to diagnose depression in women? It is likely that each of these questions is important. One thing is clear: Much more research is needed to fully understand the higher incidence of depression in women.

Alcoholism

It is well documented that men are more likely than women to drink and to abuse alcohol (American Psychiatric Association, 1994; National Center for Health Statistics, 2005; Simon, 2002). This finding holds even though women, because they have less body mass and less of the stomach enzyme that breaks down alcohol than men do, become impaired more easily and for longer periods of time than men do when they drink (Graham, Wilsnack, Dawson, & Vogeltanz, 1998). Data from both the United States and Canada indicate that among problem drinkers the ratio of men to women is about 3 to 1. The groundwork for this gender difference may be laid very early; research shows that even among adolescents males report more use of all drugs (National Center for Health Statistics, 2005). These findings fit even antiquated gender stereotypes about drinking. When people think of a skid row alcoholic, they usually think of a man; the image of a temperance advocate is inevitably female.

Women have traditionally received more negative societal responses than men have for heavy drinking, although these negative responses have been lessening over recent years. When a drug is regulated by a society, a common tradition exists that the rules of access, both formal and informal, are different for men and women, and alcohol is no exception (Gomberg, 1982). Female drunkenness is viewed with less tolerance than male drunkenness, and alcoholism is judged more negatively in women than in men. Part of the gender difference in alcohol abuse may well stem from social rules that encourage women to find expressions other than drinking for their distress (Simon, 2002). Thus, for instance, the finding that male relatives of alcoholics often become alcoholics whereas female relatives of alcoholics show a greater tendency toward depression (Cotton, 1979) might be interpreted to mean that alcoholism and depression are gender-specific expressions of similar underlying problems.

There are some differences in the routes to alcoholism for women and men. For example, women are more likely than men to abuse alcohol at home (Corrigan & Butler, 1991). A significant proportion of women with alcohol problems have also experienced sexual abuse. A national survey revealed that women with a history of childhood sexual abuse were significantly more likely than women without a history of childhood sexual abuse to report recent alcohol use, intoxication, drinking-related problems, alcohol dependence symptoms, and lifetime use of psychoactive drugs and illegal drugs. They were also more likely to report symptoms of anxiety and depression (Wilsnack, Vogeltanz, Klassen, & Harris, 1997). Other studies showed that between one-third and two-thirds of women in substance-abuse treatment programs suffer from **posttraumatic stress disorder (PTSD)**—a disorder that is caused by exposure to an extreme traumatic event such as abuse, rape, or domestic violence and is characterized by symptoms such as anxiety, depression, flashbacks, nightmares, and somatic symptoms (Rabasca, 1999).

Ethnocultural factors may interact with gender in the development of alcohol dependency. For example, alcohol dependency is a serious health problem for Native Americans, and Native American women have the same rates of alcoholism as Native American men (Manson, Shore, Baron, Ackerson, & Neligh, 1992). Although researchers disagree about the reasons for the problem, there is no doubt about its consequences: a tragically high death rate among young Native American women and men and an increasing incidence of fetal alcohol syndrome among their children (Lafromboise et al., 1994).

Women often face difficulties in alcohol treatment programs that are designed for men (Duckert, 1989); programs that incorporate or focus only on the specific needs of women have been developed. African American women may face additional difficulties seeking help in predominantly European American therapeutic environments (Amaro, Beckman, & Mays, 1987).

Eating Disorders

Two eating disorders, anorexia nervosa and bulimia nervosa, have been the objects of a surge of professional and public interest over the past two decades. Both disorders are typified by severe disturbances in eating behavior. The fundamental characteristics of **anorexia nervosa** are that the individual refuses to maintain minimally normal body weight, has an intense fear of gaining weight, and demonstrates a significant disturbance in perception of body shape and size (American Psychiatric Association, 1994). **Bulimia nervosa,** which involves a pattern of "binge" eating followed by self-induced "purging" through a variety of means, including dieting, vomiting, or laxative use, is also characterized by a preoccupation with body shape and weight. Both syndromes are far more common among women than men, with most studies indicating that females make up 90% of cases (American Psychiatric Association, 1994). The "typical" sufferer from one of these disorders is a White, middle-class woman under the age of 25; however, the disorders appear to be rising among ethnic groups. Subgroups of young women for whom thinness is especially important, such as modeling students, athletes, and professional dancers, show a higher than average incidence of eating disorders (Brooks-Gunn, Burrow, & Warren, 1988; Szymanski & Chrisler, 1990/91).

A number of writers have suggested that sociocultural factors, particularly the current emphasis on thinness, play a part in the development of eating disorders (e.g., Boskind-White, 1985; Chernin, 1981; Wooley & Wooley, 1985). An increase in the incidence of eating disorders over the past 20 years has occurred simultaneously with a shift toward thinness in the ideal of feminine beauty and a rise in interest in diets and weight reduction. Fat people, especially fat women, are disparaged as unattractive in our culture. The more dependent a person is on physical attractiveness for self-esteem, the more vulnerable she or he is to such cultural messages. Because women tend to be identified more in terms of their appearance than men are, it is perhaps not surprising that more women than men fall victim to eating disorders. Moreover, research shows that, in contrast to males, females tend to see their bodies as heavier than the ideal figure or than the figure that would appeal to the other sex (Fallon & Rozin, 1985). Among college students, women are more likely than men to see themselves as overweight and to diet. One survey found that nearly one-third of a sample of college females reported either self-induced vomiting or laxative use as a weight-loss strategy (Connor-Greene, 1988). The pressures to be thin and to match some media vision of attractiveness have affected American women from all cultural groups. Eating disorders have been reported frequently among African American women (Hsu, 1987), Native American and Hispanic women (Snow & Harris, 1989), mixed-race women (Root, 1990), and Asian American women (Yi, 1989).

Research by Harvard medical anthropologist Anne Becker (reported in Goodman, 1999) offered suggestive support for the notion that the obsession with thinness that characterizes eating disorders is fueled by cultural notions of attractiveness. Becker studied teenage girls on the South Pacific island nation of Fiji before and after the introduction of television to the island in 1995. Before the introduction of television, big was considered beautiful in Fiji, and women often complimented each other by saying things like, "You look wonderful! You've put on weight." In fact, when someone lost weight, it was a cause for concern, referred to as "going thin" and thought to be a sign of social or emotional problems. However, all that apparently began to change when the girls of this tiny country began to watch programs such as *Melrose Place, ER,* and *Beverly Hills 90210.* Thirty-eight months after the introduction of television, the number of teenaged girls at risk for eating disorders had more than doubled to 29%, and the number of high school girls who vomited for weight control had quintupled to 15%. At that time, 74% of the young women in the study reported that they felt "too big or fat," and 62% said they had dieted during the previous month.

Some theorists have suggested that eating disorders are associated with rigid adherence to or anxiety about the feminine gender role—a role that includes thinness and attractiveness. In a test of this hypothesis, researchers administered the Feminine Gender Role Stress Scale to female inpatients at a psychiatric hospital and to female college students (Martz, Handley, & Eisler, 1995). They found that scores on the scale, which measures the tendency of respondents to appraise certain situations as highly stressful because they threaten the individual's femininity, could distinguish women with eating disorders from those with other psychiatric diagnoses and from normal college women. This research suggests that women with eating disorders have internalized the requirements of femininity more strongly than other women have and may be willing to starve themselves to comply with these requirements.

What about eating disorders in men? According to researchers, men make up about 10% of people with anorexia and bulimia nervosa and up to 25% of people with binge eating disorder (Weltzin, Weisensel, Franczyk, Burnett, Klitz, & Bean, 2005). For men, as for women, eating disorders may be fostered by a societal emphasis on an idealized physique. One study of action figures found that, over the last 25 years, male action figures have become larger (except at the waist) and more muscular in appearance, thus helping to promote a lean, muscular body type as the ideal for men (Baghurst, et al., 2006). The risk factors for eating disorders in men are somewhat similar to those in women: youth, athletic participation, sexuality, and the presence of other psychological problems (Weltzin et al., 2005).

Because eating disorders are less prevalent in men than in women, they are more likely to be overlooked (Baum, 2006). Men with eating disorders are less likely than women to overestimate body size; in fact, they are often desirous of a more muscular body, not a thinner one. Thus men are less likely than women to engage in behaviors such as vomiting and more likely to engage in excessive exercise (Weltzin et al., 2005). Men may also abuse anabolic steroids (Baum, 2006). As with other disorders, men are less likely than women to seek treatment.

The cultural premium on idealized bodies, then, may stimulate the unhealthy preoccupation with food and weight that helps to generate the distortions of body image and eating patterns characteristic of eating disorders. How can we fight back against the pervasive messages to young women that they must be thin at all costs and to young men that they must be lean and muscular? Poet Marilou Awiakta (1993) has an idea: Instead of heeding the message to "starve your power," she recommends that young women remember that

> . . . if you was to take on weight
> you might start throwin' it around.
> No way they can handle
> a full-grown woman
> With a full-grown dream. No way. (p. 194)

Agoraphobia

Specific phobias are persistent, irrational fears of, and a desire to avoid, specific objects, activities, or situations, and they are more common among females than males (American Psychiatric Association, 1994). **Agoraphobia,** the most common, involves "anxiety about, or avoidance of, places or situations from which escape might be difficult (or embarrassing) or in which help may not be available in the event of having a panic attack or panic-like symptoms" (American Psychiatric Association, 1994). Sufferers from this disorder may fear situations such as busy streets, crowded stores, elevators, or public transportation; thus, they may literally be trapped in their own homes by the fear of venturing out. Women are far more likely than men to be diagnosed as agoraphobic; in the United States, women account for up to 82% of cases (Clum & Knowles, 1991).

Researchers are still unsure of the reasons for the female preponderance among agoraphobics, but existing theories center on the different expectations for coping with fear that are built into the masculine and feminine roles. Research has shown that girls and boys are fairly similar in fearfulness until adolescence. But from adolescence onward, males admit to many fewer fears than females do (Macfarlane, Allen, & Honzik, 1974). Masculine socialization encourages boys to confront and master their fears, whereas girls are reinforced not for mastery but for expressing their fears and remaining helpless and dependent (Hoffman, 1972).

Another theory is that agoraphobia, which often begins in the mid-20s and often within a few years of marriage, may be triggered when an individual experiences the conflicting demands of the feminine role to be submissive and nurturing in the home but competent, independent, and assertive in the public world (Watkins & Lee, 1997). The resulting stress may cause some women who have been conditioned by a lifetime pattern of avoidance to become increasingly helpless and dependent—a reaction that may be reinforced by the attention and sympathetic responses of those around them. Although men may have similar reactions of fear and helplessness, they are far less likely than women to be reinforced for them. Moreover, the men are more likely than the women in this group to be employed and to be the major financial provider for the family, so they simply cannot afford to avoid leaving the house. Subsequently, men who have a tendency toward agoraphobia may instead display symptoms of substance abuse or anxiety.

For agoraphobia, then, as for the other disorders discussed in this section, at least part of the explanation for the gender difference in incidence may be found in gender-role expectations. Psychological distress is manifested by different symptoms and diagnosed differently for women and men. The differences seem to derive not from a differential vulnerability to mental illness but from the different patterns of behaviors that are reinforced for the two sexes and the different kinds of pressures built into the masculine and feminine roles.

Antisocial Personality

Antisocial personality disorder, which is characterized by a lack of ethical or moral sensitivity and the absence of guilt or anxiety about hurting others, is more frequently diagnosed among males than females by a ratio of about 3 to 1 (American Psychiatric Association, 1994). Individuals who fall into this category often have difficulty forming interpersonal relationships and frequently show indifference to relationships. They also display a general disregard for authority and behave in impulsive and thoughtless ways toward others—including lying, stealing, and engaging in unwarranted aggression and physical cruelty.

The characteristics of this disorder sound like an exaggerated and distorted version of the masculine role; perhaps it is not surprising that men outnumber women with this diagnosis. Male socialization is frequently in the direction of aggression, dominance, uncommunicativeness, competitiveness, and a suppression of tender emotions. Such an orientation may provide the groundwork for the development of antisocial behavior patterns and for the personality characteristics associated with this disorder in adulthood. There is some concern that antisocial personality disorder may be underdiagnosed in women. This concern stems from the emphasis on aggressive items used to define conduct disorder, which is required to receive a diagnosis of antisocial personality disorder (American Psychiatric Association, 1994).

The Politics of Diagnosis

We have already seen one of the implications of deciding how to diagnose and "count" mental illness. When certain categories of mental illness are excluded from the tally, women appear to suffer more from mental illness than men do. However, when these categories are included, the overall gender difference in mental illness rates tends to disappear. It is important to remember that sexist biases built into the diagnostic categories may well influence perceptions of whether women and men are psychologically healthy. If the categories are based on an idea that male behavior represents the norm or standard for health, then women who are behaving in ways that are normal, given their socialization and the situation of women in society, may be diagnosed as mentally ill.

There is a danger that the mental health system will apply diagnostic categories in gender-stereotypic ways (Hartung & Widiger, 2002). Indeed, the diagnoses that are most commonly applied to members of specific subgroups of the population tend to embody the roles and stereotypes attributed to those groups (Landrine, 1987, 1989). Landrine (1987) gave stereotyped descriptions of lower-class men, single middle-class women, married middle-class women, and married upper-class men to a sample of clinical psychologists and psychiatrists. The clinicians were asked to provide diagnoses for these "cases" and were explicitly reminded that the cases might be normal. Landrine found that the stereotype of the lower-class man was labeled *antisocial*, the stereotype of the married middle-class woman was labeled *dependent*, that of the single middle-class woman was labeled *histrionic/hysterical*, and the stereotype of the married upper-class man was labeled *prototypically normal*. There were no differences in the ways male and female clinicians or psychoanalytic and feminist therapists labeled the cases—suggesting that all were influenced by prevailing social stereotypes.

Researchers have found a general pattern of gender bias in the way physicians diagnose psychological disturbance. Women tend to be overdiagnosed (identified as having psychological disorders they *do not* have), whereas men tend to be underdiagnosed (not identified as having disorders that they *do* have). This study found no differences between interns and practicing physicians in these patterns of gender bias, suggesting that the bias is not disappearing (Redman, Webb, Hennrikus, & Sanson-Fisher, 1991). The findings seem to underline the presence of a stereotype in which women are more easily regarded as "sick" and men as being in control of their lives.

An example of the politics of diagnosis occurred in the controversy over the inclusion of several new diagnostic categories in the *Diagnostic and Statistical Manual* (DSM) of the American Psychiatric Association (1994). Two of these categories, premenstrual dysphoric disorder (earlier called **late luteal phase**

dysphoric disorder) and self-defeating personality disorder, have the effect of labeling female experiences and stereotypically feminine traits as signs of mental illness. Controversy over the inclusion of these diagnostic categories in the manual was intense; more than 6 million North Americans signed petitions and wrote letters opposing their inclusion. However, late luteal phase dysphoric disorder was assigned an official number and included in an Appendix to the fourth edition of the DSM-IV.

What if stereotypically male traits were grouped together and labeled "sick"? In an article that satirizes the labeling of gender-related behavior patterns as "disorders," Kaye-Lee Pantony and Paula Caplan (1991) highlighted the bias implicit in diagnostic politics. They propose inclusion of a new diagnostic category—"delusional dominating personality disorder"—in the diagnostic manual. The "symptoms" of this disorder (first detailed by Caplan & Eichler, 1989) include, among others, the "tendency to use power, silence, withdrawal, and/or avoidance rather than negotiation in the face of interpersonal conflict or difficulty" and a "tendency to feel inordinately threatened by women who fail to disguise their intelligence" (Pantony & Caplan, 1991, p. 121). The incidence of this disorder is, according to the authors, highest among males but occasionally present in females and tends to be pronounced among "leaders of traditional mental health professions, military personnel, executives of large corporations, and powerful political leaders of many nations"

Overview   Gender and diagnoses of mental illness

- Women are more likely than men to be diagnosed with and treated for depression.

- Men are more likely than women to abuse alcohol.

- The eating disorders anorexia nervosa and bulimia nervosa are much more common among women than men.

- Agoraphobia, the most common of the specific phobias, is much more likely to be diagnosed in women than in men.

- Antisocial personality disorder is more commonly diagnosed among men than women.

- Stereotypical gender roles are likely implicated both in the ways women and men experience and express emotional distress and in the ways their symptoms are classified into particular diagnoses.

(p. 121). The "disorder" proposed by Pantony and Caplan seems absurd precisely because it characterizes as "sick" the attitudes and behaviors of powerful and successful people. Their approach underlines the point that mental health policy as it relates to gender and other social categories is not value neutral but tends to define the behavior of powerful groups as normative and that of other groups as sick.

GENDER AND MENTAL HEALTH

Good mental health is more than the absence of serious mental illness; it is often viewed as satisfaction, or as adjustment to, acceptance of, and ability to cope with one's life situation. Women, on average, report greater life satisfaction and happiness than men do—a seemingly paradoxical finding in view of women's higher rates of depression (W. Wood, Rhodes, & Whelan, 1989). It is not clear whether this gender difference represents a difference in experience, in perception, in the willingness to report extreme emotional responses, or in sensitivity to internal emotions. One study indicated that women respond with greater emotional intensity to stimuli than men do, suggesting that women's more intense positive emotions may help balance their higher levels of negative feelings (Fujita, Diener, & Sandvik, 1991).

There is a catch-22 in the "adjustment" definition of mental health: The more difficult and stressful one's situation, the more problematic it is to adjust to it. Although most of us would consider it mentally healthy for a person to accept and adjust to the necessity of working for a living rather than clinging to the improbable hope of winning a lottery, we would not counsel a person who is being beaten regularly by a spouse or partner that it is mentally healthy to "adjust" to the situation. The conception of mental health as adjustment must be tempered by a keen awareness of both the situation to which a person is being expected to adjust and whether an acceptance of that situation will ultimately be beneficial or harmful to him or her.

In the past, gender roles figured strongly in psychologists' notions of what represented proper adjustment—and thus good mental health—for women and men. People who conformed to gender expectations, masculine men and feminine women, were considered healthier than those who did not. Indeed, "rejecting" one's femininity or masculinity was considered cause for psychotherapy. Over the years, however, three major problems with this approach have been recognized. The first is that the traditional gender role to which women are expected to adjust is inherently less healthy, in terms of coping abilities and a sense of self-worth, than is that to which men are expected to conform. The second is that rigid adherence to one's gender role, like too much rigidity in any area, interferes with a person's capacity to cope with a variety of situations and thus can be counterproductive for mental health. The third is that society's gender roles channel women and men into situations that differ in the kinds of stress they exert and the requirements for coping they demand. An acceptance of one's gender role often means not just acceptance of a certain style of interpersonal behavior but of a certain position in the family, in the workplace, and so on.

A Double Standard of Mental Health?

The influence of gender stereotypes on standards of mental health for women and men was demonstrated in a landmark study of the ideals of mental health professionals (psychologists, psychiatrists, and social workers) for healthy adult men and women (Broverman, Broverman, Clarkson, Rosenkrantz, & Vogel, 1970). These researchers found that clinicians actually held different ideals for a healthy, fully functioning adult male than for a healthy, fully functioning adult female. The ideal healthy woman was described as being more submissive, less independent and adventurous, more easily influenced, less aggressive and competitive, more easily excitable in minor crises, more easily hurt, more emotional, more vain about her appearance, less objective, and less interested in math and science than the ideal healthy man. Also, the clinicians' ideal of the healthy man was similar to that of a healthy, mature adult (gender unspecified), but their ideal of a healthy woman was quite different from both. It appeared, then, that women were caught in a double bind. If they met the mental health standards for their own gender, they automatically fell short of those for the general adult population. If they met the standards for a healthy adult, they were automatically defined as unfeminine—and thus poorly adjusted.

The double standard of mental health seems to have gone underground to some extent. Therapists no longer list very different characteristics as desirable for mentally healthy women and men (Phillips & Gilroy, 1985). Therapists may have become sensitive to the issue of gender bias and less likely to respond in a biased way to a questionnaire or a hypothetical situation presented to them on paper. A meta-analysis of 30 studies of gender bias in counseling and therapy found little overall evidence for the existence of bias, and the greatest bias that was shown was found in the earlier studies (M. Smith, 1980). However, naturalistic studies, in which the therapist is confronted with a real live client instead of a hypothetical one, suggest that gender bias may still occur (Hare-Mustin, 1983). Even some studies that involve hypothetical case vignettes presented on paper still show gender bias. For example, in a more recent study, psychologists, along with university professors and students, showed a bias in favor of individualism for men but not for women (Tredinnick & Fowers, 1997). In another study, mental health trainees overestimated gender differences in emotional expressiveness, mistakenly anticipating that female and male clients would differ significantly in their willingness to express specific emotions and in their comfort with talking about emotions (Vogel, Wester, Heesacker, Boysen, & Seeman, 2006).

Cultural pressure on women to adjust to the stereotypical feminine role is antithetical to development of the healthy behaviors of independence and competence, just as pressure on men to adjust to the male role interferes with the healthy behaviors of expressiveness and warmth. Moreover, the association of good adjustment with gender-role conformity may mask problems for both women and men. For instance, when men exhibit the aggressiveness and disregard for others characteristic of the antisocial personality, they may be perceived as acting within the boundaries of the normal masculine role (Doyle, 1995).

Gender-Role Flexibility and Mental Health

Research over the past two decades has increasingly challenged the notion that conformity to gender stereotypes is associated with good mental health. Indeed, for both women and men, the rigidity associated with strong adherence to gender roles may interfere with coping and adaptability in a variety of situations. For example, Pleck (1981) has argued that many men overconform to the masculine role out of anxiety about possible violations. Such overconformity prevents the exploration of potentially satisfying behaviors and interests. Women too may suffer adverse consequences from conforming too closely to traditional feminine roles. One study that followed a group of women from the 1950s to the early 1980s found that, although traditionality of role was related to positive well-being and effective functioning at age 21, such traditionality was related to negative changes in psychological and physical health by age 43 (Helson & Picano, 1990).

A series of studies by Sandra Bem and her colleagues using the BSRI (discussed in Chapter 1) indicated that strong gender-typing in the direction of either masculinity or femininity was associated with restricted behavior in certain settings. For example, in a situation that required the "feminine" behavior of nurturing a small baby, they demonstrated that participants of both sexes who were classified as either feminine or androgynous performed significantly better than masculine men and women (Bem et al., 1976). In another study, Bem (1975) demonstrated that masculine and androgynous participants of both sexes performed better than feminine subjects at a task that required the stereotypically "masculine" behavior of independence in the face of social pressure. A third study (Bem & Lenney, 1976) demonstrated that masculine men and feminine women were more likely than androgynous women or men to choose activities that were "appropriate" for their own gender and to reject out-of-role activities. After performing cross-gender activities, masculine men and feminine women also reported experiencing more discomfort and feeling worse about themselves than did androgynous participants of either sex. These findings were taken as evidence that "appropriate" gender-typing, as measured by the BSRI, is related to behavioral inflexibility and a tendency not to adapt one's role to the requirements of unfamiliar situations—hardly a hallmark of good mental health.

Later research indicates, however, that the relationship between gender stereotypes and mental health cannot be summarized adequately by the motto that "androgyny is good; sex typing is bad." For one thing, androgyny may be more of an advantage for women than for men in this culture (A. B. Heilbrun, 1984; Wiggins & Holzmuller, 1981). Some studies have found that people with masculine qualities—those who score either androgynous or masculine on the BSRI or other scales—show the most adaptive behavior and social effectiveness, have higher subjective well-being and self-esteem, and report lower

Reflections   Is There a Gender Difference in Happiness?

Although it is well documented that women are more likely than men to be depressed, recent research shows that they are also, as a group, happier than men. This paradoxical finding comes from a large international study in which more than 38,000 people in 44 countries were interviewed about their feelings, expectations, and hopes for the future (Pew Research Center for People and the Press, 2002).

This large survey found that, all over the world, women are happier with their lives than men are. The results held in both rich and poor countries; however, the "happiness gap" was largest in less developed countries—particularly India, the Philippines, Pakistan, and Argentina—and in Japan (Chatterjee, 2003). The gap was less pronounced in North America and Western Europe.

Happiness was not necessarily linked to optimism or with a lack of concern about potentially stressful and difficult issues. More than half the women interviewed in North America, Western Europe, and eastern and southern Africa said they think the future will be worse, not better, for their children. And, all over the world, women and men clearly worried about different things. Women said they worried about their health, their children, and education. For them, the most important threat to their lives was disease. Men, on the other hand, reported more worry about government and politics, and they said that the most important threat was weapons of mass destruction.

It is not surprising that women and men differ in their concerns. In every part of the world, women are the ones most heavily charged with overseeing the well-being of children, the elderly, and the sick. Yet it *is* surprising that women report more satisfaction with their lives than men do. Women are frequent victims of discrimination, family violence, and a variety of stressful conditions linked to their gender.

What accounts for the gender gap in happiness? Could it be that women do not compare themselves to men when they assess their satisfaction? That they have lower expectations than men do and so are more easily satisfied? Or could it be that women are more attuned to the satisfactions as well as the concerns in their lives?

stress (V. Long, 1991; Lubinski, Tellegen, & Butcher, 1981; O'Heron & Orlofsky, 1990). The instrumental qualities tapped by contemporary measures of masculinity, then, are apparently very important for successful social functioning in our culture. Research is inconclusive about whether androgyny is preferable to masculinity (at least as assessed by current tests) in terms of behavioral flexibility or other aspects of mental health. It seems safe to conclude, however, that there is no mental health advantage to women to being "properly" sex typed as feminine. In fact, feminine sex-typed individuals, especially women, show more depression, anxiety, and low self-esteem than do those scoring as masculine or androgynous (Burchardt & Serbin, 1982; Heiser & Gannon, 1984; Tinsley, Sullivan-Guest, & McGuire, 1984). Although rigid adherence to gender roles may interfere with behavioral flexibility for both women and men, the consequences for women, at least in a culture that is structured so that most rewards are obtainable only through the instrumental behaviors we associate with masculinity, may be more serious.

Gender Roles and Environmental Stress

It is sometimes argued that the environments in which women and men are expected to function differ in terms of stress, a difference that would help explain women's higher rate of certain mental health problems. **Stressors** are events or conditions that are appraised as threatening by an individual and thus are the source of upset, worry, discomfort, and general distress. Researchers examining this issue have looked at both life events and life conditions. Traditionally, they have found little evidence to suggest that women and men differ in the quantity or quality of stressful life events they experience; however, this may be because, until recently, studies have not focused on the stressful events that are particular to each gender. There is strong evidence that women are more likely than men to experience stressful long-term life conditions.

STRESSFUL LIFE EVENTS   A great deal of research shows that life events, either positive or negative, that involve change or disruption are experienced as stressful and that the onset of both physical and mental illness is often preceded by a cluster of such events: an accident, job loss, promotion, pregnancy, marriage, divorce, wage increase, family discord, and so on. Because women and men differ in both their daily lives and their patterns of mental illness, it seems reasonable to ask whether they experience different numbers of stressful life events. As it turns out, most research shows no gender differences in the number of stressful life events reported (Makosky, 1980; Mulvey & Dohrenwend, 1983). How, then, can we explain women's apparently higher rate of stress-related mental illness? Perhaps the contents of the life-events lists are biased so as to include more of the stressful events that men rather than women face. Perhaps the life changes faced by men are more likely to be positive ones and thus less distressing than those faced by women. Or perhaps women experience more stress than men do in response to the same life events. Each of these possibilities has received some attention from researchers.

There are good arguments for the notion that the item content of the life-change lists used in stress research may produce misleading life-change scores for women (Makosky, 1980). For example, most lists do not include items about events happening to significant others that may be stressful to oneself (e.g., spouse fired or promoted, child changed schools), yet some research has shown that women are far more likely than men to report the occurrence of such events (Dohrenwend, 1976, as cited in Makosky, 1980). Also missing from most lists are some items of particular concern to women: rape, changes in child-care arrangements, incidents of sexual harassment, and physical abuse by spouse. It is difficult to define a list of life changes that is equally appropriate to everyone; yet if group comparisons are to be made, the list must reflect fairly the changes likely to be important for each group.

The same stressor may result in different amounts of stress for women and men. For example, when respondents were asked to imagine how much stress they would be experiencing at the present time if specific events (e.g., deaths, separations, arguments, threats to self-image, financial setbacks, general changes) had occurred 1 week ago, 1 month ago, and so on up to 3 years ago, women rated all the sets of events as more stressful than men did (Horowitz, Schaefer, & Cooney, 1974). Similarly, a study of college students found that the women reported that they found more events stressful than men did— although women and men said they used similar methods for coping with stress (Ptacek, Smith, & Zanas, 1992). A recent meta-analysis revealed that women seem consistently to rate stressors as more severe than men do (Tamres, Janicki, & Helgeson, 2002). It has been argued as well that such events as separation, divorce, and childbearing are not only perceived as more stressful by women, but actually *are* more stressful for women than for men because women tend to experience greater financial loss, are less likely to remarry, and are more likely to have the major burden of child care (Makosky, 1980).

One type of stressful event that women are more likely to experience than men is sexist treatment. Two researchers who developed a new scale, the Schedule of Sexist Events (SSE), to measure the incidence of such treatment found that 99% of the women they sampled had experienced a sexist event at least once in their lives (Klonoff & Landrine, 1995). The most common events experienced at least once were being forced to listen to sexist or sexually degrading jokes, being sexually harassed, being called sexist names, being treated with a lack of respect because of being female, and wanting to tell someone off for being sexist. More than half the sample reported being picked on, hit, shoved, or threatened because of being a woman; 40% said they had been denied a raise or promotion because they were women, and over 19% reported they had filed a lawsuit or grievance or taken other drastic action in response to sexist discrimination. A fairly similar pattern appeared when women were asked to describe events that had occurred in the past year. White women and women of color reported experiencing the same kinds of sexist discrimination; however, women of color reported significantly more sexist discrimination, both in their lifetimes and in the past year, than White women did. When the women's scores on the SSE were examined in relation to their self-reported psychiatric and physical symptoms, the researchers found that experience of sexist discrimination was significantly linked to women's symptoms. Knowing women's SSE scores as well as their scores on more traditional measures of stressful events enabled the researchers to predict their symptoms with significantly greater accuracy than simply knowing their scores on the traditional measures (Landrine, Klonoff, Gibbs, Manning, & Lund, 1995). Consequently, it appears that the traditional measures have inadequately captured at least one source of stress for women.

STRESSFUL LIFE CONDITIONS   In contrast to stressful life events, stressful life conditions are chronic environmental factors that have a long-term impact on individuals. In terms of such conditions, we have already noted that women are more likely than men to be poor; they are also more likely than men to be employed in low-status, low-paying jobs and to be heading single-parent families. They are also more likely than men to be victims of unpredictable, uncontrollable family violence. Finally, they are more likely than men to be trying to perform two concurrent full-time jobs: homemaker/mother within the home and paid employee outside the home. It is fairly easy to argue that, on average, life conditions are more stressful for women than for men.

Particular groups of women and men may be exposed to different kinds of chronic stressors. One measure of stress for African American women (Watts-Jones, 1990) includes items that reflect the following chronic stressors: inadequate resources (e.g., unable to afford your own place, living in a neighborhood with high crime), work-related stress (e.g., working at a boring job), relationship conflict/dissatisfaction (e.g., man is possessive/jealous), difficult role functioning (e.g., being a single parent), racism (e.g., working with prejudiced coworkers), and personal health problems (e.g., being overweight).

Poverty is associated with mental health problems, and the combination of poverty with responsibility for young children is devastating for women (Doyal, 1995). One study of married women living in central London showed that the rate of mood disorders was 5% for middle-class women, 25% for working-class women, and 42% for working-class women with preschool children (W. B. Brown, Bhrolchain, & Harris, 1975). Other research indicated that women who are single parents are at even greater risk for emotional problems (Pearlin & Johnson, 1977). It is unlikely that there is anything specifically "feminine" about this pattern of reactions; men living in poverty with sole responsibility for preschool children would probably get depressed too.

One reason chronic conditions such as poverty, discrimination, and fear of violence are linked to emotional problems such as depression is the lack of control over one's life that these conditions engender. It is difficult to maintain a sense of well-being and self-esteem when it is impossible, despite one's best efforts, to feed and clothe one's children properly or to keep the household running smoothly. However, for some women, one potentially stressful life condition can add to their sense of control and self-esteem instead of detracting from it: combining having a family with outside employment.

Employment is certainly a potential source of a variety of stressors for both women and men. However, it is also a potential source of satisfaction, accomplishment, and mastery as well as a reason for leaving the isolation of one's own home. Some evidence seems to suggest that people with few roles are vulnerable to mental and physical health problems. For example, Verbrugge (1983) found that the women with the poorest health profile were those without employment, husband, or children. Others (Barnett & Hyde, 2001; Baruch, Barnett, & Rivers, 1983; Hong & Seltzer, 1995) found the highest overall indications of mental health among women and men with the most roles. Among employed African American and European American women and men, job satisfaction is positively related to life satisfaction, and occupational status is positively linked to perceived control for women of both racial groups (Crohan, Antonucci, Adelmann, & Coleman, 1989).

However, lack of outside employment is not necessarily linked to discontent for women. Some researchers have found that married, full-time homemakers with young children express more pleasure and satisfaction with their lives and have fewer worries than other women (Baruch et al., 1983; Veroff,

Douvan, & Kulka, 1981). The ability to *choose* roles, not just the *number* of roles, seems to be crucial to mental health (Sales & Frieze, 1984). Perhaps most important, the working conditions and economic status associated with an individual's work roles are predictive of mental health. For example, married women who are employed as professionals report less depression that do married women who are homemakers or those who are employed in sales, clerical, or blue-collar occupations (Riley & Keith, 2003). The difference between the professionals and the other groups seems to be accounted for by the economic advantages enjoyed by the professional women. Thus combining roles may be more stressful for women in some occupations than others.

For women who have good marriages and who have adequate resources to handle child care, employment during the early child-rearing period may be less stressful than staying home. The additional demands imposed by juggling two roles can be balanced by the fact that the satisfactions of one role can act as a buffer for the problems and frustrations encountered in the other (W. B. Brown et al., 1975; Stewart & Salt, 1981). Just as men have traditionally been able to forget temporarily about failures and anxieties at work by coming home to families in which the relationships and tasks are different, so employed mothers may be able to avoid becoming trapped in feelings of frustration and anxiety about child rearing by having the additional set of goals, rewards, and concerns that the workplace provides. In addition, outside employment reduces the isolation often experienced by new mothers. For both women and men, the quality of their experiences at work and at home as well as the meanings they assign to their work and family roles mediate the effect of these roles on their well-being (Lennon, 1994; Pugliesi, 1995; R. W. Simon, 1995). For men, control over their work and positive marital interactions promote a less risky, healthier lifestyle (Wickrama, Conger, & Lorenz, 1995). For women, less routinized work (Lennon, 1994), spousal support (Matsui, Ohsawa, & Onglatco, 1995), equality in decision making and companionship in marriage (Hibbard & Pope, 1993), and perceived equity in the performance of housework (Glass & Fujimoto, 1994) are associated with better mental and physical health.

In general, researchers have found that employed women, both middle class and working class, are in better mental and physical health than those who stay at home, at least on some dimensions (Elstad, 1996; Glass & Fujimoto, 1994). Women who work outside the home report fewer symptoms and use mental health services less than do women who stay home (Wheeler, Lee, & Loe, 1983). They also report greater feelings of mastery but not more positive feelings about life (Baruch et al., 1983). Thus employment may be linked to only certain aspects of mental health. For example, employed women may have stronger feelings of competence and self-esteem but be no happier on the whole than other women (Sales & Frieze, 1984). Furthermore, researchers cannot yet say unequivocally that employment *causes* women to be more mentally healthy; it may be simply that healthier women choose to seek employment. Yet, as we will see in Chapter 13, it is a long time since employed women represented an elite or unusual minority; women enter the workforce out of economic necessity. The fact that the positive relationship between employment and mental health has remained stable with increasing numbers of women entering the labor force suggests that employment does make a contribution to women's well-being (Sales & Frieze, 1984).

For women with unsatisfying marriages, inadequate resources to guarantee good child care in their absence, or jobs that are stultifying or unpleasant, the mental health costs of combining employment and motherhood may sometimes outweigh the benefits. Moreover, there may be an "overload" point at which the positive relationship between role involvement and mental health reverses; beyond a certain limit, it may be unhealthy to juggle many roles at once (Glass & Fujimoto, 1994; Verbrugge, 1983). Single working mothers, for example, are often overstressed and vulnerable to illness.

In summary, women tend to have to cope with more stressful life conditions than men do, a difference that may help explain why women are more likely than men to become depressed. Paradoxically, however, women who add, by choice or necessity, to their potential stressors by combining employment with motherhood often report fewer symptoms of stress than do women who stay at home, perhaps because employment confers an additional source of self-worth and control. Heavily overloaded women, however, may be very distressed by the demands of multiple roles.

Treatment of Emotional Problems

PSYCHOTHERAPY   A common response to mental or emotional distress is to seek psychotherapy. An individual who enters therapy has often failed to find solutions to problems using other strategies and hopes that the therapist will be able to provide help, support, and guidance in dealing with painful, difficult situations. Often, these hopes are realized. Therapy has helped many people solve serious problems. However, therapy as an institution can reflect some of the same sexist biases that are found in the diagnostic arm of the mental health system. The potential consumer of therapy services is well-advised to evaluate therapists with care before choosing one.

Women are much more likely than men to consult a therapist, and some writers have argued that psychotherapy as an institution, like marriage as an institution, poses some inherent dangers for women (Chesler, 1972; Greenspan, 1983; Tennov, 1975). The danger stems partly from reinforcement of the dependency and helplessness that are built into the feminine role. Therapy, like marriage, can put a woman into a dependency relationship with an authority figure. If the therapist is male, the process may further reinforce the notion that a woman needs a man to solve her problems. Effective therapists will recognize any dependency that develops, however, and will address this as part of the therapy. This may help break the dependency cycle in all areas of a client's life. Further, it should be remembered that female therapists may be just as likely as their male counterparts to adhere to gender stereotypes, although they may not endorse the same ones.

A therapist may hold strongly to particular values that work against the growth and problem-solving capacity of the client. If a client is trying to transcend gender-role stereotypes, a therapist who believes implicitly in the appropriateness of these stereotypes is unlikely to provide much support. For example, a woman struggling to find the courage to leave or renegotiate a stifling marital relationship is unlikely to be helped much by a therapist who adheres strongly to the belief that the man is the natural head of the family. Likewise, a man whose relationships are failing because he is unable to express any warmth and tenderness may receive little useful advice from a therapist who believes the most important qualities for male adjustment are autonomy and independence.

However, most therapists do not view themselves as authority figures but rather as helping professionals trying to empower their clients as they work through specific problems and issues. An effective therapist works with her or his clients to define the problems and/or issues that are to be addressed; the therapist does not do this without the participation of the client. A critical goal for therapists is to identify not only the weaknesses of clients but also their strengths. A good therapist–client relationship is a collaborative and very personal partnership that can help produce constructive behavioral change and positive outcomes (Gilbert & Kearney, 2006).

However, not every therapeutic relationship meets these ideals. Sexism can sometimes affect the psychotherapeutic process. There have been many reported instances of therapists fostering traditional gender roles, telling sexist jokes, refusing to take violence against women seriously, and initiating sexual or other nonprofessional relationships with their clients (American Psychological Association, 1975). Furthermore, therapists simply may be uninformed about the psychology of women and about sexual and reproductive issues (Sherman, Koufacos, & Kenworthy, 1978). Ignorance about women's experience may be particularly serious when the client is a minority or low-income woman (Comas-Díaz & Greene, 1994). Clinicians may limit their attention to intrapsychic issues, ignoring such potential contributors to emotional distress as inadequate income, poor health, substandard housing, unsafe neighborhoods, and racial discrimination. In recent years, however, training programs have emphasized the importance of these and other environmental stressors. These have helped decrease the ignorance and/or denial of these important environmental factors that may have led some therapists to stereotype negatively low-income women, women who are victims of violence, and other individuals exhibiting stress-related emotional problems.

It is becoming increasingly clear that gender and ethnocultural factors interact in the ways that clients and therapists perceive and interact with each other (Brown & Root, 1990; Comas-Díaz & Greene, 1994). Race and gender of client and therapist influence diagnosis and treatment (Loring & Powell, 1988). However, psychologists are only beginning to gather the information needed to provide therapy that acknowledges and respects the differences among women and men of different ethnic and cultural groups. This issue is especially problematic because the therapy profession in the United States and Canada is still predominantly European American and middle class, making it difficult for an individual who belongs to another group to find a therapist whose ethnocultural background matches her or his own. Nonetheless, the number of therapists from different ethnic and cultural groups is increasing. Also, training programs that incorporate and/or specialize in gender and ethnocultural issues already exist and continue to develop based on the growing demands in North America.

One area in which therapist knowledge and understanding is often crucial to the success of treatment is sexual assault. According to some surveys, anywhere from 13% to 48% of female psychiatric patients have histories of being sexually assaulted (Dye & Roth, 1990). Women who have been sexually victimized may suffer psychological distress for years. They may develop depression, phobias, sexual dysfunction, social withdrawal, and other symptoms. Yet victims of sexual assault are often the targets of negative social attitudes: blame for the assault and social derogation. If therapists hold such negative attitudes, their reactions to female clients who have experienced sexual assault will not be helpful.

Some research shows that therapists are not very likely to endorse rape myths (e.g., "Every woman secretly wants to be raped"). Younger age and being female are associated with less acceptance of such myths; psychiatrists are more likely than other mental health professionals to accept rape myths. Therapists who hold more negative stereotypes about sexual assault victims are more likely to endorse and to employ treatment approaches that blame the victim for the assault (Dye & Roth, 1990).

Many efforts have been made to reduce bias in psychotherapy through education. Both the American and the Canadian psychological associations published guidelines for therapy with women (American Psychological Association, 1978; Canadian Psychological Association, 1980). The Canadian Psychological Association also prepared a handbook of educational materials geared to help therapists confront and deal with their own gender biases and to practice nonsexist therapy or "sex-fair" counseling (Canadian Psychological Association, 1982). The *Ethics Code* of the American Psychological Association addresses standards of conduct for psychologists treating women in therapy as well as all individuals and groups in some detail; furthermore, these issues are confronted in the *General Principles* and *Ethical Standards* sections of the APA's *Ethics Code* (2002). Nonsexist therapy is based on the idea that women and men should be treated in similar ways and should be viewed as individuals rather than as members of a particular gender. Some excellent examples of such nonsexist therapy and counseling approaches have appeared in the psychological literature (Pyke, 1979; Rawlings & Carter, 1977). Because of the availability of such materials, it has become easier for people seeking therapy to find a therapist who has struggled to overcome sexist (and racist) biases.

FEMINIST THERAPY   Awareness of the potential problems in the therapeutic relationship, particularly with respect to gender roles, gave impetus to the development of feminist therapy (Butler & Wintram, 1991; Rosewater & Walker, 1985; Worrell & Remer, 1992). There are many versions of feminist therapy, but they tend to share the following features. Feminist therapy explicitly discards traditional gender-stereotypic assumptions about behavior, and the stereotypes themselves are openly discussed rather than ignored or assumed. The female perspective is explored and valued. The therapist is aware of the impact of ethnic and cultural differences between herself and the client. Therapy incorporates instead the assumption that the differential roles and statuses prescribed for women and men are potentially harmful to both sexes, particularly women. The approach rejects the notion of the therapist as an authority figure, emphasizing instead empowerment of the client. Moreover, instead of focusing only on individual difficulties and failings, this approach encourages the client to see her or his problem in its sociopolitical context. Most important of all, the client, not the therapist, defines the changes that are desirable.

Both female and male therapists can adopt the principles of feminist therapy. However, in the current context of lower status for women, some debate has surrounded the issue of whether women should be treated by male therapists at all. Beginning with Phyllis Chesler (1971), many feminists have argued that a female therapist provides a better role model for female clients and also that women seeing female therapists are spared the opportunity to reinforce feelings of dependency on men—feelings that may be the source of problems. Also, as Lynne Rosewater (1984) noted, "Women therapists share with their women clients the experiences of being second-class citizens" (p. 271), making it easier to develop mutual understanding and respect. It may be advantageous to women to have a female therapist, given the current intergroup relations between women and men. For some of the same reasons, there may be advantages for a man in having a male therapist—someone who can empathize with the difficulty of shedding some aspects of the male gender role and who can provide a good model of the possibilities for male nurturance and self-disclosure. This is not to say, however, that a woman cannot be helped by seeing a feminist male therapist or that a female feminist therapist cannot do useful work with a male client. A significant minority of male therapists identify themselves as feminist and report using a feminist perspective in their work (Dankoski, Penn, Carlson, & Hecker, 1998). Personal as well as social contextual variables influence the success of any client–therapist relationship; individuals must seek a therapist whose style meshes successfully with their own.

HETEROSEXISM IN PSYCHOTHERAPY   The problem of finding a suitable therapist may be especially difficult for gays and lesbians. Research shows that therapists, particularly males, tend to rate gay and lesbian clients as less healthy than heterosexual clients and to set different therapeutic goals for them (Garfinkle & Morin, 1978). A therapist may show such biases by devaluing same-sex relationships, by emphasizing a search for the cause of the homosexuality rather than dealing with current problems, or even by expecting the client to be able to be impervious to the widely publicized negative images of homosexuality (Riddle & Sang, 1978; Rigby & Sophie, 1990). It is difficult for a gay or lesbian client to be helped by interactions with a therapist who defines homosexuality as the problem or who does not help the client see her or his difficulties in a social context. Because of the negative attitudes toward homosexuality in our culture, lesbians and gay men lead more stressful and often more isolated lives than many heterosexual individuals—a difference that must be acknowledged in the therapeutic process. For therapists to work effectively with gay and lesbian clients, they must have examined their own heterosexist biases, have an understanding of the oppression and invisibility their clients may be experiencing, and be knowledgeable about community resources available to provide support (Fassinger & Richie,

1997). Because much of the stress on individuals is created by negative social responses to a sexual orientation that is considered strange or unhealthy, the promotion of mental health for all groups of women and men involves changing homophobic and sexist attitudes in society.

Drug Prescriptions

Psychotherapy is not the only treatment for emotional or mental distress. A common clinical response to such problems is to prescribe psychoactive (mood-altering) drugs such as antidepressants. Women are proportionally far more likely than men to receive drug prescriptions for psychological problems (Cafferata & Meyers, 1990; Fidell, 1982). Physicians' biases in this direction are reinforced by drug advertisements in psychiatric journals. Most of the clients depicted in such advertisements are women, and the messages can be extremely gender stereotypic (Prather & Fidell, 1978). Other factors such as age and race interact with gender in physicians' readiness to prescribe mood-altering drugs. Older women (Doyal, 1995) and women of color (Jacobsen, 1994) are often more likely than other women to be treated with drugs than other methods for emotional symptoms. In addition to reflecting stereotypic expectations, this propensity to overmedicate older women and women of color presents some danger. Most of the drugs being prescribed were tested on younger, European American populations, and they may have different effects on members of different groups (Jacobsen, 1994). Another issue is that many physicians prescribing psychoactive medications are not psychiatrists, who are specifically trained to work with such medications.

One negative aspect of a treatment response to mental or emotional problems that centers completely on prescription drugs may be the lack of opportunity for the person experiencing the illness to find ways of increasing a sense of effectiveness and control. Instead, the person becomes dependent on a drug to alleviate her symptoms. A study by Deanna Gammell and Janet Stoppard (1999) explored the experiences of women who had been diagnosed and treated for depression by physicians. In interviews, the women discussed how they came to be diagnosed as depressed, how they experienced their treatment, how they understood the causes of their depression, and how the diagnosis had affected their views of themselves and of their futures. These women all provided accounts of their depression that emphasized its medical, biological aspects, and most of them had, in conjunction with the treatment, made changes in their lives that lessened rather than increased their sense of personal empowerment. The researchers concluded that "a medicalized understanding and treatment of women's depressive experiences cannot readily co-exist with personal empowerment" (p. 112) and argued that treatment strategies must be developed that combine the benefits of a medical approach with the possibility of personal empowerment.

In the realms of both psychotherapy and drug treatment, the presence of gender bias has been highlighted by concerned researchers and therapists. Yet breaking down these biases is a continuing process. For the present, mental health, mental illness, and the treatment of mental illness may continue to be gender defined by many health professionals.

SUMMARY

The "strong man–fragile woman" stereotype is far too simplistic to describe gender differences in physical and mental health. Males are more vulnerable than females to death and serious physical illness across the life span, and they have a shorter life expectancy. Women, however, report more physical and emotional symptoms and seek treatment for physical and mental illnesses more often than men. Men are muscularly stronger than women and have higher fitness levels (at least in North America), but women can outperform men in some endurance situations.

An examination of the patterns of gender differences in health and illness suggests strongly that gender roles and stereotypes make a significant contribution to these differences. Part of men's higher death rate from disease and accidents, for example, is attributed to the dangers of trying to live up to the competitive, achievement-oriented, risk-taking masculine role. Women's higher rates of depression and agoraphobia are linked to the lack of independence and control built into the feminine role.

Not only role expectations but the whole social and physical environment may provide different stressors and be the source of different problems for women and men. Women are more likely than men to be poor and to be single parents. Marriage often involves a loss of status and autonomy for women but not for men and a larger gain in social support for men than for women. Employment, which often means the addition of one full-time job to another for a woman with children, may have different health implications for women and men. Even the health care system, strongly influenced by gender stereotypes, responds differently to women and men and sometimes labels people as unhealthy when they violate norms of femininity, masculinity, or heterosexuality. The promotion of good physical and mental health for women and men requires, in many instances, that such stereotypic thinking be confronted, questioned, and changed.

KEY TERMS

hysteria

gender-specific medicine

depression

posttraumatic stress disorder (PTSD)

anorexia nervosa

bulimia nervosa

specific phobias

agoraphobia

antisocial personality disorder

late luteal phase dysphoric disorder

stressors

10

Sex and Gender and Childhood
Constructing Gender

A researcher tells the following story about her own experience of discovering the seriousness with which young children take gender stereotypes. While interviewing 3 to 6 year olds about their career aspirations, she asked each of them what they would want to be when they grew up if they were members of the other sex. Their responses showed that not only did most of the children choose careers that fit the stereotypes for the other gender but also that their perceptions of the limitations imposed by gender were sometimes quite extreme. One little girl confided with a sigh that her true ambition was to fly like a bird, but she could never do it because she was not a boy! One little boy put his hands on his head, sighed deeply, and said helplessly that if he were a girl he would have to grow up to be nothing (Beuf, 1974).

A study of the way 3- to 5-year-old children made up stories in response to such story beginnings as "Two children are playing outside one day. They discover a secret door" showed that, given the same starts, girls and boys developed very different fantasies (Libby & Aries, 1989). The girls' stories tended to involve caregiving and responding to others' needs. Their stories often contained friendly figures who offered assistance to female characters. The stories told by the boys centered more often on aggression and on attempts to master challenging situations. At this early age, these children were already reflecting gender-stereotypic expectations.

The general notion one gets from reading the responses of 3rd- to 12th-grade students, collected by Baumgartner (1983), is that a change from male to female would involve a restriction of activities and horizons, whereas a change in the opposite direction would involve a widening of possibilities. For instance, girls noted that as boys they would be more outspoken, noisier, rowdier and would have to adhere to fewer rules, would worry less about their appearance, and would be closer to their fathers. Boys thought that as girls they would have to be quieter and more reserved, less active, and more restricted in what they were allowed to do, and they would have to worry more about their appearance, worry about safety, and do fewer things with their fathers. The boys, especially the younger ones, tended to view the possibility of becoming a girl with revulsion; girls, however, were likely to see advantages to being male.

Clearly, the impact of gender roles and rules on a child's social world begins very early, and one big part of that impact is that males learn to expect more choices and more power and control over their lives than females do. Chapters 1 and 2 discussed some of the mechanisms through which this impact occurs. Children learn quickly that gender categories are important and pervasive, and they develop gender schemas for processing information according to those categories. Certain activities, certain clothes, and certain toys are found to be appropriate only for girls or only for boys and are duly assigned to "masculine" or "feminine" categories. The child's efforts to categorize things correctly are helped along by modeling, reinforcement, and explicit instruction. In short order, children become quite confident that "boys don't play with dolls" or "girls can't be pilots," and their social relationships reflect and strengthen these expectations.

In this chapter we examine the social forces that contribute to this gendering of children's conceptions of themselves and the world. We also explore ways in which female and male children learn to handle differently three basic life tasks: developing an identity, forming relationships, and selecting and achieving goals. In particular, we ask these questions:

- How do parents contribute to children's early gender learning?
- What role do the media play in teaching children about gender?

- How does our use of language reinforce these messages about gender?
- Are boys and girls encouraged to construct different kind of "selves"?
- Is the process of forming friendships gendered?
- Are girls and boys encouraged to take different approaches to choosing and achieving goals for themselves?

We shall see that gender stereotypes and gendered expectations are pervasive and that children learn the lessons of gender from a wide variety of sources.

"GETTING THE WORD": SOURCES OF EARLY GENDER LEARNING

Parents and Children

Parents are the first source of children's gender learning; they hold and communicate different expectations for males and females. Researchers who interviewed 30 first-time parents within 24 hours after childbirth found that parents of boys and girls had already begun to view their infants differently (J. Rubin, Provenzano, & Luria, 1974). Those with daughters saw their babies as softer, finer featured, and more delicate than those with sons did; those with sons saw them as firmer, stronger, better coordinated, hardier, and more alert. These differences in describing male and female infants were most marked among fathers. Objective measures of the size and health of the infants showed no differences between females and males, so it appears that parental perceptions were influenced by gender-stereotyped expectations. Such expectations probably, in fact, take hold before the child is born. One study (Sweeney & Bradbard, 1988) found that parents who saw an ultrasound picture of their fetus still in the womb and who knew its sex rated female fetuses as softer, littler, calmer, weaker, more delicate, and more beautiful than male fetuses.

The culture encourages parents in these stereotypes. In a study of the birth congratulations cards being sold in four diverse communities, one researcher found gender stereotypes embedded in the congratulatory messages (Bridges, 1993). Cards intended for the parents of baby boys had more active visual images: active babies and action-oriented toys. Cards intended for parents of baby girls contained more verbal messages of emotional expressiveness, including themes of sweetness and sharing. The baby was more often described as "little" in girl cards than in boy cards, and parental emotions were more often described as happy in boy cards.

Once parents get to know their infants, do the stereotyped perceptions and expectations give way to ones that more accurately reflect the children's individual differences? The answer to this question seems to be mixed. Strong differences in the way parents treat their daughters and sons have not been found in all studies (e.g., Bee et al., 1984; Bellinger & Gleason, 1982). Researcher Carol Jacklin commented on the surprising lack of evidence in the Stanford Longitudinal Study for the existence of parental pressure on preschoolers to conform to gender stereotypes. For example, she described the burly father who looked sheepish but made no protest as his hair was rolled into curlers by his young son (Jacklin, 1985). A meta-analysis on studies of parents' different socialization of girls and boys found that on most dimensions (such as amount of interaction, discipline, warmth) differences in the ways parents treat their sons and daughters appear small and insignificant (Lytton & Romney, 1991). Some tendency was found for parents to inflict more physical punishment on boys than on girls and to stimulate motor behavior in sons more than in daughters. And parents who have traditional gender schemas seem to pass them along to their children: Children of such parents are more likely to have strong gender-typed ideas about themselves and others (Tenenbaum & Leaper, 2002).

However, many studies do indicate that parents treat daughters and sons differently in areas specifically related to gender expectations: giving them different toys, dressing them differently, and assigning them different tasks (Lytton & Romney, 1991). One study of middle-class preschoolers' bedrooms showed that boys' rooms were filled with sports equipment, toy vehicles, military toys, and toy and live animals; girls' rooms were more likely to contain dolls and dollhouses and to be decorated with floral wallpaper and lace (Rheingold & Cook, 1975). A later study suggested that the situation had changed little in 15 years (Pomerleau, Bolduc, Malcuit, & Cossette, 1990). Before the age of 2, girls' and boys' environments were found to be very different: Boys had more sports equipment, tools, and vehicles; girls had more dolls and children's furniture. Girls were more likely to be dressed in pink or multicolored clothes and to have pink pacifiers and jewelry; boys wore blue, red, and white clothing and were given blue pacifiers.

A study of the household tasks performed by boys and girls between the ages of 2 and 17 found that the boys were mowing the lawn, shoveling snow, taking out the garbage, and doing other yard work; girls were cleaning the house, washing dishes, cooking, and babysitting for younger children (L. White & Brinkerhoff, 1981). Even Halloween costumes are gendered. Girls' costumes emphasize the traditional feminine heroes: beauty queens, princesses, brides, and cheerleaders. Boys' costumes often have warrior themes and include plenty of law enforcement agents and cowboys as well as macabre villains (Nelson, 2000).

There is evidence that parents play and interact with boys and girls differently. They are more likely to talk with their daughters and to roughhouse and play actively with their sons (Tauber, 1979). When they play with boys, parents spend most of their time with "masculine" toys; they are more flexible about the toys they choose when they are playing with girls (Wood, Desmarais, & Gugula,

2002). Parents asked to work on a jigsaw puzzle with their 6 year olds and to teach them to remember a series of picture cards were found to use different strategies for sons and daughters. They were more performance and task oriented with sons, tried to teach them more general problem-solving strategies, and were both more directive and more approving and more disapproving of sons than daughters. With daughters, parents interacted in a more cooperative, concrete way, and daughters were given more feedback about their performance (Frankel & Rollins, 1983).

It is quite possible that parents have no idea of the extent to which they are treating boys and girls differently. For example, one study examined the way 11 mothers interacted with a 6-month-old infant. Five of the mothers played with an infant who was dressed in blue pants and called "Adam," and 6 later played with the *same* infant wearing a pink dress and called "Beth" (Will, Self, & Datan, 1976). These mothers were more likely to offer a doll to Beth and a toy train to Adam and to smile at and hold the baby more closely when they thought they were dealing with Beth than when they thought they had Adam. Actually, the infant was male, yet 2 of the mothers later commented that Beth was a "real girl" because she was sweet and cried so softly. Moreover, in later interviews every one of the 11 mothers said that boys and girls were alike at this age and should not be treated differently and that they would not treat their own sons and daughters differently. Gender socialization by parents may not, however, be as straightforward as parents simply treating girls and boys differently. Rather, what happens may be a transactional process in which children's characteristics or behaviors evoke particular reactions from parents—and these reactions in turn affect children's behavior (Pomerantz, Ng, & Wang, 2004). Complicating the issue still further is that each child may respond differently to parental behaviors, depending on that child's sensitivity to feedback, motivation to please the parent, and a variety of other factors. Thus some children may be more responsive than others to gender role socialization.

If girls and boys are even a little different, this transactional model of parental socialization may explain how such differences can be magnified through parent–child interactions. And research does suggest that boys and girls have some early differences in temperament. A recent meta-analysis shows that from a very early age girls seem more oriented than boys toward effortful control: the tendency to focus attention, inhibit certain actions, and persist at tasks. Boys, on the other hand, appear more temperamentally oriented toward something called surgency: a cluster of dimensions that includes high-intensity pleasure, smiling and laughing, activity, impulsivity, and not being shy (Else-Quest, Hyde, Goldsmith, & Van Hulle, 2006). It is easy to imagine how children who differ even a little in qualities such as the tendency to focus on tasks or smiling and laughing might elicit different responses from their caretakers—which would, in turn, reinforce certain patterns of behavior.

Within North America, there is some evidence that parents in different social classes and racial groups do not follow identical patterns of gender-role socialization. For example, research on African American families showed that parents in this group socialize their daughters more toward economic responsibility and a commitment to employment than European American parents do (Greene, 1994a; E. J. Smith, 1982). African American women report androgynous patterns of gender-related traits, suggesting that they are socialized to have a mixture of instrumental and expressive qualities (Binion, 1990). One reason for this less rigid pattern of gender-role socialization may be the extended kinship bonds that characterize African American families. For example, many women in African American families may be involved in the socialization of children who are not their biological children, a situation that provides the children with several alternative role models (Greene, 1994a).

Shirley Hill (2002) interviewed 35 African American parents about the gender socialization of children in their families. Her research was guided by the idea that "Racial and gender socialization intersect. . . . Just as Black boys learn a racialized form of masculinity consistent with their social class position, Black girls learn racialized gender roles that often emphasize a combination of traditional gender-typed values along with teaching the value of economic self-reliance, community activism, and assertiveness" (p. 496).

Hill found wide and strong verbal support for gender equality in her sample of parents. For example, parents commented that "I will definitely teach my son that men and women are equal; he is not the head of anybody" (p. 497) and "I'm teaching my daughter to have a career" (p. 498). However, support for gender equality was related to social class: Securely middle-class parents were more supportive of gender equality than working-class or first-generation middle-class parents. In the latter group, there was some ambivalence about gender roles; for example, parents said they would teach their daughters that women and men had equal rights and responsibilities, but they also emphasized that their daughters should behave in ladylike ways and that, within the family, they should expect a man to take care of them. They were teaching their daughters to be strong warriors for racial justice but also to be demure in certain circumstances. The working-class parents she interviewed tended to support gender equality in the workplace, but they expressed some concern that if they did not instill proper masculinity in their sons, the sons might become homosexual. Clearly, gender socialization is not "one pattern fits all" but is shaped by racial and class attitudes.

It is not only in North America that parents socialize their sons and daughters differently. Cross-cultural studies indicate that it is not uncommon for parents to pay more attention to boys than to girls, to interact more sociably with girls, and to emphasize more achievement and autonomy with boys. For example, in a study of Mexican families, fathers but not mothers were found to differ in their behavior toward daughters and sons:

> Boys were listened to and shown how to do things, which would seem to convey the message that what they have to say is important and that they are capable of mastering new skills. Girls, on the other hand, were treated especially gently, and at the same time, with a lack of full attention and an imposing of opinions and values. The gentle treatment would seem to convey the message that they are

fragile and docile. . . . The inattention and imposing of opinion would seem to communicate the view that what females have to say is less valuable than what males have to say, so that females need to be told what to think and do, and can more readily be interrupted or ignored. (Bronstein, 1984, p. 1001)

Further evidence for differential socialization of boys and girls comes from an examination of child-rearing data from more than 100 societies (Zern, 1984). This research confirmed that boys are more strongly pressured in the direction of self-reliance, achievement, and general independence than girls are, although both sexes receive some pressure in this direction.

Media

Children in the United States watch more than 44 hours per week of television. Even very young children spend a significant amount of time in front of the TV set (Rideout, Roberts, & Foehr, 2005). Some of the time a child spends staring at a television screen may be used to interact with fantasy characters in video games—particularly if the child is male (Oldenburg, 1994). Add to this the time spent listening to the radio, watching movies and music videos, and reading, and it becomes very clear that for most children beyond infancy the media is the most potent and pervasive source of information about their social world. Gender stereotypes form a significant component of the media message.

TELEVISION　By the age of 20, the typical American adolescent has viewed some 600,000 television commercials (Black, 1997). What messages about gender are touted along with the products in these commercials? That males are the authorities, for one thing. One study revealed that approximately 90% of the narrators in commercials are male and that women were still more likely

Overview　　Parents and gender-role socialization

- Parental expectations for girls and boys begin to differ even before a child is born.

- On many dimensions there are only small and insignificant differences in the ways parents treat their sons and daughters. However, they do treat boys and girls differently in areas specifically associated with gender expectations, such as toys, clothing, and participation in household tasks.

- Some research shows that parents interact differently with sons and daughters: talking more to daughters and playing more actively with sons.

- Ethnicity and race interact with gender in the ways parents socialize their children.

than men to be seen in domestic settings and less likely than men to be shown as employed (Bretl & Cantor, 1988). A more recent study found that women continue to be underrepresented as main characters in prime-time commercials except for those touting health and beauty products. Women tend to be cast in supportive roles to men, and older women are underrepresented (Ganahl, Prinsen, & Netzley, 2003). In the United States, one study of the portrayal of women on prime-time network television showed that the proportion of women in prime-time shows had changed little since the 1950s (D. M. Davis, 1990). In this study, about 65% of the characters in prime time were male, and 35% were female. Differences in the ways females and males were portrayed were also evident. Males were far more likely than females to be included in action-adventure shows and to be of indeterminate marital and parental status. Females were far more likely than males to be shown in provocative dress (nightwear, underwear, swimsuits, tight clothing) and to be blonde or red haired.

Commercials that are directed specifically at children and adolescents also convey gender-stereotypic messages. In commercials shown on MTV, male characters outnumber females more than 2 to 1 (Signorielli, McLeod, & Healy, 1994). The female characters are more likely to have beautiful bodies, wear skimpy clothing, and be looked at by others. In televised toy advertisements, sharp distinctions between boys' toys and girls' toys continue to be portrayed (Rajecki, Dame, Creek, Barrickman, et al., 1993). All-boy ads also tend to have a practical message; all-girl ads are more emotional in tone. Thirty-seven percent of commercials aimed at children contain aggression, and those featuring groups of White boys are particularly likely to contain aggression against objects (e.g., smashing things) and physical aggression (e.g., arm twisting) (Larson, 2003).

Studies of the content of children's television have consistently shown that males are overrepresented among the characters and that males and females are usually portrayed in gender-stereotypic ways (Durkin, 1985). In one early study, Sternglanz and Serbin (1974) analyzed 10 commercially produced children's programs and found striking differences in the depictions of male and female characters. Males were shown as more aggressive and constructive and were more likely than females to be portrayed as rescuing others from dangerous and distressing situations; females were depicted as submissive and inactive. In addition, males both showed more behaviors and received more rewards for their behavior, whereas the behavior of female characters often seemed devoid of consequences. A study of first- and second-grade children's favorite programs showed that a lot of gender neutrality was included in the programs preferred by children but that many gender stereotypes persisted. In the programs children liked, male characters were more likely than female characters to give orders, show ingenuity, achieve goals, and eat (Aubrey & Harrison, 2004). Reports written by children in the second through sixth grade about their favorite television programs contained more male than female characters, used more masculine than feminine pronouns, and described more typically masculine than feminine behaviors (Calvert, Kotler, Zehnder, & Shockey, 2003).

Animated cartoons, the programs that children prefer beginning around 2 years of age, convey a message about gender that can be fraught with stereotypes. In these cartoons, male characters are given more prominence, appear more often, talk more, and engage in a wider range of behaviors than female characters do (Thompson & Zerbinos, 1995). The male characters tend to be more independent, assertive, athletic, important, attractive, technical, and responsible than the female characters. The females, by contrast, are more likely to be emotional, warm, romantic, affectionate, sensitive, frail, mature, and domestic. Male characters show more ingenuity, anger, leadership, bravery, and aggression. Female characters ask for advice or protection, emphasize relationships, are helpless, serve others, and show affection. Male characters are more likely than females to express opinions, give orders, brag, interrupt, insult, threaten, and laugh at others.

An interesting aspect of the gender stereotyping presented on television involves appearance: It is emphasized more for female characters. Men in prime-time television programs are more likely than women to be average in appearance and physical fitness; female characters are more likely to be attractive and fit (Davis, 1990; Signorielli & Bacue, 1999). Comments about appearance also reflect a gendered pattern: Female characters are twice as likely as male characters to receive comments from other characters about their appearance (Lausen & Dozier, 2002). Female characters who are overweight tend to be targets of negative comments about their bodies from male characters— and these comments are usually followed by audience laughter (Fouts & Burggraf, 1999). However, there is no relationship between a male character's weight and negative comments he receives from female characters (Fouts & Vaughan, 2002).

Both women and men are affected by such stereotypic portrayals. After viewing TV ads that portray women as slender, attractive sex objects, women in one study judged their own body size as larger and more discrepant from their ideal size than did women who viewed nonsexist advertisements. Similarly, men who were exposed to these ads revealed more dissatisfaction with their own body size—believing their bodies were smaller than the ideal (Lavine, Sweeney, & Wagner, 1999). In another study, high school students who viewed more talk shows and "sexy" prime-time shows reported more agreement with sexual stereotypes, and exposing students in the lab to stereotypical televised content led students to endorse more gender and sexual stereotypes (Ward & Friedman, 2006).

There is little doubt that children notice the different ways female and male characters and feminine and masculine content are portrayed on television. When children ages 8 to 13 were asked, in one study, to rate the behavior of the characters in Saturday morning cartoons, they evaluated the characters in ways consistent with extreme gender stereotypes. Male characters were described as brave, dominant, intelligent, making decisions easily, not having to be rescued, independent, keeping out of trouble, acting as leaders, harsh, aggressive, and unconcerned about appearance. Female characters, conversely, were rated as needing to be rescued, easily excited in a crisis, having a strong need for security, and crying easily (Mayes & Valentine, 1979).

But children's comprehension of gender-related messages on television is not limited to the content of those messages: It also encompasses form—the different ways feminine and masculine content are presented. Form of presentation includes visual techniques such as cuts, fades, and dissolves; auditory features such as music, sound effects, and types of speech; and variables such as action level and pacing of the presentation. Masculine and feminine content on children's television tends to be presented with different formal features. For example, commercials designed for boys have rapid action, frequent cuts, loud music, sound effects, and many scene changes, whereas those designed for girls have background music, fades and dissolves, and female narration (Welch, Huston-Stein, Wright, & Plehal, 1979). As early as first grade, children seem to be aware of the connotations of these different forms. When presented with pseudocommercials in which the content was identical but the formal features were either "masculine" or "feminine," 6- to 12-year-old children were able to identify correctly each form as appropriate for advertising either a toy truck or a baby buggy and for advertising directed to girls or to boys (Huston, Greer, Wright, Welch, & Ross, 1984). It is possible, then, that the form of presentation of various objects and activities on television influences children's attention and interest in subtle ways, cueing them as to the gender appropriateness of particular content. If this is indeed the case, television can act as a powerful agent of gender-role socialization even in the absence of content that explicitly defines certain activities as appropriate only for girls or only for boys.

Research has made it quite clear that television viewing is related to gender-stereotypic attitudes among children and teenagers. Research shows that the more television children, teenagers, and adults watch, the more they subscribe to male–female stereotypes (Eisenstock, 1984; Eron, Huesmann, Brice, Fischer, & Mermelstein, 1983; Frueh & McGhee, 1975; McGhee & Frueh, 1980; M. Morgan, 1982; Sternglanz & Serbin, 1974; Zemach & Cohen, 1986). Does watching television actually contribute to children's gender stereotypes, or is it just that those who already hold strong stereotypes spend more time than their counterparts do in front of the television set? At least one study suggests that heavy TV viewing may contribute to an increase in gender stereotyping. Teenagers responded twice (2 years apart) to a questionnaire measuring sexism so that researcher Michael Morgan (1982) could assess whether heavy viewing was associated with an increase in sexism. What the research revealed was that those subjects who were the least sexist to begin with, high-IQ girls, seemed to be most affected by watching television. After 2 years, girls in this group who had watched a lot of television showed more sexist attitudes than they had earlier; those who were light viewers showed no increase in sexism.

Some studies have shown that television messages have a direct effect on children's attitudes. A mere 5 minutes of viewing commercials about either traditional (housewives and mothers) or nontraditional (professional career) women affected third- and eighth-grade children's attitudes toward women (Pingree, 1978). Similarly, 5 minutes of exposure to two television Muppets labeling a toy as appropriate only for the other sex was enough to make 4 to 6 year olds refuse to play with the toy (Cobb, Stevens-Long, & Goldstein, 1982).

In adolescence, much of the TV viewing is focused on music videos. These videos frequently enshrine gender stereotypes, portraying women as emotional, frivolous, and passive and men as aggressive, "cool," and adventuresome (J. D. Brown, 1985; Hansen & Hansen, 1988). Many such videos are far more blatant in their sexual stereotyping than current television programming and commercials are, often portraying women as aloof seductresses and men as angry, macho conquerors or brooding, rejected introverts. The words of the rock songs that accompany these visual presentations frequently reinforce the sexist message. A content analysis of videos shown on MTV and other television music channels showed that young White males appeared in these videos twice as often as females, that Whites appeared 4 times as frequently as persons of color, and that most of the videos contained both violent acts and sexual imagery (Sherman & Dominick, 1986). More frequent viewing of music videos has been linked to more traditional gender-role attitudes (Ward, Hansbrough, & Walker, 2005). Also, time spent watching music videos is related to the drive for muscularity in boys: male viewers apparently want to look more like the men they see in these videos (Tiggemann, 2005).

Music videos sometimes portray rape and other forms of sexual aggression against women. One analysis of the content of 40 MTV videos found that men appeared nearly twice as often as women and that men engaged in significantly more aggressive and dominant behavior. Women were portrayed significantly more often in implicitly sexual and subservient behavior, and they were more frequently the objects of implicit, explicit, and aggressive sexual advances (Sommers-Flanagan, Sommers-Flanagan, & Davis, 1993). Is there a cumulative effect of exposure to such material? Apparently "Yes." Frequent viewing of music videos increases the probability that the viewers will later judge women's and men's behavior in gender-stereotypic ways (Hansen & Hansen, 1988). Even listening to heavy-metal music, without the video, has been found to increase young men's gender stereotyping and negative attitudes toward women (St. Lawrence & Joyner, 1991). And violent videos have been found to foster a greater acceptance of stereotypical beliefs about rape (D. L. Peterson & Pfost, 1989). The tradition of gender stereotyping continues with rap music. Themes of misogyny are common in rap music (Adams & Fuller, 2006), and these anti-woman sentiments apparently have an impact on young women. One study of African American female adolescents showed that those who reported greater exposure to rap music were more likely than their counterparts to have been arrested, to have had multiple sexual partners, to have acquired a sexually transmitted disease, and to have used drugs and alcohol over a 12-month follow-up period (Wingwook, DiClemente, & Bernhardt, 2003).

Adolescents also watch many hours of televised sports. Here, too, they are exposed to gender stereotypes. One study analyzed the verbal commentary of televised coverage of the "Final Four" of the women's and men's National Collegiate Athletic Association basketball tournaments and the women's and men's singles and mixed-doubles matches of the U.S. Open tennis tournament (Messner, Duncan, & Jensen, 1993). Commentators tended to "mark" the gender of female athletes but not male athletes (i.e., male players were simply players, but female players were female players), implicitly treating females as outsiders or special in sports and treating their accomplishments ambivalently. An analysis of broadcast commentary on the NCAA Final Four basketball championships revealed that men's games generated more commentary and that male athletes were discussed more in terms of physicality and athleticism, whereas female athletes were discussed more in terms of their personality, appearance, and background. These researchers also found that male sportscasters tended to monopolize airtime for both men's and women's games, even in the presence of female commentators (Billings, Halone, & Denham, 2002). Interestingly, commentary on golf, although still showing differences by gender, exemplifies a different pattern of gender stereotypes: Women are more likely to be described in terms of reasons for their success or failure (especially luck), and men's personality or physical attributes are more likely to be described (Billings, Angelini, & Eastman, 2005).

Interestingly, television viewing is strongly correlated with depression among college students, and depressed women watch more hours than depressed men do (Dittmar, 1994). There is no evidence at all that television *causes* college women's depression; however, given the messages that television sends out about women, watching it is unlikely to do anything to alleviate their depression.

VIDEO GAMES AND THE INTERNET   For many children and adolescents, the video screen is no longer something only to stare at passively. Rather, the screen has become an interactive playing field for a variety of fantasy games. Eighty-three percent of children ages 8 to 18 have a video game console at home, a majority have two or more consoles, and they spend an average of 50 minutes a day playing video games (Rideout, Roberts, & Foehr, 2005). In the media realm of video games, gender stereotyping is rampant. Years ago, 99% of video games were bought by or for boys; more recently, 21% of the purchases and main users of video games were female (Oldenburg, 1994). The games are still overwhelmingly oriented toward a hypermasculine stereotype, focusing on search-and-destroy missions, kicking and fighting contests, fighter pilot fantasies, or male sports. The few that explicitly target females are either equally stereotypic (shopping games and games featuring Minnie Mouse or Barbie) or create "female warrior" characters that are simply slightly feminized versions of the male characters. Almost 33% of the video games sampled in one study included no female characters, and only 15% showed women as heroes. In fact, when female characters were included, 21% of the time they played the role of "damsel in distress"—requiring rescue (Dietz, 1998). Female characters are not only underrepresented but often sexualized (Ivory, 2006). Not only does this pattern make it unlikely that girls will be attracted to video games, but it also has implications for what boys learn about gender (Anderson & Cavallaro, 2002). A few companies are marketing games meant to be gender inclusive rather than oriented to boys or girls; however, for now, the world of video games remains largely a bastion of gender stereotypes.

Most young people also make significant use of the Internet, and there are gender disparities to be found there as well. Young people ages 8 to 18 spend an average of just over an hour per day using computers (not counting schoolwork); most of that time is spent online (Rideout et al., 2005). One thing they may encounter online is pornography; one survey found that 71% of male and 40% of female adolescents had been exposed to sexually explicit materials online in the previous 6 months (Jochen & Valkenburg, 2006). In general, however, boys' and girls' online activities seem to be more similar than different (Gross, 2004).

THE PRINTED WORD   Stereotyped portrayals of females and males abound in the print media. Even the comic pages of newspapers show a preponderance of male characters (Chavez, 1985). The gender stereotyping in children's books parallels that found on television. Male characters outnumber females; far more stories are boy centered than girl centered; and males are portrayed as adventurous, brave, competent, and clever, whereas females are depicted as incompetent, fearful, and dependent on others (usually males) to solve their problems (A. J. Davis, 1984; S. B. Peterson & Lach, 1990). Despite some improvement in recent years in the ratio of males to females portrayed and some avoidance of obvious sexism, children's books continue, for the most part, to reflect gender stereotypes (Crabb & Bielawski, 1994; Davis, 1984; Gooden & Gooden, 2001; Kortenhaus & Demarest, 1993; Pursell & Stewart, 1990). However, "traditional" gender roles are now more fictional than real. For instance, books written for children continue to show many mothers working only in the home, but the majority of North American mothers in fact hold outside jobs.

Like television, books appear to influence children's behavior. For instance, nursery-school boys worked longer and harder on a task after hearing a story about achievement behavior by a male character than after hearing about the same behavior by a female character, and the reverse trend is found for nursery-school girls (McArthur & Eisen, 1976). And preschoolers are more likely to choose a gender-stereotypic toy after exposure to a stereotypic picture book and a nonstereotypic toy after exposure to a nonstereotypic book (Ashton, 1983).

The stereotyped view of males and females presented to children in books and other media may well have a strong influence on the children's capacity or willingness to imagine a world that is free of such stereotypes. A disturbing finding is that children's own writing reflects the very same stereotypic thinking evident in the books written *for* them. When the creative writing of children from grades 1 to 6 attending a "young authors conference" in Michigan was examined, it was found to reflect social perceptions of gender roles (Trepanier & Romatowski, 1985). Male characters outnumbered female ones in the stories written by both girls and boys, although the girls did include more female characters in their stories than the boys did. Not only did male characters outnumber females, but more attributes—both positive ones, such as courageous and determined, and negative ones, such as mean and nasty—were ascribed to male than to female characters. Moreover, when occupational roles were considered, there were dramatic differences in the number of such roles assigned to male and female characters. Of 127 occupational roles assigned to their characters by these young authors, 111 (87%) were assigned to male characters and only 16 (13%) to female characters. The roles themselves were stereotypic. For example, a female could be a princess, cook, teacher, babysitter, or nurse; a male could be a doctor, astronaut, dentist, clown, professor, or police officer. Even at this young age, then, children seem to have "gotten the message" that females are less interesting, are less important, and have narrower horizons than males do.

Language

Most of an individual's relations with the social world are mediated by language, and the learning of language is one of the first and most important tasks facing a developing child. Furthermore, children's development of gender identity and gender role is inextricably bound up with the acquisition of language. The labels that children learn—*boy, girl, man, woman, daddy, mommy*—help them form the categories around which they build a fundamental understanding of gender and help guide their thinking about this concept.

A problem with the role language plays in children's learning about gender is that language contains built-in biases about gender—biases that reflect the sexism and gender stereotypes of the culture. In English at least, these biases are reflected in the way language ignores females or labels them as special cases. The masculine gender is used to refer to people in general (e.g., mankind, the nature of man, sons of God, everyone must do his part). Females are labeled in ways that indicate they are exceptions, often with the additional implication of inferiority. A male, for instance, is a "real" poet, whereas his female counterpart is a "poetess." And a female colleague and I were once referred to as "professorettes."

Does the sexism built into language affect children's learning and thinking about gender? The evidence is clear that it does. Children in kindergarten, first, third, and fifth grades give male-biased responses to story cues that contained the pronoun "he," as did college students (Fisk, 1985; Gastil, 1990; Hyde, 1984a). In Hyde's study, when the pronoun in the sentence cue "When a kid goes to school, _____ often feels excited on the first day" was "he," only 12% of the stories the students went on to create were about females as compared to 18% when the pronoun was "they" and 42% when the pronoun was "he" or "she."

Clearly, the masculine pronoun makes children think of males. Moreover, fewer than half the children, even by fifth grade, indicated an awareness that "he" could be used as a generic term referring to people in general. Perhaps even more telling is the impact of masculine, feminine, or neutral pronouns on children's evaluation of how well women or men could perform the fictional job of "wudgemaker." When the pronoun used in the job description was "he," children's ratings of how well a woman could perform the job were lowest. The ratings were intermediate when neutral pronouns were used and highest when "she" was used. It appears that the choice of pronoun influenced children's perception and gender categorization of the neutral, fictional wudgemaker job. The implications for children's gender stereotyping of occupations labeled *policeman, draftsman,* or *chairman of the board* are obvious.

Hyde concluded that most elementary schoolchildren have learned to think of males when they hear "he" in a gender-neutral context and do not know that "he" can refer to both males and females. Because they are exposed to a constant stream of information using the masculine gender as normative, they learn to think of the typical person as male—an important step toward the cultural assumption that the male is normative and the female atypical or deviant. Such thinking is probably reinforced in many schoolrooms. In one study of teacher behavior in preschool classrooms, teachers regularly used masculine pronouns in a generic way, particularly to refer to animals and to gender-ambiguous characters (Gelb, 1989). In their instructions and storytelling sessions, these teachers used 3 times as many male as female pronouns.

Some steps have been taken toward a more gender-egalitarian language. Publishers of textbooks now frequently use guidelines to eliminate sexist writing, advising their authors to avoid the use of "he" when they really mean "he" or "she" and to use gender-neutral terms to refer to occupations. Teachers attend workshops on the use of nonsexist language. A few writers, such as Marge Piercy in her science fiction novel *Woman at the Edge of Time,* have experimented with the use of a neutral singular pronoun (Piercy used "per").

A study of speeches given by male business leaders across three decades showed that the use of gender-exclusive language had dropped sharply in the 1970s and remained low (Rubin, Greene, & Schneider, 1994). However, ironically, the tendency to use gender-biased language persists in academic circles. High school and college students receive little training in using nonsexist language (Kennedy, 1993), and college professors sometimes show little awareness of sexist language (Stewart, Verstraate, & Fanslow, 1990). It may be many years before gender-inclusive language becomes the norm. In the meantime, children are using gender-biased language as the cornerstone of their initial concepts of sex and gender.

Language joins parental socialization and the media as a potent source of information and social pressure with respect to gender roles. As described in Chapter 2, children use the information and reinforcement provided by these and other sources to build an understanding of gender and a set of behaviors congruent with that understanding. These cognitive and behavioral aspects of gender affect virtually all areas of a child's life. The remainder of this chapter looks at how gender-role socialization in childhood and adolescence affects two major aspects of the developing individual's life: the formation of friendships and the emergence of achievement goals.

CONSTRUCTING AN IDENTITY: THE RELATIONAL AND INDIVIDUAL SELF

A developmental task faced by every person is the construction of an **identity,** or sense of self. This sense of self includes the sense of belonging to particular social groups, such as the individual's gender, ethnic, racial, social class, sexual-orientation, and religious groups. It encompasses the qualities the person sees as part of the self as well as the acceptance for the self of labels or identities, such as *feminist* (Freedman & Lips, 2002; Lips & Freedman, 1992). A racial identity might, for instance, be defined as "the significance and qualitative meaning that individuals attribute to their membership with the . . . racial group within their self-concepts. This definition can be broken into two questions: 'How important is race in the individual's perception of self?' and 'What does it mean to be a member of this racial group?'" (Sellers, Smith, Shelton, Rowley, & Chavous, 1998). Ethnic or racial identity is often a well-articulated, important aspect of the self-concept (Shorter-Gooden & Washington, 1996).

Identities are not static; they tend to alter in response to changes in an individual's social environment and life stage. For example, the formation of the ethnic aspect of identity takes place over time, as young people explore and make decisions about the role of ethnicity in their lives. This process may occur in several stages, beginning with a phase in which ethnicity is largely unexamined and is taken for granted, moving through a period of questioning

Table 10.1   Four dimensions of racial identity.

Racial salience	The extent to which one's race is a relevant part of one's self-concept in a particular moment or situation.
Racial centrality	The extent to which a person normatively defines himself or herself with regard to race.
Racial regard	A person's affective and evaluative judgments of her or his own race in positive-negative terms; the extent to which a person feels positive about her or his own race.
Racial ideology	A person's beliefs, opinions, and attitudes with respect to how she or he feels members of the race should behave.

Source: Sellers et al. (1998).

and exploring the meaning of one's ethnicity, leading finally to a committed ethnic identity (Phinney, 1989, 1990). The exploration stage may be triggered by a significant event that awakens the person to an awareness of the implications of her or his ethnicity (Helms, 1993; Kim, 1981). Identities may also have several different dimensions. For example, one recent model of African American identity postulates four dimensions, as seen in Table 10.1. Similar dimensions might be assumed for other identities.

Gender-related expectations may play a part in the way a person responds to ethnic identity issues and vice versa. For example, in some cultures there is an assumption that women are the carriers of ethnic traditions. Also, for any individual, the relative importance of one identity, such as race, in comparison to other identities may have important implications for the meaning that she or he ascribes to other identities. "For instance, an African American woman for whom both gender and race are important to her definition of self is more likely to incorporate gender with her conceptualization of what it means to be Black than an African American woman for whom gender is not a central part of her identity" (Sellers et al., 1998, p. 23).

Earlier in this book, we considered the question of gender identity: the sense of oneself as female or male. However, there are issues in gender identity that go beyond simple identification or categorization: Is the individual proud of her or his gender? How important is gender in the individual's sense of self? Laura Abrams (2003) explored these issues in semistructured interviews with young women in two high schools: one in a wealthy, suburban White community and the other in an urban, working-class community of color. She wanted to find out how these young women felt about being girls and how they went about negotiating their gendered identities.

Abrams found that context made a big difference in the way girls experienced their femininity and in the ways they responded to stereotypes about what girls *should* be like. Girls in both communities were aware of power differences between women and men, and this awareness of women's second-class status made them unhappy and dissatisfied. They spoke of men's disrespect and violence toward women and of pervasive sex discrimination. And they felt that women had harder lives. For example, one young woman noted that ". . . you have to have babies. That's hard. I mean guys don't have to get pregnant. And then, a lot of opportunities, like hard, hard work—like the ones you make the good money at—they don't want women, they want men" (p. 69).

Girls in both groups resisted the prescription that they should conform to stereotypes. Those in the affluent suburb tended to resist cultural norms for femininity by adopting more tough, "masculine" behavior such as aggression and drug abuse—behaviors that got them into trouble. Girls in the working-class community worked to resist a different stereotype: that they were promiscuous "bad girls." Their resistance often took the form of delaying sexual intercourse.

Being a girl was not all about power struggles with boys and resistance to stereotypes, though. Girls in both communities had strategies for developing and protecting positive self-concepts. For minority girls in the working-class community, part of the negativity associated with gender was offset by strong positive cultural and ethnic identities. For the economically privileged White girls in the suburban community, positive feelings about being female came from being different from (and better than) men. For example, one girl commented that

> I like being a girl because I can really think about things. I think that guys just don't really examine things, and think about how people feel. And don't perceive what other people are thinking. I think that's a real advantage that women have. That they can just really perceive things well and understand other people better. (p. 69)

Clearly, the process of forming an identity as a woman is shaped, not only by a sense of female–male power relations, but also by such social contextual issues as the social class and ethnic composition of one's community.

Traditional theories about how a person forms an identity or sense of self have tended to emphasize separation-individuation as the basic task of human development (e.g., Erikson, 1950). To develop a clearly defined, separate sense of self, this approach stresses, the person must disconnect to some extent from relationships. Thus, for example, a child must weaken ties with the mother, must gradually become less dependent and more self-reliant, and must develop an individual set of goals and sense of purpose. Contemporary theorists argue, however, that this traditional conception of development is based largely on masculine role expectations and ignores a different and equally important aspect of identity: the development of a sense of **self-in-relation** (Calloni & Handal, 1992; Surrey, 1983, as cited in A. G. Kaplan & Surrey, 1984). The sense of oneself as a relational being, someone who is developing and growing in the ability to connect with and relate to others, is arguably as much a core aspect of identity as is the sense of oneself as a separate, independent being striving for one's own particular goals. Although theorists have noted that the self-in-relation aspect of identity may be an especially important factor in women's psychological development, it must be important to men as well. It is likely that both males and females construct identities that include both individuated and relational aspects, although gender-related expectations may lead them to place differential emphasis on the two components. The following discussion of development focuses on both relational and individual achievement issues.

FRIENDSHIP

Childhood

From the beginning, girls and boys learn different expectations about friendship. Girls receive many messages that personal relationships are an important, perhaps *the* most important, life priority. They are encouraged to develop the qualities on which relationship skills are built: empathy, nurturance, expressiveness, and sensitivity to others. They are urged to consider the needs of others when making their own decisions and plans. Boys, although not taught that relationships are unimportant, are often more strongly encouraged to be independent, self-reliant, assertive, and achievement oriented than to give high priority to friendships. This difference in emphasis for girls and boys is probably related to the traditional expectations for females and males: that, for females, security and success ultimately reside in their ability to form and maintain relationships with others, and that, for males, they reside in individual achievements.

Beginning in early childhood, boys and girls tend to separate into same-sex play groups, and best friends are almost always of the same sex (Howes & Phillipsen, 1992; P. A. Katz & Boswell, 1984; Maccoby, 1990, 1998). This division is no doubt influenced by cultural norms that encourage girls and boys to play different games and to engage in different kinds of activities; however, segregation prevails even during gender-neutral activities. The reason for children's strong preference for same-sex play appears to be twofold. First, the rough-and-tumble play and orientation toward competition and dominance that characterize boys' interactions seem to make girls wary. Second, girls find boys unresponsive to their influence attempts and so do not enjoy interacting with them (Maccoby, 1990).

The same-sex peer groups that develop during childhood reinforce cultural norms and play a powerful role in maintaining gender differences. Children make harsh judgments about peers who do not conform to gender-role standards (Fagot, 1984; Hartup, 1983); two of the most deprecating epithets that can be flung at one child by another are "sissy" and "tomboy." For boys in particular, the same-sex peer group seems to play an important role in reinforcing masculine gender identity and male dominance, a process that occurs largely through the derogation of girls and all things feminine.

The kinds of relationships that characterize girls' and boys' friendship groups differ in some respects, perhaps in response to gender roles that stress intimacy for females and adventurousness for males (Berndt & Hoyle, 1985; M. L. Clark & Ayers, 1991; Humphreys & Smith, 1987). Boys' groups tend to be larger, providing them with more friends but less intimacy and giving them a "gang" with which to embark on explorations of their world. Certainly, this is the image of male childhood friendships that has been celebrated in movies and television. Girls, however, limit the size of their friendship groups and tend to have fewer, more intense friendships—relationships that provide the arena for exploring interpersonal concerns (S. M. Rose, 1995). A recent review of studies on children's peer relationship styles revealed a pattern in which boys interacted with same-sex peers in groups more than girls did, and girls, at least at some ages, engage in longer two-person interactions than boys did (A. J. Rose & Rudolph, 2006). These reviewers also found that boys tended to have social networks that were of higher density than those of girls; in other words, boys' friends were more likely than girls' friends to become friends with one another.

Even in childhood, girls seem to be more comfortable than boys are with intimacy. In one study of 7- and 8-year-olds, same-sex pairs of children either sat close together and drew pictures of each other (high-intimacy condition) or sat with a screen separating them (low-intimacy condition). The girls smiled more and laughed less than boys did in the high-intimacy condition—an indication, according to the researchers, that they were more comfortable than the boys were in this situation (Foot, Chapman, & Smith, 1977). The same study found similarities for boys and girls in the effects of being with a friend. Children who watched a cartoon when paired with a friend showed more social responsiveness—laughing, smiling, talking, looking at their partner, and touching—than did those who were paired with a stranger. Clearly, there are gender similarities as well as differences in children's friendships.

The different kinds of activities encouraged for school-age boys and girls may help to maintain the pattern of small intimate friendship groups for girls and larger "gangs" for boys. Team sports such as softball, hockey, and football form a large part of boys' recreational activities. The boys who play these sports may well learn to associate having fun with being in the company of a fairly large, diverse group of peers. Until recent decades, only a minority of girls had been given the opportunity to engage in team sports. Researchers have yet to examine the interesting question of whether there is a relationship between overall friendship patterns and participation in team sports.

Another male–female difference in recreational activities is in the use of computer games, a pastime much more common among boys than girls. This activity, far from fostering the development of a large friendship group, promotes a one-on-one relationship of boy to machine. It is difficult to say what impact the widespread use of this form of recreation may have on boys' friendship patterns in the future. However, casual observation suggests that although boys play these games as individuals, they often come and go from the game situation in groups, and their individual success with the games is a matter of status in the group.

One of the most interesting aspects of children's preference for all-boy and all-girl groups is that different styles of interaction develop in groups of boys and groups of girls. Boys' groups show more concern with dominance and agency. Boys are more likely than girls are to interrupt one another, command and threaten, boast, refuse to comply, give information, and call other boys names. Girls, conversely, are more connection-oriented and seem more interested in sustaining social relationships (A. J. Rose & Rudolph, 2006). They are more likely than boys to say they agree with another speaker, acknowledge points made by other speakers, and pause to allow another to speak (Maltz & Borker, 1983). The interaction styles characterizing boys' and girls' groups have been labeled, respectively, **constricting** and **enabling** (Hauser, Powers, Weiss-Perry, Follansbee, Rajapark, & Greene, 1987, as cited in Maccoby, 1990). Because groups of girls and boys differ in their habitual interaction styles, and because children spend so much time interacting in same-sex groups, girls and boys are socialized by their peers into different ways of relating. These different styles of interaction apparently carry over into adolescence and adulthood.

As Maccoby (1990) noted, the different ways males and females have learned to interact with others from childhood onward have implications for later, cross-sex relationships:

> What happens . . . when individuals from these two distinctive "cultures" attempt to interact with one another? People of both sexes are faced with a relatively unfamiliar situation to which they must adapt. Young women are less likely to receive the reciprocal agreement, opportunities to talk, and so on that they have learned to expect when interacting with female partners. Men have been accustomed to counterdominance and competitive reactions to their own power assertions, and they now find themselves with partners who agree with them and otherwise offer enabling responses. It seems evident that this new partnership should be easier to adapt to for men than for women. (p. 517)

Adolescence

Adolescence is a time when friendships often become very intense, perhaps because it is a time of personal transition and uncertainty. The pattern of fewer, more intimate friendships for girls and larger, less intimate friendship groups for boys persists. Moreover, there is some evidence that relationships are more important to girls than to boys during this period (A. J. Rose & Rudolph, 2006). When teenagers were asked to rank-order a number of concerns according to their importance, both sexes ranked identity and sexuality at the top of the list, but girls placed interpersonal relationships third, whereas boys chose autonomy as their third most important concern (Strommen, 1977). Researchers have also found that high school girls express greater concerns about their friendships than high school boys do (Schneider & Coutts, 1985). Adolescent girls are more likely than their male counterparts to share information about their emotional state with their parents and friends (Papini, Farmer, Clark, Micka, & Barnett, 1990). Male friends tend to be more similar to one another than female friends on status variables such as nominations for the neatest and nicest clothes, and female friends tend to be more similar in personality and verbal achievement (M. L. Clark & Ayers, 1991). These researchers also found that African American adolescents, both females and males, choose friends who are less similar to themselves on achievement and academic status than White adolescents do.

Boys may be less concerned with friendship, *or* boys may simply be inhibited about admitting an interest in same-sex friendships. College males are significantly more reluctant than females to volunteer for studies listed as investigations of same-sex friendship and are even unwilling to sign up for studies of issues unrelated to friendship that require them to bring along a same-sex friend (Lewis, Winstead, & Derlega, 1989). Furthermore, teenage boys who are highly affiliative (that is, very interested in being with other people) report more negative emotional states, both when they are alone and when they are with friends, than do teenage girls who are highly affiliative (Wong & Csikszentmihalyi, 1991). This finding may reflect boys' expectations that they should be independent, coupled with the suspicion of homosexuality that our culture imposes on male-male friendships.

A pioneering study of adolescent friendships points to gender differences in the focus and quality of these relationships (Douvan & Adelson, 1966). For girls in their midteens, sensitivity to others and mutual trust were cited as important qualities in a friend. Girls in this age range described a friend as someone who will provide emotional support during personal crises and who will not gossip behind one's back. By contrast, boys in the same age range listed relatively impersonal qualities (e.g., easy to get along with, does favors) as the important ones for a friend to have. In addition, boys were more likely than girls to view the friendship group as a source of support against adult authority and to mention that a friend is someone who stands by you when you are in trouble with that authority.

It appears that friendships during childhood and adolescence tend to follow patterns that support girls and boys as they follow the paths laid down by traditional gender roles. Girls' friendships are geared to helping them explore and deal with personal relationships. Boys' friendships provide support for defiance of authority and assertion of independence. Of course, the differences in emphasis are not always so pronounced, particularly in later adolescence. Some studies of college student friendships have found more gender similarities than differences (Caldwell & Peplau, 1982; Rose, 1985).

One factor that may influence social relationships in different ways for girls and boys during adolescence is the timing of physical maturity. In general, girls reach puberty sooner than boys do. Maturing earlier or later than one's peers has different implications for the two sexes. For a girl, early development of breasts and a more sexually mature appearance are likely to be associated with early pressures in the direction of the traditional feminine role. Parents may place new restrictions on her, and older boys may begin to pressure her for sexual behavior (Golub, 1983; Katz, 1986). The early maturing girl may be dating at an age when her cohorts are still relying heavily on same-sex friendships to explore interpersonal issues. In fact, dating may actively interfere with a girl's same-sex friendships. To the extent that males keep the role of initiator in the heterosexual dating situation, females simply react to male invitations. Thus a girl may find herself unable to pick the times when she can get together with a boy. Rather, her only control in the situation lies in saying yes or no to a specific invitation. Under these circumstances, girls often find themselves forced to choose between previously established plans with their girlfriends and the chance to go out with a boy they like. It is perhaps not surprising, then, that girls sometimes break plans with same-sex friends to accept a date.

Some evidence shows that such early dating is disadvantageous to girls' self-esteem (Golub, 1983; Simmons, Blyth, Van Cleave, & Bush, 1979), perhaps because girls are not yet equipped emotionally to handle the sexual and affective pressures of the dating situation, or perhaps because of the loss of control over her life that waiting to be asked out can involve for a girl. Moreover, some have speculated that a girl who is physically well developed at an early age receives more reinforcement for following a traditional feminine script, making it less likely that she will explore alternatives such as a career (Katz, 1986). Early-maturing girls also tend to be dissatisfied with their weight and their appearance, causing them to focus more on these issues. Overall, early physical maturation appears to be linked to changes in the pattern of girls' social relationships—changes that involve increased pressure to be "feminine."

For a boy, early maturation is not likely to be associated with increased parental restrictiveness, although it may be associated with an increase in responsibilities. Also, since our culture has traditionally placed males "in charge" of the dating situation, there is less likelihood that early dating will cause problems for them. The boy who is quicker than his peers to develop the muscularity, strength, and physique of the adult is likely to be regarded with envy. If he begins to cultivate relationships with girls, it is still unlikely that he will significantly loosen his ties with his male friendship group. He may, to the contrary, gain increased status in that group and be expected to provide leadership. These pressures are in line with masculine role expectations.

In comparing the experiences of the early maturing girl and the early maturing boy, it is clear that both involve earlier than usual stress on gender-role conformity. However, this early pressure has quite different implications for girls and boys. For girls, it means more curtailment of their activities, significant loss of control over their social relationships, and being placed in the role of sexual object before having a chance to explore their own sexual feelings. For boys, it often means less rather than more curtailment of their activities, increases in responsibility and status, and the frequently unnerving challenge of initiating (or, at least, appearing to initiate) heterosexual relationships.

Given the gender segregation of activities that occurs through childhood and adolescence, it is not surprising to find that cross-sex friendships are relatively rare. Some do appear in adolescence; however, the cultural inclination to define any female–male relationship in sexual terms makes it difficult for them to thrive.

In middle and late adolescence, there is an increased focus on sexuality, and dating becomes a prominent concern. Girls who feel they must attract boys become very concerned with physical appearance and social skills. Although boys display a parallel concern with their attractiveness to girls, the development of heterosexual relationships is far from their only priority. Boys receive a great deal of reinforcement for other activities such as athletic pursuits and scholarly achievement. Nonetheless, for both females and males at this stage, peers of the other sex become quite important as sources of social approval and status. This pattern seems to hold even for those individuals who will eventually identify themselves as gay or lesbian. In fact, the relationship between adolescent sexuality and adult sexual preference is not particularly clear-cut (Bidwell & Deisher, 1991). As the early Kinsey surveys show, although up to

10% of adolescents who engage in homosexual behavior go on to identify themselves as gay in adulthood, most do not. Regardless of their sexual orientation, then, it appears that male and female adolescents tend to form some cross-sex attachments and to experience the gender-role pressures involved in dating.

For young women and men who are moving toward affirmation of an identity as lesbian or gay, dealing with gender-role pressures in relationships is only part of the task they must face. If they embrace a lesbian or gay identity, they are embracing a self-definition that is stigmatized by the dominant culture (Herdt, 1989; H. P. Martin, 1991). One model of the formation of a gay or lesbian identity (Cass, 1979, 1984) proposed a series of six steps, beginning with the initial realization that particular thoughts, feelings, or behavior can be identified as homosexually oriented. This realization feels incongruous, given that the person and the environment have assumed the person is heterosexual. Gradually, the individual begins to come to terms with the social alienation that the new identity represents and then to establish contacts with other lesbians and gays to obtain a sense of community and a validation of this identity. The individual develops a sense of pride in the new identity but must still confront the incongruity between strong self-acceptance and society's negative labeling of homosexuality. The incongruity produces anger; the person may become interested in confronting the dominant heterosexual culture. At this stage, she or he may become increasingly open about homosexuality. Finally, the model suggests, the person reaches a stage at which public and personal sexual identities can be synthesized. Identifying as lesbian, gay, or bisexual then becomes not an all-encompassing identity but only one aspect of the self. The whole process embodies a gradual movement from denial of a self-view that is seen as negative to embracing an identity that is ultimately seen as positive.

This model, encompassing a movement from an initially negative to an eventual positive reaction to one's sexual identity, may not adequately represent the experience of every person who forms a lesbian or gay sexual identity. Research on a national sample of over 2,000 lesbians suggests that many women experience their lesbian identity as positive and comfortable from their first recognition of it (Rabin & Slater, 2004). Clearly, there is a good deal of diversity in the ways such identities are developed.

The intersection of sexual identity with ethnic, religious, or other aspects of identity may be complicated and difficult in some cases. For instance, Espín (1987) noted that Latina lesbians sometimes feel they must make a choice to emphasize either their ethnic or their sexual orientation because the lesbian identity is labeled even more negatively in Latin cultures than in mainstream North American society. For lesbian women of color, the risk of alienation from their families and friends if they come out publicly as lesbian may be especially frightening because the social support from these networks provides an important buffer against the racism they encounter in the larger society (Greene, 1994b).

- Beginning in early childhood, children tend to separate into same-sex play groups that reinforce different relational styles: a constricting style for boys and an enabling style for girls.

- Boys tend to have larger friendship groups with whom they share activities; girls are more likely to have fewer, more intimate friendships. These patterns continue into adolescence.

- For both girls and boys, peers of the other sex become more important at adolescence.

- Early physical maturation produces an early emphasis on compliance with adult gender roles. This emphasis may affect the self-esteem and relationships of adolescent girls and boys differently. Early maturing girls may be pulled away from their female friendships toward an emphasis on heterosexual relationships.

- Sexual identity issues may arise during adolescence, leading to changes in self-esteem and relationships.

It is clear that on the interpersonal dimensions of affiliation, friendship, and sexuality, the developing child and adolescent are strongly influenced by gender roles and expectations. Does gender play a role of comparable importance in the more individualistic dimension of achievement? As the following section will show, the answer is a resounding "Yes."

ACHIEVEMENT

From an early age, children are expected to respond to the query, "What do you want to be when you grow up?" They soon learn that their gender is relevant to the answer; indeed, the influence of gender exists at every stage in the development of achievement goals and orientation. The different ways girls and boys are treated in task-oriented situations result in different levels of self-confidence, expectations for success, and feelings of self-efficacy and control for the two sexes. The kinds of expectations for their future that are portrayed for them by parents, teachers, school counselors, peers, and the media and the kinds of interests in which they are encouraged or discouraged help shape the specific achievement pathways girls and boys choose to follow and the tasks they try to accomplish.

Socialization for Achievement

When psychologists discuss achievement motivation, they usually mean a person's disposition to seek success: a stable, general personality disposition to strive for success in any situation in which standards of excellence are applied (McClelland et al., 1953). Many researchers have stressed the importance of the parent–child relationship in the development of the child's motivation to achieve. For example, parents may have higher achievement expectations for sons than for daughters. Parents are more satisfied with their daughters' grades than with their sons' grades—even when there is no actual difference between girls' and boys' academic performance (McGrath & Repetti, 2000).

Strangely, the conclusions about the best way to socialize a child to be achievement oriented differ for boys and girls. For example, parental warmth (accepting, affectionate, child-centered behaviors) has more often been found to be related positively to the achievement orientation of males than to that of females (Manley, 1977). Whereas high levels of maternal warmth and affection were associated with strong achievement orientation in boys, moderate warmth and slight hostility related most strongly to girls' achievement orientation.

A number of explanations for the apparently paradoxical situation have been offered. Crandall, Katkovsky, and Preston (1960) suggested that girls who do not receive as much maternal affection turn to achievement as an alternate source of satisfaction. These authors also suggested that the less nurturing mother may be more involved with her own achievement and thus be providing her daughter with a female achieving role model. However, some of the research results themselves may be suspect on the grounds that behavior labeled "hostility" when directed toward girls might not be so labeled when directed toward boys (Hoffman, 1972). Finally, if parental warmth does relate differently to girls' and boys' achievement orientation, the existence of the relationship does not specify cause and effect. It is just possible that parents who see a daughter becoming independent and achievement oriented may withdraw a small portion of their warmth from her, but a son exhibiting similar behavior may be the recipient of extra praise and approval. In other words, nurturing parents may be reinforcing accepted cultural definitions of appropriate behavior for girls and boys.

There are, in fact, indications that such a pattern is sometimes present in the interactions of children with their teachers. For example, a preschool child's compliance with a teacher predicts the teacher's evaluation of the child's intellectual competence—if the child is a girl (Gold, Crombie, & Noble, 1987). Less compliant girls are evaluated as less intellectually competent; compliance does not affect teacher evaluation of boys' competence, however. It appears that female intellectual competence is most likely to be rewarded in the classroom if it is manifested in an "appropriately feminine" way.

An important factor in the socialization of achievement is the presence of models. We have already noted the scarcity of achieving female role models in the media; the presence of real live role models is also important. In fact, when asked who their role models or heroes are, both children (Anderson & Cavallaro, 2002) and young adults (Parsley & Lips, 2007) most frequently list their parents. Where girls are provided with achieving female models, their attitude toward success and career attainment seems to be favorably affected. Girls who attend single-sex schools, where they are exposed to many high-status female role models, have higher career aspirations than do girls in coeducational schools (Watson, Quatman, & Edler, 2002). In middle-class families, daughters of employed women have higher educational and occupational aspirations than do daughters of women who are full-time homemakers (Betz & Fitzgerald, 1987; Etaugh, 1974; Stein & Bailey, 1973). Daughters of employed women also regard the professional competence of women more highly than do those whose mothers work in the home (Baruch, 1972), and there is a correspondence between mothers' and daughters' career interests and aspirations (Zuckerman, 1981). Among African American female college students, those pursuing nontraditional careers were more likely than their more traditional counterparts to have mothers who were well educated and working in nontraditional fields themselves (Burlew, 1982). One study found that as early as kindergarten and first grade girls whose mothers are working in nontraditional fields also tend to aspire to less gender-stereotypic careers (Selkow, 1984). In fact, in the same study, both girls and boys whose mothers were currently employed chose a greater number of future occupations and showed less gender-stereotypic vocational aspirations than did children of non-employed mothers. College women report being inspired more often by outstanding female than male role models; however, the gender of the model appears to make little difference to college men (Lockwood, 2006). Role models may be especially important when it comes to encouraging young women and men to choose nontraditional career paths. One study of female science majors found that almost all of them identified guides such as role models, mentors, or sponsors who had been influential in their choice of science as a career (Downing, Crosby, & Blake-Beard, 2005). These guides were most often women, although men were also cited as important guides.

A gradual reduction in the strength and pervasiveness of occupational stereotyping by gender may be occurring. Indeed, one survey by a task force of the American Psychological Association showed that adolescent girls are more concerned with their future careers and financial responsibilities than with questions of marriage and children (Murray, 1998). Daughters whose parents hold less rigid gender stereotypes are more likely to feel capable of moving in this direction: These young women have a stronger sense that they control their lives, more independent coping skills, and higher achievement test scores (Hoffman & Kloska, 1995). However, many social forces still support the stereotype that men are more achievement oriented, intelligent, competent, and independent than women.

Self-Confidence, Self-Esteem, and Expectations for Success

In adolescence and early adulthood, males show higher self-esteem than females do (Dukes & Martinez, 1994; Keltikangas-Jarvinen, 1990; Richards, Gitelson, Petersen, & Hurtig, 1991). One survey of 2,400 girls and 600 boys in the 4th through 10th grades suggested that the gender gap in self-esteem may widen during adolescence (American Association of University Women [AAUW], 1990). Among children aged 8 and 9, 60% of the girls and 67% of the boys reported feeling confident and positive about themselves. Among high schoolers, however, the percentage who reported feeling positive about themselves was 29% for girls and 46% for boys, leaving a considerably larger gap between the two groups. When the findings were broken down by race, it became clear that many more African American girls maintained high self-esteem in high school than did their European American or Hispanic counterparts. This fits with other findings suggesting that African American female adolescents have higher self-esteem than young Hispanic, Native American, Asian American, and European American women (Dukes & Martinez, 1994). However, the older African American girls showed less positive feelings about their teachers and schoolwork. Hispanic girls expressed less confidence in themselves than African American girls did, and the confidence gap between elementary school and high school was greater for them than that for either of the other two groups.

What is responsible for the apparent gender gap in self-esteem and self-confidence in adolescence, and how do African American girls manage to resist the trend? One researcher who interviewed many girls making this transition argued that, as girls move from childhood to adolescence, they become aware that there is a conflict between the way they see themselves and the way others (teachers, authorities) view them. They suddenly confront a message of female inferiority, exclusion, and subordination (Gilligan, 1990). They can respond to this conflict by submerging their own feelings and accepting the view of reality conveyed by adult authorities or by insisting on their own feelings and knowledge. Many girls follow the first strategy. However, a substantial number of African American girls, buoyed perhaps by the support of their families, choose the second. In so choosing, they may become alienated from the educational system, but their self-esteem apparently remains intact.

Socialization and the presence of gender stereotypes have an impact on the way females and males react to their own achievements. As early as the third grade, boys begin to predict more successful task outcomes for themselves than girls do, a difference that seems to last into adulthood (Crandall, 1969; Vollmer, 1984). The gender difference reflects both an overestimation of their performance by males and an underestimation of their performance by females. Some factors limit this effect. For example, there is evidence that expectations are affected by the gender-role appropriateness of the task. Davies (1989/90) found that, when presented with the same tasks, girls predicted better performance for themselves when the task was labeled "girls generally do better," and boys expected more success when the task was labeled "boys do better"—a finding that is similar to the impact of stereotype threat discussed in Chapter 1. Among a sample of college students, women reported lower occupational performance expectations than men did for male-dominated occupations but higher expectations for female-dominated occupations (Bridges, 1988). More recently, researchers have found that high school girls' occupational aspirations have become more ambitious (Francis, 2002); however, even among gifted students, boys still tend to aspire to careers that are higher in prestige and in educational requirements (Mendez & Crawford, 2002).

The tendency for boys to have higher achievement expectations than girls do may be mainly a European American middle-class phenomenon. African American females tend to have higher career aspirations and expectations than both African American males and European American females (Harris, 1993; E. J. Smith, 1982). Gender differences in achievement expectations and educational attainment do not appear among Asian American students (Brandon, 1991).

The different pattern of gender differences for European American and African American children may relate to teachers' expectations. Both African American and European American elementary school teachers may hold lower expectations for African American males than females (Grant, 1984; Neal, McCray, Webb-Johnson, & Bridgest, 2003; Washington, 1982). Even when teachers are presented with hypothetical case histories in which all qualities are held constant except gender, the teachers consistently hold lower expectations for African American males than for African American females (Ross & Jackson, 1991).

CLASSROOM LESSONS IN SELF-CONFIDENCE   In elementary school classrooms, teachers allow boys more than girls to talk and interrupt them—a practice that ensures not only that more time will be spent on boys' than girls' problems but that both groups will learn that male concerns take first priority. Apparently getting this message, girls ask fewer questions than boys (Pearson & West, 1991). African American girls may escape this pattern in the earliest grades, often receiving more attention and feedback than European American girls. However, by the middle of elementary school, African American girls have apparently been socialized into the same pattern of inconspicuousness to the teacher as their European American counterparts (Irvine, 1986).

Teachers are apparently unaware that they are treating boys and girls differently. The pattern of greater teacher attention to males carries through to college, where women experience the classroom atmosphere as less encouraging for themselves than for men because of an aggregation of small, nonconscious discriminatory actions on the part of professors. Students report that instructors know the names of more male than female students and that female students are more likely than males to be squeezed out of lab projects and demonstrations and are more hesitant to intrude on an instructor's time by asking for help (Schnellmann & Gibbons, 1984; Seymour, 1995). However, male students may also be targets of sexism. One study of medical students found that male students reported being excluded from learning opportunities connected with obstetrics and gynecology, whereas female students reported difficulties in finding supportive mentoring from teaching staff (Nicholson, 2002).

The study of how gender-differentiated patterns of self-confidence in achievement situations are transmitted to children has occupied researchers for many years. One of their chief findings has been that girls and boys are treated differently in the classroom, and the differences produce relatively more feelings of control among boys and relatively more feelings of helplessness among girls (Dweck, 1975; Dweck, Davidson, Nelson, & Enna, 1978; Dweck, Goetz, & Strauss, 1980; Dweck, & Leggett, 1988; Elliott & Dweck, 1988).

Teachers tend to punish boys and girls for different kinds of behavior—boys for being unruly and girls for academic mistakes. However, when praise is handed out to girls, it is likely to be for good appearance or conduct, whereas for boys it is more likely to be for good academic performance. The lessons are obvious: Girls learn that the route to appreciation is by being "good," and boys learn that they are appreciated for their academic efforts. Most damaging of all, perhaps, is the way teachers encourage girls and boys to react to their own mistakes. A boy giving the wrong answer is encouraged to keep trying until he gets it right. A girl is frequently told not to worry about a mistake, and the teacher spends less time suggesting new approaches and encouraging her to keep working on a problem until it is solved. In fact, girls are more likely than boys simply to be left in the dark about the quality of their answers. Teachers often do not tell them whether their answers are excellent, need improvement, or are completely wrong (Sadker & Sadker, 1985). The differences in teacher interactions with boys and girls may communicate that teachers expect more and better thinking from boys. Thus boys are more likely to learn to respond to an unsolved problem as a challenge, whereas girls are given the message that failure is beyond their control.

The consequences of these gender-differentiated patterns of responses by teachers may, paradoxically, be especially severe for high-achieving girls. When students who have been succeeding at problem-solving tasks are then exposed to a task on which they fail, Carol Dweck and her colleagues (summarized in Dweck, 1999) have shown that the highest-achieving girls—the A students—tend to show the most helpless response of any group, trying fewer strategies to solve the new problem and giving up more quickly.

Why are high-achieving girls so vulnerable? Dweck noted that, because girls mature earlier and often cope better and perform better in elementary school than boys do, they are often praised for being good and for being smart. In receiving this praise, the girls are also receiving the message that their traits (such as "goodness" and intelligence) are discernible from their performance outcomes. A diet of early success and praise may encourage these high-achieving girls to adopt what Dweck calls an **entity approach to abilities:** the notion that each individual has a fixed amount of ability, which is revealed by her or his performance. The girl learns to think of herself as smarter than others, a self-description that becomes an important part of her identity. If high-achieving girls accept this belief that intelligence is a fixed entity, and Dweck's research showed that they do in large numbers, they will find failure devastating because failure is taken as a sign that they are "not smart" after all. They will also be reluctant to enter into achievement situations that put them at risk of failure and will concentrate on performance goals (performing well, to demonstrate their ability) rather than learning goals (learning to master something new). As Dweck noted, this motivational pattern may not be a problem for high-achieving girls in elementary school, but

> after grade school, the game changes. Now students that are challenge-seeking and persistent and can tolerate periods of confusion have the advantage. This is because the work becomes more rigorous, as new and different subjects, such as algebra and geometry, are introduced. If bright girls doubt their ability when they encounter challenging tasks, then the occasions for ability doubting and helpless responses will become more numerous. . . . [Furthermore, if] bright girls are most attracted to tasks they're sure they'll do well on (so they can keep on feeling intelligent), then they may opt for easier programs of study, avoiding advanced math and science because these may feel too risky. (p. 124)

Dweck (1999) argued that it is much more important to emphasize challenge, effort, and strategy attributions for both success and failure than to praise students for their ability. Boys are often exhorted to "try harder" in school because they tend to be less attentive and diligent and more disruptive than girls are. Girls are perceived as working well and paying attention and are not given such feedback. Girls learn to make ability attributions for success and failure, which leaves them reluctant to try tasks on which they may fail. According to Dweck,

> Our analysis implies . . . that an emphasis on challenge, effort, and strategy is absolutely essential for girls. Their successes should indeed be praised but for the effort and the strategies that went into them. They should be taught that challenges are exciting and should be praised for taking on challenges and sticking with them. They must learn that the hallmark of intelligence is not immediate perfection, but rather the habit of embracing new tasks that stretch your skills and build your knowledge. (p. 125)

SEXUAL HARASSMENT   Sexual harassment is a common problem faced by female students, and it has a potential impact on self-confidence and achievement. A survey of 8th- to 11th-grade students, sponsored by the American Association of University Women, found that 1 in 3 students fears being sexually harassed in school. After they have been harassed, students tend to avoid the person who harassed them, talk less in class, change their seats, and be reluctant to go to school (AAUW, 2001). A study of secondary school students in the Netherlands found that 72% of the girls reported they had been harassed (Timmerman, 2002). A study of a large, nationally representative sample in Israel, however, revealed that boys were more vulnerable than girls to sexual maltreatment (Khoury-Kassabri, 2006).

Many schools do not have an adequate system for dealing with student reports of sexual harassment, and the absence of such a system communicates to students that the problem is not considered common or serious. Yet the impact on a student's self-confidence of being sexually harassed can be dramatic. One young high school student who had been on the honor roll, a flag corps captain, and a soloist in the school chorus found herself the target of advances from one of her teachers. He stared at her breasts, told her to wear sexier clothes, hugged her, and threatened her with social ostracism if she told anyone about his behavior. This formerly enthusiastic, confident student fell behind in her classes and dropped out of school just before graduation. She said, "I was scared of him, scared of what he might do or say, scared to be alone with him. He ruined high school for me" (T. Moore, 1996, p. 59).

The cumulative effect of the differential experiences of females and males in the educational system is a decrease in the self-confidence of female students—this despite the fact that females generally obtain higher grades than males at every academic level. It is difficult for education to have an empowering effect on girls and women as long as the subtle messages behind teacher–student interactions remain that females are valued less than males, that females are valued more for their appearance and good behavior than for their competence and intellectual skill, and that sexuality can be used as a weapon against female students.

Competition and Cooperation

Much of what is labeled "achievement" in our society is linked to competition, to winning. Gender stereotypes suggest that boys are more competitive than girls, and some research supports the stereotypes. For example, one study of preschoolers found that females preferred cooperative social values, and males preferred competition even before the age of 6 (Knight & Chao, 1989). Among college students, males have been found to perform best in competitive task situations, whereas females perform better in cooperative task situations (S. A. White, 1991). A study of African American sixth and seventh graders found that girls reported a higher preference for cooperative learning than boys did (C. Johnson & Engelhard, 1992). Interestingly, in this study, girls' preference for competition increased as their GPA increased, whereas boys' preference for competition *decreased* as their GPA increased. These are some indications, then, of support for the notion that girls tend toward cooperation and males tend toward competition. However, there are some indications that cooperation and competition may mean different things to boys and girls, so the gender difference may not be as straightforward as it appears.

One study examined the possibility that cooperation and competition in school might be linked with somewhat different attitudes for girls and boys (Ahlgren, 1983). The results showed that during the early school years competition was a more positive construct for boys than for girls. For elementary school boys, competitive attitudes were positively related to a sense of personal worth as a student and to internal motivation, but no such relationships were observed for elementary school girls. In the same age range, however, both sexes showed a positive relationship between cooperative attitudes and personal worth. By senior high school, the sexes were similar in some respects: Both showed a positive link between competition and sense of personal worth and internal motivation, and neither females nor males showed any links between cooperation and negative school attitudes. Nevertheless, some differences still existed. Although boys lost all negative correlates of competition, for girls competition retained some negative associations. Also by senior high school, boys showed no correlation between cooperative attitudes and a sense of personal worth, but girls still showed a link between these two attitudes.

In summary, then, by senior high school, cooperation has become completely positive for both sexes, but girls link it more strongly than boys do to their sense of personal worth. Competition has also become positive for both sexes, but girls retain some negative associations with it. Thus girls seem to end up feeling less comfortable with competition and more conscious of the importance of cooperation than boys do. In view of the strength of gender stereotypes that characterize boys as task oriented and competitive and girls as relationship oriented and cooperative, these findings are not surprising. Girls may find themselves more uneasy than boys are in the

Overview   Gendered patterns of achievement

- Some researchers have found that parental warmth is negatively related to girls' achievement and positively related to boys' achievement, but the reasons for this pattern are unclear.

- Parental and other role models are important for children's achievement. Daughters of employed women have higher and less traditional occupational aspirations than do daughters of women who are not employed.

- Girls and boys do not differ in self-esteem during childhood, but in adolescence and adulthood a difference favoring men appears in some groups.

- At least among European Americans, boys and girls seem to differ in their self-confidence: Boys predict more successful task outcome for themselves than girls do.

- Teachers tend to treat girls and boys differently, placing more emphasis on mastery for boys than for girls.

- Girls and boys develop somewhat different attitudes about cooperation and competition: By the end of high school, girls seem to feel less comfortable with competition and more aware of the importance of cooperation than boys do.

- Sexual harassment in school interferes with academic achievement for a significant number of students, particularly girls.

many achievement situations in our society that stress competition at the expense of cooperation. When cooperation is the requisite orientation for success, however, girls may have the advantage.

Choosing Career Paths

Even in elementary school, children are quizzed about "what they are going to *be*"; by high school, there is considerable pressure on adolescents to choose a career path. It is a truism in vocational psychology that the choice of an occupation is the choice of a means to implement one's self-concept (Super, 1951); thus it is not surprising that such choices reflect gender-role socialization.

Social pressure against choosing occupations that are seen as gender inappropriate is strong. Parents expect their sons to be better at math than their daughters are, and when daughters do succeed in math their parents attribute the success to hard work rather than ability (Räty, Vänskä, Kasanen, & Kärkkäinen, 2002). Children and adolescents continue to express gender-traditional career choices (Eccles, 1994; Hammond & Dingley, 1989; Houston, 1991; Lips, 2004). The high rewards associated with traditionally male occupations are not a sufficient inducement for most young women to follow a nontraditional path. Even among very gifted students, female adolescents indicate career preferences for occupations paying considerably less than the occupations to which their male peers aspire (Kelly & Cobb, 1991; Mendez & Crawford, 2002).

What factors are related to the choice of nontraditional career aspirations? For both African American and European American college women, choosing a nontraditional career is related to holding nontraditional gender-role attitudes and having high educational aspirations. African American women display less conflict over combining professional and family roles in such careers than their European American counterparts do (Murrell, Frieze, & Frost, 1991).

Vocational counselors play a part in guiding males and females into traditional careers. One study, for example, found that practicing counselors reacted more negatively to and were less willing to work with a hypothetical male client who aspired to a "feminine" (nurse) than to a "masculine" (physician) occupation (Fitzgerald & Cherpas, 1985). However, a number of other factors also serve to orient males and females toward traditional career paths, not the least of which may be an awareness of the very real difficulties associated with breaking from the traditional route.

Young women's choices to avoid certain male-dominated fields may be mediated by the ways they have learned to view themselves. For example, if math is a masculine field, why would a woman who thinks of herself as "feminine" want to be part of it? Female college students who implicitly stereotype mathematics as masculine have trouble associating math with their selves, even when they are in math-intensive majors (Nosek, Banaji, & Greenwald, 2002).

Reflections : **Gender and Technology**

Is computing technology one more thing that will give boys an advantage over girls as they prepare for future careers? Some people are afraid so. After all, only about 25% of professionals in information technology fields are women, and there has been a steady decline in the percentage of undergraduate computer science degrees awarded to women over the past two decades. What is more, the shortage of women in computing seems primed to continue: A recent survey of UCLA freshmen found that the women were only half as likely as the men to rate their computer skills as above average, and that they were significantly less likely than the men to use the Web (Hayes, 2002).

For some time, researchers have been concerned that boys seem to take to computers more easily than girls—perhaps because so many computer games involve the traditional masculine entertainments of smashing things, explosions, and physical combat. Once hooked on these games, they may become motivated to write their own programs. Since many girls are not attracted to these games, they do not have a comparable entrée to computing careers.

Computer games are clearly not the only important issue here. As we have seen in this chapter, girls anticipate discrimination when they aim for academic and career fields that are male dominated. However, attraction to technology and its uses would clearly be a way to motivate girls to enter such potentially daunting situations. Is there not a way to attract girls to computing technology?

Yes, there is. In fact, according to a recent study by the Girl Scouts of the USA (2002), it is already in place: instant messaging and e-mail. The majority of girls surveyed reported that they were online seven days a week, usually two or three times a day. The girls viewed being computer savvy as a positive thing, and almost 60% of them said they were the most computer-savvy person in their household. They spent their online time mainly in communication with friends and described such communication as, in the words of one 13-year-old, "an excellent way to become closer to people, talk to people who are far away, talk to people you are scared of talking to in person, and ask questions you need to ask but can't in person or on the phone" (p. 17). Many of them used e-mail for discussing potentially emotional subjects and for confrontations with friends. They also said they were more self-confident when interacting with boys online than face-to-face.

Does the enthusiasm with which girls have adopted instant messaging and e-mail mean that we will soon see more women in information technology careers? It is too soon to say. But at least one observer predicts that instant messaging will be a "gateway addiction" for girls—drawing them inexorably toward self-designed Web pages, JavaScript, and full-blown programming (Hayes, 2002).

And even if young women feel comfortable thinking of themselves as mathematical, they may still resist the idea of adopting a career path in this field. In other words, they may see their current selves as mathematical, but they still do not envision "mathematician" or "physicist" as possible selves for them. In one study, women who saw themselves as positively inclined toward mathematics and science could not or would not endorse the idea of a future career in the realm of engineering and the physical sciences. This might be because such careers were at odds with their notions about femininity or perhaps because they had no female role models in these areas to help them articulate a possible self (Lips, 1993). Whatever the reason, there is more divergence between male and female high school and college students in their views of their possible future academic selves than in their views of their current abilities (Lips, 2004).

Young women may be hindered from staking their futures on male-dominated fields by discrimination. Female university students in male-dominated academic areas report higher levels of current and anticipated future discrimination than do either women or men in female-dominated academic areas (Steele, James, & Barnett, 2002). Perhaps not surprisingly, such women are more likely than other women to think about changing their majors.

Steele and her colleagues also found that female students in male-dominated areas reported experiencing more stereotype threat (which we discussed in Chapter 1) than men in female-dominated areas. For example, they were more likely to agree with statements that, because of their gender, people expected them to have less ability, or professors expected them to do poorly.

Clearly, for adolescents planning their future, there is a potential conflict between career and family life. The conflict is more intense for females, who are more likely than males to anticipate having to juggle two sets of responsibilities (Eccles, 1994; Singer, Cassin, & Dobson, 2005). Yet one national survey of high school students suggested that adolescent girls are now beginning to envision their futures not primarily in terms of getting married but in terms of being able to take care of themselves financially and find the "right" career (Murray, 1998).

There are many signs that young women are aspiring in greater (though still small) numbers to traditionally masculine careers (e.g., National Science Foundation, 2002); however, the reverse trend is much weaker for young men. If gender-role socialization becomes less restrictive, perhaps both boys and girls will learn to base their occupational aspirations more heavily on their individual talents and the needs of the marketplace and less on the arbitrary limitations of masculine and feminine roles.

SUMMARY

Beginning in early childhood, girls and boys learn a different set of expectations. Parents are the first to communicate these expectations, but their influence is quickly built on by the media. Even the patterns of everyday language reinforce the notion that different tasks and occupations are more suitable for one gender than the other and that males represent the norm and females are the exceptions.

In developing a sense of identity, the growing child must develop both a sense of self-in-relation to others and a sense of separateness and individual purpose. Traditionally, the relationship aspect of development has been stressed for girls, and the individualistic, achievement-oriented aspect has been emphasized for boys. Although some research does support the idea that, probably as a result of gender-role socialization, relationships are more important to girls and achievement to boys, other research indicates that for both sexes concern with either of these two domains can interfere with the other. Boys sometimes allow interpersonal concerns to inhibit their achievement strivings, and girls may permit concern over achievements in the social arena (e.g., getting a date for Saturday night) to interfere with ongoing important relationships.

Girls and boys differ in their friendship patterns, with girls having fewer, more intense friendships than boys do and boys more than girls depending on their friends to back them up in conflicts with authority. They also differ in their achievement patterns. Despite a tendency to get better grades at every scholastic level, girls display less confidence than boys in their ability and seem more easily discouraged by failure. Perhaps this is because teachers tend to pay more attention to boys than to girls, to reward boys more for good performance and girls more for good behavior, and to encourage boys more than girls to make "effort" attributions for success and failure.

Finally, as girls and boys begin to develop their occupational goals, they are influenced by gender-role expectations. Boys assume they will someday work to support a family; girls are more likely to assume that their paid work will take second priority to domestic responsibilities. Perhaps with these assumptions in mind, girls report less confidence than boys do that they will achieve their career goals. By adolescence, then, the impact of gender-role expectations has had its effect—through parental admonishments, cartoons and children's books that show men in a wide variety of occupational roles and women in very few, teacher expectations, and counselor bias—on the life goals of girls and boys. Girls and boys have been taught to expect different amounts of control over their lives, and they have been channeled in different directions; as adults, their lives will consequently differ in many respects.

KEY TERMS

identity	constricting interaction	entity approach to
self-in-relation	style	ability
	enabling interaction	
	style	

Family and Friends
Attachment, Intimacy, and Power

*J*n a village in the remote Himalayas, it is common practice for a woman to have several husbands—all brothers. The system ensures that most men will find wives in this land where men outnumber women 4 to 3. It also holds advantages for the women, who need not endure being left alone for long periods of time while one husband is away from home and whose children have several fathers to care for them. Because women are in short supply, they need not put up with an intolerable family situation. Divorce is easy, and every time a woman changes husbands she commands a larger bride-price, usually in recognition of her increased experience and proven fertility (Zorza, 1986).

This example is often surprising to North American observers, yet it is only one of a variety of reasonably satisfactory ways human beings have devised to structure their family and other intimate relationships. Depending on the culture, various versions of **polygyny** (one husband having several wives at the same time), **polyandry** (one wife having several husbands at the same time), or **serial monogamy** (an individual having a series of mates, one at a time) may be taken for granted as accepted practice. People may have most of their needs for intimacy met by their mates, other kin, or same-sex friends. Fathers may be expected to become deeply involved with their children or to have only distant, formal relationships with them. No single arrangement of important relationships is uniformly preferred across human societies (Ingoldsby, 1995).

Relationships with family and friends both reflect and reinforce the gender stereotypes and roles of a society. They help to define the amount and kinds of influence and power available to men and women, and they shape the quality of people's social lives and their sense of personal well-being.

This chapter focuses on the ways close relationships are experienced by women and men, how those experiences are influenced by cultural understandings about gender, and how they are related to the actual and felt control that women and men have in their social environments. In particular, we ask these questions:

- How do women and men form same-sex friendships, and are friendships between women different from those between men?
- How important are cross-sex friendships? What obstacles are there to such friendships?
- How do women and men go about choosing, forming, and maintaining intimate couple relationships? How do expectations about gender influence this process?
- How do men and women use power in their intimate relationships?
- In what ways are the experiences of loneliness and loss of relationships gendered?
- When intimate relationships are formalized into legal marriage, are there different consequences for women and men?
- How large a problem is violence with marriage? How are this problem and society's responses to it shaped by gendered expectations?
- What are the differences and similarities in the ways men and women approach parenthood?

By the chapter's end, we will see that many aspects of adult relationships are shaped by cultural expectations about how women and men should behave.

....

CLOSE RELATIONSHIPS IN ADULTHOOD

Relationships serve important needs for women and men alike. Close relationships fill emotional needs for intimacy and sharing; both close and more casual relationships can fill social needs for companionship, social stimulation, and status. A variety of types of relationships can provide the individual with many forms of social support—everything from comfort in times of deep emotional distress to investment advice to the confidence that someone else will be around to restock the refrigerator when she or he has the flu and cannot venture out. Clearly, such forms of support are important to both women and men, yet the two gender groups have been found to differ somewhat in their expectations of relationships and, to some extent, in whom they count on for what.

Same-Sex Friendships

A pervasive stereotype has held that friendships between males are stronger and deeper than those between females. The notion was eloquently expressed by Montaigne: "The ordinary capacity of women is inadequate for the communion and fellowship which is the muse of the sacred bond of friendship, nor does their soul feel firm enough to endure the strain of so tight and durable a knot." In more recent times, anthropologist Lionel Tiger (1969) proposed that men have a genetically based tendency, reinforced by society, to form nonerotic bonds with other males and that these male bonds are stronger and more stable than those formed between females.

Despite the credence often given the superiority of male-male ties, however, research generally has failed to support them. Enduring, passionate friendships between women have been well documented as forming an important support for women as they have challenged societal rules and restrictions on feminine roles (e.g., Faderman, 1981; Lapsley, 1999). Psychological research indicates that men tend to be lower in affiliation motivation and affiliation values than women (Mazur, 1989). Although young men report more same-sex friendships than women do, these male friendships tend to be different and perhaps less intimate than female friendships (Bank & Hansford, 2000; Claes, 1992).

Researchers who have studied friendship agree that self-disclosure leads to close relationships: Individuals form closer bonds by sharing information about themselves (Dindia, 2002). Gender is related to self-disclosure: Women tend to disclose more about themselves than men do (Dindia & Allen, 1992; Hargie, Tourish, & Curtis, 2001), and women are also more likely than men to be the recipients of self-disclosures (Hargie et al., 2001). Men in the United States are less expressive toward and offer less support to their friends than women do (Bank & Hansford, 2000; Burleson, 2003) and are less likely to ask for support from friends when having problems (Rubin, 1986). A gender difference in the same direction has been found in Russia (Sheets & Lugar, 2005).

Not only gender but also sexual orientation may play a role in self-disclosure, particularly for men (Bliss, 2000). Whereas lesbian and heterosexual women differ little in their reported self-disclosures, gay men report more intimate self-disclosures overall than heterosexual men do. Heterosexual men say they disclose more to their female than male friends, but gay men say the reverse. These findings suggest that gay men move away from cultural norms and male socialization that inhibit men from forming close relationships.

How do women and men view their friendships? When women and men are questioned about their friendships, strong similarities appear in their responses

(Caldwell & Peplau, 1982; Gibbs, Auerbach, & Fox, 1980). However, there are some differences. Women place more emphasis on talking and sharing emotions, and men focus on shared activities (Caldwell & Peplau, 1982; Rose, 1995). In conversations with their best friends, men are more likely to discuss what is going on in the external world—current events, sports, business—and women are more likely to include discussions of feelings and personal concerns (Davidson & Duberman, 1982). Although the kinds of things women and men do with their friends are different, their reports of subjective satisfaction with such friendship activities are about the same (Mazur, 1989). Friendship is ranked among the most significant aspects of life by both women and men (Blais, Vallerand, Briere, Gagnon, et al., 1990). The things that are important to young women and men in these relationships may differ, however. One study examined middle adolescents' ranking of the importance of expressions of and desires for companionship, control, and intimacy in relationships. Males ranked the expression of control highest and expression of affection lowest; females reversed the order (Bakken & Romig, 1992). Although the research on self-disclosure suggests to some that male friendships are less intimate than those of females, some researchers argue that men and women simply define and try to achieve intimacy in different ways (Inman, 1996). Could it be that when men engage in activities with friends and women spend time telling friends about their feelings, both are trying to accomplish the same thing—to build intimacy? Researchers continue to debate this conclusion. Both women and men say they regard self-disclosure and expressiveness as important to building intimate, supportive relationships (Fehr, 2004); however, men seem less likely to engage in such behaviors with their same-sex friends, leading some researchers to conclude that men want less intimate friendships than women do (Burleson, 2003; Fehr, 2004).

An in-depth interview study of friendship attitudes among young, middle-aged, and older adults provides some insights into the differences in female and male friendships in adulthood and the ways these differences may change with age (Fox, Gibbs, & Auerbach, 1985). The researchers found that males consistently tended to be more instrumental, or goal oriented, in their friendships, and females tended to be more expressive, or emotion centered. This difference was particularly noticeable among the young adults (ages 18 to 22). Young men described their friendships as dating back to childhood, often formed through playing on sports teams together, and as durable in the face of disagreements over dissimilarities or disagreements in attitudes or behavior. They avoided confronting friends who did or said things they did not like, preferring to preserve the friendship than to challenge the friend's behavior. Young women, conversely, described their friendships as less durable and more fragile. They were more willing than males to confront their friends over things that disturbed them, and they felt it was important to express their feelings even if it meant sacrificing the friendship. Thus, it appears, young men were more able to enjoy friendships with people with whom they disagreed, perhaps because, as earlier research showed, their major emphasis was on shared activities rather than shared talk. Young women were much more sensitive to disagreement with their friends, feeling perhaps that their definition of true friendship—emotion sharing—could not be achieved with someone whose beliefs or values differed strongly from their own.

Young men appeared to be less aware than young women of the emotional needs that friendship could fill. They spoke far less than the women did about the role of empathy and altruism in friendship; women, however, stressed the importance of being able to reveal themselves and of accepting their friends' innermost feelings.

Among midlife respondents (ages 35 to 55), the instrumental-expressive difference in men's and women's friendship attitudes was still evident. However, men in this age group were more concerned and thoughtful about friendship than younger men were, and the women were more tolerant and less confrontational than younger women. Both sexes expressed a desire to hold on to their friends. Men were negative about too much dependency in friendships, and their concept of need—an instrumental one that included various kinds of concrete help—differed from women's more expressive emphasis on the need to talk, to be comforted, and to share.

Among the older sample (56 and older), both women and men held long-term friendships and were less likely than the midlife sample to be confrontational with their friends. In this age group, men's attitudes toward friendship appeared more idealistic than those of their midlife counterparts. However, men's friendships still differed from those of women in the sense that they tended to originate at work and to focus on shared activities and discussions of such externals as taxes and politics. Women continued to emphasize expressiveness in their friendships.

The authors of this study concluded that major differences exist between women and men in their experience and expression of empathy and altruism in friendship. Women are more likely than men to consider the sharing of feelings a central aspect of friendship. As the authors themselves commented, "Men as well as women defined a friend as someone you could talk to about anything, but when questioned further, the 'anything' for men was sports, politics, and business, and for women was feelings and problems" (Fox et al., 1985, p. 499). Clearly, women and men both have strong needs for friendship, but their friendships differ in the extent to which they provide emotional intimacy.

Various explanations have been suggested for the gender differences in friendship orientation just described. Perhaps men do not need as much emotional intimacy as women do, or perhaps they focus more of these needs on their female friends or partners or perhaps the competitiveness that is socialized into the masculine role is a problem. Competition may make it difficult for men to be open with other men, to "let down their guard," lest it provide these other men with a competitive advantage. It is seen as safer, perhaps, for a man to disclose his feelings to a female friend or partner—someone who is not perceived as a competitor.

Another barrier to intimacy in male friendships is **homophobia,** negative attitudes toward and fear of homosexuality (Morin & Garfinkle, 1978). Although data that demonstrate a causal connection are not available, many writers on the subject of male friendship speculate that the fear of being labeled homosexual inhibits the development of emotional intimacy in men's relationships (Kilmartin, 2000; Rubin, 1986). Still other writers have argued that men *do* achieve emotional intimacy via their friendship style of shared activity. Masculine styles of communicating closeness are simply different—not less intimate—than the more verbally oriented styles favored by women, according to these researchers (Wood & Inman, 1993).

Cross-Sex Friendships

In North America a strong emphasis is placed on having an intimate, loving, sexually exclusive relationship with another person: being part of a heterosexual couple. In fact, the pairing of women and men into such intimate relationships is taken so much for granted that people seem to find it difficult to conceive of female-male relationships that do not fit this pattern. Often we assume any friendly overture from a woman to a man or vice versa is an expression of sexual interest or that any strong bond between a man and woman must have a sexual component. One case in point: When Canadian mountain climber Sharon Wood, the first North American woman to reach the summit of Mount Everest, was interviewed on television, the male interviewer began the session by focusing eagerly on how sleeping arrangements had been managed during the ascent. Had she shared a tent with the men or had she had one to herself? When Wood responded patiently (no doubt she had faced this question before) that she had slept in her sleeping bag, in the same tent as her male coclimbers, who were all her good friends, the interviewer produced a knowing leer. Clearly, he had no conception of the possibility that a woman could live and work closely with a group of men as partners in a challenging expedition without sexuality becoming a big issue—even in the cold, exhausting, oxygen-poor environment of high-altitude climbing.

This tendency to assume a sexual aspect to male-female relationships seems to be stronger in men than women and was illustrated experimentally by Antonia Abbey (1982). Inspired by her own experience and by the anecdotes of other women about having their gestures of friendliness misinterpreted by men as indications of sexual interest, Abbey devised an experiment to see whether the phenomenon was a prevalent one. In the experiment, a series of male-female pairs participated in 5-minute, unstructured conversations in the laboratory, while a hidden female and male observed the interaction. After the interaction, both actors and observers were asked to rate the actors on a number of trait adjectives and to respond to questions about their sexual attraction to and interest in dating the other-sex actor.

The college males in Abbey's study did indeed show a tendency to misperceive female friendliness as an indication of sexual interest. Male actors and observers rated the female actor as more promiscuous and seductive than female actors and observers did. Males were also more sexually attracted to the other-sex actor than females were. Surprisingly, males also rated the *male* actor in a more sexualized way than females did, suggesting that men may be more likely than women to view the world in sexual terms. The tendency for men to perceive less friendliness but more "sexiness" in women's behavior than women do has also been demonstrated in a series of three studies that included not only peer interactions but also videotaped exchanges between a male store manager and a female cashier and between a male professor and a female student (Saal, Johnson, & Weber, 1989).

Cross-sex friendships are common among college students (Bleske & Buss, 2000) and are more likely to be reported by young adults than by middle-aged and older adults (Fox et al., 1985). Is this because the latter groups are more likely to be married, and marriage makes it difficult to pursue cross-sex relationships except as part of a couple? Perhaps, but this remains to be demonstrated. At least one study suggested that being in a committed partnership does not lead to less verbal intimacy in cross-sex friendships (Patford, 2000).

Some research suggests that cross-sex friendships are experienced as less satisfactory than same-sex friendships, especially by women (McWilliams & Howard, 1993; Parker & de Vries, 1993). Among a sample of young adults, cross-sex friendships were reported by both men and women as providing less help and loyalty than same-sex friendships, and the women said cross-sex relationships were less accepting and intimate but provided more companionship than same-sex ones did (Rose, 1985). Members of a diverse sample of urban adolescent girls reported that they were open and honest with their female peers but felt uncomfortable and nervous about speaking their minds to their male peers (Way, 1995). The girls felt it was dangerous to share their feelings with boys and literally silenced themselves in these cross-sex relationships. Among college students, men in one study were more likely to cite sexual attraction and a desire for sex as reasons for initiating cross-sex friendships, whereas

Overview — Gender differences and similarities in adult friendships

Self-Disclosure

- Women disclose more about themselves than men do.

- Women are more likely than men to be recipients of self-disclosures.

- Women's friendships may provide more emotional intimacy.

What Is Important

- Both women and men have strong needs for friendship.

- Both say that it is important to be able to talk to a friend about anything, although they may mean different things by "anything."

- Shared activities may be more important for men than for women.

women were more likely than men to cite physical protection (Bleske-Rechek & Buss, 2001). However, both women and men agreed that kindness, good conversation, and companionship were important reasons for beginning such a friendship and reported that honesty, humor, and dependability were among the most positive characteristics for a cross-sex friend. Both genders also agreed that distrust and betrayal were among the problems most likely to lead to the dissolution of this type of friendship.

Couple Relationships

For many adults, the most important close relationship is a romantic-sexual one in which two individuals develop strong bonds and think of themselves as a couple. Whether the couple is dating, cohabiting, or married and whether it is a mixed-gender or same-gender relationship, gender is one of the most important influences on the structure and functioning of the couple relationship.

CHOOSING A PARTNER AND FALLING IN LOVE   Heterosexual women and men give different responses when asked what characteristics are desirable in a mate. Both women and men are drawn to partners who are physically attractive, but men tend to place greater value on physical attractiveness than women do (Buss, 1989; Feingold, 1990). In one study of adult married couples, the women rated the following characteristics as significantly more desirable for a spouse than the men did: considerate, honest, dependable, kind, understanding, fond of children, well liked by others, good earning capacity, ambitious and career oriented, good family background, and tall. The men rated these qualities as significantly more desirable for a spouse than the women did: physically attractive, good looking, good cook, and frugal (Buss et al., 1990).

Social factors affect the way people perceive attractiveness in potentially eligible romantic partners. A study of unattached bar patrons found that men rated the attractiveness of female patrons higher as the evening wore on, and women showed a similar pattern in their ratings of male patrons (Gladue & Delaney, 1990). This effect was unrelated to the amount of alcohol consumed and suggests that people's perceptions of attractiveness are influenced by the availability of a potential partner. The "availability" effect may work in reverse as well: Individuals who are already involved in romantic relationships see other potential partners as less attractive than do individuals who are unattached (Simpson, Gangestead, & Lerma, 1990).

Interestingly, the sexes differ in the way their expressed preference for particular spousal qualities relates to the type of mate with whom they end up. In this study, the wives of husbands who preferred kind/considerate spouses tended to be agreeable, extroverted, and gregarious, whereas husbands of wives who preferred kind/considerate spouses tended to be submissive, unassertive, and socially passive. In a similar vein, wives of men who preferred spouses to be domestic tended to be warm, agreeable, submissive, and feminine, whereas husbands of wives who preferred domestic spouses were low on dominance and ambition but showed no special evidence of warmth and agreeableness. It appears that a trait such as kindness/considerateness can mean different things in women than in men or that the pool of available people seen to possess a particular characteristic is different or more restricted within one gender group than within the other.

There is a widely held stereotype that, in the interpersonal attraction sweepstakes, "nice guys finish last" with women. Supposedly, women want a man who will take charge and be dominant; they are less interested in someone who is kind, caring, and gentle. According to one group of researchers, nothing could be further from the truth. In three successive studies, they found that men who expressed altruism or who were described as considerate, cooperative, kind, and sympathetic were rated by women as more physically and sexually attractive, socially desirable, and desirable as dates than were men who appeared less caring or agreeable. By contrast, men's dominance alone did not affect women's attraction to them, although dominance did interact with men's prosocial qualities to increase attraction under some conditions (Jensen-Campbell, Graziano, & West, 1995).

Once a relationship has begun, the individuals explore the possibilities for increased commitment. The influence of gender on this process can be considerable. For one thing, young men seem more ready to fall in love than their female counterparts—perhaps because the men are focusing on the woman's physical attractiveness, and the women are looking more pragmatically at the man's education and earning potential (T. L. Huston & Ashmore, 1986). If men do fall in love more quickly, it may mean that early in the relationship men are more motivated than women to try to make a good impression and to work at maintaining the relationship (T. L. Huston & Ashmore, 1986). At any rate, for both women and men, creating a good impression often involves fulfilling gender-role expectations (Zanna & Pack, 1975).

COMMUNICATING   Although there is a great deal of evidence that women prefer more self-disclosure in intimate relationships than men do, reciprocity may dictate similar levels of disclosure between partners. Thus the amount of self-disclosure in a relationship may reflect a compromise between the preferences of both partners (Peplau, 1983). When differences do exist, it is usually the woman who discloses more. Gender differences in the content of self-disclosure have been observed by some researchers, with men being more likely than women to reveal strengths and to hide weaknesses.

In mixed-gender intimate couples, women provide more support to male speakers than men provide for women. Women ask more questions and use "mm's" and "oh's" more to indicate attention and interest than men do (Fishman, 1978). After analyzing more than 50 hours of spontaneous conversations between the members of three couples, Fishman found that 96% of the topics introduced by males "succeeded" (resulted in a conversation in which they were discussed), but only 36% of those introduced by the females did so. Men frequently did not respond or responded minimally to topics raised by women, but women almost always responded to those raised by men. Perhaps because talking does not always get the results they want, women often turn to nonverbal communication to get their point across. Wives have also been found to be better at sending nonverbal messages to their husbands than vice versa (Noller, 1980).

PERMANENCE/STABILITY AND EXCLUSIVITY   There is little direct evidence as to whether women and men differ in their concern with stability or permanence in intimate relationships. Some research suggests that men are more devastated by breakups of intimate relationships than women are (Nolen-Hoeksema & Girgus, 1994; Z. Rubin et al., 1981).

Comparisons of mixed-gender and lesbian cohabiting couples have found that heterosexuals express greater confidence than lesbians do that their relationship will continue in the future (Schneider, 1986). A factor that may be either a cause or an effect of this difference in confidence is the difference in degree of financial interdependence described by the two sets of couples. Mixed-gender couples were more likely than lesbian couples to have joint bank accounts and to have life insurance and wills naming the partner as beneficiary. Perhaps this difference in confidence about relationship longevity will disappear along with the legal and social barriers to joint financial arrangements between same-sex couples. Among both lesbian and gay male couples, high values placed on dyadic attachment (desire for intimacy in close relationships) are associated with expectations of permanence in the relationship and with willingness to move if necessary to maintain the relationship (Peplau & Cochran, 1981; Peplau, Cochran, Rook, & Padesky, 1978).

It is in the area of exclusivity that a striking difference among the relationships of gay men, lesbians, and mixed-gender couples has appeared in the past. When samples of these three groups were asked whether they had had sex with someone other than their primary partner during the past 2 months, 54% of the gay men said yes, compared to only 13% of the lesbians and 14% of college-age dating men and women (Peplau & Cochran, 1981). In the age of AIDS, awareness of the dangers of casual sex has reduced the number of sexual partners for many gay males. However, gay men still report more sexual contacts outside their primary relationship and more permissive attitudes about such contacts than lesbians do (Peplau & Cochran, 1990).

RELATIONSHIP QUALITY AND SATISFACTION   One of the qualities related to the success of a close relationship is **trust**—a multifaceted construct that includes faith that one's partner will act in loving ways whatever the future holds and belief in the partner's behavioral predictability and personal dependability (Rempel, Holmes, & Zanna, 1985). Both women and men view trust as crucial in close heterosexual relationships. However, they view it somewhat differently. For women, the three components of trust are integrally related. For them, trust includes not only faith in the partner's future caring but also belief that the partner is a dependable person, as consistently confirmed by predictable behavioral evidence. For men, the three components of trust appear to be less integrated; they can, for instance, focus on faith in a partner's future caring without putting too much emphasis on the more pragmatic concerns of dependability and predictability. John Rempel and his colleagues (1985) offer two possible explanations for the gender difference. First, women may be more concerned with the practical aspects of interpersonal behavior because they are often in positions of greater dependency in close relationships. Men, being less dependent, can perhaps afford to take a more romantic viewpoint. Second, and equally plausible, is the possibility that women are more sensitive to relationship issues than men are and so are more likely to evaluate the future of a relationship with reference to its past and present. For both women and men, however, trust seems to evolve in a reciprocal cycle in which trust leads to positive attributions about their partners, and positive attributions lead to greater trust (Miller & Rempel, 2004).

Many similarities exist among heterosexual, gay, and lesbian couples in the factors that relate to relationship quality. For example, poor relationship quality has been linked in all three groups of couples to arguing about money management, intrusion of work into the relationship, spending much time apart, and nonmonogamy (Blumstein & Schwartz, 1983). Also, love for partner has been linked to the perception of many barriers to leaving the relationship and to high dyadic attachment (Kurdek & Schmitt, 1986b). Gay male couples often endorse conventional heterosexual notions that relationships should be romantic and monogamous, worry about sexual infidelity, and are reluctant to disclose sexual encounters outside the relationship (Worth, Reid, & McMillan, 2002). However, some differences are evident among the different kinds of couples. Reciprocal dependency and equality of power have been found to be particularly important for the relationship quality of lesbian couples, whereas financial equality and similarity of educational level have emerged as especially important for the relationship quality of gay male couples (Blumstein & Schwartz, 1983).

In a comparison of married, mixed-gender cohabiting, gay, and lesbian relationships, Kurdek and Schmitt (1986b) found that the four partner types differed both in relationship quality and in the variables that predicted relationship quality. Cohabiting mixed-gender partners had the lowest love for partner and relationship satisfaction scores relative to the other three groups, who were indistinguishable from one another on these scores. Married partners reported the most barriers to leaving the relationship, and cohabiting mixed-gender partners reported the fewest. Gay male partners were more likely than the other groups to believe in "mindreading"—a belief that partners should know each other's thoughts without having to say them out loud. Lesbian couples exceeded all other groups in shared decision making. Gay and lesbian couples perceived less social support from friends and family for the relationship than did either the married or unmarried mixed-gender couples. Despite these differences, however, the major correlates of relationship quality were similar across the different groups of couples. Dyadic attachment was an important predictor of love for each partner type and an important predictor of liking for married, gay, and lesbian partners. For each partner type, relationship satisfaction was predicted by seeing few good alternatives to the relationship, high shared decision making, and few beliefs that disagreement is destructive to the relationship.

A study of relationship satisfaction in 275 dual-career lesbian couples showed that the strains of pursuing careers and couplehood are not limited to heterosexual couples. In this study, the more role conflict and need for personal autonomy were experienced by individuals, the lower was their satisfaction with the relationship (Eldridge & Gilbert, 1990). Differences between the partners' levels of career commitment were also associated with lower relationship satisfaction. Shared attachment, power, and intimacy were all positively related to satisfaction with the relationship.

Men are more likely than women to be satisfied with their marriages (Fowers, 1991). However, wives and husbands have a tendency to emphasize different things when determining satisfaction. For example, as a knowledge of traditional gender roles might lead one to expect, husbands' satisfaction is related more strongly to their wives' performance of household activities than it is to how affectionate their wives are; the reverse pattern is found for wives' satisfaction (Huston & Ashmore, 1986). In a similar vein, wives' satisfaction is related to husbands' employment stability and income, but the reverse is not consistently found for husbands' satisfaction (Karney & Bradbury, 1995). Although such findings are likely a direct consequence of gender-role expectations that the husband should be the main provider and the wife the main caretaker of the home, researchers do not seem to have directly tested this question. Perhaps partly because of such gendered expectations, there are gender differences in the sources of annoyance that heterosexual partners report as a result of each other's behavior. Women are more annoyed by behaviors that threaten the relationship and by aggressive behaviors, men by behaviors that threaten their autonomy and by the withholding of sex (Laak, Olthof, & Aleva, 2003).

How do individuals decide how satisfactory their relationship is? One of the most powerful standards applied by both women and men in evaluating a relationship is that of fairness or justice. According to this model, the partners ask themselves whether they are getting benefits out of the relationship that are fair with respect to their contributions and to their partner's benefits and contributions. The contributions and benefits that partners put into their implicit equations may include such intangibles as love, understanding, and sympathy as well as more concrete factors such as money, status, and the performance of needed tasks.

The difficulty with studying fairness is that what seems perfectly fair to one person may appear profoundly unjust to someone else. Indeed, many of us have observed close relationships in which the participants seem quite satisfied despite what appears to be a most inequitable arrangement. Nonetheless, researchers have shown that perceived **equity**—the extent to which the ratio of each partner's contributions to rewards is seen to be equal—predicts marital satisfaction for both women and men (Burley, 1995; Utne, Hatfield, Traupmann, & Greenberger, 1984).

Equity theorists argue that it is the participants' weighting of the contributions and benefits that determines perceived equity, not some outside observer's assessment of the situation. Thus, for example, one couple may think it a perfectly fair exchange for the wife to do all the housework and child care while the husband earns all the income and looks after the car. But such an arrangement might appear grossly unjust to another couple.

Attitudes about how particular contributions and benefits should be weighted are influenced to some extent by self-interest (e.g., each individual may see the tasks she or he performs as being more important or more difficult than those that the other performs) and by cultural and peer attitudes and expectations (e.g., in a social environment that takes traditional gender roles for granted, the arrangement described in the preceding example would seem more fair than it would in a less traditional environment). In fact, women and men both seem to be influenced by traditional gender roles in their perceptions of what is a fair division of household labor, which in turn affects marital satisfaction (Wilkie, Ferree, & Ratcliff, 1998).

POWER AND INFLUENCE IN INTIMATE RELATIONSHIPS   Even in the most intimate of relationships, both partners do not always want the same thing. Thus each partner must face the problem of asserting his or her own wishes and of getting the other partner to comply or at least not interfere with them. The problem is a difficult one, for it implies possibility of conflict—and conflict, if not handled well, can be the enemy of love. For example, people who perceive their partners as engaging in bullying tactics are likely to report low relationship satisfaction and to predict that the relationship will not last (Howard, Blumstein, & Schwartz, 1986).

Conflict does not have the same implications for women and men in intimate relationships. Wives are more likely than husbands to say that marital conflict interferes with their feelings of love for their partner (Huston, McHale, & Crouter, 1986; Kelly, Huston, & Cate, 1985). Could this difference be a result of greater power held by men in these relationships? Or perhaps of the different ways women and men *use* power in intimate relationships?

Those who study gender and power in intimate relationships focus on exactly these issues. They ask whether gender is related to the amount of success one partner has in influencing the other and whether gender is related to the *way* one partner goes about trying to influence the other. These are questions of **interpersonal power**: the ability of one person to get another person to do what the first person wants in the face of resistance from the second person.

As noted in several earlier chapters, men are often seen to hold more status and power, as a group, than women. It might be reasonable to expect that this power asymmetry would be reflected in the intimate relationships between individual women and men. Perhaps, too, same-gender intimate relationships would be characterized by greater equality of influence between the partners than would mixed-gender relationships. Furthermore, it might be expected that, given female–male differences in status, access to resources, and learned gender roles, the influence tactics used in intimate relationships might differ for women and men. Are such expectations confirmed by the research? The answer is "Yes," to some extent, but, as usual, the pattern of gender differences is not as simple as the theory predicts.

Before examining the research findings on power in intimate relationships, we need to look briefly at theories of power in general. One of the basic ideas in this area is that power is based on control of resources (French & Raven, 1959; Raven, 1965) and, thus, on one person's ability to affect the outcomes that occur to the other person (Thibaut & Kelley, 1959). The more resources relevant to another person's life that you control, the more you are able to affect what happens to that person and the more power you have relative to that person.

It is important to remember, though, that the translation of power into the ability to influence another is based on both individuals' perceptions of the situation. If the other person does not realize, for instance, how much power you have to affect his or her life, your attempt to influence that person may not work. However, if the other person imagines that you have control over resources or outcomes that you really do not have, that person may give way to your influence despite your objective lack of power.

The kinds of resources on which power can be based include various types of rewards and punishments, expertise, legitimacy of position, the ability to inspire identification and liking (referent power), and information (French & Raven, 1959; Raven, 1965). In any intimate relationship, each partner has some resources on which to base power, but one partner may have more than the other. The situation is made even more complex by what social exchange theorists call the **principle of least interest;** that is, the person who is least dependent on the other for rewards—who needs the relationship least—has the most power (Homans, 1974).

In intimate relationships, we might expect that access to bases of power and the amount of interpersonal dependence would affect both the amount of influence and the influence tactics employed by the partners. We might also expect that such issues of power and dependence would be related to the gender of the partners involved—that, for instance, in heterosexual couples, men would be likely to control more resources such as money, expertise, and status by virtue of their privileged position in society. In most mixed-gender couples, the man is also bigger and stronger than the woman—a not insignificant power advantage. Finally, in a patriarchal society, the man is seen, normatively, as the dominant partner or the "head of the house," and this perception endows him with power based on legitimacy. Power based on liking or attraction may be distributed equally between the partners or may favor the woman. In same-gender couples, there is less reason to expect particular power asymmetries, although particular imbalances may exist in individual couples.

Toni Falbo and Anne Peplau (1980) examined the influence strategies that members of heterosexual, gay, and lesbian couples reported they used in their intimate relationships. They were able to categorize the strategies along two dimensions: **directness** (direct-indirect) and **interactiveness** (unilateral-bilateral).

The directness dimension refers to the openness or obliqueness that character-izes an influence attempt. A straightforward request or order would be a direct influence tactic, for instance, whereas a behind-the-scenes manipulation of the situation to favor one's own preferred outcome would be an indirect tactic. The interactiveness dimension refers to the degree of mutual engagement with the partner required in the influence attempt. An extremely unilateral strategy, such as giving an order or walking out on the other person, involves no mu-tual engagement at all; a bilateral strategy, such as arguing or bargaining, re-quires considerable engagement and interchange.

Using these dimensions, Falbo and Peplau found that influence strategies varied according to the partners' perceptions of power in the relationship. In heterosexual, gay, and lesbian couples, individuals who preferred and per-ceived themselves as having more power than their partner said they used more direct and bilateral influence strategies. Conversely, those who saw them-selves as having less power than their partner reported using more unilateral and indirect tactics to get their way. Finally, as suggested by the intergroup gender differences in power and status, gay and lesbian partners were less likely than were mixed-gender partners to want more power than their part-ners or to view themselves as having such a power advantage, and women in heterosexual relationships were more likely than men were to feel at a power disadvantage. Across the groups, women showed a greater preference than men did for equal power in their relationships. Further research has confirmed that spouses who see themselves as equal partners are more satisfied with their relationships (Aida & Falbo, 1991; Kulik, 2002).

Perceptions of power are situational and may vary from interaction to in-teraction for the same couple. One study showed that both wives and hus-bands were more likely to be demanding (exerting pressure through emotional requests, criticisms, or complaints) when discussing a change that *they* wanted and to be withdrawing (retreating into defensiveness and passive inaction) when discussing a change that the *partner* wanted. On the whole, however, men were more likely than women to withdraw from their spouses during marital conflict (Christensen & Heavey, 1990).

Another study of the connection between gender and power in intimate relationships examined the relative importance of the following on the in-fluence tactics used in same-sex and cross-sex intimate relationships: gen-der, gender-role orientation, control over structural resources (money, education, age), physical attractiveness, and dependence on the relation-ship (Howard et al., 1986). Unlike Falbo and Peplau, whose respondents were undergraduates in relationships that were relatively new, these re-searchers studied a cross-section of adults in long-term relationships. They identified six categories of influence strategies: (1) manipulation (e.g., drop-ping hints, flattering, behaving seductively), (2) supplication (e.g., pleading, crying, acting ill or helpless), (3) bullying (e.g., threatening, insulting, be-coming violent), (4) autocracy (e.g., insisting, claiming greater knowledge, asserting authority), (5) disengagement (e.g., sulking, leaving the scene), and (6) bargaining (e.g., reasoning, offering to compromise). Stereotypically, manipulation and supplication are weak strategies, and bullying and autocracy are strong ones.

The researchers expected that the use of the "weak" strategies of manipulation and supplication would be linked to being female, being relatively less masculine and more feminine, having relatively less structural power, and being more dependent on the relationship than one's partner was. What they found was that, although the *actor's* gender did not relate to influence tactics, the *partner's* gender did. Both females and males with male partners were more likely to use the weak influence strategies than were females and males with female partners. As the authors suggest, "The power associated with being male thus appears to be expressed in behavior that elicits weak strategies from one's partner" (p. 107).

The researchers also found that having control of fewer resources, such as having less income or seeing oneself as less attractive than one's partner, is linked to greater reported use of supplication and manipulation, as is greater dependence on the relationship. However, these differences in structural power did not themselves account for the effects of gender on influence tactics. In other words, gender was related to power in these intimate relationships above and beyond other forms of power and dependence. Men's capacity to elicit deferential behavior cannot be completely explained by their access to money and expertise; rather, being male in our culture is correlated with so many sources of power (e.g., status, legitimate authority, size, strength) that it would be difficult to measure them all in one study. Moreover, growing up with all these indicators of power, males may develop behavior patterns, perhaps without even realizing it, that tend to elicit deference and "weak" influence strategies from others. There is much yet to learn about the dynamics of interpersonal power and influence, but it is certainly clear that gender and power are linked in intimate relationships—a link that is probably both caused by and supportive of the intergroup gender differences in power and status.

Finally, influence strategies may be shaped by gender expectations and by the quality of the couple relationship. In one study of actual negotiation behaviors in heterosexual dating couples, women and men used relationship referencing (e.g., "you should do this for the good of the relationship") equally when trying to influence their partners, and being subjectively close to their partner was associated with more use of relationship referencing by both men and women (Oriña, Wood, & Simpson, 2002). Interestingly, when women or men who were subjectively closer to their partners were trying to initiate change in the relationship, their partners were more likely to use relationship referencing to resist the change (e.g., "My position is consistent with keeping our relationship healthy"). However, women were more likely to use coercion (e.g., punishment, expressing negative emotions, or derogating the partner), and men were more likely to use logic and reasoning strategies (e.g., "If we do it this way it will be consistent with values you have always said are important to you"). The latter difference is consistent with gendered expectations for women to be more emotional and men more logical.

Loneliness

We have seen that gender has implications for both friendship and intimate "couple" relationships. It seems also to have implications for the way perceived scarcity or deficiency in such relationships—loneliness—is experienced. Given the differences in males' and females' orientation to close relationships, we might expect that females would be more likely than males to notice and to be bothered by deficiencies in their relationships and thus to feel lonely.

Some researchers have indeed found that women report more loneliness than men do (e.g., Weiss, 1973). However, given the difficulties with intimacy that some researchers have noted among men, it might be expected that men would report more loneliness than women do—and some researchers have found this pattern as well (e.g., Schultz & Moore, 1986).

In an effort to make sense of the evidence on this issue, Shelley Borys and Daniel Perlman (1985) classified the existing studies into those that had used a standard questionnaire measure of loneliness, the UCLA Loneliness Scale (D. Russell, Peplau, & Cutrona, 1980), and those that had used a self-labeling measure of loneliness (responses to questions such as "How often do you feel lonely?"). Although most studies using the UCLA scale showed no gender differences in loneliness, those that did find a difference almost always found males scoring lonelier than females. However, among the 11 self-labeling studies, 9 showed that women were more apt than men to label themselves lonely. Borys and Perlman suggested that the incongruent results for the two types of studies derive from the way questions were asked. The UCLA scale asks respondents about the quality of their relationships but does not ask them whether they would label themselves lonely. Perhaps men, because of social influence pressures, are simply more reluctant than women to admit to being lonely. In support of this explanation, Borys and Perlman (1985) offered the results of their own study indicating that college students are more rejecting of a lonely male than of a lonely female. Their findings suggest that the negative consequences of admitting loneliness are less for women than for men, at least among young adults.

One study (Schultz & Moore, 1986) has shown that there may be qualitative as well as quantitative gender differences in loneliness. These researchers examined the factors that were associated with loneliness for female and male college students. They found that lonely males were more likely than lonely females were to suffer from negative mood and negative self-evaluations—a finding that may mean that males tend to blame loneliness on their own failures, whereas females are more likely to blame it on external circumstances. This study also showed that loneliness was more strongly linked to a reported lack of social risk taking for males than it was for females. This finding is not surprising, the authors suggested, given that gender roles place more of the onus for initiating social contact, especially cross-gender contact, on males than on females.

Taken together, the two findings suggest that, at least for college students, the relatively greater degree of control over heterosocial relationships that is assigned to the masculine role can backfire on men. Charged with the responsibility for making contacts, men who are hesitant to take social risks may not only feel lonely but also blame their own inadequacies for their loneliness. Women, whose feminine role gives them more support for waiting to be approached, can at least blame some of their loneliness on the social ineptitude of their male acquaintances. In the realm of close relationships, then, it appears that even reactions to the *absence* of such relationships is influenced by gender-related expectations.

The finding that lonely young men are more likely than lonely young women to feel depressed and self-critical is echoed in a later finding: Male and female high school students differ in the music they enjoy when they are lonely (Gibson, Aust, & Zillman, 2000). Lonely young women are more likely than their nonlonely counterparts to enjoy listening to songs that celebrate love. The opposite is true for young men: When they are lonely, they are *less* likely to enjoy songs that celebrate love. Maybe these songs encourage the young women to hope that eventually the right man will come along, but they are heard by young men as reminders of their inadequacies.

AGING, THE LOSS OF RELATIONSHIPS, AND WIDOWHOOD   For both women and men, aging is often associated with the loss of important relationships—a situation that can lead to loneliness. Gender is an important variable here, not only because women outlive men and so are more likely to be widowed but also because gender stereotypes and expectations shape the ways elderly people cope with loss and loneliness.

Most studies find that widowers have an advantage over widows in their practical resources, such as income, education, and freedom from health restrictions. They are also more likely than widows to remarry. However, widows seem to have more interpersonal resources and varied sources of support, including close female friends and involved neighbors. Women who have been widowed report greater life satisfaction than their male counterparts do—an effect that goes counter to women's generally greater financial stress and more frequent somatic symptoms (Stevens, 1995). Widowed men are more vulnerable to depression than women are, and the strains associated with widowhood differ for women and men (Siegel & Kuykendall, 1990; Umberson, Wortman, & Kessler, 1992). In general, it appears that widowed men are more likely than widowed women to feel alone and lonely. (Figure 11.1 shows numbers of widowed and divorced males and females.)

Among the elderly in general, women may feel more unhappy about aging and more lonely (Imamoglu, Kuller, Imamoglu, & Kuller, 1993). Both women and men may experience the loss of the work role at retirement as isolating and depressing (Perkins, 1992) and may feel alone and depressed because of physical

Figure 11.1   Widowed and divorced males and females 15 years and older, all races, 1993–2005.

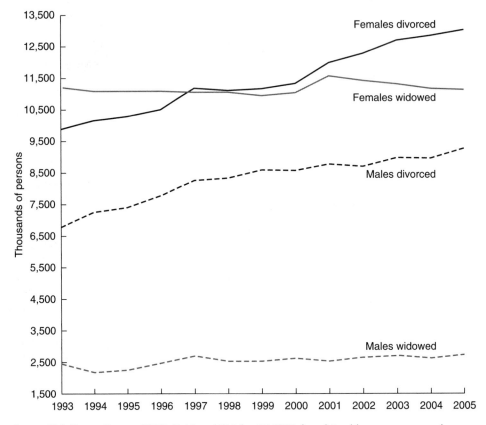

Source: U.S. Census Bureau (2006). Retrieved October 17, 2006, from http://www.census.gov/population/www/socdemo/hh-fam.html

limitations. In one sample of elderly African Americans, women were more likely than men to report memory problems, and loneliness was found to be the strongest predictor of such self-reports (Bazargan & Barbre, 1992).

For older women, marital status has an important impact on friendship networks and the exchange of social support. Among single, older, childless women, those who have never married report more life satisfaction, even though they do not necessarily have more social contacts (Rice, 1989). In this study, never-married women reported fewer social contacts than widowed women did; however, they were less affected by the absence of such contact. Never-married women are more likely than married women to have pursued careers; their sources of life satisfaction may include a variety of nonrelational factors. Marriage also shapes the ways that older women relate to friends and family. Older married women provide more help and support to family members

Overview — Gender differences and similarities in intimate couple relationships

Choosing a partner
- Men are more likely to say physical attractiveness is important.
- Women are more likely to say it is important that their partner be considerate, honest, fond of children, and a good earner.

Communicating
- Self-disclosure in a couple is a compromise between the preferences of the two individuals.
- In mixed-gender couples, women tend to provide more support for male speakers than vice versa.

Stability and exclusivity
- Men may be more devastated than women by breakups.
- Gay men are more likely than members of mixed-gender or lesbian couples to say they have recently had sex with someone other than their primary partner.

Relationship satisfaction
- Women tend to have a more integrated view of trust in their partner than men do.
- For all types of couples, poor relationship quality is linked to arguing about money; good relationship quality is linked to high attachment to the partner and the perception that there are many barriers to leaving the relationship.
- Men are more likely than women to be satisfied with their marriages.
- Equity is important to both men and women in all kinds of couple relationships.

Power and influence
- In couple relationships, the principle of least interest implies that the person who needs the relationship least has the most power in the relationship.
- Women are more likely than men to say that conflict with their partner interferes with love.
- Men and women are likely to have access to different bases of interpersonal power.
- Women are more likely than men in mixed-gender couples to see themselves as having a power disadvantage.
- Gay and lesbian partners report less desire than mixed-gender partners for having more power than their partners.
- Both women and men with male partners may be more likely to use "weak" influence strategies with their partners.

Loneliness
- Women are more apt than men to label themselves lonely.
- Men seem more likely than women to blame themselves for their loneliness.

than widows do; however, widows spend more time and give more practical help to friends than wives do (Gallagher & Gerstel, 1993). Gallagher and Gerstel suggest that marriage "privatizes women's help to others—it provides them with both the resources and opportunity to help those related, while it reduces help—both its breadth and intensity—to those not related" (p. 675). Here again, it appears that relationships are influenced by role expectations.

MARRIAGE:
THE INTIMATE ECONOMIC PARTNERSHIP

When an intimate heterosexual relationship is legally formalized through marriage or acknowledged by the partners to be a permanent living-together arrangement, new issues must be faced. Besides such emotional concerns as love, trust, and satisfaction, the spouses must now confront problems of dividing up the household work, sharing income, and making joint decisions regarding employment, housing, children, and so on. The partnership is more than a close personal relationship: It is an economic and legal one as well. If a couple is formally married or, in some jurisdictions, become common-law spouses simply by living together for a specified length of time, they have agreed, albeit often without realizing it, to abide by the terms of a marriage contract.

The terms of the marriage contract are not negotiable by the two partners; they are legal rights and responsibilities spelled out by the government. The terms cover such things as how property is shared during the marriage and divided upon divorce, sexual exclusivity, financial support, inheritance, responsibilities for children, and even the woman's right to keep her own name. As Sapiro (1986) noted, the marriage contract is virtually the only one that most people enter without knowing the terms and that can be changed by a third party (the government) while it is in force and without notification of the involved parties. Moreover, private agreements between a wife and husband that contravene the terms of the marriage contract are not enforceable by law.

Although the marriage contract used to be based on the notion that a woman, upon marriage, came under the more or less complete authority and ownership of her husband, legal changes, such as the introduction of community property laws, have removed some of the inequality built into the marriage contract. However, the idea that women are subordinate to their husbands is still built into the marriage contract in many jurisdictions. Many brides still promise to obey their husbands. In many countries, women's groups are still working to effect changes that would equalize the rights of wives and husbands in marriage. For example, Thai women have been lobbying for passage of legislation that would allow a woman to keep her birth name when she marries instead of being required to take her husband's name (*Washington Post*, 1999), and in India women are resisting the traditional practice in which the bride's parents pay a large dowry to the groom's family—essentially buying a husband for their daughter (Duff-Brown, 2003). And in Mexico the law only recently changed so that officials performing marriage ceremonies do not have to include wording mandating that the groom treat the bride "with the magnanimity and generous benevolence that the strong must have for the weak, essentially when this weak creature gives herself unto him" (Dellios, 2006, p. A18).

The economic laws and customs surrounding marriage are still largely based on assumptions about family structure and stability that do not fit current social patterns. The core of these assumptions is that women and children will have a man to provide for them. However, instead of a relatively permanent arrangement that includes one employed spouse, one homemaker, and children, families now must often respond to divorce, remarriage, out-of-wedlock births, and the necessity for two incomes. When family-disruptive events such as divorce, job loss, or disability occur, women are more likely than men to experience significant drops in their access to resources and well-being (Burkhauser & Duncan, 1989).

The Division of Labor

Until the 1970s, the basic assumptions of the marital economic arrangement in middle-class urban families were that the husband was responsible for the economic support of the wife and children and the wife was responsible for most of the domestic labor. It was even suggested that our society measured a man's masculinity by the size of his paycheck (Gould, 1973). The husband's breadwinner role was often considered his most important function by men and women alike, and a survey by Yankelovich (1974) suggested that for about 80% of employed married men the provider role gave purpose and meaning to life and to jobs that were otherwise not very satisfying. The assumption that the man should be the chief breadwinner and the woman his helpmate and homemaker has been widely questioned or rejected outright as women move into the paid workforce in large numbers. In fact, what appears to have happened in many cases is that the woman has kept most of the domestic role while taking on an increasingly larger share of the breadwinner role. Yet in married couples the employment of both spouses is clearly linked to the economic well-being of the family, as shown in Figure 11.2.

Studies show that the movement of wives into the paid labor force has not been accompanied by an equal shift of husbands into greater participation in housework (Baxter, 1992; Biernat & Wortman, 1991; Golding, 1990). Women still spend twice as many hours as men do on family-related work (U.S. Bureau of Labor Statistics, 2006a). Employed married women spend fewer hours doing household tasks than unemployed married women do, and husbands put in some time on household chores to compensate for their wives' busier schedule. Recent time use studies show that on an average day 53% of women but only 19% of men reported doing housework, such as cleaning or laundry, and that 66% of women but only 19% of men reported doing food preparation (U.S. Bureau of Labor Statistics, 2006a). For adults living in households with children under the age of 6 years, women spent an average of 1.1 hours per day in the physical care of children (e.g., bathing, dressing, feeding), whereas men spent an average of 30 minutes in such activities. Although women still do twice as much child care and housework as men do, the amount of such work

Figure 11.2 Married couples' total money income in 2005 by husband's and wife's patterns of work experiences and number of related children under 18 years of age for all races.

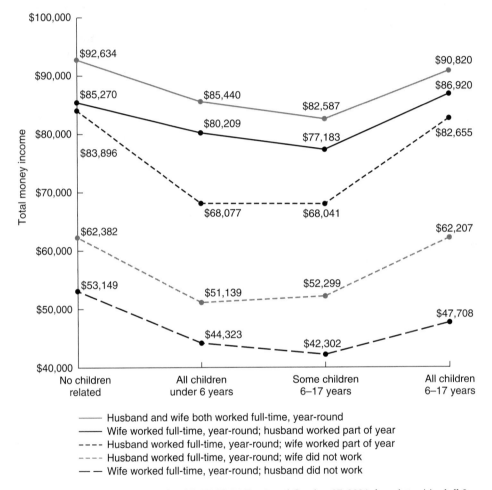

Source: U.S. Census Bureau (2006), table FINC-04. Retrieved October 27, 2006, from http://pubdb3 .census.gov/macro/032006/faminc/new04_000.htm

done by men *has* increased over the years. For example, married fathers spent an average of 9.7 hours a week on housework in 2000, compared with only 4.4 hours per week in 1965, and the time they spent on child care (including physical care, play, and other child-centered activities) more than doubled, from 2.6 hours to 6.5 hours a week (Bianchi, Robinson, & Milkie, 2006).

Although the gender gap in housework is widest among married persons, women do more housework than men do in every type of family living situation: never married and living with parents, never married and living independently, cohabiting, married, divorced, and widowed. The impact of gender is multigenerational; that is, an adult son living at home increases women's housework, whereas an adult daughter living at home decreases housework for both women and men (South & Spitze, 1994).

What affects the relative contributions of women and men to household labor? The number of children increases women's domestic labor but has no effect for men. Men with liberal gender-role attitudes spend more time on housework, but women's gender-role attitudes have no relationship to the amount of domestic work they do. Economic power also plays a role. The more the husband's earnings exceed those of the wife, the larger is the wife's share of the housework (Baxter, 1992).

Both African American and Hispanic American men are less likely than Anglo men to view the division of household labor as unfair. However, African American and Anglo women are more likely than their spouses to perceive unfairness (John, Shelton, & Luschen, 1995). It appears that, at least under some conditions, African American men spend more time doing household work than either Hispanic or Anglo men do (Hossain & Roopnarine, 1993; John et al., 1995).

An obvious explanation for the continuation of a fairly traditional spousal division of household labor in the face of changing ideologies about gender roles is that women and men each feel more skilled at the tasks that fall within their traditional spheres. Indeed, women are less likely to see the lopsided division of family work as unfair when they enjoy doing it and when their spouses view them as especially competent at doing such work (Grote, Naylor, & Clark, 2002). Although they do different kinds of work, women and men often find themselves putting in similar amounts of time and effort. Susan Bianchi and her colleagues (2006) found that in two-parent families the total hours of work put in by mothers and fathers was roughly equal when both paid and unpaid work were considered. However, women do more of the unpaid (and lower status) household work, as seen in Figure 11.3.

Beginning in childhood, females and males are assigned tasks on the basis of their gender appropriateness (L. White & Brinkerhoff, 1981), so it is not surprising if men and women each have more confidence in their skill at gender-traditional chores. However, life repeatedly confronts us with the necessity of learning new activities, and most household tasks are far from impossible for an intelligent adult to master. Why, then, does the traditional division of labor persist? Part of the answer lies in an examination of power inside and outside the marital relationship.

Issues of economics and exchange cannot be separated from issues of power and control, and one factor that slows down the change away from the traditional division of economic responsibilities in marriage is that the change threatens men's "legitimate" power as head of the household. Social norms are such that a man can still feel that his masculinity is impugned if he does too much housework or if he appears too responsive to his wife's demands for sharing in the area of domestic chores. One comprehensive review of the literature on power in marriage showed that the lowest marital satisfaction and happiness were reported in couples in which the wife was dominant in decision making—perhaps because both partners were acutely conscious of the extent to which their

𝓕𝑖𝑔𝑢𝑟𝑒 11.3   Percentage of time per day spent by married persons with spouse present on selected primary activities, by gender, 2005.

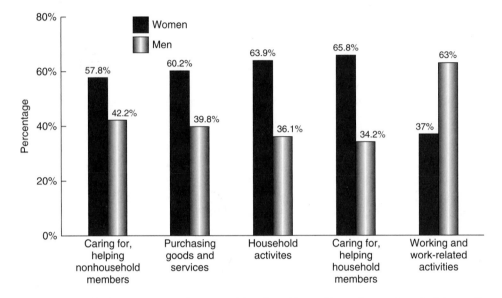

Source: Bureau of Labor Statistics (2005). Retrieved from http://www.bls.gov/news.release/pdf/atus.pdf

arrangement violated social norms (Gray-Little & Burks, 1983). Another study revealed that men's feelings of subordination at work were negatively related to the amount of housework they were willing to do at home: The more subordinated they felt at work, the less housework they did (Arrighi & Maume, 2000).

Most people will agree that housework is generally not "fun." If a person can get away with letting someone else do it, she or he will. In many marriages, men *can* get away with letting their wives do the housework by using power based on the legitimacy of gender roles ("It's not my job—it's the wife's job") or helplessness ("I can't do it as well as you can"). The assignment of the bulk of household tasks to women is further supported by the imbalance of financial contributions brought to the marriage by each spouse. Even when both spouses are employed, the husband usually earns more than the wife, making her more economically dependent on the relationship and hence more influenceable and more likely to try to maintain equity in the relationship by contributing in nonfinancial ways (Scanzoni, 1972). Increased sharing of domestic chores within a marriage is intricately bound up with changes in gender-related ideology and actual gender equality in the larger society.

NONTRADITIONAL FAMILIES   Some families have broken dramatically with tradition in their division of labor. According to some estimates, for instance, in about 3 of every 10 dual-earner couples, the wife earns more than the husband (Wenner, 2000), and there are between 1 million and 2 million men in the United States who have taken on the role of "househusband" (Doyle, 1995). These men stay at home and take the major responsibility for housework and child care, while their wives are employed full-time. The few studies of these men that have been done suggest that their role is experienced as a positive one. Not surprisingly, those who have freely chosen the role are most happy with it (Lutwin & Siperstein, 1985), and fathers who become the primary care-givers experience an improved relationship with their children (Tillitski, 1992).

Many families are not based on the unions of female-male couples. Same-gender couples, like mixed-gender couples, often form permanent re-lationships, involving economic interdependence and the rearing of chil-dren. One such family is described in an article by Lindsy Van Gelder (1991). Two women in a committed lesbian relationship wanted to have a child. They searched for and found a man who was willing to be the biological father of that child. That man, also gay, ended up making a commitment to maintaining a relationship, both emotional and financial, with the child he had fathered. The child, Sarah—a little girl of 6 at the time the article was written—consequently has a family of three adults: Nancy, her mother; Amy, her mother's partner; and Doug, her father. The three adults are good friends, and all share the par-enting of Sarah. The arrangement produces some difficulties in terms of ex-plaining the family to the rest of the world, but it has many advantages as well. Three adults rather than two share the responsibilities, and barriers exist that prevent the family from falling into the stereotypical divisions of labor and power often found in more traditional families.

The legal system in the United States has generally been hostile to gay and lesbian parents, often making it difficult for them to retain or gain custody of their children (Falk, 1989). For this reason, gay- and lesbian-headed families have often, by design, remained relatively invisible. However, estimates of the num-ber of lesbian mothers in the United States range from 1 million to 5 million; those for gay fathers range from 1 million to 3 million. These gay and lesbian par-ents are raising an estimated 6 million to 14 million children (Patterson, 1992).

Research on such families suggests that there is no psychological justification for the legal reluctance to safeguard lesbians' and gay men's marital or parental rights (Herek, 2006). One reviewer noted that not a single study has found chil-dren of gay or lesbian parents to be disadvantaged in any way relative to the chil-dren of heterosexual parents (Patterson, 1992). Children of gay and lesbian parents are no more likely than other children to have difficulty with gender identity or gender-role acquisition, and they are no more likely to be homosexual in their orientation than children of heterosexual parents (Patterson, 1992; Tasker & Golombok, 1995) although they may be less constrained by gender roles (Stacey & Biblarz, 2001). Children of gay, lesbian, and heterosexual parents show no dif-ferences in frequency of emotional disturbance, self-concept, locus of control, moral maturity, intelligence, peer relations, social relations with adults, or other measures of cognitive functioning and behavioral adjustment (Anderssen, Amlie, & Ytteroy, 2002; Flaks, Ficher, Masterpasqua, & Joseph, 1995; Gartrell, Deck, Rodas, Peyser, & Banks, 2005; Patterson, 1992).

Marital Violence

More frequently than we care to admit, coercive power within the marriage relationship is exercised through physical violence. In 18% of all violent crimes against women in the United States, the perpetrator is an intimate (husband, ex-husband, partner, boyfriend, or ex-boyfriend). Only 3% of violent crimes against men are committed by intimates (Catalano, 2006). In 2004 about 33% of female murder victims were killed by an intimate, whereas about 3% of male murder victims were killed by an intimate (Fox & Zavitz, 2006). Figure 11.4 shows rates for murder victims of intimate partners. The preponderance of female victims in violent crimes against intimates is striking—particularly when this pattern is contrasted with that for victims of violent crimes perpetrated by casual acquaintances or strangers. As illustrated

Figure 11.4 Murder victims of an intimate partner by gender and race, 1976–2004.

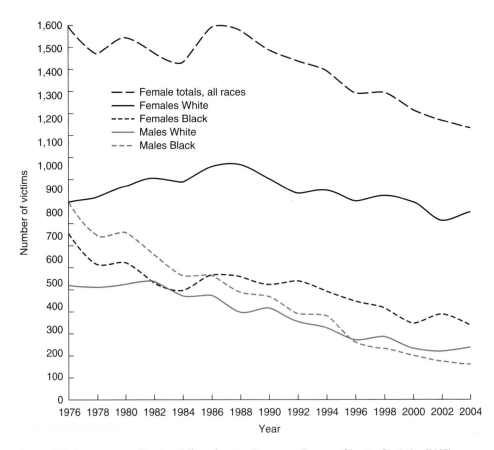

Source: U.S. Department of Justice, Office of Justice Programs, Bureau of Justice Statistics (2005). Retrieved October 17, 2006, from http://www.ojp.usdoj.gov/bjs/homicide/intimates.htm

Figure 11.5 Victimization rates for persons age 12 and over, by types of crime, relationship to offender, and gender of victim, 2003.

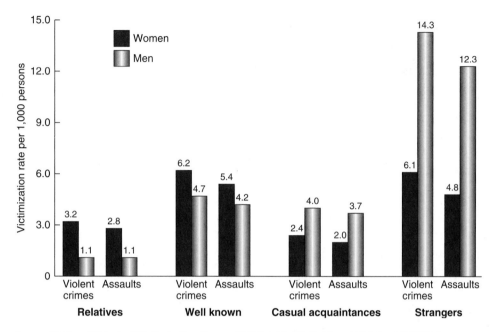

Source: National Criminal Victimization Survey (2003), table 35. Retrieved October 23, 2006, from http://www.ojp.usdoj.gov/bjs/pub/sheets/cvsprshts.htm

in Figure 11.5, males are far more likely than females to be the targets of violent crime by strangers.

Physical violence in intimate relationships can begin even before marriage. Studies have found that about 20% of courting couples report that physical violence has occurred in their relationships (Silverman, Raj, Mucci, & Hathaway, 2001), and this violence tends to continue as couples progress from dating to marriage (Murphy & O'Leary, 1989).

Domestic violence is a worldwide problem. For example, in one survey of Nicaraguan women, 52% of those who had ever been married reported that they had been abused physically by a partner at some point in their lives (Ellsberg, Caldera, Herrera, Winkvist, & Kullgren, 1999). In Chile, where domestic violence is often called "private violence" or "la violencia privada," one survey suggests that 1 of every 4 women is beaten by her partner (McWhirter, 1999). In Japan, a husband's violence is the second most frequent reason given by women who petition the courts for divorce (Kozu, 1999). In post–Soviet Russia, it is reported that between 14,000 and 16,000 women are killed each year by male partners (Horne, 1999). And in India, where one estimate suggests that every 6 hours a young married woman is beaten or burned to death or driven to commit suicide, a law forbidding domestic violence has only recently taken effect (BBC, 2006).

Violence within marriage is linked historically to a legal definition of the family that made it acceptable for a man to exercise his authority over his wife by beating her (MacLeod, 1980). From ancient Greece and Rome to Europe in the Middle Ages, men could beat or kill their wives with impunity. As late as the 19th century, British law books stated that the husband could exercise his power and dominion over his wife by beating her, although the beating must not be cruel and violent! Even in the present day, there is some tendency for judges to avoid "interfering" in wife abuse cases because family matters are supposed to be private.

Marital violence is usually initiated by the husband, but, as the pattern continues, the wife will often fight back (Saunders, 1986). The violence usually increases in severity over time (Frieze, 1986), becoming so dangerous that in about one-third of the cases the victim must seek medical treatment for her injuries (MacLeod, 1980). The female victim often becomes isolated from other people and faces a growing sense of powerlessness and helplessness as she tries and fails to change the situation in some way that will stop the violence (L. E. Walker, 1979). Eventually, the woman may try to leave the relationship but often returns because she has nowhere to go or feels too frightened and inadequate to make it on her own. As the violence becomes even more extreme, she may finally leave because she fears for her life or the lives of her children, or she may actually try to kill her husband.

People who do not know the facts about wife abuse often believe women stay in abusive relationships because they are masochistic. In fact, the reasons for staying in a violent marriage have much more to do with situationally determined issues of power and control in the family than with personality dispositions. The woman who wants to leave an abusive marriage often faces a lack of external resources for doing so: no monetary resources to draw on, no way to protect herself against violent retaliation from her husband if he comes after her, no friends or family who can help her, and no accessible shelter for battered women (Frieze, 1986). Moreover, her sense of self-confidence has been drained by the relationship. Physically abusive husbands are usually verbally abusive as well, and wives often endure long strings of insults about their competence, their appearance, and their sexuality along with the beatings (Walker, 1979). All of these factors conspire to place the abused woman at a huge power disadvantage with respect to her husband. Add to this some common beliefs, such as that all men are violent anyway or that her violent husband needs her, and it becomes easy to see how strong are the pressures on an abused woman to remain in the relationship (Frieze, 1986). Once a woman has left the relationship temporarily by escaping to a shelter for battered women, her reported exposure to psychological abuse is a better predictor of intentions to leave her spouse than is her reported exposure to physical violence (Arias & Pape, 1999).

When a woman does try to separate from or divorce an abusive partner, she risks further violence. Risks of extreme violence and murder are highest when the victim seeks freedom (Pagelow, 1993), and restraining orders are not always effective. If a wife reveals, during separation or divorce proceedings, that she has been abused by her husband, she may not be able to substantiate her claims because she and her husband have hidden the violence over the years. Thus the violence-based power dynamics that characterized the marriage may not end with the couple's separation.

Although both men and women may behave violently toward their partners, men are more likely than women to be perpetrators of domestic violence (Bornstein, 2006), and it is men who inflict the most serious abuse (Holtzworth-Munroe & Stuart, 1994). Moreover, the factors associated with violent behavior toward a spouse or intimate partner are quite different for men and women. Men who have a high need for power are more likely to abuse their partners, but women's need for power is unrelated to abusive behavior (Mason & Blankenship, 1987). Assaultive men are often not only high in the need for power but also low on verbal assertiveness toward their spouses, suggesting that violence may sometimes stem from the frustration of not having the verbal skills to exert influence (Dutton & Strachan, 1987).

Some research indicates that within violent marriages husbands with less power are more physically abusive toward their wives—another indication that violence may sometimes serve as a replacement for other kinds of male power (Babcock, Waltz, Jacobson, & Gottman, 1993; Sagrestano, Heavey, & Christensen, 1999). In line with such findings, researchers have shown that, in dating couples, men who are dissatisfied with the amount of power they have in the relationship are most likely to engage in both psychologically and physically abusive behaviors toward their partners (Ronfeldt, Kimerling, & Arias, 1998). One in-depth interview study of the experiences of 9 male batterers suggested that for some men being violent in a domestic relationship comes from their desire to assert a preferred identity—perhaps the identity of being the one in charge or in control—and avoid a devalued identity (Reitz, 1999). Important themes that emerge in violent relationships are attachment and dependency. One study of couples' reactions to breakups revealed that individuals who were physically violent with their partners were higher in attachment anxiety (i.e., insecurity about their relationships and their ability to elicit care from others) than those who were not violent (Davis, Shaver, & Vernon, 2003). And an overview of research on domestic violence showed that economic dependency in women and emotional dependency in men both contribute significantly to the likelihood that a woman will be abused by her domestic partner (Bornstein, 2006). Women who depend on their partners for economic support have less power in and fewer alternatives to their relationships and so are more vulnerable to abuse; they are also less likely to terminate an abusive relationship. This relationship becomes circular because an abusive relationship often restricts or reduces a woman's ability to establish economic independence. Men who are emotionally dependent on their partners and who are prone to become jealous when they perceive their partner is becoming close to someone else (even if this perception is incorrect) are more likely than other men to abuse their partners.

Women who report behaving violently toward their spouses are usually being treated violently by these same spouses; however, men who report being physically or psychologically abusive toward their partners are frequently not receiving the same kind of abuse (Mason & Blankenship, 1987). Lenore Walker (1999) noted that the most frequent type of aggression reported by women in some surveys is biting, "which is obviously used as a defensive strategy to get out of a stronghold" (p. 24). Also, young women's expression of and receipt of violence in adult love relationships appears to be correlated more strongly with having been abused as children than does young men's violent behavior in such relationships (Marshall & Rose, 1990).

Studies of men who repeatedly assault their wives suggest that the men tend to blame their wives or external circumstances for their aggressive behavior. One analysis of wives' reports of their husbands' behavior after a "typical" battering incident showed that only 8% of the men apologized, and 80% acted as though nothing had happened (Dobash & Dobash, 1984). A study of 75 men with histories of repeated wife assault found that about one-fifth of them excused their assault as not their responsibility but accepted that the act was wrong. The other four-fifths of the men accepted personal responsibility but found ways to justify their actions—by blaming the victim, saying that they had been too angry to control themselves, or claiming that their behavior was in line with the norms of their particular subcultural or ethnic group (Dutton, 1986). In this study, men who blamed their wife for the assault were more likely than other men to minimize the frequency, severity, and consequences of their violence.

General comparisons between violent and nonviolent partners may sometimes obscure important differences among types of batterers. An understanding of the different types of male batterers may increase the effectiveness of treatment programs. One review suggested that there are three major types: the *family-only batterer,* who focuses his violence on family members and who may have a passive/dependent personality; the *dysphoric/borderline batterer,*

Overview   Marital violence

- Women are many times more likely than men to be assaulted violently by an intimate.

- Individuals who are targets of marital violence often stay in the relationship because of a lack of resources and support.

- Although both men and women are sometimes violent toward their partners, men inflict the most serious damage.

- Abusers often justify their actions by blaming their partners.

who exhibits high levels of depression and anger, whose violence may sometimes extend outside the family, and who may have a borderline personality disorder; and the *generally violent/antisocial batterer,* whose levels of extrafamilial violence and criminal behavior are high and who has a marked tendency toward alcohol or drug abuse (Holtzworth-Munroe & Stuart, 1994). Another study, based on an examination of 200 seriously violent couples, classified male batterers as either "pit bulls," whose emotions quickly boil over into violence when they are angry, or "cobras," who are cold and methodical in their violence (Jacobson & Gottman, 1998). Different factors may be correlated with violent behavior from men in each group; more research is needed to develop interventions that may be useful with the various groups.

It is clear that intimate relationships involve issues of power as much as issues of attachment and caring. Couple relationships exist not in a social vacuum but against a background of social norms and legal rules that encourage or tolerate certain kinds of behavior. As long as those norms continue to encourage inequality between husbands and wives and to tolerate the use of violence as a way of exercising power in these relationships, marital violence, particularly wife abuse, will continue to be a problem.

WOMEN AND MEN AS PARENTS

In the popular imagination, one of the largest assumed gender differences is in parent–child relationships. Many people think of women as naturally nurturant, with a built-in instinct for mothering, and of men as second-class parents, more clumsy and less involved with their children. In fact, the notion that women have an inborn maternal instinct played a large role in shaping the history of psychologists' study of human caregiving behavior (Shields, 1984). Many early psychologists saw motherhood as women's most important function, and, until recently, psychologists concerned with the study of parenting examined only mother–child relationships (Silverstein & Phares, 1996).

Our culture abounds with images of mother nurturance. Anthropologist Ashley Montagu's (1952) comments are representative: "The sensitive relationships which exist between mother and child belong to a unique order of humanity, an order in which the male may participate as a child, but from which he increasingly departs as he leaves childhood behind" (p. 142). Michelle Hoffnung (1995) describes what she calls the "motherhood mystique"—a constellation of romanticized attitudes about motherhood that has influenced women to feel guilty or inadequate if they do not have children or if they do not devote themselves full-time to their children. The mystique says that only by having a child can a woman actualize her full potential and achieve the ultimate meaning of her life. Motherhood, according to this myth, is complementary with and does not interfere with the other traditional feminine roles of wife and homemaker. Furthermore, a "good" mother is always patient and content, never resentful, and available to her child 24 hours a day.

This mystique surrounding motherhood, which dates only from the 18th century (B. Harris, 1979), has formed the basis for what Adrienne Rich (1976) calls the institution of motherhood: the set of social prescriptions and norms that limit women's choices in and shape their experience of motherhood. Our society has institutionalized motherhood in such a way that mothers are assumed to have primary responsibility for children, are given little recognition and almost no support in this task, are isolated with their children much of the time, and are expected to experience nothing but fulfillment and a self-sacrificial glow as they live out this role. Rich attempts to convey some of the ambivalence experienced by a woman caught in this institution of motherhood:

> The physical and psychic weight of responsibility on the woman with children is by far the heaviest of social burdens. It cannot be compared with slavery or sweated labor because the emotional bonds between a woman and her children make her vulnerable in ways which the forced laborer does not know; he can hate and fear his boss or master; loathe the toil; dream of revolt or of becoming a boss; the woman with children is a prey to far more complicated, subversive feelings. Love and anger *can* exist concurrently; anger at the conditions of motherhood can become translated into anger at the child, along with the fear that we are not loving"; grief at all we cannot do for our children in a society so inadequate to meet human needs becomes translated into guilt and self-laceration. This "powerless responsibility," as one group of women has termed it, is a heavier burden even than providing a living—which so many mothers have done, and do, simultaneously with mothering—because it is recognized in some quarters, at least, that economic forces, political oppression, lie behind poverty and unemployment; but the mother's very character, her status as a woman, are in question if she has "failed" her children. (pp. 35–36)

The motherhood role may be institutionalized differently in different cultures. In Japan, for example, traditionally the role of mother has been associated with independence and power. Mothers have had almost complete control over child rearing, have directed their children's education, and have been able to influence government and community leaders when speaking as guardians of the new generation. Japanese women have perhaps been able to gain status, respect, and a personal sense of self-worth from their role as mothers (Bankart, 1989). As the options open to women in Japan increase, however, young women appear to be very realistic about the amount of work involved in motherhood and reluctant to accept motherhood as their sole route to fulfillment.

One of the goals of the feminist movement has been to gain for women the right to choose or refuse motherhood. Although the advent of effective contraception and safe access to abortion has made it much easier than it used to be for women to put off or avoid motherhood, the social expectations that continue to surround motherhood still make it difficult for women to combine motherhood with other goals. Whereas men rarely face a choice between career and parenthood, that choice is still a painful reality for many women. Women with paid jobs face this conflict starkly with their first pregnancy. For those who cannot afford sufficient maternity leave, depression stemming from over-load is a real risk (Hyde, 1995). Greater child-care responsibility is associated with lower well-being and greater psychological distress among professional women who have just had their first child (Ozer, 1995).

Immediately after the birth of a first child, trying to balance family and oc-cupational roles can be overwhelming if a woman does not have practical help and support from a spouse or other family members and institutional support from her employer. Many women cannot count on such support. As Betty Friedan (1981), who argued persuasively that feminism must not deny or de-value the human importance of love, parenthood, and family, noted,

> The price of motherhood is still too high for most women; the stunting of abilities and earning power is a real fear, because professions and careers are still struc-tured in terms of the lives of men whose wives took care of the parenting and other details of life. The point is that *equality*—the rights for which women have been fighting for over a century—was, is, necessary, for women to be able to affirm their own personhood, and in the fullest sense of choice, motherhood. The point is, the movement to equality and the personhood of women isn't finished until motherhood is a fully free choice. (p. 87)

As women approach motherhood, they are not oblivious to the problems associated with it. Among first-time expectant parents, age and duration of marriage are positively linked to good feelings about the pregnancy for men but not for women (Lips, 1983). Apparently, the older and more established in her life a woman is, the more she knows she will have to give up in becoming a mother. The older the woman in this sample, the more likely she was to agree that she could have a fulfilling life without children. Despite this awareness, however, women were more likely than men to link having children with ful-fillment of their gender roles and with having a satisfying life.

Parenthood is, however, a potential source of joy and transformation for both mothers and fathers. Expectant and new parents—female and male—often report strong feelings of happiness, hope for the future, and a change in their concept of relationship from "couple" to "family" (Lips, 1982c; Lips & Morrison, 1986). Yet, in general, the behavioral correlates of these attitudes are quite dif-ferent for mothers and fathers. Despite claims that father nurturance is on the rise, studies have estimated the amount of time fathers spend with children at 12 minutes a day (Lamb, 1987), 26 minutes a day (Gottfried & Gottfried, 1988), 36 minutes a day (Robinson, Andreyenkov, & Patrushev, 1988), 1.7 hours a day (Sanik, 1990), just over 2 hours a day (Hossain & Roopnarine, 1993), and 2.3 hours a day (Bond, Galinsky, & Swanberg, 1998). Even in the latter study, which included only dual-earner families, wives spent about an hour more per day with their children, and both parents worried that they did not have enough time to spend with their children. Recent time use survey data show that, in families where there are children under the age of 6, married fathers spend an average of 1.16 hours per day caring for children; in families with children aged 6 to 17, fathers spend an average of 22 minutes per day on their care (U.S. Bureau of Labor Statistics, 2006a).

From the beginning of a baby's life, fathers are more likely to be found playing with the baby, and mothers are more likely to be found feeding, changing, dressing, or cleaning him or her. In fact, regardless of the espousal of egalitarian ideals by couples or of social class or dual- or single-earner status, the birth of a baby is the occasion for a shift toward a gender-traditional division of roles (Lewis & Cooper, 1988; Moss, Bolland, Foxman, & Owen, 1987). This shift is associated with more stress and dissatisfaction among mothers than fathers.

The amount of time fathers spend with their children sometimes increases as the children grow older. This increase has been noted especially in the case of male children, with whom fathers often become involved in particularly "masculine" aspects of socialization such as sporting activities (Starrels, 1994).

Division of child-care work is an issue for gay and lesbian couples too. Lesbian parents report more satisfaction with their relationship when involvement in child care is more evenly divided (Patterson, 1995). Gay male parents, like heterosexual parents, report euphoria when the baby first arrives, followed by stress as they try to redesign their relationship to accommodate the demands on time and energy associated with a new baby (Silverstein, 1996). Parents of all persuasions must "learn on the job," and they become more skilled with practice (Lamb, 1987). Perhaps parents in nontraditional families sometimes try harder to develop the appropriate skills. One study showed lesbian couples to have more parenting awareness skills than heterosexual parents (Flaks et al., 1995).

Despite the "motherhood mystique" and the lack of adequate child-care participation by fathers, mothers of young children have entered the paid labor force in large numbers. Although "working mothers" often experience a great deal of conflict and guilt about the harm they may be doing to their children, research on the effects of maternal employment indicates that school-age children suffer no emotional or intellectual deprivation as a result of maternal employment (Hoffman, 1974). In addition, preschoolers often benefit socially and intellectually from child care outside the home (Clarke-Stewart, 1991), and some women are better mothers when they are employed (Schubert, Bradley-Johnson, & Nuttal, 1980).

Even infants do not seem to be adversely affected by being cared for extensively by caregivers other than the mother (Mott, 1991). One large-scale study, which followed thousands of children, found that children whose mothers worked during the first 3 years of their lives were not significantly different from children whose mothers were not employed during their first 3 years on the outcome variables of the study: obedience, behavior problems, cognitive development, self-esteem, and academic achievement (Harvey, 1999).

Of course, the impact of maternal employment must vary with the kind of child-care arrangements mothers are able to make (Scarr, 1998), as well as with such variables as the mother's attitude toward employment and the support she gets from her partner. When women are given the same supports that men are for working—the knowledge that their children are being well cared for in their absence and that their paid work is valued by other family members—maternal employment is apparently a positive, rewarding choice for women and their families. However, only a lucky minority of women have access to such support.

Gender differences in parental behavior, like so many other gender differences, can be understood at least partially with reference to learned social roles, ongoing social expectations, and access to power. First, the socialization process tends to strengthen the female's and minimize the male's attachment to children; the feminine and masculine roles have a strong influence on responsiveness to the young (Silverstein, 1996). Second, the social arrangements that support these feminine and masculine roles—the unavailability of paternity leave, the demand that "work" take place from 9 to 5 each day—make it difficult for people to be flexible, even if they are so inclined.

In a study of new parents, Susan McHale and Ted Huston (1984) found that the more the mother worked outside the home, the less central was the child to her activities when she was at home, and the more competent and interested a man was in child care before becoming a father, the more he actually did with his child later on. As the authors noted, these findings could be explained as stemming from social norms that give mothers little leeway with respect to child care and fathers little freedom of choice with respect to employment. In other words, individual differences in attitude are more likely to influence behavior when the person is free to decide whether to engage in the behavior.

The McHale and Huston (1984) study has some practical implications for increasing fathers' involvement in child care. The strong correlations they found between fathers' perceived skill at child-care tasks before their babies' birth and these fathers' later involvement in child care suggest that giving fathers practice or training in child-care activities may increase their participation in the care of their infants. The researchers also found that the extent to which the mothers were nontraditional in their gender-role attitudes and role preferences was positively related to their spouses' involvement in child care—suggesting, perhaps, that "women must be willing to step back from the role of primary caregiver if fathers are to become more involved in caring for their sons and daughters" (p. 1360). Women may be unwilling to step back, however, if they feel that child care is their major sphere of influence and expertise in the family. Moreover, the "motherhood mystique" ensures that a woman will feel guilty at first for giving up any aspect of the traditional mothering role, no matter how competent and willing her partner is.

Many fathers are motivated to be involved with their children and to do well in their paternal roles. Recently released data from a large government survey in the United States showed that almost 94% of men ages 15 to 44 either agreed or strongly agreed with the statement that "the rewards of being a parent are worth it, despite the cost and the work it takes" (Martinez, Chandra,

Abma, Jones, & Mosher, 2006). The same survey reveals that men are generally aware of the importance of shared parental and economic roles within marriage. A majority of men (almost 60%) either disagreed or disagreed strongly with the statement that "it is much better for everyone if the man earns the main living and the woman takes care of the home and family." And more than three-quarters of the men surveyed either agreed or strongly agreed that "it is more important for a man to spend a lot of time with his family than to be successful at his career."

Although most of the research on parenting has focused on women and men in two-parent, heterosexual families, parenting obviously takes place in a variety of family contexts. Besides dual-earner and wife-as-sole-earner families—the more commonly acknowledged variations on the traditional family—parenting takes place in stepfamilies and single-parent families, by parents who do not live with their children and see them only on weekends, and by

---

Reflections The Importance of Fatherhood

For years, mothers felt guilty about their inadequacies at child rearing and often blamed themselves if their children did not "turn out" well. Meanwhile, fathers, secure in their role as breadwinners, were not encouraged to worry about the impact their absence or relative lack of involvement might be having on their children. All that has begun to change as researchers have delved into the importance of fathers to their children.

Longitudinal studies of the impact of fathers on children show what many people have suspected all along: The way fathers interact with their children matters a great deal. Children grow up to form closer, more trusting relationships with others if their fathers played with them in sensitive, supportive, and challenging ways when they were toddlers (Grossman, Kindler, & Strasser, 2003). Indeed, the quality of fathers' play is as important or more important than the mother–child bond in predicting children's later ability to form healthy relationships. And the quality of a child's attachment to a father at age 5 predicts a whole host of variables at age 9—including anxiety, self-confidence,

and the likelihood of being accepted by peers (Verschueren & Marcoen, 2003).

But to form those important bonds with their children, fathers have to be available, and many of them have not yet figured out how to do this. The more hours fathers spend at work and the more money they make, the less time they spend with their children—an effect that is not found for mothers (Hofferth & Anderson, 2003). Fathers are increasingly searching for ways to spend time being engaged with their children, but they may feel that they cannot afford to take the unpaid paternity leave that is available under the Family Medical Leave Act. A survey by the U.S. Department of Labor found that the most common reason given by employees for not taking parental leave is that they cannot afford to (Waldfogel, 2001).

Those who do take time off work to spend in child care often find the experience rewarding—and they may be bolstered by these new findings that suggest it will be rewarding for their babies too.

gay fathers and lesbian mothers. All of these groups encounter special difficulties, but perhaps their greatest shared problem is their invisibility.

We continue to think of families in traditional terms and to assume that families that differ from the "normal," two-biological-parent model generate problems for their members. Such an assumption has, for example, been behind the notion that any problems experienced by the high percentage of African American families that are headed by women stem from the way the family is structured rather than, as seems more likely, from the fact that female-headed families are much more likely than are two-parent families to be living below the poverty line (Kemp, 1995). Similarly, the assumption that families should conform to the "man as provider, woman as nurturer" model has been responsible over past decades for the insistence that Native American groups abandon their own family traditions and conform to those of the dominant White culture (Almquist, 1995). The idea that children cannot be raised well by same-gender parents is one of the arguments sometimes used to deny legal recognition of gay and lesbian partnerships—even though researchers have found no relationship between parents' sexual orientation and their ability to provide children with a healthy family environment (Herek, 2006). Families are changing, and our vision of the family and our research have not kept pace with these changes.

SUMMARY

The influence of gender on peer and family relationships is rooted in our socialization into feminine and masculine patterns of behavior and maintained by social arrangements that favor these patterns. Girls learn at an early age that intimate, self-disclosing friendships are rewarding and socially approved. Boys learn equally early that too much intimacy with another male is often regarded with suspicion in a society influenced by competitive and homophobic attitudes. The narrow emphasis on sexuality in female–male relationships makes it difficult for cross-sex friendships to develop, and the separation of males and females into different kinds of jobs and even different domestic roles contributes further to this situation.

Intimate sexual/affectional relationships between women and men share many features with intimate sexual/affectional relationships between men or between women. However, a major difference between same-gender and mixed-gender intimate relationships is that there tends to be more emphasis on equality between the partners in lesbian and gay relationships than in heterosexual relationships. This difference probably derives from the difficulty mixed-gender couples have in separating their relationship from a social context in which men are accorded more status and have access to more bases of power than women do. The influence of this context is particularly apparent in the institution of marriage, in which the authority of husband over wife is legally entrenched in some respects. The impact of assumptions about gender differences and the man's right to have authority over the woman can be seen in the problems that beset many heterosexual couples: inequitable division of household labor and the use of violence by men against their partners.

Relationships between parents and their children are also conditioned by gender-role ideology and the power differences between women and men. Women are supposed to be naturally interested in and good at parenting, by virtue of their sex. The motherhood mystique encourages them to feel guilty if they find motherhood uninteresting or problematic or if they try to combine it with other goals. Men, in contrast, have often not been expected to be particularly interested or involved in child care, although there is evidence that these expectations are changing.

Changes in families over the past two decades—the increase in employment among mothers and the rise in single-parent families—have led to fears that the family is disintegrating. Some have even accused the feminist movement of destroying the family. Perhaps what is being destroyed is the monolithic conception of the family as a patriarchal structure in which the husband is the breadwinner and head, the wife is the caregiver and supporter, and the children grow up lacking all but the most superficial contact with adults other than their parents.

Betty Friedan (1981) once wrote that the family is a "feminist frontier"—an institution that must be not destroyed but changed to accommodate the full personhood of both women and men. Such an accommodation would no doubt mean, in part, that many different kinds of families would be considered "normal" and that, within such families, women and men would not be locked into expectations of submission and dominance and caregiver and breadwinner, as they have been in the past. Although some movement in this direction has certainly happened, it remains to be seen how readily this particular "feminist frontier" can be crossed.

KEY TERMS

polygyny	trust	principle of least interest
polyandry	equity	
serial monogamy	interpersonal power	directness
homophobia		interactiveness

Economic and Political Life
Power, Status, and Achievement

A common retort to advocates of equality between the sexes is, "If women are as capable as men, why are there so few great women artists? Where are the eminent women novelists, composers, philosophers, economists, chemists, politicians?" Writer Virginia Woolf would have provided a swift and decisive answer to such questions. In her haunting essay *A Room of One's Own* (1929/1957), she describes the obstacles of prejudice and economic hardship that beset women would-be writers until the 20th century. What, she muses, would have become of a sister to William Shakespeare, a sister whose talent rivaled that of the famous bard?

> It seemed to me that any woman born with a great gift in the sixteenth century would certainly have gone crazed, shot herself, or ended her days in some lonely cottage outside the village, half witch, half wizard, feared and mocked at. For it needs little skill in psychology to be sure that a highly gifted girl who had tried to use her gift for poetry would have been so thwarted and hindered by other people, so tortured and pulled asunder by her own contrary instincts, that she must have lost her health and sanity to a certainty. (p. 51)

Woolf is only one of many individuals who have argued persuasively that women's invisibility relative to men in terms of recognized achievements is due not to a lack of talent but to barriers imposed by discrimination and other external factors.

In this chapter, we examine the reasons for the difference in recognition accorded the achievements of women and men and the different success rates of the two gender groups in reaching positions of status and power. In particular, we ask these questions:

- What is the current situation with respect to positions of power and eminence for women and men?
- What role does motivation play in determining high achievement and access to powerful positions?
- Are the very definitions of *achievement* and *power* gendered?
- To what extent do women and men differ in their access to the resources on which power is based?
- Do men and women differ in the ways they use influence?
- How do women and men compare in the realm of political power?
- What role does gender play in the distribution of power in organizations and institutions?
- How do power differences become entrenched and self-perpetuating?

We will see that, in many instances, cultural expectations dictate that power and gender be intertwined.

WHERE WE ARE NOW: A SHORTAGE OF WOMEN AT THE TOP

It is clear that in most fields few women relative to men have managed to achieve positions of eminence and power.

Women make up half the world's enfranchised population, but worldwide their parliamentary representation is far lower than men's. Women account for only 16.9% of seats in national parliaments and legislatures around the world. In 1995, the United Nations set a goal for women to hold 30% of parliamentary seats. By 2006, only 18 countries had met that goal, led by Sweden at 45% (Inter-Parliamentary Union, 2006). By contrast, the level of participation by women had reached only 21% in Canada and just over 15% in the United States, (rising to 16% in the 2006 election). See Figure 12.1.

Women make up an extremely low percentage of the conductors of major orchestras, the directors of major motion pictures, the members of the National Academy of Sciences, or the recipients of the Nobel prize. When Nadine Gordimer was awarded the Nobel prize for literature in 1991, she became the first woman novelist in a quarter of a century to receive this honor. (Three women, Toni Morrison, Wislawa Szymborska, and Elfriede Jelinek, have won this prize since 1991.) Men received almost 98% of the Nobel prizes

Figure 12.1 Percentage of women in selected national parliaments, December 31, 2005.

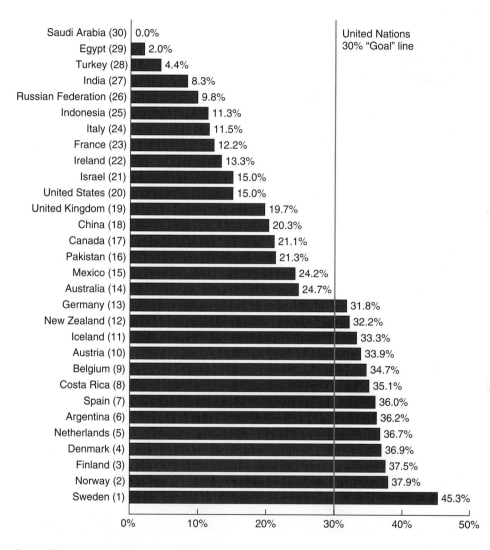

Source: Situation as of 31 December 2005, Women in National Parliaments, Statistical Archive. Retrieved October 30, 2006, from http://www.ipu.org/wmn-e/classif-arc.htm

in science areas and 99% of the prestigious awards in mathematics during the 20th century. The Nobel prize for literature has been awarded to men rather than women at a ratio of greater than 9.5 to 1, and other prestigious literary prizes show a pattern of male dominance that is almost as strong (Lips, 1999).

Across all fields, the Nobel prize has been awarded to only 33 women since 1901. In 2004 a record three women won prizes: Linda Buck for physiology or medicine, Elfriede Jelineck for literature, and Wangari Maathai for peace. However, in 2005 and 2006 no women were awarded Nobel prizes (Nobel Foundation, 2006).

Women of color, often the targets of double discrimination, have even less representation in the ranks of the eminent than do their ethnic majority counterparts. For instance, the first PhD in mathematics awarded to an African American woman, Evelyn Boyd Collins, was not granted until 1946; the first African American woman to earn a PhD in physics, Shirley Jackson, received it in 1976; and only in 1987 did the NASA astronaut training program select its first African American female astronaut, Dr. Mae Jemison (V. L. Thomas, 1989).

In the corporate world, highly visible women are still scarce. There are only 10 female CEOs of Fortune 500 companies. In addition, women comprise only 15.7% of corporate officers and 14.7% of board members in Fortune 500 companies. Since 1995, when women held only 9.6% of Fortune 500 board seats, women's presence on boards has increased only 0.5% per year. And women of color, who face the double barrier of racial and gender discrimination, have an even lower representation: In 2005 women of color held just 3.4% of Fortune 500 board seats (Catalyst, 2006a; "Glass Ceiling Remains," 2006).

This pattern is not unique to North America. There is only one female CEO and one female board chair among Britain's FTSE 100 companies, and women make up only 10.5% of directorships in that group of top companies (Women & Equality Unit, 2006). Women occupy only 8.5% of the 4,535 corporate boardroom seats in Europe—although this number rises to over 28% in Norway, where the government has introduced quotas for female representation (European Professional Women's Network, 2006). Women hold only 12% of directorships in Canada, 10.7% in South Africa, and 8.6% in Australia (Catalyst, 2006b).

In the realm of athletics, women are also far less visible and less well-rewarded than men. Talented female athletes and their teams receive far less media coverage and much lower earnings than their male counterparts. In 2002 the entire payroll for the Women's National Basketball Association was $12 million—about 56% of star NBA player Shaquille O'Neal's $21.5 million annual salary (Caputo, 2002). In professional tennis, female players earn 67 cents for every dollar a male player makes; women golfers make only 36 cents for every dollar male golfers make (Murray, 2002). Annika Sorenstam, arguably the best (and best-known) woman golfer in the world, earned about $1.9 million in 2002 (LPGA, 2003); by comparison, three male professional golfers—Vijay Singh, Tiger Woods, and Davis Love—earned over $6 million each in winnings in 2003 (Budnick, 2003).

An understanding of the large gender gap in positions of eminence, prestige, and influence requires that we examine the psychological and social issues surrounding power and achievement. In earlier chapters, we noted that females and males are socialized differently with respect to achievement, that males are often automatically accorded more status than females, and that women and men frequently differ in their access to the resources on which power is based. How are such differences translated into a social structure in which men occupy a disproportionate number of the positions of prestige and eminence and dominate most aspects of economic and political activity? Could it be that "Women aren't as motivated as men are to get to the top?"

MOTIVATION: THE DRIVING FORCE?

Many psychological theories are based on the assumption that individuals differ in the strength of their motives—their tendencies to need and to seek particular outcomes. Psychologists looking for clues to explain individual differences in behavior have studied both the achievement motive and the power motive. The **achievement motive** is defined as a general personality disposition to strive for success in any situation in which standards of excellence are applied (McClelland et al., 1953). The **power motive** is defined as the tendency to strive to feel that one is having an impact on others (Winter, 1973). Both motives are measured using the Thematic Apperception Test (TAT), a projective test in which the respondent is asked to tell stories about a series of pictures (Murray, 1937). The stories are then scored for the presence of themes indicating an orientation toward or concern with achievement or power.

The Achievement Motive

Almost all of the original research on the achievement motive was done with male respondents. David McClelland and his colleagues (1953) found that for men achievement motivation could be shown to relate to performance in competitive situations in the lab as well as to later career performance. They also found that men's achievement motivation scores tended to rise, often dramatically, when men were given "achievement-involving" task instructions—that is, instructions that stressed that their performance would reflect their intelligence, organizational ability, or leadership capacity.

These relationships did not hold for female respondents, however. McClelland and his colleagues paid scant attention to women's achievement motivation. However, they summarized their findings on gender differences in achievement motivation as follows: (1)Women get higher achievement motive scores than men do under neutral conditions. (2) Women do not show an increase in achievement motive scores when given achievement-involving instructions. (3)Women's achievement motive scores relate to their performance in the same way that men's do (p. 178).

If women's achievement motivation was not easily aroused by the instructions that worked for men, did this mean that women simply had less need for achievement than men did? Many researchers thought so. There was a prevailing assumption that women did not have great achievements because they were not particularly interested. And since achievement appeared to be mainly a male preserve, researchers focused on males. John Atkinson's (1958) classic work on achievement motivation mentions women in only a single footnote, and McClelland's book, *The Achieving Society* (1961), omits any mention of women. It was only in the context of interest generated by the feminist movement that researchers again turned their attention to achievement orientation in females.

When researchers finally tackled the problem of why women, who seemed to have the same basic amount of achievement motivation as men, did not pursue achievement in many situations, they zeroed in on the differing rewards attached to success for women and men. They began to realize, for example, that women and men might each attach higher value to performing well in gender-appropriate than in gender-inappropriate areas of achievement. For instance, social skills were somewhat unique in being viewed as "feminine" skills—and women tended to respond with increased achievement arousal when given achievement-involving instructions emphasizing social skills (Stein & Bailey, 1973). The research that brought the most attention to how people's motivation to achieve might be affected by their awareness of the gender-linked consequences of success focused on a motive that was labeled **fear of success**.

FEAR OF SUCCESS   According to a widely accepted analysis of achievement motivation (Atkinson & Feather, 1966), the motivation to achieve that is aroused in a given situation depends on three things: the strength of the person's underlying achievement motivation, the probability of success, and the incentive or reward value of success in that situation. So, even if a person has a very strong motivation to achieve, this motivation might not be aroused in a particular situation if, for example, the person perceives that the consequences of such success would be negative (that is, if the incentive value of success is low).

Matina Horner (1968) hypothesized that because achievement in many areas is considered inappropriate or at least unusual for women, a woman achieving in one of these areas might feel she was jeopardizing her femininity. Thus success for a woman would be an ambivalent experience, having both the positive consequences of self-respect and external recognition and the negative consequences of the real or imagined disapproval of others for being unfeminine. If the negative consequences appeared to outweigh the positive ones, motivation to achieve in a given situation would be low.

Horner's theory arose from her own observations that successful career women often seemed to feel a need to demonstrate that besides being successful in their vocational sphere they were also successful as "real" women—that they were loving mothers, devoted wives, marvelous cooks, and impeccable housekeepers. These women perceived that a woman outstandingly successful at her career would encounter disapproval if that success led her to give short shrift to her "proper" feminine role. Such observations led Horner to postulate that for women the negative consequences would often outweigh the positive consequences of success, leading to a situation in which the woman developed a motive to *avoid* success. Because success for a man rarely implies any loss of masculinity, Horner predicted that a motive to avoid success would appear much less frequently in men than in women.

Horner began testing her predictions on a group of University of Michigan students by giving them a projective test that she hoped would measure fear of success (the anticipation of negative consequences for success). In the test, female students were asked to complete a story beginning with the following sentence: "After first-term finals, Anne finds herself at the top of her medical school class" (Horner, 1970, p. 59). Males completed a similar story about a medical student named John. As Horner predicted, many of the women (65%) told stories that incorporated either negative consequences of Anne's success (social rejection, anxiety over her normality or femininity) or denied the possibility of that success by attributing it to an error in marking, cheating, and so on. A common theme in many of the stories was that Anne's success threatened her relationship with the man in her life or with men in general. In contrast, fewer than 10% of the men told stories in which any negative consequences came to John because of his success.

Horner's findings at first appeared to support her theory that gender-role socialization had produced different amounts of the motivation to avoid success in women and men. The theory struck a chord with the popular media, and magazine articles glibly explained that the reason women so seldom achieved eminence was that they had a basic flaw: They were afraid of success. The ready acceptance of the theory was not surprising in an era when discrimination against women in many areas was just beginning to be questioned seriously. After all, it blamed women in large part for their failure to make an impact. However, the acceptance turned out to be premature, as researchers who followed up on Horner's work were quick to discover (Condry & Dyer, 1976; Tresmer, 1976).

First, some critics argued that there was no certainty that Horner's projective test actually tapped a stable internal motive (Sancho & Hewitt, 1990). Perhaps the negative consequences described in the stories represent not a personal fear of success but simply an awareness that negative consequences can result from success, particularly for women (Pfost & Fiore, 1990). Male students given the opportunity to tell a story about Anne instead of John also tend to include many negative consequences for her success. Similarly, women as well as men tend more often to complete the story about John without negative consequences (Monahan, Kuhn, & Shaver, 1974). Thus the results of this type of test may reflect a cultural stereotype that success is often aversive for women instead of (or as well as) an actual motive to avoid success. Research does show that successful individuals, male or female, are described as more masculine than unsuccessful individuals (Gerber, 1984). In addition, women are apparently more sensitive than men to others' evaluations of their performance (Roberts, 1991), making it likely that they will be bothered by any negative reactions others might have.

Second, some argued that the gender difference in fear of success was more apparent than real. In a summary of 64 studies, Paludi (1984) found that the proportion of females showing fear of success ranged from 6% to 93%, with a median of 49%, whereas for males the proportions ranged from 7% to 95%, with a median of 45%. The reason for the wide variation may lie partly in the story cues used. Cherry and Deaux (1978) found that men indicated more fear of success when writing about John in nursing school than in medical school, whereas the reverse was true for women writing about Anne. They concluded that although both women and men have an awareness and perhaps a fear of the negative consequences of succeeding in a "gender-inappropriate" situation, there is little reason to believe that women fear success in general more than men do.

Research using African American female and male graduate students also supports the interpretation that fear of success represents a flight from inappropriate situations (Fleming, 1982). Both the men and the women in Fleming's sample showed fear of success that could be interpreted as motivation to avoid subjectively role-inappropriate behaviors. Women who showed fear of success were trying to develop career interests compatible with a strong commitment to home and husband, and the men who showed fear of success "seemed to be reacting to negative racial stereotypes and attempting to live up to a new image of the black male" (p. 339). Fear of success, then, may be a situational rather than a motivational variable, with women or men showing more fear depending on the particular situation described. In fact, when no situation was described and subjects were merely told that "Anne (or John) succeeded," no difference in fear of success was seen between male and female stories (Gravenkemper & Paludi, 1983).

In summary, there is no reason to believe women and men differ in the strength of their basic motivations toward success. However, the research stimulated by the fear of success concept has shown clearly that individuals are sensitive to the social consequences of their achievement behavior and that such consequences are perceived to be different for women and men in particular situations. Perceived institutional and social barriers rather than internal motivational ones are responsible for the different achievement behaviors of women and men.

The Power Motive

Research on the power motive has followed much the same pattern as that for achievement. Early research was conducted on males, but when females were eventually studied, it was found that the two gender groups did not differ in their power motive scores under neutral conditions. Also, both women and men responded with increased power motivation scores to power-arousing procedures (Stewart & Winter, 1976; Winter & Stewart, 1978). For both women and men, a high need for power is associated with acquiring formal institutionalized power through leadership roles or offices and with choosing careers

- Women and men do not differ in achievement motivation or power motivation under neutral conditions.

- Both women and men show arousal of these motives when the scenario or stimulus is gender appropriate.

- There is no evidence for a gender difference in "fear of success."

that involve having direct, legitimate interpersonal power over others (Winter & Stewart, 1978). Once again, then, it appears that the difference in men's and women's ascendance to positions of prestige and influence cannot be attributed to gender differences in motivational variables.

DEFINING ACHIEVEMENT AND POWER

Some research suggests that women and men may differ in the way they define *achievement* and *power* and, thus, in the ways they find to satisfy these needs. For example, for women more than for men success at social relationships may be experienced as an achievement because the area of social relations is one in which it has traditionally been acceptable for women to excel (Stein & Bailey, 1973). Early research showed that women oriented toward the traditional feminine role showed high achievement motivation only under conditions designed to arouse affiliation, whereas women who accepted achievement behavior as part of the feminine role responded to the same kinds of achievement-arousing conditions that men do (Gralewski & Rodgon, 1980).

The definition of *achievement* used in most psychological measures of motivation is likely too narrow, tapping only the traditional, male-oriented factors of direct, competitive achievement. People view not only public mastery situations but also personal and interpersonal events in achievement terms (Travis, Phillippi, & Henley, 1991). In fact, when separate components of the achievement motive have been studied, males tend to score higher than females on the drive to compete with and be better than others, and females tend to outscore males on orientation to work for its own sake (Spence & Helmreich, 1978).

Where differences do exist between women and men in the outlets they find for their achievement needs, such differences may be due not so much to definition as to opportunity and self-confidence. We have seen that people are quite sensitive to the social approval or disapproval elicited by their achievement behavior.

Women trying to achieve in a masculine-oriented arena hold overly negative self-evaluations (Beyer, 1990). No doubt many women have found that they face fewer negative and more positive consequences for achievement when they avoid competition with men and when they support the achievement efforts of their families rather than themselves.

Certainly, many women in professional and managerial careers have experienced the negative responses and exclusion that sometimes accompany competition with men. In a survey of top-level female executives in the United States, a majority of the respondents said that an important factor in their success was adjusting their personal style so they would not threaten male executives. One respondent to the survey summed up the narrow path she saw as necessary for a women in her position: "Don't be attractive. Don't be too smart. Don't be assertive. Pretend you're not a woman" (Grimsley, 1996, p. C1).

Men may discover that competition and winning is a core aspect of the masculine role and that such an approach to achievement gains them more points than does a strictly task-oriented approach. Among women, however, achievement satisfaction often comes from the intrinsic satisfaction of task accomplishment, from the vicarious satisfaction of helping others reach their goals, and from exerting influence (Offermann & Beil, 1992). Thus differing styles of achievement for women and men reflect, to some extent, a reaction to social expectations imposed by gender roles. However, constraints are forged by more than simple approval or disapproval. A woman who is at home caring for children may find few opportunities for externally validated achievement other than through her husband; a secretary may find it more practical to bask in the satisfaction of her boss's successes than to find any source of public recognition for herself.

The stereotypically masculine and feminine patterns of meeting achievement needs can both be problematic. The early literature of the feminist movement is filled with examples of women's dissatisfaction with the expectation that they limit their achievement drives to achieving social success or to achieving through the lives of those they nurture (e.g., Bernard, 1974; Friedan, 1963). For men, however, the emphasis on competition and the material rewards of achieving can be the source of considerable stress and can interfere with personal relationships and the exploration of less prestigious but potentially more satisfying lifestyles. An interesting perspective on the male side of the problem can be gleaned from an examination of the "fear of success" stories told by males. Although the stories told by females tend to stress fear of social rejection as a result of success, those told by males often involve discovering the emptiness of success (Basow, 1986).

Women and men may also differ in the ways they define and experience power. Some theorists suggested that women and men may conceive of and seek power differently: men by dominating others and women by developing a sense of their own abilities and strengths (J. B. Miller, 1977; Rich, 1976). Research has shown, though, that when asked explicitly about what power means to them, college women and men do not differ in the proportions of each group that include themes of influence over others and achievement/self-worth in their definitions (Lips, 1985a). However, certain types of experiences are more linked to feelings of power for men than for women: having material possessions, being physically strong, and participating in sports. One study has shown that women tend to define power for themselves most often as "personal authority" and that they perceive society as defining power most often as "control over others" (Miller & Cummins, 1992). Other researchers have noted that men and women may satisfy their power motives differently, according to how the two gender groups are expected to behave (McClelland, 1975). The expression of a need for power is somewhat more likely to be tempered by socialization toward responsibility in females than in males (Winter & Barenbaum, 1985).

Women in the United States may have a more difficult time than men imagining themselves as holders of powerful positions. Two studies asked college students to imagine themselves in turn as "a person with power," a president of a major corporation, an important political leader, and the director of a major scientific research center (Lips, 2000a; Lips & Rogers, 1999). Women tended to view the possibilities as both less positive and less possible than men did. However, parallel gender differences did not appear in samples of college students in Spain or Argentina. Young women in many countries apparently can envision ambitious leadership possibilities for themselves. However, they must struggle to reconcile those possibilities with feminine role expectations that dictate compliance, cooperation, and "niceness" rather than the stereotypically masculine behaviors of taking charge, taking credit, and insisting that others fall into step with one's personal vision (Lips, 2001).

In considering gender differences in the ways needs for achievement and power are expressed, it is important to remember that the value and prestige assigned to particular positions and accomplishments are not decreed by some absolute authority but are decided by social consensus. That consensus in a male-centered culture reflects a tendency to value traditionally masculine accomplishments more than feminine ones. Thus, in our society, becoming a corporation president, writing a best-selling novel, reaching the million mark in record sales, hitting a record number of home runs, or getting a large research grant are considered achievements; raising three children is not. The popular definition of *achievement* has emerged in such a way that success in the traditionally feminine domain of home and family is simply taken for granted rather than treated as an accomplishment. When asked what she does, the woman who is a full-time homemaker has learned to answer diffidently that she is "just a housewife," although her job may well involve more work and higher levels of skill than many others that are more prestigious.

Perhaps nowhere can the disregarding of traditional feminine achievements be seen more clearly than in the difficult quest for the history of women. A reading of traditional history books might well give one the impression that women had not even been present during most major historical events or at least that they had made no noticeable impact on the way things turned out. In North American history, one reads references to "the pioneer and his wife" (is the wife not also a pioneer?) with the realization that, even when working against terrible odds and under the most difficult and dangerous conditions, a woman devoting herself to her home and family is considered merely to be doing her duty rather than accomplishing anything special. Thus, although men and women have been encouraged to pursue achievement and power in different ways, these ways are neither equally visible nor equally valued.

ACCESS TO RESOURCES

Power and achievement merge to some extent into a single concept when power is conceptualized as the ability to get things done (Goodchilds, 1979). As noted in Chapter 11, the exercise of power depends on access to certain types of resources: the capacity to reward or punish others, credentials of expertise, legitimacy of authority or position, being identified with or liked by others, and information (French & Raven, 1959). Within these categories fall such specific resources as money, education, employment, physical health and strength, status, legal rights, and time. Individuals differ widely in their access to resources, but the group differences between women and men are consistent: In almost every category of resource, men have more access and control than women do. In addition, when women try to increase their access to these resources, their efforts are often regarded as illegitimate because they are violating established norms.

Let us look at some ways in which women and men differ in their access to the resources on which power can rest:

- There is a persistent wage gap between women and men (Institute for Women's Policy Research, 2005; Lips, 2003). In the United States, full-time women workers ages 16 to 50 earn less than 77 cents for every dollar men earn (Webster & Bishaw, 2006). A significant gender wage gap exists within every ethnic group, every educational level, and almost every occupation. A similar pattern can be demonstrated worldwide (International Labor Office, 2004).

- There is also a "time gap" between women and men. As we saw in the previous chapter, women do more housework and child care than men do, leaving them less time to pursue economic or achievement-related goals (Bond, Galinsky, & Swanberg, 1998).

- All over the world, women are much more likely than men to live in poverty, and the gender disparity has increased over the past decade (International Labor Office, 2004; United Nations Population Fund, 2002). Among developed countries, the United States has the highest ratio of women to men living in poverty: Women in this country are 38% more likely than men to live in poverty, and single women are almost 100% more likely than single men to live in poverty (Christopher, England, McLanahan, Phillips, & Smeeding, 2000). The gender gap is compounded by ethnicity: African American and Puerto Rican women are especially likely to be poor (Elmelech & Lu, 2003).

- Women have less access to political power than men do. Of the 11 oldest democracies in the world, 10 waited until the 20th century to give women the right to vote, ending with Switzerland in 1971. In some countries, such as Kuwait and the United Arab Emirates, women still do not have full rights to vote.

- Girls' and boys' access to education is about equal in North America; however, from a global perspective, the situation is anything but egalitarian. Worldwide, almost 23% of women and almost 13% of men are illiterate (UNESCO, 2006). See Figure 12.2.

Figure 12.2   Female and male illiteracy rates by global region in 2004 as percentage of adult persons 15 years and older.

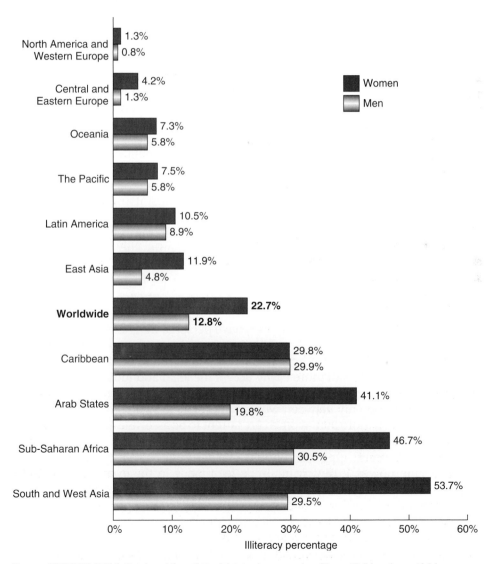

Source: UNESCO (2006). Retrieved from http://stats.uis.unesco.org/ReportFolders/reportfolders.aspx

These statistics could go on for pages, but the ones already listed make the point: Men as a group have more access than women do to the resources on which power is based. Yet women who complain about these inequities are still frequently treated as if they are being unreasonable, and those who have pioneered women's entry into the many arenas that have been closed to them have been, at every stage, the subject of disapproval and ridicule. Sometimes this disapproval has come, and continues to come, from other women. While the British suffragists were struggling to gain the vote for women, they were being opposed by Queen Victoria herself, who was, she said, "most anxious to enlist everyone to join in checking this mad wicked folly of Women's Rights, with all its attendant horrors" (as quoted in Nunes & White, 1973, p. 10). While North American feminists have been struggling to improve women's access to resources, they have been vigorously opposed by an antifeminist women's movement in the United States (Marshall, 1995) and by the REAL (Realistic, Equal, Active for Life) women in Canada (Dubinsky, 1985).

A conflict theory perspective on the opposition to the feminist movement suggests that such opposition stems from the fact that certain groups benefit while others are systematically deprived under the traditional pattern of gender relations. Those who benefit are more likely to be men than women, but many women may be convinced that a system in which males hold most of the authority is ultimately beneficial for all concerned. In fact, for a group to exert effective control over a society, that group must not merely secure power but must also establish, in the eyes of subordinate groups, its *right* to wield such power (Weber, 1965). In Max Weber's words, the group needs to "legitimate" its power, thus achieving authority over—or the right to dominate—subordinate groups. It appears that men have been and remain quite successful at convincing women that male dominance of society is legitimate.

Weber's analysis, which lists three basic sources for legitimizing power, offers some clues as to how male authority became so entrenched. Authority can stem from tradition (ruling groups may rule because they have always done so), from charisma (leaders of ruling groups have personal magnetism or charm that induces others to follow them), or from rational means (the use of legal and judicial mechanisms). Male authority certainly has tradition on its side, and, once in authority, a person can more easily access the legal and judicial mechanisms to reinforce that authority. Even charisma, which might reasonably be expected to be distributed evenly between women and men, may lie more strongly with men because men more than women are taught to be assertive and to expect others to follow them. Thus all three sources of authority can work to make male dominance of society appear legitimate. Furthermore, as Weber also notes, once a group is in power, it can maintain its legitimacy in the eyes of subordinate groups partly through the control and dissemination of ideas—and we have already noted the difficulties that have traditionally greeted women writers, politicians, and other activists. Once in place, the dominance of one group by another is reinforced by so many factors that it is extremely difficult to dismantle, and the pattern of differential access to resources is not easily changed.

Women's and men's differential access to resources has implications at both group and individual levels. It affects the capacity that each group has to make an impact, and it affects the chances female and male individuals have to achieve particular goals. For example, a female politician, even if she does not want to be identified with so-called women's issues, must deal with the fact that she is in a minority position. This minority position will color her acceptance by others and affect her ability to be effective in her job. As Agnes Macphail, the first woman elected to the Canadian House of Commons, recalled about her 14 years as the lone woman in that institution,

> I found that I couldn't quietly do my job without being ballyhooed like the bearded lady. . . . I couldn't open my mouth to say the simplest thing without it appearing in the papers. I was a curiosity, a freak. And you know the way the world treats freaks. (as quoted in Cochrane, 1977, p. 42)

Men, too, cannot evade the implications of their gender group membership when it comes to achievement and power. In mixed-sex situations, men are more likely than women to be assigned leadership roles, whether they seek them or not (Lockheed & Hall, 1976; Nyquist & Spence, 1986), and unsuccessful men are subject to more negative evaluations than unsuccessful women are (Fogel & Paludi, 1984). Perhaps because more resources are assigned to men, more is expected of them.

Thus both genders carry the weight of their intergroup differences in access to resources when they are in situations involving power and achievement. These differences influence not only what women and men can accomplish but how they try to accomplish it and how they and others evaluate their accomplishments. As described in the following section, the strategies women and men employ to gain influence and to make an impact are shaped by the fact that women, more often than men, are operating from a position of weakness in terms of resources and that people tend to see efforts to change the accepted distribution of resources as illegitimate and threatening.

Strategies of Influence

People use a bewildering array of strategies in their attempts to use their resources to exert influence and to acquire more resources. Psychologists have made various attempts to categorize these strategies and to examine the relationship between the resources a person controls and the particular interpersonal influence strategies she or he favors. They find that persons who operate from positions of relative strength (that is, who control more resources) tend to use "strong" authoritative influence techniques, whereas those in weak positions rely on "weaker" tactics based on accommodation and dependency (Howard et al., 1986; Kipnis, 1984). Furthermore, those who control more resources or who are in initially dominant positions tend to use a greater variety of influence strategies than do those with less power (Kipnis, Schmidt, & Wilkinson, 1980).

The extent to which such findings on interpersonal influence would generalize to intergroup influence is not certain. However, when groups are in a hierarchical power relationship, as men and women are, group membership itself becomes a resource for interpersonal influence. Not surprisingly, then, researchers have examined the relationship between gender and influence tactics.

Paula Johnson (1976), a pioneer in research on gender and power, suggested that there are three major dimensions on which the use of power to exert influence is affected by gender stereotypes: **directness, concreteness,** and **competence.** According to her analysis, gender norms dictate that men's influence styles can be direct, concrete, and competent, but women's should be indirect, personal, and based on helplessness or dependence.

INDIRECT VERSUS DIRECT INFLUENCE   Direct influence is demonstrated when a person uses power openly, by giving an order or making a request. Indirect influence is exercised when the individual obtains the desired outcome while trying to keep the other person unaware of the influence. Indirect influence is often called "manipulation." Johnson (1976) suggested that in middle-class, North American society there are many constraints against directness by women and that, consequently, women more than men tend to rely on indirect influence. Many feminist writers have noted that a woman who uses direct power is quickly labeled "unfeminine," "castrating," and "bitchy." Furthermore, even a casual perusal of the popular magazines devoted to advising women about interpersonal relationships shows that women are sometimes actually instructed to use manipulative rather than direct strategies to get what they want ("Let him think it was his idea").

The use of indirect influence, although potentially effective in the short run, may have negative long-term consequences for the user. When the source of influence is concealed, the person wielding it may not be regarded as powerful, may be kept in a subordinate position, and is not likely to see her- or himself as a strong person. A person who is actually wielding a good deal of influence indirectly may get little credit for it. Being the "power behind the throne" or the woman behind the successful man may have its gratifications but probably not as many as being *on* the throne or claiming the success for oneself.

PERSONAL VERSUS CONCRETE RESOURCES   An individual's attempt to exercise influence is given weight by the amount and nature of resources that the person controls. The implied threat in any influence attempt is that a refusal will be met by invoking the resources at the power holder's command to induce compliance. Johnson (1976) suggested that resources can be divided into two categories: those that depend on personal relationships, such as liking and approval, and those that are concrete and independent of relationships, such as money, knowledge, and physical strength. She argued that men have considerably more control over concrete resources than women do (an argument borne out by the statistics given at the beginning of this section) and that women therefore rely on personal resources more than men do.

Personal resources are certainly not unimportant. The threat of a denial of love, affection, or sex can be a very powerful way to induce cooperation from a person to whom that denial matters deeply. Nonetheless, as Johnson pointed out, this type of influence is effective only in the context of a personal relationship. Also, it has the disadvantage of leaving the influencer highly dependent on others. Although a woman may hold great personal power in an individual relationship, it is often not the sort that generalizes beyond the relationship or holds up in a court of law. For example, a woman may hold a great deal of power based on personal resources such as affection and sexuality with respect to her husband, easily gaining his compliance to her wishes. However, if the affection between the spouses wanes, this same woman could find herself fighting in court for child support or an equal share of the couple's financial resources. This aspect of her power is based on the affection her husband holds for her; when that disappears, her power disappears as well.

HELPLESSNESS VERSUS COMPETENCE   It is sometimes possible to get others to do things for us either by acting competent, taking charge, and giving orders or by acting incompetent and helpless and throwing ourselves on their mercy. A major theme in our gender stereotypes is that men are strong and competent and women are weak and helpless—a theme that is reinforced in everything from children's stories about the handsome prince rescuing the damsel in distress to television serials in which, week after week, fearless male heroes save hapless women from pursuit by crazed killers or international terrorists. Johnson (1976) suggested that because women are often in situations in which they are not regarded as or do not feel competent, they tend to rely on helplessness as a mode of influence more than men do. By acting helpless, women can get men to take on responsibilities and do tasks for them, particularly those tasks that fit society's expectations for the masculine role. It should be mentioned, though, that men are not above using helplessness themselves as an influence tactic, as many women have discovered when they first asked their spouse to do laundry, cook supper, or change the baby's diaper.

Johnson suggested that helplessness, though effective in the short run, does not establish its users as strong influencers and may contribute to both low status and low self-esteem.

Do Women and Men Really Use Power Differently?

Johnson's (1976) research on people's reactions to power use in a hypothetical situation (one student trying to get another to change his or her opinion on a legal case) suggested that men and women are *expected* to use power in different ways. Given a list of 15 different methods of influence in the hypothetical situation, respondents were asked to indicate whether the influencer was male or female. Results showed the following:

- Respondents expected certain strategies to be used more by men than by women: coercion based on concrete resources, competence based on legitimacy or expertise, and direct use of informational power.

- They expected women to make more use of sexuality and reward based on personal resources.

Based on these findings, Johnson concluded that men are allowed to use many different forms of influence, depending on the situation, but women are more severely restricted to the less aggressive types. Since then, many researchers have documented that people do expect women and men to base their influence on different resources (Carli, 1999):

- Men are more likely than women to be thought of as competent and thus to rely on expert power.
- Men are more likely than women to command respect and authority over others and thus to have access to legitimate power.
- Women, who are liked more than men, have more access to referent power.

If men really are allowed to use more kinds of influence strategies than women are, perhaps it is no wonder that some women resist the changes in gender roles advocated by feminists. These women may fear that if they are "liberated" their traditional feminine modes of influence may no longer be effective (e.g., if women are recognized as being as competent as men are, they cannot get their way by acting helpless). These women do not anticipate being comfortable with, good at, or allowed to use the more direct, competent tactics. Consequently, they may foresee a "liberation" that results in a net loss rather than a net gain of power for women.

Although Johnson's (1976) research addressed the question of what influence styles are stereotypically expected of women and men, it did not answer the question of whether women and men actually do use power differently. Earlier research by Johnson herself and more recent studies by other researchers indicate that different influence strategies tend to be favored by the two gender groups and that the target of the influence makes a difference as to the choice of strategy. Paula Johnson (1974) gave male and female group leaders a choice of six influence messages to persuade their group to work faster at a task. The male leaders often chose the persuasive message that stressed their own expertise, whereas female leaders avoided it. The female leaders were more likely to use the persuasive message that emphasized their own helplessness and dependency on the workers—a strategy that male leaders, without exception, rejected.

In a study using a simulated organizational setting, another group of researchers placed women and men in positions of equal power and investigated whether they would use different strategies to influence their subordinates (Instone, Major, & Bunker, 1983). They found that, relative to males, females made fewer influence attempts, used fewer types of influence strategies, and relied more on coercion and less on reward. These differences seemed to be mediated by lower self-confidence among the women than the men. Other organizational research also showed that males are more likely to use direct, assertive strategies, whereas females are more likely to use indirect, submissive ones (Ansari, 1989; Fairhurst, 1985; Goodyear, 1990).

Certainly, women are more likely than men to *report* using more obliging and compromising and less assertive supervisory styles (Carli, 1999; Goh, 1991; Korabik, Baril, & Watson, 1993). However, in at least one laboratory study (Korabik et al., 1993), such gender differences in self-reports did not match any observed differences in supervisory behavior. And the gender difference in self-reported influence styles may be sensitive to context. One study of employees in a business environment found that men were more likely than women to report that they relied on charm, manipulation, and appearance to achieve personal and organizational objectives (DuBrin, 1989).

Although the frequency with which women and men report using various strategies differs, women and men do not seem to differ overall in their order of preference for particular strategies. For both men and women, the influence strategy ranked highest in order of preference is "use reason and logic," followed by "simply state my desires," "offer to compromise," and "convince, persuade, and coax" (J.W. White & Roufail, 1989). Yet, in terms of absolute frequency of reported use, men are more likely than women to use high-pressure tactics such as arguing and yelling, threatening force, and asserting forcefully as first-choice strategies; women are more likely than men to report using negative emotion (pleading, crying, acting cold, getting angry, and demanding) as their first choice. Furthermore, some differences in the use of influence strategies may begin when people are quite young. In one study of Israeli eighth graders the boys reported that they would use *all* types of influence strategies more than girls did—obviously feeling justified in using whatever methods were necessary to exert their influence (Schwarzwald & Koslowsky, 1999).

One reason for a gender difference in influence strategies may be the impact of social expectations for women and men. As Linda Carli (1999) pointed out, a wealth of research shows that women are less likely than men to be perceived as competent experts, making them less able to use competence-based influence strategies. Furthermore, she noted, even when women are perceived as competent, they are often not perceived as having legitimate authority, and their efforts to exert influence in a directive manner are viewed as illegitimate and often resisted. Direct, assertive influence attempts by women often engender social disapproval in a way that similar strategies by men do not (Eagly, Makhijani, & Klonsky, 1992; Gervasio & Crawford, 1989), and assertive, self-promoting women produce reactions of distaste in some situations (Rudman, 1998). Men are more likely than women to resist being influenced by a woman who uses competence (Carli, 2001). Since, in their professional lives, women often work with male colleagues and since competence is what is valued in most jobs, women are in something of a quandary when it comes to exerting influence.

Clearly, gender-role expectations produce real differences in the amount of initial power, in the form of expertise and legitimacy, available to women and men. Add these differences to those in such concrete resources as money and position and it is not at all surprising that women and men differ in the way they approach certain influence situations. In fact, gender is so strongly linked to power and status that it is impossible to understand how gender relates to the use of influence strategies without considering how women and men differ in their power and status (Lips, 1991; Sagrestano, 1992a).

What happens when women violate the expectation that they will generally be agreeable and will mainly use personal, subtle, indirect influence strategies? Linda Carli (1998) explored this question in an experiment in which she paired participants with confederates who were trained to express either agreements or direct disagreements during group discussions. She found that participants increased their own disagreements when confronted with a partner who disagreed with them. However, this increased disagreement was much more pronounced when the partner was female than male, and participants expressed more open hostility toward the disagreeing woman than the disagreeing man. As Carli (1999) noted, these "results indicate that as long as a woman behaves in the expected manner, that is, pleasantly and agreeable, people use pleasant influence tactics when interacting with her. However, if she appears direct and resistant to their ideas, they react with much more direct and aggressive influence strategies than they would use with a man" (p. 92).

When researchers manipulate the situation so that women hold as much or more power than men, the gender differences in influence strategies tend to be obscured by power differences. People who hold more power use more direct influence strategies (Sagrestano, 1992b). An interesting case in point revolves around the resource of legitimacy. In many cultures, including our own, men hold more of the positions of authority than women do—positions that give them a legitimate right to make decisions and command obedience. In fact, in a culture that tends to ascribe higher status to males than to females and to consider that the man is the head of the family, even men who are not in formal positions of authority are still viewed as having some rights to exert authority over women. Obviously, a position of authority lends considerable force to any attempt to exercise influence directly. On the other hand, a person who tries to exercise a significant amount of influence independent of authority is regarded as manipulative, disruptive, and troublesome and is generally not taken seriously as a powerful person. Thus women must be cautious about open attempts to exercise influence from subordinate positions in organizations, and the woman who allows her power in the marriage relationship to show in public may risk an unflattering label (Bernard, 1972).

Legitimacy may vary according to the situation, of course, and with it the acceptability of certain kinds of influence tactics for females and males. Johnson and Goodchilds (1976) found that in a dating situation in which the issue of sexual intimacy occurs men were seen as using direct methods to influence a woman to have sexual intercourse, and women were perceived as being capable of equal directness in turning a man down. In a reversal of this situation, however, participants suggested that a woman would be quite indirect in her efforts to seduce a man, and the man would be correspondingly indirect in refusing her. The researchers use these results to suggest that a person engaging in an out-of-role influence attempt is likely to be less direct than

someone operating within his or her role expectations. A more general explanation might be, however, that the more legitimate a person perceives his or her
demands to be, the more direct will be the mode of influence used.

Pat Mainardi's (1970) essay on the politics of housework provides a good
example of the way the perceived legitimacy of a person's argument can affect
the influence tactics that are used. She outlines the helpless and indirect tactics
her husband used in his attempts to avoid doing his share of the housework.
Of course, as a man in the 1960s, he was well within the rights of the traditional
masculine role to refuse to do many household chores. However, in the course
of the marriage, he had acknowledged the legitimacy of his wife's argument
that housework should be shared, and this acknowledgment disallowed him
the use of direct means of influence such as flat refusal. The arguments that he
did use were as indirect ("Housework is too trivial to even talk about"), irrelevant ("Women's liberation isn't really a political movement"), and helpless ("I
don't mind doing the housework, but I don't do it very well") as one might
ever hope to find.

If the legitimacy of one's position increases one's capacity to use direct
modes of influence, it would seem that feminist attempts to legitimize the demands of women for equal status will eventually make it easier for women to
exercise direct power in a wide range of situations. However, because a challenge to men's authority is a challenge to a system that is considered by many
to be not only normative but natural, such attempts may have trouble com-
manding the resource of legitimacy. They are bound to be regarded by some as
merely disruptive, troublesome, and annoying.

In fact, research shows that it can be extraordinarily difficult for a woman
to gain legitimacy in certain situations. Janice Yoder and her colleagues (1998)
devised a laboratory experiment in which women were placed in leadership
positions with all-male groups on a masculine-stereotyped task. This procedure was meant to simulate the position in which women find themselves
when they acquire leadership positions in male-dominated organizations. In
all three experimental conditions, group members were told that the woman
had been randomly appointed by the experimenters to lead the group. In two
of the three conditions, the women leaders received special pretask training to
give them expertise on the group task. However, in one of these two conditions the women were told *not* to reveal that they had been trained, and in the
other condition a male experimenter informed the group that the woman who
would be leading them had come in early for special training and that she had
information that could be useful to the group as they made their decisions.
Thus the experiment compared the group outcomes for an appointed-only
leader, an appointed and trained leader, and an appointed, trained, and "legitimated as credible" leader.

What happened? Only the women who had been appointed and trained
and were legitimated as credible by the male experimenter were effective in influencing the performance of their all-male groups. Women who had simply
been appointed leaders tended to be relegated to secretarial roles in their

groups. Women who had been appointed and trained but not introduced by the experimenter as experts were continually frustrated in their attempts to share their expertise with their groups: "These women's added expertise gave them the background to influence the group without the power base from which to do it effectively. They interrupted in vain to try to make relevant points; they pleaded for acknowledgment using tag questions, yet they went unheeded" (p. 219). The women who had been trained but had not had legitimacy bestowed on them externally were apparently seen by the male group members as ineffectual and contributing little to the group. The researchers argued, based on these findings, that no matter how competent they are women in male-dominated organizations often cannot overcome the stereotype that women are not expected to be leaders unless they are empowered by an external endorsement from the organization.

SOME IMPLICATIONS OF THE DIFFERENCES   The definition of *power* implicitly includes some freedom to decide how to act. *Powerlessness* implies a situation in which one is not free to decide or to act. When a person feels free to behave in a certain way and then senses a threat to that freedom, the reaction is predictable: what psychologists label reactance (Brehm, 1966). **Reactance** is basically an effort to protect or regain the behavioral freedom that is threatened. It can manifest itself as anger and hostility toward the individual or institution that is doing the threatening. Because a threat to a person's freedom to behave in a particular way often comes from an influence attempt that is directed at that person, reactance is an important concept for understanding the effects of different influence tactics.

When a person is the target of influence based on coercion or expertise, he or she may feel a threat to behavioral freedom and be motivated to regain control by resisting the influence attempt (Rodin & Janis, 1979). However, when persons do comply with expert, coercive, or reward-based influence, they tend to attribute their compliance to external reasons and to suffer some loss of their sense of control. Both these patterns are helpful in understanding the impact of stereotypically masculine and feminine influence styles on their users and targets. Women, often operating from a weaker power base, may not be able to afford to provoke reactance in their influence targets. They use more subtle, indirect influence strategies that are less likely to make the target feel threatened. Men frequently have access to more resources with which to back their influence attempts and can be direct enough to arouse anger, hostility, and resistance.

In a male–female relationship, if the woman uses an indirect and personal style of influence and the man tends to be more direct and concrete, it is likely that the two people will attribute their compliance to very different causes. When the woman complies with the man's wishes, she will attribute her behavior to pressure from him, and she may feel little sense of control over or responsibility for her behavior. When the man complies with the woman, however, he may not even view his behavior as compliance. Instead, he may be responding

Overview   Gender and influence strategies

- Women and men are stereotyped as using different kinds of influence. Men are expected to make more use of coercion, competence, expertise, and direct persuasion; women are expected to make more use of sexuality and personal reward.

- Men are allowed by societal gender expectations to use a wider range of influence strategies than women are.

- Men report using more direct influence strategies than women do.

- Studies of actual influence behavior do not always find that men use more direct influence strategies. The mixed results may occur because of differences in context or because gender and power are confounded in some studies. Gender-role expectations can produce initial differences in the amount of legitimate and expert power available to women and men.

- When women violate gender expectations by trying to exert influence using direct, competent strategies, they often meet with disapproval and resistance, particularly from men.

- Gender differences in power and influence can be self-perpetuating because both women and men learn to rely on strategies that they find comfortable and effective.

to a manipulation that allows him to see his behavior as stemming from his own decision. He is thus able to maintain a sense of control and responsibility, and the couple's initial difference in the sense of power is reinforced. Under certain conditions gender differences in influence styles can become a self-perpetuating cycle.

RESOURCES, STRATEGIES, AND POLITICAL POWER

For some people, the word *power* is synonymous with *politics*. Can the psychological analysis of power differences between women and men be applied to their behavior in the political arena? The answer to this question must begin with an examination of gender differences in political behavior.

In a democracy, one of the most basic political behaviors is voting in elections. In most democracies, women have had to fight and to wait much longer than men for the opportunity to engage in this behavior. However, once women are allowed to vote, they have generally begun to vote at a rate comparable to that of men. Data are not available from every country, but in the Scandinavian countries, Chile, Nepal, Malta, the Barbados, and Puerto Rico, the percentage of women turning out to vote is at least as high as the percentage of men (International Institute for Democracy and Electoral Assistance, 2003a). Nonetheless, in some countries, such as India and Guatemala, men's voter turnout rates are still considerably higher than women's.

In Canada and the United States, women have been enfranchised since 1920, and any tendency for men to vote more than women disappeared years ago. A higher proportion of eligible women than eligible men have voted in every U.S. presidential election since 1980 (Center for American Women in Politics, 2006a).

Women are as active as men in grassroots-level politics; both groups do a lot of campaigning and behind-the-scenes work for political parties. At the citizen level, then, there is little difference between the political participation levels of women and men. Politics may still be seen as a male endeavor by many people (Mayer & Schmidt, 2004; Rosenwasser & Dean, 1989) and past research has indicated that female, but not male, high school political activists see future family life as limiting the possibility of their involvement in politics in adulthood (Romer, 1990). On the other hand, girls surpass boys in political interest and activity in the United States, and this difference persists through the teen years (Alozie, Simon, & Merrill, 2003); young women who are aware of gender inequality tend to be more politically engaged than women who are not (Bernstein, 2005).

At levels of politics above the grassroots level, gender differences are quite dramatic. Women make up only a small percentage of the holders of public office and are less likely than men to be in leadership or elected governmental positions (Center for Women in Government and Civil Society, 2006; Inter-Parliamentary Union, 2006). Some changes are evident, however. In 2005 Ellen Johnson-Sirleaf became the first woman to be elected president of an African country: Liberia. In the United States a record number of women ran for state legislative seats in 2006, and the results of that election also produced record numbers of women elected to the U.S Congress and as governors (Center for American Women in Politics, 2006b). Margaret Wilson became New Zealand's first female Speaker of the House in 2005, and Nancy Pelosi became the first woman Speaker of the U.S. House of Representative in 2007. A number of countries have instituted new quota systems to ensure that women are represented in legislative offices. For example, in France and South Africa recent laws require that political parties include women as 50% of their electoral candidates. In Tanzania, 20% of seats in the national legislature and 25% of local government seats are reserved for women (UNIFEM, 2003).

Yet progress for women in politics is not inexorable. In the United States, the number of women running for state political office declined in 2003, after rising steadily for several decades (Center for American Women in Politics,

2003). In 40% of U.S. states, women's overall share of the top executive, legislative, and judicial posts either fell, remained stable, or increased by less than
.01% between 1998 and 2005 (Center for Women in Government and Civil Society, 2006). In Jordan, the first-ever female member of parliament, Toujan
el-Faisal, was jailed in 2002 for criticizing the government. Women's share of
parliamentary seats fell in 22 countries between 2000 and 2002 (UNIFEM,
2003).

A power analysis of the situation described here suggests many reasons
women's and men's relatively equal participation in citizen-level politics does
not translate into more equal participation at the higher levels. First, gender
ideology and custom still give men more legitimacy than women as leaders,
political or otherwise (Butler & Geis, 1990; Porter & Geis, 1981). Specifically in
the realm of politics, male candidates are still perceived as more electable than
female candidates, and men are less likely than women to say they would vote
for a woman (Ogletree, Coffee, & May, 1992; Shvedova, 2002). So women may
have more trouble getting on the ballot than men; however, once on the ballot,
they are no less successful than male candidates at being elected (Huddy &
Capelos, 2002).

To avoid being handicapped by gender stereotypes, female candidates
must work hard to provide information about themselves as individuals. People exposed to such information (at least in the lab) tend to see candidates as
distinct individuals rather than in terms of their gender (Huddy & Capelos,
2002). Yet in real life many voters fail to receive or notice such individuating information—leaving them to judge candidates based on stereotypes. Interestingly, when "voters" in a laboratory study are presented with information that
a political candidate has been involved in a scandal, male candidates are more
negatively affected than female candidates. Regardless of their "prescandal"
ratings, postscandal ratings of male candidates on competence, leadership,
and warmth are more adversely affected for male than female candidates
(Huddy & Capelos, 2002).

Women running for office are now increasingly likely to have backgrounds
in elective, appointive, or political staff positions (Mandel, 1995). When women
do run for office, they are often hampered by a lack of access to funds, a concrete resource that is now the *sine qua non* of an effective campaign. Elizabeth
Dole's run for the presidency of the United States was cut short in 1999, not because she did not appeal to voters but because she could not raise enough funds
to mount an effective challenge against her rivals for the nomination. Moreover,
there are often few structural opportunities for women to gain office. In the
United States, incumbents are rarely defeated, so there are relatively few open-
ings for new faces at high levels.

In many countries political parties have started to put more emphasis on
women as an interest group. Over the past two decades, women have organized to increase their power as a pressure group—by increasing their political skills and expertise, by setting up funds to support women candidates or to
lobby for specific issues, and by organizing mutually supportive coalitions

among groups of women. Women's caucuses within the political parties push for the adoption of policies important to women as platform planks. When they use this kind of collective action, women increase their control over the resources that matter most to politicians: votes. Through giving or withholding their votes and convincing others to do likewise, women can use reward and coercive power collectively to influence public policy. The political system is still largely dominated by men, but women are building the power to make an increasing impact.

POWER IN ORGANIZATIONS AND INSTITUTIONS

As indicated in the preceding discussion of political power, even when women's and men's access to particular institutions is nominally equal or almost so, women are more likely than men to be relegated to marginal positions within the institution and to wield relatively less power. Sometimes it is suggested that men have more of "what it takes" to hold leadership positions than women do. However, the reasons for the gender differences in organizational power are more complex than that. They are built into the structure of the organizations themselves and into the social context in which these organizations exist.

Research within organizations shows that particular constraints and requirements in the way organizations run affect the power available to individuals within them. Rosabeth Moss Kanter's (1975) research began as an attempt to isolate the variables that separate women from career success in organizations. It showed, however, that leadership behavior of individuals was more strongly related to the position they held than to their gender. Poor leadership and success skills were found among people in token positions, people in dead-end jobs, and people in positions of nominal leadership that carried no real power. People in these positions were rigid and hostile toward outsiders and powerful superiors, and they appeared to have more concern for socializing than for advancement. The combination of relative powerlessness and responsibility (or "blameability") may produce these unproductive behavior patterns. Unfortunately for women, women tend to hold more of these problematic positions than men do. Kanter concluded that the stereotypes about women being poor managers were based on women's relegation to powerless organizational positions.

One thing researchers have found to be an important determinant of an individual's power and success in an organization is that person's access to informal networks of communication and exchange. Managers must coordinate the activities of many people within a work group, as well as negotiate with members of other groups or organizations. In performing these functions, managers cannot rely solely on the formal power that goes with their positions. They must also use informal power based on reciprocation of favors and sharing of information. Doing this successfully requires maintaining a large number of good relationships. However, for a number of reasons, the maintenance of such networks may be more difficult for women than for men.

First, if a woman is in a minority or token status, she does not easily fit into the informal networks of her male colleagues. In fact, in what Bernard (1976) has called the "stag effect," women may find that the most important informal meeting places for their male colleagues are off-limits or at least unwelcoming to women. Second, women are more likely than men to be doing double duty as homemakers and businesspersons and so simply have less time for informal discussions after work or other "optional" activities. Third, informal organizational networks may be based on male modes of communication and shared experiences, making it more difficult for women, with less background in common, to fit in (Hennig & Jardim, 1977). For these and other reasons, women often lack access to the networks that foster organizational power.

Within organizations, men are more likely than women to form strong same-gender ties across many networks. Women, too, form same-gender ties, but they are more likely to use these networks for support and friendship and to rely on their ties with men to obtain access to resources (Ibarra, 1992). Perhaps because they are more likely than men to see interpersonal bonds as friendship oriented rather than business oriented, women are less tolerant than men of politically manipulative behavior in the workplace (Drory & Beaty, 1991). However, both women and men are more tolerant of such behavior from a member of their own gender and toward a member of the other gender.

Women's relative lack of access to informal networks within and outside an organization limits their influence. They may have more trouble obtaining rewards for their subordinates, for instance. Such a situation can become a vicious circle, as subordinates may lose respect for a manager who appears powerless, thus further diminishing her power (Kanter, 1979; Ragins & Sundstrom, 1989).

In looking at the larger culture that provides the setting for organizations, it is not difficult to see how the ideology surrounding gender contributes to the maintenance of male dominance of them. As Barbara Polk (1974) noted in an article on the sources of male power, because men have shaped society's institutions, they tend to fit the value structure of such institutions. For example, masculine gender expectations match certain professional and business roles (lawyer, business executive, university president) better than feminine gender expectations do. In a pattern that would be comic if it were not so aggravating, women trying to fit their behavior to the requirements of such roles are sometimes accused of acting masculine.

Certain institutions are imbued so strongly with the notion of male dominance that women are barred from even trying to fit into leadership roles. Many religions, for example, explicitly promote the idea of a male god ruling the universe from outside. Such an image serves to legitimize male control of worldly institutions and acts very specifically as a barrier to women's participation in such formal and ceremonial leadership positions as priest, minister, rabbi, or imam. Feminist theologians have argued that the pervasive image of

"God the Father" runs deeply in Western cultures affecting even people who have consciously rejected religious dogmas, and that such imagery must be replaced if these cultures are to develop a new vision of women and men (e.g., Daly, 1973; Ruether, 1983). Religion and the ideas it promotes have a large impact on people's values and their conceptions of what is right and wrong. The pervasive acceptance of male dominance within major institutional religions is not a trivial matter for women and men.

MAINTAINING THE STATUS QUO: HOW HIERARCHIES PERPETUATE THEMSELVES

Although many people, female and male, say that they believe in equality between the sexes, their behavior does not always match this belief. Many of women's and men's habits of thought and behavior act to perpetuate the power difference between them. Learned patterns of verbal and nonverbal behavior perpetuate status distinctions. Implicit stereotypes bias perceptions before they even register in awareness, and the metamorphic effects of holding power have sometimes caused men to justify their dominance by inflating their sense of their own worth and devaluing that of women.

Verbal and Nonverbal Behavior

In an earlier chapter, we noted the role played by language in maintaining the status difference between women and men. The habitual use of *he* to mean "any person" and of *man* to mean "people" makes people feel as if females are exceptions. Women who have changed their linguistic habits to avoid the generic "he" actually think more easily of females in response to sex-indefinite cues than do those who use traditional linguistic forms (Khosroshahi, 1989). The terms of address used for males and females also help reinforce the status difference. Men are men, but women are girls or gals, chicks, or broads. It is not uncommon to hear 50-year-old women referred to as "the girls" or to hear a male manager refer to his middle-aged secretary as "my girl." Even a woman's name often incorporates her marital status (Miss or Mrs.), and when a woman marries she is still often expected to take her husband's name rather than vice versa. Finally, the use of the term *ladies,* with its implied delicacy, for adult females is incompatible with the idea of those adult females holding jobs as construction workers, police officers, and perhaps even politicians.

Dominance is also conveyed by the degree to which one can control a conversation: how successfully one can interrupt another speaker and how much attention and response one is able to draw from others. Researchers have found that men talk more than women and that they maintain this difference partly by interrupting women and by not listening or responding to them (Makri-Tsilipakou, 1994; Malamuth & Thornhill, 1994). Such tactics, commonly used by men in cross-gender conversations, tend to discourage women and subdue their efforts at participation, facilitating male conversational control. These patterns of verbal participation tend to reinforce status differences between women and men. The conversational dominance patterns are so well ingrained that when women interrupt men they are seen as rude and disrespectful—as if their behavior is undermining established power relations (LaFrance, 1992).

Communication involves more than words, however, and psychologist Nancy Henley (1977; see also Henley & Freeman, 1995) was one of the first to suggest that nonverbal communication is even more influential than language in maintaining the power differential between women and men. Henley theorized that much of the nonverbal communication that characterizes male–female relationships follows a pattern parallel to that characterizing superior–subordinate relationships. She suggested that subordinates and women, for example, tend to show controlled, circumspect nonverbal behavior, to contract into a small amount of space, and to be touched by other people. Men and powerful people tend to be more relaxed and expansive in their nonverbal behavior and to "touch downward" in the status hierarchy. Henley further suggested that when women break these rules by staring, touching men, or loosening their demeanor, their actions are interpreted not as power plays, which are unexpected in females, but as sexual invitations.

Henley's theory is fascinating, and it has attracted a great deal of attention to the possible "gendering" of nonverbal communication. Yet research support for parallels between gender and dominant–subordinate status in nonverbal communication has been limited. One recent meta-analysis revealed strong evidence that people believe there is a link between nonverbal behavior and such vertical interpersonal dimensions as power, status, and dominance; however, the actual effects of these vertical dimensions on nonverbal behavior were fairly weak. The initiation of nonreciprocal touch, for example, was believed to indicate higher status, but studies showed no consistent link between high status and this behavior. Moreover, these authors concluded that masculine–feminine differences in nonverbal behaviors are not always the same as high status–low status differences. For example, men do show more bodily openness, louder voice, and more visual dominance in mixed-gender interactions than women do—and these differences match differences between high status and low status individuals—but some nonverbal behaviors associated with higher status are more likely to be shown by women than men: more facial expressiveness, smaller distances, and better skill at sending and receiving nonverbal information. And some nonverbal behaviors on which women and men have been found to differ (such as smiling, gazing, touching others, and gesturing) do not seem to be related to such vertical dimensions as power, status, or dominance (Hall, Coats, & LeBeau, 2005).

Thus nonverbal communication may signal and reinforce power differences between women and men in some situations, but the patterns are not always clear. Women and men should probably pay attention to their nonverbal communication, but it is difficult to predict how easy or effective it would be to try to change such behavior.

Some research shows that because of gender stereotypes the same nonverbal cues that communicate power for men may not work for women. Porter and Geis (1981) found that, for a man, sitting at the head of the table is associated with being viewed as the leader of the group, but this same cue has no impact on the perception of a woman as the leader in mixed-sex groups. They suggested that nonconscious gender stereotypes bias people's perceptions, making it difficult to "see" women as leaders, even when they engage in the very same nonverbal behavior that has helped men establish leadership. Other research shows that the way a person delivers a persuasive message—using a nonverbal style that is task oriented, social, submissive, or dominant—has more impact on the degree to which participants are influenced than the speaker's gender does (Carli, LaFleur, & Loeber, 1995). However, when the audience is male, likeableness is a more important determinant of influence for female than for male speakers. Thus, when trying to influence men, women's adoption of a task-oriented style is not necessarily effective.

On the positive side, some research indicates that conscious manipulation of nonverbal cues can sometimes affect power-related aspects of the way a person is viewed and treated. Both female and male observers can accurately interpret different levels of visual dominance displayed by a woman who is interacting with either a man or another woman, rating her as more powerful in the conditions in which her use of visual dominance cues is high (Ellyson, Dovidio, & Fehr, 1981). Thus, with some nonverbal behaviors at least, it may be possible to change the perception of one's status by changing one's nonverbal behavior. Nonverbal communication, then, can act either as a barrier to or as a facilitator of change in the power relationship between females and males.

The Metamorphic Effects of Power

One more factor that tends to perpetuate status hierarchies is the effect of power on the power holder. According to a model developed by David Kipnis (1972; Kipnis, Castell, Gergen, & Mauch, 1976; Rind & Kipnis, 1999), if power holders use strong, controlling means of influence to gain compliance, they tend to believe they have caused the other person's compliance. This belief leads them to devalue the other person, take credit for that person's performance, and try to increase social and psychological distance from that person. A powerful person, gaining a lot of compliance and a lot of (perhaps false) feedback that his or her ideas are good, easily develops an inflated sense of self-worth.

Kipnis's model can readily be applied to male–female relationships. In many situations, men hold power over women, and women are taught to build up men's egos to keep them happy. In such a situation, it is quite likely that men develop an exaggerated sense of superiority with respect to women—a feeling that has the potential to become addictive. One of the reasons the cycle

Reflections

Gender Quotas and Women's Political Power

The issues discussed in this chapter show how difficult it can be to change entrenched power arrangements between women and men. Because the process of change is so slow, many have looked to a new method for balancing power between women and men in the political arena: gender quotas. The basic idea underlying gender quotas is that certain spots (in political parties, on ballots, in legislative bodies) will be reserved for women. The rationale for this approach is that it encourages women to run for political office by providing them with more chance of success, undercuts the impact of negative stereotypes that say women are unsuited for politics, and causes political parties to take women seriously as potential candidates.

Countries around the world have employed a variety of different forms of quotas to implement gender balance in political representation (International Institute for Democracy and Electoral Assistance, 2003b). In some countries, political parties have voluntarily adopted rules that ensure a certain number of women will stand for elected office. For example, Britain's Labour Party insists on a certain number of women-only short lists when deciding on candidates—ensuring that female candidates are selected to stand for some of the most "winnable" seats. The African National Congress party of South Africa has a 33.3% quota for female candidates. Since 1994, the major parties in Sweden have systematically alternated women's and men's names on their nomination lists.

Other countries have laws that require parties to field a certain minimum number of female candidates. For example, in Argentina, parties must present nomination lists with at least 30% women; in France, a 1999 law mandates that nomination lists must include 50% women. Putting more women on the ballot can have a dramatic effect: In France the parity law more than doubled the number of women elected to municipal office between the 1995 and 2001 elections.

Some gender quotas go beyond shaping the lists of candidates and actually reserve a proportion of legislative seats for women. For example, in Tanzania, 20% of national seats and 25% of local government seats are reserved for women.

The use of quotas is clearly an efficient way to get more women into political decision-making positions, but it remains controversial (Dahlerup, 1998). Supporters of quotas argue that they are necessary to get around the negative stereotypes that keep women out of political positions, they minimize the stress on lone "token" women by ensuring that there is at least a critical minority of women in legislative bodies and committees, and they ensure that women are well represented. Opponents argue that quotas are inherently unfair because they interfere with equal opportunity, qualified candidates may be pushed aside, and women who are elected under such systems will be looked down upon.

At the core of the controversy lies the definition of *equality*. If *equality* means "equality of opportunity," then quotas interfere with equality. But could *equality* mean "equality of result"? If so, then quotas might be an entirely appropriate way of ensuring equality. They compensate for barriers that continue to keep women out of politics and ensure that women and men are equally represented. These issues continue to provoke discussion all over the world.

of power differences between women and men is difficult to break, then, is that the very existence of a power difference probably has a tendency to make men feel they are superior to women.

The converse of this pattern is that women, having so frequently been given second-class status, may have learned to accept it as a true reflection of their worth. It appears that the power difference between men and women will be difficult to wipe out, even when many people consciously see it as anachronistic. Narrowing the gender gap in power requires reshaping many habits of thought and behavior.

SUMMARY

Women are much less visible than men in positions of eminence and power. Research has established that no gender differences in basic achievement or power motivation account for these differences in visibility. However, social barriers against achievement and power are often different for women and men. Both sexes are sensitive to these barriers and tend to adjust their behavior accordingly. Consequently, attempts to change patterns of gender-related achievement without altering the social structure in which these patterns are embedded will probably not be very effective at getting more women into positions of visible eminence or power.

Power comes in many forms, and women and men may tend to use it differently. Men hold more of the concrete resources, such as wealth, than women do. Thus men have more opportunities than women to wield power that involves threats or rewards based on these resources and to wield that power openly and directly. Women often find themselves in positions in which the only way they can exert influence is through subtle manipulation or an appeal to personal, relationship-based resources. However, there is not necessarily any built-in gender difference in styles of influence. Rather, the difference is a result of a social structure that awards men higher status and stereotypes them as more competent than women. When women are in positions of authority or are making a demand that is perceived as legitimate, they can more easily use strong, direct influence styles.

It is no small task to make a dramatic increase in the proportion of women holding positions of authority or eminence. The male–female status differences tend to be self-perpetuating, not only because of stereotyping but also because of women's relative exclusion from the "old boy" networks of influence in business, politics, and the professions and because of habits of thought and behavior that frequently place women and men in complementary submissive–dominant roles. Such subtleties as who controls the conversation and which pronoun is used to refer to humans in general help to create a climate in which power differences between women and men go unquestioned.

Status hierarchies, power differentials, and dominance–submission are not necessarily "natural" aspects of the human condition. As Erich Fromm (1973) noted in his classic work on human destructiveness, many so-called primitive hunting-gathering societies have been characterized by an absence of dominance or even permanent leadership associated with high-status qualities or skills. He suggested that the social structure adopted by a group of people determines, in large measure, their need for power differences and status hierarchies among themselves and that the psychology of dominance–submission is an adaptation to a social order rather than a natural human condition that generates a particular social structure. Fromm's argument is a good one to keep in mind when contemplating the kind of future society that might emerge in which *female* is not automatically associated with lower status than *male*. Men themselves now sometimes complain that the traditional masculine role, with its built-in authority, can be restrictive and burdensome. Perhaps, in the process of making changes in the power relationship between the sexes, the social structure will be altered in ways that make the dominance aspect of power less important.

KEY TERMS

achievement motive   directness   competence

power motive   concreteness   reactance

fear of success

13

Issues in the Workplace
Hilary Lips and Nina Colwill

In 1990 Houston's chief of police, Elizabeth Watson, only 3 months into her new job, discovered that she was pregnant. As she prepared to leave her position, she braced herself for what she felt would be the inevitable flood of comments along the lines of, "That's what you get when you put a woman in the job." Instead, to her surprise, her announcement was greeted with arguments that she should *not* quit—strong promises of support from the mayor, her five-member board of assistant chiefs, community members, and her husband. She stayed in the job, becoming probably the first American big-city police chief to have a baby during her tenure (Ryan, 1992).

Chief Watson's case is noteworthy because it is still unusual, not only for a woman to be so visibly successful in a male-dominated line of work, but also for that woman to receive so much public encouragement and support for combining career and family responsibilities in such a position. Women have always worked, even in male-dominated fields, but rarely has their work achieved the same status and recognition as men's, and they have frequently been penalized for trying to "have it all."

To work, to be judged as competent in one's line of endeavor, and to be recognized as a contributing member of society are important ingredients of the self-concept. Employment forms such a critical part of an individual's identity that it is common practice to ask new acquaintances to disclose their occupation within seconds of being introduced to them. This question often takes the form of "What do you do?" indicating that it is a basic question, the answer to which will classify the speaker. This very question provides a clue to the impact of gender stereotypes on social attitudes about work, for it is still probably more likely to be addressed to a man than to a woman. Women are sometimes asked, "Do you work?" or "What does your husband do?"—questions that reveal an expectation that women are unlikely to be in the workforce. Such an expectation is based on ignorance of the facts. About 60% of American women over the age of 16 are employed outside the home or are actively looking for a job, and women make up more than 46% of those employed in the United States (U.S. Bureau of Labor Statistics, 2005b). The frequency with which women are asked, "Do you work?" also reveals a pervasive bias in the way *work* is defined. No activity can be counted as work unless one gets paid for it. Unpaid work in the home, an activity to which many women devote a significant portion of their time and energy, is not granted the status of "real" work.

In this chapter, we examine some of the issues facing women and men in the workplace. In particular, we ask these questions:

- How and why is work divided into "men's work" and "women's work," and how do people fare when they violate these distinctions?
- Is there sex discrimination in pay? In hiring and evaluation?
- What happens to women and men who are "tokens" in workplaces dominated by the other sex?
- How do couples balance job and family when both are employed outside the home?
- How do family roles affect the career paths of women and men?
- What impact do issues of sexuality and power have in the workplace?

DIVISION OF LABOR BY SEX

Women's Entry Into Male-Dominated Professions

Figure 13.1 shows the changes in women's participation in the labor force. Perhaps more telling than the overall increase in women's employment shown in this figure is their increased representation in managerial and professional

Figure 13.1 Employment status of the civilian noninstitutional population 16 years and over by sex, 1971–2005.

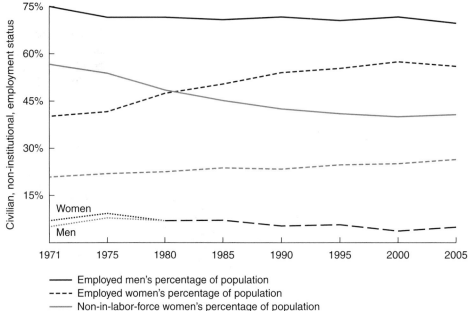

Source: Employment status, Bureau of Labor Statistics, U.S. Department of Labor (2006). Retrieved November 13, 2006, from http://www.bls.gov/cps/#empstat

occupations that have traditionally been male dominated. For example, between 1996 and 2005 in the United States, the percentage of dentists who are women rose from 10.5% to 32.3%, and the percentage of female physicians increased from 30.8% to 32.3%. In the same time period, the percentage of architects who are women rose from 19.4% to 24.4%, and the percentage of female funeral directors went from 9.1% to 21.5% (U.S. Bureau of Labor Statistics, 2006b).

During the 1960s, only 3% of law school students were women. Members of the Harvard Law School class of 1964 remember that there were no women's restrooms, that male students sometimes refused to sit next to them, and that they were asked why they were "wasting" the resources of the law school by taking places that could be used by men. They recall that one professor refused to call on women or allow them to speak in class except on one day, dubbed "Ladies Day," when all the women were put on stage and quizzed about a case involving underwear (Hope, 2003). Women have stormed the legal profession since that time. More than half of all law school students are women; women made up over 30% of lawyers and 41.2% of judges and magistrates in 2005 (U.S. Bureau of Labor Statistics, 2005c).

In some professional fields, however, women's inroads have been slow. For example, despite a number of initiatives to recruit young women into scientific and technical careers, women still make up less than 15% of engineers, and the percentage of female computer scientists and systems analysts has actually dropped slightly in recent years (U.S. Bureau of Labor Statistics, 2005b).

Women are gradually gaining access to a wide range of professional and managerial occupations, but they still have difficulty reaching the top levels of those occupations. Women entering male-dominated professions regularly encounter what some have termed a **glass ceiling.** What is a glass ceiling? It is a barrier that keeps people from rising past a certain point—but a barrier that is transparent and therefore virtually invisible until the person crashes into it. *Glass ceiling* is an apt label for the phenomenon faced by women who aspire to positions of leadership. In 1997 women made up just 2.5% of the top earners in Fortune 500 companies and held only two of the CEO positions (Catalyst, 1998a), and change has been slow since then. Currently, only 10 women are CEOs of Fortune 500 companies. Between 2002 and 2005, the number of women corporate officers in Fortune 500 companies increased by less than 1% and now totals only 16.4% (Catalyst, 2006b). In 2005 women held only 9.4% of titles higher than vice president and only 6.4% of top earner positions in these companies. Women of color held a mere 1.7% of corporate officer positions and comprised only 1% of top earners. In Canada, women hold only 14.4% of corporate office positions in the 500 largest companies and only 7.1% of the top positions. Only 4.5% of Canada's top wage earners are women (Catalyst, 2005).

Even women who do make it past the glass ceiling into top executive positions apparently do not reach a place where gender equity is the norm. One study of executives in a multinational corporation showed that the women who had reached this level faced a *second* glass ceiling (Lyness & Thompson, 1997). These women made the same pay and received the same bonuses as their male counterparts. However, they managed fewer people, were given fewer stock options, and obtained fewer overseas assignments than the men did. They had reached the same level as the men, but being in the same position does not necessarily imply having the same level of status and clout in the organization. When surveyed, the women reported more obstacles and less satisfaction than the men did with their future career opportunities. Clearly, they had gotten the message that they had moved up as far as they could in their company, whereas the men were more likely to see new opportunities ahead. The differences in the ways the two groups were rewarded were subtle, but they apparently signaled to men that they were valued for the long-term and to women that they were not.

Women in management jobs are all too aware of gender discrepancies. A survey of managers and executives by the American Management Association and the Business and Professional Women's Foundation (AMA/BPW, 1999) showed that women were less likely than men to view their compensation as fair and equitable and as equivalent to that of others doing essentially the same work. Women executives surveyed in 2003 reported that they still face exclusion from informal networks, negative stereotyping, and preconceptions about their roles and abilities because they are women (Catalyst, 2003c).

Given the problems women encounter when they enter male-dominated professions, what incentives are likely to attract them? Responses to the AMA/BPW survey indicated that women are more likely than men to work for companies that offer a variety of benefits such as parental leave, flexible work hours, and child-care assistance, that they place a higher value on these benefits than men do, and that they are more likely than men to take advantage of the benefits. Ironically, however, women feel that the use of these benefits carries negative career fallout. For example, over 38% of the women but less than 26% of the men said that using unpaid leave would have a negative impact on their status or career advancement within the company.

Even if senior-level women are willing to opt for working conditions that give them flexibility rather than financial incentives, it appears they are unlikely to get what they want. A survey of Canadian women executives revealed that they overwhelmingly preferred such incentives as a shorter work week or the flexibility to work from home for part of the week to a huge paycheck (Tedesco, 2001). However, these benefits were not available to most of the women surveyed.

If women continue to enroll in programs that train them for the male-dominated professions, the gender composition of business, law, medicine, and architecture will soon change, but that of engineering, computing, and the physical sciences have further to go. The male-dominated professions control much of the power in society and thus have a strong impact that extends beyond a narrow occupational sphere, but they employ a minority of North American men and women. Perhaps more telling to those who study the division of labor by sex is the fact that women are not entering male-dominated blue-collar occupations and that men are not entering any of the female-dominated occupations fast enough to warrant our notice.

The Forgotten People

Although there have been millions, probably billions, of words written about gender-related issues in the workplace over the past 25 years, most of these words have been addressed to two visible but small groups of people: women in management and male-dominated professions and the people who study them. Hundreds of articles have reported research on female professionals and female managers. Dozens of books have advised them on their clothing, their family lives, and their sex lives. Yet relatively little attention has been paid to the women who enter male-dominated blue-collar jobs or to the men who enter female-dominated occupations. Even more surprising, researchers' and the media's seemingly insatiable interest in employed women has rarely extended itself to the majority of employed women who work in female-dominated occupations.

WOMEN IN FEMALE-DOMINATED OCCUPATIONS   Most nurses, book-keepers, nursery-school teachers, secretaries, typists, and receptionists share a common characteristic: their femaleness. These are the women who work in female-dominated occupations, the women who are doing "women's work." They do not enjoy the prestige that their formal education, on-the-job training, and responsibility would suggest; their pay is lower and their opportunities for advancement fewer than those of women in male-dominated occupations. Yet every year young women enter the female-dominated occupations in large numbers.

Table 13.1 shows the percentage of women who work in the leading occupations for women. The occupations that employ the largest numbers of women—secretary, receptionists, registered nurse, bookkeeper—are also heavily

Table 13.1   Leading occupations for women in 2005, sorted by women's percentages of the total for each occupation. Occupations that employ the most women tend to be female-dominated and low paid relative to the median weekly earnings for men working full-time. This chart shows the percentage of women, their median weekly earning in the leading occupations for full-time women workers in the United States, and each occupation's average earning as a percentage of all men's weekly median earnings for 2005.

Occupations	*Percent Women*	*Median Weekly Salary*	*Percent of All Men's Median Weekly Salary*[1]
Secretaries and administrative assistants	97.3	$559	86%
Receptionists and information clerks	91.7	$463	92%
Registered nurses	91.6	$930	92%
Bookkeepers, accounting & auditing clerks	89.3	$551	95%
Nursing, psychiatric, and home health aides	88.5	$385	95%
Elementary and middle school teachers	82.0	$813	89%
Social workers	78.6	$682	87%
Cashiers	74.5	$322	83%
Managers, medical and health services	71.3	$1,026	77%
Adjusters, appraisers, examiners, investigators	63.0	$706	73%
Accountants and auditors	61.8	$784	73%
Managers, food preparation/serving workers	59.0	$398	76%
Secondary school teachers	55.6	$841	89%
Sales supervisors/managers, retail sales	41.4	$525	73%
Women's median weekly salary, for all occupations[1]		**$585**	**81%**

[1]Median usual weekly earnings of full-time wage and salary workers, 16 years and older, by detailed occupation and sex, 2005 annual averages.

Source: U.S. Department of Labor (2006). Retrieved November 21, 2006, from http://www.bls.gov/cps/wlf-table 18-2006.pdf female dominated (U.S. Bureau of Labor Statistics, 2006b). To improve the lives of working women, it would make sense to pay special attention to such occupations. Yet there has been surprisingly little public relations aimed at improving the image of these occupations and surprisingly little effort aimed at lowering their female domination by recruiting men.

Educational data indicate that women who enter the female-dominated professions have planned their choice; they tend to follow gender-typed patterns of preparation and entry. The educational choices that many women make at the college level (for example, their disproportionate representation among degree recipients in education, healthcare, and library science) suggest that they anticipate entry into one of the female-dominated professions. Furthermore, a majority of young women expect to combine employment and motherhood during their adult lives (Hoffnung, 2004) and may view female-dominated occupations as providing more flexibility (e.g., shorter preparation time, more opportunities for part-time work) for such a combination.

Not just individual but also structural factors act to guide women into the female-dominated professions. Women are more likely than men to be deterred from attending college because of financial concerns (Mcqueen, 1999). Gender stereotyping of academic areas such as mathematics and science may channel female students away from courses needed to pursue the male dominated professions. The perceived lack of availability of parental leave and child-care alternatives may discourage women from pursuing careers that require a 60-hour workweek, as some of the male-dominated professions do. The male domination of some professions means that a woman needs an extra dose of courage just to claim her place in that world. Sex discrimination, both blatant and subtle, still blocks women's entry into some professions. All of these structural factors are discussed in more detail later in this chapter.

More than one-fifth of the female workforce in the United States is employed in administrative support and clerical jobs (U.S. Bureau of Labor Statistics, 2005b). Most organizations could not function without these women: A full 97.3% of secretaries, 92.4% of receptionists, and 91.3% of financial records processors are women (US Bureau of Labor Statistics, 2005b). Yet secretaries and other administrative support workers are often unappreciated, laboring invisibly in a world in which all eyes are on their sisters in management. North American organizations are still reaping the benefits from the days when women seldom extended their occupational choices beyond nurse, teacher, and secretary, and managers have come to expect highly talented people to fill top-level secretarial and other clerical positions. However, the stereotype of a secretary as a bright young woman temporarily marking time in a job while she waits to get married is no longer (if it ever was) accurate. The average secretary is 43 years old, likely to be married, with children, and with a job tenure of, on average, more than 4 years (Texas Workforce Commission, 2005). She is most likely expected to possess a wide variety of skills that go well beyond keyboarding and filing; in addition to strong organizational and interpersonal skills, many employers expect extensive knowledge of various software applications such as word processing, accounting programs, Web design, spreadsheets, and database management. Despite these requirements, however, she is likely to be undercompensated: secretaries working full-time earn an average of $562 per week—less than, for example, postal service clerks, couriers and messengers, reservation ticket agents, and computer operators (U.S. Bureau of Labor Statistics, 2005b). This future is not an attractive one for young women currently making occupational choices.

As more and more highly intelligent, highly motivated women enter male-dominated fields in which they can expect to be better paid for their efforts, recognized for their talents, and given opportunities for advancement, however, a critical shortage of good secretaries may threaten the job market. It is difficult to predict the changes this shortage will engender, but one optimistic possibility is that to attract first-rate secretarial help, top management of large organizations will increasingly envision the secretarial position as a training ground for management and offer secretaries with some management training or secretaries who are prepared to gain management training the opportunities for advancement that have always been offered to entry-level men. The secretarial position requires many skills required of middle managers—skills such as independence, organization, the ability to take orders, and the ability to gain satisfaction from the accomplishments of others. It also offers an ideal location to learn the workings of the organization, and a case could be made for establishing the secretarial position as a common route into management for women and men.

WOMEN IN BLUE-COLLAR JOBS   It is no accident that more women are entering male-dominated professions than are entering male-dominated blue-collar jobs. Women have long benefited from a gender-role stereotype that labels them as good students, and women who enter occupations based largely on "book learning," even though they may be considered "uppity," can take advantage of this stereotype. But technical, spatial, and mechanical abilities and physical strength—the characteristics deemed necessary for male-dominated blue-collar work, particularly the trades—are characteristics that women have been believed to be lacking (Colwill & Colwill, 1985). Furthermore, professional women come to their jobs equipped with degrees that serve as recognized proof of their competence—degrees they earned in an atmosphere in which everyone else was equally naive. Because a blue-collar woman learns most of her visible skills on the job rather than in the classroom, she must undergo her training in an extremely vulnerable situation, often as the only neophyte in the group. Thus there are few visible skills by which the entry-level female blue-collar worker can be assessed. In situations such as this, in which there are few cues available to evaluate ability, evaluators may tend to rely more heavily on external characteristics, such as gender, as a means for judging a worker's competence.

Given these problems, it is not surprising that blue-collar women have remained in lower-paying female-dominated industries. Women are the sewing machine operators, making just over minimum wage, rather than the highly paid construction workers (U.S. Bureau of Labor Statistics, 2005b), and when they do enter the higher-paying industries, it is often into different and lower-paying jobs than men have traditionally occupied. For example, in the United States, men hold 98.2% of the automobile mechanic positions, and women hold 60% of the less lucrative jobs assembling electrical and electronic equipment. Women make up only 1.7% of electricians, 0.36% of plumbers, 1.4% of carpenters, and 7% of precision equipment repairers. They are 72.5% of sewing machine operators but less than 1% of excavating and loading machine operators (U.S. Bureau of Labor Statistics, 2005b). Furthermore, as shown in Table 13.2, women are far less likely than men to be in supervisory positions in these blue-collar occupations, and perhaps because they are clustered at the bottom levels of these occupations, they earn less than men.

The gender segregation of blue-collar occupations begins early. In high school vocational and technical courses across 12 states, a recent report showed that girls make up 96% of students enrolled in cosmetology courses, 87% of students in child-care courses, and 86% of students in courses training participants to become health care aides (National Women's Law Center, 2002). Meanwhile, boys dominate in courses that teach plumbing and electrical work (94%), welding and carpentry (93%), and automotive technology (92%). According to the report, these lopsided distributions reflect the results of discriminatory practices in which girls and boys are steered into different fields. For example, one vocational

Table 13.2   Women held 29% of these jobs in 2005, but some lower-level blue-collar production occupations appear to be disproportionately occupied by women and women hold fewer supervisory or manager positions than might be expected.

Production Occupations	Percent of workers who are women	Women's median weekly earnings	Women's percentage of men's earnings
First-line supervisors/managers of production and operating workers	20	$545	67
Inspectors, testers, sorters, samplers, and weighers	38	486	72
Bakers	50	357	74
Packaging and filling machine operators and tenders	55	384	85
Electrical, electronics, and electromechanical assemblers	60	441	84
Packers and packagers, hand	64	358	88
All Production Occupations	**29**	**423**	**70**

Source: Bureau of Labor Statistics (2006), table 18. Retrieved November 21, 2006, from http://www.bls.gov/cps/wlf-table18-2006.pdf

high school in New York prominently displayed a banner that read "Builds Mechanical Men"—implying that "its mission is to education male students in mechanical fields" (p. 6).

When a woman does venture into a male-dominated trade, her sense of isolation resembles that of the top-level female executive. She is unlikely to have a female peer and even less likely to have a female boss (Cantrell, 1996; Colwill & Colwill, 1985). As a recent hire, her advancement, which probably will be based solely on seniority, will be slow, and her potential for layoff is high (O'Farrell, 1995). In addition, virtually every study of women in the trades shows some evidence of resentment among coworkers and first-line supervisors; these women are subjected to practical jokes, threats of violence, sexual harassment, and actual violence—although few men actually participate in these activities (Mansfield, Koch, Henderson, Cohn, & Young, 1991; O'Farrell, 1995). The woman who enters a male-dominated blue-collar job when a woman before her has failed at that job is particularly likely to experience the resentment of this small minority of male coworkers.

Brigid O'Farrell (1995) argued that the slow pace of integration is due in large part not to the choices of individual women but to employer resistance, organizational barriers, government policies, and lack of opportunities. During World War II, when women were needed for factory work, the government did not simply suggest that companies lift previous restrictions on hiring women. Rather, they undertook a massive recruitment drive and established child-care centers for women workers. When such opportunities were clearly made available, women were responsive to them. Under current conditions, the opportunities for women in blue-collar jobs are neither aggressively marketed nor even clearly supported in many companies. However, a small but determined group of women is making some inroads.

MEN IN FEMALE-DOMINATED OCCUPATIONS   There is no doubt that women in male-dominated occupations suffer discrimination from people who feel that their reach exceeds their grasp, and women in female-dominated occupations suffer from association with that which is female and therefore low in prestige. But do the few men who enter the female-dominated occupations—nurses, child-care workers, elementary school teachers, and secretaries—sometimes have an even tougher row to hoe? To emulate one's status superiors, as women do when they enter male-dominated occupations, is a forgivable deviation from the norm in an achieving society, but to emulate one's status inferiors, as men do when they enter female-dominated occupations, tends to draw highly negative responses.

The situation is far from bleak for men in most female-dominated occupations, however. Regardless of the occupation, from clerical work to such professions as nursing and librarianship, men have tended to be represented disproportionately for their numbers in senior and administrative positions (Kaufman, 1995). In nursing, a field that is heavily female dominated, many of the small number of men hold administrative positions, and the usually female chief nursing executives are rarely tapped for top hospital administration positions (Kalist, 2002). Similarly, although women numerically dominate the field of education, they tend to occupy lower-prestige-level jobs and are underrepresented in administrative positions. Although women make up the vast majority of public school teachers, 66% of school principals in Canada (O'Haire, 2004) and 56% in the United States (National Center for Education Statistics, 2005) are men. Similar patterns are found in social work and librarianship. Moreover, the tendency for men to make more money than women do carries over into female-dominated occupations. Even among clerical workers, males get paid more than their female counterparts with similar education and job qualifications (U.S. Bureau of Labor Statistics, 2005b). It appears that even when men do enter female-dominated occupations, the division of labor along gender lines is maintained through the clustering of men in the higher-status, higher-paid segments of these occupations.

One researcher who studied the career progress of men in the female-dominated occupations of nursing, librarianship, elementary school teaching, and social work found what she termed a **glass escalator**—a systematic set of hidden advantages for men in such occupations. In her interviews with men in these positions, Christine Williams (1992) found that they experienced discrimination in hiring but that it was usually a positive discrimination, a *preference* for hiring

Overview   Occupational gender segregation

- Women's labor force participation has increased steadily in recent decades. Women have also steadily increased their participation in such male-dominated professions as medicine, law, and business.

- Women's gains have been slow in certain scientific and technical professions, such as engineering, computing, and the physical sciences.

- Women frequently encounter a "glass ceiling" in business and professional fields; thus there is a shortage of women in top positions.

- Many women work in female-dominated occupations, which are often characterized by low pay and low status.

- Most highly paid blue-collar jobs, such as the construction trades, continue to be dominated by men.

- Men in female-dominated occupations also experience discrimination; however, it is more likely to be positive discrimination and to involve a "glass elevator" instead of a "glass ceiling."

Reflections   Women in the Military

The military used to be a bastion of occupational gender segregation. In the first place, it was an institution run by and almost totally dominated by men. Although women had been in combat (usually in disguise) since the Revolutionary War, women were not formally a part of the U.S. Armed Forces until the formation of the Army Nurse Corps in 1901. In the second place, women's role within the military services was parallel to the role of civilian women: subordinate to men and restricted to traditionally feminine occupations. During World War I, about 74% of enlisted women served in the nursing corps; most of the rest served as clerks, translators, munitions workers, and recruiters. During World War II, women's roles expanded through the formation of the Women's Auxiliary Corps (WAC), and WACs could be found in most positions that did not involve direct combat (Wilgoren, 2003). However, just after that war, legislation imposed a 2% ceiling on the number of women in each service and excluded women from combat.

During the Vietnam War, traditional gendered division of labor persisted within the military: Almost 84% of women who served in that war were nurses. However, during that war, the 2% ceiling on women was eliminated, and women made up 7.7% of those deployed. Later, in 1981, many of the restrictions on the kinds of military jobs women could have were abolished. Women formed 18.5% of those deployed in the 1991 Gulf War and fought in combat support positions.

It is painful to think that war advances women's opportunities, but war is what the military is all about, and wars create the necessity to fill a wide range of military occupations. In the ongoing Iraq War more women are serving in more positions than ever before. Most of the restrictions on female soldiers have been lifted; women are formally barred only from submarines, the Special Forces, and the infantry, armor, and artillery divisions of the Army. A majority of Americans say they support the idea of having women in combat positions and that women should be allowed in submarines and on fighter planes (Wilgoren, 2003). However, many seem to feel a lingering unease: They are more uncomfortable about women in combat than men in combat.

The idea of anyone participating in any war provokes distress and controversy, as befits an endeavor with such serious and painful consequences to so many. Yet the particular discomfort that many people still feel with the idea of women in combat shows the strength of gender stereotypes. Are women really in need of more protection than men? Is war really worse for female than for male soldiers? And do the people who object to women in combat understand that most victims of war are, in fact, women and children who are civilians? That women are already on the front lines, whether or not they are soldiers (Nordstrom, 2004)?

men, because men were in such short supply in those occupations. The men also reported that they faced subtle pressures to "move up" in their professions. For example, one talented kindergarten teacher who loved teaching was encouraged continually to consider administration or to teach at a higher level, and one librarian had to struggle to remain in his preferred field of children's collections as his supervisors told him that he was not aiming high enough. In contrast to women in token positions, the men were likely to be supervised by someone of their own sex because males are disproportionately represented among supervisors in these occupations. This meant that it was sometimes easier for the token men than for their female colleagues to form bonds of friendship with supervisors—another reason they were often tapped for advancement.

The main discrimination faced by men in female-dominated professions came from the public. For instance, male elementary school teachers encountered suspicion about their interest in children and had to monitor their behavior carefully to guard against charges of sexual abuse. One librarian reported that "Some of the people . . . complained that they didn't want to have a man doing the storytelling scenario. And I got transferred here to the central library in an equivalent job" (p. 295). These men also encountered negative stereotypes about their competence and motivation, particularly from other men. An elementary school teacher reported, "If I tell men that I don't know, that I'm meeting for the first time, that that's what I do . . . sometimes there's a look on their faces that, you know, 'Oh, couldn't get a real job?'" (p. 294).

If history repeats itself, men's entry into female-dominated occupations will raise the status of the jobs and the salaries of the incumbents, but not without pain for the men who are treated as gender-role deviants and for the women whose jobs are lost. Only when this transition is complete—only when jobs cease to be identified as "men's work" and "women's work"—will it be possible to evaluate objectively the contribution to the labor market made by any particular occupation.

SEX DISCRIMINATION

Pay Equity

In the not too distant past, it was considered perfectly acceptable to pay women less than men for the same work. Anyone arguing against the unfairness of such a system was told that supporting a family was the primary responsibility of the man of the house and that even single men must prepare financially for that responsibility. There were, of course, single women with children; there were women who supported their husbands and their children; and there were single men and women who never married or had children. The social conscience of North America was not easily activated by gender equity issues in those days, however, and social policy was rarely affected by deviations from the norm.

In more recent times, society's collective conscience has been activated by gender inequalities, and two new concepts have been introduced into the workplace. The first is the notion that women and men should be paid the same wage for the same work. Although this concept, known as **equal pay for equal work,** is supported by legislation, it has yet to become reality for all women and men throughout the labor force. Another idea, the widespread acceptance of which started only in the 1980s and 1990s, is the notion that the work traditionally done by women and that traditionally done by men can be considered equal in value and should be remunerated accordingly. Implementation of this idea requires that the value—the composite of skill, effort, responsibility, and working conditions—of jobs normally filled by women and jobs normally filled by men within the same organization be established and compared. For example, how does the value of the work of a mail clerk (usually male) compare with that of a secretary (usually female)? How does the work of a grocery store shelving clerk (usually male) compare in value to the work of a cashier (usually female) in the same store? If the values of the jobs are determined to be similar, the salaries should be similar, according to the principle of **comparable worth** or equal pay for work of equal value.

Despite decades of debate, discussion, and activism around the issue of pay equity, women continue to earn less than men do (see Figure 13.2). The U.S. Census Bureau (2006) reported that in 2005 full-time women workers age 15 and over earned 76.98% of what their male counterparts earned. And the higher the income, the greater the ratio of men to women at that level. Among

Figure 13.2 Median wage and salary income in 2004 dollars for full-time, year-round workers 15 years and older.

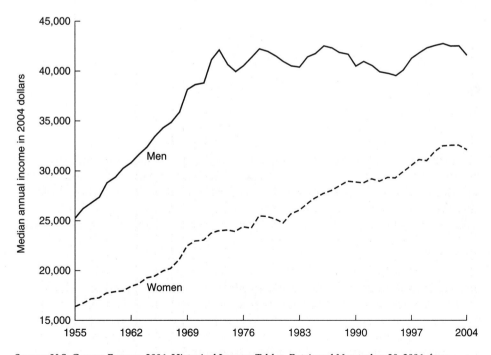

Source: U.S. Census Bureau. 2006. Historical Income Tables. Retrieved November 20, 2006, from http://www.census.gov/hhes/www/income/histinc/p36ar.html

these full-time workers, the ratio of men to women earning $100,000 or more per year is 4.15 to 1. Among all people age 15 and over who have income, the ratio of men to women earning $250,000 or more is 6.35 to 1 (U.S. Census Bureau, 2006). Furthermore, within every age range, there are more women than men among workers paid hourly rates below the federal minimum wage (U.S. Bureau of Labor Statistics, 2005a).

The gender pay gap shows up within all the major racial/ethnic groups in the United States and within every educational level; there are few signs that it is closing (Lips, 2003). It is not confined to either male-dominated or female-dominated occupations, as seen in Table 13.3. People often believe that the gender pay gap is closing, but there is little evidence that it is moving consistently or quickly in that direction (Lips, 2003). In fact, as recently as 2004, the U.S. Census Bureau issued a report documenting a significant widening of the gap due to a drop in the earnings of women (DeNavas-Walt, Proctor, & Mills, 2004).

The fight for equal pay goes back to the 19th century. In the United States, it began in 1868 with a resolution backed by workers seeking justice (Freeman, 1989) and was enshrined in legislation in 1963 with the passage of the Equal

Table 13.3   Women's 2005 median weekly earnings as a percentage of men's in six highly female-dominated and six highly male-dominated occupations.

	Percent of participants who are women	Women's percentage of men's earnings
Female-Dominated Occupations		
Secretaries and administrative assistants	97.3	86
Receptionists and information clerks	91.7	92
Registered nurses	91.6	92
Bookkeepers, accounting and auditing clerks	89.3	95
Teaching assistants	90.8	100
Nursing, psychiatric, and home health aides	88.5	95
Male-Dominated Occupations		
Computer software engineers	21.2	81
Driver/sales workers and truck drivers	3.7	75
Engineering technicians, except drafters	18.9	85
Supervisors/managers, production and operating workers	19.7	67
Laborers and freight, stock, and material movers, hand	15.2	87
Police and sheriff's patrol officers	14.5	87

Source: Bureau of Labor Statistics (2006), table 18. Retrieved November 21, 2006, from http://www.bls.gov/cps/wlf-table18-2006.pdf

Pay Act. Yet in the more than 40 years since the passage of that law guaranteeing equal pay for equal work, the gender pay gap has not closed. When times get tough, pay equity is sometimes the first goal to be sacrificed. For example, in 2004 the government of the Canadian province of Newfoundland successfully argued to the provincial Supreme Court that a budget crisis during the 1990s justified cancellation of pay equity raises for thousands of female hospital workers—saying the budget problems had to take precedence over constitutionally guaranteed equality rights (Tibbetts, 2004).

Although the concept of equal pay for work of equal value is considered to be an economic issue, it is also a symptom of a much broader social psychological phenomenon that manifests itself in the devaluation of women and of what women do (Colwill, 1984; Lips, 2003). Because women and men are valued differently, work that is labeled "masculine" has a different connotation attached to it than work that is labeled "feminine." It is extremely difficult, if not impossible, for anyone who has been conventionally socialized in North American society to evaluate the worth of an occupation independent of the gender labeling of that occupation. To tackle pay equity is to tackle the most basic tenets of our gender-role socialization, the most basic assumptions behind sex discrimination.

Discrimination in Hiring and Evaluation

Although sex discrimination in the workplace has been illegal for decades, researchers continue to find evidence of its existence. Most of this discrimination is directed at women, who are more likely than men to be seen as stepping out of their "place." However, men in female-dominated occupations also complain of discrimination.

One basis for sex discrimination in hiring and evaluation is the tendency to devalue work that is associated with women. A disconcerting example of this tendency can be seen in the statistics on literary awards. Women are stereotyped as being good with words and, as discussed in Chapter 6, when gender differences in verbal performance are found they tend to favor women. Yet prestigious literary awards such as the Pulitzer prizes, the Nobel Prize for literature, and the Booker prizes have historically gone much more often to male than to female writers (Lips, 2003). Another example can be found in research showing that people rate occupations as having less prestige and deserving less pay when they perceive them as having more women or as requiring feminine-stereotyped skills (Cejka & Eagly, 1999; Glick, 1991; Glick et al., 1995).

But how would the tendency to devalue women's work cause discrimination against men in female-dominated occupations? Sex discrimination against women and sex discrimination against men seem to take different forms. Women tend to be the targets of prejudice and discrimination in situations in which their competence and credibility, particularly to do malelike things, are at stake. Men, conversely, tend to have discriminatory attitudes and behaviors directed at them when they do femalelike things that are considered to be beneath them. Thus, as suggested earlier, women are punished as incompetents for trying to emulate their social superiors, and men are punished as deviants for trying to emulate their social inferiors. This difference was probably best demonstrated in Levinson's (1975) field study, in which men who applied for traditionally female jobs were often told that the job was too simple, too dull, or too low paying. Women applying for "men's jobs" were more likely to be told that the job was too difficult or that it required too much strength or time commitment for a woman.

But have prejudice and discrimination not been reduced dramatically in the years since 1975, when Levinson's research was published? Surveys show that negative attitudes toward female managers persist, especially among men (Heilman, 2001; Schein, 2001) and especially if the female manager uses a stereotypically masculine, "directive" leadership style (Eagly et al., 1992; Rudman & Glick, 2001). Furthermore, women managers in line management positions tend to receive lower performance evaluations than women in staff management positions and than men in either type of position (Lyness & Heilman, 2006). The researchers suggested that this discriminatory pattern is based on the perception that line positions, which involve the direction and control of essential organizational activities, are more suited to the masculine role, whereas staff positions, which involve the provision of support and expertise to line managers, are a better fit to the feminine role. Thus women in line positions appear to be evaluated more negatively because their gender makes them a poorer fit for such positions.

Data concerning the career paths of managers continue to show that women in high-status male-dominated occupations are the targets of prejudice and discrimination. One study of 1,000 top female and male managers at the top 20 U.S. companies showed that even when women had the same qualifications as men—the same education, similar levels of job tenure, equivalent work experience in the same industries and job areas, similar willingness and ability to relocate—they received smaller salary increases and fewer opportunities to relocate over a 5-year period. Over that 5-year period, women received pay increases and bonuses averaging 54% of their salaries, compared to 65% for men (Stroh, Brett, & Reilly, 1996). A survey of top executives by the American Management Association and the Business and Professional Women's Foundation (1999) showed that, among this group of high-level managers, women's base compensation averaged less than 70% of men's. Moreover, the gender discrepancy was greatest at the highest levels. Women at the top (CEO) level of management made 60.8% of what their male counterparts made, women in the next two levels made 68.7% of male earnings, and women at the fourth and fifth levels of management made 71% and 74.4% of male earnings, respectively. And it is very difficult for women to reach these top positions. Relative to men, women receive fewer promotions—their advancement slows down—as they move up the organizational ladder (Lyness & Judiesch, 1999). One reason women's advancement slows down is that women need to have higher performance evaluations than men do to receive the same promotions (Lyness & Heilman, 2006).

What processes are responsible for the difficulties women face as they try to advance in their careers? Madeline Heilman (2001) argued that gender stereotypes interfere with the way women are evaluated, meaning that "being competent provides no assurance that a woman will advance to the same organizational levels as an equivalently performing man" (p. 657).

First, she noted, there are description-based biases. Stereotypically masculine qualities are thought to be necessary qualifications for successful managers, leaders, or executives, and most women are not expected to have these qualities. Thus women are, almost by definition, expected not to fit in executive positions. Heilman's **lack of fit** model postulates that a major factor in personnel decisions is the expectation of how successful an individual will be in a particular job. This performance expectation is guided by the perceived match between the individual's abilities and the requirements of the job. Performance expectations, shaped by perceptions of how well or poorly an individual fits the job, in turn have a strong influence on the evaluation of the individual's performance.

A second factor that can work against women is the presence of prescription-based biases (Heilman, 2001). Even if a woman is seen to have the qualities needed to perform well in a job that is perceived to require masculine qualities, she is not home free. Rather, she is regarded with dislike or suspicion for not behaving in ways a woman *should* behave. After all, how can she be, for example, as tough and competitive as a "masculine" executive and *also* as nice and relationship oriented as a woman is supposed to be?

Heilman argued that certain organizational conditions pave the way for descriptive and prescriptive biases to depress the evaluation of women's performance:

- *Ambiguity in evaluation criteria:* It is harder to argue with successful performance when it is measured by something as concrete as dollars earned or number of clients than when it is measured by vague criteria such as being an inspiring leader. Women are often penalized in evaluations on the basis of such vague criteria.

- *Lack of structure in the evaluation process:* If the evaluation process is not carefully structured, it enables the same aspects of performance to be given different weights for different individuals or particular sources of information to be considered for some individuals but not for others. For example, evaluators may consider personal comments or anecdotes that reflect badly on a woman but brush similar comments aside when they concern a man.

- *Ambiguity about the source of successful performance:* Even when a woman performs very well, it may be difficult to identify her contribution to a final product that is produced jointly with other workers. Thus people may be able to acknowledge the success of her project without necessarily acknowledging her competence.

- *Ambiguity about the reason for successful upward mobility:* A woman who is promoted to a high level may encounter the belief that she reached her position only because of affirmative action or a special relationship with a powerful person. Thus her success can be explained away as due to something other than her own competence.

The consequences of gender stereotypes can be very negative for women in the workplace. First, it is difficult for their competence to shine. Second, when their competence is evident, they are often derogated and disliked because they are violating prescriptive stereotypes of femininity.

It appears that the strongest prejudice against women in a traditionally male occupation is likely to occur when people are considering hypothetical situations, among men who have had little exposure to women in that particular job, or in situations in which people are lacking data that would help them make an informed decision about the worth of a woman's work. Women and men who have been managed by women have fewer negative stereotypes about female managers (Ezell, Odewahn, & Sherman, 1981; Wheeless & Berryman-Fink, 1985), and discrimination against women is more likely to occur if managers are given insufficient information to make a personnel decision based on competence (Davison & Burke, 2000; Gerdes and Garber, 1983) or if the evaluators are not experienced managers (Marlowe, Schneider, & Nelson, 1996).

There has been a tendency in the past for both men and women to show prejudice against women, leading many people to believe everyone prefers to work with and for men. However, numerous studies now show that women are more accepting of female managers than men are (Die, Debbs, & Walker, 1990; Lortie-Lussier & Rinfret, 2002; Stevens & DeNisi, 1980; Wheeless & Berryman-Fink, 1985). In one such study, female employees expressed a preference for female coworkers (Haefner, 1977), and in another, female managers evaluated managerial women more positively than they evaluated comparably qualified men (Jabes, 1980). Female managers in the latter study were judged as being more intelligent, more likable, more successful, and more able than their male counterparts, and the future of female managers was seen as more satisfying.

Stereotypes almost invariably lead to discrimination. However, there is increasing evidence that stereotypes may have other deleterious effects. They may actually motivate the stereotyped person to behave in a manner consistent with the stereotype. This process, known as the **self-fulfilling prophecy,** was demonstrated in a study by von Baeyer, Sherk, and Zanna (1981) in which women were interviewed by men whom they were led to believe held either traditional or nonstereotypical views about women. Women who were interviewed by the "traditional" men dressed for the interview in a more "feminine" manner and were more likely to wear jewelry, scarf, and makeup than were women who were interviewed by the "nontraditional" men. In addition, women who thought they were being interviewed by men with traditional attitudes were more likely to adopt subservient nonverbal gestures: to stare at the interviewer when he was talking and to look away when they answered his questions.

Stereotypes may create a vicious circle. We have certain attitudes about a person, she or he becomes aware of these attitudes and behaves in a manner consistent with our stereotypes, and our stereotypes are reinforced. The von Baeyer, Sherk, and Zanna (1981) study demonstrated the link between perceived stereotypes and the stereotyped person's behavior. A second study by Towson, MacDonald, and Zanna (1981) demonstrated the reinforcement of the stereotyper's original attitudes. In this study, the researchers had male actors conduct interviews with female actors playing one of two roles: the role of a "feminine" woman (jewelry, scarf, makeup, and subservient nonverbal communication) or the role of a "nonfeminine" woman (same clothing, but no jewelry, scarf, or makeup, and the actor looked at the interviewer when he *and* she were speaking). In addition, the feminine woman said that she would quit work to raise her family; the nonfeminine woman said that if she were to get married and have children she would organize her life so that family commitments and career advancement would not conflict. Videotapes of these interviews were shown to men who had been tested as having either traditional or nontraditional gender-role attitudes. Men with traditional attitudes were less likely to predict job success for any of the female applicants. Furthermore, feminine women were seen as being better fitted for jobs in female-dominated occupations, and nonfeminine women were judged as being more appropriate candidates for traditionally male jobs.

How do women react to being the targets of discrimination? Sometimes they simply refuse to acknowledge it. Perhaps because they cannot bear to face the reality of its unfairness, women tend to underrate the amount of sex discrimination that is visited on them personally, even when they are quite aware that women in general experience sex discrimination. This phenomenon is known as **denial of personal discrimination** (Crosby, 1984). Women, and probably all people who are the objects of discrimination, adopt cognitive strategies that protect them from feeling deprived, using reference groups similar to themselves (other women in similar situations) rather than facing the incongruity associated with comparisons to more privileged groups. Clearly, people prefer to protect themselves from feelings that they are being treated unfairly.

Despite their lower salaries, women are less likely than men to report dissatisfaction with their pay (Buchanan, 2005; Jackson, 1989; Steel & Lovrich, 1987; Williams, McDaniel, & Nguyen, 2006). When given the opportunity to compare their pay with that of other workers, participants in one study chose to see the pay of the same-sex and same-job group first (Major & Forcey, 1985). The same study also showed that both men and women assigned to a "feminine" job expected less pay and rated their obtained pay as fairer than those in "masculine" jobs did. In addition, women thought they deserved less pay for their work than men did, regardless of their job assignment. People are apparently so used to evaluating their own and others' pay expectations by making implicit same-sex comparisons that they do not question the fairness or appropriateness of restricting their comparisons in this way. Interestingly, for women at least, looking beyond one's own sex for comparison purposes may be linked to discontent. One study of professional women indicated that women with male reference groups perceived a greater gap between what they had and wished to have, were more pessimistic about their futures, and were more dissatisfied than were their counterparts who compared themselves to other women (Zanna, Crosby, & Loewenstein, 1987).

Minorities and Tokenism

Women and men in nontraditional occupations often find themselves holding **token positions**—positions in which they are treated as symbols or representatives of their sex. Kanter (1977) made a clear distinction between tokens and minority members. She argued that in skewed groups, in which there is a large preponderance of one sex over the other (a ratio of 85 to 15, for example), the minority members are truly tokens or symbols of their group. It is only when their proportions rise to a ratio of, say, 65 to 35, that we can speak of *minorities* and *majorities* rather than of *tokens* and *dominants,* for only then do the minority members have the opportunity to be seen as individuals, differentiated from one another. At this point, they can form coalitions and have the opportunity to affect the group culture.

Kanter's sociological study of "Indsco," a pseudonymous company in which she conducted research in the 1970s, provided a great deal of information about people in token positions. Her research made it clear that tokens tend to be perceived as members of the outgroup rather than as individuals. Their every action tends to be seen either as typical outgroup behavior or as behavior that is unusual for a member of the outgroup rather than as the action of one unique person.

The token status places one in a particularly visible and thus vulnerable position, and both male and female tokens may find it difficult to relax and do their jobs as competently as they would under less adverse circumstances. In a study that attempted to duplicate the situation in which tokens find themselves, participants believed they were interacting, via television screen, with three other people, discussing opinions on several noncontroversial topics (Lord & Saenz, 1985). In reality, they were being videotaped giving their opinions as they watched prerecorded videotapes of three confederates. In the nontoken condition of this experiment, the confederates were the same sex as the participant; in the token condition, the three confederates were the other sex. The results indicated that tokens seemed to exhibit a memory deficit. Even in this relatively nonthreatening situation of expressing opinions on everyday topics and even though they were treated no differently than nontokens, they could not remember as well as nontokens what they had said or what the three others had said.

In a second part of the experiment, participants serving as observers watched the four videotapes—the three videotapes watched by the participant plus a videotape of the participant him- or herself. These observers were more likely to remember the opinions of the token than they were to remember the opinions of the nontokens or confederates. The authors argued that the tokens' memory difficulties resulted from the feeling of being scrutinized by an audience of other-sex peers. If this phenomenon generalizes to the work situation, and there is no reason to believe it does not, the token is in a particularly vulnerable position: She or he is unable to remember the details of interactions that take place in a situation in which she or he is obviously the center of attention, and a memorable one at that. Moreover, if tokenism alone is enough to cause cognitive difficulties, the added pressure of differential treatment in the workplace may well compound the problem.

Because most of the tokens at Indsco were women, Kanter's (1977) research focused mainly on the roles that token women found themselves playing in organizational settings in which they were seen primarily as "women" rather than "workers":

- the *mother* to men in the group—the comforter, the button sewer, the emotional specialist;
- the *seductress* or sex object—the object of sexual competition or male "protection" from the sexual advances of other men;
- the *pet* or mascot of the organization—the good-humored cheerleader whose competencies are fussed over as being exemplary performance for a woman; and
- the *iron maiden* who expects full rights of group membership—the "feminist" for whom no passages are smoothed.

These four roles share two commonalities: They are blatant caricatures of the female gender role, and they rob the role players of the chance to be seen in their worker role. Thus, Kanter argued, every effort should be made not to introduce lone employees into a work situation in which they are surrounded solely by members of the other sex. It is equally important that managers not postpone the integration of their organization until the day when they can introduce two or more employees into nontraditional work situations, for there is evidence that mere exposure to a token can create more positive attitudes toward the group to which the minority member belongs. In one particularly dramatic study, Shomer and Centers (1970) found more positive attitudes toward feminism among men in a group with one woman than among men in an all-male group, even though group members did not have the opportunity to talk to one another. In a more recent study, however, male employees were found to have more positive attitudes toward their female colleagues only when women made up at least 20% of the workers in the organization (Lortie-Lussier & Rinfret, 2002).

The workplace stresses associated with token experiences are numerous because the token position contains several dilemmas and contradictions. Tokens are treated as representatives of their group yet as exceptions to their group; they are visible yet backstage; they stand apart yet are stereotyped; they can relax least in "relaxing" situations in which formal organizational roles are dropped (Kanter, 1977).

Either women or men can be tokens in a workplace setting dominated by the other group. Is the token experience the same for men as it is for women? Some studies suggest it is not—that, in fact, for men gender stereotypes act to ameliorate the negative aspects of being a token. A study of young concession stand workers revealed that the token man did not experience the negative consequences—high visibility, contrast, and assimilation—that the token woman did. Rather, token men identified with (male) supervisors and advanced more quickly than nontoken men and women did (Yoder & Sinnett, 1985). In a second study, a comparison of the experiences of female police officers and male nurses, the female but not the male tokens reported that they did not feel accepted by their peers, that they felt extremely visible, and that they had been sexually harassed (Ott, 1989). Another study suggested that male nurses do not have to play the subordinate role to physicians to the same extent that female nurses do (Floge & Merrill, 1986). Male nurses interacted more with male physicians and were more likely to voice their opinions and have those opinions accepted than female nurses were. However, tokens of either gender can experience some disadvantages. Both male nurses and female physicians reported that they were excluded from conversations among the dominant group.

One thing that tokens, minority members, or new members of a group may do to reduce stress is to search for solidarity among themselves. They may isolate themselves from majority group members, interacting more frequently and positively with one another than with more established members of the group (Schein, 1968). Although such solidarity can be helpful, it also has a major drawback: It can slow down the process by which newcomers are assimilated

$\mathcal{O}$ verview   Sex discrimination

- A persistent gender pay gap exists between women and men of various educational levels and ethnicities and within almost every type of occupation. This gap seems to be at least partially the result of the undervaluing of work done by women.

- Gender-based discrimination in employment can exist against both women and men. Women are discriminated against in employment situations that require "masculine" qualities; men are sometimes targets of hostility or ridicule when they "settle" for feminine jobs.

- One important factor in sex discrimination is the perception of a lack of fit between individuals and the requirements of certain jobs. This perceived lack of fit is often influenced by gender stereotypes.

- Gender stereotypes can become self-fulfilling prophecies, shaping the behavior of the targets of the stereotypes.

- Individuals in "token" positions may suffer from the stress of being under constant observation; this stress can impair their performance. However, research suggests that, at least in some situations, being a token woman is a more negative experience than being a token man.

into the group (Moreland, 1985). This finding underlines the dilemma inherent in the position of women or men entering an occupation or workplace in which their sex is underrepresented. Not only must they cope with the many problems associated with token or minority status, but even their attempts to seek support from others in the same position may present a danger to their ultimate acceptance. The brave souls who persevere in such situations surely deserve the label *pioneers*. These pioneers are not the only people who experience workplace stress, however. In the next section, we turn to an examination of the stresses inherent in the interface between work and family.

TWO SPHERES IN CONTACT:
THE INTERACTION OF FAMILY
AND EMPLOYMENT ISSUES

How simple (and how dull) life would be for the average working person if the only responsibilities he or she faced were those connected with the job. For most of us, however, a job represents only one of the sets of tasks and sources of worry, pride, frustration, and fulfillment in our lives. No serious examination of gender-related issues in the workplace can ignore the fact that when women and men leave the workplace and head for home they are faced with different amounts and kinds of responsibilities.

Combining Job and Family: Stresses and Rewards

It used to be expected that women would set aside their own work and achievement needs to provide support for those of their husbands. Consider the comments, made in 1972, of one of the gifted women from Terman's longitudinal study of high-IQ individuals:

> A person of Henry's talent and drive desperately needs a partner to take care of family, home, and all of the social needs and other involvement. . . . My husband's multifaceted career has been the central factor in my life. Ours has been a partnership in many ways, as I have carried most of the home, family, and social responsibilities. This has enabled him to devote full time to his creative work, his teaching, etc. I wish I could have achieved creatively myself, but what small talent I might have had was absorbed in his great gifts. (as quoted in Tomlinson-Keasey, 1990, p. 217)

Traditional gender roles, by assigning women to the home and men to the working world, facilitated a certain amount of separation between the employment and family spheres. The entry of women in large numbers into the labor force now means that the tidy separation is crumbling. In the United States, more than 70% of mothers with children under the age of 18 are in the labor force. Nearly 63% of mothers with children under the age of 6 and 59% of mothers with children less than 3 years old participate in the labor force (U.S. Bureau of Labor Statistics, 2006b; see Figure 13.3).

Figure 13.3   Changes in civilian labor force participation among mothers with children under 3 years of age, under 6 years, and 6 to 17 years old, 1975 to 2005.

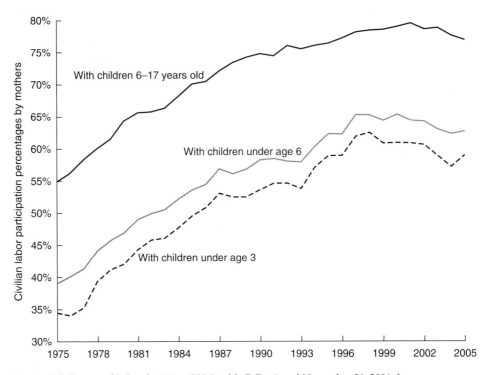

Source: U.S. Bureau of Labor Statistics (2006), table 7. Retrieved November 21, 2006, from http://www.bls.gov/cps/wlf-table7-2006.pdf

For women, especially, this situation is likely to result in increased stress. Mothers who work outside the home usually find themselves faced with another full-time job in their "off" hours: cooking, cleaning, and caring for children. Even in dual-career families, mothers continue to assume the major responsibility for the care and socialization of young children and for housework (Bielby & Bielby, 1988; Hoffnung, 1995; South & Spitze, 1994). Employed women report more absences from work due to personal or family responsibilities than men do (Statistics Canada, 1995), and they also report that a major source of stress is the conflicting set of demands generated by work and family roles (Duxbury & Higgins, 1991; Phillips-Miller, Morrison, & Campbell, 2001). Women garment workers interviewed in one study reported that worry over finding adequate day care for their children was more stressful than the unhealthy working conditions at their plant (de Koninck, 1984). Studies of some populations show that women are more likely than men to report work-family role conflict (Mashal & Kalin, 1985; Wiersma, 1990).

Compounding the stress of juggling job and family responsibilities for women are the social stereotypes associated with motherhood. For all the lofty words that have been written and spoken about the value of motherhood, the primary caretaker role is viewed as low in status. In fact, sociologists have argued that motherhood is associated with a downward bias in workers' evaluations: Workers who are mothers are considered to be less competent and less suitable for positions of authority (C. Ridgeway & Correll, 2004). In addition, whereas the knowledge that a male worker is an involved father adds a positive dimension to the way people view him (he is not only competent but warm and caring), the knowledge that a female worker is an involved and caring mother apparently adds nothing—and may even detract from the estimation of her competence (Cuddy, Fiske, & Glick, 2004).

Perhaps partly because of such stereotypes and partly because of the lopsided share of caretaking responsibilities assigned to mothers, motherhood has a big economic cost. Employed mothers earn only 60% of what employed fathers earn—a gap that is much larger than the broader gender pay gap and seems even more intransigent (Crosby, Williams, & Biernat, 2004). In fact, the glass ceiling that has apparently kept so many women from advancing into top positions may turn out to be, in part, a "maternal wall" (J. C. Williams, 2001).

All this does not mean, however, that only women are stressed by trying to combine employment and child rearing. As women and men increasingly share employment responsibilities, they may also begin to share more family-related stress. Research now shows that parent-role stress and negative parent–child relationships are equally likely to be associated with psychological distress among employed mothers and employed fathers (Barnett, Brennan, & Marshall, 1994). Furthermore, for both women and men, a positive family climate is associated with less work-family conflict. A positive family climate, including a readiness to talk things out, provide moral support, and do things together, also correlates with less time spent on domestic chores by women and less free time spent on career-related activities by men (Wiersma & Van den Berg, 1991).

Sharing household tasks is associated with lower levels of role strain for women, and many employed women expect their husbands to adjust to a higher level of participation in domestic work. One study of Mexican American women in dual-earner couples, for example, found that these women perceived themselves as coproviders (Herrera & DelCampo, 1995). They did not subscribe to the myth that they should be "superwomen"—able to work full-time and manage all aspects of the housework and child care. Even among women at the very top levels of management in Fortune 1,000 companies, stress is ameliorated by adjustments in the family. In a Catalyst survey of female executives who earned an average of $248,000 a year, three-quarters of the married women were their family's primary breadwinner. These women noted the importance of having a supportive husband (Grimsley, 1996).

In recent years a new load has been added to the domestic side of women's double burden by an emerging demographic phenomenon: increasing longevity and the concomitant demand that middle-aged people spend years caring for their elderly parents. The people called on to be the caregivers in this situation are usually women, as are most of the dependent elderly because women live longer than men (Kramer & Kipnis, 1995). These female caregivers who are also mothers have been characterized as "women in the middle" by gerontologist Elaine Brody (1981), not only because their age places them in the position of being expected to care for both their parents and their children but also because they are juggling so many competing demands on their time and energy: job, husband, health problems, and children. According to Brody's research, three-fifths of these heavily burdened women felt guilty about not doing enough for their mothers.

If the strain of combining work and family responsibilities is so great for women, what is there to be said in favor of doing it, other than the obvious financial reasons? It is clear that women can reap psychological and physical as well as economic benefits from the effort of juggling two roles, particularly if they have support from family and friends (Amatea & Fong, 1991; Epstein, 1983). In fact, employed women appear to be happier and healthier than homemakers, except when they have infants to care for (L. O. Walker & Best, 1991). One study of women in the 40 to 59 age range found that work outside the home may play an important role in the psychological well-being of middle-aged women. Employed women at midlife had higher self-esteem and less psychological anxiety than homemakers did, and they also reported being in better physical health (Coleman & Antonucci, 1983).

Taken alone, these correlational data do not prove that holding jobs caused women to feel happier, healthier, more self-confident, and less anxious; perhaps happy, healthy, self-confident, calm women are simply more likely to seek and find jobs. However, in the Coleman and Antonucci study, employment was the only significant predictor of self-esteem in midlife women, in contrast to income, education, marital status, and family life-cycle stage. This finding led the researchers to speculate that employment in and of itself may affect women's well-being. They suggested that the stabilizing impact of employment enables women to avoid some of the possible negative effects of family-role loss that occur at midlife: empty-nest syndrome, feelings of inadequacy, and loss of purpose. They further suggested that working outside the home may have a similar stabilizing influence at other crucial transition periods of the life cycle, such as early parenthood, divorce, or death of a spouse.

Perhaps it simply helps to keep life in perspective when one can look at it from the viewpoints of two very different roles. This suggestion received support from Crosby's (1990) study of divorce and work life among women managers. She noted that work was explicitly recognized by the women managers as a source of pride and repair to damaged self-esteem. In further support of the notion that multiple roles can be healthy is a study of Swedish employed parents. In this study, the researchers found that the sharing of roles was a key factor: Only in families in which both partners were employed *and* both shared the domestic and financial responsibilities did both parents report satisfaction with the work-family interface and positive psychological well-being (Haerenstam & Bejerot, 2001).

For men stress in the workplace has long been recognized as a problem. For example, researchers studying male workers have found a link between job strain (a combination of high demands and low control at work) and high blood pressure for men in low socioeconomic status groups (Landsbergis, Schnall, Pickering, Warren, & Schwartz, 2003) and have demonstrated that high levels of work fatigue are associated with high levels of drinking (Lallukka et al., 2004).

Some research indicates that a major source of stress for men may be that, because of expectations linked to the masculine role, they rely too heavily on their job and their breadwinner role for their sense of identity (Buzzanell & Turner, 2003; Willott & Griffin, 2004). When this role is threatened through unemployment, men may show increased symptoms of stress, such as ulcers, heart attacks, elevated blood pressure, and strokes (Liem & Rayman, 1982). Moreover, these negative effects of unemployment are not limited to the out-of-work men themselves; stress and ill health are common among the wives of men who have lost their jobs (Grayson, 1983). It is likely that the benefits of combining two roles are not limited to women who add employment to their traditional domestic tasks. Perhaps men can also gain from dividing their commitment more evenly between the spheres of work and family. Certainly there is a good deal of evidence that men who increase their involvement with parenting find the experience to be a positive and rewarding one, as discussed in Chapter 11. It is quite likely that, given mutual support, both men and women can benefit by not putting all their eggs in one basket—by finding sources of identity and satisfaction in both job and family.

Dual-Career Couples: Finding a New Job—Family Balance

For the growing number of families in which the two adult partners are pursuing careers, many of the traditional expectations about the division of household tasks, the supportive role played by the wife for the husband, and family mobility to accommodate the career moves of the male partner become unworkable. Even in the absence of any ideology about female–male equality, the pressures on a two-career couple force them in the direction of a more equitable division of family tasks. As this type of family structure has become more common, the male members of these couples have discovered firsthand two of the major difficulties that have traditionally plagued career women: (1) the limitations imposed on career accomplishment by the necessity to perform such survival activities as shopping, cooking, cleaning, and laundry and (2) the frequent assumption by employers that anyone who takes family responsibilities seriously lacks career commitment.

A well-worn assumption in the corporate world used to be that men bring two people to their jobs, but women bring less than one (Kanter, 1977). According to this assumption, men come equipped with wives, whose unpaid work enhances men's productivity on the job. Wives not only free their husbands from the necessity of spending energy on daily concerns such as clean shirts and school lunches but also help host business associates and maintain smooth social relations among the husbands' colleagues and coworkers. Although expectations are changing, the average female employee rarely has anyone doing these things for her and, indeed, is often trying to do them for someone else. Clearly, a single man or one whose partner spends her energy on her own career rather than on supporting his is at a disadvantage similar to that faced by most women. Although he is not likely to be in the desperate situation faced by many married career women, who juggle employment and the greater share of domestic responsibilities, he is still denied the opportunity to focus all his energy on his career and leave the details of daily living to someone else.

When men do try to take on a serious share of family duties, they may run into trouble at work. Although an employer may show some understanding and flexibility in making adjustments to accommodate a female employee whose work and family responsibilities conflict, a man experiencing similar conflicts can expect a less sympathetic response and a lower salary (Schneer & Reitman, 1993). Traditionally, people who have allowed family considerations to "distract" them from their jobs have been judged to be less than serious about their work and have been passed over for promotions and raises. In fact, women have often been stereotyped as having less "commitment" to their careers simply because of being married and having children, and some have identified such stereotypes as the main obstacles to women's advancement (Cuddy et al., 2004; Grimsley, 1996; Shellenbarger, 1995). Some companies, in an attempt to erase stereotypes about the interference of family responsibilities with work, have made flexible work arrangements available to all employees who need to manage "multiple commitments" and speak of a "life outside work" instead of work-family conflict. Such programs counter the notion that an employee must have a completely single-minded focus on his or her career to be successful and undermine the idea that women need a special "mommy track." Some organizations are recognizing that fewer and fewer of their employees can make career decisions independent of family considerations or can blithely leave all family responsibilities in the hands of a spouse. Indeed, in her inaugural address as president of the American Psychological Association in 2004, Dianne Halpern (2005) outlined the arguments and research findings that suggest the world of work must be redesigned to accommodate workers' family roles, noting that employees must be able to manage work and family obligations without having to make impossible choices between the two. Noting that many aspects of public policy regarding employment are still based on a fast-disappearing family model in which there is a stay-at-home caregiver, Halpern argued for such changes as flexibility in work hours, family-related leave, job sharing, and telecommuting.

These changes are long overdue. In the years since 1978, the number of married couples in which both spouses work full-time, year-round has increased from less than 60% to more than 70% for couples with no children, and from under 40% to more than 55% for couples with one or more children under

18, although recent years have seen a slight tendency for this increase to level off—and perhaps even to reverse direction (U.S. Census Bureau, 2006a). A Catalyst (1998b) study of dual-career couples in the United States found that the majority said that the chief benefit of having two earners is higher income. However, they also cited personal fulfillment, intellectual equality, and emotional support as important advantages, and most said they would continue working even if the financial need to do so was not there. Both members of such dual-career couples said that their top choice for benefits they would look for if they were switching companies was flexibility: the freedom to arrange their own day-to-day schedules. They also said they would like the option to customize the pace of their career advancement—being able to slow down when family responsibilities were very pressing without hurting their chances for eventual success.

The concern about work-family balance is not surprising for couples engaged in a two-career lifestyle. Such couples must wrestle with questions of whether and when to have children; they face enormous challenges each time one spouse is asked to relocate; and they sometimes spend years in long-distance "commuter" relationships. Because some of the differences in salary levels between men and women with the same educational background seem to be explained by geographical relocations based on the husband's career (Felmlee, 1995), the option of living apart is seen as preferable to relocation by some couples. This solution is still considered a drastic departure from society's expectations about marriage, and couples who adopt it may have to face the disapproval of family and friends along with the inevitable difficulties of the separation. However, studies of these couples reveal some advantages to this difficult lifestyle: The suspension of spousal-role demands allows individuals to devote long hours to their work; the absence of a better-established spouse allows the other to begin a career without relying on or being overshadowed by him or her; and individuals find opportunities for personal growth and development independent of their spouse (Douvan & Pleck, 1978; Farris, 1978; Gross, 1980). The disadvantages, though, are equally compelling: loneliness, the expense of maintaining two residences, long-distance phone calls, commuting, and the lack of a partner with whom to share domestic responsibilities (Green & Zenisek, 1983). When couples do not make such drastic compromises, however, it is often the woman's career that suffers. In the Catalyst (1998b) survey cited, fully one-third of the men in the dual-career couples viewed their careers as primary in the household, whereas only 6% of the women said their own careers were primary.

Career Paths of Women and Men

In past decades, the pattern of labor force participation for North American women has been quite different from that of men. Although men have tended to enter the workplace and continue employment until they retire, women's participation used to show a sharp dip during childbearing years, followed by a rise as women whose children were grown returned to work. Because of its shape on the graph and its significance, this pattern was sometimes labeled the M curve—M for *mother* (Farley, 1980). With each passing year, however, the M curve has been disappearing; fewer women are leaving the labor force during their child-rearing years, and the so-called women's pattern of employment participation is increasingly like men's. Between 1975 and 1991, White married women with children under age 6 increased their participation rate in the labor force from just over 34% to 59%. For African American women in the same category, the participation rate rose from just under 55% to over 73% (Thornborrow & Sheldon, 1995). The current labor force participation rate for all women with children under the age of 6 is about 63% (U.S. Bureau of Labor Statistics, 2006b).

As Figure 13.3 shows, labor force participation of mothers, even those with toddlers, is high. However, for women who do leave the workforce, the break is a costly one. Labor force discontinuity is one of the factors responsible for the salary and status differentials between employed women and men (Felmlee, 1995; Waldfogel, 1997). Not only does discontinuity limit a woman's opportunity to build experience and seniority, but it also places her in a poor bargaining position when she wishes to reenter the job market. She is likely to find, despite her experience, that her opportunities are limited to entry-level jobs. Research supports a link between labor force discontinuity and job advancement. Women without children tend to be in the labor force continuously and experience more upward mobility in occupational status (Felmlee, 1995). Even women with continuous labor force participation do not achieve upward mobility levels comparable to those of men, however, so this variable alone cannot account for the female–male differences.

In recent years, despite a minor flurry of cautionary tales in the popular press about the dangers for women of trying to "have it all," the trend of women combining family and employment shows few signs of slowing down. Indeed, for many families, losing the wife's income, even for a few years, would mean the impossibility of adequate housing, occasional family vacations, and college education for the children. Moreover, should marriage breakdown occur, as it does in one-third to one-half of cases in Canada and the United States, the woman who has been out of the labor force is at an extreme economic disadvantage. For women, divorce is one of the strongest predictors of downward economic mobility (Teachman & Paasch, 1994). Researchers have found that after a divorce the woman's standard of living typically drops about 30%, but the man's rises about 10% (Peterson, 1996, as cited in Webster, 1996). Finally, the choice of staying home with children rarely means being in a completely ideal setting, with adequate resources and an available, supportive male partner. For most people, the home comes no closer to perfection than the workplace does; if both were restructured to accommodate the needs of people who are seriously committed to both family and employment responsibilities, women and men would have less stress and more time with their children and each other.

What if solutions could be found to all the dilemmas faced by women and men in trying to fulfill both work and family roles? Would sex and gender no longer be important issues in the workplace? The answer is "No," for there is at least one other major arena in which gender expectations can interact with work roles: sexuality.

WORK, SEXUALITY, AND POWER

One of the traditional concerns about integrating women and men in the workplace has been that sexuality will interfere with job performance. In 1978, the assignment of women to work alongside men on U.S. Navy ships at sea caused a public outcry, fueled by the specter of sailors having romantic liaisons when they should be swabbing the decks. Husbands and wives of male and female managers may feel stabs of jealousy when business meetings last late into the evening or when their mates take business trips with a member of the other sex. Because changes in the gender composition of the workplace have most frequently involved the addition of women to a previously all-male preserve, these worries about sexuality have most commonly been used as arguments for keeping women out.

However, the issue of sexuality in the workplace is not a simple matter of women's presence turning men's thoughts to love (or lust). Men and women have learned ritualized ways of relating to one another, often adopting reciprocal gender roles based partially on sexuality, and these roles are not easily shed at the entrance to the workplace. Who, for example, has not encountered the man or woman who cannot seem to relate to members of the other sex without flirting? And who has not observed a change come over a group of men or women at coffee when they are joined by a single member of the other sex? It would be extremely naive to ignore the impact that sexuality can have on our perceptions of and responses to the people with whom we work.

Sexuality has implications for both women's and men's power and achievement in the workplace and also for the smooth functioning of the workplace itself. An individual can use sexuality as a power resource for influence or advancement at work or, coercively, as a weapon to keep others in line. The intimate bonds that can form in noncoercive sexual relationships at work, although sometimes good for individuals' morale and motivation, can promote the formation of coalitions that interfere with group decision making in the workplace. Moreover, public awareness of the existence of such a relationship has a variety of implications for the participants. Let us look briefly at the implications of both coercive and noncoercive sexuality in the workplace.

Coercive Sexuality: Sexual Harassment on the Job

In 1991 one of the first female neurosurgeons, Dr. Frances Conley, a professor at Stanford University School of Medicine, shocked students and colleagues when she announced her resignation. The 51-year-old physician had established an outstanding reputation over the 17 years of her career. Why was she leaving? She said that she had endured a career-long pattern of sexual harassment from her medical colleagues and superiors. She was tired of being asked, for effect, in jest, to go to bed with her colleagues. She was tired of being called "honey" by male doctors in front of her patients. She was tired of the constant sexual innuendos and putdowns to remind her that she was not a real member of the "club" (Jacoby, 1998).

Dr. Conley's experience is far from unique, nor is sexual harassment something that no longer happens now that there are more women in medicine. In one national survey 36.9% of female physicians reported they had experienced sexual harassment (Frank, Brogan, & Schiffman, 1998). In another study, 39% of medical students reported experiencing sexual harassment (Mangus, Hawkins, & Miller, 1998). The problem shows up in many workplaces: It is common to find that as many as 50% of women in particular samples say they have experienced unwanted, offensive sexual behavior (Magley, Hulin, Fitzgerald, & DeNardo, 1999). Women learn to be wary of harassment even before they enter the workplace: Nearly two-thirds of U.S. college students say they have experienced some type of sexual harassment (Tascio, 2006).

Sexual harassment, now recognized as a major problem in the workplace, can take two forms. In the first, commonly labeled **quid pro quo,** an individual is pressured to submit to unwelcome sexual advances or other unwelcome sexual conduct as a condition of employment, or employment decisions that affect the individual, such as promotion or raises, are based on her or his submission to or rejection of such conduct. The second form of sexual harassment involves the creation of a **hostile environment:** making unwelcome sexual advances or engaging in other conduct of a sexual nature that unreasonably interferes with an individual's work performance or creates an intimidating, hostile, or offensive atmosphere.

Although both female and male workers can be harassed sexually, females are the most frequent victims. The U.S. Merit Systems Protection Board (1981) found that 42% of women workers, as compared to 15% of men workers, reported experiencing sexual harassment. A more recent study of workers in five organizations revealed that about 47% of workers reported one or more experiences of sexual harassment, that women were more likely than men to be targets of harassment, and that minority women were significantly more likely than White women, White men, or minority men to experience sexual harassment (Berdahl & Moore, 2006).

Women from virtually every age, racial, and marital status group report sexual harassment to some extent. The people doing the harassing are preponderantly male: 95% of the female victims and 22% of the male victims in a large survey of federal employees in the United States reported harassment by males only (Tangri, Burt, & Johnson, 1982). In both the United States and Canada, sexual harassment is now recognized as a form of sex discrimination.

Reports by women who are pioneers in male-dominated jobs suggest that they may be at special risk for sexual harassment. Studies of blue-collar women indicate that they face resentment from coworkers and supervisors—resentment that is manifested in practical jokes, threats, violence, and sexual harassment (Cantrell, 1996; Colwill & Colwill, 1985). Years ago, six female members of the Royal Canadian Mounted Police (RCMP) caused a sensation with complaints to the press about years of being propositioned and victimized by crude sex jokes. As one woman who quit the force after 5 years commented, "I got tired of being propositioned by senior officers who thought you were a lesbian if you didn't or a slut if you did" (*Winnipeg Free Press,* 1986). Not surprisingly, RCMP records at the time showed that the resignation rate for women was 5 times higher than that of their male counterparts. In the intervening years, police forces have become more aware of the problem of sexual harassment. However, one recent international study indicated that 38% of female police officers in Australia and Britain and 57% of those in the United States have experienced sexual harassment (Brown, 1996).

The consequences of sexual harassment can be serious, in terms of both the victim's personal well-being and her or his job performance and advancement. Gutek and Nakamura (1983) reported that 17.3% of the women and 4.8% of the men in their samples had quit a job because of sexual harassment; 7.1% of the women and 2.4% of the men had missed work for the same reason. In another study, 96% of the victims of sexual harassment reported emotional stress manifested in nervousness, fear, anger, or sleeplessness; 63% developed physical reactions such as headaches, nausea, and weight losses and gains (Crull, 1980). Data from college women indicate that sexual harassment is associated with psychological distress that ultimately relates to lower academic satisfaction, more physical illness, and disordered eating. All this leads women to disengage from their studies and to earn lower grades (Huerta, Cortina, Torges, Pang, & Magley, 2006). Quid pro quo sexual harassment, with its implicit message that noncompliance will lead to reprisals, creates an intimidating and unhealthy work environment for the victim. In a precedent-setting decision, the Workers Compensation Board in Quebec ruled that extreme stress, depression, and physical symptoms caused by sexual harassment from a coworker during working hours is a work-related injury for which compensation should be paid (Lipovenko, 1985).

For victims of sexual harassment, the economic consequences may be as severe as the emotional ones. Noncompliance with the quid pro quo harasser or lodging a complaint may lead to retaliation: workloads increased, raises and promotions withheld, jobs lost, and references jeopardized. Victims who are fired or leave their jobs report that prospective employers tend to be skeptical when they cite sexual harassment as their reason for leaving previous jobs, and some have even been refused unemployment benefits (Crull, 1980). One study showed that persons who used confrontation to cope with the harassment tended to experience worse job outcomes than did others (Stockdale, 1998).

Governments, unions, and researchers acknowledge that sexual harassment is a serious problem for workers, but there is still disagreement about the kinds of behaviors that should be included as sexual harassment. Behaviors reported as harassment include actual or attempted rape or sexual assault; unwanted letters, phone calls, or materials of a sexual nature; unwanted pressure for sexual favors or for dates; unwanted deliberate touching, leaning over, cornering, or pinching; unwanted sexually suggestive looks or gestures; and unwanted sexual teasing, jokes, remarks, or questions (Tangri et al., 1982). The U.S. Equal Employment Opportunity Commission (1980) defined sexual harassment as follows:

> Unwelcome sexual advances, requests for sexual favors, and other verbal or physical conduct of a sexual nature constitutes sexual harassment when (1) submission to such conduct is made either explicitly or implicitly a term or condition of an individual's employment, (2) submission to or rejection of such conduct by an individual is used as the basis for employment decisions affecting such individual, or (3) such conduct has the purpose or effect of unreasonably interfering with an individual's work performance or creating an intimidating, hostile, or offensive work environment. (p. 746)

Despite the presence of this and other "official" definitions of sexual harassment, individuals may disagree about whether a specific incident constitutes harassment, and victims of unambiguous harassment are reluctant to report it. Research findings provide some explanations of why sexual harassment is often unrecognized by anyone but the victim and why the whole problem was ignored for so long. In one study (Cohen & Gutek, 1985), college students who were interpreting a possible case of sexual harassment placed little emphasis on variables directly related to the sexual and harassing nature of the incident (relative power of the individuals, appropriateness of the behavior) and paid more attention to the personal aspects of the incident (the degree to which the behavior in question was friendly, complimentary, or insulting) and the interpersonal relationship (amount of liking and respect) between the two parties. Furthermore, they focused on the positive aspects of the incident and tended to ignore the problematic aspects.

Behavior is most likely to be labeled sexual harassment when it violates the ordinary expectations of the actor's social role—expectations that often include the perceived power of the actor over the target. Participants in a study by Pryor (1985) rated the same comment as more harassing when made by a professor than when made by a fellow student. In addition, if the actor behaved consistently toward the target over time and similarly toward other women, Pryor's research showed that participants had a greater tendency to label the behavior sexual harassment. Finally, one study showed that the frequency of the behavior is related to its perceived offensiveness, which is, in turn, related to the likelihood of reporting the harasser (Brooks & Perot, 1991).

Taken together, these studies show that observers (and victims) are reluctant to conclude that sexual harassment is taking place. However, people are most likely to notice and label it harassment when the behavior seems out of role or surprising, when it is performed consistently by a particular individual, and when it occurs with more than one target person. Almost everyone perceives sexual bribery, explicit propositions, unwanted touching, or pressure for sexual activity as harassment (Frazier, Cochran, & Olson, 1995). There is more disagreement about behaviors such as sexist comments, suggestive looks, sexual jokes, and coarse language; however, these behaviors too are perceived as sexually harassing by many individuals.

Some have argued that women and men perceive incidents differentially as sexually harassing, and this argument has led to the adoption of a "reasonable woman" (as opposed to a "reasonable person") standard in the courts for determining whether a work environment is hostile enough to warrant legal action. In other words, is the work environment sufficiently hostile that a reasonable woman would find it hostile or abusive? Research shows little difference in the ways women and men define sexual harassment (Frazier et al., 1995; Gutek & O'Connor, 1995), so the reasonable woman standard may not be particularly useful.

The sense of ambiguity surrounding what constitutes sexual harassment may have a subtle negative consequence—the inhibition of cross-sex friendships in the workplace. Researchers who interviewed a sample of professionals in one workplace found that their awareness of sexual harassment issues led them to worry about how friendly overtures to colleagues of the other sex would be interpreted, and to dampen such overtures (Elsesser & Peplau, 2006). If such concerns lead workers to avoid cross-sex friendships, women may suffer the most negative consequences because they form the minority at the top levels of many professional work situations and would benefit from integration into workplace social networks.

Some people have argued that sexual harassment is simply a normal result of biology: Put women and men together in the workplace and what can you expect? Tangri, Burt, and Johnson (1982) examined the responses of a stratified random sample of more than 20,000 federal employees to questions about their experience of sexual harassment in an effort to assess the adequacy of three explanations for its widespread existence:

- natural social-sexual attraction,
- the hierarchical way organizations are structured, and
- the way society stratifies power and status between women and men.

They concluded that sexual harassment was not a single, unitary phenomenon and that each of the explanations was probably applicable, alone or in combination, to certain cases. The fact that women who sexually harass men are likely to be young, single, and subordinate suggests that the first explanation, social-sexual attraction, is operating in many of these cases. The fact that for both sexes being a "pioneer" in the job, being young, and needing the job badly are related to being sexually harassed supports the second explanation. Finally, the fact that women are, so much more often than men, the victims of sexual harassment lends support to the third explanation. The authors concluded that sexual harassment of women conforms more to an intimidation explanation, whereas that of men conforms more to an attraction explanation.

Other researchers have suggested that sexual harassment stems from ambivalent attitudes and stereotypes about gender that pervade many workplaces (Fiske & Glick, 1995). They note that women often encounter male coworkers whose attitudes combine **hostile sexism** (dominance-oriented paternalism, the notion that women are inferior, and hostile, dominance-oriented heterosexuality) and **benevolent sexism** (protective paternalism, the notion that women and men are different and complementary, and heterosexual intimacy motives). Both attitudes, discussed in Chapter 1, can promote harassment, albeit of different kinds. These attitudes are reinforced by organizational contexts that emphasize a masculine culture in the workplace, a scarcity of information about women, power asymmetries between women and men in the workplace, and the entry of women on a one-at-a-time, solo basis into the workforce. Each of these contextual problems can be addressed by an organization that is serious about reducing sexual harassment.

There is a popular myth that coercive and exploitative sexuality is not limited to sexual harassment but is widespread in another area: women deliberately exploiting and "selling" their sexuality for gain. Women are said to be able to reap huge professional and financial rewards by "sleeping their way to the top." Does this really happen, or is it a myth that serves mainly to undermine perceptions of women's competence? Little solid data exist, but one recent Tulane University study found that 49% of a sample of 164 female MBA graduates reported that they had used at least 1 of 10 sexual behaviors (e.g., flirting, crossing their legs provocatively, leaning over a table to let men look

Overview   Sexual harassment

- Quid pro quo sexual harassment involves pressuring an individual to submit to unwanted sexual behaviors as a condition of employment, promotion, salary increases, or other workplace outcomes.

- Hostile environment sexual harassment involves making unwelcome sexual advances or engaging in other behavior such as sexual jokes and innuendos that interfere with an individual's work performance by creating a hostile or intimidating atmosphere.

- Women are more likely than men to be targets of sexual harassment; men are more likely than women to be perpetrators of sexual harassment.

- Sexual harassment may have its roots in both hostile and benevolent sexism, but these two kinds of sexism may produce different types of harassment.

- Observers are more likely to label an unwanted sexual behavior sexual harassment when
  - the behavior seems out of role and surprising,
  - it is performed consistently by the same person, and
  - it occurs with more than one target person.

down their shirt) to try to get ahead in their careers (Jones, 2005). Interestingly, such strategies do not appear to be effective; in fact, they may even backfire on their users. Respondents who said they had never used sexuality had been more successful than those who had in terms of both promotions and salary: nonusers averaged three promotions, in comparison to two for those who had used sexual tactics, and women who had not used sexuality were more likely than those who had to have reached an income range of $75,000 to $100,000. Perhaps the reasons for these discrepancies can be understood by looking at the built-in dangers of relying on sexuality to maneuver through workplace power hierarchies. As Backhouse and Cohen (1978) noted years ago, not only do people who obtain their promotions, raises, and so on through sexual pay-offs experience self-doubts about their own abilities, but they are frequently the objects of vicious office gossip and sabotage. Moreover, for a person in this position, the end of the affair may also mean the end of the job. It appears that sexuality is only a temporary passport to power in the workplace.

Noncoercive Sexuality: Romance at Work

A survey by the American Management Association (2003) revealed that 25% of men and 35% of women in their sample of members and their customers had dated a colleague in their workplace. Over two-thirds of the respondents said that dating another employee was acceptable; however, most were more disapproving of dating between a superior and subordinate.

Although the actual number of "office romances" is difficult to determine, the amount of concern generated by the possibility of such liaisons is great (Mainiero, 1986, 1989). Some authors, in fact, have argued that the fear of sexual entanglements can lead to such extreme interpersonal vigilance that normal friendly relationships between female and male coworkers cannot develop (Elsesser & Peplau, 2006; Eyler & Baridon, 1992).

Not surprisingly, proximity is a major factor in the development of romantic relationships at work (Quinn, 1977). People whose work throws them together have more opportunities to develop intimate relationships with each other. Motivation also plays a role. Robert Quinn's research showed that observers attribute office romances to three types of motives: ego (excitement, adventure, conquest), job security or advancement, or love. Three kinds of relationships were described most frequently: (1) the "fling," characterized by ego motives on the part of both participants; (2) the "utilitarian relationship," in which the female was pursuing job-related goals and the male was seeking ego satisfaction; and (3) true love, in which both participants had sincere feelings for each other. Such attributions may often be completely off base. However, there are some data on the likely correctness of the third one: Two-thirds of respondents in the American Management Association (2003) survey who had dated at the office reported that the dating had resulted in a continuing long-term relationship or marriage.

The impact of romance in the workplace is not limited to the participants. Observers are quick with stories of how the participants in workplace romances changed for better or for worse—becoming, for example, more efficient and competent or less available than previously (Quinn, 1977). Such changes have a ripple effect on other relationships in the workplace, sometimes with disastrous results. Quinn argued that the disasters typically result from a distortion of the power and reward system created by the new relationship. He reported several cases of romances involving a male superior and a female subordinate in which the male informally increased the female's power, ignored complaints about her, and became inaccessible except through her. Coworkers who found such situations frustrating and unfair felt powerless and demoralized and resorted to tactics ranging from complaining and ostracizing to blackmailing and quitting. Some of the hostility in such cases stems from the perception that a lower ranking person has unfairly been given authority to interfere with people who are technically her superiors. Resentment may also flare when coworkers perceive that their confidences have been violated by one of the romantic partners—that, because of the special relationship, one partner is privy to information that other employees do not or should not have. The situation is fraught with potential not only for ruining employee morale but also for torpedoing the career of the subordinate in question. Apparently viewed as more dispensable, the female, who is usually subordinate, is twice as likely to be fired as the male.

Even when the office romance is between two equals, it may generate problems. It may cause traditional superior-subordinate gender roles to interfere with the equality that has been established in the workplace between, say, two vice presidents—one female and one male. The sexual double standard may cause the woman to lose status and respect in the eyes of coworkers, and the man may feel angry and out of control because of his inability to protect her from slurs and gossip (E. Collins, 1983).

It is with a view to dangers such as these that Margaret Mead (1980) proposed a new taboo on sex at work: "You don't make passes at or sleep with the people you work with" (p. 55). Arguing that ruling out coworkers as potential sexual partners would enable women and men to develop honest, respectful working relationships, Mead suggested that giving up sex in the workplace was an important step toward developing true equality between women and men. Whether or not her solution is workable, Mead's article clearly summarized the problem: As long as women and men relate to each other mainly in sexual terms, their attempts to work together will be filled with tension.

SUMMARY

Although both women and men have always worked, the traditional division of labor in industrialized societies used to mandate that they work in different spheres: women in the private sphere of the home, men in the public (and paid) sphere of employment outside the home. Until recently, when women ventured into the world of paid employment, they were automatically relegated to low-status, low-paying jobs. Although vertical and horizontal segregation of the workforce by gender still keeps most women in a few clerical and service occupations, a significant minority of women are now entering male-dominated professions. By contrast, there is a much less noticeable influx of men into female-dominated occupations.

A strong factor in the maintenance of the division of labor along gender lines has been discrimination. Sex discrimination has been manifested in a tendency to pay women less than men for the same or comparable work, to evaluate women's work performance less highly than men's, and to give preference to men over women when hiring. Some research shows that men also sometimes can be the victims of sex discrimination in evaluation and hiring when the job is defined specifically as female appropriate. Legislation has been introduced to counteract sex discrimination in hiring and to promote pay equity between women and men. Although these legislative approaches have solved some problems (for instance, by making it more difficult for employers to practice obvious sex discrimination), they have opened the door to others. Controversies now simmer about the extent to which male-dominated and female-dominated jobs are comparable in worth, and women who have been hired into male-dominated occupations find themselves dealing with all the pressures that go with token or minority status.

A second factor that helps to maintain gender-based occupational segregation is the assignment of most homemaking and child-care tasks to women, even in dual-career families. Many employed women carry a double burden of responsibility; the consequent stress, fatigue, and time pressure may well limit their capacity to take the steps necessary to move out of female-dominated occupations. However, research indicates that both women and men benefit when they take on a balance of occupational and family responsibilities. A growing minority of two-career couples are dividing family tasks more equitably and trying to place equal priority on the careers of both partners. Under pressure from such people, some employers are beginning to make structural changes that acknowledge and allow for the family responsibilities of their employees.

A third barrier to gender equality in the workplace has been the emphasis on sexuality in male–female relationships. Concern over the development of sexual liaisons at work has been the reason sometimes voiced for resistance to the integration of women into male-dominated occupations. Some people have little practice relating to members of the other gender on an equal footing in ways that are task oriented and businesslike, and they fear the necessity of doing so. When sexual liaisons *do* develop between people at work, problems sometimes result—and those problems can lead to job loss for the member of the couple who has the least seniority (usually the woman). Moreover, sexual harassment is a common problem in the workplace, especially for women and even more especially for minority women and women in token or "pioneer" positions. Such harassment can serve to keep the gender-based division of labor in place by forcing the victims from their jobs or interfering with their job performance.

Despite the barriers to gender equality in the workplace, significant steps in the direction of equality have been and continue to be achieved. Perhaps the most important change has been recognition and questioning of the barriers—a process that may eventually transform the work situation for women and men.

KEY TERMS

glass ceiling

glass escalator

equal pay for equal work

comparable worth

lack of fit

self-fulfilling prophecy

denial of personal discrimination

token positions

quid pro quo

hostile environment

hostile sexism

benevolent sexism

chapter 14

Justice, Equity, and Social Change

Justice is often depicted in the form of a woman—a blindfolded woman holding the scales on which human deeds are balanced by their outcomes. The image says a lot about society's dominant conception of justice: the equity-based notion that people deserve outcomes (rewards or punishments) in proportion to their actions. However, the depiction of justice as a woman is more than a little ironic. A long history of pronouncements by male "experts" asserts that women are morally inferior to men and less able to develop a strong, clear sense of justice unclouded by personal emotional biases. In the field of psychology, this tradition began with Sigmund Freud (1925/1974) who argued that women's weaker superego made them less capable than men of impersonal justice. Echoes of this attitude have appeared in some of the most widely accepted psychological theories of moral development.

There is another sense in which the depiction of justice as a woman is ironic. Society's formal institutions of justice—the laws and the judicial system—have been developed and dominated by men. Most lawyers and judges are still men. Women have had to struggle to be considered equal with men under the law, and many of those struggles are still under way. In Canada women were not legally considered "persons" until 1929. In the United States it has proved impossible so far to amend the Constitution with the words "Equality of rights under the law shall not be denied or abridged by the United States or any state on account of sex." Although 185 countries have ratified the United Nations Convention on the

Elimination of All Forms of Discrimination Against Women, some nations including the United States have not yet agreed to it. It appears that, as Florynce Kennedy (1970) once noted, justice really is blind—blind to the existence of sexism.

This chapter examines various issues of justice as they pertain to gender. In particular, we ask these questions:

- Do women and men differ in their notions of what is a fair and just way to allocate rewards to themselves and others?
- How do men and women perceive the fairness of affirmative action?
- Are there gender differences in moral development and moral reasoning?
- To what extent are legal systems gendered—encoding different rules or allowing different degrees of participation for women and men?
- Are men and women treated differently when they encounter the justice system as criminals or victims of crime?
- How has feminist activism changed laws to facilitate gender justice? What principles have guided such activism?

The chapter begins with an overview of research on gender differences and similarities in the perception and actualization of justice. Included here is a discussion of the ways the desire to see the world as fair and just shapes people's perceptions of social arrangements, helping them to "see" the treatment of women and men as equal even when clearly it is not. A section on gender and the law then examines some concrete results of the formal application of the justice system to women and men. Finally, the chapter closes with a discussion of the social change that might result from the challenges posed by the feminist movement to society's traditional notions of justice.

GENDER AND CONCEPTIONS OF JUSTICE

Two streams of research within the field of psychology have examined the relationship between gender and conceptions of justice: studies of reward allocation and studies of moral development. Both areas reveal evidence for both differences and similarities between women and men.

Reward Allocation and Personal Entitlement: Equity or Equality?

Differences between women and men in the way they allocate rewards to themselves and to others have been found consistently. In general, women tend to pay themselves less than men do when dividing rewards between themselves and others (Kahn, O'Leary, Krulewitz, & Lamm, 1980; Major, 1987; Major & Deaux, 1982). Women report as much satisfaction with their jobs as men do, despite the fact that they tend to hold jobs that are lower in status and more poorly paid than men's (AMA/BPW, 1999; Cox & Harquail, 1991; Williams, McDaniel, & Nguyen, 2006). In fact, Brenda Major (1994) noted that many women experience a "paradoxical contentment": They report being satisfied with their situation and seemingly do not regard as illegitimate any gender inequalities they may notice.

Some researchers have found a tendency for women to favor an equality norm in the distribution of rewards for task performance, allocating the same degree of reward to each participant, and a tendency for men to favor an equity norm, allocating rewards differentially according to task performance (Brockner & Adsit, 1986; Major & Adams, 1983). It is difficult to disentangle these gender differences from a number of other variables on which women and men may differ, such as status, political attitudes, and social versus task orientation. For example, when a situation involves persons of different status, there is often a preference for equity over equality (Wagner, 1995). People who express a social orientation have been found to prefer equal allocations; people who express a task orientation favor equity (Meeker & Elliott, 1996). Indeed, it has been argued that these differences in reward allocation stem from the socialization of women to be more interpersonally oriented than men are, so that women place more emphasis on maintaining good relationships with their coworkers than on getting a fair share of the reward (Kahn et al., 1980). Another possible explanation is that women and men differ in their own personal feelings of entitlement—of what is a fair reward for their efforts (Major, 1987; Major, McFarlin, & Gagnon, 1984). Women do not always opt for equality, however. Under certain conditions, women rely more heavily on equity, distributing rewards more in proportion to merit than men do (Major & Adams, 1984). The crucial factor is whether people are dividing a shared reward between themselves and their partners or whether they are allocating independent rewards to themselves and their partners (that is, when the allocation they make to themselves does not affect the allocation to their partners and vice versa). Major and Adams (1984) found that both women and men divided the reward more equally when asked to divide a joint reward than when asked to allocate independent rewards to themselves and their partners. Surprisingly, however, when participants were allocating rewards separately to themselves and their partners, women allocated the rewards more in proportion to merit than men did. The researchers speculated that women do not ignore merit or different levels of performance when giving out rewards; rather, they are uncomfortable when rewarding themselves for better performance means their partners will receive less. When some of the stigma of taking more for the self is removed by making the two allocations independent, women are more comfortable differentiating between their performance and that of their partners by giving themselves a larger reward.

This study did not explain *why* women should be more sensitive than men to the negative connotations of taking more for oneself at the expense of someone else, even in the case in which this can be justified by better performance. It does, however, point to the importance of such situational factors as the privacy of allocation decisions, the expectation of future interactions with a partner, and the nature of the reward on the justice decisions of both men and women. It may be that situational factors in reward allocation settings provide cues about what behavior is appropriate for both genders.

Finally, there is some evidence that the domain in which the reward allocation is taking place makes a difference: Women and men show similar distributive justice preferences when asked to consider relationship contexts, but they tend to differ when considering workplace contexts. When considering workplace contexts, women favor a more benevolent distribution of rewards (one in which they contribute more than they gain) than men do (Major, Bylsma, & Cozzarelli, 1989). Taking these findings together, it appears that it is too simple to suggest that women always prefer equality and men prefer equity in reward allocations. Rather, gendered distributive justice preferences in any situation may reflect a complex interaction of gender socialization and context.

Studies have shown that women's standards of what is fair pay for themselves are lower than those of men (Callahan-Levy & Messe, 1979; Major et al., 1984). When women and men are asked to work on a task for a period of time and then to assign themselves fair pay for their performance, women pay themselves significantly less money than men pay themselves, and they also report that less money is fair pay for their work. This happens even when men and women do not differ in their evaluations of their own performance. Moreover, when asked to do as much work as they think is fair for a given amount of money, women work longer, do more work, and perform more correctly and efficiently than men do (Major et al., 1984). In the world outside the laboratory, women anticipate lower salaries than men do at both career entry and peak salary levels (Jackson, Gardner, & Sullivan, 1992; Kaman & Hartel, 1994).

Many plausible explanations have been offered for these findings. Perhaps women have lower expectations for pay because of the history of wage discrimination against them. Or perhaps women tend to compare themselves to other women—a lower reference group standard than men because women typically are paid less than men. A third possibility is that women and men place different values on rewards. Women may value money less and interpersonal relationships more than men do. Yet another perspective is that women are more likely than men to devalue their own work and hence to underreward it or, conversely, that men overvalue and overreward their own work. Finally, it has been suggested that gender-role socialization leads women to see a weaker connection than men do between their work and pay.

All of these explanations may have some merit in particular situations, and several have received some experimental support. Major and her colleagues (1984) found that gender differences in personal entitlement did not occur when information was available about the pay of other people—a finding that suggests that women are no more likely than men to pay themselves less than others whom they see as comparable. These researchers did find evidence, however, that when no obviously appropriate comparison group was available people tended to use generalized same-sex comparisons. People seemed to match their behavior to what they thought others of their own sex would do— and both women and men thought women would pay themselves less than men for the same work and that women would work longer than men given the same pay.

This study also provides evidence that women tend to undervalue and men to overvalue their own work. Although women did more and better work than men for the specified amount of pay, men and women did not differ in the value they assigned to their own work or in their satisfaction with their pay. However, no evidence was found to support the notion that men value money more than women do; there were no gender differences in the importance ascribed to the money earned.

Finally, this research also showed that gender differences, not only in personal entitlement but also in interpersonal orientation, may have something to do with women's and men's allocation of rewards to themselves. Women but not men worked longer when they knew they were being observed by the experimenter—a finding that suggests that women's balancing of work inputs with pay outcomes was more influenced by concerns about making a good impression or pleasing the experimenter than men's was. However, the fact that women overworked or underpaid themselves relative to men in all conditions, even when not being observed, indicates that gender differences in interpersonal orientation are not enough to explain the tendency for men to allocate more rewards to themselves than women do.

Continuing research in this area has shown that people tend to prefer same-sex wage comparison information when deciding whether they are being paid fairly. In one study, even when the disadvantaged status of their own gender group was made clear and when wage comparison information for both females and males was equally available (and equally unavoidable), women were more influenced by same-sex than by cross-sex comparisons in deciding the amount they thought they should be paid, how well they thought they had performed, and how satisfied they were with their pay (Bylsma & Major, 1994). However, there are apparently some limits to the tendency to rely on same-gender comparisons. When participants in one study were led to believe wage allocation procedures were biased, their entitlement beliefs were weighted more heavily by their perceptions of their own performance than by comparisons with other women (Bylsma, Major, & Cozzarelli, 1995).

The tendency for women and men, when not provided with any comparison information, to think that they deserve differing amounts of pay for the same work apparently does not have a single cause but many. Most of these causes are probably traceable to a social structure that has traditionally provided fewer tangible rewards to women than to men for their work. If there is a norm, accepted by both sexes, that women expect less pay than men do for the same amount of work, that norm did not emerge in a vacuum but from many generations of social consensus.

On the whole, research on the way females and males allocate rewards to themselves and others shows that men and women have learned to take different perspectives toward distributive justice in particular situations. The differences in behavior may reflect differences in the sense of personal entitlement or deserving, differences in interpersonal orientation, or differential sensitivity to particular social cues—but what these latter differences reflect is not yet clear. Major and her colleagues' (1984) argument that the gender differences stem from individuals' attempts to match their behavior with their awareness of norms for their own sex is a persuasive one—and, as long as it is normative to reward women at lower rates than men, it signals real, not theoretical, problems for women. Research shows that initial expectations for pay tend to be self-confirming; that is, expecting and requesting a high salary tends to be associated with *receiving* a higher salary (Major, Vanderslice, & McFarlin, 1984). Women, expecting lower salaries, may keep on getting exactly what they expect.

GENDER INEQUALITY AND THE PERCEPTION OF JUSTICE   The finding that both women and men tend to subscribe to norms that women will be rewarded less for their work or will do more work for less pay is congruent with many of the other findings discussed in this book. There appear to be a great deal of acceptance and rationalization of situations that amount to sex discrimination. How are people able to square their acceptance of such situations with their notions of justice?

If cognitive social psychology has demonstrated one general principle, it is that human beings are capable of Olympic feats of rationalization. When people see a situation that they either cannot or do not wish to change, they are extremely good at thinking up reasons that situation is fair. For example, research has shown that people have a need to believe the world is a just place where people generally get what they deserve (Lerner, 1970, 1974). Individuals often seem to satisfy this need by seeing victims as, by definition, deserving of the harm inflicted on them. Such a general tendency may provide a partial explanation for accepting discrimination against women. Men and women may justify discrimination by believing women's work is less valuable than men's and that women are less competent, need money less, or are less interested in their work than men are. As long as people can think of reasons women *deserve* less than men, their belief in a just world can coexist comfortably with their awareness of sex discrimination.

A parallel explanation for the acceptance of female subordination stems from the study of the relationship between power and justice. As noted in Chapter 12, the group with the most power in a hierarchy not only gains control of more resources than other groups but also evolves a social philosophy that supports its right to monopolize these resources (Walster & Walster, 1975). According to equity theory, this philosophy will tend to become accepted by the entire community as justification for the status quo; if the entire group accepts the status quo, everyone avoids the discomfort of a relationship viewed as inequitable or unfair. Research has shown that both exploiters and victims can and frequently do convince themselves that even the most unbalanced of

$\mathcal{O}verview$ Gender and entitlement

- Under certain conditions, men prefer to distribute rewards using an equity principle, rewarding people in proportion to how hard they have worked or how well they have performed, whereas women prefer to distribute rewards equally.

- In lab experiments, women have been shown to work longer and better than men for the same amount of reward and to assign themselves lower pay than men do for the same amount of work.

- These findings suggest that women feel less entitled than men do to rewards for their work.

- One possible explanation for these differences is that a historical pattern of wage and other forms of discrimination against women has led women to feel less deserving of reward for their work than men feel.

- Another possibility is that gendered socialization practices have emphasized interpersonal relationships more for girls than boys, leading women to place less importance on (their own or others') individual competence and more on maintaining interpersonal relationships.

- Gender differences in entitlement may also reflect a rationalization of the ideology of male dominance and superiority.

exchanges is perfectly fair (Walster, Berscheid, & Walster, 1973). The ideology of dominance tends to be self-perpetuating: The more power a group obtains, the more its members convince themselves and others that such power is deserved and stems from superiority. For many people, recognizing that a system that discriminates against women is unfair is tantamount to admitting that their own decisions and actions have been unfair or that they have been victims of unfair treatment—possibilities that, according to equity theory, can result in considerable discomfort for individuals on both sides of the equation.

The Perceived In/Justice of Affirmative Action

If women feel uncomfortable taking more reward for themselves, even when their performance is better, how do they respond to a system that gives them any form of special treatment just because they are women? If people have learned to rationalize a situation in which men dominate the positions that are highest in status and pay by thinking that men are more competent, more ambitious, and more suitable for leadership than women, how do they react to a system that is explicitly designed to wear down such gender inequalities? Researchers who have studied the social psychology of affirmative action have found a complex set of answers to these questions.

Affirmative action refers to a set of strategies to increase the proportion of women and minorities hired by organizations or admitted into universities, particularly in fields from which they have traditionally been excluded. Such strategies may include special outreach programs and recruitment efforts and special opportunities for training directed at underrepresented groups. The programs are designed to bring the level of opportunity for underrepresented groups up to the level that it has been historically for well-represented groups.

Not surprisingly, research shows that the men who are most likely to be supportive of affirmative action for women are those who are aware of and unhappy about the discrimination directed at women (Konrad & Hartmann, 2001; Tougas & Veilleux, 1989). However, these men do not support all affirmative action programs equally. They are more supportive of programs in which the main goals involve elimination of systematic barriers against women than of those that involve preferential hiring or promotion.

Despite years of sex discrimination, women may be less comfortable than men are with accepting the preferential treatment implied by affirmative action. In one laboratory study, women and men were told that they had been selected as task leaders either on the basis of merit or preferentially on the basis of their gender (Heilman, Simon, & Repper, 1987). Women's but not men's self-perceptions and self-evaluations were negatively affected by the gender-based preferential selection method in comparison to the merit-based method. When told they had been selected as leaders because of their gender, women devalued their leadership performance, took less credit for success, described themselves as more deficient in leadership skills, and reported less interest in continuing as leader. Men were plagued by no such self-doubts when told they had been selected on the basis of their gender.

The doubts that can plague beneficiaries of affirmative action come not only from themselves but also from those around them. Research shows that people tend to stigmatize those they believe have been hired because of affirmative action. Respondents in one study evaluated an affirmative action hiree as less competent and less likely than other hirees to have been hired because of qualifications, regardless of the person's actual qualifications. Furthermore, simply being associated with affirmative action produced negative evaluations in terms of competence and career progress (Resendez, 2002). In fact, this researcher found that attitudes toward affirmative action had a stronger impact on the way an individual was evaluated than did the person's actual qualifications.

Women are the largest group to benefit from affirmative action, yet they are often not vocal in their support of it. One explanation for this silence is suggested by the studies just described. Perhaps women, who have been socialized to have more doubts about their competence than men do, are especially vulnerable to the adverse effects of preferential selection based on non-work-related criteria because they want and need the assurance and self-confidence that come with the knowledge that they have been selected or promoted on their merits. Other possible explanations lie in women's lower sense of entitlement and their preference for equality-based rather than equity-based reward distribution. It appears that one key factor lies in whether women are aware that they themselves and women as a group are targets of discrimination.

Faye Crosby (1984) argued that women often engage in a **denial of personal discrimination:** the perception by individual women that they themselves are being treated fairly, even though they may acknowledge the existence of discrimination against women as a group. There are a number of possible reasons for this denial, including the lack of relevant comparison information, such as the salaries and work histories of comparable male employees, and the unwillingness to believe that a well-regarded supervisor has supported or tolerated discriminatory treatment. However, if a woman is confronted with the necessary information, she may experience **personal relative deprivation:** a sense of dissatisfaction stemming from a comparison with others who are being more highly rewarded. She may also, if she has not already done so, experience a sense of **collective relative deprivation:** a feeling of dissatisfaction due to perceived inequities between one's own and a more advantaged group (Runciman, 1966).

Research shows that women who feel personally and collectively deprived relative to men are likely to support affirmative action policies (Beaton & Tougas, 1997; Tougas, Brown, Beaton, & St-Pierre, 1999; Tougas & Veilleux, 1988). What leads to this sense of deprivation? Women who identify strongly with women as a group are more likely to feel a sense of collective relative deprivation (Tougas & Veilleux, 1988) as are women who have been in organizations in which affirmative action policies that have been in place for some time have still not produced significant progress in women's representation (Beaton & Tougas, 1997). Finally, the experience of personally encountering discriminatory barriers when trying to move into nontraditional jobs or higher-level positions leads to the experience of collective relative deprivation, which leads, in turn, to support for affirmative action (Tougas et al., 1999).

Women often resist seeing the injustices of discriminatory treatment directed against them, and they may also resist remedies for these injustices that, because they involve preferential treatment, themselves appear unjust. Yet women's tendency to be more than fair to others and their caution about taking "more than they deserve" is modified when they are confronted with clear instances of personal or group discrimination. Under such circumstances, women become more likely to view affirmative action policies as legitimate mechanisms for rectifying injustices toward women.

Moral Development and Moral Reasoning

Several psychological theories have postulated that men and women differ in the way they develop moral reasoning, the ability to make judgments about right and wrong. Freud's (1925/1974) psychoanalytic theory suggested that because of differences in the resolution of the Oedipal complex (see Chapter 2) boys develop a superego that is more internalized, rigid, and demanding than that of girls, with the consequence that the moral character of men is more strongly defined than is that of women. Piaget's (1965) cognitive developmental theory of morality posited a similar belief in male moral superiority. He argued that equity, which involves taking into account the personal circumstances of each individual, was a more useful and advanced form of justice than equality, and Piaget noted that boys prefer equity and girls prefer equality.

Perhaps the best known theory of moral development was elaborated by Lawrence Kohlberg (1964, 1984). This theory proposed that moral development progresses through three levels in six stages, the highest of which is not reached until adulthood or may never be reached. Individuals progress from basing moral judgments on fear of consequences to themselves, to basing them on concern for social approval, harmony, and law and order, to basing them on abstract principles of universal rights for all persons. Kohlberg indicated that most women and men develop at least to the middle, conventional level of moral reasoning, but that, within this level, women prefer Stage 3 reasoning based on good intentions and social approval and men prefer the more advanced Stage 4 reasoning based on maintaining the social order. Furthermore, men are more likely than women to reach the highest level of moral reasoning; women supposedly do not reach these top two stages unless they take on occupational positions similar to men's. Otherwise, "while girls are moving from high school or college to motherhood, sizeable proportions of them are remaining at Stage 3, while their male agemates are dropping Stage 3 in favor of the stages above it. Stage 3 morality is a functional morality for housewives and mothers; it is not for businessmen and professionals" (Kohlberg & Kramer, 1969, p. 108).

Kohlberg's theory reflects some strong biases, not only about men and women and the moral requirements of their respective roles but also about the superiority of certain kinds of moral reasoning. The possibility that different forms of moral reasoning might be equally useful and valid is not acknowledged in his theory. It does not include the possibility that culture may affect moral development; cross-cultural data now suggest that respondents from outside North America cannot always be categorized predictably into the stages delineated by Kohlberg (Al-Ansari, 2002; Baek, 2002). Furthermore, the theory was developed using data only from males; thus males provide the standard for what is humanly normal. Psychologist Carol Gilligan (1982) proposed a new cognitive developmental theory of morality in an effort to correct the masculine bias of this and other theories.

GILLIGAN'S THEORY: TWO MORAL PRINCIPLES   When Gilligan analyzed the responses made by girls and women to questions about morality, she did not limit herself to looking for the kinds of themes that would indicate stages of moral development identified by Kohlberg's theory. Rather, she tried to find out whether there were themes in women's moral reasoning that had been missed by Kohlberg's scoring system. Her research revealed that, besides the principle of rights that had emerged as the basis of moral reasoning in Kohlberg's work, another principle was frequently invoked as her respondents struggled to explain why a particular decision was right or wrong: the principle of caring and responsibility. Moral judgments based on the principle of caring

Reflections   Is Affirmative Action Fair?

ffirmative action in employment is a policy that has been in place in the United States since the signing of an Executive Order by President Lyndon Johnson in 1965. In response to this order, the federal government and organizations that do business with it are required to monitor their own employment records with respect to women and people of color. If, through this monitoring of their own records, they detect that their employment of members of these designated groups falls short of the availability of such individuals (e.g., if they have few women accountants and there are many women accountants available for employment), they are supposed to take corrective measures.

Affirmative action in education follows a similar pattern: Universities take corrective steps if they determine that particular groups are underenrolled relative to their availability in the pool of qualified applicants.

Because affirmative action is proactive, and institutions do not wait for people to complain that they are victims of discrimination, the policy has had a broad and substantial effect on both employment and education. Women and people of color have made important gains in both arenas, and it is estimated that affirmative action applies to one of every four American workers. Cleary it is a policy that has benefited many—yet it remains extremely controversial. Results vary, but polls tend to show that at least a third of Americans do not support affirmative action policies (Crosby & Franco, 2003).

Why do so many people resist affirmative action and argue that such policies are unfair? In part, it may be because they believe, wrongly, that affirmative action policies are quota systems that allow the hiring or acceptance of unqualified individuals (Crosby & Franco, 2003). And it may be in part because the whole idea of preferential selection makes many people uneasy (Crosby, Iyer, Clayton, & Downing, 2003). Yet, as Crosby and her colleagues asked, is affirmative action really a system of preferential selection or is it a way of dismantling a (largely unacknowledged) system of preferential selection that already exists?

Research suggests that one reason people oppose affirmative action is that they see it as "changing the rules" after the game has started, particularly if the respondents have not been convinced that the old rules were unfair (Crosby & Franco, 2003). Some people argue that the "new rules" of affirmative action are unfair because they place a higher priority on diversity than on individual merit and constitute an abandonment of merit-based selection. The debate will likely last for years to come, and it should make us question our notions about how the "best" candidate for any job or educational slot is chosen. As Crosby and her colleagues noted, "groups, teams, organizations, and societies may function best if they include and make use of many different types of talent. Thus, in the end, the merit of the group may depend on the diversity of talented individuals within it" (p. 109).

stressed the necessity to be responsible in one's relationships, to be sensitive to the needs of others, and to avoid giving hurt. Gilligan's research led her to conclude that there were stages in the development of the care orientation to morality just as there were stages in the development of the rights orientation. Individuals moved from an initial stage of caring only for the self, to a middle stage of trying to be "good" by caring for others (sometimes called *maternal morality* by Gilligan because it is the type of morality that is urged on women in their maternal role), to a mature stage of caring for truth, which involves achieving a balance of care for the self and others.

Although both the **rights orientation** and the **care orientation** can be found in the moral reasoning of women and men, Gilligan argued that men tend to place more emphasis on rights, and women place more emphasis on care. The difference in emphasis, she suggested, is due to the different goals of development for women and men: attachment and relationship for women and separation and achievement for men. The goals are different because the problems and challenges faced by women are different from those faced by men, partly because society expects different things from them and partly because their biological differences make them vulnerable to different experiences in the area of reproduction. Gilligan argued, however, that neither the rights orientation nor the care orientation represents a superior type of moral reasoning. Rather, they are different and in some sense complementary orientations: "two disparate modes of experience that are in the end connected. . . . In the representation of maturity, both perspectives converge in the realization that just as inequality adversely affects both parties in an unequal relationship, so too violence is destructive for everyone involved" (p. 174).

Many people have found Gilligan's theory appealing, but others have criticized it for reifying the stereotype that women are emotional and nurturant and men are logical and clearheaded. Although agreeing that her contribution has been immense in drawing attention to the dimension of care and responsibility in moral judgments, many investigators have been more cautious in accepting her claim that women and men differ in their reliance on this orientation. In recent years, careful investigations have been made of both Kohlberg's and Gilligan's theories with respect to gender differences.

L. J. Walker (1984) performed a meta-analysis of studies on moral reasoning as measured by Kohlberg's interview method in 106 samples of children, adolescents, and adults. Of all these samples, only 8 clearly indicated significant differences favoring males. Moreover, several of these 8 were inconclusive because gender was confounded with occupational-educational differences. Walker suggested that rather than arguing over the extent to which gender bias is inherent in Kohlberg's theory it would be more appropriate to ask why, in the face of so little evidence, the myth persists that males are more advanced in Kohlberg's levels of moral reasoning than females are. He concluded that, in fact, the moral reasoning of men and women is remarkably similar, especially given publication and reporting biases that make differences more likely to be reported.

The failure to find empirical confirmation for the notion that males operate at higher levels of moral reasoning than females do is echoed in a meta-analysis of 56 samples including more than 6,000 subjects (Thoma, 1986). The findings showed that at every age and educational level small but reliable gender differences appear—with females scoring significantly higher than males on moral reasoning.

Another review of the literature on moral development, this one including not only studies using Kohlberg's measure but also those using a variety of other measures, found that 60% of the studies showed no differences between males and females with respect to moral development (Lifton, 1985). Among the studies that did report a significant male–female difference in moral development, most used Kohlberg's measure, and the differences sometimes favored females, particularly for children. In his own research, Lifton (1985) found no evidence of male–female differences in moral development among adolescents or adults, using either Kohlberg's measure of moral judgment or his own measure of moral character. He did, however, find significant differences in stage of moral judgment between masculine and feminine persons of both sexes, suggesting that Kohlberg's measure may favor masculine over feminine persons.

Researchers who have taken a longitudinal approach to the development of moral and prosocial reasoning among adolescents suggest that gender differences in maturity may be mistaken for differences in moral reasoning (Eisenberg, Miller, Shell, McNalley, & Shea, 1991). When they followed a sample of adolescents over an 11-year period, they found that girls used other-oriented, self-reflective modes of reasoning earlier than boys did, but within 2 years the boys had caught up. Girls did show a higher level of moral reasoning overall, a finding the researchers attributed partly to the tendency of high school boys to use more hedonistic reasoning and to make fewer socially responsible choices than girls at this age.

Some researchers have tried specifically to evaluate Gilligan's theory that an ethic of care is more prevalent among women and an ethic of rights is more prevalent among men. Gilligan and Attanucci (1988), using real-life dilemmas, found that women and men used both care and justice orientations. But care-focus dilemmas were more likely to be presented by women, and justice-focus dilemmas were more likely to be presented by men. Stiller and Forrest (1990) also found that men emphasized justice and women emphasized care in their moral reasoning. Similar findings were reported by Yacker and Weinberg (1990) using hypothetical childhood dilemmas. Skoe and Diessner (1994) found that use of the ethic of care was more strongly related to identity for women than for men. However, another study by Skoe and her colleagues found that gender-role orientation was a better predictor of care-oriented moral reasoning than gender was (Sochting, Skoe, & Marcia, 1994). Other studies that examined individuals' moral reasoning about competitive athletic encounters (Crown & Heatherington, 1989) and interpersonal relationships (Pratt, Pancer, & Hunsberger, 1990) found no gender differences in such reasoning. One study that investigated moral reasoning among African American working-class adolescents and adults found no evidence for a gender difference in care and rights orientations (Stack, 1997). More recent studies of African American (Weisz & Black, 2003) and Mexican American (Gump, Baker, & Roll, 2000) youths found a small tendency for young women to use more care-based reasoning than young men, but they found no differences in the use of justice-based moral reasoning. Researchers have also found that, among elementary school children, girls judge both physical and relational aggression as more morally wrong than boys do—and rate relational aggression as more harmful than boys do (Murray-Close, Crick, & Galotti, 2006). Like some other findings, these results suggest some tendency for girls to place more emphasis on relationships than boys do when making moral judgments.

Ford and Lowery (1986) conducted a study specifically designed to compare women and men on their use of the principles of rights and care in their moral judgments. They asked male and female undergraduates to describe three important moral conflicts in their lives and to rate the importance of those conflicts and the degree of difficulty they experienced in deciding what to do. Next, the students read summary descriptions of the rights and care orientations to moral judgment and rated, on a 7-point scale, the degree to which each orientation was a part of their own approach to the conflicts they had described. They also completed a measure of gender-role orientation and a scale evaluating the two moral orientations along good-bad, powerful-weak, and active-passive dimensions. The results of the study offered some but not overwhelming support for Gilligan's theory. Men and women did not differ significantly in the degree to which they used the rights and care orientations. However, women were more consistent from one conflict to the next in their use of the care orientation than in their use of the rights orientation; men were more consistent in their use of the rights than of the care orientation. Interestingly, for both female and male participants, the importance and difficulty ratings for the conflict situations were significantly associated with care ratings but not with rights ratings. For this college student sample, the most important and difficult moral decisions encountered so far were related more to issues of care than to issues of rights.

One longitudinal study that examined the possibility of gender differences in care and responsibility orientations suggested that, for most individuals, there is little consistency in these orientations over time (L. J. Walker, 1989). This study, in which persons ages 5 to 63 were interviewed twice, 2 years apart, revealed no gender differences in justice and care orientations for children and adolescents and none at any age using standard moral dilemmas. The only gender difference found was among adults using real-life dilemmas—for whom there was a tendency among women to use the care orientation more frequently. This gender difference in orientation appeared to be confounded with a gender difference in the content of the real-life dilemmas recalled by the respondents. Women were more likely to recall personal, as opposed to impersonal, real-life moral dilemmas—and, for both women and men, personal dilemmas were strongly associated with the use of the care orientation.

In the Ford and Lowery (1986) study, although females and males did not differ significantly in their use of the care and rights orientations, both groups rated the care orientation as a feminine response and the rights orientation as a masculine response. It appears that the belief in different styles of moral judgment for women and men existed even in this sample in which only minimal evidence for such female–male differences could be found. This finding brings us back to the question posed by L. J. Walker (1984): Why does the belief in gender differences in moral reasoning persist so strongly in the face of such weak or contradictory evidence? Brabeck (1983) addressed the question of why so many people find an intuitive appeal to Gilligan's theory despite its lack of clear empirical support. She noted that stereotypes about gender differences in morality abound; for instance, studies have found that girls and boys develop different reputations for altruism, even when their actual behavior is very similar (Shigetomi, Hartmann, & Gilford, 1981). In some way, she suggested, a belief that males and females are morally different meets our cultural and emotional needs—but it does so by distorting our vision of human beings:

> There is an essential tension between autonomy and interdependence, between the requirements of justice and the demands of mercy, between absolute moral principles and situation specific moral action, between reason and affect. To resolve this tension by assigning half to males and half to females when evidence does not support that division is to reduce the complexity of morality, to cloud truth with myth, to do an injustice to the capacities of both sexes and to lose an opportunity to revise and modify our theories of morality. (Brabeck, 1983, p. 287)

Although the last word is certainly not in on the possibility of gender differences in moral orientation (for example, it may be that the situations men experience as moral conflicts are more likely to involve rights, and those women experience as conflicts are more likely to involve care), the evidence to date suggests that women and men are unlikely to bring very different principles of moral judgment to any particular moral dilemma. The controversy continues to stimulate research, and thus far it has had the effect of broadening our understanding of moral reasoning and of conferring new respect on a dimension of morality that, whether it actually differentiates the sexes or not, has always been trivialized because it was stereotyped as feminine.

GENDER AND THE LAW

Social notions of justice are formalized into a legal system of laws and courts that, in the tradition of justice as "blind," are supposed to treat everyone with equal favor, regardless of economic, social, or political status. Not surprisingly, however, this formal justice system reflects and even perpetuates the prevalent stereotypes and prejudices about gender. Such biases are evident in the induction of lawyers and judges into the system, in laws concerning the rights of women and men, and in the treatment of male and female criminals and victims who come into contact with the legal system.

Participation in the Legal System: Lawyers and Judges

Early in the 1900s, when women in Canada were petitioning for the opportunity to become lawyers, one judge ruled that their exclusion was perfectly reasonable. His rationale was that a "lady lawyer" would have to subject her delicate ears to courtroom testimony concerning rape—a subject about which no woman should have to hear (L. Smith, 1987). In 1873, a woman named Myra Bradwell was barred from practicing law in Illinois because, the judge said, a woman's natural

Gender and moral reasoning

- Several theorists (Freud, Piaget, Kohlberg) proposed that women tend to be less advanced than men in their capacity for moral reasoning.

- Research by Gilligan challenged this idea by demonstrating that earlier theories may have been too focused on rights-based moral reasoning and thus overlooked an entire dimension of moral reasoning: care-based reasoning.

- Studies using either Kohlberg's approach or Gilligan's approach have not found consistent, large differences between boys and girls and women and men in moral development.

- Some studies found a small tendency for women to use more care-based moral reasoning than men do; however, both women and men use both care- and rights-based moral reasoning.

place was in the home (Agate & Meacham, 1977) and also because the state restricted the right of married women to make legally binding contracts. No client would want to deal with an attorney who could not be held accountable for the agreements she signed. The law in this case placed women in a frustrating double bind: first by limiting their accountability for their actions and second by acting to protect others from the consequences of this lack of accountability.

Although women have now been admitted to the practice of law, they are still hampered by the stereotype that women are more emotional and less rational than men in their orientation toward justice. Women are still a definite minority among lawyers and judges, although their numbers are increasing. In 1990, 21% of U.S. lawyers and judges combined were women (Kaufman, 1995). By 2003, women made up 29.1% of lawyers in the United States and 50% of law students. Women represented more than 25% of tenured law school faculty, 16.3% of partners in major law firms, and 15% of general counsels to Fortune 500 companies. Women have also become more visible as judges: 17.4% of U.S. Courts of Appeal judges and 16.2% of judges in U.S. District Courts were women by 2003 (American Bar Association, 2006a). However, women of color have fared less well: In 2004 only 4% of law partners were women of color, and a 2005 survey showed that 81% of minority women lawyers had left their law firms within 5 years of being hired (American Bar Association, 2006b).

Female lawyers face different career patterns than their male colleagues. They tend to be clustered in the less prestigious areas of the law: family law, trust and estates, and tax law (Kaufman, 1995). In addition, they face discrimination, gender stereotypes, and sexual harassment on the job (American Bar

Association, 2006a; Rosenberg, Perlstadt, & Phillips, 1993). Female lawyers report feeling marginalized by behavior that emphasizes their "token" status in the profession: receiving compliments for their appearance but not for their handling of a case, hearing sexist jokes and remarks from judges and attorneys, and being patronized, called by their first names, and asked whether they are lawyers (MacCorquodale & Jensen, 1993).

Sheila McIntyre (1987), in a searching and painful description of her first year on the faculty of a prestigious Canadian law school, described experiences of hostility and harassment from male students and colleagues in response to her feminist views. Particularly instructive, in view of the issues of power already discussed in this book, is her description of how female law students were silenced and intimidated when they tried to articulate feminist arguments or when they challenged traditional legal approaches to particular problems. For example, two women in her seminar on labor law expressed discomfort with the assumptions of adversarial relations and conflict built into the working model of labor law and labor relations that the class was using. They were interrupted, contradicted, and shouted down by male students:

> I . . . asked the class to reflect on what had just happened. Two usually silent women had spoken and explained why they had trouble participating. One was interrupted and called "wrong"; then the subject was changed; then their contribution was characterized as non-law. I suggested their contributions introduced an alternative model of law and labor relations which we might try to explore. Again there was an uproar. I was shouted down by the left-wing male and denounced as a "bourgeois feminist". . . . I proposed we draw up two models for a first contract: one under the working model premised on conflict, power, inequality, and private property; the other premised on code-termination, communal interests, and equality. . . . About five male students put down their pens, pulled back their chairs, and glared at me, refusing to participate. No one invited the two women who had advanced an alternative model to articulate what their vision might include. They went silent. A few men ventured some possibilities but were met with open anger from other men who interrupted, laughed, or talked over them. (p. 8)

This example illustrates just how difficult it can be for female students, even with the support of a female professor, to challenge the structure or built-in assumptions of a legal system that has always been articulated and dominated by men.

Such difficulties are not unique to law schools, of course, but they may be aggravated in the law school atmosphere of adversarial justice. A reading of McIntyre's article makes it painfully clear that women who survive law school may have had much of their interest in questioning established legal assumptions and priorities ground out of them in the process. And progress since her article appeared has been slow. In 1994–1995 hearings at 58 law schools, the American Bar Association's Commission on Women in the Profession found persistent reports of gender stereotyping, sexual harassment, and hostile and disrespectful behavior toward female faculty. They heard descriptions of a male faculty member calling his female students "little girl" and "sweetie" and stories of male students calling female faculty members inadequate and bitchy and testing them with repeated interruptions (American Bar Association, 1998). Another set of hearings, conducted in 2003 (American Bar Association, 2006a), showed that problems still persist: Respondents testified that female attorneys are often viewed as "bossy, too aggressive, not aggressive enough, too emotional, or too strident" (p. 5), and some women lawyers reported that judges and bailiffs addressed them as "baby" and "honey" or used women's first names but addressed men by their titles. It appears that women entering the legal profession, although increasing in numbers, still face considerable resistance.

Sex, Gender, and Legal Rights

In 1986 the Ontario Court of Appeal in Canada ruled that Justine Blainey, a 12-year-old girl who had been chosen to play on a first-class hockey team in Toronto but had been barred from play by the Ontario Hockey Association, could legally play on the team. This was the first sex equality case to be decided by an appeal court under Canada's then new *Charter of Rights and Freedoms,* and it is one highly publicized example of how sex discrimination can be fought by legal means (Brodsky, 1986).

Several years later, in a decision with far-reaching implications, the U.S. Supreme Court ruled that companies may not use "fetal protection" as a reason to bar women of childbearing age from jobs that pose reproductive hazards (Marcus, 1991). The case involved a Milwaukee-based battery manufacturer that barred female employees from jobs that exposed them to high levels of lead. (Lead can damage a developing fetus.) The legal action was brought on behalf of a 50-year-old divorced woman who was transferred from her position and another who chose to be sterilized to keep her job. The Court held that it was illegal for a company to force a woman to decide between having a child and having a job and noted that discrimination on the basis of a person's ability to become pregnant amounted simply to a form of sex discrimination.

In recent years we have seen an escalation of efforts, international in scope, to achieve equal rights under the law for women and men. A major push has been made toward the adoption by all countries of the United Nations Convention on the Elimination of All Forms of Discrimination Against Women (CEDAW). This convention includes, among other things, the assurance that women and men will be equal before the law, including laws governing property and contracts, have equal rights to family benefits and bank credit, have the same rights and responsibilities during marriage and its dissolution, and have equal pay for work of equal value. At this writing, 185 countries, including Canada but not including the United States, have ratified this convention (United Nations, 2006). By ratifying the convention, a country makes a commitment to pass legislation and promote policies congruent with the treaty's conditions and to submit periodic progress reports on the status of women and the implementation of the treaty. Canada ratified this treaty in 1981; the most recent country to ratify it is San Marino, in 2003. The United States signed but did not ratify the treaty in 1980. By this action, this country agreed to do nothing in contravention of the treaty's terms but did *not* agree to implement the treaty actively.

Within North America, attempts to promote equality under the law for men and women have frequently foundered on arguments about what definition of *equality* is most appropriate. This argument turns on the perception of justice: Although a group of individuals may agree that women and men should be treated the same way under the law in many circumstances, they may disagree about which legal distinctions between the sexes, if any, should be preserved. The problem is a difficult one because, as discussed earlier in this chapter, perceptions of fairness are so often conditioned by what we are used to and by "the way things have always been." To illustrate this point, consider the following list of situations in which the law, in certain jurisdictions, has discriminated on the basis of sex:

- Certain social service benefits were available to mothers who stayed home with their children but not to fathers who did the same thing.

- The child of a married couple could be given the father's surname but not the mother's.
- The father of a child born out of wedlock could be sued by the mother for the support of the child; however, a father who had custody of a child born out of wedlock could not initiate similar proceedings against the mother.
- "Protective" labor laws in some jurisdictions established a maximum number of hours a woman could work.

For years such laws seemed so "natural" that few people considered them unfair, despite their discrimination on the basis of sex. It is only in consciously stepping back from traditional assumptions about sex differences and gender roles that people become aware of the arbitrariness of laws such as these.

Within the legal system, a debate is still going on about how gender equality should be defined under the law. There are at least three perspectives (Lahey, 1984). The first is *absolute equality,* which would require legislation to be sex blind and gender neutral and to deny the existence of any meaningful differences between women and men, with the exception of reproductive differences. A feminist-inspired variation on this perspective is the *sex-specific/gender-neutral* approach, which would try to achieve equality by drafting legislation specifically geared to the needs of women as a disadvantaged group but written using such neutral terms as "parent" and "spouse" so that protections and benefits would be available to both women and men. A second alternative is the *gender-specific* approach, which acknowledges biological, social, and economic differences between the sexes and recognizes women as a disadvantaged group. This approach would strike down legislation that was detrimental to women but would retain provisions that were beneficial to women to redress the inequalities between women and men. The third possibility is *equality with recognition of real differences.* This would involve a standard in which equal treatment was the norm, but strong statistical evidence that women and men were in unequal positions could be used to uphold unequal treatment. This third standard reflects the current reasoning applied by the U.S. Supreme Court.

All of these approaches to gender equality have potential pitfalls. The problem with a gender-specific approach to equality is that gender-specific legislation can be used in the service of inequality as well as equality. For example, the recognition that women as a group are physically weaker than men has in the past been used to construct gender-specific legislation that "protects" women from being hired for jobs that require lifting heavy loads. The sex-specific/gender-neutral approach, despite its neutral language, could possibly reinforce existing gender stereotypes. For instance, laws designed to meet the needs of employed mothers may reinforce the stereotype that child care is "naturally" women's work, even though the actual wording of the legislation is in terms of "parental" rather than "maternal" leave. Even the absolute equality approach has its share of potential problems. Absolute equality denies male–female differences but does so in the context of a legal system that was designed with males in mind, so that females and female experiences end up being judged according to a male standard. An example of how ludicrous this "gender-neutral" approach to justice can become in the hands of an unsympathetic judge can be found in the ruling on a sexual assault case in Canada. A young woman had been approached by a man who, against her will, grabbed and fondled her breasts. The man was charged with sexual assault. The court ruled, however, that because breasts are female secondary sex characteristics, just as beards are male secondary sex characteristics, for a man to fondle a woman's breasts was no more a case of sexual assault than it would be for a woman to stroke a man's beard (L. Smith, 1987). This ruling was eventually overturned by the Supreme Court of Canada. However, it is clear that attempts to make the law treat both sexes fairly can backfire against either women or men and that, because laws are interpreted in courts by judges, gender bias can be a factor in the justice system even when the laws themselves are unbiased.

Gender and Crime

An important aspect of society's concern with justice has to do with preventing and punishing criminal behavior. In this area as well, gender has an impact on justice. Women and men differ in their criminal behavior, in which of their behaviors are considered criminal, and in the ways their crimes are punished. Women and men also differ in their experiences as victims of crime.

WOMEN AND MEN AS CRIMINALS   Men commit more crimes than women, and men's crimes tend to be more serious and violent than women's crimes. Women account for only 17.8% of those arrested for violent crimes and 31.9% of those arrested for property crimes (U.S. Bureau of Justice Statistics, 2004). The reported incidence of crimes by women, particularly property crimes, has increased at a faster rate than that by men in recent years, but all over the world most crimes, especially violent ones, are still committed by men.

It is difficult to evaluate how well the statistics on crime reflect gender differences in criminal behavior because there are gender biases in the criminal justice system's treatment of offenders. Among adolescents, females but not males tend to be charged with so-called status offenses, such as curfew violations or running away from home (U.S. Bureau of Justice Statistics, 2004). These behaviors are violations of social norms for young women.

Among adults, women have traditionally been less likely to be arrested and have tended to be given more lenient sentences than their male counterparts (U.S. Bureau of Justice Statistics, 2004; Weisberg, 1982), perhaps because gender stereotypes support the notion that women cannot really be as "bad" as men. The stereotypes can backfire for women accused of particularly unfeminine crimes, however; these women occasionally receive particularly punitive sentences (Chesney-Lind, 1987). Most evidence now suggests that when women receive lesser sentences it is because they have fewer and less violent previous convictions (Mauer & Huling, 1995). However, women face laws that specifically criminalize their behavior. The use of illegal drugs by pregnant women has been deemed a delivery of controlled substances to the unborn child, and women can be arrested and prosecuted for this offense (Cooper, 1992). In addition, poor and homeless women and men now frequently become entangled in the criminal justice system as many cities pass laws prohibiting begging or sleeping in public places.

Recent years have seen an increase in the number of women who are imprisoned, as seen in Figure 14.1. Between 1977 and 2004, the population of women prisoners increased by 75.7%, a yearly growth rate nearly twice that of men prisoners (Frost, Greene & Pranis, 2006). One reason for this increase is the introduction of mandatory minimum sentencing laws for a variety of non-violent, drug-related crimes. Since women are more often convicted for this type of crime than for other crimes, these sentencing laws have had an enormous impact on women.

The imprisonment of more women has had a ripple effect on children, families, and neighborhoods. One significant difference between women and men in prison is that women are more likely than men to have children of whom they have custody. More than three-quarters of the women in prison have children; two-thirds have children under the age of 18 (American Bar Association, 1998; The Sentencing Project, 2005).

For many female prisoners, incarceration is only the latest in a string of problems. More than half of women in prison say that they have been physically or sexually abused (The Sentencing Project, 2005). According to one study, nearly half of women prisoners ran away from home as girls (American Correctional Association, 1990).

Certain criminal laws discriminate directly on the grounds of sex. For example, in some jurisdictions, both statutory rape and homosexual acts are legally considered crimes only when performed by males, whereas, in others, prostitution is an exclusively female crime. Other laws, for the most part now changed, were based on the double standard with respect to sexuality in marriage. For

Figure 14.1   Number of female prisoners within jurisdiction of state and federal correctional authorities, 1990 to 2004. The number of persons in prison has risen rapidly in recent years, but the increase has been especially high for women.

Source: U.S Bureau of Justice Statistics (2006), table 6.41. Retrieved November 28, 2006, from http://www.albany.edu/sourcebook/pdf/t6412004.pdf

example, in some jurisdictions, murder was considered a justifiable reaction for a man who found his wife in bed with another man but not for a wife who found her husband in bed with another woman. Clearly, criminal law as well as civil law contains built-in inequalities with respect to gender, and these inequalities are related to social stereotypes about women and men.

An aspect of the criminal law that has been the target of much criticism for its inequitable treatment of women and men is that surrounding prostitution: the selling of sex for money. Most prostitutes are women, although there are gay male prostitutes and there are also men who sell sex and companionship to women—but not usually on the street. Although the law in most jurisdictions defines soliciting or prostitution as a crime, not all the participants in the crime are usually charged or even liable to be charged. Generally, the woman who sells sex is charged with breaking the law if she is caught; the man purchasing her services may not be charged. For example, in Toronto, a jurisdiction in which both prostitutes and their customers are liable for prosecution, over a 4-year period from 1979 to 1982, 71% of the charges for soliciting as prostitutes or customers were laid against women and only 29% were laid against men (Canadian Advisory Council on the Status of Women, 1984). A study of prostitution-related arrests in Buffalo, New York, between 1977 and 1979 showed a similar pattern: Only 12.9% of the female prostitutes but 73% of the men arrested for patronizing them were released after the arrest to await trial (Bernat, 1984). According to one estimate, the average pattern of prostitution arrests in U.S. cities is 70% female prostitutes, 20% male prostitutes, and 10% customers (Prostitutes Education Network, 1999). Certainly, more women (69.2%) than men (30.8%) continue to be charged for prostitution-related offenses in the United States (U.S. Bureau of Justice Statistics, 2004). However, the Canadian Center for Justice Statistics reports that prostitutes and customers have been at equal risk of prosecution since 1986 (Duchesne, 1997).

The sex discrimination shown in applying the law on prostitution has always been very blatant, perhaps because it fits so well with the double standard of sexual behavior (discussed in Chapter 7) and with the established power differences between women and men. The following comment, made in a 1914 report on prostitution in Europe, reflects a sentiment that has changed little in the intervening years:

> The professional prostitute being a social outcast may be periodically punished without disturbing the usual course of society. . . . The man, however, is something more than a partner in an immoral act: He discharges important social and business relations, is as father and brother responsible for the maintenance of others, has commercial or industrial duties to meet. He cannot be imprisoned without deranging society. (Flexner, 1914, p. 108)

The existence of prostitution and its lopsided gender distribution and punishment is to some extent a symptom of the inequality between the sexes. In one version of a gender-equal society, women and men would be equally likely to be prostitutes and customers, to sell and purchase sex. In another version, prostitution would not exist at all because there would be no market or social support for impersonal, commercialized sexual relations. However, prostitution will continue to be the path of least resistance for a large number of women until the economic and social pressures that disadvantage women are changed. Women's poverty and low socioeconomic status with respect to men and the gender-role socialization of both sexes make prostitution one of the very few alternatives for some women. The impact of these pressures is highlighted by the difficulties women encounter when they try to get out of prostitution. Some women who are unsuccessful in their attempts to leave prostitution have commented that, even though they can find legal jobs, there is no way to earn money that is as "easy" or lucrative as prostitution. Yet those who exit the profession successfully note that there can be rewards for finding a way to earn their livelihoods legally. As one former sex worker commented when interviewed by researcher Rochelle Dalla (2006):

> Before, I just lived day by day, didn't think about the future. And here it is. I'm just starting to work—and keep in mind just about ready to retire. You can't hustle all your life. What are you going to do when you get old, you know? You can't draw Social Security. (p. 283)

Traditional gender-role socialization with respect to work does not help young women come to terms with issues such as Social Security. Some young women still expect that their employment, whatever it is, will be an unimportant and temporary stage in their lives before they take on their "real" job as mothers. The young women who go into prostitution are no exceptions. As one 15-year-old Winnipeg prostitute said wistfully when asked in a television interview what she would ideally like to do with her life, "I want to have children and a husband to look after me." This is a fantasy that is supported by myths and fairy tales and movies such as *Pretty Woman.*

Clearly, prostitution is one area of the law in which justice is not meted out equally to women and men. However, the inequality in the law has roots that stretch deeply into other, even more basic inequalities between women and men.

VICTIMS OF CRIME   On December 6, 1989, in a tragedy that has since become known as the Montreal Massacre, Marc Lepine rampaged through the school of engineering at the University of Montreal with an assault rifle, killing 14 women and wounding 9 other women and 4 men. The preponderance of females among Lepine's victims was no coincidence. He ordered men out of the way and rounded up women to be shot, screaming at his victims that they were "all fucking feminists." Found among his belongings after he turned his gun on himself were a suicide note blaming all his failures on women as well as a "hit list" of prominent Canadian women (Caputi & Russell, 1990). More recently other men have entered schools with the apparent objective of killing girls or women only: In 2006 Carl Charles Roberts shot 10 girls in an Amish school in Pennsylvania, killing 5 of them, and Duane Morrison took 6 girls hostage at a Colorado high school and killed 1 of them. These terrible incidents reflect the disastrous intersection of three destructive forces: bitter, angry, troubled assailants; the easy availability of guns to these individuals; and a cultural context that sometimes seems to legitimize male entitlement and male anger and violence toward females.

Yet despite the horror of such incidents, and despite what some experts argued are increasing levels of viciousness in crimes against women (Caputi & Russell, 1990), homicide statistics show a decrease in the rate of violent crimes against women (Rennison & Rand, 2003). Across countries, time, and age groups, studies show that men are more often victimized by violent crime than women are (U.S. Bureau of Justice Statistics, 2006c) but women express greater fear of being victimized than men do—perhaps because the crimes of which women are victims are more likely to be personal ones such as sexual assault or violent attacks by known assailants (American Bar Association, 1998; Statistics Canada, 1995). Men are about equally likely to be victims of assault or other crimes of violence perpetrated by strangers as of such crimes perpetrated by nonstrangers, whereas women are far more likely to be assaulted or violently victimized by persons they know than by strangers (U.S. Bureau of Justice Statistics, 2006b).

Women are more than twice as likely as men to say that being victimized has made it difficult or impossible to carry out their normal activities, and many more women than men report that they feel unsafe walking alone in their neighborhood after dark or being home alone at night (Statistics Canada, 1995).

Women's greater fear may stem from their socialization that they are incapable of protecting themselves, but it probably also relates to the type of crimes to which women are most vulnerable. Women are considerably more likely than men to live in fear of physical violence from a person in their own household. Women are most likely to be killed by people they know intimately and are more likely to be murdered in their own homes than anywhere else. Victimization surveys also show that women are up to 7 times as likely as men to experience a sexual assault. Not only are such victimization experiences especially traumatic in themselves, but reporting them tends to expose the victim to stigmatization. Women who have been raped or who have been beaten by their husbands are often assumed to have done something to encourage or provoke their attacker. The possibility of encountering such attitudes often causes a female victim not to report the crime. Estimates are that only 1 of every 4 rapes and 1 of every 10 incidents of wife assault are reported; the Canadian national Violence Against Women Survey indicated that only 14% of cases of wife assault or nonspousal physical or sexual assault were reported to police, and 22% of the victimized women had told no one about their experience (Statistics Canada, 1995). In the United States, the National Crime Victimization Survey indicates that in 2004 fewer than 37% of women who had experienced rape or sexual assault had reported the incident to the police (U.S. Bureau of Justice Statistics, 2006a).

Gender prejudice has played an important role in the legal treatment of victims of rape and wife assault. For many years, a wife was considered the property of her husband, and it was legally permissible for him to beat her (see Chapter 11). Rape of a wife by her husband was considered a contradiction in terms: A husband had the right to have sex with his wife with or without her consent. This law has now been changed in North America and in many of the world's nations.

The assumption that a female rape victim enticed her attacker or actually consented to have intercourse with him was built into the rules of evidence for rape trials. It used to be routine for the victim's prior sexual history to be brought up in court to establish that she was promiscuous and therefore had probably consented to the intercourse. Laws have now made such evidence inadmissible in most U.S. and Canadian jurisdictions; however, this legislation was struck down in Canada in 1991 on the ground that it might deny a fair trial to the accused (Fulton, 1991). Newer "rape-shield" laws place the burden of proof for the woman's consent to sexual relations on the man, rather than making it incumbent on the rape victim to prove that she did *not* consent. These laws also prohibit bringing up a rape victim's sexual history in court. However, the laws are far from foolproof, and victims can still find themselves and their reputations on trial when they charge someone with rape.

If a female victim kills her attacker while defending herself against rape, she is often regarded as having used unnecessary force and is sometimes jailed, whereas men who have killed while protecting themselves from rape by another man have generally been acquitted (Sapiro, 1986). One-half of this pattern may reflect a lack of understanding about how traumatic and dangerous rape can be for the female victim. As one person is reported to have commented during the 1977 trial of Inez Garcia, a woman who killed her rapist, "You can't kill someone for trying to give you a good time" (as quoted in Sapiro, 1986). The other half of the pattern may relate to homophobia: A man defending himself against homosexual rape may be seen as defending himself from something unnatural, whereas heterosexual rape, in some people's perceptions, falls within the range of normal heterosexual experience.

A final twist on the gender bias that affects the treatment of victims is that when men find themselves the victims of sexual assault or physical abuse by women they are likely to receive very unsympathetic treatment if they report the incident. A man who cannot successfully defend himself against a woman is not much of a man according to the prevailing norms of masculinity, and the male victim of female violence is more likely to be the target of jokes than sympathy.

In summary, gender ideology plays a large part in the justice system's treatment of victims, particularly when the crime is related to sexuality or male–female relationships. Some changes in the direction of increased sensitivity and fairness have begun to occur, such as better training for police officers who must handle rape and spousal assault cases. However, it may be many years yet before the criminal justice system is equally responsive to the needs of female and male victims.

SOCIAL CHANGE: JUSTICE FOR ALL?

The Feminist Movement and Legislative Change

Feminist movements have generated the power to produce significant changes in the laws governing the treatment of the sexes in work, education, and the allocation of resources. In Canada, a national coalition of feminist groups lobbied successfully to have gender equality under the law built into the new Charter of Rights and Freedoms. Section 15 of the Charter, which took effect on April 17, 1985 (fondly referred to by Canadian feminists as "a date with equality"), guarantees equality under the law to women and men and provides the basis for challenging discriminatory statutes and practices. In the United States, some important legislation has made sex discrimination more difficult in several areas. An example of the difference that such legislation can make can be seen in the impact of Title IX of the Education Amendments of 1972, which prohibited sex discrimination in federally funded educational institutions. Before this legislation came into effect, girls and women could routinely be excluded from certain educational programs on the basis of their gender, and there was no requirement that equal resources and facilities be available to both genders.

Before the passage of Title IX, educational institutions routinely discriminated against women students and faculty. Female students were excluded from certain courses or were subject to a quota system for admission into certain programs. Female faculty members were often excluded from faculty clubs and encouraged to join faculty wives clubs instead. Female teachers were often forced to resign or take unpaid leave when they were pregnant. Colleges could and did require higher test scores for female than for male applicants to gain admission. Young women had a very difficult time finding athletic scholarships to support their university education.

Since the implementation of Title IX, there have been many dramatic changes. The number of female high school graduates going on to college rose from 43% in 1972 to 63% in 1997 (American Bar Association, 1998). Dramatic effects have been seen in the influx of girls and women in two previously male-dominated areas: sports and certain vocational education programs. In 1971, just before passage of Title IX, 294,015 girls were participating in high school sports as compared to more than 3.5 million boys. By 1997, 25 years after passage of the legislation, the gap had narrowed: almost 2.5 million high school girls were participating in sports as compared to about 4 million boys (Women's Sports Foundation, 2001). A parallel growth in female participation was obvious in college sports. In 1967, 5 years before passage of Title IX, women made up fewer than 10% of participants in sports and recreation programs in U.S. universities and colleges; currently women make up 42.9% of participation in NCAA championship sports (National Collegiate Athletic Association, 2006). Similarly, the average number of varsity women's NCAA intercollegiate teams per school has grown from 2.5 in 1970 to 8.5 in 2006 (Women's Sports Foundation, 2006). This unprecedented growth in girls' sports participation is attributable in large part to Title IX's requirement that colleges put equivalent money into women's and men's sports, thus making it possible for more high school girls to aspire to college sports scholarships. Figure 14.2 shows the changes in young women's athletic participation.

Title IX also provided the impetus for large changes in vocational education. Females could no longer be excluded from particular vocational programs and, as provided by a later law (Title II of the Education Amendments of 1976), each state appointed a full-time sex-equity coordinator to work on broadening the range of vocational education opportunities for women. In the 10 years between 1972 and 1982, both the number and the percentage of female students increased in the traditionally male programs of agriculture, technical, and trade and industry. By the early 1980s, within programs training students for office occupations, women constituted over half the students in the supervisory and management programs, whereas in 1971 only about one-quarter of these students were women (Vetter & Hickey, 1985).

Although Title IX has had a large effect in promoting gender equity in education, its force was blunted considerably in 1984 when the Supreme Court ruled that the law applied only to the actual programs that were directly receiving federal money within an institution and not to entire institutions ("Supreme Court," 1984). The Civil Rights Restoration Act, passed by Congress in 1988, broadened the definition of "program," however, so that it applied to the whole institution. The lesson is clear: Although much positive change can be generated through good legislation, vigilance is necessary to make sure the legislation survives and works well.

Figure 14.2 Women's participation in championship, nonchampionship, and emerging intercollegiate (NCAA) sports, 1981–82 to 2005–06, at 4-year colleges and universities. Women's participation in college sports has increased dramatically since the passage of Title IX in 1972.

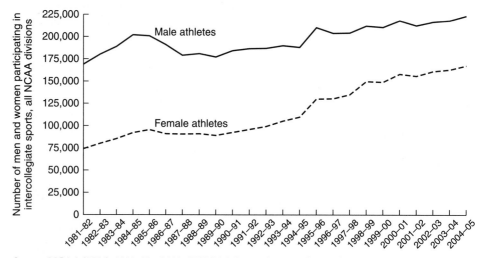

Source: NCAA (2006). 1981–82—2004–05 NCAA Sports Sponsorship and Participation Rates Report. Retrieved November 29, 2006, from http://www.ncaa.org/library/research/participation_rates/ 1982-2005/1982_2005_participation_rates.pdf

Clearly, feminism as a social movement has already had a large impact on the way females and males are treated in North America. Many instances of unfairness remain, however, and, as the following discussion will show, supporters of feminist social change do not always agree on the best way to rectify them.

How should the situation in which resources are distributed unfairly between the sexes and in which the law often supports that unfairness be rectified? How might we come up with a society that meets the ideals of justice held by both women and men? A variety of perspectives have been offered in response to such questions. Some have suggested that change will come faster if we recognize differences between women and men rather than denying them. Others have argued that what is needed is a de-emphasis on gender as an organizing principle in society. Still others have stressed the importance of making people aware of the existence of sex discrimination and its impact on them. Finally, it has been argued that tinkering with the reward structure is not enough: There must be a transformation of social values and the institutions that represent them so that society's rewards are linked less strongly to competition and more strongly to behavior that emphasizes interpersonal harmony and cooperation. Let us look in turn at examples of each of these arguments.

Recognizing Differences

There is and has been a continuing debate among feminist legal scholars about whether it is good for women to have complete equality under the law (e.g., Chesney-Lind, 1995). One participant in this debate, Alice Kessler-Harris (1985), in an examination of the historical failure to achieve equality in the workplace for women, argued that the major reason these attempts have failed is that they assume women must adjust to the male-structured workplace. If women are to achieve equal status with men, the assumption has been, they must be prepared to make it in a man's world. Kessler-Harris suggested that, whether for reasons of preference or necessity, many women are not prepared to make this kind of adjustment in their priorities. If we want gender equality in the workplace, she said, we must make some accommodations in the workplace for women. Such accommodations may benefit both women and men by making the workplace more amenable to the special needs of all.

The following example was given by Kessler-Harris as a strategy that acknowledges gender-related differences but encompasses them in a policy that extends rights to all workers. In 1984 the Women's Rights Project of the American Civil Liberties Union (ACLU) filed a brief opposing Montana's Maternity Leave Act—an act that granted pregnant women the right to unpaid leave for a time before and after the birth of a child. The ACLU argued that such a law would place women in a special category, making them less attractive to employers as workers. The ACLU proposed instead that the law be extended to cover health-related unpaid leave for all workers. In this way, an act that was potentially discriminatory could be turned into a gain for all workers, and the special needs of women with respect to pregnancy could still be met. (This example also fits the "sex-specific/gender-neutral" approach to equality under the law discussed earlier in this chapter.) In 1987, in the *California Federal S. & L. v. Guerre* decision, the U.S. Supreme Court rejected the ACLU position in favor of a stance that it is permissible for states to treat women workers equally with men by establishing a maternity leave policy (an example of the "equality plus real differences" approach discussed earlier).

The main aspect of the approach advocated by Kessler-Harris is that the work that has traditionally been done by women—child care and the maintenance of home and family life—is important work that, in the quest for gender equality, must be publicly recognized and shared. Issues that have previously been considered private must be placed on the public stage. Family and relationship responsibilities are recognized as a necessary adjunct to the wage-work process, for men as well as women, and it is essential to consider family issues when designing the workplace:

> At its most optimistic, this approach is nothing less than a belief that gender equality will be achieved only when the values of the home (which have previously been assumed to keep women out of the workplace or to assign them to inferior places within it) are brought to the workplace where they can transform

work itself. It opens the possibility that an ethic of compassion or tolerance, a sense of group responsibility to the world at large (instead of to self) might in fact penetrate the workplace. (p. 157)

A Nongendered Social Order

Although it is currently necessary to draw attention to the issue of gender to combat it as a discriminative status, some people have argued that such strategies are likely to be effective only in the short term. At least one writer (Lorber, 1986) argued that the long-term goal of feminism should be to eradicate gender as an organizing principle in society. As long as we continue to make gender an important category and to view women and men as essentially different, gender will be used to make distinctions—between workers, voters, political candidates, criminals, and so on.

Judith Lorber tried to articulate what our society might be like if restructured to de-emphasize gender. Policies regarding families would change, for instance. Each adult would be treated as a single unit for purposes of income, taxation, and legal responsibilities. Family and kinship would not be based on gender; groups of differing size and gender composition would make up households. Parenting would not be gender linked; women and men would be equally likely to take responsibility for dependent children. There would be no support for a division of labor along sexual lines within the family. The wage structure for workers would not discriminate on the basis of workers' gender or of the gender linkage of certain jobs; thus the man would not automatically be the main financial support of the family. All adults would receive support allowances for themselves and their dependents, and professional caretaking of children would no longer be treated and paid as a low-status occupation but would be compensated according to its skill level. Women would no longer be kept out of positions of power and authority by a sex-stratified occupational structure or by powerful men's perception of them as "different."

Lorber (1986) argued that drastic steps to change the gender structuring of society are necessary because political and legal equality between women and men will not necessarily ensure social equality:

> In my mind, gender equality is too limited a goal. Unless women and men are seen as socially interchangeable, gender equality does not challenge the concept of sex differences that leads to separate spheres in the family and marketplace division of labor, which in turn results in women's lesser access to control of valued resources and positions of power. Scrupulous equality of categories of people considered essentially different needs constant monitoring. I would question the very concept of gender itself, and ask why, if women and men are social equals in all ways, there needs [sic] to be two encompassing social statuses at all. (p. 577)

Lorber's argument was based on the idea that our notions of gender are socially constructed and that the differences between women and men are largely a product of the emphasis we as a society place on gender. Her proposal is not likely to be put into effect in the near future, so we cannot be sure of the extent to which her basic premise was correct. Yet, as discussed at many points in this book, research shows that social expectations about gender have a strong impact on male–female differences in many areas of behavior. De-emphasizing gender as a relevant category in the way society is structured is no doubt a necessary aspect of weakening those social expectations.

Raising Awareness of Discrimination

Lucy Stone, a 19th-century American suffragist and abolitionist, declared passionately in a speech delivered in 1885, "In education, in marriage, in religion, in everything disappointment is the lot of women. It shall be the business of my life to deepen this disappointment in every woman's heart until she bows down to it no longer."

Stone's recognition that a deep and clear awareness of injustice must precede action to correct the injustice is a well-accepted one. Before society can get very far with grand schemes for equality between women and men, individuals within society must be made aware of the fact that gender inequalities exist and affect them personally. People are simply more likely to mobilize for change if they feel that the current system is unjust, particularly if it is seen as disadvantageous to them. Yet researchers have found that people often do not recognize sex discrimination and that even among women who recognize that discrimination against women in general exists there is little recognition that they have been affected personally by it (Crosby, 1982; Unger & Sussman, 1986).

Some researchers have concentrated on the question of how best to raise awareness of discrimination (Crosby, Clayton, Alksnis, & Hemker, 1986). What they have found is that, at least some of the time, the failure to recognize discrimination is linked to the format in which information is presented. Crosby and her colleagues presented information about women and men in a fictitious corporation to male college students. Half the time, the information was presented in aggregated form, providing students with an overall picture of the situation in the company; the rest of the time, students were shown case-by-case comparisons of women and men in particular departments. The researchers suggested that the first type of presentation is comparable to learning about discrimination through the media, whereas the second is more like what occurs when we hear of a particular case or consider our own situation relative to that of another person.

The results of this study confirmed the researchers' hypothesis that the perception of discrimination is influenced by information processing considerations. Apparently, it is easier to see patterns of discrimination when many cases are presented together, perhaps because the quantity of data is more compelling or because, when information is aggregated, irrelevant differences among departments are averaged out, making the salary difference between women and men more obvious.

The results of this study indicated clearly that when trying to demonstrate that sex discrimination exists in a particular setting it is more effective to present an overall view than a trickle of case comparisons. The findings also demonstrated that cognitive factors—the way human beings process information—can have an impact on people's readiness to see discrimination above and beyond such attitu-dinal factors as prejudice or misogyny or the desire to see the world as a just place. Attempts to rectify sex discrimination must take this factor into account.

Transformation of Institutions

Many feminists have argued that society's institutions must be transformed fundamentally rather than simply made more open to women's participation. They argue that the hierarchical, competitive, and individualistic values that permeate most institutions are fundamentally opposed to designing a system that would stress equality among groups. For instance, some groups of women have tried to challenge the male dominance of the health care system, not by getting more women into medical school but by a variety of tactics that ques-tion the doctor's place at the top of a medical hierarchy. Some groups have fought for the legalization of midwifery. Others have challenged traditional physician–nurse power relationships that make it difficult for a nurse to ques-tion a doctor's instructions with respect to a patient (Fletcher, 2006). Still oth-ers have started self-care clinics or information services to make people less dependent on medical experts for their health.

Other institutions have also felt the brunt of this approach. For example, in many universities, the introduction of women's studies courses has meant not just a new content area but a questioning of the way things are done in acade-mia as well as in the outside world. As Roberta Hamilton (1985) noted, femi-nists in the academy tend to be political subversives: "They have challenged not only the structure of the university, and the limited place of women within it, but also the very parameters of what constitutes knowledge, and many of the assumptions underlying the traditional academic disciplines" (p. 3).

The transformational approach to social change is based on the idea that gender bias may be present even in areas in which it has not yet been recog-nized: in the way we think about issues that have no obvious connection to gender. It thus forces a scrutiny of the status quo that goes beyond even that encouraged by the other approaches cited here. It is a difficult and often un-comfortable approach to social change, but, as Hamilton (1985) noted, "Stu-dents of society surely deserve challenge, not consolation, and this is especially true . . . in the questions that we pose about those aspects of human relation-ships that we have hitherto taken for granted" (p. 20).

SUMMARY

We have seen that strong prescriptive stereotypes exist that women and men should rely on different standards of justice and morality and that women's and men's experiences tend to push them in the direction of those stereotypes. For example, the power differences between women and men often mean that women have fewer resources than men, and the very prevalence of this situation may lead people to accept it as normal. As a result, women may come to believe that they *deserve* less and men to believe that *they* deserve more. This difference in feelings of personal entitlement may cause what appears to be a gender difference in selfishness: Women sometimes stress equality and take less for themselves and give more to others, and men sometimes stress equity and are ready to reward themselves at the expense of others. Research shows, however, that such differences are ephemeral. If the situation is changed by giving individuals an appropriate comparison group, if the situation is deliberately structured to emphasize either interpersonal concerns or task concerns, and if individuals can reward their own superior performance without penalizing others, the traditional gender differences disappear. It appears that in the area of justice behavior, as in so many other areas discussed in this book, males and females are sensitive to situational cues about what behavior is appropriate, that these cues often differ for the two sexes, and that the difference relates to the power difference between women and men.

Studies of the way women and men actually think about justice and morality have not unequivocally supported the idea that women emphasize equality and interpersonal concerns and men stress equity and rights. However, both the manner in which that field of inquiry developed and the findings of the studies themselves indicated that there is a pervasive belief in the existence of the gender difference just described. Women are expected to emphasize care and interpersonal concerns and men to emphasize rights. A reading of the early psychological writings on justice and morality leaves no doubt that the stereotypically feminine morality of care and interpersonal responsibility has been devalued. Perhaps this devaluation has acted in a circular fashion to cause the dissociation of such an orientation from men and thus to ensure that it would continue to be devalued in a society that assigns more status to men than to women.

The idea that women and men differ in their tendency to be emotional or rational with respect to justice has been reflected in the male dominance of the judicial system and is entrenched, along with other gender stereotypes, in the fabric of the law itself. For years, civil laws gave men authority over women, even within the family; some of these laws have yet to be changed. These laws have restricted women's legal and political rights and their access to economic resources, thus maintaining a power difference between women and men that, in turn, has helped to maintain behavioral differences. In criminal law as well, gender stereotypes, particularly those concerning sexuality and marital roles, have made for inequities between women and men, both as criminals and as victims. The law itself, supposedly the embodiment of justice, sometimes perpetuates injustice on the basis of gender.

Many approaches have been offered as directions for social change that would redress the unbalanced distribution of resources and other injustices based on gender. These approaches range from practical suggestions about how to educate people with respect to sex discrimination to attempts to develop the best possible vision of the ultimate goals of change. They include strategies for how to make the system work for women and strategies for a radical transformation of that system. All of them have in common a basis of passionate concern for gender justice. Although the debate goes on about the relative merits of these various approaches to social transformation, it advances, through a series of small changes, the notion that the real needs of both sexes must weigh equally in any consideration of justice.

KEY TERMS

affirmative action

denial of personal
   discrimination

personal relative
   deprivation

collective relative
   deprivation

rights orientation

care orientation

The Ties That Bind
The Future of Sex and Gender

Sex and gender together have formed one of the most important distinctions human beings have made about one another. Awareness of another person's femaleness or maleness shapes our reactions to that person from the moment she or he is born. We judge ourselves and others according to the degree to which we and they fit the expectations of femininity and masculinity; most of us cannot imagine what it would be like to have the body of the other sex or the role expectations and identity of the other gender.

As distinctions go, however, there is something unique about the one based on sex and gender. Although we insist on the division, on the importance of the distinction between female and male, feminine and masculine, we tend to argue not that the two genders should be kept separate but that they should go together—that they complement and complete each other. We speak of situations needing a "woman's touch" or a "man's hand," and, as a society, we espouse one ideal of intimacy that involves a shared, lifelong commitment between a woman and a man. Despite the talk about how different men and women are and how little they understand each other, a large number of North American adults would count their closest, most important relationship as one with a spouse or partner of the other gender.

The gender division is somewhat unique, then, in that the two genders, though divided, are thought to "go together." But both as individuals and as groups women and men have tended to go together not as equal partners but

585

as participants in a hierarchical arrangement, with men holding the top positions. Our culture's ideas about male–female differences reflect this hierarchy. Stereotypes of femininity and masculinity split up human qualities between females and males. The qualities assigned to females are devalued—a devaluation that is linked to females' subordinate position in the gender hierarchy. Interestingly, a quality that is stereotyped as feminine may in fact be equally prevalent in both women and men, but because it is associated with femininity it may be devalued and thus unacknowledged in men. A clear example of this phenomenon comes from the research on moral reasoning discussed in Chapter 14. An ethic of care and responsibility, ignored in previous male-centered research on moral reasoning, was proposed as a principle that was especially characteristic of women's moral reasoning (Gilligan, 1982). However, as researchers began to include this hitherto ignored element of morality in their studies of moral reasoning, most found to their surprise that it was prevalent among both women and men. Why had no one noticed it before? The tendency to base decisions on concern for relationships is stereotyped as feminine. Perhaps male researchers and research participants were not noticing or acknowledging this tendency in themselves, and women were simply accepting men's definition of the situation. The hierarchical social context in which women and men perceive and relate to each other makes it impossible for us to be completely clear-eyed about what gender similarities and differences exist. Yet, when we try to nail down such differences and similarities, we are confronted with the realization that gender is socially constructed and is, to some extent, a figment of our expectations and our imagination. The more carefully we do our research, the more it appears that women and men share, or have the potential to share under conditions of social equality, most qualities.

The realization that we need not be limited to present cultural definitions of femininity and masculinity can be empowering for both women and men. However, it can also be frightening. Social change is now occurring at such a rapid rate that individuals or whole societies may freeze in "future shock" rather than adapt comfortably to new possibilities. Part of this inability or refusal to adapt may well involve holding on with grim determination to traditional gender roles. And there are, of course, good reasons for not discarding the qualities that are associated with traditional gender roles. As Joan Rabin (1987) argued, under conditions of rapid social change, we human beings are especially in need of the communal qualities usually associated with women to maintain a sense of comfort and connection—to ensure our survival as a social species. Indeed, traditions form important anchors in a rapidly changing world, and they often help us maintain our sense of meaning and connection with one another. Women, whose communal, family roles often make them the guardians of tradition and social bonds, may feel especially guilty as they redefine their roles and cannot devote as much energy to activities that bring family and friends together. Yet such feelings of guilt are based on the assumption that only women can fulfill these functions—an assumption that is simply wrong. As a society, we may finally come to the realization that the functions and qualities stereotypically associated with each gender are valuable and necessary—and much more interchangeable and shareable than we used to think.

Glossary

achievement motive a general personality disposition to strive for success in any situation in which standards of excellence are applied

acquired immunodeficiency syndrome (AIDS) a condition caused by the human immunodeficiency virus (HIV), characterized by destruction of the immune system and consequent vulnerability to life-threatening diseases

affirmative action a set of strategies to increase the proportion of women and minorities hired by organizations or admitted to universities, particularly in fields from which they have traditionally been excluded

agoraphobia a persistent, irrational fear of being in public places from which escape might be difficult or in which help might be unavailable in case of sudden incapacitation

alpha bias a tendency toward exaggerating differences between women and men

anal stage the second of Freud's psychosexual stages, in which pleasure is linked to defecation

androcentric norms the use of male behavior as the norm against which to measure females

androcentric centered on men and shaped by masculine values

androgen insensitivity syndrome (AIS) a genetically transmitted disorder in which cells are partially or completely unable to respond to androgens

androgyny a blend of stereotypically feminine and masculine qualities in a person

andropause a transition experienced by men in their 70s and 80s that is characterized by a thinning of the ejaculate, a reduction of ejaculatory pressure, and a decrease in the levels of FSH and LH

anorexia nervosa a mental disorder that involves self-starvation in an effort to maintain an unrealistically low body weight, characterized by an intense fear of becoming obese and by a disturbed body image—a tendency to "feel fat" even when severely underweight

anthropomorphism the tendency to interpret animal behavior in terms of human customs and ideology

antisocial personality disorder a mental disorder characterized by a lack of ethical or moral sensitivity and the absence of guilt or anxiety about hurting others

benevolent sexism a type of sexism that includes protective paternalism, idealization of women, and desire for intimate relations, measured by the Ambivalent Sexism Inventory

beta bias an inclination to ignore or minimize differences between women and men

biosocial theory argues that male–female differences and similarities derive from interactions between the physical attributes of men and women and the social contexts in which they live

bisexual a person who can be sexually and/or emotionally attracted to partners of either sex

bulimia nervosa a mental disorder characterized by an obsession with food and with body weight, involving a pattern of "binge" overeating followed by self-induced "purging" through a variety of means, including dieting, vomiting, or laxatives

care orientation a stress on the necessity to be responsible in one's relationships, to be sensitive to the needs of others, and to avoid giving hurt

case history method a research method that involves gathering many details about one or several individuals, usually through interviews, to support, develop, or refine a particular explanation of behavior

cerebral cortex the outermost part of the brain, divided into lobes (or sections) that fulfill different sensory and motor functions

cognitive developmental theory a theory that proposes that gender, like other concepts, cannot be learned until a child reaches a particular stage of intellectual development

collective relative deprivation a feeling of dissatisfaction due to perceived inequities between one's own and a more advantaged group

comparable worth the principle that persons should earn equal pay for work of equal value, even when their jobs are not identical

competence a dimension on which influence styles are described and that refers to the degree to which a person tries to gain compliance by acting knowledgeable and confident as opposed to helpless

components of gender stereotypes a distinct aspect of gender stereotypes that can be identified, such as personality traits, role behaviors, occupations, and physical appearance

concreteness a dimension on which influence styles are described and that refers to the degree to which the resources on which influence attempts are based is independent of relationships

congenital adrenal hyperplasia (CAH) a genetically transmitted syndrome in which the adrenal glands of the fetus malfunction, resulting in a release of excess androgens from the prenatal period onward

consciousness (or conscious mind) according to Freudian theory, the part of the mind available to awareness that contains the thoughts and feelings people know they have

constricting interaction style a style in which participants in an interaction are more likely to interrupt one another, command and threaten, boast, refuse to comply, or give information

corpus callosum a mass of nerve fibers that connects the two hemispheres of the cerebral cortex

correlational method a research method capable of showing that two things are related to each other, or go together, but incapable of showing that either one caused the other

couvade rituals used in some cultures to express father involvement in the birth process and to protect the mother and infant

couvade syndrome a syndrome in which expectant fathers suffer from physical symptoms during their wife's pregnancy or labor

cumulative continuity the process through which an individual, beginning in childhood, selects and creates environments that fit her or his preferred forms of behavior; these selected environments, in turn, reinforce and sustain that behavior

denial of personal discrimination the tendency for women to underrate the amount of sex discrimination visited on them personally, even when they are quite aware that women in general experience sex discrimination

dependent variable the variable that is measured in an experiment

depression a mental illness signaled by feelings of extreme sadness and hopelessness and by a loss of interest in most activities

descriptive stereotypes stereotypes that describe beliefs about what the typical woman and man are like

devaluation according to Karen Horney, one of two major environmental dangers to a child's development: parents' lack of respect for the child as a unique and worthwhile individual

directness a dimension on which influence strategies are categorized and that refers to the openness or obliqueness that characterizes an influence attempt

discourse analysis the analysis of the language in various texts, such as interview responses, discussions, and essays

distribution the frequency with which certain responses or scores are obtained when a group of individuals is studied

diversity-mindfulness mindset that includes openness to differences among people, appreciation and receptiveness to varied perspectives, and respect for others

double standard the use of two different standards of acceptable sexual behavior, one for women and one for men

dysmenorrhea pain and discomfort during menstruation

effect size the amount of variation in a criterion variable that is attributable to a particular treatment or category variable (such as gender) in one study or a group of studies

ego according to Freudian theory, the rational part of the personality structure that handles transactions between an individual's subjective needs and the objective world of reality

Electra complex according to Freud, girls' realization in the phallic stage that they cannot have a penis and their replacement of this wish for a penis with a wish for a child, focusing on father as a love object and on mother as a rival

enabling interaction style a relational style in which interactants seem most interested in sustaining social relationships and are likely to say they agree with another speaker, acknowledge points made by other speakers, and pause to allow another to speak

endometriosis a condition in which endometrial tissue (the type of tissue that normally lines the uterus) grows outside the lining of the uterus

entity approach to ability the notion that each individual has a fixed amount of ability, which is revealed by her or his performance

equal pay for equal work the principle that women and men should be paid the same salaries when they perform the same jobs

equity in relationships, the extent to which the ratio of each partner's contributions to rewards is seen to be equal

essentialism the idea that gender differences in behavior stem from qualities that are resident in, or possessed by, women and men

ethnocentrism the tendency to interpret observations of another culture or group in terms of our own culture

evolutionary psychology theoretical approach that tries to explain the development of the mind and mental abilities by means of adaptation to selection pressures in the environment

evolutionary theory a theory that human nature (including human sex differences) has evolved in certain ways because of pressures to adapt and survive as a species

excitement phase the first phase of sexual response, according to Masters and Johnson's model, characterized by the onset of vasocongestion

experiment a research method in which the researcher directly manipulates (that is, sets at different levels) one variable, called the **independ-**ent variable, while measuring its effects on another variable, the **dependent variable**

expressiveness an orientation toward emotion and relationships

fear of success the anticipation of negative consequences of success, such as social disapproval

follicular phase the first phase of the menstrual cycle, in which the pituitary secretes follicle-stimulating hormone (FSH), stimulating a follicle in one of the ovaries to secrete estrogen and to bring an egg to maturity

G-spot an area on the anterior wall of the vagina that some researchers think is especially sensitive to sexual stimulation

gay an alternative for the term **homosexual,** often used to describe a lifestyle rather than just sexuality

gender the nonphysiological aspects of being female or male inculcated in cultural expectations for femininity and masculinity

gender aschematic having a weak gender schema

gender belief system set of ideas that people have about gender, including sterotypes about the characteristics of women and men, attitudes about the social roles occupied by women and men, and views about their own gender identity

gender constancy an understanding that a person's gender is fixed and cannot be altered by a change in hairstyle, dress, or name and that is achieved by a child, according to cognitive developmental theory, sometime between the ages of 3 and 5

gender dysphoria unhappiness or dissatisfaction with one's given gender or sexual identity

gender identity an individual's private experience of the self as female or male

gender role a set of behaviors socially defined as appropriate for one's sex

gender-role strain difficulty in conforming to expected gender roles because such roles are often contradictory and inconsistent

gender schema theory a theory that children early on develop a network of cognitive associations (schema) for gender based on the degree to which the gender dichotomy is emphasized during socialization and that they use this to organize incoming information about themselves and others

gender schematic having a strong gender schema and having a tendency to spontaneously sort people, characteristics, and behaviors into masculine and feminine categories

gender-specific medicine new branch of medicine in which the focus is on how diseases and treatment may progress differently for women and men

genital stage the fifth of Freud's psychosexual stages, that of mature sexuality, beginning at puberty

glass ceiling an invisible barrier that keeps women from advancing into high-level positions in organizations

glass escalator a systematic set of hidden advantages for men in female-dominated occupations

gonadotropins hormones that stimulate the gonads (sex glands) to activity

group socialization theory a theory that children become socialized primarily by identifying with their peer group and taking on that group's norms for attitudes and behavior

gynocentric literally, centered on the female womb or female-centered

heterosexism the tendency to view heterosexuality as the norm and to ignore or render invisible the alternatives of homosexuality and bisexuality

heterosexual a person who prefers sexual and affectional partners of the other sex

homophobia negative attitudes toward and fear of homosexuality

homosexual a person who prefers sexual and affectional partners of the same sex

hostile environment a form of sexual harassment that involves making unwelcome sexual advances or engaging in other conduct of a sexual nature that unreasonably interferes with an individual's work performance or creates an intimidating, hostile, or offensive atmosphere

hostile sexism a type of sexism that includes dominance-oriented paternalism, derogatory beliefs about women, and heterosexual hostility as measured by the Ambivalent Sexism Inventory

human immunodeficiency virus (HIV) a virus that produces AIDS, damaging the immune system and leaving the body open to opportunistic diseases

hysteria (from the Greek word meaning *uterus*) a mysterious "disease of the uterus" often diagnosed in women until early in the 20th century, marked by fainting or fits and a variety of symptoms such as loss of voice or partial paralysis, with no apparent physical cause

id according to Freudian theory, the part of the personality structure that includes the individual's biological heritage and sexual and aggressive instincts and that provides a reservoir of psychic energy that powers the other two systems

identity the significance and qualitative meaning that individuals attribute to their membership in a particular group (such as a gender or ethnic or racial group) within their self-concept

independent variable a variable that is manipulated in an experiment

instrumentality an orientation toward action, accomplishment, and leadership

interactional continuity two-way transactions between the person and the social environment in which the person's behavior elicits reactions from others and in which those reactions promote continuity in the original behavior through reinforcement, confirmation of expectations, and confirmation of the person's self-concept

interactive model of gender-related behavior a model built on the proposition that an individual's gender-related behaviors in a given social interaction are influenced by what others expect, what the individual believes about her- or himself, and situational cues

interactiveness a dimension on which influence strategies are categorized and that refers to the degree of mutual engagement with the partner required in the influence attempt

interpersonal power the ability of one person to get another person to do what he or she wants in the face of resistance from the second person

intersexed individuals people whose sexual differentiation was disrupted *in utero* by hormonal imbalance and who are born with some biological indicators of both sexes

intimate career the sequence and patterns of a person's intimate relationships across the life span

lack of fit theory that women are not expected to succeed in executive positions because they do not have the stereotypically masculine qualities needed for such positions

late luteal phase dysphoric disorder an earlier label for **premenstrual dysphoric disorder,** a formal diagnosis included in an appendix of the *Diagnostic and Statistical Manual of the American Psychiatric Association* that lists a set of psychological symptoms that may occur during the week prior to menstruation

latency phase the fourth phase of psychosexual development, according to Freud, during which erotic impulses are repressed until just before puberty

lateralization (or *cerebral lateralization* or *hemispheric lateralization*) the degree to which particular functions are localized in one side of the brain

lesbian a woman who is sexually and affectionally attracted to other women

logical positivism an approach to knowledge that assumes reality is independent of the knower and can be discerned "objectively" under the proper conditions

longitudinal study a study that follows the same research participants over an extended period of time, usually years, and obtains data from them repeatedly during that time

luteal phase the third phase of the menstrual cycle, in which the luteinizing hormone stimulates the follicle to turn into a glandular mass of cells called the *corpus luteum,* which in turn manufactures progesterone

menarche a girl's first menstrual period

menopause the cessation of a woman's menstrual periods during middle age

menstrual cycle the cyclic pattern of sex hormone levels in women, maintained through a negative feedback system involving the hypothalamus, the pituitary gland, and the ovaries

menstruation the final phase of the menstrual cycle when the inner uterine lining (the endometrium) is shed and flows out through the cervix and the vagina

mental rotation a type of spatial ability that involves being able to quickly visualize objects from different perspectives than the one shown

meta-analysis the use of statistical methods to combine the findings of a large number of different studies of the same behavior to evaluate the overall pattern of findings

misogyny hatred of women

modern sexism a constellation of attitudes characterized by a denial that women are still targets of discrimination, antagonism toward women's demands, and a lack of support for policies designed to improve women's status

Müllerian ducts primitive ducts in the human embryo that eventually, in females, become the fallopian tubes, uterus, and vagina

myotonia one of the physiological processes in sexual response: the contraction of muscles

narrative approach a research approach that gathers a lot of information from a single individual and allows the research participant the opportunity to react to the meanings and interpretations the researcher gives to the participant's life story

naturalistic observation a research method in which a researcher spends a lot of time watching individuals in their normal setting, keeping track of the number and type of certain kinds of behaviors displayed

neosexism a constellation of attitudes characterized by a denial that women are still targets of discrimination, antagonism toward women's demands, and a lack of support for policies designed to improve women's status

Oedipus complex a system of feelings and stage of development, named by Freud for the mythical Greek character who unwittingly killed his own father and married his own mother, during which boys develop an intense attachment for mother and begin to see father as a rival

oral stage the first of Freud's psychosexual stages, in which pleasure is centered in the mouth and sucking

orgasm the third phase of human sexual response, according to Masters and Johnson, in which arousal reaches a critical point and triggers orgasm, a series of involuntary rhythmic contractions of the pelvic organs

overt aggression aggression that physically hurts or threatens another person

ovulation the second phase of the menstrual cycle, in which the follicle ruptures to release the mature egg

penis envy according to Freud, girls' realization during the phallic stage that they lack a penis and their development of a sense of inferiority and contempt for their own sex

personal relative deprivation a sense of dissatisfaction stemming from a comparison with others who are being more highly rewarded

phallic stage the third of Freud's psychosexual stages, in which erotic pleasure is obtained from the penis for boys and the clitoris for girls

phallocentric literally, centered on the male penis or male-centered

phenomenological method a research method oriented toward understanding behavior from the perspective of the person being studied, often based on in-depth, subjective information collected in interviews

plateau phase the second phase of human sexual response, according to Masters and Johnson's model, in which a peak level of **vasocongestion** is reached, and the rate of breathing, pulse rate, and blood pressure increase further

polyandry the situation of one wife having several husbands at the same time

polygyny the situation of one husband having several wives at the same time

postpartum depression mild to serious negative emotions experienced by women in the days, weeks, or months after childbirth

posttraumatic stress disorder (PTSD) a disorder caused by a traumatic event that is characterized by anxiety, depression, flashbacks, nightmares, and somatic symptoms

power motive the tendency to strive to feel that one is having an impact on others

prejudice the negative evaluation of persons or their activities because they belong to a particular group

premenstrual dysphoric disorder (PMDD) a formal diagnosis included in an appendix of the *Diagnostic and Statistical Manual of the American Psychiatric Association* that lists a set of psychological symptoms that may occur during the week prior to menstruation

premenstrual syndrome (PMS) a period of high tension, depression, irritability, and assorted physical symptoms that is said to occur during the days immediately preceding the onset of menstruation

prescriptive stereotypes stereotypes about what women and men *should* be like

principle of least interest in a relationship the theory that the person who is least dependent on the other for rewards—who needs the relationship least—has the most power

prostaglandins hormonelike substances from the lining of the uterus that cause excessive contractions in the uterine muscles, decreased blood flow, and increased sensitivity to pain, all of which contribute to menstrual cramps

prototypical traits the traits associated with the clearest examples of a particular category

pseudocyesis pseudopregnancy, characterized by physical symptoms similar to those associated with pregnancy: menstrual disturbance, abdominal enlargement, swelling and tenderness of the breasts, softening of the cervix, enlargement of the uterus, nausea and vomiting, and weight gain

psychoanalytic theory a theory first developed by Freud that emphasized the importance of unconscious motivations in personality development

quid pro quo a form of sexual harassment in which an individual is pressured to submit to unwelcome sexual advances or other unwelcome sexual conduct as a condition of employment or in which employment decisions that affect the individual, such as promotion or raises, are based on her or his submission to or rejection of such conduct

rape the forcing of sexual relations on someone against that person's choice

reactance a reaction to a perceived threat to a behavioral freedom, constituting an effort to protect or regain the freedom that is threatened and that is manifested as resistance, anger, and hostility toward the individual or organization viewed as threatening

refractory period a period lasting from a few minutes to 24 hours after **orgasm** during which a man typically cannot be restimulated to erection and **orgasm**

relational aggression aggression that hurts or threatens another person by damaging his or her relationships

resolution phase the fourth phase of human sexual response, according to Masters and Johnson's model, in which muscular tension is relaxed and blood is released from the engorged blood vessels

rights orientation a perspective that stresses an attention to principles and questions what choices are legitimate in particular situations

schema a cognitive structure (a network of associations or set of interrelated ideas) that guides and organizes the way an individual processes and makes sense of information

self-fulfilling prophecy a process in which the presence of a stereotype may actually motivate the stereotyped person to behave in a manner consistent with the stereotype

self-in-relation the sense of oneself as a relational being, someone who is developing and growing in the ability to connect with and relate to others

serial monogamy the condition of having a series of mates, one at a time

sex a person's biological maleness or femaleness

sex chromosomes the 23rd pair of chromosomes in humans: if the individual is female, the sex chromosomes are represented as XX; if male, the pair is designated as XY

sex drive sexual motivation or desire for sex

sex-limited traits the traits carried on genes that are not on either of the **sex chromosomes** but are, nonetheless, generally manifest in only one sex because they require the presence of certain levels of male or female sex hormones to appear

sex-linked traits the traits for which the genes are carried partially or totally on one of the **sex** (X or Y) **chromosomes**

sex-of-experimenter effects the effects of using a female or male experimenter to carry out research because people react differently to men and women

sex stereotypes the socially shared beliefs that certain qualities can be assigned to individuals based on their membership in the female or male half of the human race

sexism prejudice based on a person's sexual category

sexual objectification set of attitudes that define female bodies in terms of ideals of beauty and sexual attractiveness

sexual orientation an individual's preference for sexual and affectional partners of the same or other sex

sexual prejudice prejudice against persons because of their sexual orientation

sexualization according to Karen Horney, one of two major environmental dangers to a child's development: a sexual approach to the child, an emotional "hothouse" atmosphere

social cognitive theory a modification of **social learning theory** that suggests that, although children may initially learn gender roles through external rewards and punishments, as they mature they begin to regulate their own actions through internal rewards and punishments

social constructionism an approach to knowledge that assumes researchers do not discover independently existing facts through objective observation; rather, they construct knowledge that is influenced by the social context of their inquiry

social dominance theory postulates that, in societies that emphasize group dominance, women and men tend to differ on social dominance orientation such that women adhere more to hierarchy-attenuating values and men adhere more to hierarchy-enhancing values

social learning theory a theory states that the child develops both **gender identity** and **gender role** through a learning process that involves modeling, imitation, and reinforcement

social role theory a theory that differential role occupancy by women and men is mediated by the formation of **gender roles** in which persons of each sex are expected to have qualities that equip them for the tasks typically carried out by that group

social structure theories theories that female–male differences in behavior are driven by the ways societies are organized, in particular by gender differences in power and status and the division of labor by sex

sociobiology the approach to the study of biology that perceives sex differences in human behavior to have evolved because of different reproductive strategies adopted by males and females to maximize the chances that their genes will be passed on to future generations

spatial perception a type of spatial performance that involves determining spatial relationships with respect to one's own body orientation despite distracting information

spatial visualization a type of spatial performance that involves complicated, multistep mental manipulations of spatial information such as "disembedding" a simple figure from a complex background or imagining how a piece of paper would look when folded a certain way

spatiotemporal ability a type of spatial ability that involves making judgments about moving visual displays, such as predicting when a moving object will reach a particular spot

specific phobia a persistent, irrational fear of and desire to avoid specific objects, activities, or situations

spermarche a boy's first ejaculation

statistically significance the probability that a particular result occurred by chance alone, based on tests that consider sample size and variability; by convention, if the probability of the result occurring by chance alone is less than 5%, the finding is accepted as statistically significant

stereotype threat the awareness that one may be judged by or may self-fulfill negative stereotypes about one's group

straight an alternative term for **heterosexual**

stressors the external events or conditions that are appraised as threatening by an individual and thus are the source of upset, worry, discomfort, and general distress

superego according to Freudian theory, a part of the personality structure that acts as the moral aspect of the personality, striving for perfection rather than pleasure and persuading the **ego** to substitute moralistic goals for realistic ones

survey methods methods of data collection that use a standardized questionnaire or interview to collect information from a large number of people

theory a formalized set of ideas about how and why things happen that is used in science to guide research and generate hypotheses (propositions) that can be tested against observed reality

token positions the role of individuals who are treated as symbols or representatives of their sex, race, or other underrepresented group

transformationism an approach to understanding the way biology and environment work together, with neither being more fundamental than the other to an organism's development but both combining to transform the organism so that it responds differently to other concurrent or subsequent biological or environmental influences

transgendered community people who refuse to live within a particular set of gender expectations and who, in various ways, transgress gender boundaries

transgenders people who live all or part of the time in the identity of the other sex but who have no intention of having surgery to change their bodies

transsexuals people whose gender identity does not match their biological sex and who have had or want to have surgery to change their bodies to match those of the other sex

transvestites (cross-dressers) people who enjoy dressing in the clothing of the other sex

trust in intimate relationships, a multifaceted construct that includes faith that one's partner will act in loving ways whatever the future holds and a belief in the partner's behavioral predictability and personal dependability

unconscious (or unconscious mind) according to Freudian theory, the part of the mind that contains the unacceptable urges, passions, ideas, and feelings that people do not know they have and cannot acknowledge and that can be explored only indirectly through dreams, free association, symptoms, mistakes (now sometimes called "Freudian slips"), or other "leaks" of the unconscious into conscious awareness

vasocongestion a physiological process in sexual response that results in accumulation of blood in the blood vessels of a particular region

Wolffian ducts a primitive duct system in the human embryo that eventually, in males, develops into the vas deferens, seminal vesicle, epididymides, urethra, and prostate

References

Abbey, A. (1982). Sex differences in attributions for friendly behavior: Do males misperceive females' friendliness? *Journal of Personality and Social Psychology, 42*(5), 830–838.

Abbey, A. (2002). Alcohol-related sexual assault: A common problem among college students. *Journal of Studies on Alcohol, Supplement 14* (Special Issue), 118–128.

Abplanalp, J. M. (1983). Premenstrual syndrome: A selective review. *Women & Health, 8*(2/3), 107–123.

Abrams, L. S. (2003). Contextual variations in young women's gender identity negotiations. *Psychology of Women Quarterly, 27*, 64–74.

Abreu, J. A., Goodyear, R. K., Campos, A., & Newcomb, M. D. (2000). Ethnic belonging and traditional masculinity ideology among African Americans, European Americans, and Latinos. *Psychology of Men and Masculinity, 1*(2), 75–86.

Adams, C. G., & Turner, B. F. (1985). Reported change in sexuality from young adulthood to old age. *Journal of Sex Research, 21*(2), 126–141.

Adams, D. O., Johnson, T. C., Cole, S. P., Matthiasson, H., et al. (1990). Physical fitness in relation to amount of physical exercise, body image, and locus of control among college men and women. *Perceptual and Motor Skills, 70*(3), 1347–1350.

Adams, K. A. (1980). Who has the final word? Sex, race and dominance behavior. *Journal of Personality and Social Psychology, 38*, 1–8.

Adams, K. A. (1983). Aspects of social context as determinants of Black women's resistance to challenges. *Journal of Social Issues, 39*, 69–78.

Adams, S., Kuebli, J., Boyle, P. A., & Fivush, R. (1995). Gender differences in parent-child conversations about past emotions: A longitudinal investigation. *Sex Roles, 33*(5–6), 309–323.

Adams, T. M., & Fuller, D. B. (2006). The words have changed but the ideology remains the same: Misogynistic lyrics in rap music. *Journal of Black Studies, 36*(60), 938–957.

Addis, M. E., & Mahalik, J. R. (2003). Men, masculinity, and the contexts of help seeking. *American Psychologist, 58*(1), 5–14.

Adler, N. E. (1975). Emotional responses of women following therapeutic abortion. *American Journal of Orthopsychiatry, 45*(3), 446–454.

Adler, N. E., David, H. P., & Major, B. N. (1992). Psychological factors in abortion: A review. *American Psychologist, 47*(10), 1194–1204.

Adler, N. E., Ozer, E. J., & Tschann, J. (2003). Abortion among adolescents. *American Psychologist, 58*(3), 211–217.

Adler, T. (1990). NIH opens office on women's issues. *APA Monitor, 21*(12), 5.

Agate, C., & Meacham, C. (1977). Women's equality: Implications of the law. In A. Sargent (Ed.), *Beyond sex roles* (pp. 434–450). St. Paul: West.

Ahlgren, A. (1983). Sex differences in the correlates of cooperative and competitive school attitudes. *Developmental Psychology, 19*(6), 881–888.

Aida, Y., & Falbo, T. (1991). Relationships between marital satisfaction, resources, and power strategies. *Sex Roles, 24*(1/2), 43–56.

Alan Guttmacher Institute. (1999). *Facts in brief: Teen sex and pregnancy.* Retrieved from www.agiusa.org/pubs/

Alan Guttmacher Institute. (2003a). Teenagers' sexual and reproductive health: Developed countries. Retrieved from http://www.agi-usa.org/pubs/fb_teens.html

Alan Guttmacher Institute. (2003b). In their own right: Addressing the sexual and reproductive health needs of American men. Retrieved from http://www.agi-usa.org/pubs/exs_men.html

Alan Guttmacher Institute. (2005). *Facts in brief: Contraceptive use.* Retrieved July 31, 2006, from http://www.guttmacher.org/pubs/fb_contr_use.html

Al-Ansari, E. M. (2002). Effects of gender and education on the moral reasoning of Kuwait university students. *Social Behavior and Personality, 30*(1), 75–82.

Alexander, G. M., Altemus, M., Peterson, B. S., & Wexler, B. E. (2002). Replication of a premenstrual decrease in right-ear advantage on language-related dichotic listening tests of cerebral laterality. *Neuropsychologia, 40*(8), 1293–1299.

Allen, B. P. (1995). Gender stereotypes are not accurate: A replication of Martin (1987) using diagnostic vs. self-report and behavioral criteria. *Sex Roles, 32*(9/10), 583–600.

Allen, L. S., Richey, M. F., Chai, Y. M., & Gorski, R. A. (1991). Sex differences in the corpus callosum of the living human being. *Journal of Neuroscience, 11*(4), 933–942.

Allen, P. G. (1986). *The sacred hoop: Recovering the feminine in American Indian traditions.* Boston: Beacon.

Almquist, E. M. (1995). The experiences of minority women in the United States: Intersections of race, gender, and class. In J. Freeman (Ed.), *Women: A feminist perspective* (pp. 573–606). Mountain View, CA: Mayfield.

Alozie, N. O., Simon, J., & Merrill, B. D. (2003). Gender and political orientation in childhood. *Social Science Journal, 40*(1), 1–18.

Alvarez, L. (2003, October 21). Norway leads industrial nations back to breastfeeding. *New York Times*, p. A3.

Alzate, H., & Hoch, Z. (1986). The "G spot" and "female ejaculation": A current appraisal. *Journal of Sex and Marital Therapy, 12*, 211–220.

Amaro, H., Beckman, L., & Mays, V. (1987). A comparison of Black and White women entering alcoholism treatment. *Journal of Studies on Alcohol, 48*(3), 220–228.

Amatea, E. S., & Fong, M. L. (1991). The impact of role stressors and personal resources on the stress experience of professional women. *Psychology of Women Quarterly, 15*(3), 419–430.

American Association of University Women. (1990). *Shortchanging girls, shortchanging America: A call to action.* Washington, DC: Author.

American Association of University Women. (2001). *Hostile hallways: Bullying, teasing, and sexual harassment in school.* Washington, DC: Author.

American Bar Association. (1998). *Facts about women and the law.* Retrieved from www.abanet.org/media/factbooks/womenlaw.pdf

American Bar Association. (2003). A current glance of women in the law. Retrieved from http://www.abanet.org/women/glance2003.pdf

American Bar Association. (2006a). *Charting our progress: The status of women in the professsion today.* Retrieved November 28, 2006, from http://www.abanet.org/women/ChartingOurProgress.pdf

American Bar Association. (2006b). *Visible invisibility: Women of color in law firms.* Retrieved November 28, 2006, from http://www.abanet.org/women/VisibleInvisibility-ExecSummary.pdf

American Correctional Association. (1990). *The female offender: What does the future hold?* Washington, DC: St. Mary's Press.

American Lung Association. (2005). *Trends in lung cancer morbidity and mortality.* Retrieved September 1, 2006, from http://www.lungusa.org/atf/cf/{7A8D42C2-FCCA-4604-8ADE-7F5D5E762256}/lc1.pdf

American Lung Association. (2006). *Women and smoking fact sheet.* Retrieved September 1, 2006, from http://www.lungusa.org/site/pp.asp?c=dvLUK9O0E&b=33572

American Management Association. (2003). AMA's 2003 survey on workplace dating. Retrieved from http://www.amanet.org/research/pdfs/dating_workplace03.pdf

American Management Association, and Business and Professional Women's Foundation. (1999). *1999 AMA/BPW survey. Compensation and benefits: A focus on gender.* Retrieved from http://www.amanet.org

American Medical Association. (2006). *Women Physicians Congress. Statistics and history.* Retrieved September 4, 2006, from http://www.ama-assn.org/ama/pub/category/12916.html

American Psychiatric Association. (1994). *Diagnostic and Statistical Manual of Mental Disorders* (4th ed.). Washington, DC: Author.

American Psychological Association. (1975). Report of the Task Force on Sex Bias and Sex-Role Stereotyping in Psychotherapeutic Practice. *American Psychologist, 30,* 1169–1175.

American Psychological Association. (1978). Guidelines for therapy with women. *American Psychologist, 13,* 1122–1123.

American Psychological Association. (1994). *Ph.D. recipients in psychology from U.S. universities by sex and subfield: 1920–1993.* Compiled by the Research Office, APA. Washington, DC: Author.

American Psychological Association. (1999). Women in the American Psychological Association: 1999. Retrieved from http://www.apa.org/pi/wpo/wapa/homepage.html

American Psychological Association. (2000). *Women in academe: Two steps forward, one step back.* Retrieved from http://www.apa.org/pi/wpo/academe/report.html

American Psychological Association. (2002). Ethical principles of psychologists and code of conduct. *American Psychologist, 57*(12), 1060–1073.

Amey, A. L., & Bishai, D. (2002). Measuring the quality of medical care for women who experience sexual assault with data from the National Hospital Ambulatory Medical Care Survey. *Annals of Emergency Medicine, 39*(6), 631–638.

Anastasi, A. (1958a). *Differential psychology: Individual and group differences in behavior.* New York: Macmillan. (Original work published 1937)

Anastasi, A. (1958b). Heredity, environment, and the question "how?" *Psychological Review, 65,* 197–208.

Anastasi, A. (1981). Sex differences: Historical perspectives and methodological implications. *Developmental Review, 1,* 187–206.

Andersen, B. L., & Cyranowski, J. M. (1994). Women's sexual self-schema. *Journal of Personality and Social Psychology, 67,* 1079–1100.

Andersen, B. L., Cyranowski, J. M., & Aarestad, S. (2000). Beyond artificial, sex-linked distinctions to conceptualize female sexuality. Comment on Baumeister (2000). *Psychological Bulletin, 126*(3), 380–384.

Andersen, B. L., Cyranowski, J. M., & Espindle, D. (1999). Men's sexual self-schema. *Journal of Personality and Social Psychology, 76*(4), 645–661.

Anderson, K. J., & Cavallaro, D. (2002). Parents or pop culture? Children's heroes and role models. *Childhood Education* (Spring), 161–168.

Anderssen, N., Amlie, C., & Ytterøy, E. A. (2002). Outcomes for children with lesbian or gay parents: A review of studies from 1978 to 2000. *Scandinavian Journal of Psychology, 43*(4), 335–351.

Angier, N. (1990, July 20). Scientists find sex differentiation gene. *International Herald Tribune,* p. 3.

Angier, N. (1999). *Woman: An intimate geography.* Boston: Houghton Mifflin.

Angold, A., & Rutter, M. (1992). Effects of age and pubertal status on depression in a large clinical sample. *Development and Psychopathology, 4*(1), 5–28.

Ansari, M. A. (1989). Effects of leader sex, subordinate sex, and subordinate performance on the use of influence strategies. *Sex Roles, 20*(5/6), 283–293.

Antill, J. K., & Cunningham, J. D. (1982). Sex differences in performance on ability tests as a function of masculinity, femininity and androgyny. *Journal of Personality and Social Psychology, 42,* 718–728.

Archer, J. (1979). *Animals under stress.* London: Edward Arnold.

Archer, J. (1984). Gender roles as developmental pathways. *British Journal of Social Psychology, 23,* 245–256.

Archer, J. (2000). Sex differences in aggression between heterosexual partners: A meta-analytic review. *Psychological Bulletin, 126,* 651–680.

Archer, J., & Coyne, S. M. (2005). An integrated review of indirect, relational, and social aggression. *Personality and Social Psychology Review, 9*(3), 212–230.

Arias, I., & Pape, K. T. (1999). Psychological abuse: Implications for adjustment and commitment to leave violent partners. *Violence and Victims, 14*(1), 55–67.

Arias, I., Samios, M., & O'Leary, K. D. (1987). Prevalence and correlates of physical aggression during courtship. *Journal of Interpersonal Violence, 2,* 82–90.

Aries, E. (1976). Interaction patterns and themes of male, female, and mixed groups. *Small Group Behavior, 7*(1), 7–18.

Aries, E. (2002). Gender differences in interaction: A reexamination. In A. E. Hunter & C. Forden (Eds.), *Readings in the psychology of gender: Exploring our differences and commonalities* (pp. 69–82). Boston: Allyn & Bacon.

Arie, S. (2004, February 4). Armed with aprons, Italian "househusbands" unite, *Christian Science Monitor*. Retrieved June 26, 2006, from http://www.csmonitor.com/2004/0204/p01s04-woeu.html

Armitage, K. J., Schneiderman, L. J., & Bass, R. A. (1979). Response of physicians to medical complaints in men and women. *Journal of the American Medical Association, 241*(20), 2186–2187.

Aronson, J., Lustina, M. J., Good, C., Keough, K., Steele, C. M., & Brown, J. (1999). When White men can't do math: Necessary and sufficient factors in stereotype threat. *Journal of Experimental Social Psychology, 35*(1), 29–46.

Arrighi, B. A., & Maume, D. J., Jr. (2000). Workplace subordination and men's avoidance of housework. *Journal of Family Issues, 21*(4), 464–487.

Ashton, E. (1983). Measures of play behavior: The influence of sex-role stereotyped children's books. *Sex Roles, 9*, 43–47.

Astin, S., Redston, P., & Campbell, A. (2003). Sex differences in social representations of aggression: Men justify, women excuse? *Aggressive Behavior, 29*(2), 128–133.

Astrachan, A. (1989). Dividing lines. In M. S. Kimmel & M. A. Messner (Eds.), *Men's lives* (pp. 63–73). New York: Macmillan.

Associated Press. (2006, May 1). Health care tricky for transgendered. *Roanoke Times*, p. 5.

Atkinson, J., & Huston, T. L. (1984). Sex role orientation and division of labor early in marriage. *Journal of Personality and Social Psychology, 46*(2), 330–345.

Atkinson, J. W. (Ed.). (1958). *Motives in fantasy, action and society*. Princeton, NJ: Van Nostrand.

Atkinson, J. W., & Feather, N. T. (1966). *A theory of achievement motivation*. New York: Wiley.

Aubrey, J. S., & Harrison, K. (2004). The gender-role content of children's favorite television programs and its links to their gender-related

perceptions. *Media Psychology, 6*(2), 111–146.

Aubuchon, P. G., & Calhoun, K. S. (1985). Menstrual cycle symptomatology: The role of social expectancy and experimental demand characteristics. *Psychosomatic Medicine, 47*(1), 35–45.

Aulin, K. P. (1995). Gender-specific issues. *Journal of Sports Sciences*, 13, S35–S39.

Avis, N. E., & McKinlay, S. M. (1991). A longitudinal analysis of women's attitudes toward the menopause: Results from the Massachusetts Women's Health Study. *Maturitas, 13*, 65–69.

Awiakta, M. (1993). Anorexia bulimia speaks from the grave. In M. Awiakta, *Selu* (pp. 193–194). Golden, CO: Fulcrum.

Azar, B. (1998, October). Sex differences may not be set at birth. *APA Monitor, 29*(10), 25.

Babcock, J. C., Waltz, J., Jacobson, N. S., & Gottman, J. M. (1993). Power and violence: The relation between communication patterns, power discrepancies, and domestic violence. *Journal of Consulting and Clinical Psychology, 61*(1), 40–50.

Baca Zinn, M. (1989). Chicano men and masculinity. In M. S. Kimmel & M. A. Messner (Eds.), *Men's lives* (pp. 87–97). New York: Macmillan.

Backhouse, C., & Cohen, L. (1978). *The secret oppression: Sexual harassment of working women*. Toronto: Macmillan of Canada.

Baek, H.-J. (2002). A comparative study of moral development of Korean and British children. *Journal of Moral Education, 31*(4), 373–391.

Baenninger, M., & Newcombe, N. (1989). The role of experience in spatial test performance: A meta-analysis. *Sex Roles, 20*(5/6), 327–344.

Bagemihl, B. (1999). *Biological exuberance: Animal homosexuality and natural diversity*. New York: St. Martin's Press.

Baghurst, T., Hollander, D. B., Nardella, B., & Haff, G. G. (2006). Change in sociocultural ideal male physique: An examination of past and present action figures. *Body Image, 3*(1), 87–91.

Bailey, J. M., Pillard, R. C., Neale, M. C., & Agyei, Y. (1993). Heritable factors influence sexual orientation in women. *Archives of General Psychiatry, 50*, 217–223.

Bailey, J. M., & Zucker, K. J. (1995). Childhood sex-typed behavior and sexual orientation: A conceptual analysis and quantitative review. *Developmental Psychology, 31*(1), 43–55.

Baird, A. L., & Grieve, F. G. (2006). Exposure to male models in advertisements leads to a decrease in men's body satisfaction. *North American Journal of Psychology, 8*(1), 115–121.

Baker, L. A., Pearcey, S. M., & Dabbs, J. M., Jr. (2002). Testosterone, alcohol, and civil and rough conflict resolution strategies in lesbian couples. *Journal of Homosexuality, 42*(4), 77–88.

Baker, S. W. (1980). Biological influences on human sex and gender. *Signs: Journal of Women in Culture and Society, 6*, 80–96.

Bakken, L., & Romig, C. (1992). Interpersonal needs in middle adolescents: Companionship, leadership and intimacy. *Journal of Adolescence, 15*(3), 301–316.

Bancroft, J., Loftus, J., & Long, J. S. (2003). Distress about sex: A national survey of women in heterosexual relationships. *Archives of Sexual Behavior, 32*(3), 193–208.

Bandura, A. (1973). *Aggression: A social learning analysis*. Englewood Cliffs, NJ: Prentice-Hall.

Bandura, A. (1977). *Social learning theory*. Englewood Cliffs, NJ: Prentice-Hall.

Bandura, A. (1986). *Social foundations of thought and action: A social cognitive theory*. Englewood Cliffs, NJ: Prentice-Hall.

Bandura, A., & Bussey, K. (2004). On broadening the cognitive, motivational, and sociostructural scope of theorizing about gender development and functioning: Comment on Martin, Ruble, and Szkrybalo (2002). *Psychological Bulletin, 130*(5), 691–701.

Bank, B. J., & Hansford, S. L. (2000). Gender and friendship: Why are men's best same-sex friendships less intimate and supportive? *Personal Relationships, 7*(1), 63–78.

Bankart, B. (1989). Japanese perceptions of motherhood. *Psychology of Women Quarterly, 13*, 59–76.

Barash, D. (1979). *The whisperings within*. New York: Harper & Row.

Barbee, A. P., Cunningham, M. R., Winstead, B. A., Derlega, V. J., et al. (1993). Effects of gender role expectations on the social support process. *Journal of Social Issues, 19*(3), 175–190.

Barclay, R. I., & Barclay, M. L. (1976). Aspects of the normal psychology of pregnancy: The midtrimester. *American Journal of Obstetrics and Gynecology, 125,* 207.

Barfield, A. (1976). Biological influences on sex differences in behavior. In M. S. Teitelbaum (Ed.), *Sex differences: Social and biological perspectives* (pp. 62–121). Garden City, NY: Anchor Books.

Barglow, P., & Brown, E. (1972). Pseudocyesis. To be and not to be pregnant: A psychosomatic question. In J. G. Howells (Ed.), *Modern perspectives in psycho-obstetrics* (pp. 53–67). New York: Brunner/Mazel.

Barnett, R. C., Brennan, R. T., & Marshall, N. L. (1994). Gender and the relationship between parent role quality and psychological distress. *Journal of Family Issues, 15*(2), 229–252.

Barnett, R. C., & Hyde, J. S. (2001). Women, men, work, and family. *American Psychologist, 56*(10), 781–796.

Baron-Cohen, S. (2003). *The essential difference: The truth about the male and female brain.* New York: Basic Books.

Barres, B. A. (2006, July 13). Does gender matter? *Nature, 442,* 133–136.

Bart, P. (1971). Depression in middle-aged women. In V. Gornick & B. Moran (Eds.), *Women in sexist society.* New York: Basic Books.

Bart, P. (1980, March). *Socialization and rape avoidance: How to say no to Storaska and survive.* Paper presented at the National Conference on Feminist Psychology, Santa Monica, CA.

Bart, P. (1993). Protean women: The liquidity of female sexuality and the tenaciousness of lesbian identity. In S. Wilkinson & C. Kitzinger (Eds.), *Heterosexuality: A feminism and psychology reader* (pp. 246–252). London: Sage.

Baruch, G. K. (1972). Maternal influences upon college women's attitudes toward women and work. *Developmental Psychology, 6,* 32–37.

Baruch, G. K., Barnett, R., & Rivers, C. (1983). *Lifeprints: New patterns of love and work for today's women.* New York: McGraw-Hill.

Baslington, H. (2002). The social organization of surrogacy: Relinquishing a baby and the role of payment in the psychological detachment process. *Journal of Health Psychology, 7*(1), 57–71.

Basow, S. A. (1986). *Gender stereotypes: Traditions and alternatives.* Pacific Grove, CA: Brooks/Cole.

Baum, A. (2006). Eating disorders in the male athlete. *Sports Medicine, 36*(1), 1–6.

Baumeister, R. F., & Sommer, K. L. (1997). What do men want? Gender differences and two spheres of belongingness: Comment on Cross and Madson (1997). *Psychological Bulletin, 122*(1), 38–44.

Baumeister, R. F. (2000). Gender differences in erotic plasticity: The female sex drive as socially flexible and responsive. *Psychological Bulletin, 126*(3), 347–374.

Baumeister, R. F., Catanese, K. R., & Vohs, K. D. (2001). Is there a gender difference in strength of sex drive? Theoretical views, conceptual distinctions, and a review of relevant evidence. *Personality and Social Psychology Review, 5*(3), 242–273.

Baumgartner, A. (1983). *"My daddy might have loved me": Student perceptions of differences between being male and being female.* Denver: Institute for Equality in Education.

Baxter, J. (1992). Power attitudes and time: The domestic division of labour. *Journal of Comparative Family Studies, 13*(2), 165–179.

Bayley, N., & Oden, M. (1955). The maintenance of intellectual ability in gifted adults. *Journal of Gerontology, 10,* 91–107.

Bayley, T. M., Dye, L., Jones, S., DeBono, M., & Hill, A. J. (2002). Food cravings and aversions during pregnancy: Relationships with nausea and vomiting. *Appetite, 38*(1), 45–51.

Bazargan, M., & Barbre, A. R. (1992). Self-reported memory problems among the Black elderly. *Educational Gerontology, 18*(1), 71–82.

Bazzini, D. G., McIntosh, W. D., Smith, S. M., Cook, S., et al. (1997). The aging women in popular film: Underrepresented, unattractive, unfriendly, and unintelligent. *Sex Roles, 36*(7/8), 531–543.

BBC. (2006). India tackles domestic violence. *BBC News.* Retrieved October 26, 2006, from http://news.bbc.co.uk/1/hi/world/south_asia/6086334.stm

Beaton, A. M., & Tougas, F. (1997). The representation of women in management: The more the merrier? *Personality and Social Psychology Bulletin, 23*(7), 773–782.

Beaton, A. M., Tougas, F., & Joly, S. (1996). Neosexism among male managers: Is it

a matter of numbers? *Journal of Applied Social Psychology, 26,* 2189–2203.

Beck, C. T. (2001). Predictors of postpartum depression: An update. *Nursing Research, 50*(5), 275–285.

Becker, B. J., & Hedges, L. N. (1984). Meta-analysis of cognitive gender differences: A comment on an analysis by Rosenthal and Rubin. *Journal of Educational Psychology, 76,* 583–587.

Becker, B. J., & Hedges, L. N. (1988). The effects of selection and variability in studies of gender differences. *Behavioral and Brain Sciences, 11*(2), 183–184.

Bee, H. L., Mitchell, S. K., Barnard, K. E., Eyres, S. J., & Hammond, M. A. (1984). Predicting intellectual outcomes: Sex differences in response to early environmental stimulation. *Sex Roles, 10,* 783–803.

Beier, M. E., & Ackerman, P. L. (2003). Determinants of health knowledge: An investigation of age, gender, abilities, personality, and interests. *Journal of Personality and Social Psychology, 84*(2), 439–447.

Bell, A. P., & Weinberg, M. S. (1978). *Homosexualities.* New York: Simon & Schuster.

Bell, A. P., Weinberg, M. S., & Hammersmith, S. K. (1981). *Sexual preference.* Bloomington: Indiana University Press.

Bell, I. P. (1989). The double standard: Age. In J. Freeman (Ed.), *Women: A feminist perspective* (4th ed., pp. 236–244). Mountain View, CA: Mayfield.

Bell, L. (1999, November 9). Hispanic mothers face risks. *Washington Post,* Health section, p. 21.

Bell, L. C. (2004). Psychoanalytic theories of gender. In A. H. Eagly, A. E. Beall & R. J. Sternberg (Eds.), *The psychology of gender* (2nd ed., pp. 145–168). New York: Guilford Press.

Belle, D. (1984). Inequality and mental health: Low-income and minority women. In L. Walker (Ed.), *Women and mental health policy* (pp. 135–150). Beverly Hills, CA: Sage.

Bellinger, D. C., & Gleason, J. B. (1982). Sex differences in parental directives to young children. *Sex Roles, 8,* 1123–1139.

Bem, S. L. (1974). The measurement of psychological androgyny. *Journal of Consulting and Clinical Psychology, 42,* 155–162.

Bem, S. L. (1975). Sex-role adaptability: One consequence of psychological androgyny. *Journal of Personality and Social Psychology, 31,* 634–643.

Bem, S. L. (1981). Gender schema theory: A cognitive account of sex typing. *Psychological Review, 88,* 354–364.

Bem, S. L. (1985). Androgyny and gender schema theory: A conceptual and empirical integration. In T. B. Sonderegger (Ed.), *Nebraska Symposium on Motivation: Psychology of gender* (pp. 179–226). Lincoln: University of Nebraska Press.

Bem, S. L. (1993). *The lenses of gender.* New Haven, CT: Yale University Press.

Bem, S. L., & Lenney, E. (1976). Sex-typing and the avoidance of cross-sex behavior. *Journal of Personality and Social Psychology, 33*(1), 48–54.

Bem, S. L., Martyna, W., & Watson, C. (1976). Sex-typing and androgyny: Further exploration of the expressive domain. *Journal of Personality and Social Psychology, 34,* 1016–1023.

Benbow, C. P. (1986). Physiological correlates of extreme intellectual precocity. *Neuropsychologia, 24,* 719–725.

Benbow, C. P. (1988). Sex differences in mathematical reasoning ability in intellectually talented preadolescents: Their nature, effects, and possible causes. *Behavioral and Brain Sciences, 11*(2), 169–232.

Benbow, C. P., Lubinski, D., Shea, D. L., & Eftekhari-Sanjani, H. (2000). Sex differences in mathematical reasoning ability at age 13: Their status 20 years later. *Psychological Science, 11*(6), 474–480.

Benbow, C. P., & Stanley, J. C. (1980). Sex differences in mathematical ability: Fact or artifact? *Science, 210,* 1262–1264.

Benbow, C. P., & Stanley, J. C. (1982). Consequences in high school and college of sex differences in mathematical reasoning ability: A longitudinal perspective. *American Educational Research Journal, 19,* 598–622.

Benbow, C. P., & Stanley, J. C. (1983). Sex differences in mathematical reasoning ability: More facts. *Science, 222,* 1029–1031.

Benjamin, J. (1995). *Like subjects, love objects: Essays on recognition and sexual difference.* New Haven, CT: Yale University Press.

Berdahl, J. L., & Moore, C. (2006). Workplace harassment: Double jeopardy for minority women. *Journal of Applied Psychology, 91*(2), 426–436.

Berenbaum, S. A. (1998). How hormones affect behavioral and neural development: Introduction to the special issue on "Gonadal hormones and sex differences in behavior." *Developmental Neuropsychology, 14,* 175–196.

Berenbaum, S. A. (1999). Effects of early androgens on sex-typed activities and interests in adolescents with congenital adrenal hyperplasia. *Hormones and Behavior, 35,* 102–110.

Berenbaum, S. A., & Hines, M. (1992). Early androgens are related to childhood sex-typed toy preferences. *Psychological Science, 3,* 203–206.

Berenbaum, S. A., & Resnick, S. M. (1997). Early androgen effects on aggression in children and adults with congenital adrenal hyperplasia. *Psychoneuroendocrinology, 22*(7), 505–515.

Berenbaum, S. A., & Snyder, E. (1995). Early hormonal influences on childhood sex-typed activity and playmate preferences: Implications for the development of sexual orientation. *Developmental Psychology, 31*(1), 31–42.

Berkley, K. J. (2005). A life of pelvic pain. *Physiology and Behavior, 86*(3), 272–280.

Berman, P. W. (1976). Social context as a determinant of sex differences in adults' attraction to infants. *Developmental Psychology, 12,* 365–366.

Berman, P. W. (1980). Are women more responsive than men to the young? A review of developmental and situational variables. *Psychological Bulletin, 88,* 668–695.

Bernard, J. (1972). *The future of marriage.* New York: World.

Bernard, J. (1974). *The future of motherhood.* New York: Dial Press.

Bernard, J. (1976). Where are we now? Some thoughts on the current scene. *Psychology of Women Quarterly, 1*(1), 21–37.

Bernat, F. P. (1984). Gender disparity in the setting of bail: Prostitution offenses in Buffalo, NY, 1977–1979. *Journal of Offender Counseling, Services and Rehabilitation, 9*(1/2), 21–47.

Berndt, T. J., & Hoyle, S. G. (1985). Stability and change in childhood and adolescent friendships. *Developmental Psychology, 21*(6), 1007–1015.

Bernstein, A. G. (2005). Gendered characteristics of political engagement in college students. *Sex Roles, 52*(5), 299–310.

Bernstein, L., Henderson, B. E., Hanisch, R., Sullivan-Halley, J., & Ross, R. K. (1994). Physical exercise and breast cancer in young women. *Clinical Journal of Sports Medicine, 5*(2), 144.

Berzins, J., Welling, M., & Wetter, R. (1975). *The PRF Andro scale user's manual.* Unpublished manual, University of Kentucky.

Besser, A., Priel, B., & Wiznitzer, A. (2002). Childbearing depressive symptomatology in high-risk pregnancies: The roles of working models and social support. *Personal Relationships, 9*(4), 395–413.

Betz, N. E., & Fitzgerald, L. E. (1987). *The career psychology of women.* New York: Academic Press.

Beuf, A. (1974). Doctor, lawyer, household drudge. *Journal of Communication, 24*(2), 142–145.

Beyer, S. (1990). Gender differences in the accuracy of self-evaluations of performance. *Journal of Personality and Social Psychology, 59*(5), 960–970.

Beyer, S. (1999). The accuracy of academic gender stereotypes. *Sex Roles, 40*(9), 787–813.

Bianchi, S. M., Robinson, J. P., & Milkie, M. A. (2006). *Changing rhythms of American family life.* New York: Russell Sage Foundation.

Bibring, G. (1959). Some considerations of the psychological process of pregnancy. In *The psychoanalytic study of the child* (Vol. 14, pp. 113–121). New York: International Universities Press.

Bickman, L. (1974). Sex and helping behavior. *Journal of Social Psychology, 93*(1), 43–53.

Bidwell, R. J., & Deisher, R. W. (1991). Adolescent sexuality: Current issues. *Pediatric Annals, 20,* 293–302.

Bielby, D. D., & Bielby, W. T. (1988). She works hard for the money: Household responsibilities and the allocation of work effort. *American Journal of Sociology, 83*(5), 1031–1059.

Biernat, M., & Wortman, C. B. (1991). Sharing of home responsibilities between professionally employed women and their husbands. *Journal of Personality and Social Psychology, 60*(6), 844–860.

Billings, A. C., Angelini, J. R., & Eastman, S. T. (2005). Diverging discourses: Gender differences in televised golf announcing. *Mass Communication and Society, 8*(2), 155–171.

Billings, A. C., Halone, K. K., & Denham, B. E. (2002). "Man, that was a pretty shot": An analysis of gendered broadcast commentary surrounding the 2000 Men's and Women's NCAA Final Four Basketball Championships. *Mass Communication and Society, 5*(3), 295–315.

Binion, V. (1990). Psychological androgyny: A Black female perspective. *Sex Roles, 22,* 487–507.

Bishop, P., Cureton, K., Conerly, M., & Collins, M. (1989). Sex difference in muscle cross-sectional area of athletes and non-athletes. *Journal of Sport Sciences, 7,* 31–39.

Black, E. (1997, October 6). TV 101: Teaching kids how to watch wisely. *Minneapolis Star Tribune,* pp. A1, A10.

Black, S. L., & Koulis-Chitwood, A. (1990). The menstrual cycle and typing skill: An ecologically-valid test of the "raging hormones" hypothesis. *Canadian Journal of Behavioural Science, 22*(4), 445–455.

Blais, M. R., Vallerand, R. J., Briere, N. M., Gagnon, A., et al. (1990). Significance, structure, and gender differences in life domains of college students. *Sex Roles, 22*(3/4), 199–212.

Blakemore, J. E. O. (1998). The influence of gender and parental attitudes on preschool children's interest in babies: Observations in natural settings. *Sex Roles, 38,* 73–94.

Blanchard, R. (1985). Gender dysphoria and gender reorientation. In B. W. Steiner (Ed.), *Gender dysphoria: Development, research, management* (pp. 227–257). New York: Plenum Press.

Blanchard, R., Steiner, B. W., & Clemmensen, L. H. (1985). Gender dysphoria, gender reorientation, and the management of transsexualism. *Journal of Consulting and Clinical Psychology, 53*(3), 295–304.

Bledsoe, S. E., & Grote, N. K. (2006). Treating depression during pregnancy and the postpartum: A preliminary meta-analysis. *Research on Social Work Practice, 16*(2), 109–120.

Blee, K. M., & Tickamyer, A. R. (1995). Racial differences in men's attitudes about women's gender roles. *Journal of Marriage and the Family, 57,* 21–30.

Bleeker, M. M. (2003, April). *Children's attraction to math and science: The importance of parents' gender stereotypes and activities.* Paper presented at the biennial meeting of the Society for Research in Child Development, Tampa, FL.

Bleier, R. (1984). *Science and gender: A critique of biology and its theories on women.* New York: Pergamon Press.

Bleske, A. L., & Buss, D. M. (2000). Can men and women be just friends? *Personal Relationships, 7*(2), 131–151.

Bleske-Rechek, A. L., & Buss, D. M. (2001). Opposite-sex friendship: Sex differences and similarities in initiation, selection, and dissolution. *Personality and Social Psychology Bulletin, 27*(10), 1310–1323.

Bliss, G. K. (2000). Self-disclosure and friendship patterns: Gender and sexual orientation differences in same-sex and opposite-sex friendships. *Dissertation Abstracts International, 61*(5-A), 1749.

Block, J. H. (1973). Conceptions of sex roles: Some cross-cultural and longitudinal perspectives. *American Psychologist, 28,* 512–526.

Blough, P. M., & Slavin, L. K. (1987). Reaction time assessments of gender differences in visual-spatial performance. *Perception and Psychophysics, 41*(3), 276–281.

Blumstein, P., & Schwartz, P. (1976). Bisexual women. In J. P. Wiseman (Ed.), *The social psychology of sex.* New York: Harper & Row.

Blumstein, P., & Schwartz, P. (1983). *American couples.* New York: Morrow.

Bohan, J. S. (1992). Contextual history: A framework for replacing women in the history of psychology. In J. S. Bohan (Ed.), *Replacing women in psychology: Readings toward a more inclusive history* (pp. 44–56). Dubuque, IA: Kendall/Hunt.

Bohan, J. S. (1996). *Psychology and sexual orientation: Coming to terms.* New York: Routledge.

Bohan, J. S. (1997). Regarding gender: Essentialism, constructionism, and feminist psychology. In M. M. Gergen & S. N. Davis (Eds.), *Toward a new psychology of gender* (pp. 31–48). New York: Routledge.

Bond, J., Galinsky, E., & Swanberg, J. (1998). *National study of the changing workforce.* New York: Families and Work Institute.

Bonen, A. (1994). Exercise-induced menstual cycle changes: A functional, temporary adaptation to metabolic stress. *Sports Medicine, 17*(6), 373–392.

Boonstra, H. D., Gold, R. B., Richards, C. L., & Finer, L. B. (2006). *Abortion in women's lives.* Retrieved August 25, 2006, from http://www.guttmacher.org/pubs/2006/05/04/AiWL.pdf

Booth, A., & Dabbs, J. M. (1993). Testosterone and men's marriages. *Social Forces, 72*(2), 463–477.

Booth, A., Shelley, G., Mazur, A., Tharp, G., & Kittock, A. (1989). Testosterone and winning and losing in human competition. *Hormones and Behavior, 23*(4), 556–571.

Boring, E. (1929). *A history of experimental psychology* (Vol. 1). New York: Appleton-Century.

Borman, J., & Biordi, D. (1992). Female nurse executives: Finally, at an advantage? *Journal of Nursing Administration, 22*(9), 37–41.

Bornstein, K. (1994). *Gender outlaw: On men, women, and the rest of us.* New York: Vintage Books.

Bornstein, R. A. (1984). Unilateral lesions and the Wechsler Adult Intelligence Scale–Revised: No sex differences. *Journal of Consulting and Clinical Psychology, 52,* 604–608.

Bornstein, R. F. (2006). The complex relationship between dependency and domestic violence: Converging psychological factors and social forces. *American Psychologist, 61*(6), 595–606.

Borowy, T., & Goebel, R. (1976). Cerebral lateralization of speech: The effects of age, sex, race, and socioeconomic class. *Neuropsychologia, 14,* 363–370.

Borys, S., & Perlman, D. (1985). Gender differences in loneliness. *Personality and Social Psychology Bulletin, 11*(1), 63–74.

Boskind-White, M. (1985). Bulimarexia: A sociocultural perspective. In S. W. Emmett (Ed.), *Theory and treatment of anorexia nervosa and bulimia: Biomedical, sociocultural, and psychological perspectives* (pp. 113–126). New York: Brunner/ Mazel.

Boswell, H. (1997). The transgender paradigm shift toward free expression. In B. Bullough & V. L. Bullough (Eds.), *Gender blending* (pp. 53–57). New York: Prometheus Books.

Boswell, S. L. (1985). The influence of sex-role stereotyping on women's attitudes and achievement in mathematics. In S. F. Chipman, L. R. Brush, & D. M. Wilson (Eds.), *Women and mathematics: Balancing the equation* (pp. 175–198). Hillsdale, NJ: Erlbaum.

Bouchard, T. J., Lykken, D. T., McGue, M., Segal, N. L., & Tellegen, A. (1990). Sources of human psychological differences: The Minnesota study of twins reared apart. *Science, 25,* 223–228.

Boulis, A. K., & Long, J. A. (2004). Gender differences in the practice of adult primary care physicians. *Journal of Women's Health, 13*(6), 703–712.

Bourne, L. E., Healy, A. F., & Beer, F. A. (2003). Military conflict and terrorism: General psychology informs international relations. *Review of General Psychology, 7*(2), 189–202.

Bowen, C-C, Swim, J. K., & Jacobs, R. R. (2000). Evaluating gender biases on actual job performance of real people: A meta-analysis. *Journal of Applied Social Psychology, 30*(10), 2194–2215.

Bowen, D. J., & Grunberg, N. E. (1990). Variations in food preference and consumption across the menstrual cycle. *Physiology and Behavior, 47*(2), 287–291.

Boyd, N. (1979). Black families in therapy: A study of clinicians' perceptions. *Sandoz Psychiatric Spectator, 11*(7), 21–25.

Brabeck, M. (1983). Moral judgment: Theory and research on differences between males and females. *Developmental Review, 3,* 274–291.

Bradley, C. F. (1983). Psychological consequences of intervention in the birth process. *Canadian Journal of Behavioral Science, 15*(4), 422–438.

Bradley, P. H. (1981). The folk-linguistics of women's speech: An empirical examination. *Communication Monographs, 48,* 73–90.

Bradley, S. J., Oliver, G. D., Chernick, A. B., & Zucker, K. J. (1998). Experiment of nurture: Ablatio penis at 2 months, sex reassignment at 7 months, and a psychosexual follow-up in young adulthood. *Pediatrics, 102*(1), e9.

Brandon, P. R. (1991). Gender differences in young Asian Americans' educational attainment. *Sex Roles, 25*(1/2), 45–61.

Brannock, J. C., & Chapman, B. E. (1990). Negative sexual experiences with men among heterosexual women and lesbians. *Journal of Homosexuality, 19*(1), 105–110.

Brannon, R. (1976). The male sex role: Our culture's blueprint for manhood and what it's done for us lately. In D. David & R. Brannon (Eds.), *The forty-nine percent majority.* Reading, MA: Addison-Wesley.

Breathnach, C. S. (1990). The secondary sexual characteristics of the brain. *Irish Journal of Psychological Medicine, 7*(1), 59–63.

Brehm, J. W. (1966). *A theory of psychological reactance.* New York: Academic Press.

Bretl, D. J., & Cantor, J. (1988). The portrayal of men and women in U.S. television commercials: A recent content analysis and trends over 15 years. *Sex Roles, 18*(9/10), 595–609.

Bridges, J. S. (1988). Sex differences in occupational performance expectations. *Psychology of Women Quarterly, 12*(1), 75–90.

Bridges, J. S. (1993). Pink or blue: Gender-stereotypic perceptions of infants as conveyed by birth congratulations cards. *Psychology of Women Quarterly, 17*(2), 193–206.

Briere, J., Corne, S., Runta, M., & Malamuth, N. (1984, August). *The rape arousal inventory: Predicting actual and potential sexual aggression in a university population.* Paper presented at the meeting of the American Psychological Association, Toronto.

Briere, J., & Malamuth, N. (1983). Self-reported likelihood of sexually aggressive behavior: Attitudinal versus sexual explanations. *Journal of Research in Personality, 17,* 315–323.

Brockner, J., & Adsit, L. (1986). The moderating impact of sex on the equity-satisfaction relationship: A field study. *Journal of Applied Psychology, 71*(4), 585–590.

Brodsky, G. (1986, Fall). LEAF's legal cases: An update. *LEAF Letter,* p. 4.

Brody, E. M. (1981). "Women in the middle" and family help to older people. *Gerontologist, 21,* 471–479.

Bronstein, P. (1984). Differences in mothers' and fathers' behaviors toward children: A cross-cultural comparison. *Developmental Psychology, 20*(6), 995–1003.

Bronstein, P., Black, L., Pfenning, J., & White, A. (1986). Getting academic jobs: Are women equally qualified and equally successful? *American Psychologist, 41,* 318–322.

Brooks, J., Ruble, D. N., & Clarke, A. E. (1977). College women's attitudes and expectations concerning menstrual-related changes. *Psychosomatic Medicine, 39*(5), 288–298.

Brooks, L., & Perot, A. R. (1991). Reporting sexual harassment: Exploring a predictive model. *Psychology of Women Quarterly, 15*(1), 31–48.

Brooks-Gunn, J., Burrow, C., & Warren, M. P. (1988). Attitudes toward eating and body weight in different groups of

female adolescent athletes. *International Journal of Eating Disorders, 7,* 749–757.

Brooks-Gunn, J., & Ruble, D. (1980). Menarche. In A. J. Dan, E. A. Graham, & C. P. Beecher (Eds.), *The menstrual cycle* (Vol. 1). New York: Springer.

Brotman, S., Ryan, B., & Cormier, R. (2003). The health and social service needs of gay and lesbian elders and their families in Canada. *Gerontologist, 43*(2), 192–202.

Broverman, I. K., Broverman, D. M., Clarkson, F. E., Rosenkrantz, P. S., & Vogel, S. R. (1970). Sex role stereotypes and clinical judgments of mental health. *Journal of Consulting and Clinical Psychology, 34*(1), 1–7.

Brown, J. (1996). *Women, policing and the millennium.* Paper presented at the First Australasian Women Police Conference, Sydney, New South Wales, Australia.

Brown, J. D. (1985). Race and gender in rock video. *Social Science Newsletter, 70*(2), 82–86.

Brown, J. D., Childers, K. W., & Waszak, C. S. (1990). Television and adolescent sexuality. *Journal of Adolescent Health Care, 11*(1), 62–70.

Brown, L. S. (1989). New voices, new visions: Toward a lesbian/gay paradigm for psychology. *Psychology of Women Quarterly, 13*(4), 445–458.

Brown, L. S., & Root, M. P. P. (Eds.). (1990). *Diversity and complexity in feminist therapy.* Binghamton, NY: Haworth Press.

Brown, M., Amoroso, D. M., & Ware, E. E. (1976). Behavioral effects of viewing pornography. *Journal of Social Psychology, 98,* 235–245.

Brown, W. B., Bhrolchain, M., & Harris, T. (1975). Social class and psychiatric disturbance among women in an urban population. *Sociology, 9*(2), 225–254.

Brownmiller, S. (1975). *Against our will: Men, women, and rape.* New York: Simon & Schuster.

Brownmiller, S. (1984). *Femininity.* New York: Fawcett Columbine.

Bryan, A. D., Aiken, L. S., & West, S. G. (1999). The impact of males proposing condom use on perceptions of an initial sexual encounter. *Personality and Social Psychology Bulletin, 25*(3), 275–286.

Buchanan, M., & Robbins, C. (1990). Early adult psychological consequences for males of adolescent pregnancy and its resolution. *Journal of Youth and Adolescence, 19*(4), 413–424.

Buchanan, T. (2005). The paradox of the contented female worker in a traditionally female industry. *Sociological Spectrum, 25*(6), 677–713.

Buckwalter, G. A., & Galen, G. J. (2000). Associations between circulating sex steroid hormones and cognition in normal elderly women. *Neurology, 54*(3), 599–603.

Budnick, T. (2003, November 9). Notes: Campbell makes history at THE TOUR championship. *Golfweb.* Retrieved from http://www.golfweb.com/u/ce/multi/0,1977,6818645,00.html

Budoff, P. W. (1980). *No more menstrual cramps and other good news.* New York: Putnam.

Burchardt, C. J., & Serbin, L. A. (1982). Psychological androgyny and personality adjustment in college and psychiatric populations. *Sex Roles, 8,* 835–851.

Burkhauser, R. V., & Duncan, G. J. (1989). Economic risks of gender roles: Income loss and life events over the life course. *Social Science Quarterly, 70*(1), 3–23.

Burleson, B. R. (2003). The experience and effects of emotional support: What the study of cultural and gender differences can tell us about close relationships, emotion and interpersonal communication. *Personal Relationships, 10*(1), 1–23.

Burlew, A. K. (1982). The experiences of Black females in traditional and nontraditional professions. *Psychology of Women Quarterly, 6*(3), 312–326.

Burley, K. A. (1995). Family variables as mediators of the relationship between work-family conflict and marital adjustment among dual-career men and women. *Journal of Social Psychology, 135*(4), 483–497.

Burns, R. B. (1977). Male and female perceptions of their own and the other sex. *British Journal of Social and Clinical Psychology, 16,* 213–220.

Buss, D. M. (1989). Sex differences in human mate preferences: Evolutionary hypotheses tested in 37 countries. *Behavioral and Brain Sciences, 12,* 1–49.

Buss, D. M. (1994). *The evolution of desire: Strategies of human mating.* New York: Basic Books.

Buss, D. M. (1995). Psychological sex differences: Origins through sexual selection. *American Psychologist, 50,* 164–168.

Buss, D. M., et al. (1990). International preferences in selecting mates: A study of 37 cultures. *Journal of Cross-Cultural Psychology, 21,* 5–47.

Buss, D. M., Larsen, R., Westen, D., & Semmelroth, J. (1992). Sex differences in jealousy: Evolution, physiology, and psychology. *Psychological Science, 3,* 251–255.

Bussey, K., & Bandura, A. (1984). Influence of gender constancy and social power on sex-linked modeling. *Journal of Personality and Social Psychology, 47,* 1292–1302.

Bussey, K. & Bandura, A. (1992). Self-regulatory mechanisms governing gender development. *Child Development, 63,* 1236–1250.

Bussey, K., & Bandura, A. (1999). Social cognitive theory of gender development and differentiation. *Psychological Review, 106,* 676–713.

Bussey, K., & Bandura, A. (2004). Social cognitive theory of gender development and functioning. In A. H. Eagly, A. E. Beall, & R. J. Sternberg (Eds.), *The psychology of gender* (2nd ed., pp. 92–119). New York: Guilford Press.

Bussey, K., & Perry, D. G. (1982). Same-sex imitation: The avoidance of cross-sex models or the acceptance of same-sex models? *Sex Roles, 8,* 773–784.

Butler, D., & Geis, F. L. (1990). Nonverbal affect responses to male and female leaders: Implications for leadership evaluations. *Journal of Personality and Social Psychology, 58*(1), 48–59.

Butler, R., & Lewis, M. I. (2002). *The new love and sex after 60.* New York: Ballantine.

Butler, S., & Wintram, C. (1991). *Feminist groupwork.* Newbury Park, CA: Sage.

Buzzanell, P. M., & Turner, L. H. (2003). Emotion work revealed by job loss discourse: Backgrounding-foregrounding of feelings, construction of normalcy, and (re)instituting of traditional masculinities. *Journal of Applied Communication Research, 31*(1), 27–57.

Bylsma, W. H., & Major, B. (1994). Social comparisons and contentment: Exploring the psychological costs of the gender wage gap. *Psychology of Women Quarterly, 18*(2), 241–249.

Bylsma, W. H., Major, B., & Cozzarelli, C. (1995). The influence of legitimacy appraisals on the determinants of entitlement beliefs. *Basic and Applied Social Psychology, 17*(1/2), 223–237.

Byne, W., Bleier, R., & Houston, L. (1988). Variations in human corpus callosum do not predict gender: A study using magnetic resonance imaging. *Behavioral Neuroscience, 102*(2), 222–227.

Cafferata, G. L., & Meyers, S. M. (1990). Pathways to psychotropic drugs: Understanding the basis of gender differences. *Medical Care, 28*(4), 285–300.

Caldera, Y. M., Huston, A. C., & O'Brien, M. (1989). Social interactions and play patterns of parents and toddlers with feminine, masculine, and neutral toys. *Child Development, 60,* 70–76.

Caldwell, M. A., & Peplau, L. A. (1982). Sex differences in same-sex friendships. *Sex Roles, 8,* 721–732.

Callahan-Levy, C. M., & Messe, L. A. (1979). Sex differences in the allocation of pay. *Journal of Personality and Social Psychology, 37,* 433–446.

Calloni, J. C., & Handal, P. J. (1992). Differential parental attachment: Empirical support for the self-in-relation model. *Perceptual and Motor Skills, 75*(3, Pt. 1), 904–906.

Calvert, S. L., Kotler, J. A., Zehnder, S. M., & Shockey, E. M. (2003). Gender stereotyping in children's reports about educational and informational television programs. *Media Psychology, 5*(2), 139–162.

Campbell, A. (2002). *A mind of her own: The evolutionary psychology of women.* New York: Oxford University Press.

Campbell, A., & Muncer, S. (1987). Models of anger and aggression in the social talk of women and men. *Journal for the Theory of Social Behavior, 17,* 489–511.

Campbell, J. R. (1991). The roots of gender inequity in technical areas. *Journal of Research in Science Teaching, 28*(3), 251–264.

Canadian Advisory Council on the Status of Women. (1984). *Prostitution in Canada.* Ottawa: Author.

Canadian Human Rights Commission. (1983). *Unwanted sexual attention and sexual harassment: Results of a survey of Canadians.* Ottawa: Author.

Canadian Press. (2004). David Reimer, 38, subject of the John/Joan case, dies. *New York Times.* Retrieved May 12, 2006, from http://www.nytimes.com/2004/05/12/international/americas/12REIM.html?ex=1399694400&en=8f0108b49acb766b&ei=5007&partner=USERLAND

Canadian Psychological Association. (1980). *Guidelines for therapy and counselling with women*. Ottawa: Author.

Canadian Psychological Association. (1982). *Therapy and counselling with women: A handbook on educational materials*. Ottawa: Author.

Canli, T., Desmond, J. E., Zhao, Z., & Gabrieli, J. D. E. (2002). Sex differences in the neural basis of emotional memories. *Proceedings of the National Academy of Sciences, 99*(16), 10789–10794.

Cann, A., & Garnett, A. K. (1984). Sex stereotype impacts on competence ratings by children. *Sex Roles, 11*, 333–343.

Canetto, S. S. (2001). Older adult women: Issues, resources, and challenges. In R. K. Unger (Ed.), *Handbook of the psychology of women and gender* (pp. 183–197). New York: Wiley.

Cantrell, P. (1996, January/February). Blue-collar workers: Breaking through the brick ceiling. *Ms., 6*(4), 34–38.

Caplan, P. J. (1993). Premenstrual syndrome DSM-IV diagnosis: The coalition for a scientific and responsible DSM-IV. *Psychology of Women: Newsletter of Division 35, 20*(3), 4–5, 13.

Caplan, P. J., & Eichler, M. (1989). *A proposal for the delusional dominating personality disorder*. Toronto: Authors.

Caplan, P. J., MacPherson, G. M., & Tobin, P. (1985). Do sex-related differences in spatial ability exist? A multilevel critique with new data. *American Psychologist, 40*(7), 786–799.

Caputi, J., & Russell, D. E. H. (1990, September/October). "Femicide": Speaking the unspeakable. *Ms., 1*(2), 34–37.

Caputo, A. (2002, April 22). WNBA rookies shoot for bigger money. *Columbia Chronicle Online*. Retrieved from http://www.ccchronicle.com/back/2002-04-22/sports3.html

Carbonell, J. L. (1984). Sex roles and leadership revisited. *Journal of Applied Psychology, 53*, 377–382.

Carli, L. L. (1990). Gender, language, and influence. *Journal of Personality and Social Psychology, 59*(5), 941–951.

Carli, L. L. (1998, June). *Gender effects in social influence*. Paper presented at the meeting of the Society for the Study of Social Issues, Ann Arbor, MI.

Carli, L. L. (1999). Gender, interpersonal power, and social influence. *Journal of Social Issues, 55*(1), 81–99.

Carli, L. L. (2001). Gender and social influence. *Journal of Social Issues, 57*(4), 725–741.

Carli, L. L., LaFleur, S. J., & Loeber, C. C. (1995). Nonverbal behavior, gender, and influence. *Journal of Personality and Social Psychology, 68*(6), 1030–1041.

Carlson, A. (1991, March). When is a woman not a woman? *Women's Sports & Fitness*, pp. 24–29.

Carlson, B. E., & Videka-Sherman, L. (1990). An empirical test of androgyny in the middle years: Evidence from a national survey. *Sex Roles, 23*(5/6), 305–324.

Carlton, C. L., Nelson, E. S., & Coleman, P. K. (2000). College students' attitudes toward abortion and commitment to the issue. *Social Science Journal, 37*(4), 619–625.

Carrel, L., & Willard, H. F. (2005). X-inactivation profile reveals extensive variability in X-linked gene expression in females. *Nature, 434*(7031), 400–404.

Carroll, J., Volk, K. D., & Hyde, J. S. (1985). Differences between males and females in motives for engaging in sexual intercourse. *Archives of Sexual Behavior, 14*, 131–139.

Carter, F. A., Frampton, C. M. A., & Mulder, R. T. (2006). Cesarean section and postpartum depression: A review of the evidence examining the link. *Psychosomatic Medicine, 68*(2), 321–330.

Carunungan-Robles, A. (1986). Perceptions of parental nurturance, punitiveness and power by selected Filipino primary school children. *Philippine Journal of Psychology, 19*, 18–28.

Carver, C. S., & de la Garza, N. H. (1984). Schema-guided information search in stereotyping of the elderly. *Journal of Applied Social Psychology, 14*(1), 69–81.

Cash, T. F., Gillen, B., & Burns, D. S. (1977). Sexism and "beautyism" in personnel consultant decision making. *Journal of Applied Psychology, 62*, 301–310.

Cash, T. F., & Henry, P. E. (1995). Women's body images: The results of a national survey in the U.S.A. *Sex Roles, 33*(1/2), 19–28.

Caspi, A. (2000). The child is father of the man: Personality continuities from childhood to adulthood. *Journal of Personality and Social Psychology, 78*(1), 158–172.

Caspi, A., Bem, D., & Elder, G. H., Jr. (1989). Continuities and consequences of interactional styles across the life course. *Journal of Personality, 57*(2), 375–406.

Cass, V. C. (1979). Homosexual identity formation: A theoretical model. *Journal of Homosexuality, 4*, 219–235.

Cass, V. C. (1984). Homosexual identity formation: Testing a theoretical model. *Journal of Sex Research, 20*, 143–167.

Catalano, S. M. (2005). *Criminal victimization, 2004*. Retrieved August 4, 2006, from http://www.ojp.usdoj.gov/bjs/pub/pdf/cv04.pdf

Catalano, S. M. (2006). *Criminal victimization, 2005*. Retrieved October 20, 2006, from http://www.ojp.usdoj.gov/bjs/pub/pdf/cv05.pdf

Catalyst (1998a, March 10). NBC breakfast addresses work/life balancing act. Press release. Retrieved from www.catalystwomen.org/press/

Catalyst. (1998b, March 10). *NBC breakfast addresses work/life balancing act*. Press release. Retrieved May 10, 2001, from http://www.catalystwomen.org/press

Catalyst. (2003a, May 21). *Catalyst study outlines strategies for companies to capitalize on Latinas in the workplace*. Press release. Retrieved from http://www.catalystwomen.org/press_room/press_releases/woc_20030521.htm

Catalyst. (2003b, August 7). *Catalyst study highlights the unique challenges Asian women face in the workplace*. Press release. Retrieved from http://www.catalystwomen.org/press_room/press_releases/WOC%20Asia%20Press%20Release%20Final.pdf

Catalyst. (2003c, June 3). *Catalyst study finds women need experience in the business of the business to claim leadership roles*. Press release. Retrieved from http://www.catalystwomen.org/press_room/press_releases/20030603.htm

Catalyst. (2005). Latest count of women in Canadian business serves as call to action for companies. *Perspectives*. Retrieved November 20, 2006, from http://www.catalystwomen.org/bookstore/perspective/05June.pdf

Catalyst. (2006a). *2005 Catalyst census of women board directors of the Fortune 500: Ten years later: Limited progress, challenges persist*. New York: Catalyst.

Catalyst. (2006b). Rate of women's advancement to top corporate officer positions slow, new Catalyst tenth anniversary census reveals. Retrieved July 26, 2006, from http://www.catalystwomen.org/pressroom/press_releases/7_26_06%20%202005%20COTE%20release.pdf

Cattell, J. M. (1903). A statistical study of eminent men. *Popular Science Monthly, 62,* 359–377.

Cazenave, N. A., & Leon, G. H. (1987). Men's work and family roles and characteristics: Race, gender, and class perceptions of college students. In M. S. Kimmel (Ed.), *Changing men: New directions in research on men and masculinity* (pp. 244–262). Newbury Park, CA: Sage.

Ceballo, R. (1999). Negotiating the life narrative: A dialogue with an African American social worker. *Psychology of Women Quarterly, 23*(2), 309–322.

Cejka, M. A., & Eagly, A. H. (1999). Gender-stereotypic images of occupations correspond to the sex segregation of employment. *Personality and Social Psychology Bulletin, 25*(4), 413–423.

Center for American Women in Politics. (2003, October 27). *Fewer women running in state elections than in previous years.* Press release. Retrieved from http://www.cawp.rugers.edu/News/CAWP press10-03.html

Center for American Women in Politics. (2006a). *Facts and findings: Gender gap and voting behavior.* Retrieved November 12, 2006, from http://www.cawp.rutgers.edu/Facts5.html

Center for American Women in Politics. (2006b). *Facts and findings: Women candidates in election 2006.* Retrieved November 12, 2006, from http://www.cawp.rutgers.edu/Facts3.html

Centers for Disease Control and Prevention. (1998a, September). National data on HIV prevalence among disadvantaged youth in the 1990s. *CDC Update,* pp. 1–2.

Centers for Disease Control and Prevention. (1998b). *HIV/AIDS surveillance report, 10*(2).

Centers for Disease Control and Prevention. (2002). *Cases of HIV infection and AIDS in the United States and dependent areas, 2002.* Retrieved August 14, 2006, from http://www.cdc.gov/hiv/topics/surveillance/resources/reports/index.htm#surveillance

Centers for Disease Control and Prevention. (2003). *Cases of HIV infection and AIDS in the United States and dependent areas, 2003.* Retrieved August 14, 2006, from http://www.cdc.gov/hiv/topics/surveillance/resources/reports/index.htm#surveillance

Centers for Disease Control and Prevention. (2004a). *Cases of HIV infection and AIDS in the United States, 2004.* Retrieved July 31, 2006, from http://www.cdc.gov/hiv/topics/surveillance/resources/reports/2004report/commentary.htm

Centers for Disease Control and Prevention. (2004b, December 10). Use of contraception and use of family planning services in the United States: 1982–2002. *Advance Data from Vital and Health Statistics, 350.* Retrieved August 30, 2006, from http://www.cdc.gov/nchs/data/ad/ad350.pdf

Centers for Disease Control and Prevention. (2005a). Abortion surveillance—United States, 2002. Surveillance summaries. *MMWR, 54*(7), 1–31. Retrieved September 13, 2006, from http://www.cdc.gov/mmwr/preview/mmwrhtml/ss5407al.htm

Centers for Disease Control and Prevention. (2005b). Teenagers in the United States: Sexual activity, contraceptive use, and childbearing, 2002. *Vital and Health Statistics, 23*(25). Retrieved September 19, 2006, from http://www.cdc.gov/nchs/data/series/sr_23/sr23_025.pdf

Centers for Disease Control and Prevention. (2006). Youth risk behavior surveillance—United States, 2005. Surveillance summaries. *MMWR, 55*(5).

Center for Women in Government and Civil Society. (2006). *Women in state policy leadership, 1998–2005: An analysis of slow and uneven progress.* Albany: State University of New York.

Charlton, R. (2004). Ageing male syndrome, andropause, androgen decline or mid-life crisis? *Journal of Men's Health and Gender, 1*(1), 55–59.

Chatterjee, S. (2003, November 9). Report finds women worldwide are generally happier than men. *Roanoke Times,* p. A19.

Chavez, D. (1985). Perpetuation of gender inequality: A content analysis of comic strips. *Sex Roles, 13*(1/2), 93–102.

Chen, J. C. H. (2005). Students' conceptualizations of gender in Taiwan and the U.S. *Visual Arts Research, 31*(2), 10–25.

Chernin, K. (1981). *The obsession: Reflections on the tyranny of slenderness.* New York: Harper & Row.

Cherrin, A. (2003, Fall). Same-sex marriage: The fight for equality gains momentum. *National NOW Times, 35*(2), 3.

Cherry, F., & Deaux, K. (1978). Fear of success versus fear of gender-inappropriate behavior. *Sex Roles, 4,* 97–101.

Chertok, L. (1969). *Motherhood and personality.* London: Tavistock.

Chesler, P. (1971). Patient and patriarch: Women in the psychotherapeutic relationship. In V. Gornick & B. Moran (Eds.), *Women in sexist society: Studies in power and powerlessness* (pp. 251–275). New York: Basic Books.

Chesler, P. (1972). *Women and madness.* New York: Doubleday.

Chesney-Lind, M. (1987). Female offenders: Paternalism reexamined. In L. Crites & W. Hepperle (Eds.), *Women, the courts, and equality.* Newbury Park, CA: Sage.

Chesney-Lind, M. (1995). Rethinking women's imprisonment: A critical examination of trends in female incarceration. In B. R. Price & N. Sokoloff (Eds.), *Women, crime, and criminal justice.* New York: McGraw-Hill.

Chivers, M. L., Rieger, G., Latty, E., & Bailey, J. M. (2004). A sex difference in the specificity of sexual arousal. *Psychological Science, 15*(11), 736–744.

Chodorow, N. (1978). *The reproduction of mothering: Psychoanalysis and the sociology of gender.* Berkeley: University of California Press.

Chodorow, N. (1989). *Feminism and psychoanalytic theory.* New Haven, CT: Yale University Press.

Chodorow, N. J. (1995). Gender as a personal and cultural construction. *Signs, 20*(3), 516–544.

Chrisler, J. C., Johnston, I. K., Champagne, N. M., & Preston, K. E. (1994). Menstrual joy: The construct and its consequences. *Psychology of Women Quarterly, 18*(3), 375–388.

Chrisler, J. C., & Levy, K. B. (1990). The media construct a menstrual monster: A content analysis of PMS articles in the popular press. *Women and Health, 16*(2), 89–104.

Chrisler, J. C., & Zittell, C. B. (1998). Menarche stories: Reminiscences of college students from Lithuania, Malaysia, Sudan, and the United States. *Health Care for Women International, 19,* 303–312.

Christensen, A., & Heavey, C. L. (1990). Gender and social structure in the demand/withdraw pattern of marital conflict. *Journal of Personality and Social Psychology, 59*(1), 73–81.

Christiansen, K., & Knussman, R. (1987). Androgen levels and components of aggressive behavior in men. *Hormones and Behavior, 21,* 170–180.

Christopher, K., England, P., McLanahan, S., Phillips, K. R., & Smeeding, T. M. (2000). *Gender inequality in poverty in affluent* nations: The role of single motherhood and the state. Joint Center for Poverty Research Working Paper 108. Retrieved from http://www. jcpr.org/research_summaries/vol1 _num1.html

Cicchetti, D., & Toth, S. L. (1998). The development of depression in children and adolescents. *American Psychologist, 53*(2), 221–241.

Cjeka, M. A., & Eagly, A. H. (1999). Gender-stereotypic images of occupations correspond to the sex segregation of employment. *Personality and Social Psychology Bulletin, 25*(4), 413–423.

Claes, M. E. (1992). Friendship and personal adjustment during adolescence. *Journal of Adolescence, 15*(1), 39–55.

Clark, M. L., & Ayers, M. (1991). Friendship similarity during early adolescence: Gender and racial patterns. *Journal of Psychology, 126*(4), 393–405.

Clark, R., & Hatfield, E. (1989). Gender differences in receptivity to sexual offers. *Journal of Psychology and Human Sexuality, 2*(1), 39–55.

Clarke, E. (1873). *Sex in education; or, a fair chance for girls.* Boston: Osgood and Co.

Clarke, L. C. H. (2002). Beauty in later life: Older women's perceptions of physical attractiveness. *Canadian Journal on Aging, 21*(3), 429–442.

Clarke-Stewart, K. A. (1991). A home is not a school: The effects of child care on children's development. *Journal of Social Issues, 47*(2), 105–124.

Clinton, J. F. (1987). Physical and emotional responses of expectant fathers throughout pregnancy and the early postpartum period. *International Journal of Nursing Studies, 24*(1), 59–68.

Clum, G. A., & Knowles, S. (1991). Why do some people with panic disorders become avoidant?: A review. *Clinical Psychology Review, 11,* 295–313.

Coats, S., & Smith, E. R. (1999). Perception of gender subtypes: Sensitivity to recent exemplar activation and ingroup/out-group differences. *Personality and Social Psychology Bulletin, 25*(4), 515–526.

Cobb, N. J., Stevens-Long, J., & Goldstein, S. (1982). The influence of televised models on toy preference in children. *Sex Roles, 8,* 1075–1080.

Cochran, S. D., & Peplau, L. A. (1985). Value orientations in heterosexual relationships. *Psychology of Women Quarterly, 9*(4), 477–488.

Cochrane, J. (1977). *Women in Canadian politics.* Toronto: Fitzhenry & Whiteside.

Cohen, A. G., & Gutek, B. A. (1985). Dimensions of perceptions of social-sexual behavior in a work setting. *Sex Roles, 13*(5/6), 317–328.

Cohen, D., Nisbett, R. E., Bowdle, B. F., & Schwarz, N. (1996). Insult, aggression, and the southern culture of honor: An "experimental ethnography." *Journal of Personality and Social Psychology, 70*(5), 945–960.

Cohen, D., & Wilkie, F. (1979). Sex-related differences in cognition among the elderly. In M. A. Wittig & A. C. Petersen (Eds.), *Sex-related differences in cognitive functioning: Developmental issues* (pp. 145–159). New York: Academic Press.

Cohen, L. L., & Swim, J. K. (1995). The differential effect of gender ratios on women and men: Tokenism, self-confidence, and expectations. *Personality and Social Psychology Bulletin, 21,* 876–884.

Coker, D. R. (1984). The relationship among concepts and cognitive maturity in preschool children. *Sex Roles, 10,* 19–31.

Colapino, J. (1997, December 11). The true story of John/Joan. *Rolling Stone,* pp. 55–73, 92, 94–97.

Coleman, A., & Coleman, L. (1971). *Pregnancy: The psychological experience.* New York: Seabury.

Coleman, B. G. (1999, June 1). *Study: Andro may grow breasts.* Retrieved from http://search.washingtonpost.com/wp-srv/WAPO/19990601/V000907–060199-idx.html

Coleman, L. M., & Antonucci, T. C. (1983). Impact of work on women at midlife. *Developmental Psychology, 19*(2), 290–294.

Coley, R. L., & Chase-Lansdale, P. (1998). Adolescent pregnancy and parenthood: Recent evidence and future directions. *American Psychologist, 53*(2), 152–166.

Collaer, M. L., & Hines, M. (1995). Human behavioral sex differences: A role for gonadal hormones during early development? *Psychological Bulletin, 118*(1), 55–107.

Colley, A., Ball, J., Kirby, N., Harvey, R., & Vingelen, I. (2002). Gender-linked differences in everyday memory performance: Effort makes the difference. *Sex Roles, 47*(11–12), 577–582.

Collin, C. A., Di Sano, F., & Malik, R. (1994). Effects of confederate and subject gender on conformity in a color classification task. *Social Behavior and Personality, 22*(4), 355–364.

Collins, E. G. C. (1983, September/October). Managers and lovers. *Harvard Business Review,* pp. 142–153.

Collins, P. H. (1991). *Black feminist thought: Knowledge, consciousness, and the politics of empowerment.* Boston: Unwin Hyman.

Collis, B. (1985). Psychosocial implications of sex differences in attitudes toward computers: Results of a survey. *International Journal of Women's Studies, 8*(3), 207–213.

Colwill, N. L. (1984, November). Direction for future research. *Proceedings of Colloquium on the Economic Status of Women in the Labour Market.* Ottawa: Economic Council of Canada.

Colwill, N. L., & Colwill, H. D. (1985). Women with blue collars: The forgotten minority. *Business Quarterly, 50*(2), 15–17.

Colwill, N. L., & Lips, H. M. (1978). Masculinity, femininity, and androgyny: What have you done for us lately? In H. M. Lips & N. L. Colwill, *The psychology of sex differences* (pp. 125–144). Englewood Cliffs, NJ: Prentice-Hall.

Comas-Díaz, L., & Greene, B. (1994). Overview: Gender and ethnicity in the healing process. In L. Comas-Díaz & B. Greene (Eds.), *Women of color: Integrating ethnic and gender identities in psychotherapy* (pp. 185–193). New York: Guilford Press.

Condon, J. T. (1987). Psychological and physical symptoms during pregnancy: A comparison of male and female expectant parents. *Journal of Reproductive and Infant Psychology, 5*(4), 207–219.

Condry, J., & Condry, S. (1976). Sex differences: A study of the eye of the beholder. *Child Development, 47,* 812–819.

Condry, J., & Ross, D. (1985). Sex and aggression: The influence of gender label on the perception of aggression in children. *Child Development, 56,* 225–233.

Condry, S. M., & Dyer, S. (1976). Fear of success: Attribution of cause to the victim. *Journal of Social Issues, 32*(3), 63–83.

Connellan, J., Baron-Cohen, S., Wheelwright, S., Batki, A., & Ahluwalia, J. (2000). Sex differences in human neonatal social perception. *Infant Behavior and Development, 23*(1), 113–118.

Connor, J. M., & Serbin, L. A. (1985). Visual-spatial skill: Is it important for mathematics? Can it be taught? In S. Chipman, L. Brush, & D. Wilson (Eds.), *Women and mathematics: Balancing the equation* (pp. 151–174). Hillsdale, NJ: Erlbaum.

Connor-Greene, P. A. (1988). Gender differences in body weight perception and weight-loss strategies of college students. *Women and Health, 14*(2), 27–42.

Constantinople, A. (1973). Masculinity-femininity: An exception to a famous dictum? *Psychological Bulletin, 80*(3), 389–407.

Cooper, E. B. (1992). When being ill is illegal: Women and the criminalization of HIV. *Health/PAC Bulletin,* Winter, 10–14.

Cooper, K. L., & Guttmann, D. L. (1987). Gender identity and ego mastery style in middle-aged pre- and post-empty nest women. *Gerontologist, 27,* 347–352.

Corrigan, E., & Butler, S. (1991). Irish alcoholic women in treatment: Early findings. *International Journal of the Addictions, 26*(3), 281–292.

Costello, C. B., Miles, S., & Stone, A. J. (1998). *The American woman 1999–2000.* New York: W. W. Norton.

Costos, D., Ackerman, R., & Paradis, L. (2002). Recollections of menarche: Communication between mothers and daughters regarding menstruation. *Sex Roles, 46*(1/2), 49–59.

Cotton, N. S. (1979). The familial incidence of alcoholism: A review. *Journal of Studies on Alcohol, 40*(1), 89–116.

Coulomb-Cabagno, G. V., Rascle, O., & Souchon, N. (2005). Players' gender and male referees' decisions about aggression in French soccer: A preliminary study. *Sex Roles, 52*(7), 547–553.

Cox, T. H., & Harquail, C. V. (1991). Career paths and career success in the early career stages of male and female MBAs. *Journal of Vocational Behavior, 39,* 54–75.

Cozzarelli, C., Tagler, M. J., & Wilkinson, A. V. (2002). Do middle-class students perceive poor women and poor men differently? *Sex Roles, 47*(11/12), 519–530.

Crabb, P. B., & Bielawski, D. (1994). The social representation of material culture and gender in children's books. *Sex Roles, 30*(1/2), 69–79.

Craig, S. C., Kane, J. G., & Martinez, M. D. (2002). Sometimes you feel like a nut, sometimes you don't: Citizens'

ambivalence about abortion. *Political Psychology, 23*(2), 285–301.

Craig, T. J., & Lin, S. P. (1984). Sex differences in mortality rate among long-stay psychiatric inpatients. *Sex Roles, 10,* 725–732.

Cramer, R. E., Dragna, M., Cupp, R. G., & Stewart, P. (1991). Contrast effects in the evaluation of the male sex role. *Sex Roles, 24*(3/4), 181–193.

Crandall, V. C. (1969). Sex differences in expectancy of intellectual and academic reinforcement. In C. P. Smith (Ed.), *Achievement-related motives in children* (pp. 11–45). New York: Russell Sage Foundation.

Crandall, V. C., Katkovsky, W., & Preston, A. A. (1960). A conceptual foundation for some research on children's achievement development. *Child Development, 31,* 787–797.

Crews, D. (1993). The organizational concept and vertebrates without sex chromosomes. *Brain Behavior and Evolution, 42,* 202–214.

Crocker, L., Schmitt, A., & Tang, L. (1988, January). Test anxiety and standardized achievement test performance in the middle school years. *Measurement and Evaluation in Counseling and Development, 20*(4), 149–157.

Crohan, S. E., Antonucci, T. C., Adelmann, P. K., & Coleman, L. M. (1989). Job characteristics and well-being at midlife: Ethnic and gender comparisons. *Psychology of Women Quarterly, 13*(2), 223–236.

Crooks, R., & Bauer, K. (1987). *Our sexuality* (3rd ed.). Menlo Park, CA: Benjamin/Cummings.

Crosby, F. J. (1982). *Relative deprivation and working women.* New York: Oxford.

Crosby, F. J. (1984). The denial of personal discrimination. *American Behavioral Scientist, 27*(3), 371–386.

Crosby, F. J. (1990). Divorce and work life among women managers. In H. Y. Grossman & N. L. Chester (Eds.), *The experience and meaning of work in women's lives* (pp. 121–142). Hillsdale, NJ: Erlbaum.

Crosby, F. J., Clayton, S., Alksnis, O., & Hemker, K. (1986). Cognitive biases in the perception of discrimination: The importance of format. *Sex Roles, 14*(11/12), 637–646.

Crosby, F. J., & Franco, J. L. (2003). Connections between the ivory tower and the multicolored world: Linking

abstract theories of social justice to the rough and tumble of affirmative action. *Personality and Social Psychology Review, 7*(4), 362–373.

Crosby, F. J., Iyer, A., Clayton, S., & Downing, R. A. (2003). Affirmative action: Psychological data and the policy debates. *American Psychologist, 58*(2), 98–115.

Crosby, F. J., Williams, J. C., & Biernat, M. (2004). The maternal wall. *Journal of Social Issues, 60*(4), 675–682.

Cross, S., & Bagilhole, B. (2002). Girls' jobs for the boys? Men, masculinity and nontraditional occupations. *Gender, Work and Organization, 9*(2), 204–226.

Crown, J., & Heatherington, L. (1989). The costs of winning? The role of gender in moral reasoning and judgments about competitive athletic encounters. *Journal of Sport and Exercise Psychology, 11*(3), 281–289.

Crull, P. (1980). The impact of sexual harassment on the job: A profile of the experiences of 92 women. In D. A. Neugarten & J. M. Shafritz (Eds.), *Sexuality in organizations: Romantic and coercive behaviors at work* (pp. 67–71). Oak Park, IL: Moore.

Cuddy, A. J. C., Fiske, S. T., & Glick, P. (2004). When professionals become mothers, warmth doesn't cut the ice. *Journal of Social Issues, 60*(4), 701–718.

Cummings, S. M., Kropf, N. P., & De Weaver, K. L. (2001). Knowledge of and attitudes toward aging among non-elders: Gender and race differences. *Journal of Women and Aging, 12*(1–2), 77–91.

Cutrona, C. E. (1982). Nonpsychotic postpartum depression: A review of recent research. *Clinical Psychology Review, 2,* 487–503.

Dabbs, J. M., Jr. (1992). Testosterone measurements in social and clinical psychology. *Journal of Social and Clinical Psychology, 11*(3), 302–321.

Dabbs, J. M., Jr., Alford, E. C., & Fielden, J. A. (1998). Trial lawyers and testosterone: Blue-collar talent in a white-collar world. *Journal of Applied Social Psychology, 28,* 84–94.

Dabbs, J. M., Jr., Carr, S., Frady, R., & Riad, J. (1995). Testosterone, crime, and misbehavior among 692 male prison inmates. *Personality and Individual Differences, 18,* 627–633.

Dabbs, J. M., Jr., Frady, R. L., Carr, T. S., & Besch, N. F. (1987). Saliva testosterone and criminal violence in young adult prison inmates. *Psychosomatic Medicine, 49,* 174–182.

Dabbs, J. M., Jr., & Hargrove, M. F. (1997). Age, testosterone, and behavior among female prison inmates. *Psychosomatic Medicine, 59,* 477–480.

Dabbs, J. M., Jr., Karpas, A. E., Dyomina, N., Juechter, J., & Roberts, A. (2002). Experimental raising or lowering of testosterone level affects mood in normal men and women. *Social Behavior and Personality, 30*(8), 795–806.

Dabbs, J. M., Jr., de La Rue, D., & Williams, P. M. (1990). Testosterone and occupational choice: Actors, ministers, and other men. *Journal of Personality and Social Psychology, 39*(6), 1261–1265.

Dabbs, J. M., Jr., & Morris, R. (1990). Testosterone, social class, and antisocial behavior in a sample of 4,462 men. *Psychological Science, 1*(3), 209–211.

Dabbs, J. M., Jr., Riad, J. K., & Chance, S. E. (2001). Testosterone and ruthless homicide. *Personality and Individual Differences, 31*(4), 599–603.

Dabrow, A., & Ameci, G. (1991, August). What you should know about pregnancy and the law. *Management Review,* pp. 38–40.

Dahlerup, D. (1998). Using quotas to increase women's political representation. In *Women in parliament: Beyond numbers* (chapter 4). Stockholm, Sweden: International Institute for Democracy and Electoral Assistance. Retrieved from http://www.idea.int/ women/parl/ ch4b.htm

Dalla, R. L. (2006). "You can't hustle all your life": An exploratory investigation of the exit process among street-level prostituted women. *Psychology of Women Quarterly, 30*(3), 276–290.

Dalton, H. (1989). AIDS in blackface. *Daedalus, 118,* 205–277.

Dalton, K. (1964). *The premenstrual syndrome.* Springfield, IL: Thomas.

Daly, M. (1973). *Beyond God the Father.* Boston: Beacon Press.

Dan, A. J. (1976). Patterns of behavioral and mood variations in men and women: Variability and the menstrual cycle. *Dissertation Abstracts International, 37*(6-B), 3145–3146.

Dan, A. J. (1979). The menstrual cycle and sex-related differences in cognitive variability. In M. A. Wittig & A. C. Petersen (Eds.), *Sex-related differences in cognitive functioning: Developmental issues* (pp. 241–260). New York: Academic Press.

Daniluk, J. C. (1993). The meaning and experience of female sexuality: A phenomenological analysis. *Psychology of Women Quarterly, 17,* 53–69.

Daniluk, J. C. (1998). *Womens' sexuality across the lifespan: Challenging myths, creating meanings.* New York: Guilford Press.

Dankoski, M. E., Penn, C. D., Carlson, T. D., & Hecker, L. L. (1998). What's in a name? A study of family therapists' use and acceptance of the feminist perspective. *American Journal of Family Therapy, 26,* 95–104.

Darley, J. M., & Fazio, R. H. (1980). Expectancy confirmation processes arising in the social interaction sequence. *American Psychologist, 35,* 867–881.

Darwin, C. (1967). *The descent of man.* New York: Modern Library. (Original work published 1871)

Davidson, J. K., & Moore, N. B. (1994). Masturbation and premarital sexual intercourse among college women: Making choices for sexual fulfillment. *Journal of Sex and Marital Therapy, 20,* 178–199.

Davidson, J. M. (1989). Sexual emotions, hormones, and behavior. *Advances, 6*(2), 56–58.

Davidson, L. R., & Duberman, L. (1982). Friendship: Communication and interactional patterns in same-sex dyads. *Sex Roles, 8,* 809–822.

Davies, D. R. (1989/90). The effects of gender-typed labels on children's performance. *Current Psychology: Research and Reviews, 8,* 267–272.

Davies, M. (1975). Women's place is at the typewriter: The feminization of the clerical work force. In R. C. Edwards, M. Reich, & D. Gordon (Eds.), *Labor market segmentation* (pp. 279–296). Lexington, MA: Heath.

Davies, P. G., Spencer, S. J., Quinn, D. M., & Gerhardstein, R. (2002). Consuming images: How television commercials that elicit stereotype threat can restrain women academically and professionally. *Personality and Social Psychology Bulletin, 28*(12), 1615–1628.

Davis, A. (1981). *Women, race and class.* New York: Random House.

Davis, A. J. (1984). Sex-differentiated behaviors in nonsexist picture books. *Sex Roles, 11,* 1–16.

Davis, B. M., & Gilbert, L. A. (1989). Effect of dispositional and situational influences on women's dominance expression in mixed-sex dyads. *Journal of Personality and Social Psychology, 57*(2), 294–300.

Davis, D., Shaver, P. R., & Vernon, M. L. (2003). Physical, emotional, and behavioral reactions to breaking up: The roles of gender, age, emotional involvement, and attachment style. *Personality and Social Psychology Bulletin, 29*(7), 871–884.

Davis, D. M. (1990). Portrayals of women in prime-time network television: Some demographic characteristics. *Sex Roles, 23*(5/6), 325–332.

Davis, M. D., & Kennedy, E. L. (1990). Oral history and the study of sexuality in the lesbian community: Buffalo, New York, 1940–1960. In E. C. DuBois & V. L. Ruiz (Eds.), *Unequal sisters: A multicultural reader in U.S. women's history* (pp. 387–399). New York: Routledge.

Davis, S. (1990). Men as success objects and women as sex objects: A study of personal advertisements. *Sex Roles, 23*(1/2), 43–50.

Davis, S. F., Byers, R. H., Lindegren, M. L., Caldwell, M. B., Karon, J. M., & Gwinn, M. (1995). Prevalence and incidence of vertically acquired HIV infection in the United States. *Journal of the American Medical Association, 274*(12), 952–955.

Davison, H. K., & Burke, M. J. (2000). Sex discrimination in simulated employment contexts: A meta-analytic investigation. *Journal of Vocational Behavior, 56,* 225–248.

Davydov, D. M., Shapiro, D., Goldstein, I. B., & Chicz-DeMet, A. (2005). Moods in everyday situations: Effects of menstrual cycle, work, and stress hormones. *Journal of Psychosomatic Research, 58*(4), 343–349.

Dawson, D., Hendershot, G., & Fulton, J. (1987, June 10). *Aging in the eighties: Functional limitations of individuals age 65 years and over.* Advance Data No. 133. Hyattsville, MD: National Center for Health Statistics.

Deaux, K. (1977). Sex differences. In T. Blass (Ed.), *Personality variables in social behavior* (pp. 357–378). Hillsdale, NJ: Erlbaum.

Deaux, K. (1984). From individual differences to social categories: Analysis of a decade's research on gender. *American Psychologist, 39*(2), 105–116.

Deaux, K., & Emswiller, T. (1974). Explanations of successful performance on sex-linked tasks: What's skill for the male is luck for the female. *Journal of Personality and Social Psychology, 29*, 80–85.

Deaux, K., & LaFrance, M. (1998). Gender. In D. T. Gilbert, S. T. Fiske, & G. Lindzey (Eds.), *The handbook of social psychology* (4th ed., Vol. 1, pp. 788–827). Boston: McGraw-Hill.

Deaux, K., & Lewis, L. L. (1984). Structure of gender stereotypes: Interrelationships among components and gender label. *Journal of Personality and Social Psychology, 46*(5), 991–1004.

Deaux, K., & Major, B. (1987). Putting gender into context: An interactive model of gender-related behavior. *Psychological Review, 94*(3), 369–389.

De Cecco, J. P., & Shively, M. G. (1983/84). From sexual identity to sexual relationships: A contextual shift. *Journal of Homosexuality, 9*(2/3), 1–26.

de Koninck, M. (1984). Double work and women's health. *Canada's Mental Health, 32*(3), 28–31.

de Lacoste-Utamsing, C., & Holloway, R. L. (1982). Sexual dimorphism in the human corpus callosum. *Science, 216*, 1431–1432.

Delaney, J., Lupton, M. J., & Toth, E. (1987). *The curse: A cultural history of menstruation* (rev. ed.). Urbana, IL: University of Illinois Press.

De Lisi, R., & Soundranayagam, L. (1990). The conceptual structure of sex role stereotypes in college students. *Sex Roles, 23* (11/12), 593–611.

Dellios, H. (2006, May 28). Small blow to Mexican machismo. *Arizona Daily Star*, p. A18.

Demaré, D., Briere, J., & Lips, H. M. (1988). Violent pornography and self-reported likelihood of sexual aggression. *Journal of Research in Personality, 22*, 140–153.

Demaré, D., Lips, H. M., & Briere, J. (1993). Violent pornography, anti-women attitudes, and sexual aggression: A structural equation model. *Journal of Research in Personality, 27*, 285–300.

DeNavas-Walt, C., Proctor, B. D., & Mills, R. J. (2004). *Income, poverty, and health insurance coverage in the United States: 2003*. Retrieved November 21, 2006, from http://www.census.gov/prod/2004pubs/p60-226.pdf

Denmark, F. L. (1998). Women and psychology: An international perspective. *American Psychologist, 53*(4), 465–473.

Department of Defense. (2006). *Sexual assault and prevention program report*. Retrieved August 4, 2006, from http://www.defenselink.mil/news/Mar2006/d20060316SexualAssault Report.pdf

DeSteno, D., Bartlett, M. Y., Braverman, J., & Salovey, P. (2002). Sex differences in jealousy: Evolutionary mechanism or artifact of measurement? *Journal of Personality and Social Psychology, 83*(5), 1103–1116.

Deutsch, H. (1945). *The psychology of women* (Vol. 2). New York: Grune & Stratton.

De Wolf, V. A. (1981). High school mathematics preparation and sex differences in quantitative abilities. *Psychology of Women Quarterly, 5*, 555–567.

Dexter, C. R. (1985). Women and the exercise of power in organizations: From ascribed to achieved status. In L. Larwood, A. H. Stromberg, & B. A. Gutek (Eds.), *Women and work: An annual review* (Vol. 1, pp. 239–258). Beverly Hills, CA: Sage.

Diamond, L. M. (2003a). Was it a phase? Young women's relinquishment of lesbian/bisexual identities over a 5-year period. *Journal of Personality and Social Psychology, 84*, 352–364.

Diamond, L. M. (2003b). What does sexual orientation orient? A biobehavioral model distinguishing romantic love and sexual desire. *Psychological Review, 110*(1), 173–192.

Diamond, L. M., & Savin-Williams, R. C. (2000). Explaining diversity in the development of same-sex sexuality among young women. *Journal of Social Issues, 56*(2), 297–313.

Diamond, M., & Sigmundson, H. K. (1997). Sex reassignment at birth: Long-term review and clinical implications. *Archives of Pediatric Medicine, 151*(3), 298–304.

Dickason, A. (1976). Anatomy and destiny: The role of biology in Plato's views of women. In C. C. Gould & M. W. Wartofsky (Eds.), *Women and philosophy: Toward a theory of liberation* (pp. 45–53). New York: Putnam.

Die, A. H., Debbs, T., Jr., & Walker, J. L., Jr. (1990). Managerial evaluations by men and women managers. *Journal of Social Psychology, 130*(6), 763–769.

Diekman, A. B., & Eagly, A. H. (2000). Stereotypes as dynamic constructs: Women and men of the past, present, and future. *Personality and Social Psychology Bulletin, 26*(10), 1171–1188.

Dietz, T. L. (1998). An examination of violence and gender role portrayals in video games: Implications for gender socialization and aggressive behavior. *Sex Roles, 38*(5), 425–442.

Dindia, K. (2002). Self-disclosure research: Knowledge through meta-analysis. In M. Allen & R. W. Preiss (Eds.), *Interpersonal communication research: Advances through meta-analysis* (pp. 169–185). Mahwah, NJ: Erlbaum.

Dindia, K., & Allen, M. (1992). Sex differences in self-disclosure: A meta-analysis. *Psychological Bulletin, 112*(1), 106–124.

Dinnerstein, D. (1976). *The mermaid and the minotaur: Sexual arrangements and human malaise*. New York: Harper Colophon.

DiPietro, J. A. (1981). Rough and tumble play: A function of gender. *Developmental Psychology, 17*, 50–58.

Dittmar, M. L. (1994). Relations among depression, gender, and television viewing of college students. *Journal of Social Behavior and Personality, 9*(2), 317–328.

Dobash, R. E., & Dobash, R. P. (1984). The nature and antecedents of violent events. *British Journal of Criminology, 24*, 269–288.

Dodge, H. H. (1995). Movements out of poverty among elderly widows. *Journal of Gerontology-B-Psychol-Sci-Soc-Sci, 50*(4), S240–249.

Dodson, B. (1974). *Liberating masturbation: A meditation on self love*. (Available from Bodysex Designs, P.O. Box 1933, New York, NY 10001)

Doering, C. H., Brodie, H. K. H., Kraemer, H. C., Becker, H. B., & Hamburg, D. A. (1974). Plasma testosterone levels and psychological measurements in men over a 2-month period. In R. C. Friedman, R. M. Richart, & R. L. Vande Wiele (Eds.), *Sex differences in behavior* (pp. 413–421). New York: Wiley.

Donnerstein, E. (1980). Aggressive-erotica and violence against women. *Journal of Personality and Social Psychology, 3*, 269–277.

Donnerstein, E. (1983). Erotica and human aggression. In R. Green & E. Donnerstein (Eds.), *Aggression: Theoretical and empirical reviews* (Vol. 2). New York: Academic Press.

Doty, R. L., & Silverthorne, C. (1975). Influence of the menstrual cycle on volunteering behavior. *Nature, 254,* 139–140.

Doucette, J. (1986). Violent acts against disabled women. In *The future is now* (Appendix A). Report of the conference of the Ontario Disabled Women's Network. (Available from D.A.W.N., 122 Galt Ave., Toronto, Ontario, Canada, M4M 2Z3)

Douvan, E., & Adelson, J. (1966). *The adolescent experience.* New York: Wiley.

Douvan, E., & Pleck, J. (1978). Separation as support. In R. Rapoport & R. N. Rapoport (Eds.), *Working couples* (pp. 138–146). New York: Harper Colophon.

Dovidio, J. F. E., Ellyson, S. L., Keating, C. F., Heltman, K., & Brown, C. E. (1988). The relationship of social power to visual displays of dominance between men and women. *Journal of Personality and Social Psychology, 54,* 233–242.

Downing, R. A., Crosby, F. J., & Blake-Beard, S. (2005). The perceived importance of developmental relationships on women undergraduates' pursuit of science. *Psychology of Women Quarterly, 29*(4), 419–426.

Doyal, L. (1995). *What makes women sick: Gender and the political economy of health.* New Brunswick, NJ: Rutgers University Press.

Doyle, J. A. (1995). *The male experience* (3rd ed.). Madison, WI: Brown & Benchmark.

Drory, A., & Beaty, D. (1991). Gender differences in the perception of organizational influence tactics. *Journal of Organizational Behavior, 12*(3), 249–258.

Dubinsky, K. (1985). *Lament for a "patriarchy lost"? Anti-feminism, anti-abortion, and R.E.A.L. women in Canada.* Ottawa: Canadian Research Institute for the Advancement of Women.

DuBrin, A. J. (1989). Sex differences in endorsement of influence tactics and political behavior tendencies. *Journal of Business and Psychology, 4*(1), 3–14.

Duchesne, D. (1997). *Street prostitution in Canada.* Juristat Service Bulletin 17, no. 2. Ottawa, Ontario: Canada: Canadian Center of Justice Statistics.

Duckert, F. (1989). The treatment of female problem drinkers. In Nordic Council for Alcohol and Drug Research, *Women, alcohol and drugs in the Nordic countries.* Helsinki: NAD.

Duff-Brown, B. (2003, May 18). Indian woman garners attention in dowry dispute. *The Arizona Republic,* p. A25.

Dugger, K. (1991). Social location and gender-role attitudes: A comparison of Black and White women. In J. Lorber & S. A. Farrell (Eds.), *The social construction of gender* (pp. 38–59). Newbury Park, CA: Sage.

Dukes, R. L., & Martinez, R. (1994). The impact of ethgender on self-esteem among adolescents. *Adolescence, 29*(113), 105–115.

Dumas, M. C., Calliet, L. L., Tumblin, I. G., & King, A. R. (1984). Menstrual cycle influence on alcohol consumption among Blacks. *Journal of Black Psychology, 11*(1), 9–18.

Dunkle, J. H., & Francis, P. L. (1990). The role of facial masculinity/femininity in the attribution of homosexuality. *Sex Roles, 23*(3/4), 157–167.

Durkin, K. (1985). Television and sex-role acquisition. I. Content. *British Journal of Social Psychology, 24,* 101–113.

Dutton, D. G. (1986). Wife assaulters' explanations for assault: The neutralization of self-punishment. *Canadian Journal of Behavioural Science, 18*(4), 381–390.

Dutton, D. G. (1987a). The criminal justice response to wife assault. *Law and Human Behavior, 11*(3), 189–206.

Dutton, D. G., & Strachan, C. E. (1987). Motivational needs for power and spouse-specific assertiveness in assaultive and nonassaultive men. *Violence and Victims 2*(3), 145–156.

Duxbury, L. E., & Higgins, C. A. (1991). Gender differences in work-family conflict. *Journal of Applied Psychology, 76*(1), 60–74.

Dweck, C. S. (1975). The role of expectations and attributions in the alleviation of learned helplessness. *Journal of Personality and Social Psychology, 31,* 674–685.

Dweck, C. S. (1999). *Self-theories: Their role in motivation, personality, and development.* Philadelphia, PA: Psychology Press.

Dweck, C. S., Davidson, W., Nelson, S., & Enna, B. (1978). Sex differences in learned helplessness. II. The contingencies of evaluative feedback in the classroom. III. An experimental analysis. *Developmental Psychology, 14,* 268–276.

Dweck, C. S., Goetz, T. E., & Strauss, N. L. (1980). Sex differences in learned

help-lessness IV. An experimental and naturalistic study of failure generalization and its mediators. *Journal of Personality and Social Psychology, 38,* 441–452.

Dweck, C. S., & Leggett, E. L. (1988). A social-cognitive approach to motivation and personality. *Psychological Review, 95,* 256–273.

Dye, E., & Roth, S. (1990). Psychotherapists' knowledge about and attitudes toward sexual assault victim clients. *Psychology of Women Quarterly, 14*(2), 191–212.

Eagly, A. H. (1983). Gender and social influence: A social psychological analysis. *American Psychologist, 38,* 971–981.

Eagly, A. H. (1987). *Sex differences in social behavior: A social-role interpretation.* Hillsdale, NJ: Erlbaum.

Eagly, A. H. (1995). The science and politics of comparing women and men. *American Psychologist, 50*(3), 145–158.

Eagly, A. H., & Carli, L. L. (1981). Sex of researchers and sex-typed communications as determinants of sex differences in influenceability: A meta-analysis of social influence studies. *Psychological Bulletin, 90,* 1–20.

Eagly, A. H., & Crowley, M. (1986). Gender and helping behavior: A meta-analytic review of the social psychological literature. *Psychological Bulletin, 100,* 283–308.

Eagly, A. H., & Johnson, B. T. (1990). Gender and leadership style: A meta-analysis. *Psychological Bulletin, 108,* 233–256.

Eagly, A. H., & Karau, S. J. (1991). Gender and the emergence of leaders: A meta-analysis. *Journal of Personality and Social Psychology, 60*(5), 685–710.

Eagly, A. H., Makhijani, M. G., & Klonsky, B. G. (1992). Gender and the evaluation of leaders: A meta-analysis. *Psychological Bulletin, 11*(1), 3–22.

Eagly, A. H., & Mladinic, A. (1989). Gender stereotypes and attitudes toward women and men. *Personality and Social Psychology Bulletin, 15*(4), 543–558.

Eagly, A. H., & Mladinic, A. (1994). Are people prejudiced against women? Some answers from research on attitudes, gender stereotypes, and judgments of competence. In W. Stroebe & M. Hewstone (Eds.), *European review of social psychology* (Vol. 5, pp. 1–35). New York: Wiley.

Eagly, A. H., Mladinic, A., & Otto, S. (1991). Are women evaluated more favorably than men? An analysis of attitudes, beliefs, and emotions. *Psychology of Women Quarterly, 15,* 203–216.

Eagly, A. H., & Steffen, V. J. (1984). Gender stereotypes stem from the distribution of women and men into social roles. *Journal of Personality and Social Psychology, 46*(4), 735–754.

Eagly, A. H., & Steffen, V. J. (1986). Gender and aggressive behavior: A meta-analytic review of the social psychological literature. *Psychological Bulletin, 100,* 309–330.

Eagly, A. H., & Wood, W. (1982). Inferred sex differences in status as a determinant of gender stereotypes about social influence. *Journal of Personality and Social Psychology, 43,* 915–928.

Eagly, A. H., & Wood, W. (1985). Gender and influenceability: Stereotype versus behavior. In V. O'Leary, R. Unger, & B. Wallston (Eds.), *Women, gender, and social psychology* (pp. 225–256). Hillsdale, NJ: Erlbaum.

Eagly, A. H., & Wood, W. (1991). Explaining sex differences in social behavior: A meta-analytic perspective. *Personality and Social Psychology Bulletin, 17*(3), 306–315.

Eagly, A. H., & Wood, W. (1999). The origins of sex differences in human behavior: Evolved dispositions versus social roles. *American Psychologist, 54*(6), 408–423.

Eagly, A. H., Wood, W., & Fishbaugh, L. (1981). Sex differences in conformity: Surveillance by the group as a determinant of male nonconformity. *Journal of Personality and Social Psychology, 40,* 384–394.

Eakins, B. W. & Eakins, R. G. (1978). *Sex differences in human communication.* Boston: Houghton Mifflin.

Eaton, W. O., & Enns, L. R. (1986). Sex differences in human motor activity level. *Psychological Bulletin, 100*(1), 19–28.

Eccles, J. (1985). Sex differences in achievement patterns. In T. B. Sonderegger (Ed.), *Psychology and gender. Nebraska Symposium on Motivation, 1984* (pp. 97–132). Lincoln: University of Nebraska Press.

Eccles, J. (1987). Gender roles and women's achievement-related decisions. *Psychology of Women Quarterly, 11*(2), 135–172.

Eccles, J. S. (1989). Bringing young women to math and science. In M. Crawford & M. Gentry (Eds.), *Gender and thought: Psychological perspectives* (pp. 36–58). New York: Springer-Verlag.

Eccles, J. S. (1993). School and family effects of the ontogeny of children's interests, self-perceptions, and activity choice. In J. Jacobs (Ed.), *Nebraska Symposium on Motivation: Vol. 40. Developmental perspectives on motivation* (pp. 145–208). Lincoln: University of Nebraska Press.

Eccles, J. S. (1994). Understanding women's educational and occupational choices: Applying the Eccles et al. model of achievement-related choices. *Psychology of Women Quarterly, 18*(4), 585–610.

Eccles (Parsons), J., Adler, T. F., Futterman, R., Goff, S. B., Kaczala, C. M., Meece, J. L., & Midgley, C. (1983). Expectations, values and academic behaviors. In J. T. Spence (Ed.), *Achievement and achievement motives* (pp. 75–146). San Francisco: W. H. Freeman.

Eccles, J. S., Wigfield, A., Harold, R. D., & Blumenfeld, P. (1993). Ontogeny of children's self-perceptions and subjective task values across activity domains during the early elementary school years. *Child Development, 64,* 830–847.

Edwards, C. P. (2002). Behavioral sex differences in children of diverse cultures: The case of nurturance to infants. In M. E. Pereira & L. A. Fairbanks (Eds.), *Juvenile primates: Life history, development, and behavior* (pp. 327–338). Chicago: University of Chicago Press.

Edwards, J. R., & Williams, J. E. (1980). Sex-trait stereotypes among young children and young adults: Canadian findings and cross-national comparisons. *Canadian Journal of Behavioural Science, 12,* 210–220.

Efron, R. (1990). *The decline and fall of hemispheric specialization.* Hillsdale, NJ: Erlbaum.

Ehrenreich, B. (1983). *The hearts of men: American dreams and the flight from commitment.* Garden City, NY: Anchor.

Ehrenreich, B., & English, D. (1979). *For her own good: 150 years of the experts' advice to women.* Garden City, NY: Anchor.

Ehrhardt, A. A. (1985). Gender differences: A biosocial perspective. In T. Sonderegger (Ed.), *Nebraska Symposium on Motivation: Psychology of gender* (pp. 37–57). Lincoln: University of Nebraska Press.

Ehrhardt, A. A., & Baker, S. W. (1974). Fetal androgens, human central nervous system differentiation, and behavior sex differences. In R. M. Richart & R. L. Vande Wiele (Eds.), *Sex differences in behavior* (pp. 33–52). New York: Wiley.

Ehrhardt, A. A., & Baker, S. W. (1976). *Prenatal androgens and future adolescent behavior.* Paper presented at the International Conference of Sexology, Montreal.

Eichler, M. (1983). *Sexism in research and its policy implications.* Ottawa: Canadian Research Institute for the Advancement of Women.

Eichler, M., & Lapointe, J. (1985). *On the treatment of the sexes in research.* Ottawa: Social Sciences and Humanities Research Council of Canada.

Eichstedt, J. A., Serbin, L. A., Poulin-Dubois, D., & Sen, M. G. (2002). Of bears and men: Infants' knowledge of conventional and metaphorical gender stereotypes. *Infant Behavior and Development, 25*(3), 296–310.

Eisenberg, M. (2001). Differences in sexual risk behaviors between college students with same-sex and opposite-sex experience: Results from a national survey. *Archives of Sexual Behavior, 30*(6), 575–589.

Eisenberg, N., Fabes, R., & Shea, C. (1989). Gender differences in empathy and prosocial moral reasoning: Empirical investigations. In M. M. Brabeck (Ed.), *Who cares? Theory, research, and educational implications of the ethic of care* (pp. 127–143). New York: Praeger.

Eisenberg, N., & Lennon, R. (1983). Sex differences in empathy and related capacities. *Psychological Bulletin, 94*(1), 100–131.

Eisenberg, N., Miller, P. A., Shell, R., McNalley, S., & Shea, C. (1991). Prosocial development in adolescence: A longitudinal study. *Developmental Psychology, 27*(5), 849–857.

Eisenstock, B. (1984). Sex-role differences in children's identification with counterstereotypic televised portrayals. *Sex Roles, 10,* 417–430.

Eisler, R. M. (1995). The relationship between masculine gender role stress and men's health risk: The validation of a construct. In R. F. Levant & W. S. Pollack (Eds.), *A new psychology of men* (pp. 207–225). New York: Basic Books.

Eisler, R. M., & Skidmore, J. R. (1987). Masculine gender role stress: Scale development and component factors in the appraisal of stressful situations. *Behavior Modification, 11*(2), 123–136.

Eldridge, N. S., & Gilbert, L. A. (1990). Correlates of relationship satisfaction in lesbian couples. *Psychology of Women Quarterly, 14*(1), 43–62.

Elias, M. (1981). Serum cortisol, testosterone and testosterone-binding globulin responses to competitive fighting in human males. *Aggressive Behavior, 7*, 215–224.

Eliason, M. J. (1995). Accounts of sexual identity formation in heterosexual students. *Sex Roles, 32*(11/12), 821–834.

Eliason, M. J., Donelan, C., & Randall, C. (1992). Lesbian stereotypes. *Health Care for Women International, 13*(2), 131–144.

Elliott, E. S., & Dweck, C. S. (1988). Goals: An approach to motivation and achievement. *Journal of Personality and Social Psychology, 54*, 5–12.

Ellis, L. (1982). Developmental androgen fluctuations and the dimensions of mammalian sex (with emphasis upon the behavioral dimension and the human species). *Ethology and Sociobiology, 3*, 171–179.

Ellis, L., & Ames, M. A. (1987). Neurohormonal functioning and sexual orientation. *Psychological Bulletin, 101*(2), 233–258.

Ellis, L., Burke, D., & Ames, M. A. (1987). Sexual orientation as a continuous variable: A comparison between the sexes. *Archives of Sexual Behavior, 16*(6), 523–529.

Ellsberg, M., Caldera, T., Herrera, A., Winkvist, A., & Kullgren, G. (1999). Domestic violence and emotional distress among Nicaraguan women. *American Psychologist, 54*(1), 30–36.

Ellyson, S. L., Dovidio, J. F., & Fehr, B. J. (1981). Visual behavior and dominance in women and men. In C. Mayo & N. M. Henley (Eds.), *Gender and nonverbal behavior* (pp. 63–79). New York: Springer-Verlag.

Elmelech, Y., & Lu, H-H. (2003). *Race, eth-nicity, and the gender-poverty gap.* Economics Working Paper # 351, Levy Economics Institute. Retrieved from http://ideas.repec.org/p/lev/wrkpap/351.html

Else-Quest, N. M., Hyde, J. S., Goldsmith, H. H., & Van Hulle, C. A. (2006). Gender differences in temperament: A meta-analysis. *Psychological Bulletin, 132*(1), 33–72.

Elsesser, K., & Peplau, L. A. (2006). The glass partition: Obstacles to cross-sex friendships at work. *Human Relations, 59*(8), 1077–1100.

Elsner, C. W., Buster, J. E., Schindler, R. A., Nessim, S. A., & Abraham, G. E. (1980). Bromocriptine in the treatment of premenstrual tension syndrome. *Obstetrics and Gynecology, 56*, 723–726.

Elstad, J. I. (1996). Inequalities in health related to women's marital, parental, and employment status: A comparison between the early 70s and the late 80s, Norway. *Social Science and Medicine, 42*(1), 75–89.

Enman, C. (2000, November 28). Men don't seem to listen? Well, they only use half a brain. *Ottawa Citizen*, pp. A1, A2.

Entwisle, D. R., & Baker, D. P. (1983). Gender and young children's expectations for performance in arithmetic. *Developmental Psychology, 19*(2), 200–209.

Epstein, C. F. (1983, April). The new total woman. *Working Woman*, pp. 100–103.

Erchull, M. J., Chrisler, J. C., Gorman, J. A., & Johnston-Robledo, I. (2002). Education and advertising: A content analysis of commercially produced books about menstruation. *Journal of Early Adolescence, 22*(4), 455–474.

Erikson, E. (1950). *Childhood and society.* New York: Norton.

Eron, L. D., Huesmann, L. R., Brice, P., Fischer, P., & Mermelstein, R. (1983). Age trends in the development of aggression, sex typing, and related television habits. *Sex Roles, 19*(1), 71–77.

Espín, O. M. (1987). Issues of identity in the psychology of Latina lesbians. In The Boston Lesbian Psychologies Collective (Eds.), *Lesbian psychologies* (pp. 35–55). Urbana, IL: University of Illinois Press.

Espín, O. M. (1997). *Latina realities: Essays on healing, migration, and sexuality.* Boulder, CO: Westview.

Etaugh, C. (1974). Effects of maternal employment on children: A review of recent research. *Merrill Palmer Quarterly, 20*, 71–98.

Etaugh, C., & Kasley, H. C. (1981). Evaluating competence: Effects of sex, marital status, and parental status. *Psychology of Women Quarterly, 6*, 196–203.

Ethington, C. A., & Wolfle, L. M. (1984). Sex differences in a causal model of mathematics achievement. *Journal for Research in Mathematics Education, 15*, 361–377.

European Professional Women's Network. (2006). *Second bi-annual European PWN board women monitor 2006.* Retrieved November 10, 2006, from http://www.aipbw.no/Attachment/060610%20BoardWomenPressReleaseFINAL!!without%20embargo1.doc

Evans, E. M., Schweingruber, H., & Stevenson, H. W. (2002). Gender differences in interest and knowledge acquisition: The United States, Taiwan, and Japan. *Sex Roles, 47*(3–4), 153–167.

Eyler, D. R., & Baridon, A. P. (1992, Winter). Managing sexual attraction in the workplace. *Business Quarterly*, pp. 19–26.

Ezell, H. F., Odewahn, C. A., & Sherman, J. D. (1981). The effects of having been supervised by a woman on perceptions of female managerial competence. *Personnel Psychology, 34*(2), 291–299.

Fabes, R. A., & Martin, C. L. (1991). Gender and age stereotypes of emotionality. *Personality and Social Psychology Bulletin, 17*(5), 532–540.

Faderman, L. (1981). *Surpassing the love of men: Romantic friendship between women from the Renaissance to the present.* New York: Morrow.

Fagot, B. I. (1984). Teacher and peer reactions to boys' and girls' play styles. *Sex Roles, 11*, 691–702.

Fagot, B. I. (1985). Beyond the reinforcement principle: Another step toward understanding sex role development. *Developmental Psychology, 21*(6), 1097–1104.

Fagot, B. I., & Hagan, R. (1985). Aggression in toddlers: Responses to the assertive acts of boys and girls. *Sex Roles, 12*(3/4), 341–351.

Fagot, B. I., & Leinbach, M. D. (1993). Gender-role development in young children: From discrimination to labeling. *Developmental Review, 13*, 205–224.

Fairchild, S. R. (2002). Women with disabilities: The long road to equality. *Journal of Human Behavior in the Social Environment, 6*(2), 13–28.

Fairhurst, G. T. (1985). Male–female communication on the job: Literature review and commentary. In M. McLaughlin (Ed.), *Communication yearbook* (Vol. 9, pp. 83–115). Beverly Hills, CA: Sage.

Fairweather, H. (1976). Sex differences in cognition. *Cognition, 4*, 231–280.

Fairweather, H., & Hutt, S. J. (1972). Sex differences in a perceptual motor skill in children. In C. Ounsted & D. C. Taylor (Eds.), *Gender differences: Their ontogeny and significance.* Edinburgh: Churchill Livingstone.

Falbo, T., & Peplau, L. A. (1980). Power strategies in intimate relationships. *Journal of Personality and Social Psychology, 38,* 618–628.

Falk, P. (1989). Lesbian mothers: Psychosocial assumptions in family law. *American Psychologist, 44,* 941–947.

Fallon, A. E., & Rozin, P. (1985). Sex differences in perceptions of desirable body shape. *Journal of Abnormal Psychology, 94*(1), 102–105.

Fannin, N., & Dabbs, J. M., Jr. (2003). Testosterone and the work of firefighters: Fighting fires and delivering medical care. *Journal of Research in Personality, 37*(2), 107–115.

Farley, J. (1980). Worklife problems for both women and men. In D. A. Neugarten & J. M. Shafritz (Eds.), *Sexuality in organizations: Romantic and coercive behaviors at work* (pp. 29–37). Oak Park, IL: Moore.

Farris, A. (1978). Commuting. In R. Rapoport & R. N. Rapoport (Eds.), *Working couples* (pp. 100–107). New York: Harper Colophon.

Fassinger, R. E., & Richie, B. S. (1997). Sex matters: Gender and sexual orientation in training for multicultural competency. In D. B. Pope-Davis & H. I. K. Coleman (Eds.), *Multicultural counseling competencies: Assessment, education and training, and supervision* (pp. 83–110). Thousand Oaks, CA: Sage.

Fausto-Sterling, A. (1992). *Myths of gender* (rev. ed.). New York: Basic Books.

Favreau, O. E. (1977). Sex bias in psychological research. *Canadian Psychological Review, 18*(1), 56–65.

Favreau, O. E. (1993). Do the Ns justify the means? Null hypothesis testing applied to sex and other differences. *Canadian Psychology, 34*(1), 64–78.

Feather, N. T. (2004). Value correlates of ambivalent attitudes toward gender relations. *Personality and Social Psychology Bulletin, 30*(1), 3–12.

Federal Bureau of Investigation. (2001). *Crime in the United States 2001.* Washington, DC: U.S. Government Printing Office.

Fedigan, L. M. (1982). *Primate paradigms: Sex roles and social bonds.* Montreal: Eden Press.

Feeney, J. A., Hohaus, L., Noller, P., & Alexander, R. P. (2001). *Becoming parents: Exploring the bonds between mothers, fathers, and their infants.* New York: Cambridge University Press.

Fehr, B. (2004). Intimacy expectations in same-sex friendships: A prototype interaction-pattern model. *Journal of Personality and Social Psychology, 86*(2), 265–284.

Feingold, A. (1988). Cognitive gender differences are disappearing. *American Psychologist, 43*(2), 95–103.

Feingold, A. (1990). Gender differences in effects of physical attractiveness on romantic attraction: A comparison across five research paradigms. *Journal of Personality and Social Psychology, 59*(5), 981–993.

Feingold, A. (1993). Cognitive gender differences: A developmental perspective. *Sex Roles, 29*(1/2), 91–112.

Feingold, A. (1994a). Gender differences in personality: A meta-analysis. *Psychological Bulletin, 116*(3), 429–456.

Feingold, A. (1994b). Gender differences in variability in intellectual abilities: A cross-cultural perspective. *Sex Roles, 30*(1/2), 81–92.

Feldman, S. S., & Nash, S. C. (1978). Interest in babies during young adulthood. *Child Development, 49,* 617–622.

Feldman, S. S., Nash, S. C., & Cutrona, C. (1977). The influence of age and sex on responsiveness to babies. *Developmental Psychology, 13,* 675–676.

Felmlee, D. H. (1995). Causes and consequences of women's employment discontinuity, 1967–1973. *Work and Occupations, 22*(2), 167–187.

Fenelon, J., & Megargee, E. (1971). Influence of race on the manifestation of leadership. *Journal of Applied Psychology, 55,* 353–358.

Fennema, E., Peterson, P. L., Carpenter, T. P., & Lubinski, C. A. (1990). Teachers' attitudes and beliefs about girls, boys, and mathematics. *Educational Studies in Mathematics, 21,* 55–69.

Fennema, E., & Sherman, J. (1977). Sex-related differences in mathematics achievement, spatial visualization and affective factors. *American Educational Research Journal, 14,* 51–71.

Fidell, L. S. (1982). Gender and drug use and abuse. In I. Al-Issa (Ed.), *Gender and psychopathology* (pp. 221–236). New York: Academic Press.

Field, T., Sandberg, D., Garcia, R., Vega-Lahr, N., Goldstein, S., & Guy, L. (1985). Pregnancy problems, postpartum depression, and early mother-infant interaction. *Developmental Psychology, 21*(6), 1152–1156.

Fielden, J., Lutter, C., & Dabbs, J. (1994). *Basking in glory: Testosterone changes in World Cup soccer fans.* Psychology Department, Georgia State University.

Filardo, E. K. (1996). Gender patterns in African American and White adolescents' social interactions in same-race, mixed-gender groups. *Journal of Personality and Social Psychology, 71*(1), 71–81.

Fine, M. (1991, March). *Women with disabilities.* Paper presented at the national conference of the Association for Women in Psychology, Hartford, CT.

Finer, L. B., & Henshaw, S. K. (2006). *Estimates of U.S. abortion incidence, 2001–2003.* Retrieved August 25, 2006, from http://www.guttmacher.org/pubs/2006/08/03/ab_incidence.pdf

Fink, D. (1983, April 19). The sexes agree more about sex. *USA Today,* pp. 1D–2D.

Finkelhor, D. (1986). *A sourcebook on child sexual abuse.* Beverly Hills, CA: Sage.

Finn, J. D. (1980). Sex differences in educational outcomes: A cross-national study. *Sex Roles, 6,* 9–26.

Fischbein, S. (1990). Biosocial influences on sex differences for ability and achievement test results as well as marks at school. *Intelligence, 14*(1), 127–139.

Fishbein, J. (1988, December). Teenage girls know about AIDS, but don't act accordingly. *The Nation's Health, 18*(12).

Fisher, B. S., Cullen, F. T., & Turner, M. G. (2000). *The sexual victimization of college women.* Washington, DC: U.S. Department of Justice, National Institute of Justice and Bureau of Justice Statistics.

Fisher, T. D., Pollack, R. H., & Malatesta, V. J. (1986). Orgasmic latency and subjective ratings of erotic stimuli in male and female subjects. *Journal of Sex Research, 22,* 85–93.

Fishman, P. M. (1978). Interaction: The work women do. *Social Problems, 25,* 397–406.

Fisk, W. R. (1985). Responses to "neutral" pronoun presentations and the development of sex-biased responding. *Developmental Psychology, 21*(3), 481–485.

Fiske, S. T., & Glick, P. (1995). Ambivalence and stereotypes cause sexual harassment: A theory with implications for organizational change. *Journal of Social Issues, 51*(1), 97–115.

Fitch, R. H., & Denenberg, V. H. (1998). A role for ovarian hormones in sexual differentiation of the brain. *Behavioral and Brain Sciences, 21,* 311–352.

Fitzgerald, L. F. (1980). Nontraditional occupations: Not for women only. *Journal of Counseling Psychology, 27,* 252–259.

Fitzgerald, L. F., & Cherpas, C. C. (1985). On the reciprocal relationship between gender and occupation: Rethinking the assumptions concerning masculine career development. *Journal of Vocational Behavior, 27,* 109–122.

Flaks, D. K., Ficher, I., Masterpasqua, F., & Joseph, G. (1995). Lesbians choosing motherhood: A comparative study of lesbian and heterosexual parents and their children. *Developmental Psychology, 31*(1), 105–114.

Fleischer, R. A., & Chertkoff, J. M. (1986). Effects of dominance and sex on leader selection in dyadic work groups. *Journal of Personality and Social Psychology, 50*(1), 94–99.

Fleming, J. (1982). Fear of success in Black male and female graduate students: A pilot study. *Psychology of Women Quarterly, 6*(3), 327–341.

Fleming, J. (1983a). Black women in Black and White college environments: The making of a matriarch. *Journal of Social Issues, 39*(3), 41–54.

Fletcher, K. (2006). Beyond dualism: Leading out of oppression. *Nursing Forum, 41*(2), 50–59.

Flexner, A. (1914). *Prostitution in Europe.* New York: Century.

Flicker, E. (2003). Between brains and breasts—women scientists in fiction film: On the marginalization and sexualization of scientific competence. *Public Understanding of Science, 12*(3), 307–318.

Floge, L., & Merrill, D. M. (1986). Tokenism reconsidered: Male nurses and female physicians in a hospital setting. *Social Forces, 64*(4), 925–947.

Flugstad, K. D. (2002, April). Decision-making in abortion: Men's experiences. *Dissertation Abstracts International: Section B: The Sciences and Engineering.* 62(9-B), 4217.

Fogel, R., & Paludi, M. A. (1984). Fear of success and failure, or norms for achievement? *Sex Roles, 10,* 431–443.

Foot, H. C., Chapman, A. J., & Smith, J. R. (1977). Friendship and social responsiveness in boys and girls. *Journal of Personality and Social Psychology, 35,* 401–411.

Forbes, G. B., Adams-Curtis, L. E., Rade, B., & Jaberg, P. (2001). Body dissatisfaction in women and men: The role of gender-typing and self-esteem. *Sex Roles, 44*(7–8), 461–484.

Forbes, G. B., Adams-Curtis, L., Jobe, R. L., White, K. B., Revak, J., Zivcic-Becirevic, I., et al. (2005). Body dissatisfaction in college women and their mothers: Cohort effects, developmental effects, and the influences of body size, sexism, and the thin body ideal. *Sex Roles, 53*(3), 281–298.

Ford, M. R., & Lowery, C. R. (1986). Gender differences in moral reasoning: A comparison of the use of justice and care orientations. *Journal of Personality and Social Psychology, 50*(4), 777–783.

Foushee, H. C., Davis, M. H., & Archer, R. L. (1979). Empathy, masculinity, and femininity. *JSAS Catalogue of Selected Documents in Psychology, 9,* 85 (Ms. no. 1974).

Foushee, H. C., Helmreich, R. L., & Spence, J. T. (1979). Implicit theories of masculinity and femininity: Dualistic or bipolar? *Psychology of Women Quarterly, 3,* 259–269.

Fouts, G. T., & Burggraf, K. K. (1999). Television situation comedies: Female body images and verbal reinforcements. *Sex Roles, 40,* 473–481.

Fouts, G. T., & Vaughan, K. (2002). Television situation comedies: Male weight, negative references, and audience reactions. *Sex Roles, 46*(11/12), 439–442.

Fowers, B. J. (1991). His and her marriage: A multivariate study of gender and marital satisfaction. *Sex Roles, 24*(3/4), 209–221.

Fox, J. A., & Zawitz, M. W. (2001). *Homicide trends in the United States.* Washington, DC: U.S. Department of Justice, Bureau of Justice Statistics.

Fox, J. A., & Zavitz, M. W. (2006). *Homicide trends in the United States.* Retrieved September 12, 2006, from http://www.ojp.usdoj.gov/bis/homicide/homtrnd.htm

Fox, L. H. (1981). *The problem of women and mathematics.* New York: Ford Foundation.

Fox, M., Gibbs, M., & Auerbach, D. (1985). Age and gender dimensions of friendship. *Psychology of Women Quarterly, 9,* 489–502.

Franceschi, S., Dal Maso, L., La Vecchia, C., Negri, E., & Serraino, D. (1994). AIDS incidence rates in Europe and the United States. *AIDS, 8*(8), 1173–1177.

Francis, B. (2002). Is the future really female? The impact and implications of gender for 14–16 year olds' career choices. *Journal of Education and Work, 15*(1), 75–88.

Frank, E., Brogan, D. & Schiffman, M. (1998). Prevalence and correlates of harassment among U.S. women physicians. *Archives of Internal Medicine, 158,* 352–358.

Frank, R. T. (1931). The hormonal causes of premenstrual tension. *Archives of Neurological Psychiatry, 26,* 1053.

Frankel, L. (2002). "I've never thought about it": Contradictions and taboos surrounding American males' experiences of first ejaculation (semenarche). *Journal of Men's Studies, 11*(1), 37–54.

Frankel, M. T., & Rollins, H. A., Jr. (1983). Does Mother know best? Mothers and fathers interacting with preschool sons and daughters. *Developmental Psychology, 19*(5), 694–702.

Franken, M. (1983). Sex role expectations in children's vocational aspirations and perceptions of occupations. *Psychology of Women Quarterly, 8,* 59–68.

Franklin, C. W., II. (1984). *The changing definition of masculinity.* New York: Plenum.

Franklin, C. W., II. (1988). *Men and society.* Chicago: Nelson-Hall.

Franklin, U. M. (1985). *Will women change technology or will technology change women?* Ottawa: Canadian Research Institute for the Advancement of Women.

Franzoi, S. L., Anderson, J., & Frommelt, S. (1990). Individual differences in men's perceptions of and reactions to thinning hair. *Journal of Social Psychology, 130*(2), 209–218.

Frayne, S. M., Skinner, K. M., Lin, H., Ash, A. S., & Freund, K. M. (2004). Effect of patient gender on late-life depression management. *Journal of Women's Health, 13*(8), 919–925.

Frazier, P. A., Cochran, C. C., & Olson, A. M. (1995). Social science research on lay definitions of sexual harassment. *Journal of Social Issues, 51*(1), 21–38.

Fredricks, J. A., & Eccles, J. S. (2002). Children's competence and value beliefs from childhood through adolescence:

Growth trajectories in two male-sex-typed domains. *Developmental Psychology, 38*(4), 519–533.

Fredrickson, B. L., Roberts, T., Noll, S. M., Quinn, D. M., & Twenge, J. M. (1998). That swimsuit becomes you: Sex differences in self-objectification, restrained eating, and math performance. *Journal of Personality and Social Psychology, 75*(1), 269–284.

Freedman, S. A., & Lips, H. M. (1996). A response latency investigation of the gender schema. In R. Crandall, (ed.), Handbook of gender research [Special issues]. *Journal of Social Behavior and Personality, 11*(5), 41–53.

Freedman, S. A., & Lips, H. M. (2002). Harsh judgements and sharp impressions: Audience response to participants in a study of heterosexual feminist identities. *Feminism and Psychology, 12*(2), 275–281.

Freeman, E. W., Rickels, K., Sondheimer, S. J., & Polansky, M. (1990, July 18). Ineffectiveness of progesterone suppository treatment for premenstrual syndrome. *Journal of the American Medical Association, 264*(3), 349–353.

Freeman, J. (1989). The legal revolution. In J. Freeman (Ed.), *Women: A feminist perspective* (4th edition, pp. 371–394). Mountain View, CA: Mayfield.

French, J. R. P., Jr., & Raven, B. H. (1959). The bases of social power. In D. Cartwright (Ed.), *Studies in social power* (pp. 150–167). Ann Arbor: University of Michigan Press.

Freud, S. (1960). *A general introduction to psychoanalysis.* (J. Riviere, Trans.). New York: Washington Square Press. (Original work published 1924)

Freud, S. (1961). *Letters of Sigmund Freud, 1873–1939.* (E. L. Freud, Ed.). London: Hogarth Press.

Freud, S. (1974). Some psychical consequences of the anatomical distinction between the sexes. In J. Strachey (Ed. and Trans.), *The standard edition of the complete psychological works of Sigmund Freud* (Vol. 19, pp. 241–260). London: Hogarth Press and the Institute of Psycho-Analysis. (Original work published 1925)

Frey, K. A. (1981). Middle-aged women's experience and perceptions of menopause. *Women and Health, 6*(1/2), 25–36.

Fried, R., & Major, B. (1980). *Self-presentation of sex-role attributes to attractive others.*

Paper presented at the meeting of the Eastern Psychological Association, Hartford, CT.

Friedan, B. (1963). *The feminine mystique.* New York: Dell.

Friedan, B. (1981). *The second stage.* New York: Summit Books.

Friederich, M. A. (1983). Dysmenorrhea. *Women and Health, 8*(2/3), 91–106.

Friedman, H. S., Tucker, J. S., Schwartz, J. E., Tomlinson-Keasey, C., Martin, L. R., Wingard, D. L., & Criqui, M. H. (1995). Psychosocial and behavioral predictors of longevity: The aging and death of the "Termites." *American Psychologist, 50*(2), 69–78.

Friedman, L. (1989). Mathematics and the gender gap: A meta-analysis of recent studies on sex differences in mathematical tasks. *Review of Educational Research, 59*(2), 185–213.

Friedman, R. C., Hurt, S. W., Aronff, M. S., & Clarkin, J. (1980). Behavior and the menstrual cycle. *Signs: Journal of Women in Culture and Society, 5,* 719–738.

Frieze, I. H. (1979). Perceptions of battered wives. In I. H. Frieze, D. Bar-Tal, & J. S. Carroll (Eds.), *New approaches to social problems: Applications of attribution theory* (pp. 79–108). San Francisco: Jossey-Bass.

Frieze, I. H. (1986, August). *The female victim: Rape, wife battering, and incest.* American Psychological Association Master Lecture, presented at the annual meeting of the American Psychological Association, Washington, DC.

Frodi, A., & Lamb, M. (1978). Sex differences in responsiveness to infants: A developmental study of psychophysiological and behavioral responses. *Child Development, 49,* 1182–1188.

Frodi, A., Macaulay, J., & Thome, P. R. (1977). Are women always less aggressive than men? A review of the experimental literature. *Psychological Bulletin, 84,* 634–660.

Fromm, E. (1973). *The anatomy of human destructiveness.* Greenwich, CT: Fawcett.

Frost, N., Greene, J., & Pranis, K. (2006). *The punitiveness report: Hard hit: The growth in the imprisonment of women, 1977–2004.* Retrieved November 29, 2006, from http://www.wpaonline.org/institute/hardhit/index.htm

Frueh, T., & McGhee, P. (1975). Traditional sex role development and amount of time spent watching television. *Developmental Psychology, 11,* 109.

Fujita, F., Diener, E., & Sandvik, E. (1991). Gender differences in negative affect and well-being: The case for emotional intensity. *Journal of Personality and Social Psychology, 61*(3), 427–434.

Fulton, E. K. (1991, September 2). Rape and the court. *Maclean's,* p. 45.

Fulton, S. A., & Sabornie, E. J. (1994). Evidence of employment inequality among females with disabilities. *Journal of Special Education, 28*(2), 149–165.

Funk and Wagnalls Corporation. (1994). *The world almanac and book of facts: 1995.* New York: St. Martin's.

Furey, E. M. (1994). Sexual abuse of adults with mental retardation: Who and where. *Mental Retardation, 32*(3), 173–180.

Furomoto, L., & Scarborough, E. (1986). Placing women in the history of psychology: The first women psychologists. *American Psychologist, 4*(1), 35–42.

Gaddis, A., & Brooks-Gunn, J. (1985). The male experience of pubertal change. *Journal of Youth and Adolescence, 14*(1), 61–69.

Gage, J. D., & Kirk, R. (2002). First-time fathers: Perceptions of preparedness for fatherhood. *Canadian Journal of Nursing Research, 34*(4), 15–24.

Gallagher, S. K., & Gerstel, N. (1993). Kin keeping and friend keeping among older women: The effect of marriage. *Gerontologist, 33*(5), 675–681.

Gammell, D. J., & Stoppard, J. M. (1999). Women's experiences of treatment of depression: Medicalization or empowerment? *Canadian Psychology, 40*(2), 112–128.

Ganahl, D. J., Prinsen, T. J., & Netzley, S. B. (2003). A content analysis of prime time commercials: A contextual framework of gender representation. *Sex Roles, 49*(9), 545–551.

Gannon, L., & Ekstrom, B. (1993). Attitudes toward menopause: The influence of sociocultural paradigms. *Psychology of Women Quarterly, 17*(3), 275–288.

Garfinkle, E. M., & Morin, S. F. (1978). Psychotherapists' attitudes toward homosexual psychotherapy clients. *Journal of Social Issues, 34*(3), 101–112.

Garner, P. W., & Estep, K. M. (2001). Empathy and emotional expressivity. In J. Worrell (Ed.), *Encyclopedia of women and gender* (pp. 391–402). San Diego: Academic Press.

Garrison, D. (1981). Karen Horney and feminism. *Signs: Journal of Women in Culture and Society, 6*(4), 672–691.

Gartrell, N., Deck, A., Rodas, C., Peyser, H., & Banks, A. (2005). The national lesbian family study: 4. Interviews with the 10-year-old children. *American Journal of Orthopsychiatry, 75*(4), 518–524.

Gastil, J. (1990). Generic pronouns and sexist language: The oxymoronic character of masculine generics. *Sex Roles, 23*(11), 629–643.

Gavey, N., & McPhillips, K. (1999). Subject to romance: Heterosexual passivity as an obstacle to women initiating condom use. *Psychology of Women Quarterly, 23*(2), 349–368.

Geffner, D. S., & Hochberg, I. (1971). Ear laterality performance of children from low and middle socioeconomic levels on a verbal dichotic listening task. *Cortex, 7,* 193–203.

Geiger, B., Fischer, M., & Eshet, Y. (2004). Date-rape-supporting and victim-blaming attitudes among high school students in a multiethnic society: Israel. *Journal of Interpersonal Violence, 19*(4), 406–426.

Gelb, S. A. (1989). Language and the problem of male salience in early childhood classroom environments. *Early Childhood Research Quarterly, 4*(2), 205–215.

General Accounting Office. (2000). *Gender equity: Men's and women's participation in higher education.* Report to the Ranking Minority Member, Subcommittee on Criminal Justice, Drug Policy and Human Resources, Committee on Government Reform, House of Representatives. Retrieved from http://www.gao.gov

Gerber, G. L. (1984). Attribution of feminine and masculine traits to opposite sex dyads. *Psychological Reports, 55*(3), 907–918.

Gerdes, E. P., & Garber, D. M. (1983). Sex bias in hiring: Effects of job demands and applicant competence. *Sex Roles, 9*(3), 307–319.

Gervasio, A. H., & Crawford, M. (1989). Social evaluations of assertiveness: A critique and speech act reformulation. *Psychology of Women Quarterly, 13*(1), 1–26.

Geschwind, N., & Behan, P. (1982). Left-handedness: Association with immune disease, migraine, and developmental learning disorder. *Proceedings of the National Academy of Sciences, 79,* 5097–5100.

Geschwind, N., & Galaburda, A. M. (1985). Cerebral lateralization: Biological mechanisms, associations, and pathology. I. A hypothesis and a program for research. *Archives of Neurology, 42,* 428–459.

Gibbs, M., Auerbach, D., & Fox, M. (1980). A comparison of male and female same-sex friendships. *International Journal of Women's Studies, 3*(3), 261–272.

Gibson, R., Aust, C. F., & Zillman, D. (2000). Loneliness of adolescents and their choice and enjoyment of love-celebrating versus love-lamenting popular music. *Empirical Studies of the Arts, 18*(1), 43–48.

Gilbert, L. A., & Kearney, L. K. (2006). The psychotherapeutic relationship as a positive and powerful resource for girls and women. In J. Worrell & C. D. Goodheart (Eds.), *Handbook of girls' and women's psychological health* (pp. 229–238). New York: Oxford University Press.

Gilbert, L. A., Lee, R. N., & Chiddix, S. (1981). Influence of presenter's gender on students' evaluations of presenters discussing sex fairness in counseling: An analogue study. *Journal of Counseling Psychology, 28,* 258–264.

Gilligan, C. (1982). *In a different voice: Psychological theory and women's development.* Cambridge, MA: Harvard University Press.

Gilligan, C. (1990). Teaching Shakespeare's sister: Notes from the underground of female adolescence. In C. Gilligan, N. P. Lyons, & T. J. Hanmer (Eds.), *Making connections* (pp. 6–29). Cambridge, MA: Harvard University Press.

Gilligan, C., & Attanucci, J. (1988). Two moral orientations: Gender differences and similarities. *Merrill Palmer Quarterly, 34*(3), 223–237.

Ginorio, A. B., Gutiérrez, L., Cauce, A. M., & Acosta, M. (1995). Psychological issues for Latinas. In H. Landrine (Ed.), *Bringing cultural diversity to feminist psychology: Theory, research, practice* (pp. 241–263). Washington, DC: American Psychological Association.

Ginorio, A., & Huston, M. (2001). *Si, se puede!/Yes, they can: Latinas in school.* Washington, DC: American Association of University Women.

Ginsburg, F. (1996, January 26). The anthropology of abortion activism. *Chronicle of Higher Education,* p. A48.

Girl Scouts of the USA. (2002). *The net effect: Girls and the new media. Executive summary.* New York: Author.

Gjerdingen, D. K., Froberg, D. G., & Kochevar, L. (1991). Changes in women's mental and physical health from pregnancy through six months postpartum. *Journal of Family Practice, 32*(2), 161–166.

Gladue, B. A., Boechler, M., & McCaul, K. D. (1989). Hormonal response to competition in human males. *Aggressive Behavior, 15,* 409–422.

Gladue, B. A., & Delaney, H. J. (1990). Gender differences in perception of attractiveness of men and women in bars. *Personality and Social Psychology Bulletin, 16*(2), 378–391.

Gladwell, M. (1990, November 26). Public health experts turn to economic ills. *Washington Post,* p. A3.

Glass, J., & Fujimoto, T. (1994, June). Housework, paid work, and depression among husbands and wives. *Journal of Health and Social Behavior, 35,* 179–191.

Glass ceiling remains a tough one for women to crack. (2006, April 9). *Roanoke Times,* pp. 1, 4.

Glassner, B. (1989). Men and muscles. In M. S. Kimmel & M. A. Messner (Eds.), *Men's lives* (pp. 310–320). New York: Macmillan.

Glick, P. (1991). Trait-based and sex-based discrimination in occupational prestige, occupational salary, and hiring. *Sex Roles, 25*(5/6), 351–378.

Glick, P., Diebold, J., Bailey-Werner, B., & Zhu, L. (1997). The two faces of Adam: Ambivalent sexism and attitudes toward women. *Personality and Social Psychology Bulletin, 32*(12), 1323–1334.

Glick, P., & Fiske, S. T. (1997). Hostile and benevolent sexism: Measuring ambivalent sexist attitudes toward women. *Psychology of Women Quarterly, 21*(1), 119–135.

Glick, P., & Fiske, S. T. (1999). The Ambivalence toward Men Inventory: Differentiating hostile and benevolent beliefs about men. *Psychology of Women Quarterly, 23*(3), 519–536.

Glick, P., Lameiras, M., Fiske, S. T., Eckes, T., Masser, B., Volpato, C., et al. (2004). Bad but bold: Ambivalent attitudes toward men predict gender inequality in 16 nations. *Journal of Personality and Social Psychology, 86*(5), 713–728.

Glick, P., Wilk, K., & Perreault, M. (1995). Images of occupations: Components of gender and status in occupational stereotypes. *Sex Roles, 32*(9/10), 565–582.

Go, C. G., Brustrom, J. E., Lynch, M. F., & Aldwin, C. M. (1995). Ethnic trends in survival curves and mortality. *Gerontologist, 35*(3), 318–326.

Goh, S. C. (1991). Sex differences in perceptions of interpersonal work style, career emphasis, supervisory mentoring behavior, and job satisfaction. *Sex Roles, 24*(11/12), 701–710.

Gold, A. R., & Adams, D. B. (1981). Motivational factors affecting fluctuations of female sexual activity at menstruation. *Psychology of Women Quarterly, 5,* 670–680.

Gold, D., Crombie, G., & Noble, S. (1987). Relations between teachers' judgments of girls' and boys' compliance and intellectual competence. *Sex Roles, 16*(7/8), 351–358.

Gold, R. (1981). Women entering the labor force draw attention to reproductive hazards for both sexes. *Family Planning/ Population Reporter, 10*(1), 10–13.

Goldberg, D. C., Wipple, B., Fishkin, R. E., Waxman, H., Fink, P. J., & Weisberg, M. (1983). The Grafenberg spot and female ejaculation: A review of initial hypotheses. *Journal of Sex and Marital Therapy, 9,* 27–37.

Goldberg, P. H. (1968). Are women prejudiced against women? *Trans-action, 5,* 28–30.

Golden, C. (1987). Diversity and variability in women's sexual identities. In The Boston Lesbian Psychologies Collective (Eds.), *Lesbian psychologies* (pp. 18–34). Urbana, IL: University of Illinois Press.

Golding, J. M. (1988). Gender differences in depressive symptoms. *Psychology of Women Quarterly, 12*(1), 61–74.

Golding, J. M. (1990). Division of household labor, strain, and depressive symptoms among Mexican Americans and non-Hispanic Whites. *Psychology of Women Quarterly, 14,* 103–117.

Golub, S. (1976). The effect of premenstrual anxiety and depression on cognitive function. *Journal of Personality and Social Psychology, 34,* 99–104.

Golub, S. (1983). Menarche: The beginning of menstrual life. *Women and Health, 8*(2/3), 17–36.

Golub, S., & Catalano, J. (1983). Recollections of menarche and women's subsequent experiences with menstruation. *Women and Health, 8,* 49–61.

Gomberg, E. S. L. (1982). Historical and political perspective: Women and drug use. *Journal of Social Issues, 38*(2), 9–23.

Gonsiorek, J. C., Sell, R. L., & Weinrich, J. D. (1995). Definition and measurement of sexual orientation. *Suicide and Life-Threatening Behavior, 25*(Suppl.), 40–51.

Good, P. R., & Smith, B. D. (1980). Menstrual distress and sex-role attributes. *Psychology of Women Quarterly, 4,* 482–491.

Goodchilds, J. D. (1979). Power: A matter of mechanics? *Society for the Advancement of Social Psychology Newsletter, 5*(3), 3.

Gooden, A. M., & Gooden, M. A. (2001). Gender representation in notable children's picture books: 1995–1999. *Sex Roles, 45*(1), 89–101.

Goodman, E. (1999, May 30). TV arrived in Fiji in 1995, and the islands' women changed forever. *Arizona Daily Star,* p. F2.

Goodyear, R. K. (1990). Gender configurations in supervisory dyads: Their relation to supervisee influence strategies and skill evaluations of the supervisee. *Clinical Supervisor, 8*(2), 67–79.

Gooren, L. (1990). The endocrinology of transsexualism: A review and commentary. *Psychoneuroendocrinology, 15,* 3–14.

Gordon, H. W., & Lee, P. A. (1986). A relationship between gonadotropins and visuospatial function. *Neuropsychologia, 24*(4), 563–576.

Gottfried, A. E., & Gottfried, A. W. (1988). *Maternal employment and children's development.* New York: Plenum.

Gouchie, C., & Kimura, D. (1991). The relationship between testosterone levels and cognitive ability patterns. *Psychoneuroendocrinology, 16,* 323–334.

Gould, R. M. (1973). Measuring masculinity by the size of a paycheck. *Ms., 1*(12), 18–21.

Gould, S. (1981). *The mismeasure of man.* New York: Norton.

Goy, R. W. (1968). Organizing effects of androgen on the behavior of rhesus monkeys. In R. P. Michael (Ed.), *Endocrinology and human behaviour* (pp. 12–31). London: Oxford University Press.

Goy, R. W. (1970). Experimental control of psychosexuality. In G. W. Harris & R. G. Edwards (Eds.), *A discussion on the determination of sex.* London: Philosophical Transactions of the Royal Society.

Graham, C. A., Janssen, E., & Sanders, S. A. (2000). *Psychophysiology, 37*(1), 76–84.

Graham, K., Wilsnack, R., Dawson, D., & Vogeltanz, N. (1998). Should alcohol consumption measures be adjusted for gender differences? *Addiction, 93*(8), 1137–1147.

Gralewski, C., & Rodgon, M. M. (1980). Effect of social and intellectual instruction on achievement motivation

as a function of role orientation. *Sex Roles, 6,* 301–309.

Grant, L. (1984). Black females' "place" in desegregated classrooms. *Sociology of Education, 57,* 98–111.

Grant, M. J., Button, C. M., Hannah, T. E., & Ross, A. S. (2002). Uncovering the multidimensional nature of stereotype inferences: A within-participants study of gender, age, and physical attractiveness. *Current Research in Social Psychology, 8*(2), 19–39.

Gravenkemper, S. A., & Paludi, M. A. (1983). Fear of success revisited: Introducing an ambiguous cue. *Sex Roles, 9,* 897–900.

Gray, C. (1997). Tackling the mid-life crisis. *British Medical Journal, 315,* 2–3.

Gray-Little, B., & Burks, N. (1983). Power and satisfaction in marriage: A review and critique. *Psychological Bulletin, 93,* 513–538.

Grayson, J. P. (1983). The effects of a plant closure on the stress levels and health of workers' wives: A preliminary analysis. *Journal of Business Ethics, 2,* 221–225.

Green, D. H., & Zenisek, T. J. (1983). Dual career couples: Individual and organizational implications. *Journal of Business Ethics, 2,* 171–184.

Green, R. (1974). *Sexual identity conflict in children and adults.* Baltimore: Penguin Books.

Greene, B. (1994a). African American women. In L. Comas-Díaz & B. Greene (Eds.), *Women of color: Integrating ethnic and gender identities in psychotherapy* (pp. 10–29). New York: Guilford Press.

Greene, B. (1994b). Lesbian women of color: Triple jeopardy. In L. Comas-Díaz & B. Greene (Eds.), *Women of color: Integrating ethnic and gender identities in psychotherapy* (pp. 389–427). New York: Guilford Press.

Greenfeld, L. A., & Snell, T. L. (1999). *Women offenders.* Bureau of Justice Statistics Special Report (NCJ 175688). Washington, DC: U.S. Department of Justice.

Greenglass, E. R. (1976). *After abortion.* Toronto: Longman Canada.

Greenspan, M. (1983). *A new approach to women and therapy.* New York: McGraw-Hill.

Greenwald, A. G., & Farnham, S. D. (2000). Using the Implicit Association Test to measure self-esteem and self-concept. *Journal of Personality and Social Psychology, 79*(6), 1022–1038.

Griffitt, W. (1987). Females, males, and sexual responses. In K. Kelley (Ed.), *Females, males and sexuality* (pp. 156–173). Albany: State University of New York Press.

Grimes, J. M., Ricci, L. A., & Melloni, R. H., Jr. (2006). Plasticity in anterior hypothalamic vasopressin correlates with aggression during anabolic-androgenic steroid withdrawal in hamsters. *Behavioral Neuroscience, 120*(1), 115–124.

Grimsley, K. D. (1996, February 28). From the top: The women's view. *Washington Post,* pp. C1, C4.

Grodstein, F., Manson, J. E., & Stampfer, M. J. (2001, July). Postmenopausal hormone use and secondary prevention of coronary events in the Nurses' Health Study. *Annals of Internal Medicine, 135,* 1–8.

Gross, E. F. (2004). Adolescent Internet use: What we expect, what teens report. *Journal of Applied Developmental Psychology, 25*(6), 633–649.

Gross, H. E. (1980). Dual-career couples who live apart: Two types. *Journal of Marriage and the Family, 42,* 567–576.

Grossman, F. K., Eichler, L. S., & Winickoff, S. A. (1980). *Pregnancy, birth, and parenthood.* San Francisco: Jossey-Bass.

Grossman, K., Kindler, H., & Strasser, K. (2003, April). *Father support during early childhood: Effects on their adolescents' representation of attachment and partnership.* Paper presented at the biennial meeting of the Society for Research in Child Development, Tampa, FL.

Grote, N. K., Naylor, K. E., & Clark, M. S. (2002). Perceiving the division of family work to be unfair: Do social comparisons, enjoyment, and competence matter? *Journal of Family Psychology, 16*(4), 510–522.

Guadagno, R. E., & Cialdini, R. B. (2002). Online persuasion: An examination of gender differences in computer-mediated interpersonal influence. *Group Dynamics: Theory, Research, & Practice, 6*(1), 38–51.

Gump, L. S., Baker, R. C., & Roll, S. (2000). Cultural and gender differences in moral judgment: A study of Mexian Americans and Anglo-Americans. *Hispanic Journal of Behavioral Sciences, 22*(1), 78–93.

Gupta, A. (1991). Gender stereotypes and self-concepts in college students. *Psychological Studies, 36*(3), 180–186.

Gurwitz, S. B., & Dodge, K. A. (1975). Adults' evaluation of a child as a function of sex of adult and sex of child. *Journal of Personality and Social Psychology, 32,* 822–828.

Gutek, B., & Nakamura, C. (1983). Gender roles and sexuality in the world of work. In E. R. Allgeier & N. B. McCormick (Eds.), *Changing boundaries: Gender roles and sexual behavior* (pp. 182–201). Palo Alto, CA: Mayfield.

Gutek, B. A., & O'Connor, M. (1995). The empirical basis for the reasonable woman standard. *Journal of Social Issues, 51*(1), 151–166.

Guthrie, R. V. (1976). *Even the rat was white: An historical view of psychology.* New York: Harper & Row.

Gutierres, S. E., Kenrick, D. T., & Goldberg, L. (1983, August). *Adverse effect of popular erotica on judgments of one's mate.* Paper presented at the meeting of the American Psychological Association, Anaheim, CA.

Gutmann, D. (1972). Ego psychological and developmental approaches to the "retirement crisis" in men. In F. M. Carp (Ed.), *Retirement* (pp. 267–305). New York: Behavioral Publications.

Haddock, G., & Zanna, M. P. (1994). Preferring "housewives" to "feminists." Categorization and the favorability of attitudes toward women. *Psychology of Women Quarterly, 18*(1), 25–52.

Haefner, J. E. (1977). Sources of discrimination among employees: A survey investigation. *Journal of Applied Psychology, 62*(3), 265–270.

Haerenstam, A., & Bejerot, E. (2001). Combining professional work with family responsibilities—A burden or a blessing? *International Journal of Social Welfare, 10*(3), 202–214.

Halbreich, U., & Karkun, S. (2006). Cross-cultural and social diversity of prevalence of postpartum depression and depressive symptoms. *Journal of Affective Disorders, 91*(2), 97–111.

Hall, J. A. (1978). Gender effects in decoding nonverbal cues. *Psychological Bulletin, 85,* 845–875.

Hall, J. A. (1984). *Nonverbal sex differences: Communication accuracy and expressive style.* Baltimore: Johns Hopkins University Press.

Hall, J. A., Coats, E. J., & LeBeau, L. S. (2005). Nonverbal behavior and the vertical dimension of social relations: A meta-analysis. *Psychological Bulletin, 131*(6), 898–924.

Halpern, D. F. (1992). *Sex differences in cognitive abilities* (2nd ed.). Hillsdale, NJ: Erlbaum.

Halpern, D. F. (1997). Sex differences in intelligence: Implications for education. *American Psychologist, 52,* 1091–1102.

Halpern, D. F. (2005). Psychology at the intersection of work and family: Recommendations for employers, working families, and policymakers. *American Psychologist, 60*(5), 397–409.

Hamburg, D. A., Moos, R. H., & Yalom, I. D. (1968). Studies of distress in the menstrual cycle and the postpartum period. In R. P. Michael (Ed.), *Endocrinology and human behaviour* (pp. 94–116). London: Oxford University Press.

Hamilton, B. E., Martin, J. A., & Sutton, P. D. (2004). *Births: Preliminary date for 2003.* Retrieved July 31, 2006, from http://www.cdc.gov/nchs/data/nvsr/nvsr53/nvsr53_09.pdf

Hamilton, D. L. (1979). A cognitive-attributional analysis of stereotyping. *Advances in Experimental Psychology, 12,* 53–81.

Hamilton, J. A., & Gallant, S. J. (1990). Problematic aspects of diagnosing premenstrual phase dysphoria: Recommendations for psychological research and practice. *Professional Psychology Research and Practice, 2*(1), 60–68.

Hamilton, J. A., Gallant, S. A., & Lloyd, C. (1989). Evidence for a menstrual-linked artifact in determining rates of depression. *Journal of Nervous and Mental Disease, 177*(6), 359–365.

Hamilton, M. C. (2001). Sex-related difference research: Personality. In J. Worrell (Ed.), *Encyclopedia of women and gender* (pp. 973–981). San Diego: Academic Press.

Hamilton, R. (1985). Feminists in the academy: Intellectuals or political subversives? *Queen's Quarterly, 92*(1), 3–20.

Hammond, D., & Dingley, J. (1989). Sex differences in career preferences of lower sixth formers in Belfast grammar schools. *Journal of Occupational Psychology, 62,* 263–264.

Hampson, E. (1990a). Estrogen-related variations in human spatial and articulatory-motor skills. *Psychoneuroendocrinology, 15*(2), 97–111.

Hampson, E. (1990b). Variations in sex-related cognitive abilities across the menstrual cycle. *Brain and Cognition, 14*(1), 26–43.

Hampson, J. L., & Hampson, J. G. (1961). The ontogenesis of sexual behavior in man. In W. C. Young (Ed.), *Sex and internal secretions* (Vol. 1, pp. 1401–1432). Baltimore: Williams and Wilkins.

Hampson, E., & Moffat, S. D. (2004). The psychobiology of gender: Cognitive effects of reproductive hormones in the adult nervous system. In A. H. Eagly, A. E. Beall & R. J. Sternberg (Eds.), *The psychology of gender* (2nd ed., pp. 38–64). New York: Guilford Press.

Hansen, C. H., & Hansen, R. D. (1988). How rock music videos can change what is seen when boy meets girl: Priming stereotypic appraisal of social interactions. *Sex Roles, 19,* 287–316.

Harding, J. J. (1989). Postpartum psychiatric disorders: A review. *Comprehensive Psychiatry, 30,* 109–112.

Hardman, A. E., & Hudson, A. (1994). Brisk walking and serum lipid and lipoprotein variables in previously sedentary women: Effect of 12 weeks of regular brisk walking followed by 12 weeks of detraining. *British Journal of Sports Medicine, 28*(4), 261–266.

Hare-Mustin, R. (1983). An appraisal of the relationship between women and psychotherapy: 80 years after the case of Dora. *American Psychologist, 38,* 593–601.

Hare-Mustin, R. T., & Maracek, J. (1990). Gender and the meaning of difference: Postmodernism and psychology. In R. T. Hare-Mustin & J. Maracek (Eds.), *Making a difference: Psychology and the construction of gender* (pp. 22–64). New Haven, CT: Yale University Press.

Hargie, O. D., Tourish, D., & Curtis, L. (2001). Gender, religion, and adolescent patterns of self-disclosure in the divided society of Northern Ireland. *Adolescence, 36,* 665–679.

Hargreaves, D. J., Bates, H. M., & Foot, J. M. C. (1985). Sex-typed labelling affects task performance. *British Journal of Social Psychology, 24,* 153–155.

Harris, B. (1979). Careers, conflict, and children. In A. Roland & B. Harris (Eds.), *Career and motherhood* (pp. 55–86). New York: Human Sciences Press.

Harris, J. F. (1991, October 19). Va. to drop its ban on gay bars. *Washington Post,* p. C1.

Harris, J. R. (1995). Where is the child's environment? A group socialization theory of development. *Psychological Review, 102*(3), 458–489.

Harris, L. J. (1992). Left-handedness. In I. Rapin & S. J. Segalowitz (Eds.), *Handbook of neuropsychology* (pp. 145–208). Amsterdam: Elsevier Science.

Harris, S. M. (1993). The influence of personal and family factors on achievement needs and concerns of African-American and Euro-American college women. *Sex Roles, 29*(9/10), 671–689.

Harris, S. M. (1995). Family, self, and sociocultural contributions to body-image attitudes of African-American women. *Psychology of Women Quarterly, 19*(1), 129–145.

Harrison, J. (1978). Warning: The male sex role may be dangerous to your health. *Journal of Social Issues, 34*(1), 65–86.

Harry, B., & Balcer, C. M. (1987). Menstruation and crime: A critical review of the literature from the clinical criminology perspective. *Behavioral Sciences and the Law, 5*(3), 307–321.

Hartung, C. M., & Widiger, T. A. (1998). Gender differences in the diagnosis of mental disorders: Conclusions and controversies of the DSM-IV. *Psychological Bulletin, 123*(3), 260–278.

Hartup, W. W. (1983). The peer system. In P. Mussen & E. Heatherington (Eds.), *Handbook of child psychology* (4th ed., Vol. 4, pp. 103–196). New York: Wiley.

Harvey, E. (1999). Short-term and long-term effects of early parental employment on children of the National Longitudinal Survey of Youth. *Developmental Psychology, 35*(2), 445–459.

Harvie, K., Marshal-McCaskey, J., & Johnston, L. (1998). Gender-based biases in occupational hiring decisions. *Journal of Applied Social Psychology, 28*(18), 1698–1711.

Haslam, D. M., Pakenham, K. I., & Smith, A. (2006). Social support and postpartum depressive symptomatology: The mediating role of maternal self-efficacy. *Infant Mental Health Journal, 27*(3), 276–291.

Haslam, N., & Levy, S. R. (2006). Essentialist beliefs about homosexuality: Structure and implications for prejudice. *Personality and Social Psychology Bulletin, 32*(4), 471–485.

Hatcher, R. A., Trussell, J., Stewart, F., Stewart, G., et al. (1994). *Contraceptive technology.* New York: Irvington.

Hatfield, E., Sprecher, S., Pillemer, J. T., & Greenberger, D. (1988). Gender differences in what is desired in the sexual relationship. *Journal of Psychology and Human Sexuality, 1*(2), 39–52.

Hausmann, M., Becker, C., Gather, U., & Guentuerkuen, O. (2002). Functional cerebral asymmetries during the menstrual cycle: A cross-sectional and longitudinal analysis. *Neuropsychologia, 40*(7), 808–816.

Havemann, J. (1999, April 29). Birth rate of teens is down. *Washington Post,* p. A3.

Hawkins, R. S., & Hart, A. D. (2003). The use of thermal biofeedback in the treatment of pain associated with endometriosis: Preliminary findings. *Applied Psychophysiology and Biofeedback, 28*(4), 279–289.

Hayes, F. (2002, February 18). Girls warm up to IT. *Computerworld,* p. 62.

Hayes, J. A., & Mahalik, J. R. (2000). Gender role conflict and psychological distress in male counseling center clients. *Psychology of Men and Masculinity, 1*(2), 116–125.

Hazzard, W. R. (1986). Biological basis of the sex differential in longevity. *Journal of the American Geriatric Society, 34*(6), 455–471.

Healey, S. (1993). The common agenda between old women, women with disabilities and all women. *Women and Therapy, 14*(3/4), 65–77.

Hebl, M. R. & Mannix, L. M. (2003). The weight of obesity in evaluating others: A mere proximity effect. *Personality and Social Psychology Bulletin, 29*(1), 28–38.

Hedges, L. V., & Nowell, A. (1995). Sex differences in mental test scores, variability, and numbers of high-scoring individuals. *Science, 269*(5220), 41–45.

Heilbrun, A. B., Jr. (1984). Sex-based models of androgyny: A further cognitive elaboration of competence differences. *Journal of Personality and Social Psychology, 46,* 216–229.

Heilbrun, C. (1973). *Toward a recognition of androgyny.* New York: Harper & Row.

Heilman, M. E. (2001). Description and prescription: How gender stereotypes prevent women's ascent up the organizational ladder. *Journal of Social Issues, 57*(4), 657–674.

Heilman, M. E., Martell, R. F., & Simon, M. C. (1988). The vagaries of sex bias: Conditions regulating the undervaluation, equivaluation, and overvaluation of female job applicants. *Organizational Behavior and Human Decision Processes, 41,* 98–110.

Heilman, M. E., Simon, M. C., & Repper, D. P. (1987). Intentionally favored, unintentionally harmed? Impact of sex-based preferential selection on self-perception and self-evaluations. *Journal of Applied Psychology, 72*(1), 62–68.

Heilman, M. E., Wallen, A. S., Fuchs, D., & Tamkins, M. M. (2004). Penalties for success: Reactions to women who succeed at male gender-typed tasks. *Journal of Applied Psychology, 89*(3), 416–427.

Heiman, J. R. (1977). A psychophysiological exploration of sexual arousal patterns in females and males. *Psychophysiology, 14*, 266–274.

Heise, L., Pitanguy, J., & Germain, A. (1993). *Violence against women: The hidden health burden.* Washington, DC: World Bank.

Heiser, P., & Gannon, L. (1984). The relationship of sex-role stereotypes to anger expression and the report of psychosomatic symptoms. *Sex Roles, 10*, 601–611.

Helfrich, C. A., & Simpson, E. K. (2006). Improving services for lesbian clients: What do domestic violence agencies need to do? *Health Care for Women International, 27*(4), 344–361.

Helms, J. E. (Ed.). (1993). *Black and White racial identity: Theory, research, and practice.* Westport, CT: Praeger.

Helson, R., & Mitchell, V. (1990). Women's prime of life: Is it the fifties? *Psychology of Women Quarterly, 14*, 451–470.

Helson, R., & Picano, J. (1990). Is the traditional role bad for women? *Journal of Personality and Social Psychology, 59*(2), 311–320.

Hendrick, S., Hendrick, C., Slapion-Foote, M. J., & Foote, F. H. (1985). Gender differences in sexual attitudes. *Journal of Personality and Social Psychology, 48*(6), 1630–1642.

Henley, N. (1973). Power, sex and nonverbal communication. *Berkeley Journal of Sociology, 18*, 1–26.

Henley, N. (1977). *Body politics: Power, sex, and nonverbal communication.* Englewood Cliffs, NJ: Prentice-Hall.

Henley, N., & Freeman, J. (1995). The sexual politics of interpersonal behavior. In J. Freeman (Ed.), *Women: A feminist perspective* (5th ed., pp. 79–91). Mountain View, CA: Mayfield.

Hennig, M., & Jardim, A. (1977). *The managerial woman.* New York: Doubleday.

Henshaw, S. K. (2003, May). *U.S. teenage pregnancy statistics, with comparative statistics for women aged 20–24.* Alan Guttmacher Institute. Retrieved from

http://www.guttmacher.org/pubs/teen_stats.html

Hepburn, C. (1985). Memory for the frequency of sex-typed versus neutral behaviors: Implications for the maintenance of sex stereotypes. *Sex Roles, 12*(7/8), 771–776.

Herdt, G. (1989). Introduction: Gay and lesbian youth, emergent identities, and cultural scenes at home and abroad. In G. Herdt (Ed.), *Gay and lesbian youth* (pp. 1–42). New York: Harrington Park Press.

Herek, G. M. (1988). Heterosexuals' attitudes toward lesbians and gay men: Correlates and gender differences. *Journal of Sex Research, 25*(4), 451–477.

Herek, G. M. (1993). Documenting prejudice against lesbians and gay men on campus: The Yale sexual orientation survey. *Journal of Homosexuality, 25*(4), 15–28.

Herek, G. M. (2000a). The psychology of sexual prejudice. *Current Directions in Psychological Science, 9*, 19–22.

Herek, G. M. (2000b). Sexual prejudice and gender: Do heterosexuals' attitudes toward lesbians and gay men differ? *Journal of Social Issues, 56*(2), 251–266.

Herek, G. M. (2006). Legal recognition of same-sex relationships in the United States: A social science perspective. *American Psychologist, 61*(6), 607–621.

Herman, J. L. (1981). *Father-daughter incest.* Cambridge, MA: Harvard University Press.

Herrera, R. S., & DelCampo, R. L. (1995). Beyond the superwoman syndrome: Work satisfaction and family functioning among working-class, Mexican American women. *Hispanic Journal of Behavioral Sciences, 17*(1), 49–60.

Herring, S., & Reitan, R. M. (1984, August). *Sex similarities in neuropsychological sequelae of lateralized cerebral lesions.* Paper presented at the meeting of the American Psychological Association, Toronto, Ontario.

Herrmann, D. J., Crawford, M., & Holdsworth, M. (1992). Gender-linked differences in everyday memory performance. *British Journal of Psychology, 83*(2), 221–231.

Herscher, E. (1999, January 15). Health Institute confirms need for lesbian studies/ Doctors in the dark about gay women's medical needs. *San Francisco Chronicle,* p. A2.

Herzog, A., & Detre, T. (1976). Psychotic reactions associated with childbirth. *Diseases of the Nervous System, 37*, 229–235.

Hibbard, J. H., & Pope, C. R. (1993). The quality of social roles as predictors of morbidity and mortality. *Social Science and Medicine, 36*(3), 217–225.

Hibbeln, J. R. (2002). Seafood consumption, the DHA content of mothers' milk and prevalence rates of postpartum depression: A cross-national ecological analysis. *Journal of Affective Disorders, 69*(1–3), 15–29.

Hill, C. T., Rubin, Z., & Peplau, L. A. (1976). Breakups before marriage: The end of 103 affairs. *Journal of Social Issues, 32*, 147–168.

Hill, S. A. (2002). Teaching and doing gender in African American families. *Sex Roles, 47*(11/12), 493–506.

Hines, M. (1990). Gonadal hormones and human cognitive development. In J. Balthazart (Ed.), *Hormones, brain and behavior in vertebrates. Vol. 1. Sexual differentiation, neuroanatomical aspects, neurotransmitters and neuropeptides* (pp. 51–63). Basel: Karger.

Hines, M. (1998). Adult testosterone levels have little or no influence on dominance in men. *Behavioral and Brain Sciences, 21*, 377–378.

Hines, M. (2004). Androgen, estrogen, and gender: Contributions of the early hormone environment to gender-related behavior. In A. H. Eagley, A. E. Beall, & R. J. Sternberg (Eds.), *The psychology of gender* (2nd ed., pp. 9–37). New York: Guilford Press.

Hines, M., Golombok, S., Rust, J., Johnston, K. J., Golding, J., & Avon Longitudinal Study of Parents and Children Study Team. (2002). Testosterone during pregnancy and gender role behavior of preschool children: A longitudinal, population study. *Child Development, 73*(6), 1678–1687.

Hines, M., & Shipley, C. (1984). Prenatal exposure to diethylstilbestrol (DES) and the development of sexually dimorphic cognitive abilities and cerebral lateralization. *Developmental Psychology, 20*(1), 81–94.

Hirsch, K. (1990, September/October). Fraternities of fear. *Ms., 1*(2), 52–56.

Hiscock, M., Inch, R., Jacek, C., Hiscock-Kalil, C., & Kalil, K. M. (1994). Is there a sex difference in human laterality? I. An exhaustive survey of auditory laterality studies from six neuropsychology journals. *Journal of Clinical and Experimental Neuropsychology, 16,* 423–435.

Hiscock, M., Israelian, M., Inch, R., Jacek, C., & Hiscock-Kalil, C. (1995). Is there a sex difference in human laterality? II. An exhaustive survey of visual laterality studies from six neuropsychology journals. *Journal of Clinical and Experimental Neuropsychology, 17,* 590–610.

Hite, S. (1976). *The Hite report.* New York: Macmillan.

Hite, S. (1981). *The Hite report on male sexuality.* New York: Knopf.

Hochleitner, M. (2000). Coronary heart disease: Sexual bias in referral for coronary angiogram: How does it work in a state-run system? *Journal of Women's Health and Gender Based Medicine, 9,* 29–34.

Hofferth, S. L., & Anderson, K. G. (2003). Are all dads equal? Biology versus marriage as a basis for paternal investment. *Journal of Marriage and the Family, 65*(1), 213–232.

Hoffman, J. C. (1982). Biorhythms in human reproduction: The not-so-steady states. *Signs: Journal of Women in Culture and Society, 7*(4), 829–844.

Hoffman, L. W. (1972). Early childhood experiences and women's achievement motives. *Journal of Social Issues, 29*(2), 120–155.

Hoffman, L. W. (1974). Effects of maternal employment on the child: A review of the research. *Developmental Psychology, 10,* 204–228.

Hoffman, L. W., & Kloska, D. D. (1995). Parents' gender-based attitudes toward marital roles and child rearing: Development and validation of new measures. *Sex Roles, 32*(5/6), 273–295.

Hoffman, P. (2003, August). Chess queen. *Smithsonian Magazine, 34*(5), 73–79.

Hoffmann, M., Hammar, M., Kjellgren, K. I., Lindh-Åstrand, L., & Brynhildsen, J. (2005). Changes in women's attitudes towards and use of hormone therapy after HERS and WHI. *Maturitas, 52*(1), 11–17.

Hoffnung, M. (1995). Motherhood: Contemporary conflict for women. In J. Freeman (Ed.), *Women: A feminist perspective* (5th ed., pp. 162–181). Mountain View, CA: Mayfield.

Hoffnung, M. (2004). Wanting it all: Career, marriage, and motherhood during college-educated women's 20s. *Sex Roles, 50*(9), 711–723.

Hofman, M. A., & Swaab, D. F. (1989). The sexual dimorphic nucleus of the preoptic area in the human brain: A comparative morphometric study. *Journal of Anatomy, 164,* 55–72.

Hofmann, S. G., Suvak, M., & Litz, B. T. (2006). Sex differences in face recognition and influence of facial affect. *Personality and Individual Differences, 40*(8), 1683–1690.

Hohman, M. M., & Hagan, C. B. (2001). Satisfaction with surrogate mothering: A relational model. *Journal of Human Behavior in the Social Environment, 4*(1), 61–84.

Hokanson, J. E., & Edelman, R. (1966). Effects of three social responses on vascular processes. *Journal of Personality and Social Psychology, 3,* 442–447.

Hokanson, J. E., Willers, K. R., & Koropsak, E. (1968). The modification of autonomic responses during aggressive interchange. *Journal of Personality, 36,* 386–404.

Hollingworth, L. (1914). *Functional periodicity: An experimental study of the mental and motor abilities of women during menstruation.* New York: Teachers College, Columbia University.

Hollingworth, L. (1916). Sex differences in mental traits. *Psychological Bulletin, 13,* 377–385.

Hollingworth, L. (1918). Comparison of the sexes in mental traits. *Psychological Bulletin, 25,* 427–432.

Hollingworth, L. (1922). Differential action upon the sexes of forces which tend to segregate the feebleminded. *Journal of Abnormal Psychology and Social Psychology, 17,* 35–57.

Hollingworth, L., & Montague, H. (1914). The comparative variability of the sexes at birth. *American Journal of Sociology, 20,* 335–370.

Holtzworth-Munroe, A., & Stuart, G. L. (1994). Typologies of male batterers: Three subtypes and the differences among them. *Psychological Bulletin, 116*(3), 476–497.

Homans, G. C. (1974). *Social behavior: The elementary forms.* New York: Harcourt Brace Jovanovich.

Hong, J., & Seltzer, M. M. (1995). The psychological consequences of multiple roles: The non-normative case. *Journal of Health and Social Behavior, 36,* 386–398.

Hooker, E. (1993). Reflections of a 40-year exploration: A scientific view on homosexuality. *American Psychologist, 48*(4), 450–453.

Hopcroft, R. L. (2002). Is gender still a status characteristic? *Current Research in Social Psychology, 7*(20), 339–347.

Hope, J. R. (2003). *Pinstripes and pearls: The women of the Harvard Law class of '64 who forged an old-girl network and paved the way for future generations.* New York: Scribner.

Hopkins, H. R., & Klein, H. A. (1993). Multidimensional self-perception: Linkages to parental nurturance. *Journal of Genetic Psychology, 154*(4), 165–173.

Hopkins, J., Marcues, M., & Campbell, S. B. (1984). Postpartum depression: A critical review. *Psychological Bulletin, 95,* 498–515.

Horne, S. (1999). Domestic violence in Russia. *American Psychologist, 54*(1), 55–61.

Horner, M. (1968). *Sex differences in achievement motivation and performance in competitive and noncompetitive situations.* Unpublished doctoral dissertation, University of Michigan.

Horner, M. (1970). Femininity and successful achievement: A basic inconsistency. In J. Bardwick, E. Douvan, M. Horner, & D. Guttman (Eds.), *Feminine personality and conflict* (pp. 45–76). Pacific Grove, CA: Brooks/Cole.

Horney, K. (1939). *The neurotic personality of our time.* New York: Norton.

Horney, K. (1973). The flight from womanhood. In J. B. Miller (Ed.), *Psychoanalysis and women* (pp. 5–20). Baltimore: Penguin Books. (Original work published 1926)

Horowitz, M. J., Schaefer, C., & Cooney, P. (1974). Life event scaling for recency of experience. In E. K. E. Gunderson & R. H. Rahe (Eds.), *Life stress and illness* (pp. 125–133). Springfield, IL: Charles C. Thomas.

Hort, B. E., Fagot, B. I., & Leinbach, M. D. (1990). Are people's notions of maleness more stereotypically framed than their notions of femaleness? *Sex Roles, 23*(3/4), 197–212.

Horwitz, E. L. (1990, October). For your health's sake. *AAUW Outlook,* p. 5.

Hossain, Z., & Roopnarine, J. L. (1993). Division of household labor and child care in dual-earner African-American families with infants. *Sex Roles, 29*(9/10), 571–583.

Houston, M. (1991, May 7). Girls opt for pink ghetto. *Winnipeg Free Press,* pp. 1, 4.

Howard, J. A., Blumstein, P., & Schwartz, P. (1986). Sex, power, and influence tactics in intimate relationships. *Journal of Personality and Social Psychology, 51*(1), 102–109.

Howes, C., & Phillipsen, L. (1992). Gender and friendship: Relationships within peer groups of young children. *Social Development, 1*(3), 230–242.

Hoyenga, K. B., & Hoyenga, K. T. (1993). *Gender-related differences: Origins and outcomes.* Boston: Allyn & Bacon.

Hrdy, S. B. (1981). *The woman that never evolved.* Cambridge, MA: Harvard University Press.

Hrdy, S. B. (1999). *Mother nature: Maternal instincts and how they shape the human species.* New York: Ballantine Books.

Hsu, L. K. G. (1987). Are the eating disorders becoming more common in Blacks? *International Journal of Eating Disorders, 6,* 113–124.

Huang, J. (1993). An investigation of gender differences in cognitive abilities among Chinese high school students. *Personality and Individual Differences, 15*(6), 717–719.

Hubbard, R. (1990). *The politics of women's biology.* New Brunswick, NJ: Rutgers University Press.

Huddy, L., & Capelos, T. (2002). Gender stereotyping and candidate evaluation. In V. C. Ottati, R. S. Tindale, & J. Edwards (Eds.), *The social psychology of politics* (pp. 29–53). New York: Kluwer.

Huerta, M., Cortina, L. M., Pang, J. S., Torges, C. M., & Magley, V. J. (2006). Sex and power in the academy: Modeling sexual harassment in the lives of college women. *Personality and Social Psychology Bulletin, 32*(5), 616–628.

Hudgens, G. A., Fatkin, L. T., Billingsley, P. A., & Mazurczak, J. (1988). Hand steadiness: Effects of sex, menstrual phase, oral contraceptives, practice, and handgun weight. *Human Factors, 30*(1), 51–60.

Huesmann, L. R., Guerra, N. G., Zelli, A., & Miller, L. (1992). Differing normative beliefs about aggression for boys and girls. In K. Bjorkqvist & P. Niemela (Eds.), *Of mice and women: Aspects of female aggression* (pp. 77–87). New York: Academic Press.

Humphreys, A. P., & Smith, P. K. (1987). Rough and tumble friendship and dominance in school children: Evidence for continuity and change with age in middle childhood. *Child Development, 58,* 201–212.

Hunt, M. (1974). *Sexual behavior in the 1970s.* Chicago: Playboy Press.

Hunter, M. S. (1990). Psychological and somatic experiences of the menopause: A prospective study. *Psychosomatic Medicine, 52,* 357–367.

Huston, A. C., Greer, D., Wright, J. C., Welch, R., & Ross, R. (1984). Children's comprehension of televised formal features with masculine and feminine connotations. *Developmental Psychology, 20*(4), 707–716.

Huston, T. L., & Ashmore, R. D. (1986). Women and men in personal relationships. In R. D. Ashmore & F. K. Del Boca (Eds.), *The social psychology of female-male relations* (pp. 167–210). Orlando, FL: Academic Press.

Huston, T. L., McHale, S. M., & Crouter, A. C. (1986). When the honeymoon is over: Changes in the marriage relationship over the first year. In R. Gilmour & S. Duck (Eds.), *The emerging field of personal relationships* (pp. 109–132). Hillsdale, NJ: Erlbaum.

Hyde, J. S. (1981). How large are cognitive gender differences? A meta-analysis using ω^2 and *d. American Psychologist, 36,* 892–901.

Hyde, J. S. (1984a). Children's understanding of sexist language. *Developmental Psychology, 20*(4), 697–706.

Hyde, J. S. (1984b). How large are gender differences in aggression? A developmental meta-analysis. *Developmental Psychology, 20,* 722–736.

Hyde, J. S. (1986). *Understanding human sexuality.* New York: McGraw-Hill.

Hyde, J. S. (1994). Should psychologists study gender differences? Yes, with some guidelines. *Feminism and Psychology, 4*(4), 507–512.

Hyde, J. S. (1995). Women and maternity leave: Empirical data and public policy. *Psychology of Women Quarterly, 19*(3), 299–314.

Hyde, J. S. (2005). The gender similarities hypothesis. *American Psychologist, 60*(6), 581–592.

Hyde, J. S., & Ashby Plant, E. (1995). Magnitude of psychological gender differences: Another side to the story. *American Psychologist, 50*(3), 159–161.

Hyde, J. S., Fennema, E., & Lamon, S. J. (1990). Gender differences in mathematics performance: A meta-analysis. *Psychological Bulletin, 107*(2), 139–155.

Hyde, J. S., Fennema, E., Ryan, M., Frost, L., & Hopp, C. (1990). Gender comparisons of mathematics attitudes

and affect. *Psychology of Women Quarterly, 14,* 299–324.

Hyde, J. S., & Linn, M. C. (1988). Gender differences in verbal ability: A meta-analysis. *Psychological Bulletin, 104*(1), 53–69.

Hyde, J. S., Rosenberg, B. G., & Behrman, J. (1974). *Tomboyism: Implications for theories of female development.* Paper presented at the annual convention of the Western Psychological Association, San Francisco.

Hynie, M., & Lydon, J. E. (1995). Women's perceptions of female contraceptive behavior. *Psychology of Women Quarterly, 19*(4), 563–581.

Iacuone, D. (2005). "Real men are tough guys": Hegemonic masculinity and safety in the construction industry. *Journal of Men's Studies, 13*(2), 247–266.

Ibarra, H. (1992). Homophily and differential returns: Sex differences in network structure and access in an advertising firm. *Administrative Science Quarterly, 37*(3), 422–447.

Ike, N. (2000). Current thinking on XYY syndrome. *Psychiatric Annals, 30*(2), 91–95.

Imamoglu, E. O., Kuller, R., Imamoglu, V., & Kuller, M. (1993). The social psychological worlds of Swedes and Turks in and around retirement. *Journal of Cross Cultural Psychology, 24*(1), 26–41.

Imperato-McGinley, J., Guerrero, L., Gautier, T., & Peterson, R. E. (1974). Steroid 5-alpha-reductase deficiency in man: An inherited form of male pseudohermaphroditism. *Science, 186,* 1213–1215.

Imperato-McGinley, J., Miller, M., Wilson, J. D., Peterson, R. E., Shackleton, C., & Gajdusek, D. C. (1991). A cluster of male pseudohermaphrodites with 5-alpha-reductase deficiency in Papua New Guinea. *Clinical Endocrinology, 34,* 293–298.

Imperato-McGinley, J., Peterson, R. E., Gautier, T., & Sturla, E. (1979). Androgens and the evolution of male gender identity among male pseudohermaphrodites with a 5-alpha-reductase deficiency. *New England Journal of Medicine, 310,* 839–840.

Impett, E., & Peplau, L. A. (2003). Sexual compliance: Gender, motivational, and relationship perspectives. *Journal of Sex Research, 40,* 87–100.

Independent Sector. (2001). *Giving and volunteering in the United States: Key findings.* Retrieved June 16, 2006, from http://www.independentsector.org/PDFs/GV01keyfind.pdf

Ingoldsby, B. B. (1995). Marital structure. In B. B. Ingoldsby & S. Smith (Eds.), *Families in multicultural perspective* (pp. 117–137). New York: Guilford Press.

Inman, C. (1996). Friendships among men: Closeness in the doing. In J. T. Wood (Ed.), *Gendered relationships* (pp. 95–110). Mountain View, CA: Mayfield.

Institute for Women's Policy Research. (2005). *The gender wage ratio: Women's and men's earnings.* Retrieved November 10, 2006, from http://www.iwpr.org/pdf/C350.pdf

Instone, D., Major, B., & Bunker, B. B. (1983). Gender, self-confidence, and social influence strategies: An organizational simulation. *Journal of Personality and Social Psychology, 44,* 322–333.

International Institute for Democracy and Electoral Assistance. (2003a). Voter turnout by gender. Retrieved November 23, 2003, from http://www.idea.int/gender/turnout.htm.

International Institute for Democracy and Electoral Assistance. (2003b). Gender quotas. Retrieved from http://www.idea.int/gender/quotas.htm

International Labor Office. (2004). *Global employment trends for women.* Retrieved November 10, 2006, from http://www.ilo.org/public/english/employment/strat/download/trendsw.pdf

Inter-Parliamentary Union. (2006). *Women in politics: 60 years in retrospect.* Retrieved November 10, 2006, from http://www.ipu.org/PDF/publications/wmninfokit06_en.pdf

Irvine, J. J. (1986). Teacher-student interactions: Effects of student race, sex, and grade level. *Journal of Educational Psychology, 78*(1), 14–21.

Itakura, H., & Tsui, A. B. M. (2004). Gender and conversational dominance in Japanese conversation. *Language in Society, 33*(2), 223–248.

Ivory, J. D. (2006). Still a man's game: Gender representation in online reviews of video games. *Mass Communication and Society, 9*(1), 103–114.

Jabes, J. (1980). Causal attributions and sex-role stereotypes in the perceptions of women managers. *Canadian Journal of Behavioural Science, 12*(1), 52–63.

Jacklin, C. N. (1985, June). *Stalking the development of sex differences.* Invited address to the Canadian Psychological Association, Halifax, Nova Scotia.

Jacklin, C. N., Maccoby, E. E., & Doering, C. H. (1983). Neonatal sex-steroid hormones and timidity in 6–18-month-old boys and girls. *Developmental Psychobiology, 16*(3), 163–168.

Jackson, L. A. (1989). Relative deprivation and the gender wage gap. *Journal of Social Issues, 45*(4), 117–133.

Jackson, L. A., Gardner, P. D., & Sullivan, L. A. (1992). Explaining gender differences in self-pay expectations: Social comparison standards and perceptions of fair pay. *Journal of Applied Psychology, 77*(5), 651–663.

Jacobs, J., & Weisz, V. (1994). Gender stereotypes: Implications for the gifted. *Roeper Review, 16,* 152–155.

Jacobsen, F. M. (1994). Psychopharmacology. In L. Comas-Díaz & B. Greene (Eds.), *Women of color: Integrating ethnic and gender identities in psychotherapy* (pp. 319–338). New York: Guilford Press.

Jacobson, N., & Gottman, J. (1998). *When men batter women: New insights into ending abusive relationships.* New York: Simon & Schuster.

Jacoby, S. (1998, April 26). Hospital harassment. A woman neurosurgeon writes about sexism among doctors. *New York Times.* Retrieved April 10, 2007, from http://www.nytimes.com/books/98/04/26/reviews/980426.26jacobyt.html

James, W. (1890). *The principles of psychology.* New York: Holt.

Jazzman Billy Tipton revealed as a woman. (1989, February 1). *Tucson Citizen,* p. 3A.

Jelen, T. G., Damore, D. F., & Lamatsch, T. (2002). Gender, employment status, and abortion: A longitudinal analysis. *Sex Roles, 47*(7/8), 321–330.

Jemelka, J. R., & Downs, C. (1991). The social support construct in an experimental context: A reexamination. *Psychology: A Journal of Human Behavior, 28*(3), 35–46.

Jenkin, N., & Vroegh, K. (1969). Contemporary concepts of masculinity and femininity. *Psychological Reports, 25,* 679–697.

Jensen, J. M. (1990). Native American women and agriculture: A Seneca case study. In E. C. DuBois & V. L. Ruiz (Eds.), *Unequal sisters: A multicultural reader in U.S. women's history* (pp. 51–65). New York: Routledge.

Jensen-Campell, L. A., Graziano, W. G., & West, S. G. (1995). Dominance, prosocial orientation, and female preferences: Do nice guys really finish last? *Journal of Personality and Social Psychology, 68*(3), 427–440.

Jobson, S., & Watson, J. S. (1984). Sex and age differences in choice behaviour: The object-person dimension. *Perception, 13*(6), 719–724.

Jochen, P., & Valkenburg, P. M. (2006). Adolescents' exposure to sexually explicit online material and recreational attitudes toward sex. *Journal of Communication, 56*(4), 639–660.

Johansson, E. E., Risberg, G., Hamberg, K., & Westman, G. R. (2002). Gender bias in female physician assessments: Women considered better suited for qualitative research. *Scandinavian Journal of Primary Health Care, 20*(2), 79–84.

John, D., Shelton, B. A., & Luschen, K. (1995). Race, ethnicity, gender, and perceptions of fairness. *Journal of Family Issues, 16*(3), 357–379.

Johnson, C. (1994). Gender, legitimate authority, and leader-subordinate conversations. *American Sociological Review, 59,* 122–135.

Johnson, C., & Engelhard, G. (1992). Gender, academic achievement, and preference for cooperative, competitive, and individualistic learning among African-American adolescents. *Journal of Psychology, 126*(4), 385–392.

Johnson, H. J. (1974). *Executive life styles: A Life Extension Institute report on alcohol, sex and health.* New York: Crowell.

Johnson, H. L., Johnson, P. B., Nusbaum, B. J., Glassman, M. B., Bejarano, A., & Rosen, T. S. (1999). Depressive symptomatology in African-American, Dominican, Irish-American, and Puerto Rican women. *Journal of Gender, Culture, and Health, 4*(1), 49–60.

Johnson, M. J., Jackson, N. C., Arnette, J. K., & Koffman, S. D. (2005). Gay and lesbian perceptions of discrimination in retirement care facilities. *Journal of Homosexuality, 49*(2), 83–102.

Johnson, P. (1974). *Social power and sex role stereotypes.* Paper presented at the meeting of the Western Psychological Association, San Francisco.

Johnson, P. (1976). Women and power: Toward a theory of effectiveness. *Journal of Social Issues, 32,* 99–110.

Johnson, P., & Goodchilds, J. D. (1976, October). How women get their way. *Psychology Today,* pp. 69–70.

Jones, D. (2003, January 27). Few women hold top executive jobs, even when CEOs are female. *USA Today*, p. B1.

Jones, D. (2005, August 5). Study says flirtatious women get fewer raises, promotions. *USA Today*, p. 6B.

Jones, J. C., & Barlow, D. H. (1990). Self-reported frequency of sexual urges, fantasies and masturbatory fantasies in heterosexual males and females. *Archives of Sexual Behavior, 19*(3), 269–279.

Jones, M. G., Howe, A., & Rua, M. J. (2000). Gender differences in students' experiences, interests, and attitudes toward science and scientists. *Science Education, 84*(2), 180–192.

Jordan, P. L. (1990). Laboring for relevance: Expectant and new fatherhood. *Nursing Research, 39*(1), 11–16.

Joseph, C. A., McKay, T., & Joseph, C. R. (1982). Sex effects on free recall and recognition of orally presented nouns into imagery form. *Journal of General Psychology, 106,* 213–217.

Kaats, G., & Davis, K. (1971). Effects of volunteer biases in studies of sexual behavior and attitudes. *Journal of Sex Research, 7,* 26–34.

Kahn, A. S., O'Leary, V., Krulewitz, J. E., & Lamm, H. (1980). Equity and equality: Male and female means to a just end. *Basic and Applied Social Psychology, 1,* 173–197.

Kahn, A. S., & Yoder, J. D. (1989). The psychology of women and conservatism: Rediscovering social change. *Psychology of Women Quarterly, 13*(4), 417–432.

Kahn, J. (1998, April 4). Journal: Cross-dressing kickboxer is a big hit in Thailand. *The New York Times on the Web.* International section. Retrieved from http://www.ishipress.com/thaikick.htm

Kaij, L., & Nilsson, A. (1972). Emotional and psychotic illness following childbirth. In J. G. Howells (Ed.), *Modern perspectives in psycho-obstetrics* (pp. 364–384). London: Oliver & Boyd.

Kaiser Family Foundation. (2005). *Sex on TV 4.* Retrieved July 27, 2006, from http://www.kff.org/entmedia/7398.cfm

Kalist, D. E. (2002). The gender earnings gap in the RN labor market. *Nursing Economics, 20*(4), 155–162.

Kaman, V. S., & Hartel, C. E. J. (1994). Gender differences in anticipated pay negotiation strategies and outcomes. *Journal of Business & Psychology, 9*(2), 183–197.

Kanayama, G., Gruber, A. J., Pope, H. G., Jr., Borowiecki, J. J., & Hudson, J. I. (2001). Over-the-counter drug use in gymnasiums: An underrecognized substance abuse problem? *Psychotherapy and Psychosomatics, 70*(3), 137–140.

Kane, P. (1991). *Women's health.* New York: St. Martin's.

Kanter, R. M. (1975). Women and the structure of organizations: Explorations in theory and behavior. In M. Millman & R. M. Kanter (Eds.), *Another voice* (pp. 34–74). Garden City, NY: Anchor.

Kanter, R. M. (1976). Why bosses turn bitchy. *Psychology Today, 9*(2), 56–59, 88–91.

Kanter, R. M. (1977). *Men and women of the corporation.* New York: Basic Books.

Kanter, R. M. (1979). Power failure in management circuits. *Harvard Business Review, 57,* 65–75.

Kantner, J. F., & Zelnick, M. (1972). Sexual experience of young unmarried women in the United States. *Family Planning Perspectives, 4*(4), 9–18.

Kaplan, A. G. (1980). Human sex-hormone abnormalities viewed from an androgynous perspective: A reconsideration of the work of John Money. In J. E. Parsons (Ed.), *The psychobiology of sex differences and sex roles* (pp. 81–94). Washington, DC: Hemisphere.

Kaplan, A. G., & Surrey, J. L. (1984). The relational self in women: Developmental theory and public policy. In L. E. Walker (Ed.), *Women and mental health policy* (pp. 79–94). Beverly Hills, CA: Sage.

Kaplan, B. J. (1986). A psychobiological review of depression during pregnancy. *Psychology of Women Quarterly, 10,* 35–38.

Kaplan, H. S. (1974). *The new sex therapy.* New York: Brunner/Mazel.

Kaplan, H. S., & Sager, C. (1971, June). Sexual patterns at different ages. *Medical Aspects of Human Sexuality, 5,* 10–23.

Karabenick, S. A. (1983). Sex-relevance of content and influenceability: Sistrunk & McDavid revisited. *Personality and Social Psychology Bulletin, 9,* 243–252.

Karney, B. R., & Bradbury, T. N. (1995). The longitudinal course of marital quality and stability: A review of theory, method, and research. *Psychological Bulletin, 118*(1), 3–34.

Kaschak, E. (1992). *Engendered lives: A new psychology of women's experience.* New York: Basic Books.

Katz, E. J., & Madden, J. M. (1984). Using policy capturing to measure prejudicial attitudes of women toward women. *Bulletin of the Psychonomic Society, 22,* 90–91.

Katz, J. B. (1977). *I am the fire of time: The voices of Native American women.* New York: E. P. Dutton.

Katz, P. A. (1986). Gender identity: Development and consequences. In R. D. Ashmore & F. K. Del Boca (Eds.), *The social psychology of female-male relations* (pp. 21–67). Orlando, FL: Academic Press.

Katz, P. A., & Boswell, S. L. (1984). Sex-role development and the one-child family. In T. Falbo (Ed.), *The single-child family* (pp. 63–116). New York: Guilford Press.

Kaufman, D. R. (1995). Professional women: How real are the recent gains? In J. Freeman (Ed.), *Women: A feminist perspective* (5th ed., pp. 287–305). Mountain View, CA: Mayfield.

Kawakami, K., Dovidio, J. F., Moll, J., Hermsen, S., & Russin, A. (2000). Just say no (to stereotyping): Effects of training in the negation of stereotypic associations on stereotype activation. *Journal of Personality and Social Psychology, 78*(5), 871–888.

Keller, C. (2001). Effects of teachers' stereotyping on students' stereotyping of mathematics as a male domain. *Journal of Social Psychology, 141*(2), 165–173.

Keller, E. F. (1985). *Reflections on gender and science.* New Haven, CT: Yale University Press.

Keller, J. (2002). Blatant stereotype threat and women's math performance: Self-handicapping as a strategic means to cope with obtrusive negative performance expectations. *Sex Roles, 47*(3–4), 193–198.

Keller, M., & Taylor, S. (2003, Fall). Supreme Court rules on landmark cases. *National NOW Times, 35*(2), 5.

Kelly, C., Huston, T. L., & Cate, R. M. (1985). Premarital relationships correlates of the erosion of satisfaction in marriage. *Journal of Social and Personal Relationships, 2*(2), 167–178.

Kelly, K. R., & Cobb, S. J. (1991). A profile of the career development characteristics of young gifted adolescents: Examining gender and multicultural differences. *Roeper Review, 13*(4), 202–206.

Kelly, R. H., Russo, J., & Katon, W. (2001). Somatic complaints among pregnant women cared for in obstetrics: Normal pregnancy or depressive and anxiety symptom amplification revisited? *General Hospital Psychiatry, 23*(3), 107–113.

Keltikangas-Jarvinen, L. (1990). The stability of self-concept during adolescence and early adulthood: A six-year follow-up study. *Journal of General Psychology, 117*(4), 361–368.

Kemp, A. A. (1995). Poverty and welfare for women. In J. Freeman (Ed.), *Women: A feminist perspective* (5th ed., pp. 458–480). Mountain View, CA: Mayfield.

Kennedy, D. (1993). Nonsexist language: A progress report. *Canadian Journal of Education, 18*(3), 223–238.

Kennedy, F. (1970). Institutionalized oppression vs. the female. In R. Morgan (Ed.), *Sisterhood is powerful* (pp. 438–446). New York: Vintage Books.

Kessler, R. C., McGonagle, K. A., Zhao, S., & Nelson, C. B. (1994). Lifetime and 12-month prevalence of DSM-III–R psychiatric disorders in the United States: Results from the national comorbidity study. *Archives of General Psychiatry, 51*(1), 8–19.

Kessler, S. J. (1990). The medical construction of gender: Case management of inter-sexed infants. *Signs: Journal of Women in Culture and Society, 16*(1), 3–26.

Kessler-Harris, A. (1985). The debate over equality for women in the workplace: Recognizing differences. In L. Larwood, A. H. Stromberg, & B. Gutek (Eds.), *Women and work: An annual review* (Vol. 1, pp. 141–161). Beverly Hills, CA: Sage.

Khosroshahi, F. (1989). Penguins don't care, but women do: A social identity analysis of a Whorfian problem. *Language in Society, 18*(4), 505–525.

Khoury-Kassabri, M. (2006). Student victimization by educational staff in Israel. *Child Abuse and Neglect, 30*(6), 691–707.

Kiefer, I., Rathmanner, T., & Kunze, M. (2005). Eating and dieting differences in men and women. *Journal of Men's Health and Gender, 2*(2), 194–201.

Kilianski, S. E., & Rudman, L. A. (1998). Wanting it both ways: Do women approve of benevolent sexism? *Sex Roles, 39*(5/6), 333–352.

Kilmartin, C. T. (2000). *The masculine self.* Boston: McGraw-Hill.

Kim, J. (1981). *The process of Asian-American identity development: A study of Japanese American women's perceptions of their struggle to achieve positive identities.* Unpublished doctoral dissertation, University of Massachusetts.

Kimball, M. M. (1989). A new perspective on women's math achievement. *Psychological Bulletin, 105,* 198–214.

Kimball, M. M. (1995). *Feminist visions of gender similarities and differences.* Binghamton, NY: Haworth.

Kimble, C. E., Yoshikawa, J. C., & Zehr, H. D. (1981). Vocal and verbal assertiveness in same-sex and mixed-sex groups. *Journal of Personality and Social Psychology, 40,* 1047–1054.

Kimura, D. (1985, November). Male brain, female brain: The hidden difference. *Psychology Today,* pp. 50–52, 54, 56–58.

Kimura, D. (1987). Are men's and women's brains really different? *Canadian Psychology, 28*(2), 133–147.

Kimura, D. (1993). Sex differences in the brain. In *Mind and brain: Readings from Scientific American magazine* (pp. 79–89). New York: W. H. Freeman.

Kimura, D. (2002). Sex differences in the brain. *Scientific American, 12*(1), 32–37.

Kimura, D., & Clarke, P. G. (2002). Women's advantage on verbal memory is not restricted to concrete words. *Psychological Reports, 9*(3, Pt. 2), 1137–1142.

Kimura, D., & Hampson, E. (1994). Cognitive pattern in men and women is influenced by fluctuations in sex hormones. *Current Directions in Psychological Science, 3,* 57–61.

Kinsey, A. C., Pomeroy, W. B., & Martin, C. E. (1948). *Sexual behavior in the human male.* Philadelphia: Saunders.

Kinsey, A. C., Pomeroy, W. B., Martin, C. E., & Gebhard, P. H. (1953). *Sexual behavior in the human female.* Philadelphia: Saunders.

Kipnis, D. (1972). Does power corrupt? *Journal of Personality and Social Psychology, 24,* 33–41.

Kipnis, D. (1984). The use of power in organizations and in interpersonal settings. In S. Oskamp (Ed.), *Applied social psychology annual* (Vol. 5, pp. 179–210). Beverly Hills, CA: Sage.

Kipnis, D., Castell, P. J., Gergen, M., & Mauch, D. (1976). Metamorphic effects of power. *Journal of Applied Psychology, 61,* 127–135.

Kipnis, D., Schmidt, S. M., & Wilkinson, I. (1980). Intraorganizational influence tactics: Explorations in getting one's way. *Journal of Applied Psychology, 65,* 440–452.

Kissane, B. V. (1986). Selection of mathematically talented students. *Educational Studies in Mathematics, 17,* 221–241.

Kissling, E. A. (2002). On the rag on screen: Menarche in film and television. *Sex Roles, 46*(1/2), 5–12.

Kite, M. E., Deaux, K., & Miele, M. (1991). Stereotypes of young and old: Does age outweigh gender? *Psychology and Aging, 6,* 19–27.

Kite, M. E., Stockdale, G. D., Whitley, B. E., Jr., & Johnson, B. T. (2005). Attitudes toward younger and older adults: An updated meta-analytic review. *Journal of Social Issues, 61*(2), 241–266.

Kitzinger, C., & Wilkinson, S. (1995). Transition from heterosexuality to lesbianism: The discursive production of lesbian identities. *Developmental Psychology, 31*(1), 95–104.

Klein, M. (1960). *The psychoanalysis of children.* New York: Grove Press. (Original work published 1932)

Kleinpeter, C. H., & Hohman, M. M. (2000). Surrogate motherhood: Personality traits and satisfaction with service providers. *Psychological Reports, 87,* 957–970.

Klerman, G. L., & Weissman, M. M. (1980). Depressions among women: Their nature and causes. In M. Guttentag, S. Salasin, & D. Belle (Eds.), *The mental health of women* (pp. 57–92). New York: Academic Press.

Klohn, L. S., & Rogers, R. W. (1991). Dimensions of the severity of a health threat: The persuasive effects of visibility, time of onset, and rate of onset on young women's intentions to prevent osteoporosis. *Health Psychology, 10*(5), 323–329.

Klonoff, E. A., & Landrine, H. (1995). The Schedule of Sexist Events: A measure of lifetime and recent sexist discrimination in women's lives. *Psychology of Women Quarterly, 19*(4), 439–472.

Knight, G. P., & Chao, C. (1989). Gender differences in cooperative, competitive, and individualistic social values of children. *Motivation and Emotion, 13*(2), 125–141.

Knight, G. P., Guthrie, I. K., Page, M. C., & Fabes, R. A. (2002). Emotional arousal and gender differences in aggression: A meta-analysis. *Aggressive Behavior, 28*(5), 366–393.

Knussman, R., Christiansen, K., & Couwenbergs, C. (1986). Relations between sex hormone levels and sexual behavior in men. *Archives of Sexual Behavior, 15*(5), 429–445.

Koeller, O., Baumert, J., & Schnable, K. (2001). Does interest matter? The relationship between academic interest and achievement in mathematics. *Journal for Research in Mathematics Education, 32*(5), 448–470.

Koenig, A. M., & Eagly, A. H. (2005). Stereotype threat in men on a test of social sensitivity. *Sex Roles, 52*(7), 489–496.

Koeske, R. K., & Koeske, G. F. (1975). An attributional approach to moods and the menstrual cycle. *Journal of Personality and Social Psychology, 31*, 474–478.

Koff, E., Rierdan, J., & Stubbs, M. L. (1990). Conceptions and misconceptions of the menstrual cycle. *Women and Health, 16*(3/4), 119–136.

Kohlberg, L. (1964). Development of moral character and moral ideology. In M. Hoffman & L. Hoffman (Eds.), *Review of child development research* (Vol. 1, pp. 383–431). New York: Russell Sage Foundation.

Kohlberg, L. (1966). A cognitive-developmental analysis of children's sex-role concepts and attitudes. In E. E. Maccoby (Ed.), *The development of sex differences* (pp. 82–173). Stanford, CA: Stanford University Press.

Kohlberg, L. (1984). *The psychology of moral development.* San Francisco: Harper & Row.

Kohlberg, L., & Kramer, R. (1969). Continuities and discontinuities in childhood and adult moral development. *Human Development, 12*, 93–120.

Kohlberg, L., & Ullian, D. Z. (1974). Stages in the development of psychosexual concepts and attitudes. In R. C. Friedman, R. M. Richart, & R. L. Vande Wiele (Eds.), *Sex differences in behavior* (pp. 209–222). New York: Wiley.

Kolata, G. (2003, April 22). Hormone studies: What went wrong? *New York Times,* pp. D1, D6.

Konrad, A. M., & Harris, C. (2002). Desirability of the Bem Sex-Role Inventory items for women and men: A comparison between African Americans and European Americans. *Sex Roles, 47*(5/6), 259–272.

Konrad, A. M., & Hartmann, L. (2001). Gender differences in attitudes toward affirmative action programs in Australia: Effects of beliefs, interests, and attitudes toward women. *Sex Roles, 45*(5/6), 415–432.

Korabik, K., Baril, G. L., & Watson, C. (1993). Managers' conflict management style and leadership effectiveness: The moderating effects of gender. *Sex Roles, 29*(5/6), 405–420.

Kortenhaus, C. M., & Demarest, J. (1993). Gender role stereotyping in children's literature: An update. *Sex Roles, 28*(3/4), 219–232.

Koss, M. P. (1993). Detecting the scope of rape: A review of prevalence research methods. *Journal of Interpersonal Violence, 8*, 98–122.

Koss, M. P., Gidycz, C. A., & Wisniewski, N. (1987). The scope of rape: Incidence and prevalence of sexual aggression and victimization in a national sample of higher education students. *Journal of Consulting and Clinical Psychology, 55*, 162–170.

Koss, M. P., Heise, L., & Russo, N. F. (1994). The global health burden of rape. *Psychology of Women Quarterly, 18*(4), 509–537.

Kozu, J. (1999). Domestic violence in Japan. *American Psychologist, 54*(1), 50–54.

Kramer, B. J., & Kipnis, S. (1995). Eldercare and work-role conflict: Toward an understanding of gender differences in caregiver burden. *Gerontologist, 35*(3), 340–348.

Kreuz, L. E., & Rose, R. M. (1972). Assessment of aggressive behavior and plasma testosterone in a young criminal population. *Psychosomatic Medicine, 34*, 321.

Kreuz, L. E., Rose, R. M., & Jennings, J. R. (1972). Suppression of plasma testosterone levels and psychological stress. *Archives of General Psychiatry, 26*, 479–482.

Krupnick, C. G. (1985, May). Women and men in the classroom: Inequality and its remedies. *On Teaching and Learning: The Journal of the Harvard-Danforth Center,* pp. 18–25.

Kulik, L. (2002). Marital equality and the quality of long-term marriage in later life. *Ageing and Society, 22*(4), 459–481.

Kunzig, R. (2004). The hidden history of men. *Discover, 25*(12), 33–39.

Kurdek, L. A., & Schmitt, J. P. (1986a). Interaction of sex role self-concept with relationship quality and relationship beliefs in married, heterosexual, cohabiting, gay, and lesbian couples. *Journal of Personality and Social Psychology, 51*(2), 365–370.

Kurdek, L. A., & Schmitt, J. P. (1986b). Relationship quality of partners in heterosexual married, heterosexual cohabiting, and gay and lesbian relationships. *Journal of Personality and Social Psychology, 51*(4), 711–720.

Laak, J. J. F. T., Olthof, T., & Aleva, E. (2003). Sources of annoyance in close relationships: Sex-related differences in annoyance with partner behaviors. *Journal of Psychology: Interdisciplinary and Applied, 137*(6), 545–559.

Laan, E., & Everaerd, W. (1995). Determinants of female sexual arousal: Psychophysiological theory and data. *Annual Review of Sex Research, 32*–76.

Laberge, L., Carrier, J., Lesperance, P., Lambert, C., Vitaro, F., Tremblay, R. E., et al. (2000). Sleep and circadian phase characteristics of adolescent and young adult males in a naturalistic summertime condition. *Chronobiology International, 17*(4), 489–501.

Lacoursiere, R. (1972). Fatherhood and mental illness: A review and new material. *Psychiatric Quarterly, 46*, 105–124.

Laessle, R. G., Tuschl, R. J., Schweiger, U., & Pirke, K. M. (1990). Mood changes and physical complaints during the normal menstrual cycle in healthy young women. *Psychoneuroendocrinology, 15*(2), 131–138.

LaFrance, M. (1992). Gender and interruptions: Individual infraction or violation of the social order. *Psychology of Women Quarterly, 16*(4), 497–512.

Lafromboise, T. D., Berman, J. S., & Sohi, B. K. (1994). American Indian women. In L. Comas-Díaz & B. Greene (Eds.), *Women of color: Integrating ethnic and gender identities in psychotherapy* (pp. 30–71). New York: Guilford Press.

Lahey, K. (1984). *Equality and specificity in feminist thought.* Paper presented to the Charter of Rights Educational Fund Statute Audit Project of Ontario. (Summarized in the *Newsletter of the National Association of Women and the Law, 5*(8), 24–25)

Lallukka, T., Sarlio-Lahteenkorva, S., Roos, E., Laaksonen, M., Rahkonen, O., & Lahelma, E. (2004). Working conditions and health behaviours among employed women and men: The Helsinki health study. *Preventive Medicine: An International Journal Devoted to Practice and Theory, 38*(1), 48–56.

Lamb, M. (1987). The emergent American father. In M. Lamb (Ed.), *The father's role: Cross-cultural perspectives* (pp. 3–25). Hillsdale, NJ: Erlbaum.

Lamb, M. E., Owen, M. T., & Chase-Lansdale, L. (1979). The father-daughter relationship: Past, present, and future. In C. B. Kopp (Ed.), *Becoming female: Perspectives on development* (pp. 89–112). New York: Plenum.

Landrine, H. (1985). Race x class stereotypes of women. *Sex Roles, 13*(1/2), 65–75.

Landrine, H. (1987). On the politics of madness: A preliminary analysis of the relationship between social roles and psychopathology. *Psychology Monographs, 113,* 341–406.

Landrine, H. (1989). The politics of personality disorder. *Psychology of Women Quarterly, 13*(3), 325–340.

Landrine, H., Klonoff, E. A., & Brown-Collins, A. (1995). Cultural diversity and methodology in feminist psychology: Critique, proposal, empirical example. In H. Landrine (Ed.), *Bringing cultural diversity to feminist psychology: Theory, research, and practice* (pp. 55–75). Washington, DC: American Psychological Association.

Landrine, H., Klonoff, E. A., Gibbs, J., Manning, V., & Lund, M. (1995). Physical and psychiatric correlates of gender discrimination: An application of the Schedule of Sexist Events. *Psychology of Women Quarterly, 19*(4), 473–492.

Landsbergis, P. A., Schnall, P. L., Pickering, T. G., Warren, K., & Schwartz, J. E. (2003). Lower socioeconomic status among men in relation to the association between job strain and blood pressure. *Scandinavian Journal of Work, Environment and Health, 29*(3), 206–215.

Lapsley, H. (1999). *Margaret Mead and Ruth Benedict: The kinship of women.* Amherst, MA: University of Massachusetts Press.

Laqueur, T. (1990). *Making sex: Body and gender from the Greeks to Freud.* Cambridge, MA: Harvard University Press.

Larson, M. S. (2003). Gender, race and aggression in television commercials that feature children. *Sex Roles, 48*(1/2), 67–75.

Laumann, E. O., Michael, R. T., Gagnon, J. H., & Michaels, S. (1994). *Social organization of sexuality.* Chicago: University of Chicago Press.

Lauzen, M. M., & Dozier, D. M. (2002). You look mahvelous: An examination of gender and appearance comments in the 1999–2000 prime-time season. *Sex Roles, 46*(11/12), 429–437.

Lavine, H., Sweeney, D., & Wagner, S. H. (1999). Depicting women as sex objects in television advertising: Effects on body dissatisfaction. *Personality and Social Psychology Bulletin, 25*(8), 1049–1058.

Law, D. J., Pellegrino, J. W., & Hunt, E. B. (1993). Comparing the tortoise and the hare: Gender differences and experience in dynamic spatial reasoning tasks. *Psychological Science, 4,* 35–40.

Lawson, W. (2003, July/August). Aging's changing face: Science is reshaping the way we think about the older body, memory, and sex drive. *Psychology Today, 36*(4), 26.

Leahy, R. L., & Shirk, S. R. (1984). The development of classificatory skills and sex-trait stereotypes in children. *Sex Roles, 10,* 281–292.

Lebrun, C. M., McKenzie, D. C., Prior, J. C., & Taunton, J. E. (1995). Effects of menstrual cycle phase on athletic performance. *Medicine and Science in Sports and Exercise, 27*(3), 437–444.

Leder, G. (1990). Teacher/student interactions in the mathematics classroom: A different perspective. In E. Fennema & G. C. Leder (Eds.), *Mathematics and gender* (pp. 149–168). New York: Teachers College Press.

Lee, S. (2002). Health and sickness: The meaning of menstruation and premenstrual syndrome in women's lives. *Sex Roles, 46*(1/2), 25–35.

Leifer, M. (1980). *Psychological effects of motherhood: A study of first pregnancy.* New York: Praeger.

Leinbach, M. D., & Fagot, B. I. (1993). Categorical habituation to male and female faces: Gender schematic processing in infancy. *Infant Behavior and Development, 16,* 317–332.

Leinbach, M. D., Hort, B. E., & Fagot, B. I. (1997). Bears are for boys: Metaphorical associations in young children's gender stereotypes. *Cognitive Development, 12,* 107–130.

Leitenberg, H., Detzer, M. J., & Srebnik, D. (1993). Gender differences in masturbation and the relation of masturbation experience in preadolescence and/or early adolescence to sexual behavior and sexual adjustment in young adulthood. *Archives of Sexual Behavior, 22,* 87–98.

Leitenberg, H., & Henning, K. (1995). Sexual fantasy. *Psychological Bulletin, 117*(3), 469–496.

Lennane, K. J., & Lennane, R. J. (1973). Alleged psychogenic disorders in women: A possible manifestation of sexual prejudice. *New England Journal of Medicine, 288,* 288–292.

Lenney, E. (1977). Women's self-confidence in achievement settings. *Psychological Bulletin, 84,* 1–13.

Lennon, M. C. (1987). Is menopause depressing? An investigation of three perspectives. *Sex Roles, 17*(1/2), 1–16.

Lennon, M. C. (1994). Women, work, and well-being: The importance of work conditions. *Journal of Health and Social Behavior, 35,* 235–247.

Lerner, M. J. (1970). The desire for justice and reactions to victims. In J. Macaulay & L. Berkowitz (Eds.), *Altruism and helping behavior* (pp. 205–230). New York: Academic Press.

Lerner, M. J. (1974). Social psychology of justice and interpersonal attraction. In T. L. Huston (Ed.), *Foundations of interpersonal attraction* (pp. 331–351). New York: Academic Press.

Lerner, R. M. (1998). Theories of human development: Contemporary perspectives. In W. Damon (Series Ed.) & R. M. Lerner (Vol. Ed.), *Handbook of child psychology: Vol 1. Theoretical models of human development* (5th ed., pp. 1–23). New York: Wiley.

Levant, R. F. (1996). The new psychology of men. *Professional Psychology, Research and Practice, 27,* 259–265.

Levant, R. F., & Majors, R. G. (1997). Masculinity ideology among African American and European American college women and men. *Journal of Gender, Culture, and Health, 2,* 33–43.

Levant, R. F., Majors, R. G., & Kelley, M. (1998). Masculinity ideology among young African American and European American women and men in different regions of the United States. *Cultural Diversity and Mental Health, 4,* 227–236.

LeVay, S. (1991). A difference in hypothalamic structure between heterosexual and homosexual men. *Science, 253,* 1034–1037.

Levin, R. J., & Levin, A. (1975, October). The *Redbook* report on premarital and extramarital sex. *Redbook,* p. 38.

Levine, S. (1966). Sex differences in the brain. *Scientific American, 214*(4), 84–90.

Levinson, D. J. (1978). *The seasons of a man's life*. New York: Ballantine.

Levinson, R. M. (1975). Sex discrimination and employment practices: An experiment with unconventional job inquiries. *Social Problems, 22*(4), 533–543.

Levy, G. D., & Haaf, R. A. (1994). Detection of gender-related categories by 10-month-old infants. *Infant Behavior and Development, 17,* 457–459.

Levy, J. (1972). Lateral specialization of the human brain: Behavioral manifestations and possible evolutionary basis. In J. A. Kiger (Ed.), *The biology of behavior* (pp. 159–180). Corvallis: Oregon State University Press.

Lewin, M. (1984). "Rather worse than folly?" Psychology measures femininity and masculinity, 1: From Terman and Miles to the Guilfords. In M. Lewin (Ed.), *In the shadow of the past: Psychology portrays the sexes* (pp. 155–178). New York: Columbia University Press.

Lewis, M., & Weinraub, M. (1979). Origins of early sex-role development. *Sex Roles, 5,* 135–153.

Lewis, R. J., Winstead, B. A., & Derlega, V. J. (1989). Gender differences in volunteering for friendship research. *Journal of Social Behavior and Personality, 4*(5), 623–632.

Lewis, S. N., & Cooper, C. L. (1988). The transition to parenthood in dual-earner couples. *Psychological Medicine, 18*(2), 477–486.

Libby, M. N., & Aries, E. (1989). Gender differences in preschool children's narrative fantasy. *Psychology of Women Quarterly, 13,* 293–306.

Liem, R., & Rayman, P. (1982). Health and social costs of unemployment: Research and policy considerations. *American Psychologist, 37,* 1116–1123.

Lifton, P. D. (1985). Individual differences in moral development: The relation of sex, gender, and personality to morality. *Journal of Personality, 53*(2), 306–334.

Lightdale, J. R., & Prentice, D. A. (1994). Rethinking sex differences in aggression: Aggressive behavior in the absence of social roles. *Personality and Social Psychology Bulletin, 20*(1), 34–44.

Linn, M. C., & Petersen, A. C. (1985). Emergence and characterization of gender differences in spatial ability: A meta-analysis. *Child Development, 56,* 1479–1498.

Linz, D., Donnerstein, E., & Penrod, S. (1984). The effects of multiple exposure to filmed violence against women. *Journal of Communications, 34*(3), 130–147.

Lipman-Blumen, J. (1984). *Gender roles and power*. Englewood Cliffs, NJ: Prentice-Hall.

Lippa, R. A. (2005). How do lay people weight information about instrumentality, expressiveness, and gender-typed hobbies when judging masculinity-femininity in themselves, best friends, and strangers? *Sex Roles, 53*(1), 43–55.

Lipovenko, D. (1985, April 11). Compensation decision sets precedent: Sexual harassment ruled work injury. *Toronto Globe and Mail,* pp. 1–2.

Lips, H. M. (1980, March). *Pregnancy as a stimulus factor in the perception of women's moods and their causal attribution.* Paper presented at the Seventh Annual Conference on Feminist Psychology, Santa Monica, CA.

Lips, H. M. (1982a). Somatic and emotional aspects of the normal pregnancy experience: The first five months. *American Journal of Obstetrics and Gynecology, 142*(5), 524–529.

Lips, H. M. (1982b, June). *Symptom-reporting among expectant fathers: A new look at the couvade syndrome.* Paper presented at the annual meeting of the Association for Birth Psychology, Halifax, Nova Scotia.

Lips, H. M. (1982c, June). *Themes of the pregnancy experience: A content analysis of personal reports.* Paper presented at the Institute of the Section on Women and Psychology, Canadian Psychological Association meeting, Montreal.

Lips, H. M. (1983). Attitudes toward childbearing among women and men expecting their first child. *International Journal of Women's Studies, 6*(2), 119–129.

Lips, H. M. (1984, September). *University women's causal attributions for participation in math and science.* Paper presented at the annual meeting of the American Psychological Association, Toronto.

Lips, H. M. (1985a). Gender and the sense of power: Where are we and where are we going? *International Journal of Women's Studies, 8*(5), 483–489.

Lips, H. M. (1985b). A longitudinal study of the reporting of emotional and somatic symptoms during and after pregnancy. *Social Science and Medicine, 21*(6), 631–640.

Lips, H. M. (1986). *Self-schema theory and gender-related behaviours: Research on some correlates of university women's participation in mathematics, science and athletic activities.* (ERIC Document ED 263517, ERIC Clearinghouse on Counseling and Personnel Services)

Lips, H. M. (1991). *Women, men and power*. Mountain View, CA: Mayfield.

Lips, H. M. (1992). Gender and science-related attitudes as predictors of college students' academic choices. *Journal of Vocational Behavior, 40,* 62–81.

Lips, H. M. (1993). Bifurcation of a common path: Gender splitting on the road to engineering and physical science careers. *Initiatives, 55*(3), 13–22.

Lips, H. M. (1996). Predicting university women's participation in mathematics and science: A causal model. *Journal of Women and Minorities in Science and Engineering, 2*(4), 193–206.

Lips, H. M. (1999, February). *Awards, rewards, and gender: The invisibility of women's achievements.* Invited address, University of Auckland, Auckland, NZ.

Lips, H. M. (2000a). College students' visions of power and possibility as mediated by gender. *Psychology of Women Quarterly, 24*(1), 37–41.

Lips, H. M. (2000b, August). *Gender and ethnic differences in students' academic self-views among New Zealand university students.* Paper presented at the XXVII International Congress of Psychology, Stockholm, Sweden.

Lips, H. H. (2001). Envisioning positions of leadership: The expectations of university students in Virginia and Puerto Rico. *Journal of Social Issues, 57*(4), 799–814.

Lips, H. M. (2002). The gendering of possible futures: How female and male students map out divergent paths of accomplishment. *Women in a knowledge-based society: Proceedings of the Twelfth International Congress on Women in Engineering and Science.* Paper #88. [On CD].

Lips, H. M. (2003). The gender pay gap: Concrete indicator of women's progress toward equality. *Analyses of Social Issues and Public Policy, 3*(1), 87–109.

Lips, H. M. (2004). The gender gap in possible selves: Divergence of academic self-views in high school and university students. *Sex Roles 50*(5/6), 357–371.

Lips, H. M., & Asquith, K. (1995). Students' possible selves as scientists. *GATES: An International Journal Promoting Greater Access to Technology, Engineering, and Science, 2*(1), 1–7.

Lips, H. M., & Freedman, S. A. (1992). Heterosexual feminist identities: Private boundaries and shifting centers. *Feminism & Psychology, 2*(3), 441–444.

Lips, H. M., & Keener, E. (In press). *Effects of gender and dominance on leadership emergence: Sex Roles.*

Lips, H. M., & Morrison, A. (1986). Changes in the sense of family among couples expecting their first child. *Journal of Social and Personal Relationships, 3*(3), 393–400.

Lips, H. M., & Rogers, M. (1999, March). *Powerful roles and relationships: An uneasy combination?* Paper presented at the annual meeting of the Southeastern Psychological Association, Savannah, GA.

Lips, H. M., & Temple, L. (1990). Majoring in computer science: Causal models for women and men. *Research in Higher Education, 31*(1), 99–113.

Littig, L. W., & Branch, D. (1993). Exposure frequencies and sensation-seeking: No novelty effect but an unexpected experimenter-subject sex interaction. *Social Behavior and Personality, 21*(1), 25–31.

Lloyd, E. A. (2005). *The case of the female orgasm: Bias in the science of evolution.* Cambridge, MA: Harvard University Press.

Lloyd, J. E. V., Walsh, J., & Yailagh, M. S. (2005). Sex differences in performance attributions, self-efficacy, and achievement in mathematics: If I'm so smart, why don't I know it? *Canadian Journal of Education, 28*(3), 384–408.

Lock, M. (1993). *Encounters with aging: Mythologies of menopause in Japan and North America.* Berkeley: University of California Press.

Lockheed, M. E. (1985). Sex and social influence: A meta-analysis guided by theory. In J. Berger & M. Zelditch Jr. (Eds.), *Status, rewards, and influence: How expectations organize behavior* (pp. 406–429). San Francisco: Jossey-Bass.

Lockheed, M. E., & Hall, K. P. (1976). Conceptualizing sex as a status characteristic: Applications to leadership training strategies. *Journal of Social Issues, 32*(3), 111–124.

Lockwood, D. (1980). *Prison sexual violence.* New York: Elsevier.

Lockwood, P. (2006). "Someone like me can be successful": Do college students need same-gender role models? *Psychology of Women Quarterly, 30*(1), 36–46.

Loeber, R., & Stouthamer-Loeber, M. (1998). Development of juvenile aggression and violence: Some common misconceptions and controversies. *American Psychologist, 53*(2), 242–259.

Logothetis, M. L. (1991). Women's decisions about estrogen replacement therapy. *Western Journal of Nursing Research, 13*(4), 458–474.

Long, L. S., & Simon, R. J. (1974). The roles and statuses of women on children's and family programs. *Journalism Quarterly, 51,* 107–110.

Long, P. (1991, March/April). A woman's heart. *In Health, 5*(2), 53–58.

Long, V. O. (1991). Masculinity, femininity, and women scientists' self-esteem and self-acceptance. *Journal of Psychology, 125*(3), 263–270.

Lopez-Claros, A., & Zahidi, S. (2005). *Women's empowerment: Measuring the global gender gap.* Geneva, Switzerland: World Economic Forum.

Lorber, J. (1986). Dismantling Noah's Ark. *Sex Roles, 14*(11/12), 567–580.

Lord, C. G., & Saenz, D. S. (1985). Memory deficits and memory surfeits: Differential cognitive consequences of tokenism for tokens and observers. *Journal of Personality and Social Psychology, 49*(4), 918–926.

Loring, M., & Powell, B. (1988). Gender, race and DSM-III: A study of the objectivity of psychiatric diagnostic behavior. *Journal of Health and Social Behavior, 29,* 1–22.

Lortie-Lussier, M., & Rinfret, N. (2002). The proportion of women managers: Where is the critical mass? *Journal of Applied Social Psychology, 32*(9), 1974–1991.

Lott, B. (1985). The devaluation of women's competence. *Journal of Social Issues, 41*(4), 43–60.

Low, B. S. (2000). *Why sex matters: A Darwinian look at human behavior.* Princeton, NJ: Princeton University Press.

Lowe, M. (1983). The dialectic of biology and culture. In M. Lowe & R. Hubbard (Eds.), *Woman's nature: Rationalizations of inequality* (pp. 39–62). New York: Pergamon Press.

LPGA. (2003). *Statistics.* Retrieved from http://www.lpga.com/statistics/statcenter.cfm?sort=money_s

Lubinski, D., Tellegen, A., & Butcher, J. N. (1981). The relationship between androgyny and subjective indicators of emotional well-being. *Journal of Personality and Social Psychology, 40,* 722–730.

Lueptow, L. B., Garovich-Szabo, L., & Lueptow, M. B. (2001). Social change and the persistence of sex typing: 1974–1997. *Social Forces, 80*(1), 1–36.

Luker, K. (1984). *Abortion and the politics of motherhood.* Berkeley: University of California Press.

Lummis, M., & Stevenson, H. W. (1990). Gender differences in beliefs and achievement: A cross-cultural study. *Developmental Psychology, 26*(2), 254–263.

Lundberg, S., & Rose, E. (2002). The effects of sons and daughters on men's labor supply and wages. *Review of Economics and Statistics, 84*(2), 251–268.

Lundberg, S., & Rose, E. (2003). Child gender and the transition to marriage. *Demography, 40*(2), 333–349.

Lurie, N., Slater, J., McGovern, P., Ekstrum, J., et al. (1993). Preventive care for women: Does the sex of the physician matter? *New England Journal of Medicine, 329*(7), 478–482.

Lutchmaya, S., & Baron-Cohen, S. (2002). Human sex differences in social and non-social looking preferences. *Infant Behavior & Development, 25*(3), 319–325.

Lutwin, D. R., & Siperstein, G. N. (1985). Househusband fathers. In S. M. H. Hanson & F. W. Bozett (Eds.), *Dimensions of fatherhood* (pp. 269–287). Beverly Hills, CA: Sage.

Lyness, K. S., & Heilman, M. E. (2006). When fit is fundamental: Performance evaluations and promotions of upper-level female and male managers. *Journal of Applied Psychology, 91*(4), 777–785.

Lyness, K. S., & Judiesch, M. K. (1999). Are women more likely to be hired or promoted into management positions? *Journal of Vocational Behavior, 54*(1), 158–173.

Lyness, K. S., & Thompson, D. (1997). Above the glass ceiling? A comparison of matched samples of female and male executives. *Journal of Applied Psychology, 82*(3), 359–375.

Lyons, R. D. (1983, October 4). Sex in America. *New York Times,* p. C1.

Lytton, H., & Romney, D. M. (1991). Parents' differential socialization of boys and girls: A meta-analysis. *Psychological Bulletin, 109*(2), 267–296.

Ma, X. (2001). Participation in advanced mathematics: Do expectation and influence of students, peers, teachers, and parents matter? *Contemporary Educational Psychology, 26*(1), 132–146.

Maccoby, E. E. (1990). Gender and relationships: A developmental account. *American Psychologist, 45*(4), 513–520.

Maccoby, E. E. (1992). The role of parents in the socialization of children: An historical overview. *Developmental Psychology, 28*(6), 1006–1017.

Maccoby, E. E. (1998). *The two sexes: Growing up apart, coming together.* Cambridge, MA: Harvard University Press.

Maccoby, E. E., Doering, C. H., Jacklin, C. N., & Kraemer, H. (1979). Concentrations of sex hormones in umbilical cord blood: Their relation to sex and birth order. *Child Development, 50*(3), 632–642.

Maccoby, E. E., & Jacklin, C. N. (1974). *The psychology of sex differences.* Stanford, CA: Stanford University Press.

Maccoby, E. E., Snow, M. E., & Jacklin, C. N. (1984). Children's dispositions and mother-child interaction at 12 and 18 months: A short-term longitudinal study. *Developmental Psychology, 20*(3), 459–472.

MacCorquodale, P., & Jensen, G. (1993). Women in the law: Partners or tokens? *Gender and Society, 7*(4), 582–593.

Macfarlane, J., Allen, L., & Honzik, M. A. (1974). *Developmental study of the behavioral problems of normal children.* Berkeley: University of California Press.

Mackey, W. C. (2001). Support for the existence of an independent man-to-child affiliative bond: Fatherhood as a biocultural invention. *Psychology of Men and Masculinity, 2*(1), 51–66.

MacLeod, L. (1980). *Wife battering in Canada: The vicious circle.* Hull, Quebec: Canadian Government Publishing Centre.

Macrae, C., Bodenhausen, G., & Milne, A. (1995). The dissection of selection in person perception: Inhibitory processes in social stereotyping. *Journal of Personality and Social Psychology, 69,* 397–407.

Macy, C. (1986). Psychological factors in nausea and vomiting in pregnancy: A review. *Journal of Reproductive and Infant Psychology, 4*(1/2), 23–55.

Madson, L. (2000). Inferences regarding the personality traits and sexual orientation of physically androgynous people. *Psychology of Women Quarterly, 24*(2), 148–160.

Maffeo, P. A., Ford, T. W., & Lavin, P. F. (1990). Gender differences in depression in an employment setting. *Journal of Personality Assessment, 55*(1/2), 249–262.

Magazanik, M. (1991, August 9). Rape trauma less for prostitute, says judge. *The Age* (Melbourne, Australia), p. 1.

Magley, V. J., Hulin, C. L., Fitzgerald, L. F., & DeNardo, M. (1999). Outcomes of self-labeling sexual harassment. *Journal of Applied Psychology, 84,* 390–402.

Mainardi, P. (1970). The politics of housework. In R. Morgan (Ed.), *Sisterhood is powerful* (pp. 447–454). New York: Vintage Books.

Mainiero, L. A. (1986). A review and analysis of power dynamics in organizational romances. *Academy of Management Review, 11*(4), 750–762.

Mainiero, L. A. (1989). *Office romance.* New York: Rawson Associates/Macmillan.

Major, B. (1987). Women and entitlement. *Women and Therapy, 6*(3), 3–19.

Major, B. (1994). From social inequality to personal entitlement: The role of social comparisons, legitimacy appraisals, and group membership. In M. P. Zanna (Ed.), *Advances in experimental social psychology* (Vol. 6, pp. 293–335). San Diego: Academic Press.

Major, B., & Adams, J. B. (1983). The role of gender, interpersonal orientation and self-presentation in distributive justice behavior. *Journal of Personality and Social Psychology, 45,* 598–608.

Major, B., & Adams, J. B. (1984). Situational moderators of gender differences in reward allocations. *Sex Roles, 11*(9/10), 869–880.

Major, B., Bylsma, W. H., & Cozzarelli, C. (1989). Gender differences in distributive justice preferences: The impact of domain. *Sex Roles, 21*(7), 487–497.

Major, B., & Cozzarelli, C. (1992). Psychosocial predictors of adjustment to abortion. *Journal of Social Issues, 48*(3), 121–142.

Major, B., Cozzarelli, C., Cooper, M. L., Zubek, J., Richards, C., Wilhite, M., & Gramzow, R. H. (2000). Psychological responses of women after first-trimester abortion. *Archives of General Psychiatry, 57,* 777–784.

Major, B., & Deaux, K. (1982). Individual differences in justice behavior. In J. Greenberg & R. L. Cohen (Eds.), *Equity and justice in social behavior* (pp. 43–76). New York: Academic Press.

Major, B., & Forcey, B. (1985). Social comparisons and pay evaluations:

Preferences for same-sex and same-job wage comparisons. *Journal of Experimental Social Psychology, 21,* 393–405.

Major, B., McFarlin, D. B., & Gagnon, D. (1984). Overworked and underpaid: On the nature of gender differences in personal entitlement. *Journal of Personality and Social Psychology, 47*(6), 1399–1412.

Major, B., Schmidlen, A. M., & Williams, L. (1990). Gender patterns in social touch: The impact of setting and age. *Journal of Personality and Social Psychology, 58,* 634–643.

Major, B., Spencer, S., Schmader, T., Wolfe, C., & Crocker, J. (1998). Coping with negative stereotypes about intellectual performance: The role of psychological disengagement. *Personality and Social Psychology Bulletin, 24*(1), 34–50.

Major, B., Vanderslice, V., & McFarlin, D. B. (1984). Effects of pay expected on pay received: The confirmatory nature of initial expectations. *Journal of Applied Social Psychology, 14*(5), 399–412.

Maki, P. M., Rich, J. B., & Rosenbaum, R. S. (2002). Implicit memory varies across the menstrual cycle: Estrogen effects in young women. *Neuropsychologia, 40*(5), 518–529.

Makosky, V. P. (1980). Stress and the mental health of women: A discussion of research and issues. In M. Guttentag, S. Salasin, & D. Belle (Eds.), *The mental health of women* (pp. 111–128). New York: Academic Press.

Makri-Tsilipakou, M. (1994). Interruption revisited: Affiliative vs. disafilliative intervention. *Journal of Pragmatics, 21*(4), 401–426.

Malamuth, N. M. (1981). Rape proclivity among males. *Journal of Social Issues, 37*(4), 138–157.

Malamuth, N. M. (1984). Aggression against women: Cultural and individual causes. In N. Malamuth & E. Donnerstein (Eds.), *Pornography and sexual aggression* (pp. 19–52). New York: Academic Press.

Malamuth, N. M. (1996). The confluence model of sexual aggression: Feminist and evolutionary perspectives. In D. M. Buss & N. M. Malamuth (Eds.), *Sex, power, conflict: Evolutionary and feminist perspectives* (pp. 269–295). New York: Oxford University Press.

Malamuth, N. M., & Check, J. V. P. (1981). The effects of mass media exposure on acceptance of violence against women: A field experiment. *Journal of Research in Personality, 15,* 436–446.

Malamuth, N. M., Haber, S., & Feshbach, S. (1980). Testing hypotheses regarding rape: Exposure and sexual violence, sex differences and the "normality" of rapists. *Journal of Research in Personality, 14*(1), 121–137.

Malamuth, N. M., & Thornhill, N. W. (1994). Hostile masculinity, sexual aggression, and gender-biased domineeringness in conversations. *Aggressive Behavior, 20*(3), 185–193.

Maloiy, G. M. O., Heglund, N. C., Prager, L. M., Cavagna, G. A., & Taylor, C. R. (1986, February). Energetic costs of carrying loads: Have African women discovered an economic way? *Nature, 319*(6055), 668–669.

Maltz, D. N., & Borker, R. A. (1983). A cultural approach to male-female miscommunication. In J. A. Gumperz (Ed.), *Language and social identity* (pp. 195–216). New York: Cambridge University Press.

Mamiya, T. (1984). Aging and sex. *Japanese Psychological Review, 27*(3), 295–306.

Mancini, J. A., & Orthner, D. K. (1978). Recreational sexuality preferences among middle-class husbands and wives. *Journal of Sex Research, 14*(2), 96–106.

Mandel, R. B. (1995). A generation of change for women in politics. In J. Freeman (Ed.), *Women: A feminist perspective* (5th ed., pp. 405–429). Mountain View, CA: Mayfield.

Mangus, R. S., Hawkins, C. E., & Miller, M. J. (1998). Prevalence of harassment and discrimination among 1996 medical school graduates: A survey of eight US schools. *Journal of the American Medical Association, 280,* 851–853.

Manley, R. O. (1977). Parental warmth and hostility as related to sex differences in children's achievement orientation. *Psychology of Women Quarterly, 1*(3), 229–246.

Mann, J. (1999, July 6). Things could be better for women at the top. *Washington Post,* p. C10.

Mann, V. A., Sasanuma, S., Sakuma, N., & Masaki, S. (1990). Sex differences in cognitive abilities: A cross-cultural perspective. *Neuropsychologia, 28*(10), 1063–1077.

Manning, W. D., Longmore, M. A., & Giordano, P. C. (2000). The relationship context of contraceptive use at first

intercourse. *Family Planning Perspectives, 32*(3), 104–110.

Mansfield, P. K., Hood, K. E., & Henderson, J. (1989). Women and their husbands: Mood and arousal fluctuations across the menstrual cycle and days of the week. *Psychosomatic Medicine, 51*(1), 66–80.

Mansfield, P. K., Koch, P. B., Henderson, J., Vicary, J. R., Cohn, M., & Young, E. W. (1991). The job climate for women in traditionally male blue-collar occupations. *Sex Roles, 25*(1/2), 63–79.

Manson, S., Shore, J., Baron, A., Ackerson, L., & Neligh, G. (1992). Alcohol abuse and dependence among American Indians. In J. E. Helzer & G. J. Canimo (Eds.), *Alcoholism in North America, Europe, and Asia* (pp. 113–130). Oxford, England: Oxford University Press.

Marcus, R. (1991, March 21). "Fetal protection" plan ruled biased. *Washington Post,* pp. A1, A14, A15.

Margolin, L. (1992). Beyond maternal blame: Physical child abuse as a phenomenon of gender. *Journal of Family Issues, 13*(3), 410–423.

Markides, K. S. (1989). Consequences of gender differentials in life expectancy for Black and Hispanic Americans. *International Journal of Aging and Human Development, 29*(2), 95–102.

Marks, B. L., Ward, A., Morris, D. H., Castellani, J., & Rippe, J. M. (1995). Fat-free mass is maintained in women following a moderate diet and exercise program. *Medicine and Science in Sports and Exercise, 27*(9), 1243–1251.

Markush, R., & Favero, R. (1974). Epidemiologic assessment of stressful life events, depressed mood, and psychophysiological symptoms: A preliminary report. In B. P. Dohrenwend & B. S. Dohrenwend (Eds.), *Stressful life-events: Their nature and effects* (pp. 171–190). New York: Wiley.

Marlowe, C. M., Schneider, S. L., & Nelson, C. E. (1996). Gender and attractiveness biases in hiring decisions: Are more experienced managers less biased? *Journal of Applied Psychology, 81*(1), 11–21.

Marsh, H. W., & Yeung, A. S. (1998). Longitudinal structural equation models in academic self-concept and achievement: Gender differences in the development of math and English constructs. *American Educational Research Journal, 35,* 705–738.

Marshall, D. S. (1971). Sexual behavior on Mangaia. In D. S. Marshall & R. C.

Suggs (Eds.), *Human sexual behavior* (pp. 103–162). New York: Basic Books.

Marshall, L. L., & Rose, P. (1990). Premarital violence: The impact of family of origin on violence, stress, and reciprocity. *Violence and Victimology, 5*(1), 51–64.

Marshall, S. E. (1995). Keep us on the pedestal: Women against feminism in twentieth-century America. In J. Freeman (Ed.), *Women: A feminist perspective* (5th ed., pp. 547–560). Mountain View, CA: Mayfield.

Martel, R. F., Lane, D. M., & Emrich, C. (1996). Male-female differences: A computer simulation. *American Psychologist, 51,* 157–158.

Martin, C. L. (1987). A ratio measure of gender stereotyping. *Journal of Personality and Social Psychology, 52,* 489–499.

Martin, C. L. (1989). Children's use of gender-related information in making social judgments. *Developmental Psychology, 25,* 80–88.

Martin, C. L. (1990). Attitudes and expectations about children with nontraditional and traditional gender roles. *Sex Roles, 22*(3/4), 151–165.

Martin, C. L. (1993). New directions for investigating children's gender knowledge. *Developmental Review, 13,* 184–204.

Martin, C. L., & Halverson, C. F. (1981). A schematic processing model of sex typing and stereotyping in children. *Child Development, 52,* 1119–1134.

Martin, C. L., & Halverson, C. F., Jr. (1983). Gender constancy: A methodological and theoretical analysis. *Sex Roles, 9,* 775–790.

Martin, C. L., & Little, J. K. (1990). The relation of gender understanding to children's sex-typed preferences and gender stereotypes. *Child Development, 61,* 1427–1439.

Martin, C. L., Ruble, D. N., & Szkrybalo, J. (2002). Cognitive theories of early gender development. *Psychological Bulletin, 128*(6), 903–933.

Martin, C. L., Wood, C. H., & Little, J. K. (1990). The development of gender stereotype components. *Child Development, 61*(6), 1891–1904.

Martin, D. S., & Huang, M. (1984). Effects of time and perceptual orientation on actors' and observers' attributions. *Perceptual and Motor Skills, 58,* 23–30.

Martin, E. (1987). *The woman in the body: A cultural analysis of reproduction.* Boston: Beacon Press.

Martin, H. P. (1991). The coming-out process for homosexuals. *Hospital and Community Psychiatry, 42,* 158–162.

Martin, J. (2001, December). *Gender bias on a lower track: A look at gender bias in lower academically tracked classrooms.* Senior seminar paper, Trinity College. Retrieved from http://www.trincoll.edu/depts/educ/Research/MartinJ%20GenderBias.pdf

Martin, J. A., Maccoby, E. E., & Jacklin, C. N. (1981). Mother's responsiveness to inter-active bidding and nonbidding in boys and girls. *Child Development, 52*(3), 1064–1067.

Martinez, G. M., Chandra, A., Abma, J. C., Jones, J., & Mosher, W. D. (2006). *Fertility, contraception, and fatherhood: Data on men and women from Cycle 6 (2002) of the National Survey of Family Growth. National Center for Health Statistics.* Retrieved November 3, 2006, from http://www.cdc.gov/nchs/data/series/sr_23/sr23_026.pdf

Martz, D. M., Handley, K. B., & Eisler, R. M. (1995). The relationship between femi-nine gender role stress, body image, and eating disorders. *Psychology of Women Quarterly, 19*(4), 493–508.

Marván, M. L., Cortés-Iniestra, S., & Gonzalez, R. (2005). Beliefs about and attitudes toward menstruation among young and middle-aged Mexicans. *Sex Roles, 53*(3), 273–279.

Mashal, M. M. S., & Kalin, R. (1985, June). *The development of an interrole strain measure for dual-worker couples.* Paper presented at the 46th Annual Conven-tion of the Canadian Psychological Association, Halifax, Nova Scotia.

Masica, D., Money, J., & Ehrhardt, A. A. (1971). Fetal feminization and female gender identity in the testicular feminiz-ing syndrome of androgen insensitivity. *Archives of Sexual Behavior, 1*(2), 131–142.

Maslow, A., & Sakoda, J. (1952). Volunteer-error in the Kinsey study. *Journal of Abnormal and Social Psychology, 47,* 259–267.

Mason, A., & Blankenship, V. (1987). Power and affiliation motivation, stress, and abuse in intimate relationships. *Journal of Personality and Social Psychology, 52*(1), 203–210.

Masson, J. (1984, December). The persecu-tion and expulsion of Jeffrey Masson. *Mother Jones,* pp. 34–37, 42–47.

Masters, B. A. (1991, May 18). A rite of passage, a matter of rights. *Washington Post,* pp. B1, B7.

Masters, W. H., & Johnson, V. (1966). *Human sexual response.* Boston: Little, Brown.

Masters, W. H., & Johnson, V. (1970). *Human sexual inadequacy.* Boston: Little, Brown.

Mathes, E. W., Brennan, S. M., Haugen, P. M., & Rice, H. B. (1985). Ratings of physical attractiveness as a function of age. *Journal of Social Psychology, 125*(2), 157–168.

Matsui, T., Ohsawa, T., & Onglatco, M. (1995). Work-family conflict and the stress-buffering effects of husband support and coping behavior among Japanese married working women. *Journal of Vocational Behavior, 47,* 178–192.

Matthews, G. F. (1985). Mirror, mirror: Self-image and disabled women. *Resources for Feminist Research, 14*(1), 47–50.

Mauer, M., & Huling, T. (1995). *Young Black Americans and the criminal justice system five years later.* Washington, DC: The Sentencing Project.

Mauthner, N. S. (1999). "Feeling low and feeling really bad about feeling low": Women's experiences of motherhood and postpartum depression. *Canadian Psychology, 40*(2), 143–161.

Mayer, J. D., & Schmidt, H. M. (2004). Gendered political socialization in four contexts: Political interest and values among junior high school students in China, Japan, Mexico, and the United States. *Social Science Journal, 41*(3), 393–407.

Mayes, S., & Valentine, K. (1979). Sex-role stereotyping in Saturday morning cartoon shows. *Journal of Broadcasting, 23,* 41–50.

Mayo Clinic. (2001, October 9). *Headline watch: New evidence of ERT risks.* Retrieved from www.mayoclinic.com/home?id=NE00254

Mazur, A., & Booth, A. (1998). Testosterone and dominance in men. *Behavioral and Brain Sciences, 21,* 353–397.

Mazur, A., Booth, A., & Dabbs, J. M. (1992). Testosterone and chess competition. *Social Psychology Quarterly, 55*(1), 70–77.

Mazur, A., & Lamb, T. A. (1980). Testos-terone, status, and mood in human males. *Hormones and Behavior, 14,* 236–246.

Mazur, E. (1989). Predicting gender differences in same-sex friendships from affiliation motive and value. *Psychology of Women Quarterly, 13,* 277–291.

McArthur, L. Z., & Eisen, S. V. (1976). Achievements of male and female storybook characters as determinants of achieving behavior by boys and girls. *Journal of Personality and Social Psychology, 33,* 467–473.

McAuley, E., Courneya, K. S., & Lettunich, J. (1991). Effects of acute and long-term exercise on self-efficacy responses in sedentary, middle-aged males and females. *Gerontologist, 31*(4), 534–542.

McClelland, D. C. (1961). *The achieving society.* Princeton, NJ: Van Nostrand.

McClelland, D. C. (1975). *Power: The inner experience.* New York: Irvington.

McClelland, D. C., Atkinson, J. W., Clark, R. A., & Lowell, E. L. (1953). *The achievement motive.* New York: Appleton.

McCormick, N. B. (1994). *Sexual salvation: Affirming women's sexual rights and pleasure.* Westport, CT: Praeger.

McCray, C. A. (1980). The Black woman and family roles. In L. Rodgers-Rose (Ed.), *The Black woman* (pp. 67–78). Beverly Hills, CA: Sage.

McCreight, B. S. (2004). A grief ignored: Narratives of pregnancy loss from a male perspective. *Sociology of Health and Illness, 26*(3), 326–350.

McDonnell, K. (1984). *Not an easy choice: A feminist re-examines abortion.* Toronto: Women's Press.

McEwan, C. (1985). Crying the blues: Male postpartum depression explained. *Great Expectations, 14*(3), 56, 59.

McFadden, D. F. S. (2000). Body image and its relation to self-esteem and depression in heterosexual and gay men. *Disserta-tion Abstracts International: Section B: The Sciences and Engineering, 60*(9-B), 4896.

McFarland, C., Ross, M., & DeCourville, N. (1989). Women's theories of menstrua-tion and biases in recall of menstrual symptoms. *Journal of Personality and Social Psychology, 57*(3), 522–531.

McFarland, J. (2003, March 13). Women still find slow rise to power positions: Hold only 14% of corporate officer jobs in Canada. *Globe and Mail,* p. B1.

McFarlane, J., Martin, C. L., & Williams, T. M. (1988). Mood fluctuations: Women versus men and menstrual versus other cycles. *Psychology of Women Quarterly, 12*(2), 201–223.

McFarlane, J., & Williams, T. M. (1990). The enigma of premenstrual syndrome. *Canadian Psychology, 31,* 95–108.

McFarlane, J., & Williams, T. M. (1994). Placing premenstrual syndrome in perspective. *Psychology of Women Quarterly, 18,* 339–373.

McGhee, P. E., & Frueh, T. (1980). Television viewing and the learning of sex-role stereotypes. *Sex Roles, 6,* 179–188.

McGrath, E. P., & Repetti, R. L. (2000). Mothers' and fathers' attitudes toward their children's academic performance and children's perceptions of their academic competence. *Journal of Youth and Adolescence, 29*(6), 713–723.

McGraw, R., Lubienski, S. T., & Strutchens, M. E. (2006). A closer look at gender in NAEP mathematics achievement and affect data: Intersections with achievement, race/ethnicity, and socioeconomic status. *Journal for Research in Mathematics Education, 37*(2), 129–150.

McGuinness, D. (1972). Hearing: Individual differences in perceiving. *Perception, 1,* 465–473.

McGuinness, D. (1976). Away from a unisex psychology: Individual differences in visual perception. *Perception, 5,* 279–294.

McGuinness, D. (1985). Sensorimotor biases in cognitive development. In R. L. Hall (Ed.), *Male-female differences: A bio-cultural perspective.* New York: Praeger.

McGuinness, D. (1988). Socialization versus biology: Time to move on. *Behavioral and Brain Sciences, 11*(2), 203–204.

McGuinness, D., & Courtney, A. (1983). Sex differences in visual and phonetic search. *Journal of Mental Imagery, 7*(1), 95–104.

McGuinness, D., & McLaughlin, L. (1982). An investigation of sex differences in visual recognition and recall. *Journal of Mental Imagery, 6*(1), 203–212.

McGuinness, D., & Pribram, K. (1979). The origins of sensory bias in the development of gender differences in perception and cognition. In M. Bortner (Ed.), *Cognitive growth and development: Essays in honor of Herbert G. Birch* (pp. 3–56). New York: Brunner/Mazel.

McGuinness, D., & Symonds, J. (1977). Sex differences in choice behaviour: The object-person dimension. *Perception, 6,* 691–694.

McHale, S. M., & Huston, T. L. (1984). Men and women as parents: Sex role orientations, employment, and parental roles with infants. *Child Development, 55,* 1349–1361.

McHugh, M. D., Koeske, R. D., & Frieze, I. H. (1986). Issues to consider in conducting nonsexist psychological research: A guide for researchers. *American Psychologist, 41,* 879–890.

McIntyre, S. (1987). Gender bias in a Canadian law school. *Canadian Association of University Teachers Bulletin, 34*(1), 7–11.

McKinlay, J. B., McKinlay, S. M., & Brambilla, D. (1987). The relative contributions of endocrine changes and social circumstances to depression in mid-aged women. *Journal of Health and Social Behavior, 28*(4), 345–363.

McManus, A. J., Hunter, L. P., & Renn, H. (2006). Lesbian experiences and needs during childbirth: Guidance for health care providers. *Journal of Obstetric, Gynecologic, and Neonatal Nursing, 35*(1), 13–23.

Mcqueen, A. (1999, June 10). *Debt blocks some women from college.* Retrieved from search.washingtonpost.com/wpsrv/WAPO/19990610/V000122-061099-idx.html

McWhirter, P. T. (1999). La violencia privada: Domestic violence in Chile. *American Psychologist, 54*(1), 37–40.

McWhirter, N., & McWhirter, R. (1975). *Guinness book of world records.* New York: Sterling.

McWilliams, S., & Howard, J. A. (1993). Solidarity and hierarchy in cross-sex friendships. *Journal of Social Issues, 49*(3), 191–202.

Mead, M. (1935). *Sex and temperament in three primitive societies.* New York: Morrow.

Mead, M. (1980). A proposal: We need taboos on sex at work. In D. A. Neugarten & J. M. Shafritz (Eds.), *Sexuality in organizations: Romantic and coercive behaviors at work* (pp. 53–56). Oak Park, IL: Moore.

Meeker, B. F., & Elliott, G. C. (1996). Reward allocations, gender, and task performance. *Social Psychology Quarterly, 59*(3), 294–301.

Megargee, E. (1969). Influence of sex roles on the manifestation of leadership. *Journal of Applied Psychology, 53,* 377–382.

Melges, F. T. (1968). Postpartum psychiatric syndromes. *Psychosomatic Medicine, 30,* 95–108.

Mendez, L. M. R., & Crawford, K. M. (2002). Gender-role stereotyping and career aspirations: A comparison of gifted early adolescent boys and girls. *Journal of Secondary Gifted Education, 13*(3), 96–107.

Meredith, N. (1984, January). The gay dilemma. *Psychology Today,* pp. 56–62.

Messenger, J. C. (1971). Sex and repression in an Irish folk community. In D. S. Marshall & R. C. Suggs (Eds.), *Human sexual behavior* (pp. 3–37). New York: Basic Books.

Messner, M. A., Duncan, M. C., & Jensen, K. (1993). Separating the men from the girls: The gendered language of televised sports. *Gender and Society, 7*(1), 121–137.

Meyer-Bahlburg, H. F. L. (1980). Homosexual orientation in women and men: A hormonal basis? In J. Eccles Parsons (Ed.), *The psychobiology of sex differences and sex roles* (pp. 105–130). Washington, DC: Hemisphere.

Meyer-Bahlburg, H. F. L., Boon, D. A., Sharma, M., & Edwards, J. A. (1974). Aggressiveness and testosterone measures in man. *Psychosomatic Medicine, 36,* 267–274.

Meyer-Bahlburg, H. F. L., Ehrhardt, A. A., Rosen, L. R., Gruen, R. S., Veridiano, N. P., Vann, F. H., & Neuwalder, H. F. (1995). Prenatal estrogens and the development of homosexual orientation. *Developmental Psychology, 31*(1), 12–21.

Micciolo, R., Zimmerman-Tansella, C., Williams, P., & Tansella, M. (1989). Seasonal variation in suicide: Is there a sex difference? *Psychological Medicine, 19*(1), 199–203.

Michael, R. T., Gagnon, J. H., Laumann, E. O., & Kolata, G. (1994). *Sex in America.* Boston: Little, Brown.

Mieres, J. H., Shaw, L. J., Arai, A., Budoff, M. J., Flamm, S. D., Hundley, W. G., et al. (2005). Role of noninvasive testing in the clinical evaluation of women with suspected coronary artery disease: Consensus statement from the Cardiac Imaging Committee, Council on Clinical Cardiology, and the Cardiovascular Imaging and Intervention Committee, Council on Cardiovascular Radiology and Intervention, American Heart Association. *Circulation, 111*(5), 682–696.

Miller, C. L. (1983). Developmental changes in male/female voice classification by infants. *Infant Behavior and Development, 6,* 313–330.

Miller, C. L., & Cummins, A. G. (1992). An examination of women's perspectives on power. *Psychology of Women Quarterly, 16,* 415–428.

Miller, C. T., & Downey, K. T (1999). A meta-analysis of heavyweight and self-esteem. *Personality and Social Psychology Review, 3*(1), 68–84.

Miller, J. B. (1977). *Toward a new psychology of women*. Boston: Beacon Press.

Miller, P. J. E., & Rempel, J. K. (2004). Trust and partner-enhancing attributions in close relationships. *Personality and Social Psychology Bulletin, 30*(6), 695–705.

Miller, W. E., & Friedman, S. (1988). Male and female sexuality during pregnancy: Behavior and attitudes. *Journal of Psychology and Human Sexuality, 1*(2), 17–37.

Mirandé, A. (1997). *Hombres y machos: Masculinity and Latino culture*. Boulder, CO: Westview Press.

Mirandé, A., & Enriquez, E. (1979). *La Chicana: The Mexican-American woman*. Chicago: University of Chicago Press.

Mischel, W. (1970). Sex-typing and socialization. In P. H. Mussen (Ed.), *Carmichael's manual of child psychology* (Vol. 2, pp. 3–72). New York: Wiley.

Mohler-Kuo, M., Dowdall, G. W., Koss, M. P., & Wechsler, H. (2004). Correlates of rape while intoxicated in a national sample of college women. *Journal of Studies on Alcohol, 65*(1), 37–45.

Moir, A., & Jessel, D. (1991, May 5). A test: How female is your brain? *Washington Post*, p. K3.

Molloy, B. L., & Herzberger, S. D. (2002). Body image and self-esteem: A comparison of African-American and Caucasian women. In A. E. Hunter & C. Forden (Eds.), *Readings in the psychology of gender: Exploring our differences and commonalities* (pp. 111–122). Needham Heights, MA: Allyn & Bacon.

Monahan, L., Kuhn, D., & Shaver, P. (1974). Intrapsychic versus cultural explanations for the "fear of success" motive. *Journal of Personality and Social Psychology, 29*, 60–64.

Money, J., & Daley, J. (1977). Hyperadrenocortical 46 XX hermaphroditism with penile urethra: Psychological studies in seven cases, three reared as boys, four as girls. In P. A. Lee et al. (Eds.), *Congenital adrenal hyperplasia* (pp. 433–446). Baltimore: University Park Press.

Money, J., & Ehrhardt, A. A. (1972). *Man and woman, boy and girl*. Baltimore: Johns Hopkins University Press.

Money, J., & Mathews, D. (1982). Prenatal exposure to virilizing progestins: An adult follow-up study on 12 young women. *Archives of Sexual Behavior, 11*, 73–83.

Money, J., & Ogunro, B. (1974). Behavioral sexology: Ten cases of genetic male intersexuality with impaired prenatal and pubertal androgenization. *Archives of Sexual Behavior, 3*(3), 181–205.

Money, J., & Schwartz, M. (1977). Dating, romantic and nonromantic friendships, and sexuality in 17 early-treated adrenogenital females, aged 16–25. In P. A. Lee et al. (Eds.), *Congenital adrenal hyperplasia* (pp. 419–431). Baltimore: University Park Press.

Money, J., Schwartz, M., & Lewis, V. G. (1984). Adult erotosexual status and fetal hormonal masculinization and demasculinization: 46,XX congenital virilizing adrenal hyperplasia and 46,XX androgen-insensitivity syndrome compared. *Psychoneuroendocrinology, 9*, 405–414.

Monk, T. H., Moline, M. L., Fookson, J. E., & Peetz, S. M. (1989). Circadian determinants of subjective alertness. *Journal of Biological Rhythms, 4*(4), 393–404.

Montagu, A. (1952). *The natural superiority of women*. New York: Macmillan.

Montaigne, M. de (1580). *Essays* I. Chapter 27—Of friendship. Quoted in M. Gibbs, D. Auerbach, & M. Fox, A comparison of male and female same-sex friendships. *International Journal of Women's Studies, 3*(3), 270.

Moon, M., & Hoffman, C. D. (2000). References on men and women in psychology (1887–1997): PsycINFO as an archival research tool. *Psychology of Men and Masculinity, 1*(1), 16–20.

Moore, T. (1996, January/February). Willow Farey: For believing in the right of girls to be treated with honesty and respect. *Ms., 6*(4), 58–60.

Morawski, J. G. (1994). *Practicing feminisms, reconstructing psychology: Notes on a liminal science*. Ann Arbor: University of Michigan Press.

Moreland, R. L. (1985). Social categorization and the assimilation of "new" group members. *Journal of Personality and Social Psychology, 48*(5), 1173–1190.

Morgan, B. (1998). A three generational study of tomboy behavior. *Sex Roles, 39*(9/10), 787–800.

Morgan, M. (1982). Television and adolescents' sex role stereotypes: A longitudinal study. *Journal of Personality and Social Psychology, 43*, 947–955.

Morgan, S. P., Lye, D., & Condran, G. (1988). Sons, daughters, and the risk of marital disruption. *American Journal of Sociology, 94*, 110–129.

Morgan, S. P., & Pollard, M. S. (2002, May). *Do parents of girls really have a higher risk of divorce?* Paper presented at the annual meeting of the Population Association of America, Atlanta, Georgia.

Morin, S. F., & Garfinkle, E. M. (1978). Male homophobia. *Journal of Social Issues, 34*(1), 29–47.

Morrell, M. J., Dixen, J. M., Carter, S., & Davidson, J. M. (1984). The influence of age and cycling status on sexual arousability in women. *American Journal of Obstetrics and Gynecology, 148*, 66–71.

Morris, J. (1974). *Conundrum*. New York: Harcourt Brace Jovanovich.

Morris, S. (1978, May). Do men *need* to cheat on their women? A new science says YES: Darwin and the double standard. *Playboy*, pp. 109ff.

Morrison, D. M., Gillmore, M. R., Hoppe, M. J., Gaylord, J., Leigh, B. C., & Rainey, D. (2003). Adolescent drinking and sex: Findings from a daily diary study. *Perspectives on Sexual and Reproductive Health, 35*(4). Retrieved from http://www.guttmacher.org/pubs/journals/3516203.html

Morry, M. M., & Staska, S. L. (2001). Magazine exposure: Internalization, self-objectification, eating attitudes, and body satisfaction in male and female university students. *Canadian Journal of Behavioural Science, 33*(4), 269–279.

Moser, D., & Dracup, P. K. (1993). Gender differences in treatment-seeking delay in acute myocardial infarction. *Progress in Cardiovascular Nursing, 8*(1), 6–12.

Mosher, W. D., Anjani, C., & Jones, J. (2005). *Sexual behavior and selected health measures: Men and women 15–44 years of age, United States, 2002*. Retrieved July 24, 2006, from http://www.cdc.gov/nchs/data/ad/ad362.pdf

Moss, P., Bolland, G., Foxman, R., & Owen, C. (1987). The division of household work during the transition to parenthood. *Journal of Reproductive and Infant Psychology, 5*(2), 71–86.

Mott, F. L. (1991). Developmental effects of infant care: The mediating role of gender and health. *Journal of Social Issues, 47*(2), 139–158.

Moyer, K. E. (1974). Sex differences in aggression. In R. C. Friedman, R. M. Richart, & R. L. Vande Wiele (Eds.), *Sex differences in behavior* (pp. 149–163). New York: Wiley.

Muller, C. F. (1990). *Health care and gender*. New York: Russell Sage.

Mulvey, A., & Dohrenwend, B. S. (1983). The relation of stressful life events to gender. *Issues in Mental Health Nursing,* 5(1–4), 219–237.

Mumenthaler, M. S., O'Hara, R., Taylor, J. L., Friedman, L., & Yesavage, J. A. (2001). Relationship between variations in estradiol and progesterone levels across the menstrual cycle and human performance. *Psychopharmacology,* 155(2), 198–203.

Munroe, R. H., Shimmin, H. S., & Munroe, R. L. (1984). Gender understanding and sex role preference in four cultures. *Developmental Psychology, 20,* 673–682.

Murphy, C. M., & O'Leary, K. D. (1989). Psychological aggression predicts physical aggression in early marriage. *Journal of Consulting and Clinical Psychology, 57,* 579–582.

Murray, B. (1998, October). Survey reveals concerns of today's girls. *APA Monitor,* 29(10), 12.

Murray, H. A. (1937). Techniques for a systematic investigation of fantasy. *Journal of Psychology, 3,* 115–143.

Murray, S. J. (2002, April 10). Posting up in the pink ghetto. *Women's Sports Foundation.* Retrieved from http://www .womenssportsfoundation.org/cgi-bin/iowa/issues/disc/article.html?record=884

Murray-Close, D., Crick, N. R., & Galotti, K. M. (2006). Children's moral reasoning regarding physical and relational aggression. *Social Development, 15*(3), 345–372.

Murrell, A. J., Frieze, I. H., & Frost, J. L. (1991). Aspiring to careers in male- and female-dominated professions: A study of Black and White college women. *Psychology of Women Quarterly, 15*(1), 103–126.

Musselman, K., & Brouwer, B. (2005). Gender-related differences in physical performance among seniors. *Journal of Aging and Physical Activity, 13*(3), 239–253.

Myers, A. M., & Gonda, G. (1982). Utility of the masculinity-femininity construct: Comparison of traditional and androgyny approaches. *Journal of Personality and Social Psychology, 43,* 514–523.

Narrow, W. E., Rae, D. S., Moscicki, E. K., Locke, B. Z., & Regier, D. A. (1990). Depression among Cuban Americans. The Hispanic Health and Nutrition Examination Survey. *Social Psychiatry and Psychiatric Epidemiology, 25*(5), 260–268.

Nash, S. C., & Feldman, S. S. (1981). Sex-role and sex-related attributions: Constancy and change across the family life cycle. In M. E. Lamb & A. L. Brown (Eds.), *Advances in developmental psychology* (Vol. 1, pp. 1–36). Hillsdale, NJ: Erlbaum.

National Academy of Sciences. (2006a). *Membership listing.* Retrieved June 22, 2006, from http://www.nasonline .org/site/Dir/253659042?pg=rslts

National Academy of Sciences. (2006b). *To recruit and advance: Women students and faculty in U.S. science and engineering.* Retrieved June 22, 2006, from http:// www.nap.edu/books/0309095212/ html/index.html

National Center for Education Statistics. (2005). *Digest of education statistics tables and figures 2005.* Retrieved July 13, 2006, from http://nces.ed.gov/programs/ digest/d05/lt3.asp#19

National Center for Health Statistics. (1998). *Health, United States, 1998.* Washington, DC: Author.

National Center for Health Statistics. (1999, April 29). *Teen birth rate down in all states.* Press release. Retrieved from www.cdc .gov/nchswww/releases/99news

National Center for Health Statistics. (2001). *Mental health disorders.* Retrieved from http://www.cdc.gov/nchs/fastats/ mental.htm

National Center for Health Statistics. (2002). *Health: United States, 2002.* Author: Hyatsville, MD. Retrieved from http:// www.cdc.gov/nchs/data/hus/hus02 .pdf

National Center for Health Statistics. (2003d, August 11). *Advanced data from vital and health statistics.* Numbers 332, 335, 337 and 338. Retrieved from http://www .cdc.gov/nchs/about/major/ahcd

National Center for Health Statistics. (2005). *Health, United States, 2005.* Retrieved July 31, 2006, from http://www.cdc .gov/nchs/hus.htm

National Center on Addiction and Substance Abuse. (2006). *Women and prescription and illegal drugs.* Retrieved September 7, 2006, from http://www.casacolumbia .org/absolutenm/templates/Publications .aspx?articleid=421&zoneid=52

National Collegiate Athletic Association. (2006). *Participation: 1981–82—2004-05 NCAA sports sponsorship and participation rates report.* Retrieved November 30, 2006, from http://www.ncaa.org/ library/research/participation_rates/ 1982-2005/1982_2005_participation_ rates.pdf

National Institutes of Health. (2006, April 14). *Women's health initiative.* Retrieved September 5, 2006, from http://www .nhlbi.nih.gov/whi/

National Opinion Research Center. (2005). *Doctorate recipients from United States universities: Summary report 2004.* Retrieved from http://www.norc.org/ issues/sed-2004.pdf

National Science Foundation. (2002). *Science and engineering indicators 2002.* Retrieved from http://www.nsf.gov/sbe/srs/ seind)2/pdfstart.htm

National Science Foundation. (2003). *Web-CASPAR database.* Retrieved from http://caspar.nsf.gov

National Science Foundation. (2004a). *Science and engineering doctorate awards: 2003.* NSF 05-300. Retrieved June 20, 2006, from http://www.nsf.gov/ statistics/nsf05300/dst.htm

National Science Foundation. (2004b). *Women, minorities, and persons with disabilities in science and engineering: 2004.* Retrieved June 22, 2006, from http:// www.nsf.gov/statistics/wmpd/start. htm

National Women's Law Center. (2002, June). *Title IX and equal opportunity in vocational and technical education. A promise still owed to the nation's young women.* Retrieved from http://www .nwlc.org/pdf/TitleIXCareerEducation Report.pdf

Neal, L. V. I., McCray, A. D., Webb-Johnson, G., & Bridgest, S. T. (2003). The effects of African American movement styles on teachers' perceptions and reactions. *Journal of Special Education, 37*(1), 49–57.

Neff, J. A., Prihoda, T. J., & Hoppe, K. (1991). Machismo, self-esteem, education and high maximum drinking among Anglo, Black and Mexican-American male drinkers. *Journal of Studies on Alcohol, 52,* 458–463.

Neft, N., & Levine, A. D. (1997). *Where women stand: An international report on the status of women in 140 countries, 1997–1998.* New York: Random House.

Nelson, A. (2000). The pink dragon is female. *Psychology of Women Quarterly, 24*(2), 137–144.

Nesselroade, J. R., & Thompson, W. W. (1995). Selection and related threats to group comparisons: An example comparing factorial structures of higher and lower ability groups of adult twins. *Psychological Bulletin, 117*(2), 271–284.

Neugarten, B. L., & Kraines, R. J. (1965). "Menopausal symptoms" in women of various ages. *Psychosomatic Medicine, 27,* 266.

New, C. (2001). Oppressed and oppressors? The systematic mistreatment of men. *Sociology, 35*(3), 729–748.

Newcombe, N., & Arnkoff, D. B. (1979). Effects of speech style and sex of speaker on person perception. *Journal of Personality and Social Psychology, 37*(8), 1293–1303.

Newcombe, N., Bandura, M. M., & Taylor, D. G. (1983). Sex differences in spatial ability and spatial activities. *Sex Roles, 9,* 377–386.

Newton, E. (1984). The mythic mannish lesbian: Radclyffe Hall and the new woman. *Signs: Journal of Women in Culture and Society, 9,* 557–575.

Newton, N. (1971). Trebly sensuous woman. *Psychology Today, 5,* 68–71, 98–99.

Nichols, M. (1990). Lesbian relationships: Implications for the study of sexuality and gender. In D. McWhiter, S. A. Sanders, & J. Reinisch (Eds.), *Homosexuality/heterosexuality: Concepts of sexual orientation* (pp. 350–364, Kinsey Institute Series). New York: Oxford University Press.

Nicholson, J. (1984). *Men and women: How different are they?* Oxford: Oxford University Press.

Nicolson, P. (1999). Loss, happiness and postpartum depression: The ultimate paradox. *Canadian Psychology, 40*(2), 162–178.

Nicholson, S. (2002). "So you row, do you? You don't look like a rower." An account of medical students' experience of sexism. *Medical Education, 36*(11), 1057–1063.

Nobel Foundation. (2003). *Laureates.* Retrieved from http://www.nobel.se/

Nobel Foundation. (2006). *Laureates.* Retrieved November 7, 2006, from http://nobelprize.org/nobel_prizes/

Nolen-Hoeksema, S. (1987). Sex differences in unipolar depression: Evidence and theory. *Psychological Bulletin, 101*(2), 259–282.

Nolen-Hoeksema, S., & Girgus, J. S. (1994). The emergence of gender differences in depression during adolescence. *Psychological Bulletin, 115*(3), 424–443.

Noller, P. (1980). Misunderstandings in marital communication: A study of couples' nonverbal communication. *Journal of Personality and Social Psychology, 39,* 1135–1148.

Nordstrom, C. (2004, March). *Voices from the front lines: Women on war.* Keynote address to the annual meeting of the Southeastern Women's Studies Association, Savannah, GA.

Norman, R. L., & Spies, H. G. (1986). Cyclic ovarian function in a male macaque: Additional evidence for a lack of sexual differentiation in the physiological mechanisms that regulate the cyclic release of gonadotrophins in primates. *Endocrinology, 118,* 2608–2610.

Nosek, B. A., Banaji, M. R., & Greenwald, A. G. (2002). Math = male, me = female, therefore math ≠ me. *Journal of Personality and Social Psychology, 83,* 44–59.

Nowell, A., & Hedges, L. V. (1998). Trends in gender differences in academic achievement from 1960 to 1994: An analysis of differences in mean, variance, and extreme scores. *Sex Roles, 39*(1/2), 21–43.

Nunes, M., & White, D. (1973). *The lace ghetto.* Toronto: New Press.

Nyborg, H. (1983). Spatial ability in men and women: Review and a new theory. *Advances in Behaviour Research and Therapy, 5,* 89–140.

Nyquist, L., & Spence, J. (1986). Effects of dispositional dominance and sex role expectations on leadership behaviors. *Journal of Personality and Social Psychology, 50*(1), 377–382.

Oakhill, J., Garnham, A., & Reynolds, D. (2005). Immediate activation of stereotypical gender information. *Memory and Cognition, 33*(6), 972–983.

O'Connell, H. E., Hutson, J. M., Anderson, C. R., & Plenter, R. J. (1998). Anatomical relationship between urethra and clitoris. *Journal of Urology, 159*(6), 1892–1897.

O'Connor, D. B., Archer, J., Hair, W. M., & Wu, F. C. W. (2002). Exogenous testosterone, aggression, and mood in eugonadal and hypogonadal men. *Physiology and Behavior, 75*(4), 557–566.

Oden, M. H. (1968). The fulfillment of promise: 40-year follow-up of the Terman gifted group. *Genetic Psychology Monographs, 77,* 3–93.

O'Donnell, B. L., O'Donnell, C. R., & Stueve, A. (2001). Early sexual initiation and subsequent sex-related risks among urban minority youth: The Reach for Health study. *Family Planning Perspectives, 30*(6), 268–275.

OECD/UNESCO. (2003). *Literacy skills for the world of tomorrow: Further results from PISA 2000.* Paris, France: Authors.

O'Farrell, B. (1995). Women in blue-collar occupations: Traditional and nontraditional. In J. Freeman (Ed.), *Women: A feminist perspective* (5th ed., pp. 238–261). Mountain View, CA: Mayfield.

Offermann, L. R., & Beil, C. (1992). Achievement styles of women leaders and their peers: Toward an understanding of women and leadership. *Psychology of Women Quarterly, 16*(1), 37–56.

Ogletree, S. M., Coffee, M. C., & May, S. A. (1992). Perceptions of female/male presidential candidates: Familial and personal situations. *Psychology of Women Quarterly, 16*(2), 201–208.

O'Hagan, F. T., Sale, D. G., MacDougall, J. D., & Garner, S. H. (1995). Response to resistance training in young women and men. *International Journal of Sports Medicine, 16,* 314–321.

O'Haire, N. (2004). CTF surveys gender composition of Canada's teaching populations. *PD Perspectives, 4.* Retrieved November 20, 2006, from http://www.teachers.ab.ca/Quick+Links/Publications/Magazine/Volume+85/Number+3/Articles/Gender+and+Leadership.htm

O'Hara, M. W. (1985). Depression and marital adjustment during pregnancy and after delivery. *American Journal of Family Therapy, 13*(4), 49–55.

O'Hara, M. W. (1997). The nature of postpartum depressive disorders. In L. Murray, P. J. Cooper, et al. (Eds.), *Postpartum depression and child development* (pp. 3–31). New York: Guilford Press.

O'Hara, M. W., & Swain, A. M. (1996). Rates and risk of postpartum depression: A meta-analysis. *International Review of Psychiatry, 8*(1), 37–54.

O'Heron, C. A., & Orlofsky, J. L. (1990). Stereotypic and nonstereotypic sex role trait and behavior orientations, gender identity, and psychological adjustment. *Journal of Personality and Social Psychology, 58*(1), 134–143.

Ohira, T., Tanigawa, T., Iso, H., Odagiri, Y., Takamiya, T., Shimomitsu, T., et al. (2000). Effects of shift work on 24-hour ambulatory blood pressure and its variability among Japanese workers. *Scandinavian Journal of Work, Environment and Health, 26*(5), 421–426.

O'Kelly, C. G., & Carney, L. S. (1986). *Women and men in society: Cross-cultural perspectives on gender stratification.* Belmont, CA: Wadsworth.

Okorodudu, C. (1999, April). Statement of the task force on mental health of the NGO committee on the status of women. *SPSSI Newsletter, 208,* 14–15.

Oldenburg, D. (1994, November 29). The electron gender gap. *Washington Post,* p. D5.

O'Leary, V. E., & Harrison, A. O. (1975, September). *Sex role stereotypes as a function of race and sex.* Paper presented at the annual convention of the American Psychological Association, Chicago.

Olian, J. D., Schwab, D. P., & Haberfeld, Y. (1988). The impact of applicant gender compared to qualifications on hiring recommendations: A meta-analysis of experimental studies. *Organizational Behavior and Human Decision Processes, 41,* 180–195.

Oliver, M. B., & Hyde, J. S. (1993). Gender differences in sexuality: A meta-analysis. *Psychological Bulletin, 114*(1), 29–51.

O'Neill, W. L. (1998). Sex scandals in the gender-integrated military. *Gender Issues,* 16(1–2), 64–86.

Oppenheimer, V. K. (1970). *The female labor force in the United States: Demographic and economic factors governing its growth and changing composition* (Population Monograph Series No. 5). Berkeley: University of California.

Oriña, M. M., Wood, W., & Simpson, J. A. (2002). Strategies of influence in close relationships. *Journal of Experimental Social Psychology, 38*(5), 459–472.

Ott, E. M. (1989). Effects of the male-female ratio at work: Policewomen and male nurses. *Psychology of Women Quarterly, 13*(1), 41–58.

Owens, L., Shute, R., & Slee, P. (2000). "I'm in and you're out. . . ." Explanations for teenage girls' indirect aggression. *Psychology, Evolution and Gender, 2*(1), 19–46.

Ozer, E. M. (1995). The impact of childcare responsibility and self-efficacy on the psychological health of professional working mothers. *Psychology of Women Quarterly, 19*(3), 315–336.

Padgett, V. R., Brislin-Slutz, J. A., & Neal, J. A. (1989). Pornography, erotica, and attitudes toward women: The effects of repeated exposure. *Journal of Sex Research, 26,* 479–491.

Padian, N. S., Shiboski, S. C., & Jewell, N. P. (1991). Female-to-male transmission of human immunodeficiency virus. *Journal of the American Medical Association, 266*(12), 1664–1667.

Pagelow, M. D. (1993). Justice for victims of spouse abuse in divorce and child custody cases. *Violence and Victims, 8*(1), 69–83.

Paige, K. E. (1971). The effects of oral contraceptives on affective fluctuations associated with the menstrual cycle. *Psychosomatic Medicine, 33,* 515–537.

Pajntar, M. (1972). Obstetrical complications: Personality changes and emotional tension during pregnancy. In N. Morris (Ed.), *Psychosomatic medicine in obstetrics and gynecology* (Third International Congress, London, 1971). Basel: Karger.

Paludi, M. A. (1984). Psychometric properties and underlying assumptions of four objective measures of fear of success. *Sex Roles, 10,* 765–781.

Paludi, M. A., & Strayer, L. A. (1985). What's in an author's name? Differential evaluations of performance as a function of author's name. *Sex Roles, 12*(3/4), 353–362.

Pantony, K., & Caplan, P. J. (1991). Delusional dominating personality disorder: A modest proposal for identifying some consequences of rigid masculine socialization. *Canadian Psychology, 32*(2), 120–135.

Papini, D. R., Farmer, F. F., Clark, S. M., Micka, J. C., & Barnett, J. K. (1990). Early adolescent age and gender differences in patterns of emotional self-disclosure to parents and friends. *Adolescence, 25,* 959–976.

Parke, R. D. (1981). *Fathers.* Cambridge, MA: Harvard University Press.

Parke, R. D., & Sawin, D. B. (1976). The father's role in infancy: A reevaluation. *Family Coordinator, 25,* 365–371.

Parker, S., & de Vries, B. (1993). Patterns of friendship for women and men in same- and cross-sex relationships. *Journal of Social and Personal Relationships, 10*(4), 617–626.

Parlee, M. B. (1973). The premenstrual syndrome. *Psychological Bulletin, 80,* 454–465.

Parlee, M. B. (1982). Changes in moods and activation levels during the menstrual cycle in experimentally naive subjects. *Psychology of Women Quarterly, 7,* 119–131.

Parlee, M. B. (1983). Menstrual rhythms in sensory processes: A review of fluctuations in vision, olfaction, audition, taste, and touch. *Psychological Bulletin, 93,* 539–548.

Parsley, P. C., & Lips, H. M. (2007, February). *Role models and student aspirations.* Paper presented at the South-eastern Psychological Association Meeting, New Orleans, LA.

Parsons, T., & Bales, R. F. (1955). *Family, socialization, and interaction process.* Glencoe, IL: Free Press.

Patford, J. L. (2000). Partners and cross-sex friends: A preliminary study of the way marital and defacto partnerships affect verbal intimacy with cross-sex friends. *Journal of Family Studies, 6*(1), 106–119.

Patterson, C. J. (1992). Children of lesbian and gay parents. *Child Development, 63,* 1025–1042.

Patterson, C. J. (1995). Families of the baby boom: Parents' division of labor and children's adjustment. *Developmental Psychology, 31*(1), 115–123.

Patterson, C. J. (1998). Family lives of lesbians and gay men. In S. Bellack & M. Hersen (Eds.), *Comprehensive clinical psychology* (Vol. 9, pp. 253–273). Amsterdam: Elsevier.

Paul, J. P. (1985). Bisexuality: Reassessing our paradigms of sexuality. *Journal of Homosexuality, 10*(3/4), 21–34.

Paulsen, K., & Johnson, M. (1983). Sex role attitudes and mathematical ability in 4th-, 8th-, and 11th-grade students from a high socioeconomic area. *Developmental Psychology, 19*(2), 210–214.

Pauly, I. (1968). The current status of the change of sex operation. *Journal of Nervous and Mental Disorders, 147,* 460–471.

Pearlin, L., & Johnson, J. (1977). Marital status, life-strains and depression. *American Sociological Review, 42,* 704–715.

Pearlstein, T., Yonkers, K. A., Fayyad, R., & Gillespie, J. A. (2005). Pretreatment pattern of symptom expression in premenstrual dysphoric disorder. *Journal of Affective Disorders, 85*(3), 275–282.

Pearson, J. A., Burkhart, E., Pifalo, W. B., Palaggo-Toy, T., & Krohn, K. (2005). A lifestyle modification intervention for the treatment of osteoporosis. *American Journal of Health Promotion, 20*(1), 28–33.

Pearson, J. C., & West, R. (1991). An initial investigation of the effects of gender on student questions in the classroom: Developing a descriptive base. *Communication Education, 40*(1), 22–32.

Pennebaker, J. W. (1982). *The psychology of physical symptoms.* New York: Springer-Verlag.

Peplau, L. A. (1981, March). What homosexuals want in relationships. *Psychology Today, 15*(3), 28–38.

Peplau, L. A. (1983). Roles and gender. In H. H. Kelley, E. Berscheid, A. Christensen, J. H. Harvey, T. L. Huston, G. Levinger, E. McClintock, L. A. Peplau, & D. R. Peterson (Eds.), *Close relationships* (pp. 221–264). New York: W. H. Freeman.

Peplau, L. A. (2003). Human sexuality: How do men and women differ? *Current Directions in Psychological Science, 12*(2), 37–40.

Peplau, L. A., & Amaro, H. (1982). Understanding lesbian relationships. In W. Paul, J. D. Weinrich, J. C. Gonsiorek, & M. E. Hotvedt (Eds.), *Homosexuality: Social, psychological, and biological issues* (pp. 233–247). Beverly Hills, CA: Sage.

Peplau, L. A., & Cochran, S. D. (1981). Value orientations in the intimate relationships of gay men. *Journal of Homosexuality, 6*(3), 1–19.

Peplau, L., & Cochran, S. D. (1990). A relationship perspective on homosexuality. In D. P. McWhirter, S. A. Sanders, & J. M. Reinisch (Eds.), *Homosexuality/ heterosexuality: Concepts of sexual orientation* (pp. 321–349). New York: Oxford University Press.

Peplau, L. A., Cochran, S., Rook, K., & Padesky, C. (1978). Loving women: Attachment and autonomy in lesbian relationships. *Journal of Social Issues, 34*(3), 7–27.

Peplau, L. A., & Conrad, E. (1989). Beyond nonsexist research: The perils of feminist methods in psychology. *Psychology of Women Quarterly, 13*(4), 379–400.

Peplau, L. A., & Garnets, L. D. (2000). A new paradigm for understanding women's sexuality and sexual orientation. *Journal of Social Issues, 56*(2), 329–350.

Peplau, L. A., Spalding, L. R., Conley, T. D., & Veniegas, R. C. (1999). The development of sexual orientation in women. *Annual Review of Sex Research, 10*, 70–99.

Percival, E. (1991). *Thinking about gender similarities and differences: A discussion paper*. Paper presented at the annual meeting of the Association for Women in Psychology, Hartford, CT.

Perkins, K. (1992). Psychosocial implications of women and retirement. *Social Work, 37*(6), 526–532.

Perry, D. G., & Bussey, K. (1979). The social learning theory of sex differences: Imitation is alive and well. *Journal of Personality and Social Psychology, 37*, 1699–1712.

Perry, D. G., Perry, L. C., & Weiss, R. J. (1989). Sex differences in the consequences children anticipate for aggression. *Developmental Psychology, 25*, 312–319.

Perry, J. D., & Whipple, B. (1981). Pelvic muscle strength of female ejaculators: Evidence in support of a new theory of orgasm. *Journal of Sex Research, 17*, 22–39.

Pesmen, C. (1991, November). Love and sex in the '90s: Our national survey. *Seventeen*, pp. 63–68.

Petersen, A. C., & Wittig, M. A. (1979). Sex-related differences in cognitive functioning: An overview. In M. A. Wittig & A. C. Petersen (Eds.), *Sex-related differences in cognitive function: Developmental issues* (pp. 1–17). New York: Academic Press.

Petersen, A. E. (1983). Menarche: Meaning of measures and measuring meaning. In S. Golub (Ed.), *Menarche*. Lexington, MA: D. C. Heath.

Peterson, A., & Jenni, C. B. (2003). Men's experience of making the decision to have their first child: A phenomenological analysis. *Family Journal: Counseling and Therapy for Couples and Families, 11*(4), 353–363.

Peterson, D. L., & Pfost, K. S. (1989). Influence of rock videos on attitudes to violence against women. *Psychological Reports, 64*, 319–322.

Peterson, G. H., Mehl, L. E., & Leiderman, P. H. (1979). The role of some birth-related variables in father attachment. *American Journal of Orthopsychiatry, 40*, 330–338.

Peterson, S. B., & Lach, M. A. (1990). Gender stereotypes in children's books: Their prevalence and influence on cognitive and affective development. *Gender and Education, 2*(2), 185–197.

Peterson, T. (2003, April 15). What if women ran the world? *BusinessWeek Online*. Retrieved from http:// www.businessweek.com/bwdaily/ dnflash/ apr2003/nf20030415_4958 _db028.htm

Pew Research Center for People and the Press. (2002). *What the world thinks in 2002*. Retrieved from http://people-press.org/reports/pdf/165.pdf

Pfost, K. S., & Fiore, M. (1990). Pursuit of nontraditional occupations: Fear of success or fear of not being chosen. *Sex Roles, 23*(1/2), 15–24.

Phillips, R. D., & Gilroy, F. D. (1985). Sex-role stereotypes and clinical judgements of mental health: The Brovermans' findings reexamined. *Sex Roles, 12*, 179–193.

Phillips-Miller, D., Morrison, C., & Campbell, N. J. (2001). Same profession, different career: A study of men and women in veterinary medicine. In F. Columbus (Ed.), *Advances in psychology research* (Vol. V, pp. 1–53).

Phinney, J. S. (1989). Stages of ethnic identity in minority group adolescents. *Journal of Early Adolescence, 9*, 34–49.

Phinney, J. S. (1990). Ethnic identity in adolescents and adults: Review of research. *Psychological Bulletin, 108*(3), 499–514.

Phoenix, C., Goy, R. W., & Resko, J. A. (1968). Psychosexual differentiation as a function of androgenic stimulation. In M. Diamond (Ed.), *Reproduction and sexual behavior*. Bloomington: Indiana University Press.

Piaget, J. (1954). *The construction of reality in the child*. New York: Basic Books.

Piaget, J. (1965). *The moral judgment of the child*. New York: Free Press. (Original work published 1932)

Pidano, A. E., & Tennen, H. (1985). Transient depressive experiences and their relationship to gender and sex-role orientation. *Sex Roles, 12*, 97–110.

Piliavin, J. A., & Unger, R. K. (1985). The helpful but helpless female: Myth or reality? In V. O'Leary, R. Unger, & B. Wallston (Eds.), *Women, gender, and social psychology* (pp. 149–189). Hillsdale, NJ: Erlbaum.

Pillard, R. C., & Bailey, J. M. (1991). A genetic study of male sexual orientation. *Archives of General Psychiatry, 48*, 1089–1096.

Pillard, R. C., & Weinrich, J. D. (1986). Evidence of familial nature of male homosexuality. *Archives of General Psychiatry, 43*(8), 800–812.

Pingree, S. (1978). The effects of nonsexist TV commercials and perceptions of reality on children's attitudes about women. *Psychology of Women Quarterly, 2*, 262–277.

Pleck, J. H. (1981). *The myth of masculinity*. Cambridge, MA: MIT Press.

Pleck, J. H. (1995). The gender role strain paradigm: An update. In R. F. Levant & W. S. Pollock (Eds.), *A new psychology of men* (pp. 11–32). New York: Basic Books.

Plummer, D. C. (2001). The quest for modern manhood: Masculine stereotypes, peer culture and the social significance of homophobia. *Journal of Adolescence, 24*(1), 15–23.

Polk, B. B. (1974). Male power and the women's movement. *Journal of Applied Behavioral Science, 10*(3), 415–431.

Pomerantz, E. M., Ng, F. F.-Y., & Wang, Q. (2004). Gender socialization: A parent x child model. In A. H. Eagly, A. E. Beall, & R. J. Sternberg (Eds.), *The psychology of gender* (2nd ed., pp. 120–144). New York: Guilford Press.

Pomerleau, A., Bolduc, D., Malcuit, G., & Cossette, L. (1990). Pink or blue: Environmental gender stereotypes in the first two years of life. *Sex Roles, 22*(5/6), 359–367.

Pope, H. G., Jr., Kouri, E. M., & Hudson, J. I. (2000). Effects of supraphysiologic doses of testosterone on mood and aggression in normal men: A randomized controlled trial. *Archives of General Psychiatry, 57*(2), 133–140.

Popenow, D., & Whitehead, B. D. (1999). *The state of our unions: The social health of marriage in America.* Rutgers, NJ: The National Marriage Project, Rutgers University.

Porter, N., & Geis, F. (1981). Women and nonverbal leadership cues: When seeing is not believing. In C. Mayo & N. Henley (Eds.), *Gender and nonverbal behavior* (pp. 39–59). New York: Springer-Verlag.

Poulin-Dubois, D., Serbin, L. A., Eichstedt, J. A., Sen, M. G., & Beissel, C. F. (2002). Men don't put on make-up: Toddlers' knowledge of the gender stereotyping of household activities. *Social Development, 11*(2), 166–181.

Poulin-Dubois, D., Serbin, L. A., Kenyon, B., & Derbyshire, A. (1994). Infants' intermodal knowledge about gender. *Developmental Psychology, 30*(3), 436–442.

Powlishta, K. K. (1990). *Children's biased views of male and female traits.* Paper presented at the second annual convention of the American Psychological Society, Dallas.

Prather, J. E. (1971). When the girls move in: A sociological analysis of the feminization of the bank teller's job. *Journal of Marriage and the Family, 33*(4), 777–782.

Prather, J. E., & Fidell, L. S. (1978). Drug use and abuse among women: An overview. *International Journal for the Addictions, 13*, 863–885.

Pratt, M. W., Pancer, M., & Hunsberger, B. (1990). Reasoning about the self and relationships in maturity: An integrative complexity analysis of individual differences. *Journal of Personality and Social Psychology, 59*(3), 575–581.

Pratto, F. (1996). Sexual politics: The gender gap in the bedroom, the cupboard, and the cabinet. In D. M. Buss & N. M. Malamuth (Eds.), *Sex, power, conflict: Evolutionary and feminist perspectives* (pp. 179–230). New York: Oxford University Press.

Pratto, F., Sidanius, J., & Siers, B. (1997). The gender gap in occupational role attainment: A social dominance approach. *Journal of Personality and Social Psychology, 72*(1), 37–53.

Pratto, F., & Walker, A. (2004). The bases of gendered power. In A. H. Eagly, A. E. Beall, & R. J. Sternberg (Eds.), *The psychology of gender* (2nd ed., pp. 242–268). New York: Guilford Press.

Prentice, D. A., & Carranza, E. (2002). What women and men should be, shouldn't be, are allowed to be, and don't have to be: The contents of prescriptive gender stereotypes. *Psychology of Women Quarterly, 26*(4), 269–281.

Price, W. H., & Whatmore, P. B. (1967a). Behavior disorders and pattern of crime among XYY males identified at a maximum security prison. *British Medical Journal, 1*, 533–536.

Price, W. H., & Whatmore, P. B. (1967b). Criminal behavior and the XYY male. *Nature, 213*, 815.

Pringle, P. (2003, July 27). College Board scores with critics of SAT analogies. *Los Angeles Times.* Retrieved from http://www.latimes.com/news/education/la-me-sat27jul27002421, 1,2926050.story?coll=la-news-learning

Prostitutes' Education Network (1999). *Prostitution in the United States: The statistics.* Retrieved from http://www.bayswan.org/stats.html

Prybock, D. J. (2000). Body dissatisfaction as a predictor of eating, exercise, and anabolic-androgenic steroid use among males. *Dissertation Abstracts International, Section B: The Sciences and Engineering, 60*(7-B), 3577.

Pryor, J. B. (1985). The lay person's understanding of sexual harassment. *Sex Roles, 13*(5/6), 273–286.

Ptacek, J. T., Smith, R. E., & Zanas, J. (1992). Gender, appraisal, and coping: A longitudinal analysis. *Journal of Personality, 60*, 747–770.

Pugliesi, K. (1995). Work and well-being: Gender differences in the psychological consequences of employment. *Journal of Health and Social Behavior, 36*, 57–71.

Pursell, P., & Stewart, L. (1990). Dick and Jane in 1989. *Sex Roles, 22*(3/4), 177–185.

Pyke, S. (1979). Cognitive templating: A technique for feminist (and other) counselors. *Personnel and Guidance Journal, 57*(6), 315–318.

Quaiser-Pohl, C., & Lehmann, W. (2002). Girls' spatial abilities: Charting the contributions of experience and attitudes in different academic groups. *British Journal of Educational Psychology, 72*(2), 245–260.

Quill, T. E., Lipkin, M., & Lamb, G. S. (1984). Health-care seeking by men in their spouse's pregnancy. *Psychosomatic Medicine, 46*(3), 277–283.

Quinn, R. E. (1977). Coping with Cupid: The formation, impact, and management of romantic relationships in organizations. *Administrative Science Quarterly, 22*, 30–45.

Rabasca, L. (1999, February). Women addicts vulnerable to trauma. *APA Monitor,* p. 32.

Rabin, J. S. (1987, March). *Adaptation across the lifespan: Evolution, sex roles, and social change.* Paper presented at the Conference of the Association for Women in Psychology, Denver, CO.

Rabin, J. S. (1998, March). *Using developmental-interactionist and feminist perspectives in teaching ethology and comparative psychology.* Paper presented at the annual national conference of the Association for Women in Psychology, Baltimore, MD.

Rabin, J. S. (2006, March). *New feminist and multicultural frameworks for understanding evolution, genetics, sexual orientation diversity, and gender identity.* Paper presented at the national conference of the Association for Women in Psychology, Ypsilanti, MI.

Rabin, J. S., & Slater, B. R. (2004, February). *Feminist psychology, science and practice: The Lesbian Development Study.* Presentation at the annual meeting of the Association for Women in Psychology, Philadelphia, PA.

Radloff, L. S. (1980). Risk factors for depression: What do we learn from them? In M. Guttentag, S. Salasin, & D. Belle (Eds.), *The mental health of women* (pp. 93–109). New York: Academic Press.

Ragins, B. R., & Sundstrom, E. (1989). Gender and power in organizations: A longitudinal perspective. *Psychological Bulletin, 105*(1), 51–88.

Rajecki, D. W., Dame, J. A., Creek, K. J., Barrickman, P. J., et al. (1993). Gender casting in television toy advertisements: Distributions, message content analysis, and evaluations. *Journal of Consumer Psychology, 2*(3), 307–327.

Ramey, E. (1972). Men's cycles. *Ms., 1*(8), 8, 11–12, 14–15.

Randall, W., Parrila, R., & Sobsey, D. (2000). Gender, disability status, and risk for sexual abuse in children. *Journal on Developmental Disabilities, 7*(1), 1–15.

Raskin, P. A., & Israel, A. C. (1981). Sex-role imitation in children: Effects of sex of child, sex of model, and sex-role appropriateness of modeled behavior. *Sex Roles, 7*, 1067–1077.

Räty, H., Vänskä, J., Kasanen, K., & Kärkkäinen, R. (2002). Parents' explanations of their child's performance in mathematics and reading: A replication. *Sex Roles, 46*, 121–128.

Rauhala, A. (1987, April 2). Religion is key for anti-abortionists, study finds. *Toronto Globe and Mail*, pp. A1, A5.

Rauramo, L. (1986). A review of study findings of the risks and benefits of estrogen therapy in the female climacteric. *Maturitas, 8*, 177–186.

Ravelli, G., Stein, Z., & Susser, M. (1976). Obesity in young men after famine exposure in utero and early infancy. *New England Journal of Medicine, 295*, 349–353.

Raven, B. H. (1965). Social influence and power. In I. D. Steiner & M. Fishbein (Eds.), *Current studies in social psychology* (pp. 371–381). New York: Holt, Rinehart & Winston.

Rawlings, E. I., & Carter, D. K. (1977). *Psychotherapy for women: Treatment toward equality.* Springfield, IL: Charles C. Thomas.

Raymond, J. (1979). *The transsexual empire: The making of the she-male.* Boston: Beacon Press.

Reboussin, B. A., Rejeski, W. J., Marint, K. A., Callahan, K., Dunn, A. L., King, A. C., & Sallis, J. F. (2000). Correlates of satisfaction with body function and body appearance in middle- and older-generation aged adults: The Activity Counseling trial (ACT). *Psychology and Health, 15*(2), 239–254.

Redman, S., Webb, G. R., Hennrikus, D. J., & Sanson-Fisher, R. W. (1991). The effects of gender upon diagnosis of psychological disturbance. *Journal of Behavioral Medicine, 14*, 527–540.

Reid, P., & Finchilescu, G. (1995). The disempowering effects of media violence against women. *Psychology of Women Quarterly, 19*(3), 397–411.

Reid, P. T. (1993). Poor women in psychological research: Shut up and shut out. *Psychology of Women Quarterly, 17*, 133–150.

Reilly, J., & Kremer, J. (2001). PMS: Moods, measurements and interpretations. *Irish Journal of Psychology, 22*(2), 22–37.

Reinisch, J. (1981). Prenatal exposure to synthetic progestins increases potential for aggression in humans. *Science, 211*, 1171–1173.

Reis, E., Frick, U., & Schmidtbleicher, D. (1995). Frequency variations of strength training sessions triggered by the phases of the menstrual cycle. *International Journal of Sports Medicine, 16*, 545–550.

Reis, H. T., Wheeler, L., Spiegel, N., Kernis, M. H., Nezlek, J., & Perri, M. (1982). Physical attractiveness in social interaction: II. Why does appearance affect social experience? *Journal of Personality and Social Psychology, 43*, 979–996.

Reitz, R. R. (1999). Batterers' experiences of being violent: A phenomenological study. *Psychology of Women Quarterly, 23*, 143–165.

Rellini, A. H., McCall, K. M., Randall, P. K., & Meston, C. M. (2005). The relationship between women's subjective and physiological sexual arousal. *Psychophysiology, 42*(1), 116–124.

Rempel, J. K., Holmes, J. G., & Zanna, M. P. (1985). Trust in close relationships. *Journal of Personality and Social Psychology, 49*(1), 95–112.

Rennison, C. M. (2002, August). *Rape and sexual assault: Reporting to police and medical attention, 1992–2000.* NCJ 194530. Washington, DC: U.S. Department of Justice. Retrieved from http://www.ojp.usdoj.gov/bjs/pub/ascii/rsarp00.txt

Rennison, C. M. (2003, February). *Intimate partner violence, 1993–2001.* Bureau of Justice Statistics Crime Data Brief. NCJ 197838. Washington, DC: U.S. Department of Justice.

Rennison, C. M., & Rand, M. R. (2003, August). *Criminal victimization, 2002.* NCJ 199994. Washington, DC: U.S. Department of Justice. Retrieved from http://www.rainn.org/ncvs_2002.pdf

Resendez, M. G. 2002. The stigmatizing effects of affirmative action: An examination of moderating variables. *Journal of Applied Social Psychology, 32*(1), 185–206.

Rheingold, H., & Cook, K. (1975). The contents of boys' and girls' rooms as an index of parents' behaviors. *Child Development, 46*, 459–463.

Rice, S. (1989). Single, older childless women: Differences between never-married and widowed women in life satisfaction and social support. *Journal of Gerontological Social Work, 13*(3/4), 35–47.

Rich, A. (1976). *Of woman born.* New York: Norton.

Richards, M. H., Gitelson, I. B., Petersen, A. C., & Hurtig, A. L. (1991). Adolescent personality in girls and boys: The role of mothers and fathers. *Psychology of Women Quarterly, 15* (1), 65–81.

Richardson, J. T. (1989). Student learning and the menstrual cycle: Premenstrual symptoms and approaches to studying. *Educational Psychology, 9*(3), 215–238.

Richman, J. A., Raskin, V. D., & Gaines, C. (1991). Gender roles, social support, and postpartum depressive symptomatology. The benefits of caring. *Journal of Nervous and Mental Disorders, 179*(3), 139–147.

Ricketts, M. (1989). Epistemological values of feminists in psychology. *Psychology of Women Quarterly, 13*(4), 401–416.

Riddle, D. I., & Sang, B. (1978). Psychotherapy with lesbians. *Journal of Social Issues, 34*(3), 84–100.

Rideout, V., Roberts, D. F., & Foehr, U. G. (2005). *Generation M: Media in the lives of 8- to 18-year-olds: A Kaiser Family Foundation study.* Retrieved October 3, 2006, from http://www.kff.org/entmedia/7250.cfm

Ridgeway, C. L., & Correll, S. J. (2004). Motherhood as a status characteristic. *Journal of Social Issues, 60*(4), 683–700.

Ridgeway, R. T., & Tylka, T. L. (2005). College men's perceptions of ideal body composition and shape. *Psychology of Men and Masculinity, 6*(3), 209–220.

Rigby, D. N., & Sophie, J. (1990). Ethical issues and client sexual preference. In H. Lerman & N. Porter (Eds.), *Feminist ethics in psychotherapy* (pp. 165–175). New York: Springer.

Riley, A. L., & Keith, V. M. (2003). Work and housework conditions and depressive symptoms among married women: The importance of occupational status. *Women and Health, 38*(4), 1–17.

Rind, B., & Kipnis, D. (1999). Changes in self-perception as a result of successfully persuading others. *Journal of Social Issues, 55*(1), 141–156.

Ritter, B. A., & Yoder, J. D. (2004). Gender differences in leader emergence persist even for dominant women: An updated confirmation of role congruity theory. *Psychology of Women Quarterly, 28*(3), 187–193.

Robbins, M. B., & Jensen, G. D. (1977). Multiple orgasm in males. In R. Gemme & C. C. Wheeler (Eds.), *Progress in sexology* (pp. 323–334). New York: Plenum.

Roberts, S. L., Bushnell, J. A., Collings, S. C., & Purdie, G. L. (2006). Psychological health of men with partners who have post-partum depression. *Australian and New Zealand Journal of Psychiatry, 40*(8), 704–711.

Roberts, T. (1991). Gender and the influence of evaluations on self-assessments in achievement settings. *Psychological Bulletin, 109*(2), 297–308.

Roberts, T.-A. (2004). Female trouble: The menstrual self-evaluation scale and women's self-objectification. *Psychology of Women Quarterly, 28*(1), 22–26.

Roberts, T.-A., Goldenberg, J. L., Power, C., & Pyszczynski, T. (2002). "Feminine protection": The effects of menstruation on attitudes towards women. *Psychology of Women Quarterly, 26*(2), 131–139.

Robinson, G. E., & Garfinkel, P. E. (1990). Problems in the treatment of premenstrual symptoms. *Canadian Journal of Psychiatry, 35*(3), 199–206.

Robinson, J. P., Andreyenkov, V. G., & Patrushev, V. D. (1988). *The rhythm of everyday life: How Soviet and American citizens use time.* Boulder, CO: Westview.

Robinson, J. P., & Godbey, G. (1993). Sport, fitness, and the gender gap. *Leisure Sciences, 15*, 291–307.

Rodin, J., & Janis, I. (1979). The social power of health-care practitioners as agents of change. *Journal of Social Issues, 35*(1), 60–81.

Rodin, J., Silberstein, L., & Striegel-Moore, R. (1985). Women and weight: A normative discontent. In T. B. Sonderegger (Ed.), *Psychology and gender: Proceedings of the Nebraska Symposium on Motivation, 1984* (pp. 267–307). Lincoln: University of Nebraska Press.

Rodin, J., & Striegel-Moore, R. H. (1984, September). *Predicting attitudes toward body weight and food intake in women.* Paper presented at the 14th Congress of the European Association of Behavior Therapy, Brussels.

Roe, K. V., Drivas, A., Karagellis, A., & Roe, A. (1985). Sex differences in vocal interaction with mother and stranger in Greek infants: Some cognitive implications. *Developmental Psychology, 21*(2), 373–377.

Rogers, D. S., Harkrider, A. W., Burchfield, S. B., & Nabelek, A. K. (2003). The influence of listener's gender on the acceptance of background noise. *Journal of the American Academy of Audiology, 14*(7), 372–382.

Rojahn, J., & Naglieri, J. A. (2006). Developmental gender differences on the Naglieri Nonverbal Ability Test in a nationally normed sample of 5- to 17-year-olds. *Intelligence, 34*(3), 253–260.

Romance Writers of America. (2002). *2002 romance statistics.* Retrieved from http://www.rwanational.org/Statistics.pdf

Romer, N. (1990). Is political activism still a "masculine" endeavor? Gender comparisons among high school political activists. *Psychology of Women Quarterly, 14*(2), 229–244.

Ronfeldt, H. M., Kimerling, R., & Arias, I. (1998). Satisfaction with relationship power and the perpetration of dating violence. *Journal of Marriage and the Family, 60*, 70–78.

Root, M. P. P. (1990). Disordered eating in women of color. *Sex Roles, 22*, 525–536.

Rosaldo, M. Z. (1974). Woman, culture and society: A theoretical overview. In M. Z. Rosaldo & L. Lamphere (Eds.), *Woman, culture and society* (pp. 1–16). Stanford, CA: Stanford University Press.

Rose, A. J., & Rudolph, K. D. (2006). A review of sex differences in peer relationship processes: Potential trade-offs for the emotional and behavioral development of girls and boys. *Psychological Bulletin, 132*(1), 98–131.

Rose, R. M. (1969). Androgen excretion in stress. In P. G. Bourne (Ed.), *The psychology and physiology of stress* (pp. 117–147). New York: Academic Press.

Rose, S. M. (1985). Same-sex and cross-sex friendships and the psychology of homosociality. *Sex Roles, 12*, 63–74.

Rose, S. M. (1995). Women's friendships. In J. C. Chrisler & A. Huston Hemstreet (Eds.), *Variations on a theme: Diversity and the psychology of women* (pp. 79–105). Albany: State University of New York Press.

Rosenbaum, J. E. (2006). Reborn a virgin: Adolescents' retracting of virginity pledges and sexual histories. *American Journal of Public Health, 96*(6), 1098–1103.

Rosenberg, J., Perlstadt, H., & Phillips, W. R. (1993). Now that we are here: Discrimination, disparagement, and harassment at work and the experience of women lawyers. *Gender and Society, 7*(3), 415–433.

Rosenberg, R. (1982). *Beyond separate spheres: Intellectual origins of modern feminism.* New Haven, CT: Yale University Press.

Rosenthal, R. (1966). *Experimenter effects in behavioral research.* East Norwalk, CT: Appleton-Century-Crofts.

Rosenthal, R. (1990). How are we doing in soft psychology? *American Psychologist, 45*, 775–777.

Rosenthal, R., Archer, D., DiMatteo, M. R., Kowumaki, J. H., & Rogers, P. O. (1974, September). Body talk and tone of voice: The language without words. *Psychology Today, 8*, 64–68.

Rosenthal, R., & DePaulo, B. M. (1979). Sex differences in eavesdropping on nonverbal cues. *Journal of Personality and Social Psychology, 37*, 273–285.

Rosenthal, R., Persinger, G. W., Mulry, R. C., Vikan-Kline, L., & Grothe, M. (1964). Changes in experimental hypotheses as determinants of experimental results. *Journal of Projective Techniques and Personality Assessment, 28*, 465–469.

Rosenthal, R., & Rubin, D. B. (1982). Further meta-analytic procedures for assessing cognitive gender differences. *Journal of Educational Psychology, 74*, 708–712.

Rosenwasser, S. M., & Dean, N. G. (1989). Gender role and political office: Effects of perceived masculinity/femininity of candidate and political office. *Psychology of Women Quarterly, 13*(1), 77–86.

Rosenweig, S. (1933). The experimental situation as a psychological problem. *Psychological Review, 40*, 337–354.

Rosewater, L. B. (1984). Feminist therapy: Implications for practitioners. In L. E. Walker (Ed.), *Women and mental health policy* (pp. 267–280). Beverly Hills, CA: Sage.

Rosewater, L. B., & Walker, L. E. (Eds.). (1985). *Handbook of feminist therapy: Women's issues in psychotherapy.* New York: Springer.

Ross, M. T., Grafham, D. V., Coffey, A. J., Scherer, S., McLay, K., Muzny, D., et al. (2005). The DNA sequence of the human X chromosome. *Nature, 434*(7031), 325–337.

Ross, S. I., & Jackson, J. M. (1991). Teachers' expectations for Black males' and

Black females' academic achievement. *Personality and Social Psychology Bulletin, 17*(1), 78–82.

Rossi, A. S., & Rossi, P. E. (1977). Body time and social time: Mood patterns by menstrual cycle phase and day of week. *Social Science Research, 6,* 273–308.

Rossi, J. D. (1983). Ratios exaggerate gender differences in mathematical ability. *American Psychologist, 38,* 348.

Rothert, M., Rovner, D., Holmes, M., Schmitt, N., Talarczyk, G., Kroll, J., & Gogate, J. (1990). Women's use of information regarding hormone replacement therapy. *Research in Nursing and Health, 13,* 355–366.

Rothman, B. K. (1982). *In labor: Women and power in the birthplace.* New York: Norton.

Rotkin, K. F. (1972). The phallacy of our sexual norm. *RT: A Journal of Radical Therapy, 3*(11). Reprinted in A. G. Kaplan & J. D. Bean (Eds.) (1976), *Beyond sex-role stereotypes: Readings toward a psychology of androgyny* (pp. 154–162). Boston: Little, Brown.

Roughgarden, J. (2004). *Evolution's rainbow: Diversity, gender, and sexuality in nature and people.* Berkeley: University of California Press.

Rousso, H. (1986, March). Confronting the myth of asexuality: The networking project for disabled women and girls. *SIECUS Report,* pp. 4–6.

Royer, J. M., & Garofoli, L. M. (2005). Cognitive contributions to sex differences in math performance. In A. M. Gallagher & J. C. Kaufman (Eds.), *Gender differences in mathematics: An integrative psychological approach* (pp. 99–120). New York: Cambridge University Press.

Rubin, D. L., Greene, K., & Schneider, D. (1994). Adopting gender-inclusive language reforms: Diachronic and synchronic variation. *Journal of Language and Social Psychology, 13*(2), 91–114.

Rubin, J., Provenzano, F., & Luria, Z. (1974). The eye of the beholder: Parents' views on sex of newborns. *American Journal of Orthopsychiatry, 44,* 512–519.

Rubin, L. B. (1976). *Worlds of pain.* New York: Basic Books.

Rubin, L. B. (1979). *Women of a certain age: The mid-life search for self.* New York: Harper & Row.

Rubin, L. B. (1986). On men and friendship. *Psychoanalytic Review, 73*(2), 165–181.

Rubin, Z., Peplau, L. A., & Hill, C. T. (1981). Loving and leaving: Sex differences in romantic attachments. *Sex Roles, 7,* 821–835.

Ruble, D. N. (1977). Premenstrual symptoms: A reinterpretation. *Science, 197,* 291–292.

Ruble, D. N., Greulich, F., Pomerantz, E. M., & Gochberg, B. (1993). The role of gender-related processes in the development of sex differences in self-evaluation and depression. *Journal of Affective Disorders, 29*(2/3), 97–128.

Ruddick, S. (1989). *Maternal thinking: Toward a politics of peace.* New York: Ballantine.

Rudman, L. A. (1998). Self-promotion as a risk factor for women: The costs and benefits of counter-stereotypical impression management. *Journal of Personality and Social Psychology, 74,* 629–645.

Rudman, L. A., & Glick, P. (2001). Prescriptive gender stereotypes and backlash toward agentic women. *Journal of Social Issues, 57*(4), 743–762.

Ruether, R. R. (1983). *Sexism and god-talk: Toward a feminist theology.* Boston: Beacon Press.

Runciman, W. G. (1966). *Relative deprivation and social justice: A study of attitudes to social inequality in twentieth-century England.* Berkeley: University of California Press.

Rush, F. (1980). *The best kept secret: Sexual abuse of children.* New York: McGraw-Hill.

Russell, D., Peplau, L. A., & Cutrona, C. E. (1980). The revised UCLA loneliness scale: Concurrent and discriminant validity evidence. *Journal of Personality and Social Psychology, 39,* 472–480.

Russell, D. E. H. (1983). The incidence and prevalence of intrafamilial and extrafamilial sexual abuse of female children. *Child Abuse and Neglect, 7,* 133–146.

Russell, D. E. H. (1984). *Sexual exploitation: Rape, child sexual abuse and workplace harassment.* Beverly Hills, CA: Sage.

Russell, D. E. H., & Howell, N. (1983). The prevalence of rape in the United States revisited. *Signs: Journal of Women in Culture and Society, 8,* 688–695.

Russell, G. M., & Bohan, J. S. (1999). Hearing voices: The uses of research and the politics of change. *Psychology of Women Quarterly, 23*(2), 403–418.

Russell, K., Wilson, M., & Hall, R. (1992). *The color complex: The politics of skin color among African Americans.* New York: Harcourt Brace Jovanovich.

Russell, S. (1985). Social dimensions of disability: Women with MS. *Resources for Feminist Research, 14*(1), 56–58.

Russo, N. F., Amaro, H., & Winter, M. (1987). The use of inpatient mental health services by Hispanic women. *Psychology of Women Quarterly, 11*(4), 427–441.

Russo, N. F., Horn, J. D., & Schwartz, R. (1992). U.S. abortion in context: Selected characteristics and motivation of women seeking abortions. *Journal of Social Issues, 48*(3), 183–202.

Russo, N. F., & Vaz, K. (2001). Addressing diversity in the decade of behavior: Focus on women of color. *Psychology of Women Quarterly, 25*(4), 280–294.

Rust, P. C. (1992). The politics of sexual identity: Sexual attraction and behavior among lesbian and bisexual women. *Social Problems, 39*(4), 366–386.

Rust, P. C. (2000). Bisexuality: A contemporary paradox for women. *Journal of Social Issues, 56*(2), 205–221.

Ryan, M. (1992, January 5). Don't quit on us. *Parade,* pp. 8–9.

Saal, F. E., Johnson, C. B., & Weber, N. (1989). Friendly or sexy? It may depend on whom you ask. *Psychology of Women Quarterly, 13,* 263–276.

Sadker, D., & Sadker, M. (1994). *Failing at fairness.* New York: Charles Scribner's Sons.

Sadker, M., & Sadker, D. (1985, March). Sexism in the schoolroom of the '80s. *Psychology Today,* pp. 54–57.

Sadler, A. G., Booth, B. M., Cook, B. L., & Doebbeling, B. N. (2003). Factors associated with women's risk of rape in the military environment. *American Journal of Industrial Medicine, 43*(3), 262–273.

Sagrestano, L. M. (1992a). The use of power and influence in a gendered world. *Psychology of Women Quarterly, 16*(4), 439–447.

Sagrestano, L. M. (1992b). Power strategies in interpersonal relationships: The effects of expertise and gender. *Psychology of Women Quarterly, 16*(4), 481–495.

Sagrestano, L. M., Heavey, C. L., & Christensen, A. (1999). Perceived power and physical violence in marital conflict. *Journal of Social Issues, 55*(1), 65–79.

Sales, E., & Frieze, I. H. (1984). Women and work: Implications for mental health policy. In L. E. Walker (Ed.), *Women and mental health policy* (pp. 229–246). Beverly Hills, CA: Sage.

Sancho, A. M., & Hewitt, J. (1990). Questioning fear of success. *Psychological Reports, 67*(3, Pt. 1), 803–806.

Sanday, P. R. (1981a). *Female power and male dominance: On the origins of sexual inequality*. Cambridge: Cambridge University Press.

Sanday, P. R. (1981b). The socio-cultural context of rape: A cross-cultural study. *Journal of Social Issues, 37*, 5–27.

Sanfilipo, M. P. (1994). Masculinity, femininity, and subjective experiences of depression. *Journal of Clinical Psychology, 50*(2), 144–157.

Sanger, M. (1938). *Margaret Sanger: An autobiography*. New York: Dover.

Sanik, M. M. (1990). Parents' time use: A 1967–1986 comparison. *Lifestyles: Family and Economic Issues, 11*(3), 299–316.

Sapiro, V. (1986). *Women in American society*. Palo Alto, CA: Mayfield.

Saris, R. N., & Johnston-Robledo, I. (2000). Poor women are still shut out of mainstream psychology. *Psychology of Women Quarterly, 24*(3), 233–235.

Sarrel, P., & Masters, W. (1982). Sexual molestation of men by women. *Archives of Sexual Behavior, 11*, 117–132.

Saunders, D. G. (1986). When battered women use violence: Husband-abuse or self-defense? *Victims and Violence, 1*, 47–60.

Savage, R. M., & Gouvier, D. D. (1992). Rey Auditory-Verbal Learning Test: The effects of age and gender, and norms for delayed recall and story recognition trials. *Archives of Clinical Neuropsychology, 7*, 407–414.

Scamarella, T. J., & Brown, W. A. (1978). Serum testosterone and aggressiveness in hockey players. *Psychosomatic Medicine, 40*, 262–265.

Scanzoni, J. (1972). *Sexual bargaining: Power politics in the American marriage*. Englewood Cliffs, NJ: Prentice-Hall.

Scarf, M. A. (1979). The more sorrowful sex. *Psychology Today, 12*(11), 44–52, 89–90.

Scarr, S. (1988). How genotypes and environments combine: Development and individual differences. In N. Bolger, A. Caspi, G. Downey, & M. Moorhouse (Eds.), *Persons in context: Developmental processes* (pp. 217–244). Cambridge: Cambridge University Press.

Scarr, S. (1991, February 25). *How genes and environments work together*. Colloquium presentation at Radford University, Radford, VA.

Scarr, S. (1998). American child care today. *American Psychologist, 53*(2), 95–108.

Schacter, S., & Singer, J. E. (1962). Cognitive, social, and physiological determinants of emotional state. *Psychological Review, 69*, 379–399.

Schein, E. H. (1968). Organizational socialization and the profession of management. *Industrial Management Review, 9*, 1–15.

Schein, V. E. (2001). A global look at psychological barriers to women's progress in management. *Journal of Social Issues, 57*(4), 675–688.

Schmidt, R. M., Wiemann, C. M., Rickert, V. I., & Smith, E. O. B. (2006). Moderate to severe depressive symptoms among adolescent mothers followed four years postpartum. *Journal of Adolescent Health, 38*(6), 712–718.

Schneer, J. A., & Reitman, F. (1993). Effects of alternate family structures on managerial career paths. *Academy of Management Journal, 36*(4), 830–843.

Schneider, F. W., & Coutts, L. M. (1985). Person orientation of male and female high school students: To the educational disadvantage of males? *Sex Roles, 13*(1/2), 47–63.

Schneider, M. S. (1986). The relationships of cohabiting lesbian and heterosexual couples: A comparison. *Psychology of Women Quarterly, 10*(3), 234–239.

Schnellmann, J., & Gibbons, J. L. (1984, August). *The perception by women and minorities of trivial discriminatory actions in the classroom*. Paper presented at the annual meeting of the American Psychological Association, Toronto.

Schubert, J. B., Bradley-Johnson, S., & Nuttal, J. (1980). Mother-infant communication and maternal employment. *Child Development, 51*(1), 246–249.

Schultz, N. R., & Moore, D. (1986). The loneliness experience of college students: Sex differences. *Personality and Social Psychology Bulletin, 12*(1), 111–119.

Schwartz, J. (1998, April 3). Teens are lighting up in increasing numbers. *Washington Post*, p. A2.

Schwartz, J. M., & Begley, S. (2002). *The mind and the brain: Neuroplasticity and the power of mental force*. New York: Regan Books.

Schwarzwald, J., & Koslowsky, M. (1999). Gender, self-esteem, and focus of interest in the use of power strategies by adolescents in conflict situations. *Journal of Social Issues, 55*(1), 15–32.

Scott, W. B., & Webster, S. K. (1984, August). *Gender differences in the attributional effect of videotape self-observation*. Paper presented at the annual meeting of the American Psychological Association, Toronto.

Seattle Post-Intelligencer. (2003). If it's a boy, the dad's more apt to say 'I do.' Reprinted in the *Roanoke Times*, May 10, p. A12.

Selgado de Snyder, V. N., Cervantes, R. C., & Padilla, A. M. (1990). Gender and ethnic differences in psychosocial stress and generalized distress among Hispanics. *Sex Roles, 22*(7/8), 441–453.

Selkow, P. (1984, August). *Maternal employment: Effects on daughters' and sons' early career aspirations*. Paper presented at the annual meeting of the American Psychological Association, Toronto.

Sellers, R. M., Smith, M. A., Shelton, J. N., Rowley, S. A. J., & Chavous, T. M. (1998). Multidimensional model of racial identity: A reconceptualization of African American racial identity. *Personality and Social Psychology Review, 2*(1), 18–39.

The Sentencing Project. (2005). *Factsheet: Women in prison*. Retrieved November 29, 2006, from http://www.sentencing project.org/pdfs/1032.pdf

Serbin, L., & O'Leary, K. (1975). How nursery schools teach girls to shut up. *Psychology Today, 9*(7), 56–58ff.

Serbin, L. A., Poulin-Dubois, D., Colburne, K. A., Sen, M. G., & Eichstedt, J. A. (2001). Gender stereotyping in infancy: Visual preferences for and knowledge of gender-stereotyped toys in the second year. *International Journal of Behavioral Development, 25*(1), 7–15.

Serbin, L. A., Poulin-Dubois, D., & Eichstedt, J. A. (2002). Infants' response to gender-inconsistent events. *Infancy, 3*(4), 531–542.

Serbin, L. A., Powlishta, K. K., & Gulko, J. (1993). The development of sex typing in middle childhood. *Monographs of the Society for Research in Child Development, 58*(2, Serial No. 232), 1–73.

Serbin, L. A., Zelkowitz, P., Doyle, A. B., Gold, D., & Wheaton, B. (1990). The socialization of sex-differentiated skills and academic performance: A mediational model. *Sex Roles, 23*, 613–628.

Seymour, E. (1995). The loss of women from science, mathematics, and engineering undergraduate majors: An explanatory account. *Science Education, 79*(4), 437–473.

Shah, R., & Ogden, J. (2006). "What's in a face?" The role of doctor ethnicity, age and gender in the formation of patients' judgements: An experimental study.

Patient Education and Counseling, 60(2), 136–141.

Shapiro, J. L. (1987, January). The expectant father. *Psychology Today, 21*(1), 36–42.

Sheets, V. L., & Lugar, R. (2005). Friendship and gender in Russia and the United States. *Sex Roles, 52*(1), 131–140.

Sheffield, C. J. (1995). Sexual terrorism. In J. Freeman (Ed.), *Women: A feminist perspective* (5th ed., pp. 1–21). Mountain View, CA: Mayfield.

Shellenbarger, S. (1995, December 20). Work and family: Shedding light on women's records dispels stereotypes. *Wall Street Journal*, p. B1.

Shephard, R. J. (2000). Exercise and training in women, Part I: Influence of gender on exercise and training responses. *Canadian Journal of Applied Physiology, 25*(1), 19–34.

Sherfey, M. J. (1966). The evolution and nature of female sexuality in relation to psychoanalytic theory. *Journal of the American Psychoanalytic Association, 14,* 28–128.

Sherman, B. L., & Dominick, J. R. (1986). Violence and sex in music videos: TV and rock 'n' roll. *Journal of Communication, 36*(1), 79–93.

Sherman, J. A., & Fennema, E. (1977). The study of mathematics by high school girls and boys: Related variables. *American Educational Research Journal, 14,* 159–168.

Sherman, J. A., Koufacos, C., & Kenworthy, J. A. (1978). Therapists: Their attitudes and information about women. *Psychology of Women Quarterly, 2,* 299–313.

Sherrill, K., & Yang, A. (2000). From outlaws to in-laws: Anti-gay attitudes thaw. *Public Perspective, 11*(1), 20–23.

Sherwin, B. B. (1988). A comparative analysis of the role of androgen in human male and female sexual behavior: Behavioral specificity, critical thresholds, and sensitivity. *Psychobiology, 16*(4), 416–425.

Shields, S. A. (1975). Functionalism, Darwinism and the psychology of women: A study in social myth. *American Psychologist, 30*(7), 739–754.

Shields, S. A. (1984). "To pet, coddle, and 'do for'": Caretaking and the concept of maternal instinct. In M. Lewin (Ed.), *In the shadow of the past: Psychology portrays the sexes* (pp. 256–273). New York: Columbia University Press.

Shigetomi, C. C., Hartmann, D. P., & Gilford, D. M. (1981). Sex differences in children's altruistic behavior and reputations for helpfulness. *Developmental Psychology, 17*(4), 434–437.

Shively, M. G., Jones, C., & De Cecco, J. P. (1983/84). Research on sexual orientation: Definitions and methods. *Journal of Homosexuality, 9*(2/3), 127–136.

Shomer, R. W., & Centers, R. (1970). Differences in attitudinal responses under conditions of implicitly manipulated group salience. *Journal of Personality and Social Psychology, 15*(2), 125–132.

Shorter-Gooden, K., & Washington, N. C. (1996). Young, Black and female: The challenge of weaving an identity. *Adolescence, 19,* 465–475.

Shusterman, L. R. (1976). The psychosocial factors of the abortion experience: A critical review. *Psychology of Women Quarterly, 1*(1), 79–106.

Shute, V. J., Pellegrino, J. W., Hubert, L., & Reynolds, R. W. (1983). The relationship between androgen levels and human spatial abilities. *Bulletin of the Psychonomic Society, 21,* 465–468.

Shvedova, N. (2002). Obstacles to women's participation in parliament. *Women in parliament: Beyond numbers* (Chapter 2, Updated 2002). Stockholm, Sweden: International Institute for Democracy and Electoral Assistance. Retrieved from http://www.idea.int/gender/ wip/PDF/English/ Updates_2002/ Chapter2_Shvedova.pdf

Sidanus, J., Pratto, F., & Rabinowitz, J. L. (1994). Gender, ethnic status, and ideological asymmetry: A social dominance interpretation. *Journal of Cross Cultural Psychology, 25*(2), 194–216.

Siegel, D. M., Aten, M. J., & Roghmann, K. J. (1998). Self-reported honesty among middle and high school students responding to a sexual behavior questionnaire. *Journal of Adolescent Health: Official Publication of the Society for Adolescent Medicine, 23*(1), 20–28.

Siegel, J. M., & Kuykendall, D. H. (1990). Loss, widowhood, and psychological distress among the elderly. *Journal of Consulting and Clinical Psychology, 58*(5), 519–524.

Signorella, M., Bigler, R. S., & Liben, L. (1993). Developmental differences in children's gender schemata about others: A meta-analytic review. *Developmental Review, 13*(2), 147–183.

Signorielli, N., & Bacue, A. (1999). Recognition and respect: A content analysis of prime-time television characters across three decades. *Sex Roles, 40,* 527–544.

Signorielli, N., McLeod, D., & Healy, E. (1994). Gender stereotypes in MTV commercials: The beat goes on. *Journal*

of Broadcasting and Electronic Media, 38(1), 91–101.

Silverman, J. G., Raj, A., Mucci, L. A., & Hathaway, J. E. (2001). Dating violence against adolescent girls and associated substance use, unhealthy weight control, sexual risk behavior, pregnancy, and suicidality. *Journal of the American Medical Association, 286*(5), 572–579.

Silverman, L. K. (1989). It all began with Leta Hollingworth: The story of giftedness in women. *Journal for the Education of the Gifted, 12*(2), 86–98.

Silverstein, L. B. (1996). Fathering is a feminist issue. *Psychology of Women Quarterly, 20*(1), 3–38.

Silverstein, L. B., & Auerbach, C. F. (1999). Deconstructing the essential father. *American Psychologist, 54*(6), 397–407.

Silverstein, L. B., & Phares, V. (1996). Expanding the mother-child paradigm: An examination of dissertation research 1986–1994. *Psychology of Women Quarterly, 20*(1), 39–54.

Simmons, R. G., Blyth, D. A., Van Cleave, E. F., & Bush, D. M. (1979). Entry into early adolescence: The impact of school structure, puberty, and early dating on self-esteem. *American Sociological Review, 44,* 948–967.

Simon, B., Glässner-Bayerl, B., & Stratenwerth, I. (1991). Stereotyping and self-stereotyping in a natural intergroup context: The case of heterosexual and homosexual men. *Social Psychology Quarterly, 54*(3), 252–266.

Simon, R. W. (1995). Gender, multiple roles, role meaning, and mental health. *Journal of Health and Social Behavior, 36,* 182–194.

Simon, R. W. (2002). Revisiting the relationships among gender, marital status, and mental health. *American Journal of Sociology, 107*(4), 1065–1096.

Simpson, J. A., Gangestead, S. W., & Lerma, M. (1990). Perception of physical attractiveness: Mechanisms involved in the maintenance of romantic relationships. *Journal of Personality and Social Psychology, 59*(6), 1192–1201.

Singer, A. R., Cassin, S. E., & Dobson, K. S. (2005). The role of gender in the career aspirations of professional psychology graduates: Are there more similarities than differences? *Canadian Psychology, 46*(4), 215–222.

Singh, S., & Darroch, J. E. (2000). Adolescent pregnancy and childbearing: Levels and trends in developed countries. *Family Planning Perspectives, 32*(1), 14–23.

Sistrunk, F., & McDavid, J. W. (1971). Sex variables in conforming behavior. *Journal of Personality and Social Psychology, 17,* 200–207.

Six, B., & Eckes, T. (1991). A closer look at the complex structure of sex stereotypes. *Sex Roles, 24*(1/2), 57–71.

Skaalvik, E. M., & Rankin, R. J. (1994). Gender differences in mathematics and verbal achievement, self-perception and motivation. *British Journal of Educational Psychology, 64*(3), 419–428.

Skinner, K. M., Kressin, N., Frayne, S., Tripp, T. J., Hankin, C. S., Miller, D. R., & Sullivan, L. M. (2000). The prevalence of military sexual assault among female Veterans' Administration outpatients. *Journal of Interpersonal Violence, 15*(3), 29–49.

Skinner, P. H., & Shelton, R. L. (1985). *Speech, language, and hearing: Normal processes and disorders* (2nd ed.). New York: Wiley.

Skoe, E. E., & Diessner, R. (1994). Ethic of care, justice, identity, and gender: An extension and replication. *Merrill Palmer Quarterly, 40*(2), 272–289.

Skrypnek, B. J., & Snyder, M. (1982). On the self-perpetuating nature of the stereotypes about women and men. *Journal of Experimental Social Psychology, 18,* 277–291.

Slaby, R. G., & Frey, K. S. (1975). Development of gender constancy and selective attention to same-sex models. *Child Development, 46,* 849–856.

Sloane, E. (2002). *Biology of women* (4th ed.). Albany, NY: Delmar.

Smith, D. (2003). Women and sex: What is "dysfunctional"? *Monitor on Psychology, 34,* 54–56.

Smith, E. J. (1982). The Black female adolescent: A review of the educational, career, and psychological literature. *Psychology of Women Quarterly, 6*(3), 261–288.

Smith, J. E., Waldorf, V. A., & Trembath, D. L. (1990). "Single White male looking for thin, very attractive . . ." *Sex Roles, 23*(11/12), 675–685.

Smith, J. L., & White, P. H. (2002). An examination of implicitly activated, explicitly activated, and nullified stereotypes on mathematical performance: It's not just a woman's issue. *Sex Roles, 47*(3/4), 179–191.

Smith, L. (1987, January). *A feminist approach to legal research.* Paper presented at the conference on the Effects of Feminist Approaches on Research Methodologies, Calgary Institute for the Humanities, Calgary, Alberta.

Smith, M. (1980). Sex bias in counseling and psychotherapy. *Psychological Bulletin, 87,* 392–407.

Smith-Rosenberg, C., & Rosenberg, C. (1976). The female animal: Medical and biological views of women. In C. Rosenberg, *No other gods: On science and American social thought* (pp. 54–70). Baltimore: Johns Hopkins University Press.

Smolak, L. (2006). Body image. In J. Worell & C. D. Goodheart (Eds.), *Handbook of girls' and women's psychological health: Gender and well-being across the lifespan* (pp. 69–76). New York: Oxford University Press.

Snodgrass, S. E. (1985). Women's intuition: The effect of subordinate role upon interpersonal sensitivity. *Journal of Personality and Social Psychology, 49,* 146–155.

Snodgrass, S. E. (1992). Further effects of role versus gender on interpersonal sensitivity. *Journal of Personality and Social Psychology, 62,* 154–158.

Snodgrass, S. E., Hecht, M. A., & Ploutz-Snyder, R. (1998). Interpersonal sensitivity: Expressivity or perceptivity? *Journal of Personality and Social Psychology, 74*(1), 238–249.

Snow, J. T., & Harris, M. B. (1989). Disordered eating in Southwestern Pueblo Indians and Hispanics. *Journal of Adolescence, 12,* 329–336.

Snow, M. E., Jacklin, C. N., & Maccoby, E. E. (1981). Birth-order differences in peer sociability at thirty-three months. *Child Development, 52*(2), 589–595.

Snow, W. G., & Sheese, S. (1985). Lateralized brain damage, intelligence, and memory: A failure to find sex differences. *Journal of Consulting and Clinical Psychology, 33*(6), 940–941.

Sochting, I., Skoe, E. E., & Marcia, J. E. (1994). Care-oriented moral reasoning and prosocial behavior: A question of gender or sex-role orientation. *Sex Roles, 31*(3/4), 131–147.

Sommer, B. (1973). The effect of menstruation on cognitive and perceptual-motor behavior: A review. *Psychosomatic Medicine, 35,* 515–534.

Sommer, B. (1975). *Mood and the menstrual cycle.* Paper presented at the annual meeting of the American Psychological Association, Chicago.

Sommer, B. (1983). How does menstruation affect cognitive competence and psychophysiological response? *Women and Health, 8*(2/3), 53–90.

Sommer, B. (1984, August). PMS in the courts: Are all women on trial? *Psychology Today,* pp. 36–38.

Sommer, B. (1992). Cognitive performance and the menstrual cycle. In J. T. E. Richardson (Ed.), *Cognition and the menstrual cycle* (pp. 39–66). New York: Springer-Verlag.

Sommers-Flanagan, R., Sommers-Flanagan, J., & Davis, B. (1993). What's happening on Music Television? A gender role content analysis. *Sex Roles, 28*(11/12), 745–753.

Sorenson, R. C. (1973). *Adolescent sexuality in contemporary America.* New York: World.

South, S. J., & Spitze, G. (1994). Housework in marital and nonmarital households. *American Sociological Review, 59,* 327–347.

Spelke, E. S. (2005). Sex differences in intrinsic aptitude for mathematics and science?: A critical review. *American Psychologist, 60*(9), 950–958.

Spence, J. T., & Buckner, C. E. (2000). Instrumental and expressive traits, trait stereotypes, and sexist attitudes. What do they signify? *Psychology of Women Quarterly, 24*(1), 44–62.

Spence, J. T., & Helmreich, R. L. (1978). *Masculinity and femininity: The psychological dimensions, correlates and antecedents.* Austin: University of Texas Press.

Spence, J. T., Helmreich, R., & Stapp, J. (1974). The personal attributes questionnaire: A measure of sex-role stereotypes and masculinity-femininity (Ms. no. 617). *JSAS Catalog of Selected Documents in Psychology, 4,* 43.

Spencer, S. J., Steele, C. M., & Quinn, D. M. (1999). Stereotype threat and women's math performance. *Journal of Experimental Social Psychology, 31*(1), 4–28.

Spender, D. (1980). *Man made language.* London: Routledge & Kegan Paul.

Sperry, R. (1982). Some effects of disconnecting the cerebral hemispheres. *Science, 217,* 1223–1226.

Springer, S. P., & Deutsch, G. (1998). *Left brain, right brain* (5th ed.). New York: Freeman.

St. Lawrence, J. S., & Joyner, D. J. (1991). The effects of sexually violent rock music on males' acceptance of violence against women. *Psychology of Women Quarterly, 15*(1), 49–64.

Stacey, J., & Biblarz, T. J. (2001). (How) does the sexual orientation of parents matter? *American Sociological Review, 66*(2), 159–183.

Stack, C. B. (1997). Different voices, different visions: Gender, culture, and moral reasoning. In M. Baca Zinn,

P. Hondagneu-Sotelo, & M. Messner (Eds.), *Through the prism of difference: Readings on sex and gender* (pp. 51–57). Boston: Allyn & Bacon.

Stake, J., & Lauer, M. L. (1987). The consequences of being overweight: A controlled study of gender differences. *Sex Roles, 17,* 31–47.

Stallings, J. (1985). School, classroom, and home influences on women's decisions to enroll in advanced mathematics courses. In S. F. Chipman, L. R. Brush, & D. M. Wilson (Eds.), *Women and mathematics: Balancing the equation* (pp. 199–223). Hillsdale, NJ: Erlbaum.

Staples, R. (1978). Masculinity and race: The dual dilemma of Black men. *Journal of Social Issues, 34*(1), 169–183.

Stark-Adamec, C., & Kimball, M. (1984). Science free of sexism: A guide to the conduct of nonsexist research. *Canadian Psychology, 25*(1), 23–34.

Starrels, M. E. (1994). Gender differences in parent-child relations. *Journal of Family Issues, 15*(1), 148–165.

Statistics Canada. (1995). *Women in Canada: A statistical report* (3rd ed.). Ottawa, Canada: Author.

Steel, B. S., & Lovrich, N. P. (1987). Comparable worth: The problematic politicization of a public personnel issue. *Public Personnel Management, 16*(1), 23–36.

Steele, C. M. (1997). A threat in the air: How stereotypes shape intellectual identity and performance. *American Psychologist, 52,* 613–629.

Steele, J., James, J. B., & Barnett, R. C. (2002). Learning in a man's world: Examining the perceptions of undergraduate women in male-dominated academic areas. *Psychology of Women Quarterly, 26,* 46–50.

Stein, A. H., & Bailey, M. M. (1973). The socialization of achievement orientation in females. *Psychological Bulletin, 80*(5), 345–366.

Steinbacher, R., & Gilroy, F. (1990). Sex selection technology: A prediction of its use and effect. *Journal of Psychology, 124*(3), 283–288.

Steinem, G. (1983). *Outrageous acts and everyday rebellions.* New York: Holt, Rinehart and Winston.

Sternglanz, S. H., & Serbin, L. A. (1974). Sex-role stereotyping in children's television programs. *Developmental Psychology, 10,* 710–715.

Stevens, G. E., & DeNisi, A. S. (1980). Women as managers: Attitudes and attributions for performance by men and women. *Academy of Management Journal, 23*(2), 355–360.

Stevens, N. (1995). Gender and adaptation to widowhood in later life. *Ageing and Society, 15,* 37–58.

Stevenson, H. W., Lee, S., & Stigler, J. (1986, February 14). Mathematics achievement of Chinese, Japanese, and American children. *Science,* pp. 693–699.

Stewart, A. J., & Ostrove, J. M. (1998). Women's personality and middle age: Gender, history, and midcourse corrections. *American Psychologist, 53*(11), 1185–1194.

Stewart, A. J., & Salt, P. (1981). Life stress, life-styles, depression and illness in adult women. *Journal of Personality and Social Psychology, 40*(6), 1063–1069.

Stewart, A. J., & Winter, D. G. (1976). Arousal of the power motive in women. *Journal of Consulting and Clinical Psychology, 44*(3), 495–496.

Stewart, D. E. (1989). Positive changes in the premenstrual period. *Acta Psychiatrica Scandinavica, 79*(4), 400–405.

Stewart, D. E., Abbey, S. E., Shnek, Z. M., Irvine, J., & Grace, S. L. (2004). Gender differences in health information needs and decisional preferences in patients recovering from an acute ischemic coronary event. *Psychosomatic Medicine, 66*(1), 42–48.

Stewart, M. W., Verstraate, C. D., & Fanslow, J. L. (1990). Sexist language and university academic staff: Attitudes, awareness and recognition of sexist language. *New Zealand Journal of Educational Studies, 25*(2), 115–125.

Stiller, N. J., & Forrest, L. (1990). An extension of Gilligan and Lyon's investigation of morality: Gender differences in college students. *Journal of College Student Development, 31*(1), 54–63.

Stockard, J., & Johnson, M. (1979). The social origins of male dominance. *Sex Roles, 5*(2), 199–218.

Stockard, J., Schmuck, P. A., Kempner, K., Williams, P., Edson, S. K., & Smith, M. A. (1980). *Sex equity in education.* New York: Academic Press.

Stockdale, M. S. (1998). The direct and moderating influences of sexual harassment pervasiveness, coping strategies, and gender on work-related outcomes. *Psychology of Women Quarterly, 22,* 521–535.

Stone, D. L., & Colella, A. (1996). A model of factors affecting the treatment of disabled individuals in organizations. *Academy of Management Review, 21,* 352–401.

Storey, A. E., Walsh, C. J., Quinton, R. L., & Wynne-Edwards, K. E. (2000). Hormonal correlates of paternal responsiveness in new and expectant fathers. *Evolution and Human Behavior, 21*(2), 79–95.

Storms, M. D. (1973). Videotape and the attribution process: Reversing actors' and observers' points of view. *Journal of Personality and Social Psychology, 27,* 165–175.

Storms, M. D. (1980). Theories of sexual orientation. *Journal of Personality and Social Psychology, 38,* 783–792.

Straus, M. A. (1999). The controversy over domestic violence by women: A methodological, theoretical, and sociology of science analysis. In X. Arriaga & S. Oskamp (Eds.), *Violence in intimate relationships* (pp. 17–44). Thousand Oaks, CA: Sage.

Stroh, L. K., Brett, J. M., & Reilly, A. H. (1996). Family structure, glass ceiling, and traditional explanations for the differential rate of turnover of female and male managers. *Journal of Vocational Behavior, 49*(1), 99–118.

Strommen, E. A. (1977). Friendship. In E. Donelson & J. Gullahorn (Eds.), *Women: A psychological perspective* (pp. 154–167). New York: Wiley.

Studies show women 50% more likely to die of heart attacks than men. (1998, April 2). *Roanoke Times,* p. A6.

Stuenkel, C. A. (1989). Menopause and estrogen replacement therapy. *Psychiatric Clinics of North America, 12*(1), 133–152.

Stuhlmacher, A. F., & Walters, A. E. (1999). Gender differences in negotiation outcome: A meta-analysis. *Personnel Psychology, 52*(3), 653–677.

Sulloway, F. J. (1979). *Freud, biologist of the mind.* New York: Basic Books.

Summers, L. H. (2005, January 14). *Remarks at NBER conference on diversifying the science and engineering workforce.* Retrieved July 17, 2006, from http://www.president.harvard.edu/speeches/summers/2005/nber.html

Super, D. L. (1951). Vocational adjustment: Implementing a self concept. *Occupations, 30,* 88–92.

Suplee, C. (1991, August 30). Brain may dictate sexuality. *Washington Post,* pp. A1, A13.

Supreme Court delivers mixed decisions on key cases. (1984, May). *NEA Today, 2*(7), 23.

A surgeon cuts to the heart of the matter. (1991, October 28). *People,* p. 50.

Surrey, J. L., Scott, L., & Phillips, E. L. (1975). Menstrual cycle and the decision to seek psychological services. *Perceptual and Motor Skills, 40,* 886.

Susman, E. J., Inoff-Germain, G., Nottlemann, E. D., Loriaux, D. L., Cutler, G. B., & Chrousos, G. P. (1987). Hormones, emotional dispositions, and aggressive attributes in young adolescents. *Child Development, 58,* 1114–1134.

Swaab, D. F., & Hofman, M. A. (1988). Sexual differentiation of the human hypothalamus: Ontogeny of the sexually dimorphic nucleus of the preoptic area. *Developmental Brain Research, 44*(2), 314–318.

Swardson, A. (1991, June 18). Women and the sporting life. *Washington Post,* p. D3.

Swartzman, L. C., Edelberg, R., & Kemmann, E. (1990). The menopausal hot flush: Symptom reports and concomitant physiological changes. *Journal of Behavioral Medicine, 13*(1), 15–30.

Sweeney, J., & Bradbard, M. R. (1988). Mothers' and fathers' changing perceptions of their male and female infants over the course of pregnancy. *Journal of Genetic Psychology, 149*(3), 393–404.

Swetkis, D., Gilroy, F. D., & Steinbacher, R. (2002). Firstborn preference and attitudes toward using sex selection technology. *Journal of Genetic Psychology, 163*(2), 228–238.

Swim, J. K. (1994). Perceived versus meta-analytic effect sizes: An assessment of the accuracy of gender stereotypes. *Journal of Personality and Social Psychology, 66*(1), 21–36.

Swim, J. K., Aikin, K. J., Hall, W. S., & Hunter, B. A. (1995). Sexism and racism: Old-fashioned and modern prejudices. *Journal of Personality and Social Psychology, 68*(2), 199–214.

Swim, J., Borgida, E., Maruyama, G., & Myers, D. G. (1989). Joan McKay versus John McKay: Do gender stereotypes bias evaluations? *Psychological Bulletin, 105,* 409–425.

Swim, J. K., Cohen, L. L., & Hyers, L. L. (1998). Experiencing everyday prejudice and discrimination. In J. K. Swim & C. Stangor (Eds.), *Prejudice: The target's perspective* (pp. 37–60). San Diego: Academic Press.

Swim, J. K., Ferguson, M. J., & Hyers, L. L. (1999). Avoiding stigma by association: Subtle prejudice against lesbians in the form of social distancing. *Basic and Applied Social Psychology, 21*(1), 61–68.

Swim, J. K., & Hyers, L. L. (1999). Excuse me—What did you just say?!: Women's public and private responses to sexist remarks. *Journal of Experimental Social Psychology, 35*(1), 68–88.

Swim, J. K., Hyers, L. L., Cohen, L. L., & Ferguson, M. J. (2001). Everyday sexism: Evidence for its incidence, nature, and psychological impact from three daily diary studies. *Journal of Social Issues, 57*(1), 31–53.

Symons, D. (1979). *The evolution of human sexuality.* Oxford: Oxford University Press.

Szymanski, L. A., & Chrisler, J. C. (1990/91). Eating disorders, gender-role, and athletic activity. *Psychology, 27*(4) & *28*(1), 20–29.

Tamir, L. M. (1982). *Men in their forties: The transition to middle age.* New York: Springer.

The Tampax Report. (1981). (Available from Ruder, Finn & Rotman, 110 E. 59th Street, New York, NY 10022.)

Tamres, L. K., Janicki, D., & Helgeson, V. S. (2002). Sex differences in coping behavior: A meta-analytic review and an examination of relative coping. *Personality and Social Psychology Review, 6*(1), 2–30.

Tangri, S., Burt, M. R., & Johnson, L. B. (1982). Sexual harassment at work: Three explanatory models. *Journal of Social Issues, 38*(4), 33–54.

Tascio, L. (2006, September). Sexual harassment on campus. *AAUW Outlook,* 8–9, 24.

Tasker, F., & Golombok, S. (1995). Adults raised as children in lesbian families. *American Journal of Orthopsychiatry, 65*(2), 203–215.

Tauber, M. A. (1979). Parental socialization techniques and sex differences in children's play. *Child Development, 50,* 225–234.

Taylor, S. E., & Langer, E. J. (1977). Pregnancy: A social stigma? *Sex Roles, 3,* 27–35.

Taywaditep, K. J. (2001). Marginalization among the marginalized: Gay men's anti-effeminacy attitudes. *Journal of Homosexuality, 42*(1), 1–28.

Teachman, J. D., & Paasch, K. M. (1994). Financial impact of divorce on children and their families. *Future of Children, 4*(1), 63–85.

Tedesco, T. (2001, July 17). Executive women want a life: Survey. *National Post.* Retrieved from http://www.pollara.ca/new/LIBRARY/SURVEYS/wsnNatpost.htm

Tenenbaum, H. R., & Leaper, C. (2002). Are parents' gender schemas related to their children's gender-related cognitions? A meta-analysis. *Developmental Psychology, 38*(4), 615–630.

Tennov, D. (1975). *Psychotherapy: The hazardous cure.* New York: Abelard-Schuman.

Terman, L. M. (1925). *Genetic studies of genius: Vol. 1. Mental and physical traits of a thousand gifted children.* Stanford, CA: Stanford University Press.

Terman, L. M. (1951). Correlates of orgasm adequacy in a group of 556 wives. *Journal of Psychology, 32,* 115–172.

Terman, L. M., & Miles, C. C. (1936). *Sex and personality: Studies in masculinity and femininity.* New York: McGraw-Hill.

Terman, L. M., & Oden, M. (1947). *The gifted child grows up.* Stanford, CA: Stanford University Press.

Terman, L. M., & Oden, M. (1959). *The gifted group at mid-life.* Stanford, CA: Stanford University Press.

Terrelonge, P. (1989). Feminist consciousness and Black women. In J. Freeman (Ed.), *Women: A feminist perspective* (4th ed., pp. 556–566). Mountain View, CA: Mayfield.

Tersman, Z., Collins, A., & Eneroth, P. (1991). Cardiovascular responses to psychological and physiological stressors during the menstrual cycle. *Psychosomatic Medicine, 53*(2), 185–197.

Testa, R. J., Kinder, B. N., & Ironson, G. (1987). Homosexual bias in the perception of loving relationships of gay males and lesbians. *Journal of Sex Research, 23*(2), 163–172.

Texas Workforce Commission. (2005). *Occupational profile: SOC 43-6011 executive secretaries and administrative assistants.* Retrieved November 20, 2006, from http://socrates.cdr.state.tx.us/iSocrates/occprofiles/occprofile.asp?soc=43-6011&reptype=T&lwda=20 Alamo

Thibaut, J., & Kelley, H. (1959). *The social psychology of groups.* New York: Wiley.

Thomas, M. D., Henley, T. B., & Snell, C. M. (2006). The Draw a Scientist Test: A different population and a somewhat different story. *College Student Journal, 40*(1), 140–148.

Thoma, S. J. (1986). Estimating gender differences in the comprehension and preference of moral issues. *Developmental Review, 6*(2), 165–180.

Thomas, V. G., & Miles, S. E. (1995). Psychology of Black women: Past, present, and future. In H. Landrine (Ed.), *Bringing cultural diversity to feminist psychology: Theory, research, practice* (pp. 303–330). Washington, DC: American Psychological Association.

Thomas, V. L. (1989). Black women engineers and technologists. *Sage: A Scholarly Journal on Black Women, 6*(2), 24–32.

Thompson, A. P. (1983). Extramarital sex: A review of the research literature. *Journal of Sex Research, 19*, 1–22.

Thompson (Woolley), H. B. (1903). *The mental traits of sex: An experimental investigation of the normal mind in men and women.* Chicago: University of Chicago Press.

Thompson, T. L., & Zerbinos, E. (1995). Gender roles in animated cartoons: Has the picture changed in 20 years? *Sex Roles, 32*(9/10), 651–673.

Thornborrow, N. M., & Sheldon, M. B. (1995). Women in the labor force. In J. Freeman (Ed.), *Women: A feminist perspective* (5th ed., pp. 197–219). Mountain View, CA: Mayfield.

Thorndike, E. L. (1910). *Educational psychology* (2nd ed.). New York: Columbia University, Teacher's College.

Tibbetts, J. (2004, October 29). Cash crisis justified viiolating rights: Court. *Ottawa Citizen*, p. A3.

Tiefer, L. (1995). *Sex is not a natural act and other essays.* Boulder, CO: Westview.

Tiger, L. (1969). *Men in groups.* New York: Random House.

Tiggemann, M. (2005). Television and adolescent body image: The role of program content and viewing motivation. *Journal of Social and Clinical Psychology, 24*(3), 361–381.

Tillitski, C. J. (1992). Fathers and child custody: Issues, trends, and implications for counseling. *Journal of Mental Health Counseling, 14*(3), 351–361.

Timmerman, G. (2002). A comparison between unwanted sexual behavior by teachers and by peers in secondary schools. *Journal of Youth and Adolescence, 31*(5), 397–404.

Tinsley, E. G., Sullivan-Guest, S., & McGuire, J. (1984). Feminine sex role and depression in middle-aged women. *Sex Roles, 11*, 25–32.

Tobacco Information and Prevention Source. (2006). *Fact sheet: Youth and tobacco use: Current estimates.* Retrieved September 1, 2006, from http://www.cdc.gov/ tobacco/research_data/youth/ Youth_Factsheet.htm

Tobias, S. (1982, January). Sexist equations. *Psychology Today*, pp. 14–17.

Tolman, D. L., & Szalacha, L. A. (1999). Dimensions of desire: Bridging qualitative and quantitative methods in a study of female adolescent sexuality. *Psychology of Women Quarterly, 23*(1), 7–39.

Tomlinson-Keasey, C. (1990). The working lives of Terman's gifted women. In H. Y. Grossman & N. L. Chester (Eds.), *The experience and meaning of work in women's lives* (pp. 213–240). Hillsdale, NJ: Erlbaum.

Tonkinson, R. (1974). *The Jigalong Mob: Aboriginal victors of the desert crusade.* Menlo Park, CA: Cummings.

Tooby, J., & Cosmides, L. (2005). Conceptual foundations of evolutionary psychology. In D. M. Buss (Ed.), *The handbook of evolutionary psychology* (pp. 5–67). New York: Wiley.

Top, T. J. (1991). Sex bias in the evaluation of performance in the scientific, artistic, and literary professions: A review. *Sex Roles, 24*(1/2), 73–106.

Tougas, F., Brown, R., Beaton, A. M., & Joly, S. (1995). Neosexism: Plus ça change, plus c'est pareil. *Personality and Social Psychology Bulletin, 21*, 842–849.

Tougas, F., Brown, R., Beaton, A. M., & St-Pierre, L. (1999). Neosexism among women: The role of personally experienced social mobility attempts. *Personality and Social Psychology Bulletin, 25*(12), 1487–1497.

Tougas, F., & Veilleux, F. (1988). The influence of identification, collective relative deprivation, and procedure of implementation on women's response to affirmative action: A causal modeling approach. *Canadian Journal of Behavioral Science, 20*, 16–29.

Tougas, F., & Veilleux, F. (1989). Who likes affirmative action: Attitudinal processes among men and women. In F. A. Blanchard & F. Crosby (Eds.), *Affirmative action in perspective.* Boston: Springer-Verlag.

Touhey, J. C. (1974a). Effects of additional women professionals on ratings of occupational prestige and desirability. *Journal of Personality and Social Psychology, 29*, 86–89.

Touhey, J. C. (1974b). Effects of additional men on prestige and desirability of occupations typically performed by women. *Journal of Applied Social Psychology, 4*(4), 330–335.

Towson, S. M. J., MacDonald, G., & Zanna, M. P. (1981, June). *Confirming sex-role stereotypes in the job interview: Payoffs and pitfalls.* Paper presented at the annual convention of the Canadian Psychological Association, Montreal.

Trahan, D. E., & Quintana, J. W. (1990). Analysis of gender effects upon verbal and visual memory performance in adults. *Archives of Clinical Neuropsychology, 5*, 325–334.

Travis, C. B., Phillippi, R. H., & Henley, T. B. (1991). Gender and causal attributions for mastery, personal, and interpersonal events. *Psychology of Women Quarterly, 15*, 233–249.

Tredinnick, M. G., & Fowers, B. J. (1997). Gender bias and individualism: Responses to case vignettes among psychologists, professors, and students. *Current Psychology: Developmental, Learning, Personality, Social, 15*(4), 291–299.

Treffke, H., Tiggemann, M., & Ross, M. (1992). The relationship between attitude, assertiveness, and condom use. *Psychology and Health, 6*, 45–52.

Trepanier, M. L., & Romatowski, J. A. (1985). Attributes and roles assigned to characters in children's writing: Sex differences and sex-role perceptions. *Sex Roles, 13*(5/6), 263–272.

Trescott, J. (1991, August 17). Anthology of a mother's grief. *Washington Post*, pp. C1, C5.

Tresmer, D. (1976). Do women fear success? *Signs: Journal of Women in Culture and Society, 1*(4), 863–874.

Trethowan, W. H. (1972). The couvade syndrome. In J. G. Howells (Ed.), *Modern perspectives in psycho-obstetrics* (pp. 68–93). New York: Brunner/Mazel.

Tuck, R. (1975). The relationship between a mother's menstrual status and her response to illness in her child. *Psychosomatic Medicine, 37*, 388–394.

Tucson Citizen. (1989, February 1). Jazzman Billy Tipton revealed as a woman. p. 3A.

Turell, S. C., Armsworth, M. W., & Gaa, J. P. (1990). Emotional responses to abortion: A critical review of the literature. *Women and Therapy, 9*(4), 49–68.

Turkle, S., & Papert, S. (1990). Epistemological pluralism: Styles and voices within the computer culture. *Signs: Journal of Women in Culture and Society, 16*(1), 128–157.

TV debates may prompt Pakistan to change laws on reporting rape. (2006, July 9). *Roanoke Times*, p. 8A.

Twenge, J. M. (1997). Changes in masculine and feminine traits over time: A meta-analysis. *Sex Roles, 36*(5/6), 305–325.

Twenge, J. M. (2001). Changes in women's assertiveness in response to status and roles: A cross-temporal meta-analysis, 1931–1993. *Journal of Personality and Social Psychology, 81*(1), 133–145.

Tyler, L. (1965). *The psychology of human differences.* New York: Appleton-Century-Crofts. (Original work published 1947)

Udry, J. R. (2000). Biological limits of gender construction. *American Sociological Review, 65,* 443–457.

Ugarriza, D. N. (2002). Postpartum depressed women's explanation of depression. *Journal of Nursing Scholarship, 34*(3), 227–233.

Umberson, D., Wortman, C. B., & Kessler, R. C. (1992). Widowhood and depression: Explaining long-term gender differences in vulnerability. *Journal of Health and Social Behavior, 33,* 10–24.

UNAIDS. (1996–2001, annual). *Report on the global HIV/AIDS epidemic.* Geneva: Author.

UNAIDS. (2002). *UNAIDS/WHO Regional estimates as of end 2002.* Geneva: Joint United Nations Programme on HIV/AIDS. Retrieved from http://www.unaids.org/html.pub/Topics/Epidemiology/RegionalEstimates2002_en_pdf

UNAIDS. (2003). *Epidemiological fact sheets on HIV/AIDS and sexually transmitted infections: United States of America.* Geneva: Joint United Nations Programme on HIV/AIDS. Retrieved from http://www.unaids.org/html/pub/Publications/Fact- Sheets)1/USA_EN_pdf.htm

UNAIDS. (2006a). *2006 report on the global AIDS epidemic.* Retrieved July 31, 2006, from http://www.unaids.org/en/HIV_data/2006GlobalReport/default.asp

UNAIDS. (2006b). *Uniting the world against AIDS: Regions, countries: United States of America.* Retrieved July 31, 2006, from http://www.unaids.org/en/Regions_Countries/Countries/united_states_of_america.asp

UNESCO Institute for Statistics. (2002, December). *Estimated illiteracy rate and illiterate population aged 15 years and older, by region, 1970–2015.*

UNESCO. (2006). *Literacy rates, 2006 assessment.* Retrieved November 10, 2006, from http://stats.uis.unesco.org/ReportFolders/reportfolders.aspx

Unger, R. (1979). Toward a redefinition of sex and gender. *American Psychologist, 34,* 1085–1094.

Unger, R., & Crawford, M. (1993). Commentary: Sex and gender: The troubled relationship between terms and concepts. *Psychological Science 4*(2), 122–124.

Unger, R. K., & Sussman, L. E. (1986). "I and thou": Another barrier to societal change? *Sex Roles, 14*(11/12), 629–636.

UNIFEM. (2003). *Progress of the world's women: Gender equality and the millennium development goals.* Retrieved from http://www.unifem.org/index.php?f_page_pid=10

United Nations. (1995). *Statistical yearbook for Asia and the Pacific.* New York: Author.

United Nations. (2000). *The world's women 2000. Trends and statistics.* New York: Author.

United Nations. (2002). *Concise report on world population monitoring, 2002: Reproductive rights and reproductive health with special reference to HIV/AIDS.* E/CN.9/2002/2. New York: Author.

United Nations. (2006). *CEDAW—States parties.* Retrieved November 29, 2006, from http://www.un.org/womenwatch/daw/cedaw/states.htm

United Nations Development Program. (2005). *Nepal: Gender and social development.* Retrieved August 28, 2006, from http://www.undp.org.np/gender/

United Nations Population Fund. (2002). *State of world population, 2002: People, poverty and possibilities.* Retrieved from http://www.unfpa.org/swp/2002/english/ch4/index.htm

United Nations Statistics Division. (2005). *The world's women, 2005: Progress in statistics.* New York: Author.

United Nations Womenwatch Program. (2003, October 30). *Data.* Retrieved from http://www.un.org/womenwatch/resources/

Urry, M. (2005, February 6). Diminished by discrimination we scarcely see. *Washington Post,* p. B4.

U.S. Bureau of Labor Statistics. (2002). Table 39: Median weekly earnings of full-time wage and salary workers by detailed occupation and sex. In *Labor force statistics from the current population survey.* Retrieved from http://www.bls.gov/cps/home.htm#tables

U.S. Bureau of Labor Statistics. (2003a). *Labor force statistics from the Current Population Survey.* Retrieved from http://www.bls.gov/cps/home.htm#charemp

U.S. Bureau of Labor Statistics. (2003b, July 9). *Employment characteristics of families in 2002.* USDL 03-369. Washington, DC: U.S. Department of Labor.

U.S. Census Bureau. (2001, October). *Fertility of American women, June 2000.* Retrieved from http://www.census.gov/prod/2001pubs/p20-543rv.pdf

U.S. Census Bureau. (2002b). *Historical income tables—People. Table P-38. Full-time year-round workers (all races) by median earnings and sex: 1960 to 2000.* Retrieved from http://www.census.gov/hhes/income/histinc/p38.html

U.S. Census Bureau. (2002c). *Historical income tables—People. Table P-36. Wage or salary workers (all races) by median age and salary income (2001 dollars) and sex: 1955 to 2001.* Retrieved from http://www.census.gov/hhes/income/histinc/p36.html

U.S. Census Bureau, Population Division. (2002d). *Table A-1. Marital status of people 15 years and over, by age, sex, personal earnings, race, and Hispanic origin.* Retrieved from http://www.census.gov/population/www/socdemo/ms-la.html

U.S. Census Bureau. (2003). *Annual demographic supplement to the March 2002 Current Population Survey, Current Population Reports, Series P20-547, "Children's living arrangements and characteristics: March 2002."* Retrieved from http://www.census.gov/population/www/socdemo/ms-la.html

U.S. Census Bureau. (2003b). *Annual demographic survey, March supplement. Table POV01.* Retrieved from http://ferret.bls.census.gov/macro/032003/pov/new01_000.htm

U. S. Census Bureau. (2005). *American community survey.* Retrieved August 31, 2006, from http://factfinder.census.gov/servlet/DatasetMainPageServlet?_program=ACS&_lang=en&_ts=143471788982

U.S. Census Bureau. (2006a). *CPS 2006 annual social and economic supplement.* Retrieved November 20, 2006, from http://pubdb3.census.gov/macro/032006/perinc/toc.htm

U.S. Census Bureau. (2006b). *Historical income tables—Families.* Retrieved

November 21, 2006, from http://www
.census.gov/hhes/www/income/
histinc/incfamdet.html

U. S. Census Bureau. (2006c). *Statistical abstract of the United States, 2006*. Retrieved June 22, 2006. from http://www .census.gov/compendia/statab/ 2006edition.html

U.S. Bureau of Justice Statistics. (2004). *Sourcebook of criminal justice statistics online, 31st edition (2003)*. Retrieved June 27, 2006, from http://www .albany.edu/sourcebook/index.html

U.S. Bureau of Justice Statistics. (2005). *Criminal offender statistics*. Retrieved June 27, 2006, from http://www.ojp .usdoj.gov/bjs/crimoff.htm

U.S. Bureau of Justice Statistics. (2006a). *Criminal victimization in the United States—Statistical tables index*. Retrieved November 30, 2006, from http://www .ojp.usdoj.gov/bjs/abstract/cvus/ index.htm

U.S. Bureau of Justice Statistics. (2006b). *Criminal victimization in the United States, 2004: Statistical tables, National Crime Victimization Survey*. Retrieved December 1, 2006, from http://www .ojp.usdoj.gov/bjs/pub/pdf/ cvus0402.pdf

U.S. Bureau of Justice Statistics. (2006c). *Violent crime rates declined for both males and females since 1994*. Retrieved November 30, 2006, from http://www .ojp.usdoj.gov/bjs/glance/vsx2.htm

U.S. Bureau of Labor Statistics. (2005a). *Characteristics of minimum wage workers: 2005*. Retrieved November 21, 2006, from http://www.bls.gov/cps/ minwage2005tbls.htm

U.S. Bureau of Labor Statistics. (2005b). *Employed persons by detailed occupation, sex, race, and Hispanic origin*. Retrieved June 16, 2006, from http://www.bls .gov/cps/cpsaat11.pdf

U.S. Bureau of Labor Statistics. (2005c). *Labor forces statistics from the current population survey*. Retrieved November 20, 2006, from http://www.bls.gov/cps/

U.S. Bureau of Labor Statistics. (2005d). *Median weekly earnings of full time wage and salary workers by detailed occupation and sex*. Retrieved June 16, 2006, from http://www.bls.gov/cps/cpsaat39.pdf

U.S. Bureau of Labor Statistics. (2006a). *American time use survey—2005 results*. Retrieved October 16, 2006, from http://www.bls.gov/news.release/ pdf/atus.pdf

U.S. Bureau of Labor Statistics. (2006b). *Women in the labor force: A databook (2006 edition)*. Retrieved November 21, 2006, from http://www.bls.gov/cps/ wlf-databook2006.htm

U.S. Department of Education, National Center for Education Statistics. (2002). *Digest of education statistics, 2002*. Retrieved from http://nces.ed.gov/ pubsearch/pubsinfo.asp? pubid= 2003060

U.S. Department of Health and Human Services. (1998, September). Trends in sexual risk behaviors among high school students—United States, 1991–1997. *Morbidity and Mortality Weekly Report, 47*(36), 749–752.

U.S. Department of Health and Human Services. (2000). *Healthy people 2010: Understanding and improving health* (2nd ed.). Washington, DC: U.S. Government Printing Office.

U. S. Department of Justice. (1994, June 22). *Half of wmen raped during 1992 were younger than 18 years old*. Press release. Washington, DC: Author.

U.S. Department of Justice. (2001). *National criminal victimization survey*. NCJ 197064. Retrieved from http://www.ojp .usdoj.gov/bjs/abstract/cvus/number_ of_incidents745.htm

U.S. Department of Justice. (2004). *Homicide trends in the United States: Trends by gender*. Retrieved June 23, 2006, from http://www.ojp.usdoj.gov/bjs/ homicide/tables/osextab.htm

U.S. Department of Justice, Federal Bureau of Investigation. (1999a, May). *Uniform crime reports: 1998 preliminary annual release*. Washington, DC: Author.

U.S. Department of Justice, Federal Bureau of Investigation. (1999b). *The structure of family violence: An analysis of selected incidents*. Washington DC: Author.

U.S. Department of Justice, Office of Justice Programs. (1995). *Violence against women: Estimates from the redesigned survey, August 1995*. Washington, DC: Author.

U.S. Department of Labor, Women's Bureau. (2003, November 26). *20 leading occupations of employed women, full-time wages and salary workers, 2002 annual average*. Retrieved from http://www .dol.gov/wb/factsheets/20lead2002_txt .htm

U.S. Equal Opportunity Commission. (1980). Guidelines on discrimination because of sex. *Federal Register, 45*(219), 74676–74677.

U.S. Merit Systems Protection Board. (1981). *Sexual harassment in the federal workplace: Is it a problem?* Washington, DC: U.S. Government Printing Office.

U.S. National Institutes of Health. (1992). *Opportunities for research on women's health* (NIH Publication no. 92–3457). Washington, DC: U.S. Department of Health and Human Services.

USA Today. (2003, April 17). Outdated sex-crime laws leave military women at risk. p. 12A.

Utne, M. K., Hatfield, E., Traupmann, J., & Greenberger, D. (1984). Equity, marital satisfaction, and stability. *Journal of Social and Personal Relationships, 1*, 323–332.

Vaccarino, V., Krumholz, H. M., Yarzebski, J., Gore, J. M., & Goldberg, R. J. (2001). Sex differences in 2-year mortality after hospital discharge for myocardial infarction. *Annals of Internal Medicine, 134*(3), 173–181.

Valois, R. F., & Waring, K. A. (1991). An analysis of college students' anonymous questions about human sexuality. *Journal of American College Health, 39*(6), 263–268.

Vance, E. B., & Wagner, N. N. (1976). Written descriptions of orgasm: A study of sex differences. *Archives of Sexual Behavior, 5*, 87–98.

Van Den Akker, O. (2003). Genetic and gestational surrogate mothers' experience of surrogacy. *Journal of Reproductive and Infant Psychology, 21*(2), 145–161.

Vandenberg, S. G. (1987). Sex differences in mental retardation and their implications for sex differences in ability. In J. M. Reinisch, L. A. Rosenblum, & S. A. Sanders (Eds.), *Masculinity/femininity: Basic perspectives* (pp. 157–171). New York: Oxford University Press.

van der Sluis, S., Posthuma, D., Dolan, C. V., de Geus, E. J. C., Colom, R., & Boomsma, D. I. (2006). Sex differences on the Dutch WAIS-III. *Intelligence, 34*(3), 273–289.

Van Gelder, L. (1985). The strange case of the electronic lover: A real-life story of deception, seduction, and technology. *Ms., 14*(4), 94–95, 99, 101–104, 117, 123–124.

Van Gelder, L. (1991, March/April). A lesbian family revisited. *Ms., 1*(5), 44–47.

Van Goozen, S. H., Wiegant, V. M., Endert, E., Helmond, F. A., et al. (1997).

Psychoendocrinological assessment of the menstrual cycle: The relationship between hormones, sexuality, and mood. *Archives of Sexual Behavior, 26*(4), 359–382.

Van Preagh, P. (1982). The Hamilton birth control clinic: In response to need. *News/Nouvelles, Journal of the Planned Parenthood Federation of Canada, 3*(1), 2.

Vartanian, L. R., Giant, C. L., & Passino, R. M. (2001). "Ally McBeal vs. Arnold Schwarznegger": Comparing mass media, interpersonal feedback and gender as predictors of satisfaction with body thinness and muscularity. *Social Behavior and Personality, 29*(7), 711–723.

Vasquez, M. J. T. (2002). Complexities of the Latina experience: A tribute to Martha Bernal. *American Psychologist, 57*(1), 880–888.

Verbrugge, L. (1982a). Sex differences in legal drug use. *Journal of Social Issues, 38*(2), 59–76.

Verbrugge, L. (1983, March). Multiple roles and physical health of women and men. *Journal of Health and Social Behavior, 24,* 16–30.

Vergano, D. (1999, May 27). *Pumping iron lowers women's cholesterol.* Medical Tribune News Service. Retrieved from www.drkoop.com/healthnews/latest/may/strong_women.html

Veroff, J., Douvan, E., & Kulka, A. (1981). *The inner American: A self-portrait from 1957–1976.* New York: Basic Books.

Verschueren, K., & Marcoen, A. (2003, April). *Kindergartners' representations of attachment to father and mother: Different effects on later socioemotional functioning.* Paper presented at the biennial meeting of the Society for Research in Child Development, Tampa, FL.

Vetter, L., & Hickey, D. R. (1985, October). Women in vocational education: Changes since Title IX. *Vocational Education Journal, 60,* 26–29.

Viss, D. C., & Burn, S. M. (1992). Divergent perceptions of lesbians: A comparison of lesbian self-perceptions and heterosexual perceptions. *Journal of Social Psychology, 132*(2), 169–177.

Voda, A. M., & Eliasson, M. (1983). Menopause: The closure of menstrual life. *Women and Health, 8*(2/3), 137–156.

Vogel, D. L., Wester, S. R., Heesacker, M., Boysen, G. A., & Seeman, J. (2006). Gender differences in emotional expression: Do mental health trainees overestimate the magnitude? *Journal of Social and Clinical Psychology, 25*(3), 305–332.

Vollmer, F. (1984). Sex differences in personality and expectancy. *Sex Roles, 11,* 1121–1139.

von Baeyer, C. L., Sherk, D. L., & Zanna, M. P. (1981). Impression management in the job interview. When the female applicant meets the male "chauvinist" interviewer. *Personality and Social Psychology Bulletin, 7,* 45–51.

Voyer, D. (1996). On the magnitude of laterality effects and sex differences in functional lateralities. *Laterality: Asymmetries of Body, Brain and Cognition, 1*(1), 51–83.

Voyer, D., Nolan, C., & Voyer, S. (2001). The relation between experience and spatial performance in men and women. *Sex Roles, 43*(11–12), 891–915.

Voyer, D., Voyer, S., & Bryden, M. P. (1995). Magnitude of sex differences in spatial abilities: A meta-analysis and consideration of critical variables. *Psychological Bulletin, 117*(2), 250–270.

Wada, J. A., Clark, R., & Hamm, A. (1975). Cerebral hemisphere asymmetry in humans. *Archives of Neurology, 32,* 239–246.

Wade, R. (1978). *For men, about abortion.* (Available from Roger C. Wade, P.O. Box 4748, Boulder, CO, 80306)

Wagner, D. G. (1995). Gender differences in reward preference: A status-based account. *Small Group Research, 26*(3), 353–371.

Waldfogel, J. (1997). Working mothers then and now: A cross-cohort analysis of the effects of maternity leave on women's pay. In F. D. Blau & R. G. Ehrenberg (Eds.), *Gender and family issues in the workplace.* New York: Russell Sage.

Waldfogel, J. (2001). Family and medical leave: Evidence from the 2000 surveys. *Monthly Labor Review, 124*(9), 17–23. Retrieved April 2, 2007, from http://www.bls.gov/opub/mlr/2001/09/contents.htm

Walker, E., Bettes, B. A., Kain, E. L., & Harvey, P. (1985). Relationship of gender and marital status with symptomatology in psychotic patients. *Journal of Abnormal Psychology, 94,* 42–50.

Walker, L. E. (1979). *The battered woman.* New York: Harper & Row.

Walker, L. E. (1999). Psychology and domestic violence around the world. *American Psychologist, 54*(1), 21–29.

Walker, L. J. (1984). Sex differences in the development of moral reasoning: A critical review. *Child Development, 55,* 677–691.

Walker, L. J. (1989). A longitudinal study of moral reasoning. *Child Development, 60,* 157–166.

Walker, L. O., & Best, M. A. (1991). Well-being of mothers with infant children: A preliminary comparison of employed women and homemakers. *Women and Health, 17*(1), 71–89.

Walkerdine, V., & The Girls and Mathematics Unit. (1989). *Counting girls out.* London: Virago Press.

Wallen, J., Waitzkin, H., & Stoeckle, J. D. (1979). Physician stereotypes about female health and illness: A study of patients' sex and the informative process during medical interviews. *Women and Health, 4,* 135–146.

Wallen, K. (1996). Nature needs nurture: The interaction of hormonal and social influences on the development of behavioral sex differences in rhesus monkeys. *Hormones and Behavior, 30,* 364–378.

Wallston, B. S., DeVellis, B. M., & Wallston, K. (1983). Licensed practical nurses' sex role stereotypes. *Psychology of Women Quarterly, 7,* 199–208.

Walster, E. (1974). Passionate love. In Z. Rubin (Ed.), *Doing unto others* (pp. 150–162). Englewood Cliffs, NJ: Prentice-Hall.

Walster, E., Berscheid, E., & Walster, G. W. (1973). New directions in equity research. *Journal of Personality and Social Psychology, 25,* 151–176.

Walster, E., & Walster, G. W. (1975). Equity and social justice. *Journal of Social Issues, 31*(3), 21–43.

Walters, V., Avotri, J. Y., & Charles, N. (1999). "Your heart is never free": Women in Wales and Ghana talking about distress. *Canadian Psychology, 40*(2), 129–142.

Ward, L. M., & Friedman, K. (2006). Using TV as a guide: Associations between television viewing and adolescents' sexual attitudes and behavior. *Journal of Research on Adolescence, 16*(1), 133–156.

Ward, L. M., Hansbrough, E., & Walker, E. (2005). Contributions of music video exposure to Black adolescents' gender and sexual schemas. *Journal of Adolescent Research, 20*(2), 143–166.

Wardle, M. G. (1976). Women's physiological reactions to physically demanding work. *Psychology of Women Quarterly, 1*(2), 151–159.

Washington Post. (1991, June 7). PMS defense successful in Va. drunken driving case. p. A1.

Washington Post. (1999, June 12). Thai women want to keep maiden name. Retrieved from http://www.search.washingtonpost.com/wpsrv/WAPO/19990612

Washington, V. (1982). Racial differences in teacher perceptions of first- and fourth-grade pupils on selected characteristics. *Journal of Negro Education, 51,* 60–72.

Watkins, P. L., & Lee, J. (1997). A feminist perspective on panic disorder and agoraphobia: Etiology and treatment. *Journal of Gender, Culture, and Health, 2*(1), 65–87.

Watson, C. M., Quatman, T., & Edler, E. (2002). Career aspirations of adolescent girls: Effect of achievement level, grade, and single-sex school environment. *Sex Roles, 46*(9/10), 323–335.

Watts-Jones, D. (1990). Toward a stress scale for African-American women. *Psychology of Women Quarterly, 14*(2), 271–276.

Wauchope, B., & Straus, M. (1990). Age, gender and class differences in physical punishment and physical abuse of American children. In M. Straus & R. J. Gelles (Eds.), *Physical violence in American families: Risk factors and adaptations in 8,145 families* (pp. 133–148). New Brunswick, NJ: Transaction.

Waxman, B. F. (1994). Up against eugenics: Disabled women's challenge to receive reproductive health services. *Sexuality and Disability, 12*(2), 155–171.

Way, N. (1995). "Can't you see the courage, the strength that I have?" Listening to urban adolescent girls speak about their relationships. *Psychology of Women Quarterly, 19*(1), 107–128.

Webb, N. M., & Kenderski, C. M. (1985). Gender differences in small-group interaction and achievement in high- and low-achieving classes. In L. C. Wilkinson & C. B. Marrett (Eds.), *Gender influences in classroom interactions* (pp. 209–236). Orlando, FL: Academic Press.

Weber, M. (1965). *The Protestant ethic and the spirit of capitalism.* London: Unwin.

Weber, R., & Crocker, J. (1983). Cognitive processes in the revision of stereotypic beliefs. *Journal of Personality and Social Psychology, 45,* 961–977.

Webster, B. H., & Bishaw, A. (2006). *Income, earnings, and poverty: Data from the 2005 American community survey.* Retrieved November 10, 2006, from http://www.census.gov/prod/2006pubs/acs-02.pdf

Webster, K. (1996, May 17). New analysis disproves oft-quoted divorce statistic. *Roanoke Times,* p. A5.

Wegner, K. E. (2005). *Bias in perceptions of parenting roles: Analysis of gender and socioeconomic status.* Ann Arbor, MI: University Microfilms International.

Weideger, P. (1977). *Menstruation and menopause.* New York: Dell.

Weidner, G., & Helmig, L. (1990). Cardiovascular stress reactivity and mood during the menstrual cycle. *Women and Health, 16*(3/4), 5–21.

Weinberg, G. (1972). *Society and the healthy homosexual.* New York: St. Martin's Press.

Weinstock, H., Berman, S., & Cates, W. (2004). Sexually transmitted diseases among American youth: Incidence and prevalence estimates, 2000. *Perspectives on Sexual and Reproductive Health, 36*(1), 6–10.

Weir, E. (2004). Hot flashes . . . in January. *Canadian Medical Association Journal, 170*(1), 39–40.

Weis, D. L. (1983). Affective reactions of women to their initial experiences of coitus. *Journal of Sex Research, 19,* 209–237.

Weisberg, D. K. (Ed.). (1982). *Women and the law: The social historical perspective: Vol. 1. Women and the criminal law.* Cambridge, MA: Schenkman.

Weiss, R. S. (1973). *Loneliness: The experience of emotional and social isolation.* Cambridge, MA: MIT Press.

Weiss, R. (2005, March 17). Human X chromosome coded. *Washington Post,* p. A3.

Weisse, C. S., Sorum, P. C., & Dominguez, R. E. (2003). The influence of gender and race on physicians' pain management decisions. *Journal of Pain, 4*(9), 505–510.

Weisstein, N. (1971). *Psychology constructs the female or, the fantasy life of the male psychologist.* Boston: New England Free Press.

Weisz, A. N., & Black, B. B. (2003). Gender and moral reasoning: African American youths respond to dating dilemmas. *Journal of Human Behavior in the Social Environment, 6*(3), 17–34.

Weitz, R. (1989). What price independence? Social reactions to lesbians, spinsters, widows, and nuns. In J. Freeman (Ed.), *Women: A feminist perspective* (4th ed., pp. 446–456). Mountain View, CA: Mayfield.

Weitzman, N., Birns, B., & Friend, R. (1985). Traditional and nontraditional mothers' communication with their daughters and sons. *Child Development, 56,* 894–898.

Welch, R., Huston-Stein, A. C., Wright, J. C., & Plehal, R. (1979). Subtle sex-role cues in children's commercials. *Journal of Communication, 29,* 202–209.

Wells, B. E., & Twenge, J. M. (2005). Changes in young people's sexual behavior and attitudes, 1943–1999: A cross-temporal meta-analysis. *Review of General Psychology, 9*(3), 249–261.

Weltzin, T. E., Weisensel, N., Franczyk, D., Burnett, K., Klitz, C., & Bean, P. (2005). Eating disorders in men: Update. *Journal of Men's Health and Gender, 2*(2), 186–193.

Wenner, S. (2000, March 1). Wives make more than husbands. *Medill News Service.* Retrieved from http://xavier.cs.northwestern.edu:8000/article.asp?articleID=1663

Wentworth, D. K., & Anderson, L. R. (1984). Emergent leadership as a function of sex and task type. *Sex Roles, 11,* 513–524.

Westbrook, M. T. (1997). Gender differences in the perceptions of psychosocial experiences reported by persons with disabilities. *Australian Occupational Therapy Journal 49*(4), 25–41.

Westkott, M. (1986). *The feminist legacy of Karen Horney.* New Haven, CT: Yale University Press.

Weyant, R. G. (1979). The relationship between psychology and women. *International Journal of Women's Studies, 2*(4), 358–385.

Wheeler, A., Lee, E. S., & Loe, H. (1983). Employment, sense of well-being, and use of professional services among women. *American Journal of Public Health, 73*(8), 908–911.

Wheeless, V. E., & Berryman-Fink, C. (1985). Perceptions of women managers and their communicator competencies. *Communication Quarterly, 33*(2), 137–148.

Whelan, C. I., & Stewart, D. E. (1990). Pseudocyesis—a review and report of six cases. *International Journal of Psychiatry in Medicine, 20,* 97–108.

Whipple, B. (2000). Beyond the G spot. *Scandinavian Journal of Sexology, 3*(2), 35–42.

Whitbeck, C. (1976). Theories of sex difference. In C. C. Gould & M. W. Wartofsky (Eds.), *Women and philosophy: Toward a theory of liberation* (pp. 54–80). New York: Putnam.

White, J. W., & Kowalski, R. M. (1994). Deconstructing the myth of the nonaggressive woman: A feminist analysis. *Psychology of Women Quarterly, 18,* 487–508.

White, J. W., & Roufail, M. (1989). Gender and influence strategies of first choice and last resort. *Psychology of Women Quarterly, 13*(2), 175–189.

White, L., & Brinkerhoff, D. (1981). The sexual division of labor: Evidence from childhood. *Social Forces, 60,* 170–181.

White, S. A. (1991). Effects of gender and competitive coaction on motor performance. *Perceptual and Motor Skills, 73*(2), 581–582.

Whitehead, T. (1981). Sex hormone treatment of prisoners. In P. Brain & D. Benton (Eds.), *Multidisciplinary approaches to aggression research* (pp. 503–511). Amsterdam: Elsevier.

Whiteley, B. E., Jr. (2002). Gender-role variables and attitudes toward homosexuality. *Sex Roles, 45*(11/12), 691–721.

Whiten, A., Goodall, J., McGrew, W. C., Nishida, T., Reynolds, V., Sugiyama, Y., Tutin, C. E. G., Wrangham, R. W., & Boesch, C. (1999). Cultures in chimpanzees. *Nature, 399,* 682–685.

Whiting, B., & Edwards, C. P. (1973). A cross-cultural analysis of sex differences in the behavior of children aged three through eleven. *Journal of Social Psychology, 91* (second half), 171–188.

Whitley, B. E., Jr., & Kite, M. E. (1995). Sex differences in attitudes toward homosexuality: A comment on Oliver and Hyde (1993). *Psychological Bulletin, 117*(1), 146–154.

Wickrama, K., Conger, R. D., & Lorenz, F. O. (1995). Work, marriage, lifestyle, and changes in men's physical health. *Journal of Behavioral Medicine, 18*(2), 97–111.

Wiersma, U. J. (1990). Gender differences in job attribute preferences: Work-home role conflict and job level as mediating variables. *Journal of Occupational Psychology, 63,* 231–243.

Wiersma, U. J., & Van den Berg, P. (1991). Work-home role conflict, family

climate, and domestic responsibilities among men and women in dual-earner families. *Journal of Applied Social Psychology, 21,* 1207–1217.

Wigfield, A., & Eccles, J. S. (1992). The development of achievement task values: A theoretical analysis. *Developmental Review, 12,* 265–310.

Wiggins, J. S., & Holzmuller, A. (1981). Further evidence on androgyny and interpersonal flexibility. *Journal of Research in Personality, 15,* 67–80.

Wikan, U. (1977). Man becomes woman: Transsexualism in Oman as a key to gender roles. *Man, 12,* 304–319.

Wilbur, J., Dan, A., Hedricks, C., & Holm, K. (1990). The relationship among menopausal status, menopausal symptoms, and physical activity in midlife women. *Family and Community Health, 13*(3), 67–78.

Wilcox, E., Finlay, W. M., & Edmonds, J. (2006). "His brain is totally different": An analysis of care-staff explanations of aggressive challenging behaviour and the impact of gendered discourses. *British Journal of Social Psychology, 45*(1), 197–216.

Wilder, G., Mackie, D., & Cooper, J. (1985). Gender and computers: Two surveys of computer-related attitudes. *Sex Roles, 13*(3/4), 215–228.

Wildman, B. G., & White, P. A. (1986). Assessment of dysmenorrhea using the Menstrual Symptom Questionnaire: Factor structure and validity. *Behaviour Research and Therapy, 24,* 547–551.

Wilgoren, J. (2003, March 28). A new war brings new role for women. *New York Times,* pp. B1, B11.

Wilkie, J. R., Ferree, M. M., & Ratcliff, K. S. (1998). Gender and fairness: Marital satisfaction in two-earner couples. *Journal of Marriage and the Family, 60*(3), 577–594.

Wilkinson, L. C., Lindow, J., & Chiang, C. P. (1985). Sex differences and sex segregation in students' small-group communication. In L. C. Wilkinson & C. B. Marrett (Eds.), *Gender influences in classroom interaction* (pp. 185–207). Orlando, FL: Academic Press.

Will, J., Self, P., & Datan, N. (1976). Maternal behavior and perceived sex of infant. *American Journal of Orthopsychiatry, 46,* 135–139.

Williams, C. L. (1992). The glass escalator: Hidden advantages for men in the "female" professions. *Social Problems,*

39(3), 253–267. Reprinted in M. S. Kimmel & M. A. Messner (Eds.). (1998). *Men's lives.* Boston: Allyn & Bacon.

Williams, D. (2002, November 3). The strange tale of unlucky Luciano. *Washington Post,* pp. F1, F3.

Williams, D. A., & King, P. (1980, December 15). Do males have a math gene? *Newsweek,* p. 73.

Williams, J. B., & Spitzer, R. L. (1983). The issue of sex bias in DSM-III. *American Psychologist, 38,* 793–798.

Williams, J. C. (2001). *Unbending gender: Why work and family conflict and what to do about it.* Oxford, UK: Oxford University Press.

Williams, J. E., & Bennett, S. M. (1975). The definition of sex stereotypes via the adjective check list. *Sex Roles, 1,* 327–337.

Williams, J. E., & Best, D. L. (1982). *Measuring sex stereotypes: A thirty-nation study.* Beverly Hills, CA: Sage.

Williams, J. E., & Best, D. L. (1990). *Measuring sex stereotypes: A multination study.* Newbury Park, CA: Sage.

Williams, L. R. (1983). Beliefs and attitudes of young girls regarding menstruation. In S. Golub (Ed.), *Menarche.* Lexington, MA: D. C. Heath.

Williams, M. L., McDaniel, M. A., & Nguyen, N. T. (2006). A meta-analysis of the antecedents and consequences of pay level satisfaction. *Journal of Applied Psychology, 91*(2), 392–413.

Williams, S. W., Ogletree, S. M., Woodburn, W., & Raffeld, P. (1993). Gender roles, computer attitudes, and dyadic computer interaction performance in college students. *Sex Roles, 29*(7/8), 515–525.

Williamson, D. A., White, M. A., Newton, R., Jr., Alfonso, A., & Stewart, T. M. (2005). Association of body size estimation and age in African-American females. *Eating and Weight Disorders, 10*(4), 216–221.

Willis, S. L., & Schaie, K. W. (1988). Gender differences in spatial ability in old age: Longitudinal and intervention findings. *Sex Roles, 18*(3/4), 189–203.

Willott, S., & Griffin, C. (2004). Redundant men: Constraints on identity change. *Journal of Community and Applied Social Psychology, 14*(2), 53–69.

Wilmoth, G. H., de Alteriis, M., & Bussell, D. (1992). Prevalence of psychological risks following legal abortion in the U.S.: Limits of the evidence. *Journal of Social Issues, 48*(3), 37–66.

Wilsnack, S. C., Vogeltanz, N. D., Klassen, A. D., & Harris, T. R. (1997). Childhood sexual abuse and women's substance abuse: National survey findings. *Journal of Studies on Alcohol, 58*(3), 264–271.

Wilson, L., Kahan, M., Liu, E., Brewster, J. M., Sobell, M. B., & Sobell, L. C. (2002). Physician behavior towards male and female problem drinkers: A controlled study using simulated patients. *Journal of Addictive Diseases, 21*(3), 87–99.

Wingwood, G. M., DiClemente, R. J., & Bernhardt, J. M. (2003). A prospective study of exposure to rap music videos and African American female adolescents' health. *American Journal of Public Health, 93*(3), 437–439.

Winnipeg Free Press. (1986, January 20). RCMP accused of sexual abuses. p. 20.

Winnipeg Free Press. (1986, May 28). Male hormones key to math. p. 38.

Winnipeg Free Press. (1986, July 24). Women's intuition linked to thicker nerves in brain. p. 34.

Winnipeg Free Press. (1987, January 17). Paralyzed woman in beauty pageant. p. 73.

Win-O'Brien, M. (1980). Law in conflict: Another view. *Journal of Occupational Medicine, 22*(8), 509–510.

Winter, D. G. (1973). *The power motive.* New York: Free Press.

Winter, D. G., & Barenbaum, N. B. (1985). Responsibility and the power motive in women and men. *Journal of Personality, 53*(2), 335–355.

Winter, D. G., & Stewart, A. J. (1978). Power motivation. In H. London & J. Exner (Eds.), *Dimensions of personality* (pp. 391–448). New York: Wiley.

Wirth, L. (2001). *Breaking through the glass ceiling: Women in management.* Geneva: International Labor Office.

Witkin, H. A., Mednick, S. A., Schulsinger, F., Bakkestrom, E., Christiansen, K. O., Goodenough, D. R., Hirschhorn, K., Lundsteen, C., Owen, D. R., Philip, J., Rubin, D. B., & Stocking, M. (1976). Criminality in XYY and XXY men. *Science, 193,* 547–555.

Wittig, M. A. (1985). Metatheoretical dilemmas in the psychology of gender. *American Psychologist, 40*(7), 800–811.

Wolfe, J., Sharkansky, E. J., Read, J. P., Dawson, R., Martin, J. A., & Ouimetter, P. C. (1998). Sexual harassment and assault as predictors of PTSD symptomatology among U.S. female Persian Gulf War military personnel. *Journal of Interpersonal Violence, 13*(1), 40–58.

Wolfson, S. L. (1981). Sex, dependency and volunteering. *British Journal of Social Psychology, 20,* 293–294.

Wollman, N., Griggs, G., & Stouder, R. (1990). The effects of bystander sex and visibility of victim on intended helping. *Imagination, Cognition and Personality, 9*(2), 141–146.

Women's Sports Foundation. (2001). *Playing fair: A guide to Title IX in high school & college sports.* Retrieved December 1, 2006, from http://www.womenssportsfoundation.org/cgi-bin/iowa/issues/geena/record.html?record=829

Women's Sports Foundation. (2006, February 17). *Women in intercollegiate sport: A longitudinal, national study twenty-nine year update: 1977–2006.* Retrieved November 30, 2006, from http://www.womenssportsfoundation.org/cgi-bin/iowa/issues/part/article.html?record=1107

Women & Equality Unit. (2006). *Getting women on to UK boards.* Retrieved November 10, 2006, from http://www.womenandequalityunit.gov.uk/boardroom_diversity/index.htm

Wong, M. W., & Csikszentmihalyi, M. (1991). Affiliation motivation and daily experience: Some issues on gender differences. *Journal of Personality and Social Psychology, 60*(1), 154–164.

Wood, E., Desmarais, S., & Gugula, S. (2002). The impact of parenting experience on gender stereotyped toy play of children. *Sex Roles, 47*(1/2), 39–49.

Wood, J. T., & Inman, C. C. (1993). In a different mode: Masculine styles of communicating closeness. *Journal of Applied Communication Research, 21*(3), 279–295.

Wood, W., & Eagly, A. H. (2002). A cross-cultural analysis of the behavior of women and men: Implications for the origins of sex differences. *Psychological Bulletin, 128*(5), 699–727.

Wood, W., Rhodes, N., & Whelan, M. (1989). Sex differences in positive well-being: A consideration of emotional style and marital status. *Psychological Bulletin, 106*(2), 249–264.

Wooley, S. C., & Wooley, O. W. (1985). Intensive outpatient and residential treatment for bulimia. In D. M. Garner & P. E. Garfinkel (Eds.), *Handbook of psychotherapy for anorexia and bulimia* (pp. 391–430). New York: Guilford Press.

Woolf, V. (1957). *A room of one's own.* New York: Harcourt, Brace & World. (Original work published 1929)

World Health Organization. (2006). *Estimates of child and adult mortality and life expectancy at birth by country.* Retrieved August 28, 2006, from http://www.who.int/healthinfo/statistics/mortlifeexpectancy/en/index.html

World Resources Institute. (2005, August 25). *The many measures of poverty: Life expectancy.* Retrieved August 28, 2006, from http://pubs.wri.org/pubs_maps_description.cfm?ImageID=2264

Worrell, J., & Remer, P. (1992). *Feminist perspectives in therapy: An empowerment model for women.* Chichester, England: Wiley.

Worth, H., Reid, A., & McMillan, K. (2002). Somewhere over the rainbow: Love, trust and monogamy in gay relationships. *Journal of Sociology, 38*(3), 237–253.

Wu, J. H., & Eichmann, M. A. (1988). Fetal sex identification and prenatal bonding. *Psychological Reports, 63*(1), 199–202.

Yacker, N., & Weinberg, S. L. (1990). Care and justice moral orientation: A scale for its assessment. *Journal of Personality Assessment, 55*(1/2), 18–27.

Yahr, P. (1988). Sexual differentiation of behavior in the context of developmental psychobiology. *Handbook of behavioral neurobiology* (pp. 197–243). New York: Plenum.

Yakushko, O. (2005). Ambivalent sexism and relationship patterns among women and men in Ukraine. *Sex Roles, 52*(9), 589–596.

Yankelovich, D. (1974). The meaning of work. In J. Rosow (Ed.), *The worker and the job* (pp. 19–48). Englewood Cliffs, NJ: Prentice-Hall.

Yee, D. K., & Eccles, J. S. (1988). Parent perceptions and attributions for children's math achievement. *Sex Roles, 19*(5/6), 317–333.

Yengoyan, A. (1982, Spring). Transvestitism and the ideology of gender. *Newsletter of the Committee for Gender Research* (no. 1), pp. 1, 3, 6–7.

Yi, K. Y. (1989, April). Symptoms of eating disorders among Asian-American college female students as a function of acculturation. *Dissertation Abstract International, 50,* 10.

Yoder, J. D. (1991). Rethinking tokenism: Looking beyond numbers. *Gender and Society, 5*(2), 178–192.

Yoder, J. D. (1994). Looking beyond numbers: The effects of gender status, job prestige, and occupational gender-typing on tokenism processes. *Social Psychology Quarterly, 57*(2), 150–159.

Yoder, J. D., & Berendsen, L. L. (2001). "Outsider within" the firehouse: African American and White women firefighters. *Psychology of Women Quarterly, 25*(1), 27–36.

Yoder, J. D., Schleicher, T. L., & McDonald, T. W. (1998). Empowering token women leaders: The importance of organizationally legitimated credibility. *Psychology of Women Quarterly, 22,* 209–222.

Yoder, J. D., & Sinnett, L. M. (1985). Is it all in the numbers? A case study of tokenism. *Psychology of Women Quarterly, 9*(3), 413–418.

Zanna, M., Crosby, F., & Loewenstein, G. (1987). Male reference groups and discontent among female professionals. In B. A. Gutek & L. Larwood (Eds.), *Women's career development* (pp. 18–41). Beverly Hills, CA: Sage.

Zanna, M. P., & Pack, S. J. (1975). On the self-fulfilling nature of apparent sex differences in behavior. *Journal of Experimental Social Psychology, 11,* 583–591.

Zarbatany, L., Hartmann, D. P., Gelfand, D. M., & Vinciguerra, P. (1985). Gender differences in altruistic reputation: Are they artifactual? *Developmental Psychology, 21,* 97–101.

Zeichner, A., Parrott, D. J., & Frey, F. C. (2003). Gender differences in laboratory aggression under response choice conditions. *Aggressive Behavior, 29*(2), 95–106.

Zellman, G. L., & Goodchilds, J. D. (1983). Becoming sexual in adolescence. In E. R. Allgeier & N. B. McCormick (Eds.), *Changing boundaries: Gender roles and sexual behavior* (pp. 49–63). Mountain View, CA: Mayfield.

Zelnick, M., & Kantner, J. (1980). Sexual activity, contraceptive use, and pregnancy among metropolitan-area teenagers: 1971–1979. *Family Planning Perspectives, 12,* 230–237.

Zemach, T., & Cohen, A. A. (1986). Perception of gender equality on television and in social reality. *Journal of Broadcasting and Electronic Media, 30,* 427–444.

Zerjal, T., Xue, Y., Bertorelle, G., Wells, R. S., Bao, W., Zhu, S., et al. (2003). The genetic legacy of the Mongols. *American Journal of Human Genetics, 72,* 717–721.

Zern, D. S. (1984). Relationships among selected child-rearing variables in a cross-cultural sample of 110 societies. *Developmental Psychology, 20*(4), 683–690.

Zickmund, W. G., Hitt, M. A., & Pickens, B. A. (1978). Influence of sex and scholastic performance on reactions to job applicant résumés. *Journal of Applied Psychology, 63,* 252–254.

Ziegler, R., Scheidt-Nave, C., & Scharla, S. (1995). Pathophysiology of osteoporosis: Unresolved problems and new insights. *Journal of Nutrition, 125* (7 Suppl.), 2033S–2037S.

Zilbergeld, B. (1978). *Male sexuality.* Boston: Little, Brown.

Zillman, D., & Weaver, J. B. (1989). Pornography and men's sexual callousness toward women. In D. Zillman & J. Bryant (Eds.), *Pornography: Research advances and policy considerations* (pp. 95–125). Hillsdale, NJ: Erlbaum.

Zimmerman, D. H., & West, C. (1975). Sex roles, interruptions and silence in conversation. In B. Thorne & N. Henley (Eds.), *Language and sex: Difference and dominance* (pp. 105–129). Rowley, MA: Newbury House.

Zorza, V. (1986, September 1). Wife-sharing works in the remote Himalayas. *Toronto Globe and Mail,* p. A7.

Zuckerman, D. (1981). Family background, sex-role attitudes, and life goals of technical college and university students. *Sex Roles, 7,* 1109–1126.

Author Index

Subject Index

Credits

Chapter 1

Page 9. Table 1.2 Prentice & Carranza (2002), "What Women and Men Should Be, Shouldn't Be, Are Allowed to Be, and Don't Have to Be: The Contents of Prescriptive Gender Stereotypes." *Psychology of Women Quarterly,* Blackwell Publishing, 26(4), pp. 269–281. Reprinted with permission.

Page 14. Table 1.3 Cjeka and Eagly, *Personality & Social Psychology Bulletin* (25/4) p. 416, © 1999. Reprinted by Permission of Sage Publications, Inc

Page 15. Table 1.4 Reprinted from *Journal of Experimental Social Psychology,* Vol 35, No 1, 1999, pp. 68–77, Swim and Hyers, "Excuse me—What did you just say?!: Women's public and private responses to sexist remarks," with permission from Elsevie. Reprinted with permission.

Page 28. Figure 1.1 Costello, Miles, & Stone (1998). *American Women, 1999–2000: A Century of Change—What's Next?* p. 294: "Labor force participation rates of married women by race and Hispanic origin, 1976–1996."

Chapter 2

Page 62. Figure 2.1 From "Putting Gender Into Context: An Interactive Model of Gender-Related Behavior" by K. Deaux and B. Major, 1987, *Psychological Review,* 94(3), p. 372. Copyright 1987 by the American Psychological Association. Reprinted with permission.

Page 75. Table 2.1 Adapted from Pratto, F. & Walker, A. (2004), "The Bases of Gendered Power." In A. Eagly, A. E. Beall & R. Sternberg (eds.), *The Psychology of Gender,* The Guilford Press. Reprinted with permission.

Chapter 5

Page 185. Figure 5.2 Money, John and Anke A. Aherhardt. *Man and Woman, Boy and Girl: Differentiation and Dimophism of Gender Identity from Conception to Maturity.* p. 44, Fig. 3.2 © 1973 The John Hopkins University Press. Reprinted with permission of The Johns Hopkins University Press.

Page 191. Table 5.1 Reprinted from *Hormones and Behavior,* Vol 35, Berenbaum, "Effects of early androgens on sex-typed activities and interests in adolescents with congenital adrenal hyperplasia." pp. 102–110, © 1999, with permission from Elsevier.

Page 199. Table 5.2 Adapted from Table 1 from p. 448 of Udry, J. R. (2000) Biological Limits of Gender Construction. *American Sociological Review,* 65, 443–457. Reprinted with permission.

Page 200. Figure 5.3 Udry, J. R. (2000) Biological Limits of Gender Construction. *American Sociological Review,* 65, 443–457. Reprinted with permission.

Chapter 6

Page 230. Figure 6.2 Ellis, W. D. (1997) A source book of Gestalt Psychology. Reprinted with permission.

Page 237. Figure 6.3 From *The Brain: The Last Frontier* by Richard Restak, copyright 1979 by Richard M. Restak. Used by permission of Doubleday, a division of Random House, Inc.

Chapter 7

Page 259. Figure 7.1 Hyde, J. (2003) *Understanding Human Sexuality,* 8th Edition. With permission from the McGraw-Hill Companies.

Page 260. Figure 7.2 Hyde, J. (2003) *Understanding Human Sexuality,* 8th Edition. With permission from the McGraw-Hill Companies.

Chapter 8

Page 314 Figure 8.1 A. Hyde, J. (2003) *Understanding Human Sexuality, 8th Ed.* With permission from the McGraw-Hill Companies.

Page 322. Table 8.1 Lee. S. (2002) "Health and Sickness: The meaning of menstruation and premenstrual syndrome in women's lives." *Sex Roles,* 46 (1/2), 25–35. Reprinted with permission from Springer Science and Business Media.